14th Edition

GOVERNMENT BY THE PEOPLE

Bill of Rights Edition

James MacGregor Burns

Williams College

J. W. Peltason

University of California, Irvine

Thomas E. Cronin

The Colorado College

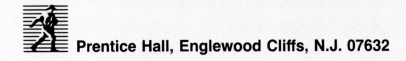

Prentice Hall, Englewood Cliffs, N.J. 07632

Library of Congress Cataloging-in-Publication Data

Burns, James MacGregor.
    Government by the people / James MacGregor Burns, J.W. Peltason,
Thomas E. Cronin. -- 14th ed., Bill of Rights ed., national version.
        p.   cm.
    Includes bibliographical references.
    ISBN 0-13-361999-0
    1. United States--Politics and government.   I. Peltason, J. W.
(Jack Walter).   II. Cronin, Thomas E.   III. Title.
    JK274.B853 1990
    320.973--dc20   89-23152
                                                                     CIP

Acquisitions editor: Karen Horton
Editorial/production supervision: Serena Hoffman
Interior and cover design: Jayne Conte and Lee Cohen
Manufacturing buyers: Peter Havens and Bob Anderson
Page Makeup: Jayne Conte
Photo editor: Lorinda Morris-Nantz
Photo Research: Joelle Burrows
Cover photo: Walter J. Choroszewski/The Stock Market

Printed in the United States of America
10 9 8 7 6 5 4 3 2 1

ISBN 0-13-361999-0

Prentice-Hall International (UK) Limited, *London*
Prentice-Hall of Australia Pty. Limited, *Sydney*
Prentice-Hall Canada Inc., *Toronto*
Prentice-Hall Hispanoamericana, S.A., *Mexico*
Prentice-Hall of India Private Limited, *New Delhi*
Prentice-Hall of Japan, Inc., *Tokyo*
Simon & Schuster Asia Pte. Ltd., *Singapore*
Editora Prentice-Hall do Brasil, Ltda., *Rio de Janeiro*

Contents

ABOUT THE AUTHORS   viii

PREFACE   ix

PART ONE: CONSTITUTIONAL
DEMOCRACY IN AMERICA

1 **LIBERTY AND ORDER:
THE GRAND EXPERIMENT**   1
The Roots of the Bill of Rights   4
The Philadelphia Convention, 1787   7
To Adopt or Not to Adopt?   13
What Kind of Constitution   17

THE CONSTITUTION
OF THE UNITED STATES OF AMERICA

Into the Third Century—And Some
    Questions   23
Notes 24

2 **THE LIVING CONSTITUTION**   25
Checking Power with Power   26
Judicial Review and
    the "Guardians of the
    Constitution   28
Checks and Balances—
    Does It Work?   31
The Constitution as an Instrument
    of Government   34
Changing the Letter of the
    Constitution   37
Ratification Politics: ERA and the D.C.
    Amendment   42
Summary 44/Further Reading 44/Notes 45

3 **AMERICAN FEDERALISM:
PROBLEMS AND PROSPECTS**   46
Why Federalism?   48

Constitutional Structure of American
    Federalism   51
Triumph of the Nationalist
    Interpretation   56
Umpires of the Federal System   60
Federal Grants   62
Federal Regulations   64
Two Levels or Three? Crazy-Quilt
    Federalism   65
The Politics of Federalism 66
Summary 70/Further Reading 70/Notes 71

PART TWO: CIVIL LIBERTIES

4 **FIRST AMENDMENT RIGHTS**   72
A Wall of Separation   74
All Persons May Worship as They
    Choose   76
Free Speech and Free People   78
Freedom of the Press   83
Other Media and Other
    Messages   85
Libel, Obscenity, and Fighting
    Words   89
Right of the People Peaceably
    to Assemble, to Petition the Govern-
    ment, and to Associate   93
Subversive Conduct and Seditious
    Speech   96
Summary 98/Further Reading 98/Notes 99

5 **EQUAL RIGHTS
UNDER THE LAW**   101
Equality and Equal Rights   102
Equal Protection of the Laws—
    What Does It Mean?   112
How to Prove Discrimination   115
Barriers to Voting   118

Barriers to Public Accommodations,
 Jobs, and Homes 121
Affirmative Action—
 Is It Constitutional? 125
Summary 127/Further Reading 128/Notes 129

6 RIGHTS TO LIFE, LIBERTY, AND PROPERTY 131

How Citizenship Is Acquired and
 Lost 131
Rights of Aliens—Admission to the
 United States 133
Constitutional Protection
 of Property 138
Freedom from Arbitrary Arrest,
 Questioning, and
 Imprisonment 143
Rights of Persons Accused
 of Crime 148
How Just Is Our System
 of Justice? 152
The Supreme Court and Civil
 Liberties 155
Summary 156/Further Reading 156/Notes 156

PART THREE: THE PEOPLE IN POLITICS

7 POLITICAL CULTURE AND IDEOLOGY 158

Political Culture 159
The Never-Ending Quest for Additional
 Rights 166
Liberalism, Conservatism, and Public
 Policy 168
A Central Ideological Tension—
 Political Equality versus
 Capitalism 179
Ideology and Tolerance 182
Summary 184/Further Reading 185/Notes 185

8 INTEREST GROUPS: THE POLITICS OF FACTION 186

The Maze of Group Interests 187
Major Interests: Size and Scope 191
Weapons of Group Power 194

PACs: Interest Groups
 in Combat 198
Lobbying, Old and New 201
Controlling Factions—Two Hundred
 Years Later 204
Summary 208/Further Reading 209/Notes 209

9 MOVEMENTS: THE POLITICS OF CONFLICT 210

Movements: The Why and How 211
American Indians: The Oldest
 Movement? 213
Blacks: Freedom Now 214
Women: The Continuing
 Struggle 218
The Politics of Peace 225
Movements and the Constitution 227
Summary 228/Further Reading 228/Notes 229

10 POLITICAL PARTIES: INSTITUTIONS UNDER CHANGE 230

Parties: Their Rise and Their
 Role 233
Party Functions: Then and Now 237
How the Parties Are Organized 245
Parties on Trial 248
Saving the Parties: Reform, Renewal,
 and Realignment 257
Summary 266/Further Reading 266/Notes 267

11 PUBLIC OPINION AND VOTING 269

How We Learn Our Political
 Beliefs 269
The Fabric of Public Opinion 273
Taking the Pulse of the People 277
How We Vote: Electoral
 Patterns 280
Nonvoting: Who Doesn't Vote and
 Why 287
Summary 292/Further Reading 292/Notes 293

iv

12 MEDIA POLITICS: REALITY OR ILLUSION? 294

The Power of the Mass Media 295
The Media and Public Opinion 298
The Image Campaign: The Mass
Media Election 303

Summary 310/Further Reading 311/Notes 311

13 ELECTIONS: THE DEMOCRATIC STRUGGLE 313

Running for Office 314
Running for President 318
Is This the Way to Pick
Presidents? 327
Campaign Money 331
Interpreting the 1988 Elections 336

Summary 340/Further Reading 340/Notes 341

PART FOUR: THE POLICY MAKERS

14 CONGRESS: THE PEOPLE'S BRANCH? 343

Congress: An Overall View 345
The Powers of Congress 347
The Houses of Congress 350
Who Are the Legislators? 354
Getting to and Remaining in
Congress 355
The Job of the Legislator 357
Committees: The Little
Legislatures 365
Getting It Together: Conference
Committees and Senate-House
Coordination 369
Is Congress Effective?—
Congressional Reform 370

Summary 373/Further Reading 374/Notes 375

15 THE PRESIDENCY: THE LEADERSHIP BRANCH? 376

An Effective Presidency? 377
Is the Presidency Too Strong—Or Not
Strong Enough? 379
The Job of the President 380
Presidents as Crisis Managers 382

Presidents as Morale-Building
Leaders 384
Presidents as Recruiters 385
Presidents as Priority Setters 386
Presidents as Legislative and Political
Coalition Builders 389
Presidents as Administrators 393
Can the Modern Presidency Survive
the Modern Media? 396
The Vice-Presidency 398
Making the Presidency Safe and
Effective 399

Summary 404/Further Reading 404/Notes 404

16 CONGRESS AND THE PRESIDENT: THE POLITICS OF SHARED POWERS 406

Presidential Influence in
Congress 408
The Imperial Presidency
Argument 410
Congress Reasserts Itself 416
The President and Congress:
The Continuing Struggle 428
The Imperial Congress
Argument 429

Summary 432/Further Reading 432/Notes 433

17 JUDGES: THE BALANCING BRANCH 434

The Scope of Judicial Power 435
Federal Justice 437
Prosecution and Defense:
Federal Lawyers 442
How Federal Judges Are
Selected 443
How the Supreme Court
Operates 448
Judicial Power in a Democracy 455

Summary 459/Further Reading 459/Notes 460

18 BUREAUCRATS: THE REAL POWER?

Who Are the Bureaucrats? 464
The United States Civil Service:
A Brief History 467

Bureaucracy in Action:
The Classical or Textbook
Model 468
Bureaucrats as Administrators—
Some Realities 470
Administrators in Action: Case
Studies 473
What the Public Thinks
of Bureaucrats 477
The Case Against Big Bureaucracy
and Its Waste 479
The Case for Bureaucracy 483
Controlling the Bureaucrats: Who and
How? 485
Summary 492/Further Reading 492/Notes 493

**PART FIVE: THE POLITICS OF NATIONAL
POLICY**

19 MAKING PUBLIC POLICY 494
Getting Things Done in Washington:
The Players 495
Competing Models of Policy
Making 497
National Policy Formation 504
Policy Implementation 511
Summary 514/Further Reading 515/Notes 515

20 MAKING FOREIGN POLICY 517
Defining and Defending Our Vital
Interests 519
The Cold War and Its Legacy 520
Foreign Policy Strategies 526
The Politics of Making Foreign
Policy 529
The Policy Machinery 535
International Organizations and the
UN 540
Summary 542/Further Reading 542/Notes 592

**21 PROVIDING FOR THE COMMON
DEFENSE 544**
The Nation's Defense
Objectives 545
How Much Is Enough? 549

Will U.S. Conventional Forces Be
Strong Enough to Win? 553
Reorganizing for a More Effective
Defense 556
Arms Build-Up and Arms
Control 560
Security and Liberty:
Not by Force Alone 564
Summary 565/Further Reading 565/Notes 656

**22 MAKING ECONOMIC AND SOCIAL
POLICY 566**
The Politics of Taxation and
Spending 566
Managing the Economy 572
Fiscal Policy: Remedies 574
Government Subsidies: How and
Why 577
Helping Business 578
Helping Farmers 579
Helping Retirees and the
Disabled 583
Helping the Needy 584
Summary 587/Further Reading 587/Notes 588

**23 THE POLITICS OF
REGULATION 589**
What Is Regulation? 590
Regulating Business 595
Regulating Labor-Management
Relations 599
Regulation to Protect the
Environment 603
Regulating Occupational Safety and
Health: A Case Study 606
Regulatory Outcomes and
Issues 609
The Deregulation Debate 611
Summary 614/Further Reading 615/Notes 615

24 THE DEMOCRATIC FAITH 616
The Case for Government by the
People 618
Participation and Representation 619
The Role of the Politician 621

What Kind of Political
  Leadership? 622
Thinking about Leadership 623
Democratic Leadership 626
The Democratic Faith 626
Notes 628

APPENDIX 629
The Declaration
  of Independence 629
The Federalist, No. 10, James
  Madison 630

The Federalist, No. 51, James
  Madison 633
The Federalist, No. 78, Alexander
  Hamilton 635
Presidential Election Results, 1798–
  1988 638

GLOSSARY 640

PHOTOGRAPHS 651

INDEX 653

About the Authors

James MacGregor Burns, a native and lifelong resident of Massachusetts, is Woodrow Wilson Professor of Political Science at Williams College, where he has taught for the past forty years. He has written several books, including *The Power to Lead* (1984); *The Vineyard of Liberty* (1982); *Leadership* (1979); *The Deadlock of Democracy: Four Party Politics in America* (1963); *Roosevelt: The Lion and the Fox* (1956); and *Roosevelt: The Soldier of Freedom* (1970). His most recent book is *The Crosswinds of Freedom* (1989). Active in professional and civic life, Burns is a past president of the American Political Science Association and a former congressional candidate. Although his major love is writing (for which he has won numerous prizes, including the Pulitzer Prize and the National Book Award), he can sometimes be found chopping wood, running, skiing, or playing tennis in his own cherished Berkshire community of Williamstown.

J. W. Peltason is one of the country's leading scholars on courts, judicial process, and public law. Educated at the University of Missouri and Princeton University, he has taught political science at Princeton, Midwestern University, Smith College, and the University of Illinois. He is at present Chancellor and Professor of Political Science at University of California, Irvine; he is Chancellor Emeritus of the University of Illinois, Urbana-Champaign, and was president of the American Council on Education in Washington, D.C. He has represented higher education before Congress and state legislatures, and his writings include *Federal Courts in the Political Process* (1955); *Fifty-Eight Lonely Men: Southern Federal Judges and School Desegregation* (1961); and *Understanding the Constitution* (1988). Among his awards are the James Madison Medal from Princeton University (1982) and the American Political Science Association's Charles E. Merriam award in 1983 to "the person whose published work and career represents a significant contribution to the art of government. . . ." He is a member of the American Academy of Arts and Sciences.

Tom Cronin is a leading student of the American presidency and national leadership and policymaking processes. He earned his Ph.D. from Stanford University and served as a White House Fellow and White House staff aide. Cronin was the 1986 recipient of the American Political Science Association's Charles E. Merriam Award for "significant contribution to the art of government." Cronin's writings include *The State of the Presidency* (1980); *U.S. v. Crime-in-the-Streets* (1981); and *Direct Democracy: The Politics of Initiative, Referendum, and Recall* (1989). He is the McHugh Distinguished Professor of American Institutions and Leadership at The Colorado College. A former candidate for the U.S. Congress and President of the Presidency Research Group, Cronin has lectured at over 200 colleges and universities. He has appeared as a political analyst on *Nightline*, *Late Night America*, *The Today Show*, C-SPAN, CNN, and several PBS and network documentaries.

Preface

A PERSONAL MESSAGE FROM THE AUTHORS

You are using this book during a time of celebration of old and newly claimed freedoms around the world. In July of 1989 the French enjoyed the two-hundredth birthday of their Declaration of the Rights of Man, which was issued a few weeks after the outbreak of their Revolution. Soviet citizens have been experimenting in recent years with *glasnost* and *perestroika*—with relaxing oppressive rules and trying out democratic processes. Eastern European countries have been allowing opposition forces to criticize their regimes and even nominate candidates for high office. And in America we are celebrating the two-hundredth anniversary of the final ratification in December of 1791 of our Bill of Rights, the first ten amendments to the Constitution.

This Bill of Rights Edition of *Government by the People* focuses on past and present struggles for liberty in America, the extension of the original Bill of Rights to embrace a broad range of political, economic, and social rights, and the current conflict over new rights.

The framers of our Constitution warned that we must be vigilant in safeguarding our rights and liberties, and we are reminded of that warning even as we celebrate the birthday of our Bill of Rights. In the spring of 1989 one nation—the most populous in the world—suddenly plunged back into the darkness of suppression of the freedoms of speech, press, and assembly. A few months before the bloody suppression of protest in Beijing and other Chinese cities, two of the authors of this volume met with hundreds of students and scholars in Chinese universities. The third author heads a university that has admitted many Chinese and large numbers of Chinese-American students. We three authors know of their aspirations for political liberty, democracy, human rights.

We dedicate this Bill of Rights Edition of *Government by the People* to our fellow teachers in China and to the students there who still carry the torch of liberty and democracy toward a new era of freedom some day in China.

ACKNOWLEDGMENTS

We wish to acknowledge the indispensible help we have received from many scholars. Professors Lois L. Duke of the University of Alabama, L. Sandy Maisel of Colby College, and Mark Petracca of the University of California at Irvine contributed their extensive knowledge of American politics and government to the redrafting of several chapters in this revision. Professor Duke made substantive contributions to Chapters 11, 12, and 13; Professor Maisel helped enormously in revising Chapters 10 and 13; Professor Petracca provided important fresh insights to Chapters 19 and 22.

We were indeed fortunate to have had an outstanding group of professors prepare the instructional aids that accompany this text. James V. Calvi, West Texas State College, wrote the margin annotations for the instructor's edition. Michael F. Digby, Georgia College, and Raymond L. Lee and Dorothy A. Palmer of Indiana University of Pennsylvania prepared the revised Instructor's Manual. Larry Elowitz of Georgia College prepared the Instructor's Guide to the transparency package. Simulations were devised by Robert Loevy of Colorado College, and Barbara Feinberg wrote the Test Item File. Our thanks to them all.

We wish to thank Pat Dennis, Kathy North, and Harriett Speegle for first-class editorial assistance. We also thank David N. Lowland for superb research assistance, Ann B. Armstrong for careful proofreading; and Marj Billings for secretarial assistance. David Sandford, Sean Gallup, and other members of a winter study course at Williams College in Editing and Writing Political Science contributed useful critiques; Sandford and Gallup made further contributions to the new edition. Michael Dawson and Milton Djuric proofread various chapters, and the Faculty Secretarial Office at Williams College helped immensely with manuscript preparation.

More than anyone else, we thank our outstanding production editor, Serena Hoffman, for pushing, coaching, and leading us to complete this major undertaking. Also, we again thank Senior Editor Karen Horton and President Ed Stanford at Prentice Hall for their encouragement and guidance. Special thanks to Dolores Mars for all her kindnesses and good cheer, and to all these other highly skilled professionals at Prentice Hall: Ann Marie McCar-

Ed Stanford at Prentice Hall for their encouragement and guidance. Special thanks to Dolores Mars for all her kindnesses and good cheer, and to all these other highly skilled professionals at Prentice Hall: Ann Marie McCarthy, senior managing editor; Peter Havens and Bob Anderson, manufacturing buyers; Terri Peterson and Roland Hernandez, marketing managers; Lori Morris and Joelle Burrows, photo researchers; Lee Cohen and Jayne Conte, designers; and Kim Bryne and Colette Conboy, supplements.

Finally, we thank the scores of students and professors who have sent us letters or called us with suggestions for improving *Government by the People*. Please know we welcome your calls and notes concerning specific matters in the book that you like or dislike; they will help make this an even better book in future editions.

As we record our debt to all these people for their help, the three of us also hereby absolve them of any responsibility for what we have written. We would appreciate it if you, our readers, would point out errors and send comments, suggestions, and advice to us at our addresses below, or care of the Political Science Editor, Prentice Hall, Englewood Cliffs, New Jersey 07632.

JAMES MACGREGOR BURNS
Williams College
Williamstown, MA 01267

J. W. PELTASON
University of California, Irvine
Irvine, CA 92717

THOMAS E. CRONIN
The Colorado College
Colorado Springs, CO 80903

REVIEWERS

Each edition of this comprehensive text profits from the informed and sometimes sharp criticisms of our political science colleagues around the country. This Fourteenth Edition benefitted from the critical suggestions, most but not all of which we have taken, from these reviewers:

David Gray Adler, Idaho State University
Dean Alger, Moorhead State University
Howard Ball, The University of Utah
Gerald Benjamin, State University of New York at New Paltz
Judith A. Best, State University College at Cortland
Chris Bosso, Northeastern University
Robert Browning, Purdue University
Gregory Caldeira, Ohio State University
James V. Calvi, West Texas State University
Allan Ciglar, University of Kansas
Raymond W. Cox, II, New Mexico State University
Doug Crane, DeKalb College
Robert E. DiClerico, West Virginia University
Larry Elowitz, Georgia College
Kathy Foley, Long Island University
Edward Fuchs, University of Texas at El Paso
Michael Genovese, Loyola-Marymount University

Mark Gibney, Purdue University
George Gordon, Illinois State University
Mark Greer, Laramie County Community College
James F. Herndon, Virginia Polytechnic Institute and State University
Shanto Iyengar, State University of New York at Stony Brook
Michael Johnston, Colgate University
Richard A. Joslyn, Temple University
Thomas J. Kehoe, Union County College
John C. Kilkelly, St. Cloud State University
Jack Knott, Michigan State University
Dale Krane, University of Nebraska at Omaha
Carol Lewis, University of Connecticut
William M. Lunch, Oregon State University
Cecilia G. Manrique, Slippery Rock University
Andrew Milnor, State University of New York at Binghamton
Matthew L. Moen, University of Maine

Stephen L. Percy, University of Virginia
Gary Prevost, St. John's University
Donald R. Ranish, Antelope Valley College
Donald R. Reichard, James Sprunt Community College
Craig A. Rimmerman, Hobart and William Smith Colleges
Leonard Ritt, Northern Arizona University
Jerel A. Rosati, University of South Carolina
Victor G. Rosenblum, Northwestern University School of Law
Andrew L. Ross, University of Kentucky
Howard E. Shuman, Arlington, Virginia
Rogers M. Smith, Yale University
Raymond Tatalovich, Loyola University of Chicago
Thomas Walker, Emory University
Darrell M. West, Brown University
Thomas Phillip Wolf, Indiana University Southeast
Nancy Zingale, College of St. Thomas

1

Liberty and Order: The Grand Experiment

If you had been in New York City (the new nation's temporary capital) in the spring or summer of 1789 and looking for young Congressman James Madison, you might have spotted him during the day on the floor of the recently established House of Representatives debating tax and tariff bills with his fellow legislators. But "after hours" you would most likely have found him at his lodgings in Mrs. Elsworth's boardinghouse on Maiden Lane, laboring over his writing desk piled with letters from state capitals and a big scrapbook of his own. It was hardly a dramatic sight—this slight, rather nondescript man writing slowly with a goosequill pen, amid sounds of fishmongers and draymen coming through the open windows from the nearby waterfront. But the situation was momentous, for Madison was composing the early drafts of what would become the Bill of Rights.

James Madison (1751–1836), a Virginian, was a key member of the Constitutional Convention of 1787, authored several impressive *Federalist* essays advocating ratification, served as speaker of the House of Representatives, and later became our fourth president. He is sometimes called the "father of the Constitution" and chief architect of the Bill of Rights.

Why momentous? Because nothing touches your life—whether you are a student or not, foreign or native born, under or over eighteen—more intimately than the freedoms guaranteed in the Bill of Rights. Most of humankind throughout history have not been free to say or hear what governments forbade, to worship as they wished, to put up posters on a wall, or to edit a newspaper without fear of arrest or censorship. But when you see a police car, you do not tremble in fear—unless you are breaking the speed limit or otherwise violating the law— that you will be taken into custody or thrown into jail. Millions and millions of people today do not enjoy such luxuries of freedom.

You are reading this book at the time of the celebration of the birth of the Bill of Rights, the first ten amendments to the Constitution. What we are really celebrating are not only these ten amendments but the Constitution itself, for this great charter, drafted in Philadelphia in the historic convention of 1787, and its later amendments form a structure of liberty.

The Constitution divides governmental power in order to restrain it from sweeping away our liberties. An elaborate system of checks and balances, which

The ideal of liberty still inspires people today, as it did in the recent demonstrations in China that were so brutally repressed.

we will analyze in depth, curbs the arbitrary use of governmental power. Provisions in the 1787 Constitution and later amendments—especially the "Big Ten" and the Thirteenth, Fourteenth, and Fifteenth adopted after the Civil War—restrict the government and seek to guarantee to all the people an array of fundamental rights.

In 1789, Madison had little time for diversion—for strolling down Broad Street to Fraunces' Tavern, or watching an American comedy on John Street, or listening to Handel's *Messiah* in famous old Trinity Church at the end of Wall Street. Sitting at his writing desk, he faced a daunting task—culling the provisions for essential rights and liberties from scores of proposals that had been sent to him from a dozen new states, and making a package of these rights for Congress to consider. He had to work quickly too. Some members of Congress were pressing for a *second* constitutional convention, which Madison and others feared might become a runaway caucus of radicals. "The business goes on still very slowly," he wrote to his father in Virginia. "We are in a wilderness without a single footstep to guide us."[1]

Not far from young Madison, however, lived and worked a man who *was* seeking to guide the nation—George Washington. Inaugurated as the nation's first president only a few weeks earlier in April 1789, Washington believed in freedom of religion, speech, and the other liberties, but he was far more concerned about another great aim—holding the struggling young nation together, maintaining order and stability, strengthening the unity of states that had often quarreled with one another and were now still living uneasily under a common constitution.

Take a coin out of your pocket and you will note how Madison's prime concern, *liberty*, and Washington's prime concern, *unity* or *union*, have formed parallel ideas throughout our history. As you study your quarter or dime or nickel, you will find the word LIBERTY in relatively large letters. This is appropriate, for liberty (or freedom) has been the central value or end for Americans throughout our national experience. You will also find the Latin words, E PLURIBUS UNUM, meaning unity out of diversity, or union out of many.

Most Americans recognized that liberty could not survive except in a unified, stable, orderly society. But how could these two great values, *liberty* and *order*, be reconciled when they came into collision with each other—for example, when freedom of speech or religion led to riots and bloodshed in the streets? This was the challenge that faced the founding fathers and has confronted us ever since. How did they meet it? In brief, by establishing a constitutional system that would realize *both* great ideals. Their way of doing that will be described fully in this and later chapters.

But how were they able to establish such a properly balanced constitutional system? In part because they were brilliant scholars of politics who at the same time had been deeply immersed in the day-to-day, nuts-and-bolts problems of governing. In part because they had long worked together and shared, or at least understood, one another's views, whether as revolutionaries or later as constitutionalists. And in part because they were men of moderation who understood the need for both liberty and order. Just as Washington was willing to accept a Bill of Rights, Madison understood the need for order, as he had already shown in his brilliant writings.

Above all, these founders of the republic were a team of like-minded but independent thinkers and politicians, and each had a "support staff" who supplied ideas and advice. Washington worked closely with his vice-president, John Adams, and his Treasury secretary, Alexander Hamilton. Madison had the support of hundreds of state leaders who submitted proposals for the amendments he was drafting.

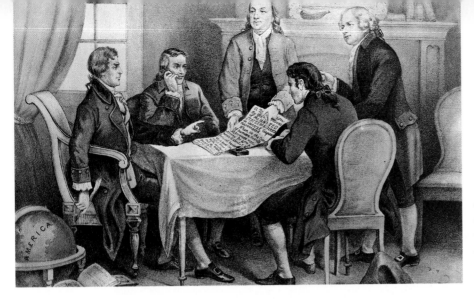

The Declaration of Independence Committee set down on paper the ideals and goals that were later incorporated in the Constitution. Shown here are Thomas Jefferson, Roger Sherman, Benjamin Franklin, Robert Livingston, and John Adams.

These were young, or at least youthful-minded, men in 1789: Madison was 38, Hamilton, 34, others even younger; Washington was a patriarch at 57. It was, in Michael Kammen's words, a "season of youth."[2]

Of course these old-time revolutionary comrades did not always agree on specifics. Washington wanted primarily to establish the presidency as an office of special honesty and integrity, an office that would transcend politics; some of his old friends found him too stiff and standoffish in dealing with everyday political matters. Vice-President John Adams wanted the president's title to be "His Highness" or the like to give the presidency more dignity; his old comrades believed that the one-time youthful revolutionary was becoming more and more conservative, or at least pompous. Treasury Secretary Alexander Hamilton wanted the new national government to take a strong lead in economic matters; many of those who had fought with him against King George did not want to create an overly centralized and powerful government like the British system. James Madison wanted above all to put through his Bill of Rights amendments. Washington gave him modest encouragement, writing his good congressional friend that the proposals would do no harm and some of them might even do some good.[3]

These four men—Washington, Adams, Hamilton, Madison—played commanding roles, as revolutionaries, constitution framers, political brokers, as policy makers, during the whole founding period of the new national government, from the 1770s until the end of the century.

A fifth man, Thomas Jefferson, not yet present in New York, probably had the greatest long-run influence of all. During those formative months of 1789, Thomas Jefferson was still minister to France, where he had a front row seat for the unfolding drama of the French Revolution. At the age of 33 Jefferson had won fame in the Old World as well as the New as the main drafter of the Declaration of Independence in 1776. He staunchly supported his close friend Madison in pressing for a Bill of Rights to be added to the Constitution. Soon he was sailing home across the Atlantic to become Washington's—and the nation's—first secretary of state.

These five men worked closely in establishing the new government, until they fell out in the rising partisan conflict of the 1790s. Each had a special role: Washington as the soldier, statesman, and unifier; Adams as the intellectual leader of the increasingly conservative Federalists; Hamilton as the political economist who favored government-business cooperation in expanding the economy; Jefferson as the nation's first great political philosopher to hold high office; Madison as the preeminent political scientist. Of course this is an oversimplification, for each of these men shared the others' roles. These five men, moreover, were only the "tip of the iceberg" of several hundred brilliant and creative national, state, and local leaders of that period. (Certain women, lacking the right to vote or hold office, still found ways to exert some influence).

Whatever the conflicts among these leaders, two goals, two values, united them: liberty and order. How liberty and order were defined, how they could be attained, how they could be secured—these paramount questions had occupied Americans ever since the first settlers arrived, and they are still troubling us in the era of President George Bush.

Let us now turn back briefly to the early struggle for liberty in America and discuss the new order established by the 1787 Constitution. Then we will pick up again the framing and adoption of the Bill of Rights in the crucial years 1787 to 1791 that are being commemorated in the current bicentennial celebrations.

The Roots of the Bill of Rights

History records that James Madison labored alone, day after day, drafting the Bill of Rights in his boarding house lodgings. But in a broader sense we know Madison was not alone. Helping him wield his pen were the barons who gathered at Runnymede in 1215 to extract from King John liberties "to all free men of our kingdom" (or at least to barons). Present too were Lord Coke and others who, in the 1628 Petition of Right, established certain rights of Englishmen as law; the English revolutionaries who curbed the power of the King in the Bill of Rights of 1689 and gained such rights as freedom of speech and debate in Parliament; the framers of the earlier Habeas Corpus Act of 1679, designed to put checks on the power of the British government and guarantee such rights as those against self-incrimination and "punishments equal to offences." The fact that these rights on paper had not always been carried out in practice only strengthened Madison's determination to spell out Americans' rights clearly and boldly.

Standing at Madison's elbow too were the great thinkers of ancient and of more recent times, some of whom he had read as a student at Princeton: the Greek philosophers who spoke out for the rights of the *aristoi*—literally the best people—although not of course for slaves and others of low rank; Martin Luther and John Calvin, who fought for religious liberty from Catholic authority but then suppressed the liberties of fellow Protestants; and John Locke and the other great thinkers of the seventeenth and eighteenth centuries who built the philosophical foundations for the protection of individual liberty against the state.

THE AMERICAN ROOTS

Above all, Madison had the American experience to guide him. For almost two centuries Europeans had been sailing to the New World in search of liberty—especially religious liberty—as well as land and jobs. While still aboard their *Mayflower*, the Pilgrims had drawn up a compact to protect their religious freedom and to make possible "just and equale laws." In America editors found that they could speak out freely in their columns; dissenters could distribute leaflets; agitators could protest in taverns or in the streets. But the picture of freedom in America was a mixed one. The Puritans in Massachusetts soon estab-

"You know, the idea of taxation *with* representation doesn't appeal to me very much either."

Drawing by Handelsman; © 1970 The New Yorker Magazine, Inc.

CHAPTER 1 // Liberty and Order: The Grand Experiment

lished a **theocracy,*** and not all religious sects in the colonies were granted equal religious liberty. Dissenters were occasionally chased out of town, and some printers had their shops closed or were even physically attacked.

Americans, in short, were struggling through these early centuries with the basic questions of the balance of unity and diversity, stability and dissent, order and liberty. Puritan theocrats continued to worry, in Joyce Appleby's words, "about what would maintain order in a society lacking an established church, an attachment to place, and the uncontested leadership of men of merit."[4] Nine of the thirteen colonies eventually set up a state church. Throughout the 1700s Massachusetts Puritans barred a man from voting unless he belonged to the proper church in town (women could not vote at all). To the Anglican establishment in Virginia, campaigns for toleration were in themselves subversive.

Still, most colonial Americans in most places enjoyed a wide array of liberties. When Peter Zenger, a New York newspaper printer, was jailed in 1737 by royal authority on the charge of seditious libel and his conviction upheld in court, Zenger's attorney appealed to a jury and won a "not guilty" verdict. Increasingly the question arose as to how the people could secure American liberties, rather than leave them in the hands of mobs, sheriffs, or religious establishments. The answer was to bind liberties tightly into colonial acts and constitutions. The Maryland Act for the Liberties of the People legislated that "all the inhabitants of this Province being Christians (slaves excepted) should have such rights liberties immunities priviledges and free customs" as any natural born subject of England. The Massachusetts Body of Liberties of 1641, which served somewhat as a model for later New York and Pennsylvania charters, guaranteed freedom of speech and petition at public meetings, right of counsel, trial by jury, "the same justice and law" for every person.[5]

As feeling against the British mounted during the 1770s and revolutionary fervor sharpened, Americans were more and more determined to fight for their rights against the British and for their liberties in general. A year after fighting with the Redcoats broke out in Lexington, Concord, and other areas, the Declaration of Independence proclaimed in ringing tones that all men are created equal, endowed by their Creator with certain unalienable rights; that among those are life, liberty, and the pursuit of happiness; that to secure those rights governments are instituted among men; and that whenever a government became destructive of those ends, it is the right of the people to alter or abolish it.

We know these great ideals so well that we almost take them for granted, but the revolutionary leaders did not. They were deadly serious about these rights and willing to fight for them, willing to pledge their lives, fortunes, and sacred honor for them. They determinedly set about guaranteeing liberty in the constitutions that the states adopted as they broke away from the Crown. All the bills of rights in the new state constitutions guaranteed free speech, freedom of religion, and the natural rights to life, liberty, and property. All the declarations spelled out rights of persons accused of crime, such as knowing the nature of the accusation, being confronted by the accusers, and receiving a timely and public trial by jury.[6]

TOWARD UNITY AND ORDER

The quest for liberty, for rights, for "pluribus" could go only so far. As the war against the British widened, the need arose for a stronger central government that could rise above the states and conduct a revolutionary war. For a time the

---

* Words that appear in boldfaced type throughout the text are defined in the Glossary at the end of the book.

The Grand Union—1776

First Stars and Stripes—1777

Continental Congress, which had led the way toward revolution, tried to direct hostilities against the British, but it took a man of George Washington's iron resolve to unify and direct the war effort. Sensing the need for more unity, Congress established a new national government under the **Articles of Confederation.** At first hardly worthy of the term "government," the Articles were not approved by all the state legislatures until 1781, after Washington's troops had been fighting for five years.

The new Confederation was a move toward a stronger national government, but a limited and inadequate one. Having fought a war against a strong central government in London, Americans were reluctant to create another one. The Articles established more of a fragile league of friendship than a national government. From 1777 to 1788 Americans made some progress under this confederation. But with the end of the war in 1783, the sense of urgency that had produced unity began to fade. Within the states, conflict between creditors and debtors grew intense. And foreign threats by no means disappeared with the defeat of the Redcoats. The English, French, and Spanish surrounded the new nation, which—internally divided and lacking a strong central government—made a tempting prize.

As pressures on the Confederation mounted, many leaders became convinced that it would not be enough merely to revise the Articles of Confederation. To create a union strong enough to deal with internal diversity and factionalism, as well as resist external threats, they needed to set up a stronger central government with adequate powers. They therefore set out to establish a republican government that could be made to work by and for *ordinary people.*[7]

Although many Americans increasingly recognized the need to give Congress authority to regulate commerce and collect a few taxes, they were still suspicious of central government. But finally, in the late summer of 1786, under the leadership of Alexander Hamilton, those who favored a truly national government took advantage of a meeting in Annapolis, Maryland (on problems of trade and navigation, attended by delegates from five states) to issue a call for a "plenipotentiary Convention." Such a convention would have full authority to consider basic amendments to the Articles of Confederation. The delegates to the **Annapolis Convention** requested the legislatures of their states to appoint commissioners to meet in Philadelphia on the second Monday of May, 1787, "to devise such further provisions as shall appear to them necessary to render the Constitution of the Federal Government adequate to the exigencies of the Union." This convention, held in August 1786, issued the call for what became the Constitutional Convention. The Annapolis Convention itself, attended by delegates from only five states, was unable to deal with these broader problems.

For a short time all was quiet. Then, late in 1786, messengers rode into George Washington's plantation at Mr. Vernon with the kind of news that he and other leaders had dreaded. Led by Daniel Shays, some farmers in western Massachusetts, crushed by debts and taxes, were rebelling against foreclosures, forcing judges out of their courtrooms, and freeing debtors from jails. Washington was appalled. Ten years before he had been leading Americans in a patriots' war against the British. Now Americans were fighting Americans!

"What, gracious God, is man?" Washington exclaimed. Clearly liberty as license had been allowed to go too far. Indeed, such disorder was a threat to liberty itself. If government could not check such disorders, he wrote to his friend Madison, "what security has a man for life, liberty or property?" It was obvious that without a stronger central government, "thirteen Sovereignties pulling against each other, and all tugging at the federal head will soon bring ruin on the whole." Not all Americans reacted as Washington did to what came to be known as **Shays's**

Rebellion. When Abigail Adams, the politically knowledgeable wife of John Adams, sent news of the rebellion to Thomas Jefferson, the Virginian replied, "I like a little rebellion now and then," adding later that the "tree of liberty must be refreshed from time to time" with "the natural manure" of the blood of patriots and tyrants.

Shays's Rebellion petered out after the farmers attacked an arsenal and were cut down by cannon fire. But this "little rebellion" had sent a stab of fear into the established leadership. It also acted as a catalyst. The message now was clear. Some kind of action must be taken to strengthen the machinery of government. Spurred on by Shays's Rebellion, seven states appointed commissioners to attend a convention in Philadelphia to strengthen the Articles of Confederation. Congress, rightly suspicious, finally issued a cautiously worded call to the states to appoint delegates for the "sole and express purpose of revising the Articles of Confederation." The cautious legislators specified that no recommendation would be effective unless approved by Congress and confirmed by all the state legislatures, as provided by the Articles.

At this point, in the long American search for the right balance between liberty and order, between "pluribus" and "unum," between diversity and unity, the impulse was decidedly toward order and unity.

The Great Seal–1782

Constitution Flag–1789

The Philadelphia Convention, 1787

The delegates who assembled in Philadelphia that summer were presented with a condition, not a theory. They had to establish a national government powerful enough to prevent the nation from dissolving. What these men did continues to have a major impact on how we are governed. It also provides an outstanding lesson in political science.

THE DELEGATES

Seventy-four delegates were appointed by the various states, but only fifty-five arrived in Philadelphia. Of these, approximately forty took a real part in the work of the convention. It was a distinguished gathering. Many of the most important men of the nation were there: successful merchants, planters, bankers and lawyers, and former and present governors and congressional representatives (thirty-nine of the delegates had served in Congress). As theorists, most had read widely in the classics of political thought. As activists, most were interested in the practical task of constructing a national government.

The convention was as representative as most political gatherings at the time. Of course, there were no women or blacks. These well-read, well-fed, well-bred, and often well-wed delegates were mainly state or national leaders, for in the 1780s ordinary people were not likely to participate in politics. Even today farm laborers, factory workers, and truck drivers are seldom found in Congress, although a self-styled peanut farmer and a movie actor have made their way to the White House. While most of the leaders in attendance eventually supported the Constitution in the ratification debates, only eight of the fifty-six signers of the Declaration of Independence were present at the Constitutional Convention. Among those who did *not* come were Jefferson, Thomas Paine, Patrick Henry, Richard Henry Lee, Sam and John Adams, and John Hancock. Of the active participants at the convention, several men stand out as the prime movers.

Under the leadership of Daniel Shays, a group of farmers forcibly restrained the Massachusetts courts from foreclosing their mortgages. The uprising was known as Shays's Rebellion.

Alexander Hamilton had been the engineer of the Annapolis Convention, and as early as 1778 he had been urging that the national government be made stronger. Hamilton had come to the United States from the West Indies, and while still a student at Kings College (now Columbia University) had won national attention for his brilliant pamphlets in defense of the Revolutionary cause. During the war he served as General Washington's aide, and his experiences confirmed his distaste for a Congress so weak it could not even supply the Revolution's troops with enough food or arms.

From Virginia came two of the leading delegates: General George Washington and James Madison. Although active in the movement to revise the Articles of Confederation, Washington had been extremely reluctant to attend the convention. He accepted only when persuaded that his prestige was needed for its success. He was selected unanimously to preside over the meetings. According to the records, he spoke only twice during the deliberations, but his influence was felt in the informal gatherings as well as during the sessions. The assumption that Washington would become the first president under the new constitution inspired confidence in it. James Madison was only 36 years old at the time of the convention, but he was one of the most learned members present. He had helped frame Virginia's first constitution and had served both in the Virginia Assembly and in Congress. Madison was also a leader of those who favored the establishment of a strong national government.

The Pennsylvania delegation included Benjamin Franklin and Gouverneur Morris. Franklin, at 81, was the convention's oldest member and, as one of his fellow delegates said, "He is well known to be the greatest philosopher of the present age." Franklin enjoyed a world reputation unrivaled by that of any other American. Gouverneur Morris of Pennsylvania was more eloquent than brilliant. He addressed the convention more often than any other person. The elegance of the language of the Constitution is proof of his literary ability; he was responsible for the final draft.

Luther Martin of Maryland, John Dickinson of Delaware, and William Paterson of New Jersey did not agree with a majority of the delegates, but they ably defended the position that all states should have equal representation.

The proceedings of the convention were kept secret. In order to encourage everyone to speak freely, delegates were forbidden to discuss the debates with outsiders. It was feared that if a member publicly took a firm stand on an issue, it would be harder for him to change his mind after debate and discussion. Also the members knew that if word of the inevitable disagreements got out, it would provide ammunition for the many enemies of the convention. There were critics of this secrecy rule, but without it agreement might have been impossible.

Benjamin Franklin (1706–1790), early American statesman, writer, printer, scientist. Franklin helped draft the Declaration of Independence and served as a delegate to the Continental Congress, postmaster general, a diplomat, and a delegate to the 1787 Constitutional Convention. He served his country with distinction in its early days.

Washington presiding over the Constitutional Convention.

The **Constitutional Convention** is usually discussed in terms of three famous compromises: the compromise between large and small states over representation in Congress, the compromise between North and South over the counting of slaves for taxation and representation, and the compromise between North and South over the regulation and taxation of foreign commerce. But this emphasis obscures the fact that there were many other important compromises, and that on many of the more significant issues, most of the delegates were in agreement.

Although a few delegates might have personally favored a limited monarchy, all supported a republican form of government; and this was the only form seriously considered. It was, indeed, the only form that would be acceptable to the nation. Equally important, all the delegates were constitutionalists who opposed arbitrary and unrestrained government, in whatever form.

The common philosophy accepted by most of the delegates was that of *balanced government*. They wanted to construct a national government in which no single interest would dominate. Because the delegates represented those alarmed by the tendencies of desperate farmers to interfere with property, they were primarily concerned with balancing the government in the direction of protection for property and business. Most of them respected the remark of Elbridge Gerry (delegate from Massachusetts): "The evils we experience flow from the excess of democracy. The people do not want virtue, but are dupes of pretended patriots." Likewise, there was substantial agreement with Gouverneur Morris's statement that property was the "principal object of government."

Benjamin Franklin favored extending the right to vote to all white males but most of the delegates agreed that owners of land were the best guardians of liberty. James Madison voiced the fear that those without property, if given the right to vote, either would combine to deprive property owners of their rights or would become the "tools of **demagogues.**" The delegates agreed in principle on restricted suffrage, but differed over the kind and amount of property one must own in order to vote. Because the states were in the process of relaxing qualifications for the vote, the framers recognized they would jeopardize approval of the constitution if they made the federal **franchise** more restricted than the franchises within the states.[8] As a result, each state was left to determine the qualifications for electing members of the House of Representatives, the only branch of the national government in which the electorate was given a direct voice.

Within five days of its opening, the convention—with only Connecticut dissenting—voted to approve the Fourth Virginia Resolve, which stated that "a national government ought to be established consisting of a supreme legislative, executive, and judiciary." This decision to establish a national government resting on and exercising power over individuals profoundly altered the nature of the central government and changed it from a league of states to a national government.

Few dissented from proposals to give the new Congress all the powers of the old plus all other powers necessary to ensure that the harmony of the United States not be disrupted by the exercise of state legislation. The framers agreed that a strong executive, which had been lacking under the Articles, was necessary to provide energy and direction. An independent judiciary was also accepted without much debate. Franklin favored a single-house national legislature, but most states had had two-chamber legislatures since colonial times, and the delegates were used to the system. **Bicameralism**—the principle of the two-house legislature—also expressed the delegates' belief in the need for balanced government.

U.S. Population Growth, 1790–1990	
1790	3,929,214
1810	7,239,881
1830	12,860,692
1850	23,191,876
1870	38,558,371
1900	75,994,575
1920	105,710,620
1940	131,669,275
1960	179,323,175
1980	226,504,825
1990	250,000,000

One chamber would represent the aristocracy and offset the more democratic House of Representatives.

CONFLICT

There were serious differences among the various groups, especially between the representatives of the large states, who favored a strong national government (which they expected they could dominate), and the delegates from the small states, who were anxious to avoid being dominated. The Virginia delegation took the initiative. It had met during the delay before the convention and, as soon as the convention was organized, presented fifteen resolutions. These resolutions, the **Virginia Plan,** called for a strong central government. The legislature was to be composed of two chambers. The members of the more representative chamber were to be elected by the voters; those of the smaller and more aristocratic chamber were to be chosen by the larger chamber from nominees submitted by the state legislatures. Representation in both houses was to be on the basis of either wealth or numbers, which gave the more populous and wealthy states—Virginia, Massachusetts, and Pennsylvania—a majority in the national legislature.

The Congress thus created was to be given all the legislative power of its predecessor under the Articles of Confederation, as well as the right "to legislate in all cases in which the separate States are incompetent." Further, it was to have the authority to veto state legislation in conflict with the proposed constitution. The Virginia Plan also called for a national executive, to be chosen by the legislature, and a national judiciary with rather extensive jurisdiction. The national Supreme Court, along with the executive, was to have a qualified veto over acts of Congress.

For the first few weeks the Virginia Plan dominated the discussion. But by June 15 additional delegates from the small states had arrived, and they began to counterattack. They rallied around William Paterson of New Jersey, who presented a series of resolutions known as the **New Jersey Plan.** Paterson did not question the need for a greatly strengthened central government, but he was concerned about how this strength would be used. The New Jersey Plan would give Congress the right to tax and regulate commerce and to coerce states, but it would retain a single-house legislature in which all states, regardless of size, would have the same vote. The plan contained the germ of what eventually came to be a key provision of our Constitution: the *supremacy* clause. The national Supreme Court was to hear appeals from state judges, and the supremacy clause would require all the judges, state and national, to treat laws of the national government and the treaties of the United States as superior to the laws of each of the states.

Paterson maneuvered to force concessions from the larger states. He favored a strong central government, but not one the big states could control. Further, he raised the issue of practical politics; to adopt the Virginia Plan—which created a powerful national government dominated by Massachusetts, Virginia, and Pennsylvania and eliminated the states as important units of government—would guarantee defeat in the coming ratification struggle. But the large states resisted, and for a time the convention was deadlocked. The small states believed states should be represented equally in Congress, at least in the upper house. The large states insisted that representation in both houses be based on population or wealth, and that national legislators be elected by the voters rather than by state legislatures. Finally, a Committee of Eleven was elected to devise a compromise. On July 5 it presented its proposals.

Because of the prominent role of the Connecticut delegation, this plan has since been known as the **Connecticut Compromise.** It called for one house

"Remember, gentlemen, we aren't here just to draft a constitution. We're here to draft the best damned constitution in the world."

Drawing by Steiner, © 1982 The New Yorker Magazine, Inc.

The signing of the Constitution in Independence Hall, Philadelphia.

in which each state would have an equal vote, and a second house in which representation would be based on population and all bills for raising or appropriating money would originate. This was a setback for the large states, who agreed to it only when the smaller states made it clear that this was their price for union. After equality of representation in the Senate was accepted, most objections to establishing a strong national government dissolved.

Slavery was already an issue in 1787. The southern states wanted slaves to be counted in determining representation in the House of Representatives. It was finally agreed that a slave should count as three-fifths of a free person, both in determining representation in the House and apportioning direct taxes. Southerners were also fearful that a northern majority in Congress might discriminate against southern trade. They had some basis for this concern. John Jay, secretary of foreign affairs for the Confederation, had proposed a treaty with Great Britain that would have given advantages to northern merchants at the expense of southern exporters. To protect themselves, the southern delegates insisted that a two-thirds majority be required in the Senate before presidents could ratify treaties.

The delegates, of course, found other issues about which to argue. Should the national government have lower courts, or would one federal Supreme Court be enough? This issue was resolved by postponing the decision; the Constitution states that there *shall* be one Supreme Court and that Congress *may* establish inferior courts. How should the president be selected? For a long time the convention accepted the idea that the president should be elected by Congress. But it was feared either that Congress would dominate the president, or vice versa. Election by the state legislatures was rejected, because these bodies were distrusted. Finally, the electoral college system was devised. This was perhaps the most novel and contrived contribution of the delegates; today it is one of the most criticized provisions in the Constitution.

After three months the delegates stopped debating. On September 17, 1787, they assembled for the impressive ceremony of signing the document they were recommending to the nation. All but three of those still present signed; others who opposed the general drift of the convention had already left. Their work over, the delegates adjourned to the City Tavern to relax and celebrate a job well done.

THE FRAMERS: WHAT MANNER OF MEN?

Were the delegates an inspired group of men who cast aside all thoughts of self-interest? Were they motivated by the desire to save the nation or by the desire to save themselves? Was the convention the inevitable result of the weaknesses of the Articles? Was it a carefully maneuvered coup on the part of certain elites?

Was the difference between those who favored and those who opposed the Constitution mainly economic? Or was the difference mainly regional?

Students of history and government disagree on these and other questions. During the early part of our history, the members of the convention were the object of uncritical praise; the Constitution was the object of almost universal reverence. Early in the twentieth century a more critical attitude was inspired by J. Allen Smith and Charles A. Beard. Smith, in *The Spirit of American Government* (1911), painted the Constitution as the outgrowth of an antidemocratic reaction, almost a conspiracy, against the rule of majorities. Beard's thesis was that the Constitution represented the platform of the propertied groups who wanted to limit state legislatures and strengthen the national government as a means of protecting property. In his influential book, *An Economic Interpretation of the Constitution* (1913), Beard described the economic holdings of the delegates and argued that their support or opposition to the Constitution could best be explained in terms of their financial interests. He explicitly denied he was charging the founders with writing the Constitution for their personal benefit. Rather, he contended that individuals' political behavior reflects their broad economic interests.

Many, but not all, recent historical works have questioned the soundness of Beard's scholarship and interpretation. Some historians have pointed out that in 1787 there was no great propertyless mass in the United States.[9] Even the poor were interested in protecting property. The founders, they argue, were too smart politically to think they could get away with a plan designed merely to protect their own wealth—even if that had been their motive.[10] Certainly, they were anxious to build a strong national government so that it could promote economic growth. Such a government would win the support of all classes of people.[11] These historians contend that the political differences over the merits of the Constitution, just like political arguments today, cut through economic class divisions. The struggle, it is argued, was between differing **ideologies.**[12]

Political scientist Martin Diamond took issue with those who portray the Constitutional Convention as a reactionary attempt by aristocrats to curtail the brave democratic beginnings proclaimed in the Declaration of Independence. He called this interpretation the "conventional wisdom of those who give academic and intellectual opinions to the nation." "The fact is," he wrote, "the Declaration . . . is neutral on the questions of forms of government; any form is legitimate, provided it secures equal freedom and is instituted by popular consent." The framers of our Constitution gave us a democratic form of government. "Of course, the Founders," Diamond comments, "criticized the defects and dangers of democracy and did not waste much breath on the defects and dangers of the other forms of government. For a very good reason. They were not founding any other kind of government; they were establishing a democratic form, and it was the dangers peculiar to it against which all their efforts had to be bent."[13]

The various interpretations of the American Revolution and of the framing of the Constitution reflect changing styles of thought; current political debates are read backward, into our past. But the various interpretations also reflect the fact that "the American Revolution . . . was so complex and contained so many diverse and seemingly contradictory currents that it can support a wide variety of interpretations and may never be comprehended in full."[14]

Beard himself recognized that people are motivated by a complex of factors, both conscious and unconscious. Self-interest, economic or otherwise, and principles are inextricably mixed in human behavior. The founders were neither gods for whom self-interest or economic considerations were of no importance, nor selfish elitists who thought only in terms of their own pocketbooks. They were, by and large, aristocrats fearful of the masses, but committed to an aristocracy of merit, education, and accomplishment—not of birth or wealth. The framers wanted to protect the nation from aggression abroad and dissension at home. Stability and strength were needed not only to protect their own interests, but also to secure the unity and order necessary for the operation of a democracy.

On one point almost all students of the founding era are agreed: The framers offered in the Constitution perhaps the most brilliant example of collective intellectual genius—of combining both theory and practice—in the history of the Western world. How could an America seventy times smaller in population than today produce several dozen men of genius in Philadelphia, and probably another hundred or so equally talented political thinkers who did not attend? The lives of the two main authors of *The Federalist*, Alexander Hamilton and James Madison, help explain the origins of that collective genius.

Like most of the other framers, Hamilton and Madison were superbly educated. Both had extensive private tutoring—a "one-to-one teacher-student ratio." As a young man Hamilton had free access to a patron's library. A graduate of the famed University of Edinburgh drilled the early-teenage Madison in Greek, Latin, logic, and the whole Edinburgh curriculum. Both young men attended leading institutions of higher education: Hamilton at what is now Columbia, and Madison at what is now Princeton.[15]

Both men—again, like scores of other thinkers of the day—combined extensive practical experience with their schooling. Both were active in their political and religious groups; both took part in political contests and electoral struggles; both helped build political coalitions. Madison in particular saw much of the very political factions that he analyzed so brilliantly in *The Federalist*.

Both men were "moral philosophers" as well as political thinkers. They had strong views of the supreme value—liberty—as well as current issues. But instead of simply sermonizing about liberty, they *analyzed* it: They debated what *kind* of liberty, how to *protect* it, how to *expand* it. They also thought hard about other values enshrined in the Declaration of Independence, such as the virtues and dangers of equality and the nature of that "Happiness" Americans should pursue.

Finally, these men were "children of conflict." Because the stakes were so high—Hamilton and the others risked execution as traitors during the Revolution—every issue took on personal and passionate overtones. Thus their political and moral education was nourished by almost continuous controversy. After independence there was sharp conflict over state issues and elections. The question of *religious* liberty was also acute. In a neighboring county in Virginia the young Madison found some Baptists languishing in jail simply because they had opposed the established Church of England. "I shall not be silent," he promised the Baptists—and he was not.

Alexander Hamilton (1755–1804), Revolutionary leader, lawyer, aide to General Washington, delegate to the Constitutional Convention of 1787, author of many *Federalist* essays, and the leader of the Federalist party in its early years. Hamilton served for several years as President Washington's secretary of the treasury.

To Adopt or Not To Adopt?

The delegates had gone far. They had not hesitated to disregard Congress's instruction about ratification or to ignore Article XIII of the Articles of Confederation. This article declared the Union to be perpetual and prohibited any alteration in the Articles unless agreed to by Congress and *by every one of the state legislatures*, a provision that had made it impossible to amend the Articles. But the convention delegates boldly declared that the Constitution should go into effect when ratified by *popularly elected conventions in nine states*. They turned to this method of ratification for practical considerations and for reasons of principle. Not only were the delegates aware that there was little chance of securing approval of the new Constitution in all state legislatures, many also believed the Constitution should be ratified by an authority higher than a legislature. A constitution based on popular approval would have a higher legal and moral status. The Articles of Confederation had been a compact of state governments, but the Constitution was to be a "union of people."

Nevertheless, even this method of ratification would not be easy. The nation was not ready to adopt the Constitution without a thorough debate. The supporters of the new government, by cleverly appropriating the name **Federalists,** took some of the sting out of the charges that they were trying to destroy the states and establish an all-powerful central government. By calling their opponents **Antifederalists,** they pointed up the negative character of the arguments of those who opposed ratification.

The split was in part geographical. The seaboard and city regions tended to be Federalist strongholds. The vast back-country regions from Maine through Georgia, inhabited by farmers and other relatively poor people, were generally Antifederalist. But, as in most political contests, no single factor completely accounted for the division between Federalists and Antifederalists. For example, in Virginia the leaders of both sides came from the same general social and economic class. New York City and Philadelphia strongly supported the Constitution, but so did predominantly rural New Jersey.

The great debate was conducted with pamphlets, papers, letters to the editor, and speeches. The issues were important, but the argument, in the main, was carried on in a quiet and calm manner. Out of the debate came a series of essays, known as *The Federalist,* written by Alexander Hamilton, James Madison, and John Jay to persuade the voters of New York to ratify the Constitution. *The Federalist* is still "widely regarded as the most profound single treatise on the Constitution ever written and as among the few masterly works in political science produced in all the centuries of history."[16] [Three of the most important *Federalist* essays, Numbers 10, 51, and 78 are found in the Appendix of this book.] The great debate stands even today as an outstanding example of free people using the techniques of discussion and debate to determine the nature of their fundamental laws.

The Antifederalists' most telling criticism of the proposed Constitution was its failure to include a bill of rights.[17] The Federalists believed a bill of rights would be unnecessary. The general government had only delegated powers, and there was no need to specify that Congress could not, for example, abridge freedom of the press. It had no power to regulate the press. Moreover, the Federalists argued, to guarantee *some* rights might be dangerous, because it would then be thought that rights *not* listed could be denied. The Constitution already protected some important rights—trial by jury in federal criminal cases, for example. Hamilton and others also insisted that paper guarantees were weak reeds on which to depend for protection against governmental tyranny.

The Antifederalists were unconvinced. If some rights were protected, what could be the objection of providing constitutional protection for others? Without a bill of rights, what was to prevent Congress from using one of its delegated powers in such a manner that free speech would be abridged? If bills of rights were needed in state constitutions to limit state governments, why was one not needed in the national constitution to limit the national government? This was a government farther from the people and with a greater tendency, it was argued, to subvert natural rights. The Federalists, forced to concede, agreed to add a bill of rights if and when the new Constitution was approved.

The lack of a bill of rights in the proposed constitution dominated the struggle over its adoption. "There is no Declaration of Rights," was the first sentence of an attack on the document by Virginia delegate George Mason. We can assume that in taverns and church gatherings and newspaper offices up and down the Eastern seaboard people were muttering, "No bill of rights—no bill of rights."[18] So strong was this feeling that some Antifederalists who were far more concerned with *states'* rights than *individual* rights joined forces with Bill of Rights advocates in order to try to defeat the proposed constitution.

The Federalists were first off the mark in the struggle over the Constitution that opened as soon as the delegates left Philadelphia in mid-September 1787. The Federalists' immediate tactic was to secure ratification in as many states as possible before the opposition had time to organize. The Antifederalists were handicapped. They lacked access to the newspapers, most of which supported ratification. Their main strength was in the rural areas, underrepresented in some state legislatures and difficult to arouse to political action. They needed time to perfect their organization and collect their strength. The Federalists, composed of a more closely knit group of leaders throughout the colonies, moved in a hurry.

In most of the small states, now satisfied by equal Senate representation, ratification was gained without difficulty. Delaware was the first state to ratify. The first large state to take action was Pennsylvania. The Federalists presented the Constitution to the state legislature immediately after the Philadelphia convention adjourned in September 1787. But the legislature was about to adjourn, and the Antifederalist minority thought this was moving with too much haste (Congress had not even formally transmitted the document to the legislature for its consideration!). They wanted to postpone action until after the coming state elections, when they hoped to win a majority and so prevent calling a ratifying convention. When it became clear the Federalists were going to move ahead, the Antifederalists left the legislative chamber. Because the legislature was now two members short of a quorum, business was brought to a standstill. But Philadelphia, the seat of the legislature, was a Federalist stronghold. The next morning two Antifederalists were roused from their quarters, carried into the legislative chamber, and forced to remain. The resolution calling for election of delegates to a ratifying convention was adopted. Under the generalship of James Wilson, the Pennsylvania convention ratified by a vote of 46 to 23 in December 1787.

By early 1788 New Jersey, Georgia, and Connecticut had also ratified. There seemed to be few Americans, in the view of the grass-roots political observer Mercy Warren of Massachusetts, who did not "unite in the general wish for the restoration of public faith, the revival of commerce, arts, agriculture, and industry, under a lenient, peaceable and energetik government."[19] Reports were coming in from Massachusetts, however, that opposition was broadening, especially in the hinterland of the state. The position of such key leaders as John Hancock and Samuel Adams was in doubt. The debate in the ratifying convention in Boston pitched some of the most polished Federalist leaders against an array of eloquent but plain-spoken Antifederalists. The debate raged for most of January 1788 and into February. At times it looked as though the Constitution would lose, as Antifederalists raised the cry of "Why no Bill of Rights?" and other objections. But in the end the Constitution narrowly won out, 187 to 168.

The Federalists were elated, but in fact both sides had won. To gain votes for the Constitution, its advocates had had to make a deal—one of the most

Ratification of the Constitution

State	Date	Vote
Delaware	Dec. 7, 1787	Unani.
Pennsylvania	Dec. 12, 1787	46–23
New Jersey	Dec. 19, 1787	Unani.
Georgia	Jan. 2, 1788	Unani.
Connecticut	Jan. 9, 1788	128–40
Massachusetts	Feb. 6, 1788	187–168
Maryland	April 28, 1788	63–11
South Carolina	May 23, 1788	149–73
New Hampshire	June 21, 1788	57–47
Virginia	June 25, 1788	89–79
New York	July 26, 1788	30–27
North Carolina	Nov. 21, 1789	194–77
Rhode Island	May 29, 1790	34–32

Samuel Adams (1722–1803), Revolutionary leader, signer of the Declaration of Independence, and a major pamphleteer. Adams was the moving spirit behind the Boston Tea Party. Sometimes viewed as a radical, he nonetheless was elected governor of Massachusetts (1794–1797).

John Hancock (1737–1793), Revolutionary patriot and signer of the Declaration of Independence. Hancock served as president of the Continental Congress (1775–1777) and later as governor of Massachusetts, both before and after the ratification of the Constitution.

important compromises in American history. The Federalists adopted the strategy of accepting their opponents' most convincing argument—the lack of a bill of rights—and offered to add a bill of rights to the Constitution, but only *after* the new government under the Constitution was set up. Thus the Federalists sidetracked proposals for a *second* convention, which might have turned into a "runaway" gathering; and the Antis, led by such notables as Samuel Adams, won a promise for bill of rights amendments—a promise that was later honored by Madison and his fellow Federalist leaders. John Hancock, it was said, came over to the Federalist side after hints that he might be selected vice-president under the new government.

The struggle over the Constitution continued through the spring of 1788. By June 21st, Maryland, South Carolina, and New Hampshire had ratified, putting the Constitution over the top in the number (nine) required for ratification. But two big hurdles remained: Virginia and New York. Virginia was crucial, as the most populous state, the home of Washington and other heroes, a link between North and South. The Virginia ratifying convention rivaled the Constitutional Convention in the caliber of its delegates. Madison, who had only recently switched to a pro-bill of rights position after saying earlier it was unnecessary, captained the Federalist forces. The fiery Patrick Henry led the opposition. In an epic debate, Henry cried that liberty was the issue—"Liberty, the greatest of earthly possessions . . . that precious jewel!" But Madison quietly rebutted him and then played his trump card, a promise that a bill of rights embracing the freedoms of religion and speech and assembly would be added to the Constitution. At a critical moment Washington himself tipped the balance with a letter urging ratification. News of the Virginia vote, 89 to 79 for the charter, was rushed to New York.[20]

The great landowners along the Hudson, unlike their southern planter friends, were opposed to the Constitution. They feared federal taxation of their holdings, and they did not want to abolish the profitable tax New York had been levying on the trade and commerce of other states. When the convention assembled, the Federalists were greatly outnumbered, but they were aided by the strategy and skill of Hamilton and by word of Virginia's ratification. New York approved by a margin of three votes. Although North Carolina and Rhode Island still remained outside the Union (the former ratified in November 1789, and the latter six months later), the new nation was created. In New York a few members of the old Congress assembled to issue the call for elections under the new Constitution. Then Congress adjourned without setting a day for reconvening.

DRAFTING THE BILL OF RIGHTS

As we saw at the start of this chapter, Madison handsomely redeemed the Federalist promise that bill of rights amendments would be an early item of business for the new government. Rights advocates, however, had to wait for some time; over a year passed after New York's ratification, while the Senate and House opened for business, Washington took office, and the government dealt with immediate problems. Soon after that Madison was at work. It was a daunting task. The bill of rights advocates had sent in scores of proposed amendments and were pressing for action. But neither President Washington nor many members of Congress were very interested. And Madison had to operate through the cumbersome amendment process just established in the new Constitution. Counting on a groundswell of support to push the amendments through, Congress chose the amending process requiring two-thirds support in both House and Senate and endorsement by legislatures in three-quarters of the states.

CHAPTER 1 // Liberty and Order: The Grand Experiment

Madison moved step by step. First, he and other House leaders distilled a small group of amendments out of the huge pile of rights proposals. With immense patience and fine legislative skill, Madison steered amendments through the House, which sent them on to the Senate. The Senate made some changes, which meant that a joint **conference committee** had to be set up to iron out the differences. As chairman of the House conferees, Madison took a leading role in this phase, and then the agreed upon bill, consisting now of twelve amendments, had to go back to both houses for passage.

By then it was late September 1789, and the most difficult steps lay ahead— ratification by the necessary number of states. We do not have full information on this phase, for the amendments wound their way through the labyrinths of state legislatures. But somehow, with the united backing of many Federalists and Antifederalists, the amendments, now reduced to ten, were ratified by the end of 1791, with Virginia providing the final endorsement.

You will find the complete ten amendments in the copy of the Constitution later in this chapter. But nothing would be more appropriate, in concluding a discussion of the shaping of the Bill of Rights, than to quote here the first and foremost article of the "Big Ten," with its bold and absolute provisions:

> Congress shall make no law respecting an establishment of religion, or prohibiting the free exercise thereof; or abridging the freedom of speech, or of the press; or the right of the people peaceably to assemble, and to petition the Government for a redress of grievances.

Ratification of The Constitution by The States

Federalist (For)

Antifederalist (Against)

Divided

What Kind of Constitution?

By the end of 1791 the essence of the constitutional system was in place. Americans had achieved—at least for a time—the balance they wanted between order and liberty. The Constitution, framed in 1787 and ratified in 1788, established a firm, stable, orderly government. The Bill of Rights, drafted in 1789 and ratified as amendments by fall 1791, established the basic liberties of Americans against intrusion by the new federal government.

Two centuries later, during the bicentennials of these years, we are commemorating both the Constitution of 1787–88 and the Bill of Rights of 1789–91. Thus we are still celebrating the idea of a balance between liberty and order. But maintaining the balance is still a challenge. It calls not only for birthday celebrations with parades and fireworks, but also for continuing hard thought. Today's students, who can expect to live well into the twenty-first century, might ponder how well the balance of liberty and order—indeed, the whole constitutional system—will be working on the Constitution's *250th* anniversary.

This chapter, and those that follow, deal with key aspects of these and related problems, because a constitutional system embraces the whole range of laws, institutions, politics, and procedures that make up our political universe today. But two elements of the Constitution of 1787 are so crucial that they need to be highlighted at the very start: the division of powers between the national and state governments, and the separation of powers among the legislative, executive, and judicial branches.

Division of powers means **federalism.** Virtually all nations divide power between the central and regional governments. Federalism is unique because power is not granted by the central government to the states, and hence cannot be withdrawn from them. Rather, a *constitution* divides the powers, delegating

John Jay (1745–1829), a New York lawyer, diplomat, and author of five *Federalist* essays. He served at various times as president of the Continental Congress, peace negotiator with Britain, and secretary for foreign affairs during the last years of the Articles of Confederation; he was also the first chief justice of the United States.

some to the national government and reserving others to the states. This arrangement seems to work most of the time. But will it hold up during the twenty-first century under intense pressures to centralize authority in the national government?

Separation of powers means more than allocating legislative powers to the Congress, executive powers to the president, and judicial powers to the Supreme Court and other federal courts. It also means giving each branch constitutional and political *independence*, and *checks and balances* that allow the various branches to delay or block the actions of the other branches. This was the supreme creation of the framers in 1787. Although the concept was not new, the framers built the idea into a system of government so ingeniously that it has become a lasting and central part of our system. But again the question arises: Can a governmental system so divided cope with the challenges that lie ahead?

Most other democracies operate on a principle quite different from checks and balances—that of majority rule, through a parliamentary system. Typically, if one party or a coalition of parties wins a majority of seats in parliament, that majority wins control of the government. This has been true in essence of the (conservative) Thatcher government in Britain and the (socialist) Mitterand government in France. The victorious party, the majority party in the parliament, the cabinet, and the prime minister are fused together for joint decision and action, though of course there are many variations in practice.

Contrast the American system. It was carefully designed to delay or block majority action, for even though the framers wanted energetic and competent government, they did not want the "masses"—people like those led by Daniel Shays—to take control of the government. Thus, they fixed it so that a majority **faction** cannot govern just by winning control of the House of Representatives. Rather, such a faction must, in a series of elections, win control of the Senate and of the presidency—and perhaps ultimately of the Supreme Court. Further, countless antimajoritarian devices have subsequently been built into the system, for example, the right to **filibuster** bills to death in the Senate.

Is this the "government of the people, by the people, and for the people" that Lincoln celebrated in his Gettysburg address? Some critics contend that our constitutional system is fundamentally undemocratic, antimajoritarian, and antipopular, that the framers were elitists who deliberately designed a system to protect their property. Defenders of the system reply that in the long run the people do control their government. Congress, the presidency, and even the judiciary—in fact all the checks and balances—merely cushion the impact of popular demands and passions; they cannot ultimately prevent the public will from being carried out. Moreover, they claim, the system protects minority rights—and minority rights are just as important as majority rule.[21]

Obviously, questions need to be raised as we reappraise the Constitution. As we note, these questions involve some of our most basic goals and values, including liberty, equality, and justice. We can hardly hope today to match the wisdom of the framers, one of the most talented groups in Western history. But perhaps we can match their commitment to rigorous study and reasoned analysis. The first step is to define relevant terms with care.

A REPUBLIC OR A DEMOCRACY?

The American political system can be called either a constitutional republic or a constitutional democracy. Is there any real difference? The term *democracy* comes from two Greek roots: *demos*, the people, and *kratis*, authority. The word was used by the Athenians to mean government by the many, as contrasted with govern-

---

Constitutional Checks on Public Officials

Written constitution

Regular elections

Separation of powers

Federalism

Judicial review

Minority rights

Right to petition for redress of grievances

Impeachment process

Rule of law, making public officials subject to criminal prosecution

Freedom of the press to criticize public officials

Freedom of speech

Enumeration of powers

Doctrine of checks and balances

ment by the few (**oligarchy**) or by one (**autocracy**). At one time democracy meant only the kind of *direct* or *pure* democracy used in some Greek city-states, or in New England town meetings today, in which all citizens may take part in making laws. Today democracy is more likely to mean a **representative democracy**—or, in Plato's term, a *republic*—in which all the people do not actually make the laws or administer them but choose the ones who do.

The framers preferred to use the term *republic* to avoid any confusion with pure democracy. For them democracy meant mob rule and demagogues appealing to the "masses."

Here we define **democracy** or **republic** to mean a system of government in which those who have the authority to make decisions that have the force of law acquire and retain this authority either directly or indirectly as the result of winning free elections in which the great majority of adult citizens are allowed to participate.

CONSTITUTIONAL GOVERNMENT

Ours is not only a democratic system; it is a *constitutional* one as well. Although these two concepts are related, they are also different. Democracy refers to how power is *acquired* and *retained*. Constitutionalism refers to how power is *granted*, *dispersed*, and *limited*. A government can be constitutional without being democratic, as it was in seventeenth-century England. It can also be democratic without being constitutional, as it was in Athens at the time of Pericles. All governments have constitutions in the sense of agreed-upon ways by which they proceed. But the term **constitutional government** now has a more restricted meaning: government which enforces clearly recognized and regularly applied limits on the powers of those who govern. By this definition Great Britain, Canada, and the United States are constitutional democracies, but the Soviet Union is not, for there are few popular checks on the powers of Soviet rulers.

"When my distinguished colleague refers to the will of the 'people,' does he mean his people or my people?"

Drawing by Richter, © *1976 The New Yorker Magazine, Inc.*

Our founders created a system in which the first great safeguard against abuse of authority was to be reliance on the *people*—the democratic principle. But they also established a variety of checks on the power of officeholders, recognized and routinely enforced limits on what public officials—even those elected by the people—may do.

In the chapters that follow we look at our constitutional republic in greater detail. It is a complex system, difficult to describe and even harder to operate. Constitutional republics such as ours exist in only a few nations. Yet to democrats—or, if you prefer, to republicans—our system is precious because it is committed to protecting and expanding liberty. That commitment rests on certain fundamental convictions.

BASIC PREMISES OF DEMOCRACY

First, democrats recognize the fundamental dignity and importance of the *individual*. Individuals, democrats insist, have important rights, and, collectively, are the root source of legitimate governmental authority and power. These notions pervade all democratic thought. They are woven into the writings of Thomas Jefferson, especially in the Declaration of Independence: *All men are endowed by their Creator with certain unalienable rights.* Individualism makes the person—rich or poor, black or white, male or female—the *central* measure of value. The state, the union, and the corporation are measured in terms of their usefulness to individuals. Not everyone, of course, believes in putting the individual first. Some

April 1775	American Revolution begins at Lexington and Concord (Mass.)
June 1775	George Washington assumes command of Continental forces
July 1776	Declaration of Independence approved
Nov. 1777	Articles of Confederation adopted by Continental Congress
March 1781	Articles of Confederation ratified by the states
Oct. 1781	British defeated at Yorktown
April 1784	Congress ratifies Peace Treaty with British
Late 1786	Shays's Rebellion in western Massachusetts
May 1787	Constitutional Convention begins in Philadelphia
Sept. 1787	Constitution for United States adopted by Convention
June 1788	Constitution for United States ratified by nine states
Early 1789	First national elections
March 1789	United States Congress meets for the first time in New York
April 1789	George Washington inaugurated as first president
Sept. 1789	John Jay becomes first chief justice of the United States
Sept. 1789	Congress proposes Bill of Rights
Dec. 1791	Bill of Rights (first 10 amendments) ratified and becomes part of the U.S. Constitution

Note: It took about 15 years to win independence, form an interim government that tried to govern, fashion a "more perfect union," and actually get a three-branched government functioning.

believe in **statism,** considering the state supreme. Democrats, however, believe that the state, or even the community, is less important than the individuals who compose it.

Second, democrats recognize the right of each individual to be treated as a unique and inviolable human being. They do not insist that all are equal in talents or virtues; they do insist that one person's claim to life, liberty, and property must be recognized as much as another's. Although this right raises difficult questions about how equal rights can be secured, the *principle* of equality of right is clear.

Third, democrats are convinced that freedom is good in itself. *Liberty* or *freedom* (used interchangeably here) means that all individuals must have the opportunity to realize their own goals. The core of liberty is *self-determination*. Liberty is not simply the absence of external restraint on a person; it is the individual's power to act positively to reach his or her goals. Moreover, both history and reason suggest that individual liberty is the key to *social progress*. The greater people's freedom, the greater the chance of discovering better ways of life.

The basic values of democracy do not necessarily coexist happily in a particular society. The concept of individualism may conflict with the older tradition of public virtue and collective welfare—of the citizen as a participant in the general welfare. Freedom as the *liberation* of the individual may conflict with freedom as the *alienation* of people from friends or communities. Individual self-determination may conflict with collective decision making for the national welfare or the public good. The right of mill owners to run their factories as they please, as compared to the right of millhands in those factories to join unions or even to share in the running of the plants, illustrates this type of conflict in everyday life.

LIBERTY AND EQUALITY: DEMOCRATIC GOALS

Probably the single most powerful idea in American history has been that of liberty. It was for life, liberty, and the pursuit of happiness that independence was declared; it was to secure the blessings of liberty that the Constitution was drawn up and adopted. Consider our patriotic anthems: It is of the "sweet land of liberty" that we sing.

Liberty is a fuzzy as well as a compelling concept; much depends on how Americans define it as they make practical decisions. During the early decades of the republic, the American concept of liberty was essentially negative. The main aim of Jeffersonian democracy was to throw off the burdens of established governments, churches, and other institutions. These negative liberties were made explicit in the Bill of Rights of the Constitution, which granted free speech, free press, freedom of religion, and freedom of assembly. The main role of the Bill of Rights was to remove governmental constraints on individual liberties.

During most of the nineteenth century, liberty as "freedom *from*" meshed with the dominant economic and social doctrine of laissez faire. Under this doctrine individuals must be free of governments that might stop them from reaching maximum efficiency and productivity. The state, it was argued, must intervene no more than is absolutely necessary to protect life and property. Further intervention, in the form of minimum wages, health protection, or even compulsory vaccination, it was contended, is both immoral in theory and improper in fact. The idea is simple: The less governmental power, the more individual liberty.

But what did liberty (or freedom) mean when not governments but other

CHAPTER 1 // Liberty and Order: The Grand Experiment

individuals—employers, lynch mobs, plantation owners—deprived persons of this right? Slavery forced Americans to rethink their ideas. "The world has never had a good definition of the word liberty," Abraham Lincoln said during the Civil War, "and the American people, just now, are in want of one. We all declare for liberty; but in using the same word we do not all mean the same thing. With some the word liberty may mean for each man to do as he pleases with himself, and the product of his labor; while with others the same word may mean for some men to do as they please with other men. . . ."[22]

With the coming of industrialization, urbanization, and agrarian and labor discontent; of unions, depressions, and social protest; and of leaders like William Jennings Bryan, Theodore Roosevelt, Robert La Follette, Eugene Debs, and Woodrow Wilson, liberty came to have far more positive meanings. Americans slowly came to understand that men and women, crowded more and more together, lived amid webs of all kinds: personal and private, institutional and psychological. To abolish one type of restraint (such as black slavery) might mean increasing another type of restraint (such as wage slavery). To cut down on governmental restraint of liberty might simply mean increasing private economic and social power. The question was not simply how to liberate people from *government*; it was how to use government to free people from *non*governmental curbs on liberty as well.

But what about the idea of *equality*, next to liberty probably the most vital concept in American thought. "All men are created equal and from that equal creation they derive rights inherent and unalienable, among which are the preservation of liberty and the pursuit of happiness." So read Jefferson's first draft of the Declaration, and the words indicate the primacy of the concept. Alexis de Tocqueville, James Bryce, Harold Laski, and other foreigners who investigated American democracy were struck by the strength of egalitarian thought and practice in both our political and social lives.

What did equality mean? What *kind* of equality? Economic, political, legal, social, or something else? Equality for *whom*? For blacks as well as whites? For children and teenagers as well as adults? Equality of *opportunity*—almost all Americans said they wanted that—but also of *condition*? This last question was the toughest. Did equality of opportunity simply mean that everyone should have the *same place at the starting line*? Or did it mean that an effort should be made to equalize most or all the factors that during the course of a person's life might determine how well he or she would fare socially or economically? (See also Chapter 5.)

Herbert Hoover posed the issue when he said: "We, through free and universal education, provide the training of the runners; we give to them an equal start; we provide in government the umpire of fairness in the race. . . ."[23] Franklin D. Roosevelt sought to answer the question when he proclaimed first the **Four Freedoms**—freedom from *want* and *fear* as well as freedom of speech and religion—and later a "second Bill of Rights." Under this second bill of rights, he said, Americans accepted the idea that a new basis of security and prosperity could be established for all, regardless of position, race, or creed. This meant good housing, health, jobs, and social security for all. The New Deal and its successor programs, in both their achievements and failures, have tried to advance the egalitarian intentions of the second bill of rights.

Thus, two concepts once considered opposites have coalesced into a philosophy that calls for government to help broaden people's *social* and *economic* liberties while it prevents other institutions (corporations or unions or landlords) from infringing on those liberties. At the same time, the government must prevent *itself* from interfering with liberty. This is no small task, and it is not always

---

What Are Our Basic American Values?

*GOALS**
Liberty
Personal freedom
Dignity of the individual
Property rights
Equality before the law
Equality of opportunity
An open society
Justice

MEANS
Constitutionalism
Representative processes
Free and frequent elections
Majority rule, minority rights
Checks and balances
Bill of Rights
Federalism
Separation of powers
Due process
Judicial review

* Not everyone agrees on these goals, and people naturally weigh them differently according to their own values. How would you rank these goals? Would you elevate some of what we label as "means" to "goals"? A nation's values plainly have much to do with what kinds of processes, institutions, and political practices are encouraged and sustained.

On September 17, 1787, after four months of heated debate, all but three of the delegates to the Constitutional Convention signed their names to the constitution they had prepared. While they were doing so, Benjamin Franklin, pointing out the rising sun painted on the back of the president's chair, observed that painters had found it difficult to distinguish, in their art, a rising from a setting sun.

"I have," said he, "often, and often in the course of the session, and the vicissitudes of my hopes and fears as to its issue, looked at that sun behind the president, without being able to tell whether it was a rising or setting; but now, at length, I have the happiness to know that it is rising and not a setting sun."

More than two hundred years later the Constitution they wrote—amended only twenty-six times—remains the operating charter of our Republic. It is neither self-explanatory nor a comprehensive description of our constitutional rules. Still, it remains the starting point. Yet many Americans who swear by the Constitution have never read it. Copies can be found in the backs of most American government and American history textbooks, but who reads an appendix? (We hope, incidentally, that *you* will do so, for the appendix in this text contains three great essays written to explain and defend the Constitution: *The Federalist*, Nos. 10, 51, and 78.)

Justice Hugo Black, who served on the Supreme Court for thirty-four years, kept a copy of the Constitution with him at all times. He read it often. We think that, especially in this Bicentennial era, reading the Constitution as amended would be a good way for you to begin (and end) your study of the government of the United States. Thus, we have included a copy of it at this point in the book. Please read it carefully.

performed well—but the idea is exciting. It means that Americans, perhaps without being wholly conscious of it, have brought together the values of liberty and equality. No longer can we say flatly: "The more government, the less liberty"; yet neither can we say the opposite.

Liberty and equality interlock and stimulate each other at some points, and oppose each other at others. Sometimes they do not relate at all. Pushed too far, liberty could become license and unbridled individualism, and equality could mean leveling, a dull mediocrity, and even the erosion of liberty. Much of our political combat revolves around how to strike a balance.

DEMOCRACY AS POLITICAL MEANS

Some favor democracy not only because they believe it stands for such goals as liberty and equality but also because they see it as the best way to govern a complex society. Those who admire democracy for the human ends it represents are called **principle democrats;** those who consider democracy a technique of self-government are called **process democrats.** Process democrats grant that democratic processes do not guarantee justice will be done, but they contend the chances are better under "government by the people" than under any other system. Note what is *not* included in the concept of democracy as a process for making decisions: Process democrats do not judge a democracy by its policy output; their concern is with the *procedures* for making policy, and not with the rightness of the policy that is made.

Process democrats contend that government *by* the people usually produces government *for* the people. They reject the notion that it is possible to define the public interest "scientifically." If one believes, as did Plato, that decisions about public policy are of the same nature as, say, decisions about how to build a boat, then the best way to make policy is to turn everything over to a group of specialists or experts. Then, like Plato, one would favor a system that places authority in the hands of philosopher-kings or, in today's terms, in the hands of the "best and the brightest." Process democrats, on the other hand, take their stand with Aristotle, who argued that although bakers know best how to bake a cake, people who eat the cake are the better judges of how it tastes.

Most Americans do not trust experts very much. As President Dwight Eisenhower stated in his farewell address: "Yet in holding scientific research and discovery in respect, as we should, we must also be alert to the equal and opposite danger that public policy could itself become the captive of a scientific-technological elite." Few democrats—especially process democrats—wish to shift the control of our destinies from voters and their elected leaders to some new priesthood of policy analysts.

FUNDAMENTAL DEMOCRATIC PROCESSES

The crucial mechanism in all genuinely popular governments is a system of free, fair, and open elections. Democratic governments take many different forms, but democratic elections have at least four essential elements:

1. *All citizens should have equal voting power*. This does not mean that all must or will have equal political influence. Some persons, because of wealth, talent, or position, have much more power than others. How much extra

The Constitution of the United States of America

THE PREAMBLE

We the People of the United States, in Order to form a more perfect Union, establish Justice, insure domestic Tranquility, provide for the common defence, promote the general Welfare, and secure the Blessings of Liberty to ourselves and our Posterity, do ordain and establish this Constitution for the United States of America.

ARTICLE I—THE LEGISLATIVE ARTICLE

Legislative Power

Section 1 All legislative Powers herein granted shall be vested in a Congress of the United States, which shall consist of a Senate and House of Representatives.

House of Representatives: Composition; Qualifications; Apportionment; Impeachment Power

Section 2 The House of Representatives shall be composed of Members chosen every second Year by the People of the several States, and the Electors in each State shall have the Qualifications requisite for Electors of the most numerous Branch of the State Legislature.

No Person shall be a Representative who shall not have attained to the Age of twenty five Years, and been seven Years a Citizen of the United States, and who shall not, when elected, be an Inhabitant of that State in which he shall be chosen.

Representatives and direct Taxes[1] shall be apportioned among the several States which may be included within this Union, according to their respective Numbers, *which shall be determined by adding to the whole Number of free Persons, including those bound to Service for a Term of Years, and excluding Indians not taxed, three fifths of all other Persons.*[2] The actual Enumeration shall be made within three Years after the first Meeting of the Congress of the United States, and within every subsequent Term of ten Years, in such Manner as they shall by Law direct. The Number of Representatives shall not exceed one for every thirty Thousand, but each State shall have at least one Representative; and until each enumeration shall be made, the State of New Hampshire shall be entitled to chuse three, Massachusetts eight, Rhode-Island and Providence Plantations one, Connecticut five, New-York six, New Jersey four, Pennsylvania eight, Delaware one, Maryland six, Virginia ten, North Carolina five, South Carolina five, and Georgia three.

When vacancies happen in the Representation from any State, the Executive Authority thereof shall issue Writs of Election to fill such Vacancies.

The House of Representatives shall chuse their Speaker and other Officers; and shall have the sole Power of Impeachment.

Senate Composition: Qualifications, Impeachment Trials

Section 3 The Senate of the United States shall be composed of two Senators from each State, *chosen by the Legislature thereof,*[3] for six Years; and each Senator shall have one Vote.

Immediately after they shall be assembled in Consequence of the first Election, they shall be divided as equally as may be into three Classes. The Seats of the Senators of the first Class shall be vacated at the Expiration of the second Year, of the second Class at the Expiration of the fourth Year, and of the third Class at the Expiration of the sixth Year, so that one third may be chosen every second Year; *and if Vacancies happen by Resignation, or otherwise, during the Recess of the Legislature of any State, the Executive thereof may make temporary Appointments until the next Meeting of the Legislature, which shall then fill such Vacancies.*[4]

No person shall be a Senator who shall not have attained to the Age of thirty Years, and been nine Years a Citizen of the United States, and who shall not, when elected, be an inhabitant of that State for which he shall be chosen.

The Vice President of the United States shall be President of the Senate, but shall have no Vote, unless they be equally divided.

The Senate shall chuse their other Officers, and also a President pro tempore, in the Absence of the Vice President, or when he shall exercise the Office of President of the United States.

The Senate shall have the sole Power to try all Impeachments. When sitting for that Purpose, they shall be on Oath or Affirmation. When the President of the United States is tried, the Chief Justice shall preside: And no Person shall be convicted without the Concurrence of two thirds of the Members present.

Judgment in Cases of Impeachment shall not extend further than to removal from Office, and disqualification to hold and enjoy any Office of honor, Trust or Profit under the United States; but the Party convicted shall nevertheless be liable and

[1]Modified by the 16th Amendment
[2]"Other Persons" refers to black slaves. Replaced by Section 2, 14th Amendment
[3]Repealed by the 17th Amendment
[4]Modified by the 17th Amendment

subject to Indictment, Trial, Judgment and Punishment, according to law.

Congressional Elections: Times, Places, Manner

Section 4 The Times, Places and Manner of holding Elections for Senators and Representatives, shall be prescribed in each State by the Legislature thereof; but the Congress may at any time by Law make or alter such Regulations, except as to the Places of chusing Senators.

The Congress shall assemble at least once in every Year, *and such Meeting shall be on the first Monday in December, unless they shall by Law appoint a different Day.*[5]

Powers and Duties of the Houses

Section 5 Each House shall be the Judge of the Elections, Returns and Qualifications of its own Members, and a Majority of each shall constitute a Quorum to do Business; but a smaller Number may adjourn from day to day, and may be authorized to compel the Attendance of absent Members, in such Manner, and under the Penalties as each House may provide.

Each House may determine the Rules of its Proceedings, punish its Members for disorderly Behaviour, and, with the Concurrence of two thirds, expel a Member.

Each House shall keep a Journal of its Proceedings, and from time to time publish the same, excepting such Parts as may in their Judgment require Secrecy; and the yeas and Nays of the Members of either House on any question shall, at the Desire of one fifth of those Present, be entered on the Journal.

Neither House, during the Session of Congress, shall, without the Consent of the other, adjourn for more than three days, nor to any other place than that in which the two Houses shall be sitting.

Rights of Members

Section 6 The Senators and Representatives shall receive a Compensation for their Services, to be ascertained by Law, and paid out of the Treasury of the United States. They shall in all Cases, except Treason, Felony and Breach of the Peace, be privileged from Arrest during their Attendance at the Session of their respective Houses, and in going to and returning from the same; and for any Speech or Debate in either House, they shall not be questioned in any other Place.

No Senator or Representative, shall, during the time for which he was elected, be appointed to any civil Office under the authority of the United States, which shall have been created, or the Emoluments whereof shall have been encreased during such time; and no Person holding any Office under the United States, shall be a Member of either House during his Continuance in Office.

Legislative Powers: Bills and Resolutions

Section 7 All Bills for raising Revenue shall originate in the House of Representatives; but the Senate may propose or concur with Amendments as on other Bills.

Every Bill which shall have passed the House of Representatives and the Senate, shall, before it become a Law, be presented to the President of the United States; if he approve he shall sign it, but if not he shall return it, with his Objections to that House in which it shall have originated, who shall enter the Objections at large on their Journal, and proceed to reconsider

[5]Changed by the 20th Amendment

it. If after such Reconsideration two thirds of that House shall agree to pass the Bill, it shall be sent, together with the Objections, to the other House, by which it shall likewise be reconsidered, and if approved by two thirds of that House, it shall become a Law. But in all such Cases the Votes of both Houses shall be determined by yeas and Nays, and the Names of the Persons voting for and against the Bill shall be entered on the Journal of each House respectively. If any Bill shall not be returned by the President within ten Days (Sundays excepted) after it shall have been presented to him, the Same shall be a Law, in like Manner as if he had signed it, unless the Congress by their Adjournment prevent its Return, in which Case it shall not be a Law.

Every Order, Resolution, or Vote to which the Concurrence of the Senate and House of Representatives may be necessary (except on a question of Adjournment) shall be presented to the President of the United States; and before the Same shall take Effect, shall be approved by him, or being disapproved by him, shall be repassed by two thirds of the Senate and House of Representatives, according to the Rules and Limitations prescribed in the Case of a Bill.

Powers of Congress

Section 8 The Congress shall have Power To lay and collect Taxes, Duties, Imposts and Excises, to pay the Debts and provide for the common Defence and general Welfare of the United States; but all Duties, Imposts and Excises shall be uniform throughout the United States;

To borrow Money on the Credit of the United States;

To regulate Commerce with foreign Nations, and among the several States, and with the Indian Tribes;

To establish an uniform Rule of Naturalization, and uniform Laws on the subject of Bankruptcies throughout the United States;

To coin Money, regulate the Value thereof, and of foreign Coin, and fix the Standard of Weights and Measures;

To provide for the Punishment of counterfeiting the Securities and current Coin of the United States;

To establish Post Offices and post Roads;

To promote the Progress of Science and useful Arts, by securing for limited Times to Authors and Inventors the exclusive Right to their respective Writings and Discoveries,

To constitute Tribunals inferior to the supreme Court,

To define and punish Piracies and Felonies committed on the high Seas, and Offences against the Law of Nations;

To declare War, grant Letters of Marque and Reprisal, and make Rules concerning Captures on Land and Water;

To raise and support Armies, but no Appropriation of Money to that Use shall be for a longer Term than two Years;

To provide and maintain a Navy;

To make Rules for the Government and Regulation of the land and naval Forces;

To provide for calling for the Militia to execute the Laws of the Union, suppress Insurrections and repel Invasions;

To provide for organizing, arming, and disciplining, the Militia, and for governing such Part of them as may be employed in the Service of the United States, reserving to the States respectively, the Appointment of the Officers, and the Authority of training the Militia according to the discipline prescribed by Congress;

To exercise exclusive Legislation in all Cases whatsoever, over such District (not exceeding ten Miles square) as may, by

Cession of particular States, and the Acceptance of Congress, become the Seat of the Government of the United States, and to exercise like Authority over all Places purchased by the Consent of the Legislature of the State in which the Same shall be, for the Erection of Forts, Magazines, Arsenals, dock-Yards, and other needful Buildings;—And

To make all Laws which shall be necessary and proper for carrying into Execution the foregoing Powers, and all other Powers vested by this Constitution in the Government of the United States, or in any Department or Officer thereof.

Powers Denied to Congress

Section 9 The Migration or Importation of such Persons as any of the States now existing shall think proper to admit, shall not be prohibited by the Congress prior to the Year one thousand eight hundred and eight, but a Tax or Duty may be imposed on such Importation, not exceeding ten dollars for each Person.

The privilege of the Writ of Habeas Corpus shall not be suspended, unless when in Cases of Rebellion or Invasion the public Safety may require it.

No Bill of Attainder or ex post facto Laws shall be passed.

No Capitation, or other direct, Tax shall be laid, unless in Proportion to the Census or Enumeration herein before directed to be taken.[6]

No Tax or Duty shall be laid on Articles exported from any State.

No Preference shall be given by any Regulation of Commerce or Revenue to the Ports of one State over those of another; nor shall Vessels bound to, or from, one State, be obliged to enter, clear, or pay Duties in another.

No Money shall be drawn from the Treasury, but in Consequence of Appropriations made by Law; and a regular Statement and Account of the Receipts and Expenditures of all public Money shall be published from time to time.

No Title of Nobility shall be granted by the United States; And no Person holding any Office of Profit or Trust under them, shall, without the Consent of the Congress, accept of any present, Emolument, Office, or Title, of any kind whatever, from any King, Prince, or foreign State.

Powers Denied to the States

Section 10 No State shall enter into any Treaty, Alliance, or Confederation; grant Letters of Marque and Reprisal; coin Money; emit Bills of Credit; make any Thing but gold and silver Coin a Tender in Payment of Debts; pass any Bill of Attainder, ex post facto Law, or Law impairing the Obligation of Contracts, or grant any Title of Nobility.

No State shall, without the Consent of the Congress, lay any Imposts or Duties on Imports or Exports, except what may be absolutely necessary for executing it's inspection Laws: and the net Produce of all Duties and Imposts, laid by any State on Imports or Exports, shall be for the Use of the Treasury of the United States; and all such Laws shall be subject to the Revision and Controul of the Congress.

No State shall, without the Consent of Congress, lay any Duty of Tonnage, keep Troops, or Ships of War in time of Peace, enter into any Agreement or Compact with another State, or with a foreign Power, or engage in War, unless actually invaded, or in such imminent Danger as will not admit of Delay.

[6]Modified by the 16th Amendment

ARTICLE II—THE EXECUTIVE ARTICLE
Nature and Scope of Presidential Power

Section 1 The executive Power shall be vested in a President of the United States of America. He shall hold his Office during the Term of four Years and, together with the Vice President, chosen for the same Term, be elected as follows

Each State shall appoint, in such Manner as the Legislature thereof may direct, a Number of Electors, equal to the whole Number of Senators and Representatives to which the State may be entitled in the Congress: but no Senator or Representative, or Person holding an Office of Trust or Profit under the United States, shall be appointed an Elector.

The Electors shall meet in their respective States, and vote by Ballot for two Persons, of whom one at least shall not be an Inhabitant of the same State with themselves. And they shall make a List of all the Persons voted for, and of the Number of Votes for each; which List they shall sign and certify, and transmit sealed to the Seat of the Government of the United States, directed to the President of the Senate. The President of the Senate shall, in the Presence of the Senate and House of Representatives, open all the Certificates, and the Votes shall then be counted. The Person having the greatest Number of Votes shall be the President, if such Number be a Majority of the whole Number of Electors appointed; and if there be more than one who have such Majority and have an equal Number of Votes, then the House of Representatives shall immediately chuse by Ballot one of them for President; and if no person have a Majority, then from the five highest on the List the said House shall in like Manner chuse the President. But in chusing the President, the Votes shall be taken by States, the Representation from each State having one Vote; A quorum for this Purpose shall consist of a Member or Members from two thirds of the States, and a Majority of all the States shall be necessary to a Choice. In every Case, after the Choice of the President, the person having the greatest Number of Votes of the Electors shall be the Vice President. But if there should remain two or more who have equal Vote, the Senate shall chuse from them by Ballot the Vice President.[7]

The Congress may determine the Time of chusing the Electors, and the Day on which they shall give their Votes; which Day shall be the same throughout the United States.

No Person except a natural born Citizen, or a Citizen of the United States, at the time of the Adoption of this Constitution, shall be eligible to the Office of President; neither shall any Person be eligible to that Office who shall not have attained to the Age of thirty five Years, and been fourteen Years a Resident within the United States.

In Case of the Removal of the President from Office, or of his Death, Resignation, or Inability to discharge the Powers and Duties of the said Office, the same shall devolve on the Vice President, and the Congress may by Law provide for the Case of Removal, Death, Resignation, or Inability, both of the President and Vice President, declaring what Officer shall then act as President, and such Officer shall act accordingly, until the Disability be removed, or a President shall be elected.[8]

The President shall, at stated Times, receive for his Services, a Compensation, which shall neither be encreased nor diminished during the Period of which he shall have been elected, and he shall not receive within that Period any other Emolument from the United States, or any of them.

[7]Changed by the 12th and 20th Amendments
[8]Modified by the 25th Amendment

Before he enter on the Execution of his Office, he shall take the following Oath or Affirmation:—"I do solemnly swear (or affirm) that I will faithfully execute the Office of President of the United States, and will to the best of my Ability, preserve, protect and defend the Constitution of the United States."

Powers and Duties of the President

Section 2 The President shall be the Commander in Chief of the Army and Navy of the United States, and of the Militia of the several States, when called into the actual Service of the United States, he may require the Opinion, in writing, of the principal Officer in each of the executive Departments, upon any Subject relating to the Duties of their respective Offices, and he shall have the Power to grant Reprieves and Pardons for Offences against the United States, except in Cases of Impeachment.

He shall have Power, by and with the Advice and Consent of the Senate to make Treaties, provided two thirds of the Senators present concur; and he shall nominate, and by and with the Advice and Consent of the Senate, shall appoint Ambassadors, other public Ministers and Consuls, Judges of the supreme Court, and all other Officers of the United States, whose Appointments are not herein otherwise provided for, and which shall be established by Law: but the Congress may by Law vest the Appointment of such inferior Officers, as they think proper, in the President alone, in the Courts of Law, or in the Heads of Departments.

The President shall have Power to fill up all Vacancies that may happen during the Recess of the Senate, by granting Commissions which shall expire at the End of their next Session.

Section 3 He shall from time to time give to the Congress Information of the State of the Union, and recommend to their Consideration such Measures as he shall judge necessary and expedient; he may, on extraordinary Occasions, convene both Houses, or either of them, and in Case of Disagreement between them, with Respect to the Time of Adjournment, he may adjourn them to such Time as he shall think proper; he shall receive Ambassadors and other public Ministers; he shall take Care that the Laws be faithfully executed, and shall Commission all the Officers of the United States.

Section 4 The President, Vice President and all civil Officers of the United States, shall be removed from Office on Impeachment for, and Conviction of, Treason, Bribery, or other High Crimes and Misdemeanors.

ARTICLE III—THE JUDICIAL ARTICLE

Judicial Power, Courts, Judges

Section 1 The judicial Power of the United States, shall be vested in one supreme Court, and in such inferior Courts as the Congress may from time to time ordain and establish. The Judges, both of the supreme and inferior Courts, shall hold their Offices during good Behaviour, and shall, at stated Times, receive for their Services, a Compensation, which shall not be diminished during their Continuance in Office.

Jurisdiction

Section 2 The judicial Power shall extend to all Cases, in Law and Equity, arising under this Constitution, the Laws of the United States, and Treaties made, or which shall be made, under their Authority;—to all Cases affecting Ambassadors, other public Ministers and Consuls;—to all Cases of admiralty and maritime Jurisdiction;—to Controversies to which the United States shall be a Party;—to Controversies between two or more States; *between a State and Citizens of another State;*[9]—between Citizens of different States;—between Citizens of the same State claiming Lands under Grants of different States, and between a State, or the Citizens thereof, and foreign States, Citizens, or Subjects.

In all Cases affecting Ambassadors, other public Ministers and Consuls, and those in which a State shall be Party, the supreme Court shall have original Jurisdiction. In all the other Cases before mentioned, the supreme Court shall have appellate Jurisdiction, both as to Law and Fact, with such Exceptions, and under such Regulations as Congress shall make.

The Trial of all Crimes, except in Cases of Impeachment, shall be by Jury; and such Trial shall be held in the State where the said Crimes shall have been committed; but when not committed within any State, the Trial shall be at such Place or Places as the Congress may by Law have directed.

Treason

Section 3 Treason against the United States, shall consist only in levying War against them, or in adhering to their Enemies, giving them Aid and Comfort. No Person shall be convicted of Treason unless on the Testimony of two Witnesses to the same overt Act, or on Confession in open Court.

The Congress shall have Power to declare the Punishment of Treason, but no Attainder of Treason shall work Corruption of Blood, or Forfeiture except during the Life of the Person attainted.

ARTICLE IV—INTERSTATE RELATIONS

Full Faith and Credit Clause

Section 1 Full Faith and Credit shall be given in each State to the public Acts, Records, and judicial Proceedings of every other State. And the Congress may by general Laws prescribe the Manner in which such Acts, Records and Proceedings shall be proved, and the Effect thereof.

Privileges and Immunities; Interstate Extradition

Section 2 The Citizens of each State shall be entitled to all Privileges and Immunities of Citizens in the several States.

A person charged in any State with Treason, Felony or other Crime, who shall flee from Justice, and be found in another State, shall on Demand of the executive Authority of the State from which he fled, be delivered up to be removed to the State having jurisdiction of the Crime.

No person held to Service or Labour in one State, under the Laws thereof, escaping into another, shall, in Consequence of any Law or Regulation therein, be discharged from such Service or Labour, but shall be delivered up on on Claim of the Party to whom such Service or Labour may be due.[10]

Admission of States

Section 3 New States may be admitted by the Congress into this Union; but no new State shall be formed or erected within the Jurisdiction of any other State; nor any State be formed by

[9]Modified by the 11th Amendment
[10]Repealed by the 13th Amendment

the Junction of two or more States, or Parts of States, without the Consent of the Legislatures of the States concerned as well as of the Congress.

The Congress shall have Power to dispose of and make all needful Rules and Regulations respecting the Territory or other Property belonging to the United States; and nothing in this Constitution shall be so construed as to Prejudice any Claims of the United States, or of any particular State.

Republican Form of Government

Section 4 The United States shall guarantee to every State in this Union a Republican Form of Government, and shall protect each of them against Invasion; and on Application of the Legislature, or of the Executive (when the Legislature cannot be convened) against domestic Violence.

ARTICLE V—THE AMENDING POWER

The Congress, whenever two thirds of both Houses shall deem it necessary, shall propose Amendments to this Constitution, or, on the Application of the Legislatures of two thirds of several States, shall call a Convention for proposing Amendments, which, in either Case, shall be valid to all Intents and Purposes, as Part of this Constitution, when ratified by the Legislatures of three fourths of the several States, or by Conventions in three fourths thereof, as the one or the other Mode of Ratification may be proposed by the Congress; Provided that no Amendment which may be made prior to the Year One thousand eight hundred and eight shall in any Manner affect the first and fourth Clauses in the Ninth Section of the first Article; and that no State, without its Consent, shall be deprived of its equal Suffrage in the Senate.

ARTICLE VI—THE SUPREMACY ACT

All Debts contracted and Engagements entered into, before the Adoption of this Constitution, shall be as valid against the United States under the Constitution, as under the Confederation.

This Constitution, and the Laws of the United States which shall be made in Pursuance thereof; and all Treaties made, or which shall be made, under the Authority of the United States, shall be the supreme Law of the Land; and the Judges in every State shall be bound thereby, any Thing in the Constitution or Laws of any State to the Contrary notwithstanding.

The Senators and Representatives before mentioned, and the Members of the several State Legislatures, and all executive and judicial Officers, both of the United States and of the several States, shall be bound by Oath or Affirmation, to support this Constitution; but no religious Test shall ever be required as a Qualification to any Office or public Trust under the United States.

ARTICLE VII—RATIFICATION

The Ratification of the Conventions of nine States, shall be sufficient for the Establishment of this Constitution between the States so ratifying the Same.

done in Convention by the Unanimous Consent of the States present the Seventeenth Day of September in the Year of our Lord one thousand seven hundred and Eighty seven and of the Independence of the United States of America the Twelfth. *In Witness whereof We have hereunto subscribed our Names.*

THE BILL OF RIGHTS

[The first ten amendments were ratified on December 15, 1791, and form what is known as the "Bill of Rights"]

AMENDMENT 1—RELIGION, SPEECH, ASSEMBLY, AND POLITICS

Congress shall make no law respecting an establishment of religion, or prohibiting the free exercise thereof; or abridging the freedom of speech, or of the press; or the right of the people peaceably to assemble, and to petition the Government for a redress of grievances.

AMENDMENT 2—MILITIA AND THE RIGHT TO BEAR ARMS

A well regulated Militia, being necessary to the security of a free State, the right of the people to keep and bear Arms, shall not be infringed.

AMENDMENT 3—QUARTERING OF SOLDIERS

No Soldier shall, in time of peace be quartered in any house, without the consent of the Owner, nor in time of war, but in manner to be prescribed by law.

AMENDMENT 4—SEARCHES AND SEIZURES

The right of the people to be secure in their persons, houses, papers, and effects, against unreasonable searches and seizures, shall not be violated, and no Warrants shall issue, but upon probable cause, supported by Oath or affirmation, and particularly describing the place to be searched, and the persons or things to be seized.

AMENDMENT 5—GRAND JURIES, SELF-INCRIMINATION, DOUBLE JEOPARDY, DUE PROCESS, AND EMINENT DOMAIN

No person shall be held to answer for a capital, or otherwise infamous crime, unless on a presentment or indictment of a Grand jury, except in cases arising in the land or naval forces, or in the Militia, when in actual service in time of War or public danger; nor shall any person be subject for the same offence to be twice put in jeopardy of life or limb; nor shall be compelled in any criminal case to be a witness against himself, nor be deprived of life, liberty, or property, without due process of law; nor shall private property be taken for public use, without just compensation.

AMENDMENT 6—CRIMINAL COURT PROCEDURES

In all criminal prosecutions, the accused shall enjoy the right to a speedy and public trial, by an impartial jury of the State and district wherein the crime shall have been committed, which district shall have been previously ascertained by law, and to be informed of the nature and cause of the accusation; to be confronted with the witnesses against him; to have compulsory process for obtaining Witnesses in his favor, and to have the Assistance of Counsel for his defence.

AMENDMENT 7—TRIAL BY JURY IN COMMON LAW CASES

In Suits at common law, where the value in controversy shall exceed twenty dollars, the right of trial by jury shall be preserved, and no fact tried by a jury shall be otherwise re-examined in any Court of the United States, than according to the rules of the common law.

AMENDMENT 8—BAIL, CRUEL AND UNUSUAL PUNISHMENT

Excessive bail shall not be required, nor excessive fines imposed, nor cruel and unusual punishments inflicted.

AMENDMENT 9—RIGHTS RETAINED BY THE PEOPLE

The enumeration in the Constitution, of certain rights, shall not be construed to deny or disparage others retained by the people.

AMENDMENT 10—RESERVED POWERS OF THE STATES

The powers not delegated to the United States by the Constitution, nor prohibited by it to the States, are reserved to the States respectively, or to the people.

PRE-CIVIL WAR AMENDMENTS

AMENDMENT 11—SUITS AGAINST THE STATES

[Ratified February 7, 1795]

The Judicial power of the United States shall not be construed to extend to any suit in law or equity, commenced or prosecuted against one of the United States by Citizens of another State, or by Citizens or Subjects of any Foreign State.

AMENDMENT 12—ELECTION OF THE PRESIDENT

[Ratified July 27, 1804]

The Electors shall meet in their respective states, and vote by ballot for President and Vice-President, one of whom, at least, shall not be an inhabitant of the same state with themselves; they shall name in their ballots the person voted for as President, and in distinct ballots the person voted for as Vice-President, and they shall make distinct lists of all persons voted for as President, and of all persons voted for as Vice-President, and of the number of votes for each, which lists they shall sign and certify, and transmit sealed to the seat of the government of the United States, directed to the President of the Senate;—The President of the Senate shall, in presence of the Senate and House of Representatives, open all the certificates and the votes shall then be counted;—The person having the greatest number of votes for President, shall be the President, if such number be a majority of the whole number of Electors appointed; and if no person have such majority, then from the persons having the highest numbers not exceeding three on the list of those voted for as President, the House of Representatives shall choose immediately, by ballot, the President. But in choosing the President, the votes shall be taken by states, the representation from each state having one vote; a quorum for this purpose shall consist of a member or members from two-thirds of the states, and a majority of all states shall be necessary to a choice. And if the House of Representatives shall not choose a President whenever the right of choice shall devolve upon them, *before the fourth day of March next following,* then the Vice-President shall act as President, as in the case of the death or other constitutional disability of the President.[11] The person having the greatest number of votes as Vice-President, shall be the Vice-President, if such a number be a majority of the whole numbers of Electors appointed, and if no person have a majority, then from the two highest numbers on the list, the Senate shall choose the Vice-President; a quorum for the purpose shall consist of two-thirds of the whole number of Senators, and a majority of the whole number shall be necessary to a choice. But no person constitutionally ineligible to the office of President shall be eligible to that of Vice-President of the United States.

CIVIL WAR AMENDMENTS

AMENDMENT 13—PROHIBITION OF SLAVERY

[Ratified December 6, 1865]

Section 1   Neither slavery nor involuntary servitude, except as a punishment for crime whereof the party shall have been duly convicted, shall exist within the United States, or any place subject to their jurisdiction.

Section 2   Congress shall have power to enforce this article by appropriate legislation.

AMENDMENT 14—CITIZENSHIP, DUE PROCESS, AND EQUAL PROTECTION OF THE LAWS

[Ratified July 9, 1868]

Section 1   All persons born or naturalized in the United States, and subject to the jurisdiction thereof, are citizens of the United States and of the State wherein they reside. No State shall make or enforce any law which shall abridge the privileges or immunities of citizens of the United States; nor shall any State deprive any person of life, liberty, or property, without due process of law; nor deny to any person within its jurisdiction the equal protection of the laws.

Section 2   Representatives shall be apportioned among the several States according to their respective numbers, counting the whole number of persons in each State, excluding Indians not taxed. But when the right to vote at any election for the choice of electors for President and Vice President of the United States, Representatives in Congress, the Executive and Judicial officers of a State, or the members of the Legislature thereof, is denied to any of the male inhabitants of such State, being twenty-one[12] years of age, and citizens of the United States, or in any way abridged, except for participation in rebellion, or other crime, the basis of representation therein shall be reduced in the proportion which the number of such male citizens shall bear to the whole number of male citizens twenty-one years of age in such State.

Section 3   No person shall be a Senator or Representative in Congress, or elector of President and Vice President, or hold any office, civil or military, under the United States, or under any State, who, having previously taken an oath, as a member of Congress, or as an officer of the United States, or as a member of

[11]Changed by the 20th Amendment
[12]Changed by the 26th Amendment

any State legislature, or as an executive or judicial officer of any State, to support the Constitution of the United States, shall have engaged in insurrection or rebellion against the same, or given aid or comfort to the enemies thereof. But Congress may by a vote of two-thirds of each House, remove such disability.

Section 4 The validity of the public debt of the United States, authorized by law, including debts incurred for payment of pensions and bounties for services in suppressing insurrection or rebellion, shall not be questioned. But neither the United States nor any State shall assume or pay any debt or obligation incurred in aid of insurrection or rebellion against the United States, or any claim for the loss or emancipation of any slave; but all such debts, obligations and claims shall be held illegal and void.

Section 5 The Congress shall have power to enforce, by appropriate legislation, the provisions of this article.

AMENDMENT 15—THE RIGHT TO VOTE

[Ratified February 3, 1870]

Section 1 The right of citizens of the United States to vote shall not be denied or abridged by the United States or by any State on account of race, color, or previous condition of servitude.

Section 2 The Congress shall have power to enforce this article by appropriate legislation.

AMENDMENT 16—INCOME TAXES

[Ratified February 3, 1913]

The Congress shall have power to lay and collect taxes on incomes, from whatever source derived, without apportionment among the several States, and without regard to any census or enumeration.

AMENDMENT 17—DIRECT ELECTION OF SENATORS

[Ratified April 8, 1913]

The Senate of the United States shall be composed of two Senators from each State, elected by the people thereof, for six years; and each Senator shall have one vote. The electors in each State shall have the qualifications requisite for electors of the most numerous branch of the State legislatures.

When vacancies happen in the representation of any State in the Senate, the executive authority of such State shall issue writs of election to fill such vacancies: *Provided*, That the Legislature of any State may empower the executive thereof to make temporary appointment until the people fill the vacancies by election as the legislature may direct.

This amendment shall not be so construed as to affect the election or term of any Senator chosen before it becomes valid as part of the Constitution.

AMENDMENT 18—PROHIBITION

[Ratified January 16, 1919   Repealed December 5, 1933 by Amendment 21]

Section 1 After one year from the ratification of this article the manufacture, sale, or transportation of intoxicating liquors within, the importation thereof into, or the exportation thereof

from the United States and all territory subject to the jurisdiction thereof for beverage purposes is hereby prohibited.

Section 2 The Congress and the several states shall have concurrent power to enforce this article by appropriate legislation.

Section 3 This article shall be inoperative unless it shall have been ratified as an amendment to the Constitution by the legislatures of the several states, as provided in the Constitution, within seven years from the date of the submission hereof to the States by the Congress.[13]

AMENDMENT 19—FOR WOMEN'S SUFFRAGE

[Ratified August 18, 1920]

The right of the citizens of the United States to vote shall not be denied or abridged by the United States or by any State on account of sex.

Congress shall have power, by appropriate legislation, to enforce the provision of this article.

AMENDMENT 20—THE LAME DUCK AMENDMENT

[Ratified January 23, 1933]

Section 1 The terms of the President and Vice President shall end at noon on the 20th day of January, and the terms of the Senators and Representatives at noon on the 3rd day of January, of the years in which such terms would have ended if this article had not been ratified; and the terms of their successors shall then begin.

Section 2 The Congress shall assemble at least once in every year, and such meeting shall begin at noon on the 3rd day of January, unless they shall by law appoint a different day.

Section 3 If, at the time fixed for the beginning of the term of the President, the President elect shall have died, the Vice President elect shall become President. If a President shall not have been chosen before the time fixed for the beginning of his term, or if the President elect shall have failed to qualify, then the Vice President elect shall act as President until a President shall have qualified; and the Congress may by law provide for the case wherein neither a President elect nor a Vice President elect shall have qualified, declaring who shall then act as President, or the manner in which one who is to act shall be selected, and such person shall act accordingly until a President or Vice President shall have qualified.

Section 4 The Congress may by law provide for the case of the death of any of the persons from whom the House of Representatives may choose a President whenever the right of choice shall have developed upon them, and for the case of the death of any of the persons from whom the Senate may choose a Vice President whenever the right of choice shall have devolved upon them.

Section 5 Sections 1 and 2 shall take effect on the 15th day of October following the ratification of this article.

Section 6 This article shall be inoperative unless it shall have been ratified as an amendment to the Constitution by the legislatures of three-fourths of the several States within seven years from the date of its submission.

[13]Repealed by the 21st Amendment

AMENDMENT 21—REPEAL OF PROHIBITION

[Ratified December 5, 1933]

Section 1   The eighteenth article of amendment to the Constitution of the United States is hereby repealed.

Section 2   The transportation or importation into any State, Territory, or Possession of the United States for delivery or use therein of intoxicating liquors, in violation of the laws thereof, is hereby prohibited.

Section 3   This article shall be inoperative unless it shall have been ratified as an amendment to the Constitution by conventions in the several States, as provided in the Constitution, within seven years from the date of the submission hereof to the States by the Congress.

AMENDMENT 22—NUMBER OF PRESIDENTIAL TERMS

[Ratified February 27, 1951]

Section 1   No person shall be elected to the office of the President more than twice, and no person who has held the office of President, or acted as President, for more than two years of a term to which some other person was elected President shall be elected to the Office of the President more than once. But this Article shall not apply to any person holding the office of President when this article was proposed by the Congress, and shall not prevent any person who may be holding the office of President, or acting as President, during the term within which this Article becomes operative from holding the office of President or acting as President during the remainder of such term.

Section 2   This Article shall be inoperative unless it shall have been ratified as an amendment to the Constitution by the legislatures of three-fourths of the several states within seven years from the date of its submission to the States by the Congress.

AMENDMENT 23—PRESIDENTIAL ELECTORS FOR THE DISTRICT OF COLUMBIA

[Ratified March 29, 1961]

Section 1   The District constituting the seat of Government of the United States shall appoint in such manner as the Congress may direct:

A number of electors of President and Vice President equal to the whole number of Senators and Representatives in Congress to which the District would be entitled if it were a State, but in no event more than the least populous State; they shall be in addition to those appointed by the States, but they shall be considered, for the purposes of the election of President and Vice President, to be electors appointed by a State; and they shall meet in the District and perform such duties as provided by the twelfth article of amendment.

Section 2   The Congress shall have power to enforce this article by appropriate legislation.

AMENDMENT 24—THE ANTI-POLL TAX AMENDMENT

[Ratified January 23, 1964]

Section 1   The right of citizens of the United States to vote in any primary or other election for President or Vice President, for electors for President or Vice President, or for Senator or Representative in Congress, shall not be denied or abridged by the United States or any State by reason of failure to pay any poll tax or other tax.

Section 2   The Congress shall have power to enforce this article by appropriate legislation.

AMENDMENT 25—PRESIDENTIAL DISABILITY, VICE PRESIDENTIAL VACANCIES

[Ratified February 10, 1967]

Section 1   In case of the removal of the President from office or his death or resignation, the Vice President shall become President.

Section 2   Whenever there is a vacancy in the office of the Vice President, the President shall nominate a Vice President who shall take the office upon confirmation by a majority vote of both houses of Congress.

Section 3   Whenever the President transmits to the President pro tempore of the Senate and the Speaker of the House of Representatives his written declaration that he is unable to discharge the powers and duties of his office, and until he transmits to them a written declaration to the contrary, such powers and duties shall be discharged by the Vice President as Acting President.

Section 4   Whenever the Vice-President and a majority of either the principal officers of the executive departments, or of such other body as Congress may by law provide, transmit to the President pro tempore of the Senate and the Speaker of the House of Representatives their written declaration that the President is unable to discharge the powers and duties of his office, the Vice President shall immediately assume the powers and duties of the office as Acting President.

Thereafter, when the President transmits to the President pro tempore of the Senate and the Speaker of the House of Representatives his written declaration that no inability exists, he shall resume the powers and duties of his office unless the Vice President and a majority of either the principal officers of the executive departments, or of such other body as Congress may by law provide, transmit within four days to the President pro tempore of the Senate and the Speaker of the House of Representatives their written declaration that the President is unable to discharge the powers and duties of his office. Thereupon Congress shall decide the issue, assembling within 48 hours for that purpose if not in session. If the Congress, within 21 days after receipt of the latter written declaration, or, if Congress is not in session, within 21 days after Congress is required to assemble, determines by two-thirds vote of both houses that the President is unable to discharge the powers and duties of his office, the Vice President shall continue to discharge the same as Acting President; otherwise, the President shall resume the powers and duties of his office.

AMENDMENT 26—EIGHTEEN-YEAR-OLD VOTE

[Ratified July 1, 1971]

Section 1   The right of citizens of the United States, who are eighteen years of age, or older, to vote shall not be denied or abridged by the United States or by any State on account of age.

Section 2   The Congress shall have power to enforce this article by appropriate legislation.

influence key figures should be allowed to exercise in a democracy is one of the questions that faces democrats. But a president or a pick-and-shovel laborer, a newspaper publisher or a lettuce picker, casts only one vote at the polls.

2. *Voters should have the right of access to facts, criticism, competing ideas, and the views of all candidates.* Here again, the extent to which different ideas actually receive equal attention is a problem because of the nature of the mass media, the special access of the president to television and the press, and the inability of many lower-income people to make their ideas known. Still, the principle of free competition of ideas during an election is essential.

3. *Citizens must be free to organize for political purposes.* Obviously, individuals can be more effective when they join with others in a party, a pressure group, a protest movement, or a demonstration.

4. *Elections are decided by majorities (or at least pluralities).* Those who get the most votes win, even if the winning side seems to be made up of idiots. The persons chosen by the majority take office. How much power the winners may then have over the losing minority is another problem, but there is no question that the winners take office and assume formal authority.

THE AMERICAN SYSTEM: DEMOCRATIC AND CONSTITUTIONAL

Our founders believed in democracy both as a *principle* and as a *process*. Their genius lay in how they related the *goals* of democracy to its *methods*. If the Declaration of Independence was more concerned with such *goals* as liberty and equality, the Constitution focused more on the *processes* that could help realize these goals without sacrificing such values as controlled power, stability, continuity, due process, and balanced decision making. For more than two centuries now American politicians, jurists, and other leaders have been enormously influenced by the success of the revolutionaries of 1776 and 1787 in working out effective and durable political processes. The twentieth-century civil rights denials and women's rights violations, and the **Watergate** and Iran-contra scandals, are dramatic warnings, process democrats remind us, that to abuse democratic processes is to threaten both the means and the ends of a free people.

Into the Third Century—And Some Questions

A constitution that is to endure must reflect the hard experiences and high hopes of the people for whom it is written. Those who framed our Constitution did not, of course, complete the task of constitution making. That process began long before the Constitutional Convention, and it continues still. Constitutions, even written ones, are growing and evolving organisms.

The completion of two centuries of self-government—a major accomplishment—has been a time of national celebration. However, it has also been appropriately a time of national questioning. The questions have no easy answers. They are questions to which there is no single logical response, no answer that stems easily from an analysis of facts; they are basic questions that deal with value choices. The questions in the accompanying box may help stimulate your thinking as we proceed with a more detailed investigation of the American Republic.

Following is a set of key questions about the constitutional system as it works today. You might want to refer to this checklist as you read through the following chapters, in which many of these questions are discussed.

1. *National power*: Too much or too little? Are the limits on the powers of the federal government realistic and enforceable, given the intense pressures on the government?

2. *Federalism*: Does our form of it work? Does the Constitution provide for an efficient and realistic balance between national and state power?

3. *Individual liberties*: Are they adequately protected in the Constitution?

4. *Suspects' rights*: Can representative government protect its citizens and yet uphold the rights of the criminally accused?

5. *"All men are created equal"*: What kinds of equality are—and should be—protected by the Constitution, and by what means?

6. *Women's rights*: Are they adequately protected by the Constitution today?

7. *Safeguarding minorities*: Does the Constitution adequately protect the rights of blacks, native Americans, ethnics, and recent immigrants?

8. *"Government by the people"*: Does the evolving constitutional system, including political parties and interest groups, strengthen fair and effective representation of the people?

9. *The judicial branch*: Is it too powerful? Are the federal courts exceeding their proper powers as interpreters of the Constitution?

10. *Checks and balances*: Are there too many? Does the constitutional separation of powers between the president and Congress create an ungovernable system, notably in economic policy?

11. *The Constitution*: Does it look outward? Does the president possess adequate power—or too much power—over war making and foreign policy? Should Congress have more authority in this field?

12. *Constitutional flexibility*: Should we make changing our fundamental charter of government simpler and more democratic?

We must remember, as we consider these questions, that the framers did not favor a government in which the mass of people would participate directly, or one that would be representative of or responsive to the people at-large. Rather, they sought to control both the spirit of faction and the thrust of majorities. Their prime concern was how to design a viable, yet limited, government. The framers had not seen a political party in the modern sense, and would not have liked it if they had. They did not favor an arousing, mobilizing kind of leadership, but preferred instead a stabilizing, balancing, magisterial leadership, the kind George Washington was expected to (and did) supply. Today we have *high-pressure politics* characterized by strongly organized groups and political-action committees, potent and volatile public opinion dominated by opinion-making leaders, parties vying to mobilize nationwide majorities, and celebrity officials intimately covered by the media. How responsive are our governing processes to fast-moving changes in public attitudes and moods? Will our Constitution and the political system it created be able to deal with the problems of our third century?

According to an old story, Benjamin Franklin was confronted by a woman as he left the last session of the Constitutional Convention in Philadelphia in September 1787.

"What kind of government have you given us, Dr. Franklin?" she asked, "a Republic or a Monarchy?"

"A Republic, Madam," he answered, "—if you can keep it."

Notes

1. James Madison to James Madison, Sr., July 5, 1789, quoted in Robert A. Rutland, *James Madison: The Founding Father* (Macmillan, 1987), p. 65.
2. Michael Kammen, *A Season of Youth* (Knopf, 1978).
3. George Washington to James Madison, May 1789, in John C. Fitzpatrick, ed., *The Writings of George Washington* (U.S. Government Printing Office, 1939), pp. 341–42.
4. Joyce Appleby, "The American Heritage: The Heirs and the Disinherited," *Journal of American History* (December 1987), p. 808.
5. Bernard Schwartz, *The Roots of the Bill of Rights*, vol. 1 (Chelsea House, 1980), pp. 68–73.
6. Richard L. Hillard, "Liberalism, Civic Humanism and the American Revolutionary Bills of Rights, 1775–1790." Paper prepared for delivery at the annual meeting of the Organization of American Historians, Reno, Nevada, 1988.
7. Gordon Wood, *The Creation of the American Republic, 1776–1787* (University of North Carolina Press, 1969), pp. 122, 612. See also the essays in *This Constitution* (Congressional Quarterly Press, 1986).
8. John P. Roche, "The Founding Fathers: A Reform Caucus in Action," *American Political Science Review* (December 1961), pp. 799–816, emphasizes the importance of such political considerations in the framers' deliberations.
9. Robert E. Brown, *Charles Beard and the Constitution* (Princeton University Press, 1956), pp. 197–98, and John Patrick Diggins, "Power and Authority in American History: The Case of Charles A. Beard and His Critics," *American Historical Review* (October 1981), pp. 701–30.
10. Forrest McDonald, *We the People: The Economic Origins of the Constitution* (University of Chicago Press, 1958), pp. vii, 415; see also his *Novus ordo seclorum: The Intellectual Origins of the Constitution* (University Press of Kansas, 1985).
11. Gordon S. Wood, *The Convention and the Constitution* (St. Martin's Press, 1965), p. 31.
12. Wood, *American Republic, 1776–1787*, pp. 484–85.
13. Martin Diamond, "The Declaration and the Constitution: Liberty, Democracy, and the Founders," *The Public Interest* (Fall 1975), pp. 40, 50, 52.
14. Jack P. Greene, "The Reappraisal of the American Revolution in Recent Historical Literature," in Jack P. Greene, ed., *The Reinterpretation of the American Revolution, 1763–1789* (Harper & Row, 1968), p. 2.
15. Richard B. Morris, *Witnesses at the Creation: Hamilton, Madison, Jay, and the Constitution* (Holt, Rinehart & Winston, 1985), pp. 28–30, 99–101.
16. Charles A. Beard and Mary R. Beard, *A Basic History of the United States* (New Home Library, 1944), p. 136. One of the most useful analyses of the arguments made in *The Federalist* papers can be found in David F. Epstein, *The Political Theory of The Federalist* (University of Chicago Press, 1984).
17. See Herbert J. Storing, ed., abridgement by Murray Dry, *The Anti-Federalist: Writings by the Opponents of the Constitution* (University of Chicago Press, 1985).
18. Quoted in Robert S. Peck and Ralph S. Pollock, eds., *The Blessings of Liberty* (ABA Press of the American Bar Association, 1986), p. 37.
19. Quoted in Pauline Maier, *The Old Revolutionaries* (Knopf, 1980), p. 284.
20. On the role of the promised bill of rights amendments in the ratifications of the Constitution, see Leonard W. Levy, *Constitutional Opinions* (Oxford University Press, 1986), chap. 6.
21. For treatments of this question, see Diggins, "Power and Authority in American History," pp. 701–30; James MacGregor Burns, *The Vineyard of Liberty* (Knopf, 1982), chaps. 1 and 2; and Robert A. Goldwin and William A. Schambra, eds., *How Democratic is the Constitution?* (American Enterprise Institute, 1981).
22. Speech at Sanitary Fair, 1864.
23. Herbert Hoover, *American Individualism* (Doubleday, Page, 1922), p. 9. This ancient debate continues: See also John Rawls, *A Theory of Justice* (Harvard University Press, 1971), and Robert Nozick, *Anarchy, State and Utopia* (Basic Books, 1974). See also Michael Walzer, *Spheres of Justice* (Basic Books, 1983).

2

The Living Constitution

Two hundred years after the founding era, it is hard to understand that, at the time, some people were skeptical of the proposed constitution. After watching merchants and mechanics march side by side in a parade celebrating ratification, a Bostonian remarked sourly: "It may serve to please children, but freemen will not be so easily gulled out of their liberties." On the other hand, a Philadelphian said that the procession in his city had "made such an impression on the minds of our young people that 'federal' and 'union' have now become part of the household words of every family in the city." This effect on youth was significant, for the success of the new government depended on the younger generation.

Although only a few people liked all of the recently drafted constitution, most figured it was better than the one they had. The original, unamended constitution was a skinny document of only some 4543 words (you can carry it around in your coat pocket), yet it packed a powerful constitutional punch. It was intended to be only a framework for governing; it was a document into which citizens could, if optimistic, read their hopes (or, if pessimistic, their fears). Still, most of them would be surprised indeed to learn that two hundred years later we have still not written another constitution, or two or three.

With the adoption of the Constitution, prosperity returned. Markets for American goods were opening in Europe, and business was pulling out of its postwar slump. Such events seemed to justify Federalist claims that adoption of the Constitution would correct the nation's problems. Within a surprisingly short time the Constitution lost its partisan character; both Antifederalists and Federalists honored it. Politicians differed less and less over whether the Constitution was good; they now began to argue over what it meant.

Adoption of the ten amendments comprising the Bill of Rights to maintain the great balance between liberty and order made the Constitution more popular than ever. As the Constitution won the support of Americans, it began to take on the aura of natural law: "The Fathers grew ever larger in stature as they receded

25

from view; the era in which they lived and fought became a Golden Age; in that age there had been a fresh dawn for the world, and its men were giants against the sky."[1] This early Constitution worship helped bring unity to the diverse new nation. Like the Crown in Britain, the Constitution became a symbol of national loyalty, evoking both emotional and intellectual support from all Americans, regardless of their differences. The framers' work became part of the American creed.[2] It stood for liberty, equality before the law, limited government—indeed, for whatever anyone wanted to read into it.

The Constitution, however, is more than a *symbol*. It is also a *supreme and binding law* that both *grants* and *limits* powers. "In framing a government which is to be administered by men over men," wrote James Madison in *The Federalist*, No. 51, "the great difficulty lies in this: you must first enable the government to control the governed; and in the next place oblige it to control itself." (Take a look at *The Federalist*, No. 51, which appears at the back of this book in the Appendix.) The Constitution is both a *positive* instrument of government, which enables the governors to control the governed, and a *restraint* on government, which enables the ruled to check the rulers.

In what ways does the Constitution limit the power of the government? In what ways does it create governmental power? How has it managed to serve as both a great symbol of national unity and a somewhat adaptable and changing instrument of government?

Checking Power with Power

It may seem strange to begin by stressing the ways in which the Constitution limits governmental power, but we must keep in mind the dilemma the framers faced. They wanted a more *effective* national government, yet at the same time they were keenly aware that the people would not accept too much central control. Efficiency and order were important concerns, but they were not as important as *liberty*. The framers wanted to ensure domestic tranquility and prevent future rebellions, but they also wanted to forestall the emergence of a home-grown George III. Accordingly, they allotted certain powers to the national government and reserved the rest for the states, thus establishing a system of federalism (the nature and problems of which we take up in Chapter 3). Even this was not enough. They believed they needed additional means to limit the *national* government.

The most important way to make public officials observe the constitutional limits on their powers is through *free elections*; voters have the ability to throw out of office those who abuse power. Yet the framers were not willing to depend solely on such political controls, because they did not fully trust the people's judgment. Thomas Jefferson, a firm democrat, put it this way: "Free government is founded on jealousy, and not in confidence . . . in questions of power, then, let no more be heard of confidence in man, but bind him down from mischief by the chains of the Constitution."[3]

Even more important, the framers feared that a majority faction might use the new central government to deprive minorities of their rights. "A dependence on the people is, no doubt, the primary control on the government," Madison admitted, "but experience has taught mankind the necessity of auxiliary precautions." What were these "*auxiliary precautions*" against popular tyranny?

SEPARATION OF POWERS

The first step was the **separation of powers,** that is, allocating constitutional authority to each of the three branches of the national government. In *The Federalist*, No. 47, James Madison wrote, "No political truth is certainly of greater intrinsic value, or is stamped with the authority of more enlightened patrons of liberty, than that . . . the accumulation of all powers, legislative, executive, and judiciary, in the same hands . . . may justly be pronounced the very definition of tyranny."

Logic alone, however, does not account for the inclusion of this principle in our Constitution. This doctrine had been the general practice in the colonies for over one hundred years. Only during the Revolutionary period was authority concentrated in the hands of the legislature, and that unhappy experience confirmed the framers' belief in the merits of separation of powers. Many attributed the evils of state government and the lack of energy in the central government to the fact that there was no strong executive to both check legislative abuses and give energy and direction to administration.

Still, separating power was not enough. There was always the danger—from the framers' point of view—that different officials with different powers might pool their authority and act together. Separation of powers by itself would not prevent government branches and officials from responding to the same pressures; for example, from the demand of an overwhelming majority of the voters to suppress a book they found intolerable or to impose confiscatory taxes on a few rich people. If separating power was not enough, what else could be done?

CHECKS AND BALANCES:
AMBITION TO COUNTERACT AMBITION

The framers' answer was a system of **checks and balances.** "The great security against a gradual concentration of the several powers in the same department," wrote Madison, "consists in giving to those who administer each department the necessary constitutional means and personal motives to resist encroachment on the others. . . . Ambition must be made to counteract ambition."[4]

Each branch is therefore given some role in the actions of the others. We have a "government of separated institutions sharing powers."[5] Thus, Congress enacts laws, but the president can veto them. The Supreme Court can declare unconstitutional laws passed by Congress and signed by the president, but the president appoints the justices with the Senate's approval. The president administers the laws, but Congress provides the money. Moreover, the Senate and the House of Representatives have an absolute veto over each other in the enactment of a law, because bills must be approved by both houses.

Not only does each branch have some authority over the actions of the others, but each is *politically independent of the others*. The president is selected by electors (now popularly elected). Senators are now chosen by the voters in each state, and the members of the House by voters in their districts. And although federal judges are appointed by the president with the consent of the Senate, once in office they virtually hold terms for life.

The framers also ensured that a majority of the voters could win control over only part of the government at one time. A popular majority might take control of the House of Representatives in an off-year (that is, a nonpresidential) election, but the president, representing a previous popular majority, would still have two years to go. Furthermore, senators are chosen for six-year terms, but only one-third are selected every two years.

Finally, national courts were also provided. In fact, judges have become so important in our system of checks and balances that they deserve special attention.

Judicial Review and the "Guardians of the Constitution"

Judges did not claim the power of **judicial review**—the power of a court to refuse to enforce an act of the legislature that in the opinion of the judges is in conflict with the Constitution—until some years after the Constitution was in operation. From the beginning, however, judges were expected to restrain legislative majorities. "Independent judges," wrote Alexander Hamilton in *The Federalist*, No. 78 (which also appears in the Appendix of this book), would be "an essential safeguard against the effects of occasional ill humors in society."

Judicial review is an American contribution to the art of government. If British or American citizens are thrown into prison without cause, they can appeal to the courts of their respective countries for protection. But no British judge may declare a law duly enacted by Parliament null and void because the judge believes it violates the British constitution: Parliament is the guardian of the British constitution. In the United States the courts, ultimately the Supreme Court, are the keepers of the constitutional conscience—not Congress and not the president. How did the judges get this tremendous responsibility?

ORIGINS OF JUDICIAL REVIEW

The Constitution itself says nothing about who should have the final word in disputes that might arise over its meaning. Whether the members of the Convention of 1787 intended to give the courts the power of judicial review is a question long since debated. The framers clearly intended the Supreme Court to have the power to declare *state* legislation unconstitutional, but whether they intended to give it the same power over *national* legislation is not clear. Edward S. Corwin, the outstanding authority on the American Constitution, concluded that unquestionably "the framers anticipated some sort of judicial review. . . . But it is equally without question that the ideas generally current in 1787 were far from presaging the present vast role of the court."[6] Why, then, did the framers not specifically provide for judicial review? Probably because they believed the power could readily be inferred from certain general provisions.

The Federalists—the men who wrote the Constitution and controlled the national government until 1801—generally supported a strong role for federal courts and favored judicial review. Their opponents, the Jeffersonian Republicans (called Democrats after 1832), were less enthusiastic. In 1798 and 1799 Jefferson and Madison (the latter by this time had left the Federalist party), with the Virginia and Kentucky Resolutions, came very close to the position that state legislatures—and not the Supreme Court—had the ultimate power to interpret the Constitution. These Resolutions even seemed to question whether the Supreme Court had the final authority to review state legislation, something about which there had been little doubt.

In 1857 the Supreme Court denied Dred Scott his freedom by ruling that slaves were property and protected as such by the Constitution, even in the territories. This decision declared an act of Congress—the Missouri Compromise—to be unconstitutional. The decision was later overruled by the Fourteenth Amendment.

CHAPTER 2 / The Living Constitution

When the Jeffersonians defeated the Federalists in the elections of 1800, it was still undecided whether the Supreme Court would actually exercise the power of judicial review. The idea was in the air, logical reasons to support a doctrine of judicial review were at hand, and some precedents could even be cited; nevertheless, judicial review was not an established power. Then in 1803 came *Marbury* v. *Madison*,[7] one of the most famous Supreme Court decisions of all time.

MARBURY VERSUS MADISON (1803)

The elections of 1800 marked the rise to power of the Jeffersonian Republicans. President John Adams and his fellow Federalists did not take their defeat easily. Indeed, they were greatly alarmed at what they considered to be the "enthronement of the rabble." Yet there was nothing much they could do about it before leaving office—or was there? The Constitution gives the president, with the consent of the Senate, the power to appoint federal judges to hold office during "good behavior." If the judiciary were manned by good Federalists, thought Adams and his followers, they could stave off the worst consequences of Jefferson's victory.

The Federalist **lame-duck** Congress created dozens of new federal judicial posts. By March 3, 1801, Adams had appointed, and the Senate had confirmed, Federalists to all these new positions. Adams signed the commissions and turned them over to John Marshall, the secretary of state, to be sealed and delivered. Marshall had just received his own commission as chief justice of the United States, but he was continuing to serve as secretary of state until Adams's term expired. Working right up until 9 o'clock on the evening of March 3, Marshall sealed, but was unable to deliver, all the commissions. The important ones were taken care of, however, and only those for the justices of the peace for the District of Columbia were left undelivered. The newly appointed chief justice left the remaining commissions for his successor to deliver.

Jefferson was angered by this packing of the judiciary. When he discovered that some of the commissions had not been delivered, he told the new secretary of state, James Madison, to hold up seventeen of those still in his possession. Jefferson could see no reason why the District needed so many justices of the peace, especially Federalist justices.

Among the commissions not delivered was one for William Marbury. After waiting in vain, Marbury decided to seek action from the courts. Searching through the statute books, he came across Section 13 of the Judiciary Act of 1789, which authorized the Supreme Court "to issue writs of mandamus, in cases warranted by the principles and usages of law, to . . . persons holding office, under the authority of the United States." A **writ of mandamus** is a court order directing an official to perform a duty of an office. Delivering a commission is a ministerial act; the secretary of state is a person holding office under the authority of the United States. So, thought Marbury, why not ask the Supreme Court to issue a writ of mandamus to force Madison to deliver the commission? He and his companions went directly to the Supreme Court and, citing Section 13, they made the request.

What could Marshall do? If the Court issued the writ, Madison and Jefferson would probably ignore it. The Court would be powerless, and its prestige, already low, might suffer a fatal blow. On the other hand, by refusing to issue the writ, the judges would appear to support the Republican party's claim that the Court had no authority to interfere with the executive. Would Marshall issue the writ? Most people thought so; angry Republicans even talked of impeachment.

Thomas Jefferson

Chief Justice John Marshall (1755–1835) is regarded as our most influential Supreme Court justice. Appointed in 1801, Marshall served as the fourth chief justice of the United States; he served until 1835. Earlier he had been a staunch defender of the U.S. Constitution at the Virginia ratifying convention, a member of Congress, and secretary of state. He was one of those rare people who served in all three branches of government.

"And there are three branches of government, so that each branch has the other two to blame everything on."

Dunagin's People by Ralph Dunagin. © 1978 Field Newspaper Syndicate. By permission of the News America Syndicate.

On February 24, 1803, the Supreme Court delivered its opinion. The first part was as expected. Marbury was entitled to his commission, said Marshall, and Madison should have delivered it to him; a writ of mandamus could be issued by the proper court against even so high an officer as the secretary of state.

Then came the surprise. Although Section 13 of the Judiciary Act seems to give the Supreme Court original jurisdiction in cases such as that in question, this section, said Marshall, is contrary to Article III of the Constitution, which gives the Supreme Court original jurisdiction *only* when an ambassador or other foreign minister is affected or when a state is a party. Even though this is a case of original jurisdiction, Marbury is neither a state nor a foreign minister. If we follow Section 13, wrote Marshall, we have jurisdiction; if we follow the Constitution, we have no jurisdiction.

Marshall then stated the question in a more pointed way: *Should the Supreme Court enforce an unconstitutional law?* Of course not, he concluded. The Constitution is the supreme and binding law, and the courts cannot enforce any action of Congress that conflicts with it.

The real question remained unanswered. Congress and the president also had read the Constitution, and according to their interpretation, which is also reasonable, Section 13 is compatible with Article III. Where did the Supreme Court get the right to say they were wrong? Why should the Supreme Court's interpretation of the Constitution be preferred to that of Congress and the president?

Paralleling Hamilton's argument in *The Federalist*, No. 78, Marshall reasoned: The Constitution is law; judges—not legislators or executives—interpret law. Therefore, judges should interpret the Constitution. "If two laws conflict with each other, the courts must decide on the operation of each," he said. Case dismissed.

Jefferson fumed. For one thing, Marshall had said that a court with the proper jurisdiction could issue a writ of mandamus even against the secretary of state, one of the president's closest advisors. Yet there was little Jefferson could do about what he thought was Marshall's arrogance. There was not even a court order he could refuse to obey. Thus, in a single stroke Marshall had lectured the Republicans for failing to perform their duties, and he had gone a long way toward acquiring the power for the Supreme Court to review acts of Congress. And he had done it in a manner that made it difficult for the Republicans to challenge.

Marbury v. *Madison* is a masterpiece of judicial strategy. Marshall went out of his way to declare Section 13 unconstitutional. He could have interpreted the section to mean that the Supreme Court could issue writs of mandamus in those cases in which it did have jurisdiction. He could have interpreted Article III to mean that Congress could add to, though not subtract from, the original jurisdiction the Constitution gives to the Supreme Court. He could have dismissed the case for want of jurisdiction without discussing Marbury's right to his commission. But none of these would have suited his purpose. Marshall was fearful for the Supreme Court's future; he reasoned that unless the Court spoke out, it would become subordinate to the president and Congress.

Marshall's decision, important as it was, did not by itself establish for the Supreme Court the power to review and declare acts of Congress unconstitutional. In fact it was not until the *Dred Scott* case in 1857 that another act of Congress was declared unconstitutional[8] and not until after the Civil War that the modern use of judicial review really became established.

Marbury v. *Madison* might have been interpreted in a more limited way, so that the Supreme Court had the right to determine the scope of its *own* powers under Article III, but that Congress and the president had the authority to interpret *their* own powers under Articles I and II, respectively. However, Marshall's decision has not been interpreted in this way. On the contrary, building on Marshall's precedent over the decades, the Court has taken the commanding position as the authoritative interpreter of the Constitution.

Perhaps if Marshall had not spoken when he did, the Court might not have been able to assume the power of judicial review. He created the precedent. This is a classic example of constitutional development through judicial interpretation. The Constitution gives no specific authorization for the Court to declare congressional enactments null and void; yet today this practice is a vital part of our constitutional system.

Several important consequences follow from the acceptance of Marshall's argument that judges are the official interpreters of the Constitution. The most important is that even a law enacted by the Congress and approved by the president may, under many circumstances, be challenged by a single person. Simply by bringing a lawsuit, those who lack the clout to get a bill through Congress or who cannot influence a federal agency may often secure a judicial hearing. Litigation thus supplements, and at times takes precedence over, legislation as a way to make public policy.[9]

Checks and Balances—Does It Work?

What if a majority of the people should get control of all branches of government and force through radical measures? The framers knew that if the great majority of the voters wanted to take a certain step, nothing could stop them. Nothing, that is, except despotic government, and that they did not want. They reasoned that all they could do—and this is quite a lot—is to prevent, temporarily, full control by the popular majority.

It may seem surprising that most of the people did not object to these "auxiliary precautions," which often are barriers to action by a popular majority. But early Americans (and perhaps their descendants two centuries later) did not look on government as an instrument they could seize with their votes and use for their own purposes. Rather, it was something to be handcuffed, hemmed in, and rendered harmless. The separation of powers and the system of checks and balances were intended to make it difficult for a majority to gain control of the government. Equally important, these precautionary mechanisms were intended to keep those who govern from exceeding their constitutional authority.

Distrustful of both the elites and the masses, the framers deliberately built *inefficiency* into our political system; and two hundred years after the ratification of the Constitution, Americans continue to debate whether it is desirable to maintain these limits under the vastly different conditions of our times. Crucial questions remain: Are these checks necessary or sufficient to prevent abuses of political power? Is the greater danger that governments will not do the right things, or that they will do the wrong things? Do these limitations work to prevent abuses, or do they make coherent governmental action for the general welfare difficult, if not impossible?

CHECKS AND BALANCES: MODIFICATIONS

Even though fragmentation of political power remains, several developments have modified the way the system of checks and balances actually works.

You decide!

Of the over 160 national constitutions in the world, the U.S. Constitution is the oldest and one of the most admired. A constitution cannot spell out everything, and every successful constitution has compromises. Some issues are left out, and some become less relevant over time—especially two centuries later. The bicentennial era of our Constitution's writing (1787), ratification (1788), the inauguration of the new government (1789), and the drawing up and ratification of the Bill of Rights (1789–1791) has directed attention to how we might improve it. Can you point to topics you believe should be included in our Constitution that were left out? And topics that would best be deleted or modified?

(Answer/Discussion on page 32.)

Most Americans believe we should seldom change the Constitution, but a variety of proposals for amending it "are now at various levels on the nation's agenda. . . . Accordingly, while we may commit some sins in observing the Constitution's bicentenary, they are not likely to include smugness or mindlessness."

Current proposals include:

To make flag desecration illegal

To require a balanced federal budget

To reverse Supreme Court rulings disallowing state-sponsored prayers in public schools

To provide for equal rights under the law for women

To abolish the electoral college and provide for direct election of the president

To alter the system for nominating presidential candidates

To permit national legislation by initiative petitions and direct vote of the people

To make the District of Columbia and Puerto Rico states

To provide for a single, nonrenewable, six-year term for the president

To give the president an item veto over appropriations

To bridge the separation of powers by giving cabinet members seats in Congress or requiring the president to choose cabinet members from members of Congress

To move toward a more cohesive party system by electing the president, senators, and House members at the same time for terms of the same length

Perhaps by the end of this course there will be other subjects you would like to see added or altered. Undoubtedly, however, you will appreciate that changing the Constitution, even in minor ways, is a complex task. It is also highly political.

1. *Rise of national political parties.* Parties serve as unifying factors—at times drawing together the president, senators, representatives, and sometimes even judges behind common programs. But the parties, in turn, have been splintered and weakened by having to work through a system of fragmented governmental power, so that we have never developed strong, cohesive parties. Moreover, since 1954 the electorate has chosen to put Democrats in charge of the Congress and a Republican in charge of the White House most of the time. Under such circumstances parties, rather than moderating checks and balances, intensify them to the point that no definitive action gets taken on major issues.[10]

2. *Changes in electoral methods.* The framers wanted the president to be chosen by wise, independent citizens free from popular passions and hero worship. Almost from the beginning, however, presidential electors have pledged prior to elections to cast their votes for their parties' presidential candidates. Further, senators, who were originally elected by state legislatures, are today chosen directly by the people.

3. *Establishment of agencies deliberately designed to exercise all three functions—legislative, executive, and judicial.* When the government began to regulate the economy, and detailed rules had to be made on such complex matters as policing business practices or preventing pollution of our air and water resources, it was difficult to assign responsibility to an agency without blending the powers to make and apply rules and to decide disputes.

4. *Changes in technology.* Nuclear bombs, television, computers, fax machines—these and other alterations in our environment create conditions very different from those of two centuries ago. In some ways these new technologies have added to the powers of the president; in others they have added leverage to organized interests working through Congress. They have also given greater independence and influence to nongovernmental agencies, such as the press. Governmental power remains fragmented, but the system of checks and balances operates differently from the way it did in 1789, when there were no televised congressional investigating committee hearings; no electronic listening devices or FBI; no *New York Times*, *Wall Street Journal*, *USA Today*, or nightly news programs with national audiences; no presidential press conferences; and no live coverage of wars or of Americans being held hostage in foreign places.

5. *The emergence of the United States as a world power and the existence of recurrent crises.* Today crises and problems anywhere in the world become crises and problems for the United States, and vice versa. The need to deal with perpetual emergency has concentrated power in the hands of the chief executive and the presidential staff.

6. *The office of the president has sometimes served to impose some measure of national unity.* Drawing on constitutional, political, and emergency powers, the president has sometimes been able to overcome some of the restraints imposed by the Constitution on the exercise of cohesive governmental power—to the applause of some, and the alarm of others.

THE BRITISH AND AMERICAN SYSTEMS: A STUDY IN CONTRASTS

Although many Americans question the usefulness and functions of our institutions, we tend to take the system of checks and balances for granted, considering it necessary for constitutional government. Like Madison (and especially since Watergate), we view the amassing of power by any one branch of government as leading to tyranny. Yet it is quite possible for a government to be constitutional without

American System of Separation of Powers

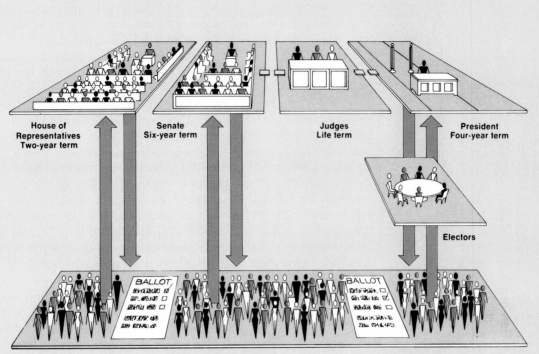

House of
Representatives
Two-year term

Senate
Six-year term

Judges
Life term

President
Four-year term

Electors

Voters

British Parliamentary System of Concentration of Responsibility

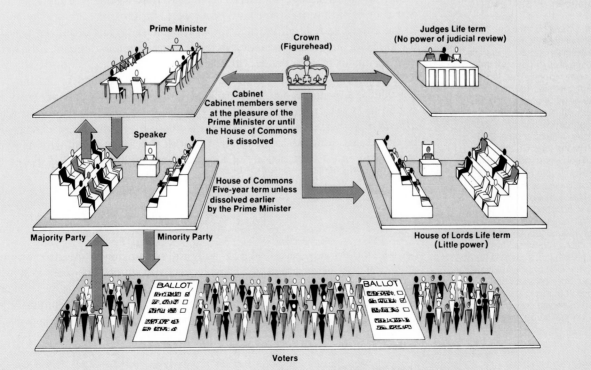

Prime Minister

Crown
(Figurehead)

Judges Life term
(No power of judicial review)

Cabinet
Cabinet members serve
at the pleasure of the
Prime Minister or until
the House of Commons
is dissolved

Speaker

House of Commons
Five-year term unless
dissolved earlier
by the Prime Minister

Majority Party

Minority Party

House of Lords Life term
(Little power)

Voters

such an apparatus. Under the British system, voters elect members of Parliament from districts throughout the nation (much as we elect members of the House of Representatives). The members of the House of Commons have almost complete constitutional power. The leaders of the majority party serve as executive ministers, who collectively form the cabinet, with the prime minister as its head. When the executive officers lose the support of the majority in the Commons on a major issue, they must resign or call for new elections. Formerly the House of Lords could check the Commons, but now it is almost powerless. There is no high court with the power to declare acts of Parliament unconstitutional. The prime minister cannot veto them (he or she may ask the Crown to dissolve Parliament and call new elections for members of the House of Commons). The British take their system as much for granted as we do our own.

The British system is based on *majority rule*; that is, a majority of the voters elects a majority of the legislators, who can put through the majority's program as long as the parliamentary majority stays together, at least until the next election. Our system usually depends on the agreement of many elements of society. The British system *concentrates* control and responsibility in the legislature; ours *diffuses* control and responsibility among several organs of government. We have a written document called the Constitution; Britain has no such single document. Yet both systems are constitutional in the sense that the rulers are subject to regular restraints. The limits our written Constitution and the conventions the unwritten British constitution impose rest on underlying values, attitudes, and norms (rules).

The Constitution as an Instrument of Government

As careful as our nation's founders were to limit the powers they gave the national government, the main reason they had assembled in Philadelphia was *to create a stronger* national government. They had learned that weak central government, incapable of governing, is a danger to liberty. They wished to establish a national government within the framework of a federal system and with enough authority to meet the needs of all times. They made general grants of power, leaving the way open for succeeding generations to fill in the details and organize the structure of government in accordance with experience.

Hence, our formal, written Constitution is only the skeleton of our system. It is filled out by numerous rules that must be considered part of our constitutional system in its larger sense. In fact, it is primarily through changes in our informal *unwritten Constitution* that our system is kept up to date. These changes are to be found in certain basic statutes and historical practices of Congress, decisions of the Supreme Court, actions of the president, and customs and usages of the nation.

CONGRESSIONAL ELABORATION

Because the framers gave Congress authority over many of the structural details of the national government, it is not necessary to amend the Constitution every time a change is needed; rather, Congress can act from year to year. Examples of congressional elaboration appear in such legislation as the Judiciary Act of 1789, which laid the foundations of our national judicial system; in the laws establish-

---

Use of Checks and Balances, 1789–1990

There have been about 2850 presidential vetoes of congressional acts. Congress subsequently overrode about 100 of those vetoes. The Supreme Court has ruled 100 congressional acts or parts of acts unconstitutional. Its 1983 decision on legislative vetoes, in *INS* v. *Chada*, affects another 200 provisions (see Chapter 16).

The Senate has refused to confirm 27 out of 140 nominees to the Supreme Court.

The House of Representatives has impeached sixteen federal officials, thirteen of whom have been federal judges; of these, the Senate has convicted five, and two are pending. The Senate has also rejected nine cabinet nominations. Many other cabinet and subcabinet level appointments have been withdrawn because of likely rejection by the Senate.

ing the organization and functions of all federal executive officials subordinate to the president; in the use of the legislative veto for three decades before it was declared unconstitutional by the Supreme Court, and in the rules of procedure, internal organization, and practices of Congress itself (These are discussed in later chapters).

Impeachment Power—An Example of Congressional Elaboration   A dramatic example of congressional elaboration of our constitutional system is the use of the impeachment power. Constitutional language is sparse. Take a look at your copy of the Constitution and note that according to Article I—the Legislative Article—it is up to Congress to give meaning to that language. Article I gives the House of Representatives the sole power of impeachment, and the Senate the sole power to try all impeachments. When sitting for that purpose, senators "shall be on oath or affirmation"; in the event the president is being tried, the chief justice of the United States presides. Article I also requires conviction on impeachment charges to have the agreement of two-thirds of the senators present. Judgments shall extend no further than removal from office and disqualification from holding any office under the United States, but a person convicted shall also be liable to indictment, trial, judgment, and punishment according to the law. In Article II—the Executive Article—the Constitution provides that the "President, Vice-President, and all civil officers of the United States, shall be removed from Office on Impeachment for, and Conviction of, Treason, Bribery, or other high Crimes and Misdemeanors." This Article also excepts cases of impeachment from the president's pardoning power. Article III—the Judicial Article—exempts cases of impeachment from the jury trial requirement. That is all the relevant constitutional language. We must look to history to answer most questions.

Fortunately, our experiences have triggered few acute constitutional disputes about the interpretation of impeachment procedures, and there is little history to go on. The House of Representatives has investigated sixty-six individuals for possible impeachment and has impeached sixteen; the Senate has convicted five (all federal judges), and two cases of federal judges are pending. (The Senate has recently decided, but not without controversy, that the entire Senate does not have to sit to hear all the evidence in the case of a federal judge but that this responsibility can be delegated to a Senate committee.) One judge resigned after being impeached, and the charges against him were dropped. One president, Andrew Johnson, was impeached in 1868, but the Senate failed by one vote to muster the two-thirds necessary to support the charges. Another president, Richard Nixon, resigned on August 9, 1974, to avoid impeachment after the House Judiciary Committee recommended three articles of impeachment against him. The House did not press the matter further, but the articles of impeachment were submitted by the committee and were "accepted" by the House.

Even though congressional precedents have rejected the *broadest* view—that the Constitution authorizes removal of officers by impeachment because of *political* objections to them or because of their unpopularity (a view that might have moved us more in the direction of a parliamentary type of government)—Congress has also rejected the *narrowest* construction—that impeachable offenses are only those that involve violations of the criminal laws. Rather, the firmly established position is that impeachment and conviction are justified if there have been serious violations of constitutional responsibilities and a clear dereliction of duty.[11]

PRESIDENTIAL PRACTICES

Although the president's formal constitutional powers have not changed, the office is dramatically more important and more central today than it was in 1789. The more vigorous presidents—Washington, Jefferson, Jackson, Lincoln, Theodore Roosevelt, Wilson, Franklin Roosevelt, Truman, and Reagan—have boldly exercised their political and constitutional powers, especially during times of national crisis. Such presidential practices have become important precedents, building the power and influence of the office. Even John Tyler made his contribution to constitutional elaboration. Upon becoming president through vice-presidential succession, Tyler established the precedent that the vice-president becomes the president, not merely the acting president.

Presidential practices discussed elsewhere include **executive privilege,** the **impoundment** of funds previously appropriated by Congress, and most important, the right to propose legislation and work actively to secure its passage by Congress.

Nuclear-age realities add force to the president's role as the nation's "final arbiter." Political scientist Richard Neustadt says: "When it comes to action risking war, technology has modified the Constitution: the President, perforce, becomes the only such man in the system capable of exercising judgment under the extraordinary limits now imposed by secrecy, complexity, and time."[12] The presidency has also become the pivotal office for regulating the economy and protecting the general welfare. Plainly, the president has also become a chief legislator as well as the nation's chief executive.

CUSTOM AND USAGE

Customs and usages have rounded out our governmental system. Presidential nominating conventions and other party activities are examples of constitutional usages. Although not specifically mentioned in the Constitution, these practices are fundamental to our system. In fact, it has been primarily through the development of national political parties and the extension of the suffrage within the states that our Constitution has become democratized. A broader electorate began to exercise control over the national government, and the presidential office has been made more responsive to the people. In addition, the nature of the relationship between Congress and the president has been altered. Further, through the growth of political parties, some constitutional blocks to popular rule were overcome.

JUDICIAL INTERPRETATION

Judicial interpretation of the Constitution, especially by the Supreme Court, has played an important part in keeping the constitutional system up to date. As social and economic conditions have changed and new national demands have developed, the Supreme Court has changed its interpretation of the Constitution to reflect these trends. In the words of Woodrow Wilson, "The Supreme Court is a constitutional convention in continuous session." Because the Constitution adapts to changing times, it does not require frequent formal amendment.

The advantages of this flexibility may be appreciated when the national Constitution is compared with the rigid and often overly specific state constitutions. Many state constitutions, more like legal codes than basic charters, are so detailed that the hands of public officials are often tied. Such constitutions must be amended frequently or replaced every generation or so.

A RIGID OR FLEXIBLE CONSTITUTION?

The idea of a constantly changing system disturbs many people. How, they argue, can you have a constitutional government when the Constitution is constantly being twisted by interpretation and changed by informal methods? This view fails to distinguish between two aspects of the Constitution. As an expression of *basic and timeless personal liberties*, the Constitution does not and should not change. For example, a government cannot destroy free speech and still remain a constitutional government. In this sense the Constitution is unchanging. But when we consider the Constitution as an *instrument of government* and a positive grant of power, we realize that if it does not grow with the nation it serves, it will soon be pushed aside. The framers could not have conceived of the problems faced by a government of a large, powerful, and wealthy nation of 250 million people in the last decade of the twentieth century. Although the general purposes of government remain the same—to establish liberty, promote justice, ensure domestic tranquility, and provide for the common defense—the powers of government adequate to accomplish these purposes in 1787 are simply insufficient two hundred years later.

"We the people"—the people of today and tomorrow, not just the people of 1787—ordain and establish the Constitution. "The Constitution," wrote Jefferson, "belongs to the living and not to the dead." So firmly did he believe this that he suggested there might be a new constitution for every generation. But new constitutions have not been necessary, because in a less formal way each generation has taken part in the process of developing and changing the original Constitution. In fact, because of its remarkable adaptability, the Constitution has survived democratic and industrial revolutions, the turmoil of civil war, the tensions of major depressions, and the dislocations of world wars.

Changing the Letter of the Constitution

The framers knew that future experiences would call for changes in the text of the Constitution and that some means of formal **amendment** was necessary. Take a look at Article V of the Constitution. Note that the framers gave the responsibility for amendment to Congress and to the states; the president has no formal authority over constitutional amendments. Presidential veto power does not extend to them, although presidential political influence is often crucial in getting amendments proposed by Congress and ratified by the states. Nor may governors veto ratification of amendments by their respective legislatures or ratifying conventions. The Constitution vests ratification in whichever body Congress designates—state *legislatures* or state ratifying *conventions*. The framers set up two ways to propose

Copyright © 1989 by Herblock in The Washington Post.

1. *Amendments whose chief importance is to add to or subtract from the power of the national government:*

    The Eleventh took some jurisdiction away from the national courts.

    The Thirteenth abolished slavery and authorized Congress to legislate against it.

    The Sixteenth enables Congress to levy an income tax.

    The Eighteenth authorizes Congress to prohibit the manufacture, sale, or transportation of liquor.

    The Twenty-first repealed the Eighteenth and gave states the authority to regulate liquor sales.

2. *Amendments whose main effect is to limit the power of state governments:*

    The Thirteenth abolished slavery.

    The Fourteenth grants national citizenship and prohibits states from abridging privileges of national citizenship, from denying persons life, liberty, and property without due process, and from denying persons equal protection of the laws. This amendment has come to be interpreted as imposing restraints on state powers in every area of public life.

3. *Amendments whose chief impact has been to expand the electorate and add to its power:*

    The Fifteenth extended the suffrage to black males in the North and South.

    The Seventeenth took the right to elect their United States senators from state legislatures and gave it to the voters in each state.

    The Nineteenth extended the suffrage to women.

    The Twenty-third gave voters of the District of Columbia the right to vote for president and vice-president.

    The Twenty-fourth forbids any state to put a tax on the right to vote (the poll tax).

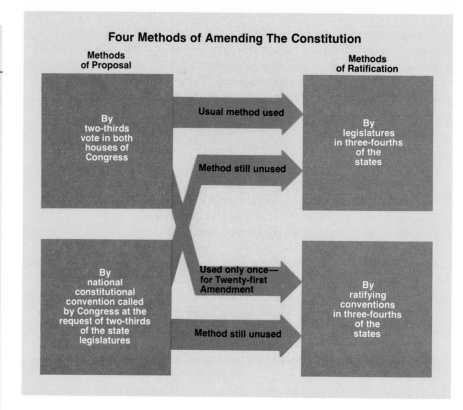

Four Methods of Amending The Constitution

amendments and two ways to ratify them, and they saw to it that amendments could not be adopted by simple majorities. Each amendment must be both *proposed and ratified.*

PROPOSING AMENDMENTS

The first method for proposing amendments—the only one that has been used so far—is by a two-thirds vote of both houses of Congress. Dozens of resolutions proposing amendments are introduced in every session. Thousands have been introduced since 1789, most of them during the last two decades. But few make any headway. Throughout our history Congress has proposed only thirty-three amendments (twenty-three plus the Bill of Rights).

In recent years there has been a flurry of congressional consideration of constitutional amendments; none have been formally proposed by both chambers. Currently under consideration are all the amendments outlined in the box on p. 32, to mention just some of them. Why has proposing possible amendments to the Constitution become such a popular pastime? In part because interest groups unhappy with Supreme Court decisions seek to overturn them. In part because groups frustrated by their inability to get things done in Congress—balancing the budget, for example—seek an amendment, even if only for symbolic reasons. And in part because scholars or interest-group representatives (not necessarily mutually exclusive categories) or public-interest institutions and centers, so-called "think tanks," and others seek to change the procedures and process of government to make the system more responsive.[13]

The second method for proposing amendments—Congress's calling a constitutional convention whenever the legislatures in two-thirds of the states so petition—has never been used. "The Constitution's Other Method"[14] presents some difficult questions. How long do state petitions remain alive? How should delegates be chosen? How should a convention be run? Recently Congress has considered bills to answer some of these questions. Most call on Congress to set the date and place for a convention whenever each chamber concludes that two-thirds of the state legislatures have petitioned about a particular subject closely enough in time to one another to reflect a "contemporaneous national request" for action. Under most proposals, each state would have as many delegates to the convention as it has representatives and senators in Congress. Finally—a crucial point—the convention would be *limited to considering only the subject specified* in the state legislative petitions and described in the congressional call for the convention. (Scholars are divided on whether Congress has this authority to limit what a constitutional convention might propose.)[15]

Despite several organized efforts to force Congress to call a constitutional convention (or else to propose the amendment itself), Congress has not yet acted. The closest we came to a convention was in the spring of 1967, when the thirty-third state legislature—only one short of the required number—petitioned Congress to call a convention to propose an amendment that would set aside a Supreme Court ruling that both chambers of a state legislature must be apportioned on the basis of population. Congress refused to propose an amendment. The thirty-fourth state never petitioned for a convention, and as state legislatures completed the process of reapportionment, pressures for an amendment abated.

In recent years Congress has received petitions for a convention to propose amendments to permit states to encourage prayer in public schools, to reverse Supreme Court decisions relating to abortions, and to deal with school busing. The most active campaign for a convention has been sponsored by the National Taxpayers Union in behalf of a Balanced Budget Amendment. Thirty-two state legislatures have petitioned Congress on this issue. (An American Bar Association committee concludes that twenty-four of these resolutions are of "questionable validity" and the Alabama legislature has rescinded its call for such a convention.)[16]

Why has Congress been so reluctant to call a convention? Members of Congress, and many other concerned citizens, are fearful of a "runaway convention" in which delegates would ignore the restraints imposed upon them and propose amendments on a variety of topics; perhaps they would even call for a new form of government. They remember what happened two hundred years ago when a reluctant Congress called into being a Constitutional Convention for the sole purpose of considering amendments to the Articles of Confederation, only to have that Convention ignore its instructions and disregard the procedures for amending the Articles. They also remember that in January 1789 James Madison expressed a strong preference that Congress propose a Bill of Rights in the form of amendments rather than call for a second convention. He wrote: "The Congress who will be appointed to execute as well as to amend the Government, will probably be careful not to destroy or endanger it. A convention, on the other hand, meeting in the present ferment of parties, and containing perhaps insidious characters from different parts of America, would at least spread a general alarm, and be but too likely to turn everything into confusion and uncertainty."[17]

The Twenty-sixth extended the suffrage to otherwise qualified persons 18 years of age or older.

4. *Amendments whose chief impact has been to subtract from the power of the electorate:*

The Twenty-second took from the electorate the right to elect any person to the office of president for more than two full terms.

5. *Amendments that have made structural changes in governmental machinery:*

The Twelfth corrected deficiencies in the operation of the electoral college that were revealed by the development of a two-party national system.

The Twentieth altered the calendar for congressional sessions and shortened the time between the election of presidents and their assumption of office.

The Twenty-fifth provides procedures for filling vacancies in the vice-presidency and for determining whether presidents are unable to perform their duties.

RATIFYING AMENDMENTS

After an amendment has been proposed, it must be ratified by the states. Again, two methods are provided: approval by the legislatures in three-fourths of the

The Child Labor Amendment, proposed in 1924, was ratified by only twenty-eight state legislatures, the last in 1937. A reasonable time for ratification has long since passed, but Supreme Court decisions since 1937 have provided Congress with other means to outlaw child labor.

states or approval by specially called ratifying conventions in three-fourths of the states. Congress determines which method is used. All amendments except one—the Twenty-first (to repeal the Eighteenth, the Prohibition Amendment)—have been submitted to the state legislatures for ratification.

Seven state constitutions require for ratification an extraordinary majority of three-fifths or two-thirds of each chamber. Although a state legislature may change its mind and ratify an amendment after it has voted against ratification, the weight of opinion is that once a state has ratified an amendment it cannot "unratify" it.[18]

Submitting amendments to legislatures rather than ratifying conventions allows changes to be made in the constitutions without any direct expressions by the voters; in fact, legislators may have been elected before the proposed amendments were submitted to the states. In any event, state legislators are chosen because of their views on schools, taxation, or other matters, or because of their personal popularity. They are almost never elected because of their stand on proposed constitutional amendments, although the candidates' position on the **Equal Rights Amendment (ERA)** did surface as a key issue in several state legislative elections.

Procedures can make a difference. The decision to submit the Twenty-first Amendment to repeal Prohibition to ratifying conventions came about because the "wets" rightly believed that repeal had a better chance of success with conventions than with the rural-dominated state legislatures. (For similar tactical reasons, southern Democrats joined with eastern Republican conservatives in an unsuccessful effort to submit the Nineteenth Amendment to give women the vote, or Susan B. Anthony Amendment, as it was called, to ratifying conventions. Let the voters decide—the male voters, that is—they argued.)[19] Congress left it up to each state legislature to determine how the ratifying conventions would be organized and delegates elected. State delegates ran at-large on tickets that pledged they would vote for or against repeal. As a result, when state conventions were called to order, they quickly ratified the decision the voters had already made. In effect, ratification was submitted to the voters.

A state must ratify proposed amendments within (what Congress considers) a reasonable time. The modern practice is for Congress to stipulate that an amend-

CHAPTER 2 / The Living Constitution

Women in the United States have been involved in a long struggle for women's rights, from the suffragettes who campaigned for the Nineteenth Amendment granting women the vote, to rallies in recent years to urge passage of the Equal Rights Amendment.

ment will not become part of the Constitution unless ratified by the necessary number of states within seven years from the date of its submission. (In fact, ratification ordinarily takes place rather quickly; see Table 2–1.)[20] Sometimes Congress places the seven-year limitation in the text of the proposed amendment, sometimes in the enabling legislation that accompanies it.

The placement of time limitations can make a difference. For example, in the autumn of 1978 it appeared that the ERA would fall three short of the necessary number of ratifying states before the expiration of the seven-year limit—March 22, 1979. After an extended debate, and after voting down provisions that would have authorized state legislatures to change their minds and rescind prior ratification, Congress, by a simple majority vote, extended the time limit until June 30, 1982. It was argued that because the time limit was in the accompanying enabling legislation, not in the body of the proposed amendment, it was subject to congres-

> **Equal Rights Amendment (ERA)**
>
> Proposed March 22, 1972.
>
> Died June 30, 1982, three state legislatures shy of the thirty-eight needed for ratification.
>
> *Section 1.* Equality of rights under the law shall not be denied or abridged by the United States or by any State on account of sex.
>
> *Section 2.* The Congress shall have power to enforce by appropriate legislation the provisions of this article.
>
> *Section 3.* This amendment shall take effect two years after date of ratification.

TABLE 2–1

The 26 Amendments: How Long They Had to Wait between Congressional Approval and Actual Ratification

AMENDMENT	TIME TO RATIFY	RATIFIED
1–10. Bill of Rights	1 year, $2\frac{1}{2}$ months	1791
11. Lawsuits against states	3 years, 10 months	1798
12. Presidential elections	$8\frac{1}{2}$ months	1804
13. Abolition of slavery	$10\frac{1}{2}$ months	1865
14. Civil rights	2 years, $1\frac{1}{2}$ months	1868
15. Suffrage for all races	1 year, 1 month	1870
16. Income tax	3 years, $7\frac{1}{2}$ months	1913
17. Senatorial elections	1 year, $\frac{1}{2}$ month	1913
18. Prohibition	1 year, $1\frac{1}{2}$ months	1919
19. Women's suffrage	1 year, $2\frac{1}{2}$ months	1920
20. Terms of office	11 months	1933
21. Repeal of prohibition	$9\frac{1}{2}$ months	1933
22. Limit on presidential terms	3 years, $11\frac{1}{2}$ months	1951
23. Washington, D.C., vote	9 months	1961
24. Abolition of poll taxes	1 year, $5\frac{1}{2}$ months	1964
25. Presidential succession	1 year, $6\frac{1}{2}$ months	1967
26. 18-year-old suffrage	4 months	1971

© 1982 Field Newspaper Syndicate, by permission of News America Syndicate.

sional modification by simple majority. (The amendment failed, even with the extension, and thus made moot the pending court test of the extension's constitutionality.)

When Congress proposed an amendment to provide full congressional representation for the District of Columbia, it pointedly reverted to earlier practice and placed the seven-year limit *in the text* of the amendment. This suggests that: (1) Congress wanted to preclude any possibility of extending the time limit for ratification of this amendment by a simple majority of both houses; and (2) Congress sought to discourage proponents of unratified amendments from seeking extensions of time limits.

Ratification Politics: ERA and the D.C. Amendment

Until the submission of ERA and the D.C. Amendment, the Child Labor Amendment was the only formally proposed amendment since the Civil War that failed to be ratified. Ordinarily the existence of a political coalition sufficient to get an amendment proposed by Congress reflects enough support in the nation to ensure ratification. The failure of the ERA and the D.C. Amendment to be ratified makes it clear that this is not always the case.

POLITICS OF THE EQUAL RIGHTS AMENDMENT

The ERA received overwhelming support in both houses of Congress. Both major political parties had repeatedly supported it in their national party platforms; not until 1980 did one party (the Republican) adopt a stance of neutrality. Every president from Truman until Reagan and many of their wives had endorsed the amendment. And, by the end of the campaign for ratification, more than 450 organizations with a total membership of over 50 million were on record in support of ERA.[21]

Soon after submission of the amendment in 1972, many legislatures quickly ratified—sometimes without hearings—and by overwhelming majorities. By the end of 1972 twenty-two states had ratified the amendment.[22] It appeared that the ERA would soon become part of the Constitution. Then the opposition organized under the articulate leadership of Phyllis Schlafly and the ERA became controversial.

Opponents argued that "women would not only be subject to the military draft but also assigned to combat duty. Full-time housewives and mothers would be forced to join the labor force. Furthermore, women would no longer enjoy existing advantages under state domestic relations codes and under labor law."[23] The ERA also became embroiled in the controversy over abortion. Many opponents contended that its ratification would jeopardize the power of states and Congress to regulate abortion in any way, and would compel public funding of abortions.[24]

After the ERA became controversial, legislatures held lengthy hearings, and floor debates became heated. Legislators hid behind parliamentary procedures and avoided making a decision for as long as possible. Opposition to ratification arose chiefly in the same cluster of southern states that had opposed ratification of the Nineteenth Amendment.

As the opposition grew more active, proponents redoubled their efforts. The National Organization for Women (NOW) called for an economic boycott of

cities in nonratifying states, and many associations refused to hold their conventions in Chicago, Kansas City, Las Vegas, Miami, Atlanta, and New Orleans. Nonetheless, on the final deadline the amendment was still three state legislatures short.

The framers intended that amending the Constitution should be difficult. The ERA ratification battle demonstrates how well they planned.[25]

POLITICS OF THE D.C. AMENDMENT

Even though the D.C. Amendment passed both chambers of Congress by large margins and with impressive bipartisan support in 1978, it had been ratified by only sixteen states by its deadline on August 22, 1985. People who live in the District of Columbia, or Washington, D.C., as it is usually called, pay federal taxes (and D.C. taxes) and are subject to federal laws. Yet the District's only congressional voice is a *nonvoting delegate* who serves on committees, attends sessions, and participates (if desired) in all debates, but casts no vote. The 1978 amendment would have given the 640,000 people of the District of Columbia two senators and the same number of representatives (one, under current law) in the House of Representatives it would have if it were a state. It would also have given the District three electoral votes, with the possibility of more if its population grew to warrant it (it has three already, under the Twenty-third Amendment), as well as a vote in the ratification of constitutional amendments. Finally, it would have repealed the Twenty-third Amendment.

Proponents charged that the current situation is "taxation without representation." Although initial hopes were high, advocates of the amendment knew that ratification would be difficult. Many people in many states view the District as being "too urban, too liberal, and too Democratic." Moreover, the coalition that pushed the D.C. Amendment through Congress failed to maintain its cohesion

The Fifteenth Amendment was ratified in 1870, yet blacks were kept from voting in many southern states until Congress implemented the amendment by the Voting Rights Act of 1965. Here, blacks lined up to register in Selma, Alabama, in 1965 are stopped by local police.

during the ratification struggle. Many proponents of the amendment, after giving up hope that it would be ratified, turned their attention to persuading Congress to admit the District to the Union as a state—except for a small portion that would remain the "seat of the Government of the United States."

Statehood for the District of Columbia and its admission as New Columbia was a plank of the 1988 Democratic Platform. Such an action would accomplish all that the D.C. Amendment could have done, and more. Moreover, it requires only a simple majority vote of both houses of Congress and the approval of the President to accomplish. However, it is not likely that such action will be approved as long as there is a Republican in the White House. Only about 8 percent of the District's voters are registered Republicans, and statehood for the District would in all probability produce two Democratic senators,[26] one of whom might well be the Reverend Jesse Jackson.

Summary

1. Our Constitution both grants powers and limits them. The framers established a government to be operated by ordinary people; they did not anticipate that Americans would be so special that they could be trusted to operate without checks and balances. The framers were suspicious of people, especially of those having political power, so they separated and distributed the powers of the newly created national government in a variety of ways.

2. The framers were also concerned that the national government be strong enough to solve public problems. They wanted it to be responsive to the wishes of the people and to carry out those wishes, that is, the matured and refined wishes of the people. Thus, they gave the national government substantial grants of power. But these grants were made with such broad strokes that it has been possible for the national government and the constitutional system to remain flexible and adapt to changing conditions.

3. Although the American governmental system has its roots in British traditions, our separation of powers and checks and balances systems differentiate our system from the British system of concentrated responsibility. It is also different because our courts have the power of judicial review.

4. The system of checks and balances has been modified over time. The Constitution has been adapted to new conditions through Congressional elaboration, modern presidential realities, customs and usages, and judicial interpretation.

5. Although adaptable, the Constitution itself needs to be altered from time to time, and the document provides for its own amendment. An amendment must be both proposed and ratified: proposed by either a two-thirds vote in each chamber of Congress or a national convention called by Congress on petition of the legislatures in two-thirds of the states; ratified either by the legislatures in three-fourths of the states or by specially called ratifying conventions in three-fourths of the states. The Constitution has been formally amended twenty-six times.

Further Reading

WILLBOURN E. BENTON, ed. *1787: Drafting the U.S. Constitution* (Texas A&M Press, 1986).

RICHARD B. BERNSTEIN. *Are We To Be a Nation? The Making of the Constitution* (Harvard Univesity Press, 1987).

JAMES BRYCE. *The American Commonwealth*, vols. 1 and 2 (Macmillan, 1889).

JAMES MACGREGOR BURNS. *The Vineyard of Liberty* (Knopf, 1982).

Congressional Research Service, Library of Congress. *The Constitution of the United States of America, Analysis and Interpretation* [Senate Document 99–16] (U.S. Government Printing Office, 1988); 1986 Supplement [Senate Document 100–9], 1987.

ALEXIS DE TOCQUEVILLE. *Democracy in America*, vols. 1 and 2 (Knopf, 1945; first published in 1835).

SANFORD LEVINSON. *Constitutional Faith* (Princeton University Press, 1988).

LEONARD W. LEVY. *Original Intent and the Framers' Constitution* (Macmillan, 1988).

DREW R. MCCOY, *The Last of the Fathers: James Madison and the Republican Legacy* (Columbia University Press, 1989).

FORREST MCDONALD. *Novus Ordo Seclorum: The Intellectual Origins of the Constitution* (University Press of Kansas, 1985).

J. W. PELTASON. *Understanding the Constitution*, 11th ed. (Holt, Rinehart & Winston, 1988).

DONALD L. ROBINSON, ed. *Reforming American Government: The Bicentennial Papers of the Committee on the Constitutional System* (Westview Press, 1985).

Subcommittee on the Constitution, Committee on the Judiciary, United States Senate. *Amendments to the Constitution: A Brief Legislative History* (U.S. Government Printing Office, 1985).

JAMES L. SUNDQUIST, *Constitutional Reform and Effective Government* (Brookings Institution, 1986).

This Constitution, a collection of essays on the framing and early debates (Congressional Quarterly Press, 1986).

CLEMENT E. VOSE. *Constitutional Change* (Lexington Books, 1972).

1. Max Lerner, *Ideas for the Ice Age* (Viking, 1941), pp. 241–42. See also "The American Public's Knowledge of the U.S. Constitution: A National Survey of Public Awareness and Personal Opinion" (The Hearst Corporation, 1987).

2. Sanford Levinson, *Constitutional Faith* (Princeton University Press, 1988), pp. 9–52.

3. Quoted in Alpheus T. Mason, *The Supreme Court: Palladium of Freedom* (University of Michigan Press, 1962), p. 10.

4. *The Federalist*, No. 51.

5. Richard E. Neustadt, *Presidential Power*, new ed. (Wiley, 1980), p. 101.

6. Edward S. Corwin, "The Constitution as Instrument and as Symbol," *American Political Science Review* (December 1936), p. 1078.

7. Cranch 137 (1803).

8. *Dred Scott* v. *Sandford*, 19 Howard 393 (1857).

9. J. W. Peltason, *Federal Courts in the Political Process* (Random House, 1955).

10. James L. Sundquist, "Needed: A Political Theory for the New Era of Coalition Government in the United States," *Political Science Quarterly* (Winter 1988–1989), pp. 613–35.

11. John R. Labovitz, *Presidential Impeachment* (Yale University Press, 1978).

12. Neustadt, *Presidential Power*, p. 280.

13. See Committee on the Constitutional System, *A Bicentennial Analysis of The American Political Structure: Report and Recommendations of the Committee on the Constitutional System* (1987) for recommendations of a committee co-chaired by Senator Nancy L. Kassebaum, C. Douglas Dillon, and Lloyd Cutler; for critical comments, see Mark P. Petracca, "To Right What the Constitution Has Wrought or to Wrong What is Right." Paper delivered at annual meeting of the American Political Science Association, September 1–4, 1988, Washington, D.C.

14. Ann Stuart Diamond, "A Convention for Proposing Amendments: The Constitution's Other Method," *Publius* (Summer 1981), pp. 113–46; Wilbur Edel, "Amending the Constitution by Convention: Myths and Realities," *State Government*, vol. 55 (1982), pp. 51–56.

15. Frank J. Sorauf, "The Political Potential of an Amending Convention," in Kermit L. Hall, Harold M. Hyman, and Leon V. Sigal, eds., *The Constitutional Convention as an Amending Device*. See also Bill Gaugush, "Principles Governing the Interpretation and Exercise of Article V Power," *Western Political Quarterly* (June 1982), pp. 212–21; and response by C. Herman Pritchett, "Congress and Article V, Conventions," *Western Political Quarterly* (June 1982), pp. 222–27.

16. *The Wall Street Journal* (October 5, 1985), p. 1; *Congressional Quarterly Weekly Report*, vol. 46 (May 28, 1988), p. 1443.

17. Letter to George Eve, quoted in Walter E. Dellinger, "The Recurring Question," *Yale Law Journal* (July 1979), p. 1634.

18. Samuel S. Freedman and Pamela J. Naughton, *ERA: May a State Change Its Vote?* (Wayne State University Press, 1979).

19. Alan P. Grimes, *Democracy and Amendments to the Constitution* (Lexington Books, 1978), p. 95. See also Clement E. Vose, *Constitutional Change* (Lexington Books, 1972), pp. 342–44, which focuses on amendment politics in the case of women's suffrage, child labor, and prohibition.

20. Gregory A. Caldeira, "Constitutional Change in America: Dynamics of Ratification under Article V," *Publius* (Fall 1985), p. 29.

21. Janet K. Boles, "Building Support for the ERA: A Case of Too Much, Too Late," *P.S.* (Fall 1982), p. 572.

22. Mark R. Daniels, Robert Darcy, and Joseph W. Westphal, "The ERA Won—At Least in the Opinion Polls," *P.S.* (Fall 1982), p. 583.

23. Janet K. Boles, *The Politics of the Equal Rights Amendment* (Longmans, 1979), p. 4.

24. Gilbert Y. Steiner, *Constitutional Inequality: The Political Fortunes of the Equal Rights Amendment* (The Brookings Institution, 1985), p. 64. See also Mary Francis Berry, *Why the ERA Failed: Politics, Women's Rights and the Amending Process of the Constitution* (Indiana University Press, 1985).

25. Margery L. Elfin, "Learning from Failures Present and Past," and Marian L. Palley, "Beyond the Deadline," in *P.S.* (Fall 1982), pp. 582–92. See also Mark R. Daniels and Robert E. Darcy, "As Time Goes By: Arrested Diffusion of the ERA," *Publius: The Journal of Federalism* (Fall 1985), p. 51; Joan Hoff-Wilson, ed., *Rights of Passage: The Past and Future of the ERA* (Indiana University Press, 1986).

26. Clifford D. May, "Rumblings Rise Anew on Status of Capital," *The New York Times* (January 11, 1989), p. B6.

3

American Federalism: Problems and Prospects

"There are two ways to empty a room in Washington: Hold a fund raiser for a defeated candidate or a debate on federalism."[1] Outside of Washington as well, when you talk about federalism you are likely to make people's eyes glaze over.

Federalism, however, closely affects our lives, as the framers clearly recognized. For early American citizens who feared governmental threats to their liberties—and most thinking Americans in the 1780s put this at the top of their worry list—both the *division* of powers between national and state governments (federalism) and the *separation* of powers at each level of government, along with the checks and balances, promised to serve as potent barriers against tyrannical action in the national or state capitals. In effect these devices "divided the enemy"—the government. If the national government threatened people's liberties, the states would protect them—and vice versa. If the executive, the legislature, or the judiciary at any level threatened people's liberties, one of the other branches would protect them. In general the more "vetoes" built into government, the more the government would keep "hands off the people's liberties," and our rights as outlined in the Bill of Rights and other provisions of the Constitution would be protected.

At the same time, for those persons who hoped that governments could be used to protect their rights and liberties—blacks or many women for example—divided government could have the reverse impact. Indeed, efforts to ban child labor in the United States had to overcome so many obstacles created in large part by our federal system, that action was delayed for over a half century. And it took decades to bring national civil rights laws into play to protect blacks against abridgment of their rights by state governments—again in large measure because of having to work through a federal system.

Thus whether federalism makes it easier to protect rights or more difficult to secure them depends upon which rights *and on* whether contending groups are seeking to protect rights *from* government or to broaden them *through* government. The framers of our Constitution, by and large, had no doubts. They believed that federalism—along with other structures of governments such as separation of powers, and checks and balances that divide governmental powers into various pockets to constrain government officials—are more important to preserving liberty and protecting our rights than is the Bill of Rights.

Imagine how the events of 1787 seemed to Americans of two centuries ago. Or to put it in modern terms, suppose you heard Congress had sent a delegation to Ottawa to meet with representatives from Canada and Mexico to draft a constitution for the United Governments of North America. Such a situation would only roughly parallel what happened in the summer of 1787, yet it gives you some idea of the worries that citizens of Massachusetts, Virginia, and the other states felt when they heard rumors about the drafting of a constitution in Philadelphia. The new government, it was rumored, was to have powers to tax and regulate the lives of the people. Citizens' apprehensions were heightened when the proposed constitution was published; most of the rumors were true.

The issues of federalism did not end with the founding period. In 1861 men and women fought and died for Virginia or Texas or for the Union (although it would be a mistake to think of the Civil War as merely a particularly heated debate over the principles of federalism).

What is a federal system? The mere existence of both national and state governments does not make our system federal. What is important is that a *constitution* divides governmental powers between the general, or national, government and the constituent governments (called states in the United States), giving substantial functions to each. Neither the central nor the constituent government receives its powers from the other; both derive them from a common source—a constitution. This constitutional distribution of powers cannot be changed by the ordinary process of legislation—for example, by an act of either a national or state legislature. Finally, both levels of government operate through their own agents and exercise power directly over individuals. Among the countries that have federal systems of government are the United States, Canada, Switzerland, Mexico, and Australia. "Nearly 40 percent of the world's population now lives within polities that are formally federal; another third live in polities that apply federal arrangements in some way."[2]

Constitutionally, our federal system consists only of the national government and the fifty states. "Cities are not," as the Supreme Court has reminded us, "sovereign entities." But in a practical sense, we are a nation of over 83,000 governmental units—from the national government to the school board district. This does not make for a tidy, efficient, easy-to-understand system, but, as we shall see, it does have its virtues.

That ours is a federal system makes a lot of difference, even if we are not always aware that this is so. Almost every aspect of our lives is affected by several layers of government. Consider your college or university, public or independent. About half of the students are likely to be receiving some form of national or state financial assistance to help pay their tuition and fees. The college itself is chartered by the state. Most of the funds that pay for the teachers, staff, and buildings come from state appropriations, state bonds, private gifts encouraged by national tax laws, or a combination of national, state, and private sources. The research your faculty is doing, especially in the sciences, and the public-service programs in which they are involved, are likely to be supported by some combination of national, state, and private (yet tax-deductible) dollars. The conditions under which students are admitted, how their grades are posted and reported, and how faculty and staff are appointed and evaluated are subject to national and state regulations. The use of experimental animals is subject to supervision by national and state governments, and national and state inspectors check to ensure that laboratories properly dispose of used chemicals.

Number of Governments	
States	50
Counties	3,042
Municipalities	19,205
Towns	16,691
School Districts	14,741
Special Districts	29,481
Total	**83,180**

Source: *1987 Census of Governments*, U.S. Department of Commerce, Bureau of the Census.

What are the alternatives to federalism? There are **unitary systems** of government in which a constitution vests all governmental power in the central government. The central government, if it so chooses, may delegate authority to constituent units, but what it delegates it may also take away. Britain, France, Israel, and the Philippines have this form of government. In the United States the relationship between states and their local governments, such as counties and cities, is usually of this sort.

Then there are **confederations** in which the constituent governments create a central government by constitutional compact, but do not give it power to regulate the conduct of individuals. The central government makes regulations for the constituent governments, but it exists and operates only at their direction. The thirteen states under the Articles of Confederation operated in this manner, as did the Southern Confederacy during the Civil War.

It complicates our understanding of federalism that the founders of our Constitution used the term *federal* to describe what we would now call a *confederate* form of government. Moreover, today "federal" is frequently used as a synonym for national. People often refer to the government in Washington as "the federal government." But, in fact, it is the states and the national government *together* that make up our federal system.

Why Federalism?

In 1787 federalism was an obvious choice. Confederation had been tried and found wanting, but a unitary system was out of the question. Most of the people were too deeply attached to their state governments to permit them to be subordinated to central rule. Even if a unitary state had been politically possible in 1787, it would not have been chosen. Federalism was, and still is, thought to be ideally suited to the needs of a heterogeneous people spread over a large continent, suspicious of concentrated power, and desiring unity but not uniformity. Federalism offered many advantages for such a people.

FEDERALISM ALLOWS UNITY WITHOUT UNIFORMITY

National politicians and parties do not have to iron out every difference on every issue in every state. Such issues as divorce, gun-control, **comparable worth,** capital punishment, and the creation, operation, and financing of community colleges are debated in state legislatures and city halls; there is no need to enforce a single national standard. As a result, it is easier to develop consensus on truly national problems.

FEDERALISM CHECKS THE GROWTH OF TYRANNY

Although in the rest of the world federal forms have not been notably successful in preventing tyranny, and many unitary governments are democratic, Americans tend to equate freedom with federalism.[3] As Madison pointed out in *The Federalist,* No. 10: "[If] factious leaders . . . kindle a flame within their particular states," national leaders can check the spread of the "conflagration into other states." Shays's Rebellion was a dramatic example. Moreover, when one political party loses control of the national government, it is still likely to hold office in a number

CHAPTER 3 / American Federalism: Problems and Prospects

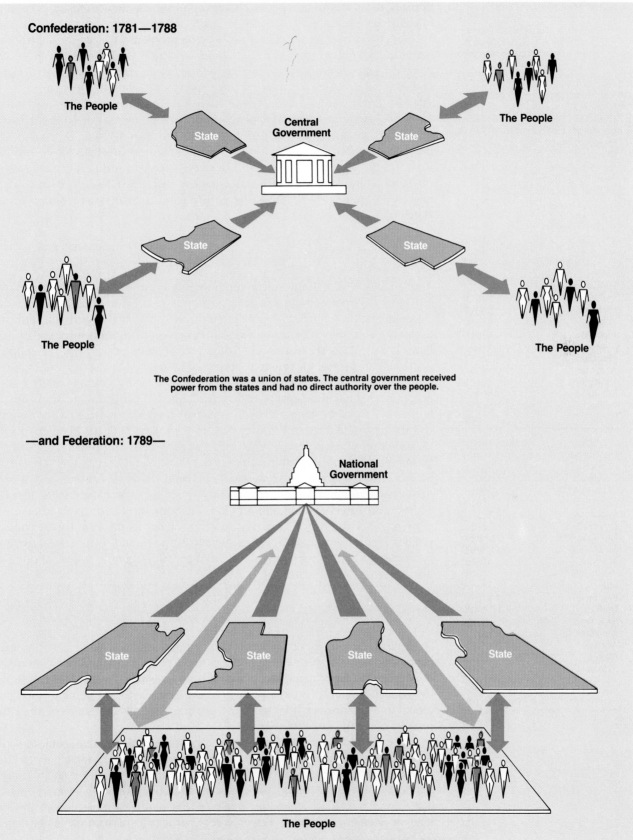

Confederation: 1781—1788

The People

The People

State

Central Government

State

State

State

The People

The People

The Confederation was a union of states. The central government received power from the states and had no direct authority over the people.

—and Federation: 1789—

National Government

State

State

State

State

The People

The Federal Union is a union of people. The national government and state governments receive power from the people and exercise authority directly over them.

Statehood (1787–1959)

This list gives dates when states either ratified the U.S. Constitution or gained formal admittance to the Union.

Delaware	12/1787
Pennsylvania	12/1787
New Jersey	12/1787
Georgia	1/1788
Connecticut	1/1788
Massachusetts	2/1788
Maryland	4/1788
South Carolina	5/1788
New Hampshire	6/1788
Virginia	6/1788
New York	7/1788
North Carolina	11/1789
Rhode Island	5/1790
Vermont	3/1791
Kentucky	6/1792
Tennessee	6/1796
Ohio	3/1803
Louisiana	4/1812
Indiana	12/1816
Mississippi	12/1817
Illinois	12/1818
Alabama	12/1819
Maine	3/1820
Missouri	8/1821
Arkansas	6/1836
Michigan	1/1837
Florida	3/1845
Texas	12/1845
Iowa	12/1846
Wisconsin	5/1848
California	9/1850
Minnesota	5/1858
Oregon	2/1859
Kansas	1/1861
West Virginia	6/1863
Nevada	10/1864
Nebraska	3/1867
Colorado	8/1876
North Dakota	11/1889
South Dakota	11/1889
Montana	11/1889
Washington	11/1889
Idaho	7/1890
Wyoming	7/1890
Utah	1/1896
Oklahoma	1/1907
New Mexico	1/1912
Arizona	2/1912
Alaska	1/1959
Hawaii	8/1959

Note: This information is not provided to be memorized (!), but to suggest the evolution and expansion of the nation.

of states. It can then regroup, develop new policies and new leaders, and continue to challenge the party in power at the national level.

Such diffusion of power creates its own problems. It makes it difficult for a national majority to carry out a program of action, and it permits those who control a state government to frustrate the consensus expressed through Congress and national agencies. To some of our country's founders this was an advantage. They were more fearful that a single-interest national majority might capture the national government and attempt to suppress the interests of others than they were that minority interests might frustrate the national will. Of course—and this point is often overlooked today (but emphasized by Madison in *Federalist,* No. 10)—the size of the nation and the many interests within it are the greatest obstacles to the formation of a single-interest majority. However, even if such a majority should form, having to work through a federal system would act as a check on it.

FEDERALISM ENCOURAGES EXPERIMENTATION

Justice Louis Brandeis, the celebrated Supreme Court justice (on the Court from 1916 to 1939), pointed out that state governments provide great laboratories for experimentation with public policy. This role "in policy experimentation may become" more important as the federal government confronts fiscal and political limits. . . . and as the nation confronts such matters as . . . the revolution in family life, including, for example, surrogate motherhood, test-tube babies, adoption, and care of the elderly."[4] States serve as proving grounds. If they adopt programs that fail, the negative effects are limited; if programs succeed, they can be adopted by other states and by the national government. Georgia, for example, was the first state to permit 18-year-olds to vote; New York has been vigorous in its assault on water pollution; California has pioneered air pollution control programs. After federal leadership waned in the 1970s, New Jersey assumed leadership in programs to handle toxic wastes; it initiated radon gas testing, and was the first state to adopt a state-wide mandatory recycling law.[5] Many states legalized abortion under certain conditions before the Supreme Court acted (whether this is progress or regression depends on one's values, as do so many questions of politics). Sunset laws, equal housing, no-fault insurance, and "lemon" laws providing consumer protection for faulty automobiles are a few other examples of programs that originated in the states.

FEDERALISM KEEPS GOVERNMENT CLOSE TO THE PEOPLE

Federalism, by providing numerous areas for decision making, involves many people and helps keep government closer to the people. Just think of the thousands of people who every night attend school board meetings, water district hearings, city council sessions, county planning board sessions, or are going to their state capitol to make presentations to their legislators. Literally thousands of Americans run our governments day by day.

We should be cautious, however, about generalizing that state and local governments are necessarily "closer to the people" than the national government is. True, more people are involved in local and state politics than in national affairs, and in recent years confidence in the ability of state governments has gone up. Yet national affairs are more on the minds of most people than are state or even local politics. Fewer voters participate in state elections than in

Although everybody is against pollution, legislating against it and establishing responsibility for the costs can arouse intense political controversy among the various levels of government.

congressional and presidential elections. Still, states and their local units remain very much a part of the political life of those concerned with public affairs.

Constitutional Structure of American Federalism

Dividing powers and responsibilities among the national and state governments requires thousands of court decisions, hundreds of books, and a million speeches to explain—and even then the division lacks precise definition. The formal constitutional framework of our federal system, however, may be stated relatively simply:

1. The national government has only those powers (with the one important exception of foreign affairs) *delegated* to it by the Constitution.
2. The state governments have the powers not delegated to the central government, except those *denied* to them by the Constitution and their state constitutions.
3. Within the scope of its operations, the national government is *supreme*.
4. Some powers are specifically denied to *both* the national and state governments; others are specifically denied *only* to the states; still others are denied *only* to the national government.

TABLE 3–1
The Most Popular Level of Government

From which level of government do you feel you get the most for your money—federal, state, or local? (Percent of U.S. public)

LEVEL	1974	1976	1978	1980	1982	1984	1986	1988
National	29	36	35	33	35	24	32	28
Local	28	25	26	26	28	35	33	29
State	24	20	20	22	20	27	22	27
Don't know	19	19	19	19	17	14	13	16

Source: Debra L. Dean, Advisory Commission on Intergovernmental Relations, "Closing the Opinion Gap: State and Local Governments Fare Well in ACIR Poll," *Intergovernmental Perspective* (Fall 1988), p. 24.

POWERS OF THE NATIONAL GOVERNMENT

The Constitution, chiefly in the first three articles, delegates legislative, executive, and judicial powers to the national government. In addition to these **express powers,** the Constitution delegates to Congress those **implied powers** that may be reasonably inferred from the express powers. The constitutional basis for the implied powers of Congress is the **necessary and proper clause** (Article I, Section 8), which gives Congress the right "to make all Laws which shall be necessary and proper for carrying into Execution the foregoing Powers, and all other Powers vested . . . in the Government of the United States."

In the field of foreign affairs, the national government has **inherent powers** that do not depend on specific constitutional grants. The national government has the same authority in dealing with other nations as if it were a unitary government. For example, the government of the United States may acquire territory by discovery and occupation, even though no specific clause in the Constitution allows such acquisition. Even if the Constitution were silent about foreign affairs—which it is not—the national government would have the right to declare war, make treaties, and appoint and receive ambassadors.

National Supremacy Clause   Article VI states: "This Constitution, and the Laws of the United States which shall be made in Pursuance thereof; and all Treaties made . . . under the Authority of the United States, shall be the supreme Law of the Land; and the Judges in every State shall be bound thereby; any Thing in the Constitution or Laws of any State to the Contrary notwithstanding." All officials, state as well as national, are bound by constitutional oath to support the Constitution of the United States. States may not use their reserved powers to override national policies. (Local units of government are agents of the states. What states cannot constitutionally do, local units cannot do. In our discussion of the constitutional structure of federalism, local units are included in all references to states.) National laws and regulations of federal agencies *preempt* the field so that conflicting state and local rules and regulations are unenforceable.

POWERS OF THE STATES

The Constitution reserves for the states all powers not granted to the national government, subject only to the limitations of the Constitution. Powers that are

Education and interstate highways are areas in which the federal government often helps state and local governments with tax dollars.

not given exclusively to the national government, by provision of the Constitution or by judicial interpretation, may be concurrently exercised by the states, as long as there is no conflict with national law. For example, each state has **concurrent powers** with the national government to levy taxes and to regulate commerce internal to each state. How federalism limits the states' taxing powers is neither simple to explain nor simple to understand. In general, a state may levy a tax on the same item as the national government, but a state cannot, by a tax, "unduly burden" commerce among the states, or interfere with a function of the national government, or complicate the operation of a national law, or abridge the terms of a treaty of the United States. Who decides whether a state tax is an "undue burden" on a national function or commerce among the states? Ultimately, the Supreme Court decides.

Federalism issues are even more complicated when states attempt to protect the public health and well-being. When Congress has not acted, states may regulate even interstate businesses, provided these regulations do not cover matters requiring uniform national treatment or are not unduly burdening interstate commerce. Who decides what requires uniform national treatment or might be an undue burden on interstate commerce? Congress does, subject to final review by the Supreme Court. When Congress is silent or does not clearly state its intentions, courts, ultimately the Supreme Court, decide if there is a conflict with the national Constitution or a national law or national regulation, or if there has been federal preemption.

CONSTITUTIONAL LIMITS AND OBLIGATIONS

To make federalism work, the Constitution imposes certain restraints on the national and state governments. States are prohibited from

1. Making treaties with foreign governments
2. Authorizing private persons to prey on the shipping and commerce of other nations—what the Constitution refers to as "granting letters of Marque and Reprisal"
3. Coining money, issuing bills of credit, or making anything but gold and silver coin a tender in payment of debts.

Nor may states, without the consent of Congress,

1. Tax imports or exports
2. Tax foreign ships
3. Keep troops or ships in time of peace (except for the state militia, now called the National Guard)
4. Enter into compacts with other states or foreign nations that "tend to increase the political power in the States, which may encroach upon or interfere" with the supremacy of the national government
5. Engage in war, unless invaded or in such imminent danger as will not admit of delay (of course, an invasion of one state would be an invasion of the United States itself).

The national government, in turn, is required by the Constitution to refrain from exercising its powers, especially its powers to tax and to regulate interstate commerce, in such a way as to interfere substantially with the ability of the states to perform their responsibilities. Making this generalization about how the princi-

CONSTITUTIONAL DISTRIBUTION OF POWERS

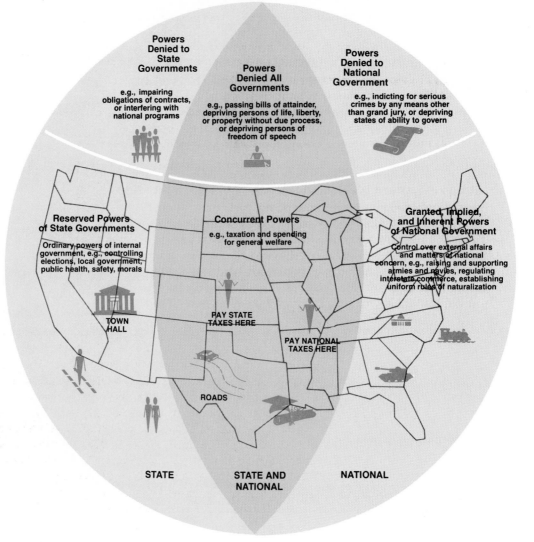

Powers
Denied to
State
Governments

e.g., impairing
obligations of contracts,
or interfering with
national programs

Powers
Denied All
Governments

e.g., passing bills of attainder,
depriving persons of life, liberty,
or property without due process,
or depriving persons of
freedom of speech

Powers
Denied to
National
Government

e.g., indicting for serious
crimes by any means other
than grand jury, or depriving
states of ability to govern

Reserved Powers
of State Governments

Ordinary powers of internal
government, e.g., controlling
elections, local government,
public health, safety, morals

Concurrent Powers

e.g., taxation and spending
for general welfare

Granted, Implied,
and Inherent Powers
of National Government

Control over external affairs
and matters of national
concern, e.g., raising and supporting
armies and navies, regulating
interstate commerce, establishing
uniform rules of naturalization

TOWN
HALL

PAY STATE
TAXES HERE

PAY NATIONAL
TAXES HERE

ROADS

STATE

STATE AND
NATIONAL

NATIONAL

ples of federalism limit national powers is easier than citing specific modern-day examples of how in fact the Supreme Court has struck down any actions of the national government because of interference with state sovereignty. Today whatever protection states have comes from the political process—the built-in restraints that our system provides because individuals elected from the states participate in the decisions of Congress—rather than from judicially enforced limitations.[6]

The Constitution also requires the national government to guarantee to each state a **republican form of government.** The framers used this term to distinguish a republic from a monarchy, on the one side, and from a pure, direct democracy, on the other. Congress, not the courts, enforces this guarantee and determines what is or is not a republican form of government. By permitting the congressional delegation of a state to take its seat in Congress, Congress is in effect deciding that the state has the republican form of government guaranteed by the Constitution.

In addition, the national government is obliged by the Constitution to protect states against *domestic insurrection*. Congress has delegated to the president the authority to dispatch troops to put down such insurrections when so requested by the proper state authorities. (If there are contesting state authorities, the president decides which ones are the proper ones.)[7] The president does not have to wait, however, for a request from state authorities to send federal troops into a state to enforce federal laws. Today it is hard to imagine a situation of domestic insurrection against a state that would not also involve federal matters.

HORIZONTAL FEDERALISM: INTERSTATE CONSTITUTIONAL RELATIONS

Three clauses in the Constitution that were taken from the Articles of Confederation require the states to give full faith and credit to one another's public acts, records, and judicial proceedings; to extend to one another's citizens the privileges and immunities of their own citizens; and to return persons who are fleeing from justice.

Full Faith and Credit   The **full faith and credit clause** is one of the more technical provisions of the Constitution. In general, it requires each state court to enforce civil judgments of other state courts and to accept their public records and acts as valid documents. (It does not require states to enforce the criminal laws of other states; in most cases, for one state to enforce the criminal laws of another would be unconstitutional.) The clause applies especially to noncriminal judicial proceedings.

Interstate Privileges and Immunities   States must extend to citizens of other states the privileges and immunities granted to their own citizens, including the protection of the laws, the right to engage in peaceful occupations, access to the courts, and freedom from discriminatory taxes. Further, because of this clause, states may not impose unreasonable "durational residency" requirements to withhold political rights such as voting or to withhold such benefits as medical help from United States citizens who move into their boundaries and thereby become state citizens. How long a residency requirement may a state impose? A day seems to be about as long as the Court will tolerate for welfare payments or medical care, fifty days or so for voting privileges, and one year for payment of in-state tuition for state-supported colleges and universities. (Persons who are financially independent who move into a state just prior to enrolling in a state-supported university or college may be required to prove that they intend to remain after finishing their schooling, and to supply proof of becoming a citizen of the state by such evidence as tax payments, driver's licenses, car registrations, voter registrations, and continuous, year-round off-campus residence.)

Extradition   The Constitution asserts that when criminals have fled from one state to another, the state to which they have fled is to deliver them to the proper officials upon the demand of the executive authority of the state from which they fled. "The obvious objective of the Extradition Clause is that no State should become a safe haven for the fugitives from a sister State's criminal justice system."[8] Congress has supplemented this constitutional provision by making the governor of the state to which fugitives have fled the agent responsible for returning them. Despite the use of the word "shall" in the Constitution, an 1861 Supreme Court decision, based on an antiquated view of federalism, controlled extradition until 1987, and federal courts would not order governors to surrender (extradite) persons wanted in other states. This is no longer so, since the 1861 decision has been reversed.[9] Usually federal courts do not become involved, and extradition is a routine matter. Recently, however, disputes over the custody of children that some-times lead to criminal charges of parental kidnapping have complicated extradition procedures.

Interstate Compacts   In addition to these three obligations, the Constitution also requires states to settle disputes with one another without the use of force. States may carry their legal disputes to the Supreme Court, or they may negotiate **inter-state compacts.** More often interstate compacts are used to establish interstate agencies to handle interstate problems. Before most interstate compacts become effective, congressional approval is required. After a compact has been signed and approved by Congress, it becomes binding on all signatory states, and its terms are enforceable by the Supreme Court. A typical state belongs to twenty compacts dealing with such subjects as environmental protection, crime control, water rights, and higher education exchanges.[10]

THE REALITIES TODAY

This outline of the constitutional structure of federalism is oversimplified and—especially in terms of the division of powers between the national government and the states—even misleading. The formal structures of our federal system have not changed much since 1787, but the political realities, especially during the last half century, have greatly altered how they are used. During the Great Depression of the 1930s, the nation debated whether Congress had the constitu-tional authority to enact legislation dealing with agriculture, labor, education, housing, and welfare. Only twenty-five years ago some questioned the constitutional authority of Congress to legislate against racial discrimination. Even today it remains technically correct that Congress lacks any general grant of authority to do whatever it thinks necessary and proper in order to promote the general welfare or preserve domestic tranquility. But as a result of the rise of a national economy, the growth of national demands on Washington, and the emergence of a world in which a nuclear attack could destroy us in a matter of minutes, our constitutional system has so evolved that the national government has authority to deal with almost every issue. Today, restraints on national power stem from constitutional provisions protecting the liberties of the people rather than from those relating to the powers of state governments.

Triumph of the Nationalist Interpretation

The preceding summary of the constitutional construction of our federal system jumps over two hundred years of conflict and proclaims victory, at least for the moment, for the nationalist interpretation. The debate between those who favor national action **(centralists)** and those who favor state and local levels **(decentral-ists)** continues, yet generally it does so outside the framework of constitutional principles. This victory for the nationalists is recent. Throughout most of our history, powerful groups have favored states' rights.

The constitutional arguments revolving around federalism grew out of specific issues: Did the national government have the authority to outlaw slavery in the territories? Did states have the authority to operate racially segregated schools? Could Congress regulate labor relations? The debates were frequently phrased in constitutional language, and appeals were made to the great principles of federalism. But they were also arguments over who was to get what, where, and how, and who was to do what to whom.

Among those favoring the states' rights interpretation, with varying emphasis, were Thomas Jefferson, John C. Calhoun, the Supreme Court from the 1920s to 1937, and, more recently, Ronald Reagan, George Bush, Chief Justice Rehnquist, and Justice O'Connor. They contend that the Constitution is a treaty among sovereign states that created the central government and gave it carefully limited authority. As a result, the national government is nothing more than an agent of the states, and every one of its powers should be narrowly defined. Any question of whether the states have given a particular function to the central government or have reserved it for themselves should be resolved in favor of the states.

States' righters hold that the national government should not be permitted to exercise its delegated powers in a way that interferes with activities reserved for the states. The Tenth Amendment, they claim, makes this clear: "The powers not delegated to the United States by the Constitution, nor prohibited by it to the States, are reserved to the States respectively, or to the people." Decentralists insist state governments are closer to the people and reflect the people's wishes more accurately than does the national government. The national government, they add, is inherently heavy-handed and bureaucratic; to preserve our federal system and our liberties, central authority must be kept under control.

The nationalist position, supported by Chief Justice John Marshall, Abraham Lincoln, Theodore Roosevelt, Franklin Roosevelt, and throughout most of our history by the Supreme Court, rejects the whole concept of the Constitution as an interstate compact. Rather, it views the Constitution as a supreme law established by the people. The national government is an agent of the people, not of the states, because it was the people who drew up the Constitution and created the national government. The sovereign people gave the national government sufficient power to accomplish the great objectives listed in the Preamble. They intended that the central government's powers should be liberally defined and that the central government should be denied authority only when the Constitution clearly prohibits it from acting.

Nationalists argue the national government is a government of all the people, and that each state speaks for only some of the people. Although the Tenth Amendment clearly reserves powers for the states, as Chief Justice Harlan Stone said: "The Tenth Amendment states but a truism that all is retained which has not been surrendered" (*United States* v. *Darby*, 1941).[11] The Amendment does not deny the national government the right to exercise to the fullest extent all the powers given to it by the Constitution. On the other hand, the supremacy of the national government, it is argued, restricts the states, because governments representing part of the people cannot be allowed to interfere with a government representing all of them.

McCULLOCH VERSUS MARYLAND

In **McCulloch v. Maryland** (1819) the Supreme Court had the first of many chances to choose between these two interpretations of our federal system.[12] Maryland had levied a tax against the Baltimore branch of the Bank of the United States, a semipublic agency established by Congress. James William McCulloch, the cashier of the bank, refused to pay on the grounds that a state could not tax an instrument of the national government. Maryland's attorneys responded that, in the first place, the national government did not have the power to incorporate a bank, but even if it did, the state had the power to tax it.

Centralists versus Decentralists

CENTRALISTS' ARGUMENTS
1. State and local governments lack expertise.
2. State and local officials tend to be parochial.
3. State and local governments are unable or unwilling to raise enough money to meet demands.
4. State and local governments are more apt to reflect race and ethnic biases.
5. State and local governments are more likely to be dominated by conservative elites.
6. State and local governments are structurally incapable of dealing with problems of redistribution from the rich to the poor.
7. Given . . . the mobility of corporate and residential taxpayers, states and localities are not able to regulate business effectively.

DECENTRALISTS' RESPONSES
1. Changes in population have made the states more competent and sensitive to urban needs.
2. Changes in tax structure have made states and local governments more flexible and progressive raisers of revenue.
3. Legal and political changes have made states and localities as sensitive to the needs of the poor and minorities as the national government.
4. Political reform movements have made state and local governments more effective governments.

Look closely at the operation of your state and city governments. Do the facts as you know them support the contentions of the centralists?

Source: Jeffrey R. Henig, *Public Policy and Federalism: Issues in State and Local Politics* (St. Martin's Press, 1985), pp. 34–41. Copyright © 1985 by St. Martin's Press, Inc. Reprinted by permission of the publisher.

Maryland was represented before the Court by some of the country's most distinguished lawyers, including Luther Martin, a delegate to the Constitutional Convention who had left early when it became apparent that a strong national government was in the making. Martin, basing his argument on the states' rights view of federalism, said the power to incorporate a bank is not expressly delegated to the national government. He contended that Article I, Section 8, Clause 18, which gives Congress the right to choose whatever means are necessary and proper to carry out its delegated powers, gives Congress only the power to choose those means and to pass those laws absolutely essential to the execution of its expressly granted powers. Because a bank is not absolutely necessary to the exercise of any of its delegated powers, Congress has no authority to establish it. As for Maryland's right to tax the bank, Martin's position was clear: The power to tax is one of the powers reserved to the states; they may use it as they see fit.

The national government was represented by equally distinguished counsel, chief among whom was Daniel Webster. Webster conceded that the power to create a bank is not one of the express powers of the national government. However, the power to pass laws *necessary* and *proper* to carry out enumerated powers is expressly delegated to Congress, and this should be interpreted to mean Congress has authority to enact any legislation convenient and useful in carrying out delegated national powers. Therefore, Congress may incorporate a bank as an appropriate, convenient, and useful means of exercising the granted powers of collecting taxes, borrowing money, and caring for the property of the United States.

Webster contended that although the power to tax is reserved to the states, states cannot use their reserved powers to interfere with the operations of the national government. The Constitution leaves no room for doubt; in cases of conflict between the national and state governments, the national is supreme.

Speaking for a unanimous Court, Marshall rejected every one of Maryland's contentions. He wrote: "We must never forget that it is a constitution we are expounding . . . a constitution intended to endure for ages to come, and consequently, to be adapted to the various crises of human affairs. . . . The government of the Union, then, . . . is, emphatically, and truly, a government of the people. In form and substance it emanates from them. Its powers are granted by them, and are to be exercised directly on them, and for their benefit. . . . It can never be to their interest and cannot be presumed to have been their intention, to clog and embarrass its execution, by withholding the most appropriate means." Marshall summarized his views on the powers of the national government in these now-famous words: "Let the end be legitimate, let it be within the scope of the Constitution, and all means which are appropriate, which are plainly adapted to that end, which are not prohibited, but consist with the letter and spirit of the constitution, are constitutional."

Having thus established the doctrine of implied national powers, Marshall set forth the doctrine of **national supremacy.** No state, he said, can use its reserved taxing powers to tax a national instrument. "The power to tax involves the power to destroy. . . . If the right of the states to tax the means employed by the general government be conceded, the declaration that the Constitution, and the laws made in pursuance thereof, shall be the supreme law of the land, is empty and unmeaning declamation."

The long-range significance of *McCulloch* v. *Maryland* in providing support for the developing forces of nationalism cannot be overstated. The arguments of the states' righters, if accepted, would have strapped the national government in a constitutional straitjacket and denied it powers needed to handle the problems of an expanding nation.

What Is the ACIR?

The Advisory Commission on Intergovernmental Relations (ACIR) was created by Congress in 1959 to monitor the operations of the federal system and to make recommendations for its improvement. By undertaking studies, issuing publications, and drafting bills, it has become a prominent part of the "intergovernmental landscape." Its twenty-six members, who serve two-year terms each, represent Congress, the federal executive branch, state and local governments, and the general public.

The formal constitutional powers of the national government are essentially the same today as they were in 1789. But the Supreme Court (building on Marshall's work in *McCulloch* v. *Maryland*), Congress, the president, and the people have taken advantage of the Constitution's flexibility to permit the national government to use whatever powers it needs to fight wars and depressions and to serve the needs of a modern industrial nation operating in a global economy. The expansion of central government functions has rested on three major constitutional pillars.

The War Power   The national government is responsible for protecting the nation from external aggression and, when necessary, for waging war. In today's world military strength depends not only on troops in the field, but also on our ability to mobilize the nation's industrial might and to apply our scientific knowledge to the tasks of defense. The national government has the power to wage war and to do what is necessary and proper to do so successfully. This means that the national government has the power to do almost anything that is not in direct conflict with constitutional guarantees.

The Power to Regulate Interstate and Foreign Commerce   Congressional authority extends to all commerce that affects more than one state and to all those activities, wherever they exist or whatever their nature, whose control Congress decides is necessary and proper to regulate interstate and foreign commerce. The term *commerce* includes the production, buying, selling, renting, and transporting of goods, services, and properties.[13] The commerce clause—Article 1, Section 8, Clause 3—packs a tremendous constitutional punch. In these few words the national government has been able to find constitutional justification for regulating a wide range of human activity and property. Few, if any, aspects of our economy today affect commerce in only one state and are thus outside the scope of the national government's constitutional authority.

Federal air traffic controllers direct air commerce among the states and internationally.

   The commerce clause can also be used to sustain legislation that goes beyond commercial matters. When the Supreme Court upheld the 1964 Civil Rights Act forbidding discrimination because of race, religion, or national origin in places of public accommodation, it said: "Congress' action in removing the disruptive effect which it found racial discrimination has on interstate travel is not invalidated because Congress was also legislating against what it considers to be moral wrongs." Discrimination restricts the flow of interstate commerce; interstate commerce was being used to support discrimination; therefore, Congress could legislate against the discrimination. Moreover, the law could be applied even to local places of public accommodation because local incidents of discrimination have a substantial and harmful impact on interstate commerce. "If it is interstate commerce that feels the pinch, it does not matter how local the operation that applies the squeeze."[14]

The Power to Tax and Spend   Congress lacks constitutional authority to pass laws solely on the ground that they will promote the general welfare, but it may raise taxes and spend money for this purpose. This distinction between legislating and appropriating makes little difference most of the time. Congress, for example, lacks constitutional power to regulate education or agriculture directly, but it does have the power to appropriate money to support education or to pay farmers subsidies. By attaching conditions to its grants of money, Congress may regulate what it cannot directly control by law.

Because Congress puts up the money, it determines how the money will be spent. By withholding or threatening to withhold funds, the national government can influence—or control—state operations and regulate individual conduct. For example, Congress has stipulated that federal funds should be withdrawn from any program in which any person is denied benefits because of race, color, or national origin; subsequently the categories of sex and physical handicap were added. Congress has also used its power of the purse to force states to raise the drinking age to 21 by tying such a condition to federal dollars for highways.

These three constitutional powers—the war power, the power over interstate commerce, and, most especially, the power to tax and spend for the general welfare—have made possible a tremendous expansion of federal functions.

Umpires of the Federal System

Today there are few doubts about the national government's constitutional authority to deal with issues affecting the nation, whether they concern civil rights, speed limits on highways, or the sale of holiday lights. Nonetheless, we still argue about (1) whether Congress intended to regulate a subject completely or to leave some regulation to state discretion, and (2) whether, in the absence of congressional action, states may deal with subjects that affect commerce or people in other states.

Although couched in terms of federalism, such arguments reflect differences between various interests. The national and state governments are the arenas in which, and through which, clashes take place between consumers and producers, workers and employers, airlines and railroads, pro-choice and right to life, pro-growth and anti-growth, and all the other contending groups that make up our political system. Although Congress and the political process ultimately decide how power shall be divided between the national and state governments, federal courthouses remain major forums where hundreds of disputes about which government should do what for and to whom are increasingly being decided daily.

THE ROLE OF THE FEDERAL COURTS

Federal judges' authority to review the activities of state and local governments expanded dramatically in recent decades as a result of modern judicial interpretations of the Thirteenth, Fourteenth, and Fifteenth Amendments (especially the Fourteenth) and the congressional legislation enacted to implement these amendments. Along with an earlier congressional and judicial expansion of the habeas corpus jurisdiction of the federal district courts (see Chapter 6), these developments ensure that almost every action by state and local officials can be challenged before a federal judge as a violation of the Constitution or of federal law. In carrying out their judgments, federal judges sometimes have, in effect, taken over the supervision of state prison systems, public hospitals, public schools, and other public facilities.

One of the major instruments for opening these matters for review by federal courts is the Supreme Court's revitalization—some would say the rewriting—during recent decades of an 1871 rights act originally written to combat the Ku Klux Klan. This Act, now called Section 1983 after its designation in Title 42 of the United States Code, permits individuals to go into federal court to sue for damages or seek injunctions against any person acting under the color of law whom they believe has deprived them of any right secured by the Constitution or by any one of the several thousands of federal laws.[15] As a result of these Section 1983 actions, cities are now facing millions of dollars worth of damage claims (states can be ordered to stop doing something, but there are Eleventh Amendment constraints upon damage suits against the states). Among other Section 1983 claims against state and local officials have been thousands of suits by state prison inmates; by Jerry Tarkanian, the Nevada (UNLV) basketball coach against the N.C.A.A. which he unsuccessfully charged was acting as an agent of Nevada; by a father who sued a school district because he was not permitted to see his children's records; and by real-estate developers who allege that county and city land-use regulations are depriving them of their rights.[16]

Over the years the decisions of federal judges, under the leadership of the Supreme Court, have favored national powers (including their own); nonetheless, few would deny the Supreme Court the power to review and set aside state actions. As Justice Oliver Wendell Holmes once remarked: "I do not think the United States would come to an end if we lost our power to declare an Act of Congress void. I do think the Union would be imperiled if we could not make that declaration as to the laws of the several States."[17]

A MESSAGE FROM GARCIA—FEDERALISM AS A POLITICAL AND NOT A LEGAL CONSTRAINT

Until 1937 the Supreme Court generally espoused the **doctrine of dual federalism,** which views national and state governments as equal sovereigns, each operating within its own restricted sphere, with the Supreme Court enforcing the boundary between the two. In 1976, echoes of this doctrine could be heard in *National League of Cities* v. *Usery*, in which the Court, by five to four, held unconstitutional a 1974 amendment of the Fair Labor Standards Act extending federal minimum wage and maximum hours provisions to employees of state and local governments.[18] Then, in 1985, again by a five to four vote, *National League of Cities* was overturned by *Garcia* v. *San Antonio Metro*. In *Garcia* the Court said, in essence, that Congress, not the courts, decides which actions of the states should be regulated by the national government. "Although *Garcia* left open the possibility that some extraordinary defects in the national political process might render congressional regulation of state activities invalid," nothing in the Tenth Amendment "authorizes courts to second-guess the substantive basis for congressional legislation 'affecting state action.' "[19] "The States," said the Supreme Court in reaffirming the *Garcia* doctrine, "must find their protection from congressional regulation through the national political process" rather than look to judges to shield them from it.[20]

All the Reagan appointees, except Justice Anthony Kennedy, who has not spoken on this issue as yet, dissented from the *Garcia* view that the political process is the states' only constitutional protection. One of them, Justice Sandra Day O'Connor, predicted "this Court will in time again assume its constitutional responsibility" of defining the scope of state autonomy protected by federalism. She is probably right, since President Bush is likely to nominate judges and justices sympathetic to her version of federalism. It seems likely that the message from Garcia is not the final word on this matter.[21] Yet even the dissenting and more conservative justices have acknowledged that even if the courts were to resume the task of protecting the states, the set of activities protected by state sovereignty from the reach of the national government "may well be negligible."[22]

Y̲ou decide!

Should Puerto Rico, with over 3 million citizens, be admitted as our 51st state? George Bush, and many Americans and many Puerto Ricans, think it should be a state. Even though they are U.S. citizens, Puerto Ricans cannot now vote in presidential elections; they have no senators and no voting members in our House of Representatives. Puerto Rica has what is called "commonwealth" status. Citizens there are exempt from paying federal income taxes, and the commonwealth also enjoys various business tax breaks that have lured more than 2000 manufacturing plants there during the past thirty years. Spanish is the language used in schools and in government circles. Do you favor or oppose statehood for Puerto Rico? And what questions do you think this issue raises?

(Answer/Discussion on page 62.)

Congress always has the most to say about whether federal or state standards or some combination of them will prevail. It authorizes programs, appropriates the funds, and establishes general rules for how the programs will operate. The president and federal administrators also get into the act. They issue the specific guidelines, decide which projects to approve, and largely determine how federal standards will be applied.

It should not be thought, however, that states and local governments are merely passive partners waiting to learn from federal officials what to do and how to do it. It is one thing to get a law through Congress; it is quite another to impose national standards on state and local officials and the people they represent. If local and state political groups fail to persuade Congress to build safeguards into a law to protect their interests, they may still use the ambiguities of the law to do what they want done, rather than what the federal agencies intend. In the implementation battles that routinely follow the enactment of legislation, the greater political power may be with state and local officials.[23]

Federal Grants

Even after the rather successful "Reagan Revolution" resulted in the "devolution" of some functions back to the states, the national government continues to do much more than it did even two decades ago, although the number of federal employees is about the same today as it was then. State and local governments have gotten larger; the federal government has not. Rather than expanding the size of the federal government, Congress has chosen to use the states, the cities, the counties, the universities—and at times even private agencies—to administer many new programs, deliver services, and carry out federal mandates.

Congress has done this by using four general types of federal grants: categorical-formula grants, project grants, block grants, and revenue sharing.

1. **Categorical-formula grants.** Congress appropriates funds for specific purposes—welfare, school lunches, the building of airports and highways. The funds are allocated by formula and are subject to detailed federal conditions, often on a matching basis; that is, the government receiving the funds must put up some of its own dollars. There are hundreds of such grant programs, but two dozen account for almost 90 percent of total spending for categoricals. These include Medicaid, child nutrition grants, wastewater treatment plant construction, Aid to Families with Dependent Children (AFDC), training and employment programs, low-rent public housing, and community development programs.)[24]

2. **Project grants.** Congress appropriates a certain sum, but the dollars are allocated to state and local units—in some instances to nongovernmental agencies—on the basis of applications from those who wish to participate.

3. **Block grants.** These grants, promoted by the Advisory Commission on Intergovernmental Relations and favored by presidents, especially Republicans, are broad grants to states for certain prescribed activities—elementary and secondary education, social services, preventive health, and health services—with only a few specific strings attached.

4. **Revenue sharing.** From 1972 to 1987, substantial federal funds were given

to state and local units of government to be used at their discretion, subject only to very general conditions. When in the second Reagan Administration federal budget deficits soared and, "there was no revenue to share," revenue sharing was terminated—to the states in 1986 and to local governments in 1987.

THE POLITICS OF FEDERAL GRANTS

Arguments about the forms of federal aid involve more than considerations of efficiency. They reflect differences about what constitutes desirable public policy, where power should be located, and who will gain or lose by the various types of grants. Republican presidents "have consistently favored fewer strings, less federal supervision, and the delegation of spending discretion to the state and local governments, whereas Democratic presidents have advocated the opposite. Congress has divided similarly, with Democrats generally voting for centralization, and Republicans decentralization."[25]

Although chief executives—governors and presidents—generally tend to urge the consolidation of categorical-formula grants into larger blocks, legislators and groups who benefit from existing programs are likely to resist, and most of the time they do so successfully. Consider the battle over libraries. "[The] Administration proposed the consolidation of several narrow library grants. The Congress resisted, and the reason is simple. It can be expressed quantitatively: 99.99% of the public is not interested in library grant reform. Of the .01 percent who are interested, all are librarians and oppose it."[26]

IRON TRIANGLES OR ISSUE NETWORKS

The debate about the form of grants is not just a dispute over whether state and local governments can be trusted to spend federal dollars wisely, but is a debate about which state and local officials should be given control over the spending. Specialists who work for state and local governments often have more in common with specialists working for the national government than they do with their own governors, mayors, or state legislators. These specialists (highway engineers, welfare administrators, educators) confer at meetings, read common journals, and jointly defend the independence of their programs from attempts by "politicians" (elected national or state officials) to regulate them.[27] When these executive branch specialists join forces with their counterparts among the interest groups and specialists working for congressional committees they create powerful "guilds."[28] The result is "iron triangles"—of interest groups, congressional committee staffers, and federal bureaucrats (who in turn are connected to state and local bureaucrats)—of great effectiveness.

FEDERAL GRANTS UNDER REAGAN AND BUSH

Ronald Reagan, during the first year of his presidency, was able to convince Congress to consolidate fifty-seven categorical grant programs consisting of 10 percent of all federal aid to state and local governments into nine block grants. But that was as far as Congress has been willing to go.

What have been the results of these consolidations? Not as much money has been saved as proponents of block grants claimed would be, but there has not been as much diversion away from the poor as the opponents of such grants feared. Most states picked up some of the slack. Nonetheless, there has been

The devastating oil spill in Alaska illustrated the ambiguities of responsibility among various government agencies and the private sector.

Purposes of Federal Grants

1. To supply state and local governments with revenue
2. To establish minimum national standards, for example, for giving aid to the blind
3. To equalize resources among the states, on the "Robin Hood principle" of taking, through federal taxes, money from people with high incomes and spending it, through grants, in states where the poor live
4. To improve the operations and levels of services of state and local governments
5. To stimulate experimentation and new approaches
6. To encourage the achievement of social objectives such as nondiscrimination
7. To attack major problems but minimize the growth of federal agencies

Source: Michael D. Reagan and John G. Sanzone, *The New Federalism*, 2d ed. Copyright © 1981 by Oxford University Press, Inc. Reprinted by permission.

some diversion of funds away from some groups targeted by the categorical grants that the block grants replaced. And after block grants were established, there was considerable pressure to reduce their funding. For "once a block grant becomes nothing more than a small fraction of a state's general program budget . . . it may seem to lose its rationale for existence."[29] Yet on balance, according to one set of experts, "The administrative rationale of block-grant consolidation, and even the political rationale for returning decision-making authority to the states, has been largely vindicated. . . ."[30]

The battle over "which piper calls the tune when one government raises the money and another spends it" tends to be cyclical. "Complaints about excessive federal control tend to be followed by proposals to shift more power to state and local governments. Then, when problems arise in state and local administration—and problems inevitably arise when any organization tries to administer anything—demands for closer federal supervision and tighter federal controls follow."[31] The trend at the moment is toward fewer federal dollars, more block grants, and fewer program-specific national controls, but despite the decentralist rhetoric, new ways have been found to impose national controls.

Federal Regulations

State and local governments have received fewer federal dollars via federal grants recently, relatively speaking, but federal controls are as strong as ever. In fact, the federal government has new ways to regulate the way states and local governments spend federal dollars, and in some instances even their own state and local dollars. State and local officials complain that these regulations are far more intrusive than the more obvious conditions a state or local government must meet in order to be eligible for a federal grant.

There are four types of federal regulations of state and local governments:

1. *Direct orders.* In a few instances, federal regulation takes the form of direct orders that must be complied with under threat of criminal or civil sanction. Examples are the Equal Opportunity Act of 1982, barring job discrimination by state and local governments on the basis of race, color, religion, sex, and national origin, and the Marine Protection Amendments of 1977, prohibiting cities from dumping sewage into the ocean. Because such direct orders raise mild constitutional concerns and more serious political ones, Congress favors other techniques to impose the federal will on the states.

2. *Cross-cutting requirements.* The first and most famous of these requirements (so-called because a condition on one federal grant is extended to all activities supported by federal funds regardless of their source) is Title VI of the 1964 Civil Rights Act, which holds that no person may be discriminated against in the use of federal funds because of race, color, national origin, sex, or handicapped status. Over sixty cross-cutting requirements concern the environment, historical preservation, contract wage rates, access to governmental information, the care of experimental animals, the treatment of human subjects in research projects, and so on.

3. *Cross-over sanctions.* These sanctions permit the "feds" to use federal dollars in one program to influence state and local policy in another. One example is the Emergency Highway Energy Conservation Act of 1974, which prohibits the Secretary of Transportation from approving federal funding for highway construction in states having a speed limit in excess of 55 miles per hour

(since amended to allow the limit to be raised to 65 in certain rural areas). Another example is a 1984 act that threatened to reduce federal highway aid by up to 15 percent for any state that failed to adopt a minimum drinking age of 21 by 1987.

4. *Partial preemption.* This kind of control rests not upon the national government's power to spend, but on its powers under the supremacy and commerce clauses to preempt conflicting state and local activities. Building on this constitutional authority, federal law in certain areas establishes basic policies but requires states to administer them. Some programs give states the option and funds to administer them, if they meet the nationally determined conditions or standards. However, if a state chooses not to participate, the national government then steps in and directly runs the programs. The Clean Air Act Amendments of 1970 calls for mandatory partial preemption; the federal government sets national air-quality standards but requires states to devise plans for their implementation and enforcement.[32]

These new forms of federal regulation accelerated during the 1970s; they abated only slightly during the 1980s. Despite the Reagan-Bush emphasis on retrenchment of federal regulations, the Reagan administration pressured for national controls to force states to adopt drunk-driving legislation, to cut off federal funds to cities enacting rent controls, and to force on states and localities certain busing, abortion, and school-prayer policies. Apparently liberals and conservatives alike favor fewer federal controls over state and local officials in the abstract, yet are willing to make exceptions in policy areas when they feel strongly that something must be done to correct or prevent an injustice. Because there are plenty of injustices, federal regulation of state and local governments remains a continuing feature of our political system.

Two Levels or Three? Crazy-Quilt Federalism[33]

During the 1960's urban crisis, the national government started in earnest to provide large-scale, direct federal aid to cities, counties, school districts, flood-control districts, and other kinds of local units. In some ways Congress "became the city council of the nation," and the "president—acting very much like a Mayor"—

Airports are built and operated through the combined efforts of the national, state, and local governments.

started "taking on the meanest housekeeping concerns of daily existence."[34] As a result, there was "virtually no function of local government from police to community arts promotion, for which there [wasn't] a counterpart federal aid program."[35] The combination of a strengthened national-city link and the corresponding state bypass resulted—at least in part—from the belief that Congress and federal authorities are more likely than state officials to ensure that the "poor and the black, especially the latter" will get their fair share from tax dollars.

Plainly, governors and state legislators do not like to see federal funds go directly to city officials; city officials of course favor such direct federal aid, or any other means by which the federal government might provide money. (Some federal programs, attempting to bypass City Hall, provided federal dollars directly to community agencies created especially to represent the poor. Because neither state nor city officials liked this approach, such programs did not last long.)

In the 1980s the number and size of federal programs providing direct federal aid to cities was dramatically reduced—by more than $30 billion a year. Abandoned by the national government, cities and counties turned once again to their own state capitols. Tensions between state and city officials started to ease. It became clear that the national government was not necessarily a more reliable source of funds for a city than its own state. Moreover, changing demographic factors and an altering political climate have made state officials more responsive to city issues. Pollution, crime, poverty, unemployment, and other problems, once thought to belong exclusively to cities, have become suburban problems as well.

The states have responded to the reduction in federal funding for urban governments with mixed results. Wealthier states such as Massachusetts and New Jersey have done more to replace the withdrawn federal funds for their cities and schools than have such economically troubled states such as Louisiana. And although state help to localities is growing, many city officials and county authorities continue to complain they have been left in the lurch.

In short, the national/city link has not been broken, but it is no longer expanding—for the moment. States are reemerging as the primary channel between Washington and local governments.

The Politics of Federalism

Americans have long argued about the "proper" division of powers between central and local governments, and from time to time various governmental commissions and "experts" have tried to set definitive criteria. But the experts discovered, as did our country's founders, that few objective standards exist. Rather, the problems are largely political. At one time or another Northerners, Southerners, business people, farmers, workers, Federalists, Democrats, Whigs, and Republicans have championed states' rights, but underlying their arguments have been such issues as slavery, labor-management relations, government regulation of business, civil rights, welfare politics, environmental regulations, and so on. Until the Civil Rights Revolution of the 1960s, for example, segregationists feared that national officials—responding to different political majorities—would work for racial integration. Thus they praised local governments, emphasized the dangers of overcentralization, and argued that the protection of civil rights was not a proper function of the national government.

Today the politics of federalism is more complicated than it was in the past. Even in the area of civil rights,[36] as a result of changing political power distributions, it is no longer safe to predict that the national government will be more favorable to the claims of minorities than most state or city governments. State and local governments, for example, "have become the principal agents for advancing the cause of comparable worth. This role challenges the conventional wisdom that only centrist alternatives can advance equal opportunity and civil rights for all citizens."[37]

Moreover, as states more actively regulate the economy, some business interests have been running back to Washington asking for preemptive federal regulation to save them not only from stringent state regulations, but from having to adjust to fifty different state laws.[38] On the whole, however, conservative ideology continues to favor state and local action, while liberal ideology continues to favor national action. Conservative theorists still tend to champion local autonomy as the "means of protecting individual freedom." Local autonomy continues to be suspect by representatives of minorities, feminists, and the disadvantaged in general as "an exclusive haven for white privilege."[39] Yet these "solid" positions about the appropriate functions of the national government versus state and local governments have begun to crumble.

THE POLITICS OF NATIONAL GROWTH

Over the past two hundred years there has been a steady drift of power from other institutions—families, churches and synagogues, the marketplace—to governments, and especially to the national government. "No one planned the growth . . . but everyone played a part in it."[40] How did this come about? For a variety of reasons. One is that many of our problems became national in scope. Much that was local in 1789, in 1860, or in 1930 is now national—even global. State governments could supervise the relations between small merchants and their few employees, but only the national government can supervise relations between an international industry and its thousands of employees, all organized in national unions. Big business, big agriculture, and big labor all add up to big government.

As industrialization progressed, powerful interests made demands on the national government. Business groups called on the government for aid in the form of tariffs, a national banking system, and subsidies to railroads and the merchant marine. Farmers learned that the national government could give more aid than the states, and they too began to demand help. By the beginning of this century, urban groups in general, and organized labor in particular, pressed their claims.

The growth of the national economy and the creation of a national transportation and communications network altered people's attitudes toward the national government. Prior to the Civil War the national government was viewed as a distant, even foreign, government. Today, in part because of television, most people identify as closely with Washington as with their state capitals.

The Great Depression of the 1930s stimulated extensive national action on such issues as relief, unemployment, and agricultural surpluses. World War II brought federal regulation of wages, prices, and employment, as well as national efforts to allocate resources, train personnel, and support engineering and inventions. After the war the national government helped veterans and inaugurated a vast system of support for university research. Moreover, the United States became the most powerful member of the free world and had to maintain substantial military forces, even during times of peace.

The **Great Society** programs of the 1960s poured out grants-in-aid to states and localities. City dwellers, including blacks who had migrated from the rural South to northern cities, began to seek federal funds for—at the very least—housing, education, and mass transportation.

Y*ou decide!*

"21 or Else" Mandate Angers States

Should the national government have used its powers to force states to make 21 the minimum age to purchase beer, wine, or distilled spirits? Or should the determination of the minimum age have been left to the states? What are the constitutional issues? What are the questions relating to federalism?

Which of the following statements sounds like Ronald Reagan, and which would you guess is from a Democratic senator?

"The problem is bigger than the individual States. It's a grave national problem, and touches all our lives. With the problem so clear-cut and the proven solution at hand, we have no misgivings about this judicious use of federal power."

"The real issue is whether the Federal Government should intrude into an area that has traditionally and appropriately been left to the States and force them into accepting its solution to the problem of drunk driving."

What's your view?

(Answer/Discussion on page 68.)

"Remember, son, we are a government of loopholes, not of men."

Drawing by Dana Fradon; © *1976 The New Yorker Magazine, Inc.*

Although economic and social conditions generated many of the pressures for expansion of the national government, so did political ones. Members of Congress, presidents, federal judges, and federal administrators have actively promoted federal initiatives. Congress in particular has encouraged this trend. True, when there is widespread conflict about what to do—how to reduce the federal deficit, regulate energy policy, reform social security, provide health care for the indigent—Congress waits for a national consensus and looks to presidents for leadership. But when an organized constituency wants something and there is no counterpressure, Congress, "responds often to everyone, and with great vigour."[41]

Once established, federal programs generate groups with vested interests in promoting, defending, and expanding them. Associations are formed; alliances are made. "In a word, the growth of government has created a constituency of, by, and for government."[42]

THE REAGAN LEGACY AND THE BUSH PROMISES

The trend toward federal expansion, like most trends, generated a reaction. In fact, the high point of federal aid in terms of real dollars occurred in 1978.[43] By the beginning of the 1980s, as national budget deficits mounted, liberals and conservatives, Republicans and Democrats, all agreed that the expansion of the national government had gone too far. First the Carter administration curtailed some federal programs. Then the Reagan and Bush administrations made the reduction of the role of the national government one of their domestic priorities. They made considerable progress. Many programs have been eliminated and even more have been sharply reduced. General revenue sharing was eliminated. Between 1980 and 1990 categorical-formula grants for states and local governments were reduced by one-third. Federal aid has dropped from almost 32 percent of all state-local own-source revenues in 1980 to an estimated 20 percent in 1990. More than half of the eighty federal regulations the National Governors' Association targeted as being especially burdensome to the states have been cut.[44] Faced with an overwhelming federal deficit, neither Congress nor President Bush will find it easy to inaugurate any substantial new federal programs.

When the national government slowed down the rate of growth of its domestic spending, states took over some of its responsibilities.[45] And "to a greater extent than almost anyone thought possible, [Reagan] . . . achieved his long-cherished goal of shifting the initiative and responsibility for domestic programs out of Washington and back to the states and cities."[46]

The national government, however, is not likely to retreat to a pre-1930 posture or even a pre-1960 one. The underlying economic and social conditions that generated the demand for federal action have not substantially altered. On the contrary, in addition to such traditional issues as jobs and preventing inflation and depressions that still require national action, countless new issues have been added to the national agenda by the transformation of our industrial economy to a global economy based on high technology, service, and information. Although it is worth remembering that in terms of gross national product, many American states are larger than many nations—California has an economy larger than that of Great Britain—and that during the last two decades the states have strengthened their governmental machinery and are more politically responsive than at any time in our history, nonetheless, the states—at least most of them—still lack the jurisdiction by themselves to clean up the air, modernize the air traffic control

CHAPTER 3 / American Federalism: Problems and Prospects

system, regulate the economy, prevent pollution of our rivers, and deal with drug abuse. There are also all the problems of public health—such as preventing the spread of AIDS and finding a cure for it, as well as issues relating to the lack of decent housing for inner-city blacks and Hispanics that are beyond the capacity of the states to solve alone.

THE FUTURE OF THE STATES AND OUR FEDERAL SYSTEM

In 1933, seeing state governments helpless during the Great Depression, one writer stated: "I do not predict that the states will go, but affirm that they have gone."[47] Thirty years later Senator Everett McKinley Dirksen from Illinois intoned that before too long, "the only people interested in state boundaries will be Rand-McNally."[48]

These prophets of doom were wrong. States are stronger than ever. "A revolution—albeit a quiet one—has transformed the states over the past quarter of a century."[49] "Almost unnoticed in Washington, there has been a revolution in state capitals from Albany to Santa Fe, from Olympia to Tallahassee, and from Richmond to St. Paul. No longer the province primarily of hangers-on and political hacks, most state governments today are remarkably sophisticated and professional, competent to address problems that only a decade ago seemed beyond their grasp."[50] Most have improved their governmental structures, taken on greater roles in funding education, launched programs to help distressed cities, and—despite new constitutional limitations—expanded their taxing bases. Outstanding men and women have been attracted to many governorships.[51] "Today, states, in formal representational, policymaking, and implementation terms at least, are more representative, more responsive, more activist, and more professional in their operations than they ever have been. They face their expanded roles better equipped to assume and fulfill them."[52]

Clearly the constitutional and political durability of our states is secure. Federalism remains strong. And considering how much federalism has changed in the last 200 years, more changes can be expected as we move into the next century.

TABLE 3–2
Which of These Statements Comes Closest to Your View about Government Power Today?

	1983		1984		1986	
	WHITES	NON-WHITES	WHITES	NON-WHITES	WHITES	NON-WHITES
The federal government:						
1. Has too much power.	41%	21%	36%	29%	29%	22%
2. Has about the right amount of power.	18	15	25	20	25	18
3. Should use its power more vigorously.	28	45	33	41	40	52
4. Don't know/No answer.	13	19	6	10	6	8

Source: Advisory Commission on Intergovernmental Relations.
Figures represent percentage of U.S. public.

Fiscal Capacity to Raise Revenue (from most able to least able)

U.S. average	100
Alaska	177
Wyoming	151
Nevada	147
Connecticut	135
Massachusetts	124
Washington, DC	122
Delaware	121
New Jersey	121
New Hampshire	119
California	118
Colorado	117
Hawaii	113
Maryland	108
New York	107
Florida	105
Texas	104
Minnesota	102
Virginia	101
Vermont	99
Arizona	99
Oklahoma	98
Washington	98
Michigan	96
Illinois	96
Kansas	96
Maine	95
Georgia	94
North Dakota	94
Oregon	93
Missouri	93
Rhode Island	92
New Mexico	91
Nebraska	91
Ohio	91
Louisiana	90
Pennsylvania	90
North Carolina	88
Montana	88
Indiana	87
Wisconsin	86
Iowa	84
Tennessee	84
Utah	80
South Carolina	79
South Dakota	78
Idaho	77
West Virginia	76
Kentucky	76
Alabama	74
Arkansas	73
Mississippi	65

Source: Advisory Commission on Intergovernmental Relations, *Intergovernmental Perspective*, 15 (Spring 1989), p. 17.

Summary

1. Our federal constitutional system has evolved into something only slightly different in form, but significantly different in operation, from the 1789 version. Whether or not we ever had a system in which it was possible to talk about neat divisions between the powers of the national and the state governments, we certainly can no longer do so accurately.

2. To recognize that the national government has the constitutional authority to do whatever Congress thinks may be necessary and proper to do is not the same as saying federalism is dead. Although during the last two centuries constitutional power has moved toward the national center, political power remains dispersed. States remain active and significant political entities.

3. Ideological bias in favor of either national or state action is likely to reflect concrete political objectives. In recent years the conservatives' stand in favor of states' rights and the liberals' stand in favor of national action are no longer as predictable. Shifting political issues continue to lead to shifting allegiances among the various levels of government.

4. The drift toward increasing federal action has been fueled more by underlying economic and social changes than by concerns about federalism, but we detect a vigorous trend toward the view that federalism as a political principle is worthy of being preserved.

5. The major instrument of federal intervention in recent decades has been various kinds of grants-in-aid, of which the most prominent are categorical-formula grants, project grants, block grants, and revenue sharing.

6. Additional forms of federal intervention to control the activities of state and local governments have become more important in recent decades; these include direct orders, cross-cutting requirements on federal funds, cross-over sanctions in the use of federal funds, and partial preemption.

7. In the 1980s there was a substantial return of policy responsibilities back to the states and a pause in the expanding role of the national government.

8. Today we no longer spend so much time debating the *law* of federalism; we have moved to the *politics* of federalism. As now interpreted, the Constitution gives us the option to decide through the political process what we want to do, who is going to pay, and how we are going to get it done.

Further Reading

Advisory Commission on Intergovernmental Relations. *An Agenda for American Federalism: Restoring Confidence and Competence* (1981). Final volume of an 11-volume study under the general title, *The Federal Role in the Federal System: The Dynamics of Growth*.

Advisory Commission on Intergovernmental Relations. *Intergovernmental Perspective*. Published four times a year (U.S. Government Printing Office).

THOMAS J. ANTON, *American Federalism and Public Policy* (Temple University Press, 1989).

RAOUL BERGER. *Federalism: The Founders' Design* (University of Oklahoma Press, 1987).

ANN O'M. BOWMAN and RICHARD C. KEARNEY. *The Resurgence of the States* (Prentice Hall, 1986).

The Center for the Study of Federalism. *Publius: The Journal of Federalism*. Published quarterly (Temple University), one of the issues is an *Annual Review of the State of American Federalism*.

TIMOTHY J. CONLAN. *New Federalism: Intergovernmental Reform from Nixon to Reagan* (The Brookings Institution, 1988).

DANIEL J. ELAZAR. *American Federalism: A View from the States*, 3d ed. (Harper & Row, 1984).

DANIEL J. ELAZAR. *Exploring Federalism* (University of Alabama Press, 1987).

PARRIS N. GLENDENING and MAVIS MANN REEVES. *Pragmatic Federalism: An Intergovernmental View of American Government*, 2d ed. (Palisades Publishers, 1984).

JEFFREY HENIG. *Public Policy and Federalism* (St. Martin's, 1985).

GOVERNOR SCOTT M. MATHESON with JAMES E. KEE. *Out of Balance* (Peregrine Smith Books, 1986).

LAURENCE J. O'TOOLE, JR., ed. *American Intergovernmental Relations* (Congressional Quarterly Press, 1985).

MICHAEL D. REAGAN and JOHN G. SANZONE. *The New Federalism*, 2d ed. (Oxford University Press, 1981).

WILLIAM H. RIKER. *The Development of American Federalism* (Kluwer Academic Publishers, 1987).

HARRY N. SCHEIBER. *Federalism: Studies in History, Law, and Policy* (Institute of Governmental Studies, University of California at Berkeley, 1985).

WILLIAM H. STEWART. *Concepts of Federalism* (University Press of America, 1984).

DAVID B. WALKER. *Toward a Functioning Federalism* (Winthrop, 1981).

Notes

1. Governor (now Senator) Charles Robb, quoted in *The New York Times* (December 15, 1985), p. A80.

2. Daniel J. Elazar, *Exploring Federalism* (University of Alabama Press, 1987), p. 6.

3. William H. Riker, *The Development of American Federalism* (Academic Publishers, 1987), pp. 14–15. Riker contends that not only does federalism not guarantee freedom, but that the framers of our federal system, as well as those of other nations, were not

animated by considerations of safeguarding freedom but by practical considerations of preservation of their unity.

4. John Kincaid, "State Constitutions in the Federal System," *The Annals of the American Academy of Political and Social Sciences, State Constitutions in a Federal System* (March 1988), p. 17. See also David Osborne, *Laboratories of Democracy: A New Breed of Governor Creates Models for National Growth* (Harvard Business School Press, 1988), p. 1.

5. Paul M. Barrett, "New Jersey, After Federal Leadership Waned, Has Become Environmental Protection Pioneer," *The Wall Street Journal* (July 5, 1988), p. 40.

6. *Garcia* v. *San Antonio Metro*, 469 U.S. 528 (1985); James R. Alexander, "State Sovereignty in the Federal System" *Publius* (Spring 1986), pp. 1–15.

7. *Luther* v. *Borden*, 7 How. 1 (1849).

8. *California* v. *Superior Court of California*, 482 U.S. 400 (1987).

9. *Puerto Rico* v. *Brandstadt*, 483 U.S. 219 (1987).

10. David C. Nice, "State Participation in Interstate Compacts," *Publius*, vol. 17, no 2 (Spring 1987), p. 70.

11. 312 U.S. 100 (1941).

12. 4 Wheaton 316 (1819).

13. *Gibbons* v. *Ogden*, 9 Wheaton 1 (1824).

14. *Heart of Atlanta Motel* v. *United States*, 379 U.S. 241 (1964).

15. *Oklahoma City* v. *Tuttle*, 471 U.S. 808 (1985); *Maine* v. *Thiboutot*, 448 U.S. 1 (1980); *Monell* v. *New York City Dept. of Social Welfare*, 436 U.S. 658 (1978). See Cynthia Cates Colella, "The United States Supreme Court and Intergovernmental Relations," in Robert J. Dilger, ed., *American Intergovernmental Relations Today: Perspectives and Controversies* (Prentice Hall, 1985), p. 66.

16. Linda Greenhouse, "1871 Rights Law Now Used for Many Causes," *The New York Times* (August 26, 1988), p. Y17.

17. Oliver Wendell Holmes, Jr., *Collected Legal Papers* (Harcourt, 1920), pp. 295–96.

18. 426 U.S. 833 (1976).

19. *South Carolina* v. *Baker*, 99 L Ed 2d 592 (1988).

20. Ibid. Whether Congress is a reliable protector of federalism is a subject of research debate among political scientists; see Rodney E. Hero, "The U.S. Congress and American Federalism: Are 'Subnational' Governments Protected?" *Western Political Quarterly*, 42 (March 1989), pp. 93–106.

21. Justice Sandra O'Connor dissenting in *Garcia* v. *San Antonio Metro*.

22. Ibid.

23. Michael J. Rich, "Distributive Politics and the Allocation of Federal Grants," *The American Political Science Review*, vol. 83 no. 1 (March 1989), p. 209.

24. George J. Gordon, *Public Administration in America*, 3d ed. (St. Martin's, 1986), p. 149.

25. John E. Chubb, "The Political Economy of Federalism," *The American Political Science Review*, vol. 79 (December 1985), p. 1005.

26. Richard P. Nathan, "Special Revenue Sharing: Simple, Neat, and Correct." Unpublished manuscript.

27. Deil S. Wright, *Understanding Intergovernmental Relations*, 3d ed. (Brooks-Cole, 1982).

28. Harold Seidman and Robert Gilmour, *Politics, Position and Power*, rev. ed. (Oxford University Press, 1985).

29. George E. Peterson et al., *The Reagan Block Grants: What Have We Learned?* (The Urban Institute Press, 1985), p. 29.

30. Ibid.

31. Donald F. Kettl, *The Regulation of American Federalism* (Johns Hopkins University Press, 1987), pp. 154–55.

32. Mel Dubnick and Alan Gitelson, "Nationalizing State Policies," in Jerome J. Hanus, ed., *The Nationalization of State Government* (D.C. Heath, 1981), pp. 56–57.

33. W. John Moore, "Crazy-Quilt Federalism," *National Journal* (November 26, 1988), p. 3004.

34. H. F. Graff, "Presidents Are Now Mayors," *The New York Times* (July 18, 1979), p. A23.

35. Neal R. Peirce, "The State of American Federalism," *Civic Review* (January 1980), p. 32.

36. Daniel J. Elazar, *American Federalism: A View from the States*, 3d ed. (Harper & Row, 1984), p. 241.

37. Debra A. Stewart, "State Initiatives in the Federal System: The Politics and Policy of Comparable Worth in 1984," *Publius* (Summer 1985), p. 93.

38. Martha M. Hamilton, "If You Want Something Done Right, Do It Yourself," *The Washington Post National Weekly Edition* (September 5–11, 1988), p. 31.

39. Gordon L. Clark, *Judges and the Cities: Interpreting Local Autonomy* (The University of Chicago Press, 1985), p. 8.

40. Advisory Commission on Intergovernmental Relations, *Restoring Confidence and Competence* (ACIR, 1981), p. 30.

41. Cynthia Cates Colella, "The Creation, Care and Feeding of the Leviathan: Who and What Makes Government Grow," *Intergovernmental Perspective* (Fall 1979), p. 9.

42. Aaron Wildavsky, "Bare Bones: Putting Flesh on the Skeleton of American Federalism," in Advisory Commission on Intergovernmental Relations, *The Future of Federalism in the 1980s* (ACIR Publication M–126, 1981), p. 79.

43. Richard P. Nathan and Fred C. Doolittle, "Federal Grants: Giving and Taking Away," *Political Science Quarterly* (Spring 1985), p. 55.

44. John Kincaid, "The State of American Federalism—1987," *Publius*, vol. 18 (Summer 1988), p. 1.

45. John Herbers, "The New Federalism: Unplanned, Innovative, and Here to Stay," *Governing* (October 1987).

46. David S. Broder, "What Reagan Did—and Didn't Do," *The Washington Post National Weekly Edition* (January 23, 1989), p. 4.

47. Luther Gulick, "Reorganization of the States," *Civil Engineering* (August 1933), pp. 420–21.

48. Quoted by Terry Sanford in *Storm over the States* (McGraw-Hill, 1967), p. 37.

49. Carl Stenberg, in Mavis Mann Reeves, *The Question of State Government Capability: A Commission Report* (Advisory Commission on Intergovernmental Relations, 1985), p. 320. See also, Ann O'M. Bowman and Richard C. Kearney, *The Resurgence of the States* (Prentice Hall, 1986).

50. Denis P. Doyle and Terry W. Hartle, "A Funny Thing Happened on the Way to New Federalism . . . ," *Washington Post National Weekly Edition* (December 2, 1985), p. 23.

51. Osborne, *Laboratories of Democracy*.

52. Ibid., p. 363.

4

Congress shall make no law respecting an establishment of religion, or prohibiting the free exercise thereof; or abridging the freedom of speech, or of the press; or the right of the people peaceably to assemble, and to petition the Government for a redress of grievances.

First Amendment Rights

"Congress shall make no law," declares the First Amendment, "respecting an establishment of religion, or prohibiting the free exercise thereof, or abridging the freedom of speech, or of the press, or the right of the people peaceably to assemble, and to petition the Government for a redress of grievances." In this one sentence our Constitution stated the fundamental supports of a free society: freedom of conscience and freedom of expression.

Although the framers drafted the Constitution, in a sense the people drafted our basic charter of liberties. As we have seen, the Constitution drawn up in Philadelphia included few specific guarantees of the basic freedoms, and the omission aroused suspicion and distrust among the people. In order to win the ratification vote, the Federalists promised to correct this deficiency. And in its very first session, the new Congress proposed amendments that were ratified by the end of 1791 and became part of the Constitution. These ten amendments are known as the Bill of Rights.

Note that the Bill of Rights literally applies *only to the national government*. As John Marshall held in *Barron* v. *Baltimore* (1833), the Bill of Rights limits the national, not the state governments.[1] Why not the states? In the 1790s the people were confident they could control their own state officials, and most of the state constitutions already had bills of rights. It was the new and distant central government the people feared. As it turned out, those fears were largely misplaced. The national government, responsive to tens of millions of voters from a variety of races, creeds, religions, and economic groups, has shown less tendency to curtail civil liberties than have state and local governments. For the most part, state judges have not used the bills of rights in their respective state constitutions to protect civil liberties.

When the Fourteenth Amendment, which *does* apply to the states, was adopted in 1868, some contended its due process clause limits states in precisely the same way the Bill of Rights limits the national government. At least, they argued, freedom of speech should be protected by the Fourteenth Amendment. For decades the Supreme Court refused to interpret the Fourteenth Amendment in this way. Then in 1925, in *Gitlow* v. *New York*, the Court announced:

> For present purposes we may and do assume that freedom of speech and of press—which are protected by the First Amendment from abridgment by Congress—are among the fundamental personal rights and 'liberties' protected by the due process clause of the Fourteenth Amendment from impairment by the States.[2]

THE NATIONALIZATION OF THE BILL OF RIGHTS

Gitlow v. *New York* was a revolutionary decision. For the first time, the national Constitution protected freedom of speech and of the press from abridgment by state and local governments. By the 1940s the other provisions of the First Amendment—religion, assembly, petition—had been brought within the scope of the Fourteenth Amendment. Today the First Amendment's restraints are applied to all who exercise governmental authority—national, state, or local.

If the First Amendment applies to the states, why not the other parts of the Bill of Rights, most of which have to do with the rights of persons accused of crimes and with restraints on police procedures? For many years a persistent minority on the Supreme Court argued that the due process clause of the Fourteenth Amendment should be interpreted to impose on states exactly the same limitations the Bill of Rights imposes on the national government. They favored "total incorporation" of the Bill of Rights into the Fourteenth Amendment. But the prevailing and persistent view of the majority of the Court is that *some,* but not *all,* provisions of the Bill of Rights should be incorporated into the due process clause. This is known as the doctrine of **selective incorporation.**

How are we to distinguish between those provisions of the Bill of Rights that are to be incorporated into the Fourteenth Amendment and those that are not? Justice Cardozo formulated the test in *Palko* v. *Connecticut.* The rights to be incorporated are those "implicit in the concept of ordered liberty," rights so important that neither "liberty nor justice would exist if they were sacrificed."[3] The rights not incorporated are those that though congenial to our system of justice, could be replaced by other procedures without necessarily resulting in a denial of justice or liberty.

Beginning in the 1930s, and continuing at an accelerated pace during the 1960s, the Supreme Court selectively incorporated provision after provision of the Bill of Rights into the due process clause.[4] Today the Fourteenth Amendment imposes on the states all the provisions of the Bill of Rights except those of the Second, Third, Seventh, and Tenth Amendments, and the grand jury requirements of the Fifth Amendment. When we talk about the Bill of Rights today, we are really talking about limits on the power of all who govern, whether they do so on behalf of the national government, the states, or local units of government.

In addition to the specific rights protected by the Constitution, the Supreme Court has found constitutional protection for other fundamental rights.

> For example, the rights of association and of privacy, the right to be presumed innocent and the right to be judged by a standard of proof beyond a reasonable doubt in a criminal trial, as well as the right to travel, appear nowhere in the Constitution or Bill of Rights. Yet these important but unarticulated rights have nonetheless been found to share constitutional protection in common with explicit guarantees.[5]

The New Judicial Federalism

Since the early 1970s there has been a dramatic increase in the number of cases where state Supreme Courts have relied on state constitutions, rather than the U.S. Constitution, to protect individual rights.

	1950-1959	1960-1969	1970-1974	1975-1979	1980-1984	1985-1988*

(y-axis: 250, 200, 150, 100, 50, 5)

* estimated
Source: Hastings Constitutional Law Quarterly, summer 1986

STATE BILLS OF RIGHTS

After the Supreme Court incorporated most of the national Bill of Rights into the Fourteenth Amendment, little attention was paid by state judges—or anybody else—to the bills of rights in their respective state constitutions. "The Supreme Court took such complete control of the field that state judges could sit back in the conviction that their part was simply to await the next landmark decision."[6] Recently, however, stimulated in large part by the United States Supreme Court's more conservative interpretation of some provisions of the national Bill of Rights, there has been a renewal of interest in state constitutions as independent sources of additional protection for civil liberties and civil rights.[7] Justice Brennan, who dissents from this more limited view of the scope of the national Bill of Rights, has led the charge by urging state supreme courts to step into the breach.[8]

Advocates of what has come to be called **new judicial federalism** contend that the national Constitution should set minimum but not maximum standards to protect our rights. There is nothing, they argue, to keep state courts from using similar provisions of the bill of rights in their own state constitution to provide even more protection than does the national Constitution. Moreover, state bills of rights sometimes have language that permits a more expansive protection of rights than does the national Bill of Rights, if state judges are inclined to so interpret them. For example, some states have an equal rights amendment in their constitutions and some explicitly protect the right of privacy.[9]

Instances of state courts' using their own bills of rights to go beyond the U.S. Supreme Court, although significant, are nevertheless unusual. Moreover, if a state supreme court provides greater protection for some rights under its state constitution than the Supreme Court of the United States provides under the United States Constitution, that state decision might be overturned by an amendment to the state constitution or, since most state judges lack lifetime tenure, even by changing the membership of the state supreme court. The Supreme Court and the federal Bill of Rights remain the dominant protectors of civil liberties and civil rights.

A Wall of Separation

The first words of the First Amendment are emphatic and brief: "Congress shall make no law respecting an establishment of religion." The framers were reacting to the English system wherein the Crown was the head not only of the government but also of the established church—the Church of England—and public officials were required to take an oath of support for the established church as a condition of holding office.

What do the words of this so-called **Establishment Clause** mean? The Supreme Court has construed the Constitution to erect a *wall of separation between church and state*, to prohibit any law or governmental action designed to confer any benefit on religion, even if all sects are treated the same.[10] However, although there can be no governmental aid for religion, with or without preference for a particular religion, sometimes the Court permits governmental *accommodations* to make religious activities possible, or even to permit some aid to flow indirectly to religious institutions.

Significantly, a different interpretation of the Establishment Clause, the non-preferentialist view, is held by, among others, four members of the Supreme Court: Chief Justice William Rehnquist, Justices Byron White, Antonin Scalia, and

Anthony Kennedy,[11] the last two being the last of the Reagan appointees. They believe the Constitution simply prohibits favoritism toward a particular religion, but it does not prohibit governmental encouragement of religious activities or even some support for religious organizations.[12]

Under prevailing doctrine, however, a law challenged for violating the Establishment Clause must meet the three-part test put forward by the Court in *Lemon* v. *Kurtzman*. First, it must have a secular legislative purpose; second, its primary effect must neither advance nor inhibit religion; and finally, it must avoid "excessive government entanglement with religion." In other words, the Establishment Clause is designed to prevent three main evils: "sponsorship, financial support, and active involvement of the sovereign in religious activity."[13]

When the *Lemon* test is given an "accommodationist" twist, a statute's purpose need not be *exclusively* secular. It is all right if the benefit to religion is slight or happens to harmonize with the tenets of some religion. Examples of this interpretation are several recent decisions trying to delineate when a display of religious symbols violates the Establishment Clause and when it does not. These rulings indicate that it depends on whether the context makes it appear that government is transmitting a religious or a secular message. Upheld have been a city display of a nativity scene together with Santa's house and other symbols of the Christmas season in a shopping district, and the Hanukkah menorah on the steps of the Pittsburgh City Hall next to a Christmas tree. These displays, concluded the Court majority, have a secular purpose of celebrating both the religious and secular dimensions of the Christmas holidays, and provide little or no benefit to religion in general or to the Christian or Jewish faiths in particular. The Constitution, said the Court in the first of these decisions, "[does not] require complete separation of church and state; it affirmatively mandates accommodation, not merely tolerance of all religions, and forbids hostility toward any."[14] On the other side, the Court ruled that the Constitution does not permit an unadorned display of the nativity scene in a court house, for in this context, the impression conveyed was that the county government was endorsing the display's specific religious message.

Because of the Establishment Clause, states (and, of course, other units of government such as state universities, colleges, and school districts) may not introduce any kind of devotional exercises into the public school curriculum. But the Supreme Court has not, as it is sometimes said, prohibited prayer in public schools. It is not unconstitutional for people to pray in a school building. What is unconstitutional is sponsorship or encouragement of prayer by public school authorities.[15] Thus, devotional reading of the Bible, recitation of the Lord's Prayer, and posting the Ten Commandments on the walls of classrooms are prohibited. Nor may a state forbid the teaching of evolution or base the teaching of it on the simultaneous teaching of "creation science."[16]

Tax exemption for church property and for other nonprofit institutions is constitutional. State legislatures and Congress may hire chaplains to open each day's legislative session—a practice that has continued without interruption since the first session of Congress. If done in a public school, this practice would be unconstitutional. Apparently, the difference is that legislators as adults are not "susceptible to religious indoctrination or peer pressure."[17] Also, as the joke goes, legislators need the prayer more.

A more troublesome area involves attempts by many states to provide financial assistance to parochial schools. The Supreme Court has tried to draw a line between permissible public aid to students, including those in sectarian schools, and impermissible public aid to religion.

At the college level the problems are relatively simple. Tax funds may be used to construct buildings and operate educational programs at church-related

"The court reached a decision on silent prayer in school. They ruled that a moment of silence is impossible."

Dunagin's People by Ralph Dunagin. © *1983 Field Enterprises, Inc. Courtesy of Field Newspaper Syndicate.*

In this and the next several chapters, we discuss constitutional rules at length. As we have noted, to talk about the Constitution is to talk about Supreme Court decisions. Many of these decisions are cited in footnotes so that you can look them up if you wish. Two forms of citation are used:

1. Official Supreme Court Reports. An example is *Gitlow* v. *New York*, 268 U.S. 652 (1925), which means that this case can be found in the 268th volume of the *United States Supreme Court Reports*, on page 652, and that it was decided in 1925. These reports are published by the United States Government Printing Office.

2. For more recent cases, the advance sheets of *United States Supreme Court Reports*, published by the Lawyers Co-operative Publishing Company of Rochester, New York. An example is *Richmond* v. *Croson*, a case concerned with affirmative action. It is cited as 102 L Ed 2d 854 (1989), which means that it can be found in volume 102 of the Lawyers' Edition, second series, on page 854, and that it was decided in 1989.

schools, as long as the money is not spent directly on buildings used for religious purposes or used to teach religious subjects. Even if students choose to attend religious schools and become ministers, governmental aid to these students is permissible. It has a secular purpose; its effect on religion is the result of individual choice; "and it does not confer any message of state endorsement of religion."[18]

At the elementary and secondary level, the constitutional problems become more complicated. Here the secular and religious parts of institutions and instruction are much more closely interwoven. Students are younger and more susceptible to indoctrination, and the chances are greater that aid given to church-operated schools might seep into aid for religion.

Despite the constitutional obstacles, some states have attempted to provide tax credits or deductions for those who send their children to private, largely church-affiliated schools. Deductions or credits available only to parents of children attending nonpublic schools are unconstitutional, but allowing taxpaying parents to deduct from their state income taxes what they paid for tuition and other costs to send their children to school—public or private—is constitutionally permissible, even if most of the benefit goes to those who send their children to private religious schools.[19]

The Supreme Court has also approved using tax funds to provide students attending primary and secondary church-operated schools (except those that deny admission because of race or religion) with textbooks, standardized tests, lunches, transportation to and from school, diagnostic services for speech and hearing problems, and other kinds of remedial help—provided such services take place away from the "pervasively sectarian atmosphere of the church-related schools."[20]

Tax funds, however, may not be used in religious schools to pay teachers' salaries, provide equipment, provide counseling for students, produce teacher-prepared tests, repair facilities, or transport students on field trips. School authorities may not permit religious instructors to come into public school buildings during the school day to provide religious instruction on a voluntary basis.

Why is it constitutional for state governments to pay for books but not for maps? For bus trips but not for field trips? For standardized tests but not for tests prepared by teachers? Those on the "approved" side meet the three-part *Lemon* test, but those on the "forbidden" side fail one of the requirements. Thus, transportation to and from school, which is permitted, involves a routine trip that every student makes every day; it is unrelated to any aspect of the curriculum. Field trips, which cannot be paid for by tax funds, are controlled by teachers and are aids to instruction. Books and standardized tests, which can be bought by tax funds, can be easily evaluated to ensure that they are not designed to promote religion, whereas maps or teacher-prepared tests cannot be so readily checked. And in cases involving teaching by public teachers in parochial schools, the supervision to ensure avoidance of religious influences creates excessive entanglement of church and state.

*Y*ou decide!

In the Adolescent Family Life Act of 1981 Congress provides for grants to charitable organizations, including religious organizations, to teach teenagers about "sexual prudence."

Does such a law violate the Establishment Clause? Do grants to religious organizations under the law violate the Establishment Clause?

(Answer/Discussion on page 78.)

All Persons May Worship as They Choose

The Constitution not only forbids the establishment of religion, but it also forbids Congress and the states from passing any law "prohibiting the free exercise thereof." "The Court has struggled to find a neutral course between the two religion clauses, both of which are cast in absolute terms, and either of which, if expanded to a logical extreme, would tend to clash with the other."[21] Thus a law that requires people to do something contrary to the teachings of their religion may interfere

CHAPTER 4 / First Amendment Rights

The right to practice one's religion covers many kinds of religious ceremonies.

with their free exercise of religion. Yet to exempt them from the law because of their religious convictions could favor religious activities in such a way as to offend the Establishment Clause. As Justice Scalia has written, "It is not always easy to determine when accommodation slides over into promotion, and neutrality into favoritism."[22]

The right to hold any or no religious belief is one of our few absolute rights. No government has authority to compel the acceptance of or to censor any creed. A state may not compel a religious belief nor deny persons any right because of their beliefs or lack of them. Requiring religious oaths as a condition of public employment or as a prerequisite to running for public office is unconstitutional. In fact, the only time the Constitution mentions the word religion is to state: "No religious test shall ever be required as a Qualification to any Office of public Trust under the United States" (Article VI).

Although carefully protected, the right to *practice* a religion has less protection than the right to hold particular beliefs. Religious convictions do not ordinarily exempt one from obeying an otherwise valid and nondiscriminatory law or government regulation, such as one imposing an obligation on parents to provide needed medical attention for children, or one prohibiting child labor, or one safeguarding people from snake handlers. However, the Supreme Court will carefully scrutinize laws alleged to infringe on religious practices, and it insists that the government provide some compelling public purpose to justify the infringement. "Only those interests of the highest order and those not otherwise served can over-balance legitimate claims to the free exercise of religion."[23]

The Supreme Court, for example, has upheld laws and regulations forbidding polygamy, outlawing business activities on Sunday as applied to Orthodox Jews, forbidding military officers to wear headgear while indoors as applied to an Orthodox Jew's wearing of a yarmulke (skullcap)—a traditional religious obligation. It has also sustained an Internal Revenue Service regulation denying tax exemption to religious schools that admit only members of one race. The Supreme Court pointedly wrote: "We deal only with religious schools, not with churches."[24]

On the other hand, a state may not require Jehovah's Witnesses (or anyone else, for that matter) to participate in public school flag-salute ceremonies. Although a state may compel parents to send their children to school, parents have a constitutional right to choose to send their children to church-sponsored rather than public schools. Further, a state's compulsory school laws cannot be applied to compel the Amish to send their children to school *beyond* the eighth grade. Through the eighth grade the interests of the state in ensuring that all children learn basic skills overbalance religious convictions; after the eighth grade religious convictions are given priority.

What is a church? What is a religion? The Constitution provides no definition, and the Supreme Court has been reluctant—understandably—to get into these questions. Unconventional religions are entitled to the same constitutional protec-

Not necessarily, said the Supreme Court by a five to four vote.

In a decision that may signal a shift in constitutional doctrine toward a much more accommodationist view, *Bowen* v. *Kendrick*, 101 L Ed 2d 520 (1988), Chief Justice Rehnquist delivered the opinion of the Court. He applied the three-pronged *Lemon* test but with a very strong accommodationist twist. The Act was, he held, clearly motivated by a legitimate secular *purpose*—the elimination or reduction of the problems caused by teenage sexuality, pregnancy. Its effect has not been to promote religion, to advance substantial federal funds to churches, or to create a crucial symbolic link between government and religion, and finally, there has been no *excessive governmental entanglement* with religion.

Justice O'Connor in a concurring opinion joined with the Chief Justice and Justices Scalia, Kennedy, and White in upholding the law on its face, but gave her vote only on the condition that the case be returned to the trial court to be sure that the law as applied in fact had not been used to permit "public funds to promote religious doctrine."

Justices Brennan, Marshall, Blackmun, and Stevens, the dissenters, argued that the law was a clear attempt by Congress to spend tax dollars to support religious teachings.

tion as are the more traditional ones. The Free Exercise Clause extends to those who act on sincerely held religious beliefs and not just those who respond to a specific command of a particular church. But, although the Court does not "underestimate the difficulty of distinguishing between religious and secular convictions and determining whether a professed belief is sincerely held,"[25] only beliefs rooted in a *religion* are protected by the Free Exercise Clause.

Disputes involving the two religion clauses promise to become even more complicated as governmental actions grow more pervasive and nontraditional religious groups grow in number. These are difficult disputes to resolve, because they involve matters about which people feel deeply. Yet despite the fact that this nation is made up of people of many differing religions, we have done better than almost any other nation in the world in removing religious disputes from politics and keeping religious tensions among us to a minimum.

Free Speech and Free People

Government by the people is based on every person's right to speak freely, to organize in groups, to question the decisions of the government, and to campaign openly against it. Only through free and uncensored expression of opinion can government be kept responsive to the electorate, and political power be transferred peacefully. Elections, separation of powers, and constitutional guarantees are meaningless unless all citizens have the right to speak frankly and to hear and judge for themselves the worth of what others have to say.

Despite the fundamental importance of free speech to a democracy, some people seem to believe that speech should be free only for those who agree with them. Americans overwhelmingly support principles of tolerance when such principles are presented in general, abstract fashion (for example, "Do you believe in freedom of speech?"). But once the questions or conflicts become more specific, Americans exhibit a much lower level of support for free speech.[26] (See also Chapter 7.) Not only do three Americans in four "draw a blank when asked if they know what the First Amendment . . . is or with what it deals," but almost 40 percent of the public would like to see strict curbs placed on newspapers.[27]

Free speech is not simply the personal right of individuals to have their say; it is also the right of the rest of us to hear them. John Stuart Mill, whose *Essay on Liberty* (1859) is the classic defense of free speech, put it this way:

> The peculiar evil of silencing the expression of opinion, is that it is robbing the human race. . . . If the opinion is right, they are deprived of the opportunity of exchanging error for truth; if wrong, they lose, what is almost as great a benefit, the clearer perception and livelier impression of truth, produced by its collision with error.[28]

Freedom of speech is not merely freedom to express ideas that differ slightly from ours. It is, as the late Justice Jackson said, "freedom to differ as to things that touch the heart of the existing order."[29] Yet some who say they believe in free speech draw the line at ideas they consider dangerous. What is a dangerous idea? Who decides? In the realm of political ideas, who can find an objective, eternally valid standard of right? Or as Chief Justice Rehnquist put it for the Supreme Court, "The First Amendment recognizes no such thing as a 'false' idea."[30] The search for truth involves the possibility—even the inevitability—of error. The search cannot go on unless it proceeds freely in the minds and speech of all. This means, in the words of Justice Holmes, not only freedom of expression for those who agree with us "but freedom for the thought we hate."[31]

Even though the First Amendment denies Congress the power to pass *any* law abridging freedom of speech, the amendment has never been interpreted in such sweeping terms. Like almost all other rights, the rights to freedom of speech and of the press are limited. In discussing the constitutional power of government to regulate speech, it is useful to distinguish among *belief*, *speech*, and *action*. At one extreme is the right to believe as we wish, a right as absolute as any can be for people living in an organized society. Despite occasional deviations in practice, the traditional American view is that *thoughts* are inviolable. No government has the right to punish a person for beliefs or to interfere in any way with freedom of conscience.

At the other extreme is *action*, which is usually restrained. The Constitution protects from governmental regulation our right to believe we should drive an automobile seventy-five miles an hour. But we have no constitutional right to drive an automobile seventy-five miles an hour. As has been said, "the right to swing your arm ends where the other person's nose begins."

Speech stands somewhere between belief and action. It is not an absolute right, as is belief, but neither is it as exposed to governmental restraint as is action. Speech that is obscene, libelous, or **seditious,** or speech that constitutes **fighting words,** is not entitled to constitutional protection, although many problems arise in distinguishing between what does and does not fit into these categories. (We discuss these problems shortly.) All other speech is entitled to constitutional protection. But are there any limits?

HISTORICAL CONSTITUTIONAL TESTS

Although the Supreme Court today uses other language, the three great constitutional tests developed earlier in this century continue to reflect basic attitudes toward governmental regulation of speech. These are the **bad tendency doctrine,** the **clear and present danger doctrine,** and the **preferred position doctrine.**

The Bad Tendency Doctrine   This doctrine, which stems from the common law, has not had the support of the Supreme Court since *Gitlow* v. *New York* in 1925. Nonetheless, many legislators, city council members, college students, and others, (including some state courts as late as 1982),[32] appear to hold this position. According to the adherents of the bad tendency doctrine, legislative bodies, which are more responsive to community feelings, and not courts have the primary responsibility to determine when speech should be outlawed. The Constitution, they argue, authorizes legislatures to forbid speech that has a tendency to lead to illegal action. Moreover, "the legislature cannot reasonably be required to measure the danger from every . . . utterance in the nice balance of a jeweler's scale. . . . It may, in the exercise of its judgment, suppress the threatened danger in its incipiency."[33]

Suppose a city council or the trustees of a public university decide that public utterances of abusive racial remarks are dangerous because they often lead to violence, and they make such remarks illegal or grounds for discipline. Those who hold to the bad tendency test argue that, because it is not totally unreasonable that abusive racial remarks could cause violence, such a law or regulation would be constitutional.

The Clear and Present Danger Doctrine   Justice Holmes announced this celebrated doctrine in *Schenck* v. *United States*. He wrote: "The question in every case is whether the words are used in circumstances and are of such a nature as to create a clear and present danger that they will bring about substantive evils that Congress has a right to prevent."[34] Justice Brandeis further elaborated in a later case, "no danger flowing from speech can be deemed clear and present, unless the incidence of the evil" that will result from that speech "is so imminent that it may befall before there is opportunity for full discussion."[35]

Supporters of the clear and present danger doctrine concede that speech is not an absolute right. Yet they believe free speech to be so fundamental that no government should be allowed to restrict it, unless it can demonstrate there is such a close connection between a speech and illegal action that the speech itself takes on the character of the action. (To shout "Fire" falsely in a crowded theater is Justice Holmes's famous example.) A government should not be allowed to interfere with speech unless it can prove, ultimately to a skeptical judiciary, that the particular speech in question presented an *immediate danger* of a *major* evil; for example, it clearly would have led to a riot, destruction of property, corruption of an election, or direct interference with recruitment of soldiers. Consider our previous example. Advocates of the clear and present danger doctrine would argue that even though a legislature had made it illegal to make abusive racial remarks in public, the law should not be applied in any specific incident unless the government presents convincing evidence that particular remarks made by a particular individual clearly and presently might have led to a riot or to some other serious evil.

TABLE 4–1
Members of the Supreme Court Since 1946

Justice	Years On Court	President Who Appointed
Hugo L. Black	1937–1971	Roosevelt
Stanley F. Reed	1938–1957	Roosevelt
Felix Frankfurter	1939–1962	Roosevelt
William O. Douglas	1939–1975	Roosevelt
Francis W. Murphy	1940–1949	Roosevelt
Robert H. Jackson	1941–1954	Roosevelt
Wiley B. Rutledge	1943–1949	Roosevelt
Harold H. Burton	1945–1958	Truman
Frederick M. Vinson*	1946–1953	Truman
Tom C. Clark	1949–1967	Truman
Sherman Minton	1949–1956	Truman
Earl Warren*	1953–1969	Eisenhower
John Marshall Harlan	1953–1971	Eisenhower
William J. Brennan, Jr.	1956–	Eisenhower
Charles E. Wittaker	1957–1962	Eisenhower
Potter Stewart	1958–1981	Eisenhower
Byron R. White	1962–	Kennedy
Arthur J. Goldberg	1962–1965	Kennedy
Abe Fortas	1965–1969	Johnson
Thurgood Marshall	1967–	Johnson
Warren E. Burger*	1969–1986	Nixon
Harry A. Blackmun	1970–	Nixon
Lewis F. Powell, Jr.	1971–1987	Nixon
William H. Rehnquist**	1971–	Nixon
John Paul Stevens	1975–	Ford
Sandra Day O'Connor	1981–	Reagan
Antonin Scalia	1986–	Reagan
Anthony Kennedy	1988–	Reagan

* Chief Justices.   ** Elevated from Associate to Chief in 1986.

CHAPTER 4 / First Amendment Rights

The Preferred Position Doctrine This was the explicit position of the Supreme Court for a brief time during the 1940s; it still represents pretty much the present Court's implicit position about speech relating to *political* matters. Those who take this view, such as the late Justice Hugo Black, come close to the position that freedom of expression—that is, the use of words and pictures—may never be curtailed. This does not mean that there is nothing left for judges to decide, for a line must still be drawn between speech and nonspeech.

The preferred position interpretation of the First Amendment gives these freedoms the highest priority in our constitutional hierarchy. Judges have a special duty to protect these freedoms and should be most skeptical about laws trespassing on them. Legislative majorities are free to experiment with and to adopt various schemes regulating our lives in general. But when they tamper with freedom of speech, they interfere with the channels of the political process. Only if the government can show limitations on speech are absolutely necessary to avoid imminent and serious substantive evils are such limitations to be allowed.

If we apply the preferred position doctrine to our example of a law against abusive racial remarks, we would declare the law itself unconstitutional. Restraints on such abusive speech are not absolutely necessary to prevent riots or other social disturbances. Whatever danger may come from such remarks does not justify restricting free comment. Moreover, supporters of the preferred position doctrine contend that the law, by imposing a "chilling effect" on speech and not merely its application, violates the Constitution.

Justice Hugo Black, a former U.S. senator from Alabama and member of the Supreme Court from 1937 to 1971, was a noted champion of First Amendment rights.

CURRENT CONSTITUTIONAL TESTS

The three historic doctrines just discussed still provide the background for debates on freedom of speech. Today, however, the Supreme Court is more apt to use the following doctrines to measure the limits of governmental power.

Prior Restraint Of all the forms of governmental interference with expression, judges are most suspicious of those that impose restraints prior to publication; these include licensing requirements before a speech can be made, a motion picture shown, or a newspaper published. The Supreme Court has refused to declare all forms of prior censorship unconstitutional, but a "prior restraint on expression comes to this court with a 'heavy presumption' against its constitutionality. . . . The Government thus carries a heavy burden of showing justification for the enforcement of such a restraint."[36]

Except as applied to motion pictures, the only examples of the Court's actual approval of prior restraints relate to the power of military commanders to regulate what is distributed in military bases, to the right of the CIA to screen what its agents and ex-agents publish, and to the right of high school authorities to exercise "editorial control over the style and content of student speech" in school newspapers and other "school-sponsored expressive activities so long as their actions are reasonably related to legitimate pedagogical concerns."[37]

Vagueness A law is unconstitutional if it "either forbids or requires the doing of an act in terms so vague that men of common intelligence must necessarily guess at its meaning and differ as to its application. . . ."[38] Laws touching First Amendment freedoms are required to pass even more rigid standards. These laws must not allow those who administer them so much discretion that they could discriminate against those whose views they dislike. The laws must also not be so vague that people are afraid to exercise protected freedoms. Such

Student editors at Hazelwood East High School in suburban St. Louis lost their battle against censorship by their school principal when the Supreme Court ruled in 1988 that school officials have broad powers over student newspapers.

You decide!

In *The New York Times Company* v. *United States* (1971) the Supreme Court set aside an injunction the attorney general had secured from a lower court against the publication by several newspapers of the *Pentagon Papers*, a classified study of the government's decision-making process on Vietnam policy. The attorney general failed to convince the Court that the publication of these documents would cause immediate and specific damage to national security.* In the Pentagon Papers case the government had asserted its right to act without any specific congressional authorization. In 1979, when federal executive officials learned that a magazine, *The Progressive*, was about to publish an article entitled "The H-Bomb Secret: How We Got It, Why We're Telling It," federal prosecutors acted pursuant to the Atomic Energy Act. They went before a federal district judge to seek an injunction prohibiting publication of this article. This act authorizes the federal government to enjoin the dissemination of restricted data concerning the design, manufacture, or use of atomic weapons. The district judge could "find no plausible reason why the public needs to know the technical details about hydrogen bomb construction," and he issued a preliminary restraining order.

What do you think the Supreme Court would do with this example of prior restraint? And how would you have ruled?

* 403 U.S. 713 (1971).

(Answer/Discussion on page 85.)

vague and overbroad laws have a "chilling effect" on freedom of speech. The Supreme Court has struck down laws that condemn "sacriligious" movies or publications of "criminal deeds of bloodshed or lust . . . so massed as to become vehicles for inciting violent and depraved crimes."[39]

Overbreadth Closely related to the vagueness doctrine is the requirement that a statute relating to First Amendment freedoms cannot be so broad that it sweeps within its prohibitions protected speech as well as nonprotected activities, for example, a loyalty oath that endangers protected forms of association along with illegal activities. Because the very existence of overbroad statutes tends to repress protected speech, such statutes may be declared unconstitutional on their face, that is, entirely and not in some particular application of the law.

Least Drastic Means Even for an important purpose, a legislature may not choose a law that impinges on First Amendment freedoms if there are other ways to handle the problem. To illustrate, a state may protect the public from unscrupulous lawyers, but it may not do so by forbidding organizations to make legal services available to their members, or by forbidding attorneys from advertising their fees for simple services. The state could adopt other ways to protect the public from such lawyers that do not impinge on freedom of association or speech.

Content Neutral Content neutral laws are much less likely to be struck down than those that restrict speech because of its content. For example, a law forbidding posting of handbills on telephone polls has been sustained. Yet a law prohibiting posting of handbills advocating racism or sexism would in all probability be declared unconstitutional, because it would relate to what is being said rather than where and how it is being said. (Justice Stevens believes the content neutral standard is of little help. He quipped: "Any student of history who has been reprimanded for talking about the World Series during a class discussion of the First Amendment knows that it is incorrect to state that a time, place, or manner restriction may not be based upon either the content or subject matter of speech."[40])

Centrality of Political Speech "Not all speech is of equal First amendment importance. It is speech on 'matters of public concern that is at the heart of the First amendment's protection.' "[41] The Court gives much greater constitutional protection to speech relating to public policy and politics than to speech relating to other matters. There is some contradiction between content neutrality and centrality of political speech. Legislatures and city councils are supposed to pass laws that are content neutral, but in determining whether or not those laws violate the Constitution judges may take into account what kind of speech is involved.

Plainly, neither doctrines nor constitutional tests decide cases: Judges do. Doctrines are judges' starting points; each case requires a judge to weigh a variety of factors. *What* was said? *Where* was it said? *How* was it said? What was the *intent* of the person who said it? *Which government* is attempting to regulate the speech—a city council speaking for a few people, or the Congress speaking for many? (Few congressional enactments have ever been struck down because of conflict with the First Amendment.) *How* is the government attempting to regulate the speech? By prior censorship? By punishment after the speech? *Why* is the government acting? To preserve the public peace? To prevent criticism of those in power? These and scores of other considerations are involved in the never-ending process of determining what the Constitution permits and what it forbids.

Hundreds of writers marched in 1989 outside the Iranian Mission to the United Nations to protest the "death sentence" imposed by Ayatollah Khomeini upon Salman Rushdie for his book *The Satanic Verses*.

Freedom of the Press

Although we still utilize street-corner meetings and public rallies to communicate ideas and influence public policies, today most of us rely on television, newspapers, radio, movies—the mass media—to tell us what is happening in the world. The Constitution, not surprisingly, also speaks of freedom of the press.

Freedom of the press is the same as freedom of speech, except that the clause relating to speech protects oral communications, and the phrase relating to the press embraces written ones. Some, however, especially the representatives of the press, contend the press has greater freedom than others. Former Chief Justice Burger acknowledged that media representatives have a valid claim to function as "surrogates for the public and thus may be provided special seating and priority of entry [at trials] so that they may report what people in attendance have seen and heard."[42] Further, the Supreme Court has been careful to protect the press from special tax burdens, even when there is no evidence of any evil intent on the part of the taxing authorities. Finally, "media defendants" appear to have more protection against libel suits than "nonmedia defendants."[43]

Still, the prevailing view is: "The First Amendment does not 'belong' to any definable category of persons or entities; it belongs to all who exercise its freedoms."[44] Representatives of the press continue to argue otherwise. They also claim not merely the constitutional right to publish but also a right of access, a right to protect their sources, and a right to secure their files against search warrants.

DOES THE PRESS HAVE A RIGHT TO KNOW?

Courts have carefully protected the press's right to publish information—no matter how it got it. But reporters, editors, and others have argued this is not enough. If reporters are excluded from places where public business is being conducted, or denied access to information in government files, they will not be able to perform the press's historic function of keeping the public informed. The Supreme Court, however, has refused to acknowledge a right to know, although it did concede there is a First Amendment right for the press, along with the public, to be at criminal trials.[45]

Although they have no constitutional obligation to do so, many states have adopted **sunshine laws** requiring public agencies to open their meetings to

During the campaign of 1988, George Bush was challenged by CBS newsman Dan Rather to explain his role in the Iran-contra affair. In the heated exchanges that followed, Bush reprimanded Rather for turning a profile interview into a confrontation.

the public and the press. And Congress, too, requires most federal executive agencies to open various types of hearings and meetings of advisory groups to the public. Congress, in fact, holds most of its committee meetings in public. Federal and state courtroom trials are open, but judicial conferences are not.

Congress has authorized the president to establish a classification system to keep some public documents and governmental files secret, and it is a crime for any person to divulge such classified information. So far, however, although they have been threatened, no newspapers have been prosecuted for doing so.

By the Freedom of Information Act of 1966 (FOIA), as amended, Congress has liberalized access to nonclassified government records. This act makes the records of federal executive agencies available, subject to certain exceptions, such as private financial transactions, personnel records, criminal investigation files, interoffice memoranda, and letters used in internal decision making. If federal agencies fail to move promptly on requests, persons are entitled to speedy judicial hearings. The burden is on an agency to explain any refusal to supply material, and if the judge decides the government has improperly withheld information, the government has to pay the legal fees.

Since the inception of FOIA more than 250,000 people have requested information and more than 90 percent of these requests have been granted. Some are concerned that FOIA has had an adverse effect on our ability to enforce laws and carry out confidential investigations and that its implementation costs too much. Others are concerned that FOIA has been used by firms to obtain competitors' secrets. But most observers, especially newspaper reporters and scholars, believe that FOIA gives real meaning to the citizen's right to know.[46]

EXECUTIVE PRIVILEGE

Most presidents have claimed a constitutional right of **executive privilege** to withhold information not only from the press but from Congress and the courts if, in the president's judgment, its release would jeopardize national security or interfere with the confidentiality of advice. In the celebrated case of *United States v. Nixon* (1974), the Supreme Court ruled that executive privilege does not shield a president from a judicial subpoena for material relevant to a criminal prosecution.[47] This historic decision, which marked the second time the Supreme Court decided a matter directly involving the president as a party to a case, rejected a claim of absolute executive privilege. The Court did, however, recognize that a president's "singularly unique role" gives the office a limited executive privilege to which judges should show the "utmost deference."

Following his nationwide television speech, President Nixon sits in his office with the transcripts subpoenaed by the Supreme Court.

DOES THE PRESS HAVE A RIGHT TO WITHHOLD INFORMATION?

Although most reporters have challenged the right of the government to withhold information, they claim a right to do so themselves, including the right to keep information from grand juries and legislative committees. Without this right, they say, they cannot assure their sources of confidentiality, and they will not be able to get the information they need to keep the public informed. But the Supreme Court has declared that reporters, and presumably scholars, have no constitutional right to ignore legal requests and withhold information from judicial authorities. Speaking for the Court, Justice White quoted from English political theorist Jeremy Bentham: "Were the Prince of Wales, the Archbishop of Canterbury, and the Lord High Chancellor, to be passing by in the same coach, while a chimney sweeper and a barrow woman were in dispute about a halfpennyworth of apples, and the chimney sweeper or the barrow woman were to think proper to call upon them for their evidence, could they refuse it? No, most certainly." The Court concluded: " 'The public has a right to every man's evidence,' except for those persons protected by a constitutional, common-law, or statutory privilege." The majority pointed out that if a reporter were allowed to withhold evidence in a criminal trial, the defendant could be injured and the public interest in the conviction of criminals adversely affected. If any privilege is to be given to newspeople, said the Court, it should be done by act of Congress and of the states.[48] Congress has not yet responded to this suggestion, but many states have passed so-called **shield laws** that provide some protection for the press from state courts.

FREEDOM OF THE PRESS VERSUS FAIR TRIALS

When newspapers and television report in vivid details the facts of a crime, interview prosecutors and police, question witnesses, and hold press conferences for defendants and their attorneys, they may so inflame the public that conducting a fair trial is difficult. In England, strict rules determine what the media may report, and judges do not hesitate to punish newspapers that comment on pending criminal proceedings. In the United States, in contrast, free comment is emphasized. The Supreme Court has even set aside contempt citations against editors who threatened judges with political reprisals unless the judges imposed severe punishments on certain named defendants. Yet the Supreme Court has not been indifferent to protecting persons on trial from inflammatory publicity. Its remedies have been to order new trials or to instruct judges to impose sanctions on prosecutors and police, not on reporters.

Federal rules of criminal procedure forbid any form of radio or photographic coverage of criminal cases in federal courts, but most states now permit electronic, including television, coverage of courtroom proceedings.[49] Defendants, however, always have the right to present evidence that television interfered with their particular trials, prevented fair hearings, and deprived them of due process.

Other Media and Other Messages

When the Constitution was written, "the press" referred to leaflets, newspapers, and books. The Constitution also protects speech that comes from other media such as the mails, motion pictures, radio, television, cable, picketing, as well as certain kinds of symbolic conduct. Because each form of communication entails special problems, each needs a different degree of protection.

THE MAILS

Seventy years ago, Justice Holmes wrote in dissent: "The United States may give up the Post Office when it sees fit, but while it carries it on, the use of the mails is almost as much a part of free speech as is the right to use our tongues."[50] In 1965 the Court adopted Holmes's views by striking down the first congressional act ever held to conflict with the First Amendment. That act had directed the postmaster general to detain foreign mailings of "communist political propaganda" and to deliver these materials only upon the addressee's request. The Court has also set aside federal laws authorizing postal authorities to exclude from the mails materials they consider obscene.

Although government censorship of the mails is unconstitutional, household censorship is not. The Court has sustained a law giving any householder the absolute right to ask the postmaster to order mailers to delete their names from all mailing lists and to refrain from sending any advertisements that householders, in their sole discretion, believe to be "erotically arousing or sexually provocative." It makes no constitutional difference if a householder includes a dry-goods catalogue in such a category. Moreover, Congress may forbid—and has forbidden—the use of mailboxes for any materials except those sent through the United States mails.

MOTION PICTURES

Films may be treated differently from books or newspapers, and prior censorship of films to prevent the showing of obscenity is not necessarily unconstitutional. However, laws calling for submission of films to a review board, or authorizing judges to issue restraining orders against showing motion pictures are constitutional only if there is a prompt judicial hearing. The burden is on the government to prove to the court that the particular film in question is in fact obscene.

RADIO AND TELEVISION

Television is the most important means of distributing news as well as the primary forum for appealing for votes. Yet of all the mass media broadcasting has received the least First Amendment protection. Congress has established a system of commercial broadcasting, supplemented by the Corporation for Public Broadcasting, which provides funds for public radio and television. The entire system is regulated by the Federal Communications Commission (FCC). Broadcasters, using publicly owned airwaves, have no constitutional right to use these facilities without licenses. The FCC grants licenses for limited periods and makes regulations for their use.

The First Amendment would prevent censorship if the FCC tried to impose it. Yet the First Amendment does not prevent the FCC from imposing sanctions on stations that broadcast "filthy words," even though such indecencies are not legally obscene. Nor does the First Amendment prevent the FCC from refusing to renew a license if in its opinion a broadcaster has not served the public interest.

The First Amendment does not, under prevailing interpretations, prevent the FCC, as it did from 1949 to 1987, from adopting what came to be known as the **fairness doctrine,** requiring broadcasters to cover issues of public significance and to reflect differing viewpoints. Thus, if licensees made editorial statements or endorsed candidates, they had to give persons representing a different point of view an opportunity to respond. Congress has imposed an additional **equal-time requirement** requiring licensees to be sure that all candidates for public office had equal air time. (Congress has modified this requirement to make possible presidential debates between only candidates of the two major parties.)[51]

Do political parties, candidates for office, or interest groups have a right to radio or television time if they are willing to pay for it? The answer divides champions of free speech: It is hard to tell the "good guys" from the "bad guys." Although a unanimous Supreme Court concluded that governments could not force newspapers to accept advertisements or print replies from those they have criticized, judges have had a much harder time finding the "right answer" to similar questions about broadcasting. Without too much trouble the justices concluded that Congress may impose on broadcast licensees an obligation to sell time to legally qualified federal candidates, and that the FCC may supervise how they do so.

On the other hand, seven justices concluded (*Red Lion Broadcasting Co.* v. *Federal Communications Commission*) that neither the First Amendment nor the Federal Communications Act gives anybody the right to buy air time. The Court, however, could not muster a majority behind any single opinion. Chief Justice Burger noted that if broadcasters had to accept the offers of all who wished to buy air time, those with the most money would monopolize radio and television. He said although the First Amendment gives no one a right of access to broadcasting facilities, Congress or the FCC could provide such access. Justice William O. Douglas, a long-time advocate of an expansive interpretation of the First Amendment, argued that refusal by broadcasters—with the sanction of the FCC—to accept paid political advertisements violates the First Amendment rights of those who are denied access to television audiences.[52]

"And here with us this evening, to skirt the issues, are Senator Tom Kirkland and Congressman Alan Sullivan."

Drawing by H. Martin; © 1988 The New Yorker Magazine, Inc.

The major argument in favor of greater regulation of broadcasters than of newspaper and magazine publishers is that the public owns the limited number of airwaves and those who have access to these airwaves have control over a limited resource. This rationale for treating broadcasting differently from the print media is under increasing attack. In a footnote to a 1984 decision the Court noted, "the prevailing rationale for broadcast regulation has come under increasing criticism in recent years" because such technological changes as cable, direct beam broadcast, and videotapes may be undermining the assumption that the scarcity of channels justifies substantial government regulation. "We are not prepared, however," wrote Justice Brennan for the majority, "to reconsider our long-standing approach without some signal from Congress or the FCC that technological developments have advanced so far that some revision of the system of broadcast regulation may be required."[53] So far Congress has not signaled its desire for change. On the contrary it has opposed attempts by the FCC under the Reagan and Bush administrations to move toward deregulation of television.

CABLE TELEVISION AND THE RIGHT OF ACCESS

Constitutional issues are never resolved; they are just applied to new situations. As new means of communication come onto the scene, they bring the old issues in new forms. Cable television is a good example. In the 1984 Cable Act Congress allowed, but did not require, free public access to channels. As a condition for getting a license, cable firms in many cities had to agree to provide free access to one or more channels on a first-come, first-served basis. Such public access channels, it was argued, would be the town meetings of the next century.

Does every group have a constitutional right to say anything they wish to any audience? For example, does the Ku Klux Klan have a right to put on a program advocating racial supremacy, or a Palestine Liberation group to sponsor a program advocating the destruction of Israel? Does the First Amendment give any person the right to say or do on public television what they can say or do on a street corner? Could a state or a city pass a law abolishing the public access channel, as did Kansas City, Missouri, in 1988 to keep the Klan off the air. And what of the First Amendment rights of the cable operators? Does the Constitution protect their right not to provide access to those whose views they find objectionable? And where does the FCC fit in?

The courts are only beginning to supply the answers and they are doing so by applying the traditional doctrines, moving slowly, watching actual experiences, and taking their clues from the FCC. As David A. Kaplan has pointed out, "It is an exquisitely vexing debate over cable television and the First Amendment. Trouble is, the First Amendment seems to be on both sides."[54]

HANDBILLS, SOUND TRUCKS, AND BILLBOARDS

Religious and political pamphlets, leaflets, and handbills have been historic weapons in the defense of liberty, and their distribution is constitutionally protected. So, too, is the use of their more contemporary counterparts, sound trucks and billboards. A state, for example, cannot restrain the passing out of leaflets merely to keep its streets clean; nor can it ban handbills that do not carry the name and address of the author. However, reasonable, content neutral regulations specifying where publications may be sold are permissible. As for sound trucks, those that emit loud and raucous noises may be banned. Furthermore, content-neutral regulations detailing the time, place, and manner in which amplification devices may be used for musical performances such as rock concerts are also acceptable. Billboards, too, are entitled to constitutional protection. Those used for noncommercial purposes, however, are more protected than those used for commercial reasons.

PICKETING

A law forbidding all peaceful picketing would be an unconstitutional invasion of speech. However, "picketing involves elements of both speech and conduct, i.e., patrolling," and "because of this intermingling of protected and unprotected elements, picketing can be subject to controls that would not be constitutionally permissible in the case of pure speech."[55]

Even peaceful picketing can be restricted if it is conducted for an illegal purpose, such as to press an employer to practice racial or sex discrimination in hiring workers. Federal regulations are so comprehensive for trade union picketing, however, that the power of states to interfere is much narrower than it might appear from First Amendment decisions.

COMMERCIAL SPEECH

Even though commercial speech is constitutionally protected, common-sense differences exist between commercial and other kinds of speech. Commercial speech is, therefore, subject to much more regulation than other speech; for example, advertising the sale of anything illegal may be forbidden, as can false and misleading commercial advertising. (A law forbidding false and misleading political speech or political advertising is clearly unconstitutional. In political debate, no one can say what is false and misleading.) Moreover, if government has a "substantial reason," it may even regulate nonfalse and nonmisleading commercial advertising about legal activities. For example, Puerto Rico has been allowed to ban local advertising for gambling casinos, which are legal in Puerto Rico, but still allowed such advertising outside the island. In this way, Puerto Rico can attract tourists from elsewhere—but not encourage residents—to come to gamble.[56] Advertising on radio and television is subject to even greater regulation than advertising transmitted in print.

Exercising the freedom of speech, this woman using a bullhorn is entitled to constitutional protection.

"We cannot accept the view," wrote Chief Justice Earl Warren, "that an apparently limitless variety of conduct can be labeled speech whenever the person engaged in the conduct intends thereby to express an idea."[57] Similarly, Chief Justice Warren Burger wrote: "Conduct that the State police power can prohibit on a public street does not become automatically protected by the Constitution merely because the conduct is moved to . . . a 'live theatre' stage, any more than a 'live' performance of a man and woman locked in a sexual embrace at high noon in Times Square is protected by the Constitution merely because they simultaneously engaged in a political dialogue."[58]

The burden is on those who engage in expressive *conduct* to show that the First Amendment applies, and even if it does, government may forbid or regulate symbolic expressive conduct: (1) if the conduct itself may be regulated; (2) if the regulation is content neutral; (3) if the regulation is narrowly drawn to further a substantial governmental interest; (4) if this interest is unrelated to the suppression of free speech; and (5) if ample alternative channels for communication of the information are left open.[59]

Of course, the line between speech and conduct is not always clear. Deliberately burning a draft card in violation of a congressional regulation is not, for example, a constitutionally protected form of speech; but burning the American flag as a form of political protest with the intent "to seriously offend" observers is constitutionally protected.

Libel, Obscenity, and Fighting Words

As we have noted, some kinds of speech are not entitled to constitutional protection. This does not mean that the constitutional issues relating to these kinds of speech are simple. On the contrary. How we prove **libel,** how we define **obscenity,** and how we determine which words are **fighting words** are hotly contested issues.

You decide!

Should the Bill of Rights be amended?

The Supreme Court's five to four decision in *Texas* v. *Johnson* (June 21, 1989) that the First Amendment protects the expressive act of burning the flag prompted President Bush to advocate a constitutional amendment that reads as follows: "The Congress and the States shall have power to prohibit the physical desecration of the flag of the United States."

Do you think Congress should propose such an amendment? Should the states ratify it?

(Answer/Discussion on page 91.)

Although this display of the American flag on the floor of the Chicago Art Institute deeply offended many people, a similar use of the flag was defended as a form of political protest protected by the First Amendment in *Texas* v. *Johnson.*

WE IN CONGRESS VOTED IN FAVOR OF DEMOCRACY IN CHINA

AND WE VOTED IN FAVOR OF THE AMERICAN FLAG

THAT'S WHAT WE WERE ELECTED FOR—

TO MAKE THE TOUGH DECISIONS!

© 1989 Boston Globe. Reprinted by permission.

LIBEL

At one time newspaper publishers and editors had to take considerable care about what they wrote, for fear they might be prosecuted for libel by the government or sued for money damages by individuals. Today, through a progressive raising of constitutional standards, it has become more difficult to win a libel suit against a newspaper or magazine.

In *The New York Times* v. *Sullivan*, and subsequent cases, the Supreme Court has established the guidelines: Neither *public officials* nor *public figures* can collect damages for any comments made about them unless they can prove the comments were made with knowledge of their falsity or with reckless disregard for whether the comments were true or false, that is, unless they can prove the comments were made with "actual malice."[60] Furthermore, public figures cannot collect damages for emotional distress even when outrageous and clearly inaccurate and false cartoons of them are published. Such was the case when *Hustler Magazine* printed an advertisement parodying the Reverend Jerry Falwell; the Court held such cartoons cannot reasonably be understood as describing actual facts or actual events.[61]

Constitutional standards for libel charges brought by *private* persons or that do not involve "matters of public concern" are not so rigid. State laws may permit private persons to collect damages without having to prove actual malice if they can prove the statements made about them are false and negligently published. Moreover, one does not lose status as a private person and become a public figure, and thus become subject to more rigid requirements for collecting libel damages merely because of newspaper publicity, for example, about getting a divorce, being accused of being a spy, or receiving a federal grant and being accused by a senator of wasting taxpayers' money.

OBSCENITY

Today, fears about obscenity and pornography (see the next section) have replaced seventeenth-century fears about heresy and 1950s fears about sedition. In 1970 a Presidential Commission on Obscenity and Pornography funded studies that, to the disappointment of the Nixon administration, found no evidence that exposure to obscenity plays a significant role in causing delinquent or criminal behavior. Then in 1986 the Attorney General's Commission on Pornography argued to the contrary: Evidence does exist that "some forms of sexually explicit material bear a causal relationship . . . to sexual violence." This Commission called for an all-out war on "smut" and made over ninety recommendations for tighter regulation and tougher punishments, especially of cable television.[62]

Obscene publications are not entitled to constitutional protection, but the members of the Supreme Court, like everybody else, have had great difficulty in defining what is obscene. Almost 100 separate opinions have been written on the matter by Supreme Court justices. In *Miller* v. *California* (1973) the Court was finally able to assemble a majority opinion. Speaking for five members of the Court, Chief Justice Warren Burger once again tried to clarify a constitutional definition of obscenity. A work may be considered legally obscene provided: (1) The average person, applying contemporary standards of the particular community, would find that the work, taken as a whole, appeals to a prurient interest in sex (that is, patently offensive interests "over and beyond those that would be characterized as normal")[63] ; (2) the work depicts or describes in a patently offensive way sexual conduct specifically defined by the applicable law or authoritatively con-

CHAPTER 4 / First Amendment Rights

strued; and (3) the work, taken as a whole, lacks serious literary, artistic, political, or scientific value.[64] Chief Justice Burger specifically rejected part of the previous test—the so-called *Memoirs* v. *Massachusetts* (1966) formula: No work should be judged obscene unless it is "utterly without redeeming social value."[65] He argued such a test would make it impossible for a state to outlaw hard-core pornography.

Did the *Miller* decision mean that local communities could ban whatever a prosecutor could persuade a jury was obscene? Many hoped they could; many others feared they could. But how far could a jury go? Could it decide to ban "Little Red Riding Hood"? After all, who really knows what went on in that bedroom? A year after the *Miller* decision, the Supreme Court warned: "It would be a serious misreading of *Miller* to conclude that juries have unbridled discretion in determining what is patently offensive."[66] Appellate courts, said then Justice Rehnquist speaking for the Court, should review jury determinations to ensure compliance with constitutional standards. And the Supreme Court itself, after such review, ruled that the movie *Carnal Knowledge* was not obscene, contrary to the conclusion of a jury in Albany, Georgia.

Obscenity, then, is not entitled to constitutional protection. But governments must proceed under laws that specifically define the kinds of sexual conduct forbidden in word or picture. Moreover, it is not a crime for booksellers to offer obscene books for sale; they must be shown to have done so *knowingly*. Otherwise, booksellers would tend to avoid placing on their shelves materials that some authorities might consider objectionable, and the public would be deprived of an opportunity to purchase anything except some person's determination of the "safe and sanitary." The mere private possession of obscene materials is not a crime either.

States are primarily responsible for regulating obscene literature. Yet ever since the 1880s when Anthony Comstock started a national crusade against "smut," Congress has been concerned with the subject. It has adopted, and the Supreme Court has upheld, laws forbidding the importation of obscene materials into the United States or the sending of such materials through the mails or interstate commerce—even to willing adults or even transported for private use in a briefcase in an airline.

What about "dirty books" and "X-rated movies" that fall short of the constitutional definition of obscenity? They are entitled to some constitutional protection, but less protection than political speech, and they are subject to greater government regulation. "Society's interest in protecting this type of expression is of a wholly different, and lesser, magnitude than the interest in untrammeled political debate. . . . The state may legitimately use the content of these materials as the basis for placing them in a different classification from other motion pictures."[67] Cities may also regulate, by zoning laws, where "adult motion picture theaters" may be located.

Sexually explicit materials either about minors or aimed at them are *not* protected by the First Amendment. Provided they act under narrowly drawn statutes, state and local governments can, for example, ban the knowing sale of "girly" magazines to minors, even if such materials would not be considered legally obscene if sold to adults. And they can make it a crime to depict sexual conduct by children, even if the depicted behavior would not be considered obscene if performed by adults. Currently being challenged before the courts by a coalition representing the publishing and entertainment world is a provision of the 1988 federal Child Protection and Obscenity Act. The provision in question requires anyone who produces sexual material to keep records of the age of the model or actor and provides that, in the absence of such records, distributors prosecuted for selling obscene materials will be presumed to have used minors.[68]

Magazines and newspapers on sale at this newsstand in New York City run the gamut from serious journalism to sensationalism.

Answer/Discussion

Before you decide, you might want to read the several decisions of the Supreme Court justices. Your reference librarian can probably find copies for you. Excerpts can be found in most metropolitan newspapers dated June 21–22, 1989.

PORNOGRAPHY

Pornography used to be merely a synonym for obscenity. In recent years, however, some feminists have defined pornographic materials as sexually explicit pictures or words that depict women as sexual objects enjoying pain and humiliation or that present abuse of women as a sexual stimulus for men. They argue that just as sexually explicit materials about minors are not entitled to First Amendment protection, so should there be no such protection for pornographic materials.

In the past, pressure for regulating pornography came primarily from political conservatives and religious fundamentalists concerned that it undermines moral standards. More recently, some feminists have joined them, arguing that "pornography is central in creating and maintaining sex as a basis for discrimination."[69] They contend pornography promotes sexual abuse of individual women and perpetuates social subordination of women as a class. They propose that civil penalties be imposed on pornographers and that women—and others who have had pornography forced upon them—be given the right to file complaints.

Not all feminists favor antipornography ordinances, yet those who do have been joined by social conservatives, and this new chapter in the battle over pornography has just begun. Women and men have differed significantly in their attitudes about pornography. Men, by a two to one ratio, do not think pornography damages adults who read it, and they are about equally divided on whether newsstands should be permitted to sell pornographic material. In contrast, women, by about a three to one ratio, say newsstands should not be allowed to sell pornographic magazines and that laws against pornography are not strict enough.[70]

For this new antipornography coalition to be successful, a substantial alteration in constitutional doctrine will be required.[71] Although several cities have been considering the adoption of antipornography ordinances, only Indianapolis has passed such a law, which was declared unconstitutional in a decision affirmed by the Supreme Court without opinion.[72] The Court has also refused to allow Congress to ban "indecent" telephone messages for commercial purposes.

Censorship of films and books may be imposed by a variety of means other than formal action. In some cities such local groups as the Legion of Decency may pressure authorities. Feminists, by threats of boycott, have pressured some stores to stop selling magazines they believe depict women in a demeaning and pornographic manner. Local police have been known to threaten booksellers with criminal prosecution if they persist in showing films or selling books of which some local people disapprove. In 1986 the Attorney General's Commission on Pornography wrote letters to various retail companies saying the commission had received testimony alleging they were supplying pornography because they sold *Playboy* or *Penthouse* magazines or adult video cassettes. Retailers were given a chance to respond to these allegations, but they were also told "failure to respond will necessarily be accepted as an indication of no objection to the allegation."[73]

Under this pressure some of the stores did stop selling the magazines, but others have carried the issue to the federal courts where it is waiting final resolution. Of course, anyone is free to stay away from pictures or books he or she dislikes, and even to try to persuade others to stay away. What the Constitution forbids is the use of coercive powers of government to keep adults from seeing or reading what they wish to see or read.

Police protected these Ku Klux Klan demonstrators whose banners displayed harsh and offensive words.

FIGHTING WORDS

Certain well-defined and narrowly limited classes of speech "by their very utterance inflict injury or tend to incite an immediate breach of peace that governments may constitutionally punish."[74] These fighting words "have a direct tendency to cause acts of violence by the person to whom, individually, the remarks are addressed."[75] That the words are abusive, harsh, or insulting is not sufficient. Thus, the four-letter word used in relation to the draft and worn on a sweatshirt is not a fighting word in the constitutional sense, at least when it is not directed to any specific person.

Right of the People Peaceably to Assemble, to Petition the Government, and to Associate

FREEDOM OF ASSEMBLY

"The right to assemble peaceably applies not only to meetings in private homes and meeting halls, but to gatherings held in public streets and parks, which since . . . time out of mind have been used for purposes of assembly . . . and discussing public questions."[76] In the winter of 1977, Frank Collins, "a self-avowed Nazi,"[77] threatened to lead his small band, dressed in brown shirts and carrying swastika regalia, in a jack-booted march through the streets of Skokie, Illinois, a Chicago suburb with a large Jewish population. Some of these citizens are themselves survivors of Hitler's extermination camps; many of them had relatives who lost their lives in the Holocaust. Many people, including the officials of Skokie and a local judge, argued that Collins and his followers should not be allowed to march. They argued that this would be like shouting "Fire!" in a crowded theater, and that to permit such a use of the streets presented a clear and present danger of inciting people to violence. These same arguments were put forward to contend that Iranian followers of the late Ayatollah Khomeini should not be allowed to protest publicly in Washington at a time when most Americans were angry about Khomeini's illegal and brutal treatment of innocent American hostages in Tehran. The right to assemble peaceably, they said, should not be extended to Iranian aliens who were abusing this right to provoke Americans to violence.

In both cases judicial authorities defended the rights of these unpopular minorities to demonstrate. (Collins never actually marched in Skokie, but he did march in another part of the Chicago area.) But it is not always the "bad guys" whose rights have to be protected by the courts: It also took occasional judicial intervention in the 1960s to preserve for Martin Luther King, Jr., and those who marched with him, their right to demonstrate in the streets of southern cities in behalf of blacks' rights.

Such incidents present the classic free speech problem of the "heckler's veto" when the audience becomes so abusive that it is impossible for the speaker to be heard. It is almost always easier, and certainly politically more prudent, to maintain order by curbing public demonstrations of unpopular groups than by moving against those who are threatening them. On the other hand, if police did not have the right to order groups to disperse, public order would be at the mercy of those who resort to street demonstrations just to create tensions and provoke street battles.

One form of protest "speech" is this farmers' tractorcade to Washington to draw attention to their economic distress.

The Supreme Court has refused to give a categorical "yes" or "no" answer to the question: "Does the Constitution require police officers always to protect unpopular groups whose public demonstrations arouse others to violence or threats of it?" In 1951, in *Feiner* v. *New York*, the Court upheld the conviction for unlawful assembly of a sidewalk speaker who, against the orders of the only two police officers present, refused to move on after his provocative remarks aroused a crowd to anger.[78] The *Feiner* case has not been overruled, but since that decision the Supreme Court has emphasized that governments must act under more precisely drawn statutes than those for disturbing the peace and unlawful assembly. The Court has refused to sustain convictions of persons whose only offenses have been to engage in peaceful but unpopular demonstrations.

It is clear, however, that the Constitution does not give persons the right to communicate their views to everyone, every place, at any time they wish. No one has the right deliberately to incite others to violence, to block traffic, or to hold parades or make speeches in public streets or on public sidewalks whenever he or she wishes. Governments may make reasonable *time*, *place*, and *manner* regulations, provided they are content neutral.

The Supreme Court has divided public property into three categories: public forums, limited public forums, and nonpublic forums. The extent to which governments may limit access depends on the nature of the forum. "Public places historically associated with the free exercise of expressive activities, such as streets, sidewalks, and parks, are considered, without more, to be 'public forums.' " Courts look closely at time, place, and manner regulations as they apply to these traditional public forums to ensure that they are being applied evenhandedly and that action is not taken because of what is being said rather than how and where or by whom it is being said. Furthermore, in these traditional public forums, no restrictive laws are permitted unless they are viewpoint neutral and the government in question can prove that they are necessary to serve a compelling governmental interest.

Other kinds of public property may be designated as "limited public forums," open for assembly and speech for *limited purposes*, a *limited amount of time*, and even for a *limited class of speakers*, provided the distinctions between those allowed access and those not allowed access are viewpoint neutral.

What of public facilities, such as airports, libraries, courthouses, schools, swimming pools, and government offices, that although public are not forums and are designed for other public purposes? As long as persons assemble to use such facilities within the normal bounds of conduct, they may not be constitutionally restrained from doing so. However, persons may be excluded from such places if they want to talk on subjects or engage in activities for which the facilities were not created. They have no right to interfere with programs or try to appropriate facilities—such as a university chancellor's office—for their own use.

What of private property? The right to assemble does not include a right to trespass on private property. A state may protect property owners against those who attempt to convert property to their own uses, even if they are doing so to express ideas. The profusion of large, privately owned shopping malls, which may cover many acres and which are larger than some towns, presents some difficult constitutional issues. The Supreme Court has set the following guidelines (*Pruneyard Shopping Center* v. *Robins*): Privately owned shopping malls are neither public streets nor places of public assembly; no one has a constitutional right to use such a mall to hand out political leaflets, to picket for political purposes, or otherwise to exercise First Amendment freedoms. On the other hand, states and cities, if they wish, and to an extent still to be defined, may legally obligate the owners of such centers to permit their use for peaceful political purposes such as distributing handbills or getting people to sign petitions. In other words, although people have no constitutional right to engage in political action in a nonpublic shopping center, neither do the owners of such centers have a constitutional right to close them to political action in the face of reasonable state or local regulations providing access that does not interfere with their primary commercial purposes.[79]

Does the right of peaceful assembly and petition include the right to violate a law nonviolently but deliberately? We have no precise answer. But in general, civil disobedience—even if peaceful—is not a protected right. When Dr. Martin Luther King, Jr., and his followers refused to comply with a state court's injunction forbidding them to parade in Birmingham without first securing a permit, the Supreme Court sustained their conviction, even though there was serious doubt about the constitutionality of the injunction and the ordinance on which it was based. Justice Stewart, speaking for the five-member majority, said: "No man can be judge in his own case, however exalted his station, however righteous his motive, and irrespective of his race, color, politics, or religion." Persons are not "constitutionally free to ignore all the procedures of the law and carry their battles to the streets."[80] The four dissenting justices insisted that one does have a right to defy peacefully an obviously unconstitutional statute or injunction.

FREEDOM OF ASSOCIATION

The right to petition the government for redress of grievances is specifically guaranteed by the Constitution; today this right is likely to be exercised in association with others. The right to organize to promote political and other causes is not specifically mentioned in the Constitution, but "it is beyond debate that freedom to engage in association for the advancement of beliefs and ideas is an inseparable aspect of the 'liberty' assured by the Due Process clause of the Fourteenth Amendment which embraces freedom of speech."[81]

The Supreme Court has written of the freedom to associate in two distinct senses. In one line of decisions it has protected people's right to enter into and maintain "certain intimate human relationships" against "undue intrusion by the State. . . . In this respect, freedom of association receives protection as a fundamental element of personal liberty."[82] In this sense freedom of association sometimes comes into conflict with the government's action to protect people against discrimination. We discuss this aspect of the freedom of association in Chapter 6. The other aspect of freedom of association relates to activities protected by the First Amendment: speech, assembly, petition, and the redress of grievances, and the free exercise of religion.

Many troublesome constitutional questions grow out of the conflict between the constitutional right to join political parties and the right of governments to regulate the conditions of public employment. Federal **Hatch Acts** (most states have similar laws) forbid nearly all federal employees from actively campaigning or taking leadership roles in political parties; these acts have been upheld as reasonable measures to ensure a neutral civil service and to free government employees from coercion in behalf of the party in power (see discussion in Chapter 18).

CAMPAIGN FINANCE

Congress, and many states, have regulated the amount of money that candidates, parties, and interest groups can raise and spend for political purposes. But many of these regulations have come into conflict with people's constitutional right to associate to promote political and social causes. In *Buckley* v. *Valeo* the Court sustained limits on the amount of money people may contribute *to candidates* and their campaign committees on the grounds that such limits only marginally restrict contributors' abilities to express political views.[83] But it has struck down limits on the amounts that may be contributed *to associations* formed to support or oppose ballot measures submitted to popular vote.

Limits on what people can *spend*, in contrast to what they can *contribute*, have fared even less well. Governments may not set limits on the amounts that people—including candidates—can spend on political matters. However, presidential candidates who accept federal funds for their campaigns may be limited in what they directly spend as a condition of receiving these public funds. Constitutionally, these limitations on what presidential candidates can spend apply only to expenditures by the candidates' party organizations and "coordinated" groups, not to "independent groups or committees," who have a constitutional right to spend as much as they wish to further the candidates' elections.[84]

Subversive Conduct and Seditious Speech

"If there is any fixed star in our constitutional constellation," Justice Robert Jackson said, "it is that no official, high or petty, can prescribe what shall be orthodox in politics, nationalism, religion, or other matters of opinion. . . ."[85] Any group can champion whatever position it wishes: vegetarianism, feminism, sexism, communism, fascism, black nationalism, white supremacy, Zionism, anti-Semitism, Americanism. But what about people who attempt through force or violence to impose their views on others?

Christopher Boyce being led into Federal court for arraignment on charges of espionage.

TRAITORS, TERRORISTS, SPIES, SABOTEURS, REVOLUTIONARIES

Laws aimed at acts of violence, terrorism, espionage, sabotage, or treason in themselves raise no constitutional questions, nor do they infringe on protected constitutional liberties. However, they can be used to intimidate if they are loosely drawn or indiscriminately administered. The framers of the Constitution, themselves considered traitors by the English Crown, knew the dangers of defining **treason** loosely. Accordingly, they carefully inserted a constitutional definition: *Treason* consists only of the overt acts of giving aid and comfort to the enemies of the United States or levying war against it. Further, in order to convict a person of treason, two witnesses to the overt treasonable acts must testify, or the defendant must confess, in open court.

The national government may also move against other conduct designed to subvert the democratic system. Congress, for example, has made it a crime to engage in espionage or sabotage, or to cross interstate boundaries or use the mails or interstate facilities to bomb buildings and schools. (This law, passed in 1960, was aimed at the white segregationists alleged to have blown up black churches and to have used force to intimidate black leaders and their white allies.) It is also a crime to cross state lines or use interstate facilities with the intent to incite a riot (passed in 1968 and aimed at black militants) or to conspire to do any of the just-described activities.

More often than not, when the government prosecutes under such laws, the charge is **conspiracy.** It is easier to prove conspiracy than to sustain a charge against named defendants that they have thrown a brick, planted a bomb, engaged in a riot, or committed an act of violence. However, conspiracy charges, although long known to Anglo-American jurisprudence, are especially threatening to civil liberties; they can be abused by prosecutors to intimidate the politically unpopular.

For the most part, the highly charged prosecutions of the late 1960s and the early 1970s against political radicals and black militants for allegedly engaging in, or conspiring to engage in, violent acts led to verdicts of not guilty, or reversals on appeal. To some this is evidence that our court system is strong and can be counted on to protect the innocent. To others it is evidence of the inability of the government to bring to justice those who should have been punished for their deeds. To still others it is evidence that governments can use legal procedures to intimidate adherents of unpopular causes. Even if defendants are finally acquitted, the effort and expense of defending themselves in court have an intimidating impact on political dissenters. Historians, journalists, political scientists, and others will be debating the lessons of these trials for many years.

SEDITIOUS SPEECH

It is one thing to punish persons for what they *do*; it is another to punish them for what they *say*. The story of the development of free government is in large measure the story of making this distinction clear. Until recent centuries seditious speech was so broadly defined that all criticism of those in power was considered criminal. As recent as the eighteenth century in England, seditious speech was said to cover any publication intended to incite disaffection against the king or the government, or to raise discontent among the people, or to promote feelings of ill will between different classes. And it made no difference if what was said was true. On the contrary: "The greater the truth the greater the libel." If one charged the king's ministers with being corrupt, and in fact they were corrupt, such a charge would more be likely to cause discontent among the people than if it were false.

The adoption of the Constitution and the Bill of Rights did not result in a quick, easy victory for those who wished to establish free speech in the United States.[86] In 1798, only seven years after the First Amendment had been ratified, Congress passed the first national **sedition** law. Those were perilous times for the young republic, for war with France seemed imminent. The Federalists, in control of both Congress and the presidency, persuaded themselves that national safety required some suppression of speech. Although the Sedition Act marked a considerable advance over English common law in that it made truth a defense and allowed the jury, not a judge, to decide the fact of sedition as well as the fact of publication, it did make it a crime to utter false, scandalous, or malicious statements intended to bring the government or any of its officers into disrepute or "to incite against them the hatred of the good people of the United States."[87]

Popular reaction to the Sedition Act helped defeat the Federalists in the elections of 1800. They had failed to grasp the democratic idea that a person may criticize the government of the day, oppose its policies, work for its downfall, but still be loyal to the nation.

THE SMITH ACT OF 1940

During World War I and the "Red scare" that followed it, a flurry of laws and prosecutions was aimed at seditious speech. Hundreds of people who expressed mildly radical ideas found themselves in trouble. Some went to jail.[88] But the first peacetime sedition law since the Sedition Act of 1798 was the Smith Act of 1940. The Smith Act forbids persons to advocate overthrow of the government with the intent to bring it about; to distribute, with disloyal intent, matter teaching or advising the overthrow of government by violence; and to organize knowingly or to help organize any group having such purposes.

In *Dennis* v. *United States* (1951) the Court agreed that the Smith Act could be applied to the leaders of the Communist party, who had been charged with conspiring to advocate the violent overthrow of the government.[89] Since then the court has substantially modified its holding. Congress may not outlaw the mere advocacy of the abstract doctrine of violent overthrow: "The essential distinction is that those to whom the advocacy is addressed must be urged to do something now or in the future, rather than merely to believe in something."[90] Moreover, advocacy of the use of force may not be forbidden "except where such advocacy is directed to inciting or producing imminent lawless action and is likely to incite or produce such action."[91]

In short, seditious speech, if narrowly defined to cover only the advocacy of immediate and concrete acts of violence, is not constitutionally protected. Such narrow interpretation of the sedition laws means people are free to work for their political objectives as long as they abandon the use of force—or its specific and immediate advocacy—as a means of bringing it about.

Summary

1. First Amendment freedoms—freedom of religion, freedom from the establishment of religion, freedom of speech, freedom of the press, freedom of assembly and petition, and freedom of association—are at the heart of the democratic process.

2. Since World War I, the Supreme Court has become the primary branch of government for giving meaning to these constitutional restraints. And since 1925 these constitutional limits have been applied not only to Congress but to all governmental agencies—national, state, and local.

3. Clashes about First Amendment freedoms are not usefully thought of as battles between the "good guys" and the "bad guys," or as dramas in which judges rush to the rescue of

liberty. Rather, these are arguments over conflicting notions of what is good. Those who argue for restraint on First Amendment freedoms do so for a variety of reasons.

4. Over the years, the Supreme Court has taken a practical approach to First Amendment freedoms. It has refused to make them absolute rights above any kind of governmental regulation, direct or indirect, or to say that they must be preserved at whatever price. But the justices have recognized that a democratic society tampers with these freedoms at great peril. They have insisted upon compelling justification before permitting these rights to be limited. How compelling the justification is, in a free society, will always remain an open question.

Further Reading

T. Barton Carter, Marc A. Franklin, and Jay B. Wright. *The First Amendment and the Fourth Estate*, 3d ed. (Foundation Press, 1985).

Zechariah Chafee, Jr. *Free Speech in the United States* (Harvard University Press, 1941).

Ellis Cose. *The Press* (William Morrow, 1989).

Edward de Grazia and Roger K. Newman. *Banned Films: Movies, Censors and the First Amendment* (R. R. Bowker, 1982).

Ithiel de Sola Pool. *Technologies of Freedom* (Bellenap Press, 1983).

Franklyn S. Haiman. *Speech and Law in a Free Society* (University of Chicago, 1981).

Nat Hentoff. *The First Freedom: The Tumultuous History of Free Speech in America* (Delacorte, 1980).

Leonard W. Levy. *The Establishment Clause: Religion and the First Amendment* (Macmillan, 1986).

Martha M. McCarthy. *A Delicate Balance: Church, State, and the Schools* (Phi Delta Kappan Educational Foundation, 1983).

John Stuart Mill. *Essay on Liberty*. First published in 1859, it is available in many editions, one of which is Arthur Burtt, ed., *The English Philosophers from Bacon to Mill* (Random House, 1939).

William Lee Miller. *The First Liberty: Religion and the American Republic* (Knopf, 1986).

Melville B. Nimmer. *Nimmer on Freedom of Speech: A Treatise on the Theory of the First Amendment* (Mathew Binder, 1987).

5

Equal Rights under the Law

Let's consider again the ringing words of the Declaration of Independence: "We hold these truths to be self-evident, that all men are created equal, that they are endowed by their Creator with certain unalienable Rights, that among these are Life, Liberty, and the pursuit of Happiness. . . ." In this one sentence the Declaration affirmed the precious rights of equality and liberty and appeared to rate equality at least on a par with liberty. The Declaration does not talk about equality of white, Christian, or Anglo-Saxon men, but of *all* men. (Undoubtedly, if the Declaration were to be written today, the framers would speak of "persons" rather than "men.") This creed of individual dignity and equality is older than our Declaration of Independence; its roots go back at least as far as the teachings of Judaism and Christianity.

What about the Constitution? What was the framers' attitude toward liberty and equality? We know that the builders of our constitutional system cherished liberty as their highest ideal. And although you will not find any reference to the idea of *equality* (not even the word itself is in the Constitution or in the array of liberties that form the Bill of Rights) we know the framers believed that all men, at least all white men, were equally entitled to their lives, liberties, and pursuit of happiness (they changed this to property in the Bill of Rights), and that there should be no noble or privileged class under the law. Like the Declaration, however, the Constitution refers to "men" or "him," not to women. And none of its lofty sentiments applied to slaves, who enjoyed neither liberty nor equality.

The framers resolved their ambiguity about what kind of equality and for whom by creating systems of government designed to protect what they called natural rights. Today we speak of human rights, but the idea is the same: the dignity and worth of all citizens. By equal rights the framers meant that every person has an equal right to protection against arbitrary treatment, an equal right to the liberties guaranteed by the Bill of Rights, and an equal right to protection by any laws passed by the new national government.

Women's History is Half of History

Lucretia Mott,
Elizabeth Cady Stanton
barred from
this convention

Sewing machine
invented

Women's Rights
Convention

Declaration of
Sentiments,
Seneca Falls

Harriet Beecher Stowe,
Uncle Tom's Cabin

Sojourner
Truth

Women's
Loyal
League

Clara Barton,
Mother
Bickerdyke,
nurses

Harriet
Tubman
leads raid

1840   1860

World
Anti-slavery
Convention

Irish immigration
begins

Gold
Rush

Dred Scott
decision

Lincoln
elected

Emancipation
Proclamation

Texas admitted
to the Union

Harper's
Ferry

Fort
Sumter

The Constitution itself provides two ways of protecting civil rights. First, it ensures that the government itself imposes no discriminatory barriers, and, second, it grants the national and state governments authority to protect civil rights against interference by private individuals. This chapter is concerned with both the protection of our rights from abuse *by* government and the protection *through* government of our rights, free from abuse by our fellow citizens.

Equality and Equal Rights

Americans are committed to equality. Equality, however, is an elusive term, and "few issues have sparked more controversy or held more sway over the course of history."[1] Part of the difficulty is that equality lacks precise meaning. The concept for which there is the greatest consensus, and that is most clearly written into the Constitution, is that everybody should have *equality of opportunity* regardless of race, ethnic origin, religion, and, in recent years, sex. Ensuring this equality of opportunity is what we mean by the struggle for civil rights.

A variation of the concept of equal opportunity is *equality of starting conditions*. There is not much equal opportunity if one person starting the race is born into a well-to-do family, lives in a quiet suburb, is well fed, and receives a good education, while another is born into a poor, broken family, lives in an inner city neighborhood, and attends inferior schools. Thus, it is argued, if we are to have equality of opportunity in a meaningful sense, we must compensate the disadvantaged to ensure that they have true equality of opportunity.

Compensating people so they will have equality of conditions can be, and is most often, accomplished in the United States by ensuring that individuals are not placed at a disadvantage because of prejudice or poverty. But such action sometimes shades into a concept of *equality among groups*. Traditional emphasis has been upon individual achievement. When large disparities in wealth and advantage exist among groups—as between blacks and whites or women and men—equality becomes a highly divisive political issue. The disadvantaged tend to emphasize those common traits that exclude them from the "mainstream." They tend to champion programs designed to provide special help to people based upon their group memberships. Whether such programs promote or deny equality is one of the most controversial current debates (see page 125).

Finally, equality sometimes means *equality of results*. One perennial debate, especially among college students, is whether social justice and "genuine" equality can coexist in a nation in which some people have so much money and so many good things in life and others have so little. Socialists and some others say they cannot. Yet such a view has had little support in the United States. There is some consensus for guaranteeing a minimum floor, a safety net, below which no one

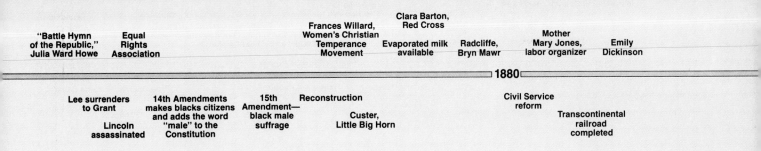

"Battle Hymn
of the Republic,"
Julia Ward Howe

Equal
Rights
Association

Frances Willard,
Women's Christian
Temperance
Movement

Clara Barton,
Red Cross

Evaporated milk
available

Radcliffe,
Bryn Mawr

Mother
Mary Jones,
labor organizer

Emily
Dickinson

1880

Lee surrenders
to Grant

Lincoln
assassinated

14th Amendments
makes blacks citizens
and adds the word
"male" to the
Constitution

15th
Amendment—
black male
suffrage

Reconstruction

Custer,
Little Big Horn

Civil Service
reform

Transcontinental
railroad
completed

should be allowed to fall, but insistence on equality of results would greatly restrict or undermine equality of opportunity. The American Dream is not that everybody should have the same amount of material goods, but that all people should be able to hope, yearn, and strive to improve their lot and, especially, the opportunities for their children. Thus, whatever a person's economic status for the moment, that person should be able to think things will get better, and that hard work and risk taking will be rewarded.

It is within the context of these concerns for equality that we need to look at the struggle for civil rights. The first phase took up the first two hundred years of our nation's existence. The struggle is not over yet, but we have largely achieved equality under the law. Basic ground rules provide equality of formal opportunity. Whether this is enough is a much debated issue in current domestic politics.

To put into perspective the court decisions, laws, and other kinds of governmental actions relating to civil rights for women and minorities, we review next the political and social contexts in which these constitutional issues are raised. Constitutional questions do not involve just a series of court decisions, laws, and constitutional amendments; they encompass the entire social, economic, and political system. Although the struggles of all groups are interwoven, they are not identical, so we comment briefly and separately on each of them. (Chapter 9 includes more detail on the movements behind these battles for legal equality.)

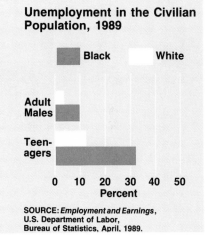

Unemployment in the Civilian Population, 1989

SOURCE: *Employment and Earnings,*
U.S. Department of Labor,
Bureau of Statistics, April, 1989.

WOMEN'S RIGHTS

The struggle for equal rights for women has long been intertwined with the battle to secure such rights for blacks (remember the obvious fact that half of African Americans are women). The Seneca Falls Women's Rights Convention (1848), which launched the women's movement, involved men and women who had long been active in the campaign to abolish slavery.

As the Civil War approached, women were urged to abandon their cause, at least temporarily, and devote their energies to getting rid of slavery.[2] The Civil War brought the women's movement to a halt. The Fourteenth Amendment even introduced into the Constitution a provision that overtly allowed discrimination against women; it provided that any state that kept males over 21 from voting should suffer a reduction of its representation in the House of Representatives. Women were no better served by the Fifteenth Amendment. For a time, the Temperance Movement diverted attention away from women's rights as well.

By the turn of the century, however, a vigorous campaign was under way for women's suffrage within the states. The first victories came in western states, where Wyoming led the way. As a territory, Wyoming had given women the right to vote. It is said that when members of Congress in Washington grumbled about

| International Council of Women | Ladies Home Journal | National American Woman Suffrage Association | Jane Addams— Hull House | | Charlotte Perkins Gilman, *Women and Economics* | Women's Trade Union League | Brandeis brief— protective legislation |

International Council of Women   *Ladies Home Journal*   National American Woman Suffrage Association   Jane Addams— Hull House   Women's Trade Union League   Brandeis brief— protective legislation

General Federation of Women's Clubs   Susan B. Anthony   Florence Kelly, reformer   Charlotte Perkins Gilman, *Women and Economics*

1900

Samuel Gompers, American Federation of Labor   Immigration from Southern Europe   Progressive Era   Panama Canal begun

Populists   Battle of Wounded Knee   Theodore Roosevelt

Women marched in 1912 to get the vote, a goal that was achieved in 1920.

this "petticoat provision," the Wyoming legislators replied that they would stay out of the Union one hundred years rather than come in without women's suffrage Congress gave in and admitted Wyoming to the Union, women's suffrage and all. By the end of World War I, over half the states had granted women the right to vote in some or all elections.

To many suffragists this state-by-state approach seemed slow and uncertain. They wanted a decisive victory—a constitutional amendment that would, with one blow, force all states to allow qualified women to vote. Finally in 1920 Congress proposed the Nineteenth Amendment. Opposition to its adoption and ratification was intertwined with opposition to the rights of blacks. Many southerners opposed the amendment. Not only would it extend the franchise to black women, but it might also bring federal officials to investigate elections to ensure that the amendment was being obeyed, which would thereby call attention to how blacks were being kept from voting.

Senator James Vardman, Democrat from Mississippi, opposed the Nineteenth Amendment and called for "repeal of the Fifteenth, the modification of the Fourteenth . . . , making this a government by white men, of white men, for all men."[3] But opposition to women's suffrage was not limited to southerners. Senator William Borah, a noted liberal Republican from Idaho, also opposed it, again on racial grounds, saying, "There are 100,000 Japanese and Chinese women in the Pacific states, and I have no particular desire to bestow suffrage upon them."[4]

With the ratification of the Nineteenth Amendment in 1920, women won the right to vote. Still, women were denied equal pay and equal rights, and they suffered numerous legal disabilities imposed by both national and state laws. During the last several decades the struggle to secure the adoption of the Equal Rights Amendment has occupied much of the attention of the women's movement. But there are now other goals, and the political clout of women is being mobilized increasingly behind issues that range from pay, through pensions, to peace.

THE STRUGGLE FOR RACIAL JUSTICE

Americans have had a painful confrontation with the problems of race before, during, and after the Civil War. As a result of the northern victory, the Thirteenth, Fourteenth, and Fifteenth Amendments became part of the Constitution. Congress also passed a series of civil rights laws to implement these constitutional provisions and established such special programs as the Freedmen's Bureau to provide educational and social services for the freed slaves.

Before these programs had any significant effect, the southern white male political community was restored to power. By 1877 Reconstruction was ending, and Northern political leaders abandoned blacks to their fate at the hands of their former white masters. The president no longer concerned himself with the enforcement of civil rights laws, and Congress enacted no new ones. The Supreme

| National Women's Party | Suffragists jailed for White House demonstration | Woman's Committee, National Council of Defense | Women get the vote | League of Women Voters | Alice Paul introduces Equal Rights Amendment (ERA) | Margaret Mead, *Coming of Age in Samoa* | Frances Perkins, Secretary of Labor | Clare Booth Luce, *The Women* |
| | | | | | The Flapper | | Frozen foods Introduced | Eleanor Roosevelt |

1920

| Woodrow Wilson | U.S. enters World War I | Treaty of Versailles | Prohibition | | | Herbert Hoover | Depression | |
| | | 19th Amendment ratified | | | | Stock market crash | FDR— New Deal | |

Court either declared old laws unconstitutional or interpreted them so narrowly that they were ineffective. The Court also gave such a limited construction to the Thirteenth, Fourteenth, and Fifteenth Amendments that they failed to accomplish their intended purpose of protecting the rights of blacks.

By 1900 white supremacy was unchallenged in the South, where most blacks lived. Blacks were kept from voting; they were forced to accept menial jobs; and they were denied educational opportunities. In 1896 in *Plessy* v. *Ferguson*, the Supreme Court gave constitutional sanction to government-imposed racial segregation.[5] Even if the Court had declared segregation unconstitutional, a decision so contrary to popular feeling and political realities would have had little impact. In 1896 blacks were lynched an average of one every four days, and few whites raised a voice in protest.

During World War I blacks began to migrate to northern cities to seek educational opportunities and jobs. These trends were accelerated by the New Deal and World War II, and the South, through urbanization and industrialization, became more like the rest of the nation. As migration of blacks out of the rural South into southern and northern cities shifted the racial composition of cities, the black vote became important in national elections. Although discrimination continued, there were more jobs and more social gains. Above all, these changes created a black middle class opposed to segregation as a symbol of servitude and a cause of inequality. By the middle of the twentieth century, urban blacks were active and politically powerful citizens. There was a growing, persistent, and insistent demand for the abolition of color barriers.

The National Government Begins to Respond   Because of the special nature of the electoral college and the pattern of our political system, by the 1930s it became more difficult for a person living in the White House—or anyone hoping to live there—to ignore the aspirations of blacks. The commitment of our presidents, and in more recent decades of our senators, to the cause of equal protection became translated into the appointment of federal judges more sympathetic to a broad construction of the Thirteenth, Fourteenth, and Fifteenth Amendments.

In the 1930s African Americans began resorting to lawsuits to secure their rights, and especially to challenge the doctrine of segregation. They emphasized litigation because they had no alternative; they lacked sufficient political power to make their demands effective before either state legislatures or Congress. By the 1950s civil rights litigation began to have an impact. Under the leadership of the Supreme Court, federal judges started to use the Fourteenth Amendment to reverse earlier decisions that rendered it and federal legislation ineffective. The Court outlawed all forms of government-imposed segregation and struck down most of the devices that had been used by state and local authorities to keep African Americans from voting. Presidents used their executive authority to fight segregation in the armed services and the federal bureaucracy, and they directed the Department of Justice to enforce whatever civil rights laws were available.

	WACS, WAVES, WASPS—Women's Service Corps	800,000 women fired by aircraft companies		Dr. Spock			Title VII prohibits sex discrimination in employment	Executive Order mandates affirmative action
Rosie the Riveter			Suburbia	Mary McCarthy, *The Group*		Betty Friedan, *The Feminine Mystique*		The "Pill"

1940 _____ **1960**

Pearl Harbor	Atomic bomb		Television		The New Frontier	Kennedy assassinated	Civil Rights Act	Vietnam
		War ends		Korea	March on Washington— Martin Luther King	The Great Society		Peace movement
				Eisenhower				

As the 1950s came to a close, the emerging national consensus in favor of governmental action to protect civil rights and the growing political voice of African Americans began to have some influence on Congress. In 1957 Congress overrode a southern filibuster in the Senate and enacted the first federal civil rights laws since Reconstruction. During the 1950s the conflict was primarily an attempt by the national government to compel Southern state governments to stop segregating African Americans into inferior schools, parks, libraries, houses, and jobs. Then came the momentous 1960s.

A Turning Point   A decade after the Supreme Court declared public school segregation unconstitutional, most black children in the South still attended segregated schools. In Northern cities segregation in housing and education remained the established pattern as well. Most legal barriers in the path of equal rights had fallen, yet most African Americans still could not buy houses where they wanted, secure the jobs they needed, find educational opportunities for their children, or walk on the streets without being insulted. What had once been thought of as a southern problem was finally recognized as a national problem. By 1963 the struggles in the courtrooms were being supplemented by a massive social, economic, and political movement.

The revolt in 1963 did not come unannounced, and its immediate background was not the struggle to desegregate the schools. In one sense it began when the first black slave was educated three hundred years ago. Its more recent origin was in Montgomery, Alabama, when seamstress Rosa Parks, who refused to give up a seat in the front of a bus, was removed from the bus. The black community of Montgomery responded by boycotting city buses. The boycott worked. And Montgomery produced a charismatic national civil rights leader: the Reverend Martin Luther King, Jr. Through his Southern Christian Leadership Conference and his doctrine of nonviolent resistance, Dr. King gave a new dimension to the struggle. By the early 1960s new organizational resources came into existence in almost every city to support and sponsor sit-ins, freedom rides, live-ins, and nonviolent demonstrations.[6] These measures were sometimes met with violence toward blacks and their civil rights allies, and at times state and local governments failed either to protect the victims or prosecute those responsible for the violence.[7]

The forces of social discontent exploded in the summer of 1963. The explosion started with a demonstration in Birmingham, Alabama, which was countered by the use of fire hoses, police dogs, and mass arrests. It ended in a march in Washington, D.C., where at least 250,000 people heard Dr. King speak in person and countless millions of others listened and watched him over television. By the time the summer was over, there was hardly a city, North or South, that had not had demonstrations, protests, or sit-ins. Some also had violence.

This direct action had some effect. Civil rights ordinances were enacted in many cities, and more schools were desegregated that fall than in any year since 1956. At the national level, President John Kennedy urged Congress to enact a

Rosa Parks was arrested in Montgomery, Alabama, in 1955 for refusing to sit at the back of a bus, sparking a bus boycott that involved thousands of blacks and lasted over a year.

CHAPTER 5 / Equal Rights under the Law

National Organization for Women (NOW) — Gloria Steinem, *Ms. Magazine* — National Women's Strike — ERA passed by Congress — Title IX prohibits sex discrimination in education — International Women's Year — Supreme Court legalizes abortion — Women's Educational Equity Act Passed — Episcopalians ordain women — National Women's Conference, Houston — ERA ratification deadline extended — Kassebaum elected to Senate

1980

Student unrest — Nixon — Resurrection City — Moon landing — Cambodia — Watergate — Carter — Mid-East peace talks — Iran

Adapted from COMMENT, A Research/Action Report on Wo/Men, June 1980

comprehensive civil rights bill. Late in 1963, the nation's grief over the assassination of President Kennedy, who had become identified with civil rights goals, added political fuel to the drive for federal action.[8] President Lyndon Johnson gave civil rights legislation his highest priority. On July 2, 1964, after months of debate, he signed into law the Civil Rights Act of 1964[9] (see page 122).

Two Societies?   At the close of the 1960s the legal phase of the civil rights movement had about come to a close. But as "things got better," discontent grew. When blacks had been completely subjugated, they had lacked resources to defend themselves. Then, as is true of almost all social revolutions, as conditions began to improve, demands became more and more insistent. Millions of impoverished African Americans, like white Americans before them, demonstrated growing impatience with the discrimination that remained. This volatile situation gave way to racial violence and disorders. By 1965, the year of the Watts riots in Los Angeles, racial disorders were clearly becoming a part of the American scene. In 1966 and 1967 the disorders increased in scope and intensity. The Detroit riot in July 1967 was the worst such disturbance in modern American history.[10]

President Lyndon Johnson appointed a special Advisory Commission on Civil Disorders to investigate the origins of the riots and to recommend measures to prevent or contain such disasters in the future. When the commission (called the Kerner Commission after its chair, then Governor Otto Kerner of Illinois) issued its report, it said in stark, clear language: "What white Americans have never fully understood—but what the Negro can never forget—is that white society is deeply implicated in the ghetto. *White institutions created it, white institutions maintain it, and white society condones it.*" The basic conclusion of the commission was that "our nation is moving toward two societies, one black, one white—separate and unequal" and that "only a commitment to national action on an unprecedented scale" could change this trend.

The commission made sweeping recommendations on jobs, education, housing, and improving the welfare system. But the Vietnam War, the partial calming of racial tensions, and a growing skepticism about the effectiveness of governmental action diverted attention from these recommendations, at least temporarily.

Today, legal barriers have been lowered, if not removed, by civil rights legislation, executive orders, and judicial decisions. Blacks can vote, get a meal where they want, and stay at hotels. Hundreds of thousands have entered the middle class. Although some people still find ways to circumvent or obstruct the force of certain civil rights laws, especially those that apply to housing, by and large the actions by governments in the 1960s opened the legal system and provide blacks with equal rights under the laws. Important as are these victories: "They were victories largely for the middle class—those who could travel, entertain in restaurants and stay in hotels. Those victories did not change life conditions for the mass of blacks who are still poor."[11]

More than a generation after the Kerner Commission issued its report, life

First Woman Supreme Court justice appointed	ERA Deadline passed without ratification	ERA reintroduced in Congress	First woman Geraldine Ferraro, nominated as vice-presidential candidate of a major political party (the Democrats)	State of Washington adopts comparable worth for some state employees	Congress reverses impact of *Grove* Supreme Court decision that had limited federal civil rights laws	Supreme Court restricts *Roe v Wade*

1990

| Reagan | | | | Challenger tragedy | Reagan-Gorbachev talks- INF Treaty | Bush |

Martin Luther King, Jr., at the Lincoln Memorial in Washington, D.C., on August 28, 1963, speaking to the 250,000 people who participated in a "march for jobs and freedom."

"I Have A Dream . . ."

Five score years ago, a great American in whose symbolic shadow we stand, signed the Emancipation Proclamation. This momentous decree came as a great beacon light of hope to millions of Negro slaves who had been seared in the flames of withering injustice. It came as a joyous daybreak to end the long night of captivity. But one hundred years later, we must face the tragic fact that the Negro is still not free. One hundred years later, the life of the Negro is still sadly crippled by the manacles of segregation and the chains of discrimination. One hundred years later, the Negro lives on a lonely island of poverty in the midst of a vast ocean of material prosperity. One hundred years later, the Negro is still languishing in the corners of American society and finds himself

for inner city blacks is worse. As middle class blacks have moved out of the inner city the remaining underclass, as they are coming to be called, has become even more isolated from the rest of the nation.[12] Children are growing up on streets where drug abuse and crime are an everyday occurrence. These Americans live in "separate and deteriorating societies, with separate economies, diverging family structures and basic institutions, and even growing linguistic separation within the core ghettos. The scale of their isolation by race, class, and economic situation is much greater than it was in the 1960's, impoverishment, joblessness, educational inequality, and housing insufficiency even more severe."[13]

NATIVE AMERICANS

Of the nearly 1,500,000 people who designate themselves as Indians (or Native Americans, as many prefer to be called), almost half live on or near a reservation and are enrolled as members of one of the 306 tribes within the continental United States or one of the 200 native Alaskan communities served by the Bureau of Indian Affairs. Native American tribes within the United States are wards of the nation. They are not states, nor are they nations possessed of the full attributes of sovereignty. Rather, they are a separate people with power to regulate their own internal affairs, subject to congressional supervision. Congress has special responsibilities to Native Americans. States are precluded from regulating or taxing the tribes or extending the jurisdiction of their courts over the tribes unless authorized to do so by Congress.[14] Native Americans living off reservations and working in the general community pay taxes like everybody else.

By act of Congress, Indians are American citizens, and by act of the states in which they live, they have the right to vote. Off reservations they have the same rights as any other Americans. If they are enrolled members of a recognized tribe, they are entitled to certain benefits created by law and by treaty. These benefits are administered by the Bureau of Indian Affairs of the Department of the Interior. Moreover, Native Americans who belong to these federally recognized tribes have preference in employment within the Bureau, a preference the Supreme Court upheld as a grant not to a "discrete racial group, but, rather, as members of quasi-sovereign tribal entities. . . ."[15]

As a result of the growing militancy of Native Americans and a greater national awareness of the concerns of minorities, more Americans are aware that most live in poverty. Native Americans "are in far worse health than the rest of the population, dying earlier and suffering disproportionately from alcoholism, accidents, diabetes and pneumonia."[16] Some reservations lack adequate health care facilities, educational opportunities, decent housing, and jobs. Congress has started to compensate native Americans for past injustices and to provide more opportunities for the development of tribal economic independence. Judges are also showing a greater vigilance in the enforcement of Indian treaty rights.

CHAPTER 5 / Equal Rights under the Law

The struggle for civil rights has by no means been limited to women, blacks, and Native Americans. Each new wave of immigrants has been considered suspect by those who arrived earlier—all the more so if its members were not white or English speaking. Formal barriers of law and informal barriers of custom have combined to deny equal rights. But as groups have established themselves—first economically, then politically—most of these barriers have been swept away and constitutionally guaranteed rights asserted.

Hispanics   Hispanics (or Latinos, as some prefer to be called) "are among the world's most complex groupings of human beings. Most . . . are white, millions . . . are mestizos, nearly half a million in the United States are black or mulatto."[17] The largest group consists of at least 12 million Mexican Americans. It is useful, however, to make distinctions among the Mexican-Americans. There are those born in Mexico who have moved to live in the United States; there are those who reside in Mexico but come to work in the United States, legally or illegally; and there are those of Mexican parentage or background born in the United States—the largest group—often called Chicanos.

Most Chicanos live in California, Texas, Arizona and New Mexico, but many now live in other parts of the nation as well. Many Chicanos speak both Spanish and English. Among those born and raised in Mexico, 84 percent speak mostly Spanish at home; by the third generation, 84 percent speak mostly English at home.[18]

The second largest group of Hispanics consists of the 2.5 million Puerto Ricans who reside on the mainland, primarily in the "barrios" of New York, Chicago, and other northern cities. Puerto Ricans are usually in worse economic condition than any other Hispanic group. They retain close ties with Puerto Rico and move back and forth from the island to the mainland.

The third subgroup of Hispanics consists of about one million who fled from Castro's Cuba early in the 1960s, and a second wave of refugees who fled in the 1980s. These Cubans, who live mainly in south Florida, include a substantial number of well-educated, successful businesspeople and professionals.

The fourth group includes a rapidly growing number of refugees from other nations in Central and South America who presently number around 2.2 million. This number is likely to grow as economic turmoil and political repression in that part of the world increase.

Hispanics are our fastest-growing minority. "The Hispanic population . . . has increased by more than one-third since the 1980 census, growing nearly five times faster than the rest of the population."[19] Nineteen million Hispanics live in our country today, as compared with about 27 million blacks. By the end of this century more than 40 million Hispanics could well be living in the United States; Martinez is already one of our most common surnames. We have the fourth largest Spanish-speaking population of any country in this hemisphere, and New York is the fifth largest Spanish-speaking city in the world.

To black power has been added "brown power"—sometimes as an ally, sometimes as an opponent.[20] Yet not only do many Hispanics lack even the patronizing ties with the white power structure that provided some help for blacks—at least prior to the civil rights movement—they have also been handicapped because English, the primary language of mainstream America, is not their native tongue. Until recent decades "no provision whatsoever was made for the education of Mexican-American children" in the Southwest. "When eventually they were allowed into the schools, they were segregated from Anglo children because of their lan-

an exile in his own land. So we have come here today to dramatize an appalling condition. . . .

I have a dream that one day this nation will rise up and live out the true meaning of its creed: "We hold these truths to be self-evident; that all men are created equal."

I have a dream that one day on the red hills of Georgia the sons of former slaves and the sons of former slaveowners will be able to sit down together at the table of brotherhood.

I have a dream that one day even the state of Mississippi, a desert state sweltering with the heat of injustice and oppression, will be transformed into an oasis of freedom and justice.

I have a dream that my four little children will one day live in a nation where they will not be judged by the color of their skin but by the content of their character. . . .

Martin Luther King, Jr.

Several hundred Navajo Indians marched through their reservation in 1986 in a show of solidarity against giving up any of their land.

Black and White: A Newsweek Poll

Neither race sees much to be gained from working less with one another, but there are significant differences between the way both view their relative positions today—and what might be done to improve things.

On the whole, do you think most white people want to see blacks get a better break or keep blacks down?

	Whites	Blacks
Better break	52%	30%
Keep down	6%	25%

Compared to five years ago, do you think the situation of black people in this country is better or worse?

	Whites	Blacks
Better	49%	33%
Worse	8%	22%

Do black children do better if they go to racially mixed schools?

	Whites	Blacks
Better	39%	48%
Worse	4%	6%
No difference	38%	41%

Would you prefer to live in a neighborhood with mostly whites, with mostly blacks or in a neighborhood mixed half and half?

	Whites	Blacks
Mostly blacks	0%	8%
Mostly white	33%	2%
Half and half	46%	68%

Would the most effective way for black people to improve their situation be working less with white people and more with other blacks? (Percent answering no)

Whites	62%	Blacks	61%

Do middle-class blacks do as much as they should to help improve conditions for poorer blacks, not as much or have they no obligation?

	Whites	Blacks
As much as they should	22%	22%
Not as much	33%	54%
No obligation	15%	11%

Why do you think poor blacks have not been able to rise out of poverty? Is it mainly the fault of blacks themselves or is it the fault of society?

	Whites	Blacks
Fault of blacks	29%	30%
Fault of society	42%	44%

Is the federal government doing too much, too little or about the right amount to help American blacks?

	Whites	Blacks
Too much	18%	5%
Too little	29%	71%
About right	36%	13%

Because of past discrimination should qualified blacks receive preference over equally qualified whites in such matters as getting into college or getting jobs or not?

	Whites	Blacks
Should	14%	40%
Should not	80%	50%

Do welfare benefits give poor people a chance to stand on their own two feet and get started again? Or do they make poor people dependent and encourage them to stay poor?

	Whites	Blacks
Get started again	18%	31%
Stay poor	66%	50%

Is it likely that there will be a black U.S. president in the next 20 years?

	Whites	Blacks
Very likely	18%	22%
Somewhat	44%	34%
Not at all	34%	39%

Compared to white people charged with crimes, are blacks people charged with crimes treated more harshly or more leniently or about the same in the U.S. justice system?

	Whites	Blacks
More harshly	34%	66%
More leniently	5%	3%
Same	50%	23%

Source: *Newsweek* (March 7, 1988), p. 23. © 1988 by NEWSWEEK, Inc.

For this *Newsweek* Poll, The Gallup Organization interviewed representative samples of 632 white adults and 305 black adults by telephone Feb. 19–22. 1988.

Gilbert Herrera, president of the Dallas Council of the League of United Latin American Citizens (LULAC) presents George Bush with a T-shirt after Bush addressed the LULAC convention.

guage handicap. Considered by school authorities to be children of an inferior race, they were often punished for speaking Spanish, heard their names involuntarily Anglicized, and saw their cultural background systematically ignored in textbooks."[21]

Taking their cue from blacks, Hispanics are becoming increasingly active in politics, although they do not yet register or vote in significant numbers as compared to blacks. Although Hispanics total 7 percent of the United States population, there are only twelve Hispanic members in the 435 member U.S. House of Representatives. "The Congressional Hispanic Caucus is but a shadow of its role model and ally, the Black Caucus."[22] However, this situation is beginning to change. Some Hispanic members of Congress have gained senority and occupy key roles, such as Henry B. Gonzalez, Democrat of Texas, chair of the Banking Committee. Hispanic mayors preside in Denver, Miami, and Tampa; Florida has a Hispanic governor and New Mexico recently had a Hispanic governor; and the number of Hispanics in other leadership positions is growing. The Mexican-American Legal Defense and Education Fund, the Puerto Rican Legal Defense and Education Fund, and the League of United Latin American Citizens (LULAC) are becoming increasingly active.

Hispanics are not all of one mind on most issues, but most give strong support for bilingual and bicultural education. In 1974, in *Lau* v. *Nichols*, a case involving Chinese students in San Francisco, the Supreme Court ruled that Title VI of the 1964 Civil Rights Act requires a school district to offer instruction to overcome language difficulties whenever it has a substantial number of non-English-speaking students.[23] Many Hispanics actively support bilingual education. Such programs, they argue, not only assist Hispanic children in gaining an education, but help preserve their heritage. Opponents of bilingual education argue that fluency in English is essential for success in American society, and that most bilingual programs retard the learning of English. Hispanics have also worked to amend civil rights laws to protect the rights of language minorities. Clearly, as the political position of Hispanics becomes more important in the years ahead, governments will be even more responsive to their claims.

In January 1983 three Japanese Americans who were jailed during World War II for resisting internment sued the United States for damages and the overturn of their 1942 conviction.

Asian Americans The term "Asian" describes individuals from many different countries and many different ethnic backgrounds. Moreover, most people from Asian backgrounds do not think of themselves as "Asians," but rather as Americans of Chinese, Japanese, Vietnamese, Cambodian, and so on, ancestry. Whatever they may call themselves, about 40 percent of our immigrants now are from Asia.

The Chinese were the first Asians to come to the United States. Beginning in 1847, when young male peasants came to get away from poverty and to work in mines, on railroads, and farms, the Chinese ran into economic and cultural fears of the white majority, who did not understand them or their culture. Facing this, and considering their intentions to return home, the Chinese seldom tried to assimilate but instead gravitated to "Chinatowns." Discriminatory immigration and naturalization restrictions, imposed beginning in 1882, were strengthened in the following years and were not removed until the end of World War II. Since that time the Chinese have moved into the mainstream of American society, and they are beginning to move into politics.

The Japanese first migrated to Hawaii in the 1860s and then into California in the 1880s. Most of the immigrants remained in the west coast states. By the beginning of the twentieth century they faced overt public hostility. In 1905 labor leaders organized the Japanese and Korean Exclusion League, and in 1906 the San Francisco Board of Education excluded all Chinese, Japanese, and Korean children from neighborhood schools. Some western states passed laws denying the right to own land to aliens who were ineligible to become citizens, that is, aliens of Asian ancestry. During World War II anti-Japanese hysteria provoked the internment of west coast Japanese, most of whom were American citizens guilty of no crimes, in prison camps, the largest of which was Manzanar, at Tule Lake, California. During this time Japanese property was confiscated or sold at confiscatory rates. Following the war, the exclusionary acts were repealed, and by congressional, presidential, and court action, laws designed to keep Japanese-Americans from participating fully in American economic and political life were set aside. In 1988 President Reagan signed a law providing $20,000 restitution to each of the approximately 60,000 surviving World War II internees.

Koreans, over 800,000 of them, are concentrated in southern California, Colorado, Honolulu, and New York City. Until recently, like other Asian Americans, they faced discrimination in jobs and housing. A Korean middle class is growing. Many Koreans are entering the learned professions, while many others continue operating their small family businesses such as dry cleaners, florists, and small grocers.[24]

When Filipinos first came to the United States in the early part of this century, they were considered American nationals, because the United States then owned

American's Ethnic Asian Population (thousands)			
	1980	1990*	2000*
Japanese	715	800	860
Chinese	810	1,260	1,680
Indian	385	680	1,000
Korean	355	820	1,320
Philippine	780	1,400	2,080
Vietnamese	245	860	1,580
Laotian	55	260	500
Cambodian	15	180	380
All Asians	**3,465**	**6,550**	**9,850**

Source: *The Economist*, June 3, 1989, p. 23.
* Projections.

their native country. Nonetheless, they were denied their rights to full citizenship and faced discrimination, including anti-Filipino riots in the state of Washington in 1928 and later in California, where nearly one-third of the approximately million and a half Filipinos live.[25] Their economic status has improved, but their influence in politics remains as small as their numbers.

The newest Asian group consists of more than a million IndoChinese refugees from Vietnam, Laos, and Cambodia, who first came to the United States in 1975 and settled in California's Los Angeles, Orange, and San Diego counties. Although this group includes middle-class people who left during the fall of Saigon, it also consists of large numbers of "boat people," mostly peasants in their homelands, who came to our shores without any financial resources. In a relatively short time most have established themselves economically. Although they are starting to have political influence (most of them apparently registered as Republicans) they remain socially and economically segregated and have not been in the United States long enough to become an effective part of the political process.

Equal Protection of the Laws— What Does It Mean?

The Fourteenth Amendment declares: "No state [including any subdivision thereof shall] deny to any person within its jurisdiction the equal protection of the laws." Although there is no **equal protection clause** limiting the national government, the Fifth Amendment's due process clause has been understood to impose the same restraints on the national government. Note, the restraints of equal protection apply only to the actions of governments, not to those of private individuals. Thus an important question is always: Is the action being challenged that of a government—known in law as "state action"—or is the challenged discriminatory action merely that of private persons unsupported and detached from the actions of a government?

The Constitution does not prevent governments from making distinctions among people, because it could not legislate without doing so. What the Constitution forbids is *unreasonable* classifications. In general, a classification is unreasonable when there is no relation between the classes it creates and permissible governmental goals. A law prohibiting redheads from voting, for example, would be unreasonable. On the other hand, laws denying to persons under 18 the right to vote, to marry without the permission of their parents, or to apply for a license to drive a car appear to be justified (at least to most persons over 18).

One of our most troublesome constitutional issues is how to distinguish between a reasonable and an unreasonable classification. The Supreme Court has developed a variety of tests: rational basis, suspect classifications, quasisuspect classifications, and fundamental rights.

THE RATIONAL BASIS TEST

The traditional test to determine whether a law complies with the equal protection requirement places the burden of proof on those attacking it. If it is free from invidious discrimination and any facts justify a classification, it will be sustained, even if it results in some inequality. Usually if the Supreme Court chooses to apply this **rational basis test,** the law in question will be upheld. Occasionally, however, a state law fails to meet even the minimal standards of this test, as when Alaska was told it could not give more from its surplus revenues to old-time citizens of the state than it gives to newcomers, and when a city was told it could not require a special-use permit for group homes for mentally retarded people when it did not require such a permit for other multiple-dwelling facilities.[26]

The Supreme Court applies a more stringent standard than the rational basis test when a law is challenged under the equal protection clause in three situations: when a suspect classification is involved, when a quasisuspect classification is involved, and when a fundamental right is involved.

SUSPECT CLASSIFICATIONS

A suspect class is a class historically suffering disabilities, subjected to purposeful unequal treatment in the past, or relegated by society to a position of such political powerlessness as to require extraordinary judicial protection.[27] Race and national origin are **suspect classifications.** So is religion, although there is no specific Supreme Court decision to this effect, probably because states have seldom classified people according to religion. Classifying people by their lack of citizenship is another suspect classification with respect to state (not national) laws' imposing *political* disabilities upon aliens.

When a law involves a suspect classification, the normal presumption of constitutionality is reversed. It is not sufficient that the law be a reasonable means to handle a particular problem. Such laws are subject to *strict scrutiny*. The Supreme Court must be persuaded that there is both a "compelling public interest" to justify such a classification and there is no other, less restrictive way to accomplish this compelling public purpose.

QUASI-SUSPECT CLASSIFICATIONS: ILLEGITIMACY AND SEX

Some contend that laws imposing disabilities on illegitimate children should be subject to the same severe tests as laws based on race. The Supreme Court has been unwilling to go that far. However, in view of the long history of treating illegitimate children less favorably than legitimate ones, the Court has subjected laws dealing with illegitimate children to a "heightened level" of scrutiny only slightly less exacting than those applied to suspect classifications such as race.

What of classifications based on sex? Not until 1971 was any classification based on sex declared unconstitutional. Prior to that time many laws that purported to provide special protection for women—such as a Michigan law forbidding any woman other than the wife or daughter of a tavern owner to serve as barmaid—were upheld. As Justice William Brennan wrote for the Court in 1973: "There can be no doubt that our nation has had a long and unfortunate history of sex discrimination. Traditionally such discrimination was rationalized by an attitude of 'romantic paternalism' which, in practical effect put women, not on a pedestal, but in a cage."[28]

Today the Court's view is that sex classifications, although not as suspect as those based on race, are subject to "heightened scrutiny." To sustain a classification based on sex, the burden is on the government to show that it serves "important governmental objectives" and is substantially related to these objectives. Treating women differently from men (or vice versa) is forbidden when supported by no more substantial justification than "archaic and overbroad generalizations," "old notions," and "the role-typing society has long imposed upon women."[29] If the government's objective is "to protect members of one sex because they are presumed to suffer from an inherent handicap or to be innately inferior," that object itself is illegitimate.[30]

In recent years the Supreme Court has struck down most, but not all, laws brought before it alleged to discriminate against women. (Those the Court has refused to strike down include the males only draft and veterans' preference in civil service jobs.) The Court has also sustained some legislation said to discriminate against men. Overall, "Except for the right to vote, U.S. women have experienced more improvement in their legal status in the last twenty years than in the last two hundred."[31]

In summary, classifications based on sex, although not suspect, require considerable justification before the Court will sustain them.[32]

Is Poverty a Suspect Classification? The Supreme Court has been pressed to treat poverty as a suspect class, but it "has never held that financial need alone identifies a suspect class for purposes of equal protection analysis."[33] Thus, a state may rely on property taxes for funds for schools even if this means that schools in "rich" districts spend more per pupil than those in poor districts.

Is Age a Suspect or Quasi-suspect Classification? Age is not a suspect or quasi-suspect class. Historically our laws and practices have commonly made distinctions based on age: to obtain a driver's license, to marry without parental consent, to attend schools, to buy alcohol, and so on. Many governmental institutions have age-specific programs: for senior citizens, for adult students, for midcareer persons. Although the Supreme Court has refused to make age a suspect classification requiring extra judicial protection, Congress, responding to "Gray Power," is treating age more and more as a protected category. Congress has made it illegal for governments or interstate employers to discriminate on the basis of old age and has prohibited mandatory retirement for most employees, except for a few specially exempt occupations. About a third of the states have passed similar laws restricting mandatory retirement. Congress has also forbidden federal funds to be given to any program or activity that denies benefits because of age, except where age is a factor in the normal operations of the program or activity, such as a program created specifically for children. Today about one-fourth of the court actions filed by the Equal Employment Opportunity Commission relate to claims of age discrimination.[34]

FUNDAMENTAL RIGHTS

In addition to subjecting state regulations to strict scrutiny when they are based on suspect classifications, the Court gives similar strict scrutiny to laws impinging on "fundamental rights." However, the justices are not too clear about what makes a right fundamental. As Justice Lewis Powell explained in *San Antonio School District* v. *Rodriguez* (1973), it is not the social importance of the right nor the justices' conclusions about the significance of the right that determines whether or not it is fundamental, but whether it is *explicitly or implicitly guaranteed by the Constitution.* Under this test the rights to travel and to vote have been held to be fundamental, as well as such First Amendment rights as the right to associate for the advancement of political beliefs. However, the right to receive an education or housing or welfare benefits has not been held to be fundamental. Important as many feel these rights to be, they are not guaranteed by the Constitution. Nor do any specific constitutional provisions protect these rights from governmental regulation.

Some Recent Governmental Actions Declared Unconstitutional by the Supreme Court Because of Sex Discrimination*

Provisions of social security laws providing benefits to families with unemployed fathers but not unemployed mothers.

A state law giving sons child support from their fathers until they are 21, but daughters only until they are 18.

A state law prohibiting the sale of beer to males under 21, but to females under 18.

A state law providing that husbands, but not wives, may be required to pay alimony.

A state law excluding males from enrolling in a professional nursing program, designed for women, offered by a public university.

* The Constitution protects men as well as women from discrimination because of sex.

CHAPTER 5 / Equal Rights under the Law

How to Prove Discrimination

Does the fact that a law or a regulation has a differential impact on persons of different race or sex by itself establish that it is unconstitutional? In one of its more important decisions, *Washington* v. *Davis* (1976), the Supreme Court said no. "The invidious quality of a law claimed to be racially discriminatory must ultimately be traced to a racially discriminatory purpose."[35] Or, as the Court said in a later case: "The Fourteenth Amendment guarantees equal laws, not equal results."[36]

What does this mean in practical terms? It means city ordinances that permit only single-family residences and thus make low-cost housing projects impossible are not unconstitutional—even if their effect is to keep minorities from moving into the city—unless it can be shown that they were adopted *with the intent to discriminate* against minorities. It means a preference for veterans in public employment does not violate the equal protection clause, even though its effect is to keep many women from getting jobs; the distinction between veterans and nonveterans was not adopted deliberately to create a sex barrier.

Still, that a law or governmental practice has a differential impact is not irrelevant. In a community with a large number of blacks or Hispanics, it would be constitutionally suspicious if only a few of them were called for jury duty. Under such circumstances the burden of proof shifts to the state or city to demonstrate that it has not engaged in unconstitutional discriminatory conduct.

What is constitutional can nonetheless be made illegal. (Things that are unconstitutional are always illegal, but what is illegal may not be unconstitutional.) Congress has made a number of employment practices illegal; for example, the use in most circumstances of tests not related to job performance, if such tests screen out members of one race or sex to a greater extent than another, regardless of the motives of the employers. Most important, the Voting Rights Act of 1965 tests the legality of voting laws and practices by their *effects* rather than by the purposes of those who passed them.

The Life and Death of Jim Crow Education

Laws requiring blacks to be segregated into separate public facilities date only from the end of the nineteenth century. Before that, social custom and economic conditions, rather than law, kept the two races apart.[37] But from the end of that century until the Supreme Court struck down such laws in the 1950s, Southern states and cities made it illegal for whites and blacks to ride in the same train cars, attend the same theaters, go to the same schools, be born in the same hospitals, or be buried in the same cemeteries. **Jim Crow laws,** as they came to be called, blanketed southern life. How could these laws stand in the face of the Equal Protection Clause?

IS SEGREGATION DISCRIMINATION? PLESSY v. FERGUSON

In 1896 in *Plessy* v. *Ferguson*, the Supreme Court endorsed the view that racial segregation did not constitute discrimination if "equal" accommodations were provided for the members of both races.[38] Even equal accommodations were

Some Recent Governmental Actions Alleged to Be Unconstitutional Discriminations against Persons Because of Sex, but Sustained by the Supreme Court

A state law granting a property tax exemption to widows but not to widowers.

A naval regulation giving women thirteen years to be promoted or discharged, but giving male officers only nine years.

A provision giving larger social security retirement benefits to women than to men.

A federal law requiring registration for a possible draft for males but not for females.

not required except for public facilities and for a limited category of public utilities, such as trains and buses. Under this *separate-but-equal* formula, southern states, and some places in the North, enforced segregation in transportation, places of public accommodation, educational facilities, swimming pools, and parks. Although the *Plessy* decision required equality as the price for compulsory segregation, the "equal" part of the formula was meaningless. States segregated blacks into unequal facilities, and blacks lacked the political power to protest.

The passage of time did not lessen the inequalities. In 1950 all the segregated states had a total of fourteen medical schools for whites, none for blacks; sixteen law schools for whites, five for blacks; fifteen engineering schools for whites, none for blacks; five dentistry schools for whites, none for blacks. Beginning in the late 1930s blacks started to file lawsuits challenging the doctrine. They cited facts to show that, in practice, separate but equal always resulted in discrimination against blacks. However, the Supreme Court was not yet willing to upset the doctrine directly. Rather, it began to undermine it. The Court scrutinized each situation and, in case after case, ordered facilities to be equalized.

THE END OF SEPARATE BUT EQUAL: BROWN v. BOARD OF EDUCATION

Finally, in the spring of 1954, in *Brown* v. *Board of Education*, the Supreme Court reversed its 1896 holding as it applied to public schools. It ruled that "separate but equal" is a contradiction in terms. Segregation is itself discrimination.[39] A year later the Court ordered school boards to proceed with "all deliberate speed to desegregate public schools at the earliest practical date."[40] In the years following the *Brown* decision, federal judges struck down a whole battery of schemes designed to evade the Court's ruling.

Beginning in 1963 the Supreme Court gradually reversed its second *Brown* decision that granted school districts time to prepare for desegregation. In 1969 the Court completed that reversal, stating: "Continued operation of racially segregated schools under the standard of 'all deliberate speed' is no longer constitutionally permissible. School districts must immediately terminate dual school systems based on race and operate only unitary school systems."[41]

In the 1960s Congress and the president joined even more directly in the battle against school segregation. Title VI of the Civil Rights Act of 1964 stipulates that federal dollars under any grant program or project must be withdrawn from an entire school or institution of higher education that discriminates "on the ground of race, color, or national origin in any program or activity receiving federal financial assistance." The Education Act of 1972 adds sex to this list; other acts have added the handicapped, the aged, Vietnam veterans, and disabled veterans. Title VI also imposes a responsibility on schools for taking affirmative action to ensure that persons in the protected categories are not denied access to any federally supported program or activity.

In 1984 the Supreme Court, in *Grove City College* v. *Bell*, limited Title VI's (and in effect similar federal laws) coverage to only those programs and activities that directly received federal funds rather than the entire institution of which they were part.[42] Then in 1988 Congress, overriding a presidential veto, set aside the impact of *Grove* and made it clear that if any part of an institution receives federal funds, the entire entity is covered. For example, if a department of computer sciences receives federal funds, then no program or activity of that college is exempt from the requirements of these acts.

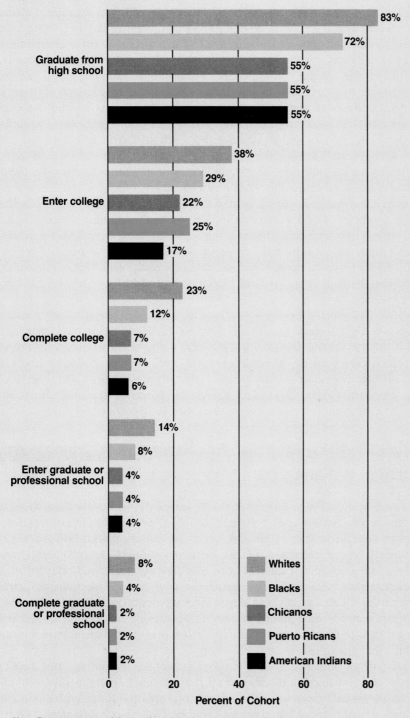

The Education Pipeline for Minority-Group Students

Graduate from high school
- 83%
- 72%
- 55%
- 55%
- 55%

Enter college
- 38%
- 29%
- 22%
- 25%
- 17%

Complete college
- 23%
- 12%
- 7%
- 7%
- 6%

Enter graduate or professional school
- 14%
- 8%
- 4%
- 4%
- 4%

Complete graduate or professional school
- 8%
- 4%
- 2%
- 2%
- 2%

Legend:
- Whites
- Blacks
- Chicanos
- Puerto Ricans
- American Indians

0   20   40   60   80
Percent of Cohort

Note: Percentages are of the number of students entering high school in each group

Source: "Colleges Urged to Alter Tests, Grading for Benefit of Minority-Group Students," *Chronicle of High School Education*, February 3, 1982, p. 11.

Half of all American students are bused to schools; of these, less than 7 percent are bused to achieve school desegregation. Still, busing has been one of the more hotly debated questions of our time.[43] The Supreme Court endorsed busing as one of the tools a federal judge might use to bring about school integration, but only to remedy the consequences of officially sanctioned, that is, **de jure segregation,** or segregation by law. It has refused to permit busing to overcome the effects of **de facto segregation.** In other words, if judges find that authorities had operated segregated schools in the past or had caused segregation by systematic and purposeful actions, judges could order a school district to bus pupils.[44] But judges may not, said the Supreme Court in a case involving the Detroit metropolitan area, order busing between suburbs and cities or any other interdistrict lines to overcome racial imbalances in schools not caused by official actions.[45]

The result has been parodoxical. There has been more integration of schools in large southern cities that previously operated legally segregated school systems than in large northern cities. In large metropolitan areas—partly as the result of white flight to the suburbs and private schools to escape court-ordered busing—many school districts in central cities are predominantly black. Without interdistrict busing it is difficult, in fact in most big cities impossible, to integrate schools by judicial decree.

". . . [T]here has been no progress in school desegregation on a national level since the Supreme Court's decision in the Detroit case."[46] Congress has been hostile to busing; the Reagan Administration sought to end court-ordered supervision of school desegregation on the grounds it is no longer necessary; the Bush Administration is carrying through with these cases and trying to take them out of the courts;[47] and black leaders have been giving more attention to improving the quality of inner city schools than to desegregating them.

Black students were bused under heavy police guard to mostly white schools in south Boston despite protests against the court-ordered busing as a means of school integration.

Barriers to Voting

States determine suffrage qualifications for all elections, but they do so subject to a variety of constitutional restraints. Article I, Section 4, gives Congress the power to supersede state regulations as to the "times, places, and manner" of elections for federal officers, that is, for members of the House of Representatives, senators, and presidential electors. Congress has used this authority to set age qualifications and residency requirements to vote in national elections, to establish a uniform day for all states to hold elections for members of Congress and presidential electors, and to give American citizens who reside outside the United States the right to vote for members of Congress and presidential electors in the states in which they previously lived.

The major limitations on the state's power to set suffrage qualifications, however, are contained in the Fourteenth and Fifteenth Amendments (forbidding unreasonable qualifications and those based on race), the Nineteenth Amendment (forbidding qualifications based on sex), and the Twenty-sixth Amendment (forbidding states to deny citizens 18 years of age or older the right to vote on account of age). These amendments also empower Congress to enact the laws necessary to enforce their provisions.

Despite fierce opposition to the Nineteenth Amendment, no organized resistance surfaced after its ratification gave all women in the North and white women in the South the right to vote. However, this was not so following ratification of the Fourteenth and Fifteenth Amendments. After their adoption, black men were allowed to participate in the political life of the southern states only because the federal government insisted upon it. As soon as federal troops were withdrawn from the South in 1877, southern Democrats regained control of state governments and set out to keep blacks from voting. They used social pressure and threats of violence, and they organized secret societies like the Ku Klux Klan that engaged in such terrorist activities as threats, midnight shootings, burnings, and whippings.

These measures "worked." But toward the end of the nineteenth century, and for the first time since the Civil War, parts of the South had two strong political parties: the Democrats and the Populists. White supremacists were fearful parties might compete for the black vote and blacks might come to hold the balance of power. White supremacists also feared that continued use of excessive force and fraud to disenfranchise blacks might cause the president and Congress to intervene.

Southern leaders reasoned that if they could pass laws depriving blacks of the vote on grounds other than race, blacks would find it difficult to challenge such laws in the courts. Some whites protested that laws could be used against whites as well as blacks. But keeping poor whites from voting did not disturb the conservative leaders of the Democratic party, for they were often just as anxious to undermine white support for the Populist party as they were to disenfranchise blacks. "The disenfranchisement movement of the 'nineties' gave the Southern states the most impressive system of obstacles between the voter and the ballot box known to the democratic world."[48]

In the 1940s the Supreme Court began to strike down one after another of the devices used to keep blacks from voting. In 1944 (*Smith* v. *Allwright*) the Court declared the **white primary** unconstitutional.[49] In 1960 it held that racial **gerrymandering** is contrary to the Fifteenth Amendment. The Twenty-fourth Amendment had eliminated the **poll tax** in *federal* elections, and in 1966 the Court held that the Fourteenth Amendment forbade the poll tax as a condition in any election.

Those wishing to deny blacks the right to vote were forced to rely on registration requirements. On the surface these requirements appeared to be perfectly proper; it was the way they were administered that kept blacks from the polls. They were often applied by white election officers while white police stood guard, with white judges hearing appeals from decisions of registration officials. These officials often seized on the smallest error in an application blank as an excuse to disqualify a voter. In one parish in the state of Louisiana, after four white voters filed affidavits in which they challenged the legality of the registration of black voters on the grounds that these voters had made an "error in spilling" [sic] in their applications, registration officials struck 1300 out of approximately 1500 black voters from the polls.[50]

In many southern areas literacy tests were used to discriminate against blacks. Some states, either as an additional requirement or as a substitute, required applicants to demonstrate to the satisfaction of election officials that they understood the national and state constitutions and, furthermore, that they were persons of good character. Whites were often asked simple questions; blacks were asked questions that would baffle a Supreme Court justice. In Louisiana, 49,603 illiterate white voters were able to persuade election officials they could understand the Constitution, but only two illiterate black voters were able to do so.

THE VOTING RIGHTS ACT OF 1965

For two decades after World War II, under the leadership of the Supreme Court, federal judges carefully scrutinized voting laws and procedures in cases brought before them. Yet this approach did not open the voting booth to blacks, especially those living in rural areas of the Deep South. Finally, in 1964, Congress began to act, after having left the major responsibility to the courts.

The Civil Rights Act of 1964 had hardly been enacted when events in Selma, Alabama, dramatized the inadequacy of depending on the courts to prevent racial barriers in polling places. A voter-registration drive in that city, led by Martin Luther King, Jr., produced arrests, marches on the state capital, and the murder of two civil rights workers. But there was no major dent in the color bar at the polls.

Responding to events in Selma, President Lyndon Johnson made a dramatic address to Congress and the nation calling for federal action to ensure that no person would be deprived of the right to vote in any election for any office because of color or race. Congress responded with the Voting Rights Act of 1965.[51] The major provisions of that act are outlined in the box on page 121. Read it carefully.

The Voting Rights Act—enacted almost a century after the Fifteenth Amendment was ratified—finally made it possible for blacks to register and vote in every district in the United States. The act has been extended and strengthened three times, most recently in 1982. Since its passage blacks now have both in form and effect the right to vote, and they are doing so.[52] Although as late as 1983 federal observers were still being sent into some places to ensure that blacks were not being intimidated, it has been unnecessary to appoint federal examiners in most areas (they have been sent to 60-some counties), because the mere threat to send them has been enough.[53]

Dilution   The Voting Rights Act goes beyond merely protecting the right to vote, especially as amended in 1982. Political units in areas covered by the act may make no change in their voting practices without pre-clearance by the attorney general. That office is to ensure that the adoption of any new practice or procedure—including a mere boundary change or, most especially, the use of at-large election electoral districts—does not have the consequence, *whether intended or not*, of diluting the voting power of minorities.[54] What precisely constitutes dilution and how it is to be measured is the subject of much litigation.

The Results   Millions of blacks now participate in our political life. More than 6500 blacks hold national, state, or local office.[55] More than 300 are mayors, including such key cities as Atlanta, Birmingham, Detroit, Los Angeles, Baltimore, Philadelphia, and Washington, D.C.[56] There are blacks in all southern legislatures, and there are more blacks in the U.S. House of Representatives than at any time since Reconstruction, including William Gray, Majority Whip in the House. And a black, Doug Wilder, was the Democratic candidate for governor of Virginia in 1989.

Has all this made any difference? "A significant disillusionment with the franchise is said to be evident among many blacks today."[57] The precise influence of black voting is a subject of much study, but the results are not clear, and the

President Lyndon Baines Johnson signs the landmark Voting Rights Act of 1965.

Black voter registration drives throughout the South attempted to activate the newly enfranchised voters.

CHAPTER 5 / Equal Rights under the Law

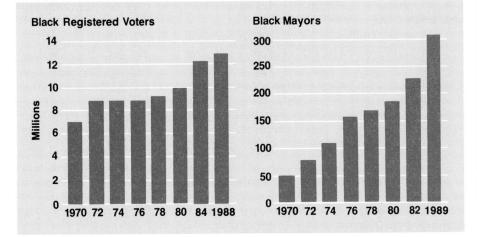

Black Registered Voters

Black Mayors

patterns are changing.[58] Yet most scholars are coming to the conclusion that "if blacks [and Hispanics] organize, compete in the electoral arena, and elect one or more of their number to city council, they can lay claim to a larger slice of the public pie."[59] In effect, minorities can convert their voting potential into public policy if they mobilize their members.

The consequences of greater participation by blacks in the political process need to be measured by means in addition to the number of black office holders.[60] When the influence of black voters is distributed over a larger number of districts, black voters may provide the margin of victory, even if they are unable to elect a black office holder. As long as candidates of any race believe they have a chance of getting enough black votes to win, they will probably find it politically profitable to be concerned about the interests of black constituents.[61]

Since the passage of the Voting Rights Act of 1965, governors and senators, especially in areas where there are large numbers of black voters, have become much more sympathetic to the concerns of black voters. The views of black constitutents have become a fact of political life and have to be taken into account by policy makers, including presidents who appoint and senators who confirm federal judges. The significance of this political fact was demonstrated by the Senate's rejection in 1987 of Robert Bork's nomination to the Supreme Court. Judge Bork was a member of the Court of Appeals for the District of Columbia and a respected constitutional authority. But his constitutional views aroused the opposition of many, including the leaders of civil rights and women's groups. Among those voting against his confirmation were many "Senators from southern states, where once, not too long ago, blacks could not register to vote. [They] voted against Bork . . . to protect the seats an enfranchised black electorate helped them to win."[62]

Barriers to Public Accommodations, Jobs, and Homes

An often overlooked point is that the Fourteenth Amendment applies only to governmental action, not to private discriminatory conduct. Moreover, our Constitution creates: "a zone of privacy which precludes government from interfering with private clubs or groups. The associational rights which our system honors permit all-white, all-black, all-brown, and all-yellow clubs to be established. They also permit all-Catholic, all-Jewish, or all-agnostic clubs. . . . Government may

Major Provisions of the Voting Rights Act of 1965 as Amended in 1974 and 1982 and Interpreted by the Supreme Court

SECTION 2

Forbids *any* government to use any procedures related to voting, regardless of intent, that result in the denial of vote to any person because of race or color or the *dilution* of the voting power of members of a protected class.

SECTIONS 3, 6, AND 7

In the areas covered by the law, those that have had a long history of discrimination against blacks, mostly but not exclusively in the South, federal courts and the United States attorney general may appoint federal examiners to register voters and to insure that all persons' votes are counted.

SECTION 4

Abolishes English literacy requirements for any person who has gone beyond the sixth grade. In addition in areas where more than five percent of the citizens are members of a single language minority, ballots and other written materials relating to the vote are to be printed in that language.

SECTION 5

Requires governmental units covered by the law to submit for pre-clearance all proposed changes in their voting laws or practices to the United States attorney general or to the United States Court of Appeals for the District of Columbia. (Note that approval of the local federal district judge will not do. Congress did not want to entrust this responsibility to anyone who might be subject to local political pressures—even a federal judge.) These changes are not to be approved until reviewed to assure that the change has neither the *purpose* nor the *effect* of denying the vote to any person because of race or color nor *diluting* the voting power of any person because of race or color.

SECTION 10

Abolishes the poll tax as a precondition of voting in any governmental election.

Black Elected Officials in 1988	
State	401
County	742
Municipal	3,341
Judicial and Law Enforcement	738
Education	1,542
Total	**6,764**

Source: Joint Center for Political Studies, Washington, D.C., January 1988. Excluding Virgin Islands.

Teaching Tip: Ask students to discuss the circumstances under which a group can legally practice private discrimination.

A Ku Klux Klan march through Houston, Texas, gets a mixed response from onlookers.

not tell a man or a woman who his or her associates must be. The individual may be as selective as he desires."[63]

However, families, churches, or private groups organized for political, religious, cultural, or social purposes or expressive purposes are constitutionally different from large associations organized along other lines, such as the United States Jaycees (the Junior Chamber of Commerce) or a large law partnership. The Supreme Court, for example, has upheld the application of state and local human relations and public accommodations laws forbidding sex or racial discrimination to organizations such as the Jaycees, the Rotary Club, and large (in this case more than 400 members) private eating clubs. Such associations and clubs are not small intimate groups. Nor were they able to demonstrate that allowing women or minorities to become members would change the content or impact of their purposes.[64]

Until recent decades serious constitutional constraints hindered Congress's authority to regulate against discriminatory conduct by private individuals. In 1883 the Supreme Court declared unconstitutional an act of Congress that made it a federal offense for any operator of a public conveyance, hotel, or theater to deny accommodations to any person because of race or color on the grounds that the Fourteenth Amendment does not give Congress authority to legislate against discrimination by private individuals.[65] In addition, for one hundred years the Court so narrowly construed the Thirteenth Amendment's grant of power to Congress to legislate against slavery and involuntary servitude that Congress could act only against physical compulsion or peonage (a condition of compulsory servitude based on indebtedness of the worker to the employer).

Since the 1960s, however, the constitutional authority of Congress to legislate against discrimination by private individuals is no longer an issue. The Court has so broadly construed **the commerce clause** that it alone justifies almost any action that Congress might want to take against discriminatory conduct by individuals. The Court has also reinterpreted the Thirteenth Amendment, at least as far as racial discrimination is concerned, to sustain congressional legislation against discrimination. Speaking for the Court, Justice Potter Stewart concluded:

> When racial discrimination herds men into ghettos and makes their ability to buy property turn on the color of their skin, then it too is a relic of slavery. . . . At the very least, the freedom that Congress is empowered to secure under the Thirteenth Amendment includes the freedom to buy whatever a white man can buy, the right to live wherever a white man can live. If Congress cannot say that being a free man means at least this much, then the Thirteenth Amendment made a promise that the Nation cannot keep.[66]

In addition to the Thirteenth and the Fourteenth Amendments, Congress may use, and has used, the power to tax and spend to prevent not only racial discrimination, but also discrimination based on ethnic origin, sex, disability, and age. It may also use the power to regulate interstate commerce, as it did in the most important and sweeping Civil Rights Act—that of 1964.

THE CIVIL RIGHTS ACT OF 1964
TITLE II: PLACES OF PUBLIC ACCOMMODATION

With this law, for the first time since Reconstruction, Congress authorized the massive use of federal authority to combat privately imposed racial discrimination. Title II makes it a federal offense to discriminate against any customer or patron in a place of public accommodation because of race, color, religion, or national origin. It applies to any inn, hotel, motel, or lodging establishment (except establishments with fewer than five rooms and occupied by the proprietor—in other words, small boardinghouses); to any restaurant or gasoline station that services interstate travelers or serves food or products of which a substantial portion have moved in interstate commerce; and to any movie house, theater, concert hall, sports arena, or other place of entertainment that customarily presents films, performances, athletic teams, or other sources of entertainment that are moved in interstate commerce.

Title II has been vigorously enforced. Blacks organized programs to test it. The Department of Justice filed more than four hundred lawsuits, and within a few months after its adoption, the Supreme Court (in *Heart of Atlanta Motel* v. *United States*) unanimously sustained its constitutionality.[67] As a result, most establishments, including those in the South, opened their doors to all customers.

"Treat people as equals, and the first thing you know, they believe they are."

Drawing by Mulligan; © 1982 The New Yorker Magazine, Inc.

THE CIVIL RIGHTS ACT OF 1964
TITLE VII: EMPLOYMENT

The Constitution forbids *governments* to deny persons employment because of race, color, religion, or sex. Under Title VII of the Civil Rights Act, Congress has made it illegal for any employer or trade union in any industry affecting interstate

---

Major Civil Rights Laws

Civil Rights Act (1957). The first civil rights bill since Reconstruction, PL 85-315 made it a federal crime to prevent persons from voting in federal elections and authorized the attorney general to bring suit when a person was deprived of his voting rights.

Civil Rights Act (1964). The most sweeping anti-bias law, PL 88-352 barred discrimination in employment on the basis of race, sex, religion, and national origin; in public accommodations and federally funded programs on the basis of race, color, religion, or national origin; and created the Equal Employment Opportunity Commission.

Voting Rights Act (1965). PL 89-110 authorized the appointment of federal examiners to register voters in areas found to have been discriminating, and strengthened penalties for those who interfered with others' right to vote.

Age Discrimination in Employment Act (1967). PL 90-202 prohibited job discrimination against workers or job applicants aged 40–65. It was amended

in 1975 (PL 94-135) to bar age bias in federally assisted programs, and in 1986 (PL 99-592) to prohibit mandatory retirement in most jobs.

Fair Housing Act (1968). PL 90-284 prohibited discrimination on the basis of race, color, religion, or national origin in the sale or rental of most housing. It also included provisions to protect civil rights workers from injury or intimidation and provided for federal penalties for those convicted of rioting or encouraging others to do so.

Rehabilitation Act of 1973. Primarily a reauthorization of programs to rehabilitate the handicapped, PL 93-112 carried two little-noted provisions whose importance became clear only after the fact. Section 503 required that recipients of federal grants greater than $2,500 institute affirmative-action programs to hire and promote "qualified handicapped individuals," while Section 504 said, "No otherwise qualified handicapped individual . . . shall, solely by reason of his handicap, be excluded from the participation in, be denied the benefits of, or be subjected to

discrimination under any program or activity receiving federal financial assistance."

Civil Rights Restoration Act (1988). Overriding President Reagan's veto, Congress in PL 100-259 overturned a 1984 Supreme Court ruling that anti sex-discrimination provisions of the 1972 Education Act Amendments applied only to the specific program or activity receiving federal aid and not to the entire institution. In reversing *Grove City College* v. *Bell*, Congress also specified that anti-bias provisions of three other laws applied to entire institutions if any segment received federal funding. The three were the 1964 Civil Rights Act, Section 504 of the 1973 Rehabilitation Act and the 1975 Age Discrimination Act.

Fair Housing Act Amendments (1988). PL 100-430 gave the Department of Housing and Urban Development greater authority to enforce the 1968 law and prohibited housing bias against the handicapped and families with children.

Source: *Social Policy*, May 13, 1989, p. 1122.

commerce and employing fifteen or more people (and, since 1972, any state or local agency such as a school or university) to discriminate in employment practices against any person because of race, color, national origin, religion, or sex.[68] Other legislation makes it illegal to engage in these activities against those with physical handicaps, veterans, or persons over 40.

There are a few exceptions. Religious institutions such as parochial schools may use religious standards. Age, sex, or handicap may be considered where bona fide occupational qualifications are necessary to the normal operation of a particular business or enterprise.

Title VII was passed to protect minorities and women; nonetheless, employers who discriminate against white males also violate its provisions. Moreover, when Congress adopted Title VII it stated that it should not be used to require any employer to grant preferential treatment to any individual or to any group on account of racial or sexual imbalance that might exist in the employer's workforce. Title VII, however, does not preclude employers, public or private, from adopting race-sensitive *affirmative action* programs designed to overcome past discrimination against minorities and women. (See page 125 for Supreme Court's growing skepticism about such programs.)

Title VII has several special features. Not only do aggrieved persons have a right of private action to sue for damages for themselves, but they can do so for other persons similarly situated—in a so-called **class action.** In addition, Congress created the *Equal Employment Opportunity Commission*, known as the EEOC, to enforce its provisions. The commission, which consists of five members appointed by the president with the consent of the Senate, works together with state authorities to try to bring about compliance with the act and may seek judicial enforcement of complaints against private employers. The attorney general prosecutes Title VII violations by public agencies. The vigor with which the EEOC as well as the attorney general have acted has varied over the years, depending on the commitment of the president in office.[69]

Title VII is supplemented, indeed in some instances even supplanted, by a 1965 presidential executive order requiring all contractors of the federal government, including universities, to adopt and implement affirmative action programs to correct for "underutilization" of women and minorities. Such programs may not establish racial or ethnic quotas for minorities or women, but they do call on contractors to establish timetables and goals; to follow open-recruitment procedures; to keep records of applicants by race, sex, and national origin; and to explain why their labor force does not reflect the same proportion of persons in the covered categories that exist within the labor market pools. Failure of contractors to file and implement an approved affirmative action plan may lead to loss of federal contracts or grants. The Reagan and Bush administrations, however, have not been vigorous in enforcing this executive order.

HOUSING: THE CIVIL RIGHTS ACTS OF 1866, 1968, AND 1988

Fair housing is the last frontier of the civil rights crusade, the area in which progress is slowest and genuine change most remote. "Blacks at every economic level are significantly segregated from whites of similar economic status."[70] "Housing segregation is serious because it is at the root of many other forms of segregation and inequality."[71] "Segregated housing contributes mightily to a vicious circle that also includes educational and employment discrimination. . . . Because of poor schools for many minorities, they cannot find well-paying jobs. Without such jobs they often cannot afford to live in nicer neighborhoods with decent housing. And because of their location in less desirable communities, good educational systems are less likely to be available."[72]

In 1948, in *Shelley* v. *Kraemer*, the Supreme Court held that judges could no longer enforce racially **restrictive covenants** (a provision in a deed to real property restricting its sale).[73] Perhaps most important, in 1968 Congress passed a Civil Rights Act relating directly to housing.

This act, amended in 1988, is now known as the Fair Housing Amendments Act and covers all housing offered for rent or sale, except that owned by private individuals who own no more than three houses, who sell or rent these houses without the services of an agent, and who do not indicate any preference or discrimination in their advertising; dwellings that have no more than four separate living units, in which the owner maintains a residence ("Mrs. Murphy boardinghouses"); and religious organizations and private clubs housing their own members on a noncommercial basis. For all other housing, the act forbids owners to refuse to sell or rent to any person because of race, color, religion, national origin, sex (since 1974), and because of handicap or because one has children (since 1988). Housing for older persons is exempted from this family provision. No discriminatory advertising is permitted.

"Thanks for coming in. It's such a relief to be able to deny someone a loan when there's no possibility of being charged with sex, race, age, or ethnic bias."

Drawing by Ed Fisher, © *1976 The New Yorker Magazine, Inc.*

"The weakest link" in the 1968 act turned out to be the sections dealing with enforcement. Prior to the 1988 amendments, primary responsibility fell upon those injured by discriminatory housing practices. Now the Department of Housing and Urban Development (HUD) is obliged to investigate and process complaints. The Department of Justice must provide an attorney for complainants who are unable to afford one. Even more important, complainants may now bring their allegations of discrimination before administrative law judges within HUD.

More than two decades after the adoption of the Housing Act of 1968, many, if not most, blacks still meet discrimination when they seek to rent a home or buy a house. "While blacks and other minorities have made strides in voting rights, education and jobs, the homes they return to each night are in communities still largely defined by race."[74] Striking back, the Department of Justice has filed hundreds of cases, especially those involving large apartment complexes. The courts have built up such "a formidable body of precedent that almost anyone who can prove discrimination, and has the determination and money to do so, can get the house he wants and even substantial damage awards."[75] And the addition in 1988 of administrative enforcement procedures gives this federal law considerably stronger teeth.

Affirmative Action—Is It Constitutional?

Prior to 1954, when white majorities were using state power to segregate blacks and impose disabilities upon them, civil rights advocates cited with approval the words of Justice Harlan, dissenting in *Plessy* v. *Ferguson*: "Our Constitution is color-blind and neither knows nor tolerates class among citizens."[76] It was not until 1954 that Justice Harlan's views triumphed. In *Brown* v. *Board of Education* the Court called racial classifications "odious to our system" and made race a suspect class—probably an outlawed one. In the years immediately following, the Court also established that although the Fourteenth Amendment was adopted to protect blacks, its provisions extend to other minorities, to women, and to white males. The Court emphasized that the rights protected belong to each and every individual, not to the group to which he or she may belong.

By the 1960s there was a new set of constitutional and national policy debates. Many began to assert that government neutrality is not enough. If governments and universities and employers merely stop discriminating against blacks, Hispanics, and women, yet change nothing else, those previously discriminated against are still kept from equal participation in American life. They have been so handicapped by past discrimination that in the competition for openings in medical schools, or for skilled jobs, or for their share of government grants and contracts, they suffer disabilities not shared by white males.

By the 1960s governments started to respond to these arguments. Presidents issued executive orders, Congress adopted programs, state legislatures created requirements, cities adopted ordinances, and university trustees issued policies. Although the details vary (and the details are constitutionally significant), these programs call on governments, governmental contractors, and in some instances private employers to take **affirmative action** to redress imbalances in work forces and govermental contracts in order to reflect more accurately the racial, sex, and ethnic diversity of employment pools and to give opportunities to minority and women contractors. These race-, ethnic-, and sex-conscious remedies to overcome the consequences of past discrimination against blacks, Hispanics, Native Americans, and women are known as affirmative action programs by those who support them but as reverse discrimination by those who oppose them.

What of the constitutionality of affirmative action programs resting on race and sex classifications, motivated not by feelings of racial hostility but by a desire to help persons handicapped by individual and institutional racism and sexism? The questions have been raised most directly with respect to affirmative action programs for blacks.

The first major statement of the Court on these perplexing issues came in a celebrated case relating to university admissions. Allan Bakke, a white male and a top student at Minnesota and Stanford Universities, as well as a Vietnam War veteran, applied in both 1973 and 1974 to the medical school of the University of California at Davis. In each of those years the school admitted 100 new students, 84 in a general admissions program and 16 in a special admissions program created for blacks, Chicanos, Asian Americans, and American Indians—groups who had been totally underrepresented there until the special admissions program was established. Bakke's application was rejected each year, but students with lower grade-point averages, test scores, and interview ratings were admitted under the special admissions program. After his second rejection Bakke brought a suit in federal court claiming he had been excluded because of his race, contrary to requirements of the Constitution and Title VI of the Civil Rights Act of 1964.

In *University of California Regents* v. *Bakke* (1978), the Supreme Court ruled the Davis plan was unconstitutional.[77] But in an opinion by Justice Lewis Powell, which no other member of the Court completely shared, the Court also declared that affirmative action programs are not necessarily unconstitutional. In order to get a diversified student body, a state university may properly take race and ethnic background into account as one of several factors in choosing students. However, the university's goal may not be to redress past misconduct by the society or to ensure that more minority members become doctors. The problem with the California plan was it created a category of admissions from which whites were excluded solely because of their race.

Following *Bakke*, the Court dealt with a variety of affirmative action programs, sustaining most, but not all of them. Yet as Justice White said, "Agreement upon a means for applying the Equal Protection Clause to an affirmative-action program

Allan Bakke, who led a landmark Supreme Court decision striking down minority admissions quotas, chatting with fellow graduates.

has eluded this Court every time the issue has come before us."[78] Then, in *Richmond v. Corson* in 1989, a Court majority, over the bitter dissents of Justices Marshall, Brennan, and Blackmun, struck down a plan of the city of Richmond requiring nonminority city contractors to subcontract at least 30 percent of the dollar amount of their contracts to one or more minority business enterprises. In doing so the Court majority appears now to adhere to the following general principles that set rather narrow boundaries to *state and local governmental* affirmative action programs, at least those based on race.

1. All racial classifications, including those justified for benign or remedial purposes are suspect, and are subject to the strict scrutiny test to insure that they are neither motivated by illegitimate notions of racial inferiority or simple racial politics.

2. Congress has much greater discretion than do states or local governments in fashioning race-sensitive remedial measures because it is empowered by Section 5 of the Fourteenth Amendment to do what is necessary and has power to enforce equal protection guarantees.

3. At the state and local levels, "When a legislative body chooses to employ a suspect classification, it cannot rest upon a generalized assertion as to the classification's relevance to its goals." Race-sensitive remedial measures are to be justified only after a strong basis in evidence has established that remedial action is necessary to overcome the consequences of past discriminatory action.

4. A race-sensitive remedy must be narrowly tailored to remedy this specific prior discrimination.

5. When a state and local government can identify in fact racial discrimination within its jurisdiction it may adopt "in the extreme case, some form of narrowly tailored racial preference . . . necessary to break down patterns of deliberate exclusion."[79]

Justice Marshall in dissent contended that there is "a profound difference separating governmental actions that themselves are racist, and governmental actions seeking to remedy the effects of prior racism." The proper test, he writes, for race conscious classifications designed to further remedial goals is merely that they have to be justified as serving important governmental objectives and must be substantially related to the achievement of those objectives. The majority, he said, "sounds a full-scale retreat from the effort to deliver on the century-old promise of equality and scuttled the efforts of a city to surmount its discriminatory past."

Richmond v. *Carson* is not the last word. It does not relate directly to private employers or to programs based on sex. And other governmental affirmative action programs differ from that of *Richmond* in what may be constitutionally important detail. There are more decisions to come as the Court—and the nation—engage in the never-ending business of clarifying constitutional guidelines.

Summary

1. The crusade for women's rights was born partly out of the struggle to abolish slavery. The fate of these two social movements has long been intertwined. Recently the struggle for equal rights under the law has been expanded to cover concerns for the rights of Native Americans, Hispanics, and Asians.

2. Progress in securing civil rights for blacks was a long time in coming. After the Civil War the national government briefly tried to secure some measure of protection for the freed slaves and to enforce the Thirteenth, Fourteenth, and Fifteenth amendments and the civil rights laws passed to implement them. But when the national government withdrew

from the field in 1877, blacks were left to their own resources, and the rights granted by the Constitution became meaningless. The Supreme Court reversed an 1896 decision and, in *Brown* v. *Board of Education*, announced that enforced racial segregation in public education was unconstitutional.

Eventually Congress and the president threw their weight behind a major effort to prevent racial segregation and discrimination against blacks.

3. The Supreme Court uses a three-tiered approach to evaluate the constitutionality of laws challenged as violating the equal protection clause. Laws touching economic concerns are sustained if they are rationally related to the accomplishment of a legitimate government goal. Laws that classify people because of sex or illegitimacy are sustained only if they meet the more rigorous test of serving important governmental objectives and if they are substantially related to achieving those objectives. The top or most stringent tier is used to review laws that touch fundamental rights or classify people because of race or ethnic origin. Such laws will be sustained only if the government can show a "compelling public interest."

4. After a long struggle women achieved the right to vote with the adoption of the Nineteenth Amendment in 1920. With the rebirth of the women's movement in the 1960s, federal courts began to interpret constitutional provisions to protect women against sex discrimination.

5. Most recently older Americans have joined with Hispanics, Native Americans, and Asian Americans to secure legislative protection for their special concerns.

6. The desirability and constitutionality of affirmative action programs that provide special benefits to those who have been subjected to past discrimination divide the nation and the Supreme Court. Remedial programs, especially those designed by Congress, closely tailored to overcome specific instances of disadvantage due to past discrimination are likely to pass the Supreme Court's suspicion of race, national origin, and sex classifications. However, such programs, at least as applied to race, enacted by state and local governments will have to survive more exacting judicial scrutiny and be subject to the strict scrutiny test as applied by the Supreme Court to laws based on racial classifications.

Further Reading

NORMAN C. AMAKER, ed. *Civil Rights and the Reagan Administration* (Urban Institute, 1988).

HARRY S. ASHMORE. *Hearts and Minds: The Anatomy of Racism from Roosevelt to Reagan* (McGraw-Hill, 1982).

RUSSEL LAWRENCE BARSH and JAMES YOUNGBLOOD HENDERSON. *The Road: Indian Tribes and Political Liberty* (University of California Press, 1980).

TAYLOR BRANCH. *Parting the Waters: America in the King Years, 1954–1963* (Simon & Schuster, 1988).

GEORGE H. BROWN, NAN L. ROSEN, and SUSAN T. HILL. *The Condition of Education for Hispanic Americans* (U.S. Government Printing Office, 1980).

PAUL BURSTEIN. *Discrimination, Jobs, and Politics: The Struggle for Equal Employment Opportunity in the United States since the New Deal* (University of Chicago Press, 1985).

LAURA L. CRITES and WINIFRED L. HEPPERLE. *Women, the Courts, and Equality* (Sage Publications, 1987).

JANET DEWART, ed. *The State of Black America 1989* (National Urban League, 1989). Published annually.

ELEANOR FLEXNER. *Century of Struggle: The Woman's Rights Movement in the United States* (Belknap, 1959).

FRED R. HARRIS and ROGER W. WILKINS. *Quiet Riots: Race and Poverty in the United States: The Kerner Report Twenty Years Later* (Pantheon Books, 1988).

RICHARD KLUGER. *Simple Justice* (Knopf, 1976).

AILEEN S. KRADITOR. *The Ideas of the Woman Suffrage Movement, 1890–1920* (Columbia University Press, 1965).

ALLAN P. SINDLER. *Bakke, DeFunis, and Minority Admissions* (Longman, 1978).

MAURILIO E. VIRGIL. *Hispanics In American Politics: The Search for Political Power* (University Press of America, 1987).

J. HARVIE WILKINSON, III. *From Brown to Bakke: The Supreme Court and School Integration, 1954–1978* (Oxford University Press, 1979).

Notes

1. From Sidney Verba and Gary R. Orren, *Equality in America: The View from the Top* (Harvard University Press, 1985), p. 1, on which this section is based. See also Jennifer L. Hochschild, *What's Fair? American Beliefs about Distributive Justice* (Harvard University Press, 1981).

2. Ellen Carol DuBois, *Feminism and Suffrage: The Emergence of an Independent Women's Movement in America, 1848–1869* (Cornell University Press, 1978); and Joan Hoff-Wilson, "Women and the Constitution," *News for Teachers of Political Science* (American Political Science Association, Summer 1985), pp. 10–15.

3. Alan P. Grimes, *Democracy and the Amendments to the Constitution* (D. C. Heath, 1979), pp. 90–91; and Nancy F. Cott, *The Grounding of Modern Feminism* (Yale University Press, 1987).

4. Grimes, *Democracy.*

5. 163 U.S. 537.

6. See David J. Garrow's prize winning account, *Bearing The Cross: Martin Luther King, Jr., and The Southern Christian Leadership Conference* (Morrow, 1986).

7. Michael R. Belknap, *Federal Law and Southern Order: Racial Violence and Constitutional Conflict in the Post-Brown South* (University of Georgia, 1987), pp. 128–204.

8. Taylor Branch, *Parting the Waters: America in the King Years, 1954–1963* (Simon & Schuster, 1988). See also Joel D. Aberbach and Jack L. Walker, "The Meanings of Black Power," *American Political Science Review* (June 1970), pp. 367–88; Harris Wofford, *Of Kennedys & Kings: Making Sense of the Sixties* (Farrar, Straus

& Giroux, 1980); and Carl M. Brauer, *John F. Kennedy and the Second Reconstruction* (Columbia University Press, 1977).

9. Charles and Barbara Whalen, *The Longest Debate: A Legislative History of the 1964 Civil Rights Act* (Sevenlocks Press, 1985).

10. Aldon D. Morris, *The Origins of the Civil Rights Movement: Black Communities Organizing for Change* (The Free Press/Macmillan, 1985); James Farmer, *Laying Bare the Heart: An Autobiography of the Civil Rights Movement* (Arbor House, 1985); and Branch, *Parting the Waters*.

11. James Farmer in Rochelle L. Stanfield, "Black Complaints Haven't Translated into Political Organization and Power," *National Journal* (June 14, 1980), p. 465. Alphonso Pinkey, *The Myth of Black Progress* (Cambridge University Press, 1984), argues that the failure of blacks to make greater progress is due to white racism; William Julius Wilson, *The Declining Significance of Race*, 2d ed. (University of Chicago Press, 1984), argues to the contrary that most of the problems are those of class, not race. See also Stuart Scheingold, "Constitutional Rights and Social Change: Civil Rights in Perspective," in Michael W. McCann and Gerald L. Houseman, eds., *Judging the Constitution* (Scott, Foresman and Company, 1989), pp. 73–91.

12. Fred R. Harris and Roger W. Wilkins, eds., *Quiet Riots: Race and Poverty in the United States: The Kerner Report Twenty Years Later* (Pantheon, 1988); and Janet Dewart, ed., *The State of Black America, 1989* (National Urban League, 1989); also National Academy of Science, *A Common Destiny: Blacks and American Society* (National Academy Press, 1989).

13. Gary Orfield, "Separate Societies: Have the Kerner Warnings Come True?" in Harris and Wilkins, *Quiet Riots*, p. 103; and Madeline Landau, "Race, Poverty & the Cities: Hyperinnovation in Complex Policy Systems," *Public Affairs Report*, Bulletin of the Institute of Governmental Studies, University of California, Berkeley, vol. 30 (January 1989), p. 1. See also Margaret C. Simms, ed., *Black Economic Progress: An Agenda for the 1990's* (The Joint Center for Political Studies, 1988).

14. Charles F. Wilkinson, *American Indians, Time, and the Law* (Yale University Press, 1987), p. 62; and Vine Deloria, Jr., and Clifford M. Lytle, *The Past and Future of American Indian Sovereignty* (Pantheon Books, 1984).

15. *Morton* v. *Mancari*, 417 U.S. 535 (1974); and Theodore W. Taylor, *The Bureau of Indian Affairs* (Westview Press, 1984).

16. Office of Technology Assessment, quoted by Spencer Rich in "Native Americans, They Can Still Get Free Health Care If They're Indian Enough," *The Washington Post National Weekly Edition* (July 14, 1986), p. 34.

17. Valdes Y. Tapia, "Hispanics Need to Unite to End Their Exile at Home," *The Denver Post* (July 19, 1980), p. 7.

18. The Bilateral Commission on the Future of United States-Mexican Relations, *The Challenge of Interdependence* (University Press of America, 1989), p. 99.

19. From the Census Bureau, as reported in *The New York Times* (September 7, 1988), p. 12.

20. Maurilio E. Virgil, *Hispanics in American Politics: Search for Political Power* (University Press of America, 1987).

21. Alan Pifer, *Annual Report of the Carnegie Corporation of New York* (1979), p. 16.

22. David Rampe, "Power Panel in Making: The Hispanic Caucus," *The New York Times* (September 30, 1988), p. 13.

23. 414 U.S. 563 (1974).

24. Won Moo Hurh, *Korean Immigrants in America* (Fairleigh Dickinson University Press, 1984).

25. Antonio J. A. Pido, *The Filipinos in America: Macro/Micro Dimensions of Immigration and Integration* (Center for Migration Studies of New York, 1986).

26. *Zobel* v. *Williams*, 457 U.S. 55 (1982); and *Cleburne* v. *Cleburne Living Center*, 473 U.S. 432 (1985).

27. *San Antonio School District* v. *Rodriquez*, 411 U.S. 1 (1973).

28. *Frontiero* v. *Richardson*, 411 U.S. 677 (1973).

29. *Califano* v. *Webster*, 430 U.S. 313 (1977).

30. *Mississippi University for Women* v. *Hogan*, 458 U.S. 718 (1982).

31. Hoff-Wilson, "Women and the Constitution," p. 14 (italics deleted from the original).

32. Deborah Rhode, "Justice, Gender, and the Justices," in Laura L. Crites and Winfred L. Hepperle, eds., *Women, the Courts, and Equality* (Sage Publications, 1987). See also Deborah L. Rhode, "Equal Protection and Justice," in Michael W. McCann and Gerald L. Houseman, eds., *Judging the Constitution* (Scott, Foresman and Company, 1989).

33. *San Antonio School District* v. *Rodriguez*.

34. Sidney P. Freedberg, "Forced Exits? Companies Confront Wage of Age-Discrimination Suits," *Wall Street Journal* (October 13, 1987), p. 39.

35. *Washington* v. *Davis*, 426 U.S. 229 (1976); and *Hunter* v. *Underwood*, 471 U.S. 522 (1985).

36. *Personnel Administrator of Massachusetts* v. *Feeney*, 442 U.S. 256 (1979).

37. C. Vann Woodward, *The Strange Career of Jim Crow* (Oxford University Press, 1968).

38. 163 U.S. 537.

39. 347 U.S. 483 (1954). See also J. W. Peltason, *Fifty-eight Lonely Men: Southern Federal Judges and School Desegregation* (University of Illinois Press, 1971), p. 248.

40. *Brown* v. *Board of Education*, 349 U.S. 294 (1955). For a comprehensive history of the events leading up to *Brown*, see Richard Kluger, *Simple Justice* (Knopf, 1976). Earl Black, *Southern Governors and Civil Rights: Racial Segregation as a Campaign Issue in the Second Reconstruction* (Harvard University Press, 1977), shows response, reaction, and eventually neutralization of race as a political issue following the *Brown* decision.

41. *Alexander* v. *Board of Education*, 396 U.S. 19 (1969).

42. *Grove City* v. *Bell*, 465 U.S. 555 (1984).

43. Gary Orfield, *Must We Bus? Segregated Schools and National Policy* (Brookings Institution, 1979); and Jennifer L. Hochschild, *The New American Dilemma: Liberal Democracy and School Desegregation* (Yale University Press, 1984).

44. *Swann* v. *Charlotte-Mecklenburg Board of Education*, 402 U.S. 1 (1971).

45. *Milliken* v. *Bradley*, 418 U.S. 717 (1974); and Bernard Schwartz, *The School Busing Case and the Supreme Court* (Oxford University Press, 1986).

46. Orfield, "Separate Societies", p. 116.

47. Julie Johnson, "Deciding What to Do Next about Civil Rights," *The New York Times* (March 12, 1989), p. E. 5; and Norman C. Amaker, ed., *Civil Rights and the Reagan Administration* (Urban Institute, 1988).

48. V. O. Key, Jr., *Southern Politics* (Knopf, 1949), p. 555. For a history of the rise and fall of black disenfranchisement, see Steven F. Lawson, *Black Ballots: Voting Rights in the South, 1944–1969* (Columbia University Press, 1976).

49. 321 U.S. 649 (1944).

50. *Report of the United States Commission on Civil Rights* (U.S. Government Printing Office, 1959), pp. 103–4.

51. David J. Garrow, *Protest at Selma: Martin Luther King and the Voting Rights Act of 1965* (Yale University Press, 1978).

52. Richard L. Engstrom, "Racial Vote Dilution: The Concept and the Court," in Lorn S. Foster, ed., *The Voting Rights Act: Consequences and Implications* (Praeger, 1985), p. 13.

53. Mack H. Jones, "The Voting Rights Act as an Intervention Strategy for Social Change: Symbolism or Substance?" in Foster, *The Voting Rights Act*, pp. 63–84 for the view that Justice Department failed to enforce these provisions with appropriate vigor.

54. See Abigail M. Thernstrom, *Whose Votes Count? Affirmative Action and Minority Voting Rights* (Harvard University Press, 1987).

55. *The Washington Post National Weekly Edition* (October 5, 1987), p. 14.

56. "Outlook Bright For More Black Mayors," *Orange County Register* (July 3, 1986), p. A12.

57. Engstrom, "Racial Vote Dilution: The Concept and the Court," in

Foster, *The Voting Rights Act*, p. 13. Engstrom cites Harrell R. Rodgers, "Civil Rights and the Myth of Popular Sovereignty," *Journal of Black Studies*, vol. 12 (1981), pp. 53–70. See also Leonard A. Cole, *Blacks in Power: A Comparative Study of Black and White Elected Officials* (Princeton University Press, 1976); and Dianne M. Pinderhughes, *Race and Ethnicity in Chicago Politics: A Reexamination of Pluralist Theory* (University of Illinois Press, 1987), p. xvi. For a skeptical evaluation of the act, see Foster, *The Voting Rights Act*.

58. Huey Perry, "Review Essay," *Publius*, vol. 18 (Fall 1988) p. 198, covering, among others, relevant work on these questions by Margaret Edds, *Free at Last: What Really Happened When Civil Rights Came to Southern Politics* (Alder and Alder, 1987); Lawrence J. Hanks, *The Struggle for Black Political Empowerment in Three Georgia Counties* (University of Tennessee Press, 1987); Foster, *The Voting Rights Act*; Abigail Thernstrom, *Whose Votes Count?*; and Harold W. Stanley, *Voter Mobilization and the Politics of Race: The South and Universal Suffrage, 1952–1984* (Praeger, 1987).

59. Kenneth R. Mladenka, "Blacks and Hispanics in Urban Politics," *The American Political Science Review*, vol. 83 (March 1989), p. 188.

60. Thernstrom, *Whose Votes Count?* p. 243.

61. Perry, "Review Essay," p. 198.

62. Charles V. Hamilton, "On Parity and Political Empowerment," in Dewart, *The State of Black America*, p. 119.

63. Justice Douglas dissenting in *Moose Lodge No. 107* v. *Irvis*, 407 U.S. 163 (1972).

64. *New York State Club Association* v. *City of New York*, 101 L Ed 2d 1 (1988).

65. *The Civil Rights Cases*, 109 U.S. 3 (1883).

66. 393 U.S. 409 (1968).

67. 379 U.S. 421 (1964).

68. Paul Burstein, *Discrimination, Jobs, and Politics: The Struggle for Equal Employment Opportunity in the United States since the New Deal* (The University of Chicago Press, 1985).

69. Hanes Walton, Jr., *When The Marching Stopped: The Politics of Civil Rights Regulatory Agencies* (State University of New York Press, 1988).

70. John O. Calmore, "To Make Wrong Right: The Necessary and Proper Aspirations of Fair Housing," in Dewart, *The State of Black America*, p. 95.

71. Orfield, "Separate Societies," p. 105.

72. Charles M. Lamb, "Housing Discrimination and Segregation," *Catholic University Law Review* (Spring 1981), p. 370.

73. 334 U.S. 1 (1948).

74. "The Racism Next Door: Segregated Housing Is Still a Blight in Most Neighborhoods," *Time* (June 30, 1986), p. 40; Alan Finder, "Housing Bias Still Pervades the New York Region," *The New York Times* (March 13, 1989), p. A16.

75. Robert Reinhold, "Race Barriers in Housing Still High 11 Years after the Civil Rights Act," *The New York Times* (June 8, 1979).

76. 163 U.S. 537 (1896).

77. 438 U.S. 265 (1978).

78. Concurring in *Wygant* v. *Jackson Board of Education*, 476 U.S. 267 (1986).

79. Justice O'Connor for the Court in *Richmond* v. *Croson*, 102 L Ed 2d 854 (1989). Justices Kennedy and Scalia, who are part of the majority, are opposed to any kind of racial classification, even as a remedy. On the other side, Justice Stevens, who also voted with the majority, believes race may properly be taken into account under some circumstances, even when not a remedy for past discrimination.

6

Rights to Life, Liberty, and Property

Public officials have great power. Under certain conditions they can seize our property, throw us into jail, and—in extreme circumstances—even take our lives. It is necessary to give power to those who govern; it is also dangerous. It is so dangerous that to keep officials from becoming tyrants, we are unwilling to depend on the ballot box alone. We know political controls mean little when a majority uses its power to deprive unpopular minorities of their rights. Because public power can be dangerous, we parcel it out in small chunks and surround it with restraints. No single official can decide to take our lives, liberty, or property: officials must act according to the rules. If they act outside the scope of their authority or contrary to the law, they have no claim to our obedience.

These are the precious rights of all who live under the American flag—rich or poor, young or old, black or white, man or woman, alien or citizen. The Constitution also confers some special rights on citizens and protects the right to become and to remain an American citizen.

Who belongs to the body politic? Who is an American? Every nation has rules that determine nationality and define who is a member of, owes allegiance to, and is a subject of the nation-state. But in a democracy citizenship is more than nationality, more than being merely a subject.[1] Citizenship is an office and, like other offices, it carries with it certain powers and responsibilities. How citizenship is acquired and retained should therefore be a matter of considerable importance to everyone.

How Citizenship Is Acquired and Lost

This basic right of membership in the body politic was not given constitutional protection until 1868, when the Fourteenth Amendment was adopted. The Fourteenth Amendment makes "all persons born or naturalized in the United States

Albert Einstein (1879–1955), his daughter (right), and his secretary (left), taking the oath of American citizenship in 1940. A brilliant physicist known for formulating the theory of relativity, Einstein was born in Germany. In 1934 the Nazi government confiscated his property and revoked his citizenship, at which time he immigated to the United States.

Dual Citizenship

Because each nation has complete authority to decide for itself the question of nationality, it is possible for a person to be considered a citizen by two or more nations. Dual citizenship is not unusual, especially for persons from nations that do not recognize the right of the individual to choose his or her own nationality, called the right of *expatriation.* (One of the issues of the War of 1812 was that England did not recognize that sailors born in England had abandoned their English citizenship on becoming naturalized American citizens.) Children born abroad to American citizens may also be citizens of the nation in which they were born. Children born in the United States of parents from a foreign nation may also be citizens of their parents' country.

Dual nationality carries negative as well as positive consequences; for example, such an individual may be subject to national service obligations and taxes in both countries.

and subject to the jurisdiction thereof . . . citizens of the United States and of the State wherein they reside." As a result, all persons born in the United States, except children born to foreign ambassadors and ministers, are citizens of this country regardless of the citizenship of their parents. (Congress has defined the United States to include Puerto Rico, Guam, the Northern Marianas, and the Virgin Islands.) Although the Fourteenth Amendment does not make native Americans citizens of the United States and of the states in which they live, Congress has done so.

The Fourteenth Amendment confers citizenship according to the principle of **jus soli**—by place of birth. In addition, Congress has granted, under certain conditions, citizenship at birth according to the principle of **jus sanguinis**—by blood. A child born to an American living abroad is an American citizen if the American parent has lived in the United States for ten years, including two after age 14.

Citizenship may also be acquired by either collective or individual **naturalization.** The granting of citizenship to the people of the Northern Marianas in 1977 by an act of Congress is an example of collective naturalization. Individual naturalization requirements are determined by Congress. Today, with minor exceptions, non-enemy aliens over age 18 who have been lawfully admitted for permanent residence and who have resided in the United States for at least five years and in a state for at least six months are eligible for naturalization.

Any state or federal court of record in the United States can grant citizenship. The Immigration and Naturalization Service (INS) makes the necessary investigations and reports to a judge. The final step is a hearing in open court. If the judge is satisfied that the applicant has met all the requirements, the applicant renounces allegiance to his or her former country, and swears to support and defend the Constitution and laws of the United States against all enemies and to bear arms in behalf of the United States when required to do so by law. Those whose religious beliefs prevent them from bearing arms are allowed to take an oath that, if called to duty, they will serve in the armed forces as noncombatants, or that they will perform work of national importance under civilian direction. The court then grants a certificate of naturalization.

Naturalized citizenship may be revoked by court order if the government can prove it was secured by deception. In addition, citizenship, however acquired, may be voluntarily renounced. But citizenship cannot be taken from people because of what they have done—for example, committed certain crimes, voted in foreign elections, or served in foreign armies. Some actions, however, such as taking out citizenship in another country or swearing allegiance to another nation, may be taken into account as "highly persuasive evidence of a purpose to abandon citizenship." Even so, the government must prove that the citizen "not only voluntarily committed the expatriating act prescribed in the statute, but also intended to relinquish his citizenship."[2]

RIGHTS OF AMERICAN CITIZENSHIP

An American citizen becomes a citizen of one of our states merely by residing in that state. (Residence, as used in the Fourteenth Amendment, means domicile, the place one calls home. The legal status of domicile should not be confused with the fact of physical presence. A person may be living in Washington, D.C., but be a citizen of California, that is, consider California home. Residence is primarily a question of intent.)

CHAPTER 6 / Rights to Life, Liberty, and Property

Many of our most important rights flow from state citizenship rather than from United States citizenship. In the *Slaughter House Cases* (1873) the Supreme Court carefully distinguished between the privileges of United States citizens and those of state citizens. It held that the only privileges attaching to national citizenship are those that "owe their existence to the Federal Government, its National Character, its Constitution, or its laws."[3] These privileges have never been completely specified, but they include the right to use the navigable waters of the United States; to assemble peacefully; to petition the national government for redress of grievances; to be protected by the national government on the high seas; to vote, if qualified to do so under state laws, and to have one's vote counted properly; and to travel throughout the United States.

The Right to Travel Abroad   Although the right of interstate travel is virtually unqualified, the right to international travel can be regulated within the bounds of due process. Under current law it is unlawful (except as otherwise provided by the president, as has been done for travel to Mexico and Canada) for citizens to leave or enter the United States without a valid passport. The president, acting through the secretary of state, may refuse to grant or may revoke a passport if the government judges that a holder's activities in foreign countries are causing or are likely to cause serious damage to our national security or foreign policy.

The Right to Live in the United States   This right, which is not subject to any congressional limitation, is perhaps the most precious aspect of American citizenship. Aliens have no such right.

Rights of Aliens—
Admission to the United States

Some Americans want the United States to live up to its heritage as a haven for people fleeing religious and political persecution. President Franklin Roosevelt is reputed to have opened his address to a convention of the Daughters of the American Revolution with the salutation, "Fellow immigrants and revolutionaries." Other Americans, however, are concerned about diluting American traditions and strongly oppose admitting so many people from abroad. Throughout our history debates have flared among those wishing to open our borders and those wishing to close them.

Congress decides how many and which aliens shall be admitted to the United States and under what conditions. By 1875 it had begun to restrict the entry of persons alleged to be "undesirable," such as prostitutes and revolutionaries. During World War I Congress, for the first time, set limits on the number of aliens who could be admitted each year. The Immigration Act of 1924 created a national origin system that discriminated against immigrants from southern Europe and southeastern Asia.

In 1965, after years of debate, a new immigration law was adopted. It remains the basic legislation, although it has often been amended. The law sets an annual ceiling of 270,000 aliens allowed to come here as *permanent residents,* but excludes relatives of permanent resident immigrants from this numerical limitation. Even within the quotas, preference is given to family members of United States residents. In fact, since current law awards visas primarily on the basis of family reunification, not many people from Western European countries and some African nations

---

Naturalization Requirements

An applicant for naturalization must:

1. Be over age 18.
2. Be lawfully admitted to the United States for permanent residence, and have resided in the United States for at least five years and in a state for at least six months.
3. File a petition of naturalization with a clerk of a court of record (federal or state) verified by two witnesses.
4. Be able to read, write, and speak English.
5. Possess a good moral character.
6. Understand and demonstrate an attachment to the history, principles, and form of government of the United States.
7. Demonstrate that he or she is well disposed toward the good order and happiness of the country.
8. Demonstrate that he or she does not now believe in, nor within the last ten years has ever believed in, advocated, or belonged to an organization that supports opposition to organized government, overthrow of government by violence, or the doctrines of world communism or any other form of totalitarianism.

A Citizenship Ceremony?

Naturalized citizens have had to prove to a judge that they understand the nature of our governmental system and the obligations of citizenship. It has been argued that native-born citizens should also be taught "what it means to be a citizen in a self-governing society," and that we should "institute a ceremony in which young native-born adults, like naturalized citizens, explicitly declare themselves parties to the system of agreements constituting our body politic."

Is this a good idea?

Martin Edelman, *Democratic Theories and the Constitution* (State University of New York Press, 1984), p. 304.

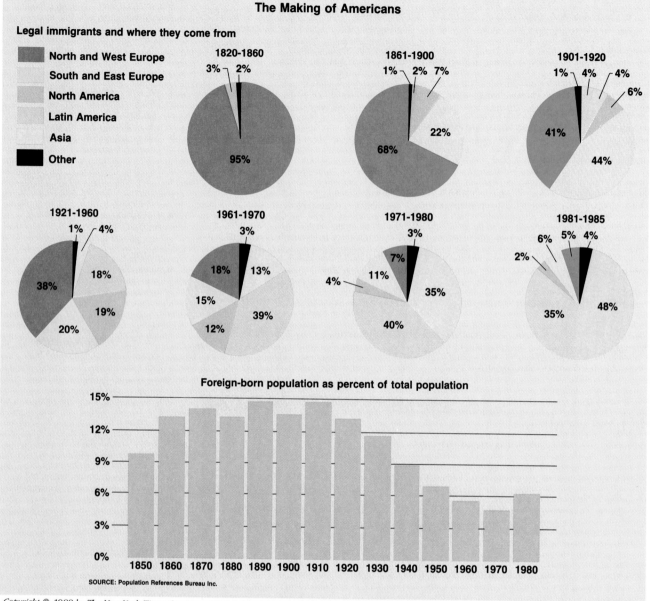

The Making of Americans

Legal immigrants and where they come from

- North and West Europe
- South and East Europe
- North America
- Latin America
- Asia
- Other

1820-1860
3% 2%
95%

1861-1900
1% 2% 7%
22%
68%

1901-1920
1% 4% 4%
6%
41%
44%

1921-1960
1% 4%
18%
38%
19%
20%

1961-1970
3%
18% 13%
15%
39%
12%

1971-1980
3%
7%
4% 11%
35%
40%

1981-1985
6% 5% 4%
2%
35%
48%

Foreign-born population as percent of total population

15% —
12% —
9% —
6% —
3% —
0% —
1850 1860 1870 1880 1890 1900 1910 1920 1930 1940 1950 1960 1970 1980

SOURCE: Population References Bureau Inc.

have been able to emigrate to the United States because they have few immediate relatives living in the United States. Congress has added a provision to the quota limits permitting 25,000 such persons to come each year. In recent times more than 600,000 immigrants each year have been given permanent resident status.

In addition, over 100,000 *political refugees* have been admitted each year. Political refugees are defined by law as persons who have well-founded fears of persecution in their own countries based on race, religion, nationality, social class, or political opinion. The base number allowed is 50,000 annually, but each year, after consultations with Congress, the president may set a higher number.

In addition, the attorney general, acting through the U.S. Immigration and Naturalization Service (INS), may grant *asylum* to persons already in the United

America, the land of liberty, was the dream of thousands of impoverished Europeans. Here a boatload of immigrants approaches New York harbor in 1906.

States, at ports of entry, or in countries other than their own if they have well-founded fears of persecution in their own countries based on race, religion, nationality, social class, or political opinion. It is not enough, however, that applicants for asylum face the same conditions, no matter how terrible, that all other citizens of their countries face or that they wish to escape from bad economic or political conditions. They must show *individual* danger of persecution. Although the Immigration and Naturalization Service may turn back at the border those seeking asylum when it considers their requests insubstantial, or hold them in detention camps, there is an elaborate and time-consuming review system of the claims for asylum.[4] But people are willing to risk great danger getting here and possible detention once they arrive, just for the possibility of asylum status.

UNDOCUMENTED ALIENS— THE IMMIGRATION REFORM AND CONTROL ACT OF 1986

Even more controversial than whom to admit is the question of how to deal with the variously estimated millions of aliens, mostly from Mexico and other nations in Central and South America, who have illegally crossed our borders, not because they fear political persecution but because they see greater economic opportunity in the United States.[5] It is not a question of constitutional power, for "over no conceivable subject is the legislative power of Congress more complete than it is over the admission of aliens."[6] Rather, the problems are more practical. The Immigration and Naturalization Service does not have the money or staff to patrol the thousands of miles of our southern and northern borders. Moreover, it is very difficult to track down undocumented aliens inside the United States, round them up, and expel them in a fashion consistent with the practices and policies of a free society. Once here, undocumented aliens do not find it hard to become invisible, especially in our larger cities, or to find jobs. Some employers prefer to hire them because they work for less money than those who are here lawfully.

In dealing with the problems presented by the large number of undocumented aliens, Congress has been faced with conflicting fears: from Hispanic groups who

Illegal aliens rushed to apply for the 1988 amnesty program that would grant them citizenship.

are concerned that making it illegal to hire undocumented workers will cause employers to hesitate to hire Hispanics; from employers who do not want to keep costly records; from employers of farm workers who want to be sure that they will have enough laborers to pick seasonal crops; from domestic workers who do not want itinerant workers from outside the United States to be used to keep wages low; from city and local governmental officials who have to find the funds to provide social services for undocumented aliens. To deal with these conflicting pressures, Congress enacted the Immigration Reform and Control Act, often known as Simpson-Rodino, in 1986.

The Act's several provisions are the outcomes of bargains designed to lessen these fears. First, the Act permitted undocumented aliens who could prove they have lived continuously in the United States since January 1, 1982, to apply for amnesty for a limited time. Second, employers who knowingly hire illegal aliens may be fined from $250 to $5,000 per alien, and repeat offenders may be given up to a six-month prison term. On the other hand, employers are also subject to penalty if they discriminate against legal residents because they were foreign born. Third, the Act allows a certain number of aliens to come into the United States to serve as temporary farm workers.

Of the estimated 2 to 3 million aliens eligible for amnesty under the Act, about 1.8 million applied for it by the May 4, 1987 deadline. Others did not apply because of costs, because of inability to document their status, and because of fear that they might expose family members to deportation. Those granted preliminary amnesty must now show minimum proficiency in English and knowledge of American government or face possible deportation. They can meet this requirement by taking forty hours of classroom instruction.

Many—especially immigrants themselves—are confused about what is to happen to those who came to the United States after the deadline and about the status of those who, although able to qualify for amnesty, did not apply for it. And since Simpson-Rodino appears not to have stemmed the tide of undocumented migration, the problems remain. Large members of undocumented aliens live and work here, and the number continues to increase.

In 1989 the Senate passed a bill that set a ceiling on the total number of aliens to be legally admitted in one year. The bill also changed the priorities used to determine who receives a visa. Preference for relatives of individuals currently living in the United States was ended, and a new category of "independent" immigrants who have special skills needed in the United States was given visa priority. The House is also considering these issues, and congressional action in the 1990s seems likely. What we do will affect not merely the internal politics of the United States, but our relations with other nations, most especially with Mexico. Whereas officials of the United States tend to view immigration policy as a matter of our sovereignty, "Mexicans see it as a bilateral process that requires a bilateral policy."[7]

RIGHTS OF ALIENS INSIDE THE UNITED STATES

While in the United States—no matter how they get here—aliens enjoy considerable constitutional protection. All aliens, it should also be noted, are "subject to the full range of obligations, including the payment of taxes, imposed by the states' civil and criminal laws."[8] Most of the provisions of the Constitution speak of the

Andres Martinez hugs his young nephew, who arrived in Miami with his family. His father, Raimundo Martinez, was one of eleven political prisoners released from Cuba with their families under a U.S.-Cuba immigration agreement.

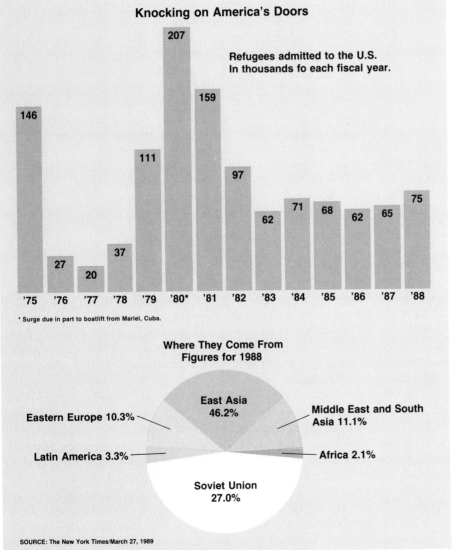

Knocking on America's Doors

Refugees admitted to the U.S. In thousands fo each fiscal year.

'75	'76	'77	'78	'79	'80*	'81	'82	'83	'84	'85	'86	'87	'88
146	27	20	37	111	207	159	97	62	71	68	62	65	75

* Surge due in part to boatlift from Mariel, Cuba.

Where They Come From
Figures for 1988

East Asia 46.2%
Middle East and South Asia 11.1%
Eastern Europe 10.3%
Africa 2.1%
Latin America 3.3%
Soviet Union 27.0%

SOURCE: The New York Times/March 27, 1989

rights of persons, not just of citizens. Congress and the states, for example, have no greater authority to interfere with an alien's freedom of religion than with a citizen's. State and local regulation of aliens is subject to "heightened" judicial scrutiny. In fact, the Supreme Court has ruled that states cannot keep children of undocumented aliens living within their boundaries from attending public schools free of charge.

Congress has wide discretion in setting the terms and conditions under which aliens come and stay in the United States. It even has the power to make retroactive conditions. Present laws make aliens, even those who are here legally, deportable for such things as conviction of two crimes involving moral turpitude, for joining organizations that advocate revolution, or for engaging in activities that the attorney general believes to be "subversive to national security."

Constitutional Protection of Property

Property does not have rights. People do. *Property rights* are the rights of an individual to own, use, rent, invest in, buy, and sell property. Historically, the close connection between liberty and ownership of property, between property and power, has been emphasized in American political thinking and American political institutions.

A major purpose of the framers of the Constitution was to establish a government strong enough to protect all people's rights to use and enjoy their own property. At the same time the framers wanted a government so limited that it could not endanger that right. They were disturbed by the efforts of some state legislatures to protect debtors at the expense of their creditors. As a result, they ensured that the Constitution forbids states from making anything except gold or silver *legal tender* for the payment of debts and from passing any law "impairing the obligation of contracts."

THE CONTRACT CLAUSE

The contract clause was designed to prevent states from extending the period during which debtors could meet their payments or otherwise get out of contractual obligations. The framers had in mind an ordinary contract between private persons. However, beginning with Chief Justice John Marshall, the Supreme Court expanded the coverage of the clause to prevent states from altering privileges previously conferred on a corporation.

In effect, the contract clause was used to protect vested property at the expense of the power of the states to guard the public welfare. In the 1880s, however, the Court gradually began to restrict the coverage of the contract clause and to subject contracts to what in constitutional law is known as **police powers**— the power to protect the public health, safety, welfare, and morals. By 1934 the Supreme Court actually held that even contracts between individuals—the very ones the contract clause was intended to protect—could be modified by state law in order to avert social and economic catastrophe.[9] Although the contract clause is still invoked occasionally to challenge a state regulation of property, it is no longer a significant limitation on governmental power.

EMINENT DOMAIN—WHAT HAPPENS WHEN THE GOVERNMENT TAKES OUR PROPERTY?

Both the national and the state governments have the power of **eminent domain**—the power to take private property for public use—but the owner must be fairly compensated. This limitation was the first provision of the Bill of Rights to be incorporated within the Fourteenth Amendment and thus to be made applicable to the states.

What constitutes a "taking" for purposes of the eminent domain clause?[10] Ordinarily, but not always, the taking must be direct, and a person must lose title and control over the property. The clause does not require compensation merely because governmental action may result in property loss; for example, if a zoning regulation restricts an area to single-family residential use and thus lowers the value of a particular property.

Sometimes, especially in recent years, the courts have found that a governmental regulation has gone "too far" and must be deemed a "taking" for which the government must pay compensation to its owners even when title is left in the hands of the owners.[11] Thus, if a government creates landing and take-off paths for airplanes over property adjacent to an airport such that the land is no longer suitable for its prior use (say, raising chickens), compensation is warranted. "Just compensation" is not always easy to define. In case of dispute, the final decision is made by the courts.

DUE PROCESS—NEW AND OLD

Perhaps the most difficult parts of the Constitution to understand are the clauses in the Fifth and Fourteenth Amendments that forbid national and state governments *to deny any person life, liberty, or property without due process of law*. These **due process clauses** have resulted in more Supreme Court decisions than any other provisions in the Constitution, although the equal protection clause runs a close second. Even so, it is impossible to explain due process precisely. The Supreme Court itself has refused to give "due process" a precise definition.

There are two kinds of due process: procedural and substantive. **Procedural due process** generally refers to the methods by which a law is enforced. But a law itself, as enacted, may violate the procedural due process requirement if it is too vague or if it creates an improper presumption of guilt. A vague statute fails to provide adequate warning and does not contain sufficient guidelines for law enforcement officials, juries, and courts (see accompanying box).

A statute that creates an improper presumption denies due process by shifting the burden from the government to prove guilt beyond a reasonable doubt. Laws presuming, for example, that all marijuana or cocaine in a person's possession must have been obtained illegally have been declared unconstitutional. Still, the Court did uphold such a presumption with respect to heroin; virtually all of it is illegally imported. It is therefore not unreasonable to presume that a person who possesses heroin obtained it illegally.

Traditionally, however, procedural due process refers to the way in which a law is applied. To paraphrase Daniel Webster's famous definition, it requires a procedure that *hears* before it condemns, proceeds upon inquiry, and renders judgment only after a trial or some kind of hearing. Originally, procedural due process was limited to criminal prosecutions, but it now applies to many different

> **Some Statutes Declared Void for Vagueness**
>
> A statute making it a crime to treat "contemptuously" the American flag.
>
> A vagrancy ordinance classifying vagrants as "rogues and vagabonds," "dissolute persons who go about begging," "common night walkers," and so on.
>
> An ordinance requiring persons who loiter or wander the streets to provide "credible and reliable" identification and to account for their presence when required by a police officer.

kinds of governmental proceedings. It is required, for instance, in juvenile hearings, disbarment proceedings, proceedings to determine eligibility for welfare payments, revocation of drivers' licenses, and disciplinary proceedings in state universities and public schools.

Procedural due process has taken on new importance with the expanded interpretation of the words "liberty" and "property." The liberty that is protected is more than freedom from being thrown into jail, and the property that is secured goes beyond mere ownership of real estate, things, or money. Rather, liberty includes "the right of the individual to contract, to engage in any of the common occupations of life, to acquire useful knowledge, to marry, to establish a home and bring up children, to worship God according to the dictates of his own conscience, and generally to enjoy those common law privileges long recognized as essential to the orderly pursuit of happiness of free men."[12] The property protected by the due process includes a variety of rights that may be conferred by state law, such as certain kinds of licenses, protection from being fired from some jobs except for cause and according to certain procedures, deprivation of certain pension rights, and so on.

This expansion of the meanings of liberty and property has blurred the distinctions between liberty rights and property rights. Moreover, it has lessened the difference between a right and a privilege. Today public welfare, housing, education, employment, professional licenses, and so on, are increasingly becoming matters of entitlement. Their denial thus involves some form of due process.

Nevertheless, "the range of interests protected by procedural due process is not infinite." Not every "grievous loss visited upon a person by the State is sufficient to invoke the procedural protections of the due process clause."[13] Whether or not an interest is protected by due process depends on the nature of the interest, not its importance to the individual. Faculty members in public institutions, for instance, are not entitled to procedural due process before being denied tenure, because they have no constitutional right to teaching jobs. However, public employees who are given tenure rights by law or institutional policies are entitled to due process before they may be deprived of property rights or jobs.[14]

"Once it is determined that due process applies, the question remains what process is due." What is due varies with the kind of interest involved, the reliability of the procedures used, and the governmental purposes to be served.[15] In a federal courtroom, due process requires the careful observance of the provisions of the Bill of Rights as outlined in Amendments Four through Eight. The question of what is due in other kinds of proceedings is what must be done to ensure *fundamental fairness.* It is hard to generalize because many kinds of proceedings are involved, but at a minimum the person involved must have *adequate notice* and *an opportunity to be heard.*

SUBSTANTIVE DUE PROCESS

Procedural due process places limits on *how* governmental power may be exercised; **substantive due process** places limits on *what* that power may be used to do, no matter how it is done. Procedural due process has to do with the *procedures* of the law; substantive due process has to do with the *content* of the law. Procedural due process mainly limits the executive and judicial branches; substantive due process mainly limits the legislative branch. Substantive due process means that an "unreasonable" law, even if properly passed and properly applied, is unconstitutional. It means that there are certain things governments should not be allowed to do, no matter how they do it.

"What's so great about due process? Due process got me ten years."

Drawing by Handelsman. © 1972 The New Yorker Magazine, Inc.

Before 1937 substantive due process was used primarily to protect "liberty of contract," that is, business liberty. Indeed, the adoption of the doctrine of substantive due process and the simultaneous expansion of the meaning of liberty and property made the Supreme Court, for a time, the final judge of our economic and industrial life. During this period the Supreme Court was dominated by conservative jurists who considered almost all social welfare legislation unreasonable. They used the due process clause to strike down laws regulating hours of labor, establishing minimum wages, regulating prices, and forbidding employers to fire workers for union membership.

The trouble with the substantive interpretation of due process is that what we think is a "reasonable" law depends on economic, social, and political views rather than on any narrow legal doctrine. In democracies, elected officials are supposed to accommodate opposing notions of reasonableness and to decide what regulations of liberty and property are needed to promote the public welfare. When the Supreme Court substitutes its own ideas of reasonableness for those of the legislature, it acts like a superlegislature.

In response to this criticism, the Supreme Court since 1937 has largely refused to apply the doctrine of substantive due process to review laws regulating our economy. The Court is now of the view that deciding what constitutes reasonable regulations of our business and commercial life is a *legislative*, not a judicial, responsibility. As long as the justices find a connection between a law and the promotion of the public welfare, the Supreme Court will not interfere.

Abandonment of substantive due process as a limit on the government's power to regulate business has not meant an abandonment of substantive due process. On the contrary. The word "liberty" in the Fifth and Fourteenth Amendments has been expanded to include the basic civil liberties. Substantive due process has been given new life as a limitation on governmental power regarding these liberties. Furthermore, since the 1950s the Supreme Court has developed a substantive interpretation of the equal protection clause to supplement the substantive interpretation of due process.

Prior to 1937 liberal justices (in dissent) and liberal commentators accused conservative justices of using substantive due process to impose their own ideas upon the nation. Today conservative judges are contending that once again the Supreme Court is going beyond the bounds of its responsibilities (see Chapter 17). Justices who support the current application of substantive due process of course deny they are merely substituting their own values for those of the legislature. They contend there is a fundamental difference between what they are doing in protecting civil liberties and what the pre-1937 conservative justices did to protect property rights. The earlier justices were writing into the Constitution the principles of laissez-faire economics, whereas the present justices are extracting from the Constitution its principles of civil liberties.

Justice Powell, in behalf of the Court, conceded:

Substantive due process has at times been a treacherous field for this Court. There are risks when the judicial branch gives enhanced protection to certain substantive liberties without the guidance of the more specific provisions of the Bill of Rights. . . . There is reason for concern lest the only limits to such judicial intervention become the predilections of those who happen at the time to be Members of this Court. . . . That history counsels caution and restraint. But it does not counsel abandonment of substantive due process.[16]

The notion that laws must be reasonable has deep roots in natural law

Some Laws Declared To Deny Substantive Due Process

A school board regulation requiring teachers to cease teaching past the fourth month of pregnancy and barring them from returning to the classroom until three months after the birth of a child.

A state law permitting confinement of nondangerous mentally ill persons against their wishes.

*Y*ou decide!

Scott E. Ewing was dismissed by the University of Michigan from a six-year combined undergraduate and medical educational program after failing an examination required to qualify for the final two years. His request to retake the examination was denied. He brought an action in a federal district court, alleging that because every other medical student who had failed the examination had routinely been given at least a second chance to take the test that he had a property interest in his continued enrollment in the program. He contended that his dismissal was arbitrary and capricious and was thus in violation of his substantive due process rights guaranteed by the Fourteenth Amendment. The University answered that he had been dismissed for proper academic reasons, that no one has a constitutional right to a second examination, and that what it had done was perfectly reasonable.

Did Ewing have a due process property interest to continued enrollment free from arbitrary state action?

Did the state of Michigan violate his substantive property right in this instance?

(Answer/Discussion on page 142)

concepts and a long history in the American constitutional tradition. For most Americans most of the time, it is not enough merely to say that a law reflects the wishes of the popular or legislative majority. We also want our laws to be just, and we continue to rely heavily on judges to decide what is just. In Chapter 17 we look again at the tensions between democratic procedures and judicial uses of substantive due process to review the constitutionality of the acts of elected officials.

THE RIGHT OF PRIVACY

Perhaps the most important part of the new interpretation of the meaning of due process in recent decades has been the expansion of the right of privacy, most especially marital privacy. Although there is no mention of the right of privacy in the Constitution, the Supreme Court has put together some elements from the First, Fourth, Fifth, Ninth, and Fourteenth Amendments to recognize that personal privacy is one of the rights protected by the Constitution. There are three aspects of this right: (1) the right to be free from governmental surveillance and intrusion, especially in marital matters; (2) the right not to have private affairs made public by the government; and (3) the right to be free in thought and belief from governmental compulsion.[17]

Congress showed some concern about privacy in the Family Educational Rights Act of 1974 and the Privacy Act of 1974. These laws limit record-keeping and record-disclosing activities of schools and universities that receive federal funds; place restraints on files kept by federal agencies; and, under certain conditions, give individuals access to government files in order to correct information about themselves. But privacy, although highly valued in the abstract, has often run afoul of other rights, for example, freedom of the press. When in conflict with these other rights, it has not fared well before either Congress or the courts.

The most controversial aspect of constitutional protection for privacy relates to marital privacy and the extent of state power to regulate abortions. In *Roe* v. *Wade*, decided in 1973, the Supreme Court ruled: (1) during the first trimester of a woman's pregnancy, it is an unreasonable and therefor unconstitutional interference with her liberty and privacy rights for a state to set any limits on her choice to have an abortion, or on her doctor's medical judgments about how to carry it out; (2) during the second trimester, the state's interest in protecting the health of women becomes compelling, and a state may make a reasonable regulation about how, where, and when abortions may be performed; and (3) during the third trimester, when the life of the fetus outside the womb becomes viable, the state's interest in protecting the unborn child is so important that the state can proscribe abortions altogether, except when necessary to preserve the life or health of the mother.

Sixteen years later, after heated public debate, a bitterly divided Rehnquist Court, although not overruling *Roe* v. *Wade*, repudiated its underlying trimester and viability rationale in *Webster* v. *Reproductive Health Services*. The Court majority held: (1) states may make reasonable regulations to insure that abortions are not performed when the fetus is viable; and (2) a state can prohibit the use of state resources in performing abortions. Thus the Supreme Court invited state regulation of abortions, and the highly charged battles between the pro-choice and pro-life groups were passed back to the state legislatures. Further lawsuits will have to determine the limits of legislative powers in this area.

Although there is debate as to how much constitutional protection is provided for marital privacy, the Supreme Court has refused to extend any such protection

Reprinted with special permission of NAS, Inc.

142

The highly emotional controversy over the Supreme Court's 1973 ruling on abortion boiled over again in 1989 when the Court agreed to rule on a challenge to that decision. Demonstrators on both sides of the question flooded Washington in an attempt to influence the Court.

to relations between gays. By a five to four vote the Court refused to declare unconstitutional a Georgia law that criminalized consensual sodomy as applied to homosexuals. The fact that homosexual conduct occurs in the privacy of the home, said the majority, does not affect the result. Justice Blackmun in dissent contended that the "Constitution embodies a promise that a certain private sphere of individual liberty will be kept largely beyond the reach of government," and that the Court has long recognized that certain *"decisions* are properly for the individual to make" and that there are certain *places*, such as the home, where the government should intrude only in extreme circumstances.[19]

Because of the strong emotions on both sides of this issue, the right of privacy as an element of substantive due process is one of the developing edges of constitutional law, one about which people both on and off the court have strong feelings. How the Supreme Court handles these issues has become front page news.

Freedom from Arbitrary Arrest, Questioning, and Imprisonment

James Otis's address in 1761 protesting arbitrary searches and seizures by English customs officials was the signal for the American Revolution. As John Adams later said of that speech: "American independence was then and there born." The Fourth Amendment states: "The right of the people to be secure in their persons, houses, papers, and effects, against unreasonable searches and seizures, shall not be violated, and no Warrants shall issue, but upon probable cause, supported by Oath or affirmation, and particularly describing the place to be searched, and the persons or things to be seized."

Edward Lawson, known as the California Walkman, brought a suit for damages against San Diego police after they had arrested him fifteen times. Lawson, who walked late at night in neighborhoods other than his own, won his case.

WHAT IS UNREASONABLE SEARCH AND SEIZURE?

Despite what we sometimes see in television police dramas and read in the press, law-enforcement officers have no general right to break down doors and invade homes. They are not supposed to search people except under certain conditions, and they have no right to arrest them except under certain circumstances. This is a highly technical area, and one in which the Supreme Court has had great difficulty in determining what the Constitution means.[20]

Arrests The Constitution does not forbid all searches and seizures, only "unreasonable" ones.[21] "Seizures," or what we now call police detentions and arrests, are in fact given less protection than searches. Police may arrest people without warrants in *public places*, provided they have *probable cause* to believe the people have committed or are about to commit crimes. Immediately after making an arrest, especially one made without a warrant, the police must take the arrested person to a magistrate so that the latter—not just the police—can decide whether probable cause existed to justify the warrantless arrest. Except in emergencies, more than probable cause is required to arrest people in their own homes without a warrant.

Deadly Force Under the common law police officers apprehending a fleeing felon could use weapons that might result in such a felon's serious injury, even death. But the Fourth Amendment places substantial limits on the use of "deadly force." It is unconstitutional to shoot at an apparently unarmed suspected fleeing felon unless the officer has probable cause to believe that the suspect poses a significant threat of death or serious injury to the officer or others. Also, when feasible, the officer must first warn the suspect—"Halt or I'll shoot."[22]

Searches For the most part (see accompanying box for exceptions), a police search without proper consent is constitutionally unreasonable, unless it has been authorized by a valid search warrant, issued by a magistrate after the police indicate under oath that they have "probable cause" to justify its issuance. Magistrates must perform this function in a neutral and detached manner and not serve merely as rubber stamps for the police.

The Constitution not only ordinarily requires a search warrant, but it also requires a specific one because **general search warrants** are unconstitutional. When a magistrate issues a warrant, the warrant must describe what places are to be searched and what things are to be seized. And a warrant is needed to search a person in any place he or she has an "expectation of privacy that society is prepared to recognize as reasonable," for example, in a hotel room, in a rented home, in a friend's apartment, or even in a telephone booth.[23] In short, the Fourth Amendment protects people, not places, from unreasonable governmental intrusions.

The Fourth Amendment protects against searches by government officers other than the police, such as public school teachers and officials, internal revenue agents, health inspectors, and occupational and safety inspectors. However, less stringent conditions apply to nonpolice searches. Although covered by the Fourth Amendment, public school officials, for example, may search a student when there

> **Search Warrants Are Not Required for Police Searches**
>
> 1. When searches are based on consent of the person searched.
> 2. Under certain conditions involving automobiles, including mobile motor homes.
> 3. When police briefly stop and quickly frisk possibly armed and dangerous persons, remove weapons from them, and search areas under their immediate control, such as the passenger compartment of an automobile. (Such a search is known as a *Terry* search because it was first sanctioned by the Supreme Court in *Terry* v. *Ohio*.*)
> 4. When police officers have a reasonable suspicion that the person in question was involved in or is wanted in connection with a felony. (This must be a "Terry" search.)
> 5. When police have an arrest warrant or probable cause to make an arrest, which allows them to make a complete search of the persons being arrested and the area under such persons' immediate control.

are "reasonable grounds for suspecting that the search will turn up evidence that the student has violated or is violating either the law or the rules of the school." Such a search is constitutionally permissible in its scope, when it is "not excessively intrusive in light of the age and sex of the student and the nature of the offense."[24]

In recent years Fourth Amendment questions have been raised about the constitutionality of testing blood and urine for drugs. Although agreeing that such tests intrude upon expectations of privacy and are searches within the meaning of the Fourth Amendment, the Supreme Court held that the federal regulations requiring such tests for railroad workers involved in accidents do not violate the Fourth Amendment, even as used without any warrant requirement. Justice Thurgood Marshall, bitterly dissenting, wrote, "the majority's acceptance of dragnet blood and urine testing ensures that the first, and worst, casualty of the war on drugs will be the precious liberties of our citizens. . . ." The Court has also upheld drug testing for some federal employees under some circumstances[25] (see Chapter 18.)

Scientific inventions have confronted judges with new problems in applying the Fourth Amendment. Obviously, the writers of the Fourth Amendment intended such physical objects as books, papers, letters, and other kinds of documents to be unseizable by police except on the basis of limited search warrants issued by magistrates. But what of overhearing phone conversations by tapping phone wires, or using electronic devices to eavesdrop, or using secret television cameras to make videotapes? In *Olmstead* v. *United States* (1928) a bare majority of the Supreme Court held there was no unconstitutional search unless seizure of physical objects or actual physical entry into a premise were involved. Justices Holmes and Brandeis, in dissent, argued that the Constitution should keep up with the times; the "dirty business" of wiretapping produced the same evil invasion of privacy the framers had in mind when they wrote the Fourth Amendment.[26]

Forty years later, in *Katz* v. *United States* (1967), the Supreme Court adopted the Holmes-Brandeis position: "The Fourth Amendment protects people—and not simply 'areas'—against unreasonable searches and seizures." "Wherever a man may be" (subsequently modified and limited to those places where one has an expectation of privacy that society is prepared to recognize as reasonable[27]), "he is entitled to know that he will remain free from unreasonable searches and seizures."[28]

THE EXCLUSIONARY RULE

Combining the Fourth Amendment prohibition against unreasonable searches with the Fifth Amendment injunction that persons shall not be compelled to be witnesses against themselves, the Supreme Court ruled, in *Mapp* v. *Ohio*, that evidence unconstitutionally obtained cannot be used in a criminal trial as part of the government's main case against persons from whom it was seized.[29] This exclusionary rule was adopted in large part to prevent police misconduct. Because police are seldom prosecuted for making illegal searches and are often unable to pay civil damages, the justices felt that the exclusionary rule was the best—and maybe the only—sanction.

Critics of the exclusionary rule, including Chief Justice Rehnquist, question why criminals should go free just because of police misconduct. So far the Supreme Court has refused to abandon the rule, yet it has started making some exceptions to it, such as when police have relied in good faith on a search warrant that subsequently turned out to be improperly granted.[30]

6. When incriminating evidence or contraband is in "plain view."

7. As part of the routine procedure incident to incarcerating an arrested person. Police can search articles in the possession of the person being arrested.

8. At international border crossings. This includes opening mail entering the country if officials have "reasonable cause" to suspect it contains merchandise imported contrary to the law. It also includes detention and bodily searches if customs officials have a reasonable ground to suspect smuggling of drugs or other contraband in bodily cavities.

9. On ships on the waterways of the United States, including inland waterways that provide access to the open seas.

10. When officers do not have time to secure a warrant to keep evidence from being destroyed or when there is a need "to protect or preserve life and avoid serious injury"; for example, when firefighters and police need to break into a burning building.

* *Terry* v. *Ohio*, 392 U.S. 1 (1968).

You decide!

At 1 A.M. on July 18, 1982, Ralph E. Watkinson was closing his shop for the night, when someone pointing a gun came toward him. Watkinson drew his own gun and fired, the fire was returned, and Watkinson was hit in the leg. He watched his assailant flee, apparently wounded on the left side. Later that night Rudolph Lee, Jr., suffering from a gunshot wound to his left chest, was identified by Watkinson as the man who shot him. Lee was charged with the crime. Shortly thereafter the Commonwealth of Virginia moved in a state court for an order directing Lee to undergo surgery to remove (in effect, search for) an object thought to be a bullet lodged under his left collarbone.

Does such a search violate the Fourth amendment?

(Answer/Discussion on next page.)

The Court has also narrowed the exclusionary rule to cover only trials of those from whom the evidence was unconstitutionally seized, as one citizen, Jack Payner, found out. Internal Revenue Service agents, aided by a private investigator and operating in the best tradition of television police dramas, broke into Payner's banker's hotel room while a female undercover agent lured the banker out to dinner. The agents "borrowed" the banker's briefcase, photographed documents, put the original documents back, and returned the briefcase. This "caper" was clearly a deliberate intrusion into the banker's privacy and a violation of his Fourth Amendment rights. Nonetheless, the evidence was allowed to be used to convict Payner, one of the banker's customers, of income tax evasion. Payner could expect neither privacy in his banker's briefcase nor any ownership of the documents taken from it.[31]

THE RIGHT TO REMAIN SILENT

During the seventeenth century certain special courts in England forced confessions of heresy and sedition from religious dissenters. The British privilege against self-incrimination developed in response to these practices. Because they were familiar with this history, the framers of our Bill of Rights included in the Fifth Amendment the provision that persons shall not be compelled to testify against themselves in criminal prosecutions. This protection against self-incrimination is designed to strengthen a fundamental principle of Anglo-American justice: No person has an obligation to prove innocence. Rather, the burden is on the government to prove guilt.

The privilege against self-incrimination applies literally only in criminal prosecutions, but it has always been interpreted to protect any person subject to questioning by any agency of government, for example a congressional committee. It is not enough, however, to contend that answers might be embarrassing or might lead to loss of a job or even to civil suits; persons must have a reasonable fear that the answers might support a criminal prosecution or "furnish a link in the chain of evidence needed to prosecute" a crime.[32]

Sometimes authorities would rather have answers from witnesses than prosecute them. Congress has established procedures so that prosecutors and congressional committees may secure a grant of immunity from a federal judge for such a witness. After immunity has been granted, a witness may no longer claim a right to refuse to testify. However, the only immunity Congress currently provides is that, except for perjury prosecution, the government cannot use the information directly derived from the testimony.

THE THIRD DEGREE

Police questioning of suspects is a key procedure for solving crimes. It can, however, be easily abused. Police officers sometimes forget or ignore the constitutional rights of suspects, especially of those who are frightened and ignorant. Unauthorized detention and sustained interrogation to wring confessions from suspects, common practices in police states, are not unknown in the United States.

What good is the presumption of innocence if, long before the accused are brought before the court, they are detained and forced to prove their innocence to the police? Judges have done much to stamp out police brutality. The Supreme Court has ruled that even though there may be sufficient evidence to support a conviction apart from a confession, the admission into evidence of a coerced confession violates the self-incrimination clause, deprives a person of the assistance of counsel guaranteed by the Sixth and Fourteenth Amendments, deprives a person of due process, and undermines the entire proceeding.

Federal and state laws require police officers to take those whom they have arrested before magistrates immediately so the magistrates may inform them of their constitutional rights and allow them to get in touch with friends and to seek legal advice. Despite these requirements, in the past police were often tempted not to take suspects directly to magistrates; if they could quiz suspects before they were informed of their constitutional right to remain silent, they could often get them to confess.

To put an end to such practices, the Supreme Court, in *Miranda* v. *Arizona* in 1966, announced that no conviction—federal or state—could stand if evidence introduced at the trial had been obtained by the police as the result of "custodial interrogation," unless the following conditions were met: Suspects have been (1) notified that they are free to remain silent; (2) warned that what they say may be used against them in court; (3) told that they have a right to have attorneys present during the questioning; (4) informed that if they cannot afford to hire their own lawyers, attorneys will be provided for them; and (5) permitted to terminate any stage of the police interrogation.

If suspects answer questions in the absence of an attorney, the burden is on the prosecution to demonstrate that the suspects knowingly and intelligently gave up their rights to remain silent and to have their own lawyers present. Failure to comply with these requirements leads to reversal of a conviction, even if other evidence is sufficient to establish guilt.[33]

Critics of the Miranda decision believe the Court has unnecessarily and severely limited the ability of the police to bring criminals to justice. The importance of pretrial interrogations is underscored by the fact that roughly 90 percent of all criminal convictions result from guilty pleas and never reach a full trial. Nevertheless, despite sustained attack, the Supreme Court has refused to reverse Miranda, although it has modified its original ruling to some extent. In order to deter perjury—lying under oath—if defendants make statements at their trials contrary to what they have previously told the police, evidence obtained contrary to the Miranda guidelines may be used to attack the credibility of such statements.

THE WRIT OF HABEAS CORPUS

Even though most of the framers did not think a Bill of Rights was necessary, they considered certain rights important enough to be included in the original Constitution. Foremost is the guarantee that the **writ of habeas corpus** will be available unless suspended in time of rebellion or invasion. Permission to suspend the writ is found in the article setting forth the powers of Congress, so, presumably, only Congress has the right to suspend it.

As originally used, the writ was merely an inquiry by a court to determine whether or not a person was being held in custody as the result of an act of a court with proper jurisdiction. But over the years it has developed into a remedy "available to effect discharge from any confinement contrary to the Constitution or fundamental law."[34] Simply stated, the writ is a court order directing any official having a person in custody to produce the prisoner in court and to explain to the judge why the prisoner is being held. Persons being held apply, usually through an attorney, for release and state why they believe they are being unlawfully held. The judge then orders the jailer to show cause why the writ should not be

---

The Crime Control and Safe Streets Act of 1968

1. Makes it a crime for any unauthorized person to tap telephone wires or use or sell in interstate commerce electronic bugging devices.
2. Empowers the United States attorney general to secure a warrant from a federal judge authorizing federal agents to engage in bugging in order to track down persons suspected of certain federal crimes.
3. Permits wiretaps without prior court approval for forty-eight hours in emergency situations involving certain crimes, such as child pornography, illegal currency transactions, offenses against crime witnesses, or immediate danger of death or serious injury.
4. Authorizes the principal prosecuting attorney of any state or political subdivision to apply to a state judge for a warrant approving wiretapping or oral intercepts for felonies. (Most state and local jurisdictions allow such intercepts.)
5. Permits judges to issue warrants only if they decide probable cause exists that a crime is being, has been, or is about to be committed, and that information relating to that crime may be obtained only by the intercept.

issued. If a judge finds a petitioner is being unlawfully detained, the judge may order the prisoner's immediate release.

The case of Messrs. Duncan and White is a good example of one use of the writ. Two years after Pearl Harbor, Duncan, a civilian shipfitter, was convicted by military authorities of assaulting two marine sentries. Eight months after Pearl Harbor, White, a stockbroker, was convicted by military authorities of embezzling stock from another civilian. Duncan and White both filed petitions for writs of habeas corpus in the district court of Hawaii, citing both statutory and constitutional reasons why the military had no right to try them and to keep them in prison. The court then asked the military to show cause why the petition should not be granted. The military replied that Hawaii had become part of an active theater of war; that the writ of habeas corpus had been suspended; that martial law had been established; and that, consequently, the district court had no jurisdiction to issue the writs. Moreover, the writ of habeas corpus should not be issued because the military trials of Duncan and White were valid. The district court, in an action eventually approved by the Supreme Court, agreed with Duncan and White and issued writs ordering their release.[35]

Although state judges lack jurisdiction to issue writs of habeas corpus to find out why persons are being held by national authorities, federal judges may do so to find out why persons are being restrained by state and local officials. Sometimes a single federal judge will set aside a conviction even after it has been reviewed by the state supreme court. Partly because of criticism by state judges, partly because of concern for the principles of federalism, and partly because of a growing overload on the federal courts, the Supreme Court has begun to restrict the use of habeas corpus by federal judges.[36] For example, if a state court has already provided an opportunity for persons to present the argument that the evidence used against them was unconstitutionally obtained, a federal district judge may no longer review the matter in a habeas corpus hearing.

Rights of Persons Accused of Crime

Considerable evidence in the popular press affirms that many people consider the rights of persons accused of crime to be less important than other civil liberties. But, as Justice Felix Frankfurter observed: "The history of liberty has largely been the history of observance of procedural safeguards." Further, these safeguards have frequently "been forged in controversies involving not very nice people."[37]

THE SHORT AND NOT TOO HAPPY LIFE OF JOHN F. (FEDERAL) CROOK

The rights of persons accused of crime by the national government can be found in the Fourth, Fifth, Sixth, and Eighth Amendments. In order to gain some idea of how these constitutional safeguards are applied, let us follow the fortunes and misfortunes of John F. Crook (a fictitious name).

John Crook sent circulars through the mails soliciting purchases of stock in a nonexistent gold mine—an action contrary to at least three federal laws. When postal officers uncovered these activities, they went to the district court and secured from a United States magistrate a warrant to arrest Crook and another warrant to search his home for copies of the circulars. They found Crook at home and read the *Miranda warning* to him, emphasizing especially his *right to remain silent* and *to have the assistance of counsel.* They showed him the warrants, arrested him for using the mails to defraud, and found and seized some of the circulars mentioned in the search warrant.

Crook was promptly brought before a federal district judge. (He could have had his preliminaries handled by a United States magistrate; see Chapter 17.) The judge again emphasized that Crook had a constitutional right to assistance of counsel. (Judges have a positive obligation to ensure that all persons subject to any kind of custodial interrogation are represented by lawyers.[38] Unless the record clearly shows that the accused were fully aware of what they were doing and gave up the right to counsel or intelligently exercised the right to represent themselves, the absence of such counsel will render criminal proceedings unconstitutional. The right extends to all trials for all offenses for which an accused was in fact deprived of liberty, whether or not a jury trial is required. Trials in which fines are the only penalty are exempt from the assistance-of-counsel requirement. This assistance is required at every stage of a criminal proceeding after the initiation of formal charges—preliminary hearings, bail hearings, trial, sentence, and first appeal.) When Crook told the judge he could not afford to hire his own counsel, the judge appointed an attorney paid for by the federal government to represent him.

At this point Crook had not been convicted of anything. In fact, he had not even been formally charged with any crime, and he was entitled to be free without having to pay *excessive bail*. Note that the Eighth Amendment does not require that bail be set, but forbids imposition of "*excessive* bail." Prior to the Supreme Court's decision in *United States* v. *Salerno* in 1987, it was generally thought that the Constitution required bail for all except capital crimes, and that bail higher than might reasonably be calculated to ensure the presence of a defendant at trial would be considered "excessive." Since persons are considered innocent until guilt has been determined by a trial, the sole constitutional justification for bail, it was thought, was to prevent flight before trial. But in *Salerno* the Court upheld the preventive detention provision of the Bail Reform Act of 1984 (there are similar laws in thirty or so states) authorizing federal judges to deny bail to "dangerous persons" charged with certain felonies. Suspects are entitled to a hearing on the matter within five days, and judges or a magistrate must explain in writing why they believe there is clear and convincing evidence that no condition of pretrial release can ensure the safety of other persons and the community.

In sustaining the law, Chief Justice Rehnquist speaking for the Court wrote, "We believe that when Congress has mandated detention on the basis of a compelling interest other than prevention of flight, as it has here, the Eighth Amendment does not require release on bail."[39] However, Crook's crime was not one covered by the Preventive Detention Act, and the judge having set his bail at $2500, Crook was held over until the convening of the next federal **grand jury**. After hiring a professional bondsman, who posted the bail and collected a 10 percent fee, Crook was free as long as he remained within the judicial district.

Except for members of the armed forces, the national government cannot require anyone to stand trial for a serious crime except *on grand jury indictment*. Grand jurors are concerned not with a person's guilt or innocence but merely with whether there is enough evidence to warrant a trial. No person has a right to appear before a grand jury, but one may be invited or ordered to do so. If a majority of the grand jurors agree that a trial is justified, they return what is known as a *true bill*, or *indictment*. When the next grand jury was convened, the United States district attorney brought evidence before the twenty-three jurors to indicate that Crook had committed a federal crime. In Crook's case the grand jury was in agreement with the United States district attorney and returned a true bill against Crook.

What Is an *Ex Post Facto Law* and a *Bill of Attainder*?

The Constitution forbids both the national and the state governments to pass ex post facto laws or enact bills of attainder (Article I, Sections 9 and 10).

An **ex post facto law** is a retroactive criminal law that works to the disadvantage of an individual. For example, a law making a particular act a crime that was not a crime when committed, increasing punishment for a crime after the crime was committed, or lessening proof necessary to convict for a crime after it was committed. The prohibition does not prevent the passage of retroactive penal laws that work to the benefit of an accused—a law decreasing punishment, for example—nor does the prohibition prevent passage of retroactive civil laws: Income tax rates as applied to income already earned may be increased.

A **bill of attainder** is a legislative act inflicting punishment, including deprivation of property, without judicial trial on named individuals or members of a specified group.

*Y*ou *decide!*

As a condition of receiving federally funded student financial aid men must attest that they have complied with the registration requirements of the selective service act.

Is this a bill of attainder?

(Answer/Discussion on next page.)

"Considering the overwhelming case load in our nation's judiciary, Your Honor, may I suggest you dismiss the charges against me?"

Drawing by Stevenson; © 1983 The New Yorker Magazine, Inc.

After a copy of the indictment was served on Crook, he was again ordered to appear before a federal district judge. The Constitution guarantees the accused *the right to be informed of the nature and cause of the accusation* so that he or she can prepare a defense. Consequently, the federal prosecutor took care that the indictment clearly stated the nature of the offense, and she saw to it that copies were properly served on Crook and his lawyer.

Actually, prior to his hearing, Crook's attorney discussed with the United States attorney's office the possibility of Crook's pleading guilty to a lesser offense. This kind of **plea bargaining** is used often. Faced with more cases than they can handle, prosecutors often prefer to accept a guilty plea to a reduced charge rather than prosecute for a more serious offense. Likewise, defendants are often willing to "cop a plea" to a lesser offense to avoid the risk of more serious punishment.

When defendants plead guilty, they are usually forever prevented from raising objections to their convictions. That is why, before accepting guilty pleas, judges question defendants to be sure that their attorneys have explained the alternatives and that they know what they are doing. It never came to this in Crook's case, however. After discussing the matter with his attorney, Crook elected to stand trial on the charge and entered a plea of not guilty.

After indictment, Crook's bail was raised to $5000. Now the federal government was obliged to give him *a speedy and public trial*. Do not, however, take the word "speedy" too literally. Crook had to be given time to prepare his defense. Defendants, in fact, often ask for delays, because delay often works to their advantage. If, in contrast, the government denies the accused a speedy trial in a constitutional sense, the remedy is drastic. Not only is the conviction reversed, but the case must be dismissed outright.

Crook's lawyer pointed out that under the Sixth Amendment, Crook had a right to trial before an *impartial jury* selected from the state and district in which the alleged crime was committed, because he was being tried for a serious crime, that is, one punishable by more than six months in prison or a $500 fine.[40] Although federal law requires juries of twelve, the Constitution requires only that juries consist of at least six persons. Conviction in federal courts must be by unanimous vote. (The Constitution permits state courts to render guilty verdicts by nonunanimous juries, provided such juries consist of six or more persons.) An impartial jury, and one that meets the requirements of due process and equal protection, consists of persons who represent a fair cross-section of the community. Although defendants are not entitled to juries on which there are necessarily members of their own race, sex, religion, or national origin, they are entitled to be tried by juries from which jurors have not been excluded for having these characteristics. (Such discriminatory action would also violate the civil rights of those denied the opportunity to serve on juries.)

In preparation for his defense, Crook told his lawyer he had dinner with George Witness on the night on which he was charged with sending the damaging circulars. The attorney took advantage of Crook's constitutional *right to obtain witnesses in his favor* and had the judge subpoena Witness to appear at the trial and testify. Although Witness could have refused to testify on the grounds that his testimony would tend *to incriminate* him, he agreed to do so. Crook himself, however, chose to use his constitutional right *not to be a witness against himself* and refused to take the stand. He knew that if he did so, the prosecution would have a right to cross-examination, and he was fearful of what might be uncovered. In order to protect Crook's right against self-incrimination, the judge conducting the trial was required to caution the jury against drawing any conclusions from Crook's decision not to testify. All prosecution witnesses appeared in court and were available for defense cross-examination; the Constitution also insists that accused persons have the *right to be confronted with the witnesses* against them.

At the conclusion of the trial, the jury brought in a verdict of guilty. The judge then raised Crook's bail to $10,000 and announced that she would hand down a sentence on the following Monday. The Eighth Amendment forbids the levying *of excessive fines* and the *inflicting of cruel and unusual punishments*. Furthermore, in the Sentencing Reform Act of 1984 Congress created a United States Sentencing Commission—whose members include three federal judges, appointed by the president with the consent of the Senate—to set sentencing guidelines to be used by all federal judges. The judge, in accordance with these guidelines, gave Crook the maximum punishment of a $10,000 fine and three years in the penitentiary. Such a sentence could not be considered cruel and unusual. Crook could have appealed both his sentence and his conviction to the Court of Appeals (see Chapter 17), but he chose not to do so.

Crook's case did not involve a capital offense. What of capital punishment in other cases? After much soul searching, and many cases, the Supreme Court has ruled that the death penalty is not necessarily cruel and unusual punishment when imposed for conviction of the crime of murder. (Such decisions are of more than passing interest to the well over one thousand people now under death sentence in thirty-two states. For about a decade after 1972, when the Supreme Court held in *Furman* v. *Georgia* that most death penalty statutes were unconstitutional because they left juries with undirected discretion, no persons were executed in the United States.[45] States have now revised their statutes, and executions are being carried out again.) The death penalty may, however, be imposed only on those convicted of crimes that have resulted in a victim's death, but the Court no longer insists that only the "triggerman" may be subject to such a penalty.[46]

A state must ensure that whoever imposes the death penalty—judge or jury—does so only after careful consideration of the character and record of the person and the circumstances of the particular crime. The automatic use of the death sentence for every person convicted of a specified capital offense is not acceptable: "It is essential that the capital sentencing decision allow for consideration of whatever mitigating circumstances may be relevant to either the particular offender or the particular offense."[47] The Court has suggested that the best procedure is first to have a jury determine guilt, and then, in a subsequent proceeding, to focus attention on whether the circumstances justify the death penalty.

RIGHTS OF PERSONS ACCUSED OF CRIMES AND THE NATIONAL BILL OF RIGHTS

While still in the federal penitentiary, Crook was taken by federal authorities before the state courts to answer charges that he had also committed a state crime. Because Crook was entitled to a speedy trial on these state charges, the state could not wait until he had been released by federal authorities before bringing him to justice.

Through his state-appointed attorney, Crook protested that he had already been tried by the federal government for using the mails to defraud. He pointed to the Fifth Amendment provision that no person shall be "subject for the same offense to be twice put in jeopardy of life or limb." This **double jeopardy** limitation, Crook's attorney pointed out, has been interpreted by the Supreme Court to be part of the Fourteenth Amendment and therefore to be a limit on the power of a state.[48] The judge answered: "The Supreme Court has said that double jeopardy prevents two criminal trials by the same government for the same criminal offense."

The ban against cruel and unusual punishments limits government in three ways:

1. It limits the kinds of punishment that may be imposed; for example, it prohibits using torture, intentionally denying medical care to prisoners, holding prisoners in inhumane conditions, or unnecessarily or wantonly inflicting pain.[41]

2. It prohibits punishments that are grossly disproportionate to the severity of the crime. However, outside the context of capital punishment—where the Court has limited the death penalty to crimes in which a life has been taken—the Court has been "reluctant to review legislatively mandated terms of imprisonment,"[42] and "successful challenges to the proportionality of particular sentences will be exceedingly rare."[43] The only noncapital punishment the Court has set aside for being cruel and unusual—and that by a vote of five to four—was a South Dakota court's sentence of a person to life in prison, without the possibility of parole, on his seventh conviction for relatively minor nonviolent felonies. The Supreme Court found that the defendant was being treated more severely by South Dakota than were criminals who had committed far more serious crimes, and more severely than he would have been in any other state, and that therefore his punishment was "significantly disproportionate."[44]

3. It limits the power of the government to decide what can be made a criminal offense. For example, the mere act of being a chronic alcoholic may not be made a crime because it is an illness. However, being drunk in public may be made a criminal offense.

(Trial by a state and one of its municipalities is trial by the same government; trial in a juvenile proceeding precludes another trial for the same offense by the state in its regular courts.) It does not prevent punishment by the national and the state governments for the same offense or for successive prosecutions for the same crime by two states, including even conviction by one government after acquital for the same offense by another sovereign.

What constitutional rights can Crook claim in the state courts? First, every state constitution contains a bill of rights listing practically the same guarantees found in the national Bill of Rights. Until recently, most state judges were less inclined than federal judges to interpret the constitutional guarantees of their own state constitutions liberally in favor of those accused of crime. Although, as we noted in Chapter 4, state judges are applying the bills of rights more liberally in their own state constitutions to protect the rights of persons accused of crimes, most cases still turn on the application of the provisions of the Bill of Rights of the national Constitution.

To what extent does the national Constitution protect courtroom procedures from state actions? As noted, the Bill of Rights does not directly apply to the states, but the Fourteenth Amendment does. The Fourteenth Amendment imposes on the states all the provisions of the Bill of Rights except those of the Second, Third, Seventh, and Tenth Amendments, and the grand jury requirements of the Fifth Amendment. No specific Supreme Court decision applies the excessive bail and fine limitation to the states. However, almost by definition, if a bail or fine is excessive, its imposition is likely to be considered a denial of due process.

The Supreme Court will probably not incorporate additional provisions; most lawyers, political scientists, and other observers believe states should be allowed to continue to indict persons for serious crimes by means other than grand juries. Eighteen states no longer require grand juries for any crimes; twenty-one require them only for felonies; and only eight require them for all except minor offenses. Other provisions not yet incorporated are really not applicable to the states.

How Just Is Our System of Justice?

What are the major criticisms of the American system of justice? How have they been answered?

TOO MANY LOOPHOLES

"The Court finds itself on the horns of a dilemma. On the one hand, wiretap evidence is inadmissable, and on the other hand, I'm dying to hear it."

Drawing by Handelsman; © *1972 The New Yorker Magazine, Inc.*

Some observers argue that by overprotecting the innocent and placing so much of a burden of proof on the government, we delay justice, encourage disrespect for the law, and allow guilty persons to go unpunished. Justice should be swift and certain without being arbitrary. But under our procedures criminals may go unpunished because: (1) the police decide not to arrest them; (2) the judge decides not to hold them; (3) the prosecutor decides not to prosecute them; (4) the grand jury decides not to indict them; (5) the jury decides not to convict them; (6) the judge decides not to sentence them; (7) an appeals court decides to reverse the conviction; (8) a judge decides to release them on a habeas corpus writ; or (9) if retried and convicted, the executive decides to pardon, reprieve, or parole them. As a result, the public never knows whom to hold responsible when laws are not enforced. The police can blame the prosecutor, the prosecutor can blame the police, and they can all blame the judges.

Police were accused of excessive use of force in putting down a demonstration in Tompkins Square Park in New York City in the summer of 1988.

Many critics blame the Supreme Court for imposing its own notions of justice on the country and for placing so many disabilities on police and prosecutors that these officials are finding it increasingly difficult to bring cases to conclusion. Others take a different view and point out that there is more to justice than simply securing convictions. All the steps in the administration of criminal laws have been developed over centuries of trial and error, and each step has been constructed to protect against particular abuses. History warns against entrusting the instruments of criminal law enforcement to a single officer. For this reason, responsibility is vested in many officials.

TOO UNRELIABLE

Critics who complain that our system of justice is unreliable often point to trial by jury as the chief source of trouble. Trial by jury, they argue, leads to a theatrical combat between lawyers who base their appeals on the prejudices and sentiments of the jurors. "Mr. Prejudice and Miss Sympathy are the names of witnesses whose testimony is never recorded, but must nevertheless be reckoned with in trials by jury."[49] No other country relies as heavily on trial by jury as does the United States. Jury trials are also time consuming and costly.

Defenders of the jury system reply that trial by jury provides a check by nonprofessionals on the actions of judges and prosecutors. Also, no evidence supports the charge that juries are unreliable. On the contrary, decisions of juries do not systematically differ from those of judges.[50] Moreover, the jury system helps to educate citizens and enables them to participate in the application of their own law.

The grand jury system has also come under attack. In theory, the grand jury has two functions: (1) to protect the innocent from having to stand trial by requiring prosecutors to demonstrate behind closed doors that they have evidence to justify trial; and (2) to provide an independent agency, not controlled by those in power, to investigate wrongdoing. Critics charge, however, that the grand jury has become a tool of the prosecutor. Said Justice Douglas: "It is, indeed, common knowledge that the grand jury, having been conceived as a bulwark between the citizen and the Government, is now a tool of the Executive."[51]

During the 1960s critics on the left of the political spectrum charged that grand juries had become instruments to intimidate radicals, blacks, and antiwar militants. However, by the 1970s grand juries were being used to investigate the executive branch. In the Watergate investigation it was through the use of the grand jury that the special prosecutor was able to present to the courts his contention that the president had no constitutional right to withhold information about wrongdoing. As the editors of the *Congressional Quarterly* pointed out:

> Liberals can applaud grand juries for investigating Watergate and denounce them for intimidating militants. Conservatives might just as easily reprove them for the former and commend them for the latter. The important question about grand juries is whether they are an effective instrument for protecting the innocent and bringing the guilty to trial. . . . On these questions, the jury is still out.[52]

DISCRIMINATION

During the last several decades, the Supreme Court has worked particularly hard to give reality to the ideal of equal justice under the law. Persons accused of crime who cannot afford attorneys must be furnished them at government expense. If transcripts are required for appeals, such transcripts must be made available to those who cannot afford to purchase them. If appeals are permitted, the government must also provide attorneys for at least one legal appeal of the decision of the trial court. Poor people cannot be imprisoned because of inability to pay a fine. Nor, once sentenced, can poor persons be kept in jail beyond the term of the sentence because they cannot afford to pay a fine. (Even for civil proceedings—divorce proceedings, for example—fees cannot be imposed that deny poor persons their fundamental rights, such as the right to obtain a divorce. A state has no obligation, however, to waive fees for those seeking to be declared bankrupt. The Court apparently believes that people have a constitutional right to be absolved of the ties that bind but not of their debts.)

Yet it remains true that racial and ethnic discrimination in the criminal justice system, especially outside the courtroom, persists. How much it persists is hard to measure. The editors of the *Harvard Law Review* believe it is significant. "Racism still pervades the United States criminal justice system," they charge, including police conduct, prosecutorial actions, bias among jurors, and in the sentencing process.[53] They blame the persistence of racism in the criminal justice system in part on the Supreme Court's requirement that, except in cases involving juror selection, litigants cannot legally prove racism through general evidence about racism in the system. They must show through direct evidence relating to their particular cases the discriminatory intent of the decision maker and the adverse consequence flowing from this intent to their case.[54] One person close to the subject comes to a different conclusion. He finds "about 80 percent of the black overrepresentation in prison can be explained by differential involvement in crime and about 20 pecent by subsequent racially discriminatory processes."[55] Or as he put it, "That is not at all to say that racial discrimination within the criminal justice system is unimportant; it certainly is important. What is suggested is only that it is relatively less important than other discriminatory pressures"[56] in society in general outside the criminal justice system.

One of the more acute problems of our society is the tension between the police and the black and Hispanic communities congregated in the ghettos and

"I TAKE THE IRAN-CONTRA DEFENSE—I WOULDN'T HAVE HAD TO BREAK ANY LAWS IF YOUR STUPID LAWS HAD FIT IN WITH WHAT I WANTED TO DO"

From Herblock at Large (*Pantheon Books, 1987*).

barrios of our large cities. Many members of minorities do not believe they have equal protection under the law. "Whether the stated belief is well founded or not is at least partly beside the point. The existence of the belief is damaging enough."[57] Blacks consider the police to be enforcers of white law. Studies proving prejudice on the part of some white police officers and examples of rough, if not brutal, police treatment of blacks are ample evidence to support their viewpoint. The general pattern, however, is that minorities are being shot by the police at rates approximately proportional to rates of minorities in street crime, but "there is a slight added increment and all you can conclude is the data support what common observation and folk tales make very clear—there is an element of racial prejudice in police shooting at minorities."[58]

In recent decades action has been taken to recruit more blacks, Hispanics, and women to police forces. Community relations programs have been established. Considerable progress has been made, and tensions between police and minority communities appear to be improving.

The Supreme Court and Civil Liberties

Clearly, judges—especially those on the Supreme Court—play a major role in enforcing constitutional guarantees. In fact, this combination of judicial enforcement and written guarantees of enumerated liberties is one of the basic features of the American system of government. As Justice Jackson wrote:

> The very purpose of a Bill of Rights was to withdraw certain subjects from the vicissitudes of political controversy, to place them beyond the reach of majorities and officials and to establish them as legal principles to be applied by the courts. One's right to life, liberty, and property, to free speech, a free press, freedom of worship and assembly, and other fundamental rights may not be submitted to vote: they depend on the outcome of no elections.[59]

This emphasis on constitutional limitations and judicial enforcement is an example of the "auxiliary precautions" James Madison believed were necessary to prevent arbitrary governmental action. In other free nations citizens rely more on elections and political checks to protect their rights; in the United States we appeal to judges when we fear our freedoms are in danger.

Such reliance on judicial protection of our civil liberties focuses attention on the Supreme Court. Yet only a small number of controversies are actually carried to the Supreme Court, and a Supreme Court decision is not the end of the policy-making process. Lower court judges as well as police, superintendents of schools, local prosecutors, school boards, state legislatures, and thousands of others give reality to the Court's doctrines.

The Supreme Court can do little unless its decisions reflect a national consensus. Judges by themselves cannot guarantee anything; neither can the First Amendment. As Justice Robert Jackson once asked:

> Must we first maintain a system of free political government to assure a free judiciary to guarantee free government? . . . It is my belief that the attitude of a society and of its organized political forces, rather than its legal machinery, is the controlling force in the character of free institutions. . . . Any court which undertakes by its legal processes to enforce civil liberties needs the support of an enlightened and vigorous public opinion. . . .[60]

Thus, the Bill of Rights—and the other procedural and substantive liberties of our Constitution—cannot rest on a foundation merely of tradition. The preservation of these rights depends on wide, continuing, and knowledgeable public support. Inevitably that public support will be tested—sometimes sorely tested—in the years to come.

Summary

1. One of the basic distinctions between a free society and a police state is that in a free society there are effective restraints on the way public officials, especially law-enforcement officials, perform their duties. In the United States these constitutional restraints are judicially enforceable.

2. The Constitution protects the acquisition and retention of citizenship. It protects the basic liberties of citizens as well as aliens.

3. The Constitution protects our property from arbitrary governmental interference, although debates about which interferences are reasonable and which are arbitrary are not easily settled.

4. The Constitution imposes limits not only on the procedures government must follow but also on the ends it may pursue. Some actions are out of bounds no matter what procedures are followed. Legislatures have the primary role in determining what is reasonable and what is unreasonable. However, the Supreme Court continues to exercise its own independent and final review of legislative determinations of reasonableness, especially on matters affecting civil liberties and civil rights.

5. The framers knew from their own experiences that in their zeal to maintain power and to enforce the laws, public officials are often tempted to infringe on the rights of those accused of crimes. To prevent such abuse, the Constitution imposes detailed procedures national officials must follow in order to make searches and arrests and to bring people to trial.

6. The Supreme Court interprets the Constitution, especially the Fourteenth Amendment, to impose on state and local governments almost the same restraints in the administration of justice as it imposes on the national government.

7. The Supreme Court continues to play a prominent role in developing public policy to protect the rights of the accused, to ensure that the innocent are not punished, and to guarantee that the public is protected against those who break the laws. The Court's decisions influence what the public believes and how police officers and others involved in the administration of justice behave. But the Court alone cannot—and should not—guarantee fairness in the administration of justice.

Further Reading

BLASI, VINCENT, ed. *The Burger Court: The Counter Revolution That Wasn't* (Yale University Press, 1983).

ABRAHAM S. BLUMBERG. *Criminal Justice: Issues and Ironies*, 2d ed. (New Viewpoints, 1979).

JAMES V. CALVI and SUSAN COLEMAN. *American Laws and Legal Systems* (Prentice Hall, 1989).

ALAN M. DERSHOWITZ. *The Best Defense* (Random House, 1982).

MACKLIN FLEMING. *The Price of Perfect Justice* (Basic Books, 1974).

NATHAN GLAZER, ed. *Clamor at the Gates: The New American Immigration* (ICS Press, 1985).

JOHN GUINTHER. *The Jury in America* (Facts on File Publications, 1988).

DAVID J. HIRSCHEL. *Fourth Amendment Rights* (Lexington Books, 1979).

MARY M. KRITZ, ed. *U.S. Immigration and Refugee Policy* (Heath, 1982).

JAMES S. KUNEN. *How Can You Defend Those People? The Making of a Criminal Lawyer* (Random House, 1983).

STUART NAGEL, ERIKA FAIRCHILD, AND ANTHONY CHAMPAGNE. *The Political Science of Criminal Justice* (Charles C Thomas, 1983).

DAVID M. O'BRIEN. *Privacy, Law and Public Policy* (Praeger, 1979).

JOSEPH E. SCOTT AND TRAFIS HIRSCHI, ed. *Controversial Issues in Crime and Justice* (Sage Publications, 1988).

CHARLES E. SILBERMAN. *Criminal Violence and Criminal Justice* (Random House, 1978).

LLOYD WEINREB. *Denial of Justice: Criminal Process in the United States*, 2d ed. (Free Press, 1979).

NORMAN L. AND NAOMI FLINK ZUCKER. *The Guarded Gate: The Reality of American Refuge Policy* (Harcourt Brace Jovanovich, 1987).

Notes

1. Martin Edelman, *Democratic Theories and the Constitution* (State University of New York Press, 1984), p. 304.
2. *Vance v. Terrazas*, 444 U.S. 252 (1980).
3. 16 *Wallace* (1873).
4. Arnold H. Leibowitz, "The Refugee Act of 1980: Problems and Congressional Concerns." *The Annals* (May 1983), pp. 163–71. See also Gil Loescher and John Scanlan, *Calculated Kindness: Refugees and America's Half-Open Door, 1945 to Present* (Free Press, 1986).

5. The National Research Council concluded that the number is between 2 to 4 million; other studies have estimated it to be as high as 12 million. Many cite 6 million as the correct number; government officials use the figure 3.9 million. See Gaylord Shaw, "Number of Illegal Aliens in U.S. May Be as Low as 2 Million, New Study Contends," *Los Angeles Times* (June 25, 1985), and The Bilateral Commission on the Future of United States-Mexican Relations, *The Challenge of Interdependence: Mexico and the United States* (University Press of America, 1989), p. 185.
6. *Kleindienst* v. *Mandel*, 408 U.S. 753 (1972).
7. Bilateral Commission, *The Challenge of Interdependence*, p. 77.
8. Justice Brennan in *Phyler* v. *Doe*, 457 U.S. 202 (1982). See also Paul Yoshihashi, "Employer Sanctions and Illegal Workers," *The Wall Street Journal*, May 26, 1989, p. B1.
9. *Home Building & Loan Assn.* v. *Blaisdell*, 290 U.S. 398 (1934).
10. Richard A. Epstein, *Taking: Private Property and the Power of Eminent Domain* (Harvard University Press, 1985).
11. *First Lutheran Church* v. *Los Angeles County*, 482 U.S. 304 (1987).
12. *Meyer* v. *Nebraska*, 262 U.S. 390 (1923).
13. *Meachum* v. *Fano*, 427 U.S. 215 (1976).
14. *Cleveland Bd. of Education* v. *Loudermill*, 470 U.S. 532 (1985).
15. *Morrissey* v. *Brewer*, 408 U.S. 471 (1972).
16. *Moore* v. *City of East Cleveland*, 431 U.S. 494 (1977).
17. Philip B. Kurland, *Some Reflections on Privacy and the Constitution* (The University of Chicago Center for Policy Study, 1976), p. 9. A classic and influential article about privacy is S. D. Warren and L. D. Brandeis, "The Right to Privacy," *Harvard Law Review* (December 15, 1890), pp. 193–220.
18. *Roe* v. *Wade*, 410 U.S. 113 (1973); *Webster* v. *Reproductive Health Services, Daily Appellate Report*, July 6, 1989, p. 8724.
19. *Bowers* v. *Hardwick*, 478 U.S. 186 (1986).
20. The most comprehensive analysis of these complicated issues is Wayne R. LaFave, *Search and Seizure: A Treatise on the Fourth Amendment*, 2d ed. (West Publishing, 1987).
21. Jeffrey A. Segal, "Predicting Supreme Court Cases Probabilistically: The Search and Seizure Cases, 1962–1981," *The American Political Science Review* (December 1984), pp. 891–900.
22. *Tennessee* v. *Garner*, 471 U.S. 1 (1985).
23. *Florida* v. *Riley*, 102 L Ed 2d 835 (1989).
24. *New Jersey* v. *T.L.O.*, 469 U.S. 365 (1985).
25. *Skinner* v. *Railway Labor Executives, Los Angeles Daily Appellate Journal*, March 22, 1989.
26. 277 U.S. 438 (1928).
27. For a recent case dealing with this standard involving the reasonableness of expecting privacy from police helicopter searches, see *Florida* v. *Riley*, 102 L Ed 2d 835 (1989).
28. 389 U.S. 347 (1967).
29. 367 U.S. 643 (1961).
30. *United States* v. *Leon*, 468 U.S. 897 (1984).
31. *United States* v. *Payner*, 447 U.S. 727 (1980).
32. *Blau* v. *United States*, 340 U.S. 332 (1951).
33. 384 U.S. 436 (1966). Liva Baker, *Miranda: Crime, Law and Politics* (Atheneum, 1983), explores every aspect of the decision, including subsequent controversy about its effects.
34. *Presier* v. *Rodriguez*, 411 U.S. 475 (1973).
35. *Duncan* v. *Kahanamoku*, 327 U.S. 304 (1946).
36. William F. Duker, *A Constitutional History of Habeas Corpus* (Greenwood Press, 1980).
37. Dissenting in *United States* v. *Rabinowitz*, 339 U.S. 56 (1950).
38. *Johnson* v. *Zerbst*, 304 U.S. 458 (1938); *Gideon* v. *Wainwright*, 372 U.S. 335 (1963). Anthony Lewis, *Gideon's Trumpet* (Random House, 1964 and 1972), has become a classic on this issue.
39. *United States* v. *Salerno*, 481 U.S. 739 (1987).
40. *Blanton et al.* v. *City of North Las Vegas*, March 8, 1989.
41. *Rhodes* v. *Chapman*, 452 U.S. 337 (1981).
42. *Hutto* v. *Davis*, 454 U.S. 370 (1982).
43. *Solem* v. *Helm*, 463 U.S. 277 (1983).
44. Ibid.
45. *Furman* v. *Georgia*, 408 U.S. 238. See Raoul Berger, *Death Penalties: The Supreme Court's Obstacle Course* (Harvard University Press, 1982), for an attack on the Court for interfering with states' rights to impose the death penalty. See also Hugo Adam Bedau, *The Death Penalty in America*, 3d ed. (Oxford University Press, 1982), for a more balanced collection of readings by an opponent of the death penalty.
46. *Tison* v. *Arizona*, 481 U.S. 137 (1987).
47. *Roberts* v. *Louisiana*, 431 U.S. 633 (1977).
48. *Benton* v. *Maryland*, 395 U.S. 784 (1969).
49. Jerome Frank, *Courts on Trial* (Princeton University Press, 1949), p. 122. See also Rita James Simon, ed., *The Jury System in America: A Critical Overview* (Sage Publications, 1975). For more recent coverage, see John Guinther, *The Jury in America* (Facts on File Publications, 1988).
50. Harry Kalven, Jr., and Hans Zeisel, *The American Jury* (University of Chicago Press, 1971), pp. 57 ff.
51. *United States* v. *Mara*, dissenting, 410 U.S. 19 (1973).
52. "The Supreme Court; Justice and the Law," *Congressional Quarterly* (1973), p. 93. See also Leroy D. Clark, *The Grand Jury: The Use and Abuse of Political Power* (Quadrangle, 1975), a critical account calling for reform of the grand jury.
53. "Race and the Criminal Process, *Harvard Law Review*, vol. 101 (May 1988), p. 1493.
54. Ibid, p. 1476.
55. Norval Morris, quoting Dean Alfred Blumstein and Joan Petersilia in "Race and Crime: What Evidence Is There That Race Influences Results in the Criminal Justice System?" *Judicature* (August–September 1988), p. 112.
56. Morris, "Race and Crime," p. 112.
57. George Edwards, *The Police on the Urban Frontier* (Institute of Human Relations Press and The American Jewish Committee, 1968), p. 28.
58. Morris, "Race and Crime," p. 113.
59. *West Virginia State Board of Education* v. *Barnette*, 319 U.S. 624 (1943).
60. Robert H. Jackson, *The Supreme Court in the American System of Government* (Harvard University Press, 1955), pp. 81–82.

7

Political Culture and Ideology

The American political tradition is based on a pragmatic ideology and characterized by optimism, idealism, and a heavy dose of nationalism. In addition to our Bill of Rights freedoms treated in the previous chapters, we Americans believe in a lot of principles—liberty, order, private property, political equality, equality of opportunity, progress, individualism, democracy, capitalism, discipline, and moderation—not all of which are wholly compatible.

But these sometimes clashing values trouble us little. "The marvelous success and vitality of our institutions is equalled by the amazing poverty and inarticulateness of our theorizing about politics," writes historian Daniel Boorstin. "No nation has ever believed more firmly that its political life was based on a perfect theory. And yet no nation has ever been less interested in political philosophy or produced less in the way of theory."[1]

Although we have more beliefs in common than we have that divide us, our politics is full of name calling and labeling of one sort or another. Thus George Bush faulted his 1988 presidential opponent as a "way-out liberal," and critics of Judge Robert Bork's nomination to the Supreme Court in 1987 said the flaw they found in him was not that he was a conservative but that he was not a "true conservative." He was, they accused, an "extremist" and "out of the mainstream." National Democratic Party Chairman Ron Brown says he prefers his party to be called "progressive," not liberal, "a party concerned about human needs . . . a party that says that we have a great country, the greatest on the face of the earth, but we're not satisfied with that and we can do better." New York Governor Mario Cuomo insists that such labels as liberal and conservative are meaningless. Cuomo calls himself "a progressive pragmatist."[2]

Confusion abounds when it comes to political categories. Thus it is said of some politicians: "His heart is on the left, but his wallet's on the right." Or, "She is a fiscal conservative but a liberal on civil rights and social issues." Labels abound: Libertarian, Marxist, Radical Feminist, Reactionary, "Tree-Hugger," Populist, Mugwump, Zealot, Liberationist, Flaming Moderate, Rightist, Leftist, Middle-winger, and on and on. Name-calling is often not an innocent activity; rather it is often designed to win votes and discredit opponents. Somehow in a democracy a line must be drawn between fair criticism and the type of mean-spirited name calling that questions a person's integrity and patriotism. We hope the following discussion meets this test.

This chapter defines and examines America's common political values as well as the beliefs and tensions that divide us. There is what can be called an American Creed—a set of beliefs about the dignity of the individual, the proper role of government, and aspirations of a government by and on behalf of the people. Yet we also highlight enduring tensions in the ideological makeup of American political life. These tensions tend to focus on the compatibility or incompatibility of liberty and equality, our simultaneous desire for political equality, and our deep-seated commitment to free-enterprise capitalism. Clearly, we differ in our views about how much of a role government should play to promote the general welfare. We differ too, and often sharply, in our tolerance about the rights of individuals and the means by which individuals should be able to exercise their constitutional rights. Ideological differences also play an important role in fights over public policy in America.

What do we mean by the term **ideology?** We use it to refer to the structure of a person's ideas or beliefs about political values and the role of government and political power. Ideology refers to the political and economic views we develop as we mature. These views are about how government works and how government should work, and they link our basic values to the day-to-day operations or policies of government. Most people are not deeply "ideological" in the sense that—unlike legislators, lobbyists, or party activists—the average citizen does not spend a lot of time thinking about government and public policies. Still, all of us have values and sometimes fiercely held views.

Our ideological values provide us with a lens through which we view politics. Our ideology helps simplify the complexities of politics, policies, personalities, and programs. Our views are acquired in a vague way when we are young, reinforced and recast in schools, churches, families, and neighborhoods, and further shaped by the media, major events, and the rhetoric of political campaigns. An ideology may be an accurate or an inaccurate description of reality, yet it is still the way we think about people, power, and society. Ideologies have consequences. Ideologies, collectively held, shape social and political institutions and help determine public policies and constitutional change.

Let's first look at several of our shared values—the political values and civic beliefs that bind us together and help define the American civic culture.

"I'm surprised, Marty. I thought you were one of us."

Drawing by Zeigler; © 1983 The New Yorker Magazine, Inc.

Political Culture

Political scientists use the term **political culture** to refer to a set of widely shared beliefs, values, and norms concerning the relationship of citizens to government and to one another. As our earlier chapters emphasized, Americans have always been united by their commitment to liberty. Equally important has been the belief that government should exist to serve the people, rather than the other way around.

No value in the American political culture is more revered than freedom or liberty. "We have always been a nation obsessed with liberty. Liberty over authority, freedom over responsibility, rights over duties—these are our historic preferences," wrote the late Clinton Rossiter, a well-known political scientist. "Not

American values are taught to children in school very early in life.

the good man, but the free man has been the measure of all things in this 'sweet land of liberty'; not national glory but individual liberty has been the object of political authority and the test of its worth."[3]

The American political culture is the sum of our most pronounced shared values. Support for the Constitution and the Bill of Rights is a hallmark of our civic culture. We may differ, as we have noted, over what certain constitutional provisions require or over precise meaning of the framers' original intentions. Yet the Constitution itself is worshiped as a national symbol, and Americans view being "unconstitutional" as exceedingly close to being "un-American."

What shapes our political culture is the persisting commitment to the individual. Political scientist Everett Carll Ladd summarizes the central features well:

> According to the ideology, society in general and government in particular exist, or should exist, to fulfill the rights of each to 'life, liberty and the pursuit of happiness.' To realize their rights fully, individuals must have freedom, the opportunity to make their own choices with a minimum of restraint. The worth of each individual should be seen as equal.[4]

What are the other values Americans share? In addition to a reverence for the Constitution and the Bill of Rights, we also strongly favor a two-party system, regular elections, and the dream—often called the "American Dream"—that everyone has an equal chance to succeed. A set of shared values that underlie our politics and give our nation strength and resilience are summarized in the box on this page. In our examination of political differences later in this chapter, it will become evident that we Americans too often ignore the values that bind us together.

Politically, Americans are often said to be moderate and pragmatic. Studies repeatedly suggest that we Americans, even though we may not vote in large numbers, are more supportive of our political system, more patriotic, and more likely to know how to influence our elected officials and political bureaucracies than people in other political democracies.[5] Thus, in contrast to citizens of most other Western democracies and presumably any authoritarian nation, most Americans believe people should be active in political life, and that they can do something about unjust public regulations or policies at all levels of our government.

CHAPTER 7 / Political Culture and Ideology

We know our system isn't perfect. We often grumble about our elected national officials losing touch with the common people. And we are disgusted by too many scandals and the slowness of the system to solve problems like the deficit and drugs. Yet we believe that people in the minority should be free to try to win majority support for their opinions. We also generally think that no matter what a person's political beliefs, he or she is entitled to the same legal rights and protections as anyone else. And most Americans also believe in free speech, no matter what another person's views might be. Clearly, however, we honor many of these rights more generously in the abstract than in particular situations. Unfortunately, intolerance of offensive views is amply documented in most public opinion polls and is observed clearly on college and university campuses as well. Liberals and conservatives alike can be intolerant of what they view as "wrongheaded" or extremist views that differ from theirs. Still, Americans can ordinarily be characterized as affirming support for democratic and constitutional values.

Indeed, recent studies, if you can believe opinion polls, indicate that Americans favor even more democracy. They would, for example, abolish the electoral college and have us vote directly for president. Americans also seem to favor constitutional amendments that would provide for a national referendum on issues and for the right to **recall** (that is, discharge officials from office before their term has expired through special elections) members of Congress and presidents who become irresponsible or corrupt.[6]

Americans, as a general rule, are also highly nationalistic. Americans are proud of their past and tend to deemphasize, or even forget, past intolerance, diplomatic and military setbacks, the shame of slavery, and denial for more than a century of suffrage to women. Americans also make a big to-do about the "American Dream." The American Dream, it is often emphasized, is all about people, not government. It is about people and citizens who believe they are above and more important than government. It is also about opportunity, choice, options, and individualism. Most of all, it is about freedom to improve oneself and to achieve success with as little interference as possible from others or the government. To its staunchest supporters the last thing the American Dream is about is taxation, governmental regulation, and bureaucratic rules.

But any serious discussion of the American Dream must quickly acknowledge that there are perhaps as many American Dreams as there are Americans. The beliefs people hold most dear are often called *myths* or *dreams*. These help hold societies together, and they can be powerful. Sometimes they are more powerful than logic, because usually they cannot be refuted. Is it any wonder that shrewd political leaders have seen the importance of myths and dreams and have often used them to acquire power? Plato argued that rulers should invent myths even when they know them to be wrong. Machiavelli, the brilliant observer of politics in Renaissance Italy, advised princes to use religion and myth as an aid to power. Dreams and myths have a different look today than in former times, yet they are no less important.

Even when the ideas people espouse are repugnant, Americans affirm their right to express them, as in the case of this demonstration by a group of "skinheads."

Ideology and the American Dream

The official philosophy in America, of course, is that America has no official philosophy. We do have a rather general body of ideas and values that serves as a rough but persisting guide to our civic and political actions and helps to define us as a people and as a nation. But we have no unified, consistent, and well-defined

Lincoln Memorial

ideology. Indeed, many of the myths and dreams by which Americans live contradict one another. In part, this is because values from one era have been carried over uncritically into new situations; it is also part of American pragmatism to hold contradictory beliefs simultaneously without bothering to resolve the potential conflicts between them.

We do not mean to stress the uniqueness of the American people, as if America were isolated from the rest of the world. The American Dream has much in common with the aspirations of most peoples: peace, prosperity, personal ownership of property, personal liberty, and the belief that individuals are free to achieve any goals, to accumulate material wealth, to live any lifestyle. Ralph Waldo Emerson wrote: "The office of America is to liberate, to abolish kingcraft, priestcraft, castle, monopoly, to pull down the gallows, to burn up the bloody statute-book, to take in the immigrant, to open the doors of the sea and the fields of the earth." All should have the chance to chart their own courses, to become rich, to be elected president, to mold their own destinies—to go as far as their abilities permit.

Some consider the "American Dream" to be a misleading term used by the middle and upper classes to fool the poor and unemployed into thinking their lives can be improved. Others point out that even though the dream has become a reality for some white Anglo-Saxon males, it has not been fulfilled for millions of others who suffer discrimination, unemployment, and substandard housing and medical care. For these millions the dream has often been a nightmare. Equality of opportunity is a bitter myth for those who cannot get a decent education, who are generally unorganized and unrepresented politically, and who do not know how to make the system work for them. These people have understandably become disillusioned and embittered. But however contradictory and paradoxical, our dream nonetheless exists, and it helps shape how most Americans conduct their lives and respond to government and its policies.

Central to the American Dream is the notion that this is the land of opportunity for the enterprising. Here the competitive, practical go-getter can make a fortune or build a dream home. The achievement, self-help, or success ethic is so strong here—and always has been—that some people believe the prime function of the state is to assist private individuals in the production of wealth and the protection of property. (See the box on Contending American Dreams.)

This part of the American Dream has doubtless shaped the American national character in several ways. Its focus is primarily self-centered, materialistic, pragmatic, and individualistic; rugged individualism and resourcefulness are celebrated in our folklore and ballads. One byproduct of this aspect of the American Dream has been the continuous quest for liberty and freedom. Often the hero is the lone cowboy—unrestrained, unregulated, and self-reliant. Often the villain is the bureaucrat—the government regulator, the tax collector, or (indeed) anyone who imposes restrictions.

Still another element of the American Dream is faith in the common sense of the ordinary person. The tradition of Abraham Lincoln and Harry Truman, that anyone can become president, has been a bold one. We prefer action to reflection; we are antitheoretical, antiexpert, and indeed antiintellectual. Stressing practicality and immediacy, the ethic of the marketplace ("street sense") has become part of our image. Poets such as Walt Whitman, Stephen Vincent Benet, and Carl Sandburg, and storytellers such as Mark Twain, Will Rogers, and Garrison Keillor helped shape this idea into tradition. This reverence for the common person helps in part to explain Americans' ambivalence toward power, politics, and government authority. In America government has always been viewed as a necessary *evil* (with a certain stress on evil).

CHAPTER 7 / Political Culture and Ideology

There remains a remarkable belief that America is better, stronger, and more virtuous than other nations. Doubtless this sense of mission is a source of discipline, an obvious builder of morale and fortifier of nationalism. But an excessive or wrongheaded sense of mission can also cause problems. The Wilsonian notion that "America is the most unselfish of nations" is an example of a romanticized and inflated sense of mission. Our dealings with native Americans, our compromises over slavery in order to get the Constitution ratified, our era of Manifest Destiny, and our intrusion into the affairs of others in the post-World War II period are all illustrative.

Some of us, of course, deride this righteousness, this false purity, this notion of the United States as an elect or redeemer nation. Critics say this **messianic spirit** or providential destiny is an illusion. No nation is sacred. America, like every country, has interests and motives that are selfish as well as generous; we have motives that are squalid as well as idealistic. We, too, are part of human history. Still, a persistent idealism and moralism at times loom large as part of the promise of America. Our efforts in the human rights area—food relief, financial support for the International Red Cross and the United Nations, our Peace Corps, and other humanitarian contributions—provide some evidence. America may not be the only hope for the world—but it is still one of the hopes.

CHALLENGING THE AMERICAN DREAM

Several years ago in a commencement speech at Harvard University, Alexander Solzhenitsyn posed a number of sharp challenges to the American Dream. The famed Soviet exile roundly criticized America's unchecked materialism, timid leadership, irresponsible press, and legalism in the face of a spiritual and moral vacuum.

Contending American Dreams

THE AMERICAN WAY

Liberty
Freedom
Rugged individualism
Private property rights
Survival of the fittest
Success to the best
Achievement, merit, excellence
Leave me alone
Don't fence me in
"Life is unfair"
People are not angels—government by the best
Emphasis on our republic

"This land became great not by what government did for the people but what the people did for themselves."

American Way refers to our traditional values and practices. We use the phrase *American Testament* to refer to many of our ideals, hopes, and aspirations. Both lists of values are part of the American Dream. Most of us have grown up conditioned by both American Dreams. The list on the left has doubtless been the primary American Dream for most Americans—as most of it was for the founders of this nation in the 1770s and 1780s. Over the years, however, elements of the list on the right have evolved to take an important place in our lives. Many of our major national public documents, and the most memorable addresses of various American

THE AMERICAN TESTAMENT

Equality
Liberation from discrimination
E pluribus unum—commonwealth
Community
Pro underdog, pro yeoman farmer
Affirmative action
Help for those who can't help themselves
Generosity
Fairness
"We can do better"
Government by the people
Emphasis on participatory democracy and the common sense of the common person

"America must educate every individual to his or her capacity, eliminate ignorance, prejudice, hate, and the squalor in which crime is bred. We must also protect against the economic catastrophies of illness, disability, and unemployment."

leaders, are associated with the list on the right: Jefferson, Lincoln, Susan B. Anthony, Franklin and Eleanor Roosevelt, Martin Luther King, Jr., John F. Kennedy. On the other hand, many of our distinguished leaders and politicians are plainly associated with the list on the left: John Adams, Madison, Hamilton, Teddy Roosevelt, and Ronald Reagan, to name just a few. How about you? Which set of values and aspirations most define your views? Are you a partisan of one list to the exclusion of the other—or do you, like most modern Americans, subscribe to a mixture of the two?

"Someone once labelled me a reactionary, and it stuck."

Drawing by Weber; © 1985 The New Yorker Magazine, Inc.

Further, he said Americans have taken freedom too far, which has led to a permissiveness that in turn encourages crime, violence, pornography, and a tasteless, third-rate culture. He plainly thinks we have lost our way, that we need some kind of moral revitalization and more central direction to overcome our softness, our decadence, our drift.[7]

Solzhenitsyn is not alone in questioning the health and viability of the American ideology. Critics from all quarters attack American beliefs as inconsistent, contradictory, or purely illusory. The most fundamental dispute concerns our most strongly held values, namely, the principles of *liberty and equality* set forth in the Declaration of Independence.

These two principles, largely complementary at the time of our nation's founding, are often in conflict today. In the late eighteenth century, equality of an individual before the law and personal liberty served as twin battle cries of the revolution. Government was viewed as the primary threat to these values, and restraining government served to enhance both. But with the concentration of vast wealth in a few hands, especially around 1900, individuals or giant corporations became threats to liberty as well; equality of opportunity became an empty promise when individuals were denied the education, political power, and economic security necessary to succeed in American society.

How do we choose when a supreme value like liberty clashes with a supreme value like equality? Part of the answer is to ask ourselves *whose* liberty or equality, how defined, in what circumstances? We might wish to give equality—or at least equality of opportunity—precedence during a period of reform like the New Deal. We might wish to put security—"freedom from fear"—first during a war. We might wish to give top priority to liberty—liberty from governmental regulation, for example—during a conservative era.

But is is not enough to answer the question of the priority of values by saying: "It depends." Ultimately the thoughtful citizen must make such a choice. There are conflicts among values, and one may have to yield to another. The authors of this book urge that you, students of government, sort out your values and establish priorities among them.

We, of course, must practice what we preach. Your three authors agree that freedom of speech in particular and the Bill of Rights in general stand at the pinnacle of our hierarchy of values. Thus we would defend the principle of liberty against all comers—against forces of aggression from abroad that might threaten all our freedoms; against would-be censors at home who would deprive us of the right to read and speak and even think as we wish; against those who would prevent our fellow-citizens—even Nazis or Stalinists—from the right to stand up on soapboxes and preach their outrageous doctrines.

So if we had to choose between the values of liberty and equality, we, along with most other Americans, put liberty first. But much depends on how we define these values. If we define equality as *equality of condition,* as the idea of leveling everyone's income and living conditions, equality might mean taking **personal property** from some to redistribute to others who need it, in a manner that might jeopardize individual liberties of the former. But if we define equality as *equality of opportunity,* it would mean providing youngsters, for example, with the kind of housing, home life, medical care, and schooling they need to expand their actual liberties, and thus give them a truly equal start. No one is more denied *all* freedoms than persons who are imprisoned in a poverty of ignorance, illness, low self-esteem, and other deprivations.

Because change is scary, and uncharted change frightening, people with certain fixed values or ideologies often cling tenaciously to simple definitions of reality, which in turn define their view of the American Dream and the kind of

CHAPTER 7 / Political Culture and Ideology

politics they want to encourage. Libertarian critics today, for example, argue that democracy, specifically majority rule, has gone too far in imposing the values of one group, due simply to their larger numbers, upon the values of others. The welfare state has gone too far, they argue, and it has undermined the American Dream and basic personal freedoms.

Critics on the left produce a different set of charges. They say the rich get richer, the poor get poorer. The rich are better treated before the law than the poor. Further, much of our tax system is regressive, and most federal laws and regulations actually benefit the more prosperous in the nation.[8] The rich are also better represented in political decision-making bodies, such as legislatures or courts. Money alone may not buy elections, they say, yet it buys just about all the political resources needed to gain information, influence voters, and shape the outcomes of public policy. Like money, freedom of expression is available to all, but in widely varying quantities. The rich have the time, the organizational knowhow, and the ability to hire experts (lobbyists, speechwriters, public relations firms), all of which allow them more access, more say, and hence more influence. The rich are more represented than the poor. It gives "them" a "louder voice" in this land of supposed political equality. A true democracy, say some of these critics, would necessitate a more equal distribution of the basic resources needed for real participation and valid representation.

Other, usually more moderate, voices have warned that the governability of America is threatened these days because of intense commitment to democratic and egalitarian ideals. They say, for example, that the effective operation of our political system requires some measure of apathy and noninvolvement. They point out that government needs to operate with a measure of secrecy, deception, and even manipulation, for in times of crisis government must have the political authority to impose upon its peoples certain necessary sacrifices. They quote John Adams, who said a democracy never lasts long: "It soon wastes, exhausts, and murders itself. There never was a democracy yet that did not commit suicide." In short, we must beware of the excesses of democracy. Just as we have come to recognize that there are potentially desirable limits to economic growth, we must realize "there are also potentially desirable limits to the indefinite extension of political democracy."[9]

We must nonetheless recognize certain realities. Many millions are still denied opportunity because of their race, ethnic background, and sex. An underclass persists in the form of impoverished families, ill-nourished and ill-educated children, and people living in the streets.[10] Many cities are actually "two cities," where thousands live in luxury, tens of thousands live in squalor. The gap between rich and poor has grown in recent years. The gap between rich farms and marginal farms has deepened. And a sharp difference between white and black income tenaciously persists. One's chances to succeed still depend, far more than we want to admit, on the neighborhood one grew up in.

To the extent we have failed to live up to our principles and the American Dream, can we identify the causes? Some may consider that the problem is the *values* themselves—their vagueness, superficiality, lack of popular support. Others might blame our *political system*—its built-in fragmentation and friction, its over-representation of the "haves" against the "have-nots," its domination by quarreling politicians rather than far-seeing leaders. Still others might point to our *leadership* as lacking the concern, the skill, and the commitment necessary to convert our principles into down-to-earth performance.

All this has important implications for one other test of values: Can they be converted into clear guidelines for politicians to convert into policy and performance? Surely, the more we think through our values, define them, and rank

"At the root of our disagreement, as I see it, is this: I hear America singing, and you *don't* hear America singing."

Drawing by D. Reilly; © 1985 The New Yorker Magazine, Inc.

them, the more effective such conversion will be. But even if our values are clear and explicit, are our politicians skillful enough to put them into practice? Are our leaders bold and creative enough? Our political system effective enough?

The Never-Ending Quest for Additional Rights

Our political values and ideology are clearly affected by historical developments and economic and technological growth. Thus our first commitment as a people was to liberty and the constitutional order. Property rights, individual rights, and the right to regularly elected representative assemblies were the primary reasons for the American Revolution.[11] In the early years we emphasized separation of powers, checks and balances, states' rights, and of course the Bill of Rights.

It would take an additional generation or two before our "ideology" would also begin to take seriously the ideal of democratic governance, the extension of the suffrage, and competitive nominations and elections. Notions of political equality and effective participation became concerns for many during the Jackson presidency and mid-nineteenth century in general. A bit later the Populists and Suffragists embraced these ideals and formed large-scale movements to achieve more democratic forms of participation and more responsive forms of governance.

By the late nineteenth century, as the agrarian society began to be gradually replaced by commercial and industrial capitalism and the rise of large corporations, American ideology became irreversibly transformed. We committed ourselves to encourage economic growth mainly by encouraging privately owned corporations. This transformation of our economic order had profound consequences for our political values, how we viewed the role of government, and how we related to one another. No one captures this reality better than political scientist Robert Dahl:

> At the time [at the turn of the century], the emerging new order surely appeared to a great many Americans as if it were no more than a re-affirmation of the first historic commitment which, after all, included an all but universal belief in private property. In time, however, despite continuing rear-guard actions by critics, the commitment came to mean de facto approval for the evolution of very large, even gigantic, privately owned corporate enterprises, the largest of which were one day to have gross incomes greater than those of most of the countries of the world. By the standards of all previous centuries, they are today themselves political systems of great opulence and power.

But it was the impact on equality that Dahl was especially concerned about, and his point is an important one for considerations of ideology.

> One of the consequences of the new order has been a high degree of inequality in the distribution of wealth and income—a far greater inequality than had ever been thought likely or desirable under an agrarian order by Democratic Republicans like Jefferson and Madison, or had ever been thought consistent with democratic or republican government in the historic writings on the subject from Aristotle to Locke, Montesquieu, and Rousseau. Previous theorists and advocates had, like many of the framers of our own Constitution, insisted that a republic could exist only if the citizen body continued neither rich nor poor. Citizens, it was, argued, must enjoy a rough equality of conditions.[12]

Noted capitalist John D. Rockefeller.

Thus, although constitutionalism or limited government and then later the democratic ideal embodied American political values in its first century and a quarter, a commitment to capitalism and free enterprise became an additional, and some would say competing or even dominant, political ideology in the early twentieth century.

With the rise and success of the American economy came the accumulation of great wealth in the hands of certain industrialists and tycoons. Many of them had taken great risks and earned their fortunes through inventions and large-scale efficiencies. And as disparities of income grew, so did disparities in political resources. As an old American maxim puts it, "Power follows property." Economic resources can be converted into political resources. Thus, "economic advantages increase one's chances of getting an education, gaining higher status, having more time available for politics, and so on," wrote Dahl. "Economic advantages also help in providing psychological resources such as confidence and optimism, which strengthens both the incentives to participate in politics and the willingness to acquire political skills."[13]

Then came the Great Depression and the near-collapse of the capitalistic system. Unrestrained capitalism and the unregulated market are faulted by many as one of the causes of the Depression. In any event, when it came, it brought the nation to the brink of disaster. There was no unemployment compensation, no guarantee on bank savings, no federal regulation of the securities exchanges, no old-age insurance. Americans everywhere became concerned with both saving the economic system and trying to improve the lot of the millions of jobless, homeless, and hurt. It was then, during FDR's New Deal era, that the idea took hold among a much wider public that government should assertively use its powers and resources in an affirmative way to ensure some measure of equality of opportunity and social justice.

In a sense the *rights revolution* of the 1780s and 1790s has never ended. The protection of property rights from an overly powerful government was followed by the quest for political rights, suffrage rights, black emancipation, and in the mid-twentieth century by campaigns for economic rights. Even later in our day we witness fights for gender rights, children's rights, gay rights, animal rights, the rights of trees and endangered species and so forth.

President Franklin Roosevelt's celebrated "Second Bill of Rights" address in 1944 was the epitome of this new ideology. Roosevelt reminded Americans that the Republic had its beginning and grew to strength under the protection of

During the Depression of the 1930s, the WPA created jobs by putting the unemployed to work improving roads and public buildings.

167

certain inalienable political rights, the rights we have examined in the past few chapters. Those were our rights to life and liberty, Roosevelt said. But as our nation matured in size and stature, and as industrialism emerged, these political rights proved inadequate to assure equality in the pursuit of happiness. Implicitly, FDR was acknowledging the tension between capitalism and democracy. That is, the effect of capitalism is to centralize wealth, and if power flows from wealth, then only the few will enjoy political power. Such a centralization of political power is at odds with a democracy that seeks to disperse political power.

In one of the boldest statements ever made by any American president, Roosevelt declared we needed to make an equally firm commitment to a whole new set of rights.

> We have come to a clear realization of the fact that true individual freedom cannot exist without economic security and independence. "Necessitous men are not free men." People who are hungry and out of a job are the stuff of which dictatorships are made. In our day these economic truths have become accepted as self-evident. We have accepted, so to speak, a second Bill of Rights under which a new basis of security and prosperity can be established for all—regardless of station, race or creed.
> Among these are:
>> The right to a useful and remunerative job in the industries or shops or farms or mines of the nation;
>> The right to earn enough to provide adequate food and clothing and recreation;
>> The right of every farmer to raise and sell his products at a return which will give him and his family a decent living;
>> The right of every businessman, large and small, to trade in an atmosphere of freedom from unfair competition and domination by monopolies at home or abroad;
>> The right of every family to a decent home;
>> The right to adequate medical care and the opportunity to achieve and enjoy good health;
>> The right to adequate protection from the economic fears of old age, sickness, accident, and unemployment;
>> The right to a good education.[14]

President Lyndon B. Johnson carried on the Roosevelt and Kennedy tradition by proclaiming a War on Poverty.

Roosevelt's proclamation and later efforts in the 1960s to pass landmark civil and voting rights legislation and launch a War on Poverty have in large measure defined the ideological political fights of the last half of the twentieth century. Modern-day liberalism and conservatism turn, in large measure, on how much of the Roosevelt "Second Bill of Rights" and how much government assistance one believes is owed to minorities, women, or others who have suffered discrimination or have been left behind by the industrial or technological revolutions of the twentieth century.

Liberalism, Conservatism, and Public Policy

Political labels have different meanings across national boundaries as well as over time. To be a liberal in certain European nations is to be on the right; to be liberal in the 1990s in the United States is to be on the political left. Many American liberals view George Bush as a conservative, yet some conservatives view Bush as too moderate. To be on the left in contemporary America is to place an important value on equality of opportunity, and to be a conservative is to value liberty as a primary goal. Yet nearly all of us believe in both, even as we may emphasize one more than the other. In short there are, as we shall suggest, all kinds of liberals and a variety of conservatives as well—and a considerable number of Americans who simply view themselves as "middle-of-the roaders." Clearly, labels have to be used with caution.

Our attitudes about politicians and public policies are not held in a highly systematic fashion. A voter may want increased spending for defense, but vote for the party that is for reducing defense spending, because he or she has always voted for that party. Or a person may favor adoption of the Equal Rights Amendment and government-financed abortions but still vote for George Bush. Consistency among various attitudes and opinions is often relatively low. Many people much of the time view political issues as isolated matters and do not apply a general standard of performance in evaluating parties and candidates. Indeed, many citizens have difficulty relating what happens in one policy situation to what happens in another. This problem becomes worse as government gets into more and more policy areas. Hence, most people, not surprisingly, have difficulty finding candidates who reflect their preferences across a range of issues.

The absence of widespread, hardened ideologies in the United States makes for markedly different kinds of politics and policy-making processes than in many European or third-world nations. Our policy making is characterized more by coalitions of the moment than by fixed alignments pitting one set of warring ideologues against another. And our politics are more a politics of moderation and accommodation than a prolonged and strained battle between two, three, or more competing philosophies of government. Elsewhere—as in countries where a strong Communist or Christian-Democratic party exists—things are different.

By no means, however, does this mean that policies or ideas are not taken into account in our politics. As a result of better and more education and better and more sources of information about political activities, we have witnessed a slight increase in ideological thinking and issue voting. Such issues as affirmative action, welfare assistance programs, the Supreme Court's abortion rulings, and the Strategic Defense Initiative (Star Wars) have aroused people who previously were relatively passive about politics and political ideas. A certain kind of modified ideology is playing an important role in our system.

Two major, yet rather broad and hazy, schools of political thinking dominate American politics: *liberalism* and *conservatism*. As Tables 7–1 and 7–2 show, most American adults are willing to say they are either liberal or conservative. Two lesser, but more defined, schools of thought, *socialism* and *libertarianism,* also help define the spectrum of ideology in America.

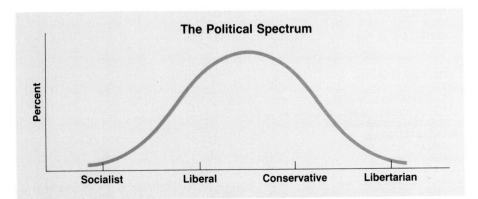

CHAPTER 7 / Political Culture and Ideology

TABLE 7–1
Liberal, Moderate, or Conservative?

Q. How do you describe your views on most political matters? Generally, do you think of yourself as liberal, moderate, or conservative?

	LIBERAL	*MODERATE*	*CONSERVATIVE*
1981	20%	40%	34%
1985	19	42	33
1989	23	37	34

Source: New York Times-CBS National Surveys, as reported in *The New York Times* during these years.

LIBERALISM

In the seventeenth and eighteenth centuries, classical liberals fought to minimize the role of government. They were stressing individual rights and perceived governments as the primary threat to these rights and liberties. Thus, they favored a small government and sought ample guarantees of protection from governmental harassment.

The emphasis on individualism has remained constant; it is the perception of government that has changed. Nowadays, proponents of **liberalism** view government as protecting individuals from being abused by a variety of nongovernmental forces (market vagaries, business decisions, and so on).

In its modern American usage, liberalism also refers to a belief in the positive uses of government to bring about justice and equality of opportunity. Modern-day liberals wish to preserve the rights of the individual and the right to own private property, but they are very willing to have the government intervene in the economy to remedy the defects of capitalism and a market economy. Contemporary American liberalism has its roots in Franklin Roosevelt's New Deal programs, designed to aid the poor and to protect people against the possibilities of unemployment, inadequate or deficient medical assistance, and inadequate or deficient housing and education. Liberals believe in affirmative action programs and in

TABLE 7–2
What the Public Thinks It Means to Be a Liberal or a Conservative

Q. What does it mean to you when someone says he or she is a liberal?

Acceptable to change/flexible	17%
Support programs that increase spending	17
Someone open-minded	13
Favor social programs	9
Believe in rights of all people	8
Other	37
Don't know	18

Q. What does it mean to you when someone says he or she is a conservative?

Resistant to change	21%
Thrifty	17
Traditional/old fashioned	8
Reasonable/practical	8
Narrow-minded/prejudiced	6
Middle-of-the-road	5
Other	38
Don't know	15

Source: The Times Mirror Study of the American Electorate, Gallup Organization in Norman Ornstein et al., *The People, the Press, and Politics* (Addison-Wesley, 1988), p. 125. Survey of 4,244 adults, Spring 1987.

progressive taxation measures and regulatory efforts that help protect the average worker's health and safety. American liberals have also favored the right of unions to organize as well as to strike.

On a more philosophical level, liberals generally believe in the possibility of progress. They believe things can be made to work, that the future will be better, that obstacles can be overcome. This positive set of beliefs may explain some of their willingness to believe also in the potential benefits of governmental action, a willingness to alter or even negate the old Jeffersonian notion that "government governs best when it governs least." Liberals contend that the character of modern technology and the side effects of industrialization cry out for at least limited governmental programs to offset the loss of liberties suffered by the less well-to-do and the weak. Liberals frequently stress the need for a politics of compassion, a politics of affirmative government.

Liberals contend conservatives will always rule in their own interest and will act on the maxim: "Let the government take care of the rich, and the rich in turn will take care of the poor." Liberals, on the other hand, prefer to believe that the government should take care of the weak, for the strong can nearly always take care of themselves. "We have rejected the discredited theory that the fortunes of the nation should be in the hands of a privileged few," said President Harry Truman. "Instead, we believe that our economic system should rest on a democratic foundation and that wealth should be created for the benefit of all . . . Every segment of our population and every individual has a right to expect from his government a fair deal."

In the liberal view, all people are equal. Equality of opportunity is essential, and toward that end, discriminatory practices must be eliminated. Some liberals favor the reduction of great inequalities of wealth that make equality of opportunity impossible. But most believe a certain minimum level of wealth is necessary to ensure equality of opportunity. Rather than placing a cap on wealth, they want a floor placed beneath the poor. In short, liberals have sought "to lessen the harsh impact of oligarchical rule in economic life, to introduce a measure of democracy within or democratic controls over the industrial-technological process, to assure freedom from arbitrary command within the economic no less than within the political sphere."[15] They ask: How can citizens be equal and free if they are dependent and necessarily servile to the powers that be?

The following defenses of liberalism were written by unrepentant and unabashed liberals—one a composer-conductor, the other a noted historian-writer.

"Harold, would you say you are left of center, right of center, center, left of left, right of left, left of right, or right of right, or what?"

Drawing by Booth; © 1972 The New Yorker Magazine, Inc.

Who fought to free the slaves? Liberals. Who succeeded in abolishing the poll tax? Liberals. Who fought for women's rights, civil rights, free public education? Liberals. Who stood guard and still stands guard against sweatshops, child labor, racism, bigotry? Lovers of freedom and enemies of tyranny: Liberals.[16]

The presidents we admire and celebrate most—Jefferson and Jackson and Lincoln and Theodore Roosevelt and Wilson and FDR and Harry Truman and JFK—were all, in the context of their times, vigorous and unashamed liberals. They were all pioneers on new frontiers, seeking out the ways of the future, meeting new problems with new remedies, carrying the message of constructive change in a world that never stops changing. From the start of the republic liberalism has always blazed the trail into the future—and conservatism has always deployed all the weapons of caricature and calumny and irrelevance to conceal the historic conservative objective of unchecked rule by those who already have far more than their fair share of the nation's treasure.[17]

Liberals share a commitment to aid the poor and the hungry.

Liberals, it should be emphasized, come in many varieties. Some stress civil and women's rights and promote quality public education. Another group of liberals emphasizes the need for government to adopt a more progressive tax system and do more to help the homeless, the handicapped, and society's "have-nots." Still others are primarily concerned about the arms race and crusade for treaties and alliances that might bring about a safer world without terrorism and war. And yet other liberals are preoccupied with environmental or consumer issues. Some liberals embrace all of these issues and place them on an equal plane.

In a sense some liberals who emphasize economic issues may be called *New Deal liberals*. Others are social or peace liberals, and so on. And, if this is not confusing enough, there are also those who call themselves **neoliberals.** Neoliberals still believe in liberty, justice, and a fair chance for everyone. They argue that the truly down-and-out must have government assistance. Yet they do not automatically favor unions and big government, nor do they automatically criticize big business or the military. Neoliberals are best characterized as liberals who have lost faith in many welfare programs and are skeptical about the efficiency and responsiveness of large Washington-based bureaucracies. They are better at diagnosing some of the deficiencies of old liberalism than they are at pointing out what should be done. Yet, in general, they favor the fair tax reforms of Senator Bill Bradley (D-NJ), the military reform initiatives of Senator Sam Nunn (D-Georgia), and the emphasis on national service championed by Virginia Senator Chuck Robb (D-Virginia). A regular sample of neoliberal thinking appears in the journal called *The Washington Monthly*.[18]

Senator Paul Simon (D-Illinois), in his brief bid to win his party's presidential nomination in 1988, announced: "I am not a neo-anything. I'm a Democrat."[19] He was trying to affirm that he was an FDR and Harry Truman liberal. Yet Simon was often "outliberaled" in the grueling primaries and caucuses of that year by Jesse Jackson and also, on occasion, by Governor Michael Dukakis.

But not everyone, by a long shot, is convinced that liberalism has the answers for the problems of the 1990s. Critics of liberalism, old and new, say it places too much reliance on governmental solutions, higher taxes, and bureaucrats. Opponents of liberalism say somewhere along the line liberals forgot that government, to serve our best interests, has to be limited. Power tends to corrupt, they add, and too much reliance or dependence on government can corrupt the spirit, can undermine self-reliance and make us forget about those cherished personal

Traditional conservatives have customarily favored dispersing power broadly throughout the political and social systems precisely to avoid great concentration of power at the national level. They favor asking the market to distribute goods rather than through government planning.

Traditional as well as libertarian conservative theorists view economic and social *equality* as a value far less to be revered than liberty and freedom. To allow the worst off to take advantage of the best off is to hurt both groups in the end, writes one conservative who advocates a minimal state.

Senator Jesse Helms (R–North Carolina)

> The minimal state treats us as inviolate individuals, who may not be used in certain ways by others as means or tools or instruments or resources; it treats us as persons having individual rights with the dignity this constitutes. Treating us with respect by respecting our rights, it allows us, individually or with whom we choose, to choose our life and to realize our ends and our conceptions of ourselves, insofar as we can, aided by the voluntary cooperation of other individuals possessing the same dignity. How *dare* any state or group or individuals do more or less.[24]

Another brand of conservatism—sometimes called the New Right, Ultraconservatism, or even the Radical Right—emerged in the past generation. It shares the love of freedom shown by the traditional conservatives, yet it wants a stronger central government to combat international communism. It has also developed an activist public policy agenda that it would like implemented by conservatives in Congress and in the White House. The New Right favors the return of organized prayer in the public schools and covert operations by the CIA, and opposes legal abortions and such policies as job quotas, busing, and any tolerance of pornography. In short, a defining characteristic of the New Right is their strong desire to impose various social controls; in effect, they are asking government to step in and help achieve what churches and families were once expected to perform.

One of the most influential leaders of the New Right has been Senator Jesse Helms (R-North Carolina). Helms built an impressive coalition in the South and elsewhere uniting fundamentalist Christians worried about "secular humanism" and favoring official school prayer, conservative Catholics opposed to abortion, white parents opposed to drugs, pornography, and forced busing, small business owners who detest government intrusion, and manufacturers who favor less governmental regulation and more defense spending.

For Senator Helms and the Moral Majority, once led by the Reverend Jerry Falwell, the answer to America's problems is not a political program but a spiritual reawakening. "As Christians we need to work with missionary zeal," wrote Helms, "to reinstate the rule of Christ in our sadly demoralized country."[25] Helms is a fundamentalist who believes the Bible is free of error. He is also an uncommonly talented fundraiser and one of the best parliamentarian tacticians in Congress. And he is, in addition, a gifted television performer. All of these skills combined with his steadfast devotion to Christianity, free enterprise, and self-styled "patriotic" principles won him a huge following in the 1980s.[26]

But there is some question over this type of activist conservatism. Former Senator Barry Goldwater, also known as an ardent conservative, worries that too much prominence and influence has been given to the New Right, especially to those he calls the "moral majority" and "checkbook clergy" types. Our Constitution, Goldwater said, seeks to allow freedom for everyone, not merely those professing certain moral or religious views of ultimate right. Goldwater pointed to the bloody divisions in Northern Ireland, the holy wars in Lebanon, and the pernicious religious righteousness in Iran as examples of the heavy-handed politicization of churches.

Reverend Jerry Falwell

"The Moral Majority has no more right to dictate its moral and political beliefs to the country than does any other group, political or religious," said Goldwater. "The same is true of pro-choice abortion or other groups. They are free to persuade us because this land is blessed with liberty, but not to assign religious or political absolutes—complete right or wrong."[27] Goldwater fears that the great danger in the new right movement is that, instead of broadening its base, it will tear itself and his beloved Republican Party apart. He is also, one gathers, opposed to moral absolutes—the kind the Moral Majority thrives on.

The past generation has also witnessed the emergence of conservatives who call themselves **neoconservatives.** Many of them are former Democrats who admired FDR and Harry Truman but left the Democratic party over issues such as Vietnam, busing, and the decisions of the liberal (overly liberal in their view) Earl Warren Supreme Court. They had special contempt for the 1972 Democratic nominee, George McGovern, whom they viewed as soft on crime, soft on communism, and a threat to mainstream values.

Those who call themselves neoconservatives often prefer to be called pragmatic conservatives. They say they want to keep or enact programs that work or are truly necessary, and reject the rest. Neoconservatives have given up on New Deal and Great Society liberalism, which they believe will lead to a paternalistic state. Though willing to interfere with the market for overriding social purposes, neoconservatives prefer to do so by "rigging" the market, or even creating new markets, rather than by increasing bureaucratic and central government controls.

Neoconservatives favor larger military expenditure than do Democrats, because they are more skeptical than liberals of the intentions of the Soviets and the Warsaw Pact nations. They also say our national leaders should favor the death penalty and be more worried about crime than the homeless. They say the courts have gone too far in protecting the rights of the criminal and are too little concerned with the safety of the victims of crime.

Neoconservatives are credited with various original writings on social policy, supply-side economics, education, and the rule of "national interest" in foreign affairs. They disparage the United Nations, "international law," and even NATO as viable solutions to American foreign-policy problems. "It is the conception of our 'national interest' that sets the terms for all our debates on foreign policy," writes neoconservative Irving Kristol. "Specifically, the debate centers on the issue

Noted liberal former senator and presidential candidate George McGovern with noted conservative writer William Buckley at a debate at Yale University.

Another Way of Looking at Ideology and Public Policy

	Extent of Policy Change	
	Incremental*	**Major**
Progressive Redistribution**	Liberalism	Socialism
Nonredistributive	Conservativism	Libertarianism

Nature of Policy Change

*Incremental here refers to small steps in policy change.
**Redistribution refers to altering opportunities and wealth in a society from the advantaged to the disadvantaged.

of if it is in our national interest to attempt actively to shape the future world order by the use of American power; or instead, to create an America that provides an example to humanity so splendid as to move other nations toward an emulation of our model."[28] Kristol's and the neoconservatives' answer is that America has to use its power to shape events, that it can't retreat to an isolationist response to world developments. Thus the neoconservatives heartily approved Reagan's invasion of Grenada, his bombing of Libya, and U.S. assertiveness in Central America.[29]

Ideology as Cause and Effect   It is important to appreciate that ideology both causes events and is affected by them. Just as the Great Depression resulted in almost a tidal wave of change in ideology, so did our involvement in World War II, Korea, and Vietnam, each in its own way. The overall effect of World War II was to provide an example of how government can work to defend freedom; it resulted in an expansion in positive views about the role of the national government. The Vietnam War probably had the opposite effect—a disillusionment with government. The antigovernment sentiment found in recent presidential elections is undoubtedly related to our experience in Vietnam.

The Reagan era experience can be exaggerated, yet there is no question that eight years of Reaganism helped the conservative cause, just as his election was shaped in part by a rise in the acceptance of conservative philosphy. By the 1988 elections "liberal", which back in Roosevelt's day had been popular, had become a word most politicians sought to avoid. George Bush found it helpful in his campaigns to charge Dukakis and congressional Democrats with being "liberal," which he equated with high taxes, softness on crime, and too much government interference in the economy.

Now a brief comment on socialism and libertarianism.

SOCIALISM

Socialism is an economic and governmental system based on public ownership of the means of production and exchange. Karl Marx once described socialism as a transitional stage of society between capitalism and communism. In a capitalist system the means of production and most of the property are privately owned, whereas in a communist or socialist system the property is "owned" by the state in common for all the people. In the ultimate socialist country justice is achieved by having participants determine their own needs and take what is appropriate from the common product of society. Marx's dictum was: "From each according to his ability, to each according to his needs."

American socialists—of whom there are probably only a million or two—favor a greatly expanded role for the government. They would nationalize certain industries. They would institute a public jobs program so that all who want work would be put to work. They would change the tax system to place a much steeper tax burden on the wealthy and eliminate all tax preferences for the rich. In short, American socialists favor policies to help the underdog and the common person by means of government redistribution programs. They also favor economic justice and stepped-up efforts toward greater equality over property rights. American socialists would drastically cut defense spending as well.[30] Most of the democracies of Western Europe are far more influenced by socialist ideas than we are in the United States.

Critics of socialism here say the last thing we need is more governmental interference in the economy. Do we want more operations like the U.S. Postal Service? They complain that there are already few incentives for efficiency in our bureaucracies. Further, socialism places too much faith in the state at the expense of individual rights and liberties. They generally add that the right to own private property and skepticism toward centralized government are key factors that have made America great—factors that would be vastly less important in a socialist scheme of things.

LIBERTARIANISM

Libertarianism is an ideology that cherishes individual liberty and insists on a sharply limited state and government. It carries some overtones of anarchism, of the English liberalism of the past, and of a 1930-style conservatism. A Libertarian party has gained a following in recent years, especially among those who believe both liberals and conservatives lack consistency in their attitude toward the power of the national government. It is now America's third largest political party. The libertarians preach opposition to government and just about all its programs. They favor massive cuts in government spending, an end to the FBI and CIA and most regulatory commissions, a minimal defense establishment (one that would defend America only if we were directly attacked), and complete disengagement of American troops from overseas missions. A poster at one of their recent national conventions read: "U.S. out of Latin America; U.S. out of North America!" Libertarians favor eliminating not only welfare programs, but also programs that subsidize business, farmers, and the rich. They opposed government-backed guaranteed loans for Chrysler and would turn the functions of the Postal Service over to private companies. Unlike most conservatives, libertarians would repeal laws regulating personal morality, such as anti-prostitution or anti-marijuana laws.

A Libertarian party candidate for president has been on the ballot in all fifty states in recent presidential elections, although never obtaining more than 1 percent of the vote. A few books on libertarianism have become best sellers.[31] The Libertarian candidate for president in 1988, former Texas Congressman Ron Paul, ran on a platform that emphasized elimination of $500 billion in corporate subsidies, social welfare, and foreign military welfare; decriminalization of drugs; abolition of the Federal Reserve Board and return of the gold standard; withdrawal of the overseas military from Japan, Korea, the Philippines, Germany, and elsewhere;

abolishment of the IRS and the income tax. The Libertarian positions are rarely timid or understated and they have, at the very least, prompted intriguing political debates.

Still, critics dismiss libertarianism as hopelessly naive, and as ignoring the failure of the market and the at least occasional need for certain public goods and services. Critics on the left say advocates of libertarianism would indeed return us to the good old days, but it would be more like the days of serfdom.

In sum, in many respects the old debates over the New Deal and about where one stands on communism are increasingly dated and perhaps increasingly irrelevant in American politics. In the 1990s there is little fear that the United States will become communist. But people of varying ideologies do indeed worry about whether America is becoming too soft and losing ground in global economic affairs. Today we are more likely to debate what will make us competitive so we can beat, or at least compete with, "those capitalists from Japan" and other Pacific Rim nations. More and more, ideological debate centers on how we can improve our schools, encourage a stronger work ethic, stop the flow of drugs into the country, educate more leaders, scientists, and inventors, and how best to instill religious values, build character, encourage cohesive and lasting families, and so on. Do our social programs and job training programs make things better or worse? Is the marketplace or reliance on the government planners a better way to make long-term policy decisions for the nation? What is the best way to balance the budget and curb inflation? We worry, too, less about the American corporation than about foreign investors and international conglomerates that are increasingly doing business in the United States and shaping our lives as well as our economic-policy decisions. Ideological debate and differences are always with us, but the nature of the issues changes. This is likely to be even more the case as we approach the end the century.

Ron Paul, 1988 Libertarian party presidential candidate.

A Central Ideological Tension— Political Equality versus Capitalism

As we have seen, nearly everyone in American political life favors liberty and equality as well as democracy and a free-enterprise market system. We have much in common. No one of importance goes around advocating abolition of elections, a one-party system, a government-controlled press, or the prohibition of dissent. Clearly, however, liberals and conservatives differ over the extent to which political and social equality should be the primary goals of government.

More specifically, Americans are divided over whether the first priority of the state (the government) is to promote individualism or to promote political and social equality.

> While most Americans favor a competitive, private economy in which the most enterprising and industrious individuals receive the greatest income, they also want a democratic society in which everyone can earn a decent living and has an equal chance to realize his or her full human potential. Since these two sets of values often conflict with each other in practice, the mood of the country may shift from one era to another as the values of one tradition or the other predominate. In one period the nation may be shocked by society's failure to fulfill the democratic promise of American life for the poor, the unemployed, and other disadvantaged groups, and may accelerate its efforts to rectify this failure; in the next period, however,

"To the rich, the very rich, and the super rich! Have I left anybody out?"

Drawing by Joe Mirachi; © 1988 The New Yorker Magazine, Inc.

many people may complain that the nation has gone too far in pursuing these goals and may advocate a shift back toward a more conservative, laissez-faire, and procapitalist course.[32]

Most Americans believe the semi-regulated or mixed free enterprise system is one of the great achievements of America. Ours is not an unbridled, unfettered system of free enterprise: we do have certain government regulations, such as antitrust laws, job safety regulations, environmental standards, minimum wage rates, and so on. We believe this mixed system gives almost everyone a fair chance, that it is necessary for free government to survive, and that our freedom depends on it. We reject communism and even modified forms of socialism and take pride in the reality that not only has communism not worked around the world, but that some Marxist nations, such as China and the Soviet Union, appear to be taking free-enterprise incentive systems more and more seriously in the 1990s.

Americans overwhelmingly tell pollsters they do not believe we have anything to learn from the Soviet system and they disagree that "some form of socialism would certainly be better than the system we have now." Further, the idea of private property enjoys extraordinary popular favor. Americans say private ownership of property is as important to a good society as is freedom, and that it is fundamental for economic progress. Moreover, people generally believe that the individuals who own property have the right to decide how it is to be used.

Central to our support for capitalism is the belief that people with more ability and people who work extremely hard should get ahead, should earn more, and should enjoy economic rewards. We also believe that those who earn a lot of money should be able to pass most of what they have earned along to their families. Americans, even those in the most marginal economic circumstances, oppose stringent inheritance taxes or limits on how much someone can earn.[33]

In the years when the American political tradition was taking shape, the United States was still predominantly an economy of independent small-scale entrepreneurs, artisans, craftsmen, and farmers who worked their own land and operated out of their own homes or shops. But this has changed. The operation of the free market system over the past hundred years has produced new class divisions, new forms of privilege, and new inequalities that have a considerable bearing on political and social opportunities. Simply put, the enormous successes of some have produced a growing division between the rich and the poor. While Americans primarily classify themselves as members of the "middle" or "working classes," there is considerable evidence that the gap between rich and poor has widened in recent decades.

Corporations have acquired great wealth and, in many instances, exercise great political clout. Political economist Charles Lindblom outlines the problem:

> It has been a curious feature of democratic thought that it has not faced up to the private corporation as a peculiar organization in an ostensible democracy. Enormously large, rich in resources, the big corporations . . . command more resources than do most government units. They can also, over a broad range, insist that government meet their demands, even if these demands run counter to those that citizens express through their polyarchal [that is, democratic] controls. Moreover, they do not disqualifty themselves from playing the partisan role of a citizen—for a corporation is legally a person. They are on all these counts disproportionately powerful . . . The large private corporation fits oddly into democratic theory and vision. Indeed, it does not fit.[34]

CHAPTER 7 / Political Culture and Ideology

TABLE 7–3
American Attitudes on Business and Fairness

	AGREE	DISAGREE	DON'T KNOW
Today it's really true that the rich get richer while the poor get poorer.	67%	31%	2%
There is too much power concentrated in the hands of a few big companies.	67%	20%	3%
Business corporations make too much profit.	61%	33%	7%
Business corporations generally strike a fair balance between making profits and serving the public interest.	42%	53%	5%
Our society should do what is necessary to make sure that everyone has an equal *opportunity* to succeed.	94%	7%	1%
The government should guarantee every citizen enough to eat and a place to sleep.	66%	31%	3%

Source: Surveys of thousands of adults conducted for the Times Mirror Corporation by the Gallup Organization, October 1988.

The rise of the huge corporation and individual wealth in American politics could not help but create division and breed a certain amount of resentment. Not surprisingly, ideological tensions have arisen. An increasing number of Americans believe the political system too often favors the rich over the poor. And it is widely believed that when it comes to taxes, corporations and wealthy people don't pay their fair share. Further, the public attitudes reported in Table 7–3 suggest that feelings about inequalities are an important feature of political life in America today.

Whatever our differences, however, most Americans favor both political equality (the right of each person to have an equal vote and an equal voice in elections and political discussion) and the free market system. These two ideologies have coexisted somewhat uneasily throughout our history as a republic. We want both, yet tension or incompatibilities exist between these values. Capitalism inevitably leads to unequal economic rewards, for it is based upon the promise that risk taking and hard work should be rewarded. Those who can create products, jobs, and profits also earn the right, in our economic system, to rich rewards. Those rewards are usually economic, yet many of the economic resources of the wealthy, as noted earlier, are convertible into political resources, thus creating disparities in political access, political influence, and the opportunity to shape public policies.

It is unrealistic to expect all our values or ideological views to coexist in perfect harmony. "While most societies aspire to a unified value system, complete unity of belief is impossible to sustain in large and complex societies experiencing rapid change and containing groups that are free to express their diverse viewpoints," write McCloskey and Zaller. "To remain viable, a free society requires not uniformity of belief, but countervailing groups and institutions that are able to check each other and to prevent any one from acquiring a monopoly of power over the nation's institutions and ideas."[35]

Still we need to appreciate that we are divided over how much equality and how much of an unrestrained free enterprise system we want. Many of us hold compromised positions on both matters. Indeed, our political system and its leaders wrestle with these tensions on a regular basis. In practice, as we have pointed out, we have a mixed free-enterprise system that combines capitalism

Marena Lopez, a United States citizen, ponders Miss Liberty while her parents file for legalization of their alien status.

with a modified welfare state; we also have a wide array of regulations that businesses must heed. And though we may yearn for political equality, we know it is an ideal that is unlikely to be wholly realized. Inequalities do exist, and we are apparently willing to live with a certain degree of inequality and unfairness. Even so, the political and ideological debates of our day and for most of the twenty-first century will undoubtedly focus on these central tensions and dilemmas.

Ideology and Tolerance

The connections betwen ideological support for civil liberties and the ideologies of liberalism and conservatism are striking. Some political scientists assert that conservatives are generally less tolerant than liberals. The reasons for these differences "can be traced in large measure to the hopes, fears and values embodied in each of the ideologies. Over the past two centuries," observe McCloskey and Brill, "conservatives have repeatedly shown their fear of political and social instability. With rare exceptions, the conservatives have been the party of tradition, stability, duty, respect for authority, and the primacy of 'law and order' over all competing values."[36]

As we noted, conservatives respect tradition, discipline, and established institutions. They prize liberty over equality, the private sector over the public sector, and they view human failure, delinquency, and crime as the fault of character deficiencies. Liberals share many of these views but place a different emphasis on the interpretation. Liberals have more faith in government and readily turn to government to help achieve greater equality of opportunity. Liberals are usually more tolerant of dissent and the expression of unorthodox opinions. However, liberals *too* can be intolerant of the anti-abortion forces or the National Rifle Association or the view of a Judge Robert Bork or the KKK.

Most liberals are strongly opposed to crime and lawbreaking, yet they are as concerned about the roots or causes of crime as they are about the punishment of criminals. Perhaps for this reason, liberals exhibit somewhat greater sympathy than conservatives for the rights of the accused and are more willing to honor the rights of due process. Conservatives usually take a harder line and, in recent years, have won widespread popular support for urging more concern for the victims of crime than for the rights of the accused.

Such differences are best shown in the responses of liberals and conservatives to a number of questions about civil rights and civil liberties. Table 7–4 has divided respondents along an ideological continuum into liberal left, liberal, conservative, and conservative right. Those involved in the survey were knowledgeable adult leaders who were active in, or associated with, ideological organizations that range from the far left to the far right. These findings confirm that, despite our common political culture and despite our widespread allegiance to constitutionalism and the Bill of Rights, many Americans sharply disagree about rather basic political matters.

As the data in Table 7–4 suggest, liberals are ordinarily more willing than conservatives to defend the rights of those who are in the minority, who may be wrong, or who take unorthodox or unpleasing stands. For example, even though the Fifth Amendment in our Bill of Rights unequivocally protects individuals from being forced to testify against themselves in our courtrooms, at least four times as many strong conservatives as strong liberals (among community leaders sampled) would deny this precious right to people accused of brutal crimes.

TABLE 7–4
Liberal-Conservative Differences in Perception of the Inalienability or Contingency of Rights

	LIBERAL LEFT	LIBERAL	CONSERVATIVE	CONSERVATIVE RIGHT
A newspaper has a right to publish its opinions—no matter how false and twisted its opinions are.	49%	38%	21%	12%
On issues of religion, morals and politics, high school teachers have the right to express their opinions in class—even if they go against the community's standards.	81%	68%	16%	14%
If minorities aren't receiving equal treatment in jobs or housing—the government should step in to see that they are treated the same as everyone else.	94%	92%	29%	31%
Keeping people in prison without a trial—is never justified.	62%	56%	26%	16%
Any American who shows disrespect for the flag—has the right to think what he pleases.	91%	78%	29%	18%

Source: Adapted from Herbert McCloskey and Alida Brill, *Dimensions of Tolerance* (Russell Sage Foundation, 1983), pp. 278–79 (N–2131).

Similar differences exist between ideological camps when they are asked about such civil liberties as freedom of the press, freedom of speech, and privacy and lifestyle concerns. Liberals or "progressives" are more pro-civil liberties than conservatives. Examine the notable differences in orientations in Table 7–5.

Conservatives nowadays believe America has become too permissive. Many conservatives, especially the new or religious right, are highly critical of homosexuals, hippies, drug users, pornographers, and prostitutes. They worry about what they claim has been a decline in moral standards and, interestingly enough, call on government to help reverse these trends.

Liberals, on the other hand, generally accept nonconformity in conduct and opinion as an inescapable byproduct of freedom. "Like John Stuart Mill [the English philosopher], contemporary liberals tend to perceive the free exchange of divergent views and attempts at social experimentation as potential harbingers of social improvement and progress. They regard the dangers to society from unorthodox beliefs and behavior as minimal compared with their potential benefits—a small price to be paid for social advancement."[37]

It is these sharp cleavages in political thinking that stir opposing interest groups into formation and action. Groups such as the Moral Majority, the American Civil Liberties Union, Amnesty International, Mothers Against Drunk Driving, and countless others came into being precisely to push their views about what is politically desirable in matters of civil rights and civil liberties. It is also these differences in ideological perspectives that reinforce party loyalties and that divide us at election time. Policy fights in Congress, between Congress and the White House, and during judicial confirmation hearings also have their roots in our uneasily coexisting ideological values.

In sum, ideologies have consequences. Although Americans share many ideas in common, we as a people also hold many contradictory ideas. Our hard-earned rights and liberties are never entirely safeguarded; they are fragile and susceptible to the political, economic, and social climate of the day. In the next few chapters we examine the pressure groups, political movements, and political parties that are ever present to advance their values and compete in the always evolving American political culture.

How Tolerant Are the Liberals on Your Campus?

Although the discussion in these pages suggests that liberals are usually more tolerant of unorthodox views and more vigorously defend freedom of speech, reflect on what would happen if a campus political group at your school invited the president of South Africa or a major spokesperson advocating pro-life and anti-ERA stands to speak. Do liberal students favor CIA recruiters on campus? Do liberals believe it is good for diversity to invite racists to teach at your college? Probably not. Tolerance is a tricky matter. It is easy, as we suggested earlier, to favor free speech in the abstract. In practice, liberals as well as conservatives are sometimes intolerant and oppose free speech for those whose views are fundamentally at odds with their own. Examine your own campus—and while you are at it—your own views. How tolerant are you? Would you ban any speakers, just a few, or none at all?

TABLE 7–5
Liberal-Conservative Differences on Civil Liberties

	LIBERAL LEFT	LIBERAL	CONSERVATIVE	CONSERVATIVE RIGHT
When it comes to free speech, extremists—should have the same rights as everyone else.	94%	92%	69%	51%
Censoring obscene books—is an old-fashioned idea that no longer makes sense.	82%	73%	17%	7%
How do you feel about movies that use foul language or show nudity and sexual acts on the screen?—They have as much right to be shown as other films.	82%	74%	25%	11%
Should a community allow the American Nazi party to use its town hall to hold a public meeting?—Yes.	57%	56%	30%	19%
Is it a good idea or a bad idea for the government to keep a list of people who take part in protest demonstrations?—A bad idea.	92%	83%	17%	12%
Searching a person's home or car without a search warrant—should never be allowed.	81%	77%	45%	44%
Freedom of sexual conduct between adults should be—left up to the individuals.	96%	95%	66%	45%

Source: Adapted from Herbert McCloskey and Alida Brill, *Dimensions of Tolerance* (Russell Sage Foundation, 1983), pp. 302–05 (N–2141).

Summary

1. The United States, like every other nation or society, has a distinctive political culture, a widely held set of fundamental political values, and accepted processes and institutions that permit it to manage conflict and resolve its problems. In the United States, for example, there is, at least in the abstract, a widespread reverence for the Constitution, the Bill of Rights, a two-party system, and the right to elect officials on the basis of majority rule.

2. Every nation also has a distinctive ideology, a collection of beliefs that its citizens hold about political power, how government works, or should work, and why.

3. Although it is often said that America is a nonideological nation primarily guided by moderate pragmatism, a closer look reveals that Americans hold a number of distinctive ideological commitments that have varied over our history. Our foremost commitment has been to individual liberty, yet we have also developed commitments to democratic rights and procedures, the free-enterprise or capitalistic market system, equality of opportunity, and a certain level of social justice.

4. Perhaps the most notable tension in the American political culture is that we simultaneously believe in capitalism and political equality. We want our economy to be relatively free from government controls and for major economic decisions to be shaped by the marketplace; yet we also want every American to enjoy the possibility of an equal voice in shaping our laws and policies. These two commitments are incompatible in certain ways and we increasingly turn to government, often in vain, to try to minimize some of the resulting inequalities in the political system.

5. Our ideological orientation has a bearing upon how tolerant we are of the views and conduct of others. Liberals tend to be more permissive whereas conservatives generally favor tradition, stability, and greater levels of "law and order." These differences have major consequences for electoral contests, judicial interpretation, and policy development in our political system.

Further Reading

LEON P. BARADAT. *Political Ideologies: Their Origins and Impact*, 2d ed. (Prentice Hall, 1984).

JAMES MACGREGOR BURNS. *Uncommon Sense* (Harper & Row, 1972).

KENNETH M. DOLBEARE and PATRICIA DOLBEARE. *American Ideologies* (Markham, 1971).

RUSSELL G. FRYER, ed. *Recent Conservative Political Thought: American Perspectives* (University Press of America, 1979).

LOUIS HARTZ. *The Liberal Tradition in America* (Harcourt, Brace & Co., 1955).

KENNETH R. HOOVER. *Ideology and Political Life* (Brooks/Cole Publishing Company, 1987).

Samuel Huntington. *American Politics: The Promise of Disharmony* (Belknap, 1981).

George Lodge. *The New American Ideology* (Knopf, 1975).

Herbert McCloskey and Alida Brill. *Dimensions of Tolerance: What Americans Believe about Civil Liberties* (Russell Sage Foundation, 1983).

Herbert McCloskey and John Zaller. *The American Ethos: Public Attitudes Toward Capitalism and Democracy* (Harvard University Press, 1984).

Notes

1. Daniel J. Boorstin, *The Genius of American Politics* (University of Chicago Press, 1953), p. 8.
2. Robert S. McElvaine, *Mario Cuomo: A Biography* (Scribners, 1988), p. 389.
3. Clinton Rossiter, *Conservatism in America* (Vintage, 1962), p. 72.
4. Everett Carll Ladd, "The American Constitution as Ideology," *The Christian Science Monitor* (February 2, 1987), p. 16. See also, in general, Sanford Levinson, *Constitutional Faith* (Princeton University Press, 1988).
5. See, for example, the classic study by Gabriel A. Almond and Sidney Verba, *The Civic Culture: Political Attitudes and Democracy in Five Nations* (Princeton University Press, 1963).
6. See Thomas E. Cronin, *Direct Democracy: The Politics of Initiative, Referendum and Recall* (Harvard University Press, 1989), Chaps. 6 and 7.
7. Alexander Solzhenitsyn, "The West Has Lost Its Courage," *The Washington Post* (June 11, 1978), p. C1.
8. See Benjamin Page, *Who Gets What from Government* (University of California Press, 1983).
9. Samuel Huntington, in Michel J. Crozier, Samuel P. Huntington, and Joji Wantanuki, *The Crisis of Democracy* (New York University Press, 1975), p. 115.
10. For an analysis of one aspect of this, see Paul M. Sniderman and Michael Hagen, *Race and Inequality: A Study in American Values* (Chatham House, 1985).
11. See, generally, Bernard Bailyn, *The Ideological Orgins of the American Revolution* (Harvard University Press, 1967).
12. Robert A. Dahl, "Liberal Democracy in the United States," in William Livingston, ed., *A Prospect of Liberal Democracy* (University of Texas Press, 1979), p. 64.
13. Ibid., pp. 59–60.
14. Franklin Roosevelt, 1944 State of the Union message, in Samuel I. Rosenman, ed., *The Public Papers and Addresses of Franklin D. Roosevelt, 1944–45* (Harper & Brothers, 1950), p. 41.
15. David Spitz, "A Liberal Perspective on Liberalism and Conservatism," in Robert Goldwin, ed., *Left, Right and Center* (Rand McNally, 1965), p. 31.
16. Leonard Bernstein, "I'm a Liberal and Proud of It," *The New York Times* (October 30, 1988), p. E23.
17. Arthur M. Schlesinger, Jr., "Hurray for the L-Word," *Wall Street Journal* (October 21, 1988), p. A10.
18. See also Charles Peters and Philip Keisling, eds., *A New Road for America: The Neoliberal Movement* (University Press of America, 1984); and Randall Rothenberg, *The Neoliberals: Creating the New American Politics* (Simon and Schuster, 1984).
19. Simon's statement comes from his own book, *Winners and Losers: The 1988 Race for the Presidency—One Candidate's Perspective* (Continuum, 1989).
20. E. J. Dionne, Jr., "A Liberal's Liberal Tells Just What Went Wrong," *The New York Times* (December 22, 1988), p. C21, quoting Congressman Barney Frank. For a book that makes this and similar points, see Robert Kuttner, *The Life of the Party: Democratic Prospects in 1988 and Beyond* (Viking, 1987).
21. Kenneth R. Hoover, *Ideology and Political Life* (Brooks/Cole, 1987), p. 34.
22. See the writings of Milton Friedman, *Capitalism and Freedom* (University of Chicago, 1962). See also Friedrich A. Hayek, *The Road to Serfdom* (University of Chicago Press, 1967; originally published in 1944).
23. Barry Goldwater, *The Conscience of a Conservative* (Victor, 1960), p. 76.
24. Robert Nozick, *Anarchy, State and Utopia* (Basic Books, 1974), pp. 333–34.
25. Jesse Helms, *When Free Men Shall Stand* (Zondervan Publishing House, 1976), pp. 17–18.
26. See Ernest B. Furgurson, *Hard Right: The Rise of Jesse Jackson* (Norton, 1987); and Garrett Epps, "The Discreet Charms of a Demagogue," *New York Review of Books* (May 7, 1987), pp. 31–35.
27. Barry Goldwater with Jack Casserly, *Goldwater* (Doubleday, 1988), p. 387.
28. See Irving Kristol, "Don't Count Out Conservatism," *The New York Times Magazine* (June 14, 1987), p. 53.
29. For a general discussion of this ideology, see Peter Steinfels, *The Neoconservatives* (Simon and Schuster, 1979). For a general text from this perspective, see Richard T. Saeger, *American Government and Politics: A Neoconservative Approach* (Scott, Foresman, 1982).
30. Irving Howe, *Socialism and America* (Harcourt, 1985); and Michael Harrington, *Socialism: Past and Future* (Arcade, 1989).
31. See, for example, Robert Ringer, *Restoring the American Dream* (QED, 1979); and Ed Clark, *A New Beginning* (Caroline House, 1980).
32. Herbert McCloskey and John Zaller, *The American Ethos: Public Attitudes toward Capitalism and Democracy* (Harvard University Press, 1984), p. 292.
33. See Robert E. Lane, *Political Ideology: Why the American Common Man Believes What He Does* (Free Press, 1962).
34. Charles Lindblom, *Politics and Markets* (Basic Books, 1977), p. 356.
35. McCloskey and Zaller, *The American Ethos*, p. 187.
36. Herbert McCloskey and Alida Brill, *Dimensions of Tolerance: What Americans Believe about Civil Liberties* (Russell Sage Foundation, 1983), pp. 274–75.
37. Ibid., p. 313.

8

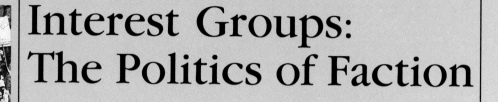

Interest Groups:
The Politics of Faction

We have focused in the last several chapters on individual liberty and people's rights and values. We have noted how the liberties of the Bill of Rights—the "Big Ten"—broadened over two centuries, amid many struggles and with successes as well as failures. And as Chapter 7 indicated, the pursuit of liberty, equality, and the other rights is only part of the American experiment. As we noted in Chapter 1, Americans have also sought *order*, whether they call it unity or stability or security.

No one two hundred years ago was more aware of the need for both liberty and order—and the dangers of both—than James Madison. When he helped draft the Constitution and later wrote the newspaper columns that would become part of *The Federalist*, the young Virginian had vivid memories of the tumult caused by Shays's Rebellion. He had also seen the power and fury of factions—especially religious factions—in Virginia politics. Perhaps, too, he remembered his friend John Adams complaining about a Boston group that met in Tom Dawes's house in a smoke-filled room where they "drank flip" and chose selectmen and assessors before the town could vote for them.

For Madison and the other framers, the daunting problem was how to establish a stable and orderly constitutional system that at the same time would respect the liberty of free citizens: in short, how to balance the great ideals of liberty and order. Writing his newspaper columns with a goose-quill pen in his small, precise handwriting, Madison warned of the tendency of popular government toward the "vice" of faction, toward "instability, injustice, and confusion." Still, he would not sacrifice the liberty that led to faction. How could this dilemma be resolved?

Madison, a good practical politician and a brilliant theorist, offered both a diagnosis and a solution. These were not secret. He summarized the diagnosis in a newspaper column that would become *The Federalist*, No. 10. The solution had already taken concrete form in the new constitution that Madison firmly believed would control the effects of factionalism; Madison summarized this solution in *The Federalist*, No. 51 (see the Appendix).

Madison diagnosed the problem so clearly in *The Federalist*, No. 10 that the authors of this text urge you to read his complete essay in the Appendix, but a summary here may be useful:

1. The main problem with popular government is violent factionalism.
2. Such factionalism has caused the downfall of many popular governments.
3. People are already complaining that "our governments" are too unstable and divided.
4. Laws are passed that simply reflect the power of the strongest factions.
5. Basic solution alternatives:
   (A) Remove causes of faction.
      (1) Abolish liberty, which is "to faction what air is to fire." *But abolish liberty? Never!*
      (2) Make all citizens have the same opinions, passions, and interests. *Impossible, out of the question! Human beings will always disagree and form factions!*
   (B) Control its effects. Establish a government with so many checks and balances built into the constitutional system that the power of factions will be cushioned and curbed, but without any sacrifice of liberty.

Madison lays out this solution in *The Federalist*, No. 51. Its application has already been examined in Chapters 2 and 3 in the discussion on the division of powers between state and national government, and the separation of powers within the national government—our system of checks and balances.

The brilliance of *The Federalist*, No. 10 lies in the manner in which Madison describes the factions of the day. No one pictured these better than Madison himself. Note how he begins with a fundamental proposition: "The latent causes of faction are thus sown in the nature of man . . ." Note also how he does not take a simplistic approach to faction; factions are not merely religious, economic, or political but a combination of these, and factions can be divided into subfactions; thus, property owners may be divided into landed, manufacturing, mercantile, moneyed, and many lesser interests. Madison demonstrated that Americans lived amid a maze of group interests.

The Maze of Group Interests

The maze of interests is even larger today. As a student you may belong to a variety of groups—an athletic team, a sorority, a debate club, a rock band, or Young Republicans. Your experience with these groups—with the coalitions and rivalries within them and among them—trains you well for "real-life" political activities.

Does this sound fanciful? Some years ago a first-year student entered the Southwest Texas State Teacher College at San Marcos, sized up the faculty and students ("who got what, when, and how"), and decided to overthrow an elite group of athletes who ran the campus. He formed a group and recruited support from other groups: "the YMCA group, the townies, the debating society, and music and art groups."[1] He mobilized the support of poor undergraduates by promising to distribute the student activities funds more equitably. After extensive campus politicking, he and his group defeated the elite athletes. It is said that his campaigning and coalition building forecast much of his later political career. His name was Lyndon B. Johnson.

In the late eighteenth century Madison was concerned about religious, political, and economic factions. What are the key groups and issues today? What are the sources of the groups' strengths and weaknesses? How do they seek to influence government? Are they as dangerous to the public interest now as Madison feared they were in his time? And, if so, what has been done about it, and what else could be done?

GROUP INTERESTS TODAY

The United States has often been called a nation of joiners. Europeans sometimes make fun of us for setting up all sorts of organizations, and we ourselves are often amused by the behavior of our groups—the noisy conventions of veterans' associations, the solemn rites of great fraternal organizations, the oratory of patriotic societies. Yet most of these groups are serious in their aims, and they play an enormous role in politics.

How many groups are there in America? There is no way of knowing accurately. The family is the most basic and important group of all, and there are over 60 million families in the United States. We have one-quarter million religious congregations, diverse farm groups, and trade unions, and over two thousand trade associations. All these are groups in the broadest sense of the term; that is, their members share some common outlook or attitude, and they interact with one another in some way.

Interest groups, groups that seek to influence public policy, are also numerous and are growing in number. Sometimes referred to as "special interests," they are viewed by many as selfish, concerned only with advancing their own well-being. Indeed, the discussion of interest groups for many conjures up images of powerful or moneyed interests pressuring legislators to retain tax loopholes or groups, such as the National Rifle Association, lobbying against controls on handguns or automatic weapons. Yet, even such "special interests" would claim that their actions promote common national interests.

The interests represented by organized groups and the methods they employ are diverse. Interest groups vary widely from business organizations to public interest groups. They are also of many types. Some are formal associations or organizations; others have no formal organization at all. Some are organized primarily to lobby; some have other goals, such as securing wage increases, conducting research, or broadly influencing public opinion by publishing reports and mass mailings.

The last two decades have witnessed a tremendous expansion of interest groups as well as changes in the scope of their activities. A growing distrust of government and big business during the 1960s led to the rise of many "public interest groups" (representing no particular economic interest), such as those pioneered by Ralph Nader. But if the 1960s was the decade for environmental and consumer groups, the 1980s was the decade in which all these interests reasserted themselves in Washington. Grass-roots lobbying became an important new legislative tactic for these interests. The decline of party loyalties, the weakening of the power of committee chairmen through congressional reforms, and the diffusion of power to junior members of Congress had by the mid-1970s led to a major alteration of lobbying strategies.[2] The campaign finance reform law of 1973 made it legal for corporations as well as labor unions to form political action committees (PACs), enabling them to make campaign contributions. New technologies also increased the reach and effectiveness of interest groups.

In May of 1986, five million Americans joined in the Hands Across America rally to win support for the poor and hungry.

One of these new technologies is the computerized and targeted *mass mailing*. For many decades interest groups have been sending out huge mailings to lists culled from telephone directories and other sources. Most of these mailings were "blind," sent out indiscriminately. Today's technology can grind out personalized letters targeted to specific groups with a special message for those groups. Thus thousands of letters could be targeted to white males over fifty living in southern California who have written to their senator during the last twelve months, subscribe to a hunting magazine, and belong to the National Rifle Association. Such targeted letters can also appeal to public interest groups who share a common concern, such as environmental groups.

Organized interest groups raise questions closely akin to the central problem addressed in this book. Do such groups fairly represent the great range and variety of interests in the United States? Do the leaders of specific associations— union presidents, for example—fairly represent the various interests of their own members? Some have argued that interests make themselves felt through organization, and that if all the relevant interests are organized, then a balance is achieved. The problem with this view is that not all the affected interests in our society are equally well organized, and, as we shall see, some sectors of our society are far more adept at pressing their interests in the political arena.

Richard Viguerie, a noted leader behind several right-wing conservative groups. A businessman and conservative political activist, Viguerie is a king of direct-mail fund raising.

GROUP THEORY

Why do Americans organize? Group theory has traditionally asserted that organizations are formed to further the common interests of groups. Rational persons combine to obtain benefits they ordinarily would not achieve without collective action. However, the logic behind group formation is far more complex than these theories would assert. Although there are benefits to joining groups, there are costs as well. Individuals must often sacrifice time, money, or their allegiances to other interests in order to participate in an organized group. Further, if all persons are rational and group activity helps promote their interests, why are citizen or consumer groups weaker than the less numerous groups? While the number of interest groups participating in American politics is astounding, not all Americans belong to one of these groups and not all groups are equally successful at raising money or influencing government officials. Important factors determining whether a group of people will organize successfully are the size of the group and the incentives that collective group action provides.

A woman is carried on a stretcher into a police van during an anti-abortion protest outside a Manhattan abortion clinic.

189

Although members of a group all have a common interest in obtaining the collective benefit of group action, they have no common interest in paying the cost of providing that benefit, whether it be a sacrifice of time or a membership fee, such as union dues, to finance the group's activities. If we apply simple economics to the problem, it is clear that people will not participate unless the benefits of joining outweigh the costs. This observation helps explain the relative success of small groups compared to large groups. Members of large groups might not rationally contribute to an organization representing them because their individual contribution is so small and would probably "not make a difference anyway." However, in a small group, where each member gets a substantial proportion of the total gain, organization to promote a common interest may be achieved through the voluntary, self-interested action of the group's members.[3]

For instance, if your neighbors formed a neighborhood clean-up committee and asked you to join, would you? If your neighborhood is of considerable size, it is unlikely that any personal contribution that you make to the clean-up effort would make a significant difference to your surroundings. Also, you are benefiting from the work that is already being done by current members of the committee. Since you would probably not be able to notice the difference between the level of cleanliness with or without your help, it is not worth your time and effort to participate. You would probably remain a "free rider," benefiting from the committee's work, without personally contributing. On the other hand, you might help out just to "do your bit."

On the other hand, suppose you were the president of one of the few yo-yo manufacturing companies of America and were invited to join the Yo-yo Makers of America, an organization consisting of the other five companies in the industry that lobbies in Washington against yo-yo regulation. You are told each company generally donates $500,000 to the association's PAC, and you are expected to donate this sum as well. You are also told that currently the association has $2.5 million to spend on its lobbying activities. With your contribution, its resources will be increased by 20 percent, enabling it to lobby much more effectively and virtually guarantee the passage of a yo-yo tariff. Therefore, joining the group would clearly give you a benefit you would not ordinarily receive. Because the group is so small in this case, your contribution is very perceptible, and the benefits of organization (a yo-yo tariff, among other things) outweigh the cost of contributing.

How can larger groups overcome the incentive problem, as in our neighborhood clean-up committee? The answer becomes clear when we contrast the success of some large organizations, such as unions or the American Association of Retired Persons (AARP), with the weakness of consumers and other large groups. Individuals will not always join an organization for the benefits of collective action. Organizations must provide selective incentives, material or otherwise, compelling enough to attract the potential free rider.[4] Unions are organized not just for the purpose of lobbying but also to perform other important services for their members. Unions derive much of their strength from their negotiating position with corporations, which they use to obtain wage increases or improved safety standards. Similarly, the AARP, in addition to lobbying against Social Security cuts and speaking out on other issues of concern to older citizens, offers incentives such as a free subscription to its magazine, *Modern Maturity*, and member discounts at certain hotels. This combination of size and strength sets these groups apart from other large organizations in their effectiveness because members derive numerous perceived benefits from joining.

Marian Wright Edelman, president of the Children's Defense Fund and one of the most respected public interest lobbyists in Washington, joins in a celebration of children.

The mobilization of business interests has been successful in recent years in large part because of the small membership of most industry groups. However, another important factor has been the sustained, economically driven interest of the nation's corporations and trade associations in the outcome of the legislative and elective process on a day-to-day basis.[5] On the other hand, large corporations today are exposed to a much broader array of specific policy impacts.[6] Often larger groups become organized only when an important issue excites the public or when effective leadership can guide public opinion.

Americans are often angered at the power of these "special interests." In the FDR and Truman eras, labor unions were often seen as greedy and power-hungry. Today corporate conglomerates more often come under attack. Occasionally—when perhaps a powerful corporation squares off against a strong union, as in the transportation field—the public may utter a "curse on both your houses."

"There's getting to be a lot of dangerous talk about the public interest"

From The Herblock Gallery *(Simon & Schuster, 1968).*

Major Interests: Size and Scope

The vast majority of gainfully employed Americans are members of at least one of the big occupational associations that have much to say about income and working conditions for employers and professional people as well as for farmers and union workers. The typical large association is a mosaic of local and state bodies, and the product of slow and painful growth over a period of decades.

MAJOR ECONOMIC INTERESTS

Probably the oldest "unions" in America were farm organizations. The earliest farm group—the South Carolina Agricultural Society—was founded even before the Constitution was written. In the late nineteenth century the National Grange, or Patrons of Husbandry, led farm rebellions against low farm prices, railroad monopolies, and middlemen. The Grange, once a fighting organization with over a million members, is today smaller and more conservative than other big farm groups. The largest farm group now is the American Farm Bureau Federation, which is especially strong in the corn belt. Originally organized around government agents who helped farmers in rural counties, the Federation today is almost a semigovernmental agency, but it retains full freedom to fight for such goals as price supports and expanded credit facilities. A number of other farm organizations are based on the interests of producers of specific commodities, such as the American Soybean Association.

Workers, too, have long been organized. The earliest trade union locals were founded during Washington's first administration. Throughout the nineteenth century workers organized political parties and local unions. Their most ambitious effort at national organization, the Knights of Labor, claimed 700,000 members. By the beginning of this century, the American Federation of Labor, a confederation of strong and independent-minded national unions mainly representing craftworkers, was the dominant organization. During the ferment of the 1930s, unions more responsive to industrial workers broke away from the AFL and formed a rival national organization, the Congress of Industrial Organizations. Later the AFL and CIO reunited in the organization that exists today, but some industrial union leaders contend that the AFL-CIO has become too conservative, and some large unions, including the United Auto Workers, remain outside the AFL-CIO.

Students from Boston University picket a Burger King restaurant in a demonstration against the subminimum (training) wage proposed by the Bush administration.

Business associations are the most varied and numerous of all. The several thousand national trade associations and local groups are as diverse as the products and services they sell. The main general agency for business is the Chamber of Commerce of the United States, organized in 1912. The chamber is a federation of federations, composed of several thousand local chambers of commerce representing tens of thousands of business firms. Loosely allied with the chamber on most issues is the National Association of Manufacturers, which, since its founding in the wake of the depression of 1893, has tended to speak for the more conservative elements of American business.

Some of the smaller and less well-known business groups nevertheless have considerable influence. The Conference Board, founded in 1916, conducts research on practical problems and seeks to inform the public on the role of business in the economy. It does not take public stands on issues but emphasizes economic and policy analysis developed through a large staff. Frequently it also holds conferences, briefings, and seminars. The Business Roundtable, organized in 1972, is an association of the heads of major corporations, banks, and utilities. Founded in the belief that top business executives need to take unified public stands on such issues as taxation, government regulation, and energy, the Roundtable seeks to ensure that the views of big business are heard in public policy debates. It was reported to have had a major role in defeating a 1977 picketing bill strongly backed by the AFL-CIO.

The large, nationwide business associations very often take up issues that involve many industries, such as opposition to a bill to give workers advance notice of plant closings that was passed in 1988. However, individual industries have their own interest groups that are often successful in achieving their goals due to their smaller size and focus. One such industry group is the Aerospace Industries Association of America, representing a number of important defense contractors, which launched an intensive lobbying campaign in the late 1980s to combat growing public distrust of the defense industry.[7] Another industry group active in the late 1980s is the alcoholic beverage industry, representing organizations such as the Distilled Spirits Council of the United States and the Beer and Wine Institutes. With support from other diverse interests and the National Association of Manufacturers, this group has been successful to date in heading off proposals to raise the excise taxes on alcohol.[8] In the endless battle of factions, however, the influence of such interests is limited. Otherwise alcohol would not be the most heavily taxed of any single commodity.

Professional people have organized some of the strongest "unions" in the nation. Some are well known, such as the American Medical Association and the American Bar Association. Others are divided into many subgroups: Teachers are organized in the National Education Association, the American Federation of Teachers, the American Association of University Professors, and also in particular subject groups, such as the Modern Language Association. Many professions are closely tied in with government, especially on the state level. Lawyers, for example, are licensed by the states, which have set up, often as a result of pressure from lawyers themselves, certain standards of admission to the state bar.

THE CRISSCROSS OF INTERESTS

Cutting across associations based on economic interest or occupation are other groups based on sex or national origin, or on religious, racial, ideological, recreational, and other ties. Few Americans are members of more than one occupational group, but because they have endless nonoccupational interests, they are often

CHAPTER 8 / Interest Groups: The Politics of Faction

emotionally and financially involved in various other groups, such as the American Legion, Veterans of Foreign Wars, or Amvets; nationality groups, such as the multitude of Irish, German, Polish, Scandinavian, Hispanic, and other organizations; or religious organizations, such as the Knights of Columbus. The variety of such groups is remarkable; more than 150 nationwide organizations are based on national origin alone.

Cutting across both economic and ethnic groups are interest-group associations focused on issues and ideology. Virtually all interest groups convince themselves that they are devoted to the public welfare and not merely to their own self-interests; issue and ideological groups usually present their cases in terms of their value to the "public interest." The Americans for Democratic Action (ADA), for example, campaigns for liberal candidates and issues, while the Young Americans for Freedom (YAF) works for conservative ones. The YAF is active on university and college campuses, where it supported Ronald Reagan and George Bush in recent campaigns; the ADA endorsed Senator Edward M. Kennedy for the Democratic nomination in 1980. Countless groups have organized around specific issues, such as civil liberties, birth control, abortion, opposition to the Panama Canal treaty, environmental protection, nuclear energy, and nuclear arms. Some highly ideological groups are thriving in the otherwise pragmatic, pluralistic politics of the 1990s, but the John Birch Society, on the extreme right, has survived with a hard-core membership only in the tens of thousands. The Libertarian party, more an interest group than a party, has also attracted a small but provocative following on the right. The Moral Majority, on the other hand, attracted large numbers and apparently had a significant impact in recent elections.

Large associations themselves are often made up of alliances of many small associations. As Tocqueville observed long ago, Americans form and reform associations for every conceivable purpose and function. And as government has become more central to Americans' lives, these associations have turned their attention to government. In Washington today the associations rival the federal bureaucracy itself in number, size, complexity, and resources.

Of special importance in recent years has been a "public interest" group that arose out of the political ferment of the 1960s. Common Cause, founded in 1970 by independent Republican John W. Gardner and later led by noted Watergate prosecutor Archibald Cox, campaigns effectively for electoral reform and for making the political process more open. Its Washington staff raises money through direct mail campaigns, oversees state chapters, issues a flood of research reports and press releases on current issues, and lobbies on Capitol Hill and in major government departments. Ralph Nader started a conglomerate of consumer organizations that investigate and report on governmental and corporate action—or inaction— relating to consumer interests. These groups have had a direct impact on legislation, for example, on the passage of the National Traffic and Motor Vehicle Safety Act and the Highway Safety Act. Public Interest Research Groups (PIRGs), also founded by Ralph Nader, today number among the largest interest groups in the country with a claimed national membership of over 400,000, and have become a major player on Capitol Hill. Chapters of these groups exist on many college campuses and are active in promoting environmental issues, safe energy, consumer protection, and good government.

Issues of domestic policy are not the only matters of concern to interest groups. More and more, groups are organizing to promote or oppose certain foreign policies. Among the most prestigious (although not uncontroversial) foreign affairs group is the Council on Foreign Relations in New York. Long denounced by critics as a center of conservative and corporate power, the Council is in fact a meeting place for mainly aging establishment types who gather to hear speakers

This protester combines opposition to American involvement in Nicaragua with a plea for government support for workers.

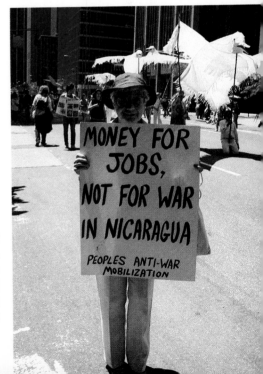

Secretary of State James A. Baker addressing the American Israel Public Affairs Committee in Washington, May 1989.

and to make use of an unusually good library of international affairs. Other groups, devoted to narrower areas of American foreign policy, exert pressure on legislators for specific policies. Among these are interests concerned with the Arab-Israeli conflict and the apartheid system in South Africa. Formal lobbies for both Israel and the Arab nations—the American Israel Public Affairs Committee and the National Association of Arab-Americans, respectively—compete to influence policy makers in Washington. Both organizations make their cases on the basis of U.S. national interests. These lobbies have been particularly articulate in debates over proposed arms sales to Israel or the Arab nations. Interest group pressure has also influenced United States policy towards South Africa. Groups ranging from student organizations to national lobbies like the American Committee on Africa have urged divestment, sanctions, or other policy measures in seeking to promote change in South Africa from the outside.

Although political factions are not a new phenomenon, in recent years there has been a virtual explosion in the number and variety of interests and associations. This is especially true of "single-cause" groups. (Again, this is not new: The Anti-Saloon League of the 1890s was single-mindedly devoted to barring the sale and manufacture of alcoholic beverages. It was said that the League did not care whether a legislator was drunk or sober as long as he voted dry.) Today single-cause groups crusade tirelessly for or against highly specialized, but politically "hot" questions, such as the National Rifle Association's opposition to regulation of the sale of firearms, or the Nuclear Freeze movement's dedication to the peace cause.

The number, intensity, and specialized nature of these single-cause groups raise a basic question about our "government by the people": Can it represent some kind of general or majority interest at the same time as it responds to a welter of narrow and particular interests?

Weapons of Group Power

Some Americans tend to overreact to organized groups, especially to ones they oppose. They view such groups as vast, well organized, well financed, and all but irresistible in political action. They should remember, however, that large and relatively well-organized groups have weaknesses as well as strengths. The larger the group, the greater the likelihood of crisscrossing interests that drain it of unity, energy, money, and singleness of purpose.

STRENGTHS AND WEAKNESSES

Obviously size is still a central test of political power; an organization representing 5 million voters will have more influence than one speaking for 50,000. Obviously, too, the unity of the membership is a key element. Unity, however, is easier to achieve in a small group that focuses on a relatively specific and concrete concern that does not noticeably affect others—for example, a tariff on steel pins. But we need to look at these and other bases of group power more closely.

A fundamental factor in group impact is the attitude and makeup of the membership. Many people join an organization for reasons that have little to do with its political objectives. They may join to secure group insurance, take advantage of travel benefits, participate in professional meetings, or get a job. If organizational leaders can depend on the political backing of their followers, the organization is able to put its full strength into pursuing its aims, and it will have an enormous advantage in the political arena. If they cannot, the organization will not be nearly as effective.

Most Americans are members of many groups; their loyalties are divided. It is this fact of *overlapping membership* that largely determines the cohesiveness of a group. Organization leaders run up against the problem time after time. Suppose a union official, for example, asks a dozen members to come to a meeting. Several may say they will come. But two others may have to be with their bowling club that night; two others may have to stay home with their families; and another may have to attend a church supper. Even those who finally do show up may not be 100 percent supporters. Perhaps they are asked to vote for a particular candidate in a coming election. Some will. But one may decide to vote for the other candidate because they are neighbors or because they are both Italian-Americans, or Republicans, or Legionnaires. Or perhaps one will not know what to do and will not vote at all.

Usually a mass-membership organization is made up of three types of members.[9] The first is a relatively small number of formal leaders who may hold full-time, paid positions or at least devote much of their extra time, effort, and money to the group's activities. The second is a hard core for those involved in the group organizationally and psychologically. They identify with the group's aims, show up at meetings, cheerfully pay dues, and do a lot of the legwork. The third type comprises people who are members in name only. They do not participate actively; they do not look on themselves as Teamsters or Rotarians or Legionnaires; and they cannot be depended on to vote in elections or otherwise act as the leadership wants. In a typical organization, for every top leader there might be a few hundred hard core activists and 10,000 more or less inactive members.

A second factor in the cohesion of a group is its organizational structure. Some groups have no formal organization. Others consist of local organizations that have joined together in some sort of loose state or national federation. The local organizations retain a measure of separate power and independence, just as the states did when they entered the Union. A sort of separation of powers may be found as well. The national assembly of an organization establishes—or at least ratifies—policy. An executive committee meets more frequently. A president or director is elected to head and speak for the group, and permanent, paid officials form the organization's bureaucracy. Power may be further divided between the organization's main headquarters and its Washington office. An organization of this sort tends to be far less cohesive than a centralized, disciplined group such as the Army or some trade unions.

Closely related to cohesion is a third factor: the nature of the leadership. In a group that embraces many attitudes and interests, leaders may either weld the various elements together or sharpen their disunity. The leader of a national business association, for example, must tread cautiously between big business and little business, between exporters and importers, between chain stores and corner grocery stores, between the makers and the sellers of competing products. Yet leaders must not be mere punching bags for different interests, for above all they must lead. They must show how to achieve whatever goals can be agreed on. The group leader is in the same position as a president or a member of Congress; he or she must know when to lead followers and when to follow them.

We have been talking about the characteristics of groups; but the power of a group is also affected by the nature of the political and governmental system in which it operates. Because of our federal system, a group consisting of 3 million

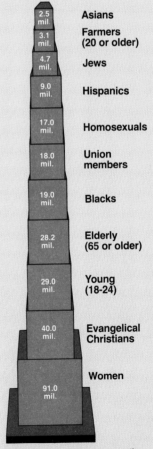

Voting Blocks—Can a Candidate Pile Them Up?

Persons Age 18 or Older

2.5 mil.	Asians
3.1 mil.	Farmers (20 or older)
4.7 mil.	Jews
9.0 mil.	Hispanics
17.0 mil.	Homosexuals
18.0 mil.	Union members
19.0 mil.	Blacks
28.2 mil.	Elderly (65 or older)
29.0 mil.	Young (18-24)
40.0 mil.	Evangelical Christians
91.0 mil.	Women

NOTE: People may belong to more than one group. Basic data: U.S. Departments of Commerce and Labor, American Jewish Committee, American Coalition for Traditional Values, National Gay Task Force.

SOURCE: Reprinted from *U.S. News & World Report* (July 16, 1984). Copyright 1984, U.S. News & World Report, Inc.

supporters concentrated in a few states will usually have less influence than another group consisting of the same number of supporters spread out in a large number of states. A group whose goals are contrary to widely accepted values will have a more difficult time than another group that can clothe its demands in acceptable ideology. And, as we shall see in later chapters, governmental structures are significant, because they allow some groups more access to decision makers and other groups less.

TECHNIQUES

The typical image of interest groups in action is that of powerful, hard-nosed lobbyists skillfully employing a combination of knowledge, persuasiveness, personal influence, charm, and money to influence legislators and bureaucrats. Interest-group representatives seeking to wield influence can often choose from a variety of political weapons and targets. These include persuasion, litigation, rule making, election activities, and lobbying.

Persuasion All interest groups exploit the communications media—television, radio, newspapers, leaflets, signs, direct mail, and word of mouth—to influence voters during elections and to motivate constituents to contact their representatives between elections. Business enjoys a special advantage in this arena, and businesspeople have the money to utilize propaganda machinery. Being advertisers on a large scale, they know how to deliver their message effectively. Most important, they generally have easy access to the means of disseminating propaganda, such as the press. When a business organization places full-page messages in newspapers across the nation, unions have to find funds to hire similar space for answers. Although labor has not yet matched the propaganda skills of business, it is devoting a good deal of money and attention to this technique.

Other groups have also become aware of the uses of propaganda. In a battle recently waged by the Recording Industry Association (RIAA) against the Home Recording Rights Coalition (HRRC) over the new DAT tape recorders developed by Japanese electronics firms, the RIAA accused the HRRC of being a puppet of Japanese business interests, and both sides conducted media campaigns supporting their views.

How effective is group propaganda? It is impossible to measure precisely the impact of propaganda campaigns, for too many other factors are involved. But we know enough to be skeptical of some of the extravagant claims made for them. For example, organized labor strongly denounced the **Taft-Hartley Act** (which banned the closed shop, slightly limited the right to strike, and restricted union activities in other ways) for years after its passage, but surveys have shown that the great majority of the public and of *union members* either wanted to keep the new law or had no opinion about it. Also, the more a group publicizes its position, the more it risks arousing opponents and stimulating *their* propaganda potential.

Litigation When groups find the usual political channels closed to them, they may seek other ways to influence public policy.[10] The courts have increasingly become the center of such efforts. The NAACP, for example, has instituted and won numerous cases in its efforts to improve legal protection for blacks. The technique is not new, of course, but in recent decades urban interests and environmental groups, feeling underrepresented in state and national legislatures, have turned to the courts. Women's groups—such as the National Organization for

Women and the American Civil Liberties Union Women's Rights Project—have also used the courts as one arena for pursuing their objectives.[11] Ralph Nader, too, has exploited this device.

Groups can gain a forum for presenting their points of view by seeking permission to file **amicus curiae (friend of the court) briefs,** even in cases in which they are not direct parties. The American Civil Liberties Union, for example, files many such briefs with the Supreme Court in cases that raise constitutional questions.

Rule Making   Groups have ready access to the rule-making process, in which executive and regulatory agencies write the rules that implement laws. Agencies publish proposed regulations in the *Federal Register* and invite responses and reactions from all interested persons before the rules are finalized. The *Federal Register* is published daily on weekdays. Well-staffed associations and corporations peruse the *Register*, ever alert for proposed agency actions that will affect their interests. You can find the publication in your school or public libraries.

The League of Women Voters sponsors presidential debates to arouse interest and clarify the candidates' positions.

Election Activities   Although nearly all large organizations say they are nonpolitical, almost all organized groups are involved in politics in one way or another. What group leaders usually mean when they say they are nonpolitical is that they are *nonpartisan*. A distinguishing feature of organized interest groups is that they try to work through one or both parties; usually this means working for individual candidates in either party. The policy labor has followed for years—helping friends and defeating enemies—is the policy of almost all interest groups.

This policy is put into action in different ways. Occasionally an organization openly endorses a candidate and actively works for that person's election. In 1924, for instance, many labor unions endorsed "Fighting Bob" La Follette for president; the CIO officially backed Roosevelt in 1944; and the AFL-CIO supported Humphrey, Carter, Mondale, and Dukakis. Some labor organizations formally stay neutral, but some prominent officials take a partisan stand. Because of such factors as overlapping membership, an organization may set up a front organization to carry on its political activities; the Committee on Political Education (COPE) of the AFL-CIO is a case in point.

Presidential primaries provide an opportunity for organized interest groups to push for the nomination of their candidates.

Individual labor unions, which have somewhat homogeneous memberships, can sometimes afford to take rather firm positions. Other organizations are handicapped by the diversity of their members. A local retailers group, for example, might be composed equally of Republicans and Democrats, and many of its members might refuse to take an open position on a candidate for fear of losing business. In such cases more subtle means may be equally effective: At meetings word may be passed around that candidate *X* is sound from the organization's point of view; perhaps the hat is passed around, too.

Ideological groups, on the other hand, may "target" candidates, seeking to change the candidates' positions or to influence voters. The Christian Voter's Victory Fund, for example, publicizes congressional candidates' "scores"—based on their roll call votes—on abortion, sex education, school busing, school prayer, and the Equal Rights Amendment. Americans for Democratic Action and Americans for Constitutional Action publish ratings of incumbents on a number of liberal and conservative issues, respectively.

How effective is electioneering by interest groups? No generalization is possible, because everything depends on the kinds of factors we have been discussing: the group's size, unity, objectives, political resources, and leadership, and the political context in which it is operating. In general, though, the power of the mass-membership organizations to mobilize their full strength in elections has been exaggerated in the press. Too many cross-pressures are operating in the pluralistic politics of America for any one group to assume a really commanding role. Some groups reach their maximum influence only by allying closely with one of the two major parties. They have placed their members on local, state, and national party committees and have helped send them to party conventions as delegates. But this means losing some of their independence and singleness of purpose.

Another interest-group strategy is to form a political party with the intent less of winning *elections* than of publicizing a *cause*. The Free Soil party was formed in 1848 to propagandize against the spread of slavery, and the Prohibition party was organized twenty years later to ban the sale of liquor. Farmers have formed a variety of such parties.

PACs: Interest Groups in Combat

In the last few years the number and impact of **political action committees (PACs)** has exploded. Technically, a PAC is simply the political arm of a business, labor, professional, or other interest group, legally entitled to raise funds on a voluntary basis from members, stockholders, or employees in order to contribute funds to favored candidates or political parties.[12] Because PACs link two vital techniques of influence—giving money and other political aid to politicians, and persuading office-holders to act or vote "the right way" on issues—we look at PACs more broadly as the means by which interest groups seek to control "who gets what, when, and how" through electoral activity and lobbying.

Candidates Who Got the Most for 1988 Election Campaigns from PACs and Other Sources

SENATE

Pete Wilson, R-Calif.	$11.4 million
Lloyd Bentsen, D-Tex.	8.3 million
George V. Voinovich, R-Ohio*	7.8 million
Pete Dawkins, R-N.J.*	7.8 million
Herb Kohl, D-Wis.	7.6 million
Howard Metzenbaum, D-Ohio	7.3 million
Frank Lautenberg, D-N.J.	7.1 million
Leo McCarthy, D-Calif.*	7.0 million
John Heinz, R-Pa.	5.3 million
Connie Mack, R-Fla.	5.2 million

HOUSE OF REPRESENTATIVES

Jane Eskind, D-Tenn.*	$ 2.6 million
Philip Bredesen, D-Tenn.*	1.9 million
Robert Dornan, R-Calif.	1.7 million
Joseph J. Dioguardi, R-N.Y.*	1.6 million
Gary K. Hart, D-Calif.*	1.5 million
Thomas Campbell, R-Calif.	1.4 million
Joseph P. Kennedy 2d, D-Mass.	1.4 million
Nita M. Lowey, D-N.Y.	1.3 million
John Miller, R-Wash.	1.3 million
Jim Moody, D-Wis.	1.3 million

Source: Federal Election Commission and *New York Times*, June 5, 1989, p. A13. Copyright © 1989 by The New York Times Company. Reprinted by permission.

* Lost election

PACs Who Gave the Most to Federal Candidates in 1988

National Association of Realtors	$ 3.0 million
International Brotherhood of Teamsters	2.9 million
American Medical Association	2.3 million
National Education Association	2.1 million
National Association of Retired Federal Employees	2.0 million
United Auto Workers	1.9 million
Association of Trial Lawyers of America	1.9 million
National Association of Letter Carriers	1.7 million
American Federation of State, County & Municipal Employees	1.6 million
International Association of Machinists and Aerospace Workers	1.5 million

Source: Federal Election Commission and *New York Times*, June 5, 1989, p. A13. Copyright © 1989 by The New York Times Company. Reprinted by permission.

Let's look at some specific cases. Between January 1987 and October 1988, Congressman Charles Rangel of New York City raised a war chest of just under half a million dollars, $301,400 of which came from PACs; Congressman John Dingell of Michigan raised just over half a million, $379,852 of which came from PACs; and Congressman Martin Frost of Texas raised $524,000, about half of which came from PACs. While this was nothing new—Rangel had raised $74,150 of PAC money in the first six months of 1985—PAC contributions escalated during the 1980s. But the most significant aspect of these donations was that *none of the above congressmen was facing opposition in 1988*. The PACs in 1988 made a total donation of almost $15 million to 59 congressmen facing token opposition or none at all. Why such interest in these men? Some were on tax-writing or other financial committees. Senate Finance Committee Chairperson Bob Packwood, the top PAC recipient, alone received $691,015 from what the president of Common Cause (representing a "special interest," too) characterized as "special interest groups intent on preserving their tax breaks, providing a sea of PAC dollars to the Congressional tax writers."[13] With crucial financial issues arising constantly in the 1989–1990 Congress as President Bush confronts a Democratic House and Senate, PAC money can be expected to have an even greater influence.

Ironically, considering that the explosion of PACs has occurred mainly in the business world, it was organized labor that invented this device. In the 1930s John L. Lewis, president of the United Mine Workers, set up the Non-Partisan Political League as the political arm of the newly formed CIO. When the CIO merged with the American Federation of Labor, the new labor group established the Committee on Political Education (COPE). This unit came to be the model for most political-action committees: "From the outset, national, state, and local units of COPE have not only raised and distributed funds, but have also served as the mechanism for organized and widespread union activity in the electoral process, for example, in voter registration, political education, and get-out-the-vote drives."[14] Some years later manufacturers formed the Business-Industry Political Action Committee, but this committee, and the small number of other PACs in the 1960s, had a limited role.

The 1970s brought a near-revolution in the role and influence of PACs. The number of PACs increased dramatically from about 150 to over 4000 today. Corporations and trade associations contributed most to this growth; today their PACs comprise the majority of all PACs. Labor PACs, on the other hand, increased only slightly in number, representing less than 10 percent of all PACs. But the increase in the number of PACs is less important than the intensity of recent PAC participation in elections and in lobbying.

"Talking with politicians is a fine thing, but with a little money they hear you better," comments Justin Dart, Chairperson of Dart Industries.[15] PACs take part in the entire election process, but their main influence lies in their capacity to contribute money to candidates. Candidates today need big money to wage their election or reelection campaigns. It is no longer uncommon for House candidates to spend over a million dollars, and many Senators or would-be Senators may spend ten times that amount.[16]

As corporate and industrial PACs increase rapidly in number, their influence grows accordingly. What counts is not so much the amounts they give but rather to whom they give: the more influential incumbents. House members receiving the largest amount of PAC contributions in the last election cycle from 1987 through the first quarter of 1988 included Budget Committee chairman William Gray III (D-Pennsylvania), Rep. Nancy Pelosi (D-California), and Rep. Mary Rose Oaker (D-Ohio).[17]

Despite lurid reports of freewheeling spending by big corporations, most business PACs proceed rather cautiously.[18] In deciding which candidates to help and with how much, PACs first consider the candidate's record and the likelihood of his or her voting as the PAC wishes. But other factors must be considered too: the likelihood that the candidate will win; how much difference the money would make in the campaign; whether the candidate is an incumbent (and hence would reasonably have more chance of winning); and the PACs' access to the candidate if elected. Party is not a major criterion for corporate-related PACs, although they do contribute somewhat more to Republican candidates than to Democratic ones. Labor PACs, on the other hand, give overwhelmingly to Democrats.

How much influence does PAC money, especially corporate PAC money, have on election outcomes, legislation, and representation? One critic has written that "Members of Congress are growing more and more dependent on PAC money

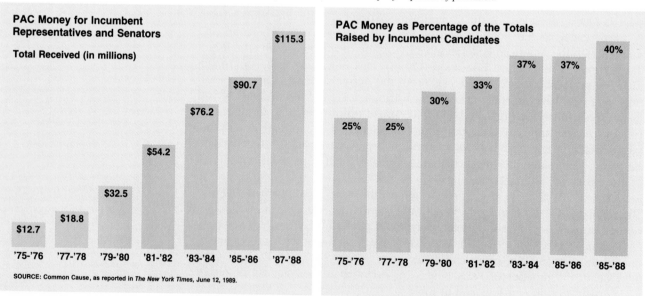

PAC Money for Incumbent Representatives and Senators

Total Received (in millions)

'75-'76	'77-'78	'79-'80	'81-'82	'83-'84	'85-'86	'87-'88
$12.7	$18.8	$32.5	$54.2	$76.2	$90.7	$115.3

SOURCE: Common Cause, as reported in *The New York Times*, June 12, 1989.

PAC Money as Percentage of the Totals Raised by Incumbent Candidates

'75-'76	'77-'78	'79-'80	'81-'82	'83-'84	'85-'86	'85-'88
25%	25%	30%	33%	37%	37%	40%

and less and less free to respond to the needs of their constituents." An organization called Citizens Against PACs publishes attacks on members who, in their opinion, accept too many out-of-state PAC contributions. Obviously, in this area, as in others, "money talks." But it is easy to exaggerate that influence. While a candidate may receive a considerable amount of PAC money, only a fraction of that total comes from any single interest. PACs are by law limited to a contribution of $5000 to a single candidate. Corporations find that raising political money from a diverse group of stockholders and/or executives is a slow venture. In fact, corporations usually do not wish to raise a great deal of political money for fear that they will be attacked in the press for their "huge slush funds." In addition, it is not clear that campaign contributions have much effect on election outcomes, that winning candidates will feel willing and able to "remember" their financial angels, or that the money in the end produces a real payoff in legislation. So even big corporate PACs have learned to be patient. Bernadette A. Budde, political education director of the Business-Industry PAC, declared: "You know you're not going to make 10 yards on the first down, so you try to make 2 or 3 or 4 yards at a time."[19]

Much depends, however, on the context within which money is given and received.[20] Many campaigns—especially congressional and state and local campaigns—are low-voltage undertakings in which a sizable amount of money seems to make a difference. Amid all the murk of campaigning, a candidate may feel grateful for so tangible and convertible a contribution as money. But much depends on whether PACs can protect their financial investment with the exercise of influence *within* government—that is, whether they can lobby effectively.

Lobbying, Old and New

Lobbying, one of the best-known weapons of group influence, is probably also the oldest; it is certainly one of the most criticized. Generations of Americans have been stirred by exposés of an "invisible government." From the time of the Yazoo land frauds 190 years ago, when a whole state legislature was bribed and the postmaster general was put on a private payroll as a lobbyist, to the latest logrolling scandals in Congress, Americans have enjoyed denouncing lobbyists. Some truly powerful lobbies flourished in the last century. One of these was the Anti-Saloon League which, after years of warring against "demon rum," actually managed to win passage of a constitutional amendment—the highest and most difficult achievement in American politics. These so-called "drys" included such famous women as Frances Willard and Carrie Nation, as well as the Women's Christian Temperance Union. An equally powerful lobby of "wets"—all male except for Pauline Morton Sabin and her Women's Organization for National Prohibition Reform—won repeal of the Prohibition Amendment, which of course required another constitutional amendment.[21]

Today lobbying is far more extensive and sophisticated, though not necessarily more effective. Thousands of lobbyists are active in Washington, but few of them are as glamorous or as unscrupulous as the media suggest, nor are they necessarily very influential. Most lobbying is a rather routine affair conducted by spokespersons for such organizations as the National Fertilizer Association, the Retired Officer Association, or the Institute of Shortening and Edible Oils. Lobbyists for these associations are usually Washington attorneys who have long experience in the agencies and on "the Hill"; they are retained to keep an eye on a handful of

Lobbyists in Washington await the results of a vote in Congress.

bills and to keep in touch with a few administrative officials and members of Congress. Because lawmaking today is highly technical, these lobbyists—or legislative counsels, as they prefer to be called—play a large role in modern government. Busy administrators or legislators, threading their way through mountains of paper and among conflicting interests, often turn to them gladly for their views and information.

All this is the traditional stuff of government, but with the rise of Big Government and the huge stakes of business and other organizations in governmental decisions, lobbying has taken on far greater importance. Lobbyists know that influence in Washington depends on influence in the precincts, and that they must use techniques of public persuasion in order to create the right political "climate" for the governmental actions they want. Hence, they must also know how to mobilize their organizations back home so that a blizzard of letters, telegrams, and petitions descends on Washington. Lobbyists have to be experts in the arts of political influence and legislative technique, as they take part in drafting laws, testifying before committees, and helping to speed some bills through while slowing down others.

Tax reform was one of the most significant legislative undertakings of the 1980s, and one in which lobbyists played a crucial role. The issue of taxation has always been an important concern of business and other interests, so they lobby actively when any tax changes are proposed. In tax legislation a simple sentence or a few lines can significantly affect the welfare of major interests. The Tax Reform Act of 1986, an extensive reworking of the tax code, was predictably a hard-fought battle among lobbyists for diverse interests, but one in which changes were made despite opposition from some powerful lobbies. Since the 1986 reform, Congress has made minor amendments to the code, and President Bush, upon his election, began to pressure key members of Congress to reduce the capital gains tax—a move heavily supported by big business. Tax lobbyists have been in rising demand, with many former congressional and Treasury aides taking positions as lobbyists. With the increased lobbying activity by former government employees, it is not surprising that there have been scandals in which these former officials have been indicted.

Legal and political skills, along with specialized knowledge, have become so crucial in executive and legislative policy making as to be a form of power in themselves. Elected representatives increasingly depend on their staffs for guidance, and these staffs in turn are linked with the staffs of executive departments and of the interest-group associations. Issue specialists will know more about Section 504 or Title IX or the amendment of 1972, and who wrote that amendment and why, than the political and administrative leaders, who are usually generalists. It is in this gray area of policy making that many interest groups play a vital role, as people move freely from congressional or agency staff to association staff and perhaps back again.

The recent growth of PACs has immensely expanded these traditional activities and sharpened the issue of their rightful place in the battle of interest groups. More than ever before, interest groups, through PACs, can organize a "triple-threat" offensive: skillful mobilization of public opinion through large, well-financed public relations campaigns; direct assistance to candidates in the form of money, campaign propaganda, "education" of voters by mailings, advertisements, and the like; and direct influence on officeholders through lobbying. The National Rifle Association (NRA), one of the most powerful medium-sized interest groups, with a membership of more than a million and a staff of 300, "has become a master at mobilizing citizens who support its cause. . . . The NRA boasts that it can

Suggested Steps To Successful Lobbying

Anticipate and analyze the political situation and the key players.

Define a realistic objective.

Understand the timing.

Target your audience.

Always tell the truth, the whole truth.

Always work with the professional staff.

Know when to play offense and when to play defense.

Support your political friends.

Be sensitive to outside strategy needs.

Be aware of the special opportunities presented by presidential campaigns.

Source: Terrence D. Straub, *Changing Faces*, published by the Graduate School of Political Management, New York University (April 11, 1988), p. 5.

CHAPTER 8 / Interest Groups: The Politics of Faction

flood Congress with 500,000 pieces of mail virtually overnight in opposition to any gun control proposals."[22]

LABOR'S POLITICAL "MACHINE"

For some years labor's COPE has been one of the most respected—and most feared—political organizations in the country.[23] In the Kennedy-Johnson years it won a reputation as the strongest national political "machine"—the word the late George Meany, AFL-CIO chief, used to describe his political arm. In many respects COPE could boast of its political effectiveness: It encouraged and supervised grass-roots political activity on the part of the tens of thousands of union locals at the base of the AFL-CIO. The national organization adopted a detailed, explicit "platform," fifty or sixty pages long, which spelled out labor's position on the issues. Labor contributed money to candidates, ran registration and get-out-the-vote campaigns, and supported its favorites with leaflets, picnics, motorcades, and television and radio programs. COPE granted, or withheld, endorsements of candidates. Finally, in Washington and in many of the state capitals, organized labor marshaled one of the largest, most experienced, and most knowledgeable lobbies of all the interest groups.

Yet this political "machine" often sputtered and faltered. Because the AFL-CIO is a federation of powerful and independent national unions, state and local groups or federations of unions were often politically divided. Also, the aging national leadership of the AFL-CIO had been in office so long that it lacked vigor and freshness of approach. When George Meany retired in 1979, he had been president of the national organization for twenty-seven years; William Green had headed it for twenty-eight years before Meany, and Samuel Gompers had been in control off and on for thirty-eight years before Green. Moreover, the AFL-CIO by no means spoke for all labor; union labor represented about 60 percent of the nation's work force, and AFL-CIO membership amounted to about 60 percent of the total number of those organized.[24] In 1982, 64 percent of the COPE-endorsed candidates for United States representative won their elections—only a fair record. In 1984, under President Lane Kirkland, the AFL-CIO took the unusual step of endorsing a Democratic presidential candidate, Walter F. Mondale, even before the primary season began. When Mondale won the nomination but lost the general election, many pundits concluded that labor's endorsement had become a liability. Nevertheless, Kirkland insisted that the AFL-CIO would once again offer an early endorsement in the 1988 presidential election. However, they did not.

Labor's political and lobbying muscle is obviously limited, and the prospects for increasing influence in the future are dim. Organized labor's membership is dwindling relative to the increase in the national work force. It has failed to unionize a large part of industry in the South and the Sunbelt generally, and the number of corporate PACs has increased greatly while the number of labor PACs has remained almost the same. Knowing that it must look for political allies, labor is increasingly working closely with the Democratic party. Still, labor is jealous of its political independence and hesitates to join a party that has its own problems and weaknesses. Another possibility is for labor to form temporary coalitions with other groups that have certain interests similar to its own. Labor often follows this tactic, working closely with consumer, public-interest, liberal, and sometimes—especially when faced with the issue of foreign imports—even with industry groups. But labor pays a price for such collaboration: watering down or even giving up some of its own goals. "We do our best when we're part of a coalition" says a top labor lobbyist, "and you don't have a coalition on a pure issue."[25]

COOPERATIVE LOBBYING

Other groups besides labor need to work with like interests without sacrificing their own goals. Business groups have worked out day-to-day, informal, flexible alliances, and some of these have developed into organizations in their own right. The Food Group, a thirty-year-old informal conference group in Washington, has, for example, represented more than sixty business and trade associations. In addition, it spawned an Information Committee on Federal Food Regulations to fight "truth-in-packaging" legislation. Although the Food Group has been fairly effective, it does run into the usual problem of differences over goals and priorities and has found it difficult to put strong and unified pressure on Congress and government agencies.

Other like-minded groups have also worked out cooperative arrangements. The Leadership Conference on Civil Rights brought together many black and other group interests in this area. Different types of environmentalists work together, as do consumers and ideological groups on the right and on the left. Women continue to be represented by a large variety of groups that reflect their diverse interests; many of these banded together as ERAmerica to support passage of the ERA. But the larger the coalition, the greater the chance that women, like other groups, may divide over such issues as abortion and equal rights.

Temporary, flexible coalitions have often been viewed as relatively ineffective, given the American political process. A recent study of women's organizations, however, challenges this view. In this case issue coalitions seem to be both the most realistic and the most common way to organize diverse interests. Cooperative lobbying allows "a great deal of diversity of opinion among cooperating groups while still combining lobbying capabilities. This is very important for an interest as varied as that of American women. Groups only need to agree on a single issue to join an ad hoc issue coalition."[26] Analysts of other common group interests might, of course, reach a different conclusion.

This stack of petitions was presented to the Supreme Court as part of a massive effort by various anti-abortion groups to reverse the *Roe* versus *Wade* ruling that legalized abortions.

AMERICANS AGAINST ABORTION
PETITION FOR LIFE
2,893,767 Signatures

Controlling Factions—Two Hundred Years Later

If James Madison were to return today, over two hundred years after writing *The Federalist*, he would not be surprised by the existence of interest groups. Nor would he be surprised by the variety of interest groups. He *would* be surprised, however, by the intense modern expression of factionalism—the varied weapons of group influence, the deep involvement of interest groups in the electoral process, and the vast number of lobbyists in Washington and the state capitals. And doubtless Madison, if he were alive today, would be more concerned than ever about the power of faction, especially its tendency toward instability and injustice.

Certainly, Americans today are worried about the power of faction, and for somewhat the same reasons. Specifically, they fear that:

1. The struggle among factions is not a fair fight; narrower, more highly organized and better-financed "single-issue" or "single-cause" groups hold a decided advantage over more general groups.

2. The interest-group battle leads to great inequities, because lower-income people are grossly underrepresented among interest groups as compared to richer, more highly organized people, many of whom are represented by a multitude of organizations and lobbyists.

3. The organization of hundreds of single-issue groups has reinforced the diffusion of power and fragmentation in government so desired by our nation's founders. The result is incoherent policies, waste and inefficiency, endless delays, and inability to plan ahead and anticipate crises.

Single-issue groups, which are intensively organized for or against particular policies—abortion, handgun control, tobacco subsidies, animal rights, for example—have aroused much concern in recent years. "It is said that citizen groups organizing in ever greater numbers to push single issues ruin the careers of otherwise fine politicians who disagree with them on one emotional issue, paralyze the traditional process of governmental compromise, and ignore the common good in their selfish insistence on getting their own way," notes Sylvia Tesh.[27] But which single issues reflect narrow, selfish interests? Women's rights—even a specific issue such as the Equal Rights Amendment—are hardly "selfish," women's rights leaders argue, because they would help over half the population. Peace groups, too, claim that they are representing the *whole* population, as do those supporting prayer in schools. These issues would seem quite different from those concerned with subsidies to dairy farmers, for example. But some doubt the feasibility of distinguishing between narrower and broader issues.

What to do, if anything? For decades Americans have been trying to find ways to keep interest groups in check. They have agreed with James Madison that the "remedy" of suppressing factions would be worse than the disease—it would be absurd to abolish liberty simply because it nourished faction. Today the existence and activity of interest groups and lobbies are solidly protected by the Constitution. By safeguarding the value of *liberty*, Americans have allowed interest groups to threaten *equality*, the second great value in our national heritage. So we are left with the question: How can interest groups be regulated in a way that (1) does not threaten their constitutional liberties yet (2) curbs their tendencies toward inequity?

"I would guess, sir, by the look on your face, that you are a single-issue person."

Drawing by Dana Fradon; © 1987 The New Yorker Magazine, Inc.

REGULATION OF INTEREST-GROUP LOBBYING

On the whole, Americans have responded to this question by seeking to regulate lobbying in general and political money in particular. Concern over the use of money—especially corporate funds—to influence politicians goes back well over a century, to the Crédit Mobilier scandals. In 1877 Georgia simply wrote into its constitution the provision that lobbying is a crime—but that provision violated the federal constitution. By the turn of the century the liberal press was charging that corporations were pouring millions into the presidential campaigns of candidates like Benjamin Harrison and William McKinley. During the "Progressive" first decade of this century, Congress passed legislation outlawing corporate contributions in federal elections and requiring disclosure as to the use of money. In 1925 Congress passed the Federal Corrupt Practices Act, requiring disclosure reports, both before and after elections, of receipts and expenditures by Senate and House candidates and by political committees seeking to influence federal elections in more than one state. Note that these were *federal* laws applying to *federal* elections; regulation of state lobbying and elections was left to the states, which often failed to act effectively or at all.

Federal legislation, including the 1946 Federal Regulation of Lobbying Act, has not been very effective either. It was, in fact, largely unenforced. Many candidates filed incomplete reports or none at all. The reform mood of the 1960s brought basic changes, "nurtured by the ever-increasing costs of campaigning, the incidence of millionaire candidates, the large disparities in campaign spending between various candidates and political parties, some clear cases of unique influence on the decision-making process by large contributors and special interests, and the apparent disadvantages of incumbency in an age of mass communications with a constant focus on the lives and activities of office-holders."[28] The upshot was the Federal Election Campaign Act (FECA) of 1971, which supplanted the earlier legislation.

Because the main significance of recent laws has been their impact on elections, we discuss them later, in Chapter 13. Here we must note the major impact of the 1971 act on interest groups themselves, especially on their political arms. Ironically, that impact was not to decrease or restrict them, but to enlarge their number and importance. The main reason for this was the new strategy of the 1971 law: to authorize direct and open participation by both labor and corporate organizations in elections and lobbying, with the hope that allowing a proper role for interest-group activity, in the clear light of day, with effective enforcement, would be constitutional under the First Amendment and effective in the world of practical politics. The 1971 act allowed unions and corporations to communicate on political matters to members or stockholders, to conduct registration and get-out-the-vote drives, and to spend union and company funds to set up "separated segregated funds" to be used for political purposes.

At last corporations could be sure that their open and regulated political activities were wholly legal—and they made the most of it. The explosion of corporate PACs followed. But organized labor, which had previously enjoyed the right to set up its PACs, had less need of the act (except to legitimate what it was already doing). There was little increase in the number of labor PACs. The result, labor leaders contend, is a greater imbalance than ever between the political action and organization of a relatively small number of corporation executives and stockholders, and the large membership, and potential membership, of labor unions.

In 1976 the Supreme Court ruled unconstitutional all limitations on individual or candidate campaign spending (*Buckley* v. *Valeo*), and in 1985 it extended this ruling to include PACs. In a series of suits initiated by Democrats who had hoped to prevent powerful right-wing PACs from avoiding federal campaign laws, the Court vetoed regulation of independent PAC spending. Over $15 million of the $16.7 million in independent expenditures in 1984 was devoted to Ronald Reagan's reelection, but the Supreme Court nevertheless decided that Congress may not constitutionally limit independent PAC spending for publicly funded presidential candidates. The decision, grounded in First Amendment guarantees of freedom of speech, did not affect separate congressional provisions limiting the amount PACs may contribute directly to candidates.[29] Since then bills to reduce PAC spending to $3000 per congressional candidate, per PAC, from the current ceiling of $5000 have been debated in Congress. These attempts have as yet been unsuccessful, but Democrats, more dependent than Republicans on PAC contributions, are facing increasing pressure from both the Republicans and voters for "house cleaning." In 1988 Republican Senators Mitch McConnell of Kentucky and Bob Packwood of Oregon offered a drastic solution—to eliminate PACs altogether—during a Senate debate on campaign finance reform.[30] Democratic Senator David Boren

Capitol Hill—or Capital Hill?

". . . No more than 20 percent of a candidate's funds should be allowed to come from PACs. . . . a voluntary ceiling must be placed on total campaign spending. The United States Supreme Court, in *Buckley* v. *Valeo* in 1976, struck down compulsory spending limits as an unconstitutional restriction of free speech. Given that, the only way to bring about reform would be to establish voluntary spending limits providing for strong inducements to comply with the limits.

Spending limits would be based on the number of voters in a candidate's state. Only candidates who comply with spending limits would be eligible for benefits such as reduced advertising and mail rates that are now available to all.

Ronald Reagan warned in his farewell address against the growing power and permanence of the 'iron triangle' in American politics—the networks formed by individual members from the executive branch, Congress, and special-interest groups. These networks control the debate on specific issues and prevent outsiders from having a voice in policymaking.

Mr. Reagan's warning is ever more urgent: Special interests and Congress are too closely connected, and the ties that bind are the millions spent on campaigns."

Source: Senator David Boren, *New York Times* (May 29, 1989), p. A19.

of Oklahoma proposes that no more than 20 percent of a candidate's funds come from PACs (see box).

Will Congress reform the PACs and campaign finance in general? Not only is reform itself complex and difficult, as we have emphasized throughout this chapter, but does Congress really *want* reform? Many members of Congress thrive on the present arrangements, and the leaders and members of both parties actually compete for PAC dollars. When the National Association of Home Builders, a richly funded lobby, began to give more and more money to Republican candidates, Democratic leaders of the House warned the home builders' lobby that, in effect, the lobby had better help Democrats too, or the "good relationship" between the lobby and the Democrats might be "damaged." One reason members of Congress become entrenched in their seats is that they become increasingly funded by PACs. Some of them reason, "Why give up such a cozy relationship?" Thus the real question may not be whether Congress can reform the interest group lobbies, but whether Congress can reform itself.[31]

LOBBYISTS: DEFENSE AND ATTACK

Lobbyists have been defended as providing a kind of "third house" of Congress. Whereas the Senate and House are set up on a geographical basis, lobbyists represent people on the basis of their main interests: their jobs or other economic interests, their issue positions, and their ideological leanings. Small but important groups, such as professional associations, can sometimes get representation in the "third house" that they might be unable to gain in the other two. In a nation of vast and important interests, this kind of functional representation, if not abused, is most useful as a supplement to geographical representation. Should the former kind of representation supplant the latter? Most analysts say no, because legislative institutions are needed to represent people in the totality of their lives and needs.

There are other arguments for "hands off the lobbyists." PACs support both Democratic and Republican candidates and hence do not favor just one party; ideological groups, especially those of a conservative cast, usually contribute more money than either business or labor, but that money does not have as direct or marked an effect on actual policy making as many outsiders suppose.[32] Another argument is that the increase in PAC corporate spending is not as great as it appears; in fact, much of the PAC money may be "old wine in new bottles"; that is, money given earlier in the form of legal or illegal personal campaign contributions by business chiefs.[33] Finally, we are reminded, in the spirit of the Bill of Rights, that whatever the evils, no action should be taken that even remotely threatens the liberties and autonomy of corporations or interest groups in general.

The usual response to this problem depends on the interest group to which one belongs. Union leaders believe that business PACs are allowed too much financial power, and business leaders hold that labor is allowed too much electoral power. Groups with insufficiently vested interests—those defined in terms of race and sex—argue that a system so grounded in economic interests discriminates against those with little access to economic power. Is a more objective position possible?

Scholars analyzing PACs and campaign financing have concluded that, on balance, the situation is serious, though not desperate. As summarized by one participant, a Harvard study group concluded that "PAC money is 'interested money'—that is, linked to a legislative lobby agenda; that reliance on PAC funds

"It's true, Dave, that I have an unsavory past, but if elected to public office I hope to hold myself to a higher standard."

Drawing by Dana Fradon; © 1987 The New Yorker Magazine, Inc.

had led to a nationalization of the sources of money available to candidates, bringing in funds from outside a candidate's state or district (particularly Washington); and that the growing role of PACs has resulted in political money becoming bureaucratically organized—that is, detached from their source and aggregated in a fashion which renders them unaccountable."[34] Others argue that PAC money helps candidates challenge incumbents, which leads to much-needed "new blood" in Congress—though, in fact, PACs overwhelmingly favor incumbents.[35]

TO REFORM OR NOT REFORM?

Some observers favor wider regulation of political money and publicly financed congressional elections. Others call for **deregulation** of the political arms of interest groups, assuming that the groups will find a natural and proper balance. Still others believe that the balance must be righted between the present wide and intensive activity of corporate PACs and the far less influential role of PACs for consumer groups, women's groups, environmental groups, and civil rights groups.[36]

A quite different school of thought holds that none of these "solutions" will work. The problem lies more outside interest groups and PACs than within them or among them. This school notes that James Madison set a good example in concluding that the *causes* of faction could not be removed, and that the *effects* could be controlled only by fundamental changes in the whole political system. His solutions (extending the sphere of government to take in "a greater variety of parties and interests"; creating federal-state-local tiers of government; and fragmenting the power of government so no majority or minority could control it) worked to some degree but also aggravated the problems. Today the main proposal for controlling interest groups by reshaping the external political system is that of proponents of stronger political parties (see Chapter 10).

Finally, there are those who believe that the main problem lies not in interest groups but in the way public opinion is made, managed, and manipulated—above all, by the rise of the barons of the electronic media in a new age of communications politics. These observers are urging Congress to limit what commercial television stations can charge for political advertising and to discourage so-called "negative targeting" of candidates in political advertising. We treat this subject in Chapter 12.

Summary

1. The dominant interest groups are economic or occupational, but a variety of other groups—religious, racial, ideological, ethnic—have memberships that cut across the big economic groupings and both reduce and stabilize their influence.

2. The sources of group power are size, unity, singleness of purpose, organization, and leadership, but the actual power of an interest group stems from the manner in which these elements relate to the political and governmental environment in which the interest group is operating.

3. For many decades interest groups have engaged in lobbying, but these efforts have become far more pervasive and significant with the deep involvement of groups in the electoral process, especially through the expanded use of political-action committees (PACs).

4. Concern about PACs centers on their ability to raise money and spend it on elections, in behalf of endorsed candidates. This concern has led to extensive regulation of interest-group political spending.

5. The key issue today in "controlling factions" is whether to allow groups to find some kind of balance of their own, to try to regulate groups, or to seek reforms outside the groups by building up balancing power in political parties or elsewhere.

Further Reading

JEFFREY BERRY. *The Interest Group Society*, 2nd ed. (Little, Brown and Company, 1989).

ALLAN J. CIGLER and BURDETT A. LOOMIS, eds. *Interest Group Politics*, 2d ed. (Congressional Quarterly Press, 1986).

CAROL S. GREENWALD. *Group Power: Lobbying and Public Policy* (Praeger, 1977).

MILDA K. HEDBLOM. *Women and American Politics: A Perspective on Organizations and Institutions*, test ed. (American Political Science Association, 1983).

ALLEN D. HERTZKE. *Representing God in Washington: The Role of Religious Lobbies in the American Polity* (University of Tennessee Press, 1988).

MICHAEL J. MALBIN, ed. *Parties, Interest Groups, and Campaign Finance Laws* (American Enterprise Institute for Public Policy Research, 1980).

ANDREW S. McFARLAND. *Common Cause: Lobbying in the Public Interest* (Chatham House, 1984).

MANCUR OLSON. *The Logic of Collective Action* (Harvard University Press, 1965).

NORMAN J. ORNSTEIN and SHIRLEY ELDER. *Interest Groups, Lobbying and Policymaking* (Congressional Quarterly Press, 1978).

LARRY J. SABATO. *PAC Power: Inside the World of Political Action Committees* (Norton, 1984).

KAY LEHMAN SCHLOZMAN and JOHN T. TIERNEY. *Organized Interests and American Democracy* (Harper & Row, 1986).

PHILIP M. STERN. *The Best Congress Money Can Buy* (Pantheon, 1988).

Notes

1. Doris Kearns, *Lyndon Johnson and the American Dream* (Harper & Row, 1976), ch. 2; Robert A. Caro, *The Years of Lyndon Johnson: The Path to Power* (Knopf, 1982), part 2.
2. Thomas Byrne Edsall, *The New Politics of Inequality* (W.W. Norton, 1984), p. 114.
3. Mancur Olson, *The Logic of Collective Action* (Harvard University Press, 1965), p. 34.
4. Robert Salisbury, "Interest Representation: The Dominance of Institutions," *American Political Science Review* (March 1984), p. 66.
5. Edsall, *The New Politics of Inequality*, p. 110.
6. Salisbury, "Interest Representation," p. 69.
7. Kirk Victor, "Shooting Back," *National Journal* (May 21, 1988), pp. 1345–1349.
8. Viveca Novak, "Under the Influence," *Common Cause* (May/June 1988), pp. 19–23.
9. V. O. Key, Jr., *Public Opinion and American Democracy* (Knopf, 1961), pp. 504–7.
10. Lucius J. Barker, "Third Parties in Litigation: A Systemic View of the Judicial Function," *Journal of Politics* (February 1967), pp. 41–69; Jethro K. Lieberman, *Litigious Society*, rev. ed. (Basic, 1983).
11. Karen O'Connor, *Women's Organizations' Use of the Courts* (Lexington Books, 1980).
12. Herbert E. Alexander, *PACs: What They Are, How They Are Changing Political Campaign Financing Patterns* (Grass Roots Guides, 1979), p. 3.
13. *Congressional Quarterly Weekly Report* (September 14, 1985), p. 1806.
14. Edwin M. Epstein, "Business and Labor under the Federal Election Campaign Act of 1971," in Michael J. Malbin, ed., *Parties, Interest Groups, and Campaign Finance Laws* (American Enterprise Institute for Public Policy Research, 1980), p. 112. See also Gary Jacobson, *Money in Congressional Elections* (Yale University Press, 1980).
15. Quoted in *The Wall Street Journal* (August 15, 1978), p. 1.
16. Senator Charles C. Mathias, *The New York Times* (February 27, 1986), p. A31.
17. *Congressional Quarterly Weekly Report* (May 7, 1988), p. 1205.
18. Gary J. Andres, "Business Involvement in Campaign Finance: Factors Influencing the Decision to Form a Corporate PAC," *PS* (Spring 1985), p. 213.
19. Quoted in *National Journal* (November 24, 1979), p. 1983.
20. Sandra Davis, "PACs in the American Political System" (unpublished manuscript).
21. See Ruth Bordin, *Women and Temperance: The Quest for Power and Liberty, 1873–1900* (Temple University Press, 1981); David E. Kyvig, *Repealing National Prohibition* (University of Chicago Press, 1979); Carol S. Greenwald, *Group Power: Lobbying and Public Policy* (Praeger, 1977); Norman J. Ornstein and Shirley Elder, *Interest Groups, Lobbying and Policymaking* (Congressional Quarterly Press, 1978).
22. Dennis S. Ippolito and Thomas G. Walker, *Political Parties, Interest Groups, and Public Policy: Group Influence in American Politics* (Prentice Hall, 1980), p. 335.
23. Harry Holloway, "Interest Groups in the Postpartisan Era: The Political Machine of the AFL-CIO," *Political Science Quarterly* (Spring 1979), pp. 117–33.
24. Ibid., p. 120.
25. *Congressional Quarterly Weekly Report* (July 19, 1975), p. 1533.
26. Anne N. Costain, "The Struggle for a National Women's Lobby: Organizing a Diffuse Interest," *Western Political Quarterly* (December 1980), p. 490.
27. Sylvia Tesh, "In Support of 'Single-Interest' Politics," *Political Science Quarterly* (Spring 1984), pp. 27–44. See also the references to other literature in this article.
28. Alexander, *PACs: What They Are*, p. 5.
29. *Congressional Quarterly Weekly Report* (March 23, 1985), p. 532.
30. Richard E. Cohen, "PACs and Perks," *National Journal* (June 11, 1988), p. 1582.
31. See Brooks Jackson, *Honest Graft: Big Money and the American Political Process* (Knopf, 1989); also Robert Kuttner, "Protection Racket," *The New Republic* (March 16, 1989), pp. 40–42, a review of the Jackson book.
32. Some of these arguments are summarized in Epstein, "Business and Labor," in Malbin, ed., *Parties, Interest Groups*, pp. 107–51.
33. Michael J. Malbin, "Campaign Financing and the 'Special Interest,' " *The Public Interest* (Summer 1979), pp. 21–42. But for a somewhat different view, see David Cohen and Wendy Wolff, "Freeing Congress from the Special Interest State: A Public Interest Agenda for the 1980s," *Harvard Journal of Legislation*, vol. 17, no. 2 (1980), pp. 253–93.
34. The Institute of Politics, John F. Kennedy School of Government, Harvard University, *An Analysis of the Impact of the Federal Election Campaign Act, 1972–78: A Report by the Campaign Finance Study Group to the Committee on House Administration of the U.S. House of Representatives*, May 1979, based in part on analysis by Xandra Kayden; summarized by Epstein in Malbin, ed., *Parties, Interest Groups*, p. 142.
35. Gary C. Jacobson and Samuel Kernell, *Strategy and Choice in Congressional Elections* (Yale University Press, 1983).
36. See David Jessup, "Can Political Influence Be Democratized? A Labor Perspective," in Malbin, ed., *Parties, Interest Groups*, pp. 26–55.

9

Movements:
The Politics
of Conflict

It was a strange sight, that January day in 1917 at the gates of the White House. A group of women—society ladies from the Washington area, eminent professionals, young college graduates, workers from a munitions plant—marched up and down, carrying banners: "MR. PRESIDENT! WHAT WILL YOU DO FOR WOMAN SUF-FRAGE?" "HOW LONG MUST WOMEN WAIT FOR LIBERTY?" As the days passed, the banners became more militant. Male hoodlums and self-styled patriots began to harass the picketers, heckling them and tearing down their banners. Then the police began to arrest the women. Over two hundred were taken into custody; almost one hundred were jailed. The picketers dramatized their plight by going on hunger strikes; prison authorities responded with brutal efforts at forced feeding. By now the whole country was aware of the women's ordeal. A small band of leaders had aroused the consciousness of a nation.

Clearly, suffragists comprised an "interest group" as described in the last chapter. Yet they were much more than a group; indeed, they can best be described as a political *movement*. They were heavily politicized and looked toward political action as the chief means of reaching their goals. They also felt excluded by law and society from full political participation on the basis of their sex. Even more, they perceived themselves as subject to a more powerful group—men—and as confined to the "private sphere" of the home while being excluded from the "public sphere."[1]

In struggling to achieve equal rights, the women's movement still finds the basic liberties of the Bill of Rights as extended by the Fourteenth and Nineteenth Amendments both necessary and inadequate. Necessary, because women even more than men depend on the First Amendment rights of free speech, press, assembly, religion, and the others. Inadequate, because those liberties (*against* government) do not always help women deal with what they see as pervasive male domination of the economy, education, politics, religion, and the professions. To deal with such "patriarchy" women need not only the "Big Ten" liberties, the equal protection clause, and the right to vote, but also education, jobs, skills, respect, and self-esteem. In addition they need political solidarity, organization, ideas, ideals, and leaders—in short they need a movement.[2]

And so do large numbers of other Americans, whether on the right or the left, who confront domination by middle-aged WASPs—white Anglo-Saxon Protestants.

Movements: The Why and the How

A **movement** is a large body of people, with varying degrees of centralized leadership and organized membership, united around a central idea of continuing significance. Interest-group politics and movement politics may overlap or resemble each other. Labor, for example, may at times act like a movement but at other times more like a pressure group. How then can we distinguish between the two? And how relevant is that distinction?

Interest groups, as we use the term, operate within the political system of daily give-and-take. They tend to have relatively focused or specific concerns, such as anti-gun control or higher pensions for veterans. The pressures they can exert, the bargains they can strike, and the **transactional** relationships they can establish with government officials and agencies usually serve their ends. Movements, on the other hand, are often unwilling or unable to engage in ordinary political activity. They may feel alienated, disenfranchised, and ignored by those in power. In addition, movements are often more moral or ethical than political in tone; hence, they may be far less willing to compromise. Their goals, unlike those of interest groups, are sometimes **transformational;** that is, they seek to change attitudes and institutions, not just policies. While movements also seek to influence the political agenda, they frequently bypass regular lobbying channels in favor of the streets and the airwaves.

The distinction between movements and interest groups may seem hazy because as a movement gains a political foothold and begins to accomplish its goal, it often *becomes* an interest group. The goal comes to be interwoven with the political thinking of people outside the movement, becoming an interest that is recognized within the mainstream of society. This is what happened with Greenpeace. It started as an ecological movement, but once it produced real changes in the ways government and business treat the environment, Greenpeace became an interest group with political viability.

Like-minded people may belong to an interest group and a movement at the same time. Although Greenpeace has become an established group, it still may use unconventional means to achieve its end. Thus Greenpeace activists have gone to the scene to block the slaying of whales and sea otters. Similarly, the New Right today retains characteristics of both a movement and an interest group. Although the movement has become established in Washington, D.C., and uses lobbying as well as campaign contributions to make itself heard, the New Right still feels left out of government and must campaign outside government circles to mobilize public support.

Another movement that quickly established itself in the 1980s, Mothers Against Drunk Driving (MADD), has also taken on characteristics of an interest group. Its founder, Candy Lightner, turned to politics in 1980 when her daughter was killed by a drunken driver. At first unable to work through ordinary government channels, she relied instead on publicity and perseverance to obtain a hearing with the governor of California and later with President Reagan. The movement succeeded in obtaining stronger penalties for drunk driving as well as helping

Some Examples of Movements in America

Abolitionist
Suffragist
Prohibitionist
Gay Rights
Populist
Progressive
Civil Rights
Anti-Vietnam War
Antitax
Moral Majority
Nuclear Freeze
Animal Liberationist
Earth First

Movements versus Interest Groups

Interest Groups in American politics tend to operate within the framework of government and the existing two-party system, to use the political tactics of lobbying, to build policy coalitions within the legislature and executive, to strive for consensus outside of government, and to advance their goals as beneficial to all groups—not just their own.

Movements tend to feel "left out" of government, to conduct political action at the grass-roots level, to put pressure on government from the outside, to build coalitions among mobilized publics, to see their causes as morally right and the opposition as wrong—even evil—and to thrive on social and political conflict.

to convince the federal government to pressure states to raise the legal drinking age to 21. Today, with hundreds of offices across the country, MADD lobbies as an interest group for legislation in its fight against drunk driving.

The histories of some political movements illustrate how groups organize and act as they attempt to bring about major changes in the political system. Other types of groups also form to challenge or regain basic values—philosophical, moral, or material—that cut across race, sex, and economic lines. A classic example is peace movements. Certain religious groups have long rejected the notion of a state possessed of the ultimate authority to use violence for its formation or preservation. Other *pacifists*, practitioners of what some call "active nonviolence," have visions of a peaceful society guided by individual and collective conscience. In matters of conscience concerning the use of violence, they refuse to cooperate with the state; they even refuse to pay fines for noncompliance. Rather, they engage in acts of civil disobedience for which they are arrested and often sent to jail.

For as long as the United States has drafted armed forces and engaged in wars, even defensive wars, organized groups—religious as well as secular—have resisted such governmental actions. These groups include the Women's Peace Party, Women's International League for Peace and Freedom, Women's Strike for Peace, Fellowship of Reconciliation, War Resisters League, American Friends Service Committee, War Tax Resistance, and New Mobilization Committee to End the War in Vietnam, to name just a few.[3] The peace movement today manifests itself in the nuclear arms race and anti-Star Wars protests. Pacifists and believers in active nonviolence have also brought their writings and tactics—mass civil disobedience, marches, demonstrations—to the abolitionist, civil rights, and women's movements.

THE ANTITAXERS

The antitax movement (not to be confused with the war tax resistance) is an attempt to institute a modern American conservative principle: "That government is best which governs—and taxes—least." California antitax crusaders helped place Proposition 13—to cut property taxes by more than half—on the California ballot in 1978 in order to reduce "unneeded" government services and bureaucratic waste. The proposition was approved by 65 percent of the voters in California and attracted nationwide media attention. Twelve other states have since followed California's lead by taking similar actions. Proposition 13 has been viewed as the start of the "Reagan Revolution," and as the 1988 election showed, the spirit of the antitax movement is alive and well today.

The antitax movement arose in part from a general feeling of impotence in political decision making and a distrust of political leadership.[4] The efforts of President Reagan and conservative senators and representatives to bring down federal spending in the nonmilitary sector of the federal budget and to institute income tax cuts were part of the tax revolt that continued even after the conservative leaders themselves came to the helm of government. After reducing overall income tax rates, the Reagan administration moved on to tax reform in an effort to make the tax code simpler and fairer. George Bush's memorable campaign promise, "Read my lips. . . . No new taxes," showed that tax concerns are still very real and no doubt contributed to his election victory.

The federal government and indeed many state governments face tremendous budget deficits today. As important social programs are threatened by deficit reduction plans, leaders have come under pressure to raise taxes. For some, the benefits

"Ecotage"—A Movement?

"Ecotage" describes activities by groups such as Earth First, Greenpeace, and Sea Shepherds that are used to delay or halt what they see as environmentally damaging projects. These activities have included throwing dye on baby seal pups to make their pelts worthless and getting in the way of netting operations on the high seas. Earth First has also erected platforms in trees for sit-in demonstrations in an effort to stop the cutting, and have damaged tires and engines of trucks used to transport the cut timber.

These actions are generally taken after other legal options are exhausted. The courts are the first place the battles are fought, and only after losing in court do these groups participate in such tactics. They realize some battles will be lost, probably most in fact. But slowing down the destruction of the environment must be fought one battle at a time. Each incident is part of a larger war to halt environmental destruction by disabling the means of that destruction.

Interest groups such as Greenpeace sometimes use unorthodox tactics in their fight to preserve the environment.

CHAPTER 9 / Movements: The Politics of Conflict

of lower taxes have been outweighed by the reduction in government services. What of the large numbers of people who do not own property or who do not earn large enough incomes to benefit from lower taxes? Will they turn to electoral politics or party politics to stem the tide of decreasing governmental services? Or will they be unable to find a party or candidates to run against the tax revolt? Movements provoke countermovements—but not necessarily of equal strength.

American Indians: The Oldest Movement?

"George Bush says he will not raise taxes. That's all I know. That's all you need to know."

Drawing by Joe Mirachi; © 1988 The New Yorker Magazine, Inc.

Centuries ago colonists sailed west looking for another India. Often holding grants of land from their own governments, they believed the land in the New World "belonged" to them. However, the land belonged by long usage to "Indians," tribal peoples who had long inhabited its mountains and valleys, meadows and plains. As settlers moved west, colonial leaders dealt with Indian representatives to obtain land for colonists, to reserve certain lands to Indians, and to gain access for Indian hunters in the ceded areas. Much was settled by negotiation and agreement; in North America the British made treaties with the Creek Confederacy, the Cherokee Nation, Wyandot, the Iroquois Confederacy, and the Seneca Nation.[5] But as the settlers aggressively pressed into Indian lands, conflicts arose, and the native Americans resisted through both violent and nonviolent means, and the rifle became an important tool of "negotiation" too.

BACKGROUND OF THE MOVEMENT

The early Indian resistance movements reflected a deep division between cultures. Early in this century a congressional committee chairperson reflected the white cultural bias: "As a race of people, the Indian is not much inclined to continuous work; he is not very ambitious; he specially enjoys fishing, hunting, racing and other sports rather than any kind of hard labor; governmentally he is naturally tribalist; he is more inclined to tribalism than to individualism. . . ."[6] White leaders, reflecting their own patriarchal society, assumed Indian tribes were patriarchal as well, and hence dealt only with Indian men. But in some tribes the braves lacked full authority.[7] Thus, the political cultures of the Europeans and the Native Americans clashed, especially with regard to patriarchy, private property, individualism, capitalism versus communalism, tribalism, nonprivate lands, and a nonprofit economy.

Historically, the federal government has followed a dual policy toward Native Americans. On the one hand, Congress did not propose to rule the tribes but simply to regulate trade with them. In fact, white settlers continued to move into tribal lands, often with backing from their local and state governments—in defiance of treaties made in Washington. According to Chief Justice John Marshall, Indians were "domestic dependent nations." "They occupy a territory to which we assert a title independent of their will, which must take effect in point of possession when their right of possession ceases. Meanwhile they are in a state of pupilage. Their relationship to the United States resembles that of a ward to his guardian."[8] Many Native Americans, however, preferred their own culture.

In 1944 some Indian leaders formed the National Congress of American Indians (NCAI), with Ruth Muskrat Bronson as its first director. In some respects the NCAI operated as a typical interest group, working on legislation affecting Indian tribes and conducting litigation in behalf of Indian voting rights, welfare, and civil rights. But the NCAI was also militant in defense of Indian culture.

Native American leaders seek changes in U.S. policy toward their people.

"Tribalism is not an association of interest but a form of consciousness," according to two authorities; it is a feeling of being born "into a family, a territory, a spiritual world . . . the mental experience" of "a warm, deep and lasting communal bond among all things in nature in a common vision of their proper relationship."[9]

This sense of "movement militance" erupted in charges that the United States government had practiced genocide in the Indian wars from 1790 to 1915—beginning with wars against the Indian tribes in the Old Northwest Territory and ending with wars against the Paiute in Colorado. Indian leaders also charged that the government had destroyed rights supposedly guaranteed by treaties, such as rights to fishing and hunting, as well as to timber and other natural resources. Such charges coincided with movements for national liberation that were surfacing in the 1960s around the world, especially in third-world nations in Asia and Africa. American Indian leaders even claimed a kind of fourth-world status, as a "colony within a nation."

MORE RECENT MOVEMENT MILITANCE

In the summer of 1961 ten young college-educated Indians, five men and five women—a Paiute, a Mohawk, a Ute, a Shoshone-Bannock, a Ponca, a Potawatomi, a Tuscarora, two Navajos, and a Crow—met in the Gallup, New Mexico, Indian Community Center. They came to decide how to carry out a Declaration of Indian Purpose adopted at a national gathering of Indian tribal leaders earlier in the summer. They formed the National Indian Youth Council (NIYC). "In the Indian way," they elected one another members of the council and chose Paiute Mel Thom as their first president. Their membership grew large in the following years. In Mel Thom's words: "The movement grew in the Indian way. We had decided what we needed was a movement. Not an organization, but a movement. *Organizations rearrange history. Movements make history. . . .* Long ago the Indians knew how to use direct action. You might say that was the traditional way that Indians got things done. We were concerned with direct action: Indians moving out and doing something."[10]

NIYC's first venture was to challenge the alleged denial of the Indians' tribal fishing rights by the state of Washington. Beginning in 1964 the NIYC and the Northwest Indian tribes held "fish-ins" on the Quillayute, Puyallup, Yakima, Nisqually, Columbia, and Green Rivers. Men, women, and children participated, and the police arrested and jailed many of them. The NIYC actions sparked a surge of Indian activism. Indians of All Tribes, first organized in the San Francisco Bay area, retook Alcatraz Island. The American Indian Movement (AIM) occupation of Wounded Knee in 1973 mobilized the Indians of many tribes and focused attention on recovering sovereignty in Indian lands.

Although differences do exist between the traditional Indian tribal leaders and the more militant advocates of Indian rights, such as Russell Means of AIM, the tribe still seems to be a focal point of concern. And as long as native Indians cherish their culture, it can be expected that their movement—militant but nonviolent—will continue.

Blacks: Freedom Now

"Ain't gonna let nobody, Lawdy, turn me 'round, turn me 'round, turn me 'round. Ain't gonna let nobody turn me 'round, gonna keep on a-walkin', keep on a-talkin', marchin' up to Freedom Land. . . ."[11]

Throughout our history, African-Americans have struggled to rise from chattel slavery to full participation in American society. African-American movements have followed several paths of development, from slave rebellions and underground escapes, to the more recent freedom rides, sit-ins, marches, and boycotts. As with other movements, intragroup disagreements over goals and strategies have always existed. Within the black community the central question has been whether to strive for equality of opportunity inside the present federal system or outside of it.

Free black men and women lived, worked, and voted in small numbers in the northern colonies, and in smaller numbers in the southern colonies, before independence. But the majority of black Africans and succeeding generations of African-Americans lived in slavery, mainly on southern farms and plantations. Europeans wrenched these African peoples from complex and sophisticated societies in West Africa—Ghana, Mali, Hausa—herded them into slave trading posts along the West African coast, and branded and packed them into the holds of ships for the treacherous six- to ten-week Atlantic crossing. This trade in humans supplied the workers and "breeders" of workers required by the whites to develop the economic staples of tobacco and cotton in the South and the textile industry in the North and in England.[12]

A HISTORY OF RESISTANCE

Coming from communal societies in which both men and women performed recognized and important functions, the Africans held their own well-developed conceptions of life, liberty, and property. In the New World Africans and their descendants began to construct their own cultures and relations anew.[13] Strategies used by slaves to overcome suppression ranged from what their owners took to be docility and ignorance to outright revolt. Many times rebellions were individual and spontaneous; at other times small groups defied their masters. Others escaped, sometimes via the Underground Railroad, engineered by people such as Harriet Tubman and Frederick Douglass. At the northern ends of the lines, greeting the escapees as they emerged from southern forests under cover of night, were Vigilance Committees—groups of free blacks who helped the escapees start new lives.

A series of slave uprisings—desperate, isolated, and abortive—broke out during the eighteenth and early nineteenth centuries, headed most notably by Gabriel Prosser in Richmond in 1800, Denmark Vesey in Charleston in 1822, and Nat Turner in Virginia in 1831. These uprisings revealed communication networks and leaders who were able to calculate opportunities and organize human and material resources.[14] The white authorities harshly put down all these revolts. Still, knowledge of the uprisings has provided black citizens with the courage and historical perspective needed to overcome continuing discrimination.

While black slaves in the South continued to resist their oppression, their brothers and sisters in the North were joined by white men and women convinced that slavery must somehow be ended. At first antislavery activists aimed to free the slaves and colonize them outside the United States—as evidenced by the formation of the American Colonization Society. But this movement soon flagged. William Lloyd Garrison later reinvigorated the movement by calling for a new direction and goal: Emancipate the slaves and grant equal rights to blacks as citizens of the United States. Such publications as Garrison's newspaper *Liberator* and Lydia Maria Child's *An Appeal in Favor of That Class of Americans Called Africans*, along with meetings of local and state antislavery societies, culminated in the formation of the American Anti-Slavery Society in 1833. By 1838 a quarter

Harriet Tubman

Frederick Douglass

William Lloyd Garrison

Harriet Beecher Stowe

of a million people belonged to the 1350 individual societies that made up the national organization.

Dissension grew within this organization because of Garrison's radical views. Not only did he castigate church ministers who did not support abolition, but he also advocated the "right" of women to speak in public. Garrison and his group became convinced, ironically, that secession of the *nonslave* states from the Union was a necessity. They argued that to continue union with the South was to support a Constitution that legitimized slavery.[15] The American and Foreign Anti-Slavery Society formed in opposition to Garrison, to pursue a more gradualist approach to ending slavery. The abolition movement continued up to the Civil War, and helped spawn the Liberty and Free Soil parties. Abolitionist agitation was a major factor in the formation of the Republican party, which emerged out of the split among the Whigs over the issue of slavery. It was finally the proslavery rather than the antislavery states that seceded from the Union; the Civil War accomplished in part what the Abolitionists began.

The contemporary black freedom movement began to surface quietly during World War I in New York City with a Silent Parade sponsored by the National Association for the Advancement of Colored People (NAACP) protesting racial segregation. The movement grew slowly as first one organization and then another formed, their leaders inspired by news of the nonviolent marches and other actions of Gandhi in India. By the 1950s the movement against racial segregation was becoming more and more public. To combat segregated public transportation, the Congress of Racial Equality (CORE) and later the Student Nonviolent Coordinating Committee (SNCC) went "freedom riding" through the South on Greyhound and Trailways buses. In Montgomery, Alabama, Mrs. Rosa Parks refused to give up her seat on a city bus to a white person. Her arrest sparked the formation of the Southern Christian Leadership Conference (SCLC) by the Reverends E. D. Nixon, Ralph Abernathy, and Martin Luther King, Jr. Black students and their parents challenged segregated schools and universities by enrolling in Little Rock High School, the University of Mississippi, and the University of Alabama, among other institutions. Federal troops had to be called in to ensure the black students' safety. (See Chapter 5 for more details on the fight for equal rights.)

The movement accelerated in the 1960s. Black college students challenged segregated public accommodations by sitting in at lunch counters in the South. As more and more people sat in or went on freedom rides, an increasing number were arrested and jailed for their nonviolent civil disobedience. SNCC advocated "jail, not bond," and these jail-ins brought many people into contact with racism and poor conditions in numerous southern jails. Activists challenged the white electoral process through the Voter Education Project (VEP), sponsored by the NAACP, CORE, SCLC, and SNCC. Black voter registration was a revolutionary action in the deep South and drew countless violent reactions by white mobs and police.[16] Throughout the nation there were other violent reverberations, including assassination of leaders associated with ideas of the movement: Medgar Evers in June 1963; Malcolm X in February 1965; and Martin Luther King, Jr., in April 1968. President John F. Kennedy was assassinated in November 1963 as he was, coincidentally, becoming more outspoken on civil rights. Shortly after Martin Luther King, Jr.'s assassination, Robert Kennedy was also shot (June 1968) just after leaving a victory celebration on the night of the California presidential primary.

During the two decades after John Kennedy's death the movement broadened as the civil rights struggle shifted to northern cities, where discrimination often rivaled or even surpassed that in the South. Lyndon Johnson's civil rights measures of 1964 and 1965 had paved the way for major changes in the South, but they had less impact in key urban areas of the North. New, more militant leaders—

Stokely Carmichael, for example, and a host of women, student, and street activists—assumed commanding roles in the movement. The black leadership, however, became more fragmented between established moderate organizations such as the NAACP and the new militant associations that sprang up to cope with specific ills. The rise of Jesse Jackson to nationwide leadership gave the black movement some unity but raised a tough strategic issue: Should black leaders continue to work mainly with the Democratic party, inheriting its weaknesses as well as its strength, or should they strike out on their own in the political arena?

KKK: COUNTERMOVEMENT

Following the Civil War many movements arose supporting or opposing reform. Two movements in particular concerned newly "freed" black people directly: the Ku Klux Klan (KKK), who lynched people and burned homes to keep blacks "in their place"; and the antilynching movement, led by one black woman, Ida Bell Wells-Barnett, who was joined by others in forming antilynching societies.

The KKK sought to preserve its version of the white southern way of life. On the one hand, Klan leaders wanted to maintain the cheap black labor pool and prevent black ownership of property. On the other, they wanted to protect the symbol of the pure white woman, whose value would be greatly diminished if women were "violated" through any kind of contact with black men. They gave no regard to black women, who literally and regularly had been violated by their white owners and masters,[17] nor to white women who might not wish to be so used and protected by being confined to a "pedestal."[18] A more complex intertwining of race, sex, and class issues can hardly be found. Black scholar and activist W. E. B. Du Bois pinpointed the very human basis of the Klan fear: "The method of force, which hides itself in secrecy, is a method as old as humanity. The kind of thing that men are afraid or ashamed to do openly, and by day, they accomplish secretly, masked, and at night."[19] Small and often violent Klan groups are still active today.

After writing antilynching editorials in her own Memphis weekly, Ida Bell Wells-Barnett went on to launch a national, even international, crusade against lynching. Her investigations into lynching incidents took her into the forbidden and murky heart of sex-race relations. She found that though the rape of white women was popularly thought to be the reason for lynching, rape was actually charged in only a third of the over 700 lynchings reported for the ten-year period she studied. Her last *Free Speech* editorial hinted at a truth on which she later elaborated in a study of lynching entitled *A Red Record*:[20] Black men lynched for "rape" often were involved in mutually affectionate, though necessarily clandestine, relationships with white women.

Continued lynchings spurred the formation of other antilynching societies and the antilynching committee of the NAACP. The Anti-Lynching Crusaders, led by Mary B. Talbert, was organized in 1922 as a national effort to draw women into the NAACP efforts. In 1930 white women formed the Association of Southern Women for the Prevention of Lynching and brought home their own "revolt against chivalry."[21] This group chose to work for state laws against lynching. Although President Truman's 1947 Committee on Civil Rights called for federal antilynching legislation—the goal of the movement—it was never passed.

THE BLACK MOVEMENT TODAY

Through direct action—both spontaneous and organized—labor leaders, workers, ministers, students, blacks and whites, and countless others brought about compre-

A KKK march in Tennessee.

Jesse Jackson, twice a presidential candidate, is one of the most prominent and effective spokesmen for minority rights.

hensive changes in the laws of the United States. But laws do not operate in a vacuum. Their implementation tends to be slow, complicated by bureaucratic politics. By the 1960s many blacks were living in poverty in large cities, without the economic and social resources to take advantage of the opportunities held out by the laws. Police incidents in black ghettos in Los Angeles, Detroit, and Newark set off riots—or what many considered rebellions against continuing racism.[22]

The legacy of the African-American movement is one of continuing activism, even though (or more likely because) racism and critical socioeconomic obstacles remain. Although the KKK is still active, by most estimates hard-core Klansmen numbered fewer than 12,000 in the mid-1980s, and their numbers are shrinking. However, racism is still an issue in American politics. In 1989 David Duke, former Imperial Wizard of the Ku Klux Klan, won election to the Louisiana state legislature as a Republican. Other racist groups, neo-fascist white supremacist organizations, were active in the 1980s and recruited young "skinheads" to their violent cause.

Black efforts continue, though, with great success. The 1980s saw a 52 percent increase in the number of black managers, professionals, technicians, and government officials.[23] In 1989 Ronald H. Brown became the first black to chair the Democratic National Committee. More and more blacks have organized and won election to public office. African American electoral strength benefited from the increased mobilization and voter registration stimulated by Jesse Jackson's 1984 and 1988 presidential campaigns. His 1988 campaign was particularly successful in bringing new life to black political aspirations. It also demonstrated that a black candidate could gain support among blacks and whites alike, at least at the national level. (Black candidates won little white support in the Chicago mayoralty election of April 1989.)

Divisions clearly remain within the black movement. However, today new issues are cutting across old cleavages; for example, the antiapartheid struggle in South Africa, similar in many ways to the 1960s Black Freedom movement, is drawing together forces and raising the consciousness of many of today's black youths. Another issue of particular significance to young blacks is the threat posed by drug-related gang warfare. The upsurge in street slayings in recent years has prompted a renewed call for black unity among youths.

Women: The Continuing Struggle

The story of women's movements in the United States is the story of a group — large in numbers but otherwise lacking in political power—who developed a sense of group consciousness, moved into politics despite countless frustrations and setbacks, and, after long struggles, achieved some of their major political goals.

Independence for America in the 1770s brought little independence for its women, who—like their sisters in western Europe—were still dependents of fathers and husbands. Women could not make legal arrangements or contracts, earn wages separate from those of their husbands, or vote. By marrying, they forfeited to their husbands legal custody of themselves as well as custody of all property and children.[24] "A wife is dead in law" was a commonly accepted doctrine. And lacking the right to vote, women could not turn to electoral politics to overcome this kind of discrimination. Rather, they "determined to foment a rebellion," in Abigail Adams's words, for "we would not hold ourselves bound by any laws in which we have no voice or representation."[25]

Women needed to become conscious of themselves as a group and to learn their rights. During the Revolution, and later during the War of 1812, many wives had to take over their husbands' work. Later, tens of thousands of women flocked to New England and other textile mill areas to work in factories.[26] This experience, along with those that women encountered on farms and on the expanding western frontier, made women more conscious of their abilities and resources, both as individuals and as a group. It also made them more aware of their legal and political powerlessness.

Initially, political activity among women was confined mainly to three areas: for literacy, and against slavery and liquor. Formal education for women was restricted to female academies in which daughters of the wealthy were taught social graces and other "female arts." Early reformers encouraged education for men and women alike. And although women were involved in the earliest campaigns against slavery, even like-minded males tried to distance themselves from the "female agitators." Seeing the effects of the "demon rum" on their families further encouraged women to form temperance societies.

Such forays into the world of politics helped lay the groundwork for the movements to come, and numerous leaders emerged to organize their sisters. Sarah Bagley, a young Lowell mill worker, organized women workers in the Massachusetts and New Hampshire textile mills and founded the Female Labor Reform Association in 1845. The FLRA, together with other labor groups, submitted a petition in favor of the ten-hour day, signed by 10,000 workers, to the Massachusetts legislature. Lucretia Mott, a Philadelphia Quaker, toured meetings of the Friends to speak on temperance, peace, antislavery, and women's rights. Elizabeth Cady Stanton, who as a child in her father's law office had heard women pour out their grievances about discrimination and oppression, devoted her life to denouncing discrimination against women. In 1821 Emma Willard founded Troy Seminary for Women, a college that offered higher mathematics as well as the more conventional arts. Most controversial of all was Frances Wright, advocate of more liberal divorce laws, birth control, equal rights, and free public education. "Fanny" was denounced for her belief in the equality of all, regardless of sex, color, and class. It was even rumored that she favored "free love."

At an international antislavery meeting in London in 1840, delegates Lucretia Mott and Elizabeth Cady Stanton suffered the humiliation of being refused seats as delegates; rather, they were sent off to the gallery to watch. Then and there they resolved to hold a women's rights convention on their return home. Eight years later such a convention was held in Seneca Falls, New York, to discuss the "social, civil, and religious conditions and rights of woman." The convention was a curious "mixture of womanly modesty and feminist militancy."[27] Because no woman would chair the meeting, Lucretia Mott's husband was asked to do so. The women's demands were radical for the times. The convention adopted resolutions calling for equal rights in marriage, property, contracts, trades, professions, and universities. Even more radical was a resolution to secure women's suffrage. Pushed by Elizabeth Cady Stanton and supported by Frederick Douglass, the measure barely passed.[28] Other conventions followed, in the East and as far west as Akron, Ohio. Women were on the march.

A CENTURY OF STRUGGLE

Between the 1850s and the 1950s, leaders of the women's movement fought their political campaigns on many fronts. They took part in the antislavery movement, organized women's suffrage associations, won the right to vote in several western states, collaborated with temperance and other reform movements, helped found

Shunning the stereotypical role as passive and apolitical, women campaigned for the vote in Washington.

the National Association of Colored Women in 1896, fought against sexist discrimination on a state-by-state basis, established their right to higher education and professional positions, cooperated with women trade union workers, encountered defeat after defeat in their efforts to win the vote state by state, and finally won the national suffrage in August 1920, after a hard campaign for the enactment of the Nineteenth Amendment.

Many believe the women's movement died after this victory. But in fact, women's organizations continued to work on "women's issues," that is, issues directly affecting women's status as women, and on other concerns, such as voter education, prison reform, antilynching measures, child welfare, and peace. Two organizations in particular continued the fight on women's issues: the National Woman's Party (NWP) and the National Federation of Business and Professional Women (NFBPW). Founded by Alice Paul, the NWP believed the vote alone would not get rid of economic inequality in the workplace, holding instead that only a constitutional amendment could establish the *principle* of sex equality. The NWP was responsible for introducing the Equal Rights Amendment in Congress in 1923 and for keeping it alive there session after session until it was embraced by the "second wave" of the women's movement in the 1960s. The NFBPW supported the Equal Rights Amendment during this period and worked generally to improve employed women's educational and employment opportunities.[29]

In contrast, during this period the Women's Bureau of the Department of Labor worked *against* the Equal Rights Amendment. Because working conditions associated with so many women's jobs were harsh and unhealthy, the Women's Bureau instead supported protective legislation for employed women.[30]

This century of struggle raised a number of questions of ends and means, of strategy and tactics—questions that also confront other major groups. What is the *goal* of the women's movement? To secure rights only for women, or to win them also for other disadvantaged groups, such as blacks, low-paid labor, immigrants, and Native Americans. If women's rights are the goal, *which* rights—to vote, to have a good education, to enjoy legal protection, to have a decent job, or to receive equal pay? To what extent should women work with other groups, at the expense possibly of having to dilute their own efforts? Should women form their own party, work within the existing two-party system, emphasize nonparty action (such as education and lobbying), or build a mass protest movement, march, and demonstrate for their demands? Should the movement concentrate on influencing the federal government, focus more on state action, or stress local, day-to-day concerns, such as education or neighborhood improvement?

Like most groups, women shifted tactics to meet new goals and circumstances. The national leaders split over whether to fight for suffrage alone or for a broader program, whether men should be allowed into the movement and on what basis, and what specific tactics should be adopted.

Today the National Organization for Women (NOW), often thought of as the primary group of the women's movement, is sometimes criticized for gaining legal and political reforms that help white middle-class women but not the poor and minority women. Many feminists contend, moreover, that political and legal reforms are not enough to restructure gender roles that limit women's economic and educational opportunities, and constrain the lives of both women and men.[31] Women's groups have met problems in mobilizing women for collective action; and even though women have become more politically conscious in the last decade, they have not identified as a group in the same way as blacks, whose group consciousness has fostered collective action for social change. Furthermore, there is growing divergence of thought within the women's movement as its goals and methods change. Women are a majority of the population in the United States, but on issues such as equal pay for equal work, pornography, civil rights, and the ERA, there is much disagreement.

In the end, using a variety of political tactics and operating at all governmental levels paid off in securing the right to vote. Because conventional political action had not worked without the right to vote, it took the arrests of picketers and the forced feeding of society women in jails to dramatize the issues. The fact that many women were organized for both national and state politics paid off when they pushed the suffrage amendment through the House and Senate, and then through three-quarters of the state legislatures. In 1920 the Senate passed the amendment by exactly the two-thirds required, and the last legislature to ratify (Tennessee's) did so by a majority of one!

A NEW CONSCIOUSNESS: ERA

Armed with the right to vote, many American women entered the 1920s with heightened self-confidence and political influence. Congress acted favorably on maternity and infancy legislation, consumer bills, and other issues of special interest to women. By the end of 1921 twenty states had granted women the right to serve on juries. A few states passed equal pay and equal rights laws. Soon came the first woman governor, woman senator, and women cabinet members, and others followed. A new organization, the League of Women Voters, educated its members on issues and urged them to exercise their hard-won right to vote.

But if women had new political clout, they also faced new handicaps. A reaction to feminist successes set in. The child-labor constitutional amendment failed to make any headway, and conservative groups put down feminist groups and women leaders, calling them communists, antifamily, and deviant lesbians. Some women who had been active in or influenced by the women's movement veered off in other directions. Most pursued "lifestyle feminism" using the opportunities opened up by the women's movement for their own personal self-development, and leaving behind the group effort that made the opportunities possible. Although fewer continued to pursue the political aspects of feminism, they kept the fire smoldering until it burst out again in the 1960s.[32]

Women's goals expanded immensely following World War II, during which women had taken on heavy responsibilities, including military service. In the late 1950s and early 1960s, the struggle for black rights involved hundreds of women leaders and precipitated a more militant political effort. In the course of the struggle for "freedom now," it began to occur to more and more women, black and white, that sex as well as race was a source of oppression. Women in the anti-Vietnam War and draft resistance movements began to realize they were being relegated to nonpolicy-making roles in those efforts. Whether black, socialist,

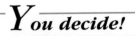

*Y*ou decide!

As a leader in the women's movement today, you are serving on a planning group considering new political strategies, in light of the failure of the Equal Rights Amendment to pass. A rank-and-file activist tells your group that movement politics has failed, that a *party* strategy is necessary—and that women must form their own party. What is your response?

(Answer/Discussion on page 223.)

or radical feminist, many broke off and joined the women's movement.[33] Women in the labor movement likewise recognized sexism in the movement as well as in the workplace and formed the Coalition of Labor Union Women (CLUW). To many women—especially middle-class housewives or those destined for that role—the appeals of Betty Friedan and other feminist writers came like fire sirens in the night.[34]

In broadening women's consciousness of their real needs and aspirations, literary and political leaders also expanded women's political and legislative goals. During the 1950s women won executive appointments in government but achieved few concrete gains. However, the Kennedy administration confronted women's issues more directly than either Truman's or Eisenhower's had. Kennedy's initiatives, such as the President's Commission on the Status of Women, contributed to the emergence of a broad-based feminist movement.[35] No longer were women content working for a small number of legislative enactments; instead they took positions, lobbied, marched, demonstrated, or "boycotted" for bills cutting across all their concerns: equal pay, discrimination on the job, legal equality, divorce and child care, welfare rights, health care, protection against brutality and rape, equal credit opportunities, and educational equity. This range of interests required women to create new general organizations such as NOW, as well as multitudes of women's liberation groups backing specific proposals or providing particular services.[36]

The women's movement of the late 1970s became more and more conscious of its own diversity; it was not just a white middle-class phenomenon. Many began to work on coalition building within the movement as well as with other groups—consumer, trade union, black, religious and educational groups—in order to push bills in Congress and the state legislatures. As in any movement, women were internally divided; some women deserted NOW because it was too radical, others because it was too conservative.

As we saw in Chapter 2, the efforts of many groups came to a focus in the battle for the Equal Rights Amendment (ERA) in the 1970s. To this struggle pro-ERA leaders brought not only moral claims and raised consciousness but also potentially vast numbers of voters and a large coalition of organizations. By the mid-1970s an alliance of younger organizations such as NOW and older groups such as the League of Women Voters and the Business and Professional Women had set up a national lobby, ERAmerica, with headquarters in Washington. Yet the battle for the ERA, like that for the vote a century before, proceeded slowly. Even though women constituted a majority of the American people, they faced opposition from well-organized minorities. Many women flatly opposed the ERA, and they formed their own organization: STOP ERA. Others favored the ERA but feared that concentrating so much on this one general issue would divert efforts from more specific and practical goals. Moreover, even though many men supported the ERA, others assailed it. And millions of Americans, both women and men, were apathetic.

By the mid-1980s supporters of the ERA were still unable to win majorities in both houses of the thirty-eight states needed to pass the amendment.[37] A striking symbolic victory occurred in 1984 when the Democrats chose Congresswoman Geraldine A. Ferraro of New York as their vice-presidential candidate, but there were not many other victories. Indeed, reaction to feminism in the 1980s strikingly paralleled that of the 1920s. A conservative Republican occupied the White House, and many conservatives viewed the women's movement as radical and antifamily. Yet as we enter the 1990s women in the movement are more politically conscious and capable of organizing around controversial issues, and they have more political and economic resources and experiences upon which to draw. Women have won numerous legislative and even several gubernatorial races at the state level.

At the same time, the women's movement, like the blacks', has tended to fragment as it has taken on a wider variety of personal and public problems. Women have begun to form unions, such as "9 to 5," which organized women office workers in Boston in 1973. They have assumed more leadership in religious and professional organizations; for example, at the annual meeting of the American Political Science Association, an active women's caucus presents a host of problems plaguing women scholars and teachers.

As the women's movement broadened, however, it confronted the same problem as the black movement—how to maintain the militance and idealism of its members while simultaneously taking part in activities that might win election victories but might further divide the movement, drain its energies, and compromise its program. For some women this has raised the specific alternatives of continuing to work closely with the national Democratic party, forming a third party, resorting to traditional pressure-group tactics, or finding another alternative. This question has become especially urgent in the early 1990s, after three Democratic presidential-election defeats in a row.

THE RISE OF THE NEW RIGHT

One of the strongest movements of the 1970s and 1980s emerged on the far right. Large numbers of Americans, disillusioned by what they saw as a gradual decline in the morality of American society, faulted the federal government for banning prayer in schools, for court-approved abortion, busing policies, and affirmative action. They faulted society for the spread of pornography, sexual liberty, the decay of the traditional family, and the acceptance of homosexuality. For many the intensity of these social upheavals was matched by a serious decline in American prestige and power as the United States seemed to retreat from its position as leader of the Western world following political defeats in Vietnam and Iran. Also, the post-war economic boom had come to an end as growth slowed and inflation hit double digits. These crises helped give rise to the New Right, an alliance of Christian fundamentalists and old-time conservatives who sought to rejuvenate the United States through an emphasis on Judeo-Christian values (as they interpret them), conservative economic policies, and a hard-line military stance.

Bennett for The St. Petersburg Times.

Although women rallied in support of ratification of the Equal Rights Amendment, they were unable to win the necessary votes in thirty-eight states, and the measure was defeated.

Answer/Discussion

You might note that women outnumber men and that this would help a party strategy. But you should also note that most women cast their vote influenced more by economic, social, religious, and even some ethnic concerns than because of gender factors. Historically third parties have often been self-defeating. They have rarely gained power because our electoral system is biased against third parties. In this case a women's party might siphon women activists away from a major party that spoke for feminists' concerns for other goals, such as peace and education. You might propose a somewhat different party strategy—that women focus their efforts in one of the existing major parties and hence benefit from that party's broader electoral support. But which major party would you select? Why?

223

Both sides in the abortion controversy believed strongly in the rightness of their cause, and they came to Washington to persuade legislators and the Supreme Court to support them.

By the late 1970s Christian fundamentalism had reasserted itself as a powerful force in American politics. The New Christian Right voiced its anger and frustration about an America "rotting from within." Television evangelists Jerry Falwell, Pat Robertson, and Jimmy Swaggart blamed America's moral decline on "secular humanists," or atheists, whose obsessions include "sex, pornography, marijuana, self-indulgence, rights without responsibilities and disillusionment with America."[38] They built highly profitable television empires that reached out to millions of Americans. By 1986 Pat Robertson's Christian Broadcasting Network was the fourth largest network of any kind.[39] Insisting that their faith demanded involvement in secular issues, the "televangelists" went beyond purely biblical themes in their sermons to rally public support against "amoral" government policies.

During the same period, hard-line conservative Richard A. Viguerie and others helped establish the political New Right. The proliferation of probusiness organizations, along with allied groups favoring "law and order" and bigger defense programs, helped the New Right take its case to a wider public. Viguerie pioneered the massive and skillful use of computerized direct mail. By the election of 1980 he had amassed the names of 4.5 million conservatives. Operating outside the major party organizations, Viguerie helped both Democrats and Republicans—if they were solid conservatives. To broaden their influence further, Viguerie and his colleagues turned to television ministers, including Jerry Falwell, Pat Robertson, and Jim Bakker. In 1979 they created the Moral Majority, thereby solidifying the alliance of the New Right and the New Christian Right. Under the leadership of Falwell, the Moral Majority sought to bring together Catholics, Mormons, fundamentalists and orthodox Jews in the struggle against liberalism.

The right-wing movement attracted intense support from "social" and "moral" conservatives concerned with such issues as abortion, prayer in the classroom, busing, and sexual freedom. One of the most effective efforts in the "profamily" movement was STOP ERA, led by Phyllis Schlafly. Schlafly took up the battle against the Equal Rights Amendment when it seemed almost certain to be ratified. In *The Power of the Positive Woman*, she urged women to "reject socialism" and defend "our Judeo-Christian civilization." Her national 50,000-member movement against ERA, which viewed the amendment as communist-inspired at worst and unnecessary at best, had a central role in defeating it. Tim LaHaye and Paul Weyrich formed the American Coalition for Traditional Values, an umbrella organization that included the Moral Majority, to press the social agenda of the New Right. In addition to social issues, the New Right supported reduced taxes, cuts in social programs, and massive military spending increases.

CHAPTER 9 / Movements: The Politics of Conflict

How has the New Right movement related to presidential and party politics? Falwell endorsed both Reagan and Bush for the presidency, yet other leaders of the New Right, such as Viguerie, were skeptical of their commitment to the movement. By skillfully moving the GOP to the right, Reagan perhaps did more for the conservative movement than the movement did for him. Although Reagan, Bush, and the movement shared opinions on such issues as busing and school prayer, each side has viewed the other with suspicion. The Republican party has come to recognize the importance of the New Right for electoral support, yet it also recognizes that it cannot win with the support of the far right alone. During the 1988 campaign Bush dismissed Viguerie and his supporters as fringe elements on the right whose support he did not need to court.[40] On the other hand, Bush saluted the Reverend Falwell during his race for the presidency. Since Bush assumed office, the signals have been equally mixed. Bush was attacked by the right for his appointment of Louis Sullivan as Secretary of Health and Human Services, a moderate whose position on abortion was unclear. On the other hand, the Bush administration challenged the 1973 Supreme Court ruling on abortion and thus pleased the New Right.

There have been indications in recent years that the New Right movement may be faltering. Attacks by the liberal opposition have successfully eroded support for the right. With a membership approaching 250,000, the People for the American Way, a liberal organization, took the initiative with television and radio spots attacking the New Christian Right and convincing many Americans of their extreme position. Opposition groups criticized Falwell for his support of the Marcos regime in the Philippines and the apartheid government in South Africa. In 1986 Falwell was forced to change the name of the Moral Majority to the Liberty Federation after it was brought to his attention that it implied all nonmembers were immoral. Falwell also modified some of his basic positions during the 1980s, taking a more moderate stance on the abortion issue and gay rights.[41] Later in 1987 he resigned from the presidency of the Liberty Federation, signaling a partial withdrawal from national politics. Finally, the scandal involving Praise the Lord network head Jim Bakker's affair with a secretary made 1988 a particularly bad year for the religious right. Bakker was forced to resign and the ministry collapsed.

Despite these setbacks, has the New Right been successful at forging a new conservative consensus in American politics? Clearly, social issues like abortion and the family won increased attention, as evidenced by the 1988 election campaign. Pat Robertson's race for the presidency, while unsuccessful, received strong support in some states. George Bush voiced a need to return to traditional values and emphasized the importance of the family. He also made clear his determination to maintain a strong national defense and promote tougher anti-crime and anti-drug efforts, as well as promising no new taxes. Some have argued, however, that apart from the election of both Reagan and Bush, there is little indication of a significant shift to the right. There is evidence that Americans became more liberal on abortion and affirmative action in the 1980s.[42] However, the Bush presidency may yet prove a victory for the New Right when Bush has the opportunity to replace aging liberal justices in the Supreme Court.

A determined band of "spirit walkers" kept a peace march going across the desert of Utah in 1986 to arouse support for world-wide nuclear disarmament.

The Politics of Peace

Peace movements—or at least antiwar campaigns—began early in American history. The Civil War and other major conflicts aroused strong opposition on a local, and sometimes on a national, basis. The Women's Peace Party and the Fellowship of Reconciliation were formed in the United States during World War I. The bloodbaths of that war brought a powerful revulsion against militarism, interventionism, and the "merchants of death" who were said to profit from wars they helped bring about. The antiwar movement of the 1930s, headed by such diverse figures as the popular hero Charles A. Lindbergh and socialist Norman Thomas, caused President Franklin Roosevelt to move warily against the gathering forces of fascism.

Concern over peace rose to a new intensity with the advent of nuclear weapons and the onset of the Korean and Vietnam Wars. Students and other activists took to the streets, disrupted classrooms, occupied administration buildings, and took part in (usually) nonviolent action against the authorities. As the superpowers stepped up their nuclear arsenals, new organizations arose—most notably the liberal Committee for a Sane Nuclear Policy (SANE) and the more activist Committee for Nonviolent Action (CNVA), and later a host of religious groups and professional organizations, such as Physicians for Social Responsibility.[43] In 1980 peace leaders joined with environmentalists behind the Citizens Party and nominated noted biologist Barry Commoner for president, but this third-party effort failed, as have a number of others throughout history.[44]

The election of Ronald Reagan in that year, and perhaps more important, his reelection in 1984, left the peace movement divided and frustrated. Campaigns continued to "ban the bomb" and to ensure a mutually verifiable nuclear "freeze," but the peace movement lacked unified leadership, a coherent policy program, and a realistic political strategy. Arguments over the proper course of action broke out, and the peace leaders sometimes appeared unable to keep peace among themselves. Individual dedication remained strong nonetheless. A 1986 peace march across the United States finished successfully in Washington, D.C. By educating people across the nation about nuclear issues, it helped raise support for the Peace Development Fund and an international peace march in the Soviet Union in 1987.

The old questions that have dogged all American movements stared these leaders in the face: Should the peace activists link themselves more closely with the two major parties or with one of the major third-party groups, in which case the smaller party might be engulfed by the larger one? Or should they link with one existing major party, presumably the Democrats, who were looking for allies? Or should they be content to serve as the junior partner in some multiparty coalition in Congress, without any hope of gaining the presidency?

Since the Bush administration came into office, peace leaders have sought to enlarge their ranks and fashion a more effective movement. Ronald Reagan, instead of galvanizing the peace movement, appears to have diffused it—especially with arms negotiations with Soviet leader Mikhail Gorbachev. President Reagan asserted that the INF treaty was the result of his deployment of Pershing II and cruise missiles in Europe, allowing the United States to negotiate from a position of strength. However, some argue that Ronald Reagan signed the INF Treaty with the Soviet Union in 1987 in partial response to a vocal peace movement. Since then negotiators from the Bush administration and the Soviet Union have been at work on treaties for the reduction of intercontinental ballistic missiles and conventional forces in Europe. Although progress may weaken the movement, the reduction of armaments will still be viewed as having been won through the efforts of the peace movement.

Today the newest focus of the peace movement is the Common Security concept, whose basic premise is that no nation can ensure its own security at the expense of another.[45] Proponents of this concept call for a restructuring of each side's military forces through gradual nuclear disarmament and a shift to nonprovocative conventional defense. This new security agenda also includes inter-

Centrist Movements?

Why is it that nearly all political movements come from either the left or right? By definition, a movement emerges not from within the mainstream of the political system, but from the fringes or from "the outside." Thus populists, moralists, and anti-Establishment activism periodically arise from the left and the right.

Centrists or mainstream political activists may temporarily lend their allegiance to a proconsumer campaign or to a short-lived cause such as the John B. Anderson independent candidacy for President in 1980. Invariably, however, such activism either dissipates or is quickly channeled back through regular political parties or existing interest groups. This is why this chapter has focused primarily on the crusades and causes of the far right and the left. If movements seldom if ever erupt from the center, are movements futile, lost causes? Centrists would often say yes. Movement leaders insist that their causes are the "causes yet to be won!"

CHAPTER 9 / Movements: The Politics of Conflict

national environmental and economic challenges and requires stronger cooperation among world powers at solving global problems.

Peace leaders remain divided over strategy and tactics. Whether the peace effort should remain a loosely connected cluster of peace *campaigns* for specific goals, such as the nuclear freeze, or become a strong movement that could directly influence parties and candidates—or something in between—remains unresolved. Some peace leaders wonder if a dramatic or even tragic event might be necessary to stimulate the movement and Americans generally—but who wishes for such an event in an era of superpower nuclear rivalry?

Movements and the Constitution

Movements face many obstacles, constitutional and otherwise. Thus the Constitution barred Congress from stopping the slave trade prior to 1808 and permitted a tax of $10 on each slave imported. It not only prohibited any amendment of this clause but also provided for the return of fugitive persons "held to service or labor"—slaves—to their owners. In fact, until the Thirteenth Amendment was ratified, the Constitution made any major movement against slavery appear to be unconstitutional.

Although the Constitution does not ignore Native Americans (it acknowledges the existence of their tribes), it offers them scant hope of operating within the constitutional system politically. Their scattered numbers, their divisions, and the overwhelming military weight of incoming settlers effectively precluded their exerting a major influence in elections.

The Constitution is all but silent concerning women. It speaks of "we the people" and "persons," but also refers to "a President . . . He." The Fourteenth Amendment specifically mentions *male* voting rights. Thus, the basic law of the land excluded women from the public sphere of government until the ratification of the Nineteenth Amendment.[46]

However, defenders of the Constitution contend that even though the constitutional system excluded blacks, Native Americans, and women from the political process in the eighteenth and nineteenth centuries, these "outside" groups worked their way into the Constitution during this century. Blacks and Native Americans, they assert, have won more through litigation and lobbying than through movement politics. Admittedly, the Constitution was not written for women, but for an eighteenth-century charter it is alleged to be rather advanced. It may delay—but it cannot forever stop—women from reaching their goals if most voters support those goals.

New movements constantly coalesce as people discover new needs and as the old ones are satisfied. A movement that has recently become increasingly vocal and militant, for example, is the one for animal rights. An automobile company has proclaimed a "bill of rights" for car owners. Perhaps one of these days millionaires will demand "rights for the rich." Where will it all end? And will our more than two-hundred-year old constitutional system be able to cope with a future tide of larger, more activist movements, each proclaiming some sacred cause? Or will the movements engulf and endanger our slow-moving, often deadlocked governmental system?

Movements polarize opinion, but they can also persuade many people to change their attitudes and raise public consciousness about social issues when government might otherwise ignore those same issues. In many countries movements are viewed as a threat to government. Indeed, they may be—to governments in South Africa, China, or Czechoslovakia, for example, which appear unable to deal peaceably with what they see as threats. Our Constitution continues to a marked degree to protect the liberties and independence of movements. The Bill of Rights guarantees movements, whether popular or unpopular, free assembly, free speech, and due process. Hence militants do not have to engage in terrorism or other extreme activities in the United States, and they need not fear persecution for demonstrating. In a democratic system that restricts the power of those in authority, movements have considerable room to operate *inside* the constitutional system.

Summary

1. Movements of large numbers of people who are frustrated with government policies have always been with us in the United States. Blacks, women, Native Americans, and the economic underdogs have at various times organized themselves into movements. The so-called "New Right" and "Religious Right" are a mix of movement and traditional interest group politics.

2. The key components of movements are negative perceptions of the political system; group consciousness of mistreatment, organization, and leadership; and direct actions involving large numbers of group members and supporters.

3. Individuals gain group consciousness through movements. They may experience direct action itself or participate in alternative educational experiences, or they may be encouraged by families or movement leaders.

4. Movement politics involves groups outside the political system who are in conflict with and confront the system in public, direct actions intended to achieve comprehensive change. In contrast, interest-group politics involves groups inside the political system who bargain privately within a framework of consensus to bring about incremental change.

5. The focal point of American Indian movements is to recover tribal sovereignty, which was first established by treaties and then abrogated continuously as settlers violated the treaties.

6. The focal point of the black movements is to change the original slave status of black Africans to freedom as persons and full-fledged citizens of the United States.

7. The focal point of women's movements is to transcend the artificially imposed dichotomy of the public and private spheres.

8. The "latest movement" is the New Right headed by television evangelist Jerry Falwell, and inspired and supported by Ronald Reagan.

9. The peace movement is fractured at a time when a cohesive strategy is most critical. Different goals, clashing methods, and conflicting priorities threaten to negate the potentially potent effect of peace activists.

Further Reading

RUSSEL LAWRENCE BARSH and JAMES YOUNGBLOOD HENDERSON. *The Road*: *Indian Tribes and Political Liberty* (University of California Press, 1980).

DAVID H. BENNETT. *The Party of Fear* (University of North Carolina Press, 1988).

RUFUS P. BROWNING, DALE ROGERS MARSHALL, and DAVID H. TABB. *Protest Is Not Enough*: *The Struggle of Blacks and Hispanics in Urban Politics* (University of California Press, 1984).

STEVE BRUCE. *The Rise and Fall of the New Christian Right* (Oxford University Press, 1988).

CLAYBORNE CARSON. *In Struggle*: *SNCC and the Black Awakening of the 1960s* (Harvard University Press, 1981).

JEAN L. COHEN, ed. "Social Movements," *Social Research* (Winter 1985).

ROBERT COONEY and HELEN MICHALOWSKI. *The Power of the People*: *Active Nonviolence in the United States* (Peace Press, 1977).

SARA H. EVANS. *Born for Liberty: A History of Women in America* (Free Press, 1989).

CYNTHIA HARRISON. *On Account of Sex: The Politics of Women's Issues, 1945–1968* (University of California Press, 1988).

STEPHEN CORNELL. *The Return of the Native*: *American Indian Political Resurgence* (Oxford University Press, 1988).

GLORIA T. HULL, PATRICIA BELL SCOTT, and BARBARA SMITH, eds. *All the Women Are White, All the Blacks Are Men, but Some of Us Are Brave: Black Women's Studies* (Feminist Press, 1982).

HOWARD JARVIS. *I'm Mad as Hell!* (Times Books, 1979).

ALDON D. MORRIS. *The Origins of the Civil Rights Movement*: *Black Communities Organizing for Change* (Free Press/ Macmillan, 1985).

BARBARA DECKARD SINCLAIR. *The Women's Movement* (Harper & Row, 1983).

U.S. COMMISSION ON CIVIL RIGHTS. *Indian Tribes: A Continuing Quest for Survival* (U.S. Government Printing Office, 1981).

RICHARD VIGUERIE. *The New Right* (Carolina House, 1981).

Notes

1. For a discussion of women as a sex-class, see Zillah Eisenstein, *The Radical Future of Liberal Feminism* (Longman, 1981). On the suffragists see Ellen Carol DuBois, *Feminism and Suffrage: The Emergence of an Independent Women's Movement in America, 1848–1869* (Cornell University Press, 1978).

2. Diane L. Fowlkes, "Feminist Theory—Reconstructing Research and Teaching about American Politics and Government," *News for Teachers of Political Science* (Winter 1987), pp. 6–9. See Andrea Dworkin, *Right-Wing Women* (Putnam's, 1983); Zillah R. Eisenstein, ed., *Feminism and Sexual Equality: Crisis in Liberal America* (Monthly Review Press, 1984); Ethel Klein, *Gender Politics* (Harvard University Press, 1984); Rebecca E. Klatch, *Women of the New Right* (Temple University Press, 1987).

3. See Helen Michalowski, "The Roots of American Nonviolence, 1650–1915," in Robert Cooney and Helen Michalowski, eds., *The Power of the People: Active Nonviolence in the United States* (Peace Press, 1977), pp. 14–37.

4. David Lowery and Lee Sigelman, "Understanding the Tax Revolt: Eight Explanations," *American Political Science Review* (December 1981), pp. 963–74. For a new look at Proposition 13, see Douglas Jeffe and Sherry B. Jeffe, "Proposition 13 Ten Years Later," *Public Opinion* (May/June 1988).

5. Dorothy V. Jones, *License for Empire: Colonialism by Treaty in Early America* (University of Chicago Press, 1982).

6. Quoted in Russel Lawrence Barsh and James Youngblood Henderson, *The Road: Indian Tribes and Political Liberty* (University of California Press, 1980).

7. On the roles of American Indian women, see Rayna Green, "Native American Women," *Signs: Journal of Women in Culture and Society* (Winter 1980), pp. 248–67.

8. *Cherokee Nation* v. *Georgia*, 5 Peters 25, 17 (1831).

9. Barsh and Henderson, *The Road*, pp. vii–viii.

10. Stan Steiner, *The New Indians* (Harper & Row, 1968), p. 40. (Emphasis added.)

11. Adaptation of traditional song by members of the Albany Movement, 1961–1962, which Bernice Reagon, then an Albany State College student, called the "Singing Movement." See Clayborne Carson, *In Struggle: SNCC and the Black Awakening of the 1960s* (Harvard University Press, 1981), especially pp. 56–65. The song is recorded on *Sing for Freedom: Lest We Forget*, vol. 3, produced by Guy and Candie Carawan of the Highlander Center, Newmarket, Tennessee, for Folkways Records, 1980. Printed in *We Shall Overcome, Songs of the Southern Freedom Movement*, compiled by Guy and Candie Carawan (Oak Publications, 1963).

12. See August Meier and Elliott M. Rudwick, *From Plantation to Ghetto* (Hill and Wang, 1966); and Lerone Bennett, Jr., *Before the Mayflower: A History of the Negro in America, 1619–1964*, rev. ed. (Penguin, 1966).

13. Herbert G. Gutman, *The Black Family in Slavery and Freedom, 1750–1925* (Vintage Books, 1977).

14. Eugene D. Genovese, *From Rebellion to Revolution: Afro-American Slave Revolts in the Making of the New World* (Vintage Books, 1981), pp. 4, 27.

15. Louis Ruchames, *The Abolitionists: A Collection of Their Writings* (Capricorn Books, 1964), pp. 13–24.

16. Carson, *In Struggle*. See also Cooney and Michalowski, *The Power of the People*.

17. Gerda Lerner, ed., *Black Women in White America: A Documentary History* (Vintage Books, 1973), especially pp. 150–93.

18. Anne Firor Scott, *The Southern Lady: From Pedestal to Politics 1830–1930* (University of Chicago Press, 1970).

19. W.E.B. Du Bois, *Black Reconstruction in America, 1860–1880* (Meridian Books, 1964, first published by Harcourt, Brace and Company, 1935), pp. 677–78.

20. Ida B. Wells, *A Red Record* (Donohue & Henneberry, n.d.; reprinted by Arno Press, 1969).

21. Jacquelyn D. Hall, *Revolt against Chivalry: Jessie Daniel Ames and the Women's Campaign against Lynching* (Columbia University Press, 1979).

22. *Report of the National Advisory Commission on Civil Disorders* (Kerner Commission) (Bantam, 1968).

23. Richard Lacayo, "Between Two Worlds," *Time* (March 13, 1989), p. 58.

24. Eleanor Flexner, *Century of Struggle* (Harvard University Press, 1975), pp. 7–8, 63–65.

25. Letter of Abigail Adams to John Adams, March 31, 1776, in Miriam Schneir, *Feminism: The Essential Historical Writings* (Vintage Books, 1972), p. 3.

26. Milton Cantor and Bruce Laurie, eds., *Class, Sex, and the Woman Worker* (Greenwood Press, 1977).

27. DuBois, *Feminism and Suffrage*, p. 23.

28. Ibid., pp. 40–41.

29. Klein, *Gender Politics*, and Susan J. Carroll, *Women as Candidates in American Politics* (Indiana University, 1985).

30. Judith Hole and Ellen Levine, *Rebirth of Feminism* (Quadrangle/The New York Times Book Company, 1971), especially pp. 77–81.

31. Eisenstein, *The Radical Future of Liberal Feminism*.

32. Rayna Rapp and Ellen Ross, " 'It Seems We've Stood and Talked Like This Before': Wisdom from the 1920s," *Ms.* (April 1983), pp. 54–56.

33. Sara Evans, *Personal Politics: The Roots of Women's Liberation in the Civil Rights Movement and the New Left* (Vintage Books, 1980).

34. Betty Friedan, *The Feminine Mystique* (Norton, 1963).

35. Cynthia Harrison, *On Account of Sex: The Politics of Women's Issues, 1945–1968* (University of California Press, 1988).

36. Jo Freeman, *The Politics of Women's Liberation* (David McKay, 1975).

37. Janet K. Boles, *The Politics of the Equal Rights Amendment* (Longman, 1979). See in general James MacGregor Burns, *The Crosswinds of Freedom* (Knopf, 1989), chap. 10.

38. Tim LaHaye, *The Battle for the Mind*, as cited in David H. Bennett, *The Party of Fear* (University of North Carolina Press, 1988), p. 378.

39. Bennett, *The Party of Fear*, p. 379.

40. Gerald M. Boyd, "Bush Says He Has Earned Support of Right Wing," *The New York Times* (June 2, 1988), p. A1.

41. Sean Wilentz, "God and Man At Lynchburg," *The New Republic* (April 25, 1988), pp. 30–36.

42. Steve Bruce, *The Rise and Fall of the New Christian Right* (Oxford University Press, 1988), p. 166.

43. Ulrike C. Wasmuht, "A Sociological Survey of American Peace Movements," *Alternatives*, vol. 9 (Spring 1984), pp. 581–91.

44. Alan Wolfe, "Why Is There No Green Party in the United States?" *World Policy Journal* (Fall 1983), p. 172.

45. *A Call to Action: Common Security and our Common Future*, (Institute for Peace and International Security, June 1989).

46. From Diane L. Fowlkes, *How Gender Politics Reconstructs American Government and Politics* (American Political Science Association, 1983). See also Sarah Slavin, *Women and the Politics of Constitutional Principles* (American Political Science Association, 1983).

10

Political Parties: Institutions under Change

In the early pages of this book we noted how our Constitution divides government by setting the legislative, executive, and judicial branches at odds with one another. The framers of 1787 did this by making the president, Senate, House, and even the judiciary (indirectly) responsive to different constituencies (see Chapter 2). The purpose, you will recall, was to limit the government's power and influence so it would not "gang up" against the people's liberties. The Bill of Rights was a powerful additional safeguard. Most early Americans favored these protections; like many of us today, they wanted to keep the government—especially the federal government—"off their backs."

But there was a flip side to this idea. Americans then also wanted efficient, orderly, and effective government—just as we do today. They wanted teamwork in government: a group of officials who could work together and collectively be held responsible for what they did or failed to do. So Americans in effect invented what could be called a "second constitution"—government by political parties. Two or more parties would compete for office, and the winning party, or coalition of parties, would put its leaders in office, both legislative and executive. These leaders would form a team capable of uniting government to carry out its party principles. The losing party would serve as a loyal—but forceful—opposition. It may seem paradoxical to call a party system a constitution. Yet in the most basic sense, political parties organize power, grant and withhold authority, and try to keep officeholders accountable, just as constitutions do.

Note the contrasts between the "first Constitution" of 1787 and the "second (party) constitution." The first Constitution was written in a single summer by the elite of the day: by the "well bred, the well read, the well fed, and the well wed." The "second constitution" was shaped over a hundred-year period by many men and women—often "common people"—meeting in taverns and town halls, caucussing wherever politics was discussed. The first Constitution went into effect as soon as it was ratified by the requisite number of states. The "party constitution" took decades to take root in people's minds and acts, and many changes took place as it grew into a full-bodied system with party leaders, whips, activists, and supporters. The Constitution of 1787 was framed by the nation's heroes—men like Washington and Franklin and Madison. The need for a "party constitution" was suggested by some of these same men as they gained experience under the first Constitution, but it was framed by local leaders and by a few national ones—notably in the 1830s by Martin Van Buren, a young man of humble origin who had absorbed politics by listening to great talkers in his father's tavern and who went on to become a Democratic party leader and president. The first Constitution was a comprehensive plan; the second developed slowly, by trial and error.

The greatest contrast between the two constitutions, however, lies in their impact on government. The party constitution is an instrument of majority rule—of "rule by the people," whereas the 1787 Constitution protects rule by a minority, or coalition of minorities. By making presidents, senators, and representatives responsive to different constituencies, the 1787 Constitution impedes teamwork in government; by making presidents and members of Congress responsive to one organized party majority, the party constitution encourages teamwork. The 1787 Constitution was accepted early on, but the very idea of parties was attacked from the start by Washington and others as divisive, fractious, turbulent, and overly democratic. The 1787 Constitution depends on checks and balances to protect the people's liberties; the party constitution relies on regular, open, and democratic elections.

You might expect that the paper Constitution—the framers' constitution of 1787—would become antiquated and feeble, and that the dynamic "people's constitution" of the political parties would endure. But this is not so. The division of power in the formal Constitution endures, as you can see every time that the House of Representatives and the Senate fail to agree, or the president vetoes a bill passed by both chambers. That Constitution has evolved to meet a changing society, but the philosophy on which it is based has persisted. Meanwhile, the party system has faced serious challenge. Questions have been raised as to whether that "party constitution" still performs its assigned duties of organizing power and keeping officeholders accountable. We will turn to those questions later. Yet merely raising questions brings to mind a most urgent query: If the health of our whole system depends upon a balance between a Constitution that divides leaders and a party system that unites them, what will happen if either of these constitutions fails to perform adequately?

What is the current state of political parties in America? We discuss this question in detail later in this chapter. Perhaps part of the question can be answered by you, the reader. How partisan are you? Your parents? Your friends and neighbors? If there is a Young Democrats or Young Republicans or some other party club in your school, are you a member of it? Chances are—statistically—that you are not strongly partisan, nor are most of the people you know.

Contrast this with the "grand old days" of American parties. A century ago you and many of your friends would have been fiercely partisan. The party was part of your way of life, part of the eternal order of things, like the family and religion. It was part of your inheritance. Belonging to the "other" party was not quite respectable. Which party you belonged to was often a regional matter. If you were white and grew up in the South, Republicans were alien beings who opposed all you stood for. If you were black and grew up in the South, Republicans were the emancipators (except that they pulled their federal troops out too soon and you lost your right to vote and hold office). If you were raised in Kansas, Democrats were people who frequented saloons and lived off a few patronage crumbs from Washington.

Things are different today. For most of the last quarter century, parties have

Seven Realities about American Parties

1. Parties began as soon as people began taking sides in the debate over ratifying the U.S. Constitution—although it took a few years for them to organize into formal bodies.

2. Political parties, and especially our two-party system, have persisted over the course of our history.

3. Ours is, and just about always has been, a two-party system, making us stand out from most nations that have a one-party or multi-party system.

4. Since 1830 we have witnessed reasonably effective competition in our national party system.

5. Our parties have historically been highly decentralized and fragmented, but there has been a marked increase in the importance of the national committees in recent years.

6. Winning office and power have been more important to party leaders than specific issues or platforms; political parties in the United States are primarily organized to win or obtain political power.

7. Our parties can be characterized as moderate, centrist, and pragmatic, with only modest ideological cohesion and voting discipline—especially when compared to European political parties.

been declining in popular support. The number of citizens who feel they are "strong" Republicans and "strong" Democrats has dropped by about a third; the number who do not support either party has grown by a similar amount. Dominant state or local party organizations are rare. Where a party is strong locally, it is often ruled by a small group of "old timers," and the extent of their power over meaningful decisions is in question. Americans are losing interest in political parties.[1]

The party as an organization no longer makes the single most crucial decision in national politics—*the choice of the presidential nominee.* Although the two winning candidates are formally chosen at the Democratic and Republican national conventions, the delegates to these conventions have not really made that choice in more than three decades. The party nominees are *actually* chosen in a string of local caucuses and state presidential primaries held throughout the winter and spring of presidential election years. In some states independents as well as partisans vote for their candidate choices at the polls. Although party leaders frequently try to exert their influence, the formal organization cannot play an active role, and the extent of leaders' influence is limited. In 1976 Jimmy Carter won the Democratic nomination, even though he had little influence with either the national Democratic party or state and local party leaders in most areas. In that same year, Ronald Reagan, then a former governor of California thought to represent an extreme element within the Republican party, nearly wrested his party's nomination from President Gerald Ford, a long-time national leader of the GOP (the Grand Old Party—the Republican party). In 1988 the Reverend Jesse Jackson exerted a great deal of influence over the Democratic National Convention because traditional party leaders recognized his popularity with a significant segment of Democratic voters, even though that popularity was feared by leaders of the organization.

Perhaps the most dramatic—and tragic—example of party weakness was **Watergate.** In his 1972 reelection campaign President Nixon bypassed the Republican party organization and depended on his personal organization, the Committee to Re-elect the President, which gained infamy under its nickname CREEP. CREEP's independence grew out of changes in campaign finance laws that required separate campaign committees, and out of President Nixon's desire to separate his own campaign from that of other Republicans who did not seem so likely to win. Thus "Watergate"—a burglary at the headquarters of the Democratic National Committee, various other dirty tricks and illegal or unethical activities performed by campaign operatives, and the attempt to cover up presidential knowledge of those activities—grew in part out of CREEP's secrecy, financing, and excessive personal loyalty to President Nixon. Political party organizations, in contrast, have a stake in our electoral system that transcends loyalty to one candidate.

Ronald Reagan, who led the GOP to sweeping national victories in 1980 and 1984, used the national party organization as an extension of his own campaign. But President Reagan, recognizing the importance of victories by his fellow Republicans, helped the party organization raise money for other Republican candidates; he was tireless in his efforts to help rebuild his party. National leaders in both parties have seen the importance of working for the election of all of their party nominees. They have seen that they must draw state and local party leaders back to the party fold. The Democratic party has done this by giving many of those leaders ex officio status as so-called *superdelegates* to the national nominating convention. But the effort to renew elected officeholders' commitment to party organization has been only partially successful. Many governors and mayors, whether Democratic or Republican, see party organization as important only insofar as it affects their own elections.

Two-party advocates, like the student below, also believe in another, very real party system.

CHAPTER 10 / Political Parties: Institutions under Change

Similarly, many Americans have mixed feelings about the parties. Critics charge that the parties evade the issues; that they fail to deliver on their promises; that they have no new ideas; that they are sources of corruption and misgovernment; that they follow public opinion rather than lead it; or that they are just one more special interest. Others favor the party system and take part in it. Most Americans believe in voting for individual candidates regardless of party label, but even this group wants party labels kept on the ballot.[2]

So the state of our political parties is not clear. They are not as strong as they once were, but party leaders have recognized the need to change. This change has only just begun, yet many involved in politics and many less active citizens seem not to care. Does this matter? Are parties relevant to "government by the people" as this nation heads into its third century under the written Constitution? If so, can the effort to breathe new life into them be successful?

Parties: Their Rise and Their Role

Before we begin, we need to make a crucial distinction between the *factions* we discussed in earlier chapters and the *parties* we now consider. If you find this question a bit baffling, you are in good company. It baffled our country's founders too. In fact, they confused the issue; we must try to clarify it.

A BRIEF LOOK AT THE HISTORY OF AMERICAN POLITICAL PARTIES

The founders did understand the nature of faction; Madison's definition of it in *The Federalist*, No. 10 (see Appendix) is still the best we have. Madison and others called the factions they opposed "cliques" or "juntos" or even "parties" (by which they meant factions). Fearing the excesses of economic, social, and other highly organized groups, they devised a federal constitution that would moderate the power of faction, as we saw in Part One of this text. And because they did not want to extinguish the freedom that stimulated faction, they provided for the fundamental liberties we examined in Chapters 4, 5, and 6.

To the leaders of the young Republic, parties usually meant bigger, better organized, and more fierce factions—and they did not want them. Benjamin Franklin worried about the "infinite mutual abuse of parties, tearing to pieces the best of characters." In his farewell address, George Washington warned against the "baneful effects of the Spirit of Party." And Thomas Jefferson said: "If I could not go to heaven but with a party, I would not go there at all."[3]

How, then, did parties get started? Largely out of practical necessity. The same early leaders who so frequently stated their opposition to political parties also recognized the need to organize officeholders sharing their views so that divided government could act. To get its measures passed through Congress, the Washington administration had to fashion a coalition among factions, that is, a rudimentary party. This job fell to Treasury Secretary Alexander Hamilton, who built an informal Federalist "team" while Washington stayed "above politics." Secretary of State Jefferson and other officials, many of whom hated Hamilton and his aristocratic ways as much as they opposed the policies he favored, were uncertain about how to deal with these political differences. The overriding factor for most was success of the new government; personal loyalty to Washington was a close second. Thus, Jefferson stayed in the cabinet, despite his opposition to administration policies, during most of Washington's first term. When he left

Although the symbols of our major parties have remained the same, their positions and bases of support have shifted, making them fundamentally different from the parties of a century ago.

the cabinet at the end of 1793, many who joined him in opposition to the administration's economic policies remained in Congress. They formed a partisan group of legislators in opposition to Federalist fiscal policies, and eventually to a foreign policy that appeared "too soft on Britain."

John Adams succeeded Washington in the presidency and gave those who opposed the Federalists an inviting target to attack, as Washington had not. In 1800 Jefferson returned to the political wars and pieced together a coalition strong enough to defeat Adams and put himself into the newly built White House. Aaron Burr helped Jefferson in Manhattan by setting up a "party ticket" of Anti-Federalist candidates, organizing rallies, and establishing get-out-the-vote committees in the wards. (Anti-Federalists were later known as Republicans, then as Democratic-Republicans, then as Democrats.) The Jeffersonians succeeded because they understood the need to carry their opposition to Federalist policies back to the voters, some of whom were old friends from the Revolution. This effort to reach the electorate, even at a time when suffrage was limited and when only representatives in Congress were directly elected by the people, marked an important step from faction to party.[4]

Soon President Thomas Jefferson, the man who had denounced parties, became for a time one of the most successful party leaders the nation has known. Again, this was a matter of practical necessity. Jefferson wanted the Louisiana Purchase and other big bills and appropriations passed by Congress. He wanted to carry on the debate against the Federalists. And he wanted to win reelection and keep the Republicans in power. So he had to maintain a coalition of group interests—southerners and northerners, farmers, laborers, and other economic interests, religious groups—and he had to assure that those who favored his views were elected to office. In effect, he invented the modern political party, an organization that held a well-considered view of the direction national policy should take, appealed to the will of the people, and linked the electorate to those who were making governmental decisions. His party was built from the center out, from elected officials at the seat of government back to the electorate.

But Jefferson as party leader turned out to be something of a flash in the pan. He did not seem very clear about his party role, nor did he understand the role of the minority party as the loyal opposition. As a strong national force his party hardly outlived him. His successor, James Madison, tried to act more as a broker among factions than as a national party leader. This resulted in a weak presidency. At the same time, the Federalists failed to attract any following in the electorate; a period of diminished parties ensued.

Party politics was reinvigorated following the election of 1824, in which the leader in the popular vote—the hero of the Battle of New Orleans, Democrat Andrew Jackson—failed to achieve the necessary majority of the electoral college and was defeated by John Quincy Adams in the run-off election in the House of Representatives. Jackson, brilliantly aided by Martin Van Buren, a veteran party builder in New York State, later knit together a winning combination of regions, group interests, and political doctrines. The Whigs succeeded the Federalists as the opposition party. By the time Van Buren followed Jackson in the White House in 1837, the Democrats had become a large, nationwide movement with national and state leadership, a clear party doctrine, and grass-roots organization. The Whigs were almost as strong; in 1840 they put their own man, General William Henry Harrison—"old Tippecanoe"—into the White House. A two-party system had been born.

We have had that two-party system ever since—one of very few; most democracies have multi-party systems. During the 1830s and 1840s Whigs and Democrats competed strenuously in almost every state in the Union, but this system differed

234

in important ways from the parties under Jefferson. The Jacksonian party system was decentralized, built from the grass roots out. Parties had become elaborate, complex organizations. They reached out for supporters and helped broaden the franchise by gradually eliminating property qualifications on voting. Political participation became more widespread, with many citizens enjoying the hoopla of election campaigns. The electoral aspects of parties became as important as the policy aspects, if not more so. The **spoils system** of rewarding those who supported the victor with government jobs and contracts provided an important incentive for political participation. During this time the national conventions and party platforms came into existence. The parties fostered cooperation between presidents and other partisans in Congress, and strong party leadership developed in the House and Senate. Still, the Whigs never achieved as broad and durable a coalition as the Democrats. And neither party was strong enough to cope with the issue of slavery as the 1850s drew to a close.

THE RISE OF THE REPUBLICANS

Out of the crisis evolved a new party: the second Republican party—ultimately the "Grand Old Party" (GOP).[5] Abraham Lincoln was elected in 1860 amid the collapse of one system of party competition and the emergence of another.[6] As the party of the Union, the Republicans won the support not only of financiers, industrialists, and merchants but also of large numbers of white and newly freed black male workers and farmers. Evoking northern loyalties and memories, many Republican candidates simply "waved the bloody shirt." For fifty years after 1860 the Republican coalition won every presidential race, except for Grover Cleveland's victories in 1884 and 1892. The Democratic party survived with its durable white male base in the South. Many presidential elections during this period were close, but either Democrats or Republicans dominated politics in most states.

For all their noisy battles during the early years of the present century, both parties remained true to the idea that under a two-party system neither side can afford to be extremist. However, both parties contained liberal and conservative elements, and both appealed for support from major economic interests, including business and labor. But the Democrats were less effective than the Republicans in building broad coalitions. They won (with Woodrow Wilson as their candidate) only in 1912 and 1916, when the Bull Moose party under Theodore Roosevelt rebelled against Republican party regulars.

The Progressive Era brought new rules in the political game. Civil service reforms shifted some of the patronage out of the hands of party officials. The direct primary election took control of nominations from party leaders and gave it to the rank and file. And in a number of cities nonpartisan governments were instituted, taking the role of party away totally. United States senators came to be popularly elected with the passage of the Seventeenth Amendment to the Constitution. Women were granted the right to vote when the Nineteenth Amendment was ratified in 1920. Thus, within a short period of time the electorate changed, the rules changed, and even the stakes of the game changed.

The Democrats were unable to build a durable winning coalition during this time. In fact they remained the minority party until the early 1930s, when the Hoover administration was overwhelmed by the Great Depression. Franklin Roosevelt strengthened the farm-labor-southern alliance that Woodrow Wilson had begun to build. He also put together a "grand coalition" of these groups plus unemployed middle-class persons, intellectuals, and national and racial minorities. This coalition reelected Roosevelt three times and brought presidential victories to the Democrats (except when Eisenhower ran) after Roosevelt died.

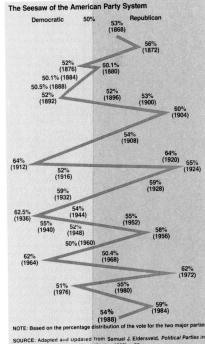

The Seesaw of the American Party System

NOTE: Based on the percentage distribution of the vote for the two major parties

SOURCE: Adapted and updated from Samuel J. Eldersveld, *Political Parties in American Society* (Basic Books, 1982) p. 38.

Although the Roosevelt or New Deal coalition dominated American politics for more than thirty years, it did not go unchallenged. The personal popularity of Dwight D. Eisenhower led to Republican presidential victories in 1952 and 1956. Four years later John Kennedy barely carried the electoral college. In 1968, the Democratic party, split by the Vietnam War, not only allowed Richard M. Nixon to forge a winning coalition, but it also called into question the party's ability to maintain its controlling coalition. Nixon brought together a coalition of predominantly white middle-class voters who feared the welfare state, "hard hat" workers who responded to appeals to patriotism, conservative southerners who opposed Democratic civil rights policies, and business elements who wanted less government intervention. The coalition was strengthened in the 1972 election when the Democrats nominated George McGovern, who was portrayed as the ultraliberal candidate of "amnesty, acid, and abortion."

Despite gains in presidential elections, however, the Republicans were unable to make a dent in Democratic control of the Congress. Voters were responding to issues on the presidential level, but to other factors in congressional campaigns.[7] In 1976 Jimmy Carter reunited the old New Deal coalition at the presidential level to wrest the presidency by a razor-thin margin from Gerald Ford, who was hindered by having pardoned President Nixon for any crimes he might have committed during the Watergate affair. But Carter's presidency was deemed ineffective.

In 1980 Ronald Reagan captured the Republican nomination and brought conservatives into dominance in the GOP. His campaign against Carter stressed his conservative views on economic and social issues. Although Reagan claimed a mandate for his right-wing agenda following his landslide victory, others felt that the election was more a referendum on the failed Carter policies than on the Reagan agenda. The Republicans gained control of the Senate during the 1980 election and made significant progress toward taking the House of Representatives. In the 97th Congress (1981–1982), many aspects of the Reagan economic program were put into place. However, congressional Democrats rebounded strongly in the 1982 election, held their own in 1984 despite Reagan's second landslide victory, and regained the Senate and strengthened their hold of the House in the 1988 election. Emboldened by these electoral successes, the Democrats resisted the "Reagan Revolution."

President Reagan had few legislative successes after his first two years in office and failed in his desired goal of realigning Americans' allegiance to party so that Republicans would form a majority in House and Senate as well as the electoral college. He was successful in helping his chosen successor George Bush capture the presidency in 1988, but the Congress was more solidly Democratic when Reagan left office than it had been when he entered. Americans seemed uninterested in setting out in a new direction, but rather content to have the divided government outlined in the Constitution reflected in the workings of the second or party constitution.

KEY ASPECTS OF PARTIES TODAY

Both parties are now middle-aged. The GOP has celebrated its centennial, and in a few years the Democrats will mark their bicentennial. (They claim the present Democratic party grew directly out of the first Republican party, born when Jefferson departed from Washington's cabinet in 1793.) The longevity of the two parties is remarkable, considering the depressions, wars, social changes, and political crises they have survived. But if the names and the symbols have stayed the same, what they represent has clearly changed. Extensive shifts have occurred in the positions of the major parties, in their social bases and electoral support, in their organizational structures, and—perhaps most important—in their role in our system of government.

Both parties are *moderate* in their policies and leadership, although the GOP shifted to the right in the 1980s.[8] Successful party leaders must be group diplomats; to win presidential elections and congressional majorities, they must find a middle ground among more or less hostile groups so that they can reach agreement on general principles. Each party takes its extremist supporters more or less for granted and seeks out the voters in the middle. This is one reason college students on the far left or far right are impatient with the leadership of the major parties. To such students both parties seem to operate in the center—and in fact they do. (Some party analysts believe the major parties have become so weak and disorganized that they are not capable of following *any* strategy—left, right, or center.)

The key characteristic of the major parties today is that they are *decentralized*. In addition, reflecting their size and importance, they exhibit a complex network of connections and allegiances among those who comprise them. Like the government itself, they have national, state, and local organizations, and each level has executive, legislative, and other elements. Each party includes: (1) a pyramid of national, state, and local organizations; (2) inner circles of leaders holding or seeking public office; (3) networks of leaders (formerly and occasionally still called "bosses") who continually tend the organizational machinery; (4) party activists who give money, time, and enthusiasm to the party's candidates; and (5) voters who identify strongly with the party, almost always support its nominees, and desert it only as a result of such disasters as an unpopular war, a scandal like Watergate, or the soaring inflation and unemployment of the late 1970s.

And interestingly, despite their long history, political parties are still *feared*—at least strong parties are. The apprehension is that a great popular majority—the kind kindled by Jefferson or Jackson or Franklin Roosevelt—might be radical or extremist and thus threaten the basic liberties that make Americans free. But these fears have been largely unrealized. In their own way, parties act as a check on extremists' bids to gain governmental power. To win a party's nomination today, a candidate must appeal to a broad spectrum of party supporters. Ronald Reagan is seen as having moved his party to the right but he also won votes from many centrist Republicans and conservative Democrats. George Bush, the heir to Ronald Reagan, was a moderate in the Republican candidate field. He had learned the lessons of Barry Goldwater, the precursor to the Republicans' move to the right, who lost a landslide election in 1964, and of George McGovern, the so-called ultraliberal Democrat who was similarly trounced in 1972.

Parties are a potential vehicle for large masses of people to use to gain power in government. Farmers in the nineteenth century, workers during the past century, women and African Americans during recent decades, Sunbelt conservatives during the 1980s—these and other movements and groups have tried to work through the major parties, with varying degrees of success. In all cases, however, they have had to work with other groups in the major parties, thus enhancing the role of the party as a balancing, mediating, stabilizing force.[9]

Party Functions: Then and Now

Our major parties have been expected to take on many heavy tasks. At times in our history they have performed admirably, and at times they have been found lacking. One of the key functions of our two-party system has been to *unify the*

"My God! I went to sleep a Democrat and I've awakened a Republican."

Drawing by Dana Fradon; © 1987 The New Yorker Magazine, Inc.

electorate and bring together groups, sections, and ideologies, to moderate conflicts within the body politic. The parties failed to bring the sections together in 1860; as a result not only did the parties break up, but the very fabric of the nation was torn apart by the vehemence of the North-South rupture over the issue of slavery. For over a century since that great break, however, the parties have managed to please various power groups. The Republicans and Democrats have continued in operation; they have held domestic conflict within acceptable bounds. Party leaders and candidates for public office seek to appeal to Hispanics, blacks, and Jews, as well as white Protestants, if only because they represent a large number of votes. Groups such as these have seen parties as an ally in their fights for social justice and equality; their faith has often been upheld. When the parties have divided on controversial social issues—as they have in recent years on civil rights, the ERA, or abortion—the conflict has still stayed within the limits of tolerance.

Parties *simplify the choices* for the electorate. For the parties this is a means to gain votes. For the system of government, it serves to provide the electorate with meaningful choices and to stimulate interest in politics. Usually the parties present the voters with two relatively different alternatives. A vigorous, clear-cut election contest is exciting. It makes politics look like a big prizefight or the World Series, and it draws millions of people into controversy. Citizens choose sides and participate.

Another function that parties perform is to *provide a loyal opposition*. Indeed, this role was the first one played by the Jeffersonians during the Washington administration. After a polite interval following an election, a time in which the administration is put into place and policies are proposed, the opposition party begins to criticize the party that controls the White House. This criticism follows whether the opposition party controls either or both houses of the Congress, though the criticism tends to take on a different character when the opposition party has a power base of its own in another branch of government.[10] At times this criticism has been most effective, as when Senate Majority Leader Lyndon Johnson criticized the Eisenhower administration's lack of response to the Soviet space program, and NASA and our own space program were conceived in the process. At other times the opposition has failed to perform this role effectively. Congressional Democrats were quick to criticize President Ford during the energy crisis of 1975, but they broke up into opposing factions and were unable to propose alternatives to solve the problem facing the nation. At other times, opposition parties have found it appropriate to mute their criticism on the grounds that some issues—foreign policy, religion, education, and so on—should be above politics.

In the past, political parties were *important socializing elements for immigrant Americans*. For much of their history city bosses were a significant source of public welfare. To win votes and gain enduring allegiances, local parties provided loans, free coal, picnics, and recreation for the needy and helped those in trouble with pensions, taxes, and licenses. The boss of the Republican organization in Philadelphia bragged that he headed "one of the greatest welfare organizations in the United States . . . without red tape, without class, religion, or color distinction." The takeover of welfare by the federal government during the New Deal and the tremendous increase in constituent services provided by congressional offices in the last thirty years have removed the functions of providing welfare and dealing with governmental bureaucracy from most city organizations, but some persist in playing this role to a more limited extent.

For some Americans local parties were not only a welfare agency but also a home away from home. Party clubhouses provided a place to meet, to talk

---

Functions of Major Parties*

Recruit candidates

Nominate candidates

Raise campaign funds

Register voters

Unify diverse interests

Mobilize voters

Help run elections

Provide some patronage

Write platforms

Oppose the incumbent party's policies

Help leaders to bridge the separation of powers

Help in the peaceful management of conflicts

Link popular wishes and government action

* Parties are expected to perform most of these functions. Some are performed well, some not so well, and some hardly at all.

---

238   *CHAPTER 10 / Political Parties: Institutions under Change*

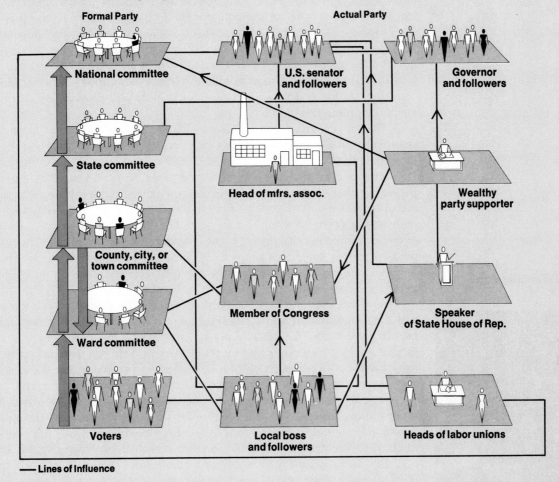

— Lines of Influence

about community and political affairs, to have a social drink, to work together on voting lists, and to enjoy a sense of belonging. It is in part because the bosses of the big cities maintained these local associations—along with their glee clubs and athletic teams—that "bossism" flourished for so long.

In the past the parties were also *important channels of upward mobility* for those "on the outside" of American public life (such as Irish Americans, Italian Americans, and African Americans). The first jobs for many immigrants were municipal service jobs provided by the local party organization. These jobs often led to roles in that organization and eventually to appointive or elective office. During the last century, a few African American men rose to leadership positions in the Republican party. With the move of southern blacks to the north in this century, many followed the same paths of upper mobility that immigrants followed, and more African Americans—men and women—attained high offices, usually within the Democratic party. Because parties are also national organizations, local associations help build personal and political bonds between local communities and the national government.[11]

While parties, especially local parties, were providing first jobs for many Americans, they were also serving as a kind of *employment agency for the govern-*

ment through their control of **patronage.** Leaders have long used their influence over government officials to obtain jobs for friends and party workers. Since Andrew Jackson's administration, they have defended this practice on the grounds that when a party wins an election, it should be able to put its own supporters into office in order to carry out the mandate of the election. Patronage has dwindled in importance in recent decades due to the rise of the civil service; moreover, government salaries have not maintained parity with those of the private sector. It is estimated that of 3 million federal civilian jobs, only a few thousand are patronage positions. Patronage has declined in similar proportions at the state, county, and municipal levels.

The patronage system was delivered a heavy blow in 1980, when the Supreme Court ruled that public employees cannot ordinarily be fired solely on the basis of party affiliation.[12] The question, said Justice John Paul Stevens, speaking for the Court, "is not whether the label 'policy maker' or 'confidential' fits a particular position; rather the question is whether the hiring authority can demonstrate that party affiliation is an appropriate requirement for the effective performance of the public office involved." Justice Lewis Powell, speaking in part for a minority of three, pointed out that many people consider that patronage helps build strong political parties and helps keep the government responsive to the voters, and that, in any case, the issue of patronage versus civil service is one for the legislature, not the judiciary, to decide.

Although the functions discussed above are important, for both the parties and our political system, by far the most crucial party task is *recruiting and selecting candidates for office.* From the very beginning, parties have been the mechanism by which candidates for public office are chosen. The earliest method, the **caucus**—a closed meeting of local leaders—was used in Massachusetts only a few years after the *Mayflower* landed, and it played an important part in pre-Revolutionary politics. For several decades after the Union was established, party groups in the national and state legislatures served as the caucus. The legislators in each party simply met separately to nominate candidates. Our first presidential candidates were chosen by senators and representatives meeting as party delegates.

But the legislative caucus brought charges of "secret deals" and "smoke-filled rooms." Moreover, it could not be representative of the people in areas where a party was in a minority, or nonexistent because only officeholders were members. There were efforts to make the caucus more representative. Thus the *mixed caucus* brought in delegates from districts in which the party had no elected legislators. Then, during the 1830s and 1840s, a system of **party conventions** was instituted. Delegates, usually chosen directly by party members in towns and cities, chose the party standardbearers, debated and adopted a platform, and provided a chance to whip up party spirit and perhaps to celebrate a bit. But the convention method soon came under criticism. It was charged that the convention was subject to control by the party bosses and their machines. Delegates were freely bought and sold, instructions from rank-and-file party members were ignored, and meetings got completely out of control.

To cut down the power of the "bosses" to pick party nominees, and to involve more voters, Wisconsin introduced the **direct primary** on a statewide basis in 1903. A direct primary election is one in which the citizens of a particular area who are permitted to vote in a party's election vote directly to choose the party's nominees for office. Primaries spread rapidly after their introduction in Wisconsin—in the North as part of the Progressive Era reforms, and in the South as a means to bring democracy into a region that had seen no meaningful elections due to one-party rule by the Democrats since the end of Reconstruction. By the end of Woodrow Wilson's second administration in 1920, direct primaries were

The Democratic and Republican Conventions in 1988.

CHAPTER 10 / Political Parties: Institutions under Change

used for at least some offices in almost all of the states. Various states also used direct primaries as a means of selecting delegates to the national nominating conventions.

Today the direct primary is the main method of picking party candidates in almost all states. However, primaries vary significantly from state to state. They differ in terms of: (1) who may run in a primary and how one qualifies for the ballot; (2) whether the party organization can or does endorse candidates before the primary; (3) who may vote in a party's primary, that is, whether or not one must demonstrate some degree of allegiance to a party in order to vote; and (4) how many votes are needed for nomination—a plurality, a majority, or some other number determined by party rule or state law. The differences among primaries are not trivial; they have an important impact on the role played by party organization and on the strategy used by competing candidates.[13] The direct primary was promoted as a major cure for party corruption and as an important contributor to democracy. But it did not cure all of the evils; in fact, it actually led to some new problems. The most notable problem is the weakening of the influence of party leaders over the party's choice of candidates—and hence a weakening of party *responsibility*.

The rise of primaries has not meant the death of caucuses or conventions. In fact, caucuses have been reborn in a number of states, as a step in the process of nominating presidential and other candidates, but they have been reborn in a much more open, democratic, and participatory form. In the states that use caucuses as the first step in selecting delegates to national conventions, party caucuses—open to all persons who meet state requirements for voting in a primary—choose delegates to higher party gatherings, which in turn select delegates to state and national conventions. The caucus today is one of the most dynamic elements in party organization. In recent elections the Iowa caucuses have been the first important test of potential presidential nominees. Hundreds of thousands of Iowans—farmers, laborers, doctors, civil servants, the elderly, college students, housewives, teachers, the wealthy, and the unemployed—have found that they could enter these caucuses and have their voices heard and their votes count equally with local VIPs. They have not only gained national media attention, but they have brought voters back to the parties.[14]

Much the same can be said for conventions, although fewer participate and they do not occur in every state. In a few states conventions still play a role in the nominating process for some offices. In Connecticut, for example, convention choices become the party nominees unless they are challenged. Anyone who attains a specified level of support in the convention has an automatic right to challenge, but this right is not always exercised. In other states convention nominees are designated as such on the primary ballot; they may or may not receive help from the party organization. In still other states conventions are used as a means to invigorate the party faithful, to let those who work for the party nominees hear from their leaders. Conventions are big "party parties." Everyone feels good. Everyone is happy to be a Democrat or a Republican. And everyone is ready to go out to work in the election campaign.

Of course, the nominees for president and vice-president are formally chosen at national nominating conventions. Although they once played decisive roles in determining the nominees, nowadays presidential conventions almost always ratify the results of earlier primaries. Conventions are still important as gatherings of the party, as occasions for uniting divided factions, as forums for emerging party leaders to be tested before a national audience, and as a place at which future courses are charted.[15] One common theme has emerged in state and national parties through nearly a century of changing practices. Party leaders no longer

Levels of Party Involvement

Leaders

Workers

Members

Primary voters

Party identifiers

General supporters

control party nominations. They may participate in the process—as they do in caucuses or even as key delegates to national nominating conventions. They may influence others. But they do not dominate the nominating process. The invention and spread of the direct primary took this most important party function out of the hands of party organization.

Parties serve as the link between the wishes of the people and the action government finally takes. By choosing candidates in an open and democratic way, parties help legitimize our elected policy makers. They help organize the machinery of government and influence the men and women they have helped put into office. The president serves as party leader; Congress is organized on party lines; even bureaucrats are supposed to respond to new party leadership. Governors and legislative majorities serve in the same way in the states. Thus, parties partly bridge the separation of powers and prevent the constitutional checks and balances from fragmenting government.

Parties have had only limited success in this role, however, especially when compared with traditionally strong European parties.[16] The European model of party government assumes that parties control their members. They control nominations and campaigns; representatives are elected as members of political parties. Once in office, they are expected to act according to party wishes. Parties, in turn, run on fairly specific platforms and are expected to be capable of implementing those platforms once they are in office.

This summary of a responsible party system presents something of an idealized view, but it contrasts markedly with the American model in which party leaders do not control nominations (and therefore cannot deny errant members renomination), in which representatives are elected largely based on their own qualifications and personal appeal, not party membership, and in which party members in the legislature cannot be made to vote the party line. As a consequence, in the American system, party leaders cannot guarantee passage of their program, even if they are in the majority; therefore, the link between opinions of the voters and actions of their representatives in government is weak.

THIRD PARTIES: PERSISTENCE AND FRUSTRATION

Although we have been focusing on major parties, we must not lose sight of all the exotic third parties in American history: the abolitionists, the populists, the prohibitionists, Theodore Roosevelt's Bull Moose party, the Communist party and its ideological offshoots, George Wallace's American Independent party, and John Anderson's National Unity party, to name but a few. Third parties are described by some scholars as "a response to major party failure," but the crucial aspect about third parties is how often they charge into the national party arena and how they never win.[17] To be sure, they have had a significant indirect influence. They have drawn attention to controversial issues the major parties wished to duck. And they have organized special-interest or "cause" groups such as the antislavery and anti-civil rights movements. They boast, sometimes correctly, that they are champions not of lost causes, but of causes yet to be won. But except for the Republican party of 1860, they have never won the presidency or more than a handful of congressional seats. They have never shaped national policy from inside the government. And their influence on national policy in general, and on the platforms of the two major parties, has been limited.[18]

Third parties have taken three forms. One type has been the *doctrinal* party, such as the small labor and socialist parties on the left and the even smaller conservative movements on the right. Most of these parties, like the Socialist

CHAPTER 10 / Political Parties: Institutions under Change

Workers party, have lived on for decades, publicizing their ideas but not expecting to win elections. The second type is the *issue* party that arises (or splinters from a major party) over a particular issue and then dies as the issue is resolved or fades away. Several issue parties, such as the Free Soilers, rose and fell before the Civil War; the Progressive party, which has reemerged a number of times in this century, has challenged the political power of big business; the States' Rights party arose from a split within the Democratic party in 1948 over President Truman's civil rights policies. The final type of third party, a variation of the issue party, revolves around a *particular political personality*. The Bull Moose party of Theodore Roosevelt, which was formally constituted as a Progressive party in most states, exemplifies this type of third party. More recently, in 1968, George Wallace's American Independent party (AIP) polled over 13 million votes and won 46 electoral votes, after he broke with the Democratic party over desegregation and conservative social issues. In 1980 John Anderson split from the Republican party, favoring many of its economic stands but taking liberal positions on social issues; he garnered 6.6 percent of the national vote, but no electoral votes.

Have you noticed that we talk about a "two-party" system and that there have been a number of "third" parties? In 1948, in fact, two "third" parties each ran serious national campaigns: the Progressive party, whose presidential candidate was Henry Wallace, and the States' Rights party, whose ticket was headed by Strom Thurmond. The difference between the campaigns run by those parties, and the causes of the failure of each, says a good deal about why third parties generally fail in our electoral system. The Progressive party ran a national campaign, attacking President Truman from the left in every state. Wallace drew nearly a million popular votes, but he won no electoral votes. In our electoral system, the winner of the popular vote in a state receives all of that state's electoral votes; this system is called *winner-take-all*.[19] Wallace's votes were divided around the nation; he failed to carry a plurality in any one state. The States' Rights party was a regional party, emerging from a southern delegate walkout from the Democratic National Convention over a civil rights plank in the platform. Thurmond ran only in southern states. Although he drew fewer total votes than did Henry Wallace nationally because his strength was concentrated regionally, and he won only a plurality in some states, he did manage to pick up 39 electoral votes. However, even those 39 votes, and the split of the normally Democratic votes caused by the Progressive party in other regions, did not prevent President Truman from winning a majority in the electoral college. Thus, both "third" parties in 1948 were losers, with little national impact, though for different reasons.

The Libertarian Party

One third party that is currently active on the national scene is the Libertarian Party. Founded in 1972, this party wants to turn all, or almost all, government services over to the private sphere. They would end the welfare state, reduce the military to a bare minimum, terminate all foreign commitments (including membership in the UN), and abolish all laws legislating morality, such as laws dealing with prostitution, drugs, gambling, abortion, and gay rights. In 1980 they polled over 1 million votes, making them the third largest party, but their strength slipped in the 1980s, leading some to think that Reagan had partially stolen some of their support and agenda. Their membership is also quite divided on the abortion issue.

TABLE 10–1
Third Parties in Presidential Elections

YEAR	PARTY	PRESIDENTIAL CANDIDATE	PERCENTAGE OF VOTE	ELECTORAL VOTE
1832	Anti-Masonic	William Wirt	7.8	7
1856	American (Know Nothing)	Millard Fillmore	21.5	8
1860	Democratic (Secessionist)	J. C. Breckinridge	18.1	72
1860	Constitutional Union	John Bell	12.6	39
1892	People's (Populist)	James B. Weaver	8.6	22
1912	Progressive	Theodore Roosevelt	27.4	88
1912	Socialist Party	Eugene V. Debs	6.0	0
1924	Progressive	Robert M. La Follette	16.6	13
1948	States' Rights	Strom Thurmond	2.4	39
1948	Progressive	Henry A. Wallace	2.4	0
1968	American Independent	George C. Wallace	13.5	46
1980	National Unity Ticket	John B. Anderson	6.6	0

Clearly our electoral rules favor the maintenance of a two-party system.[20] The presidency is our biggest prize. A party does not gain anything by finishing second. Our system has a single president; the runner-up parties receive no consolation prizes, except perhaps in Congress. The two existing parties have a distinct advantage in the race for the White House because of the winner-take-all system. Similarly our state gubernatorial elections favor the two major parties. Most of our congressional election districts have a single incumbent, and the candidate with the most votes—a plurality—wins. Again, no second prize goes to the person who comes close. Even if a third party candidate can keep each major party candidate from receiving more than 50 percent of the vote—a majority—the candidate with the most votes wins. So we have the "Catch 22" of American party politics: third parties have trouble raising funds because they aren't taken seriously, and they aren't taken seriously because they can't raise ample funds.

What would a different system look like? Most other democracies in the world have multi-party systems. In a typical multi-party system, the legislature is the most important branch of the government, and the most important individual in the government (often called the prime minister or premier) is the leader of one of the major parties in the legislature. Frequently, individual districts elect more than one member of the legislature. Parties run slates of candidates for those positions. The parties receive the proportion of the legislators corresponding to their proportion of the vote; that is, even if a party does not come in first in a district, that party does receive "a reward" proportionate to its strength in the electorate. Under such a system an incentive exists for third, fourth, or additional parties to run. They may well win some seats in the legislature. Furthermore, if no party wins a majority of seats in the legislature, as frequently happens in some countries—for example, Italy and Israel—the leading parties must form a coalition in order to govern. Minor parties can gain concessions—positions in a cabinet or particular policies that they want implemented—in return for their participation in a coalition. Major parties need the minor parties and are therefore willing to bargain. Thus, the system favors the existence of minor parties by giving them incentives to persevere.

What difference might it make if we had a different set of election rules, rules that encourage stronger and more persistent third parties? Two factors seem to distinguish two-party systems from multi-party systems. In multi-party systems, more parties form on the extremes. This means that more people's views are more accurately reflected, but it also means that those parties tend to be more doctrinaire and do not appeal to great masses of people. In a two-party system, on the other hand, parties tend to be centrist, appealing to moderate elements, but not closely reflecting the views of those with stronger positions. Second, in multi-party systems governments can be somewhat unstable as coalitions form and collapse; in addition, the swings in policy when party control changes can be quite dramatic. Two-party systems lead to majority governments; these tend to be stable and centrist. As a result, policy shifts occur more incrementally, except in very rare situations.

Which system is better? That depends largely on the social, economic, and political environment in which the party system exists. Many claim that our system suits our polity well, because our history has been replete with issues that divided the populace on one major issue, not among a great many. Other countries, with feudal histories and greater class differences, have developed party systems that reflect their history. How you evaluate our party system depends on how well it performs its most important function—recruiting and choosing candidates for office and presenting choices so that citizens can have an effective say in deciding the policies their government will pursue. Our two-party system has not impeded the carrying out of that function and has, in fact, served us well when it has been functioning effectively.

How the Parties Are Organized

Why have our parties been so decentralized? The main reason is the *federal* basis of our government. The Constitution has shaped our political system, just as the political system has shaped our governmental structure. Parties are a prime example of this circular relation. They tend to be structured around elections and officeholders. Because our federal system sets up elections and offices on a national-state-local basis, our parties are organized on a similar basis.

NATIONAL PARTY LEADERSHIP

The supreme authority in both major parties is the *national presidential convention*. The convention meets every four years to nominate candidates for president and vice-president, to ratify the party platform, and to elect officers and adopt rules. But the convention actually holds limited power. The delegates have only three or four days in which to accomplish their business, and many key decisions have been made ahead of time. As stated earlier, the convention usually simply ratifies the presidential aspirant already chosen in the presidential primaries and caucuses during the preceding months. Even so, the national presidential convention continues as the supreme legal authority in both major parties.

More directly in charge of the national party—at least on paper—is the *national committee*. In the past the national committee gave large states only a little more representation than small ones. Committee members were usually influential in their states but had little national standing, and the committees rarely met. Recently the Republicans made their national committee more representative, and the Democrats, largely as a result of the reform spirit of 1968, enlarged their national committee to make it more responsive to areas that tended to be more populous and more Democratic, and to groups that have traditionally supported Democratic candidates. Such changes, however, have not necessarily brought stronger leadership.

The chief executives of the two national parties are the *national party chairpersons*. Traditionally this top party official is elected by the national committee at the close or shortly after the national nominating convention, upon the recommendation of the party nominee. Traditionally as well, this official plays a major role in running the national campaign. These practices follow from a long history of the national party serving mainly as a vehicle to run presidential campaigns; the candidates named the chairpersons and they served the candidates' campaigns. After the election, the power of the national chairperson of the victorious party tends to dwindle. Even though he or she serves as a liaison between the national committee and the White House, the chairperson actually serves at the pleasure of the president and does the president's bidding with the national party. A defeated national candidate has little control over the national chairperson; in fact, the national committee has usually elected a new head after electoral defeats, as for example, when the Democratic National Committee elected Ron Brown as party chairman after the 1988 election.

Republican party leaders have generally been more independent of the White House than have Democrats, but they too have to cope with the White House.[21]

You decide!

How strong is the *local* Democratic or Republican party in your town or city? How would you go about finding out?

(Answer/Discussion on the next page.)

Ron Brown, chairman of the Democratic National Committee, is a Washington attorney who had been an advisor to Senator Edward Kennedy and to Jesse Jackson. He is the first black to head a national political party.

When Richard Richards retired as chairperson of the Republican party during the first Reagan term, he summed up the problems of running the party organization in competition with a Republican administration:

> It is a tough, tough job to be the National Chairman when you have the White House. . . . The unique thing that will always exist—Democrats or Republicans—is that every clerk and secretary in the White House thinks that they can do your job better than you can, and they don't even know what you do. . . . Last year you know why they wanted my job. Very simple. I had 40-million bucks and we could spend it any way we wanted to spend it.[22]

The White House, of course, wanted to control that spending; the RNC had (only slightly) different ideas.

Just as the national committees have taken on new roles, so too have the *congressional and senatorial campaign committees.* Today both Republican and Democratic senatorial campaign committees are composed of senators chosen for two-year terms by their fellow party members in the Senate; congressional campaign committees are chosen in the same manner. However, the chairs of these committees, appointed by the party leadership in Congress, are the most important players, especially in the distribution of campaign funds. Whereas these committees once offered token contributions to selected candidates for the Senate and the House of Representatives, today each committee plays a major role in congressional campaigns. Again, the Republicans saw the potential for these committees earlier than did the Democrats. In the late 1970s, in coordination with the RNC, they developed extensive fund-raising lists and raised enough money to be able to help most Republican candidates for the House or the Senate.[23] The Democrats in the House and Senate have closed the fund-raising gaps and made their campaign committees more effective. Using loopholes in the Federal Election Campaign Law, these committees are able to make important contributions to the campaigns of many of their parties' candidates for office.[24]

Do these stronger national party organizations try to influence party nominations? Very seldom. Politicians still build personal organizations and work on their own, while the party remains "neutral." In the early 1980s, the Republican national organization tried to convince a number of qualified Republicans to take on Democratic officeholders, promising them campaign help and support. This recruitment effort was soon abandoned. National organizations can help nominees once they are chosen in local areas, but they cannot intervene in party primaries or referee local rivalries. Heated primary contests may be democratic, but opponents in party primaries are often unable to patch up their differences, not even enough to present a united party in the general election. And the national parties are helpless to prevent these cracks in party unity.[25]

PARTIES AT THE GRASS ROOTS

Party organization below the national level parallels national organization in structure. Each state has a *state committee,* headed by a *state chairperson.* The composition of the state committees and rules regulating them are determined by state law. Members of the state committees normally are elected from local areas, but party auxiliaries such as the Young Democrats or the Federation of Republican Women sometimes are represented as well. In many states these committees are dominated by governors, senators, or coalitions of local elected, business, and ethnic leaders. The state chairpersons are normally elected by the state committees, although approximately one-quarter are chosen at state conventions. Those in

CHAPTER 10 / Political Parties: Institutions under Change

the party that controls the governor's chair are often agents of the governor, but others are quite independent.[26] Those who are powerful and independent have developed their roles much as national chairpersons have in recent years. Despite much state-to-state variation, the trend is toward stronger state organizations, but with significant differences between the two parties. The average annual budget of the Republican state committees has been at least three times that of the average Democratic state committee. Committees with such resources are finding a new role at the state level similar to that played by the national committees in the last decade.[27]

Below the state committees in the hierarchial organization of parties are *county committees*. They vary tremendously in function and power, yet the trend again is toward the more active, participatory committees that existed decades ago. One key role of these committees is recruiting candidates for such offices as county commissioner, sheriff, and treasurer, but the recruiting job often involves finding a candidate for the office, not deciding among competing contenders. When the job is truly valued by those seeking office, however, primaries, not the power of the county chairperson, usually decide the winner.

Few county chairpersons are powerful bosses of dominating machines, as typified by the late Richard J. Daley, mayor of Chicago and chairman of the Cook County Democratic Committee.[29] But many county organizations do maintain a significant level of activity, distributing campaign literature, organizing telephone campaigns, distributing posters and lawn signs, and canvassing door-to-door. This description of activity by some county organizations should not mislead. The fact is that in many areas county committees do not function at all, and many party leaders are just figureheads.

In recent years the efforts of county organizations have been aided by financial assistance from the party's national committee. These committees have distributed millions of dollars to county committees in so-called *soft money*, that is money that does not have to be reported under the Federal Election Campaign Law. This money must be spent for the entire ticket, not just for a particular congressional, senatorial, or presidential candidate.

It is at the base of the party pyramid—at the city, town, ward, and precinct level—that we find the grass roots of the party in all their richness and variety. In a few places party politics is a round-the-clock, round-the-year occupation. The local ward and precinct leaders do countless favors for constituents, from fixing parking tickets, to organizing clambakes, to obtaining racing passes in a state such as Arkansas. But such strong local organization is rare. Most local committees are poorly financed and inactive except during the few weeks before election day.[30]

Our party systems are complex, like the fragmented constitutional structure they fit into. For example, a state party organization may include a state committee, congressional district committees, county committees, state senatorial district committees, state judicial district committees, ward committees, and precinct committees. Despite this organizational complexity, even party politics tends to be individualistic and personalized; in fact, in recent years it has been more nearly correct to say that we have *candidate* or *officeholder* politics rather than *party* politics. Candidate organizations have been especially prevalent in campaigns for major offices, for mayor in a large city, for governor, for a seat in Congress or in the United States Senate.

Decentralization remains the most significant characteristic of our party system. One reason is that elections—the main activity of parties—are actually regulated and run by the *states*, not by the national government. Some states hold their state and local elections in different years from national elections (mostly

Lee Atwater, chairman of the Republican National Committee, has specialized in campaign management for Senator Strom Thurmond, as well as for Presidents Reagan and Bush.

in an effort to insulate state politics from national). Thus New York State elects its governors for four-year terms in even-numbered years between presidential elections, while New York City elects its mayors every four years in odd-numbered years. Most town and city elections are "nonpartisan" and often do not involve the parties as such. Thus state and local politics is separated from national politics.

Because of the intricacies of campaign finance laws, and because of the superior fund-raising capacities of national parties, the national committees have become more involved in state and local campaigns in the most recent elections. The result is a complex decentralized party system that reflects our federal government both in the independence of local units and in the interdependence among the parts.

Parties on Trial

Parties strengthen national unity by bringing conflicting groups together. They soften the impact of extremists at both ends of the political spectrum. They stimulate and channel public discussion. They find candidates for the voters and voters for the candidates. They help run elections. They both stimulate and moderate conflict. In short, parties are assigned much of the hard, day-to-day work of democracy. But, in fact, parties do not perform these tasks very well. In many cases candidates' personal campaign organizations have replaced the party organizations in performing the most important electioneering tasks.

The American party system faces three main charges: (1) parties do not take meaningful and contrasting positions on issues, especially the issues of the 1990s; (2) party membership is essentially meaningless, so that parties neither define issues critically nor are they able to prosper organizationally; and (3) parties are so concerned with accommodating those in the middle of the ideological spectrum that they are incapable of serving as an avenue for social progress. How valid are these charges today?

PARTY PLATFORMS: TWEEDLEDEE VERSUS TWEEDLEDUM?

The typical party platform, it is said, seems designed to pick up every stray vote rather than to speak out in a convincing manner on the vital questions of the day. Platforms are often so vague, and candidates' statements so ambiguous, that voters frequently have no basis on which to choose. This charge may once have been valid, but recent scholarship indicates that today it overstates the problem. By the 1960s at least, many voters saw their own party or the opposition party as standing for something. Thus, most business and professional people consider that the Republican party best serves their interests, while workers tend to look to the Democrats as the party most helpful to them. The proportion of voters discerning important differences increased sharply during the Reagan years, when parties seemed to become more polarized.

After studying recent party platforms to see how similar they were, one scholar concluded: "Democrats and Republicans are not 'Tweedledee' and 'Tweedledum.' "[31] In recent presidential elections the differences between the two parties were even sharper than has traditionally been the case. Parties share a consensus on many matters, but their policies are hardly identical, as a reading of the 1988 Democratic and Republican platforms makes clear.[32] Both party platforms, for example, emphasized the need for a strong economy. On the one hand, the Democratic party platform said that the government was not working fairly for all Americans and called for new programs to assure economic justice for all: "a first-rate full employment economy with an indexed minimum wage that can help lift and keep families out of poverty, with training and employment programs—including child care and health care—that can help people move from welfare to work, with portable pensions and an adequate Social Security System . . . that can help assure a comfortable and fulfilling old age . . ."

The Republican party platform, on the other hand, asserted that a strong economy will come from less government involvement. That document cited progress under the Reagan administration and claimed, "Government didn't work this economic wonder. The people did. Republicans got government out of the way, off the back of households and entrepreneurs, so the people could take charge." The platform stressed "free enterprise, free markets, and limited government, that tradition [which] regards people as a resource, not a problem."[33] The differences were dramatic and clear.

Key Party Differences: Excerpts from Republican and Democratic Party Platforms, 1988

	REPUBLICANS	DEMOCRATS
Abortion	"The unborn child has a fundamental individual right to life which cannot be infringed."	"The fundamental right of reproductive choice should be guaranteed regardless of ability to pay."
Minimum wage	"As an alternative to inflationary—and job-destroying—increases in the minimum wage, we will work to boost the incomes of the working poor through the earned income tax credit . . ."	The party supports "an indexed minimum wage that can help lift and keep families out of poverty . . ."
Child care	"In returning to our traditional commitment to children, the Republican Party proposes a radically different approach: establish a toddler tax credit for pre-school children as proposed by Vice President Bush, available to all families of modest means, to help them support and care for their children in a manner best suited to their families' values and traditions . . ."	"We believe that Government should set the standard in recognizing that worker productivity is enhanced . . . by major increases in assistance making child care more available and affordable to low and middle income families, helping states build a strong child care infrastructure, setting minimum standards for health, safety and quality. . ."
Budget, taxes	"We oppose any attempts to increase taxes. . . . We will reduce to 15 percent the tax rates for long-term capital gains. . . . We call for a flexible freeze on current Government spending. . . . We call for a balanced budget amendment to the Constitution. . ."	"We believe that it is time for America to meet the challenge to change priorities after eight years of devastating Republican policies . . . to reinvest in its people within a strong commitment to fiscal responsibility. . . . Investing in America and reducing the deficit requires that the wealthy and corporations pay their fair share and that we restrain Pentagon spending."
Soviet Union	"Republicans are proud that it was a Republican President who extended freedom's hand and message to the Soviet Union. It will be a new Republican President who can best build on that progress, ever cautious of Communism's long history of expansionism and false promises. We are prepared to embrace real reform, but we will not leave America unprepared should reform prove illusory."	"We believe in . . . maintaining a stable nuclear deterrent sufficient to counter any Soviet threat . . . standing up to any American adversaries whenever necessary and sitting down with them whenever possible . . . testing the intentions of the new Soviet leaders about arms control, emigration, human rights and other issues."
Middle East	"The foundation of our policy in the Middle East has been and must remain the promotion of a stable and lasting peace, recognizing our moral and strategic relationship with Israel . . . We oppose the creation of an independent Palestinian state; its establishment is inimical to the security interests of Israel, Jordan and the U.S."	". . . This country, maintaining the special relationship with Israel founded upon mutually shared values and strategic interest, should provide new leadership to deliver the promise of peace and security through negotiations that has been held out to Israel and its neighbors by the Camp David accords . . ."

Source: *The New York Times* (August 17, 1988), p. A20. Copyright © 1988 by The New York Times Company.

WEAK PARTY MEMBERSHIP?

Some party analysts believe that parties would take stronger positions, and also work more effectively, if they had a solid core of rank-and-file members with a strong and sustained loyalty to their party—indeed, a stronger loyalty to their party than to any particular issue, interest group, or area. They note that anyone 18 or over can "join" a party, although "joining" may mean nothing more than voting in a primary or attending a caucus. Such party "members" pay no dues, do no work for the party, and rarely take part in political activities or even discussions. Their commitment to their party is minimal.

Some local party organizations do have active members. What motivates these activists? Involved workers may be in the party mainly for personal or material reasons: jobs, favors, or access to government officials. Others belong mainly for social reasons: the chance to meet people at the local clubhouse. These activists are thought of as professionals or regulars; they stick with the party through thick or thin, support all of its candidates, keep the organization going between elections. Others participate in party politics to advance public policies or the candidates they support. They are often characterized as amateurs or volunteers who may be "issue purists" or "candidate loyalists," viewing party activity not as an end in itself but as a means to a greater good, such as new social programs.[34] Critics question their long-term commitment to party politics and the efficacy of parties that cannot sustain such commitment.

Those who analyzed these types of party activists during the late 1960s and early 1970s, a period of intense social upheaval and conflict over both domestic policies and especially the war in Vietnam, emphasized that tension and hostility marked the relationship between the two groups of activists. The party veterans came from middle-income backgrounds, whereas the volunteers tended to be better educated and more ideological. At first the fear was that the volunteers would "win" internal party struggles and then abandon the party after an election. Later party critics feared that, over a period of time, the volunteers would gradually assume the political style and motive patterns of the professionals, with the result that the party would become less concerned with ideology and programs.

However, the experience today reveals a changed pattern. The professional and the volunteer each offer different strengths and weaknesses. But issue activists now tend to be concerned not only with policy positions and ideological commitment, but also emphasize the goal of electoral success. They are not more likely to reject compromise and coalition-building than are party professionals. While in theory they may opt for ideological purity over compromise for electoral success, in practice they choose candidates on the basis more of "who can beat the other party's candidate" than of "who is more pure on the issues of the day."[35] Thus, while activists might not demonstrate the level of commitment some critics would favor, they do provide greater strength and durability than many fear.

PROUD TO BE A DEMOCRAT!

PARTIES VERSUS PROGRESS?

American parties, some charge, are not vehicles for social reform. That both major parties must be such inclusive and moderate organizations means neither one can act boldly for the great mass of lower-class, lower-income, and politically vulnerable people. Over the course of American history, some believe, this "party passiveness" has probably had a good effect of helping the parties to perform a peace-making or reconciling function. But in a period of exceptionally rapid and extensive change, it may enfeeble the political system.[36] Because rapid social

CHAPTER 10 / Political Parties: Institutions under Change

change seems continuous these days, it can be argued that parties were useful only in the past and are now outdated and should be scrapped.

According to this view, weak parties simply end up strengthening the status quo. The rich and powerful have plenty of political weapons of their own, such as lobbyists, money, and influence over the media. The political party could be the vehicle of collective popular action; ideally, it could be the "people's lobby." If the party is insipid in doctrine, ineffective both when in power and when in opposition, and disorganized from top to bottom, it blights people's hopes instead of realizing them. Others contend that parties are more effective than critics admit—that pluralistic, decentralized parties are appropriate for a pluralistic, individualistic society. They further maintain that parties have been effective, even if slow, in aiding minorities and those without power, and that no other institution in our government can claim equal successes.[37] That Jesse Jackson has continued to pursue his vision of a changing American society within the Democratic party, rather than as a third party candidate, is evidence that today's most eloquent spokesperson for the less privileged in our society shares this commitment to political parties as a vehicle for social progress.

DEMOCRATS VERSUS REPUBLICANS— IS THERE REALLY A DIFFERENCE?

Perhaps because they have not experienced the great party battles that their parents and teachers have, students often ask, "How do the parties really differ?" The question is an important one. The answer, as in so many other aspects of the confusing American political system, is complex. Much depends on which aspect of the parties we are looking at—their histories, their policies and platforms, their leadership, their rank-and-file membership—and which level of government—national, state, or local—is being analyzed. And much depends on our own perceptions—on what we see from where we sit.

During the New Deal, the difference between Democrats and Republicans was clear to everyone. Citizens were loyal to one political party or the other because of how they felt about President Roosevelt's efforts to respond to the Depression. In the simplest terms, those who were helped favored the Democrats and thought Roosevelt a hero; those who were hurt were Republicans and thought badly of Roosevelt and his heavy spending and "social engineering." But as the New Deal philosophy came to be accepted by both parties—symbolized perhaps by the fact that Republican President Dwight Eisenhower did not even attempt to repeal most New Deal policies when he won the White House in 1952—the lines between the parties blurred in the eyes of many citizens. Those who became politically active in the 1950s, for instance, did not know a time when they felt that what the government did would differ sharply if Democrats were in office as opposed to Republicans.

For those who entered political maturity in the 1960s and 1970s, the differences were even less apparent. To be sure, the two parties differed sharply over civil rights for blacks. But the Vietnam War, the biggest foreign policy issue of the time, was begun under the Democratic administration of John Kennedy, escalated under the Democratic administration of Lyndon Johnson, and continued under the Republican administration of Richard Nixon. What was the difference? Most critics of the war were Democrats, like Eugene McCarthy or Robert Kennedy, but some of the most forceful were Republicans like New York's Jacob Javits and Oregon's Mark Hatfield. When the Republicans nominated a "truly conservative" candidate, Barry Goldwater in 1964, he was repudiated not only by the general

TABLE 10–2
How Partisanship and Political Attitudes Are Correlated

HOW DO YOU FEEL ABOUT DEFENSE SPENDING?			
	TOO MUCH	ABOUT RIGHT	TOO LITTLE	NO. OPINION
Republicans	32%	46%	17%	5%
Independents	44	35	13	8
Democrats	54	30	10	6

DO YOU APPROVE OR DISAPPROVE OF THE WAY GEORGE BUSH IS HANDLING HIS JOB AS PRESIDENT?		
	APPROVE	DISAPPROVE	NO OPINION
Republicans	79%	6%	13%
Independents	48	27	25
Democrats	41	33	26

Source: Defense Survey, Gallup Poll, 1987; Bush rating, Gallup Poll, May, 1989.

electorate but also by his own party, as it sought more centrist candidates in subsequent years. The same can be said of the Democrats, following the defeat of George McGovern in 1972. In the 1980s, however, the differences sharpened. Today, what are those differences?

One contrast shows in the public stands the parties take in their view of the future. The 1984 Democratic platform proclaimed: "A fundamental choice awaits America, a choice between two futures. It is a choice between solving problems and pretending they don't exist; between the spirit of community and the corrosion of selfishness; between justice for all and advantage for some. . ." In 1988, the Republican platform drew equally distinct lines: "An election is about the future, about change. But it is also about the values we will carry with us as we journey into tomorrow and about continuity with the best from the past. . . . The question is: Will it be change and progress with the Republicans or change and chaos with the Democrats?"

Democrats and Republicans also hold sharply contrasting images of one another. As we enter the 1990s, Democrats consider the Republican party to be a John Wayne/Rambo/tough-guy party that talks a hard line against communists and terrorists in foreign affairs and against criminals, welfare cheats, and "draft dodgers" at home. Republicans consider the Democratic party to be the party of "the losers, the lame and the lazy"—the party that will not meet the nation's responsibilities in the world arena, the party that is too soft toward the communists abroad, and too tolerant of fringe groups at home: feminists, peaceniks, gays, and "troublemakers" in general. Reagan's shift late in his presidency toward a friendlier stance toward Moscow, and Bush's mixed approach hardly altered these contrasting images.

Some in both parties do not see the alleged "gap." For years conservative Republicans attacked top GOP leaders like Dwight Eisenhower and Nelson Rockefeller as being "me-too Republicans" cuddling up to Democratic party principles and policies. These critics have been far happier under Reagan and Bush's leadership. Today a host of Democrats attack their national party and congressional leadership as being too moderate—or at least as being too responsive to the conservative wing or enclaves in the party. Jim Hightower, the (elected) Texas agriculture commissioner, spoke for many of these critics when he assailed fellow Democrats who urge a "go along—get along" strategy and a "cautious middle

Bill Bradley (D-NJ) helped shape the 1986 tax reform bill.

CHAPTER 10 / Political Parties: Institutions under Change

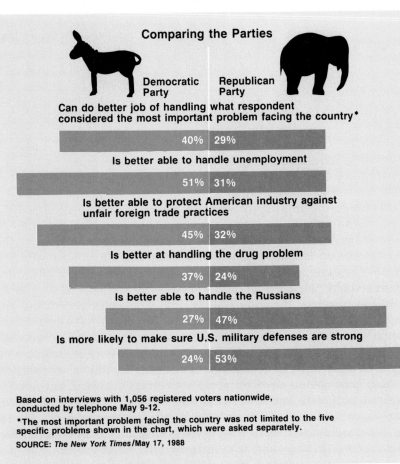

Comparing the Parties

Democratic Party

Republican Party

Can do better job of handling what respondent considered the most important problem facing the country*

40%	29%

Is better able to handle unemployment

51%	31%

Is better able to protect American industry against unfair foreign trade practices

45%	32%

Is better at handling the drug problem

37%	24%

Is better able to handle the Russians

27%	47%

Is more likely to make sure U.S. military defenses are strong

24%	53%

Based on interviews with 1,056 registered voters nationwide, conducted by telephone May 9-12.

*The most important problem facing the country was not limited to the five specific problems shown in the chart, which were asked separately.

SOURCE: *The New York Times*/May 17, 1988

Copyright © 1988 by The New York Times Company. Reprinted by permission.

New York Governor Mario Cuomo chose not to run for the Democratic presidential nomination in 1988.

Representative Richard Gephardt (D-Missouri) is majority leader of the House and a spokesman for moderate Democrats.

path." Hightower quoted a farmer friend of his: "Hell, Hightower, there's nothing in the middle of the road but yellow stripes and dead armadillos."[38]

These views tend to mask real differences in the leadership of the two parties. The principal legacy of Ronald Reagan may well be that as party leader he completed the Republicans' move to the ideological right begun by Barry Goldwater in the early 1960s. For many years, after the Roosevelt administration, the Republican party saw almost open warfare between centrist or moderately liberal Republican leaders like Thomas E. Dewey and Nelson Rockefeller and true conservatives like Senator Robert A. Taft of Ohio and Goldwater. In winning the presidency in 1980, Ronald Reagan drew millions of religious fundamentalists and social conservatives—pro-life, pro-prayer, and pro-defense activists; integration, busing, racial-quotas, and gay rights opponents—into the GOP. Although Reagan failed to convert many of his conservative ideas into law, he did realign his party toward conservatism, for years if not decades. The party leadership has become so dominated by right-wing beliefs that George Bush, President Reagan's loyal vice-president and designated heir, was viewed as one of the more moderate candidates in the 1988 Republican primaries, outflanked to the right by Pat Robertson on social issues, by Jack Kemp and Pete DuPont on economic issues, and by Alexander Haig on defense issues.

What about the Democratic party leadership? Here the story is somewhat different. No one questions that Democratic leaders are more liberal, however one defines that term, than are Republican leaders. But a serious question arises as to *how liberal* the true leaders of the Democrats of the future will be. Look merely at the United States Senate, where the Democratic party is home to liberals like Edward Kennedy, Alan Cranston, and Howard Metzenbaum, moderates like George Mitchell and Charles Robb, strong defense advocates like Sam Nunn, and even a few remaining southern conservatives like Senators Richard Shelby and John Breaux—although more and more southern conservatives are finding their home in the Republican party, with Texan Phil Gramm, who switched from the Democratic party to the Republican, serving as a most apt example. Many Democratic party leaders are populists, like Jesse Jackson, and progressives, like Michael Dukakis and Mario Cuomo. Others are more difficult to characterize, like Bill Bradley of New Jersey and Speaker of the House Tom Foley. The Democratic umbrella encompasses leadership groups that range across the ideological spectrum: the conservative Coalition for a Democratic Majority; the moderate Democratic Leadership Council, dominated by an array of southern governors and senators; and the liberal Americans for Democratic Action. And the Democratic coalition still embraces activists in the civil rights and other liberal-left movements described in Chapter 9. The group is diverse, still seeking definition, still arguing over how far from the center one can go without forfeiting any chance of electoral victory.

Are these party differences in history and policies and leadership reflected in rank-and-file members? The answer is less clear. Who are Democrats and who are Republicans? How can one even define these two groups? The best answer seems to be: Let them define themselves. This can be done in one of two ways. For years political scientists and professional pollsters have asked respondents whether they considered themselves to be Democrat, Republican, or neither.[39] Analysts have been able to characterize party members according to degree of commitment to party and a number of different demographic and attitudinal indices. The other way to define party membership is by vote, usually vote in presidential elections. Using sophisticated exit polling as voters leave the voting booths, analysts have similarly been able to define who comprised the voters for each party and how those voters felt on certain issues.

A 1988 *Times Mirror* voter survey, conducted by the Gallup Organization, found that the political parties were still important reference groups for voters, but that party followers who sided with either of the parties often did so for very different reasons. The Republicans were composed largely of two groups. The largest Republican group was categorized as "enterprisers," those for whom pro-business and antigovernment interference stands were most important; these Republicans wished to cut the deficit, but without raising taxes; to restrict government programs for health care, the homeless, the elderly and those with AIDS; and to strengthen our defense posture. The second largest component of the Republican coalition were "moralists." They opposed abortion but favored prayer in the schools, the death penalty, quarantining AIDS patients, and held anticommunist, pro-defense positions. Two additional groups in the electorate lean Republican, but not so heavily as the enterprisers and the moralists. These are the "upbeats," young, middle-income, noncollege educated voters for whom economic concerns are a top priority, and the "disaffecteds," middle-aged, middle-income voters who are antigovernment and antibusiness but pro-military and for whom unemployment and the budget deficit are the top concerns.

Four groups lean strongly toward the Democratic party. The most strongly Democratic group is the "partisan poor," a group of low-income, poorly educated, urban voters, many of whom are members of racial minorities, for whom unemployment and social justice are the top issues. The second part of the Democratic coalition is made up of the "passive poor," an older group committed to social justice but also to anticommunist stands. The other two components of the modern Democratic coalition were drawn to the party in earlier times. The "New Deal

How to Tell 'em Apart

Republicans usually wear hats. Democrats usually don't.

Democrats buy banned books. Republicans form censorship committees and read them.

Democrats eat the fish they catch. Republicans hang them on the wall.

Republicans study the financial pages of the newspaper. Democrats put them on the bottom of the bird cage.

On Saturday Republicans head for the golf course, the yacht club, or the hunting lodge. Democrats get a haircut, wash the car, or go bowling.

Republicans have guest rooms. Democrats have spare rooms filled with old baby furniture.

Republicans hire exterminators. Democrats step on the bugs.

Republicans sleep in twin beds— some even in separate rooms. That is why there are more Democrats.

Source: Adapted from the National Republican Congressional Committee newsletter.

Democrats" are older, Eastern and Midwestern voters, many of whom are Catholic; they are blue-collar workers, often union members, who favor social programs but are often intolerant of personal freedoms and programs targeted especially for minorities. Similarly drawn to the Democrats are the "60s Democrats," who identify with the peace, civil rights, and environmental movements and the Democratic leaders for whom these were important; these are the most liberal and the most well educated segments of the Democratic coalition. Two other groups lean Democratic: the "seculars" profess no religious belief, but are strongly committed to personal freedoms and opposed to antiabortion legislation, school prayer, and such matters, while the "followers" are at the midpoint on almost all issues, leaning toward Democratic candidates but without much fervor.[40]

These views of the electorate seem to give a more definitive picture than do those that emerged from the exit polls taken in 1988. For instance, of those who thought that the deficit was the most important issue facing the electorate, 57 percent voted for George Bush, but 43 percent favored Michael Dukakis; of those who thought tax increases would be necessary—remember Bush's famous lip sync, "NO NEW TAXES!"—58 percent favored Dukakis, but 42 percent favored Bush despite his pledge. Those who thought controlling illegal drugs was the most important issue split their votes evenly; so did those who believed that environmental concerns should be high on the next president's agenda. On some issues, however, the voters clearly saw partisan differences and voted accordingly. Those who favored cuts in defense spending voted for Dukakis by almost 3 to 1; those who took the opposite view favored Bush just as strongly. Those who thought crime was a major issue overwhelmingly supported the Republican candidate. On the other hand, of those who favored continuing programs to aid the middle class, the vast majority voted Democratic.

The exit polls also showed some demographic differences between the parties. The most notable contrasts: 86 percent of African Americans and 69 percent of Hispanic Americans favored Michael Dukakis, while 59 percent of white Americans voted for George Bush. Bush won 2 to 1 among white Protestants and 4 to 1 among white fundamentalists and evangelicals; Dukakis won 2 to 1 among Jewish voters, while Catholics split their vote almost evenly. Dukakis polled 62 percent of the voters from families with incomes under $12,500; Bush received similar levels of support from those with incomes over $50,000. Those who had a college education favored Bush; those with less than a high school education favored Dukakis; and, interestingly, those who were high school graduates and those who had graduate degrees split their votes about evenly.[41]

In sum, adherents of the two parties are drawn to them by a combination of factors: stands on particular issues; personal and/or party histories; religious, racial, or social peer groupings; attraction of candidates. The emphases among these factors change over time, but they are remarkably consistent with those identified by political scientists nearly thirty years ago.[42]

ARE THE PARTIES DYING?

Some party experts fear the parties are so weak they are mortally ill—or at least in a long decline. They point first to the long-run impact of the progressive reforms early in this century—reforms that robbed party organizations of their control of the nomination process by allowing masses of independents and "uninformed" voters to enter the primaries and vote for candidates who might not be acceptable to party leaders. They also point to a long series of "reforms"—nonpartisan elections in cities and towns and the staggering of national, state, and local elections—that made it harder for parties to influence the election process.

This was bad enough, say the party pessimists, but parties suffer from further ills today. The rise of television and video cassette campaigns, and the parallel rise in campaign, media, and direct-mail consultants, have denied parties their historic role of educating, mobilizing, and channeling the electorate. In addition, partly as a result of media influence, the most powerful electoral forces today are officeseeker or officeholder organizations, not party organizations. Officeseekers, supported by money and media, organize their personal followings to win nominations (while the party leaders are supposed to stand by neutrally); if they win office they are far more responsive to their personal followings than to the party leadership. This means that the party lacks clout over politicians and policy.

According to this view, the very foundations of parties are eroding away. There has been a virtual collapse of local party organizations during the past quarter century. Party membership is weaker and scarcer at the grass roots. Voters identify less with their parties and talk more about "voting the person rather than the party." Harry Truman now appears to have symbolized an earlier era; Truman "always voted for the best man," he said, "and that man is always the Democrat." Today television plays up the personality, the celebrity, the candidate who can buy media attention and advertising through colossal spending.[43]

Party optimists concede some of this diagnosis: the demise of political machines at the local level, the decline in strong partisan affiliations, the weakness of grass-roots party membership. Yet they see signs of party revival they think the pessimists ignore. The national party organizations—the national committees and the congressional and senatorial campaign committees—are significantly better funded than they were in earlier days; they even own permanent, modern headquarters in Washington, D.C. Moreover, the parties are more capable of providing assistance to candidates and to state and local party organizations, because of their increased financial bases, and because they have defined their roles as providing expertise in these areas to those who need it but cannot otherwise obtain it. Optimists hope these advances will give the national parties some leverage over the positions that officeseekers and officeholders take on party issues.[44]

How can the "party doctors" differ so widely in diagnosing the condition of the "patients"? Party pessimists have concentrated mostly on the Democratic party, which has been much weaker nationally than the Republican party, and on presidential elections, where the Democrats are weakest, rather than on congressional or gubernatorial results. Only in the last few years have the Democrats shown signs of rebirth as a viable national organization. Optimists have seen what the Republicans have been able to do for some years and projected, correctly, that the Democrats would follow suit.

These contrasting interpretations rest on differing notions of what makes for a strong and enduring party. Party pessimists tend to have an "old-fashioned" view of the party as a pyramid of local, county, and state committees culminating in national leadership; as a broad-membership, grass-roots organization at the bottom; as an organization, both democratic and disciplined, that can put forth a meaningful platform, nominate and elect politicians committed to that platform, and exercise considerable influence over the legislative and executive roles of its elected members in government. Most party optimists contend that these are idealized notions, that our parties never existed in those ways—nor could they, given our political system. They believe the primary function of parties is to help candidates be elected to office. The optimists look for a role for party organization in simplifying meaningful choices for the electorate and instituting a link between the wishes of the electorate and the actions of their government. And the national parties have begun to play that role more effectively. Moreover, they have been successful in extending their reach downward to state and local organizations and candidates. Thus, two of the optimists conclude, "Although it is still true that neither party completely controls its own destiny, and both have minimal influence on the nomination of their presidential candidates, they are beginning to emerge as the single most effective participant in electoral politics outside of the campaign organization."[45] That conclusion would hold as much for the Democrats today as it does for the Republicans.[46]

A crucial test of the effectiveness of party revolves around the coherence of party views once candidates are elected to office. Here again the evidence for those seeing a rebirth of parties is impressive. During the first year of the Reagan administration, the Republican party in Congress demonstrated a remarkable ability to vote together on issues of importance to the president's program. This can be measured by the Party Unity Score, defined as the percentage of members of a party who vote together on roll call votes in Congress on which a majority of the members of one party vote against a majority of the members of the other party. The 76 percent scored by the congressional Republicans in 1981 astounded observers; it was the highest score recorded in more than two decades. Although they did not reach that peak again, the Republicans averaged over 73 percent during the Reagan administration and never had an annual average below 70 percent. The Democrat's record was even more impressive. Democratic party unity has varied between 76 percent and 80 percent in recent congresses. No scores in this range had been achieved in modern congressional history.[47] Thus, while rank-and-file voters do not seem to be returning to strong partisan ties, party organizations and the party in government do show distinct and significant signs of life.

David Duke

Ex-Klansman Wins GOP Legislative Seat

Talk about switching parties! David Duke was an avowed Nazi in college. Later, as a Democrat, he ran unsuccessfully in some presidential primaries. A former grand wizard of the Knights of the Ku Klux Klan, he ran still later as a presidential candidate of the Populist Party. In 1989 he ran in Louisiana as a Republican state legislator—although several national Republicans like Reagan and Bush had urged his defeat. He won anyway, and was accepted into the state Republican legislative caucus. He also heads the National Association for the Advancement of White People.

Saving the Parties: Reform, Renewal, Realignment

From the start, the very idea of political parties upset some Americans. George Washington's indictment of parties in his farewell address was remarkably broad and bitter for this man of rather moderate opinions. The spirit of party, he said, "serves always to distract the Public Councils and enfeeble the Public administration. It agitates the Community with ill-founded jealousies and false alarms, kindles the animosities of one part against another, foments occasionally riot and insurrection. It opens the door to foreign influence and corruption . . . through the channels of party passions."[48] Most of the other political leaders of Washington's day strongly agreed.

These critics were really attacking big and powerful *factions*, because the party in the modern sense had not yet been born. But when sophisticated political parties developed during the Jacksonian era, they were equally controversial. Critics attacked them for granting the spoils of office to party henchmen, for exercising too much influence over the press (most of the newspapers of the day were violently partisan), and for turning lawmakers and other officials into robots hewing to the party line. But behind these criticisms was a deeper fear: that one party might become the instrument for the great mass of people to take over the government and convert it to their own purposes. This was the fear of majority rule— or majority tyranny. Whigs accused the Democratic party under Andrew Jackson and Martin Van Buren of catering to the ignorant and unwashed. The "second" or "people's" constitution of the 1830s, in short, was even more controversial than the Constitution of 1787.

Much of this distrust has persisted into the present era. A politician is suspect

Most Democratic to Least Democratic States	
Louisiana	1
Mississippi	2
Georgia	3
Alabama	4
Arkansas	5
South Carolina	6
Texas	7
Hawaii	8
North Carolina	9
West Virginia	10
Maryland	11
Rhode Island	12
Massachusetts	13
Florida	14
Virginia	15
Oklahoma	16
Kentucky	17
Tennessee	18
Missouri	19
Nevada	20
New Mexico	21
Washington	22
Minnesota	23
California	24
Connecticut	25
New Jersey	26
Oregon	27
Wisconsin	28
Montana	29
Michigan	30
New York	31
Illinois	32
Pennsylvania	33
Ohio	34
Delaware	35
Iowa	36
Maine	37
Arizona	38
Alaska	39
Indiana	40
Colorado	41
New Hampshire	42
Utah	43
Idaho	44
North Dakota	45
Nebraska	46
Wyoming	47
Kansas	48
South Dakota	49
Vermont	50

Source: Based on state and national election results from 1960 to 1984. An index of two-party competition was developed by Robert D. Loevy, "The Two Party Index: Toward a Standard Statistic for Comparing United States Elections," *Social Science Journal* (April 1984). This has been updated through the 1984 elections.

if he or she is excessively partisan. And public officials are constantly urged by editorial writers to rise above party. On the other hand, most Americans think of themselves as Democrats or Republicans. They contribute a fair amount of money to parties. They look for the "R" or the "D" on the ballot. So far, at least, they have not given much support to presidential candidates who try to run as independents, outside of the party system. They believe, at least vaguely, that you cannot run a big democracy without parties.

Americans, in short, have a love-hate attitude toward parties. The practical result of this has been curious. On the one hand, we want to maintain our parties—we even subsidize them through our taxes. On the other hand, we keep trying to change and improve them. First we tried to reform our parties. Then we tried to reorganize or renew them. Currently we are trying to realign them. Let us look at each of these efforts in turn.

PARTY REFORM

By 1900 party organizations had fastened their grip on countless American cities. These were not called organizations, however, but "machines" in the grip of party "bosses." Boss Tweed of New York City had been long dethroned and jailed, but his image lived on—the image of a crooked power wielder at the center of a vast web of influence, buying and selling legislators and councilors by the job lot, handing out spoils to party henchmen, bribing officials when he could not control them outright, making corrupt deals with business interests, living off kickbacks from contractors, and commanding a following of "toughs" and strong-arm men. The essence of the boss's power lay in his control of nominations, which he controlled by packing conventions with his own people. By the dawn of the twentieth century, as we have seen, middle-class reformers, increasingly indignant, took the nominating process "back to the people" by means of the party primary. But many party experts hold the primary responsible for the downfall not only of the "bosses" but also of parties as responsible and efficient organizations. The conventions were not just a means of picking candidates; they were also the grass-roots leadership corps of the party. In most cities and some states, the convention—and with it much of the leadership corps—simply disappeared.

The national party convention survived the onslaught, even though many reformers preferred a nationwide direct primary for choosing presidential candidates. The next great wave of reform came in the 1960s, with a dramatic effort to change the way in which conventions were managed, convention delegates chosen, and other party affairs conducted. This was particularly the case in the Democratic party, but the GOP, too, was influenced by the political reforms of the 1960s and 1970s.

The critical year was 1968—and what a year that was! Amid rising tumult over Vietnam, Senator Eugene McCarthy of Minnesota challenged President Johnson for renomination, and soon Senator Robert Kennedy of New York plunged into the fray. After suffering an image (though not an electoral) defeat in the New Hampshire Democratic primary, Johnson suddenly announced he would not run again. As the temper of the country became more and more ugly, Martin Luther King, Jr., was assassinated, as was Robert Kennedy, shortly after he won the California primary. The 1968 Democratic convention scene in Chicago dissolved into near chaos, as outside the hall Yippies conducted love-ins, anti-Vietnam protestors demonstrated, thousands of outraged people ringed the Chicago hotels, and the police responded with clubbings and tear gas. Within the convention hall insurgents and regulars fought bitterly over the nomination, which had been made almost worthless as millions of television viewers watched the Democratic party bleed.

Hardly noticed in all the commotion was the appointment of two commissions to study and improve the structure of the party and the way in which convention delegates were chosen—for many years a bone of contention at Democratic conventions. Chaired by Senator George McGovern of South Dakota, the Commission on Party Structure and Delegate Selection proposed a series of reforms.[49] State parties were to ensure that party meetings were held with proper advance notice, in public places, and at set times. Voting by proxy was to be forbidden. The other commission, chaired by Michigan Congressman James O'Hara, voted to prohibit the **unit rule,** by which the vote of a whole delegation was cast as the majority voted. Although such reforms might seem rather elementary, they were in fact a response to frequent violations of fair play.

Other guidelines were more substantive and involved efforts to broaden participation.[50] Just as proponents of party primaries at the turn of the century had charged that bosses restricted participation in conventions, the reformers of the 1960s held that countless Democrats were being excluded from party functions and decision making. Here the McGovern-Fraser Commission proposed three changes.[51] One was not controversial; it ensured that party rules barred discrimination on the basis of race, color, creed, sex, or national origin. Another was a bit controversial; it allowed and encouraged all those 18 or older to take part in party affairs (the Twenty-sixth Amendment had not yet been ratified). A third was *very* controversial; it proposed that specific steps must be taken to provide representation in party affairs (and especially in nomination decisions) of young people, women, and minorities "in reasonable relation to their presence in the state's population"; that is, it proposed enforced proportional representation of defined groups of voters.

George McGovern was nominated for president at a Democratic National Convention whose delegates were selected under these rules. The convention's delegates included more females, more nonwhites, and more young delegates than had ever been the case before. And they nominated a candidate, portrayed as an ultraliberal by his Republican opponent and by the press, who suffered the worst defeat ever endured by a Democratic candidate until that time. The commission's proposals had been hotly opposed by some Democrats at the time they were implemented, especially by those who were not at the convention, either because they had been defeated in primaries or caucuses, or because they had not followed the new guidelines and were declared to have been elected illegally, as was the case of Chicago Mayor Richard J. Daley (father of the present mayor of Chicago).

Although some commission critics favored broadening the party, centrists feared that too much effort would be made to bring in young people and women, but not enough to recruit working-class people, labor unionists, the elderly, and others. The emphasis on a participatory rank-and-file party, they declared, was really undemocratic. Those who would attend open, grass-roots caucuses were the more educated and affluent—people who had the time, the stamina, and the interest to debate all night. Working and poor people lacked the leisure, energy, or self-confidence to express their interests at meetings or even to attend them. Critics especially opposed the quota system—"democracy by demography"—as arbitrary and basically unrepresentative.

So heavy was the opposition to the quota system that it has been substantially eliminated.[52] However, it is clear that most of the essential reforms are here to stay. Party rules require nondiscrimination on the basis of "sex, race, age, religion, economic status, sexual orientation, ethnic identity, national origin, or color."[53] But despite heated debate over so-called quotas, the most lasting effect of the McGovern-Faser Commission has been that party primaries now dominate the

"Very Republican. I love it."

Drawing by B. Tobey; © 1986 The New Yorker Magazine, Inc.

process by which delegates are elected. State parties were given a number of options as to which procedures to follow. Because caucus procedures under the new guidelines were difficult to understand, and because many felt they prevented some traditional Democrats from participating, many state party organizations that had run caucuses to choose delegates under the old rules opted for primaries under the new system. At least 60 percent of the delegates to each Democratic National Convention since the reforms have been selected in primaries.

The Democrats continued to convene "reform" commissions after each presidential election, each trying to improve the process for nominating the presidential candidate. The commission formed after the 1980 election, led by former North Carolina Governor James Hunt, undid some of the McGovern-Fraser "reforms," in an attempt to bring party professionals back into the nominating process with the creation of "superdelegates," party officials and officeholders who automatically qualified as delegates by virtue of their positions. Nevertheless, most people sent to party conventions are candidate or issue enthusiasts, not party activists.[54]

In 1986 the Democratic party's Fairness Commission, the most recent "reform" commission, resisted any major changes in party rules. It did, however, respond to one of Jesse Jackson's main complaints about the democratized party rule that candidates for the presidential nomination shall be awarded delegates in proportion to the votes they receive, either in a primary or in caucuses. However, states were permitted to set a threshold; candidates were required to poll more than that percentage of votes in order to qualify for any delegates. In 1984, Jackson had won the support of over 18 percent of the voters in the primaries that he entered, but he received only 10 percent of the delegates from those states. He claimed that the 20 percent threshold in many of those primaries discriminated against his candidacy. The Fairness Commission voted to lower the threshold from 20 percent to 15 percent.

Another Democratic reform had sought to limit the nominating process to a three-month period. Some states had been granted an exemption from starting their nominating process during that three-month "window," ostensibly for historical reasons, but in reality because the national party did not have the political will to demand compliance. When Iowa held the first caucus in 1988, and New Hampshire, the first primary, they each garnered a great deal of publicity.[55] The Democrats instituted a regional primary of sorts for 1988, although this change was not instituted by party rules. A number of Southern Democrats, led by the Democratic Leadership Council, felt that the South's influence over the nominating process would be enhanced, and perhaps would even offset that of Iowa and New Hampshire, if they held their primaries early in the allowable period and all on one day. State legislatures throughout the South were persuaded to adopt this strategy; eventually twenty states, fourteen of which were southern or border states, decided to hold their 1988 primary on "Super Tuesday."

The Republicans have been more relaxed over the issue of party reform than the Democrats. For one thing, the pressure of minority elements in the GOP for recognition has not been as intense as within the Democratic party. For another, Republicans do not believe philosophically that the national party should have too much authority over state and local parties. And furthermore, the Republican National Convention is, in practice as well as in theory, the only body that can change party rules. Thus, no commissions could institute procedural changes between conventions. Because the candidates and their relative strengths and weaknesses are rarely predictable four years in advance of a nomination battle, the fact that only the quadrennial convention can change the rules has removed much of the political infighting over the matter.

Still, Republican party rules prohibit discriminatory practices, and state committees are urged—though not required—to take positive action and to encourage broad participation in the delegate-selection process by young people, women, minority and ethnic groups, and older voters.[56] More important, Republican procedures have changed as a result of Democratic reform. Many of the reforms required by the Democrats have had to be implemented through state law, which in turn affects all parties. Thus, Republicans now have many more primaries, selecting many more delegates, than they did twenty years ago. The McGovern-Fraser reforms were indirectly responsible for this shift. Similarly, Republicans throughout the South held early primaries, almost all on one day in 1988, again because of changes in state law instigated by Democrats.

PARTY RENEWAL

Some politicians and scholars, both Republican and Democrat, are more interested in party *renewal* than party reform. In their view—or at least in the view of the "party pessimists"—the party system needs to be saved and strengthened, not reformed. They may accept some of the proposed changes—especially those that fortify the party as an organization—but they would nurse both the elephant and the donkey back to health and vitality before they would teach either animal how to improve its ways.

Congressman Jack Kemp

So, while some Democrats at the 1968 and 1972 conventions were stressing the need for more participation, proper procedures, and fairer representation, other Democrats were focusing on the need to turn the party into a better structured, more active, more effective, and more policy-oriented organization. This opinion came to the fore at the 1972 convention in a successful movement to call a charter conference—a meeting that might revamp the Democratic party (just as a state constitutional convention might reorganize a state governmental system). Two years later more than two thousand delegates assembled in Kansas City for long sessions of debate on a proposed charter. Once again battles erupted between reformers and renewers, but most of the delegates were convinced that revitalization was crucial. In drawing up the first written "constitution" in American major-party history, the charter convention took the following steps:

1. It recognized the national convention as the supreme governing body of the party and required state parties to adapt their rules and practices to national party standards.
2. It enlarged the Democratic National Committee to make it stronger and more representative.
3. It strengthened the national and financial agencies in the party.
4. It authorized midterm national party conferences for the discussion of national public policy, at a point halfway through the presidential term.

The most important—and most fleeting—of these changes was the creation of the **midterm party conference.**[57] Mid term or microconventions were held by the Democrats in 1978 and 1982, although party leaders thought they were divisive and costly.[58]

Then in 1985 the Democratic National Committee moved quickly and quietly to eliminate the midterm convention. Out of fear that the conference would spawn divisiveness and destroy the unity necessary to regain the Senate in 1986 and the presidency in 1988 (and to save $1 million), newly elected Chairperson Paul

G. Kirk canceled what some Democrats viewed as an effective tool for shaping a vision and a strategy for Democratic success.

Republicans, concerned about the health of their own party, were not idle during this period. Committees proposed giving the national committee more control over presidential campaigns in an effort to avoid Watergate-type excesses, and state parties were urged to encourage broader participation by all groups, including women, minorities, youth, and the poor. The Republican party entered the 1980s with a party organization far superior to that of Democrats. The GOP emphasized grass-roots organization and membership recruitment. Seminars were held to teach Republican candidates how to make speeches and hold press conferences, and weekend conferences were organized for training young professionals. Candidates were taught how to "draw up a campaign plan, write and buy advertising, raise money, set up phone banks, recruit volunteers and schedule [their] time."[59]

A number of other factors may be strengthening the leadership of both parties. In this day of complex campaign laws and finance legislation and of sophisticated and expensive election technology, state and local parties, and candidates at all levels, have increasingly turned to the national party for technical advice and assistance. Although the national GOP will remain a federation of state parties in theory, in practice national headquarters may continue to gain more visibility and influence from its expanded services. In the Democratic party these same factors favor centralization. One analyst has predicted that both national parties "will become national bureaucracies with hierarchies, divisions of labor" and specialized experts.[60]

Must reform or renewal be alternatives, or even conflict with each other? Some party experts believe that parties can be open, representative, participatory, and fair in their procedures, *and* at the same time well organized, competently led, politically effective, and highly competitive. The key to such a fusion, they believe, may lie at the base of the party, in the *local caucus.* Properly conducted, caucuses are open to all local-area party members. All present have the same vote and the same right to speak. Decisions are made by majority vote, but minorities may still have the right to some representation, for example, in the selection of delegates to higher party meetings. Caucuses can actively recruit and involve new members of the party; they can help finance party activities through the collection of dues; they can train people in party issues and administration; they can be an active party presence in the community; and they can identify talented persons and supply leadership to the higher echelons. In short, caucuses can be the building blocks of both participation and organization. Other state parties may adopt the caucus-based model of Iowa and Minnesota. Massachusetts Democrats, for example, have adopted a party charter that requires local ward and town committees to convene open caucuses whenever candidates or public issues are voted on.

THE POLITICS OF REALIGNMENT

Ronald Reagan won both praise and criticism as chief executive, but he will rank in history as one of the more forceful and influential American party leaders. In his two terms as president, as we have noted, he transformed the Republican party from the more moderate and reactive GOP to a distinctively activist party of the right wing. Reagan accomplished in the 1980s what Barry Goldwater was unable to do in the 1960s: He narrowed his party's program without condemning the GOP to the status of a perpetual minority. And what of the Democrats? While

Reagan was redirecting and expanding his party, the Democrats were struggling to maintain the "Grand Coalition" of labor, the unemployed, minorities, the middle class, small business, intellectuals, big cities, and the South, which for five decades had defined the party and brought it consistent victory. With such a strong party leader as Reagan, the GOP has been more successful in its task than the Democrats have been in preserving the coalition and ideology they pioneered fifty years earlier under FDR.

President Reagan, most of his supporters, and many of his Democratic opponents were united in the belief that neither reform nor renewal adequately addresses the problem of party decline. They turned to the third "R" of party change—**realignment.** A party is more than an ideology; it is also a bundle of actions, a coalition drawn to a leader or to a party philosophy. Realignment in its simplest form is the reshuffling of coalitions within parties. Coalitions may reconstitute themselves—or be reconstituted by a party leader—because of new issues dominating their attention, or because of new positions taken by a party or party leaders on those issues, or because the electorate itself has changed its politics. Add to this the calculation of election gains and losses for parties and candidates, and you have the basic tools for examining one of the most fascinating and perplexing aspects of electoral politics: realignment.[61]

In the 1930s the United States faced a devastating economic collapse. After a century of sporadic government action, the New Dealers stepped in and fundamentally altered the relationship between government and society. In an unprecedented response to the unprecedented crises of massive depression, political deadlock, social disorder, urban blight, and other twentieth-century ailments, Franklin Roosevelt assumed extensive powers and responsibilities over the welfare of the citizenry. In so doing, he led the way toward transforming his party into the resourceful—and victorious—majority party it would be for the next generation. The realigned configuration of coalition and ideology acted as a safety valve, and it rewarded the party that responded positively to crisis with electoral success. For two decades the Republican opposition could do nothing but watch—and oppose.

Under the popular General Dwight Eisenhower the Republicans temporarily regained the White House, but it was the legacy of Roosevelt and Truman that shaped the political landscape.[62] When Senator Barry Goldwater of Arizona challenged the assumptions of the New and Fair Deals in 1964, he was resoundingly defeated. Even under the presidency of Richard M. Nixon, the Republicans could rarely break out of the mold of moderate opposition, or of minority party, not only in Congress but in voter identification and registration as well. That change would wait for the leadership of Ronald Reagan. Some thought that Reagan had placed the Republican party on the road to majority status; however, that was not to be.

And where are the Democrats? Although the values and objectives of the New Deal are as challenging as ever, its original coalition proved impossible to preserve. North and South, once united over FDR's attempts to heal a nation, drifted apart as the liberalism applied to poverty and unemployment in the 1930s was extended to civil rights measures in the 1950s and 1960s. Today, at the national level at least, the Republican party is alive and well in much of the formerly one-party South. Southern Democrats tend to be moderates, like Terry Sanford of North Carolina or Wyche Fowler of Georgia. More and more conservative Southerners who win in races are Republicans, like North Carolina's Jesse Helms or Mississippi's Trent Lott. Although Democrats have remained dominant in state and local races in the South, this core part of the Roosevelt coalition has drifted away.

Other elements of the Roosevelt coalition have become less committed, partly because of the impact of legislative successes. A generation that matured in union households, amidst immigrant workers, and through the distresses of the Great Depression now joins other beneficiaries of the New Deal who want to preserve their economic gains—through the Republican party! Social Security, Medicaid, GI Bills, and student loans helped to expand the middle and upper classes, but the beneficiaries of these programs have not all remained loyal to the party that brought about the programs that led to their upward mobility. The natural constituency that gave the Democrats their victories and the abilities to govern, those who would benefit from progressive programs, has been diminished by the gains brought about by those very programs.

Those pundits and party professionals who would renew the Democratic party through a polarizing realignment find inspiration in the enemy camp in the actions of their Republican opponents. The "realigners" would guide the Democrats as swiftly and surely toward a progressive posture as the GOP has been led to a conservative one. Rather than fearing the future, the proponents of polarization assert that Democrats should embrace it and reject "centrist schizophrenia." Then, perhaps, they may inspire those who are now alienated, apathetic, disempowered, and disenfranchised to aid in rejuvenating the Democratic party. Be courageous, as Reagan and the Republicans have been, they proclaim, and you too shall be victorious. But realignment is something more than a change in party ideology, or an exchange of voters or voting blocs. For that something more, and for evidence of a contemporary realignment, we must examine election results and the party preferences of the populace.

Voters today describe themselves as more conservative than they did twenty years ago. Although they liked Reagan's tax cuts and his strengthened defense policy, only 4 percent of the electorate in 1984 reported that they voted for Ronald Reagan because he was conservative. In that election, a clear electoral and popular landslide for President Reagan, the Republican party nevertheless lost two seats in the Senate and gained a scant eighteen in the House.[63] In 1988 the pattern was repeated. George Bush won a decisive popular and electoral victory, but it was more for "a man—not a message. . . . [and] reflected a lack of clear consensus among the voters about the direction the new president should take. . . . Indeed voters offered no clear rationale based on issues for why they voted the way they did."[64] Voters continued to describe themselves as more conservative than they were a generation ago, but this conservatism did not translate into votes for Republicans other than Bush.

Why has realignment moved so slowly? Why aren't all good conservatives now happily ensconced in the Republican party and all stout liberals gladly lodged in the Democratic? In part because Americans do not blithely cross party lines. If you grew up in a conservative New Hampshire family whose forebears voted Republican for a century, you are pretty much conditioned to stay with the GOP. Even if that party took a direction you disliked, you might continue to register as a Republican but quietly vote Democratic to avoid friction in the family. Or if you come from a "Yellow Dog" Democratic family in Texas (meaning a family that would vote for anyone or anything as long as it was a Democrat), you might continue to vote for Democrats locally even though you disliked various Democratic candidates for president. Much evidence indicates that this pattern is common throughout the South.

The other reason for slow realignment is the federal nature of the party. For decades conservative Democrats in the South have been voting for Republican candidates for president, not only Bush and Reagan, but before them Nixon and even Eisenhower. They have done so, however, without "crossing the aisle" from

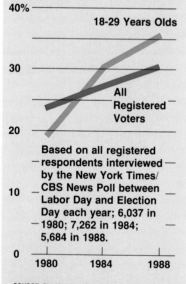

Young Voters Move to the G.O.P.

Percentage calling themselves Republican.

18-29 Years Olds

All Registered Voters

Based on all registered respondents interviewed by the New York Times/CBS News Poll between Labor Day and Election Day each year; 6,037 in 1980; 7,262 in 1984; 5,684 in 1988.

SOURCE: *The New York Times*, Oct. 31, 1988, p. B4, CBS News Poll

Copyright © 1988 by The New York Times Company. Reprinted by permission.

CHAPTER 10 / Political Parties: Institutions under Change

the Democratic party to the Republican. Why? Partly for the family attitudes noted above, but also because such voters know that the Republican party is weak organizationally throughout the South. So if candidates and voters want to have an impact on local politics, in which the only meaningful elections are the Democratic primaries in most cases, they must stay registered as Democrats. Hence the Democratic party in the South is moderate for federal offices but conservative for local offices; the Republican party is conservative for federal offices, but largely nonexistent for local offices.

What, then, are the prospects for party realignment in the 1990s? What hope— or fear—of a still "Reaganized" Republican party arrayed against a Democratic party supporting a clearly liberal-labor-left program?

Since the Republicans have been winning with their realigned party, they are not likely to change their present strategy. They have successfully realigned themselves. Clearly the realignment ball is in the Democrats' court following their third presidential election defeat in a row in 1988—and their fifth defeat in the last six presidential elections. As the Bush administration moved through its first year, Democrats were reassessing their strategy like a football team meeting with its coaches following a winless season. Several strategies were debated:

"And I promise to always be loyal to my party, even if I have to change parties to do it!"

Dunagin's People by Ralph Dunagin. Reprinted with special permission of NAS, Inc.

Strategy No. 1: Occupy the central ground abandoned by the GOP. Rebuild the ancient center-left coalition between southern moderates and conservatives and northern liberals and labor. Under this alternative the party would not undertake daring new ventures but, as a prominent Democrat has urged, reassess its outdated policies, emphasize issues such as crime and defense, and attract a wide spectrum of Democrats, "conservative as well as liberal, hawkish as well as dovish, tight-fisted as well as free-spending." Democrats, according to this view, should return to bipartisanship by working with the Bush White House on as many defense and foreign policy issues as possible.[65]

Strategy No. 2: Move strongly in a liberal-left or progressive direction, seeking to arouse support from the tens of millions of nonvoters who might be attracted to the "humane and compassionate" welfare policies of the Democratic party, such as heavily subsidized child welfare programs. The party would make a stronger pitch to blacks, women, and other "movement Democrats," as well as to Hispanic and other growing electoral blocs. Advocating this kind of strategy, Senator Edward M. Kennedy of Massachusetts called early in 1989 for the kind of activism that viewed "government as a positive instrument," and he urged Democrats to "move beyond the New Deal and the New Frontier and the Great Society" toward aggressively solving social problems.[66] Some liberal Democrats favor a greater effort in the old "progressive" states of the East and West and in the farm-industrial states of the Midwest, at the expense of the South. Others oppose what they call a "Dump Dixie" strategy.

Strategy No. 3: Adopt no strategy, except to hunker down, sit tight, wait for the Republicans to lose their way, fumble the ball, antagonize their fans. Eventually the party pendulum will swing back toward the Democrats, as it has always done in the past. Then the Democrats could take office without having made promises and commitments that would be difficult to honor. Such a strategy would be less of realignment than of dealignment; that is, a lessening of party conflict. This might be appropriate in an era of party decline.[67]

Each of these strategies came under fire. The first—preempt the center— would repudiate decades of Democratic progressivism in government. "Me-too" Democrats, moreover, could hardly offer militant opposition to the GOP. The second strategy, it was charged, would simply inflict more presidential election defeats on the Democrats. As for attracting new voters, even sizable increases of voting by blacks, Hispanics, and poor people would not have brought a Dukakis victory in 1988.[68] Hunker down? No party with a great tradition of reform and innovation could sit back and wait for the party in power to make mistakes. The party pendulum might not swing back as predictably as a clock's.

So the prospects of planned party realignment appear dim. Still, if history repeats itself, a realignment might occur in an unplanned way. Massive realignments in the past had been triggered by critical elections during the times of great conflict or crisis, as in the pre-Civil War period or in the 1930s. A sharp economic recession, environmental catastrophes, global population and migration pressures, war in the Middle East are all potential flash points of crisis and conflict.

Would most Americans approve of party realignment should it ever take place? Many voters appear to prefer nondoctrinaire parties and divided party rule, like the Democratic Congress and Republican president produced by the 1988 election. A unified left or right party in power might evoke ancient American fears of "majority tyranny." To be sure, Britain offers an example of party government under which the majority party—currently the Conservatives—has a monopoly of legislative and executive power without jeopardizing fundamental liberties.[69] But many Americans might fear that an entrenched majority would override not only the minority opposition but their most precious liberties, as set forth in the Bill of Rights.

Summary

1. American political parties have declined both in organizational strength and in the estimation of many Americans since the days in which they were described as strong political forces. In recent years both parties, at the national level and within the government, have shown renewed signs of vitality.

2. Our two major parties maintained their ascendancy in the past by bringing factions and interests together in coalitions broad enough to win the presidency and congressional elections.

3. Today some people believe that the parties are established and accepted, but basically weak and even stagnant. Others contend that we are at the start of a party resurgence, with another "golden age" of parties lying just over the horizon. Still others hold that parties are in a transitional period and the role they will play in the future will depend on the quality of their leaders at all levels.

4. For over a hundred years third parties—whether doctrinal or forming around current issues or personalities—have not been notably successful.

5. Parties have many functions, which they perform with varying degrees of adequacy: recruiting and nominating candidates; raising money for campaigns and ongoing activities; clarifying issues; mobilizing voters; providing patronage for supporters and employees for the government; uniting diverse interests; and serving as a link between the voters and their representatives in government.

6. The two major parties have been criticized as being too much alike, yet this criticism is overstated if one looks at the policies they favor, their leadership cadres, and their performance when in power. They are also said to be poorly organized and financed, a criticism that was much more valid a decade ago than it is today.

7. Whether the major parties—or any party—can survive depends on the capacity of their leaders at all levels to pursue effective strategies of reform, renewal, and realignment.

Further Reading

JOHN F. BIBBY. *Politics, Parties and Elections in America* (Nelson-Hall, 1987).

JOHN E. CHUBB and PAUL E. PETERSON, eds. *The New Direction in American Politics* (Brookings Institution, 1985).

THOMAS B. EDSALL. *The New Politics of Inequality* (Norton, 1984).

SAMUEL J. ELDERSVELD. *Political Parties in American Society* (Basic Books, 1982).

LEON EPSTEIN. *Political Parties in the American Mold* (University of Wisconsin Press, 1986).

XANDRA KAYDEN and EDDIE MAHE, JR. *The Party Goes On* (Basic Books, 1985).

WILLIAM J. KEEFE. *Parties, Politics, and Public Policy in America*, 5th ed. (Congressional Quarterly Press, 1985).

L. Sandy Maisel. *Parties and Elections in America: The Electoral Process* (Random House, 1987).

David Mayhew. *Placing the Parties in American Politics* (Princeton University Press, 1986).

Nelson W. Polsby. *Consequences of Party Reform* (Oxford University Press, 1983).

Gerald M. Pomper, ed. *Party Renewal in America* (Praeger, 1980).

David E. Price. *Bringing Back the Parties* (Congressional Quarterly Press, 1984).

Steven J. Rosenstone, Roy L. Behr, and Edward H. Lazarus. *Third Parties in America: Citizen Response to Major Party Failure* (Princeton University Press, 1984).

Larry J. Sabato. *The Party's Just Begun: Shaping Political Parties in America's Future* (Scott, Foresman, 1988).

Frank Smallwood. *The Other Candidates: Third Parties in Presidential Elections* (University Press of New England, 1983).

James Sundquist. *Dynamics of the Party System: Alignment and Realignment of Political Parties in the United States*, rev. ed. (Brookings Institution, 1983).

Notes

1. On party decline and other aspects of party, see Gerald M. Pomper, ed., *Party Renewal in America* (Praeger, 1980). For the argument that people have grown neutral, not hostile, to parties, see Martin P. Wattenberg, *The Decline of American Political Parties, 1952–1980* (Harvard University Press, 1984).

2. These mixed attitudes toward parties are summarized in Austin Ranney, *Curing the Mischiefs of Faction* (University of California Press, 1975), pp. 53–56.

3. Washington, Franklin, and Jefferson, as quoted in Richard Hofstadter, *The Idea of a Party System* (University of California Press, 1969), pp. 2, 123.

4. For a further discussion of the development of the first American parties see L. Sandy Maisel, *Parties and Elections in America* (Random House, 1987), chap. 2.

5. See William E. Gienapp, *The Origins of the Republican Party, 1852–1856* (Oxford, 1987).

6. See James L. Sundquist, *Dynamics of the Party System: Alignment and Realignment of Political Parties in the United States*, rev. ed. (Brookings, 1983).

7. See Norman H. Nie, Sidney Verba, and John R. Petrocik, *The Changing American Voter*, enlarged ed. (Harvard University Press, 1979).

8. See John E. Chubb and Paul E. Peterson, eds. *The New Direction in American Politics* (Brookings, 1985).

9. James MacGregor Burns, in Pomper, *Party Renewal in America*, pp. 194–96.

10. Charles O. Jones, *The Trusteeship Presidency: Jimmy Carter and the United States Congress* (Louisiana University Press, 1988); see also Charles O. Jones, "Ronald Reagan and the U. S. Congress: Visible Hand Politics," and Paul E. Peterson and Mark Rom, "Lower Taxes, More Spending and Budget Deficits," in Charles O. Jones, ed., *The Reagan Legacy* (Chatham House, 1988), for discussions of the role of party in Congress during the last two administrations.

11. See Wilson Carey McWilliams, "Parties as Civic Associations," in Pomper, *Party Renewal in America*, pp. 51–68. For a "revisionist" view that Irish bosses were not generous with jobs for non-Irish constituents, see Steven P. Erie, *Rainbow's End: Irish-Americans and the Dilemmas of Urban Machine Politics, 1840–1945* (University of California Press, 1989).

12. *Branti* v. *Finkel*, 445 U.S. 507 (1980).

13. See Maisel, *Parties and Elections in America*, chap. 5.

14. For appraisal of key electoral criteria in another caucus state, Minnesota, in comparison with those in primary states, see Thomas R. Marshall, "Turnout and Representation: Caucuses versus Primaries," *American Journal of Political Science* (February 1978), pp. 169–82.

15. See Byron E. Shafer, *Bifurcated Politics* (Harvard University Press, 1988).

16. See, for example, David W. Brady and Charles S. Bullock IV, "Party and Faction Within Legislatures," in G. Loewenberg, S. Patterson, and M. Jewell, eds., *Handbook of Legislative Research* (Harvard University Press, 1985), chap. 4.

17. Steven J. Rosenstone, Roy L. Behr, and Edward H. Lazarus, *Third Parties in America: Citizen Response to Major Party Failure* (Princeton University Press, 1984).

18. On the impact of third parties, see Howard R. Penniman, "Presidential Third Parties and the Modern American Two-Party System," in William Crotty, ed., *The Party Symbol* (W. H. Freeman, 1980), pp. 101–17. See also Frank Smallwood, *The Other Candidates: Third Parties in Presidential Elections* (University Press of New England, 1983).

19. The winner-take-all system of dividing electoral votes pertains in all states except for Maine, which uses a district system.

20. William H. Riker, "The Two-Party System and Duverger's Law: An Essay on the History of Political Science," *American Political Science Review* (December 1982), pp. 753–66. For a classic analysis, see E. E. Schattschneider, *Party Government* (Rinehart, 1942).

21. James Reichley, "The Rise of National Parties," in Chubb and Peterson, eds., *The New Direction in American Politics*, chap. 7.

22. Richard Richards, interviewed in *Party Line* (February 1983), quoted on p. 7.

23. The early Republican efforts and advantages over the Democrats are well documented in Thomas B. Edsall, *The New Politics of Inequality* (Norton, 1984), and in Gary C. Jacobson, "The Republican Advantage in Campaign Finances," in Chubb and Peterson, eds., *The New Direction in American Politics*, p. 6.

24. See Paul S. Herrnson, *Party Campaigning in the 1980s* (Harvard University Press, 1988). For a more critical view of these endeavors, see Brooks Jackson, *Honest Graft: Big Money and the American Political Process* (Alfred A. Knopf, 1988).

25. See L. Sandy Maisel, *From Obscurity to Oblivion: Running in the Congressional Primary*, rev. ed. (University of Tennessee Press, 1986).

26. See John F. Bibby, *Politics, Parties, and Elections in America* (Nelson-Hall, 1987). For further data on these roles, see Cornelius P. Cotter, James L. Gibson, John F. Bibby, and Robert J. Huckshorn, *Party Organizations in American Politics* (Praeger, 1984).

27. See James L. Gibson, Cornelius P. Cotter, John F. Bibby, and Robert J. Huckshorn, "Assessing Party Organizational Strength," *American Journal of Political Science* (May 1983), and Cotter et al., *Party Organizations in American Politics*.

28. See James L. Gibson, Cornelius P. Cotter, John F. Bibby, and Robert J. Huckshorn, "Whither the Local Parties?: A Cross-Sectional and Longitudinal Analysis of the Strength of Party Organizations," *American Journal of Political Science* (February 1985), pp. 139–59, and Cotter et al., *Party Organizations in American Politics*.

29. For a fascinating account of Daley's chairmanship, see Milton Rakove, *Don't Make No Waves, Don't Back No Losers* (Indiana University Press, 1975).

30. On the influence of local parties, see Xandra Kayden and Eddie Mahe, Jr., *The Party Goes On* (Basic Books, 1985).

31. Gerald M. Pomper, *Elections in America*, rev. ed. (Longman, 1980); Alan D. Monroe, "American Party Platforms and Public Opinions," *American Journal of Political Science* (February 1983), pp. 27–42.

32. Students can address this question for themselves by consulting Donald Bruce Johnson, ed., *National Party Platforms* (University of Illinois Press, 1978), vol. 1, 1840–1956; vol. 2, 1960–1976.

33. The complete texts of the national party platforms are found in

many places. See *Congressional Quarterly Weekly Report*, July 16, 1988, pp. 1967–1970 for the Democrats, and August 20, 1988, pp. 2369–2399 for the Republicans.

34. For further distinctions between volunteers and professionals, see James Wilson, *The Amateur Democrat* (University of Chicago Press, 1962); Jeane Kirkpatrick, *The New Presidential Elite* (Russell Sage Foundation/Twentieth Century Fund, 1976); Robert T. Nakamura, "Beyond Purism and Professionalism: Styles of Convention Delegate Followership," *American Journal of Political Science* (May 1980), pp. 207–32.

35. See Ronald B. Rapoport, Alan I. Abramowitz, and John McGlennon, *The Life of the Parties* (University Press of Kentucky, 1986); Douglas I. Hodgkin, "Presidential Primaries, Caucuses, and the Recruitment of 1984 State Convention Delegates." Paper delivered at the New England Political Science Association Annual Meeting, Hartford, Connecticut, April 5, 1986.

36. Everett Carll Ladd, Jr., *American Political Parties: Social Change and Political Response* (Norton, 1970), pp. 307–8. For the contention that mass-membership organizations impede rather than facilitate political action by the poor, see Frances Fox Piven and Richard A. Cloward, *Poor People's Movements* (Pantheon, 1977).

37. See Walter Dean Burnham, *Critical Elections and the Mainsprings of American Politics* (Norton, 1970).

38. Jim Hightower, "A Texan's Rx for What Ails the Democratic Party," address to the National Press Club, *Boston Globe* (June 5, 1985).

39. The classic work in this field is Angus Campbell, Philip E. Converse, Warren E. Miller, and Donald E. Stokes, *The American Voter* (Wiley, 1960). Their work was based on a survey conducted by the National Election Study project of the Survey Research Center of the University of Michigan.

40. The summaries are drawn from Norman Ornstein, Andrew Kohut, and Larry McCarthy, *The People, The Press, and Politics: The Times Mirror Study of the American Electorate* (Addison-Wesley, 1988), chaps. 1 and 3.

41. The data in these paragraphs are drawn from the *New York Times/CBS*, the *Washington Post/ABC*, and the *Wall Street Journal/NBC* polls. See also "The Issues That Mattered," *Time* (November 21, 1988), p. 37.

42. See Campbell, Converse, Miller and Stokes, *The American Voter*, and Norman Nie, Sidney Verba, and John Petrocik, *The Changing American Voter* (Harvard University Press, 1976).

43. For the "pessimistic view" of the party condition, see Wattenberg, *The Decline of American Political Parties*, and Alan Ware, *The Breakdown of Democratic Party Organization, 1940–1980* (Clarendon Press, 1985).

44. For the "optimistic" view, see Goldman, *Search for Consensus*, pp. 366–373; Kayden and Mahe, *The Party Goes On*; Larry Sabato, *The Party's Just Begun* (Scott, Foresman, 1988); Joseph A. Schlesinger, "The New American Political Party," *American Political Science Review* (December 1985), pp. 1152–69; and David E. Price, *Bringing Back the Parties* (Congressional Quarterly Press, 1984).

45. Kayden and Mahe, *The Party Goes On*, p. 11 (emphasis added).

46. See Jackson, *Honest Graft*.

47. See *Congressional Quarterly Weekly Report* (November 19, 1988), pp. 3334–3342.

48. John C. Fitzpatrick, ed., *Writings of Washington*, vol. 35 (United States George Washington Bicentennial Commission, 1940), p. 227.

49. These proposals are drawn mainly from the report of the McGovern Commission, *Mandate for Reform: A Report of the Commission on Party Structure and Delegate Selection to the Democratic National Committee* (Commission on Party Structure and Delegate Selection, Democratic National Committee, 1970).

50. William J. Crotty, *Political Reform and the American Experiment* (Crowell, 1977), pp. 241–47, offers a full listing of the resolutions of the Democratic Charter conference. See also Crotty's *Party Reform* (Longman, 1983); and Ranney, *Curing the Mischiefs of Faction*. For a general discussion of party reform and its consequences, see Bryon E. Shafer, *Quiet Revolution* (Russell Sage Foundation, 1983); and Nelson W. Polsby, *Consequences of Party Reform* (Oxford University Press, 1983).

51. Senator McGovern resigned to run for the presidency before the commission had completed its work; he was replaced by Minnesota Congressman Donald Fraser, whose name became associated with the commission's final report.

52. Coalition for a Democratic Majority, Task Force on Democratic Party Rules and Structure, "Toward Fairness and Unity for '76," mimeographed (1974).

53. *Delegate Selection Rules for the 1984 Democratic National Convention* (Democratic National Committee, 1982), p. 6. For a history of majority and minority women at the Democratic national conventions, see *Democratic Women Are Wonderful: A History of Women at Democratic National Conventions* (National Women's Political Caucus, 1980).

54. See Stephen J. Wayne, *The Road to the White House*, 3d ed. (St. Martin's Press, 1988), and John H. Kessel, *Presidential Campaign Politics*, 3d ed. (Dorsey, 1988).

55. See Garry Orren and Nelson W. Polsby, *Media and Momentum* (Chatham House, 1987).

56. Delegates and Organizations (DO) Committee, *The Delegate Selection Procedures for the Republican Party*, Part II of the DO Committee Progress Report (Republican National Committee, 1971). For a history of majority and minority women at the Republican national conventions, see *Republican Women Are Wonderful: A History of Women at Republican National Conventions* (National Women's Political Caucus, 1980).

57. Ken Bode, "Miniconvention," *The New Republic* (December 23 and 30, 1978).

58. "Democrats Meet to Pump Life into Tired Ideas," *Congressional Quarterly Weekly Report* (June 19, 1982), pp. 1467–69; and "Democrats Develop Tactics; Laying Groundwork for 1984," *Congressional Quarterly Weekly Report* (July 3, 1982), pp. 1591–95.

59. Morton Kondracke, "The G.O.P. Gets Its Act Together," *The New York Times Magazine* (July 13, 1980), p. 44.

60. Xandra Kayden, "The Nationalizing of the Party System," in Michael J. Malbin, ed., *Parties, Interest Groups, and Campaign Finance Laws* (American Enterprise Institute for Public Policy Research, 1980), pp. 257–82, quoted on p. 276.

61. For a theoretical discussion of realignment, see Sundquist, *Dynamics of the Party System: Alignment and Realignment of Political Parties in the United States*.

62. William E. Leuchtenberg, *In the Shadow of FDR: From Truman to Reagan* (Cornell University Press, 1982).

63. Nelson W. Polsby, "Did the 1984 Election Signal Major Party Realignment?" *Key Reporter* (1985).

64. Rich Jaroslovsky and John E. Yang, "Polls Show No Clear Consensus among Voters about Direction New President Should Take," *Wall Street Journal* (November 9, 1988), p. A24, in an article analyzing the *Wall Street Journal/NBC* News exit polls.

65. Joseph A. Califano, "Tough Talk for Democrats," *The New York Times Magazine* (January 8, 1989), pp. 28–9, 38–43.

66. *The New York Times* (March 7, 1989), p. 14.

67. See Wattenberg, *The Decline of American Political Parties*; Everett Carll Ladd, Jr., "On Mandates, Realignments, and the 1984 Presidential Election," *Political Science Quarterly* (Spring 1985), p. 1.

68. Ruy A. Teixeira, "End of the Rainbow," *The New Republic* (April 3, 1989), pp. 11–12.

69. See, however, James Atlas, "Thatcher Puts a Lid On: Censorship in Britain," *The New York Times Magazine* (March 5, 1989), p. 36ff.

11

Public Opinion and Voting

In previous chapters we examined interest groups, mass movements, and political parties—all groups or organizations of Americans who feel strongly enough about certain issues to combine efforts in order to promote their views. We now turn to American politics at the most rudimentary level, and examine individual viewpoints that are at the heart of our democracy, as well as the sources of consensus and conflict.

The most dynamic aspect of politics involves the political opinions people hold and how they convert those opinions to votes on election day. The study of public opinion is the study of those issues to which the public reacts, whether individually or in groups. All of us have discussed politics or have argued our viewpoints with our families, friends, or fellow students. Public opinion polls are frequently used in newspapers and magazines, and some of us may even have been surveyed on political issues. Some of us voted in the last election, and some of us did not.

In this chapter we examine how we learn our political beliefs, the factors that affect how we form our opinions, and how these opinions translate to votes on election day.

How We Learn Our Political Beliefs

No one is *born* with political views. We learn them from many teachers. The process by which we develop our political attitudes and values is called **political socialization.** When does this process start? The answer is now clear: in childhood. For centuries some philosophers held that childhood was a time of innocence, even of ignorance, about the great world of politics outside the home. But now we know that—at least for Americans—political learning starts *in* the home, that children are not cut off from the world outside, and that we begin to form opinions at an early age.

"He's trustworthy, loyal, obedient, cheerful, and all that, but he leans to the left."

Drawing by Dedini: © 1988 The New Yorker Magazine, Inc.

The noted child psychologist Robert Coles studied youngsters in American homes and elsewhere. "Children are not empty vessels into which the content of culture is poured," Coles concluded. "They are as much makers as receivers."[1] American children typically show political interest by the age of ten or even earlier, and by the early teens their interest may be fairly high. Learning experiences gradually shape the values and beliefs we acquire in childhood. As children and teenagers we begin to influence other persons' attitudes, not only to be influenced by them.

Political beliefs often stem from religious, racial, gender, ethnic, and economic attitudes. The sources of these and other views are, of course, immensely varied in the pluralistic political culture of America. But we can make one generalization quite safely: We form our attitudes in groups—not only in the major groups described in Chapter 8, but especially in close-knit groups. When we identify closely with the attitudes and interests of a particular group, we tend to see politics through the "eyes" of that group.[2]

Does this mean that an active member of a strong group, such as a family, is a captive or even a "slave" to that group? Not necessarily. Each member of a group—even a child, as noted earlier—influences the group and is influenced by it. More important, group members usually bring their own emotions, feelings, memories, and resistances to their groups. The extent to which people are captive to groups is indeed a running argument among scholars from different disciplines. Sociologists tend to emphasize the pervasive influence of groups over their members. Certain schools of psychology focus more on the developmental influences within individuals that preserve their independence and individualism. Political scientists have traditionally tended to agree with the sociological approach.[3] Political psychologists seek to combine both approaches.

The considerable variation in the factors that influence our political beliefs produces a wide array of attitudes in society. However, children at an early age also adopt common values central to American society that provide continuity with the past and legitimate the political system. Young children know what country they live in, and loyalty to the nation develops early. Although details of our political system may still elude them, most young Americans acquire a reverence for the Constitution and for the concept of participatory democracy, as well as a respect for the most visible figure in our democracy, the president.

The two greatest influences in the complex socialization process, as well as in the creation of "good citizens," are the family and schools.

THE INFLUENCE OF THE FAMILY

Consider your own political socialization. You probably formed your picture of the world listening to your parents at breakfast or absorbing the tales your older brothers and sisters brought home from school. Perhaps you heard about the family past from grandparents, aunts, and uncles. Increasingly you, in turn, influenced your family, if only by bringing some of your own hopes and problems home from school. What we first learn in the family are not so much specific political opinions but rather basic attitudes that shape our opinions—attitudes toward our neighbors, other classes or types of people, and society in general. Some of us may rebel against the ways of the close little group in which we live, but most of us conform. The family is a link between the past and the present. It translates the world to us, but it does so on its own terms. And the terms are many and varied because our families may be extended or nuclear, two-headed, female single-headed, male single-headed, or communal.

Studies of high school students indicate a high correlation between parents and children in the political parties they support. And this relatively high degree of correspondence continues throughout life. Such a finding raises some interesting questions: Does the *direct* influence of parents create the correspondence? Or are parents and children equally influenced by living in the same social environment? The answer is *both*—and one influence often strengthens the other. A daughter of Democratic parents growing up in a small southern town of strong Democratic leanings will be affected by friends, by other adults, and perhaps by youngsters in a Sunday school group, all of whom may reinforce the attitudes of her parents.[4]

Does the mother or the father have greater influence over children's political opinions? It used to be assumed that the father had the dominant impact, perhaps because it was assumed that "politics is a man's business." But the balance of influence between the two parents seems to be surprisingly equal; it may even be tipped in the mother's favor. What happens when mother and father disagree politically? Children are likely to favor the party of the parent with whom they have had closer ties.

Still, older children sometimes do not share the views of their parents. Parental influence over their offsprings' party choices has been declining. What other forces are at work?

POLITICAL IMPACT OF THE SCHOOLS

Schools also mold young citizens' values and attitudes. At an early age schoolchildren begin to pick up specific political values and acquire basic attitudes toward our system of government. Education, like the family, prepares Americans to live in society. It is a massive enterprise in the United States, which is one of the leading countries in school enrollment.

Education develops political values that enhance citizenship and legitimate the political system. In their study of American history, schoolchildren are introduced to great American figures, important events in our past, and many of the ideals of our society. Other aspects of the student's experience, such as the daily Pledge of Allegiance, have important political significance. However, education also provides the skills necessary for citizens to formulate their own opinions and to make political choices.

Do school influences give young people greater faith in political institutions? Yes and no. A classic study examined relationships between community leaders' attitudes, civics texts, and students' attitudes in three Boston communities—one upper-middle class, one lower-middle class, and one working class. The school texts in all communities stressed the right of citizens to try to influence government, but the texts used in the upper-middle-class community were the only ones to stress politics as a *conflict* process for settling differing group demands. And only the upper-class community leaders underscored politics as a conflict process, and thus reinforced the lessons in the texts. Edgar Litt concluded that the lower-class students were being brought up to view government as a process carried out by institutions in the students' behalf, while the upper-class students were learning to understand the political process in realistic terms and to take part in that process on their own behalf.[5]

Another study found no evidence that the civics curriculum has a significant effect on the political orientations of the great majority of American high school students. Of course, students differed in their interest in politics, but this resulted not from taking (or not taking) civics or government courses, but from the students' backgrounds and life plans.

A voter registration drive outside a manufacturing plant in Virginia attracts many young, first-time voters.

How does *college* influence political opinions? One study suggested that students planning to attend college are more likely to be knowledgeable about politics, more in favor of free speech, and more likely to talk and read about politics. Perhaps reflecting national trends, campus conservatism and Republicanism increased in the 1980s.[6] Is this the influence of the professors, the curriculum, or the students? It is difficult to generalize. Parents sometimes fear that professors have too much influence on their offspring in school; professors are likely to be skeptical about this.

But why talk in generalities when you who are reading this book can make your own judgments? What has influenced *you* the most—a teacher, a book (possibly even a *textbook?*), movies such as "Rambo" or "Platoon," a particular course, the Bush/Dukakis debates, discussions with other students, the televised massacre of Chinese students in Beijing? And *how* have you been influenced?

IDEOLOGY

There is thought to be a good deal of consensus in the United States regarding basic democratic values. Both the family and schools help provide continuity with the past, as well as transmit some of its lessons to subsequent generations. The Constitution stands with only minor alterations, and 1988 marked two hundred years of free elections. Few would question the ideals of our democracy expressed in general terms, or the importance of the individual freedoms shielded by the Bill of Rights. However, Americans are a diverse people, and conflict, like consensus, is an important aspect of our national character. For example, it is said that American journalists write about things that people are interested in, and journalists perceive Americans "are very interested in any sort of confrontation."[7]

Americans demonstrate their basic individualism by getting together with others of similar interests to form groups that represent particular attitudes or political interests. Groups, as we have seen, are often highly issue-oriented or represent religious, ethnic, and other backgrounds. Perhaps the two largest political groups in society, loosely defined in terms of political opinions and encompassing many other smaller groups, are those that characterize themselves as liberals and conservatives (see Chapter 7).

Liberals and conservatives are not formal groups or movements of the kind we encountered in previous chapters. Liberalism and conservatism are both ideologies that focus on the function of liberty and equality in our society and the proper role of government. The terms describe opposing attitudes on a wide range of social, political, and economic issues.

Race is often a more important factor than wealth in dividing people on the conservative and liberal continuum, especially on social issues. Scholars are also fascinated by correlations with *gender*, that is, are women more liberal than men? But we find that although there are differences on some issues, wealth is still an important variable that influences why one is a liberal or a conservative.

OTHER INFLUENCES

Family and school are not the only influences on children and adolescents. The mass media also serve as agents of socialization by providing a link for individuals to adopt the values and behavior of others. For example, the mass media present information about our society, and when we watch, listen, and read, we find out what values and role models are considered important. As an example, pause to

"Well, dear, *I'm* a woman, and I'm mad for George Bush!"

Drawing by D. Reilly; © 1988 The New Yorker Magazine, Inc.

CHAPTER 11 / Public Opinion and Voting

reflect how television presents American motherhood. Television mothers are typically pretty, loving, happy, and wholesome. Consider Mrs. Huxtable ("The Bill Cosby Show"), Mrs. Cunningham ("Happy Days"), or Ann Romano ("One Day at a Time"). This positive image of motherhood is only one example of how social values and behavior patterns are passed from the "tube" along to the individual.[8] People are now born into a televised political and social atmosphere and live with the medium throughout their lives.

Religious and *ethnic* attitudes may also serve to shape opinions, both within and outside the family. Generally, Protestant families tend to be more conservative than Catholics on economic and welfare issues, whereas Jewish families tend to be more liberal on both economic and noneconomic issues than either Catholics or Protestants. Yet Protestants are quite variable on certain social issues, and all are subject to cross pressures. Evangelicals, who include a small percentage of Catholics but who are mainly made up of Protestants and many of the more fundamentalist sects, tend to be more socially conservative then nonevangelicals (see Table 11–1). Children in ethnic families learn of the heritage and customs of other countries; they may also learn of historical or current struggles so vividly that their attitudes toward current American foreign policy are affected.

What happens when a young person's parents and friends disagree? One study revealed that when high school students were *cross-pressured* in this way, they tended to go along with parents rather than friends on party affiliations; with friends rather than parents on the issue of the vote for 18-year-olds; and somewhere in between on their actual votes in presidential elections.[9]

Adults are not simply the sum of all these early experiences. Analysts are becoming more and more interested in the ways in which adults keep modifying their views *after* completing school or college. A major factor may be a harsh experience, such as a war or depression, that shocks people out of their existing attitudes. Most people, however, keep on growing as they move into new social situations and become exposed to new newspapers, television programs, and political leaders. Democrats or Republicans, for example, may shift their party affiliations in their adult years simply because the "party of their family and forebears" no longer responds to their attitudes and interests.[10]

TABLE 11–1
Evangelicals versus Nonevangelicals on Key Social Issues

ISSUE	EVANGELICALS	NONEVANGELICALS
Favor ban on all abortions	43%	31%
Oppose ERA	44	30
Oppose homosexual teachers in the schools	84	67
Favor prayer in schools	84	56

Source: Survey by the Gallup Organization, August 1980, in *Public Opinion* (April–May 1981), p. 25. Reprinted by permission of Elsevier Science Publishing Co., Inc. Copyright © 1981 by The Trustees of Columbia University.

The Fabric of Public Opinion

In 1983 one of the most dramatically heralded and widely watched programs in television history, "The Day After," was aired. This was a dramatization of the horror and desolation caused by a fictionalized nuclear war between the United States and the Soviet Union. Viewers would long remember the stunning scenes:

a university student paying little attention to a radio report about trouble abroad; the rapid escalation of hostility and crisis; the trails left by American nuclear rockets over the peaceful Kansas terrain; the mushrooming clouds after the Soviet attack; the overburdened hospitals; people dying from radiation sickness amid the rubble of their homes.

The program raised much controversy and high expectations. Supporters of President Reagan's defense program charged that it was designed to undermine confidence in the administration. Some labeled it "blatant political propaganda" that would stimulate pacifist efforts. Some nuclear-freeze advocates, on the other hand, expected the program to make people worry about their prospects of surviving a nuclear war, stimulate grass-roots participation in antiwar movements, make voters more dubious about Reagan's ability to stay out of a nuclear war, and perhaps even cause people to feel more "politically efficacious" in preventing war. At the very least, these observers expected the program to trigger a vast flood of antiwar mail to the White House and Capitol Hill.

What happened? None of these fears or hopes was realized. Confidence in President Reagan actually increased, in a kind of "rally-around-the-flag" phenomenon. The program did not increase expectations of a nuclear war or of people's ability to survive it; did not stimulate grass-roots peace activity; did not make people feel more politically efficacious; did not produce a torrent of mail to Washington. A team of George Washington University researchers concluded that, after years of discussion and controversy, Americans' political opinions about nuclear issues and policy were so intense and stable that no single television program, no matter how graphic, could markedly change those opinions.[11]

BENEATH THE SURFACE

This episode reminds us that to understand public opinion we must look beneath the surface features—beneath the more visible little waves and eddies—and study the underlying tides and currents that continuously shape people's attitudes and opinions. Because journalists and pollsters so often look only at the surface manifestations, their analyses and predictions may go awry. They speak, for example, of "public opinion," when in fact there are *many publics*, with differing sets of opinions.

Suppose a group of students at your school invites a notorious criminal to speak on crime and punishment. Think of the public opinion this incident creates. The "public" is actually made up of a number of publics—the rest of the student body (itself divided into subpublics), the administration, the faculty, the local townspeople, parents, and taxpayers. And all react in different ways. Some don't react at all; others shake their heads and promptly forget about it; others write to the governor or their state legislator. Many approve the invitation, but for conflicting reasons.

Translate the student episode into a national issue. A president's speech about labor legislation falls differently on the ears of union leaders and members, businesspeople, farmers, Democrats, and Republicans. When a senator calls for the end of government "handouts," many businesspeople applaud because they want lower taxes, but businesspeople *receiving* subsidies are critical. They may cry out that "the American public" wants a strong (that is, subsidized) merchant marine. Instead of one public opinion, we must think in terms of the diversity of opinion within a particular population. We must ask: What portion of the people is on one side of an issue? What portion on the other? Who feels strongly? Who does not? What, in short, makes up the fabric of public opinion?

CHARACTERISTICS OF PUBLIC OPINION

By looking beneath the surface we have seen that public opinion represents a complex world comprised of many publics with many different attitudes and opinions. How strongly do individuals hold to their opinions? Have they always taken this stance and, if so, for how long? Such important qualities in public opinion assume a number of forms, and we shall consider these next.

Intensity This factor produces the brightest and deepest hues in the fabric of public opinion. People vary greatly in the fervor of their beliefs. For example, some are mildly in favor of gun-control legislation, while others are mildly opposed; still others are fanatically for or against. Some people may have no interest in the matter at all; still others may not even have heard of the issue.

Latency Political opinions may exist merely as a *potential;* they may not have crystallized. But they can still be important, for they can be evoked by leaders and converted into action. Latent opinions set rough boundaries for leaders, who know that if they take certain actions, they will trigger the opposition or support of millions of people. For example, the abortion controversy has been marked with intense periods of demonstrations, by both anti-abortion and pro-choice supporters, when there appeared to be changes in governmental policy toward this issue. In April 1989, hundreds of thousands of pro-choice supporters marched on Washington as the Supreme Court prepared to review its 1973 abortion ruling, while "Right to Lifers" continued their rallies throughout the nation.

But latent opinions are also a great opportunity for leaders. If they have some understanding of people's real wants, needs, and hopes, they will know how to motivate and mobilize them in groups or parties, and draw them to the polls on election day.

Salience What causes opinions to be stable or fluid, intense or latent? A major factor is salience. By *salience* we mean the extent to which people feel issues relate to their own lives and connect with them. Your next-door neighbor may feel intensely about abortion or gun control, whereas you may get excited about drug abuse or unemployment. Most people are more concerned about personal issues like health and jobs and families than about national issues. But connect their personal concerns with national issues, and salience rises sharply.

Salience may change over time. During the depression of the 1930s Americans were mainly concerned about jobs, wages, and economic security. By the 1940s foreign issues came to the fore. In the 1960s problems of race and poverty aroused intense feeling. Vietnam and then Watergate riveted the people's attention. By the 1990s drugs, crime in the street, the quality of our schools, the dangers from foreign competition, threatening inflation, and danger to our environment had become our leading domestic concerns.

Consensus and polarization Considering the electorate as a whole, we may find some opinions on which most people agree or most people disagree. When at least 75 percent of a sample agree on an issue—for example, that schools should be racially integrated—a *consensus* exists on that issue. But on most issues, people are divided more evenly and in various proportions. When a large portion of each side feels very intensely about the issue, the voters are *polarized* on that issue. Vietnam a few years ago and abortion today are examples of polarizing issues.

Reprinted by permission of UFS, Inc.

TABLE 11–2
How Groups Differ on Abortion

	PERCENT SAYING ABORTION SHOULD BE . . .			KNOW SOMEONE WHO HAD ABORTION	SAY IT WAS RIGHT TO DO IN THAT CASE*
	LEGAL AS IT IS NOW	LEGAL ONLY IN CERTAIN CASES	NOT PERMITTED AT ALL		
TOTAL ADULTS	49	39	9	51	57
AGE					
18–29 years	56	35	8	66	58
30–44 years	49	40	9	64	53
45–64 years	45	39	12	36	63
65 and over	39	45	9	26	52
SEX AND MARITAL STATUS					
All men	51	38	8	48	60
Unmarried	60	31	7	55	65
Married	46	41	8	45	57
All women	47	40	11	54	54
Unmarried	54	37	7	60	60
Married	42	42	14	50	50
EDUCATION					
Less than high school	37	41	16	39	56
High school graduate	47	41	9	47	54
Some college	56	35	7	60	58
College graduate	58	35	5	67	61
RACE					
White	49	39	9	51	58
Black	45	42	13	54	51
RELIGION					
All Protestants	44	44	9	51	53
Religion very important	34	49	13	46	42
Not so important	61	36	1	59	69
All Catholics	48	36	13	45	55
Religion very important	28	49	22	41	32
Not so important	72	22	4	50	76
POLITICAL PHILOSOPHY					
Liberal	65	28	5	61	66
Moderate	54	38	6	54	61
Conservative	38	46	13	46	46
EXPOSURE					
Women who say they had an abortion	79	12	9	95	81
People who know:					
Someone who had an abortion	58	34	7	100	57
No one who had abortion	39	44	12	0	—

Source: The New York Times/CBS News Poll, *New York Times,* April 26, 1989, p. A25. Copyright © 1989 by The New York Times Company. Reprinted by permission.

* Percent of those knowing someone who had abortion

Based on interviews with 1,412 adults nationwide, conducted by telephone April 13 to 16, 1989.

STABILITY AND FLUIDITY

Some of our opinions change very little; they are part of our personalities, and we hang onto them all our lives. Other opinions may change slowly, even though the world is changing rapidly. This is especially true of loyalty toward our own groups and hostility toward competing groups. In general, people who remain in the same place, in the same occupation, and in the same income group throughout their lives tend to have more stable opinions. But people can carry their attitudes with them. Families who move from cities to suburbs often retain their big-city attitudes long after they have made their moves.

Still other kinds of public opinion can change dramatically, and almost overnight. Opposition to Roosevelt's foreign policies in 1941, for example, practically disappeared following Japan's attack on Pearl Harbor. Change often comes about as a result of *events*—a depression, a sharp increase in the crime rate, a natural event like a long drought in the Southeast, the taking of hostages by Iran, or a disaster such as the Alaskan oil spill in 1989.

Sometimes even the strongest and most stable opinions are subject to change. One of the "sacred cows" of American politics twenty-five years ago was nonrecognition of the People's Republic of China. A powerful lobby, composed of leaders of both major parties, carried on a militant campaign against admitting mainland China to the United Nations. Then President Nixon, who had earlier opposed the recognition of communist China, made his dramatic trip to the People's Republic. Soon he was following a policy of détente toward Beijing. Many Americans, responding to Nixon's leadership, shifted their own position toward friendlier relations with China. Then, with the massacre of students in Tienanman Square in June 1989, American attitudes toward the *government* of China hardened again.

Similarly, public attitudes toward the Soviet Union have changed noticeably in recent years in response to Mikhail Gorbachev's efforts at reform, several highly visible summits, and the INF treaty. Although Americans are still cautious toward the Soviet Union, many see an opportunity for compromise and a healthier relationship, unless the Soviets unexpectedly revert to some form of Stalinism.

How does one measure public opinion and public perceptions? Essential tools used by both political scientists and government leaders to assess the views of the American people are public opinion polls or surveys.

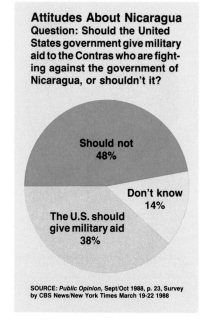

Attitudes About Nicaragua
Question: Should the United States government give military aid to the Contras who are fighting against the government of Nicaragua, or shouldn't it?

Should not 48%

Don't know 14%

The U.S. should give military aid 38%

SOURCE: *Public Opinion*, Sept/Oct 1988, p. 23, Survey by CBS News/New York Times March 19-22 1988

Copyright © 1988 by The New York Times Company. Reprinted by permission.

Taking the Pulse of the People

"What I want," Abraham Lincoln once said, "is to get done what the people desire to have done, and the question for me is how to find that out exactly." This question faces every politician, in office or out. Another president, Woodrow Wilson, once complained to the newspapers that they had no business saying that all the people out their way thought so and so: "You do not know, and the worst of it is, since the responsibility is mine, I do not know, what they are thinking about. I have the most imperfect means of finding out, and yet I have got to act as if I knew. . . ."

How can a politician find out what the people are thinking? The usual way, of course, is to look at election results. If Jane Brown wins over James Smith, presumably the people want what Jane Brown stands for. If Brown is an advocate of gun regulation and Smith is 100 percent against any form of control, evidently the majority of the people support some kind of firearms regulation. But we know that in practice things do not work this way. Elections are rarely fought on single issues, and candidates rarely take clear-cut stands. It is impossible, moreover, to separate issues from candidates. Did Bush win in 1988 because of economic conditions, his experience, opposition to Dukakis, or shifts in party support? The answer is that he won for some of these reasons, and for many others. Which brings us back to the question: What do the people want?

"One final question: Do you now own or have you ever owned a fur coat?"

Drawing by Stevens; © 1989 The New Yorker Magazine, Inc.

"Young man, I am no random sample."

© Punch/Rothco.

A woman being interviewed for a Gallup Poll survey. Scores of public opinion companies regularly ask Americans their views on policies, candidates, parties, and the general processes of government.

This is where public opinion polls come in. In this country public opinion polls are over a century old, but their main development has taken place in the last four decades. Today there are hundreds of polling organizations. We are usually aware of them because they constantly measure and report presidential popularity.

If a politician or a social scientist wants to measure opinion precisely, the first thing to be determined is the **universe,** the whole group whose opinion is being sought: every adult, all students on this campus, all students in the United States, all voters in city *X*. If the universe consists of only thirty units, the most precise way to find out what they think on a particular issue is to poll every one of them. But for most politically significant problems, this is impossible; so pollsters *sample* the universe in which they are interested. One way to develop a representative sample is to draw the sample completely at random. But this type of **random sampling** is impossible for most political surveys. Instead, we use census tracts (when these are available), which give the number of residences and their locations. By shuffling census tracts, drawing out the required number at random, and then sending interviewers to every fifth or tenth or twentieth house, we get a random sample. Another technique is random digit telephone dialing, in which a computer selects telephone numbers to be called at random.

A less reliable method is known as **nonprobability sampling.** This method is most frequently utilized by newspaper columnists or television stations who invite the public to write or call in to express their opinions. The reasons for its reduced accuracy are clear. Only those aware of the service and willing to take the initiative to respond are included in the sample.

The accuracy of the results depends largely on securing a sample representative of the total universe. If drawn properly, so that each unit in a universe has an equal chance to be included, a relatively small sample can provide accurate results. Beyond a certain point an increase in the size of the sample reduces only slightly the **sampling error,** the difference between the divisions found in the sample and those of the universe. People are often suspicious of results based on what appears to be a small sample. Is it really possible to generalize about the opinions of 250 million persons on the basis of a few thousand interviews? The answer is yes. In comparisons of demographic characteristics based on census results and those based on a carefully drawn sample, the differences in an exemplary study were very small. The census reported that 18.8 percent of the population were between the ages of 21 and 29, 23.5 percent were between 30 and 39, and 20.9 percent were between 40 and 49. The sample results were 18.4, 23.8, and 21.5, respectively.[12] Social scientists assume that if a sample chosen by modern techniques reproduces such characteristics of the population so precisely, it will reproduce the attitudes and opinions of the total population equally well.

ASKING THE RIGHT QUESTIONS IN THE RIGHT WAY

Pollsters have a lot of leeway in choosing questions. The average person may be concerned with problems that pollsters and political leaders know little about or have trouble defining. Another major difficulty is in phrasing questions. If you ask a question in a certain way, you can get the answer you want. Ask people if they favor labor unions and they may say no. But ask them if they favor organized efforts by workers to improve their well-being, and chances are more will answer yes. Also, trouble may arise in the alternatives a question presents. Clearly, asking a person "Do you favor the United States' entering a world government, or do you prefer our traditional independence in determining our own affairs?" is loading

CHAPTER 11 / Public Opinion and Voting

the dice. Polling organizations go to great efforts to make their questions fair; some conduct trial runs with differently worded questions.[13]

One way to avoid this difficulty is to ask a multiple-choice question. For example, a Gallup poll asked, "How far do you, yourself, think the federal government should go in requiring employers to hire people without regard to race, religion, color, or nationality?" The respondent could answer: all the way; none of the way; depends on type of work; should be left to state governments; or don't know. A variation of this type—the open-ended question—allows respondents to supply their own answers. They may be asked simply, "How do you think we should deal with the problem of air pollution by automobiles?" The answers to this type of question are, of course, hard to tabulate accurately.

Interviewing is a delicate task. Most interviews today are done by telephone, and the sincerity of a person's voice is important. For in-person interviews the interviewer's appearance, clothes, language, and way of asking questions may influence the replies. Inaccurate findings may result from the bias of the interviewer or from failure to do the job fully and carefully. And the persons interviewed may be the source of error. Respondents suspicious of the interviewer's motives may give false or confused answers. Their memories may be poor. To cover up ignorance they may give neutral answers or appear undecided. Or they may give the answers they think the interviewer would like them to give.

Polls may give a false impression of the firmness and intensity of opinion; as we have seen, opinions may be volatile and fleeting. Moreover, polls do not differentiate among people. They give equal weight to a follower and to an opinion leader who may in the end influence other voters. Studies suggest that public opinion is not like an iceberg; the movement of the top does not necessarily indicate the movement of the great mass underneath. The visible opinion among leaders and activists or among the more outspoken may be moving in a different direction—indeed, it may even be differently located—from that of the great mass of less-visible opinion. In short, it is far easier to measure the surface of public opinion than to gauge its depth and intensity.

INTERPRETING THE RESULTS

Election forecasting intrigues the average American; everyone likes to know in advance how an election will turn out. During the campaign pollsters submit regular "returns" on the standings of the candidates. On the whole, the record of the leading forecasters in "day-before" polling has been good, as Table 11–3 shows.

The most sensational slip came in 1948, during the presidential battle between President Truman and Governor Dewey. Most of the polls indicated that Truman was running far behind. However, in addition to the president, who denounced the polls as unreliable, a poll taken of Minnesota state fair-goers indicated that President Truman would carry that state. This poll gave President Truman 11,423 votes to Governor Dewey's 11,104.[14] Generally, the other pollsters stood pat on their predictions that Governor Dewey would win. Early in September one of them actually announced that the race was over. Gallup gave the president 44.5 percent of the popular vote in his final forecast, and Roper predicted 37.1 percent. Actually, Truman won 49.4 percent of the popular vote, and the pollsters were subjected to general ridicule. Their mistake lay in not selecting a representative sample of the universe, instead relying on nonprobability sampling to make their predictions. Since then they have been more careful in their methods and more cautious in making predictions.[15]

How You Ask It Shapes How You Answer It

Do you agree or disagree with this statement? The federal government should see to it that all people have adequate housing.

Agree: 55.1%
Disagree: 44.9%

Some people feel the federal government should see to it that all people have adequate housing, while others feel each person should provide his own housing. Which comes closest to how you feel about this?

Government responsible: 44.6%
Government not responsible: 55.4%

Some people feel each person should provide his own housing, while others feel the federal government should see to it that all people have adequate housing. Which comes closest to how you feel about this?

Government responsible: 29.5%
Government not responsible: 70.5%

Source: Adapted from Howard Schuman, *Questions and Answers in Attitude Surveys: Experiments on Question Form, Wording, and Context* (Academic Press, 1981), pp. 70–71.

Although election forecasting has generally been accurate, it has been known to miss the mark. The 1948 presidential election forecast is a classic example.

TABLE 11–3
Presidential Forecasts by the Pollsters (by percentage)

YEAR	ACTUAL DEM. VOTE	ROPER POLL	GALLUP POLL	HARRIS POLL
1944	53.8	53.6	53.3	—
1948	49.4	37.1	44.5	—
1952	45.+	43.0	46.0	—
1956	42.0	40.0	40.5	—
1960	49.4	47.0	49.0	—
1964	61.4	—	61.0	—
1968	42.7	—	40.0	43.0
1972	37.7	—	35.0	34.8
1976	51.0	51.0	46.0*	46.0*
1980	41.0	—	44.0	41.0
1984	41.0	45.0	41.0	44.0
1988	46.0	—	44.5	48

* In 1976 both Gallup and Harris said it was a "tossup" and refused to make a prediction. They also reported that more people than usual had not made up their minds. In 1988, the *Washington Post*/ABC poll predicted a 54% to 44% Bush win; *USA Today*/CNN predicted in its last poll a 55% to 44% Bush win.

Political polls have taken on increasingly significant functions in our political system. Candidates use polls to determine where to campaign, how to campaign, and even whether to campaign. In the years and months preceding a national convention, politicians watch the polls to determine who among the hopefuls has political appeal.

Surely polls are no substitute for elections. Faced with a ballot, voters must translate opinions into concrete decisions between personalities and parties. They must decide what is important and what is not. Democracy is more than the expression of views, more than a simple mirror of opinion; it is also *choosing* among leaders taking sides on certain issues, and among the governmental actions that may follow. Democracy is the thoughtful participation of people in the political process; it means using heads as well as counting them. Elections, with all their failings, at least establish the link between the many voices of "We the People" and the decisions of their leaders. So let us turn to the biggest, fairest, and most decisive "public opinion poll" of all—elections.

How We Vote: Electoral Patterns

Sometimes Americans are called fickle voters because they switch from party to party. Actually a majority of Americans stay with one party year after year, and their sons or granddaughters vote for the same party long after that. Politically, these voters are "set in their ways." Of course, there are still millions of so-called independent voters. They help make our elections the unpredicatble affairs they so often are. Still, even within the year-to-year variations, there are certain persistent elements:

1. *A pattern of sectional voting.* The South is the most famous example. The Democratic solidarity of the states that formed the Confederacy lasted over eighty years in presidential elections, and continues today in state and local elections. Republican sectionalism was not so clear-cut, but northern New

England and parts of the Midwest used to be dependable areas for the GOP. Vermont has given its electoral votes to the Democrats only once since the Civil War, and Maine only twice since 1912. More recently the South has become more Republican at the presidential level, but not so much at congressional or gubernatorial levels, and the Northeast more Democratic. Ronald Reagan won all of the South in 1984 as did Bush in 1988. Today the Republicans' "solid West" almost rivals the Democrats' "solid South" of old—at least for presidential elections.[16] Sectional patterns tend to be fuzzy and sometimes brief. Lately there has been much talk about the Sunbelt, the area from the southeastern states to California, which was considered to be the base of a rising American conservatism. But in many recent elections the divisions have tended to lie between the East and the West, and this pattern may not last long either. Sectional patterns often reflect very close election results within states, and those patterns can easily be changed by other influences.

2. *A pattern of national voting.* Traditional sectional alignments also give way to national trends. The Franklin Roosevelt administration, for example, ushered in a new age of Democratic popularity that affected even the most traditionally Republican areas, and Eisenhower's popularity accelerated the breakup of the solid South. States and sections are subject to a variety of local influences, but they cannot resist the great political tides that sweep the nation.

3. *A pattern of similar voting for different offices.* Sectional and national forces affect voting for different candidates and offices in the same election. A considerable number of voters usually vote a straight ticket; that is, they throw their support to every one of their party's candidates. If one candidate is an especially good vote getter, the party's whole slate may gain. This is the famous **coattail effect,** whose precise nature is one of the challenging problems in the study of political behavior. Evidently, popular presidential candidates like Roosevelt or Reagan have long coattails that help elect many other candidates on their party tickets. But congressional and state candidates may have helpful coattails too, and it is not easy to tell which candidates ride on whose coattails or just how important the relation is.[17] While George Bush carried 42 states in 1988, the Democrats still control Congress and most statehouses.

4. *A pattern of voting over time.* Great political tides seem to flow back and forth across the generations. Most presidential elections are **maintaining elections,** in which the existing pattern of partisan support persists. Long periods of maintaining elections are occasionally interrupted by **deviating elections,** which the "out" party wins because it has an especially attractive presidential candidate or because the existing administration has lost the nation's confidence. In such elections the underlying division of party support is not long disturbed, and the next election result returns to the old pattern. Occasionally, however, a **realigning election** brings a basic and long-lasting transformation of party loyalties. A whole new balance of parties comes into being, as it did in the 1930s.[18] Some have predicted that we are on the eve of another series of realigning elections and a historic realignment of the parties. (See Chapter 10.) Others see mainly a murky pattern of confusion and diminished party loyalties.

A traditional explanation for the great political tides is that they reflect economic conditions. A drop in business activity has often preceded a loss of congressional seats and then a presidential defeat for the party in power. But we cannot

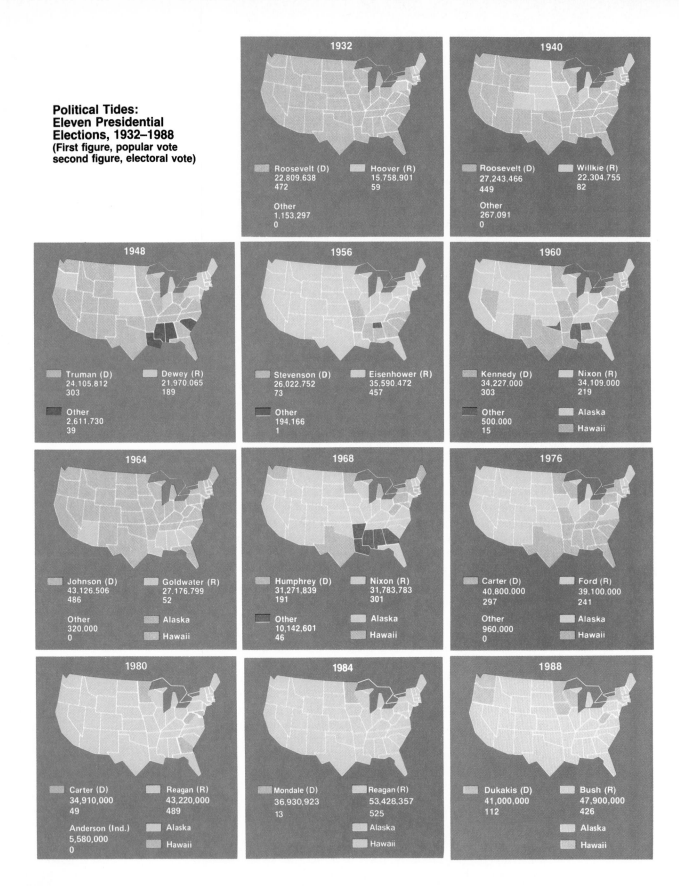

**Political Tides:
Eleven Presidential
Elections, 1932–1988**
(First figure, popular vote
second figure, electoral vote)

1932

Roosevelt (D)
22,809,638
472

Hoover (R)
15,758,901
59

Other
1,153,297
0

1940

Roosevelt (D)
27,243,466
449

Willkie (R)
22,304,755
82

Other
267,091
0

1948

Truman (D)
24,105,812
303

Dewey (R)
21,970,065
189

Other
2,611,730
39

1956

Stevenson (D)
26,022,752
73

Eisenhower (R)
35,590,472
457

Other
194,166
1

1960

Kennedy (D)
34,227,000
303

Nixon (R)
34,109,000
219

Other
500,000
15

Alaska

Hawaii

1964

Johnson (D)
43,126,506
486

Goldwater (R)
27,176,799
52

Other
320,000
0

Alaska

Hawaii

1968

Humphrey (D)
31,271,839
191

Nixon (R)
31,783,783
301

Other
10,142,601
46

Alaska

Hawaii

1976

Carter (D)
40,800,000
297

Ford (R)
39,100,000
241

Other
960,000
0

Alaska

Hawaii

1980

Carter (D)
34,910,000
49

Reagan (R)
43,220,000
489

Anderson (Ind.)
5,580,000
0

Alaska

Hawaii

1984

Mondale (D)
36,930,923
13

Reagan (R)
53,428,357
525

Alaska

Hawaii

1988

Dukakis (D)
41,000,000
112

Bush (R)
47,900,000
426

Alaska

Hawaii

282

be sure that business cycles *cause* political cycles. Psychological, political, traditional, sectional, international, and other forces may muddle the effect of economic factors.[19] It was not primarily economic issues but rather the sharply rising concern over slavery that precipitated the breakup of the Democratic-Whig party system in the 1850s. On the other hand, the Great Depression in the early 1930s was a main reason the GOP was toppled after its long period of supremacy. The Democrats won the elections of 1974 and 1976 in part because of public reaction against Watergate—a noneconomic issue. But the GOP won in 1980 at the presidential level on high inflation and interest rates, and in 1984 on having "whipped inflation" and revived the economy. In 1988, George Bush may have won in part because of his vow not to raise taxes.

Any patterns that do exist in American politics are rough and often blurred by unexplained variations. Indeed, patterns may exist for years and then disappear. Before the 1948 election a change in party control of Congress in an off-year election had regularly preceded a change in party fortunes in the following presidential election. But the Democrats, who lost control of Congress in 1946, won both houses and—to everyone's surprise, especially Thomas Dewey's and perhaps even Harry Truman's—the presidency in 1948. And despite a 1954 congressional victory for the Democrats, the GOP won the presidential election of 1956. Republicans won the White House again in 1988 after some setbacks in the 1986 congressional elections.

GROUP FACTORS IN VOTING

Despite the murkiness of voting tendencies, analysis of massive amounts of voting data has uncovered some basic patterns:

1. *Voting as members of family groups.* Most Americans vote the same way their families or friends or workmates vote. Although on election day they mark their ballots in private, voting is largely a group experience. The most homogeneous of all groups in terms of molding party identification, and ultimately the voting behavior of its members, is the family. Members of the family shape one another's attitudes (often unintentionally), and members of the same family are naturally exposed to similar economic, religious, class, and geographical influences.[20]

   As young adults move away from their families, they become members of many different groups. Some of their group memberships may mutually *reinforce* voting decisions. A young engineer who has grown up in a Democratically inclined family may marry a more conservatively inclined man, associate on her job with Republican executives, socialize a good deal with other members of a country club, and join a taxpayer's organization. The engineer will probably become a Republican, though she may long feel a Democratic tug from family years. Group memberships, however, may have conflicting impacts on a person's vote. A factory worker, for example, may associate with Democrats in his local union but with Republicans in his social group or ethnic organization. Such persons are said to be *politically cross-pressured* and sometimes take the easiest way out by not voting at all.

   Group influences on voting may change over time. Blue-collar workers, blacks, and some urban ethnic groups tended to rally round FDR and the New Deal in the 1930s, in part because they felt the Republican party had failed them and, in part because the New Deal Democrats recognized them

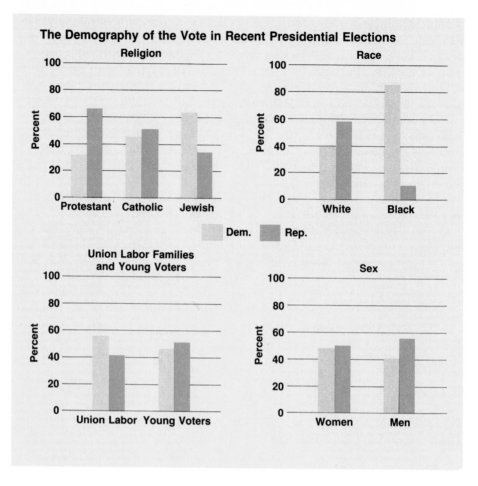

The Demography of the Vote in Recent Presidential Elections

Religion

Race

Union Labor Families and Young Voters

Sex

Dem. Rep.

Boston's Mayor Raymond Flynn addresses a group at City Hall.

and gave them concrete social and economic benefits. In the 1960s and 1970s newer issues—Vietnam, racial equality, law and order, Watergate—cut across group alignments, created new group allegiances to Republican candidates, and caused severe splits within the Democratic party coalition. Now, in the 1990s, economic, military, and such social issues as gender equality, abortion, and gay/lesbian rights have come to the fore, with different impacts on groups.

2. *Voting as members of parties.* In this century most voters have identified with one or the other of the major parties. Some support their party almost automatically, no matter who the candidate or what the issues.[21] Voting by party has been declining in recent decades, as discussed below, and continued to do so in most recent elections.

3. *Voting in terms of class, occupation, and income.* For the last several decades a strong relationship has existed among those three influences. However we define social class—by occupation, income, or social identification—the higher the class, the stronger the tendency toward Republicanism.

4. *Voting by religion.* In the 1960s "religion remained a potent source of political cleavage in the United States . . . the single most important of four predictors of political party identification, and was comparable to, if not more important than, the *combined* effects of education, occupation, and income."[22] John Kennedy's campaign for the presidency tended to align Catholics even more

with the Democrats, and Protestants with the GOP. In 1984 religious issues experienced another resurgence; emphasis on issues such as abortion and prayer in the classroom led Catholics and Protestants to vote Republican, by substantial margins. These results, heavily favoring Reagan, came despite opposition from minister's son Walter Mondale and from Geraldine Ferraro, a Catholic. In 1988, Pat Robertson, a Christian TV evangelist, ran competitive races in the Republican primaries against George Bush and Robert Dole.

Women have become a majority of the American electorate. Registration drives like this stress the importance of using that new-found clout.

5. *Voting by race. Racial* voting has been a polarizing force. During the late nineteenth century northern blacks voted heavily Republican, and southern whites almost exclusively Democratic—a carry-over from the Civil War. During Roosevelt's New Deal and Truman's Fair Deal, blacks began shifting over to the Democratic party and to the civil rights policies that party was supporting. For the same reason, southern whites began to move toward the Republican party. Blacks today are probably the most strongly Democratic of all groups. They were crucial to Carter's victory in 1976. This, in part, influenced Jesse Jackson's decisions to run for the Democratic nomination in 1984 and 1988. The support Jackson received earned black Americans an enhanced voice with the party leadership, while the shift of southern whites to the Republican party has continued.

6. *Voting by sex or gender.*[23] Women as a whole voted a bit differently from men as a whole in the 1980s; women were more likely to vote for Carter, men for Reagan and Bush. Still, in absolute numbers more women *and* men voted for Reagan. The last time such a "gender gap" occurred was in the 1950s, when women voted for Ike at higher rates than men. In terms of values, women evaluated President Reagan more negatively than did men on issues of war and peace; and these negative evaluations were related to women's greater tendency to vote against Republicans and for Democrats.[24]

The "gender gap" illustrates how people's political *behavior* can differ from their political *attitudes*. During 1984 polls reported that fewer women than men approved of Reagan's stands on economic, social and defense issues. Especially with the *first* woman nominee for vice-president on the Democratic party ticket, it was expected that women would tilt heavily toward Mondale in the election. In the voting, however, Reagan gained 56 percent of the votes cast by women—an increase of seven percentage points over 1980.[25] These results suggest that the women's vote will not be won merely by having a woman on the national ticket.[26]

7. *Voting by age.* From 1936 until recently, the younger you were the less likely you were to vote Republican; young voters who came to maturity after the Depression and the New Deal identified with Democrats. But youth, unlike race or religion, is fleeting, and as such is a less reliable voting indicator. Prior to 1980, new voters tended to be Democratic; in 1984, however, they were Ronald Reagan's strongest age group.[27] Young voters continued to provide valuable support for George Bush in 1988.

PARTISANS AND INDEPENDENTS

Plainly, party affiliation is a key factor in how people vote, yet voting is also heavily influenced by opinions on major issues, evaluations of the candidates, and the impact of events at home and abroad. The stronger people's party feeling, however, the more likely that they will look at issues and candidates through their "party lens," that is, fit those factors into the overriding party factor. Those who are worried about party influence, however, can relax, because that influence seems to be declining. Moreover, parties do not reflect totally basic social, economic, geographical, or religious differences; thus there is no "party of the poor."

Is this "party fuzziness" desirable? Some favor a situation in which neither major party can claim a monopoly of any group, because this keeps the parties from reinforcing and exaggerating differences.[28] Some party activists disagree. Parties with more clear-cut electoral support might supply national leaders with the kind of mandate they need to offer a firmer sense of direction to the American people.

In any event, although partisans are still important, independents are on the rise. Both groups are worth further examination.

Who are the partisans? We measure party identification by asking people, "Generally speaking, do you usually think of yourself as a Republican, a Democrat, an Independent, or what?" Those who name one of the two major parties are then asked, "Would you call yourself a strong Republican/Democrat or a not very strong Republican/Democrat?" By 1988, strong and weak Democrats comprised less than 40 percent of the adult population, Republican identifiers accounted for about 35 percent, and independents comprised about 28 percent.[29]

Who are the independents? Almost a third of the voters can be classified as unaffiliated or independent, but "independent" is a tricky term. Some persons are called independent because they are party switchers; they cross and recross party lines from election to election. Some are ticket splitters; at the same election they vote for candidates of different parties.[30] Some are independents because they *feel* independent. Some call themselves independents because they think it is socially more respectable, but actually they vote for one party. One study indicates that younger voters with above-average incomes and college educations tend to be more independent than other voters, but the independent vote otherwise is rather evenly distributed throughout the population.

Many who identify themselves as independents have made a conscious decision to be independent of either party; they are not merely apathetic. This category grew from almost 21 percent in 1964 to a peak of almost 29 percent in 1976, and dropped to about 24 percent in 1980. By 1988 the percentage was up a bit to 28 percent. On the other hand, some independents have no partisan preference. Although they are aware of the party system, they are much more attuned to *individual candidates*. These nonpartisans have grown from 2 percent to almost 10 percent of the electorate.[31]

Is the independent voter the more informed voter? There has been heated debate over this question, yet much of it is fruitless. The answer depends on what kind of independent we are talking about. If independents are defined as those who fail to express a preference between parties, the independent voter tends to be less well informed and less likely to vote. But if we mean those who switch parties between elections, we find some who are highly informed and who carefully pick and choose at the polls. The independent is really not all that different from the partisan. Independents seem to be neither more nor less cynical about the "system" than party supporters. Most independents seem to vote as regularly for one or the other party as do those who identify with a party. Still, in a nation in which parties seem to be losing many of their old-time supporters, candidates seek to appeal to the "independent" voter, however defined.

Nonvoting: Who Doesn't Vote? and Why?

In 1988 only 50.16 percent of the eligible voters cast their ballots in the presidential election, marking the lowest voter turnout since 1924. In 1960, turnout peaked at 62.8 percent, but it has since declined almost steadily to its recent low.[32] Although the campaign dominates television and other media for months, almost 90 million Americans have failed to vote in recent presidential elections; the nonvoting figures are even higher for congressional, state, county, and local elections.

Americans, who like to consider their country as a democratic model, have one of the poorest voter-turnout records of all the industrial democracies.[33] A few years ago, when one hundred nations were ranked on turnout, the United States was *twelfth from the bottom*. Historically, voter turnout in the United States has never approached the levels found in many other democracies (often over 90 percent in Austria and Sweden).

Why the recent concern? Because, following important legislative changes since 1960, turnout should actually have gone up rather than fallen over 10 percent. With the passage of the Voting Rights Act in 1965, state and local barriers to registration that kept blacks and other minorities from voting were removed. Registration among blacks has increased considerably since then, and women, another historically underrepresented group, have increased their voting levels to the point where, in 1988, turnout among women actually exceeded that of men. Finally, levels of education and real income, both shown to have a positive effect on voting, rose during this period.

If almost half of all eligible voters are not participating in elections, they, too, are expressing an opinion we must examine. Who fails to vote? Why? Is low voter turnout a serious problem in a democracy? If so, what can be done about it?

WHY IS TURNOUT SO LOW?

The simplest explanation of low voter turnout is sheer apathy. It is easy to criticize people as "just too lazy to vote." If people do not want to vote, a columnist wrote, "to hell with them—serves them right." The problem is not that simple. Of course some people just do not care; they would not go to the polls if King Kong were running against Snow White. But the vast majority of Americans are not like that. Paradoxically, we compare favorably with other nations in political interest and awareness,[34] but we fail to convert these qualities into votes, for a variety of *institutional* and *political* reasons.

One explanation for our low voter turnout is that the costs of voting are higher in the United States than in other industrialized democracies, while the perceived benefits are lower.[35] In our system, individuals face tough institutional obstacles to voting and must make sense out of a narrow range of political alternatives that do not necessarily meet their interests. In the United States the two major parties, having drawn closer together on many issues, do not provide enough of a choice for many individuals to give them a stake in voting.

The main institutional block is the voter registration requirement, along with absentee ballot complications. In most other democracies the state, along with the political parties, assumes responsibility for registering its citizens. While

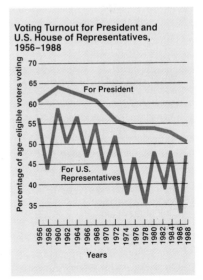

Voting Turnout for President and U.S. House of Representatives, 1956–1988

poll taxes, literacy tests, and other such obstacles were outlawed in 1965, registration can still be elusive and complex. In a number of states the cutoff date for registration is early, sometimes fifty to sixty days before the election. Few states allow registration on election day, and voters are thus forced to plan ahead. In some states, registration is conducted only at the county courthouse or another single location, requiring voters to search for it and often travel a great distance to register. Obtaining and casting an absentee ballot can also be a hassle, and is often only allowed for out-of-state voting, thus excluding the elderly or others who have trouble getting to the polls for voting.

Two other key explanations are political and psychological factors. In other large industrialized democracies the political parties shoulder much of the burden of persuading people to vote. American parties are too weak to take on this task; in particular, the Democratic party, which has an enormous stake in a heavy voter turnout from lower-income Americans, talks big but very rarely does the job. Another factor is the absence of real competition in many election contests. Americans like a good close fight in politics, just as they do in sports, but in one-party districts election outcomes are known far in advance.

Finally, there is a strong psychological factor. Some Americans believe it makes no difference who wins. They think there is no real choice between candidates or parties; that winning candidates and parties fail to carry out their promises; and that the same people run government no matter who wins.

During the 1988 election campaign, one critic pointed out that no party spoke to the interests of the lower classes. The political debate in the United States has been mostly silent on class issues, with the Democratic party fearful of appearing too liberal economically.[36] Many people are not apathetic toward politics; on the contrary, they contend American politics and government are apathetic toward *them*.[37]

A final factor in the decline in voting since the 1960s is the ratification of the 26th Amendment in 1971, which lowered the voting age from 21 to 18. The youngest voters, those from 18–24, have a poorer voting record than any other age group. Turnout in 1972 fell to 55.2 percent from 60.9 percent in 1968.[38]

WHO FAILS TO VOTE?

Nonvoting might not be a serious problem if those who do vote were a cross section of those who do not. But this is not the case. Demographically, nonvoters are different from voters. The extent of voting varies widely among different types of voters. Race and ethnicity help produce different levels of voting, with blacks in general turning out at lower rates than whites. The poor and less educated are also more likely to shun the polls on election day. Education seems by far the most important influence on voting, regardless of race and ethnicity: "Education increases one's capacity for understanding complex and intangible subjects such as politics," according to one study, "as well as encouraging the ethic of civic responsibility. Moreover, schools provide experience with a variety of bureaucratic problems, such as coping with requirements, filling out forms, and meeting deadlines."[39] The data are convincing: Those who finish elementary school are more likely to vote than those who do not; those who graduate from high school tend to turn out more than those who finish elementary school; and those who graduate from college turn out more than those who graduate from high school. Only black men and women with less than eighth-grade educations seem to contradict this finding.

"I'm undecided, but that doesn't mean I'm apathetic or uninformed."

Drawing by C. Barsotti; © 1980 The New Yorker Magazine, Inc.

Why People Don't Vote	
Did not register	38%
Do not like the candidates	14
Are not interested in politics	10
Have no particular reason	10
Are sick or disabled	7
Are not U.S. citizens	4
Are new residents in area	4
Are away from home	3
Cannot leave job	2
Have no way to get to polls	2
Other reasons	6

Source: Data from U.S. Department of Commerce and the Gallup Poll, 1980.

Income and *age* are also important factors. Those with higher family incomes are more likely to vote than those with lower incomes. Income, of course, corresponds to type of occupation, and those with higher-status careers are more likely to vote than those with lower-status jobs. The older you are (unless you are *very* old and perhaps infirm), the more likely you are to vote. Persons 18 to 24 years of age have a poor voting record; so do persons over 70. Women's increased turnout generally is attributed to higher levels of education and employment; black women in particular are influenced by their party identification and by feminism.[40]

But the most important fact remains: the poor, the uneducated, and the homeless are still seriously underrepresented in the voting booth. More specifically, according to the conclusions of a study based on a wide sample, the "least educated, the very poor, Puerto Ricans, Chicanos, and people who moved in the year before the 1974 election are all underrepresented by between one-third and one-half. In addition, people without a high school diploma or below the median income, those who live in the South, the young, the elderly, the unemployed, the unmarried, and blacks show voting strength reduced by at least 15 percent. On the other hand, college graduates are overrepresented by nearly one-third, as are people who earn more than $25,000."[41] The study added that the strength at the polls of government employees was 24 percent *greater* than their share of the population.

Why do low-income people vote in fewer numbers than the wealthy, especially when the poor would seem to have such a stake in government? For several reasons: they have less sense of involvement and confidence; they feel less of a sense of control over their political environment; they feel at a disadvantage in social contacts; and their social norms tend to deemphasize politics. Thus, nonvoting is not accidental; it is part of a larger political and psychological environment that discourages political activity.[42]

Black voting patterns, especially in the South, show another side of the voting/nonvoting equation. Since 1965 southern black voters have been turning out at higher and higher rates, but they are still not voting at the same rates as whites. Apathy accounts for only a small part of nonvoting. In fact, strong black political organization increases black voter turnout, and perception of black electoral gain probably boosts turnout.[43] But a primary factor in the South is the weakness of black political organizations. Elsewhere, the elections of Wilson Goode of Philadelphia and Tom Bradley of Los Angeles seem to be examples of the effect of organization and perceived stake on black voter turnout.

NONVOTING—HOW SERIOUS IS IT?

Some political scientists contend that nonvoting is not a critical problem. "Nonvoting is not a social disease," contends a noted student of politics. He points out that legal and extralegal denial of the vote to blacks, women, Hispanics, persons over 18, and other groups has now been outlawed, so nonvoting is *voluntary.*[44] He quotes the late Senator Sam Ervin as saying: "I don't believe in making it easy for apathetic, lazy people to vote."

Those who argue that nonvoting *is* a critical problem cite, above all, the "class bias" of those who do vote. That is, the social makeup and attitudes of nonvoters are significantly different from those of voters and hence greatly distort the representative system. Nonvoters tend to be the low-income, blue-collar, less educated, "less white" Americans, as noted earlier. The "very poor, those with incomes below $5,000 a year, have about two-thirds the representation among

Political Participation and Awareness in America in the Late 1980s	
Vote in presidential elections	50%
Vote in congressional elections	35–40
Know name of congressional representative	36
Know names of both U.S. senators	29
Occasionally contact local officials	28
Vote in local elections	10–30
Occasionally attend public meetings	19
Occasionally contact federal or state officials	16
Know name of state senator	13
Give money to candidate or party	13
Know name of state representative	12

Source: Selected polls, including Gallup, *Denver Post* Poll, University of Michigan, and *The New York Times.*

Xavier L. Suarez, the first Cuban-born mayor of Miami, Florida. The Cuban-American community of south Florida is a major influence in local politics and has voted solidly for Republican candidates in recent elections.

voters than their numbers would suggest." Thus the people who need help from the government most lack their fair share of electoral power to obtain it. And, it is argued, this situation is growing worse.[45]

Some reject this class bias argument. They admit that nonvoters are demographically different, but they cite polls that show nonvoters' attitudes are not much different from voters. One study compared the party identification of voters with that of all Americans and found that the proportion of Democrats was nearly identical: 51.4 percent of all citizens and 51.3 percent of voters, while Republicans were slightly overrepresented—36 percent of citizens and 39.7 percent of voters.[46] All other political differences are considered to be much smaller than this 3.7 percent gap. Further, voters were not found to be "disproportionately hostile" to social welfare policies. Another study asserts that the typical nonvoter is no longer just poor or a high school dropout, but is dispersed among socioeconomic and other categories. In 1960, 72 percent of nonvoters had less than a high school education, and 60 percent were poor. By 1980 the figures were 39 percent and 44 percent respectively.[47]

Those who see a class bias defend their observations. Such polls, they say, reflect "the underdevelopment of political attitudes resulting from the historic exclusion of low-income groups from active electoral participation."[48] In short, part of the problem of low-income, less educated people is their failure to be conscious of their real interests. Dynamic leadership or strong party organization, or both, would not only attract the poor to the polls but make clear their "class grievances and aspirations."

What effect might increased voter turnout have in national elections? It would make a difference, since there are partisan differences between different demographic groups. Schattschneider, while acknowledging that no political system could achieve 100 percent participation, points out that the entire balance of power in the political system could be overturned if the large nonvoter population decided to vote.[49] However, others argue that the difference may not be as pronounced as some may hope. Studies show that changes in registration laws would account for a 9 percent increase in voter turnout but only 0.3 percent increase for the Democratic party.[50]

OVERCOMING BARRIERS TO VOTING

The main target is the registration hurdle. Representatives from such organizations as the League of Women Voters and the National Association for the Advancement of Colored People have joined to challenge archaic registration laws and procedures. They have urged the use of government offices as registration places. They also favor registration by postcard. If government offices can be used to register young people for the draft, they say, why cannot they be used to register people to vote?

Registration simplifiers, however, have run into countless obstacles. Even some Democratic party officials and office holders, who would appear to have a profound interest in broadening the vote, have been resistant. Some moderate Democrats, it is alleged, fear an influx of poor voters who might "radicalize" the party.[51] The Republican party, on the other hand, appears not to fear an "influx from the right." The GOP cooperated with efforts of the Moral Majority, the Assemblies of God, and thousands of church groups to register people, bring voters to the polls, and help Ronald Reagan retain the presidency in 1984. George Bush also courted the right, though a bit more cautiously than his predecessor.

"Next time I want to vote *for* someone"

© *1988 by Herblock in The Washington Post.*

FROM OPINIONS TO VOTES

What about those who *do* vote? How does public opinion translate into individual votes, which translate into elected office holders? Let us look first at voting for presidents. Even the most sophisticated studies have concluded that the opinion most directly related to that decision is *which candidate the voter likes best*. The sophistication comes in explaining how voters come to like one candidate better than another. As we have noted, the main influences are threefold: party identification, attitudes on issues, and candidates' perceived integrity or competence as well as their past performance.

One's party identification has a lot to do with one's evaluation of the candidates—unless the favored party's candidate is assessed negatively on performance or on personal qualities. But when voters have no party identification or when they do see differences between the candidates, they tend to vote for the candidate who comes out best in their assessment of personal qualities and issues.[52] That was the plight of Democratic presidential candidates in the 1980s.

Several studies have found a relationship between "out" party gains (and "in" party losses) in congressional seats and the state of the economy,[53] but only recently have political scientists been able to locate the sources of this effect in individual voters' decision making. Voters tend to vote against candidates of the "in" party, even including incumbents, if the voters perceive that they themselves have experienced a decline or standstill in their own personal financial situations.[54] But a more recent study finds that this relationship is based on the voters' socioeconomic status. Lower-status voters tend to judge candidates on the basis of the voters' personal financial condition. Upper-status voters, who personally tend to suffer less when economic conditions decline, are more likely to watch the national performance of the economy through the newspapers and to judge candidates on that basis.[55]

Analysts of voting behavior have engaged in heated debates about the role of issues and opinions in voters' decisions. George Bush was elected even though some of his supporters preferred Mike Dukakis's issue positions. Bush's mandate was a mixture of support for his economic and defense initiatives combined with his reassuring personality. It was also, in part, a vote of no confidence in Dukakis and the national Democratic Party.

In the 1990's, new issues have come to the forefront as Americans' perceptions of future needs changed. A more pessimistic view of the future prompted increased support for social issues, such as education and the environment.[56] Inflation and security were no longer seen as the primary challenges confronting the United States.

When does a problem become a voting issue? Although opinion polls may indicate which issues the public considers most important in a campaign, a problem becomes a voting issue only when people believe the candidates differ significantly in their approach or in their ability to solve it.[57] Inflation, the greatest concern in 1980, was not only the biggest perceived threat, but was also a voting issue as Americans overwhelmingly favored a new approach in government. In 1988, no issue appeared to be clearly more important than any other.

"Would you say Attila is doing an excellent job, a good job, a fair job, or a poor job?"

Drawing by Chas. Addams; © 1982 The New Yorker Magazine, Inc.

Below are the results of a poll asking Americans what they considered the most urgent problems facing this nation.

ECONOMIC
Unemployment/recession	8%
Budget deficit	8%
The economy	7%
Poverty/hunger	4%
Homelessness	3%
Inflation/high prices	2%
Foreign trade	2%

SOCIAL
Drugs	16%
Morality	4%
AIDS	3%
Crime	2%

GOVERNMENT
The government	3%

FOREIGN
Fear of war	5%
International problems	4%
Arms control	3%

What are the implications of this data for Democratic and Republican party strategies, for voter turnout, and for party platforms?

Source: Survey by the Gallup Organization and CBS News/New York Times, May 9–12, 1988, *Public Opinion* (July/August 1988), p. 35. Reprinted with permission of the American Enterprise Institute for Public Policy Research.

Summary

1. Public opinion is not a solid unit but a loose and complex combination of views and attitudes individuals acquire through various influences from childhood on. It takes on qualities of stability, fluidity, intensity, latency, consensus, or polarization—all closely affected by people's feelings about salience of opinions to themselves.

2. Better-educated, middle-aged, and more party- and group-involved people tend to vote more; the poor tend to vote the least.

3. Voting tends to be higher in national elections than in state and local ones, and higher in executive than legislative elections.

4. Sectional, cyclical, party, economic, and other patterns can be found in American voting behavior, but these patterns are cloudy and subject to change.

5. We have fairly reliable methods for roughly measuring people's opinions at a given time, provided the polling is done carefully and responsibly, using tested procedures and safeguards.

6. People decide how to vote on the basis of complex calculations involving their party identifications, as well as comparative assessments of the candidates on the issues, the candidates' past performances, and their personal qualities.

Further Reading

HERBERT ASHER. *Polling and the Public* (Congressional Quarterly Press, 1988).

SANDRA BAXTER and MARJORIE LANSING. *Women and Politics: The Invisible Majority* (University of Michigan Press, 1983).

DORIS GRABER. *Processing the News: How People Tame the Information Tide* (Longman, 1984).

HARRY HALLOWAY and JOHN GEORGE. *Public Opinion: Coalitions, Elites and Masses* (St. Martin's Press, 1979).

V. O. KEY, JR. *Public Opinion and American Democracy* (Alfred A. Knopf, 1961).

W. RUSSELL NEUMAN. *The Paradox of Mass Politics* (Harvard University Press, 1986).

MICHAEL B. PRESTON, LENNEAL J. HENDERSON, JR., and PAUL PURYEAR, eds. *The New Black Politics: The Search for Political Power* (Longman, 1982).

JERRY L. YERIC and JOHN R. TODD. *Public Opinion: The Visible Politics*, 2nd ed. (Peacock, 1989).

See also *Public Opinion Quarterly; The Journal of Politics; The American Political Science Review.*

Notes

1. Robert Coles, *The Moral Life of Children* (Atlantic Monthly Press, 1986); and Robert Coles, *The Political Life of Children* (Atlantic Monthly Press, 1986).

2. Pamela Johnston Conover, "The Influence of Group Identifications on Political Perception and Evaluation," *Journal of Politics* (August 1984), pp. 760–85; and Henry E. Brady and Paul M. Sniderman, "Attitude Attribution: A Group Basis for Political Reasoning," *American Political Science Review* (December 1985), pp. 1061–78.

3. Shawn W. Rosenberg, "Sociology, Psychology, and the Study of Political Behavior: The Case of the Research on Political Socialization," *Journal of Politics* (May 1985), pp. 715–31.

4. See Russell J. Dalton, "Reassessing Parental Socialization: Indicator Unreliability versus Generational Transfer," *American Political Science Review* (June 1980), pp. 421–31.

5. Elizabeth Leonie Simpson, *Democracy's Stepchildren* (Jossey-Bass, 1971); M. Kent Jennings and Richard G. Niemi, *The Political Character of Adolescence* (Princeton University Press, 1974); Stanley Allen Renshon, "Personality and Family Dynamics in the Political Socialization Process," *American Journal of Political Science* (February 1975), pp. 63–80; and Frances Fitzgerald, *America Revised* (Atlantic-Little, Brown, 1979).

6. Alexander W. Astin et al., *The American Freshman: National Norms for Fall 1984* (UCLA Graduate School of Education, 1984), pp. 3–4.

7. Comment made by Jack Nelson, *Los Angeles Times* Washington bureau chief, at "The People, the Press and Politics—Discussion on the Media," sponsored by *The Los Angeles Times* and *Times Mirror,* January 19, 1988.

8. Joseph R. Dominick, *The Dynamics of Mass Communication* (Random House, 1987), p. 41.

9. Suzanne Koprince Sebert, M. Kent Jennings, and Richard G. Niemi, "The Political Texture of Peer Groups," in Jennings and Niemi, *The Political Character of Adolescence,* p. 246.

10. Charles H. Franklin, "Issue Preferences, Socialization, and the Evolution of Party Identification," *American Journal of Political Science* (August 1984), pp. 459–78.

11. William C. Adams et al., "Before and After 'The Day After': A Nationwide Survey of a Movie's Political Impact." Paper presented at the Annual Meeting of the International Communication Association, San Francisco, May 27, 1984; and Stanley Feldman and Lee Sigelman, "The Political Impact of Prime-Time Television: 'The Day After,'" *Journal of Politics* (May 1985), pp. 556–78.

12. Samuel A. Stouffer, *Communism, Conformity, and Civil Liberties* (Doubleday, 1955), p. 238.

13. See Donald J. Devine, "The Problem of Question Form in Describing Public Opinion," *Polity* (Spring 1980), pp. 522–34.

14. *The New York Times* (Sept. 10, 1948), p. 17.

15. See Harold Mendelsohn and Irving Crespi, *Polls, Television, and the New Politics* (Chandler, 1970), chap. 2.

16. Important works on southern politics are Earl Black and Merle Black, *Politics and Society in the South* (Harvard University Press, 1987); and Louis Seagull, *Southern Republicanism* (Wiley, 1975). A provocative sectional theme is found in Kirkpatrick Sale, *Power Shift: The Rise of the Southern Rim and Its Challenge to the Eastern Establishment* (Vintage, 1976).

17. For an example of some of the complex factors at work, see Barbara Hinckley, "Incumbency and the Presidential Vote in Senate Elections: Defining Parameters of Subpresidential Voting," *American Political Science Review* (September 1970), pp. 36–42. See also Gary C. Jacobson, "Presidential Coattails in 1972," *Public Opinion Quarterly* (Summer 1976), pp. 194–200; Frank B. Feigert, "Illusions of Ticket-Splitting," *American Politics Quarterly* (October 1979), pp. 470–88; Raymond E. Wolfinger, Steven J. Rosenstone, and Richard A. McIntosh, "Presidential and Congressional Voters Compared," *American Politics Quarterly* (April 1981), pp. 245–56.

18. These three types of elections are defined and discussed in Angus Campbell, Philip E. F. Converse, Warren E. Miller, and Donald E. Stokes, *Elections and the Political Order* (Wiley, 1966). See also Walter Dean Burnham, *Critical Elections and the Mainsprings of American Politics* (Norton, 1970).

19. For a noneconomic cyclical theory of presidential elections, see James David Barber, *The Pulse of Politics* (Norton, 1980).

20. See Richard E. Dawson and Kenneth Prewitt, *Political Socialization* (Little, Brown, 1969). For a specific example of an intrafamily relationship, M. Kent Jennings and Richard G. Niemi, "The Division of Political Labor between Mothers and Fathers," *American Political Science Review* (March 1971), pp. 69–82.

21. The Center for Political Studies, University of Michigan, periodically measures dimensions of party support. See also Philip E. Converse, *The Dynamics of Party Support: Cohort-Analyzing Party Identification* (Sage Library of Social Research, 1976).

22. David Knoke, "Religion, Stratification and Politics: America in the 1960's," *American Journal of Political Science* (May 1974), p. 344.

23. On the difference between sex and gender, see Reesa M. Vaughter, "Review Essay: Psychology," *Signs: Journal of Women in Culture and Society* (Autumn 1976), pp. 122–23, note 14.

24. Kathleen A. Frankovic, "Sex and Politics—New Alignments, Old Issues," *PS* (Summer 1982), pp. 439–48.

25. Jane J. Mansbridge, "Myth and Reality: The ERA and the Gender Gap in the 1980 Election," *Public Opinion Quarterly* (Spring 1985), pp. 164–78.

26. Ethel Klein, "The Gender Gap: Different Issues, Different Answers," *The Brookings Review* (Winter 1985), pp. 33–37.

27. *The New York Times* (October 16, 1984), p. 1.

28. S. M. Lipset, *Political Man* (Doubleday, 1960), p. 31.

29. Updated and adapted from Warren E. Miller, Arthur H. Miller, and Edward J. Schneider, *American National Election Studies Data Sourcebook, 1952–1978* (Harvard University Press, 1980), p. 81. See also Ellis Sandoz and Cecil V. Crabb, Jr., eds., *Election 84* (Mentor, 1985); and *The New York Times* (November 10, 1988), p. B6.

30. Walter De Vries and V. Lance Tarrance, *The Ticket-Splitter: A New Force in American Politics* (Erdmans, 1972).

31. See Arthur H. Miller and Martin P. Wattenberg, "Measuring Party Identification: Independent or No Partisan Preference?" *American Journal of Political Science* (February 1983), pp. 106–21.

32. *The New York Times* (November 9, 1988), p. A24.

33. G. Bingham Powell, Jr., "American Voter Turnout in Comparative Perspective," *American Political Science Review* (March 1986), pp. 17–43.

34. Ibid., pp. 18–22.

35. Ruy Teixeira, "Will the Real Nonvoter Please Stand Up?" *Public Opinion* (July/August 1988), pp. 41–44 and 59.

36. Stanley K. Sheinbaum, "Just Think," *New Perspectives Quarterly* (Summer 1988), p. 64.

37. See Paul R. Abramson and John H. Aldrich, "The Decline of Electoral Participation in America," *American Political Science Review* (September 1982), pp. 502–21; and Norman R. Luttbeg, "Attitudinal Components of Turnout Decline: Where Have Some States' Voters Gone?" *Social Science Quarterly* (June 1985), pp. 435–43.

38. *The New York Times* (November 9, 1988), p. A24.

39. Raymond E. Wolfinger and Steven J. Rosenstone, *Who Votes?* (Yale University Press, 1980), p. 102. See also Sandra Baxter and Marjorie Lansing, *Women and Politics: The Invisible Majority* (University of Michigan Press, 1980), pp. 35–37.

40. See Baxter and Lansing, *Women and Politics*. See also Claire Knoche Fulenwider, *Feminism in American Politics: A Study of Ideological Influence* (Praeger, 1980). On age as a key correlation with high turnout, see Lee Sigelman, Philip W. Roeder, Malcolm E. Jewell, and Michael A. Baer, "Voting and Nonvoting: A Multi-Election Perspective," *American Journal of Political Science* (November 1985), pp. 749–65.

41. Wolfinger and Rosenstone, *Who Votes?*

42. See Angus Campbell, Philip E. Converse, Warren E. Miller, and Donald E. Stokes, *The American Voter* (Wiley, 1960). This volume remains a foundation of modern voting analysis despite much new evidence and reinterpretation. See also Norman H. Nie, Sidney Verba, and John R. Petrocik, *The Changing American Voter* (Harvard University Press, 1976); and Ruy A. Teixeira, *Why Americans Don't Vote: Turnout Decline in the United States, 1960–1984* (Greenwood, 1987).

43. Douglas St. Angelo and Paul Puryear, "Fear, Apathy, and Other Dimensions of Black Voting," in Michael B. Preston, Lenneal J. Henderson, Jr., and Paul Puryear, eds., *The New Black Politics: The Search for Political Power* (Longman, 1982), pp. 109–30; and Philip L. Miller, "The Impact of Organizational Activity on Black Political Participation," *Social Science Quarterly* (March 1982), pp. 83–98.

44. Austin Ranney, "Nonvoting Is Not a Social Disease," *Public Opinion* (October/November 1983), pp. 16–19.

45. Thomas Byrne Edsall, *The New Politics of Inequality* (W. W. Norton, 1984), p. 181.

46. Wolfinger and Rosenstone, *Who Votes?* p. 109.

47. Teixeira, "Will the Real Nonvoter Please Stand Up?" p. 43.

48. Frances Fox Piven and Richard A. Cloward, "Prospects for Voter Registration Reform: A Report on the Experiences of the Human Serve Campaign," *PS* (Summer 1985), pp. 582–92.

49. E. E. Schattschneider, *The Semisovereign People* (Dryden Press, 1975), p. 96.

50. Wolfinger and Rosenstone, *Who Votes?* pp. 73 and 109–111.

51. Richard A. Cloward and Frances Fox Piven, "Trying to Break Down the Barriers," *The Nation* (November 2, 1985), pp. 433–36.

52. See Samuel Popkin, John W. Gorman, Charles Phillips, and Jeffrey A. Smith, "Comment: What Have You Done for Me Lately? Toward An Investment Theory of Voting," *American Political Science Review* (September 1976), pp. 779–849. Also of interest is Gregory B. Markus, "Political Attitudes during an Election Year: A Report on the 1980 NES Panel Study," *American Political Science Review* (September 1982), pp. 538–60.

53. See, for example, Gerald H. Kramer, "Short-Term Fluctuations in U.S. Voting Behavior, 1896–1964," *American Political Science Review* (March 1971), pp. 131–43, and the revision reprinted by Bobbs-Merrill (PS–498). See also Edward R. Tufte, "Determinants of the Outcomes of Midterm Congressional Elections," *American Political Science Review* (September 1975), pp. 812–26.

54. John R. Hibbing and John R. Alford. "The Educational Impact of Economic Conditions: Who is Held Responsible?" *American Journal of Political Science* (August 1981), pp. 423–39; and Morris P. Fiorina, "Who is Held Responsible? Further Evidence on the Hibbing-Alford Thesis," *American Journal of Political Science* (February 1983), pp. 158–64.

55. M. Stephen Weatherford, "Economic Voting and the 'Symbolic Politics' Argument: A Reinterpretation and Synthesis," *American Political Science Review* (March 1983), pp. 158–74.

56. Samuel Popkin, "Optimism, Pessimism, and Policy," *Public Opinion* (November/December 1988), pp. 51–55.

57. "Problems or Voting Issues?" Opinion Roundup, *Public Opinion* (July/August 1988), p. 33.

12

Media Politics: Reality or Illusion?

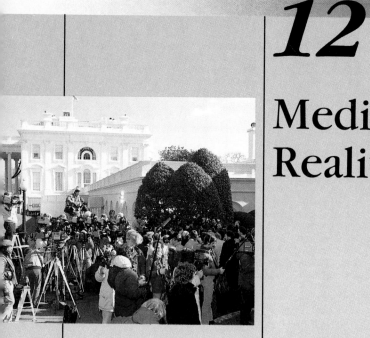

Vice-presidential nominee Dan Quayle besieged by reporters.

When presidential candidate George Bush and his political advisors met in New Orleans to select the 1988 Republican vice-presidential candidate, front-runners for the Number 2 spot were Representative Jack Kemp, Senator Bob Dole, former cabinet member Elizabeth Dole, and Senator Alan Simpson.

Some advisors have described the search as one in which Bush wanted a "Kemp without Kemp," that is, a young, conservative Republican outspoken enough to please the party's right wing, yet modest enough not to overshadow Bush. Senator Dan Quayle's name came up. Even though few in the campaign took Quayle seriously at first, Bush's pollster and media consultant wielded great influence in the final decision. Both pollster Robert Teeter and media consultant Roger Ailes had advised Quayle's campaigns in the past. They liked him. Ailes liked the image Quayle would bring to the ticket: He viewed Quayle's physical attractiveness on television as a definite plus for the campaign. Stuart Spencer, who managed the GOP's vice-presidential campaign, said of Quayle, "He's Robert Redford." Teeter saw Quayle, 41, as a candidate who would appeal to the baby-boom generation and at the same time bolster the conservative image of the Republican party.

After Quayle's background was investigated by a Bush aide and a team of Washington attorneys, Quayle completed a seventy-seven-item questionnaire dealing mostly with finances and personal matters, including marital relations and possible extramarital affairs. There was one open-ended question: "Is there anything in your background that might embarrass us?" It was during this background check that Quayle was reportedly asked about his National Guard service: "Did you pull strings?" Quayle's answer was said to be "No."

However, only two days after Bush announced his surprise choice of Quayle, *The Indianapolis News*, part of Quayle's own family's newspaper publishing empire, ran the story that a retired National Guard general had used his influence to get Dan Quayle a much sought after slot in the Guard. To fulfill his military obligation, Quayle had spent six years of weekend duty and summer camp working for the Guard as a public relations aide.

Why was this revelation so controversial that it virtually overshadowed President Bush's acclaimed acceptance speech at the GOP convention? Quayle's reputation in the Senate had largely been built on his right-wing conservative political position, his defense of Pentagon spending, and his vocal support of the Vietnam War. As it turned out, many of the news stories portrayed Quayle as a hypocrite and a draft dodger who used family connections to avoid serving in Vietnam—a war he had supported politically. At a news conference in Quayle's home town of Huntington, Indiana, Quayle said the implication of reporters' questions was that his Guard duty was unpatriotic. "No sir," responded Ellen Hume, reporter for *The Wall Street Journal*, "the implication is that people were dying . . . and you were writing press releases." The assembled crowd shouted at Hume to leave Quayle alone.

From Editor and Publisher, September 3, 1988, p. 13.

What was the outcome of this as a political issue? Did the news stories end up hurting Quayle and the Republican ticket? After receiving such play in the media for about a week, the controversy slowly died down in media importance. During this period, however, the news media continued to dig, and came up with other accusations: Quayle, on a golfing weekend, had propositioned a female lobbyist; Quayle had bought drugs while in college; Quayle had received poor grades as a college student. Only the third of these charges turned out to have a foundation in fact. In the interim, however, Bush's campaign team coached Quayle for the upcoming national election, and Bush began to take the offensive in Quayle's support.

As the 1988 election results revealed, the selection of Quayle for the vice-presidential spot did not seriously hinder Bush's election. Quayle learned his lessons well from his image coaches. The tension eased so much that within several days the polls indicated that Quayle had won sympathy even beyond Republican ranks for the battering he took from the press about his National Guard enlistment. Quayle proved that he could campaign effectively at the national level by learning to meet the mass media on their own ground. He had learned anew that the mass media are often the agenda setters in American politics. In short, within a matter of days after his nomination, Dan Quayle came to grips with the real "power of the press."[1]

The Power of the Mass Media

Whereas your parents and grandparents tended to look at politics through a Democratic or Republican "party lens," today we filter politics through a different, very real lens—that of a television camera. American politics is not only heavily influenced by the mass media, but our culture and social lifestyles are driven by the mass communication industry.

We use the term "mass media" without fully appreciating the significance of the different media represented by the term "mass." These include not only newspapers, magazines, radio, and television (including cable), but also the film, recording, and book industries.[2] The media, in particular the print media, have been called the "other government," "the fourth estate," and "the fourth branch of government"—with equal amounts of anger and appreciation.[3] Certainly the media are big business. They live off high audience ratings and substantial advertising traffic, essential to their "bottom line" of big profits.

The Media	
New	Computers
	Satellites
	Cable television
	Videocassette recorders
	Direct broadcast satellite
	Multipoint distribution service
	Satellite master antennae television
	Subscription television
	Low-power television
	VHF drop-in television
	Videotex
	Teletext
	Lasers
	Fiber optics
Old	Books
	Broadcast television
	Radio
	Newspapers
	Magazines
	Telephone
	Telegraph
Non-News Media	Direct mail
	Electronic mail
	Polling
	Videoconferencing
	Computer conferencing
	Teleconferencing

Source: Jeffrey B. Abramson, F. Christopher Arterton, and Gary R. Orren, *The Electronic Commonwealth: The Impact of New Media Technologies on Democratic Politics* (Basic Books, 1988), p. 5. Copyright © 1988 by the President and Fellows of Harvard College. Reprinted by permission of Basic Books, Inc., Publishers.

THE NEW MEDIA AND THE OLD

Technological advances in recent years have created intense competition for advertising revenues and have contributed to sweeping changes in the manner in which news is transmitted and received. Satellites, cable, lasers, computers, and videocassette recorders (VCRs) have made vast amounts of political information available twenty-four hours a day: for example, satellites eliminate the obstacles of time and distance; computers increase the volume of information that can be stored and retrieved; and cable channels and VCRs have made television an even more prevalent medium.

Other discoveries include fiber optics, an innovation that transmits voice, pictures, and other data by sending digital bursts of light down strands of super-transparent glass; and videotex, a video-computer service that can electronically publish everything from the daily newspaper to *The Encyclopedia Britannica* on the home video monitor. Teletext is a one-way technology that delivers textual and graphic information to TV screens or computer monitors after receiving data from satellite, radio, or television signals.

Technological advances are coming so rapidly that any wrap-up of the new media is almost obsolete by the time it is written. But we do know that the traditional media (radio, TV, newspapers, and magazines) have come to rely strongly on many of the new technologies. Thus most of the traditional media and many of the new technologies, especially cable, use communication satellites.[4]

Cable, which basically grew because the system improved television reception in rural and mountainous areas, offers specialized networks that include the non-commercial C–SPAN, which covers Congress and public affairs. The all-news channel (CNN) provides political news as well as entertainment.

The "new" media have not replaced the "old" media. They have, however, created keen competition among the media for the advertising dollar. The news-weeklies (*Time, Newsweek,* and *U.S. News & World Report*) have faced competition from week-in-review sections of newspapers, from television talk shows, magazine shows, and weekend "insider" programs. Where once the news magazines were the general public's primary source of news about special areas such as the law, medicine, and the environment, today all the large daily newspapers also employ writers specializing in these subjects. And where once the news magazines provided small town citizens with just about their only source of national and international developments, almost everyone in the country can get home delivery of *The New York Times* and *The Wall Street Journal*, or tune in to one of the major broadcast networks or flick on one of the many specialized cable channels—often through the use of a privately owned satellite dish.

MASS MEDIA: MASS CULTURE?

Just how powerful are the mass media? The media seem to be powerful indeed. They envelop us in information, music, symbols, and images; they provide vicarious experiences that contribute to our socialization; they serve as surrogate companions. The mass media are a growing influence in our lives and have created a mass popular culture in which our heroes are chosen by this pop culture.

What are the implications of this mass culture for politics and our democratic process? Over the past decades, the mass media and technological innovations have altered the means by which citizens participate in government, the way in which we conduct campaigns, and the manner in which public policy is made.

One could no more separate political views and opinions from the news disseminated by the electronic and print media than one could stop a city from celebrating the national victory of its hometown college basketball team. Although the information we receive through the mass media may, in fact, not be explicitly political, the content may have implicit messages about social order and politics.[5] For example, Bruce Springsteen's album "Born in the U.S.A." sold eleven million copies.[6] Can we draw a parallel between the song lyrics and the resurgence of patriotism in America at about this same time? In the same manner, do we identify with a particular candidate or issue because of a theme or an image in a TV spot, a cable broadcast, a movie, or a talk show?

WHO CONTROLS THE MEDIA?

These "media giants" have caused campaign costs to skyrocket and have placed a premium on a candidate's ability to communicate by television and radio. Media may be "the fourth branch of government," as we noted, yet they are politically unaccountable within government's ordinary structures. Who controls these "giants"—their reporters, editors, producers, anchors, or stockholders? And what have television and the print media done to political parties?

Once political parties were mediating devices that allowed leaders to communicate with their constituents. Today, the mass media serve that role. But the three networks (once dubbed "America's three political parties") no longer dominate the media industry as they once did. Cable syndicated shows, independent stations, and home videos have stolen network viewers. And, although the focus of media politics was once on newspaper editorials, today the emphasis is more on whether the newspaper picks up a story or whether a network chooses a thirty-second spot for the evening news, and if it does, the manner in which it uses and projects it.[7]

A political system must have freedom of thought and speech—in other words, competition of ideas and symbols—if it is to be considered a democracy. In America that freedom is guaranteed by the First Amendment. Can a few media conglomerates support competition of ideas?[8] But without them, can the local populations scattered around the country find out what is happening in the nation's capital, if they depend only on local media companies? Why not have government-owned media carry out educational and information functions, as well as entertainment functions, as they do in Great Britain and France?[9] Or are Americans too suspicious of the government and too jealous of their rights ever to accept this? Most observers believe that even though the media and their practices are often criticized, they are unlikely to change.

The mass media include about 1700 daily newspapers and over 7000 other newspapers, about 19,000 radio and television stations, over 9000 magazines or serial publications, over 4300 film producers and distributors, over 10,000 movie theaters, and about 1300 book publishers.[10] Ten business and financial corporations control the 3 major television and radio networks, 34 subsidiary television and radio stations, 201 cable television systems, 62 radio stations, 20 record companies, 59 magazines, including *Newsweek* and *Time*, 58 newspapers, including *The New York Times*, *The Washington Post*, *The Wall Street Journal*, and *The Los Angeles Times*, 41 book publishers, and various motion picture companies such as Columbia and Twentieth Century Fox. In addition, 75 percent of the major stockholders of ABC, CBS, and NBC are banks, such as Chase Manhattan, Morgan Guaranty Trust, Citibank, and Bank of America.[11]

Prime Time Audiences Have Shifted

Of homes with television sets on, the percent tuned to each type of station during prime time (8 P.M. to 11 P.M.) during January of each year.

1982
1989

* Including basic service and pay cable.

Note: Sums may exceed 100% due to more than one television set per home.

SOURCE: Nielsen Media Research; *The New York Times* (March 5, 1989), p. 4F.

Another growing concern among media watchers over the past several decades has been the gobbling up of American communication assets by foreign interests. In the last few years, the Japanese (Sony Corp.) bought CBS Records; West Germany's Bertelsmann, known primarily for its book division, acquired RCA Records. The Australian Rupert Murdoch owns two Texas newspapers, more than twenty magazines, including *TV Guide* and *Seventeen*, Twentieth Century Fox, and the seven TV stations that form the heart of Fox Broadcasting. Australia's Qintex Group has plans to acquire United Artists, the movie studio founded by Charlie Chaplin.[12]

Tom Brokaw was able to let worldwide viewers share a revealing conversation with Russia's Mikhail Gorbachev, himself a master of media opportunities.

These trends have accompanied a decline in local media ownership and the development of a centralized national media that is described as a diluting, homogenizing, and moderating influence on American press and television. *USA Today*, *The Wall Street Journal*, *The New York Times*, the three networks, and C-SPAN have replaced many local media outlets and lured the American reader and viewer to the national press. One of their most important functions is their ability to frame public perceptions of issues, events, and political actors.[13]

An estimated sixty million Americans watch some part of the weekday evening news programs on the three major networks or on cable. Americans buy about sixty-three million newspapers a day, countless foreign-language newspapers, thousands of weeklies, and many publications of a free-wheeling alternative press. Noted journalist Walter Lippmann called the newspaper the "bible of democracy, the book out of which a people determines its conduct." And radio continues to reach tens of millions of persons.

Television has also expanded public discussion of politics. Recent years have seen a boom in Sunday morning public-affairs shows featuring leading journalists who analyze the news and interview the newsmakers. Popular talk shows such as those hosted by Phil Donahue and Geraldo Rivera often emphasize confrontation over issues. Leaders of the Religious Right use the power and visibility that they gain from their large viewership to involve their followers in politics, as seen through their support of Ronald Reagan.

What, then, is the ultimate impact of the media on public opinion? And is it beneficial or not?

The Media and Public Opinion

Franklin Delano Roosevelt was the first president to make effective use of the media; his fireside chats reached millions of homes.

For a long time analysts tended to play down the influence of the news media in American politics, as compared with the influence of leaders using the media. Franklin D. Roosevelt's use of radio for his "fireside chats" seemed to symbolize the power of the politician as against that of the news editor. FDR spoke *directly* to his listeners over the radio in a way and at a time of his own choosing, and no network official was able to block or influence that direct connection. President Kennedy's use of the television press conference represented the same kind of direct contact with the public. President Reagan was nicknamed The Great Communicator because of his ability to take an issue directly to the people through television, and gather support for his policies.

All this has changed the way in which our elected officials govern and make decisions, and members of Congress take their case directly to the people. The presidency has also been altered by its relationship with the media.[14] Presidential events and "photo opportunities" are planned with the evening news and its format in mind. Even the Supreme Court is considering dissemination of its opinions in electronic form.[15] And the media in turn respond to such manipulation. White

House news releases are frequently exposed directly to national audiences. How the press uses government officials, how government officials use the press, and to what extent the press and television can and should be regulated are critical questions for study.

Most early studies of the media, concluding that the effect of the media as such was at best of secondary importance, came to two important conclusions. First, people are not empty vessels to be filled up with torrents of television talk or acres of newsprint. Rather, they tend to focus on those speeches and news stories that meet their interests or fit their biases; they buy the newspapers and magazines that tend to support their prejudices. The news media may present "new facts," but we have an enormous capacity to filter those "facts" and see what we want to see. This difference between exposure and effect is largely caused by *selective perception*.[16]

A second powerful opinion-making force, and thus a check on the direct influence of the news media, is group affiliation. Authoritative members of groups who consume the media act as *opinion leaders* in channeling and interpreting media content for others in the group.[17] In this way family and other primary groups who heavily influence growing children also intervene between adults and the direct impact of the media. Direct face-to-face contacts often have far more impact on people than the more impersonal tube or newspaper. Belonging to a party also acts as a powerful filter.[18] A conservative Bush Republican may watch the "liberal Eastern networks" night after night and year after year and stick to his or her own opinions—perhaps even strengthen them.

More recent studies, however, have found somewhat greater influence by the news media on public opinion in general. Also, analysts have begun to look at the different reasons people have for using the media. Some studies of television viewers found that people use the media to gain information, to relax and be entertained, to counteract boredom, fatigue, and inadequate satisfaction in other aspects of social life, to escape, to have something to talk about, and to be with their families.[19] Still, leaders with direct access to people can appeal powerfully to their needs and attitudes, thus bypassing the media.

Political messages may be found in all types of programming. Every sports event begins with the national anthem, which may encourage people to be proud of their country. Many entertainment programs include jokes about political figures. Most media content, including ever-present advertising, still portrays mostly white men and women. And the token black and Hispanic men and women who are portrayed are often shown in stereotypic gender and race roles, which subtly reinforce the cultural values of sex and race inequality.[20]

A major part of the mass media's influence is their agenda-setting function. The media ultimately filter the events that become "the news." At the least, the mass media news determines what issues people will be discussing during a particular period of time.[21]

NEWSPAPERS: WHAT KIND OF IMPACT?

As the coils of Watergate tightened around him, Richard Nixon said, "Basically, they're ultra-liberal and I am conservative. . . . The reasons for their attitudes toward the president go back many years, but they're basically ideological, and I respect that. If I would pander to their liberal views, I could be infinitely popular with some of our friends out there, and a lot of the heat would go out of Watergate." Nixon had long been battling with the press, and a year after entering the White House, had launched a campaign against the television networks. Now he was trying to shift responsibility for Watergate to the news media.

*Y*ou decide!

Do the mass media have a heavy impact on public opinion? What about your own experience? How deeply do you believe your political views have been influenced by the mass media, as compared with your parents, teachers in high school or college, siblings and friends, religious instructors?

(Answer/Discussion is on page 300.)

Media Endorsements— Do They Matter?

A survey of most of the nation's major newspapers by Editor and Publisher found that in 1988 most papers did not endorse a presidential candidate.

No endorsement	428
Endorsed Bush	243
Endorsed Dukakis	103

Influential papers, such as the Wall Street Journal, Washington Post, Los Angeles Times, and USA Today, endorsed no one. The New York Times endorsed Dukakis and the New York Daily News endorsed George Bush.

Any support and recognition is sought by the candidates, and doubtless a strong endorsement can be of assistance, but most voters make up their minds based on economic, partisan, and character considerations.

Answer/Discussion

Media do make a significant difference. How much, of course, depends on the type of person or group being influenced, the nature of the issue, and the nature of the medium, especially newspapers versus television.

How about yourself—what media not only influence you more but help make you a more thoughtful observer of events?

This was by no means the first time politicians attacked the news media, or at least tried to turn them to their own uses. Jefferson was so upset by the influence of the Federalist press that he founded a Republican newspaper. During the nineteenth century most newspapers were proudly and openly partisan. In recent decades liberals contended that the newspapers were overwhelmingly biased toward conservative policies and candidates. And because they believed the press was mainly Republican or conservative, Franklin Roosevelt turned to radio and John F. Kennedy to television.

Newspapers today do still tend, sometimes by overwhelming margins, to endorse Republican over Democratic presidential candidates. Nixon had the support of 83 percent of the daily circulation in 1960, and of 78 percent in 1968; Ronald Reagan garnered similar editorial support in 1980 and 1984. In 1988 Bush won nearly twice as many newspaper endorsements as did Dukakis (see box). But the issue today is not so much partisanship (few newspapers support a party as such) as ideology or general point of view. President Lyndon B. Johnson believed the "big" media were controlled by a handful of people in the Northeast who disliked him because he was a Texan and an outlander. Conservatives like Irving Kristol and Kevin Phillips fear that the big newspapers, television networks, wire services, and many magazines are controlled by members of the "liberal establishment." Long before he became senator from New York, Daniel P. Moynihan saw a growing tendency for journalists to be recruited from among college graduates with hostile attitudes toward middle-class Americans.[22] Others contend that although reporters may tend to be liberal, publishers take conservative positions; like other businesspeople, they worry about sales and profits. According to a recent study, although journalists as a group are liberal and Democratic in opinion, their professional behavior as news reporters does not reflect their personal opinions and partisan identification (see Table 12–3).[23]

Certain newspapers, such as The New York Times, The Washington Post, and The Wall Street Journal, have special influence because of the leaders they reach at home and abroad. They even serve as communications links among such leaders. Readers of these newspapers tend to be more affluent and more liberal than the rest of the nation. Moynihan contends that, as a result, our most influential newspapers tend "to set a tone of pervasive dissatisfaction with the performance of the national government, whoever the presidential incumbent may be and whatever the substance of the policies."[24]

Criticism of newspapers has been abundant; practical remedies have been few. Some suggest that newspaper chains be broken up through antimonopoly legislation. Others propose that the government subsidize competing newspapers. Such proposals have received little support; many Americans oppose any action that might, in their view, threaten the freedom of the press. Better a biased, commercially oriented press, they say, than a government-controlled one. As a result, the press has been allowed to "police" its own practices.

There is a long-standing regulatory asymmetry between the print and broadcast media. Newspapers are not regulated as such in this country and operate as any business enterprise. The broadcast media, however, are subject to technical, financial, and content oversight.

TELEVISION NEWS: ELECTRONIC THRONE?

People seem exceptionally vulnerable to the tube. They believe what they see on the television screen far more than they believe what they read in newspapers. Television news exposure cuts across age groups, educational levels, social classes, and races to an astonishing degree. Moreover, the TV audience is often captive, compared to newspaper subscribers, who can read selectively. And video, with all its concreteness, vividness, and drama, has an emotional impact print cannot hope to match.[25]

Some observers believe television is a threat to *representative* government. Direct television coverage of White House news bypasses the government structures through which information was traditionally passed and political conflict organized. Today the public is more likely to tune in to a debate on ABC's "Nightline." Also, television now covers congressional committee meetings, in which much dealing, swapping, and compromising occur. How will this "brokerage" play on television? Will viewers expect the committee members to be more principled and high-minded? And if the brokers hear of such reactions, will they be less willing to bargain and barter—processes at the heart of the legislative process?

Some fear "big television" will become allied with "big government." Presidents can command television networks at prime time virtually at will. They can speak directly to the nation. They do not need to answer questions, and they can minimize their press conferences, as Reagan did (see Table 12–1). During his presidency, Reagan used the electronic media more adeptly than any other president before him, while his advisors carefully crafted the images and scenes of his presidency to fit the role of television. Thus, television has been called an "electronic throne." According to former Vice-President Walter Mondale: "If I had to give up . . . the opportunity to get on the evening news or the veto power . . . I'd throw the veto power away. [Television news] is the President's most indispensable power."[26]

Other observers have been less extravagant but still concerned. A close study of a controversial news special, "The Selling of the Pentagon," found that the show led viewers to believe the American military had taken part in national politics and misled the public about Vietnam. Television journalism has a special importance, this study concluded, because it "disseminates news and information far more widely than does any other news source, bringing political information to people in the society who might never have bothered to obtain this information before television arrived, and who might still not bother, were it not for TV news." More broadly, the study suggested that reliance on television news has fostered political cynicism, distrust, and negativism.[27] (The cynicism, however, may be caused by the unhappy reality investigative reporters often reveal.)

TABLE 12–1
Presidential News Conferences with White House Correspondents, 1929–1988

PRESIDENT	AVERAGE PER MONTH	TOTAL NUMBER
Hoover (1929–1933)	5.6	268
Roosevelt (1933–1945)	6.9	998
Truman (1945–1953)	3.4	334
Eisenhower (1953–1961)	2.0	193
Kennedy (1961–1963)	1.9	64
Johnson (1963–1969)	2.2	135
Nixon (1969–1974)	0.5	37
Ford (1974–1977)	1.3	39
Carter (1977–1981)	0.8	59
Reagan (1981–1988)	0.5	44

Sources: Samuel Kernell, *Going Public* (Congressional Quarterly Press, 1986), p. 69; and "News Conferences," *Weekly Compilation of Presidential Documents* 21:1 (January 7, 1985)–22:53 (January 5, 1987), pp. 1–1685 and 23:1 (January 12, 1987)–24:52 (January 2, 1989), pp. 1–1671.

Television newscasters often command a great deal of trust among the viewers.

Peter Jennings, ABC

Dan Rather, CBS

Tom Brokaw, NBC

Diane Sawyer, ABC

TABLE 12–2
Media Believability

18–29 YEARS	30–49 YEARS	50 AND OVER
1. *Wall Street Journal*	1. MacNeil-Lehrer	1. MacNeil-Lehrer
2. CBS	2. *Wall Street Journal*	2. *Wall Street Journal*
3. *Time*	3. CNN	3. *Reader's Digest*
4. ABC	4. *Time*	4. Local TV
5. CNN	5. CBS	5. CNN
Local TV	Local TV	
	Newsweek	

Source: Michael J. Robinson, "An Absence of Malice: Young People and the Press," *Public Opinion* (November/December 1986), p. 45. Reprinted with the permission of the American Enterprise Institute for Public Policy Research.

Another study—of the CBS and NBC evening news and of *Time* and *Newsweek*—focused on the kind of people who control the news media. According to this study, the national news organizations are dominated by persons of privileged background and standing. Because the producers believe in individualism, moderation, social order, and strong national leadership, their ideas tend to be reflected in the news. In the long run, the news media cater to, and uphold the actions of, "elite individuals and elite institutions." The author of this study concluded that news has a class bias that favors the status quo.[28] This view has been extensively rebutted, especially by the media.

Diverse proposals have been offered to deal with such problems as sensationalism, overemphasis on "theater" and spectacles, obsession with violence, lack of self-criticism within the media, lack of objectivity, superficial reporting, and so on. The news media have been urged to press for more explanation, interpretation, and analysis, to look at how they report on activities of the government, to be less dependent on "packaged" news handed out by government bureaucracies, to be more aggressive in covering the White House, and to become better educated themselves about what really goes on in the Congress.[29]

Critics hesitate to propose harsh or sweeping remedies for the failures of press, television, and radio, because they fear any threat to First Amendment liberties. But they are also uncertain about how serious the problem really is and how improvement can best be accomplished.[30] Further, the seriousness of the problem varies widely with the situation. For example, in closely balanced election races, where media influence or bias might be large enough to tilt the outcome one way or the other, the opinions put forth by major press and networks might be crucial. Still, in our pluralistic nation, which is comprised of the enormous variety of groups and movements mentioned in Chapters 8 and 9, Americans have so many "filters" through which to observe events that it is extremely difficult to influence public opinion—as many a propagandist has discovered.

Our decentralized governmental system may also serve as a partial defense against undue media influence. Members of Congress may be far more concerned about what the local anchorperson reports about them than whether or not NBC's Tom Brokaw mentions them on the national news. Most congressional candidates are more dependent on local press coverage than on television, because even local channels, covering perhaps half a dozen congressional districts, cannot pay much attention to any one race. Thus, although the overall combined influence of the media is enormous, how it affects the president and several hundred members of Congress in their own political habitats is a matter for analysis, not overgeneralization.

"What'll it be—the Nightly News with Tom Brokaw, the Evening News with Dan Rather, World News Tonight with Peter Jennings, or, the heck with it, a Martini with a twist?"

Drawing by C. Barsotti; © 1985 The New Yorker Magazine, Inc.

The Image Campaign: The Mass Media Election

The campaign of 1988 was a campaign of images, yet these images were often inconsistent. In July George Bush lagged behind Michael Dukakis by as much as 17 percent. On election day Bush won by 7 percent of the vote, a 24-point turnaround in four months. What happened? While the press was mainly concerned with who was ahead and by how much, the real story was that the public images of Michael Dukakis and George Bush changed dramatically between July and November.

Before the Republican convention, George Bush was considered a weak candidate. He had been the invisible vice-president for eight years; his voice was not particularly pleasing to the ear; he was described as having been "born with a silver foot in his mouth"; and he had offered few real ideas on issues. Michael Dukakis, on the other hand, was the frugal, competent head of one of the more successful state governments in the Union. Declaring that the election was not to be about ideology, but competence, Dukakis led by a comfortable margin.

However, by November George Bush was the tough war hero, loyal servant to Reagan, a family man, a humble patrician with a conservative vision. Michael Dukakis was the intellectual elitist, the Harvard liberal who let murderers out of jail on furloughs, and who vetoed a bill to require schoolchildren to recite the Pledge of Allegiance. Dukakis was perceived as emotionless and stilted in front of the TV cameras. During the second debate, Bernard Shaw asked Dukakis what he would do if a man raped his wife. Dukakis's passionless response confirmed the image of a cold, unfeeling technocrat. It was this creation and recreation of a media image that partly accounted for the 24-point Bush turnaround.[31]

To describe the modern presidential campaign as just a battle of strategies would be like portraying the Kentucky Derby as just a collection of riders racing around a track. Both events are dominated by celebrities, crowds of spectators, big money, and endless coverage by television, radio, and the print media.[32] The mass media campaign aims to create certain images about the candidates. This campaign has two aspects: One is the intentional and unintentional impact of the mass media on the voters, especially in the primaries. The other is the effort of candidates to exploit the media in their own behalf.

THE NEWS MEDIA: ELECTION IMPACT

Long ago there was much more concern about the way candidates exploited the media than about the electronic and print media themselves. But in recent decades network television, big-circulation newspapers and magazines, and large radio chains have become huge industries with their own identities, interests, internal politics, and political biases. Even when the media try to be neutral, some critics say, they bias the outcome of campaigns. They do this by focusing public attention on certain candidates or controversies rather than others, by playing up certain issues and ignoring or playing down others, and by openly editorializing about candidates and campaign issues. A key criticism of the media—especially television—is that they often treat campaigns more as games than as serious encounters over issues. Presidential primaries are treated as "horse races," with the news media awarding attention to the most photogenic or provocative candidate, rather than to the candidate who—like Michael Dukakis in 1988—is slowly rolling up delegate votes.[33]

A reporter conducts an interview at the 1988 Democratic Convention.

"Many stories focus on who is ahead, who is behind, who is going to win, and who is going to lose, rather than examining how and why the race is as it is," according to one analysis.[34] The press "sees the electorate as a people influenced mostly by tactics and strategy," and "thus exaggerates seemingly dramatic forces such as 'momentum.' "[35] The media seem to alternate between a kind of "gee whiz" attitude toward their current hero and a tendency to pounce on a candidate's ill chosen or witty remarks and exploit them for days, as they did with Jimmy Carter's comment about lust in his heart in the 1976 *Playboy* interview, George Bush's 1980 attack on Ronald Reagan's "voodoo economics," or Senator Lloyd Bentsen's "you're no Jack Kennedy" retort to Dan Quayle in a 1988 debate.

Sensationalizing or trivializing campaigns is serious enough, but even more serious is playing down the *substance* of the campaign, especially issues. A media advertising expert says the press spends too much time reporting why a candidate chooses a speech for a particular day and place, what the candidate's staff argued about in writing the speech, and so on: "What tends to get lost is what he *said*."[36]

Studies of eight national elections concluded:

First, the data presented supported the notion that television has played a role in the gradual personalizing of American presidential elections . . . Second, the short-term elements of elections, particularly voter reactions to candidates, have become more important at the expense of long-term elements, such as party identification and citizen attitudes toward the parties . . . Third, the weight of attitudes toward the parties, as measured by open-ended questions such as those used for the candidates, was once among the best predictors of the vote, but over the eight elections has become nearly irrelevant . . .[37]

Other recent presidential races have brought a turning point in our understanding of the media and elections. According to Michael J. Robinson, although the media "dominate candidate schedules and campaign decisions,"[38] they may not affect the outcome as much as is commonly believed. Or, at least, the media—especially news coverage—may have different influences on different subgroups of the electorate. Robinson's analysis suggests that while the news reporters and commentators were covering the "horse race," the voters were focusing on the perceived differences between the candidates' stands on the economic situation and national defense.

Paid campaign advertising in congressional elections may have more influence than presidential campaign advertising. But again conditions determine the greatest effectiveness. For example, advertising, especially negative advertising, is more effective if left unanswered. A rule of thumb in the "old politics" was to ignore the charges of the opposition, thus according one's rival no importance or standing; that practice seems to be changing.

Advertising is particularly effective for the candidate whose public image is vague, and who is taking on an incumbent thought to be on the "wrong" side of issues that are salient to the electorate during the time of the campaign.[39] But even if paid political advertising (sometimes known as "polispots") lacks great influence on the voting public in general, it does significantly affect potential campaign workers, contributors, and the reporters and analysts who cover the election.[40]

A more intrusive impact of television on presidential elections is election night reporting. All national news is based in the East, three hours ahead of the West Coast. In past elections, the major networks have projected the presidential winner well ahead of poll closings in the Western states. This has discouraged

Western voters from voting since the media have already told them the winner. As a result, voter turnout in congressional and local elections, where races have not been decided and every vote does count, has been affected.

BUILDING THE CANDIDATE'S IMAGE: CAMPAIGN TECHNOLOGY

There is nothing new in office seekers' trying to improve their standing with the voters through various techniques of advertising and promotion. What is new is the rapidly expanding technology of image building and the escalating cost of doing it. So complex and elaborate is this technology that candidates regularly hire media advisers and campaign consultants. These are typically experts in mass mail promotions, "thirty-second spots" and other television advertising devices, intensive fund-raising methods, relations with the press, "targeting" special audiences, staging campaign activities for maximum media impact, and much more.[41]

This sophisticated technology has produced a new power base in the electoral process: paid political and media consultants. Since 1980 every major presidential candidate has had at least one media consultant, as do most senatorial and gubernatorial aspirants, and nearly all Senate and House candidates in contested districts have purchased at least some television and radio time, and some members of Congress publicly attribute their election victories to paid political advertising.[42]

Media consultants have prospered because their techniques have been successful. They not only shape the overall strategies of a campaign, but they also gear specific messages to a particular medium, making the end product cost effective. For example, candidates may be advised to turn to radio for the sharpest attacks on their opponents. "Radio is a guerrilla warfare technique," according to Joe Slade White, a New York media consultant. "It's underground. It's not seen. The minute you go on television, everybody writes about it. But you can do something on radio and it's a sleeper. It creeps up on you."[43] Radio spots are also economical for the candidate. Consultants can produce as many as five radio spots for the cost of one television commercial, and pay considerably less to buy time on radio stations.

A media consultant can advise a candidate how often and how early to use paid political television spots and how to gain free media—news stories about the candidates appearing on the evening news or reported as an actuality in the newspaper. The timing of key media decisions may be crucial in setting campaign themes and creating the candidate's image. As Senator Edward Kennedy concluded, "Events matter less than what is now widely referred to as spin control—who in which campaign can explain why something doesn't mean what it seems."[44]

Candidates have further need for consultants in using the technology and

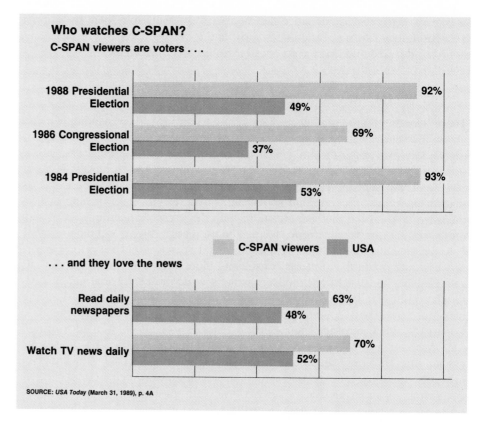

Who watches C-SPAN?

C-SPAN viewers are voters . . .

1988 Presidential Election	C-SPAN viewers	92%
	USA	49%
1986 Congressional Election	C-SPAN viewers	69%
	USA	37%
1984 Presidential Election	C-SPAN viewers	93%
	USA	53%

C-SPAN viewers   USA

. . . and they love the news

Read daily newspapers	C-SPAN viewers	63%
	USA	48%
Watch TV news daily	C-SPAN viewers	70%
	USA	52%

SOURCE: *USA Today* (March 31, 1989), p. 4A

gadgetry to get to the voters. In 1988, when Michael Dukakis wanted to make a televised, in-depth appeal to the Iowa voters, the message could not be targeted through the national networks and there was no state-wide network. Therefore, Dukakis put together his own network of stations by buying time on local cable channels, renting a broadcast-size dish antenna, and arranging to use a communication satellite orbiting 22,300 miles over the equator. Dukakis' image was beamed up to the satellite from a small studio in Des Moines, bounced back down to antennas at selected cable outlets, and then distributed via coaxial TV cables to the homes of voters. The candidate was then able to conduct a live phone-in TV program. The show reached an estimated 1.5 million homes in Iowa and neighboring states, and the total bill was $15,000—a fraction of the cost as compared to direct mail or telephone.[45] In the 1988 election, C–SPAN, the nonprofit Cable-Satellite Public Affairs Network, and Ted Turner's Cable News Network reached more than 860,000 subscribers in Iowa. The significance of these numbers is that these cable news networks attract the politically aware information seeker.[46]

The improved technology also cuts down on costs and reduces the turnaround time in producing political ads. An ad can be written in New York and the ad copy can be transmitted by facsimile (FAX) machine or computer modem to California where it is performed. Computers can also be used in "tracking polls" (polls to determine the direction or flow of public opinion late in the campaign).

Technology even permits campaign staffers to "cover" their own candidate. The staff can follow the candidate around with cassette recorders and minicams, taping anything the candidate does that resembles news. These tapes can then be delivered to radio and television stations and cable systems by hand, by telephone, or even by satellite. Speed and low cost make these electronic actualities readily available to the media, where these reports are often broadcast intact and, in many instances, without much editorial comment. These staged activities reported as news have included producing rallies against patriotic backdrops (as former President Reagan so often did) and presidential candidate Michael Dukakis riding in a tank.[47]

Some critics charge that the consultants have taken the place of the old-time party leaders. Such leaders made their judgments about possible candidates on the basis of long observation of the candidates' performances under fire, decisiveness, conviction, political skill, and other "presidential" qualities (in addition to their chances of victory). Consultants, according to the critics, think more in terms of the candidates' images, television techniques, flexibility, "salability," and the like. Some critics allege political consultants have become a new "political elite" that can virtually choose candidates by determining in advance what men and women have the right images—or at least images that can be restyled for the widest popularity.[48]

Political consultants say they are simply modernizing election techniques and adapting them to the electronic age. They also warn against exaggerating the impact of television advertising. In 1984 Senator John Glenn built his campaign around a heavily financed television advertising effort, but he ran well behind other candidates in the presidential primaries. However, the advertising consultant for Republican Howard H. Baker, Jr., sees the issue differently: "Television is more and more a dominant part of politics," he notes.[49] Critics of television advertising fear this tendency will intensify in the 1990s.

HOW EFFECTIVE ARE THE MEDIA?

The debate over the power of the press has raged for centuries in America, for Americans have had a special concern about the role of a free press in a democracy. As communication technologies have expanded over recent decades, so too has the debate over the political impact of the media on our lives. This debate includes the central questions raised in this chapter. What is the media's role in our democracy? Which media do we mean: network television or newspapers or CNN? What, if any, are their biases? Are they liberal or conservative, or something else altogether? And whose bias is most crucial—that of journalists, editors, or owners? With what type of ideas do the media deal, and upon which targets—viewers, voters, candidates—do they have the greatest influence? What are the goals of the media? And how much effect do they actually have on people's politics? Finally, do these questions affect the news that eventually emerges from television and newspapers, or the politics of the viewers and readers?

Some commentators believe the power of the press has been vastly overstated in political discussion. They say parties, interest groups, and the personalities of politicians are far more important. City, state, and federal governments, they assert, have far more impact on a person's politics than television or the press. Religion, friends, family, teachers, wars, depressions and assassinations are all more important than the media, which can only reflect the nation's wants, cater to its needs, and sometimes, perhaps, illuminate its troubles or successes. Political scientists asked people to rank the impact of various institutions on their lives; those listed as possessing "a great deal of power" appear in the marginal box.[50]

Others consider the media to be far more powerful than this popular perception. To them, the media are "an integral part of the daily functioning of government."[51] They note that 67 percent of the adult public watches some television news and reads at least one newspaper daily.[52] They argue that the media

Institutions Perceived as Possessing a Great Deal of Power	
Federal government	68%
State government	55%
City government	44%
Major corporations	43%
Organized labor	43%
Banks	41%
Local newspapers	21%
Local churches	19%
Local television stations	18%

define the issues we discuss, set the boundaries of political debate, serve as both player and referee in the game of politics, and affect the thinking and decisions of Congress, cabinet secretaries, and even the White House itself.[53] Michael K. Deaver, Ronald Reagan's former staff assistant and White House communications director, talked candidly about how he tailored the news to the media's needs: "The majority of people get their news from television, so you have to pay attention to them. You're aware of how we construct events and craft photos that are designed for 30 seconds to a minute so that it can fit into that 'bite' on the evening news. We'd be crazy if we didn't think in those terms."[54]

"Since the 1960s," asserts one critic of media power, "the press has taken on all the trappings of other elite institutions: high salaries, luxurious perks, status, top billing on the society pages."[55] And when questioned about its power, even the press agrees; it lists itself as the second most powerful American political institution after business and before the federal government.[56]

Not all those who think the media are powerful agree that their power is bad. After all, they argue, people get 45 percent of their information about issues that concern them from television, 30 percent from newspapers—the media perform a vital educative function.[57] Furthermore, they continue, almost 70 percent of the public think the press is a watchdog of government and that it keeps leaders from doing bad things.[58]

However, those people who are most susceptible to television and print media's impact are also those least likely to view these messages with a critical or skeptical set of eyes and ears. And some insist that the media's treatment of politics, particularly television's, "tends to suppress the ability to perceive significant differences between candidates," and thereby decreases election interest and turnout among the public that is exposed.[59]

Presidential candidates remain unconvinced. Every four years they dutifully allocate at least half their budgets to television advertising.[60] On a congressional level, Democrat Robert C. Byrd of West Virginia was challenged by his colleagues for his Senate leadership position in 1985 and 1987, not because he was a poor party leader, but in large part because he was not perceived as telegenic enough. At the very least, the media have the power to mold the agenda of the day, and at most, in the words of the late Theodore White, to "determine what people will talk and think about—an authority that in other nations is reserved for tyrants, priests, parties, and mandarins."[61]

THE MEDIA CANDIDATE

"Television networks are large corporations whose first and foremost concern is profit."[62] To many critics of the media this observation defines the peculiar nature of the press. It is dedicated, on the one hand, to the impartial and unadulterated reporting of "fact," and, on the other, to a search to please ratings analysts, circulation managers, advertisers, sponsors, and, ultimately, stockholders. Somewhere along the line, some say, the search for truth gets lost.[63]

Although news organizations pride themselves on their objectivity, it is becoming more difficult to distinguish what is news, what is opinion, and what is entertainment. Political jokes abound on late night comedy shows, and we get pungent political messages from the cartoon pages, prime-time network shows, and Hollywood. Actors have become politicians, and politicians have become actors. Political analysis creeps onto the front pages of most papers, and many fear that the politics of the editorial page influences the news we get in the front of the paper. When we see Sam Donaldson, ABC's political analyst, expressing his views on Sunday morning TV, can we honestly believe him when we see Sam Donaldson, reporter, covering the evening news?

Similar arguments are voiced by David Broder of the *Washington Post*, who fears that the ranks of journalism are being tainted by those who have served in government. A partial list includes William Safire, Pat Buchanan, Diane Sawyer, Ken Bode, Bill Moyers, Pierre Salinger, George Will, and Hodding Carter. According to Broder, a sacred line must divide objective journalism from partisan politics, but many in the print and television media have crossed this line. Others argue that, because of their government service, these people give us a valuable perspective on government, without losing their neutrality as professionals.

Equally disturbing to some observers is the media's alleged political bias, whether liberal or conservative. But to whom are these critics referring? To reporters, writers, editors, producers, or owners of TV and newspapers? Do they assume a journalist's personal politics will be translated into biased reporting? And does the public think so?

Journalists are more liberal than the population as a whole, although editors tend to be a bit more conservative than their reporters, and media stockholders more conservative still. Twenty-three percent of the public describe themselves as liberal, compared to 38 percent of college-educated professionals, from whose ranks most journalists are drawn. But even among the professionals, journalists' liberalism stands out. Fifty-five percent describe themselves as liberals (see Table 12–3). Even more telling are the voting patterns among journalists. The most obvious is the fact that 70 percent of journalists voted for George McGovern in 1972, although he received only 37 percent of the popular vote in a landslide election.[64] Journalists voted 92 percent for Johnson in 1964, 87 percent for Humphrey in 1968, and 81 percent for Carter in 1976.[65] Some argue, however, that liberal journalists bend over backward in their treatment of conservatives to prove that their reporting is not biased—a kind of reverse bias—and some would even argue that there has been a "media realignment" in which journalists have become less liberal.[66]

Hollywood on the Potomac

Actors Embracing Politics		Actors Embracing Politicians	Actors as Politicians	Politicians as Actors
Alan Alda	Art Linkletter	Jane Fonda (Tom Hayden)	Ronald Reagan	Richard Nixon ("Laugh-In")
Ed Asner	Shirley MacLaine	Elizabeth Taylor (John Warner)	Clint Eastwood	Ed Koch ("Saturday Night Live"—SNL)
Warren Beatty	Penny Marshall	Debra Winger (Robert Kerrey)	Fred Grandy	George McGovern ("SNL")
Marlon Brando	Marsha Mason	Phyllis George (John Y. Brown)	Sonny Bono	Jesse Jackson ("SNL")
Mike Farrell	Paul Newman	Linda Ronstadt (Jerry Brown)	Daniel Flood	Daniel Patrick Moynihan ("SNL")
Sally Field	Carroll O'Connor	Marlo Thomas (Henry Kissinger)	Robert Dornan	Richard Kneip ("SNL")
Jane Fonda	Robert Redford	Jill St. John (Henry Kissinger)	Nancy Culp	Nancy Reagan ("Diff'rent Strokes")
Lee Grant	Vanessa Redgrave	George Hamilton (Lynda Bird Johnson)		Henry Kissinger ("Dynasty")
Howard Hesseman	John Ritter	Nancy Reagan (Ronald Reagan)		George Bush (sought role on "Miami Vice")
Charlton Heston	Martin Sheen			Gerald and Betty Ford ("Dynasty")
Bob Hope	Jimmy Stewart			Gary Hart ("Cheers")
Margot Kidder	Barbra Streisand			Tip O'Neill ("Cheers")
Robert Klein	Donald Sutherland			
Jack Klugman	Marlo Thomas			
Kris Kristofferson	Ralph Waite			
Hal Linden				

Source: Victoria A. Sackett, "Statecraft as Stagecraft: Actors' and Politicians' New Roles," *Public Opinion* (May/June 1987), p. 15. Reprinted with the permission of the American Enterprise Institute for Public Policy Research.

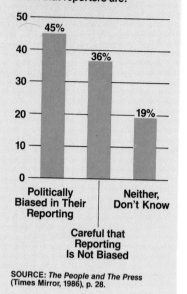

Is Reporting Biased?
Percentage of people who
think that reporters are:

- Politically Biased in Their Reporting: 45%
- Careful that Reporting Is Not Biased: 36%
- Neither, Don't Know: 19%

SOURCE: *The People and The Press*
(Times Mirror, 1986), p. 28.

TABLE 12–3
Politics of the Press

	PUBLIC	JOURNALISTS	COLLEGE-EDUCATED PROFESSIONALS
Consider self			
Liberal	23%	55%	38%
Conservative	29	17	30
Government regulation of business			
Favor	22	49	26
Oppose	50	41	57
Verifiable nuclear freeze			
Favor	66	84	79
Oppose	22	13	17
Increased defense budget			
Favor	38	18	32
Oppose	51	80	63
Allowing women to have abortions			
Favor	49	82	68
Oppose	44	14	28
Prayer in public schools			
Favor	74	25	58
Oppose	19	67	36
Death penalty for murder			
Favor	75	47	67
Oppose	17	47	26

Source: Adapted from *Public Opinion* (August/September 1985), p. 7. Reprinted with the permission of the American Enterprise Institute for Policy Research.

Another critique of bias comes from the far left. These critics contend the mainstream press is purely a propaganda device of the ruling class, which creates the boundaries of acceptable thinking, thereby shutting out left-wing viewpoints. They see the mass media as capitalist enterprises that dislike airing anticapitalist sentiments. As well as being a tool of the business class, according to these critics, the media are also a tool of government propaganda seeking to distort the facts. Others see this "conspiracy theory" as a rationalization by leftists disgruntled over the failure of their views to take hold with the American people.

Whether biased or not, the press and electronic media remain influential forces in our political and cultural system. Media power rivals that of the three branches of government, yet there is no real regulation of the activities of the media. The media are intrusive, bringing the inner workings of government closer to the people than the founding fathers would have wanted. Their desire for profits supercedes other motives. Who reports the news and how it is reported are often more important than what is reported. The media have the power to bring information to American citizens, but they also have the power to make and distort the images that we see. The way we view policy issues and politicians is usually not through personal contact or acquaintance with the subject, but rather through the filtered lens of the media.

Summary

1. The rise of new communications technologies has made the media more influential throughout American society.

2. The power of the mass media over public opinion is significant yet not overwhelming. People may not pay much attention to the media, or believe what they read or see or hear. They may be critical or suspicious of the media and hence resistant to it. They live in groups or homes or neighborhoods that "filter" opinions coming in through the media.

3. A major effect of mass media news is agenda setting, that is, determining what problems will become salient issues for people to form opinions about and to discuss.

4. The mass media are big business, but their product is information, which is protected under the First Amendment.

5. The media are under attack for sensationalism, superficial reporting, biased coverage, and overemphasis on "theater." Any efforts at comprehensive reform will be frustrated, however, by at least two factors: Reformers do not agree on what course to follow; and they, and virtually all other Americans, fear taking any action that might threaten the freedom of the press.

6. Presidential campaigns are dominated by media coverage during both the pre- and postconvention stages. One effect of media influence is that most people seem more interested in the contest as a "game" or "horse race" than as an occasion for serious discussion of issues and candidates.

Further Reading

DEAN E. ALGER. *The Media and Politics* (Prentice Hall, 1989).

W. LANCE BENNETT. *The Politics of Illusion* (Longman, 1988).

RONALD BERKMAN and LAURA W. KITCH. *Politics in the Media Age* (McGraw Hill, 1986).

DAVID S. BRODER. *Behind the Front Page: A Candid Look at How the News is Made* (Simon & Schuster, 1987).

JAMES W. CAREY, ed. *Media, Myths, and Narratives: Television and the Press* (Sage Publications, 1988).

JAMES DEAKIN. *Straight Stuff: the Reporters, the White House, and the Truth* (William Morrow, 1984).

EDWARD S. HERMAN and NOAM CHOMSKY. *Manufacturing Consent* (Pantheon Books, 1988).

MARK HERTSGAARD. *On Bended Knee* (Farrar, Strauss and Giroux, 1988).

STEPHEN HESS. *The Ultimate Insiders: U.S. Senators in the National Media* (Brookings Institution, 1986).

JOHN H. KESSEL. *Presidential Campaign Politics: Coalition Strategies and Citizen Response* (The Dorsey Press, 1988).

DOROTHY D. NESBIT. *Videostyle in Senate Campaigns* (University of Tennessee Press, 1988).

W. RUSSELL NEWMAN. *The Paradox of Mass Politics: Knowledge and Opinion in the American Electorate* (Harvard University Press, 1986).

CHARLES PRESS and KENNETH VERBURG. *American Politicians and Journalists* (Scott, Foresman, 1988).

WILLIAM RUSHER. *The Coming Battle for the Media* (William Morrow, 1988).

Notes

1. *Newsweek* (August 15, 1988), p. 21; *Newsweek* (August 29, 1988), pp. 16–20, 22–26; *The Washington Post* (September 4, 1988), pp. A1 and A8; Roy L. Behr and Shanto Iyengar, "Television News, Real-World Cues, and Changes in the Public Agenda," *Public Opinion Quarterly* (Spring 1985), pp. 38–57; and Larry Sabato, "Political Influence, the News Media and Campaign Consultants," *PS* (March 1989), pp. 15–17.

2. Leslie G. Moeller, "The Big Four: Mass Media Actualities and Expectations," in Richard W. Budd and Brent D. Ruben, eds., *Beyond Media: New Approaches to Mass Communication* (Transaction Books, 1988), p. 15.

3. William Rivers, *The Other Government* (Universe Books, 1982); Douglass Cater, *The Fourth Branch of Government* (Houghton Mifflin, 1959); Dom Bonafede, "The Washington Press—An Interpreter or a Participant in Policy Making?" *National Journal* (April 24, 1982), pp. 716–21; and Michael Ledeen, "Learning to Say 'No' to the Press," *Public Interest* (Fall 1983), p. 113.

4. Jeffrey B. Abramson, F. Christopher Arterton, and Gary R. Orren, *The Electronic Commonwealth: The Impact of New Media Technologies on Democratic Politics* (Basic Books, 1988).

5. Doris A. Graber, *Mass Media and American Politics* (Congressional Quarterly Press, 1989), pp. 153–83; and David L. Paletz and Robert M. Entman, *Media Power Politics* (The Free Press, 1981), pp. 149–67.

6. R. Dominick, *The Dynamics of Mass Communication*, (Random House, 1987), p. 260.

7. Hedrick Smith, *The Power Game* (Random House, 1988).

8. Ben H. Bagdikian, *The Media Monopoly* (Beacon Press, 1983).

9. See Graber, *Mass Media and American Politics*; and Gina M. Garramone and Charles K. Atkin, "Mass Communication and Political Socialization: Specifying the Effects," *Public Opinion Quarterly* (Spring 1986), pp. 76–86.

10. Benjamin M. Compaine, ed., *Who Owns the Media? Concentration of Ownership in the Mass Communications Industry* (Knowledge Industry Publications, 1979), p. 1; and Dominick, *The Dynamics of Mass Communication*, pp. 189, 242, 282.

11. Michael Parenti, *Inventing Reality: The Politics of the Mass Media* (St. Martin's Press, 1986), p. 27. For a further discussion of business configurations that characterize the media industry, see Graber, *Mass Media and American Politics*, pp. 41–50.

12. *Newsweek* (August 22, 1988), pp. 42–47; *The New York Times* (March 19, 1989), p. E7; *The New York Times* (April 16, 1989), pp. 1F and 8F.

13. Shanto Iyengar and Donald R. Kinder, *News that Matters* (University of Chicago Press, 1987).

14. Harvey G. Zeidenstein, "News Media Perceptions of White House News Management," *Presidential Studies Quarterly* (Summer 1984).

15. George Garneau, "Supreme Court May Go Electronic," *Editor and Publisher* (October 15, 1988), pp. 20–21.

16. See the classic works: Paul Lazarsfeld, Bernard Berelson and Hazel Gaudet, *The People's Choice: How the Voter Makes Up His Mind in a Presidential Campaign*, 3d ed. (Columbia University Press, 1968); and Bernard Berelson, Paul Lazarsfeld, and William McPhee,

Voting: A Study of Opinion Formation in a Presidential Campaign (University of Chicago Press, 1954).

17. Elihu Katz and Paul Lazarsfeld, *Personal Influence: The Part Played by People in the Flow of Mass Communications* (Free Press, 1955).

18. See another classic, Angus Campbell et al., *The American Voter* (Wiley, 1960).

19. Stuart Oskamp, ed., *Television as a Social Issue* (Sage Publications, 1988); and James W. Carey, ed., *Media, Myths, and Narratives: Television and the Press* (Sage Publications, 1988).

20. Caryl Rivers, "Women, Myth, and the Media," in *When Information Counts: Grading the Media*, Bernard Rubin, ed. (Lexington Books, 1985), pp. 3–11. See also S. Robert Lichter, Linda S. Lichter, Stanley Robinson, and Daniel Amundson, "Prime-Time Prejudice: TV's Images of Blacks and Hispanics," *Public Opinion* (July/August 1987), pp. 13–16.

21. Shanto Iyengar, Mark D. Peters, and Donald R. Kinder, "Experimental Demonstrations of the 'Not-So-Minimal' Consequences of Television News Programs," *American Political Science Review* (December 1982), pp. 848–58.

22. Daniel P. Moynihan, "The Presidency and the Press," *Commentary* (March 1971), p. 43.

23. Michael J. Robinson, "Just How Liberal Is the News? 1980 Revisited," *Public Opinion* (February/March 1983), pp. 55–60; Herbert J. Gans, "Are U.S. Journalists Dangerously Liberal?" *Columbia Journalism Review* (November/December 1985), pp. 29–33; and Aaron Wildavsky, "The Media's 'American Egalitarians,'" *The Public Interest* (Summer 1987), pp. 94–104.

24. Moynihan, p. 44.

25. Among others researching this topic, see Doris Graber, "Say It with Pictures: The Impact of Audio-Visual News on Public Opinion Formation," paper presented at the Annual Meeting of the Midwest Political Science Association, Chicago, April 1987; and Benjamin I. Page, Robert Y. Shapiro and Glenn R. Dempsey, "What Moves Public Opinion?" *American Political Science Review* (March 1987), pp. 23–43.

26. Michael J. Robinson and Margaret A. Sheehan, *Over the Wire and on TV: CBS and UPI in Campaign '80* (Russell Sage Foundation, 1983).

27. Michael J. Robinson, "Public Affairs Television and the Growth of Political Malaise: The Case of 'The Selling of the Pentagon,'" *American Political Science Review* (June 1976), pp. 409–32, quoted on p. 430.

28. Herbert J. Gans, *Deciding What's News: A Study of CBS Evening News, NBC Nightly News, Newsweek, and Time* (Pantheon, 1979), p. 61.

29. For some of these proposals, see Lewis W. Folson, *The Untapped Power of the Press* (Praeger, 1985).

30. Norman E. Isaacs, *Untended Gates: The Mismanaged Press* (Columbia University Press, 1985).

31. Steve Lilienthal, "Election '88 Media Consultants," *Public Opinion* (January/February 1989), pp. 20 and 53–55; and Larry Sabato, *The Rise of Political Consultants* (Basic Books, 1981), pp. 111–74.

32. Richard Stout, "The Pre-Pre-Campaign-Campaign," *Public Opinion* (December/January 1983), pp. 17–20, 60.

33. Thomas R. Marshall, "Issues, Personalities, and Presidential Primary Voters," *Social Science Quarterly* (September 1984), p. 750; and Kathleen C. Ruszay, "Media Coverage of the 1988 Presidential Election: Access and Emphasis." Paper presented at the Annual Meeting of the Midwest Political Science Association, Chicago, April 13–15, 1989.

34. See John H. Aldrich, *Before the Convention* (University of Chicago Press, 1980), p. 65, a study of candidates' choices and strategies. See also Thomas E. Patterson, *The Mass Media Election* (Praeger, 1980).

35. John Foley et al., *Nominating a President: The Process and the Press* (Praeger, 1980), p. 39. For the press's treatment of incumbents see James Glen Stovall, "Incumbency and News Coverage of the 1980 Presidential Election Campaign," *Western Political Quarterly* (December 1984), p. 621.

36. Ibid., p. 78. Emphasis added.

37. Scott Keeter, "The Illusion of Intimacy: Television and the Role of Candidate Personal Qualities in Voter Choice," *Public Opinion Quarterly* (Fall 1987), pp. 344–58.

38. Michael J. Robinson, "The Media in 1980: Was the Message the Message?" in Austin Ranney, ed., *The American Elections of 1980* (American Enterprise Institute for Public Policy Research, 1981), p. 178.

39. Robinson, "The Media in 1980."

40. Edwin Diamond and Stephen Bates, *The Spot: The Rise of Political Advertising on TV* (MIT Press, 1984). For a historical look at political advertising, see Kathleen Hall Jamieson, *Packaging the Presidency* (Oxford University Press, 1984).

41. See Sabato, *The Rise of Political Consultants*.

42. Frank I. Luntz, *Candidates, Consultants, and Campaigns: The Style and Substance of American Electioneering* (Basil Blackwell, 1988), pp. 72–73.

43. Richard Berke, "To Hear the Sharpest Advertising Attacks, Tune into Radio," *The New York Times* (November 6, 1988), p. Y 17.

44. *The Los Angeles Times* (December 1, 1987), as reprinted in Luntz, *Candidates, Consultants, and Campaigns*, p. 46.

45. "Beaming at the Voters," *Time* (Feb. 15, 1988), pp. 78–79.

46. Dan Hunter, "Cable's New Clout," *Columbia Journalism Review* (January/February 1988), p. 36.

47. Richard Armstrong, *The Next Hurrah: The Changing Face of the American Political Process* (Beech Tree Books, 1988), pp. 19–21.

48. See in general, Sabato, *The Rise of Political Consultants*; and James David Barber, *The Pulse of Politics: Electing Presidents in the Media Age* (Norton, 1980). See also Fred Barnes, "The Myth of Political Consultants," *The New Republic* (June 16, 1986), p. 16.

49. Douglas Bailey, quoted in William J. Lanouette, "You Can't Be Elected with TV Alone, But You Can't Win Without It Either," *National Journal* (March 1, 1980), pp. 344–48.

50. Leo Bogart, "The Public's Use and Perception of Newspapers," *Public Opinion Quarterly* (Winter 1984), p. 711.

51. Michael A. Ledeen, "Learning to Say 'No' to the Press," *Public Interest* (Fall 1983), p. 117.

52. Bogart, "The Public's Use and Perception of Newspapers," p. 710.

53. Martin Linsky, *Impact: How the Press Affects Federal Policymaking* (W. W. Norton & Co., 1986).

54. "Michael Deaver Rates the President's Press," *Washington Journalism Review* (April 1984), p. 25.

55. Ledeen, "Learning to Say 'No' to the Press," p. 114.

56. Ibid., p. 116.

57. Bogart, "The Public's Use and Perception of Newspapers," p. 712.

58. *The People and the Press* (Times Mirror, 1986).

59. Joseph Wagner, "Media Do Make a Difference," *American Journal of Political Science* (August 1983).

60. C. Don Livingston, "The Televised Presidency," *Presidential Studies Quarterly* (Winter 1986), p. 22.

61. Ibid., p. 25.

62. Fred Smoller, "The Six O'Clock Presidency: Patterns of Network News Coverage of the President," *Presidential Studies Quarterly* (Winter 1986), p. 34.

63. See Nelson Polsby, "The Subculture of News Media," *Consequences of Party Reform* (Oxford, 1983), pp. 142–46. See also "Media and Business Elites: Two Classes in Conflict!" *The Public Interest* (Fall 1982).

64. *The Washington Post* (September 29, 1976), pp. A1 and A10.

65. S. Robert Lichter and Stanley Rothman, "Media Business Elites," *Public Opinion* (October/November 1981), pp. 42–46 and 59–60.

66. Fred Barnes, "Media Realignment," *The New Republic* (May 6, 1985), p. 12.

13

Elections: The Democratic Struggle

Nothing concerned the framers in 1787 more than the manner in which elections would be conducted in the new republic. Eighteenth-century English citizens had little to say about who governed them. Elections for members of the House of Commons were tightly controlled affairs in which "rotten boroughs" and districts were bought and sold by aristocrats and landed gentry. And even though the colonists did elect their own legislators, the American colonies were governed by royal appointed governors.

Thus, it is not surprising that the framers devoted so much attention to the electoral system. Because they represented many states with diverse interests, they were forced to adopt a variety of compromises. The framers were well aware that many republics had failed because their leaders had manipulated their election systems, tampered with terms of office, or simply abolished elections altogether.

If you turn back to the text of the Constitution in Chapter 1, you will note that the framers dealt at length with some of the basic aspects of elections, especially in the long Article I—"The Legislative Article." They gave us the foundations of elections that still exist today. They specified what federal officials will be chosen, how voters will choose them, when they will be elected, how many representatives and senators each state would be entitled to, and more. However, the new Constitution left it to the states to decide the suffrage requirements and, subject to a congressional override, "the Times, Places and Manner of holding elections," which in effect paved the way for the exclusion of blacks, Native Americans, women, and the landless from the electoral process.

It did not take long—only sixteen years—before the people started to choose the president, and before long white male suffrage began to be expanded, but it did take another one hundred years before blacks and women were effectively brought into their country's political life. Despite this indefensible delay, elections today lie at the very heart of "government by the people."

1988 Electoral Votes

Bush (426)

Dukakis (111)

Electoral votes needed to win: 270

A congressional candidate campaigning door to door in the suburbs.

At first, office seeking tended to be rather genteel in the new republic. Likely candidates who were "co-opted" by local elites might run for office (or ride on horseback or by carriage) in a friendly way. But electioneering was already changing in the 1790s, particularly in the cities. By the end of the century a Jeffersonian Republican in New York City—Aaron Burr—was organizing his campaign aides on a ward-by-ward basis, card-indexing voters' names and attitudes, setting up house-to-house fundraising teams, and arranging transportation for voters on election day.

The nature of election struggles has, of course, changed immensely in the past two centuries, largely as the result of the influence of the modern media and new technologies, as described in the previous chapter. But the election struggle still lies at the heart of democratic politics. In this chapter we look more closely at modern campaigns for Congress and the presidency. We note three problems in particular that appear to be entrenched in our electoral system: the *lack of competition* for some offices, the danger and distortion inherent in the *electoral college*, and the influence of *money*.

Running for Office

How candidates run for office obviously depends largely on the nature of their district or state. We tend to focus on presidential elections because they command so much media attention. But Americans also elect 100 United States senators, 435 representatives to the United States Congress, 50 state governors, over 2000 state senators, nearly 6000 members of the lower houses of state legislatures, and more than a half million other persons to various state and local offices.[1] Each of these offices in each jurisdiction requires a different type of campaign. The nature of a campaign also depends on who the candidate is: a first-term senator or representative running for reelection, a veteran with a strong personal organization, or a novice who has never run for office before. We can, however, note certain similarities in House and Senate elections.

First, we find a relative lack of competitiveness in many elections. This phenomenon was noted more than two decades ago by those who study congressional elections, and the advantage enjoyed by sitting members of the House of Representatives has been explored in great depth.[2] In recent years scholars have begun to question how we should measure competitiveness in elections—by the closeness of the two-party vote; by the number of incumbents who are seriously challenged; by the number who are challenged at all; by the number of incumbents who lose; or by some other standard.[3] They further noted that the lack of competitiveness in congressional elections was also apparent in elections for some other offices.[4]

When low levels of competition cause more seats to become safe, these elections do not adequately perform their assigned role because they do not give the populace a chance to express their views on the issues and candidates of the day. Democratic theorists find this a most disturbing trend. Competition is more likely for higher offices and for offices viewed as important within a particular jurisdiction. Thus, elections for governor and for the United States Senate are seriously contested more than for the House of Representatives. Congressional elections tend to be more competitive than state house or senate elections in most states, but mayoral elections are often hotly contested, because politicians view the prize as more valuable.

Presidential performance also affects both House and Senate elections. For many years political scientists talked about presidential "coattails" in congressional elections, that is, popular presidential candidates help others running in their party to achieve office. Although the **coattail effect** has been less evident in recent years, presidential performance might well affect congressional elections indirectly, even in midterm elections. To a considerable degree the ballots cast in these elections reflect the voters' judgment on the performance of the president, especially his management of the economy.[5]

Technology is increasingly influencing all campaigns for office, but the influence is felt in different ways in different campaigns. Candidates for governor, United States senator, or member of the House of Representatives quickly become attuned to the need for campaign agencies, opinion pollsters, direct-mail fund raisers, computer experts, media specialists, and many other consultants. Campaigns are "packaged" as well as managed to the point that many fear that candidate personality and appearance have become more important than issues or party affiliation. Although technology is new, human nature is old. Negative campaigning—that is, focusing on an opponent's alleged failings rather than demonstrating why one's own candidate should be elected—has been with us since the beginning. But in recent years campaign strategists have carried negative campaigning to new depths of nastiness.

A congressional candidate campaigning in a rural community.

CAMPAIGNING FOR THE HOUSE

Most incumbent members of Congress seek reelection, and they usually do so successfully.[6] Incumbents usually base their decision to run again on their own career progression. Is it an opportune time to run for some other office? Has the representative served long enough to retire? Is there some concern about reelection that would lead him or her to opt out of a race? But once a decision to run is made by an incumbent, the prohibitive favorite is the incumbent. In the last twenty years, on average over 93 percent of the incumbent members of the House seeking reelection have done so successfully. In the two most recent elections, incumbents have had a successful reelection rate of over 98 percent, with only six losing in general election campaigns in 1986 and in 1988.

For a nonincumbent contemplating running for the House of Representatives, the first question is one of timing. Does the year look good for the candidate and the party? Is the incumbent running for reelection, or will the seat become open? Is there any kind of groundswell against the incumbent? If it is a presidential election year, will the party ticket be headed by an attractive national candidate? In a midterm election, will the party ticket be headed by a vote-getting statewide candidate? If either case, can the would-be representative get a firm hold on the coattails? Should the candidate wait two or four more years in order to broaden his or her own range of acquaintances? Or will it be too late by then? In short, is this the time to run? Candidates think hard about these questions, but in the final analysis they must make their decisions without fully knowing the answers.

The outcome for most potential candidates is that they will not run. However, every two years as many as 1000 candidates—including approximately 400 incumbents—decide that they will campaign for Congress. After deciding to take the plunge, the candidates must first plan a primary race, unless they face no opponents for the party's nomination. Incumbents are rarely challenged for renomination from within their own party, and when they are, the challenges are rarely serious. In 1988, for example, only one incumbent was denied renomination. The challengers who are least likely to have primary opposition are those running for seats in which the incumbents are thought least vulnerable.[7]

For would-be challengers in contested primaries or for those seeking open seats, the first step is to build a *personal* organization, because the *party* organization usually stays neutral until the nomination is decided. A candidate can build an organization while holding a lesser office, such as a seat in the state legislature, or by deliberately getting to know people, serving in civic causes, helping other candidates, and being conspicuous without being controversial.

The next step is to raise funds to hire campaign managers and technicians, to buy television and other advertising, to conduct polls, and to pay for a variety of other activities. But few candidates are able to do this effectively in primaries. Most primary campaigns are run on low budgets with limited funds.

The main hurdle a candidate faces is gaining *visibility*. Candidates work to be mentioned by the media. But in large metropolitan areas where many campaigns are going on simultaneously, congressional candidates are frequently lost in the media "noise." In rural areas the press often plays down political news. Candidates rely on personal contacts, on handshaking and door-to-door campaigning, and on identifying likely supporters and courting their favor—the same techniques used in campaigns for lesser offices. The turnout in primaries tends to be very low except in campaigns in which large sums of money were expended on advertising.

In the general election, however, campaigning for Congress becomes more sophisticated. General election campaigns can usefully be divided into four types: incumbent campaigns; serious challenger campaigns; weak challenger campaigns; and open seat campaigns. A distinguishing feature is the amount of money spent on the campaign and the consequent impact on the electorate.

Incumbents tend to win reelection because, by and large, those who run against them run weak campaigns.[8] On the average, incumbents outspend their challengers by as much as three to one. However, averages mask important differences. Most challengers spend very little money, run campaigns that are not significantly more visible than primary campaigns, contact few voters, and lose badly. A few challengers in each election mount serious challenges because of the perceived vulnerability of the incumbent, the challenger's own wealth, party or political action committee efforts, or a combination of factors. Often their campaign expenditures rival the incumbents', and still, most of them lose. In 1988, only six challengers defeated incumbents; only forty others polled more than 40 percent of the votes in the November election.

Why is keeping a House seat so much easier than gaining it? Incumbent representatives have a host of perquisites that help them gain reelection. These "perks" include free mailings to constituents (franking), the free use of studios to record radio and television tapes to be sent to local media outlets, and, perhaps most important of all, a large staff to perform countless favors and send a stream of press reports and mail, in the member's name, back to the district. These all help a House member build up not only name recognition, but also a positive image.[9] Representatives also try to win committee posts that relate especially to the needs of their districts, even if these are on relatively minor committees.[10]

Congressional careers are built on a variety of types of personal contact: shaking hands, canvassing homes, emphasizing local problems, remembering people's names, doing favors.[11] If an incumbent does this contacting well, he or she will win reelection again and again. But if incumbents have trouble with local politics, or if no incumbent is running, then other factors enter, particularly national politics and the comparative ability of candidates to run modern campaigns and build up the grass-roots support on which a long career can be based.

If incumbents win so often, how do we get any significant turnover in the House of Representatives at all? The turnover comes when incumbents die, decide

Drawing by Lorenz: © 1980 The New Yorker Magazine, Inc.

Seats Gained or Lost by White House Party in House of Representatives National Midterm Elections	
1930	−49
1934	+9
1938	−71
1942	−45
1946	−55
1950	−29
1954	−18
1958	−48
1962	−4
1966	−47
1970	−12
1974	−48
1978	−12
1982	−26
1986	−5
1990	—

to retire, or seek some other office. Potential candidates for the House as well as political action committees and political party committees all watch open seat races closely. Hence, open seat races tend to be competitive; the winners in sixteen of the twenty-six open seat races in 1988 polled less than 60 percent of the vote.

CAMPAIGNING FOR THE SENATE

Because state populations vary so widely, generalizing about Senate campaigns is difficult. But running for the Senate is big-time politics. The six-year term and the national exposure make a Senate seat a glittering prize, so competition is usually intense. A race normally costs millions of dollars. In 1984 two candidates spent over $10 million each. In 1986 the average Senate race cost $2,578,000. The average winning Senate race cost $3.5 million.[12]

Candidates for the Senate are far more visible than House candidates. They find it more important to take positions on national problems, and they cannot duck tough issues very easily. In other ways, Senate races tend to be much like those for the House. The essential tactics are to get others involved, use as much personal contact as possible (especially in the states with smaller populations), avoid giving the opposition any positive publicity, and have a simple campaign theme. Candidates for the Senate, like candidates for all offices, must persuade people by *reinforcing* their present feelings, *activating* their latent attitudes, and *converting* their opposing views to gain their support. Facts do not speak for themselves; candidates must provide an intellectual and psychological framework.

Incumbency is also an advantage for senators, although not as much as for representatives. Incumbent senators are widely known through the media, not just through their own efforts to reach their constituents. While citizens rarely hear anything negative about an incumbent representative—because almost everything they hear about these incumbents is generated from the representatives' own offices—senators' careers are examined more objectively by the media. Further, senators normally face tougher competition—challengers who frequently are already well known because of holding other office or who have the ability to raise and spend significant amounts of money.[13] Senate campaigns generally feature state-of-the-art campaign technology from both candidates.

In recent elections 76 percent of incumbent senators seeking reelection did so successfully; yet they do not enjoy the easy challenges encountered by their colleagues in the House.[14] In 1980, for example, ten of the twenty-six senators seeking reelection lost, and Republicans were able to gain control of the Senate

---

Important Factors in Winning a Contested Election

UNCONTROLLABLE FACTORS:
Incumbent rerunning or open seat
Strength of party organization
National tides or landslide possibility
Socioeconomic makeup of district

ORGANIZATIONAL FACTORS:
Registration drives
Fundraising machinery
Campaign organization
Volunteers
Effective media campaign
Direct-mail campaign efforts
Get-out-the-vote effort

PERSONAL LEADERSHIP FACTORS:
Candidate's personal appeal
Candidate's knowledge of issues
Candidate's speaking and debating ability
Candidate's commitment and determination
Candidate's ability to earn unpaid, positive media coverage

TABLE 13–1
"Big Spenders" in 1988 House and Senate Elections—and How They Fared

House	Jane G. Esking (D-Tennessee)	$2,558,003	Lost
	Philip Norman Bredesen (D-Tennessee)	$1,883,727	Lost
	Robert Kenneth Dornan (R-California)	$1,755,892	Won
	Joseph J. DioGuardi (R-New York)	$1,567,129	Lost
	Gary K. Hart (D-California)	$1,548,193	Lost
Senate	Peter B. Wilson (R-California)	$12,969,294	Won
	Lloyd Bentsen (D-Texas)	$8,829,361	Won
	Howard M. Metzenbaum (D-Ohio)	$8,547,545	Won
	George V. Voinovich (R-Ohio)	$8,233,859	Lost
	Peter Miller Dawkins (R-New Jersey)	$7,616,249	Lost

Source: Federal Election Commission.

Connecticut Attorney General Joseph I. Lieberman, a Democrat who unseated incumbent Senator Lowell P. Weicker, Jr.

for the first time in nearly three decades. While few incumbents lost in either 1982 or 1984, the 1986 election again saw a big turnaround, with the Democrats regaining control. In 1986 Republican Paula Hawkins, who had first been elected in 1980 and who was running for reelection without Ronald Reagan on the national ticket, lost to popular Florida Governor Bob Graham. Connecticut's maverick Republican Lowell Weicker was defeated by the state's attorney general, Joseph Lieberman, in 1988. On the whole, however, 1988 was again a strong year for incumbents, with only three losing.

Is there any place for rational planning in all this? Most politicians see victory as nine-tenths perspiration and one-tenth inspiration. But careful calculation may pay off, especially in the tricky business of picking a good year to run and a good presidential candidate to run with or against. In 1974 Republican candidates in most districts did their best to separate themselves from President Nixon, Watergate, and inflation. And in 1980, when many Republican candidates saw Ronald Reagan's star rising, they tried to catch on to it. But the impact of such efforts is not always predictable, nor are candidates always successful in cementing the connections they view as helpful. Most election results are also affected by factors over which candidates have little control. These include the form of the ballot (which may link presidential and congressional candidates or separate them), national trends, party registration, and the influence of local candidates.

We may be entering a period in which campaign effectiveness will become even more significant in determining election outcomes, especially for offices of prominence like United States senator or state governor. This may happen not merely because of the greater effectiveness of new political techniques, but also because a growing number of young voters, not loyal to any one party, approach campaigns ready to be persuaded. Although party loyalties will not disappear altogether, there are likely to be fewer voters to whom candidates can appeal in terms of party loyalty alone.

And modern campaign techniques, if sufficient money is available to afford them, give individual candidates the tools to forge new appeals. In the 1988 campaign, for example, the New Jersey Republicans nominated General Pete Dawkins—a Heisman Trophy-winning football star from West Point, a Rhodes Scholar and a decorated Vietnam veteran—to run against first-term Senator Frank Lautenberg. Dawkins went on the attack, and the incumbent responded with what a political scientist termed "the most nasty, dirty, vicious campaign" in memory.[15] Two weeks before the election the race was nearly even. Although Dawkins vowed to stop negative advertisements, his pledge was empty because, having already spent millions of dollars, Dawkins was out of money. Lautenberg ended his campaign with a series of positive advertisements, emphasizing his record for New Jersey. Relying on media consultants Carter Eskew and Robert Squier (whom he paid nearly $700,000) and pollster Paul Maslin (who cost the campaign more than $180,000), Lautenberg outspent Dawkins by three to one in the campaign's last week and a half and won by eight percentage points. In this and many other races the campaign team's utilization of sophisticated analysis of what the voters are looking for and a commitment to win—even if that requires questionable advertising techniques—can determine the outcome of the race.

Running for President

There are really two campaigns for the presidency. One is the "mass media election,"[16] which we examined in Chapter 12. The other is the formal election process that involves seeking the nomination of a major party and then amassing enough

Luckovitch for The Times-Picayune.

CHAPTER 13 / Elections: The Democratic Struggle

votes to win a majority in the electoral college on the first Tuesday after the first Monday in November. The "formal" campaign has three stages: winning delegates, capturing the convention, and campaigning in the fall.

STAGE ONE: WINNING DELEGATES

Presidential hopefuls must make a series of tactical decisions, any one of which might be critical. The first is when to start campaigning. Some candidates begin almost as soon as the last election is over, as several 1988 aspirants did as early as 1985. Campaigning begins well before any actual declaration of candidacy, as candidates try to line up supporters to win caucuses or primaries in key states and to raise money for their nomination effort. Presidential nominating campaigns now begin so early that some analysts see nominations as decided even before the first primary is held.

The hardest job for candidates and their strategists is calculating how to deal with the crazy-quilt system of presidential primaries and caucuses that makes up the delegate-selection system. This complex system varies from state to state and often between the two parties in the same state. Although the process is influenced somewhat by federal regulation of campaign financing and national party rules, within broad limits the states can set up the systems they prefer. The result has been a complex maze.

Presidential Primaries　State **presidential primaries** for choosing convention delegates (unknown before this century) have become the main method of choosing delegates. Today about thirty states, including most of the larger states and hence the vast majority of voters, use presidential primaries. The rest use caucuses or conventions (see the next section). Presidential primaries have two main features: the "beauty contest," in which voters indicate their choice for president, usually from a list, and the actual selection of delegates to the convention. Different combinations of these two features have produced the following systems:

1. *Proportional representation*: Delegates to the national convention are allocated on the basis of the votes candidates win in the "beauty contest." This system has been used in most of the states, including several of the largest ones.[17]

2. *Winner take all*: The results of the presidential preference poll bind all the delegates, so that whoever wins the "popularity contest" wins *all* the delegates in that state or district. To win all the delegates of a state like California, of course, is an enormous bonus to a candidate. (George Bush won all of California's delegates in 1988.) Only the Republicans use this system at the state level; the Democrats banned it in 1976, although they still use it in some districts within states.

3. *Winner take more*: This is a variation of the winner-take-all system, and the winner of a district's popular vote gets a bonus for winning; delegates are allocated proportionally after the bonus has been awarded.

4. *Delegate selection*: In several states, large and small, voters choose delegate candidates who may or may not have indicated how they will vote in the presidential convention. The names of the presidential hopefuls do not appear separately on the ballot; there is no presidential preference poll or "beauty contest." Under this arrangement the chosen delegates are more likely to feel free to exercise their independent judgment at the convention. Again, this system is used by only the Republicans.

George Bush on the campaign trail.

5. *Delegate selection and separate presidential poll*: In several states, including New Hampshire (where in recent years the first primary has been held), voters decide twice: once to state their choice for president and once to choose delegates shown on the ballot to be pledged, or at least favorable, to a presidential candidate. This is one of the oldest types of presidential primary.[18]

Caucuses and Conventions   About twenty states use a caucus and convention system for choosing delegates. This is the oldest method of choosing delegates and is fundamentally different from the primary system because it centers on the *party organization*. In principle, the caucus and convention system is far simpler than the primary method. Delegates to national conventions are chosen by delegates to state or district conventions, who themselves are chosen earlier in county, precinct, or town caucuses. A **caucus** is nothing more than a meeting of party members. The process starts at local meetings open to all party members, who discuss and take positions on candidates and issues and elect delegates to represent their views at the next level. This process is repeated until presidential convention delegates are chosen by conventions of delegates from throughout a district or state.

There are many variations of the caucus and convention system, because they are regulated by each state's parties and legislature. The most significant one may be Iowa's, because Iowa has held the earliest caucuses in most recent presidential nominating contests. Early in February 1988, on a Monday evening, Iowans held hundreds of Democratic and Republican precinct meetings. Large numbers of voters showed up at these small "party town meetings." Although an even larger number of Iowans would doubtless have voted in a primary had there been one, the thousands attending these caucuses had a chance to meet and exchange views about issues and candidates, rather than merely pulling the lever in a voting booth or placing an "X" on a ballot. A special feature of the Iowa meetings was that college students could attend local caucuses in their college or hometowns, as they preferred, with a minimum of hassle.

Strategic Considerations   Strategies for gaining delegates to the national convention through primaries and caucuses have changed over the years. As recently as 1972 and 1976, candidates often thought it wise to skip some of the earlier contests and enter first where their strength lay. This strategy was put to rest by the "go everywhere" strategy that Jimmy Carter pursued in winning the 1976 Democratic nomination. But questions still exist about emphasis and allocation of resources. Many recent candidates stressed the importance of Iowa and New Hampshire, hoping that early showings in these states, which receive a great deal of attention, would move them into the spotlight for later efforts. In 1988, however, the outcomes in these two states did not clearly forecast the final nominations. In the same year Tennessee Senator Albert Gore tried a "southern strategy," downplaying his efforts in Iowa and New Hampshire in hopes of winning Democratic delegates in his native South. His strategy failed because a number of other candidates also won states on "Super Tuesday," when most of the southern primaries were held.

In part, strategies are determined by events beyond the candidates' control. Straw polls, conducted in some states well in advance of the opening caucuses and primaries and interpreted by the press, have given some relatively unknown candidates advantages. Thus, participation in all such events becomes important, since the media deem them so. Similarly, debates—often televised—have become an important feature of the nominating process. As recently as 1980 only a few

DEMOCRATIC
NATIONAL
CONVENTION
ATLANTA 88

OMNI COLISEUM, ATLANTA
JULY 18-21, 1988

DELEGATE

PAUL G. KIRK, JR.
CHAIRMAN

JULY 19, 1988

1558

≡TUESDAY≡

CHAPTER 13 / Elections: The Democratic Struggle

of these debates were held. However, in 1988 the candidates seemed to be debating at least every week. The early debates were important for lesser-known candidates.

Conventional wisdom sets candidate strategy, but recent history has shown that conventional wisdom is often wrong. Candidates win or lose by their ability to adapt their own strengths to changing circumstances: the number of candidates running, the ideological splits among the candidates, the calendar of events, the amount of resources available for various aspects of the campaign, the ways in which the media are covering a particular state, and the events that disrupt planning.

STAGE TWO: CAPTURING THE CONVENTION

Presidential conventions compress into three or four days all the excitement of the preceding six or seven months of preconvention politics. The first convention probably was held in 1808, when a few Federalist leaders met secretly in New York to nominate candidates for president and vice-president. In the early 1830s, under the leadership of Democrats Andrew Jackson and Martin Van Buren, the first real "open" convention was held by a major party. Today the national convention is a famous and unique political institution. For about four days every four years, each party enjoys world attention; covered by batteries of cameras and battalions of newspersons, selected incidents in the convention hall are carried to millions in this country and abroad. This is very much a *party* affair; even though nominating or confirming the nomination of a president is the main event, the party has a chance to come together as a national institution, parade its leaders, adopt a platform, and indulge in oratory, hoopla, and high jinks.

Historically delegates arrived at national conventions with differing degrees of commitment, semicommitment, and noncommitment to presidential candidates. Some delegates were pledged to no candidate at all; others to a specific candidate for one or two ballots; others to their favorite "until hell freezes over." Recent conventions have seen two changes. Because of the adoption of "reforms" requiring delegates to pledge themselves to a definite presidential hopeful (in the Democratic party), and because a Reagan or a Bush, a Carter or a Dukakis has been able to amass the necessary number of delegates in advance, recent conventions have merely ratified decisions already made in the primaries and caucuses. And because of "reforms" encouraging delegates to stick to the person to whom they are pledged, there has been less room for maneuver at conventions.

How tightly should delegates be bound in the convention to presidential candidates to whom they were pledged in the primaries? This question dominated the first day of proceedings at the 1980 Democratic convention. Delegates supporting President Carter, who had won most of the primaries, argued that if delegates could violate their "pledges," primaries would be a farce, and conventions undemocratic and unrepresentative. Delegates backing Senator Edward Kennedy contended that such a rule would make delegates into "pawns" and conventions into "rubber stamps." Why have a convention at all, they asked, if delegates could not act in a deliberative—rather than merely a representative—capacity, especially because months had gone by since many delegates had been selected, and conditions had changed. A majority of the convention supported Carter's position, and party rules appeared to require that "delegates elected to the national convention pledged to a presidential candidate shall in all good conscience reflect the sentiments of those who elected them."[19]

That debate was more over practical politics than philosophy. The delegates pledged to Jimmy Carter were not merely Carter supporters; they were *ardent* Carter supporters, and many had been Carter loyalists since 1976. His campaign

The Democratic convention of 1988.

Vice presidential candidates Lloyd Bentsen and Dan Quayle act friendly enough after a hard-hitting televised debate that brought out the frequently repeated quip by Bentsen to Quayle, "You're no Jack Kennedy."

"My former opponent is supporting me in the general election. Please disregard all the things I said about him in the primary."

Dunagin's People by Ralph Dunagin. Reprinted with special permission of NAS, Inc.

had to approve their candidacy to be delegates. They ran hard *for* him. Similarly the Kennedy supporters were not just against "robot" delegates; they were *for* Senator Kennedy. They knew full well that Carter would win if delegates maintained their pledged positions, so they tried to change the rules. This episode reflects not only the debate over the role of delegates, a matter of democratic and party theory, but also the interplay between debates over rules and the positions of various candidates.

Conventions have their own rules, routines, and rituals. Usually the first day is devoted to a keynote address as well as to other speeches touting the party and denouncing the opposition; the second day to committee reports; the third day to presidential balloting; and the fourth to choosing a vice-presidential nominee.[20] Balloting for president is, of course, the highlight of the proceedings, but dramatic struggles can occur over the adoption of the rules and the platform, if one or more candidates see some advantage in challenging a convention rule or a party plank. Not long ago sharp encounters occurred over credentials, that is, over which delegates should be seated when the matter was in dispute, but recently these have dwindled because of more certain procedures in choosing delegates.

Conventions usually spend many hours debating their platforms. Why? Critics have long pointed out that the party platform is binding on no one. It has been compared to a train platform—something to get in on, not to stand on. But presidential politicians take the platform seriously. It gives a good indication of the general direction a party wants to take and provides rival candidates with a test of their convention strength. Most presidents also make considerable effort to implement their parties' platforms.[21]

The choice of the vice-presidential nominee has become increasingly important. For many years the just-elected presidential nominee has dictated the choice of a running mate; this practice is now taken for granted. Rarely does a person actually "run" for the vice-presidential nomination, because only one vote counts. But there is a good deal of maneuvering in order to capture that one vote.

Traditionally the presidential nominee has chosen a running mate who would "balance the ticket." Walter Mondale raised this tradition to a dramatic new height in 1984 by selecting a woman, Representative Geraldine A. Ferraro, to run with him. Mondale's bold decision was an effort to strengthen his appeal to women voters. In 1988 Governor Dukakis took the more traditional course by choosing a moderate Texan, Senator Lloyd Bentsen, to offset his liberal northern image, while Vice President Bush chose to appeal to younger voters by selecting a relative unknown, Indiana Senator Dan Quayle.

Why do the parties continue to have conventions if the nominee is known in advance and the vice-presidential nominee is decided by one person's choice? What role do conventions play in our system? For the parties they are a time of "coming together" to endorse a party program, and build unity and enthusiasm for the fall campaign. The potential is there to heal wounds festering from the campaign and move into the general election united. Of course, the potential is not always achieved.

STAGE THREE: THE FALL CAMPAIGN

The convention adjourns immediately after the presidential and vice-presidential candidates deliver their acceptance speeches to the delegates and the national television audience. Traditionally the time between the conventions and Labor Day was one for resting, binding post-convention wounds, gearing the party for action, and planning campaign strategy. In recent elections, however, the campaigns have hardly paused after the convention. The marathon image repeated so often by candidate Michael Dukakis has a certain true ring to it.[22]

Strategy differs from one election to another, but politicians, pollsters, and political scientists have collected enough information in recent decades to agree broadly that a number of basic factors affect election outcomes. The great bulk of the electorate votes on the basis of party, candidate appeal, and issues. Much depends on voter turnout as well as on party disposition. Nationally the Democrats have a slight advantage in party registration (see Chapter 10). But the Republicans also have an advantage, because their partisans are more likely to turn out on election day, and they have better access to money and usually a somewhat more favorable press (at least in terms of editorial endorsements). Pledges on policy and program may not arouse the mass of the electorate, but they do help activate interest groups and party organizations, which in turn help get out a favorable vote.

The course of the presidential campaign has become familiar over time. In the first stage, immediately after the conventions, the candidates and their staffs plan strategy.[23] They must determine how to allocate their financial and "people" resources. They must decide how they will get their message across to particular groups. They must build group support. Each candidate sets up veterans, farmers, and other campaign groups to operate through interest groups such as the American Legion, the AFL-CIO, and the American Medical Association.

The question of offensive or defensive strategies plagues the tacticians: Do Americans vote *for* or *against* candidates? Should the opposition be attacked or ignored? Should the candidate campaign aggressively? And how should the image of the candidate be tailored? There was a major, and evidently highly effective, effort by the 1968 Nixon campaigners to shed his old image of divisive campaigning and, indeed, of failure as a campaigner.[24] In a less dramatic way, Roger Ailes and the other consultants who shaped the Bush campaign in 1988 were concerned about transforming his image as a "wimp" and also about portraying Governor Dukakis as a northern liberal.

No one has captured the spirit of presidential campaigning better than Adlai E. Stevenson, the unsuccessful Democratic candidate in 1952 and 1956:

You must emerge, bright and bubbling with wisdom and well-being, every morning at 8 o'clock, just in time for a charming and profound breakfast talk, shake hands with hundreds, often literally thousands, of people, make several inspiring, "newsworthy" speeches during the day, confer with political leaders along the way and with your staff all the time, write at every chance, think if possible, read mail and newspapers, talk on the telephone, talk to everybody, dictate, receive delegations, eat, with decorum—and discretion!—and ride through city after city on the back of an open car, smiling until your mouth is dehydrated by the wind, waving until the blood runs out of your arm, and then bounce gaily, confidently, masterfully into great howling halls, shaved and all made up for television with the right color shirt and tie—I always forgot—and a manuscript so defaced with chicken tracks and last-minute jottings that you couldn't follow it, even if the spotlights weren't blinding and even if the still photographers didn't shoot you in the eye every time you looked at them. (I've often wondered what happened to all those pictures!) Then all you have to do is make a great, imperishable speech, get out through the pressing crowds with a few score autographs, your clothes intact, your hands bruised, and back to the hotel—in time to see a few important people.

Presidential candidates must "press the flesh" and mingle with the crowds who attend campaign events.

But the real work has just commenced—two or three, sometimes four hours of frenzied writing and editing of the next day's immortal mouthings so you can get something to the stenographers, so they can get something to the mimeograph machines, so they can get something to the reporters, so they can get something to their papers by deadline time. (And I quickly concluded that all deadlines were yesterday!) Finally sleep, sweet sleep, steals you away, unless you worry—which I do. . . .[25]

Many parts of this description are still accurate. However, xerox machines have replaced stenographers, and speechwriters usually draft the "immortal utterings" for many candidates. The tragedy of Dallas in November 1963 ended the motorcades on the backs of open cars. Nevertheless, anyone who listened to the hoarse voice of Michael Dukakis or saw the fatigue of George Bush in late October 1988 will recognize how demanding running in a presidential campaign is.

The Electoral College System: Mechanics   Americans go to the polls to choose not a president but *electors*, who in turn vote for president. In each state the voters are presented with slates of electors pledged to certain presidential candidates. Each slate consists of persons selected in a manner chosen by each state to serve in this essentially honorary role (each state has one electoral vote for every senator and representative). The slate that wins the most popular votes throughout the state casts all the electoral votes for the state in the **electoral college.** To win the presidency, a candidate must receive a combination of electoral votes that will give him or her an absolute majority in the electoral college.

The electors as a unit are referred to as the **electoral college.** This unique institution never meets and serves only the limited electoral function of electing the president. Yet it has an importance of its own. The framers of the Constitution devised the electoral college system because they wanted to remove the choice of the president from the people and invest that power in a group exercising independent judgment. In its original format, each elector cast two votes, at least one of which had to be for a resident of a state other than his own; this limitation was to prevent state parochialism. The assumption was that each elector would

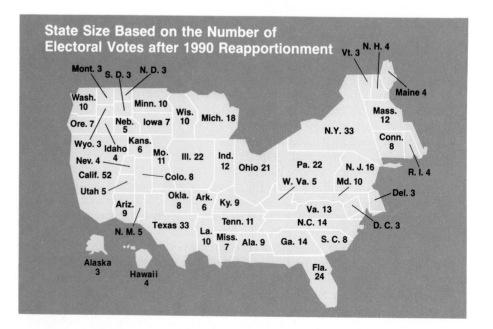

State Size Based on the Number of Electoral Votes after 1990 Reapportionment

cast one vote for a "favorite son" and the other for the true choice as the best individual to serve as president. The founders wanted a system that would guarantee the election of George Washington as the first president. They worried about subsequent choices.

The founders did not envision the party system that evolved during our nation's first decades (see Chapter 10). The election of 1800 demonstrated that the original system would not suffice; the Twelfth Amendment to the Constitution (ratified in 1804) called for separating the votes for president from those for vice-president, recognizing the reality that electors supported candidates of parties, not just meritorious individuals.

This amendment and subsequent redefinitions of voter eligibility in the various states have transformed the electors into straight party representatives who, under normal circumstances, simply register the voters' decision. The electors on the winning slate travel to their state capital on the first Monday after the second Wednesday in December; there they go through the ceremony of casting their ballots for their party's candidates, perhaps hear some speeches, and go home. The ballots are sent from the state capitals to Washington, where they are formally counted by the House and Senate in a joint session in early January. The election formally ends when the sitting vice-president, acting in his role as president of the Senate, announces the winner. In 1989 George Bush was the first vice-president since Martin Van Buren to have the privilege of announcing his own election.

The House is empowered to act when no presidential candidate secures a majority of the electoral votes. This is not likely as long as there are only two serious contending parties. Nevertheless, the House has had to act twice in our history: in 1800, before the passage of the Twelfth Amendment, and again in 1824. On a number of other occasions, the possibility of no candidate's receiving a majority because of a third party contender's receiving some electoral votes was far from remote. When no person receives a majority of the electoral votes the House chooses the president from among the top three candidates. Each state delegation has one vote, and a majority is necessary for election. (A tied delegation has no vote.)

If no person receives a majority of the electoral vote in the vice-presidential contest, the Senate chooses between the top two candidates. Each senator has one vote, and again a majority is required. This has happened only once in our history—in 1837 when Richard M. Johnson of Kentucky was selected for that office.

Although the mechanics of the electoral college system seem set, the actual workings of the system at the margins can be unpredictable. In 1988 an elector chosen on the Democratic ticket in the state of West Virginia cast her vote for Lloyd Bentsen for president to demonstrate the potential problem of "faithless electors." Such departures from custom are rare and have never affected the outcome of an election. But many people agree it is dangerous to have a system that allows individual electors to vote for whomever they wish despite the results of the popular vote in their state. They fear this faulty system could lead to an electoral crisis, or even a constitutional one.

The Electoral College System: Politics The operation of the electoral college, with its statewide electoral slates, sharply influences the presidency and presidential politics. In order to win a presidential election, a candidate must appeal successfully to urban and suburban groups in such big states as California, Texas, Ohio, and Illinois.[26] Under the electoral college system, as we have seen, a candidate wins either *all* a state's electoral votes or *none*. So presidential candidates ordinarily

George Bush and Michael Dukakis presenting their views to the electorate in a televised 1988 debate.

do not waste time campaigning in a state unless they have at least a fighting chance of carrying that state; nor do they waste time in a state in which their party is a sure winner. The fight usually narrows down to the medium-sized and big states where the balance between the parties tends to be fairly even.

The fact that less populous states enjoy extra strength in the electoral college makes it possible for a person to receive a majority of the national popular vote but not a majority of the electoral vote. This happened in 1824, when Andrew Jackson won 12 percent more of the vote than John Quincy Adams; in 1876, when Samuel Tilden received more popular votes than Rutherford Hayes; and again in 1888, when, despite his large popular vote, Grover Cleveland received fewer electoral votes than Benjamin Harrison. It has come close to happening in recent history, particularly in the close elections of 1960 and 1976, when the shift of a few votes in a few key states would have resulted in the election of a president without a popular majority.

Presidential Debates In recent years televised presidential debates have enlivened—or at least focused—the campaigns. Prior to 1960 the major television networks were reluctant to televise debates between major party candidates for the presidency because of the Equal Time Provision, which stipulated that if the networks gave time to one candidate, they would have to give time to all candidates. They feared that a debate between the major party candidates would necessitate giving free time to all minor party candidates. In 1960 John Kennedy and Richard Nixon challenged each other to a series of debates, and the Congress suspended the Equal Time Provision for that purpose. Kennedy's apparent "victory" in the first debate greatly boosted his campaign.[27]

In 1964 and 1972 incumbents Johnson and Nixon did not deign to give their opponents equal billing in debates; thus, no debates were held. But in 1976 President Ford had the courage to do so. The legal ramifications were avoided when the debates were sponsored by the nonpartisan League of Women Voters.[28]

In 1980 the question of who should debate resurfaced. Participation in the debate was particularly important for the photogenic and articulate John Anderson, who was running as a third party candidate. As the sponsoring organization, the League of Women Voters specified that he would be included if he appeared to be receiving more than 15 percent support in public opinion polls. President Carter's strategists did not want to have Anderson included because they felt such inclusion would give his campaign legitimacy—and that Anderson would be gaining votes at the expense of Carter. Thus, the first debate was between Ronald Reagan, the Republican candidate, and John Anderson, a minor party aspirant who more than held his own. The two debaters ganged up on their absent common opponent during that debate, and the Carter strategy changed. The most telling contest of 1980 was the Carter-Reagan debate in the last week of the campaign. President Carter was confident of his ability to "win" the debate because of his intellectual superiority, but he underestimated Ronald Reagan's communication skills. During the debate Reagan skillfully used his campaign theme to his advantage: "Are you better off now than you were four years ago?" In 1984 and 1988, presidential and vice-presidential debates were part of the general election campaigns. The League of Women Voters was replaced by a Commission on Presidential Debates as a sponsor of these debates.

Although the debates have not always had telling effects on the outcome of elections, they have provided important opportunities for the candidates to distinguish themselves and for the public to weigh their candidacies. Most observers feel that Governor Dukakis did not take advantage of this opportunity in 1988, failing to respond to the negative campaign that the Bush camp was waging against him and proving incapable of shedding the image that he was an emotionless technocrat.

More important, however, is general dissatisfaction with the format of the debates. The presidential candidates worry so much about avoiding errors during these highly publicized campaign events that the debates have become little more than "side-by-side" news conferences. The candidates have pat answers to anticipated questions. They do not respond to the reporters' questions, much less to each other. They appear to be more worried about the lighting, the height of the podiums, the warning lights for lengthy answers, and the makeup of the questioning panel than about substance.

Other Campaign Considerations   The inevitable mistakes that occur in presidential campaigns—and the play they receive in the national press and on television—further enliven presidential campaigns. In speaking for the "absolute and total separation of church and state," Jimmy Carter warned in a *Playboy* interview against the sin of pride. To illustrate his point, he went on: "I've looked on a lot of women with lust. I've committed adultery in my heart many times." This comment became a "nine-days' wonder" at the height of the campaign. President Ford matched this blunder by stating, in defending his record of negotiating with Russia over Eastern Europe, that each of these countries "is independent, autonomous, it has its own territorial integrity, and none was under Soviet domination." The Democrats exploited this for a full week.[29] Republicans in 1988 blew the Boston Harbor pollution far out of proportion, as Democrats did the Bush "wimp" factor. But such episodes probably have slight effect on the final vote. The major influences on election outcome are party affiliation, interest-group membership, attitudes on issues, the candidates' personalities, and the nominees' exploitation of these various factors.

Is This the Way to Pick Presidents?

Concern over how we choose presidents now centers on two main issues: (1) the rise in the number, the timing, and the power of presidential primaries, which now dominate the whole presidential selection process, and (2) the actions of the electoral college, including the slight possibility that a presidential election might be thrown into Congress, with possibly dire results. Although the American people have "lucked out" in the electoral college gamble in recent years, the threat remains.[30]

PRESIDENTIAL PRIMARIES: PROS AND CONS

The main argument for presidential primaries is that they open up the nominating process to a larger number of voters than was previously the case. Today the media play up the primary in every important state, and voters follow the race in other states as well as their own. In doing so they can judge the candidates' political qualities: their abilities to organize campaigns, communicate through the media, stand up under pressure, avoid making mistakes (or recover if they do make them), adjust their appeals to shifting events and to different regions of the country, control their staffs as well as utilize them, be decisive, articulate, resilient, informed, and ultimately successful in winning votes. In short, the primaries, it is said, test candidates on the very qualities they must exhibit in the presidency.[31]

Finally, it is said, the primaries are not only the most participatory but also the most *representative* method for choosing our presidents. With millions of voters participating in over thirty state primaries,[32] the public gets a good picture of the popular support for each candidate. As the primaries take place, some aspirants drop out. With the number of entrants thus narrowed down, the public learns who are the most popular remaining candidates. Thus, the Democratic party field was narrowed to Walter Mondale, Gary Hart, and Jesse Jackson after only a few primaries in 1984, and the Democrats' "seven dwarfs" were down to two—Michael Dukakis and Jesse Jackson—relatively early in 1988. The primary results are then converted into delegate votes at the presidential conventions, which in turn become more representative of party rank-and-file feeling than before.

Critics of primaries rebut these arguments and add some criticism of their own. They grant that more voters take part in primaries than in the caucus and convention methods of choosing delegates, but they question the *quality* of the participation. For one thing, supporters of the different candidates have no opportunity to deliberate together in public. Voters in primaries, therefore, must depend largely on the news media and advertising for their information and basis for judgment. Voters in presidential primaries tend to be more interested in or influenced by candidates' personalities and media skills than in their positions on vital issues.[33]

In addition, the primary voting mechanism—each citizen casting a vote for one candidate, often in a multi-candidate field—does not allow voters to express relative preferences. In 1976, for instance, a number of relatively liberal Democratic candidates ran in the New Hampshire primary. Jimmy Carter was the only aspirant perceived as moderate or conservative. The liberal candidates split the liberal vote; Carter received the moderate and conservative vote. The liberal voters had no opportunity to say that they preferred *any* of the liberal candidates over Carter. An electoral system in which those casting ballots vote for only one candidate among many does not allow for the kind of rank ordering that may be necessary to reflect what the electorate actually wants.[34]

A third criticism holds that the primaries are badly scheduled and last too long.[35] And the media give an undue amount of attention to the first primary, as we have noted.[36] Most of the southern states held their primaries on the same day in March 1988; in all, twenty states chose their delegates on that Super Tuesday for presidential aspirants. But primaries in some of the larger states, such as Pennsylvania, Illinois, New York, and California are traditionally held later in the spring. In many recent years this has frequently been after the contests in both parties had been virtually decided. As a result, voters in some of the most populous states have no impact on who the presidential candidates will be.

Moreover, the length of the nominating campaign exhausts the candidates and tries the patience of the voters. The "primary season" lasts more than three months—the three-month "window" for primaries declared open by the Democrats, plus the time in advance of the window granted as an exception to New Hampshire. During that period primaries are held at least twice a month, and at times weekly. Candidates campaign literally years in advance of the New Hampshire primary and the Iowa caucus, which has become the functional equivalent of a primary in terms of candidate attention and media coverage. Victory might even go to the candidates with the stronger physiques, it has been said, rather than the stronger brains.[37]

But the main criticism directed against primaries is that they do not test candidates for the qualities needed in the presidency. Candidates are tested for their ability to play a "media game" in which they must demonstrate flexibility, resourcefulness, attractiveness, and articulateness. Are these the key qualities required of a president? Thomas Jefferson, Abraham Lincoln, and Harry Truman were able presidents, critics say, but they might not have gained or retained their posts if they had had to pass the test of "media appeal." Critics point to Jimmy Carter as a little-known candidate who was generally successful in gaining media attention from unexpected successes but less successful in governing the country.

In sum, the gap between the qualities required to carry primary contests and the qualities needed to organize an administration, get support on issues, and deal with congressional leaders, governors, and mayors disturbs critics of the primary system.

PROPOSALS FOR REFORM OF THE NOMINATING PROCESS

What would the critics substitute for state presidential primaries? Some argue in favor of a *national presidential primary*. This would take the form of a single nationwide election, probably held in May or September, or of separate state primaries held in all the states on the same day. Supporters contend that a one-shot national presidential primary (though a runoff might be necessary) would be simple, direct, and representative; would cut down the wear and tear on candidates; and would attract a large turnout because of intensive media coverage. Opponents argue that this "reform" would make the present system even worse, would enhance the role of media showmanship and candidate gamesmanship, and would be enormously expensive and hence hurt the chances of candidates lacking strong financial backing.[38]

A more modest proposal—a variation of which was tried by the Democrats in 1988—is to hold *regional primaries*, possibly at two- or three-week intervals across the country. In 1988 legislators in a number of southern states organized such a primary, but a number of states in other regions held their delegate selection contests at the same time. A system of regional primaries might bring more coherence to the process, encourage more emphasis on issues of regional concern, and cut down on wear and tear. But they would retain most of the disadvantages of the present system—especially the emphasis on money and media. Clearly they would give an advantage to candidates from whatever region held the first primary; this would encourage regional candidates and might increase polarization among sections of the country.

A quite different proposal is to cut down drastically on the number of state presidential primaries and to make more use of the *caucus* system. The huge turnout of voters in the Iowa caucuses in recent elections demonstrates that participation can be high; the fact that participants had to spend some hours discussing candidates and issues proves that such participation can be thoughtful and informed. Voting mechanisms that call for the redistribution of votes among the candidates with certain minimum levels of support—and eliminating those with less support—permit a more nearly accurate reflection of the preferences of those participating in primary elections. In caucus states candidates are less dependent on the media and more dependent on their abilities to reach political activists. By centering delegate selection in party meetings, the caucus system would also enhance the role of the party.[39]

Still another idea, used by Colorado to make state nominations since 1910, would turn the process around. Beginning in May, local caucuses and then state conventions would be held in every state. These would send delegates—a certain percentage of whom would be unpledged to any presidential candidate—to the national conventions, which would be held in the summer. Deliberations at the national conventions would result in the selection of two or three candidates to compete in a national primary to be held in September. In this Colorado plan or *national preprimary convention* plan, voters registered by party would be allowed to vote for their party nominee in the September primaries.[40]

The process of choosing national party nominees for the presidency is determined by a combination of party rules and state laws. Reformers have gained consensus that the current process is flawed—though not on which aspects of it require change. They have been markedly less successful at achieving consensus on how to change the system—or even on the proposition that the system should be changed nationally. Democrats have been most unhappy with the current system, because it has produced a series of nominees by their party who have not fared well in the general election. However, Ronald Brown, the Democratic National chairman, has expressed doubt that a change of rules will result in more successful Democratic candidates. His view reflects the gap between those concerned about reforming the process because they do not believe that the procedures in place conform with how leaders should be chosen in a democracy and those who do not like the candidates existing procedures produce.

REFORMING THE ELECTORAL COLLEGE

Americans have long been concerned about the nature and workings of the electoral college. Critics argue that (1) small states and large "swing" states are overrepresented; (2) the winner-take-all aspect distorts equal representation of all voters and a candidate who receives fewer popular votes than an opponent can be elected; (3) electors can (and do) vote for a person other than the candidate for whom they were pledged to vote; (4) if no candidate wins a majority, the issue is thrown into the House of Representatives, where each state delegation, no matter how large or small, has one vote, which thus distorts the representative process even more. The electoral college has been compared to the human appendix: useless, unpredictable, and possibly dangerous.

Defenders of the system say opponents exaggerate the possible dangers; the system has not broken down so far, and probably never will. And if the electoral college is antipopular or antimajoritarian, so what? "The Electoral College avoids uncertainty when the popular vote is extremely close (as in 1960, 1968, 1976) and prevents candidates with narrow appeal from making it to the White House," says Malcolm S. Forbes, Jr.[41]

The most controversial reform proposed is *direct popular election of the president*. Presidents would be elected directly by the voters just as governors are; the electoral college and individual electors would be abolished. This kind of proposal usually provides that if no candidate receives at least 40 percent of the total popular vote, a **runoff election** be held between the two contenders with the most votes. Supporters argue that this plan would give every voter the same weight in the presidential balloting, in accordance with the one person, one vote doctrine. Winners would take on more credibility or "legitimacy" because of their clear-cut popular victories. And, of course, the dangers and complications of the present electoral system would be replaced by a simple, visible, and decisive method. Opponents argue that the plan would require a national election system, which would further undermine federalism; that it would encourage naked, unrestrained majority rule and hence political extremism; and that it would submerge the smaller states, which would lose some of their present influence. Some also fear that the plan would make presidential campaigns more remote from the voters; candidates might stress television and give up their present forays into shopping centers and city malls.[42]

From time to time Congress considers proposals for an amendment to elect presidents directly. Such proposals, however, seldom get very far because of the strong opposition of various interests who believe they may be disadvantaged by such a change, for example, such "minorities" as blacks and farmers who fear they might lose their "swing" vote power.

An ingenious proposal for a "national bonus plan" has been worked out by a group of scholars and politicians. Under this plan the electoral college would be retained, but it would be heavily weighted toward the winner of the popular vote. The plan would work like this. A pool of 102 electoral votes (two for each state and the District of Columbia) would automatically be granted to the candidate who gained the most popular votes. These bonus votes would be added to that candidate's electoral college vote gained in the election. He or she would be elected if these totaled a majority in the electoral college. If not, a runoff would be held between the two candidates who won the most popular votes. The position of elector would be eliminated. Proponents contend the plan would ensure that the popular vote winner would also be the electoral vote winner; encourage increased voter turnout and two-party competition in one-party states; and do away with the elector who votes against the decision in his or her state.[43] Opponents say minor parties and independent candidates would be discouraged by such a system.

None of these plans has garnered much public support. The failure of the effort to change the system of elections—like the failure of the attempt to change the nominating process—points to an important conclusion about procedural reform. Americans normally do not focus on procedures. Only after a major electoral college crisis is any significant change likely. Then citizens will focus on problems of the electoral system, not hypothetical problems discussed by political scientists and democratic theorists, but real problems facing them. But must we wait for a crisis to force changes?

Campaign Money

The process of change, both successful and unsuccessful reform, can be demonstrated by an examination of how we finance our electoral campaigns. Big long campaigns—especially presidential campaigns—have required big money for some time. Neil O. Staebler, who observed politics for over half a century as a state committeeman, a state chair, a national committeeman, a member of Congress, and eventually a member of the Federal Election Commission, commented, "Money corruption has been present in politics for 170 or 180 years. We've been actively working at it since Teddy Roosevelt started back in 1907. But for sixty years practically nothing useful was done. . . . Politics was very much the art of figuring out what you could get away with."[44]

EFFORTS TO REGULATE CAMPAIGN MONEY

Reformers have tried three basic strategies to prevent abuse: (1) imposing limitations on the giving, receiving, and spending of political money; (2) requiring disclosure of the sources and uses of political money; and (3) giving governmental subsidies for campaigns, including incentive arrangements. Recent campaign fi-

Typical Congressional Campaign Budget

Entertainment	$ 7,500
Travel	18,000
Hotels	2,500
Office equipment, furniture	10,000
Rent	13,000
Media consultant	45,000
Printing	46,000
Research	1,500
Television and radio advertising	200,000
Stamps	6,000
Telephone charges	14,000
Tickets for dinners, etc.	3,000
Staff payroll	80,000
Direct-mail campaign	55,000
Polls	17,000
Voter surveys	20,000
Mail and vote list computerization	12,000
Videotape machines	2,000

THE VOTE THAT REALLY COUNTS

By permission of Bill Mauldin and Wil-Jo Associates.

nance laws have tended to use all three attempts to deal with a problem that sometimes seems insoluble.

Limiting campaign spending is one of the older methods. Under the 1925 Corrupt Practices Act, a candidate for the United States House of Representatives could not spend more than certain set sums. The act was utterly unrealistic and easily evaded. Reporting was inadequate; often reports were filed after the election was over. Policing was almost nonexistent. And much of the corrupt practices legislation did not even cover primary elections. The 1925 act was "more loophole than law."

Sensitive to charges that his father's money had "bought" him the 1960 election, President Kennedy appointed a bipartisan Commission on Campaign Costs, yet little followed this commission's report. However, the climate for campaign finance reform improved later in the 1960s and in the early 1970s, as wealthy candidates like New York's Nelson Rockefeller spent millions on their own campaigns and other candidates benefited from extremely large contributions from donors with interest in government action. The public began to fear that we were getting the "best government money could buy"; politicians reacted to those fears.

In 1971 the Congress passed two significant pieces of legislation. The Federal Election Campaign Act (FECA) dealt with the problems of rich candidates "buying" their own elections and of the "Madison Avenue" approach to politics, by limiting the amounts that candidates for federal office could spend on media advertising. The FECA also called for the disclosure of the sources of campaign funds. All political committees that anticipated receiving or spending more than $1000 on behalf of federal candidates in any year were required to register with the government; periodic reports had to be filed including full data on all major contributions and expenditures; and one person was not allowed to contribute in the name of another person.

In addition, Congress passed the Revenue Act of 1971, which employed a different strategy: subsidizing campaign costs through tax incentives. The purpose was to draw into politics more money with no strings attached. The law provided that political donors might claim tax credit against their federal income taxes for part of their contributions. More recent tax laws repealed this tax credit. This 1971 law also provided a tax checkoff that allowed taxpayers to direct $1 of general revenue to a fund to subsidize presidential campaigns.

However, the experience of the 1972 election further fueled worry about how we finance our campaigns. In that election the Nixon campaign spent more than $60 million, twice what it had expended in 1968, money was "laundered" in secret bank accounts outside the country, and **Watergate** grabbed the nation's attention. As a result the Watergate break-in and Nixon's cover-up of his campaign committee's actions became symbols of the corruption of our political process caused in part by the presence of huge sums of money for which no one seemed accountable. Public concern led to new congressional efforts for reform and a new system of campaign finance.

Late in 1974, after prolonged debate, Congress passed and President Ford signed the most sweeping campaign reform measure in American history. The new act established more realistic limits on contributions and spending. The act tightened disclosure, reporting, and accountability. But what made the new measure a breakthrough was a new set of provisions for public financing of *presidential* campaigns. For example, in 1976 each presidential candidate was limited to spending $21.8 million in the general election, an amount provided through a public subsidy, but considerably less than that spent by either party in 1972. The amount of the public subsidy was linked to rises in the Consumer Price Index. Among other provisions are:

- The establishment of a Federal Election Commission appointed by the president with the advice and consent of the Senate to regulate the campaign financing of candidates for president, senator, and representative
- The requirement that all candidates designate one principal campaign committee to report all contributions and expenditures
- Provisions for public financing of presidential general election campaigns (with funds from the tax checkoff) and for partial public financing (on a matching basis) of presidential nominating campaigns
- A subsidy to the two national parties for their convention expenses
- The eligibility for a subsidy of any minor party that polled 5 percent of the total vote in the previous presidential election
- Limitations on spending by candidates for presidential nominations (on a state-by-state basis and in total) and in the presidential general elections for those candidates who accept public funding[45]
- Limitations on the amounts that national parties may spend on presidential campaigns and on individual congressional and senatorial campaigns
- A $1000 limitation on the amount that any individual can give to a candidate for the United States Senate or for the House in the primary election, a $1000 limitation per candidate in the general election, and a $5000 limit per candidate per election for multi-candidate organizations (political action committees)
- An overall limitation of $25,000 on the amount that any individual can donate to all candidates for federal office in an election cycle (no similar limitation applicable to political action committees)
- No limitation on the amount that individuals or groups can spend independently (that is, activities not coordinated with a candidate's campaign)[46]

The 1974 Act was extensively amended after the *Buckley* v. *Valeo* Supreme Court decision in 1976 overturned several of its specific provisions. However, the basic outline of the act, emphasizing limitations on contributions and full and open disclosure of all activities by candidates for the House of Representatives and the Senate and public financing of presidential campaigns, remains unchanged. Similarly, later amendments adjusted reporting requirements and encouraged volunteer activities, but they have not altered the philosophy behind the regulation of campaign money.

AN EVALUATION OF THE CAMPAIGN FINANCE REFORMS

How has all this supervising, regulating, and subsidizing worked? The 1974 law has had a marked impact on all subsequent elections. Over half the costs of a presidential campaign are covered by public subsidy. The amount of private money invested in the national election dropped from $127 million in 1972 to less than half of that in 1976.[47] Further, one standard feature of presidential campaigns almost disappeared in 1976: the desperate search for money. President Harry Truman ran so short in 1948 that he had to raise funds from day to day to keep his campaign train moving. Presidential candidates have found the task of raising money a demeaning business, and an ever-present worry that donors are trying to buy special influence, or at least access. Since 1976 all presidential campaigns have agreed to forego private fundraising during the general election. The goals

"And, unlike my opponent, I don't owe a thing to special interests . . . In fact, they still owe me two installments!"

Dunagin's People by Ralph Dunagin. © News Group Chicago, Inc. Courtesy of News America Syndicate.

of making the financial playing field even (for presidential campaigns) and of taking the influence of large contributors out of the presidential election process have thus been met. Furthermore, the reporting requirements for all federal elections have brought the subject of campaign financing out of the shadows and into the "pitiless light" of full publicity.

These are not the only consequences of the efforts at campaign finance reform. One of the goals was to reduce the overall costs of national campaigns. That goal has not been met. While accurate data are not available for the period before 1974 (when the Federal Election Commission came into operation and was charged with reporting on financial activity of all candidates for federal office), the total amount spent on all federal elections since that time has more than quadrupled. In 1988 more than $2 billion was spent on campaigns for federal office.

These are big sums, but they must be put into perspective. The $2 billion spent on national races is but a fraction of a percent of the total cost of government. One Trident submarine, for example, costs hundreds of millions of dollars. Consider, too, the money spent on commercial advertising: Procter & Gamble or General Motors each budgets more in a two-year election cycle to advertise its products than is spent in all elections for national office. Political spending per voter in the United States is also lower than political spending in other democratic countries. Americans spend a little more than one dollar per capita in a typical election year, in contrast, for example, with the $21 spent in Israel.

Campaign reform has also been criticized on the philosophical grounds that it works to the disadvantage of third party candidates. The law is frankly based on the assumption that serious presidential campaigns are likely only between Republicans and Democrats, and it discourages third parties. Most of the criticism of the 1974 law, however, does not deal with funding of presidential campaigns, but with the fact that the public finance provisions do not apply to congressional campaigns. How to fund campaigns is a constant problem both for members of Congress and for the public, especially now that PAC money has become such a key factor in congressional campaigns. The amount of such contributions has skyrocketed. Although President Carter urged Congress to extend public financing to campaigns for the House and Senate, Congress has refused to "subsidize" itself.[48]

Rather it is evident that the 1974 legislation has prompted a shift of private money from presidential to congressional races, which in turn encourages big spending on a local level. Certainly the costs of congressional and senatorial campaigns have escalated since the reform legislation was passed.

While large contributions have been eliminated, contributions by political action committees have escalated. In races for the House of Representatives, political action committees give most of their money to incumbents. Thus, the system of campaign financing has contributed to incumbents' advantages. In the 1986 election cycle, PACs gave a total of $140 million to congressional candidates; $105 million of that went to incumbents and only $15 million to those challenging incumbents. In that same election cycle, incumbents raised approximately 40 percent of their money from PACs, compared to less than 5 percent for challengers.[49]

Moreover, many question the motives of PAC contributors. People give political money for many reasons. Most givers want something specific. Business, labor, and other groups want certain laws passed or repealed, certain funds appropriated, or certain administrative decisions rendered. Many simply want access to office holders. They neither expect nor get specific governmental rewards for their "cash on the barrelhead"; what they do expect, and usually get, is the opportunity to see the office holder after the election and to present their cases. And this is an advantage reformers claim that others do not have.

Is giving worthwhile? Is there a payoff? This question is unanswerable because the relation between giving money and getting an act passed, for example, is obscure. Other factors are involved (including the giving of money by people on the other side of an issue). Yet most politicians and most donors *think* that giving money brings results. Hence, PACs will continue to be the key financial contributors to congressional campaigns—and will continue to be controversial.

In a "Declaration of War" on PACs, Common Cause, a group concerned with campaign finance, declared that "unless we change our system for financing congressional campaigns and change it soon, our representative system of government will be gone. We will be left with a government of, by and for the PACs." Common Cause would like to see rigid limits on PAC contributions. In response, the Mobil Corporation ran magazine ads that called PACs "truly the voice of the people—people who band together to make their electoral choices more emphatic by pooling their funds in support of one or more candidates." The alternative, Mobil said, might be public campaign financing, causing inequities and taxing voters without giving them the chance to name the candidate for whom their dollars were intended.[50]

The FECA has also been roundly criticized for what it fails to do. As currently written, campaign finance legislation does not restrict rich candidates—the Rockefellers, the Heinzes, the Kennedys—from giving heavily to their own campaigns. Critics claim that big money makes a big difference, and wealthy candidates can afford to spend the amounts of money required to get a decisive head start. In presidential politics this advantage can be most meaningful in the period before the primaries begin. In a similar vein, the legislation does not constrain group or individuals' expenditures separate from candidates'. This loophole has been legitimated by the Supreme Court on free speech grounds. Groups sympathetic to, but independent of, candidates are allowed to raise and spend funds to help elect them or to defeat their opponents.

Some also contend that the law fails in that it provides vast sums for presidential campaigns and relatively little—mainly for convention costs—to the national parties. Helping candidates at the expense of parties, it is said, intensifies the growing trend toward more personalistic, fragmented, and individualistic politics. Some would favor greater subsidies to parties until they can get on their feet and be self-supporting. But the law also left a loophole for political parties, and both parties have been quick to exploit it. The parties have established nonfederal accounts for money to be spent on party-building activities and efforts other than aiding candidates for federal office. As long as this money is segregated, it is unregulated because the parties are not obliged to reveal the source of the contributions and the contributors are not restricted. These funds have become known as "soft money." In 1988 each party raised over $40 million dollars in "soft money" to aid its campaign efforts.

THE OUTLOOK FOR FURTHER REFORMS

With widespread criticism of the current campaign finance system, what is the outlook for further reforms? Close observers say that reform is most needed in two areas: the influence of political action committees on congressional elections and the emergence of soft money as a means of avoiding the disclosure provisions so key to the acceptance of the 1974 reforms.

Who Gives Most to Whom

AT&T

$574,608 to 288 Democrats	$473,527 to 224 Republicans

UPS

$341,121 to 241 Democrats	$219,562 to 150 Republicans

PHILIP MORRIS

$284,294 to 162 Democrats	$195,187 to 128 Republicans

FEDERAL EXPRESS

$305,200 to 100 Democrats	$118,787 to 36 Republicans

Source: *Fortune*, November 7, 1988, p. 12. Based on data from the Federal Election Commission.

There is skepticism that Congress will ever reform itself in this area. Even if members were so inclined, consensus does not exist even among reformers on the best approach to take. Legislation to control the influence of political action committees, often tied to public financing of congressional campaigns and limitations on overall expenditures, has been on the congressional agenda for fifteen years.

On the one hand, some members fear that public subsidies might encourage opponents to run against them, and equalize the battle of the "outs" versus the "ins." On the other hand, some fear that a limit on campaign expenditures would further restrict challengers; defeating an incumbent member of Congress is all but impossible unless a challenger can spend a great deal of money to offset the advantages of incumbency.[51] Opponents of public financing also worry about citizens' response to their voting to subsidize their own campaigns. Some supporters of public funding of congressional races have urged that, if such a law is passed, government money be channeled to candidates through party organizations in order to strengthen the role of the party. During his first year in the White House, President Bush proposed a package of reforms (see box) in an effort to "free our electoral system from the grips of special interests." He sought to eliminate most PACs, strengthen the role of political parties, and cut down on noncampaign or personal use of campaign funds. Democrats in Congress responded cooly. Since Democratic incumbents received the lion's share of PAC money, they charged that the president was aiming to eliminate Democrats rather than derelictions.

Interpreting the 1988 Elections

George Bush handily won the 1988 elections by a 54 percent to 46 percent margin in the popular vote and by an even more impressive 426 to 111 margin in the electoral college (with the one "faithless elector" voting for Lloyd Bentsen). His victory was the fifth for Republicans in six presidential races. It was also the first time Republicans have won three elections in a row since 1928. Yet Bush failed to bring along with him a Republican Congress. In fact, Democrats picked up several seats in the U.S. Congress and also gained another governorship, making the margin of state chief executives 28 Democrats to 22 Republicans. As the Bush presidency began, it faced a House and Senate both solidly controlled by the opposition party.

Key Factors in the 1988 Elections How did the Bush Republicans win the 1988 elections and what did it mean? What kind of "mandate" if any arose out of the Bush victory? And what are the key questions raised by the 1988 national elections?

More than anything else, Bush benefited from the presumed good economic conditions in 1988. Most voters most of the time are influenced in how they vote by how they think the economy is doing. In 1988 voters believed that the Reagan-Bush policies deserved credit for relatively low unemployment and good economic times in general. Many people were doubtless apprehensive about the growing national debt and budget deficits and the loss of trade to other nations, yet on balance they thought that the economy had improved during the 1980s. Bush campaigned on the theme of continuing Reagan's policies and improving the economic opportunity for Americans. He also vowed not to raise taxes. His opponent, Governor Michael Dukakis of Massachusetts, pointed to those areas in the country where the economy was not booming and also focused attention on the millions of Americans who were struggling to make ends meet. But he was

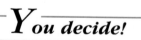

You decide!

As a member of Congress who almost lost out to a heavily PAC-financed candidate in the last election, you are urged by constituents to take a bold and simple step: Vote to abolish all PACs. A bill is introduced that would simply abolish all such committees on the grounds that through financial contributions to candidates they are gaining excessive influence over politics and policy. How do you vote?

(Answer/Discussion on p. 338.)

generally unable to persuade the vast bulk of those in the middle and upper classes that Bush should be faulted for deficits or any unevenness in the performance of the American economy or that the economy would turn on them as a result of the Reagan legacy.[52] Thus, prosperity, at least for most of those who vote, was a decisive factor in Bush's victory.

A second key factor was peace. Not only was America at peace, but the Reagan administration had recently negotiated a widely acclaimed arms reduction treaty with the Soviet Union. Reagan, moreover, had held several summits with the Soviet leader Gorbachev. The Soviets were, at election time, withdrawing troops from Afghanistan. Iran and Iraq were ending their war, and concerns about war in the Persian Gulf were easing. Chad, Angola, and other nations were ending small wars in their respective regions of Africa. On balance, the Reagan-Bush foreign policy record appeared positive, especially since both Reagan and Bush were deemphasizing their previously unpopular positions about military aid for the contras in Nicaragua.

And if "prosperity and peace" were not enough, Bush also gained strength because of his ties and "understudy" association with the then popular President Ronald Reagan. Reagan had lost popularity in 1987 when his Iran-contra scandal had been exposed and investigated. But by late 1988 his popularity was back to a point at which 60 percent of Americans approved of the way he was handling the presidency. Reagan campaigned actively for Bush and in the last weeks of the campaign made several important campaign trips to close states such as California, Illinois, Ohio, and Texas.

A fourth factor that contributed to Bush's success in 1988 was his, and his campaign's, ability to portray Michael Dukakis as an out-of-the-mainstream liberal. Polls consistently showed in 1988 that there were only 17 percent or 18 percent of the electorate who considered themselves as liberals whereas about twice as many people, thirty-four percent, considered themselves to be conservatives. The others, perhaps about 49 percent, called themselves moderates. It was therefore an effective strategy to paint Dukakis as a liberal, which in many respects he is. Bush staffers created several hard-hitting negative ads—some were even sleazy— all with the intent of raising questions about Dukakis's competence and leadership ability. Initially, Dukakis ignored the charges. He was not, he said, "a label." He preferred to talk about issues and what he would do when he became president. Yet the ads worked. Increasing numbers of voters began to have doubts about Dukakis. On the positive side, Bush reminded voters of his many years of experience in top positions in the national government, Congress, diplomatic posts, the cabinet, and as vice-president. His experience was an asset, and he understandably and convincingly turned it to his advantage. In addition, he portrayed himself as a compassionate leader, as a family man who would bring his family and family values to the White House.

Meanwhile, Dukakis ran an uninspiring campaign. As one writer aptly put it, he let the charges of the Bush campaign splatter against him and stick like glue. He looked weak and, at times, foolish—as in the commercial that portrayed him driving a tank. His campaign's strongest ads aimed at the Republican vice-presidential candidate, but voters cast their ballots for candidates for president, no matter how uneasy they might be about a running mate. After the campaign ended Dukakis acknowledged that he should have responded more vigorously and quickly to the often unfair negative attacks made against his crime and environmental records and his patriotism. He and his aides also admitted that he was often too stiff and mechanical. *Time* magazine accused him at one point of running for accountant-in-chief instead of commander-in-chief.

Dukakis said the negative advertising against him plainly worked and that

Winners in 1988—Bush and Quayle and their wives.

Who Voted for Bush?	
Men	57%
Women	50
Whites	59%
Blacks	12
Hispanics	30
Liberals	18%
Moderates	49
Conservatives	80
East	50%
Midwest	52
South	58
West	52
Family Income	
Under $12,500	37%
$12,500–$24,999	49
$25,000–$34,999	56
$35,000–$49,999	56
$50,000 and over	62

Source: The New York Times—CBS News Exit Poll. Copyright © 1988 by The New York Times Company.

Figures are percent Republican vote. N = 11,645 voters.

The "L word," the liberal label, was exploited by the Republicans against Dukakis in 1988.

Powers on the Hill: Senators Barbara Mikulski (D–Maryland) and Nancy Kassebaum (R–Kansas).

he did not respond in kind because he is basically a positive person who had tried all his life to provide positive leadership. The Dukakis campaign staff also shares in the blame for the poorly run Dukakis effort; there was considerable strife and feuding in his inner circle, and this took its obvious toll on Dukakis.[53]

In the end liberals and Democrats stuck with Dukakis, and about half of those who had been called Reagan Democrats returned to the Democratic candidate, but upper-income groups, Southerners, white males, and white Protestants continued their drift toward the Republican Party. Eighteen percent of those who call themselves Democrats did not vote for Dukakis. Fifty-five percent of the independents gave their vote to Bush and Quayle; only 43 percent voted for Dukakis and Bentsen.

Exit polling by the major television networks and leading newspapers revealed that specific issues played little role in voter decisions. Many Bush supporters were critical of Bush's attacking Dukakis rather than emphasizing what he would do to help solve major problems such as deficits, trade imbalances, and environmental pollution. Americans nonetheless voted for Bush because a vote for Bush was a vote for the status quo, a vote for continuity.

Many observers believed that Bush's relatively content-free campaign meant that his victory, despite its impressive eight point margin, was without any clear mandate. Much of the confusion over the meaning and mandates of the 1988 campaign arose because the American people were not especially excited about the appeals from either candidate or either party. Much would depend on Bush's ability during his four-year term to speak to key issues, build alliances with the Democratic leaders in Congress, and rally the American people around a sensible policy agenda.

Congressional Election Results   One of Bush's difficulties was that voters all across the country exhibited a split personality when they voted in the November 1988 elections. They voted for Bush, yet at the same time many voted to send large Democratic majorities back to Congress. The Democratic edge in the Senate was increased to fifty-five Democrats to forty-five Republicans. In the House, incumbents were again overwhelmingly successful, with only six losing in the November election.

Were voters saying that they want no party in total charge? Voters sent a Republican back to the White House yet at the same time made it nearly impossible for President Bush to whip Congress into line with any regularity. Perhaps the voters want neither party to exercise unbridled power in shaping national policies. They like the checks and balances built into our Constitution, yet just in case one branch should be inclined to overreach, the voters appear to have created an additional check or constraint—this one from the voting booth.

WHAT ABOUT THE 1990S?

The 1988 presidential election once again confirmed that the Democrats' "solid South" now generally votes Republican in presidential elections and is likely to in the near future. But the 1988 elections also suggest that if the Republicans have had a lock on the electoral college, the Democrats appear to have a stronger hold on the U.S. Congress. Neither of these trends is irreversible, yet they have surely become patterns.

Republicans believe they have regularly won the White House because they, better than the Democrats, appeal to the conservative values of family, patriotism, strong defense, and a tough stance against criminals. Republicans believe the family is the foundation of our social order and that it is important that we reflect upon and consider carefully the impact of government upon family life. Bush and the Republicans strive to cut out excessive regulations, decentralize many domestic programs, and return power and policy discretion to the state and local levels. Critics of George Bush's campaign in 1988 agree that he appealed to "traditional" American values—but these were bigotry, envy, greed, chauvinism, and fear. They also think he was unrealistic, if not dead wrong, in saying that he would not raise taxes.

As noted earlier, many feel the 1988 election was one of the worst in recent memory—with too much mud-slinging on both sides and too little thoughtful discussion of cutting-edge national issues. Others say, however, that this was a perfectly acceptable election, and that hard-hitting comparative advertising is now a standard feature in modern elections. Further, they add, the candidates did speak to the issues; it was the media that emphasized the occasional negative or personal attacks and blew these out of proportion.

Whatever the case, partisanship is likely to color many of the relations between Congress and the presidency in the next few years. A certain bitterness remains. The Democrats are already in prolonged debate about the future of their party and its chances to win back the White House in the 1990s. Jesse Jackson and liberal Democrats say the Democrats have failed because they have lost their soul and been unwilling to become the programmatic party that people would respect. Moderate Democrats such as Senator Sam Nunn, Senator Charles Robb, and Senator Lloyd Bentsen insist the Democrats have to move away from the issues and programs of the 1930s and 1960s and focus on the issues of the 1990s. They say, too, that Democrats have to move more to the center, noting that Lyndon Johnson and Jimmy Carter, both Southerners and moderate Democrats, have been the only Democrats to make it to the White House in the last twenty-five years. This Democratic debate is not new, yet it is more sharply expressed these days.

Several Democrats either have their eye on the White House or have supporters who would like them to run in 1992. Liberal Democrats, such as Jesse Jackson, New York Governor Mario Cuomo, and Senate Majority Leader George Mitchell, are regularly mentioned. Moderates, like Senators Nunn, Robb, Gore, Representative Richard Gephardt and those whom it is more difficult to classify, like Senator Bill Bradley, are also the objects of much speculation. Senator Lloyd Bentsen, who won such widespread bipartisan respect in his vice-presidential quest in 1988, will undoubtedly remain a prominent figure, although his age might be a handicap for a presidential run.

Republicans are expected to rally around President Bush in 1992 unless he suffers major political setbacks during the early 1990s. Still there are other Republicans, such as former Congressman Jack Kemp and Senator Robert Dole, back in the Senate as minority leader, who might reenter presidential politics if Bush falters.

The congressional elections are likely to follow a familiar pattern. Most incumbents will win in the House of Representatives, and the Democrats will retain control. Republicans will look to the 1992 election with the hope that redistricting following the 1990 census will add seats to states in which they are strong—and preliminary indications are that this will happen. They also hope that new district lines will make some incumbents less secure, will pit some incumbent Democrats against each other, and generally will improve their chances. But the outlook remains bleak for an early Republican takeover in the House.

The Senate elections are less predictable. Of the thirty-four seats up in 1990, sixteen are currently held by Democrats and eighteen by Republicans. Thus, the Republicans would need a massive turnaround to regain majority control. However, they are already looking to 1992, when twenty Democratic and only fourteen Republican seats will be up. Their campaign efforts in the next two elections aim at giving President Bush a Republican Senate at the start of his second term. The Democrats, of course, are just as intent on preventing that result. They hope to increase their control in 1990 and use their strong candidates in 1992 to aid a Democrat in the race for the presidency.

Meanwhile, Republican President Bush and the Democratic Congress face the major issues of the deficit, the national debt, trade, drugs, AIDS, environmental pollution, the quality of education and basic research, and continued negotiations with the Soviets. Much depends on the willingness of both institutions and both parties to reconcile their differences and work for the broad longer-term interests of the American people. The American people want innovative leadership that will rise above factional bickering; they want problems to be solved and the creative energies of the nation to be unlocked. Perhaps voters in the 1990s will judge our national leaders not on their ability to pass the buck and blame their opponents but on their records of performance.

Summary

1. Candidates for the Senate and the House tend to base their campaigns more on their personal organizations and access to the media than on their party affiliation.

2. Many House, state, and local races are not seriously contested. The extent to which a campaign is likely to be hotly contested varies with the importance of the office and the chance a challenger has of winning.

3. The race for the presidency actually consists of three campaigns: winning delegate support in presidential primaries and caucuses, gaining the formal party nomination at the presidential convention (usually predetermined by the first campaign), and winning a majority of the electoral college.

4. The present presidential selection system is under criticism because of its length and expense, and because it seems to test candidates for qualities that are less needed in the White House than the ability to govern, including the capacity to form coalitions of diverse interest groups and make decisions that may antagonize those groups.

5. Even though presidential nominations today are usually decided weeks or months before the party conventions, these conventions still have an important role in setting the parties' direction, unifying their ranks, and firing up enthusiasm. They also hold the potential for deciding nominations in some future races.

6. The electoral college has been criticized because it is unrepresentative and because it holds within it the potential for disaster. However, reform efforts have been unsuccessful because the system has worked in recent elections; thus a climate for reform has not emerged.

7. Because large campaign contributors are suspected of improperly influencing public officials, Congress has long sought to regulate political money. Campaign finance reform was vigorously pursued and implemented after the Watergate scandal of the early 1970s. The main approaches of reform have been (1) imposing limitations on receiving and spending money; (2) requiring public disclosure of the sources and uses of political money; and (3) giving government subsidies to presidential candidates, campaigns, and parties. Present regulation includes all three approaches.

Further Reading

LARRY M. BARTELS. *Presidential Primaries and the Dynamics of Public Choice* (Princeton University Press, 1988).

LINDA L. FOWLER and ROBERT D. McCLURE. *Political Ambition: Who Decides to Run for Congress* (Yale University Press, 1989).

JOHN G. GEER. *Nominating Presidents: An Evaluation of Voters and Primaries* (Greenwood Press, 1989).

GARY C. JACOBSON. *The Politics of Congressional Elections*, 2d ed. (Little, Brown, 1987).

MALCOLM JEWELL and DAVID OLSEN. *American State Political Parties and Elections*, 3d ed. (Dorsey Press, 1988).

JOHN KESSEL. *Presidential Campaign Politics*, 3d ed. (Dorsey, 1988).

L. SANDY MAISEL. *From Obscurity to Oblivion: Running in the Congressional Primary*, rev. ed. (University of Tennessee Press, 1986).

MICHAEL NELSON, ed. *The Elections of 1988* (Congressional Quarterly Press, 1989).

Neal R. Peirce and Lawrence Longley. *The People's President: The Electoral College in American History and the Direct-Vote Alternative*, 2d ed. (Yale University Press, 1981).

Gerald Pomper, et al. *The Election of 1988* (Chatham House, 1989).

A. James Reichley, ed. *Elections American Style* (The Brookings Institution, 1987).

Frank J. Sorauf. *Money in American Elections* (Scott, Foresman, 1988).

Stephen J. Wayne. *The Road to the White House: The Politics of Presidential Elections*, 3d ed. (St. Martin's, 1988).

Notes

1. "Census: Elected Officials Outnumber Bank Tellers," *The Boston Globe* (January 25, 1989), p. 9.
2. See, as examples, David Mayhew, *Congress: The Electoral Connection* (Yale University Press, 1974); Richard F. Fenno, Jr., *Home Style: House Members in their Districts* (Little, Brown, 1978); and James E. Campbell, "The Return of Incumbents: The Nature of Incumbency Advantage," *Western Political Quarterly* (September 1983), pp. 434–444.
3. L. Sandy Maisel, *From Obscurity to Oblivion*, rev. ed. (University of Tennessee Press, 1986); and Gary C. Jacobson, "Strategic Politics and the Dynamics of House Elections: 1946–1986," paper delivered at the annual meeting of the American Political Science Association, September 1988.
4. Malcolm E. Jewell and David Breaux, "The Effect of Incumbency on State Legislative Elections," *Legislative Studies Quarterly* (November 1988), pp. 495–514.
5. See Gary C. Jacobson, *The Politics of Congressional Elections*, 2d ed. (Little, Brown, 1987), chap. 6; and Alan I. Abramowitz, "Economic Conditions, Presidential Popularity, and Voting Behavior in Midterm Congressional Elections," *Journal of Politics* (February 1985), pp. 31–43.
6. Keith Drehbiel and John R. Wright, "The Incumbency Effect in Congressional Elections: A Test of Two Explanations," *American Journal of Political Science* (February 1983), p. 140.
7. See Linda L. Fowler and Robert C. McClure, *Political Ambition: Who Decides to Run for Congress* (Yale University Press, 1989); and David T. Canon, "Political Conditions and Experienced Challengers in Congressional Elections, 1972–1984," paper presented at the annual meeting of the American Political Science Association, September 1985.
8. See for example, Alan I. Abramowitz, "Party and Individual Accountability in the 1978 Congressional Election," in L. Sandy Maisel and Joseph Cooper, eds., *Congressional Elections* (Sage, 1981); and Thomas E. Mann and Raymond E. Wolfinger, "Candidates and Parties in Congressional Elections," *American Political Science Review* (September 1980), pp. 617–32.
9. See, as examples, Albert D. Cover, "One Good Term Deserves Another: The Advantages of Incumbency in Congressional Elections"; Morris P. Fiorina, *Congress: Keystone of the Washington Establishment* (Yale University Press, 1978); and R. Mayhew, *Congress: The Electoral Connection*.
10. See Mayhew, *Congress: The Electoral Connection*; Richard F. Fenno, Jr., *Congressmen in Committees* (Little, Brown, 1973); and Steven S. Smith and Christopher J. Deering, *Committees in Congress* (Congressional Quarterly Press, 1984).
11. See Fenno, *Home Style: House Members in Their Districts*.
12. Candice J. Nelson, "Campaign Finance in Presidential and Congressional Elections," *The Political Science Teacher* (Summer 1988), p. 6.
13. Alan I. Abramowitz, "Explaining Senate Election Outcomes," *American Political Science Review* (June 1988), pp. 385–403.
14. Peter Tuckel, "The Initial Re-election Chances of Appointed and Elected U.S. Senators," *Polity* (Fall 1983), p. 138.
15. Quoted in "Mudslinging in New Jersey," *The Washington Post National Weekly Edition* (February 13–19, 1989), p. 8.
16. Thomas E. Patterson, *The Mass Media Election: How Americans Choose their President* (Praeger, 1980).
17. Paul T. David and James W. Ceaser, *Proportional Representation in Presidential Nominating Politics* (University of Virginia Press, 1980), assess the influence of proportional representation on candidate support and convention balloting.
18. These types are drawn from James W. Davis, *Presidential Primaries*, rev. ed. (Greenwood Press, 1984), chap. 3. See pp. 56–63 for specifics on each state (and Puerto Rico). This material is used with the permission of the publisher.
19. *Delegate Selection Rules for the 1984 Democratic National Convention* (Democratic National Committee, 1982), p. 13.
20. Stephen J. Wayne, *The Road to the White House*, 3d ed. (St. Martin's Press, 1988).
21. Jeff Fishel, *Presidents and Promises* (Congressional Quarterly Press, 1984).
22. In fact Jules Witcover used the same image to describe the 1976 presidential campaign in his book *Marathon: The Pursuit of the Presidency, 1972–1976* (Viking, 1977).
23. See, for example, John H. Kessel, *Presidential Campaign Politics: Coalition Strategies and Citizen Response*, 3d ed. (Dorsey, 1988).
24. On the key factor of personal attributes in presidential campaigning, see David P. Glass, "Evaluating Presidential Candidates: Who Focuses on Their Personal Attributes?" *Public Opinion Quarterly* (Winter 1985), pp. 517–34. See also Herbert B. Asher, *Presidential Elections and American Politics*, 4th ed. (Dorsey Press, 1988).
25. Adlai E. Stevenson, *Major Campaign Speeches, 1952* (Random House, 1953), pp. xi–xii. Copyright 1953 by Random House, Inc.
26. George Rabinowitz and Stuart Elaine MacDonald, "The Power of the States in U.S. Presidential Elections," *American Political Science Review* (March 1986), pp. 65–87.
27. Sidney Kraus, *The Great Debates: Kennedy vs. Nixon, 1960* (Indiana University Press, 1962). See also Myles Martel, *Political Campaign Debates* (Longman, 1983).
28. See generally Austin Ranney, ed., *The Past and Future of Presidential Debates* (American Enterprise Institute for Public Policy, 1979). See also Joel L. Swerdlow, *Beyond Debate: A Paper on Televised Presidential Debates* (A Twentieth Century Fund Paper, 1984).
29. Gerald Pomper et al., *The Election of 1976* (David McKay, 1977), deals with this and other aspects of the Carter-Ford contest that have implications for the future. See also Witcover, *Marathon*.
30. See Robert Hunter, ed., *Electing the President: A Program for Reform, Final Report of the Commission on National Elections* (The Center for Strategic and International Studies, 1986); James L. Sundquist, *Constitutional Reform* (The Brookings Institution, 1986); and Edward N. Kearny, "Presidential Nominations and Representative Democracy: Proposals for Change," *Presidential Studies Quarterly* (Summer 1984), pp. 348–56.
31. Barbara Norrander and Gregg W. Smith, "Type of Contest, Candidate Strategy, and Turnout in Presidential Primaries," *American Politics Quarterly* (January 1985), p. 28.
32. Estimate of Walter Shapiro in *Time* (June 20, 1988), p. 19.
33. See John G. Geer, "Voting in Presidential Primaries," paper prepared for delivery at the annual meeting of the American Political Science Association, Washington, D.C., September 1984. See also

Albert R. Hunt, "The Media and Presidential Campaigns," in A. James Reichley, ed., *Elections American Style* (The Brookings Institution, 1987), pp. 52–74.

34. See Steven J. Brams and Peter Fishburn, *Approval Voting* (Birkhauser, 1983).

35. George S. McGovern, "Considerations on our Political Processes," *Presidential Studies Quarterly* (Summer 1984), pp. 341–47.

36. Gary R. Orren and Nelson W. Polsby, eds., *Media and Momentum: The New Hampshire Primary and Nomination Politics* (Chatham House, 1987).

37. American Enterprise Institute Memorandum (Spring, 1986), p. 10.

38. Compare "A National Agenda for the Eighties," *Report of the President's Commission for a National Agenda for the Eighties* (U.S. Government Printing Office, 1980), p. 97, which, proposes holding only four presidential primaries, scheduled about one month apart.

39. Nelson Polsby, *Consequences of Party Reform* (Oxford University Press, 1983), p. 118.

40. Thomas E. Cronin and Robert Loevy, "The Case for a National Primary Convention Plan," *Public Opinion* (December/January 1983), pp. 50–53.

41. M. S. Forbes, Jr., "Helpful, Useful Antique," *Forbes* (February 6, 1989), p. 27.

42. Neal R. Peirce and Lawrence Longley, *The People's President*, 2nd ed. (Yale University Press, 1981), describes and advocates the direct-vote alternative. Nelson W. Polsby and Aaron B. Wildavsky, *Presidential Elections*, 7th ed. (The Free Press, 1988), essentially favors the present system.

43. For a broader discussion of the plan and the problem, see Thomas E. Cronin, "Choosing a President," *The Center Magazine* (September-October 1978), pp. 5–15; *Winner Take All: Report of the Twentieth Century Fund Task Force on Reform of the Presidential Election Process* (Holmes & Meier, 1978).

44. Quoted in Herbert E. Alexander and Brian A. Haggerty, *The Federal Election Campaign Act: After a Decade of Political Reform* (Citizen's Research Foundation, 1981), p. 13.

45. Reformers had intended to limit spending on all federal campaigns—for president, the House of Representatives, and the Senate—but these provisions were ruled to be an unconstitutional abridgement of free speech in *Buckley* v. *Valeo*.

46. For an extensive discussion of recent legislation, see Herbert E. Alexander, *Financing Politics: Money, Elections, and Political Reform*, 2d ed. (Congressional Quarterly Press, 1980), or Frank J. Sorauf, *Money in American Elections* (Scott, Foresman, 1988).

47. Report of the Federal Election Commission, June 4, 1977, *The New York Times* (June 5, 1977), p. 25.

48. Bruce Bender, "An Analysis of Congressional Voting on Legislation Limiting Congressional Campaign Expenditures," *Journal of Political Economy* (October 1988), pp. 1005–21.

49. See L. Sandy Maisel, "Electoral Competition and the Incumbency Advantage in the U.S. House of Representatives." Paper presented at the Conference on Campaign Finance Reform and Representative Democracy, The Bradley Institute for Democracy and Public Values, 1989.

50. See Herbert E. Alexander, "Public Financing of Congressional Campaigns," *Regulation* (January–February 1980), pp. 27–32. On the PAC controversy, see *Campaign Practices Reports* (February 28, 1983), pp. 5–6; an advertisement by Mobil, "PACs—Consider the Alternatives," *Time* (May 9, 1983), p. 4; and especially Frank J. Sorauf, "Political Action Committees in American Politics: An Overview," and the general debate in The Twentieth Century Fund, *What Price PACs?* (Twentieth Century Fund, 1984).

51. See Gary C. Jacobson, *Money in Congressional Elections* (Yale University Press, 1980).

52. See Charles O. Jones, ed., *The Reagan Legacy* (Chatham House, 1988).

53. See "How Bush Won," *Newsweek* (November 21, 1988), pp. 112–15.

14

Congress:
The People's Branch?

In January, 1789 James Madison ran for a Congress that did not yet exist. The "Father of the Constitution," having led the great effort to draft a new Constitution in Philadelphia two years before, wanted to represent his section of Virginia in the new House of Representatives. It was not an easy contest for the young Virginian. For one thing, it was so cold that after one meeting, held outdoors in the snow, Madison had to ride twelve miles to find a place to stay overnight and suffered severe frostbite during the journey. For another, his opponent was James Monroe, another popular young Virginian. But his real enemy was the famous Patrick Henry, who feared that under the new Constitution the national government would have too much power. Using his influence in the Virginia legislature, Henry had rigged congressional districts in such a way that Madison was thrown into competition with Monroe.

Things went well for Madison. He and Monroe were personally friendly, and they agreed to journey from county to county in a series of friendly debates. Of course, Madison supported the new Constitution and Monroe opposed it, but Madison made clear he now favored adding a Bill of Rights. The young candidate had discovered that his constituents strongly supported adding a Bill of Rights. Madison won by what his friend George Washington called a "respectable majority."[1]

Madison visited Mount Vernon, then hastened to New York, where the first Congress was due to meet March 4. Held up by snow, floods, and impassable roads, he did not arrive in Manhattan until much later in the month, but no matter—other lawmakers-elect were delayed too. Nearly a month passed before both chambers in this newly fashioned **bicameral** body had enough members (a quorum) to begin business.

Madison and his fellow politicians were about to set up a brand new government in an old town. Long before, the young Virginian had become used to the sights of lower Manhattan—cows wandering up and down Broadway, hogs rooting through the garbage-clogged gutters, milkmaids carrying buckets of milk hanging from a yoke, chimney sweeps calling out "Sweep ho! Sweep ho!"—all amid a bedlam of knife grinders, ragmen, and lamp menders calling out their special cries. These familiar scenes contrasted markedly with the spacious remodeled room in City Hall that would house the new representatives.

At sunset on March 3, 1789, the struggling and now repudiated government created by the Articles of Confederation came to an end. Eighteen months had elapsed between the signing of the Constitution in Philadelphia and the first working day of the new Congress. Eleven states had ratified the Constitution, and the newly elected or selected members of Congress (senators were then appointed by state legislatures) began straggling into New York City (population 30,000), the temporary seat of the new republic.

Problems of enormous importance awaited Congress, but this first branch of government got off to an uncertain start. It was nearly a month before each chamber had a quorum; the House managed to obtain the proper number on April 1, 1789; it took the Senate until April 6.

Soon Congress moved to select its leaders and set in motion the constitutional provisions for establishing the rest of government. As you will recall from reading the Constitution, Congress was to count the ballots of the first electoral college and arrange to swear in the first president and vice-president. Congress began this task, although a few more weeks passed before it actually inaugurated the president. Even more time and more delays followed before it enacted the enabling legislation for the judiciary to come into being.

This first Congress, not unlike Congress in the 1990s, was made up of talented, experienced, and generally well-to-do elites. Eighteen senators and thirty-six members of the House of Representatives had served in previous Congresses under the Articles of Confederation. Eleven senators and nine representatives had served as delegates in Philadelphia at the Constitutional Convention. Many others had served in the Revolutionary army and in their state legislatures. Still others had participated in ratifying conventions and as local jurists. Although some of them had not been ardent supporters of the Constitution, once it was adopted they were willing to try to make it work.

James Madison arrived in New York determined to honor the promise that had been made to add a Bill of Rights. He assumed responsibility for drafting and proposing the necessary amendments. He discovered on joining the new Congress, however, that most of his fellow representatives were far more interested in questions like taxes and tariffs. Again and again Madison asked the House to turn to work on the Bill of Rights, only to be told that revenue had to come first (if only to provide money for congressional salaries!). Finally, early in June 1789, Madison gained the floor long enough to present the proposals that would constitute the first ten amendments. He spent the rest of the summer pulling together a package of amendments he steered through Congress, preparatory to their being submitted to the state legislatures.

Among the many other matters that awaited them, the most pressing was the need to raise revenue to pay the country's bills. Sound familiar? This seems to be the ever-present matter before Congress. The Continental Congress had lacked the power to raise needed funds, but the new Constitution changed all that. After just one week Congress was debating how best to impose import fees and tariffs, and Madison took part. In a sense, this new Congress picked up precisely where the Confederation's Congress had displayed its greatest incapacity.[2]

Congress: An Overall View

Two hundred years later, Congress is a much larger and different kind of institution, located in the midst of a sprawling federal government in Washington, D.C., yet most of its major functions remain the same. We still look to Congress to make the laws, raise revenues, represent the citizens, confirm top administrative and judicial appointees, investigate the abuse of power, and oversee the executive branch. Congress is still a bicameral organization, and its chambers, as we shall discuss, serve to check one another as together they check the other two major branches of government.

In its first years Congress met for several months a year. Nowadays Congress regularly meets all year. Senators (because of the Seventeenth Amendment) are directly elected by the people, and members of the House represent twenty times as many constituents as they originally did. Most members engage in continual electioneering to stay in office. As in the 1790s, many of the members appear driven by their desire to win reelection—so much so that much of what takes place in Congress—such as the angling over what committees to serve on—seems mainly designed to promote reelection. These efforts work. Most incumbents most of the time win reelection in both chambers. But these efforts, combined with the absence of strong party discipline, have also encouraged internal fragmentation and diffusion of power. More and more of the work these days is done in committees or subcommittees. Multiple, successive decision points make it much easier to prevent than to pass legislation.

How does such a Congress make any progress? In an institution where most members act as individual entrepreneurs and consider themselves leaders, the task of providing *institutional* leadership is big. This is particularly true in the U.S. Senate, which prides itself on extended debate and deliberation. With limited resources, and only sometimes aided by the president, congressional leaders are asked to bring together a fragmented, nonhierarchical institution. The congres-

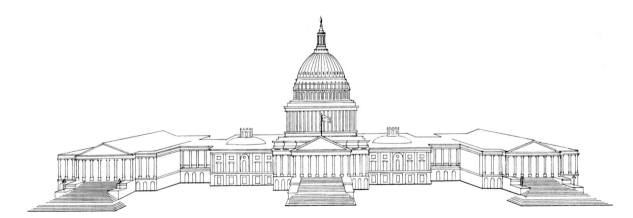

Congress is the seat of legislative authority, the center of public debate, a carry-over of folksy political traditions from earlier days—and a collection of several hundred relatively independent politicians with separate but overlapping constituencies. The architecture of the capitol bespeaks its ways: two chambers, endless corridors, ornate rotundas and galleries, and a rabbit warren of grand rooms, tiny offices, and winding passageways. There is no culminating point of authority but a multiplicity of decision centers.

"Listen pal, I didn't spend seven million bucks to get here so I could yield the floor to you."

Drawing by Dana Fradon; © 1987 the New Yorker Magazine, Inc.

sional system requires majority action and acts only when majorities can be achieved. Congress functions as an effective collective body only to the extent that leadership emerges in both parties and in both houses of Congress. The framers can well be proud that their original objective of having a Congress that would not move with undue haste has been generally well realized over the years.

Most Americans realize Congress is not a perfect institution, and we often characterize it as a bickering, timid, ignorant, selfish, or narrow-minded body. Yet we also often admire the stamina and civic responsibility of members of Congress whom we know. And incumbent members of Congress keep getting reelected—in part because people like them and their work.

The members of Congress are popular, but Congress is not. This is because we expect Congress to solve most of our national ills, yet judge individual members of Congress primarily on how well they serve the interests of their states and districts, and on their personal appeal. Much of the criticism of Congress is unjustified. Critics usually forget that our national legislature is particularly exposed. First, Congress does nearly all its work directly in the public eye. Unfortunate incidents—quarrels, name calling, evasive actions, inaccurate statements and ethical lapses—that might be hushed up in the executive or judicial branches are almost always observed by journalists. Second, Congress by its nature is controversial and argumentative. Its 535 members are found on both sides, sometimes on half a dozen sides, of every important question. The average citizen who holds one opinion is likely to be intolerant of other views and of the legislators holding them. Also, there is a considerable difference between holding an opinion and writing legislation.

The chief complaints about Congress are that it is inefficient, unrepresentative, and not accountable enough. Further, critics say it is paralyzed by personal bickering and interest-group favoritism. Some contend that many members of Congress are too beholden to special interests. Legislators are described as being obsessed with staying in office—indeed, as concentrating solely on winning reelection—often at the expense of critical national issues such as the deficit, drug abuse, foreign policy, and trade. Former House Republican leader John Rhodes was especially harsh when he said that "the majority of congressional actions are not aimed at producing results for the American people as much as perpetuating the longevity and comfort of the men who run Congress."[3]

Some of the paralysis in Congress is caused by the proliferation of subcommittees, the overlapping jurisdictions of these committees, and the great increase of congressional staff. A complicated budget process, recently made even more complicated, has also caused problems. Better-educated and more independent-minded persons are coming to Congress, often with loose or weak ties to political parties.[4] This makes it difficult for party leaders to build coalitions and to stick to an efficient agenda for Congress.

Many people allege that special interests and single-issue groups are stronger than ever, and that they are able to fragment and often delay or block proceedings in Congress. The current system of financing congressional elections has been called a scandal. It forces members of Congress to beg for money from Washington-based special-interest, political action committees whose primary purpose is to seek support for their pet legislation.

Others wonder if the problems of Congress, especially encouraging cooperation between Congress and the presidency, arise because some of our constitutional arrangements are outmoded. Certain scholars and practitioners suggest, for example, that we might be better served by having four-year terms for members of the House, and by having some members of Congress serve simultaneously in the president's cabinet. A few scholars even propose that we elect presidents and members of Congress on a team ticket; that is, send a partisan team to Washington and prevent split-ticket voting. These reformers also seek means to strengthen partisan ties and cooperative efforts to better link the two chambers with the executive branch. In short, these observers say many of Congress's flaws are the result of too much reverence for the Constitution and unwillingness to consider constitutional reform.[5]

But would a Congress that "leads" more be what everyone wants? We have to ask ourselves, too, what would happen to the presidency and the courts if Congress should "lead" more. Already many conservative critics complain that Congress is too powerful, too meddlesome in the affairs of the executive branch, and that it has usurped constitutional or practical functions in economic and national security areas that are clearly executive in nature.[6]

Criticism of Congress—its alleged incompetence, its overresponsiveness, its inefficiencies—are not issues that can be dealt with outside the context of policy preferences and democratic procedures. Sometimes criticism tells us more about the critic than it does about the effectiveness of Congress. Democracy is not supposed to be efficient. Congress was never intended to act "swiftly"; it was not created to be a rubber stamp or even a cooperative partner for presidents. Congress is supposed to reflect geographical and special interests—to register the diversity of America. The real question is whether Congress is operating effectively enough most of the time to deal with those broad national issues the general public feels require national action.

Some suggest that Congress has such a split personality that there are at least two Congresses. The first Congress is a *law-making institution*. It is asked to write laws and make policy for the entire nation. In this capacity all the members are expected to set aside their personal ambitions and perhaps even their concerns about their own constituencies. But Congress is also a *representative assembly*, made up of 535 elected officials who serve as links between their constituents and the national government. The dual roles of *making laws* and *responding to constituents' demands* were very much bound together in the minds of the framers of the Constitution when they designed a legislature elected from states and geographical districts. Since the first Congress formed, these two functions have forced members to balance national issues with the personal concerns of their constituents.

In fact, pressures mount continuously on members of Congress to help constituents deal with an increasingly complicated government. Indeed, members must spend considerable time and effort helping constituents, especially if they want to stay elected. This notion of the "two Congresses" has important implications for how Congress works and how it is organized—a subject we consider later.

The Powers of Congress

The Constitution is generous in its grant of powers to Congress. In the very first article the framers outlined the structure, powers, and responsibilities of Congress, giving it "all legislative powers herein granted." Among these are the power to spend and tax in order to "provide for the common defense and general welfare of the United States"; the power to borrow money; the power to regulate commerce with foreign nations and among the states; the power to declare war, raise and support armies, and provide and maintain a navy; the power to establish post offices and postroads; and the power to set up the federal courts under the Supreme Court. As a final catch-all, the Constitution gave the Congress the right "to make all laws which shall be necessary and proper for carrying into execution" the

HOUSE OF REPRESENTATIVES

Washington, D.C.

1 Speakers' Offices
2 Committee on Ways and Means
3 Parliamentarian
4 House Floor Library
5 Cloakrooms
6 Members' Retiring Room and Lobby
7 House Chamber
8 Committee on Appropriations
9 Minority Whip

10 House Reception Room
11 House Minority Conference Room
12 House Majority Conference Room
13 House Document Room
14 Committee Meeting Room
15 Representatives' Offices
16 Prayer Room
17 Minority Leader

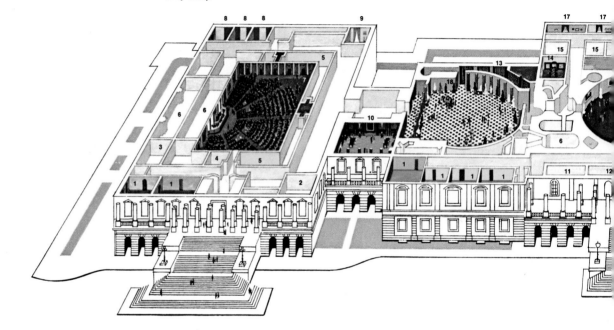

powers set out. Several nonlegislative functions were also granted, such as participating in the process of constitutional amendment and impeachment (given to the House), and trying an impeached federal officer (given to the Senate).

The Constitution confers special additional responsibilities on the Senate. The Senate has the power to confirm presidential nominations—sometimes as many as 500 key executive and judicial nominees a year. (In Chapter 16 we discuss how the Senate meets this responsibility.) The Senate must also give its consent, by a two-thirds vote of the senators present, before a president may ratify a treaty. This gives the Senate a special role in foreign policy.

The House also has some special responsibilities, but these have not proved to be as important as those given to the Senate. For example, all revenue bills must originate in the House. In fact, this has made little practical difference, because the Senate has freely amended bills that originate in the House, sometimes changing everything except the title.

The framers had no intention of making Congress all-powerful. They reserved certain authority to the states and to the people and gave other powers to the executive and judicial branches of the national government. As time passed, Congress gained power in some respects and lost it in others. The power of Congress also changes depending on the times and the president. As the role and authority of the national government have expanded, so too have the policy-making and

PUBLIC AREAS

18 Statuary Room
19 Rotunda
20 Senate Rotunda
21 Old Senate Chamber

SENATE

Washington, D.C. 20510

22 Senators' Offices
23 Executive Clerk
24 Senate Conference Room
25 Majority Leader
26 Majority Leader
27 Minority Leader
28 Office of the Vice-President
29 Senators' Reception Room

30 Cloakrooms
31 Senate Chamber
32 Marble Room
33 President's Room
34 Offices of the Secretaries
35 Chief Clerk
36 Bill Clerk and Journal Clerk
37 Official Reporters of Debates

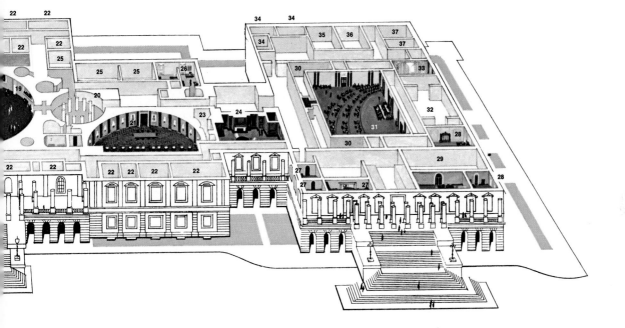

oversight responsibilities of Congress. Still, Congress has not kept pace with its great rival, the presidency, which in many respects today holds the place in our national government that many of the founders apparently desired for Congress. The president's national security responsibilities, initial preparation of the budget, media visibility, and agenda-setting influence have all enhanced the position of the presidency in recent generations. This may be part of a worldwide trend. Legislative bodies almost everywhere have become subordinate to the executive at all levels of government.

Despite its sometimes secondary role in recent decades, Congress still performs at least these six important functions: *representation, lawmaking, consensus building, overseeing, policy clarification,* and *legitimizing.* Representation is expressing the diversity and conflicting views of the regional, economic, social, racial, religious, and other interests making up the United States. Law making is enacting measures to help solve substantive problems. Consensus building is the bargaining process by which these interests are reconciled. Overseeing the bureaucracy means seeing that laws and policies approved by Congress are faithfully carried out and that they accomplish what was intended. Policy clarification, or "policy incubation," as it is sometimes called, is the identification and publicizing of issues. Legitimizing is the formal ratifying of policies through proper channels. We will examine these functions later in the chapter.

CHAPTER 14 / Congress: The People's Branch?

The Houses of Congress

The single most important fact about Congress is the dispersion of power between its two houses. The Senate and the House each has an absolute veto over the other's law making. Each house runs its own affairs, sets its own rules, and conducts its own investigations. The law-making role, however, is shared. Each house must be seen as a separate institution, even though both houses reflect somewhat similar political forces and share organizational patterns.

The Constitution's framers intended the national legislature to be divided into two chambers in order to perform different functions. As Madison says in *The Federalist*, No. 51, the protection against giving too much power to the legislature "is to divide the legislature into different branches; and to render them by different modes of election and different principles of action, as little connected with each other, as the nature or their common functions, and their common dependence on the society will admit." The House of Representatives was expected to reflect the popular will of the average citizen, whereas the Senate was to provide for stability, continuity, and in-depth policy deliberation. In fact, many of the framers hoped the Senate would stem rash populist impulses of the other chamber.

Although the Seventeenth Amendment to the Constitution, which provides for direct election of U.S. Senators, has altered the character of the Senate's membership, the two chambers still organize themselves differently, approach issues differently, and structure their actions differently. Two hundred years later the two houses of Congress are still different institutions, which have, in Madison's terms, "different principles of action." Plainly, however, the two houses are more similar today in their membership and operations than they were two hundred or even one hundred years ago, and this blurring will doubtless continue during the next one hundred years.[7]

THE HOUSE OF REPRESENTATIVES

Organization and procedure in the House are somewhat different than in the Senate, if only because the House is over four times as large as the Senate. Still, *how* things are done usually affects *what* is done. The House assigns different types of bills to different calendars. For example, finance measures—tax or appropriations bills—are put on a special calendar for quicker action. The House has worked out other ways of speeding up law making, including an electronic voting device. Ordinary rules may be suspended by a two-thirds vote, or immediate action may be taken by unanimous consent of the members on the floor. By sitting as the *committee of the whole*, the House is able to operate more informally and more quickly than under its regular rules. A quorum in this committee is only 100 members, rather than a majority of the whole chamber, and voting is quicker and simpler. Members are limited in how long they can speak. In contrast to the Senate, debate may be cut off simply by majority vote.

The Speaker The **speaker** is the presiding officer in the House of Representatives. The Constitution mandates that the House of Representatives shall choose their speaker, yet it does not say anything about any duties or powers of the office. This officer is formally elected by the House but actually selected by the majority party, usually someone with substantial seniority. Throughout most of this century House members were unwilling to vest power in their party leaders. Revolts in

1910 by the rank-and-file progressives stripped speakers of most of their authority, which included control over who served on congressional committees. In the mid-1970s, however, several changes strengthened the speakership. The 1910 changes, designed to reduce the power of the speaker, were introduced as progressive reforms; sixty years later, progressive reforms gave back to the speaker some of these powers.

The routine powers of the speaker include recognizing members who wish to speak, ruling on questions of parliamentary procedure, and appointing members to select and conference committees, that is, temporary committees, not standing committees. In general, the speaker directs the business on the floor of the House. More significant, of course, is a speaker's political and behind-the-scenes influence. (When Democrats are in the majority, the speaker chairs the influential Democratic Steering and Policy Committee. This committee consists of about twenty-four members: the speaker's lieutenants, four others appointed by the speaker, and twelve elected by regional caucuses within the House Democratic party. It devises and directs party strategy.) The speaker has the authority to refer legislation to the relevant committee and to select most members and the chair of the House Rules Committee.

The speaker, as the highest ranking officer in Congress, also represents the legislative branch on ceremonial occasions. Third in line of succession to the presidency (in case of death, resignation, or impeachment), the speaker must keep the White House informed about his whereabouts at all times.

Representative Thomas P. "Tip" O'Neill, who served as the House's speaker from 1977 until 1987, emphasized he not only had to represent the major party in Congress and continue to represent his own constituents (from the Cambridge, Massachusetts area), but he also had to be, in his words, the "guiding force behind both the development of legislation and the process of winning enough votes to get it passed." Further, adds O'Neill, the "most important power is to set the agenda." If the speaker genuinely doesn't want a bill to come up for a floor vote, it generally does not.[8] The speaker also has the key power of recognizing which members will speak from the floor.

The speaker is assisted by a **majority floor leader,** who helps plan party strategy, confers with other party leaders, and tries to keep members of the party in line. The minority party elects a **minority floor leader** who usually steps into the speakership when his or her party gains a majority in the House. Assisting each floor leader are the party **whips.** (The term comes from the whipper-in, who in fox hunts keeps the hounds bunched in the pack.) The whips serve as liaisons between the House leadership of each party and the rank and file. They inform members when important bills will come up for a vote, and prepare summaries of the bills' contents; do nose counts for the leadership; exert mild pressure on members to support the leadership; and try to ensure maximum attendance on the floor for critical votes.

At the beginning of the session and occasionally afterward, each party holds a caucus of all its members (called a conference by Republicans) to elect party officers, approve committee assignments, elect committee leaders, discuss important legislation, and perhaps try to agree on party policy.

The House Rules Committee One way in which the House differs from the Senate is in the procedure for deciding the flow of business. In the House this power is vested in the Rules Committee, one of the regular House standing committees. In the normal course of events, a bill does not come up for action on the floor without a rule from the Rules Committee. By failing to act or refusing to grant a

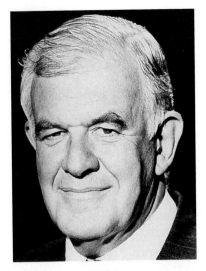

Congressman Tom Foley (D–Washington) was elected Speaker of the House in mid-1989 when Jim Wright of Texas was forced to resign because of an ethics probe. Foley, first elected in 1964, has a reputation as a fair, reasonable legislator and a top spokesman for Democratic policies.

Representative Newt Gingrich (left) is congratulated on his election as minority whip by House minority leader Bob Michel.

Senator Lloyd Bentsen (D–Texas), chairman of the important Senate Finance Committee, won widespread respect as the Democratic party's nominee for vice president in 1988.

Senate Majority Leader George Mitchell (D–Maine), elected to the post in 1989.

rule, the committee can hold up a bill. The rule granted gives the conditions under which the bill will be discussed, and these conditions may seriously affect the bill's chance of passage. The Rules Committee may grant a rule that makes it easy for a bill to be amended to death on the floor. A special rule may prohibit amendments altogether or provide that only members of the committee reporting the bill may offer amendments. The rule also sets the length of debate and specifies what can and cannot be amended.

Until the mid-1960s the Rules Committee was dominated by a coalition of Republicans and conservative Democrats. Liberals denounced it as unrepresentative, unfair, and dictatorial. Today it seldom blocks legislation unless the House leadership prefers measures to be held up. Meanwhile the Rules Committee membership—due to deaths and new appointments—has come to reflect the views of the total membership of the majority party. Because the speaker can control its membership, the Rules Committee today is usually an arm of the leadership. And rather than block legislation, it offers a "dress rehearsal" opportunity to those who are trying to press for new measures.

THE SENATE

In many respects the Senate resembles the House. It has the same basic committee structure, elected party leadership, and dispersion of power. But because the Senate is a smaller body, its procedures are more informal, and it has more time for debate. The power of television and the emergence of new issues have made the Senate an even more visible and key political forum. It has become more open and outward looking, and its members today share influence more equitably than in the past. The Senate now addresses a wider range of issues than ever before.[9]

The president of the Senate (the vice-president of the United States) has little influence. He can vote only in case of a tie and is seldom consulted when important decisions are made. The Senate also elects from among the majority party a **president pro tempore,** who is the official chairperson in the absence of the vice president. But presiding over the Senate is a thankless chore and is rotated among junior members of the chamber.

Party machinery in the Senate is somewhat similar to the House's. There are party conferences (caucuses), majority and minority floor leaders, and party whips. Each party has a *policy committee*, composed of the leaders of the party, which is theoretically responsible for the party's overall legislative program. (In the Senate the party steering committees handle only committee assignments.) Unlike the House political party steering committees, the Senate's party policy committees are formally provided for by law, and each has a regular staff and a budget. Although the Senate policy committees have some influence on legislation, they have not asserted strong legislative leadership or managed to coordinate policy.

The **Senate majority leader,** however, is usually a person of influence within the Senate and sometimes nationally. As the Senate's major power broker, the majority leader has the right to be the first senator heard on the floor. In consultation with the minority floor leader, the majority leader determines the Senate's agenda and has much to say about committee assignments for members of the majority party. The position confers somewhat less authority than the speakership in the House, and its influence depends on the person's political and parliamentary skills and on the national political situation.[10]

Senators are a somewhat different breed from most House members, and some people believe the Senate has a character all its own. Senators have more political elbow room than representatives, if only because of their six-year-terms. In addition, senators are more likely to wield power in their state parties. First-term senators become visible and politically significant earlier in their careers. This is due partly to the relative smallness of the Senate and to its easier access to the media, and partly, no doubt, to the larger staffs that senators have.[11]

To a degree the Senate is a mutual-protection society. Members tend to guard the rights and privileges of other senators so that their own rights and privileges will be protected in turn. Like many close-knit social or professional groups, the Senate has developed a set of informal folkways—standards of behavior to which new members are expected to conform. Courtesy in debate is a cardinal rule, for example, and debate takes place in the third person. By far the most important folkway is *reciprocity*. A senator requests and receives many favors and courtesies from colleagues, always with the understanding that he or she will repay the kindness. A senator may be out of town and request that the vote on a particular bill be delayed. Or a senator may ask a committee chair how a given bill will affect constituents, and rely on the colleague's judgment. Reciprocity may involve trivial pleasantries—or millions of dollars in traded votes for public works appropriations.

In times past liberal and new senators used to complain of a conservative "Establishment" or "club" that dominated the Senate through the power of these folkways and through control of key committees and processes. But the Senate has changed. An activist and mediagenic senator can sometimes become a national political figure in less than a few years, and can soon thereafter be talked about as a possible candidate for the presidency. Indeed, presidential ambition in the Senate has also led to the decline of the Senate Establishment. What is notable about the Senate today is the dispersion of power among party leaders, sixteen committee leaders, several dozen subcommittee chairs, senators from the larger states, and issue experts or activists, such as Senator Sam Nunn, Democrat of Georgia on defense issues, or Senator Phil Gramm, Republican of Texas on budget issues. The contemporary Senate is individualistic. Committee leaders have more power than regular members, but with the expanding role of subcommittee chairs and expanding staff, their influence has lessened. More and more key decisions are made on the Senate floor. The Senate is a more open, fluid, and decentralized body now than it was a generation or two ago. Indeed, it is often said that the Senate has 100 separate power centers and is so splintered that the party leaders have difficulty arranging the day-to-day schedule. "It's pretty hard to set the agenda over here," said Senator Robert Dole. "The leadership is powerless unless the senators are willing to give them authority.[12]

The Filibuster Rule A major difference between the Senate and the House is that debate is almost unlimited in the Senate. A senator who gains the floor has the right to go on talking until relinquishing it voluntarily or through exhaustion. This right to unlimited debate may be used by a small group of senators to **filibuster**—or delay the proceedings of the Senate in order to prevent a vote.

At one time the filibuster was a favorite weapon used by southern senators to block civil rights legislation. More recently the filibuster has been used less frequently. But at the end of any Senate session, when there is a fixed date for adjournment, threat of filibuster is a real danger for controversial legislation.

Differences between House and Senate

HOUSE
Two-year term
435 members
Smaller constituencies
Less staff
Equal populations represented
Less flexible rules
Limited debate
More policy specialists
Less media coverage
Less prestige
Less reliance on staff
Important Rules Committee
More powerful committee leaders
Very important committees
22 major committees
Nongermane amendments (riders) not allowed

SENATE
Six-year term
100 members
Larger constituencies
More staff
States represented
More flexible rules
Unlimited debate
Policy generalists
More media coverage
More prestige
More reliance on staff
More equal distribution of power
Less important committees
16 major committees
Less important Rules Committee
Special treaty ratification power
Special confirmation power
Nongermane amendments (riders) allowed

Senate Minority Leader Robert Dole (R–Kansas).

The knowledge that a bill might be subject to a filibuster is often just enough to force a compromise satisfactory to its opponents. Of course, if there are enough votes, the objections can be overcome—if there is enough time. But at the end of a session, senators are anxious to go home and campaign. Sometimes the leadership, knowing that a filibuster would tie up the Senate and keep it from enacting other needed legislation, does not bother to bring a bill to the floor.

Can a filibuster be defeated? The majority can keep the Senate in continuous session so that a filibustering senator will have to give up the floor. But if two or more senators cooperate, they can keep on talking almost indefinitely. They merely ask one another long questions that permit their partners to take lengthy rests.

Until 1917 the Senate could terminate debate or a filibuster only if every member agreed. That same year, however, the Senate adopted its first debate-ending or **cloture** rule. Now, as long as the senators who are doing the talking stay on their feet, debate can be shut off only by a cloture vote. The rule of cloture specifies that, two days after only sixteen members sign a petition, the question of curtailing debate must be put to a vote. If three-fifths of the total number of elected senators (60 of the 100 members) vote for cloture, no senator may speak for more than one hour. Today, too, a final vote must be taken after no more than thirty hours of debate, including all delaying tactics such as quorum calls, roll call votes on procedure, and the like. After the thirty hours debate, the motion before the Senate must be brought to a vote.

Filibusters are rare. Still, the filibuster, and the threat of it, are a delaying device available to Senate minorities that forces the majority to compromise and water down their preferences. Not surprisingly, cloture votes are relatively rare as well, yet they are more common today than in earlier years. As many as twenty attempted cloture votes (over a two-year session) have been typical in recent years, with cloture votes to end filibusters successful at least half of the time. Sponsors sometimes invoke a cloture vote hoping to expedite floor business before debate has even been seriously begun.

Who Are the Legislators?

All members of Congress are successful politicians, mostly between the ages of 35 and 70 who have risen to national office through political processes in their home communities and states. The entire membership of the House of Representatives (435) is elected every second year. Elections for the six-year Senate terms are staggered, so that one-third of the Senate's 100 members are chosen every two years. The Constitution sets up no major barriers to holding office except age and citizenship. Members of the House of Representatives must be 25 years old and have been citizens for seven years. Senators must be at least 30 and have been citizens for nine years. Yet the composition of Congress does not reflect the socioeconomic makeup of the people as a whole. The overwhelming number of national legislators are male (95 percent), well educated, middle-aged, and from upper-middle or upper-income backgrounds. Until recently members were also mainly white Anglo-Saxon Protestants (WASPs). The greater numbers of Roman Catholics and Jews in recent Congresses—about 140 Catholics and 38 Jews—now bring the religious makeup of Congress closer in line with that of the general population. But there are far fewer blacks and women in Congress

Congressional Norms and Folkways

Observers with an anthropological eye sometimes notice both houses of Congress have certain informal "rules of the game" or norms that seek to encourage civility and lessen interpersonal conflict. These folkways are never perfectly observed and are perhaps less in fashion now than they were a generation or two ago. Junior members of both houses, for example, seldom are interested in putting in a long period of *apprenticeship*. Nor are many of the younger members shy when it comes to gaining as much publicity as possible in this era of televised congressional sessions. Still, members of Congress are expected to *specialize* in some substantive policy area and to do their fair share of the demanding and often boring work of committees. Members are still expected *to defer*, at least somewhat, to senior members of their party and their committee. For the most part, too, members refer to each other in the third person and refer to each other as "distinguished colleague" even when they may not think especially highly of the previous speaker. Then, too, members are expected to display at least a bit of *institutional boosterism* and to defend their chamber of Congress against its critics. However, not everyone honors these and the several other norms of *reciprocity* and *courtesy* congressional leaders would like to see observed. On balance, however, legislative norms promote collegiality, problem solving, and enough cohesiveness for Congress to accomplish most of its complicated work.

TABLE 14–1
Profile of the 101st Congress (1989–1991)

	HOUSE		SENATE
Party			
Democrats	260	Democrats	55
Republicans	175	Republicans	45
Age	52		55
Sex			
Male	439	Male	98
Female	26	Female	2
Religion (*in recent Congresses*)			
Protestant	59%	Protestant	69%
Catholic	29%	Catholic	20%
Other	12%	Other	11%
Number of blacks	23		0
Lawyers (*by percentage*)	32%		60%

Note: Numbers reflect actual number of people within each category unless specified as percents.

Congressman Norman Y. Mineta (D–California).

than in the general public (see Table 14–1).[13] There are also a handful of members of Asian descent and about a dozen with Spanish heritage.

About 40 percent of national legislators are lawyers. Congress also includes one veterinarian, two former judges, a retired admiral, two members of the clergy, about two dozen farmers, and a large number of teachers, professors, and business people. Plainly, Congress does not mirror the nation as a whole from an occupational standpoint. Rarely does a member of Congress emerge out of trade unions or from the so-called blue-collar occupations, although a dozen or so members of the House of Representatives in the early 1980s briefly formed a "blue-collar caucus" composed of members with working-class backgrounds. Among these were a former longshoreman, a pipefitter, a warehouse worker, and an ex-riverboat captain. How important is this "misrepresentation"? Critics say it offers just one more instance of government of the elite, by the elite, and for the elite. Defenders point out that we would hardly expect to find the national percentage of high school dropouts mirrored in Congress. Whatever its makeup, an important question is whether a Congress composed of legislators drawn from a restricted segment of the population is biased in favor of certain points of view. The present makeup of Congress doubtless means that such specific questions as women's rights and antipoverty measures get somewhat less support than they would if Congress were representative in a literal sense. Still, just because most members are the products of middle- and upper-class families does not necessarily mean they are interested only in improving the position of that portion of the population.

Congresswoman Patricia Schroeder (D–Colorado) is currently the woman with the greatest seniority in Congress. Schroeder ran a brief but unsuccessful campaign for the Democratic nomination in 1988.

Getting to and Remaining in Congress

Being elected to Congress depends on a number of factors as noted in Chapter 13: party strength in the area, personal character and appeal, first-term or incumbent status, occasional national tides (such as in the 1964, 1974, or 1980 elections), and campaign strategies and fundraising abilities. An overriding factor, however, is the type of district or state in which a candidate runs. Is it a safe seat—one that is predictably won by one party or the other—or a highly competitive one? Congress has left control over the drawing of congressional districts to the state legislatures. Senators, of course, represent entire states, but House seats are distributed among the states according to population; each state receives at least one seat.

In many states the party in control of the state legislature openly engages in **gerrymandering,**—that is, it tries to draw district boundaries in such a way as to secure for its party as many representatives as possible. This is why congressional districts take on weird shapes. The once rural-dominated legislatures used to arrange the districts so as to overrepresent rural areas. But this was modified both by the population shift to the cities and suburbs and by a 1964 Supreme Court decision. The Court ruled the Constitution requires all congressional districts in a state to have precisely the same number of people (as nearly as possible), so that one person's vote is equal to that of every other person. How much difference did this and subsequent Supreme Court rulings make? Population inequalities have ended. The voice of suburban populations have been strengthened. But a certain amount of gerrymandering continues: State politicians still draw boundary lines—usually to protect incumbents.

THE INCUMBENCY ADVANTAGE

Incumbents in Congress have an excellent chance of remaining in Congress: About 80 percent of Senate incumbents and at least 95 percent of House members who run again are reelected. Most House seats are "safe" in the sense that incumbents win by such majorities that the chances of challengers defeating them are minimal. Yet, as most House members know, they can be challenged twice every two years in a party primary as well as in the general election, and defeat may be as near as a good opponent with lots of money in either their own party's primary or at the next general election.

As long as the members can keep "the folks and the interests back home" happy, they can remain reasonably independent from the president and from their party leadership. Of course, an incumbent can be voted out of office, especially if a legislator loses touch with constituents or national needs. But how would the voters know if this were the case? Few people know the names of their representatives. Senators are better known, but one-third to one-half the public do not know their names. Still fewer citizens evaluate legislators on their stands or votes on issues. Unhappily (or happily, depending on your view), members of Congress are judged on service to their constituents, communications with the district, attendance records, "small favors done over the years," and other nonlegislative matters.

Not surprisingly, most members of Congress pursue policies and assignments, and allocate their time and energy, in ways that increase their chances of being reelected. A safe seat, however, permits a legislator to serve as a national leader without having to worry too much about constantly returning home. Senator Sam Nunn, for example—as long as he does not take issue with sensitive domestic concerns of the people of Georgia—can count on the base from which he has become a national spokesperson for certain defense and foreign policy points of view. Representatives from competitive states or districts, on the other hand, find it somewhat more difficult to ignore local concerns, and tend to concentrate their time and energies on narrower issues. Doubtless the rise in the number of safe seats has increased in large part because members of Congress have skillfully organized their staffs and their own schedules to serve constituent interests.[14]

"Please, Senator Fairchild, you have to leave. You lost."

Drawing by Sauers; © 1983 the New Yorker Magazine, Inc.

CHAPTER 14 / Congress: The People's Branch?

The Job of the Legislator

National legislators lead a hectic life. Congress now meets year round, whereas two hundred years ago and even one hundred years ago it often met for just a few months each year. There is never enough time to digest all the information, letters, complaints, reports, and advice that pour in. Staying in office is a chief priority; some members seem to have few other interests. But most keep on top of their committee responsibilities, stay in touch with key leaders and activists back home, and strive to understand national problems. Most legislators work extremely hard. They drive themselves at a pace far more strenuous than that of typical professional or business persons. Their travel commitments are as demanding as those of airline pilots or cross-country truck drivers. The average member remains in Congress about twelve years. Depending on the kind of district, the personality of the member, and the issues of the day, a member of Congress emphasizes representation, lawmaking and committee work, constituency casework, external relations with interest groups or the White House, or reelection tasks.

LEGISLATORS AS REPRESENTATIVES

For whom does the representative speak? The geographical district and its immediate interests? The party? The nation? Some special clientele? His or her conscience? How legislators define their representative roles has been one of the major questions in political science—and for good reason. Congress was intended to serve as a forum for registering the interests and values that make up the nation. It was never intended that the legislative branch represent views identical with those of the executive. But to whom does the individual representative listen?

Although certain patterns are evident, their meaning is far from clear. For one thing, members of Congress perceive their roles differently. Some believe they should serve as **delegates** from their districts; they should find out what the "folks back home" need or want and serve those needs as effectively as possible. In a sense they would primarily *re-present* the views of the voters who sent them to Washington. This orientation, studies find, is often assumed by Republicans, nonleaders, non-southerners, or members with low seniority.

But most members see their role as that of **trustee.** Their constituents, they contend, did not send them to Congress to serve as mere agents or robots. They are to vote independently, on the basis of their own, more complete information and greater experience, for the welfare of the whole nation. As one member once put it: "This means that we must on occasion lead, inform, correct, and sometimes even ignore constituent opinion, if we are to exercise fully that judgment for which we were elected." This view echoes the stand once championed by famed English legislator Sir Edmund Burke, who said his judgment and conscience ought not to be sacrificed to the opinions of others. In his view a legislature was a place for deliberation and learning. It was not a mere gathering of ambassadors from localities. Interviews a few years ago with members of the House of Representatives suggest that the trustee, or national, focus is more common among Democrats, House leaders, Southerners, and high-seniority members.

Although the question of delegate versus trustee is an old one, it is somewhat misleading. Representatives cannot follow detailed instructions from their constituents because such instructions seldom exist. On many important policy questions, members hear nothing from their constituents. And they hear most often from

Why Do Incumbent Members of Congress Usually Win?

They enjoy *better name recognition*, and to be known at all is generally to be known favorably. Challengers are almost always less well known.

They enjoy *free mailings* (called the "franking privilege") to every household in the state or district. These mailings—which often resemble campaign brochures—make them known and portray them as hard working and influential.

They *raise more campaign money* more easily than challengers, because lobbyists and political-action committees seek their ears and their favor. Also many campaign contributors know incumbents are more likely than challengers to get reelected, so they give to those they know will win. Indeed $7 out of every $10 of PAC money is now given to incumbents.

They usually have had *more campaign experience*, and they can claim to have had *more experience in Congress* and in Washington.

They have *large staffs* to help and to stimulate requests for casework and constituency services for the folks back home.

They *take credit for federal monies* that get allocated to their regions.

They are in a better position than challengers to *take advantage of government research staffs*, new government studies, and even classified information.

Note: No one of these factors can guarantee a member's reelection, but skillful use of these and related resources makes it difficult to unseat a healthy incumbent.

those who agree with them. On the other hand, it is rather unrealistic to expect a legislator to be able to define the national interest if this means understanding the needs and aspirations of millions of people. Most legislators shift back and forth in their role, depending on their perception of the public interest, the electoral facts of life, and the pressures of the moment. Overall, however, most members of Congress view themselves as free agents rather than as agents under the control of their constituents.

LEGISLATORS AS LAW MAKERS

In their major role as law makers, the members of Congress are influenced by how they perceive the nation's key problems and what can be done about them; how they respond to their constituents' interests; and how they follow suggestions from colleagues, staff, the White House, and lobbies.

How a member of Congress makes up his or her mind varies according to issues and to the contexts of decision making. No single factor determines how a member votes most of the time. Members cast more than 1200 votes on a wide variety of subjects in the span of a single session. Some issues are controversial and directly affect a member's district or state. On such occasions a national legislator will more often than not heed the interests of the folks back home. On complicated issues that have little or no bearing on the home district, most members of Congress tend to rely on their own convictions and on the advice of colleagues and friends. Sometimes the president will single out an issue as crucial to the success of the administration, and this factor plus party considerations may weigh more heavily. Obviously, how a member decides to vote depends on many factors and contexts.[15]

The Influence of a Member's Policy and Philosophical Convictions Ideological or issue orientation is the best predictor of how members will vote on a variety of issues. Most members most of the time vote their own ideological beliefs, knowing constituents tend to grant them considerable leeway on policy or issues without punishing them at the polls.[16] A liberal on social issues is also likely to be a liberal on tax and national security issues. The policy convictions of Senator Bill Bradley (D-New Jersey) are reasonably consistent, as are those of Representative Newt Gingrich (R-Georgia). Thus, on controversial issues such as national health insurance, gas and oil decontrol, or defense spending and the strategic defense initiative (Star Wars), knowing the general philosophical leanings of individual members provides a helpful guide both to how they make up their minds and how they will vote. One study finds that an increasing and continuing ideological split has developed in Congress; a social and economic justice coalition is pitted against a growing coalition of free market economic conservatives.[17] In a watered down sense it is a Michael Dukakis versus George Bush split; in economic terms it pits John Kenneth Galbraith "progressives" versus a Milton Friedman "free-market" coalition. Other scholars detect flexible majorities of the moment and say ambition, publicity seeking, and emphasis on appearing competent rather than ideology are increasingly the hallmark of the new generation of members such as Congressmen Richard Gephardt and Tom Downey, or Senators Albert Gore, Tim Wirth, and Richard Lugar.[18]

The Influence of the Voters Much of the time ligislators are influenced by their perception of how their constituents feel. Party and executive branch pressures also play a role, but when all is said and done, the members' political future

The Many Meanings of Representation

Representation is one of the more troublesome concepts in political science, and one of the most important. These definitions may be helpful:

1. *Formal representation* is the authority to act in another's behalf, gained through an institutional process of arrangement such as free and open elections. The formal arrangement of selection, not the behavior of the representative, defines representation in this usage.

2. *Descriptive or demographic representation* is the extent to which a representative mirrors the characteristics of the people he or she formally represents. According to this usage of the term, a representative legislature should be an exact portrait, in miniature, of the people.

3. *Symbolic representation* is the extent to which a legislator is accepted as believable and as "one of their own" by the folks back home. This usage has a lot to do with a legislator's style and nonverbal signals.

4. *Substantive representation* is a legislator's responsiveness to constituents. Do the policy and voting views of a legislator match those of constituents, or does the legislator rely primarily on his or her own judgment? This second approach is that of a guardian or trustee, as opposed to a direct delegate of the citizens.

CHAPTER 14 / Congress: The People's Branch?

depends on how a majority of voters feel about their performance. Rarely does a person consistently and deliberately vote against the wishes of the people back home.

This commonsense observation is supported by several studies. On such domestic issues as social welfare and civil rights, there is usually a great deal of agreement between legislators and their districts. Junior members from competitive seats, in particular, often vote their constituencies' attitudes as they perceive them. But even members who win by substantial margins are not necessarily free to ignore the concerns of the voters. They may, in fact, have won precisely because people know they will follow voters' wishes on issues important to them.[19] Of course, the extent to which members try to respond to their constituents' views also depends on the measure under consideration. Legislators might pay more attention to voter attitudes when social and economic matters are involved than when mass opinion is not so well informed.

A paradox is evident here. Members of Congress sometimes think their individual law-making actions may have considerable impact on constituents. Yet the constituents' general ignorance of how their representatives vote implies that the impact can be small. Members may think their constituents like (or dislike) what they are doing, when actually the voters have little idea of what is going on in Congress. This is explained in part by the tendency of legislators to overestimate their visibility; most citizens don't even know the names of their senators and representatives. Also, members must constantly be concerned about how they will explain their votes. And some members are worried about small shifts in the vote on election day. Even if only a few voters are aware of their stands on a given issue, this group might make the difference between victory and defeat.

The Influence of Colleagues   Voting decisions are also affected by the advice members obtain from other representatives. Severe time limitations and the occasional necessity to make decisions with only a few hours' notice force legislators to depend on others. Most members develop friendships with people who think as they do. They often ask one another about a piece of pending legislation. In particular, they look to respected members of the committee working on the bill.

Unlike most of the voters back home, other members usually have detailed knowledge about many of the issues before Congress. Their views are often public. They may have voted on the matter in previous sessions or in committee, and their public statements may have been placed in the *Congressional Record*. Sometimes members are influenced to vote one way merely because they know a colleague is on the other side of the issue. On occasion, in recent years, members say they have been impressed by watching another member's speech on C-SPAN while working in their office. More often legislators find out how their friends stand on an issue, listen to the party leadership's advice, and take into account the various committee reports. If they are still in doubt, they consult additional friends and staff. The members most often consulted by their colleagues are those who represent similar districts or the same region or state, or like-minded members of the same party or faction—especially those who serve on the committee from which the legislation has come.

A member may also go along and vote with a colleague in the expectation that the colleague will later vote for a measure about which the member is highly concerned. Thus, some vote trading takes place to build coalitions so that members can "bring home the bacon" to their constituencies. This is as much a case of reciprocity in congressional relations as it is of deference to colleagues' superior information or expertise.

Whom and What Do the Representatives Represent?

SURVEY OF HOUSE MEMBERS:

Do you feel that you should be primarily concerned with looking after the needs and interests of your own district, or do you feel that you should be primarily concerned with looking after the needs and interests of the nation as a whole?

Whole nation	45%
Both nation and district	28
District	24
Not sure	3
	100%

When there is a conflict between what you feel is best and what you think the people in your district want, do you think you should follow your own conscience or follow what the people in your district want?

Follow own conscience	65%
Depends on the issue	25
Follow district	5
Not sure	3
	98%

Source: "Sample Survey of over 140 House Members," *Final Report, Commission on Administrative Review, U.S. House of Representatives*, vol. 2 (December 31, 1977), pp. 887, 890.

The Influence of Congressional Staff Today Congress has a huge staff. For years political scientists urged Congress to strengthen its staff. Without additional help, they said, representatives and senators were at a disadvantage in dealing with the executive branch and were overly dependent on information supplied them by the White House or lobbyists. Congress responded, some would say, with a vengeance. Every committee and subcommittee is now elaborately staffed. In addition, members of Congress have all enlarged the number of personal staff working for them in both their Washington and home district offices. Congress in recent years also added a Congressional Budget Office, and an Office of Technology Assessment to its already existing Library of Congress and General Accounting Office staffs.

Congress is the only legislature in the world with a vast staff. This is one of its chief sources of power; without its staffs Congress would doubtless become too much the prisoner of the executive branch and interest groups. Complexity of issues and increasingly demanding schedules have led to an explosion in congressional staffs. About 38,000 staff members, researchers, budget analysts, and others now work for Congress (this figure includes the U.S. Government Printing Office, which is nominally part of the legislative branch). This number has grown at least fourfold in the last twenty-five years. But numbers tell only part of the story of staff influence. Members of Congress have to delegate all kinds of tasks to their staffs. A few members now ask whether they or their staffs are in charge.

Increasing numbers of congressional staff members now work in the home district or state offices. About one-third of all staff of the House of Representatives, and one-fourth of the Senate, are home-based. In part this is due to the increased attention focused on constituency services and casework. It helps members stay in close communication with the voters back home. Much of the work done in these district offices is akin to a continuous campaign effort—generating favorable publicity, arranging for local appearances and newspaper interviews, scheduling and general contact with important civic and business leaders in the region.[20]

One consequence of both the increasing congressional staff and the growing demands on members of Congress is that the legislators sometimes become dependent on staff. This is especially true of senators, who tend to have a wider range of subject matter specialties than do representatives. At congressional hearings it is often the staff member who tells the legislator what to ask. Congressional staff become knowledgeable about special policy areas and deal on a day-to-day basis with their counterparts in the executive departments and interest groups. Indeed, a few observers say some of the most powerful people in Washington are congressional "staffers," as they are called. They draft bills, do the research, and often do much of the parliamentary negotiating and coalition building. No one disputes the view that professional staffers or "Hill people" often have the opportunity to influence legislative decisions. And there is doubtless some truth to the notion that the more staffers there are, the more they look for things to do, such as preparing more legislation, suggesting more investigations, and in general making work for themselves. Still, recent research suggests that when congressional aides engage in the promotion of a particular policy goal, they usually, if not always, do so at the request of the chair of the committee they work for or the member they serve.[21]

Yet we should not exaggerate the independent power base of staffers, who can be summarily fired at the whims of the people they serve. Staffers lack civil service protection, although they cannot be dismissed because of their race, sex, or national origin. And they know that if they wander too far from the views of the one person who can hire and fire them, they will quickly be called back into line.

CHAPTER 14 / Congress: The People's Branch?

The Influence of the Party Another source of influence on legislative behavior is the *political party*. Friendships tend to develop within the party. Of course, there is a fair amount of natural agreement among party colleagues. On some issues the pressure to conform to a party position is immediate and direct. Sometimes there is pressure to go along with the party even when a member does not believe in the party position.

TABLE 14–2
Senate Roll-Call Vote on Amending the Constitution to Require a Balanced Budget*

FOR AMENDMENT—66

DEMOCRATS—23

Bentsen, Tex.	Gore, Tenn.	Pell, R.I.
Bingaman, N.M.	Harkin, Iowa	Proxmire, Wis.
Boren, Okla.	Heflin, Ala.	Pryor, Ark.
Chiles, Fla.	Hollings, S.C.	Sasser, Tenn.
DeConcini, Ariz.	Johnston, La.	Simon, Ill.
Dixon, Ill.	Long, La.	Stennis, Miss.
Exon, Neb.	Melcher, Mont.	Zorinsky, Neb.
Ford, Ky.	Nunn, Ga.	

REPUBLICANS—43

Abdnor, S.D.	Grassley, Iowa	Pressler, S.D.
Andrews, N.D.	Hatch, Utah	Quayle, Ind.
Armstrong, Colo.	Hawkins, Fla.	Roth, Del.
Boschwitz, Minn.	Hecht, Nev.	Rudman, N.H.
Cochran, Miss.	Helms, N.C.	Simpson, Wyo.
D'Amato, N.Y.	Humphrey, N.H.	Specter, Pa.
Danforth, Mo.	Kasten, Wis.	Stevens, Alaska
Denton, Ala.	Laxalt, Nev.	Symms, Idaho
Dole, Kan.	Lugar, Ind.	Thurmond, S.C.
Domenici, N.M.	Mattingly, Ga.	Trible, Va.
Durenberger, Minn.	McClure, Idaho	Wallop, Wyo.
East, N.C.	McConnell, Ky.	Warner, Va.
Garn, Utah	Murkowski, Alaska	Wilson, Calif.
Goldwater, Ariz.	Nickles, Okla.	
Gramm, Tex.	Packwood, Ore.	

AGAINST AMENDMENT—34

DEMOCRATS—24

Baucus, Mont.	Eagleton, Mo.	Levin, Mich.
Biden, Del.	Glenn, Ohio	Matsunaga, Hawaii
Bradley, N.J.	Hart, Colo.	Metzenbaum, Ohio
Bumpers, Ark.	Inouye, Hawaii	Mitchell, Me.
Burdick, N.D.	Kennedy, Mass.	Moynihan, N.Y.
Byrd, W.Va.	Kerry, Mass.	Riegle, Mich.
Cranston, Calif.	Lautenberg, N.J.	Rockefeller, W.Va.
Dodd, Conn.	Leahy, Vt.	Sarbanes, Md.

REPUBLICANS—10

Chafee, R.I.	Hatfield, Ore.	Mathias, Md.
Cohen, Me.	Heinz, Pa.	Stafford, Vt.
Evans, Wash.	Kassebaum, Kan.	Weicker, Conn.
Gorton, Wash.		

* It takes a two-thirds vote to amend the Constitution, and this proposal lost in the Senate by just one vote. A vote "for" was a vote in favor of the proposed change—a change President Reagan repeatedly advocated. Also, the vote was often not a pure party vote, yet party members tended to go along with their colleagues. Liberal and moderate Republicans defected, and conservative and southern Democrats were more likely than liberal Democrats to vote in favor.

Source: Congressional Record, March 25, 1986.

The result of party pressure is a tendency, on major bills, for *most* Democrats to be arrayed against *most* Republicans. Members of the House typically vote with their party majority at least two-thirds of the time. In recent years, for example, the average Democrat voted with the party majority 79 percent of the time and the typical Republican votes with Republican forces 73 percent of the time. However, senators are slightly more independent than representatives. Party influence also varies over time. It was stronger during the nineteenth century than it has been in this century, and it is somewhat stronger in recent years than it was in the post-World War II era. Party influence varies by issue. Party differences have been stronger over domestic, regulatory, and welfare measures than over foreign policy and civil liberty issues.

In the past few years party leaders in both chambers and parties have tried to encourage more cohesive and loyal party voting. Proponents of increased party cohesion (when partisans stick together and vote with greater unity) say this is the only realistic way to achieve collective responsibility in Congress. They claim that increased partisan unity in voting would help Congress solve problems and the wheeling and dealing of ad hoc and shifting coalitions would decline. Although this tendency for members of Congress to "go their own way" or "rise above party" is still far more characteristic of U.S. national legislators than of European parliamentarians, the overall pattern of increased partisan voting in Congress has continued now for about a decade.[22]

Presidential and Other Influences Many forces—regional, local, ties of friendship—can override party influence. Members are sometimes influenced by informal groups (state delegations, ideological groups, ethnic caucuses, regional groupings, and even the class of colleagues with whom they were elected, for example, "the class of 1986"). Also, they are influenced by the more important interest groups and lobbyists—especially those who can help pay off past and future campaign debts.[23]

One voting pattern in Congress reflects a conservative coalition of Republicans and southern Democrats. In the 1950s and 1960s a majority of southern Democrats and a majority of Republicans voted against the majority of northern Democrats on about a quarter of the important roll-call votes. Although this was less the case in the 1970s, it has reappeared in recent years in a weakened form. The conservative coalition is most likely to appear on domestic issues, especially on social welfare legislation. But its strength in Congress cannot be measured by voting decisions alone, because the many committee leaders who are members of this group are often able to prevent legislation they oppose from ever being voted on.

Presidents and executive-branch officials can also influence how legislators vote. Some critics say Congress has yielded extensive policy initiation and budgetary planning to the administrative branch. They say no matter how hard Congress may struggle on one issue, it is overwhelmed by the vastly greater forces of the presidency. Even today a fair number of legislators complain (as they have throughout our history) that, as now organized and staffed, Congress cannot really come to grips with the enormously complex questions involved in making national policy.

Even if Congress were better organized or its members more expert, the growing significance of foreign policy and complicated economic issues would still make the role of the president vital. Presidents have the tools of foreign policy in their hands, and even those they share with Congress, such as the treaty-making power, are usually less significant than their overall negotiating and agenda-setting roles. Through the full use of their constitutional and political powers,

Influences on Congressional Votes*

Member's policy and philosophical convictions

Member's perception of the state's or district's needs

Constituent opinion and mail

Committee leaders

Other committee members

Members of his or her delegation

Other members of Congress

Informal caucuses

Congressional staff members

Interest groups and lobbyists

Ideological or ethnic caucuses

President's position

Party leaders

Campaign contributors

Political action committees

Congressional research publications

National editorial and public opinion

* Usually a mix of these factors is at work. Rarely is one factor alone the whole explanation for how a member votes on important legislation on budget matters.

presidents like Lyndon Johnson and George Bush became serious, full-time partners in legislation; nonetheless, members of Congress are reluctant to admit they are influenced by pressures from the White House. Some studies suggest, moreover, that presidential influence on congressional voting decisions may not be as significant as commonly believed.[24] Although a president has more impact on votes in the area of national security policy than in other areas, even on these questions power is very much a shared responsibility.[25] On key domestic issues legislators are more likely to be influenced by what the constituents want (or what they think they want) and by their own policy convictions than by what the White House wants.

THE LEGISLATIVE OBSTACLE COURSE

From the beginning Congress has been a system of multiple vetoes. This was in part the intent of the framers, who wanted to disperse powers so they could not be accumulated by any would-be tyrant. In addition, Congress has developed an elaborate set of customs that distributes political influence in different ways to different people. To follow a bill through Congress is to see this *dispersion of power*. Procedures and rules in the two houses are somewhat different, but the basic distribution of power, in its effect on shaping legislation, is roughly the same.[26]

Every bill, including those drawn up in the executive branch, must be introduced in either house by a member of that body. The vast bulk (more than 95 percent) of the 10,000 or so bills introduced every two years die in a subcommittee for lack of support. On major legislation that has significant backing, the committee or one of its subcommittees holds hearings to receive opinions. It then meets to

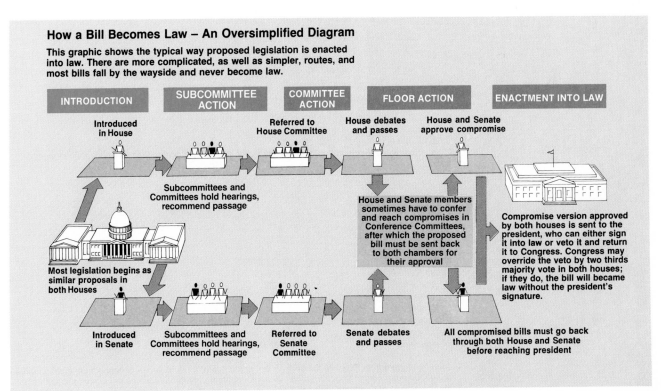

How a Bill Becomes Law – An Oversimplified Diagram

This graphic shows the typical way proposed legislation is enacted into law. There are more complicated, as well as simpler, routes, and most bills fall by the wayside and never become law.

| INTRODUCTION | SUBCOMMITTEE ACTION | COMMITTEE ACTION | FLOOR ACTION | ENACTMENT INTO LAW |

Introduced in House

Referred to House Committee

House debates and passes

House and Senate approve compromise

Subcommittees and Committees hold hearings, recommend passage

Most legislation begins as similar proposals in both Houses

House and Senate members sometimes have to confer and reach compromises in Conference Committees, after which the proposed bill must be sent back to both chambers for their approval

Compromise version approved by both houses is sent to the president, who can either sign it into law or veto it and return it to Congress. Congress may override the veto by two thirds majority vote in both houses; if they do, the bill will became law without the president's signature.

Introduced in Senate

Subcommittees and Committees hold hearings, recommend passage

Referred to Senate Committee

Senate debates and passes

All compromised bills must go back through both House and Senate before reaching president "mark up" (discuss and revise) and vote on the bill. If the subcommittee and then the parent committee vote in favor of the bill, it is reported—or sent—to the full house, where it is debated and voted on. If passed, it goes to the other chamber, where the whole process is repeated. If there are differences between the bills as passed by the House and the Senate—and there often are—the two versions must go to a conference committee for reconciliation.

In 1789 through 1790, 142 bills were introduced in the House of Representatives, and only eighty-five reports were filed from committees. Today 10,000 to 15,000 bills are introduced in each Congress; of these less than 1000 are enacted into law. These figures are lower than they were ten and twenty years ago because Congress in the 1980s and 1990s has had to focus more on budget, tax, and deficit concerns than on new programs.

OPPORTUNITIES FOR DELAY

The complexity of the congressional system provides a tremendous built-in advantage for the opponents of any measure. Those who sponsor a bill must win at every step; opponents need to win only once. Multiple opportunities for vetoes exist because of the dispersion of influence and because at a dozen points in committee or in the House or Senate, a bill may be killed or allowed to die. Whether good or bad, a proposal can be delayed by any one of the following: (1) the chairperson of the House substantive committee; (2) the House substantive committee; (3) the House Rules Committee; (4) the House; (5) the chairperson of the Senate subcommittee; (6) the Senate committee; (7) the majority of the Senate; (8) the floor leaders in both chambers; (9) a few members of the Senate in the case of a filibuster; (10) the House-Senate conference committee if the chambers disagree; and (11) the president. If the agreement of still other committees is required—appropriations, for example—the points of possible veto are multiplied.

Clearly, a controversial bill cannot get through without good legislative leadership and compromise. One tactical question at the start is whether to push for initial action in the Senate or in the House. If a bill is expected to have a rough time in the Senate, for example, its sponsors may seek passage in the House and hope that a sizable victory will spur the Senate into action. Another question concerns the committee to which the bill should be assigned. Normally referral

TABLE 14–3
Comparison of House and Senate Activity and Workload, 83rd and 98th Congresses

CATEGORY	83rd CONGRESS (1953–1954)		98th CONGRESS (1983–1984)	
	SENATE	HOUSE	SENATE	HOUSE
Standing committees	15	19	16	22
Subcommittees	63	81	102	139
Hearings	—	—	2471	5661
Days in session	294	240	281	266
Messages from president	—	5	235	179
Messages from executive departments	—	1855	3642	4164
Resolutions passed	321	519	380	397
Bills passed	2231	2129	936	978

Source: Adapted from Roger H. Davidson and Thomas Kephart, "Indicators of Senate Activity and Workload," and by the same authors, "Indicators of House of Representatives Workload and Activity," Congressional Research Service, Library of Congress (June 1985).

CHAPTER 14 / Congress: The People's Branch?

to a committee is automatic. Sometimes, however, a bill cuts across more than one jurisdiction, but it can be written in such a way that it is bound to go to one committee rather than another.

Getting a bill through Congress requires more than a majority at any one time or place. Majorities must be mobilized over and over again—in subcommittee, in committee, and in chamber. These majorities shift and change, and they involve different legislators in different situations at different points in time. New coalitions must be built again and again.

These days, almost everything Congress wants to do by legislation requires dollars. So even if a bill passes, it must go through the process again to secure appropriations. Congress may go through the entire process of authorizing a program, and then fail to appropriate money to implement it; or it may appropriate so little money that what was authorized cannot be carried out.

Committees: The Little Legislatures

It is sometimes said that Congress is a collection of committees that come together in a chamber every once in a while to approve one another's actions. There is much truth in this. Almost from the beginning Congress has relied on committees to get much of its work done.[27] The main struggle over legislation takes place in committees and especially in subcommittees, for this is where the basic work of Congress is done.[28] The House of Representatives has 22 standing committees, each with an average membership of about 35 representatives. These committees have a total of about 140 subcommittees. The committees are "the eye, the ear, the hand, and very often the brain of the House."

Standing committees have great power, for all bills introduced in the House are referred to them. They can defeat bills, pigeonhole them for weeks, amend them beyond recognition, or speed them on their way. A committee reports out favorably only a small fraction of all the bills that come to it. Although a bill can be forced to the floor of the House through a **discharge petition** signed by a majority of the membership, legislators are reluctant to bypass committees. They regard committee members as experts in their fields. Sometimes, too, they are reluctant to risk the anger of committee leaders. And there is a strong sense of reciprocity—"You respect my committee's jurisdiction, and I will respect yours." Not surprisingly, few discharge petitions gain the necessary number of signatures.

The Senate has sixteen standing committees, each composed of twelve to twenty-nine members, and at least eighty-five subcommittees. Whereas members of the House hold relatively few committee assignments, each senator normally serves on three committees and an average of seven subcommittees. Among the important Senate committees are foreign relations, budget, finance, and appropriations. Senate committees have the same powers over the framing of legislation as do those of the House, but they have somewhat less power to keep bills from reaching the floor.

CHOOSING COMMITTEE MEMBERS

Partisanship shapes the control and staffing of standing committees. The chair and a majority of the members are elected from the majority party. The minority party is represented roughly in proportion to its membership in the entire chamber. Getting on a politically advantageous committee is important to members of Con-

Types of Committees

Standing Committees are the substantive committees to which proposed bills are referred for consideration. Less than 10 percent of the more than 10,000 measures sent to committees are ever reported out of these committees, so their main job is to set priorities. They are called "standing" because they continue from one Congress to the next and hence are generally viewed as the permanent workshops of congressional lawmaking.

Select Committees are created to conduct special investigations or studies and report back to the chamber that established them. They do not ordinarily draft and report legislation. Some select committees do stay in business, however, over the course of several sessions of Congress.

Joint Committees are formed with members from both houses of Congress, partly to coordinate investigations or special studies. In practice, they are study committees set up to expedite business between the houses and help focus public attention on major matters such as the economy, taxation, or scandals.

Conference Committees are one form of joint committee set up to reconcile differences when the House and Senate have passed different versions of the same bill. No bill can be sent to the White House for a president's signature unless it has been passed in identical manner by both chambers of Congress. Many major bills thus have to be negotiated in conference committees and sent back for approval in the respective chambers before being sent to the White House.

What Committees Do

Study legislative proposals

Consider communications from the executive branch

Confirm or reject federal appointees

Conduct hearings and investigations

Review ongoing executive operations

Prepare reports and surveys, and make recommendations about corrective legislation

Review reports, documents, and research related to committee policy

Meet informally with public- and private-sector leaders about their committee domain

Conduct on-site visits/inspections

Hold hearings that send messages about preferred policies, priorities, and personnel nominees.

Standing Committees of the House of Representatives

Agriculture

Appropriations

Armed Services

Banking, Finance, and Urban Affairs

Budget

District of Columbia

Education and Labor

Energy and Commerce

Foreign Affairs

Government Operations

House Administration

Interior and Insular Affairs

Judiciary

Merchant Marine and Fisheries

Post Office and Civil Service

Public Works and Transportation

Rules

Science and Technology

Small Business

Standards of Official Conduct

Veterans' Affairs

Ways and Means

A congressional committee meeting.

gress. A representative from Kansas, for example, would much rather serve on the agriculture committee than on the merchant marine and fisheries committee. Members usually stay on the same committees from one Congress to the next, although younger members who have had undesirable assignments often bid for better committees when places become available.

How are committee members chosen? In the House of Representatives a Committee on Committees of the Republican membership allots places to new Republican members. This committee is composed of one member from each state having Republican representation in the House; the member is almost always the senior member of the state's delegation. Because each member has as many votes in the committee as there are Republicans in the delegation, the group is dominated by senior members from the large-state delegations. On the Democratic side assignment to committees is handled by the Steering Committee of the Democratic caucus in negotiation with senior Democrats from the state delegations. In the Senate veterans also dominate the assignment process; each party has a small steering committee for that purpose. In making assignments, leaders are guided by various considerations: how talented and cooperative a member is, whether his or her region is already well represented on a committee, and whether the assignment will aid in reelecting the member.

One reason Congress can cope with its huge workload is that its committees and subcommittees are organized around subject-matter specialties. This allows members to develop technical expertise in specific areas and to recruit skilled staffs, so that Congress is often able to criticize and challenge experts from the bureaucracy. Interest groups and lobbyists realize the great power a specific committee has in certain areas and focus their attention on its members. Similarly, members of executive departments are careful to cultivate the committee and subcommittee chairs and members of "their" committees. One powerful Senate committee chairperson reminded his constituents of the amount of federal tax money being spent in their state: "This does not happen by accident," the senator's campaign pamphlet said. "It takes power and influence in Congress."

COMMITTEE DIVERSITY AND PERSISTENCE

Most committees are separate little centers of power, with rules, patterns of action, and internal processes of their own. Analyzing the House appropriations committee, students of Congress discovered it is characterized by remarkable agreement among

Senator Sam Nunn (D–Georgia), chairman of the Senate Armed Services Committee.

its members on key issues and on the role the committee should play. Leadership is stable, and members tend to remain a long time. They have worked out a way of life emphasizing conformity, give-and-take, and hard work. The subcommittee chairpersons of the House Appropriations Committee become specialists on the budgets and programs of the agencies within their jurisdiction, and often exercise more influence over administrative policy than any other single representative. For example, the chair of the Appropriations Subcommittee on Foreign Aid has more influence over that program than the chair of the House Committee on Foreign Affairs. The various appropriations subcommittees defer to one another's recommendations and back up the decisions of the parent committee.

Committees, however, differ. Whereas some are powerful, others are much less important. Because of the Senate's special role in foreign policy, for example, the Senate Foreign Relations Committee is usually more influential than the House Committee on Foreign Affairs. For the two appropriations committees, however, the reverse is true: The House committee sometimes plays a more significant role than the Senate committee. However, these differences are less than they used to be. We should also note that committees differ not only for institutional reasons but also according to the goals and abilities of their members.[29]

How Congress uses committees is critical in its role as a partner in national policy making. In recent years progress has been made to open hearings to the public and to improve the quality of committee staffs, but it is difficult to modernize jurisdictions, and jurisdictional overlap is common. For example, a dozen different committees deal with energy, education, and the nation's war on drugs. Efforts to make the committee system more efficient are often considered as a threat to the delicate balance of power within the chamber.

THE IMPORTANCE OF COMMITTEE AND SUBCOMMITTEE CHAIRS

Committee and subcommittee leaders exercise influence over both the operations of their committees and the final output of Congress. A generation ago committee chairs determined the total workload of committees, hired and fired staff, and formed subcommittees and assigned them jurisdictions, members, and aides. Chairs also managed the most important bills assigned to their committees. In recent years, however, younger members have insisted they be given more authority. Subcommittee chairs have also tended to be more independent from the parent committees. It is not uncommon these days for a member of Congress of only one or two terms to be the chair of an important subcommittee, and indeed this is the tradition in the Senate.

Chairs are still usually awarded on the basis of *seniority*. The member of the majority party who has had the longest continuous service on the committee ordinarily becomes its head. The chair may be at odds with other members of the party, may oppose the party's national program, and may even be incompetent; still, he or she usually wins the chair position because of seniority.[30]

MODIFYING SENIORITY

Committee chair as well as assignments are the responsibility of the party caucuses in both chambers. The custom of seniority still prevails, but it is not a written rule, and other factors are beginning to be taken into account. In 1971, for example, the House Republican Conference decided that ranking Republicans on committees

Standing Committees of the Senate

Agriculture, Nutrition and Forestry
Appropriations
Armed Services
Banking, Housing, and Urban Affairs
Budget
Commerce, Science, and Transportation
Energy and Natural Resources
Environment and Public Works
Finance
Foreign Relations
Governmental Affairs
Judiciary
Labor and Human Resources
Rules and Administration
Small Business
Veterans' Affairs

Representative Dan Rostenkowski (D–Illinois), chairman of the House Ways and Means Committee, is widely recognized as one of the most powerful and influential House members.

Senator Alan Simpson (R–Wyoming) has served as Deputy Majority Leader.

would henceforth be elected by the conference by a secret ballot. Soon afterwards Democrats authorized a secret ballot vote on chair positions if 20 percent of the caucus demanded it. In 1975 rank-and-file House Democrats, their ranks swollen and resolve stiffened by seventy-five mostly liberal newcomers, removed from their membership three elderly committee chairpersons. In early 1985 Les Aspin of Wisconsin was elected chair of the House Armed Services Committee by a coalition of junior and older members who respected him as the best choice and believed he was right on some major issues, even though he was not next in the line of seniority.

When Republicans control the Senate, Republican members of the major committees choose each committee's chair. When their party loses control over the Senate, these same persons become the ranking minority members. As a regular practice, Republican members almost always elect the senior member to serve as their leader on a committee.

The Senate Democrats choose their committee leaders by a secret ballot of the Democratic Conference whenever requested to do so by 20 percent of the Senate Democratic membership. The Senate Democrats almost always elect the senior Democratic member of the Senate committee to serve as the ranking committee member, but that the Democratic Conference could by secret ballot do otherwise has forced senior members to make concessions to ensure their reelection.

The system of seniority tends to give the most influence in Congress to those constituencies that are politically stable or even stagnant. These are the areas where party competition is low or where a particular interest group or machine influence may be greatest. It stacks the cards against areas where the two parties are more evenly matched, where interest in politics is high, and where competition is keen.

Seniority is defended on the grounds that elevating the most experienced members to leadership positions is automatic and impersonal and prevents disputes. Seniority is also one of the important conflict-reducing norms practiced in both chambers of Congress. It facilitates the organization of Congress.

The argument over seniority is in large part over policy and political influence. Rural interests used to favor the system. And, historically, it was opposed by such groups as organized labor, civil rights advocates, and other urban-based interests, who believed it gave rural interests and their conservative representatives too much power in Congress. Yet liberal groups may also profit from the system. The passage of time may cause the seniority custom to increase the influence of suburban and urban-based northern interests. As time passes, and more women and minorities win election to Congress, they too will likely attain chairs under the seniority custom that might be denied to them under more free-wheeling selection rules.

The system of seniority remains because it supports the interests of congressional leaders. Many legislators conclude: "The longer I'm here, the better I like the system." Further, those who are most anxious to change the system have the least power to produce such changes. But as power has become dispersed, and as subcommittees have become increasingly important, the issue of seniority has diminished in importance. Subcommittee chairs tend to be members with less seniority, and they are likely to be more moderate than the committee chairs. In the Senate all but a handful of the majority party chair their own subcommittees; in the House more than 100 Democrats are subcommittee chairs. In recent years there have also been moves to strengthen the powers of the party leaders and caucuses—again at the expense of the committee chairs.

One of the most controversial activities of Congress is its investigations, especially such well-publicized open hearings as those of the Senate Foreign Relations Committee during the Vietnam War or those of various committees that investigated the Iran-contra affair in 1987. Why does Congress investigate? Hearings by standing committees, their subcommittees, or special select committees are an important source of information and opinion. They provide an arena in which experts can submit their views and statements and statistics can be entered in the record.[31]

Public hearings are an important channel of communication and influence. Senator Albert Gore of Tennessee, for example, held hearings a few years ago to investigate the record industry and allegations that many radio stations play music based on money slipped under the table, not on a record's merits. Saying a " 'new payola' is alive and well and worse than ever," Gore sought to focus public attention on these corrupt and illegal bribery practices. A committee or its chair may use a hearing to address Congress. Committee hearings may also be used to communicate with the public at-large. The Senate's Watergate Committee's televised investigations into election practices and campaign finance abuses in 1973, for example, were intended less to obtain new information than to arouse citizens and to promote public support for election reforms. Some investigations by regular committees involve overseeing the current administration. A committee can summon administration officials to testify in hearings. Some officials fear these inquiries; they dread the loaded questions of hostile members and the likelihood that some administrative error in their agency may be uncovered and publicized.

A legislative inquiry is a two-edged sword. It can spur Congress and the public to support needed laws or corrective legislation, or it can debase First Amendment principles, invade the privacy of citizens, and afford a platform for grandstanding demagogues. Congressional investigations can also diminish executive branch morale. In 1987 a joint Senate-House Committee investigated the Iran-contra activities of the National Security staff and the diversion of funds from arms sales to Iran to the rebels in Nicaragua. Their goal as an investigatory committee was to raise important questions, to encourage increased executive branch accountability to the public, and to highlight the importance of shared foreign-policy making that includes the leadership in Congress. Such hearings are critically important for reminding Americans about the basic principles of constitutionalism. They can also help set the political agenda and send messages to the executive branch regarding personnel and policy preferences.[32]

Senator "Pete" Domenici (R–New Mexico) has headed the Senate Budget Committee, where he exerted pressure on Ronald Reagan to cut spending and raise revenues to balance the budget.

Members of the joint House-Senate select committee investigating the Iran-contra affair consult with their legal counsel. Left to right are: John Nields, House counsel, Senator George Mitchell, Arthur Liman, Senate counsel, Senator Warren Rudman, and Senator Daniel Inouye.

Getting It Together:
Conference Committees and Senate-House Coordination

When the framers created a two-house national legislature, they anticipated that the two chambers would represent sharply different interests. The Senate was to be a small chamber of persons elected indirectly by the people and holding long, overlapping terms. It would have the sole power to confirm nominations. Proposed treaties required the approval of a two-thirds vote in the Senate. The Senate was to be a chamber of scrutiny, a gathering of wise leaders who would counsel and sanction a president—whether that president liked it or not.

The House of Representatives, elected anew every two years, was to be a more direct instrument of the people. The Senate was a conservative check on

A joint Senate-House conference committee works on the budget.

the House, especially in the late nineteenth and early twentieth centuries, when it was extremely conservative and something of a rich man's club. But some factors—chiefly political—have altered the character of both the House and the Senate. Sometimes now the House serves as a conservative check on the Senate. Executive departments and agencies sometimes consider the Senate to be a court of appeals for appropriations that have been shot down by the House.

Given the differences between the House and the Senate, it is not surprising that the version of a bill passed by one chamber may differ substantially from the version passed by the other. Only if both houses pass an absolutely identical measure can it become law. As a general rule, one house accepts the language of the other, but at least 15 percent of all bills passed (usually major ones) must be referred to a **conference committee.**

If neither house will accept the other's bill, a conference committee—a special committee of members from each chamber—settles the differences. Both parties are represented, but the majority party has more members. The proceedings of this committee are usually an elaborate bargaining process. When it is brought back to the two houses, the conference report can be accepted or rejected (often with further negotiations ordered), yet it cannot be amended. Each set of conference members must convince its colleagues that any concessions made to the other house were on unimportant points and that nothing basic in their own version of the bill was surrendered.

How much leeway does a conference committee have? Ordinarily the members are expected to stay somewhere between the different versions. On matters for which there is no clear middle ground, members are sometimes accused of exceeding their instructions and producing a new bill. The conference committee has even been called a "third house" of Congress, one that arbitrarily revises policy. Conference committees are also criticized on the ground that they are not representative, even of the committees approving the bill, and that they disproportionately represent senior committee leaders. Critics also complain that little can be done about biases that may creep into the bill in the conference committee, because the houses are usually confronted with a take-it or leave-it situation. Despite such criticism, some kind of conference committee is needed for a two-house legislature to work. Conference committees integrate the houses, help resolve disputes, and make compromises.

Which chamber, House or Senate, wins more often in conference committees? On the surface it appears the Senate's version wins more often, but this is partly because the Senate more often than not acts on its legislation after the House has. "However, such an outcome does not mean that the Senate has a greater impact on the final legislative product than does the House. On the contrary, by creating the original bill and setting the agenda for debate on the issue, the House is judged to have the more real impact on the final shape of legislation as it passes through conference than does the Senate."[33] In effect the House plays a dominant lawmaking role, while the Senate plays a key representational role through amendments.

Is Congress Effective?—Congressional Reform

Here are a few of the more frequent criticisms of Congress.

1. Congress is *inefficient*. The House and Senate are simply not suited to the needs of an industrial nation. Too much time is required to get bills through

the complicated legislative process, and bills are often buried or defeated by procedural devices. Members are not as well informed as they should be. The dispersion of power guarantees slowness.

Some of this criticism is exaggerated. Evaluating procedure and structure is difficult to separate from evaluating policy, about which everyone has an individual preference. For example, from the White House vantage point, Congress is inefficient when it does not process the president's bills quickly.

Congress deals with an enormous number of complex measures. Many procedures in both houses expedite handling of bills, and the committee and subcommittee system is a reasonable device for hearing arguments and compiling information. Still, the question of efficiency remains. Many members themselves feel defeated by the system. Study groups inside and outside Congress have urged the houses to reduce the number of committee assignments, establish better information systems, centralize a bit more power in their leadership positions, and strengthen majority rule. Congress has done many of these things, yet the pace is not much improved.

2. Congress is *unrepresentative.* The complaint is often made that Congress represents regional or constituents' interests over the national interest. It is also said that the committee system often is too responsive to organized special interests. The seniority system, even with its modifications, biases both houses toward conservatism. Defenders of Congress contend there should be a strong institution to guarantee minority rights and to act as a check on mindless majority rule. Critics answer by arguing that minorities should have a right to publicize and delay what the majority proposes to do, but not to defeat it.

Both houses, critics hold, overrepresent well-organized economic power structures at the expense of the average citizen. Can the members of Congress, who are so much the products of upper- or upper-middle-class backgrounds, really speak for the needs of low-income groups? Can a Congress that has only 5 percent women and 4 percent black membership truly represent our female and minority population?

Speaker of the House Jim Wright was forced to resign that post in 1989 because of various ethics charges.

In fact, we have a system of dual representation in which both Congress and the president can and do claim to speak for the people. But because "the people" seldom, if ever, speak with a single voice, the structure and character of the two systems tend to give us a Congress that speaks for one majority and a president who often speaks for another. Between the two, sometimes we get a balance—and sometimes a deadlock.

3. Congress is *unethical.* It's government by money, not government by the people—or so many people think. Critics complain that some members of Congress are too tied to the economic interests they are asked to regulate and are beholden to the political action committees that increasingly fund their campaigns. Others charge that members of Congress get too many personal privileges and that there have been too many abuses of these so-called fringe benefits. The forced departures of Speaker Jim Wright and House Majority Whip Tony Coelho in 1989 because of ethical conflicts of interest, and the indictment and conviction of a handful of other national legisators in recent years reinforced this image.

In response to occasional scandals, both houses have passed reasonably strong ethics codes and have created ethics committees. These changes require

"Early today the senator called a spade a spade. He later issued a retraction."

Drawing by Joe Mirachi; © 1989 The New Yorker Magazine, Inc.

public disclosure of income and property holdings by legislators, key aides, and spouses. They also bar gifts of over $100 to a legislator, a staff member, or a legislator's family from a registered lobbyist, an organization with a political-action committee, a foreign government, or a business with an interest in legislation before Congress. But these actions have not much improved the image of Congress as a place where power often tends to corrupt many of its members.

4. Congress *lacks collective responsibility*. The main problem in Congress is the dispersion of power among committee and subcommittee leaders, elected party officials, factional leaders, informal caucus leaders, and other legislators. It is a "nobody's in charge" system. This dispersion of power means that to get things done, congressional leaders must bargain and negotiate. The result of this "brokerage" system is that laws may be watered down, defeated, delayed, or written in vague language. Also, according to some critics, too much leeway is given to unknown bureaucrats. Accountability is confused, responsibility is eroded, and well-organized special interests who know how to work the system are given an unfair advantage.

Critics worry that if Congress responds to so many single interests, it cannot speak for the great majority or for the nation as a whole. It cannot anticipate problems, plan ahead, and put together political coalitions to deal with critical problems. Those concerned about congressional irresponsibility do not blame a few conservative interests or elite elements. They recognize that brokerage is mainly the result of a constitutional system that divides authority, checks power with power, and disperses political leadership. Yet other factors making it difficult for Congress to act as a unified branch arise from the fact that each house may be controlled by a different political party. Also, we are now electing brighter and more independent-minded individuals who are less inclined to go along with party leaders.

5. Congress *delegates too much to the executive branch*. Another charge is that Congress fails to do its job, and tends to delegate too much authority to the executive branch. Because of the complexity of modern problems and an inability to work out coalitions and compromises, there is a tendency for Congress to say to the executive branch: "Do something" about drugs; or "Do something" about AIDS and acid rain. If Congress turns a matter over to an administrative agency, the result may be that the rules and regulations issued by the administrators effectively become the law.

These critics often disagree with the policy initiatives in question. Still, the complaint is valid, for we expect our *elected* officials to hammer out public policies. Congress is aware of this criticism, but sometimes escaping responsibility is a major consideration. If Congress passed specific legislation, affected persons or groups might then blame Congress rather than the administrative agencies—and perhaps even particular members of Congress, who then might lose their seats.

6. Congress is *too responsive to organized interests that make large campaign contributions through their political-action committees*. This final charge suggests that even though few members of Congress can be bought by campaign contributions, the way Congress conducts its business—and who gets heard at its hearings and in its corridors—is influenced to too great an extent by those who can raise and disburse large sums of money. Former Senator S. I. Hayakawa put it this way: "I'm not saying my colleagues are corrupted by the system. But it isn't hard

for the recipient of a generous contribution from, let us say, the dairy industry to convince himself that what is in the interest of the dairy industry is indeed in the public interest."[34] Congressional campaign costs have skyrocketed in recent years; typical campaigns cost over $500,000 for the House, and often several million dollars for the Senate. Money buys access, so it is claimed. The 1979 ABSCAM scandals, in which FBI agents posing as Arab sheiks successfully bought several promises of influence and favors from a handful of members of Congress, provide evidence for this criticism. It is small consolation that these members were subsequently indicted and convicted by the federal courts. Former representative, senator, and Reagan cabinet member Richard S. Schweiker said, "We've reached the point where a member has to be either a millionaire or a continual fundraiser, and that's a tragic commentary on where we are going."[35]

Defenders of Congress insist these charges are overstated. They say money would hardly influence the three dozen or more millionaires who are members of the Senate and the 100 or so members of the House who are well off financially. Defenders of Congress also point out that some members of Congress regularly turn down certain types of campaign contributions. Because of various campaign reform laws, candidates for Congress must now report all major campaign contributions to the Federal Election Commission. Thus, who gives what to whom is at least part of the public record. Still, the criticism is valid, and a large number of Americans are perplexed or disturbed about the degree of influence seemingly associated with campaign contributions and most especially political action committees.

In *The Federalist*, No. 57, James Madison wrote: "Who are to be the electors of the Federal Representatives? Not the rich more than the poor; not the learned more than the ignorant; not the haughty heirs of distinguished names, more than the humble sons of obscure and unpropitious fortune." Yet as the costs of campaigning increase, and as the body of elected officials continues to come from essentially the upper or upper-middle class, one must question whether ours is the open, representative, responsive, and responsible legislative system we can point to with pride as a model for those in other parts of the world who yearn for a more democratic society.

As Congress begins its third century, the following questions have to be raised: Can Congress create majorities? Can it have a long-range view, staying power, span of attention, and the ability to make sensible laws for the whole nation? Although answers would differ, all would agree that a vital, responsive, and effective Congress is a must if we would make government by the people work.

S ummary

1. Senators and representatives come primarily from upper- and middle-class backgrounds. They are far better educated than Americans as a whole. The typical member of Congress is a middle-aged, white, male lawyer.

2. Most of the work in Congress is done in committees and subcommittees. Congress has attempted in recent years to streamline its committee system and modify its methods of selecting committee chairs. Seniority practices are still generally followed, but the threat of removal forces committee chairs to consult with younger members of the majority party. Subcommittees are now more important in an increasingly decentralized Congress.

3. Congress performs these functions: representation, law making, consensus building, overseeing, policy clarification, and legitimizing. Congress as a collective body must attempt to perform these tasks even as most of its members serve as

ombudsmen for their constituents and work for their own reelections.

4. The workload for Congress is considerable. Much could be done to make our national legislature perform its functions more effectively. Some improvements have been made in recent years: Redistricting and reapportionment have shaped a Congress that somewhat more accurately reflects the population. The filibuster in the Senate and the Rules Committee in the House are less obstructive than they once were. The role of the speaker and of party steering committees has been enhanced, and Congress is better staffed.

5. The negative image of Congress as a ponderous or sluggish institution is still common. Its greatest strengths—its diversity and deliberative character—also weaken its dealings with the more centralized executive branch. Its members will rarely be fast on their 1070 feet. The 535 members, divided into two houses, two parties, dozens of committees, and hundreds of subcommittees, will always have a difficult time arriving at a common strategy to combat a president determined to use executive powers to the fullest. How effectively can Congress assert itself, especially with respect to the presidency? How can it deal with budget deficits and national security? We return to a consideration of these questions in Chapter 16, after we have examined the modern presidency and its responsibilities.

Further Reading

ROBERT A. BERNSTEIN. *Elections, Representation, and Congressional Voting Behavior* (Prentice Hall, 1989).

WILLIAM S. COHEN and GEORGE J. MITCHELL. *Men of Zeal: A Candid Inside Story of the Iran-Contra Hearings* (Viking, 1988).

ROGER H. DAVIDSON and WALTER J. OLESZEK. *Congress and its Members*, 2d ed. (Congressional Quarterly Press, 1985).

CHRISTOPHER J. DEERING, ed. *Congressional Politics* (Dorsey, 1989).

LAWRENCE C. DODD and BRUCE I. OPPENHEIMER, eds. *Congress Reconsidered*, 4th ed. (Congressional Quarterly Press, 1989).

RICHARD F. FENNO, JR. *Home Style: House Members in their Districts* (Little, Brown, 1978).

RICHARD F. FENNO, JR. *The Making of a Senator—Dan Quayle* (Congressional Quarterly Press, 1989).

MORRIS FIORINA. *Congress: Keystone of the American Establishment* (Yale University Press, 1977).

WILLIAM J. KEEFE. *Congress and the American People* (Prentice Hall, 1988).

JOHN KINGDON. *Congressional Voting Decisions*, 3rd ed. (University of Michigan Press, 1989).

GERHARD LOEWENBERG, SAMUEL C. PATTERSON, and MALCOLM JEWELL, eds. *Handbook of Legislative Research* (Harvard University Press, 1985).

BURDETT LOOMIS. *The New American Politician* (Basic Books, 1988).

DAVID R. MAYHEW. *Congress: The Electoral Connection* (Yale University Press, 1974).

WALTER J. OLESZEK. *Congressional Procedures and the Policy Process*, 3d ed. (Congressional Quarterly Press, 1989).

GLENN R. PARKER. *Characteristics of Congress: Patterns in Congressional Behavior* (Prentice Hall, 1989).

BARBARA SINCLAIR. *The Transformation of the U.S. Senate* (The Johns Hopkins University Press, 1989).

STEVEN S. SMITH. *Call to Order: Floor Politics in the House and Senate* (Brookings Institution, 1989).

DAVID J. VOGLER. *The Politics of Congress*, 5th ed. (Allyn and Bacon, 1988).

DARRELL M. WEST. *Congress and Economic Policymaking* (University of Pittsburgh, 1987).

Notes

1. George Washington to James Madison, Feb. 16, 1789, Robert A. Rutland and Charles F. Hobson, eds., *The Papers of James Madison* (University Press of Virginia, 1977), vol. 11, p. 446.

2. On the early history of Congress, see Alvin M. Josephy, Jr., *On the Hill: A History of the American Congress from 1789 to the Present* (Touchstone, 1980), chap. 1.

3. John Rhodes, *The Futile System* (EPM Publications, 1976), p. 15. See also Gregg Easterbrook, "What's Wrong with Congress?" *The Atlantic Monthly* (December 1984), pp. 57–84.

4. See Burdett Loomis, *The New American Politician* (Basic Books, 1988).

5. See James L. Sundquist, *Constitutional Reform and Effective Government* (Brookings Institution, 1986); James MacGregor Burns, *The Power to Lead* (Simon & Schuster, 1984); and Donald L. Robinson, ed., *Reforming American Government* (Westview Press, 1985).

6. See the essays in Gordon Jones and John Marini, eds., *The Imperial Congress* (Heritage Foundation/Claremont Institute, 1989); and L. Gordon Crovitz and Jeremy Rabbin, eds., *The Fettered Presidency: Legal Constraints on the Executive Branch* (American Enterprise Institute, 1989).

7. See David C. Kozak, "House-Senate Differences: A Test among Interview Data," in David C. Kozak and John D. Macartney, eds., *Congress and Public Policy*, 2d ed. (Dorsey Press, 1987), chap. 3.

8. Thomas P. O'Neill with William Novak, *Man of the House: The Life and Political Memoirs of Speaker Tip O'Neill* (Random House, 1987), p. 273.

9. See Barbara Sinclair, *The Transformation of the U.S. Senate* (Johns Hopkins University Press, 1989).

10. For an account of Howard Baker as majority leader in the early and mid-1980s, as well as a general account of Senate life, see James A. Miller, *Running in Place: Inside the Senate* (Simon & Schuster, 1986).

11. See Stephen Hess, *The Ultimate Insiders: U.S. Senators and the Media* (Brookings Institution, 1986).

12. Steven V. Roberts, "Wheels Are Spinning over the Senate Rules," *The New York Times* (February 26, 1986), p. 8.

13. For a study of female members of Congress, see Irwin N. Gertzog, *Congressional Women: Their Recruitment, Treatment, and Behavior* (Praeger, 1984). See also Robert A. Bernstein, "Why Are There

So Few Women in the House?" *Western Political Quarterly* (March 1, 1986), pp. 155–64.

14. See John R. Johannes, *To Serve the People: Congress and Constituency Service* (University of Nebraska Press, 1984); Morris Fiorina, *Congress—Keystone of the Washington Establishment* (Yale University Press, 1977); Richard F. Fenno, Jr., *Home Style: House Members in their Districts* (Little, Brown, 1978).

15. See David C. Kozak, *Contexts of Congressional Decision Behavior* (University Press of America, 1984).

16. See Robert A. Bernstein, *Elections, Representation, and Congressional Voting Behavior* (Prentice Hall, 1989).

17. Jerrold E. Schneider, *Ideological Coalitions in Congress* (Greenwood Press, 1979).

18. See Loomis, *The New American Politician*; and Richard F. Fenno, Jr., *The Making of a Senator—Dan Quayle* (Congressional Quarterly Press, 1988).

19. John W. Kingdon, *Congressional Voting Decisions*, 3rd ed. (University of Michigan Press, 1989).

20. For a comparison of how different members serve their districts' needs, see John Johannes, *To Serve the People*. See also Steven H. Schiff and Steven B. Smith, "Generational Change and the Allocation of Congressional Staff," *Legislative Studies Quarterly* (August 1985), pp. 457–67.

21. Christine DeGregorio, "Professionals in the U.S. Congress: An Analysis of Working Styles," *Legislative Studies Quarterly* (November 1988); for a more critical view, as his title suggests, see Michael J. Malbin, *Unelected Representatives* (Basic Books, 1980).

22. See Patricia Hurley, "Parties and Coalitions in Congress," in Christopher J. Deering, ed., *Congressional Politics* (Dorsey Press, 1989), pp. 113–34; and John R. Crawford, "Party Unity Scores Slip in 1988, but Overall Pattern is Upward," *Congressional Quarterly* (November 19, 1988), pp. 3334–42.

23. See Kay Lehman Schlozman and John T. Tierney, *Organized Interests and American Democracy* (Harper & Row, 1986), especially chaps. 10 to 12.

24. George G. Edwards III, *Presidential Influence in Congress* (Freeman, 1980), chaps. 5, 6, and 7.

25. See Cecil V. Crabb, Jr., and Pat M. Holt, *Invitation to Struggle*, 3d ed. (Congressional Quarterly Press, 1988).

26. For two well written studies that follow legislation through the process, see Jeremy H. Birnbaum and Alan S. Murray, *Showdown at Gucci Gulch: Lobbyists and the Unlikely Triumph of Tax Reform* (Random House, 1988); and T. R. Reid, *Congressional Odyssey: The Saga of a Senate Bill* (Freeman, 1980).

27. See, for example, Thomas W. Skladony, "The House Goes to Work: Select and Standing Committees in the U.S. House of Representatives, 1789–1828," *Congress & the Presidency* (Autumn 1985), pp. 166–87.

28. The best books on congressional committees, their staffs, and their influential roles are: Steven S. Smith and Christopher J. Deering, *Committees in Congress* (Congressional Quarterly Press, 1984), and Joseph Unekis and Leroy N. Rieselbach, *Congressional Committee Politics* (Praeger, 1984).

29. Richard F. Fenno, Jr., *Congressmen in Committees* (Little, Brown, 1972).

30. For a good examination of the role of a subcommittee chair in the Senate, see Fenno, *The Making of A Senator*, chaps. 2 and 3.

31. For studies of the role of congressional investigations, see James Hamilton, *The Power to Probe: A Study of Congressional Investigations* (Vintage, 1976); Morris S. Ogul, *Congress Oversees the Bureaucracy* (University of Pittsburgh Press, 1976); and Loch Johnson, *A Season of Inquiry: The Senate Intelligence Investigation* (University of Kentucky Press, 1985).

32. John W. Kingdon, *Agendas, Alternatives and Public Policies* (Little, Brown, 1984).

33. David J. Vogler, *The Politics of Congress*, 5th ed. (Allyn and Bacon, 1988), p. 213.

34. Quoted in *U.S. News & World Report* (December 20, 1982), p. 24. See also The Twentieth Century Fund Task Force on Political Action Committees, *What Price PACs?* (Twentieth Century Fund, 1984).

35. David S. Broder, "Who Took the Fun out of Congress?" *The Washington Post National Weekly Edition* (February 17, 1986), p. 10. See also Philip Stern, *The Best Congress Money Can Buy* (Pantheon, 1988).

15

The Presidency: Leadership Branch?

The framers in 1787 perceived the presidency in the image of George Washington, the man they expected would first occupy the office. The American chief executive, like Washington, was to be a wise, moderate, dignified, nonpartisan "president of all the people." But should the future presidency be "above politics" or should it be a frankly political institution? Should the president *lead* the people, or wait upon a consensus? Should a president be essentially a "republican monarch" or a democratic politician, a man of the people?

No one in 1789 commanded the trust and respect that George Washington did. He had served his country in a variety of ways, most notably as commander in chief of the Continental army for eight years and as an instigator of, and later presiding officer at, the Constitutional Convention of 1787. In early 1789 he was unanimously elected the first president of the new Republic.

On April 30, 1789, after the first Congress had been in session for several weeks, George Washington was sworn in at Federal Hall in the downtown financial district of New York. Standing beside him were Vice-President John Adams and several Revolutionary generals. A crowd of artisans as well as society and business types watched as the Chancellor of New York administered the oath of office to Washington. As Washington concluded the oath, the American flag was raised on the staff above the balcony and the crowd shouted, "Long live George Washington, President of the United States!", while the guns of the battery roared their salute. After this brief ceremony, Washington stepped inside to the Senate's chamber and delivered the first presidential inaugural address. On April 30, 1989, President Bush returned to Federal Hall for the 200th anniversary reenactment of the Washington inauguration.

Washington knew the country needed more continuity and more foreign policy and emergency leadership from its fledgling government. Yet, as he set out in April 1789 for New York (the temporary seat of government), his feelings about the role of the presidency in American society were mixed. If he had doubts about his qualifications for this new post, they must have magnified as he traveled slowly up the east coast from Mt. Vernon to New York. A series of parades and fireworks greeted him as he went. His whole trip was one long ovation, a celebration of and yearning for leadership. Just as they would do in other periods of crisis or major transition, Americans turned to one strong individual to provide unity and to symbolize the best in the nation.

Washington and his compatriots were of two minds about executive power for good reasons. Today we would call this attitude an ambivalence toward power. To put it simply, the framers and their supporters admired yet feared leadership. They realized the country needed more effective, centralized governance mechanisms, yet they were suspicious of the potential abuses of power, and especially of great power vested in a single individual. They had every right to these fears after what they had lived through in the 1760s and 1770s. Moreover, people like Washington hardly wanted to jeopardize the rights and liberties they had fought so hard to win in the recent revolution.

Although Constitutional Convention delegates James Wilson and Gouverneur Morris are credited with writing many of the constitutional provisions for the presidency, George Washington also played an important role in shaping the American presidency. Since at least 1780 he had been calling for the strengthening of the leadership capacities of the new government. His experience and some of his functions as commander in chief were incorporated into the new job of the president. Other key aspects of the new invention were modifications of the office of governor in New York and Massachusetts, or variations of powers exercised by the Crown, and lessons learned from the ineffectual attempts by the Continental Congress to provide ad hoc executive leadership. But just as important, the debates in Philadelphia about what kind of presidency we would have were also debates over what powers the delegates were willing to grant to George Washington, because most of the delegates there hoped he would serve as the first national executive.

Washington's misgivings about his qualifications and about the scope of presidential power faded as he set precedents and fulfilled the hopes of the people.[1] He was sensitive to the fine line between providing stronger leadership and infringing on the individual rights and liberties of the people. He knew then, as every president after him has either known or learned, that Americans have a strong streak of anti-government and even anti-authority sentiment. We want strong presidential leadership when the times demand it or when it serves our favorite causes, yet we also insist that no elected official or governmental agency dare infringe on our rights.

We have never been wholly pleased by the reality of strong governments and centralized leadership institutions such as the presidency. Nonetheless, most Americans today accept these as necessities in our complex and highly developed modern world. We still worry about the abuses of power, the diminution of our rights and liberties, and the extent to which we have concentrated power in Washington, D.C.; yet, paradoxically, we also revere our successful presidents, and we often hunger for compelling, creative, dynamic leadership. President Bush came under heavy pressure from the media to demonstrate clear, forthright leadership during his first year in office.

An Effective Presidency?

What does it take to be an effective president? Are the constitutional powers of the presidency adequate for carrying out modern presidential responsibilities?

TABLE 15–1
Qualities Desired in a
Presidential Candidate

Honesty	94%
Intelligence	87
Ability to communicate	74
Political experience	52
Political philosophy	33
Political party	23

Source: *US News and World Report–CNN* poll of 1000 adults, 1986.

Abraham Lincoln

Theodore Roosevelt

Can the modern presidency meet our high expectations? And can it survive the grinding pressures of crises abroad and human demands at home?

Our Constitution establishes only three qualifications for the office: a president must be at least 35 years of age, have lived in the United States for fourteen years, and be a natural-born citizen. Our "unwritten presidential job description"—the one we carry around as images in our heads—says that a president has to be many things to many people. Every four years Americans search the national landscape for a new superstar who is blessed with the judgment of a Washington, the mind of a Jefferson, the steadfastness of a Lincoln, the calm of an Eisenhower, and the grace of a John F. Kennedy. Although the American presidency may not have been designed in 1787 as a leadership institution (certainly not as a party, legislative, or economic leadership post), the situation has certainly changed.

Surveys in recent years indicate voters weigh ability to *accomplish* things, their *stands on issues* and their *character* when judging presidential candidates. Presidents are expected to provide strong, able, and popular leadership. Americans want leaders who can grasp the real needs and higher aspirations of the American people and who can make our huge, fragmented system of government serve those needs and aspirations. In periods of crisis our so-called three-branch system seems to have worked best as a presidential system, that is, as a system in which the presidency has been dominant. Only strong presidents have been able to overcome the tendency toward inertia inherent in a nation so beset with checks and balances and separated powers.

But exactly what do the American people want of their president? They want leadership, but what kind of leadership?—an ability to work with Congress, to solve economic problems, to keep the peace, to gain the people's confidence, and to get things done. They also want someone who can provide a sense of purpose: someone who can remind us of our basic aspirations as a democratic and generous nation and as an innovative and experimenting people.

Voters sometimes place more emphasis on a candidate's character and integrity than they do on the candidate's *policy* preferences. This is not misguided. Presidents have enormous power, especially in emergencies. They also play an important role in making appointments, which in turn reflects their interest in upholding ethical standards of governmental performance. Thus, it is important to assess their characters. Will they become rigid or dogmatic in dealing with crises, or with Congress, the press, advisers, and critics? Will they display vision, judgment, a grasp of history, a sense of proportion, and a sense of humor? To be sure, people prefer candidates whose views on issues accord with their own; if they like a person's personality, they trust that individual's policy ideas to be acceptable. Hence, a candidate's character and policy preferences sometimes get blurred—if not reversed—in the voter's mind.

In addition, the public also wants a president to be tough, decisive, and competent. Voters recognize the need, *even in a democracy*, for strong leadership. They yearn for a leader with foresight and personal strength. Moreover, people want someone who will simplify politics, symbolize the protective role of the state, and yet seem to be concerned with *them*. We want *effectiveness*, but also *fairness*. Do we ask too much? Novelist John Steinbeck thought so: "We give the President more work than a man can do, more responsibility than a man should take, more pressure than a man can bear. We abuse him often and rarely praise him. We wear him out, use him up, eat him up. . . . he is ours and we exercise the right to destroy him."[2]

Americans applaud presidents when things go well and blame them when things go wrong. Disasters as well as triumphs are credited to presidents—Wilson's League of Nations, Hoover's Depression, Roosevelt's New Deal, Johnson's Vietnam

War, Nixon's Watergate, Carter's Iranian crisis, Reagan's debt. An exaggerated sense of presidential wisdom and power has caused us to forget that there are limits to what presidents can accomplish. Although the tragedies of American involvement in Vietnam and of presidential involvement in the Watergate scandals deglamorized the presidency, the vitality of our democracy still depends in large measure on creative presidential leadership.

Is the Presidency Too Strong— Or Not Strong Enough?

Some critics see the presidency as fast becoming inconsistent with democratic ideals. They view it as an often remote and autocratic institution, as the citadel of the status quo, as the center of the industrial-military-political complex—and as the very heart of the "Establishment." They charge that presidents are less accountable today than ever before, and that they have the power to get around the formal checks and balances designed by the Constitution's framers. Critics complain too that presidents now manipulate the public's sense of reality by relying on secrecy, emergency powers, and the "electronic throne" of television.

Many people care more about the purposes of presidential authority than about the extent or uses of it. Only when the president appears to represent interests that these people approve do they say the power should be left unchecked. Other critics are more concerned about *process*. If the president's actions reflect the wishes of the majority of the people most of the time, the process is assumed to be working properly.

Activists in both parties, on the other hand, look to the president as the potential spokesperson for the common person. Throughout the twentieth century active presidents have tended to bring about changes that have pleased the progressive forces. The New Deal and the Kennedy-Johnson initiatives on civil rights are examples. There is no guarantee, of course, that an activist president will please the progressives. Vietnam provides an example to the contrary. The Reagan tax and budget cuts are another example.

Historically the great presidents have been strong presidents who have moved outside elite power structures to reach and serve the masses. That was how Jefferson and Jackson overcame the established elites of their day; that is how the two Roosevelts overcame the "economic royalists" of their day. Although presidents often have to compromise with existing elites, sometimes the chief executive has the power to defy the "Establishment." Presidents like to quote Franklin Roosevelt who, after some businesspeople had cursed him for his "radical" New Deal policies, cried out at the height of his 1936 reelection campaign: "I should like to have it said of my first Administration that in it the forces of selfishness and of lust for power met their match. I should like to have it said of my second Administration that in it their forces met their master!"

After the Watergate scandals of the Nixon administration, many argued persuasively that our system of checks and balances needed to be strengthened. But once Watergate had faded into the past and the nation was faced with inflation, unemployment, huge federal deficits, severe trade imbalances, and countless other problems that nobody seemed able to solve—including Presidents Ford and Carter—the public seemed to demand stronger national leadership.

Ronald Reagan came to office after two short and some would say failed presidencies. He rallied "middle class" and conservative interests against the congressional establishment and enjoyed several successes during his first term. But

CHAPTER 15 / The Presidency: Leadership Branch?

379

Harry S Truman

Dwight David Eisenhower

John Fitzgerald Kennedy

Lyndon Baines Johnson

his second term witnessed soaring budget deficits, several legislative defeats, and a number of celebrated scandals, including indictments and convictions of some of his White House aides and advisors. Congress thwarted nominations and used its investigative powers to counter some of Reagan's less valued initiatives.

In 1989 George Bush came to office with an impressive electoral college victory, yet with a murky mandate. He was the first president in this century to enter the White House not only with the other party controlling both houses of Congress, but also with the other party actually gaining seats in both chambers. Divided government thus faced Bush more starkly than it had his predecessors.

Constitutional checks and balances seem to be working, but they seem to work better when, as during recent decades, one party controls Congress and one the White House. The Iran-contra hearings, the detailed investigations of presidential nominees, including the Senate's failure to confirm Robert Bork to the Supreme Court in 1987 or John Tower as Secretary of Defense in 1989, are illustrative. Still, an occasional observer suggests it might be better if we had a parliamentary system in which the president and Congress were always under the same partisan control.[3] This might help to lessen the paralysis that arises through partisan disagreement. It might also prevent the evasion of responsibility that is one of the causes of confusion in our government—confusion over who is accountable.

This may be the case, yet we are not likely to have a parliamentary system here. And this is why presidents, like Bush, are constantly calling for a bipartisan approach to major foreign and economic policy issues. But bipartisanship does not mean that the two branches must always agree. There are, and will always be, differences in approach and on substance. Surely, too, bipartisanship must mean more than Congress always giving in to a president's wishes. The duty of an opposition is to *oppose*, especially when that opposition controls an equal branch of government and that opposition believes a president's policies can be improved.[4] And this is generally how our system operates.

Public attitudes, as well as those of scholars who study the presidency, are difficult to pin down, and they change often. Everyone seems to favor strong leadership; yet this does not necessarily mean strong executive leadership. We want, apparently, strong presidents, provided they do what we want them to do. Otherwise, we want them to be limited by checks and balances. Indeed, all our checks and balances make the prospects for positive presidential leadership difficult.[5]

The Job of the President

The nation's founders created a presidency of somewhat limited powers. They wanted a presidential office that would stay clear of parties and factions, enforce the laws passed by Congress, deal with foreign governments, and help states put down disorders. They wanted a presidency strong enough to match Congress, but not so strong that it would overpower Congress. They seemed to have in mind that the president should be an elected king, with substantial personal authority, who serves the common good and minimizes the baleful influence of the worst factions. The framers of the Constitution rejected a *plural* or *collegial* executive; there would be no ceremonial head separate from an administrative one. The term of office would be four years, and presidents would be indefinitely reeligible to succeed themselves. Although independent from the legislature, presidents would still share considerable power with Congress. The essence of the arrangement would be an *intermingling*, or *sharing*, of powers with Congress. To achieve change, the separate branches would have to work in cooperation and consult with one another. A president's major appointments would have to be approved by the Senate; Congress could override the chief executive's veto by a two-thirds vote of each chamber; and the president could make treaties only with the advice and consent of two-thirds of the senators. All appropriations (the power of the purse), of course, would be legislated by Congress, not the president.

Even a presidency with such limited powers, hemmed in by the system of checks and balances, worried some Americans in 1787. The framers deliberately gave broadly outlined powers to the president. The president, they thought, should have discretionary power, so that this official could act when other governmental branches failed to meet their responsibilities or to respond to the urgencies of the day. But they were reassured by the fact that George Washington was to be the first chief executive. And they recognized that, at least on paper, Congress was truly the first branch. A relatively unified Congress could make life pretty miserable for a president. It could, for example, refuse to confirm a president's vital nominations, refuse to pass legislation suggested by a president, refuse funds for key programs, and refuse to approve treaties. It could also **override** the chief executive's vetoes. But the historical record suggests most presidents have enjoyed far greater cooperation with Congress than this implies. Nonetheless, modern-day presidents are more powerful than those of the last century, even though their constitutional powers have not changed.

After nearly two centuries our presidential "track record" is good. Perhaps in no other nation have persons with such power at their command so carefully followed the restraints imposed on them by a written Constitution. But to describe presidential power is inadequate. The exact dimensions of executive power at any given moment are partly the consequence of the incumbent's character and energy, combined with the needs of the time and the challenges to our nation's survival.[6] By and large, the history of presidential power is one of steady but uneven growth. Of the forty one individuals who have filled the office, about a third have enlarged its powers. Jackson, Lincoln, and both Roosevelts, for example, strengthened both the institution and its powers by the way they responded to crises and set priorities.

In this extension of the executive power Congress and the courts have often been willing partners. In emergencies Congress often rushes to delegate discretion to the executive branch; and the legislature sometimes seems incapable of dealing with matters that are highly technical or that require constant management or consistent judgment. Some people think what Congress lacks most is the will to use the powers it already has. But this hardly seems to be a satisfactory explanation, because Congress is not unique among legislative bodies. During the last two centuries in all democracies, and at all levels, power has drifted from legislators to executives. The English prime minister, the French president, the governors of our states, and the mayors of our cities all play more dominant roles than they did, generally speaking, 100 years ago.

The danger of war plainly increases a president's impact on the nation's affairs. The Cold War shattered most of the remaining nostalgia for **isolationism.** The combination of a substantial standing army, nuclear weapons, and the Cold War invited presidential dominance in national security matters. Television has also contributed to the growth of presidential influence. With access to prime time, presidents can take their cases directly to the people. This invitation to bypass and sometimes to ignore Congress, the Washington press, and even party leaders weakens the checks once imposed on the presidency.

Richard Milhous Nixon

Gerald Ford

Jimmy Carter

Ronald Reagan

Constitutional Responsibilities of a President

Act as commander in chief
Negotiate treaties
Receive foreign ambassadors
Nominate top federal officials, including federal judges
Veto bills
Faithfully administer federal laws
Pardon certain persons convicted of federal offenses
Address Congress and nation

Additional Presidential Responsibilities and Informal Roles

Morale builder
Party leader
Legislative leader
Coalition builder
Crisis manager
Personnel recruiter
World leader
Budget setter
Priority setter
Bargainer and persuader
Conflict resolver

In the ceremonial role of the president, George Bush visited Beijing, China, a few weeks before the historic people's protest against their government.

The great growth of the federal role in domestic and economic matters has also enlarged presidential responsibility and contributed to the swollen presidential establishment. Problems not easily delegated to any one department often get pulled into the White House. When new programs concern several federal agencies, someone near the president is asked to set a consistent policy and reconcile conflicts. White House aides, with some justification, claim the presidency is the only place in government where it is possible to establish and coordinate national priorities. And presidents constantly set up central review and coordination units. These help formulate new policies, settle jurisdictional disputes among departments, and provide access for the well-organized interest groups who want their views to be given weight in decision making.

The swelling of the presidency has also been encouraged by the public's expectations. Although we may dislike or condemn individual presidents, popular attitudes toward the institution of the presidency remain positive. We want very much to believe in and trust our presidents. Perhaps this is because we have no royal family, no established religion, and no common ceremonial leadership divorced from executive responsibilities. In an effort to live up to unrealistic expectations, some presidents overextend themselves. Maintaining presidential popularity encourages them to make frequent appeals to the general public. This may help presidents temporarily improve their public images and even win occasional fights in Congress, but they may gamble too often that they can use public support as a chip to secure bargains in their favor. They may also undermine their relations with Congress and help render the parties less important in supplying policy ideas and keeping presidents and other elected officials accountable.[7]

Today a president is asked to play countless roles that are not carefully spelled out in the Constitution. We want the chief executive to be an international peace maker as well as a national morale builder, a politician-in-chief, and a unifying representative of all the people. We want every new president to be virtually everything all our great presidents have been. Rightly or wrongly, we believe our greatest presidents were models of talent, tenacity, and optimism: persons who could clarify the vital issues of the day and mobilize the nation for action. We like to think of our great presidents as leaders who could not only symbolize the best in the nation and move the enterprise forward, but who could summon the highest kinds of moral commitment from the American people. These storybook images of our great presidents often make it tough for modern presidents to do their job.

In addition to the obvious leadership responsibilities a president has in foreign policy, economics, and domestic policy, seven broad functional kinds of leadership are expected of a president. These policy areas and functions, when examined together, permit us to develop a job profile of an American president (see Table 15–2).

Presidents as Crisis Managers

"The President shall be Commander in Chief of the Army and the Navy of the United States," reads Section 2 of Article II of the Constitution. Even though this is the first of the president's powers listed in the Constitution, the framers intended the military role to be a limited one—far less than a king's. It was as if the president would be a sort of first general and first admiral. As it turns out, the military role has become much more important: The president has a finger on the nuclear button and appears to have sole authority over limited wars as well.

TABLE 15–2
A Presidential Job Description

	EXAMPLES OF POLICY RESPONSIBILITIES		
FUNCTIONAL LEADERSHIP	FOREIGN POLICY	ECONOMICS	DOMESTIC POLICY
Crisis management	Dealing with Iranian crisis, U.S. troops in Lebanon	FDR's handling of the Depression, 1930s	Controlling immigration and drug flow
Symbolic and morale-building leadership	Bush's trip to Emperor Hirohito funeral in Tokyo	Being bullish on American productivity	Visiting flood and disaster victims, helping Alaska clean up oil spill
Recruitment of top officials	Selecting chairpersons of the Joint Chiefs of Staff	Hiring wise economic advisers	Nominating a chief justice
Priority setting and problem clarification	Defining our relations with the USSR—INF Treaty	Outlining tax-cut or revenue producing program	Setting priorities in environmental protection
Legislative and political coalition building	Fighting for aid for El Salvador and contras	Bush's veto of minimum wage legislation	Fighting over domestic spending
Program implementation and administration	Making Middle East peace accords work	Helping to reduce the federal deficit	Seeing that the laws are faithfully executed
Oversight of government performance and early detection of possible problems	Evaluating our relations with Japan and Mexico	Monitoring internal revenue service performance	Appraising the impact of federal social programs

When crises and national emergencies occur, Americans instinctively turn to the chief executive, who is expected to provide not only executive and political leadership but also the appearance of a confident, "take-charge" leader who has a steady hand at the helm. Public necessity forces presidents to do what Lincoln and Franklin Roosevelt did during the national emergencies of their day: protect the union and safeguard vital American interests.

Nearly two centuries of national expansion and recurrent crises have increased the powers of the president beyond those specified by the Constitution. The complexity of Congress's decision-making procedures, its unwieldy numbers, and its constitutional tasks make it a more public, deliberative, and divided organization than the presidency. When major crises occur, Congress traditionally holds debates, but just as predictably delegates authority to a president, charging that official to take whatever actions are necessary.

The primary factor underlying this transformation in the president's function as commander in chief has been the changed role of the United States in the world, especially since World War II. In the postwar years every president argued for and won widespread support for the position that military strength, especially military superiority over the Soviet Union, was the primary route to national security. Nations willingly grew dependent on our assistance, which rapidly became translated into a multitude of treaties, pacts, and **executive agreements.** From then on, nearly every threat to the political stability of our far-flung network of allies became a test of whether we would honor our commitments in good faith. These commitments, plus the fear of nuclear war and the importance of deterrence, prompted Congress to give great flexibility to presidents in this area.

Presidents are expected to be crisis managers in the domestic sphere as well. Whenever things go wrong, we demand presidential level planning and problem solving. When both New York City and the Chrysler Corporation were on the verge of bankruptcy, people turned to the White House for help. When

Presidential Age and Turnover

Oldest when elected: Reagan, 69 (first term), 73 (second term)
Youngest when elected: Kennedy, 43
Average age at inauguration: 55
Average service: 4.9 years
One-term presidents: 25
Two-term presidents: 14
Four terms: F. D. Roosevelt

terrorists attack U.S. citizens, people assume their president will retaliate. When a disastrous oil spill occurs, as it did off the Alaskan coast in 1989, people expect the White House to step in and assist. In many crises, however, a president is often little more than a victim of fast-breaking events and environmental forces. Presidents are sometimes surprised, overtaken by developments beyond their control, and placed on the defensive.

Presidents as Morale-Building Leaders

Presidents are the nation's number-one celebrities, almost anything they do is news. Merely by going to church or to a sports event, presidents command attention. By their actions presidents can arouse a sense of hope or despair, honor or dishonor.

The framers of the Constitution did not fully anticipate the symbolic and morale-building functions a president must perform. Certain magisterial functions, such as receiving ambassadors and granting pardons, were conferred. But over time the presidency has acquired enormous *symbolic* significance. No matter how enlightened or rational we consider ourselves, all of us respond in some way to symbols and rituals. The president often affects our images of authority, legitimacy, and confidence in our political system.

Although Americans like to view themselves as hardheaded pragmatists, they—like humans everywhere—cannot stand too much reality. Humans do not live by reason alone. Myths and dreams are an age-old form of escape. And people turn to national leaders just as tribespeople turn to shamans—for meaning, healing, empowerment, assurance, and a sense of purpose.

Americans expect many things from their presidents: honesty, credibility, crisis leadership, agenda-setting and administrative abilities, and also certain tribal-leader or priestly functions. Many people find comfort in an oversimplified image of the president as a warrior-captain at the helm of the great ship of state, as a liberator, prophet, defender of liberty and democracy, and spokesperson for the American Dream.

George Washington and his advisors recognized from the beginning, in 1789, that the job of the presidency demanded symbolic leadership. They knew that effective leadership must symbolize the best in the community, the best in our traditions, values, and purposes. Effective leadership infuses vision and a sense of meaning into the enterprise of a nation.

THE POPULAR NEED FOR LEADERSHIP

A president's personal conduct affects how millions of Americans view their political loyalties and civic responsibilities. Of course, the symbolic influence of presidents is not always evoked in favor of worthy causes, and sometimes presidents do not live up to our expectations of moral leadership. "The Presidency is the focus for the most intense and persistent emotions. . . . The President is . . . the one figure who draws together the people's hopes and fears for the political future. On top of all his routine duties, he has to carry that off—or fail."[8]

It would be much easier for everyone, some say, if our president were a prime minister, called on merely to manage the affairs of government in as efficient and practical a way as possible and not also our chief of state. But this is not the case. Americans are not about to invent a head-of-state position separate from the presidency. Moreover, to do so would weaken an already fragile institution.

Presidential head-of-state duties often seem trivial and unimportant. For example, throwing the first baseball of the season, buying Christmas or Easter seals, pressing buttons that start big power projects, and consoling the survivors of American victims of terrorist attacks do not require executive talents. Yet our president is continuously asked to champion our common heritage, to help unify the nation, and also to create an improved climate within which the diverse interests of the nation can work together.

A PRESIDENTIAL DILEMMA

Under ordinary conditions the presidential claim to be "leader of all the people," or symbolic leader of the nation, conflicts with the reality of a president who acts as party leader. Some expectations for presidents are fundamentally inconsistent with one another. On the one hand, the president is a party leader: the spokesperson and representative of a segment of the population loosely identified with a particular party. As such the chief executive not only directs the national party organization but—as chief legislator—also takes specific positions on issues for or against some groups. On the other hand, as ceremonial leader and chief of state, the president attempts to act for all the people. A chief executive must faithfully administer the laws, whether passed by Democratic or Republican majorities in Congress. Yet in choosing subordinates and in applying the law, presidents often understandably think first of the interests of those who elected them.

The relationship between these presidential roles is uneasy. For example, the president may wish to address the nation about a problem—and usually the chief executive is granted free time on radio and TV. But if an election is close, the opposition often charges the president is really acting as party chief and that the party should pay for the radio or TV time. The same question comes up in connection with a president's inspection trips, especially when they are used as occasions for political talks and general politicking.

Most of the time a president manages to combine the offices of chief of state and party leader without much difficulty. Most people accept that a president holds both roles and moves from one to the other as conditions demand. There is nothing wrong with the symbolic powers that come with the job. They become a problem only when they lead the public to believe symbolism equals accomplishment, or when ceremonial responsibilities keep presidents from performing their other demanding duties.

The morale-building job of the president involves much more than just ceremonial, cheerleading, or quasi-chaplain duties. Presidential leadership, at its finest, radiates confidence and empowers people to give their best, to unleash the vast energies for good that are at-large in the nation. Our best leaders have been able to provide this special and often intangible element. Although it may defy easy definition, we judge a president's success and popularity by it. Still, we know all too well that it is not something that the Constitution confers or something conveniently closeted in the White House for the use of each new occupant.

"They're all out taking polls to see which way you want to be led."

© 1978 Engelhardt in the St. Louis Post-Dispatch. Reprinted by permission.

Presidents as Recruiters

Often a single appointment may achieve more than scores of presidential policy initiatives. President Eisenhower's nomination of Earl Warren to be chief justice of the United States may have been the single most significant decision of his administration in the area of domestic policy. Warren served for over fifteen years and presided over vast changes in civil rights and civil liberties. President Reagan's Supreme Court appointees, William Rehnquist, Sandra O'Connor, Antonin Scalia, and Anthony Kennedy, will also have long-term effects. In a similar way selection of a secretary of state, top economic advisers, the secretary of the interior, or top White House aides can have an enormous impact on long-term national policy.

Effective presidents shrewdly use their appointment powers—presidents have control over 5000 appointments, including hundreds of federal judgeships and top positions in the military and diplomatic service—not only to reward campaign supporters and enhance ties to Congress but also to communicate priorities and policy directions. (Note, however, that since many appointments must be made with the approval of the Senate, appointment powers are limited to some extent.) Because a president's top appointees are also a major link between the White House and the millions of people who serve in the career federal and military services, the chief executive needs the best possible managers and motivators in these crucial positions. Besides identifying and recruiting them, the president must also try to keep the most talented of these officials in government as long as possible.[9]

The turnover problem is acute. Many able people come to top positions—say in the cabinet or subcabinet—and stay for eighteen months or two years. Less than a third stay for more than three years. These top federal posts do not pay as much as comparable positions in the private sector. Also, living in Washington can be expensive.

Various financial-disclosure and conflict-of-interest requirements, imposed on presidential appointees as a result of the Ethics in Government Act of 1978, discourage some potential appointees from accepting government jobs. They must fill out many forms, and they must testify (as former Senator John Tower discovered) at complicated, time-consuming, and confusing congressional hearings. Critics of these laws say they have raised the risks of personal embarrassment and subjected appointees' private lives to much greater scrutiny.[10] Media scrutiny of these citizen leaders called to government service has also become more intensive. Recruiters for recent presidents report they often go to their second or third choice before they find someone willing to accept an appointment. "No other nation relies so heavily on noncareer personnel for the management of its government. . . . If talented Americans decline the opportunity for public service, if they endure it only for brief periods, or if they are ill-prepared for the challenges they will face in the public sector, the system will not deliver on its promise."[11] This system puts another heavy burden on presidents.

A president must strengthen the hand of the ablest people working in the bureaucracy and often also promote these people to higher positions at the senior reaches of the executive branch. In short, the personnel responsibilities of a president are greater and require more time than anyone, including presidents, expects.

Presidents as Priority Setters

Presidents, by custom, have become responsible for proposing initiatives in the areas of foreign policy, economic growth and stability, and the quality of life in America. This was not always the case. But beginning with Woodrow Wilson,

---

Answer/Discussion

President Reagan said the people should be able to reelect a president as many times as they want, just as they now can reelect House and Senate members. He also hinted that the Twenty-second Amendment might weaken a president late in his second term by making him a lame duck, namely, less powerful because everyone knows he will not be around in a year or so. Advocates of repeal also say we may sometimes need to keep a veteran president in office during a crisis period, much as we retained FDR in 1940. The Twenty-second Amendment is not only a limit on the incumbent but also on the electorate; the first since the adaptation of the Constitution to restrict the power of the electorate, rather than expand it. It is based, advocates of repeal suggest, on the assumption that the voters can't be trusted.

Those who favor keeping the Twenty-second Amendment cite these reasons: First, the presidency is so powerful today that we need the Twenty-second as an additional check and balance against abuse of this power. Second, the amendment encourages both parties to seek out quality candidates to succeed to office and discourages dependence on a single ruler, as happened in the Philippines under Marcos or in Haiti under the Duvaliers. Third, few leaders are likely to have the health, the intellectual energy, and the new ideas needed to perform the demanding responsibilities of the presidency beyond eight years in office. Finally, Americans have always believed in citizen-leaders rather than career politicians, and this amendment, even if it was passed for the wrong reasons (Republican revenge against Roosevelt), encourages this noble ideal.

and especially since the New Deal, a president is expected to promote peace, prevent depressions, and propose reforms to ensure domestic progress. The long-term trend in national policy making is toward greater centralization: Federal program ideas are seized upon by a president searching for campaign issues or legislative program material, and they are refined by the executive office staff and by special presidential task forces and commissions, as well as by the Congress.

NATIONAL SECURITY POLICY

Presidents generally have more leeway in foreign policy and military affairs than they have in domestic matters. The framers foresaw a special need for speed and unity in our dealings with other nations. The Constitution vests in a president command of the two major instruments of foreign policy—the diplomatic corps and the armed services. It also gives the chief executive responsibility for negotiating treaties and commitments with other nations, although Congress, of course, gets to vote on these matters.

Congress had granted presidents wide discretion in initiating foreign policies, for diplomacy frequently requires quick action. A president can act swiftly, Congress usually does not. The Supreme Court has upheld strong presidential authority in this area. In the **Curtiss-Wright** case in 1936, the Court referred to the "exclusive power of the president as the sole organ of the federal government in the field of international relations—a power which does not require as a basis for its exercise an act of Congress, but which, of course, like every other governmental power, must be exercised in subordination to the applicable provisions of the Constitution."[12] These are sweeping words.[13] Yet a determined Congress *that knows what it wants to do,* and can agree on it, does not lack power in foreign relations. It must authorize and appropriate the funds that back up our policies abroad. It is a forum for debate and criticism. And, as it at least tried to do after the Vietnam War, it can specify the conditions of war making (more on this in Chapter 16).

ECONOMIC POLICY

Ever since the New Deal, presidents have been expected to prevent unemployment, fight inflation, keep taxes down, ensure economic growth and prosperity, and to do whatever they think necessary and proper to prevent recession. The Constitution does not place these duties on the White House, but presidents know that if they fail to act, they will suffer the fate of Herbert Hoover, who was denounced for years by the Democrats for his alleged inaction during the Great Depression. Recent elections have turned largely on economics.

The chief advisers to the president on economic policy are the secretary of the treasury, the three members of the Council of Economic Advisers, and the director of the Office of Management and Budget. Indirectly the chairperson of the Federal Reserve Board of Governors is often also a key White House adviser on the economy. Although presidents sometimes get their economic advice elsewhere, they often get advice on what actions to take from these persons. The growth and complexity of economic problems have placed even more initiative in the hands of the president. The delicate balancing required to keep a modern economy operating means that the presidency must regularly make key fiscal and budgetary policy decisions.

George Bush assembled a highly praised team for defense strategies that included (left to right): retired general Brent Scowcroft, National Security Adviser; former congressman Richard Cheney, Secretary of Defense; and James Baker, Secretary of State.

Line of Succession to the Presidency

1. Vice president.
2. Speaker of the House of Representatives.
3. Senate president pro tempore.
4. Secretary of State.
5. Secretary of the Treasury.
6. Secretary of Defense.
7. Attorney general.
8. Secretary of the Interior.
9. Secretary of Agriculture.
10. Secretary of Commerce.
11. Secretary of Labor.
12. Secretary of Health and Human Services.
13. Secretary of Housing and Urban Development.
14. Secretary of Transportation.
15. Secretary of Energy.
16. Secretary of Education.
17. Secretary of Veterans Affairs.

The Constitution leaves succession after the vice president up to Congress. This is the line according to statute. In addition, the constitutional qualifications still apply. Thus, if the secretary of state was born in a foreign country of parents who were not U.S. citizens, he or she would be bypassed in this line.

The White House

1600 Pennsylvania Ave., N.W.
Washington, D.C. 20500

EAST WING

WEST WING

MANSION

The White House is an executive office, a ceremonial mansion, and a home. Several presidents have viewed it almost as a jail, preferring to spend as much time as possible at other presidential retreats outside of Washington. But most Americans view the rather elegant White House as the center of political and social activity in the nation's capital. It is also something of a national shrine as millions of people from America as well as around the world visit and inspect it each year.

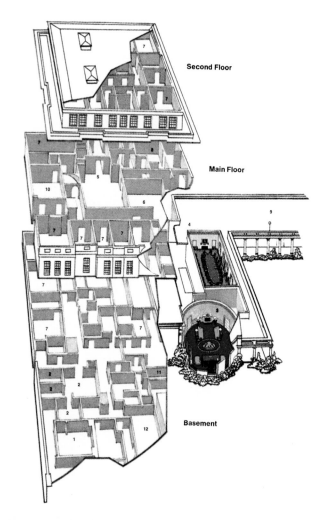

Second Floor

Main Floor

Basement

WEST WING

1 Situation Room
2 National Security Council Staff
3 Oval Office
4 Cabinet Room
5 West Lobby
6 Roosevelt Room (Conference Room)
7 Assistants to the President
8 Presidential Press Secretary
9 Press Briefing Room and Filing Center
10 Vice-President's Office
11 Photo Office
12 White House Staff Dining Room

A leader is one who knows where the followers are. Lincoln did not invent the antislavery movement. Kennedy and Johnson did not begin the civil rights movement. George Bush did not initiate the "war on drugs" crusade. But they all, in their respective times, became embroiled in these controversies, for a president cannot ignore for long what divides or inspires a nation.

The essence of the modern presidency lies in its potential capability to resolve societal conflicts. To be sure, much of the time a president will avoid conflict when possible, and will seek instead to defer, delegate, or otherwise delay controversial decisions. An effective president, however, will clarify the major issues of the day, define what is possible, and organize the governmental structure so that important goals can be realized.

A president—with the cooperation of Congress—can set national goals and propose legislation. Close inspection indicates, however, that in most instances a president's "new initiatives" in domestic policy are measures that have been under consideration in previous sessions of Congress. Just as the celebrated New Deal legislation had a fairly well-defined history extending back several years before its embrace by Franklin Roosevelt, many of the Reagan-Bush initiatives were the fruits of long campaigns by congressional activists and special interests.

"First of all, let me explain exactly what advice the president wants to hear."

Dunagin's People by Ralph Dunagin. Reprinted with special permission of NAS, Inc.

Presidents as Legislative and Political Coalition Builders

The Constitution provides that the president "shall from time to time give to the Congress information on the State of the Union, and recommend to their Consideration such Measures as he shall judge necessary and expedient." From the start strong presidents have exploited this power. Washington and Adams came in person to Congress to deliver information and recommendations. Jefferson and many presidents after him sent written messages, but Wilson restored the practice of delivering a personal, and often dramatic, message. Franklin Roosevelt used personal appearances (as have most presidents since then) to draw the attention of the whole nation to his program. Bush visited Congress soon after he was elected—and went back on several additional occasions to mingle with members of Congress or to give major reports to the nation.

Less obvious, but perhaps equally important, are the frequent written messages dispatched from the White House to Capitol Hill on a vast range of public problems. These messages may not create much stir, but they are important in defining the administration's position and in giving a lead to friendly legislators. Moreover, these messages are often accompanied by detailed drafts of legislation that members of Congress may sponsor with little or no change. These White House proposals, the products of bill-drafting experts on the president's own staff or in the executive departments and agencies, may be strengthened or diluted by Congress, but many of the original provisions survive.

An effective president is an effective politician—the most visible and potentially the strongest mobilizer of influence in the American system of power. *Politician* is a nasty word to many Americans; it denotes a scheming, evasive person out for his or her own self-interest. Little wonder many politicians claim they are "above politics." There is, however, a more constructive definition of *politician*: one who helps manage conflict; one who knows how to negotiate, bargain, and help reconcile different views in order to make the difficult and desirable become reality. Presidents cannot escape political coalition-building tasks.[14] As candidates, they have made promises to the people. To get things done and to be reelected, a president must work with many people and countless interest groups who have differing loyalties and responsibilities. Inevitably, a president becomes embroiled in legislative politics, bureaucratic politics, and lobbying politics.

Presidents make good on more of their promises than the general public appreciates. Most presidents enjoy at least partial success on most of the initiatives they favored during their campaigns or soon after they came to the White House.[15] Although presidents control most of what they decide to recommend to Congress, other institutions, especially the Congress, control what presidents can achieve. Presidents may control what and how they initiate, at least within reason, but other political leaders determine the fate, shape, and funding of these presidential initiatives.

Despite the available formal powers, presidents can rarely command; they spend most of their time *persuading* people. Potentially, presidents have enormous persuasive powers, but in the long run people think of their own self-interests, and presidential wishes often go unheeded. In a government of separated institutions that share powers, some congressional, bureaucratic, and even military leaders are beyond the political reach of the president. They have their own constituencies—a House committee, for example, or a powerful interest group. Presidents cannot simply give orders like a first sergeant. Before Dwight Eisenhower became president, Harry Truman said of him: "He'll sit here, and he'll say, 'Do this! Do that!' And nothing will happen. Poor Ike—it won't be a bit like the Army. He'll find it very frustrating."[16] *All* presidents have found it frustrating.

Many students of the presidency think the power to persuade is the chief resource of a president and that such power comes through bargaining. Bargaining, in turn, comes primarily through getting others to feel that it is in their own self-interests to cooperate. Hence, the skill of a president in communicating and in winning others over is the necessary energizing factor in moving the institutions of the national government to action. This school of thought also holds that a president cannot be shy and above the battle, or above politics. Rather, a president must enjoy the give and take of congressional-presidential relations, and the give and take between the parties and between the White House and the press. Classic examples of effective presidential political coalition building are Franklin Roosevelt's building of public support around his New Deal programs, Lyndon Johnson's successfully passing his "Great Society" legislation, and Ronald Reagan's mobilizing public and congressional support for his programs.

THE PRIME-TIME PRESIDENCY

No other politician (and few television or film stars) can achieve a closer contact with the people than can the president. Typically, the chief executive has been a prominent senator, a vice-president, or a governor, and has built up a host of followers. Having won nominations and elections, most presidents have been in the public eye for years. But the White House is the finest platform of all. A television studio that can be used for a direct appeal to the people exists right in the White House. Presidents can meet the press when they wish, arrange fireside chats or radio call-in shows, choose sympathetic audiences, or undertake "nonpolitical" speaking tours. And they can time all these moves for maximum advantage.[17]

The press conference is an example of how the president can employ the machinery of communication in a systematic manner. Years ago press conferences were rather casual affairs. Franklin Roosevelt ran his get-togethers informally and

CHAPTER 15 / The Presidency: Leadership Branch?

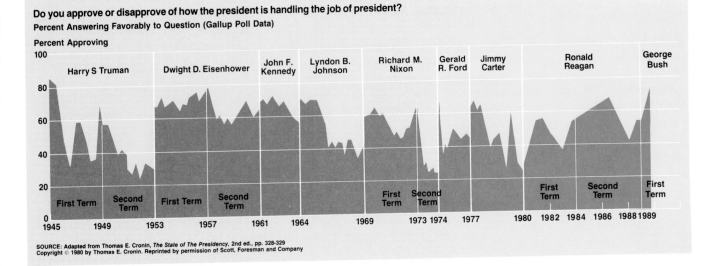

Do you approve or disapprove of how the president is handling the job of president?
Percent Answering Favorably to Question (Gallup Poll Data)

Percent Approving

Harry S Truman | Dwight D. Eisenhower | John F. Kennedy | Lyndon B. Johnson | Richard M. Nixon | Gerald R. Ford | Jimmy Carter | Ronald Reagan | George Bush

First Term Second Term | First Term Second Term | First Term Second Term | First Term Second Term | First Term

1945 1949 1953 1957 1961 1964 1969 1973 1974 1977 1980 1982 1984 1986 1988 1989

SOURCE: Adapted from Thomas E. Cronin, *The State of The Presidency*, 2nd ed., pp. 328-329
Copyright © 1980 by Thomas E. Cronin. Reprinted by permission of Scott, Foresman and Company

was a master at withholding information as well as giving it. Under Truman the conference became an institutionalized part of the presidential communications apparatus. Kennedy authorized regular live telecasts of press conferences and used them frequently for direct communication with the people. Ronald Reagan regularly and effectively used five-minute Saturday afternoon radio chats to communicate his views, ask for support, and win Sunday morning media coverage.

Presidents commission private polls to gauge public opinion; they want to be able to distinguish the public's petty whims, estimate the strength and direction of its opinions, and respond to its impatience—and they must anticipate its potential impact. Presidents must know not only what to do but when to do it. Public opinion can be unstable and unpredictable. The public generally rejects government by public opinion; they do not want a president to fall captive to the polls. President Johnson recognized that his wide popular support of the mid-1960s had melted away by 1968, when he decided not to run again. President Nixon's dramatic drop of nearly 45 percentage points in public-opinion polls, a result of the Watergate scandals, helped force his resignation. Most presidents lose support the longer they are in office. (Eisenhower and Reagan are exceptions to this rule.) Dissatisfaction sets in; interest groups grow impatient; unkept promises must be accounted for; and the president gets blamed for many of the things that go wrong.

PARTY LEADERSHIP

Another potential source of influence for the president is the political party. Most presidents since Jefferson have been party leaders, and generally the more effective the presidents, the more use they have made of party support. Wilson, the two Roosevelts, and Reagan fortified their executive and legislative influence by mobilizing support within their party. Yet no president has ever fully led a party.

The president has no formal position in the party structure, but the chief executive's influence over national policies and over thousands of appointments commands respect from party leaders. Both president and party need each other. The president needs the party's backing in order to enact a legislative program. The party needs the president's direction and prestige—and the political "gravy" that flows from the White House.

CHAPTER 15 / The Presidency: Leadership Branch?

The strings of the national organization all lie in a president's hands. Formally, the national party committee picks the national party chair; actually, the president lets the committee know the desired candidate and the members choose that person. Today presidents can hire or fire national party chairs much as they shift department heads or even their own staff. The president's pronouncements on national party policy are more authoritative than those of any party committee or the party platform itself. Presidents can give a candidate a good deal of recognition and publicity in Washington. They can grant—or deny—campaign assistance and even financial assistance.

LIMITS ON PARTY LEADERSHIP

Yet the president's practical power over the party is limited and often comes to an end precisely when it is needed most. Presidents rarely have influence over the selection of party candidates for Congress and for state and local office. Presidents also sometimes have trouble getting crucial votes from individuals in their own parties in Congress. This is due in part to the chief executive's limited control of state and local organizations. But also, party organizations themselves do not control their candidates in office: Most candidates win office less through the efforts of the organized party than through their own individual campaigning. Of course, the situation varies from place to place, but in most instances *personalized politics* emphasizing the candidate is more successful than *programmatic politics* emphasizing party and issues.

Presidents must *bargain* and *negotiate* with the party leaders in Congress and in the states just as they do with other independent power centers. Lacking full support from the whole party, presidents usually fall back on the personal organizations that enabled them to be nominated in the first place.[18]

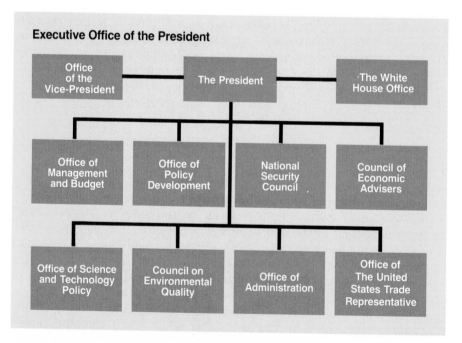

Executive Office of the President

CHAPTER 15 / The Presidency: Leadership Branch?

Presidents as Administrators

The Constitution charges the president to "take care that the laws be faithfully executed." Presidents, however, must delegate much of their administrative authority, because they are forever overscheduled and other responsibilities demand most of their attention. They are, then, dependent on their subordinates. Theoretically, at least, orders flow down an administrative *line*, from president to department heads, to bureau chiefs, and down to smaller offices. The president, like all top executives, is assisted by a *staff*, who advise the chief executive. This line and staff organization is inherent in any large administrative entity, whether it be the Army, General Motors, or the United Nations.

Presidents have come to rely heavily on their personal staffs. Nowhere else—not in Congress, not in the cabinet, not in the party—can presidents find the loyalty and single-mindedness that often develop among their closest aides.[19] Moreover, presidents come to view most cabinet heads as advocates, who advance ideas that benefit the particular friends and interest groups associated with their departments. Presidents apparently think their own aides will provide them with more neutral and objective advice. But there are substantial costs to listening only to one's closest aides. The White House can usefully be thought of as a palace court in which strong presidents create an environment that weeds out any assistant who persists in presenting irritating thoughts. "Palace-guard survivors learn early to camouflage themselves with a coating of battleship grey. . . . Inevitably in a battle between courtiers and advisers, the courtiers will win out. This represents the greatest of all barriers to presidential access to reality . . ."[20] And an astute writer notes: ". . . if a president needs to be protected by his White House staff against the departments, he also needs to be kept on guard by the departments against his White House staff, who may all too easily begin to think only they know the purposes and the needs and the mind of their president, until *he* becomes *their* creature and believes that his interests are safe with them."[21]

The number of employees in the presidential entourage has grown steadily since the early 1900s, when only a few dozen people served a president at a cost of less than a few hundred thousand dollars annually. Today a White House staff of over 500 operates at the cost of several million dollars a year. The Executive Office of the President, approved by Congress in 1939, was the recommendation of President Franklin Roosevelt's Committee on Administrative Management. The Executive Office was to provide presidents the help they obviously needed to carry out the growing responsibilities imposed by the Depression and by the enlarged role of government.

Growth of White House Staff		
1943	FDR	50
1949	Truman	240
1953	Ike	250
1962	JFK	340
1965	LBJ	300
1971	Nixon	580
1975	Ford	525
1988	Reagan	550
1990	Bush	500+

THE INSTITUTIONALIZED EXECUTIVE OFFICE

The **Executive Office of the President** consists of the Office of Management and Budget, the Council of Economic Advisers, and several other staff units. The most prominent and controversial presidential staff, of course, is the White House Office. A president's immediate staff, working out of the White House itself, does not have a fixed form; indeed, part of its value lies in its flexibility and adaptability. Most presidents, however, have an appointments secretary, a press secretary, a correspondence secretary, a legal counsel, a national security adviser, military aides, and several other legislative, administrative, and political assistants. The staff of the White House office can be categorized by functions: (1) domestic policy; (2) economic policy; (3) national security or foreign policy; (4) administration and personnel matters (as well as personal paper work and scheduling for the president); (5) congressional relations; and (6) public relations.

Presidential aides sometimes insist they are simply the eyes and ears of the president, that they make few important decisions, and that they never insert themselves between the chief executive and the heads of departments. But the burgeoning White House staff and the inevitability of a strong chief of staff have made this traditional picture nearly obsolete. Some White House aides, impatient with bureaucratic and congressional bottlenecks or even political sabotage, come to view the presidency as if it alone were the whole government. Separation of powers means little to them, and they lose sight of their location within the larger constitutional system. Listen to a Nixon aide: "There shouldn't be a lot of leeway in following the President's policies. It should be like a corporation, where the executive vice-presidents [the cabinet officers] are tied closely to the Chief Executive, or to put it in extreme terms, when he says jump, they only ask how high."[22] And a Carter aide told one of the authors that giving so much power to the cabinet members "was probably President Carter's biggest mistake."

The **Office of Management and Budget (OMB)** continues to be the central presidential staff agency. Its director advises the president in detail about the hundreds of government agencies—how much money they should be allotted in the budget, and what kind of job they are doing. The OMB seeks to improve the planning, management, and statistical work of the agencies. It makes a special effort to see that each agency conforms to presidential policies in its dealings with Congress; each agency has to clear its policy recommendations to Congress through the OMB first.

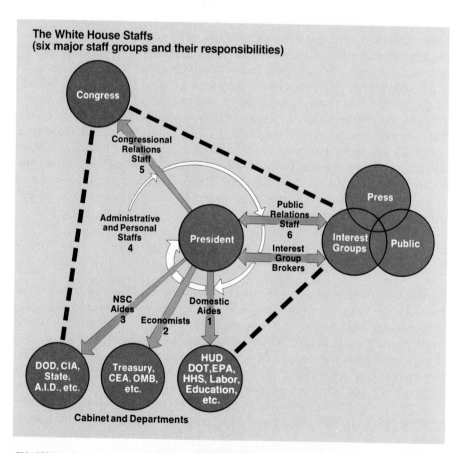

CHAPTER 15 / The Presidency: Leadership Branch?

A budget is not just a financial plan, because it reflects power struggles and indicates policy directions (and wishful thinking).[23] To the president the budget is a means of control over administrators who may be trying to join ranks with politicians or interest groups to thwart presidential priorities. Through the long budget preparing process, presidents use the OMB as a way of conserving and centralizing their own influence.

THE CABINET

It is hard to find a more unusual institution than the cabinet. It is not specifically mentioned by name in the Constitution. Yet since George Washington's administration, every president has had a cabinet. Washington's consisted of his secretaries of state, treasury, and war, plus his attorney general. Today the selection of cabinet members is just about the first major job for the president-elect. The cabinet consists of the president, the vice-president, the officers who head the fourteen executive departments, and a few others (see the accompanying box). The cabinet has always been a loosely designated body, and it is not always clear who belongs to it. In recent years, for example, certain executive-branch administrators and White House counselors have been accorded cabinet rank.

Cabinet government as practiced in parliamentary systems simply does not exist in America. In fact, a president is not required by law to form a cabinet or to hold regular meetings. Kennedy, Johnson, and Nixon all preferred small conferences with those specifically involved in a problem. Kennedy saw no reason to discuss defense department matters with his secretaries of agriculture and labor, and he thought cabinet meetings wasted valuable time for too many already busy people. During his administration crucial decisions were often reached in informal conferences between the president, the heads of two or three major departments, and senior White House staff members. Both Carter and Reagan tried to revive the cabinet, and both met often with their cabinets during their first two years. But the longer they remained in office, the less frequently they met with their cabinets as a whole. And one of Reagan's top aides actually admitted that Reagan often "dozed off" during cabinet meetings.

Personal presidential advisers and the heads of various White House based cabinet councils or review units such as the **National Security Council** and the Office of Management and Budget have gained superior status over many of the department and cabinet secretaries. This has occurred in part because these people are located physically in or next door to the White House. Further, presidents believe their department heads adopt narrow "advocate" views: the agriculture

The Cabinet, 1990
Vice President
Secretary of State
Secretary of Treasury
Secretary of Defense
Attorney General
Secretary of Interior .
Secretary of Agriculture
Secretary of Commerce
Secretary of Labor
Secretary of Health and Human Services
Secretary of Housing and Urban Development
Secretary of Transportation
Secretary of Energy
Secretary of Education
Secretary of Veterans Affairs
CIA Director
Director, Office of Management and Budget
White House Chief of Staff

The first cabinet: Knox, Jefferson, Hamilton, and Washington. Abraham Lincoln's cabinet: Stanton, Chase, Lincoln, Welles, Smith, Blair, Seward, Bates.

cabinet officer as a strident advocate for the farmers; the Housing and Urban Development cabinet officer as an ambassador for the housing industry and to some extent also for the mayors; and so on through much of the cabinet—especially those preoccupied with domestic policy matters. As good relations between presidents and these cabinet members weaken, the former, in frustration, turn more often to trusted senior White House staff aides to settle conflicts and coordinate policy. As a result, tension almost always builds between senior White House aides and their counterparts in the cabinet. Personal staff remains close to the president's ear, and more influential as a result.

Some presidents form various cabinet councils in an attempt to integrate key departmental and White House advisers around major policy matters. President Ford was pleased with this system. President Reagan, who had a notable penchant for delegating responsibility, also relied on these cabinet councils. He usually had a cabinet member or senior White House aide in charge of the council. Such councils are patterned after the National Security Council, established in 1947. Such efforts are aimed at decentralizing policy discussions and collaborative efforts while giving the various cabinet members a genuine feeling that they are being consulted and involved in important policy developments.[24] Designed to give more regard to the counsel of cabinet members, these councils generally end up centralizing more decision making in the White House or in a small select group of "inner cabinet" members.[25]

Cabinet members, as individuals, are often important advisers and administrators. But the cabinet as a decision-making body is not as important as press accounts would have us believe. Nowadays it would take a leap of imagination to think of cabinet meetings as a place where the large outlines of policy are hammered out in common, or where essential strategy is decided upon.

Can the Modern Presidency Survive the Modern Media?

Ronald Reagan once walked away from one of his news conferences, and turning to an aide, "cussed out" his press adversaries, not realizing a microphone was picking up his very words. John F. Kennedy once canceled over fifty White House subscriptions to the *New York Herald Tribune* because he was furious about how the paper was treating his decision making. Lyndon Johnson regularly planted "softball questions" (questons he could easily answer) among friendly reporters at presidential press conferences. All recent presidents have complained both that the modern media have misrepresented them and that the media report only the bad news.

Enjoying enormous First Amendment rights in this country, reporters usually go about their business of analyzing and criticizing presidents with striking gusto. Scores of media representatives are regularly stationed at the White House, and they travel everywhere the president goes, reporting on the president's every move. Presidential statements—even on the most trivial matter—are sent back to the newsrooms and are usually printed or aired. Major statements and policy initiatives are reported and subjected to interpretative analysis. The media, at the White House and elsewhere, also force to the forefront of national attention issues that might never have been discussed publicly in earlier times—and that never get discussed in many other countries. Presidents, of course, want all their initiatives printed and praised as much as possible.

But the press and the media believe they should provide a context in which presidential statements can be understood. Hence, they not only tell people what

President Bush meets the media.

CHAPTER 15 / The Presidency: Leadership Branch?

a president said but also often try to explain what the statement means. This is done primarily by columnists, editorial writers, and commentators, who are expected to agree with or to criticize a president and to provide their reasons for doing so. Furthermore, the management of most newspapers and radio and television stations in the country want to balance their stories about what presidents say—especially in presidential speeches—with an equal amount of time for the spokespersons of the opposition party or at least for persons who hold different points of view. Thus, when President Reagan spoke in support of aid to the Nicaraguan Contras or in favor of his Strategic Defense Initiative (Star Wars), the media frequently gave an almost equal amount of attention to the views of various senators who opposed him on these issues.

In recent years this kind of adversarial media coverage has often left the impression that a president's influence is more divisive than unifying. Except when a president attends a baseball game or welcomes to the White House some noted sports or arts hero, media coverage always seems to be—at best—ambivalent. No reporter has ever won a Pulitzer or any other media prize for writing a story favorable to the administration. The journalism profession honors those who uncover wrongdoing.

What have presidents done about this? Typically they have been patient and respected the critical dialogue so essential in a democracy. However, presidents and their aides have also engaged in extensive public relations efforts aimed at winning admiration and support for the president and White House policies.[26] Bush, for example, frequently invites friendly newspaper reporters for extensive interviews. Out-of-town editors are invited in for special briefings, and special efforts are made to get the President out of Washington for meetings with local and regional media representatives, who were generally viewed as less critical than Washington-based media. Special White House media experts regularly met to devise better ways to get the president's point of view out to the public, to get the president on prime-time television, or to arrange for flattering action photos.

Bush's efforts are not novel; every recent president has tried similar public relations stratagems. Presidents and their aides often conclude that unifying national leadership is almost impossible to achieve in a country that encourages such critical—even cynical—media. Some White House aides go so far as to say the media are badly hurting the nation. "They destroy every hero," said a Reagan deputy. "We don't have heroes anymore, we don't have anyone to believe in because they strip them naked."[27]

The modern media are perhaps the primary adversary of the modern presidency. Some complain the American presidency is being brutally wounded and its capacity for leadership sapped—if not paralyzed—because of excessive media criticism. Although media admit occasional abuses by the press, they rally to cherished "free press" traditions. Defenders of the press also like to quote from Thomas Jefferson, who although angered by the press when he was president, once said: "Were it left to me to decide whether we should have a government without newspapers or newspapers without a government, I should not hesitate to prefer the latter." Defenders of the media say that presidents have too often lied or manipulated the public's understanding of the issues. The media, they contend, are obligated to stand up and speak out—especially when they think a president is wrong. Defenders add, also, that even though journalists may have political sympathies, they prize their independence more, and seldom have political loyalties. "Their fault may be the opposite: seeing politicians and their handlers up close, they have no faith in any of them and are carriers, as well as recorders, of the prevailing disenchantment."[28]

"And when you're in real trouble, you press this button."

Copyright © 1988 by Herblock in the Washington Post.

No matter who is in the White House, presidents and the media will often be in conflict. This ongoing struggle is inherent in a democracy. The Watergate scandals fortified the media in their independence, and many people credited the media with playing an important role in bringing these scandals to the public's attention. Further, because the media—especially television—are viewed as more trustworthy and believable than most other American institutions, most Americans, most of the time, believe what they hear on television is as true as what presidents say. The goals of a president and of the media are often in conflict; and as long as this continues to be the case, presidents and the media will be adversaries. But the resources of the White House, especially in the hands of communicators such as FDR, John Kennedy, and Ronald Reagan, seem worthy combatants in taking on the so-called fourth branch of government.

The Vice-Presidency

Although the vice-presidency is now a part of the presidential establishment, it has not been that way for long. Most vice-presidents served mainly as president of the Senate. In most administrations the vice-president was at best a kind of fifth wheel, and at worst a political rival who sometimes connived against the president. The office was often dismissed as a joke. The main reason for the vice-president's posture as an outsider was that presidential nominees had usually chosen as running mates candidates who were geographically, ideologically, and in other ways likely to "balance the ticket."

In recent decades, however, presidential candidates have selected somewhat more like-minded persons for their running mates and have made more use of them. George Bush did his best to avoid upstaging Reagan, and Vice-President Dan Quayle appears to be following the same script. Today the vice-presidency brings both virtues and liabilities to a vice-president who aspires to the presidency. The job surely provides exposure to the issues and challenges of the office, but it is hard to appear "presidential" while at the same time not being disloyal to or upstaging the president.[29]

Ideally, a vice-president serves several roles in addition to the largely ceremonial function of acting as president of the Senate. A vice-president gets to cast the tie-breaking vote if the Senate has a tie vote—but this usually occurs less than once a year. As successor to the president should the latter die, resign, or become incapacitated, the vice-president works as an understudy who assumes some of the president's party and ceremonial duties, and thereby eases some of the president's burden. A vice-president can also perform specialized assignments, such as chairing advisory councils, cabinet-level committees, or a White House conference, or undertaking good-will missions abroad.

Tensions usually develop between top presidential aides and vice-presidents and their staffs. Part of the problem arises because presidents seldom wish to give up any ceremonial duties for which they themselves can win credit. Neither do cabinet members like to share their responsibilities with vice-presidents, which makes it very hard for vice-presidents to gain administrative experience. Then too, presidents often delegate unpleasant political chores to their vice-presidents.

The importance of the way in which we select and use vice-presidents is underscored by the fact that eight presidents have died in office—four by assassination, four by natural death—and one president has resigned. One-third of our presidents were once vice-presidents, including five of our last nine presidents.

Vice-President Dan Quayle gets advice from a former vice-president—Richard Nixon. Nixon praised Quayle, saying he is not an "intellectual midget."

Support exists for devising better ways to pick vice-presidential nominees as well as for making the vice-presidency a more significant office. Both major parties have considered practical means of making the selection procedure for the vice-presidency more democratic. Under the existing system presidential nominees have a free hand in choosing their running mates. Although there are some notable advantages to the present system—especially the possibility that the ticket will be ideologically compatible—drawbacks are also clear. Disadvantages of the present methods include the pressure of time, the lack of formalized consultation within the party, the rubber-stamp role for convention delegates, and the absence of public scrutiny of prospective vice-presidential candidates before the nomination.

The vice-presidency has been significantly affected by two post-World War II constitutional amendments. The Twenty-second Amendment, ratified in 1951, imposes a two-term limit on presidents, so that vice-presidents have a better chance of moving up to the Oval Office. The Twenty-fifth Amendment, ratified in 1967, confirms the prior practice of making the vice-president not acting president but president, in the event of the death of a president. Of greater significance, this amendment provides a procedure to determine whether an incumbent president is unable to discharge the powers and duties of the office, and it establishes procedures to fill a vacancy in the vice-presidency. For a few hours in 1985, George Bush became the first "acting president" when the first of these provisions was invoked while President Reagan underwent a minor cancer operation. The amendment also provides that in the event of a vacancy in the office of vice-president, the president nominates a vice-president, who takes office upon confirmation by a majority vote of both houses of Congress. This procedure generally ensures the appointment of a vice-president in whom the president has confidence. Thus, vice-presidents who have to take over the presidency can be expected to reflect most of their predecessor's policies, as was true when President Nixon appointed Gerald Ford to replace the resigned Spiro T. Agnew, and Ford in turn selected Nelson Rockefeller.

The vice-presidency will remain attractive to aspiring politicans if only because it is one of the major paths to the presidency. The policy-advising role of the vice-president was enhanced under Carter and Reagan. It will be interesting to watch and see if Bush provides the leadership opportunities for Quayle that Reagan at least occasionally provided for him. However, the tensions between a president and a vice-president are natural (after all, everybody else who works closely with presidents can be fired by them). It is almost certain the vice-president will continue to have an undefined role, subject to the good will and moods of the president more than to any fixed job description.[30]

"Look on the bright side . . . you're becoming obscure enough to be vice president."

Dunagin's People by Ralph Dunagin. Copyright 1984, The Orlando Sentinel, Field Newspaper Syndicate.

Making the Presidency Safe and Effective

The startling series of events of the **Watergate** and **Iran-contra** scandals sharpened the old question: How much executive power can a democracy afford? New questions were also raised: Was a bigger presidency necessarily better? Did presidential powers grow because they were usurped by presidents or handed over by Congress? Would we be better served by a six-year presidential term? Would some form of parliamentary government be better than our three-branch "presidential" system?

During the past two decades, presidents have been criticized for impounding billions of congressionally approved funds, obstructing justice, abusing the doctrine of executive privilege, lying about the conduct of the Vietnam War, and acting

Factors that Constrain Presidents

The Constitution
Federalism
Separation of powers
Congress
Federal courts
Investigative press and media
Public opinion
Opposing party
Opposing factions in president's party
Interest groups
Editorial opinion (and cartoonists)
Bureaucratic resistance
Opposing world powers and the international economy
World public opinion and UN policies
Regularly fixed elections
Unrealistic expectations
Party platforms
Independent counsels
The shape of the economy and the imperatives of economic development
Fear of losing next election for self or party

with excessive secrecy. People lost confidence first in Johnson's and then in Nixon's brand of leadership, and then, for different reasons, in Ford, Carter, and Reagan. The credibility, if not legitimacy, of the presidency itself was often tested.

How much formal authority does and should a president have? The Constitution grants broad executive authority without defining boundaries. In certain emergencies the president has powers to protect the public interest and to act before the Congress has the chance to do so. There seems to be a kind of *inherent* power in the presidency, vast but undefined, that an aggressive president can exploit in times of crisis. Unfortunately, crisis is now often the rule rather than the exception.

Franklin Roosevelt's conception of his power, in the Jefferson and Lincoln tradition—sometimes called the *prerogative theory*—was that in the face of emergencies a president had the same power once claimed by kings: the power to act according to discretion for the public good, without the prescription of the law and sometimes even against it. The World War II destroyer-bases agreement, for example, in which Roosevelt on his own initiative traded naval destroyers to England in return for some military bases, conflicted with several laws and set what some believe was a dangerous precedent that others (like Nixon) seem to have followed.

PRESIDENTIAL CHARACTER

What about presidential personality? If the presidency has too much power for the safety of the country (and the world), and yet not enough to solve some of the nation's toughest problems, what kind of person do we need in this office? Political scientist James David Barber writes that because the issues are always changing, we should be concerned somewhat less with the stands a candidate takes than with the candidate's *character*. The character, Barber claims, will stay pretty much the same.[31]

Barber claims we can classify presidents and would-be presidents according to their *activism* (how active and assertive they are) on the one hand and their *enjoyment* of politics and public service on the other. With these two dimensions, he contends, we can pretty well predict presidential performance. Table 15–3 shows Barber's classification scheme and how he assesses most twentieth-century presidents.

Barber holds that the people best suited for the presidency are politicians

TABLE 15–3
Barber's Classification of American Presidents

		ENERGY LEVEL IN THEIR POLITICAL JOB	
		ACTIVE	PASSIVE
EMOTIONAL ATTITUDE TOWARD POLITICS AND THE JOB OF THE PRESIDENCY	POSITIVE	Franklin Roosevelt Harry Truman John F. Kennedy Gerald Ford Jimmy Carter George Bush	William H. Taft Warren Harding Ronald Reagan
	NEGATIVE	Richard Nixon Lyndon Johnson Herbert Hoover Woodrow Wilson	Dwight Eisenhower Calvin Coolidge

CHAPTER 15 / The Presidency: Leadership Branch?

who creatively shape their environment and savor the give-and-take exchanges of political life. He calls them "active-positives." Beware, he tells us, of the active-negative types. They are the driven personalities, compelled to feverish activity, yet doomed by rigidity and personal frustration in the way they approach their jobs. Wilson, Hoover, Johnson, and Nixon are illustrative cases. Barber said Ford was an active-positive type, but others think of Ford as somewhat more of a passive-positive. Some observers thought Carter was as much in the negative category as in the positive. Still others thought that the contradictory conclusions about where to put them merely demonstrated that this scheme was more confusing than helpful—and more likely to tell us about the classifiers than the classified. Barber called Reagan a passive-positive. He worried that Reagan would be tempted to let things drift and that he would be overly deferential to his friends. Barber is more hopeful of the flexible George Bush.

Our understanding of personality and character, however, is not yet so developed that we can make accurate predictions about suitable presidential candidates. Moreover, critics doubt that Barber's generalizations are based on sufficient evidence.[32] Also, many people judged Reagan to be an "active" and not a "passive," type. Still others, who are at least partially persuaded by Barber's analysis, doubt that we can really put it to work during most elections. What happens, for example, if most of the candidates are "active-positive"? Further, using strict character criteria to screen candidates probably would have prevented the moody and often depressed Abraham Lincoln from winning office. Nor can we be sure that a president's character will stay the same throughout an entire term or even over the life span of an issue. In addition to a presidential candidate's character, voters want and deserve to know the issue positions of the candidates. It would also help to know the kind of people a candidate seeks out as advisers.

Perhaps too much emphasis is placed on presidential personality and character. Psychologists, of course, tend to emphasize the personal more than the institutional. But the personality of the president is but one factor, and Barber's classifications lack so much precision that they predict little. If institutions and constitutional and political arrangements matter, as we have suggested they do, then it may be a mistake to suggest that changing the personality of the individual president will have a major impact on presidential effectiveness. The causes of presidential ineffectiveness are usually due more to the shape of our political system than to the personality of our presidents. This is not to say that the president's character, integrity, and leadership or management styles are unimportant. But these considerations are only one set of concerns, and they may be less important than our institutional structures and processes. Political scientists debate these differing emphases, and we encourage you to do so as well.

NEW CHECKS AND BALANCES

Presidential power may be greater today than ever before. It is misleading, however, to infer from a president's capacity to begin a nuclear war that the chief executive has similar power to bring about positive change and solutions in policy-making areas. Seldom are presidents free agents in bringing about basic social change. As priority setter, politician, and executive, a president shares power with members of Congress, bureaucrats, and interest-group elites. The ability to set priorities is not the same as the ability to enforce laws and administer them properly. Presidents who want to be effective in implementing policy changes must know what they want to achieve and how to motivate and strengthen the bureaucracy to that end.

Should We Have a Six-Year Nonrenewable Term for Presidents?

PRO:

It might help take the politics out of the presidency, and thereby lessen the likelihood of scandals like Watergate.

Four years is too short a time to get the job done.

Presidents could concentrate on the job rather than on reelection.

During wartime a president wouldn't waste time campaigning.

Budgets are already cast for about two years ahead when a president gets into office.

Six years is enough even for the healthiest of presidents.

CON:

A six-year term would give us two more years of the "clunkers" and two fewer years of the great ones.

Four years is long enough to tell whether a president is doing the job.

The best way to be reelected is to do the job well, maintain majority support, and be an effective leader.

The four-year term forces presidents to be accountable for their promises and platforms.

Many of our great presidents served ably for more than six years: Washington, Jefferson, Wilson, FDR, and Ike.

A healthy, democratic country needs a politician in the White House: one who can bargain, persuade, build crucial political coalitions, and get diverse political factions to work together.

We should not surrender a hardwon democratic right: to kick a leader *out* of office.

More recently, some writers have called attention to the growing number of international constraints or roadblocks facing any president who wants to govern. Warnings about the age of limits, or even the age of decline, for America haunt even optimists in the White House. Historian Paul Kennedy puts it bluntly when he writes that the task facing American leaders over the next few decades must be to recognize that broad trends are under way on a global scale, and "that there is a need to 'manage' affairs so that *relative* erosion of the United States' position takes place slowly and smoothly, and is not accelerated by policies which bring merely short-term advantage but longer-term disadvantage."[33] In effect he and others are saying that our presidents and leaders have to learn to cooperate with and persuade allies, and they must have the ability to work with leaders elsewhere as well.

Less unilateral action by the United States is a reality.

While the traditional president did not participate in the international system and the modern president could dominate it, the post-modern president has no choice but to cooperate and compete, since economic and national security problems are not contained within national boundaries. There is nothing novel in this challenge. Leaders of other democratic nations long ago learned the basic fact of life: To succeed in an interdependent world requires watching the rest of the world as well as one's own country.[34]

We may still be the most important world power, but as our margin of economic influence declines, presidents will have to compensate with more creative and skilled diplomatic leadership.

This is a tough assignment in a political system held together in such large measure by compromise and contradictory goals. Not only must presidents deal with key congressional leaders, cabinet members, important bureaucrats, a vice-president, party chiefs, and even leaders of the opposition party, but they must also cope with the political forces operating around the White House: public opinion, pressures from organized interests, demands from their own party. They must negotiate endlessly among differing individuals, among clashing American values (see Chapter 7), and among competing transnational interests. They will constantly struggle with investigative reporters and muckrakers. And they must respond to public sentiment at the same time as they educate it. The fierce light of public opinion, magnified by the press and the electronic media, beats down upon the White House.

A NEW ATTITUDE TOWARD THE PRESIDENCY?

Unrealistic expectations of the presidency have helped to weaken it. Part of the reason presidents have turned to secrecy and subordinated substance to style has been that we have overburdened the office with exaggerated expectations. We elect a politician and then insist on a superhuman performance. As currently designed, the presidency is an institution that manipulates its occupants, and accentuates their *shortcomings* as well as their virtues.[35]

In one sense the best safeguard and restraint on presidential powers rest with the attitudes of the American people. Citizens have far more power than they generally realize. Presidents usually hear when citizens are "sending a message." Citizens can also "vote" between elections in innumerable ways—by changing parties, by organizing protests, by voting for the opposition party in off-year elections, by voting for or against issues in state referendums.

The Reagan Legacy

No one doubts that Reagan made the presidency work after it had been a troubled institution for several years. He possessed both the mind of an ideologue and the skill of a politician. He proved to be a natural horse trader who often seemed to relish fashioning compromises as he moved the political system toward his political ends. He proved also to be a genius at American pomp and pageantry. Americans had heard that the presidency had grown too complex for one person to manage, but Reagan seemed to reassert the force of individual leadership and make the office function with ease.

Critics say he was lucky. It's hard to tell whether he was an effective president or an average one who got lucky. But he did help to restore self-assurance to the American people and to the presidency. His presidency marked a watershed in domestic policy and signaled a fundamental shift in attitude with the federal government assuming a much smaller responsibility for social and urban issues. If the Roosevelt New Deal served as a period of ascendancy in identifying and dealing with social concerns, the

CHAPTER 15 / The Presidency: Leadership Branch?

We need a healthy skepticism toward presidential decisions. A lesson learned from the Watergate period is not that the powers of the presidency should be lessened, but that other institutions—parties, Congress, the courts—should grow in stature. Unless we can find ways to revitalize our political parties, to achieve some measure of responsiveness to the electorate and party control over public policy, we may well be destined to continue the march toward an American version of the De Gaulle model of leadership in France—a highly personalized and centralized system overly dependent on a charismatic leader.[36]

A few presidential advisers and scholars believe we need to rethink our constitutional system and our doctrine of a separation of powers. Our old constitutional restraints, they fear, too severely constrain presidential leadership, especially the ability of a president to get a program enacted. To make the presidency more effective, these "reformers" would amend the Constitution so that Congress and the president would be elected at the same time, and perhaps the voter would choose a package or unified party ticket rather than opt for a representative and senator from one party and a president from another. It has also been suggested that presidents serve a single, six-year term, and that they be able to ask a member of Congress to serve in the cabinet—as is done in parliamentary systems. Other reformers would repeal the two-term limitation imposed by the Twenty-second Amendment. Still bolder is the suggestion that presidents—failing to get support for their programs in Congress—be empowered to dissolve Congress and call for new elections as a test of strength and as a kind of referendum or vote of confidence for their programs.[37] These are radical steps, and they are not likely to win approval.

One of the persisting paradoxes of the American presidency is that on the one hand, it is always too powerful, and on the other, it is too weak. It is always too strong, because in many ways it is contrary to our ideals of government by the people and decentralization of power; yet the office seems to have inadequate powers, because presidents seldom are able to keep the promises they make. Of course, the presidency is always too strong when we dislike the incumbent. And the presidency is always too constrained when we believe a president is striving to serve the public interest as we define it.

The presidency will surely remain one of our nation's best sources for creative policy change. Americans will expect presidents to do more, not less, in the future. The presidency will almost certainly continue to be a hard-pressed office, laden with the cumulative weight of contradictory expectations. Americans' mixed views of the job of the president often put our presidents in "no-win" situations.[38] Thus, we want our president to be:

1. Gentle and kind but also forceful, cunning, and decisive
2. A common person who can give an uncommon performance
3. Above politics, yet a skilled political coalition builder
4. An inspirational leader who never promises more than can be achieved
5. A programmatic but also pragmatic and flexible leader
6. Innovative and inventive, ahead of the times, yet always responsive to popular majorities
7. A moral leader, yet not too preachy or moralizing
8. A bipartisan leader of all the people, but also a leader of one political party

History suggests there is no foolproof way to guarantee that our presidents will possess the appropriate functional skills as well as the moral character the job requires. On balance, the voters have chosen remarkably well. Still, James

Reagan presidency marked a turning away from that agenda. He had a clear idea of what he wanted to do—cut the budget on the domestic side, raise it on the military side, and cut inflation and interest rates—and often he succeeded. He was far less successful at balancing the budget and lessening our trade imbalances. And his administration will always be known for scandals—at the White House, in the Justice Department, at Housing and Urban Development, and in Defense procurement.

Reagan will be judged on the effect of his national security policies and especially on how the economy performs in the near future. He will also be evaluated in retrospect on whether he truly represented the nation as a whole or just one stratum within it. Experts say that a great or near-great president has to show that he wants the blessings of this country shared by all the people. A great president has to contribute to the soundness of our economy and to the security of the nation—both physical and psychological.

However the historians treat and assess the Reagan legacy, he left a large mark on the institution of the presidency.

Madison's advice remains useful: "A dependence on the people is, no doubt, the primary control of the government; but experience has taught mankind the necessity of auxiliary precautions."[39] We must maintain the effectiveness of these "auxiliary precautions"—Congress, parties, the courts, the press, and concerned citizens' groups—if we are to ensure a properly balanced and constitutional presidency.

Summary

1. Presidents must act as crisis-managing, morale-building, recruiting, priority-setting, coalition-building, and managerial leaders. No president can divide the job into tidy compartments. Ultimately, all the responsibilities overlap.

2. The office of the president is a combination of the huge presidential establishment, a president's personality and character, and the heavy demands and expectations on the chief executive. It is still being reshaped as new presidents with ideas and styles of their own move into the White House.

3. The expansion of presidential powers has been a continuous development during the past several decades. Crises, both foreign and economic, have enlarged the powers of the president. When there is a need for decisive action, presidents are asked to supply it. Congress, of course, is traditionally expected to share in the formulation of national policy.

Yet Congress is often so fragmented that it has been a willing partner in the growth of the presidency—at the same time that it is constantly setting boundaries on how far presidents can extend their influence. Every president must learn anew the need to work closely with the members of Congress and to enlist their support before major policy changes can be made.

4. The overriding task of American citizens is to bind presidents to the majority will without shackling them. To expect too much of our presidents may be to weaken them in the leadership tasks we need them to perform. To require immediate accountability might paralyze the presidency. Presidential leadership, properly defined, must be more than the power to persuade and less than the power to coerce: It must be the power to achieve by democratic means results acceptable to the people.

Further Reading

BRUCE BUCHANAN. *The Citizen's Presidency* (Congressional Quarterly Press, 1986).

JAMES MACGREGOR BURNS. *The Power to Lead: The Crisis of the American Presidency* (Simon & Schuster, 1984).

THOMAS E. CRONIN, ed. *Inventing the American Presidency* (University Press of Kansas, 1989).

THOMAS E. CRONIN. *The State of the Presidency*, 2d ed. (Little, Brown, 1980).

ROBERT E. DICLERICO, ed. *Analyzing the Presidency* (Dushkin, 1985).

CHARLES O. JONES, ed. *The Reagan Legacy* (Chatham House, 1988).

SAMUEL KERNELL. *Going Public: New Strategies of Presidential Leadership* (Congressional Quarterly Press, 1986).

MICHAEL NELSON, ed. *Guide to the American Presidency* (Congressional Quarterly Press, 1989).

BRADLEY PATTERSON. *The Ring of Power: The White House Staff and Its Expanding Role* (Basic Books, 1988).

SIDNEY MILK and MICHAEL NELSON. *The American Presidency: Origins and Development, 1776–1990* (Congressional Quarterly Press, 1990).

RICHARD ROSE. *The Postmodern Presidency: The White House Meets the World* (Chatham House, 1988).

LESTER G. SELIGMAN and CARY R. COVINGTON. *The Coalitional Presidency* (Dorsey Press, 1989).

HEDRICK SMITH. *The Power Game: How Washington Works* (Random House, 1988).

Notes

1. Glenn A. Phelps, "George Washington: Precedent Setter," in Thomas E. Cronin, ed., *Inventing the American Presidency* (University Press of Kansas, 1989), chap. 10.

2. John Steinbeck, *America and Americans* (Bonanza Books, 1966), p. 46.

3. For an example, see J. William Fulbright, with Seth Tillman, *The Price of Empire* (Pantheon, 1989).

4. See the essay by Michael Kinsley, *Time* (April 17, 1989), p. 84.

5. See Bert A. Rockman, *The Leadership Question* (Praeger, 1984),

and James MacGregor Burns, *The Power to Lead* (Simon & Schuster, 1984).

6. For a different point of view, see Benjamin I. Page and Mark P. Petracca, *The American Presidency* (McGraw-Hill, 1983), chap. 1.

7. See Theodore J. Lowi, *The Personal President* (Cornell University Press, 1985).

8. James David Barber, *The Presidential Character*, 3d ed. (Prentice Hall, 1985). See also George Edwards, *The Public Presidency* (St. Martin's Press, 1983).

9. See G. Calvin Mackenzie, *The Politics of Presidential Appointments* (Free Press, 1981).

10. See G. Calvin Mackenzie, ed., *The In-and-Outers: Presidential Appointees and the Problems of Transient Government in Washington* (Johns Hopkins Press, 1987), chap. 1.

11. "Leadership in Jeopardy: The Fraying of the Presidential Appointments System," *National Academy of Public Administration Report* (November 1985), p. 3.

12. *United States* v. *Curtiss-Wright Export Corp.*, 299 U.S. 304 (1936).

13. For provocative debate on presidential war powers and "prerogative power," see David Gray Adler "The President's War-Making Power," and Robert Scigliano, "The President's 'Prerogative Power,'" in Cronin, *Inventing the American Presidency*.

14. Lester Seligman and Cary Covington, *The Coalitional Presidency* (Dorsey Press, 1989).

15. Jeff Fishel, *Presidents and Promises* (Congressional Quarterly Press, 1984).

16. Richard E. Neustadt, *Presidential Power* (Wiley, 1980), p. 9.

17. Samuel Kernell, *Going Public* (Congressional Quarterly Press, 1986); and Edwards, *The Public Presidency*.

18. For a more detailed treatment see Thomas E. Cronin, "The Presidency and the Parties," in Thomas E. Cronin, ed., *Rethinking the Presidency* (Little, Brown, 1982), chap. 21; and Robert Harmel, ed., *The President as Party Leader* (Praeger, 1984).

19. This is not to suggest that all White House aides and advisors necessarily like one another or that a team spirit always emerges. For discussion of the disarray and backbiting in the Reagan White House, see David Stockman, *The Triumph of Politics* (Harper & Row, 1986).

20. George Reedy, *The Twilight of the Presidency* (World, 1970), p. 98. For another view see Bradley Patterson, *Ring of Power* (Basic Books, 1988).

21. Henry Fairlie, *The Kennedy Promise* (Doubleday, 1973), pp. 167–68. See also Stephen Hess, *Organizing the Presidency* (Brookings Institution, 1976), and Edward Weisband and Thomas M. Franck, *Resignation as Protest* (Penguin, 1975).

22. John Ehrlichman, interview published in *The Washington Post* (August 24, 1972). See also Jeb Stuart Magruder's account of White House life in the Nixon administration, *An American Life: One Man's Road to Watergate* (Atheneum, 1974), and Donald Regan's account of the Reagan White House, *For the Record* (Harcourt Brace Jovanovich, 1988).

23. See Stockman, *The Triumph of Politics*; and Howard E. Shuman, *Politics and the Budget*, 2d ed. (Prentice Hall, 1988).

24. Fred I. Greenstein, ed., *Leadership in the Modern Presidency* (Harvard University Press, 1988).

25. The notion of an "inner cabinet" is developed in Thomas E. Cronin, *The State of the Presidency*, 2d ed. (Little, Brown, 1980).

26. See Mark Hertsgaard, *On Bended Knee: The Press and the Reagan Presidency* (Farrar, Straus & Giroux, 1988).

27. Juan Williams, "Presidential Newsmaking: How Reagan's Staff Spreads His Message," *The Washington Post* (February 13, 1983), p. 18. Two books that examine Washington reporters and the White House press office are Stephen Hess, *The Washington Reporters* (Brookings Institution, 1981), and Michael B. Grossman and Martha J. Kumar, *Portraying the President* (Johns Hopkins University Press, 1981).

28. Thomas Griffith, "Goodbye to All That," *Time* (April 18, 1988), p. 47.

29. For an analysis of the recent growth of the role of the vice-president as a potential advisor to the president, see Thomas E. Cronin, "Rethinking the Vice Presidency," in Cronin, *Rethinking the Presidency*; and Report of the Twentieth Century Fund Task Force on the Vice Presidency, *A Heartbeat Away* (Priority Press, 1988).

30. Three useful books on the vice-presidency are: Paul Light, *Vice Presidential Power* (Johns Hopkins University Press, 1984); Joel Goldstein, *The Modern Vice Presidency* (Princeton University Press, 1982); and Marie Natoli, *American Prince, American Pauper* (Greenwood Press, 1985).

31. Barber, *The Presidential Character*. See evaluations of this study by Alexander L. George, "Assessing Presidential Character," *World Politics* (January 1974), pp. 234–82, and by Alan C. Elms, *Personality in Politics* (Harcourt Brace Jovanovich, 1976), chap. 4. See also Michael Nelson, "James David Barber and the Psychological Presidency," *Virginia Quarterly Review* (Autumn 1980).

32. See, for example, Fred I. Greenstein, *The Hidden-Hand Presidency* (Basic Books, 1982), which suggests Barber is wrong on Eisenhower, and Betty Glad, *Jimmy Carter in Search of the Great White House* (Norton, 1980), for a somewhat different view on Carter. For a different analysis of recent presidents, see also Hedley Donovan, *Roosevelt to Reagan* (Harper & Row, 1985).

33. Paul Kennedy, *The Rise and Fall of the Great Powers* (Random House, 1987), p. 534.

34. Richard Rose, *The Postmodern Presidency: The White House Meets the World* (Chatham House, 1988), p. 28.

35. See Bruce Buchanan, *The Presidential Experience* (Prentice Hall, 1978).

36. See the analysis in Lowi, *The Personal President*.

37. See Lloyd Cutler, "To Form a Government—On the Defects of Separation of Powers," in Cronin, *Rethinking the Presidency*. See also Burns, *The Power to Lead*; Donald Robinson, ed., *Reforming American Government* (Westview, 1985); and James L. Sundquist, *Constitutional Reform* (Brookings Institution, 1986).

38. These and related paradoxes are discussed in Cronin, *The State of the Presidency*, 2d ed., chap. 1. See also Godfrey Hodgson, *All Things to All Men* (Simon & Schuster, 1980)

39. James Madison, *The Federalist*, No. 51 (Modern Library, 1937), p. 337.

16

Congress and the President: The Politics of Shared Powers

The framers anticipated that the president and the Congress would on occasion disagree over policy, for they gave the president a veto power over legislation and they gave Congress the power to override that veto. The framers actually made such disagreement inevitable by providing that the president, Senate, and House would be elected by different constituencies acting through different electoral mechanisms. Indeed, the framers *wanted* such disagreement, because checks and balances within the government would prevent the president and Congress from "ganging up" against the people's liberties.

Oddly, however, in 1789, the first few weeks and months of the new government—run by many of the framers themselves—were a time of remarkable harmony among the branches for several reasons. Although Congress started legislating weeks before Washington, the great Revolutionary War general, even took the oath of office, it was made up largely of his admirers and was thus not disposed to challenge him. And Washington in turn respected the leaders of Congress—especially his fellow Virginian James Madison—and had no intention of using his veto power often, if at all, or of wielding undue influence in the national legislature.

Today, the high point of cooperation between the two branches in 1789 seems almost amusing—and certainly extraordinary. At Washington's request, Madison "ghost-wrote"—as we would say today—Washington's inaugural address. He then wrote the formal reply of the House of Representatives. Then president Washington asked Madison to compose his reply to the House—and also his reply to the Senate. For a week or so Madison was a man "in dialogue with himself."[1]

This early harmony was short-lived. Soon Congress and the president shifted to their historic posture of differing over legislation and other matters, and the dominant influence shifted back and forth between the White House and "the Hill." A century later conflict seemed normal. "Oh, if I could only be president and Congress too, for just ten minutes!" President Theodore Roosevelt once re-marked. Although most presidents share the same wish, our Constitution rules this out—and for good reason.

The United States is unique among major world powers because it is neither a parliamentary democracy nor a wholly executive-dominated government. Our Constitution invites both Congress and the president to set policy and govern the nation. Much of the time during the twentieth century, the main role of Congress has been to respond to executive branch leadership; the president serves as policy promoter and the Congress as a policy adapter. But this has not always been the case, and in recent years Congress has often yearned to be an equal partner in national policy formulation.

Article I of the Constitution grants to Congress "all legislative powers" but limits them to those "*herein granted*." It then sets forth in some detail the powers vested in Congress. Article II, in contrast, grants to the president "the executive power," but describes these powers only in general terms. Is this difference signifi-cant? Some scholars and most presidents have argued that a president has additional undefined power to act to promote the well-being of the United States. Therefore, they contend, a president is not limited to the powers spelled out in the Constitution, as is Congress. Other scholars and most members of Congress contend the president has no such inherent power.

Whatever the language of the Constitution, the president has often exercised powers not expressly defined in it. These powers have a variety of names: implied or inherent powers or moral, residual, and emergency powers. Implied powers are often considered more restricted in scope than inherent or emergency powers. Clear distinctions, however, are hard to establish.[2]

The framers did expect presidents to be a major influence in foreign policy. Although foreign affairs in the eighteenth century were generally thought to be an executive matter, our framers did not want the president to be the only or even the dominant agent. Several of the specific powers vested in Congress in the Constitution were designed to bring Congress into foreign policy. Indeed, a good part of the Constitution was written to carve away from executive powers control over foreign policy and foreign relations, which under the English system was vested in the King. The framers intended the Senate to serve as more of a partner in the making of foreign policy, and they gave Congress as a whole the power to declare war. "The framers meant, at the most, that the President should be a joint participant in the field of foreign affairs, but not an equal one."[3]

The framers never intended the president to be the dominant agent in domes-tic policy making either. For much of the twentieth century, however, scholars have held that we need a strong, dynamic presidency to overcome the tremendous fragmentation of power in America. The creaky machinery of our government, they contend, can be made to work only if we give a president the proper amount of help and authority. The American people have generally favored the expansion of presidential powers and with the development of radio and television, the visibility of the president has increased. Indeed, considering the publicity given presidents, it is hardly surprising that citizens look to them to solve the nation's problems.

As the roles of Congress and the presidency have changed, tensions between the branches have been inevitable. They were, as we have noted, not only anticipated but planned. The branches were designed with different constituencies, different length terms, and different responsibilities. The branches are also organized differ-ently, and they are jealous of their powers. Members of each branch are often suspicious of the other.

Rarely is a president called before a congressional committee. Here, however, President Ford faces a House judiciary subcommittee to explain why he pardoned former President Richard M. Nixon.

Gerald Ford on Congress versus the Presidency

"When I was in the House for 25 years I almost always looked down Pennsylvania Avenue at the White House, regardless of whether Democrats or Republicans were there, and wondered why they were so arrogant. Then, when I was in the White House myself, I looked up at the Congress and wondered how there could be 535 irresponsible members of Congress."

Source: Talk at Hinckley Institute of Politics, University of Utah, February 1982.

Still, even though the Constitution disperses power and invites a continuing struggle between these two branches, it also requires the two branches to integrate the fragmented parts of the system into a workable government. And usually these two branches do work together. Even when the relationship "is guarded or hostile, bills are passed and signed into law. Presidential appointments are approved by the Senate. Budgets are enacted and the government is kept afloat. This necessary cooperation goes on even when the White House and the Capitol are controlled by different parties."[4]

What are the sources of conflict and cooperation between these two branches? In dealing with this central question we look first at the legislative role of presidents and the efforts of Congress to fulfill its constitutional responsibilities.

Presidential Influence in Congress

The presidential record of dealing with Congress in recent years is a mixed one. Presidents enjoy considerable success in getting most of their nominations confirmed by the Senate. Also, relatively few presidential vetoes have been overturned by Congress, and the vast bulk of presidential budget requests eventually win approval. On the other hand, often only 50 percent of presidents' major policy initiatives are passed.[5] Even though President Reagan won more of his major legislative struggles with Congress than did his three immediate predecessors, he, like several before him, fared less well with Congress the longer he was in office. Many actions that he would have liked, such as weakening the Clean Air Act or abolishing the Departments of Energy and Education, were either defeated or shelved because they lacked support.

Why are presidents in conflict with Congress so often? In part, because the whole process was designed to maximize checks and balances and deliberation—rather than cooperation and speedy action. And Americans by and large want it that way. They do not want presidents dictating policies and laws (see Table 16–1).

Another reason for conflict is that the presidency and Congress represent different constituencies. Not only do members of Congress represent state and local citizenry—and hence reflect different geographical interests than a president—but our staggered system of electing only one third of the Senate every two

TABLE 16–1
Public Expectations of the Role of Congress and the President in Policy Making

Question: Now I would like to ask you some questions about the president and Congress. Some people think that the president ought to have the major responsibility for making policy, while other people think that Congress ought to have the major responsibility. In general, which do you think should have the major responsibility for setting policy?

WHO SHOULD HAVE THE MAJOR RESPONSIBILITY?	ECONOMIC POLICY	FOREIGN POLICY	GENERAL RESPONSIBILITY
Congress	40%	27%	36%
Equal	20	18	22
President	34	49	37
Don't know	6	6	5
	100	100	100

Source: Gallup poll, nationwide survey of over 1500 adults conducted by WHYY, Inc., Philadelphia–Wilmington (Fall 1979).

years means two-thirds of the senators are elected at times different from the president; this no doubt makes them responsible to somewhat different moods and points of view. Moreover, many members of Congress may have been there for ten or twenty years, and look forward to serving perhaps another ten. Presidents, however, think mainly about the present.

Still other factors are at work. The opposition party in Congress often tries to mount its own programs. It will, when possible, defeat a president's policy initiatives and substitute its own. Sometimes it will merely defeat White House measures. This becomes especially troublesome for a president if Congress is controlled by a majority of the opposition. This was the situation for Presidents Nixon and Ford and during part of Reagan's two terms. It is also the case for Bush.

What can and does a president do in working with Congress? What are the chief sources of influence? The greatest asset for presidents working with Congress is to have both houses controlled by members from their own political parties. Presidents often try to enlarge their parties' representation in Congress during the midterm elections, but they are seldom successful in this effort. Indeed, they almost always lose support as a result of midterm elections. Today most members of Congress prefer to run their own campaigns quite independent of the president's. Even when they do seek a president's help, it is not clear whether this aid is effective. Presidential coattails, once thought to be a significant factor in helping to elect members of a president's party to Congress, have had little effect in recent years. Members of Congress are usually reelected because of the quality of their constituency services and because they can take advantage of incumbency.

From the president's vantage point it is seldom helpful to punish party mavericks. With power dispersed and decentralized in Congress it is just too risky for a president to single out a few party "disloyalists" for retribution. White House congressional relations aides abide by the motto of "no permanent allies, no permanent enemies." Someone whose vote is lost today may cast the crucial vote on some other measure next week.

A president who wins widespread backing in the country—and in the states and congressional districts—can use this popularity to try to influence certain members of Congress. In addition, presidents are now expected to build coalitions with key interest groups. Lyndon Johnson and Ronald Reagan were often effective in this regard. Presidents today are expected to meet regularly not only with the leadership within Congress but also with the members of key committees and subcommittees.

Another big advantage presidents have in dealing with Congress is that they usually have significantly more public visibility than do even the leading members of Congress. Their influence is enhanced by their national campaigns, by presidential debates, by their inaugural addresses, by various speeches and televised press conferences, and by their ability to rally the country to support their top priorities. Members of Congress respect this advantage and often seek to win White House support for their own legislative measures because they know that with presidential assistance their own measures stand a much better chance of winning passage and being signed into law by the president.

Presidents also have the vast bureaucracy and hundreds of advisors and advisory bodies to assist them in preparing the budget and major policy initiatives. To be sure, as we noted in Chapter 14, Congress in recent decades has built its own vast network, yet it is still rather small compared to the executive branch's. Throughout the twentieth century Congress has either formally or informally given increased authority to presidents to prepare the budget and conduct day-to-day operations of foreign policy.

George Bush's Offered Hand

We need a new engagement . . . between the Executive and Congress.

The challenges before us will be thrashed out with the House and Senate. We must bring the federal budget into balance. And we must ensure that America stands before the world united . . .

We need compromise; we've had dissension. We need harmony; we've had a chorus of discordant voices . . .

We have seen the hard looks and heard the statements in which not each other's ideas are challenged, but each other's motives. And our great parties have too often been far apart and untrusting of each other.

It's been that way since Vietnam. That war cleaves us still. But, friends, that war began a quarter of a century ago; and surely the statute of limitations has been reached . . .

A new breeze is blowing—and the old bipartisanship must be made new again.

To my friends—and yes, I do mean friends—in the loyal opposition . . . I put out my hand.

. . . when our fathers were young, Mr. Speaker, our differences ended at the water's edge . . .

The American people await action. They didn't send us here to bicker. They ask us to rise above the merely partisan. . . .

Inaugural Address, 1989.

On taking office, George Bush invited Congress to work together with him.

Presidents are often in a better position to bargain and trade for votes with members of Congress than members are able to bargain with each other. In addition to receiving presidential help in their reelection campaigns, members of Congress also want federal projects for their districts, patronage for their supporters, help with their own pet legislative measures, defense contracts for their states, and similar national government help for major industries or farming interests in their districts or states. Thus, "among the currencies in the president's trading system are negative sanctions—threats to withhold favors from members who fail to go along."[6]

Still, a president's position in dealing with Congress is relatively fragile. President Nixon misused and abused many presidential powers, but he was no more able to influence Congress than other presidents. In fact, he won passage of fewer key policy initiatives than did most other recent presidents. To say a president is in a relatively weak position in dealing with Congress is to say the White House does not have a large number of resources with which to influence most members of Congress. Presidents can make stirring appeals for party unity—if their parties enjoy majorities in Congress. They can also try to educate and rally the public around their major programs.

But much of the time a president must deal with a Congress that moves according to its own pace and that responds to a variety of interests above and beyond those coming from the White House. As we have noted, members of Congress are influenced more by their own philosophical and ideological convictions, by their colleagues in Congress, and by the interests of their districts back home than they are by instructions or pleas from the White House. These realities will remain central factors in presidential-congressional relations.

The events of Watergate that resulted in the first resignation of a president in our history aroused public concern about the role of Congress. Most people wished Congress to be a more coequal branch of government, to be more assertive and alert, and to exercise its own powers. The change in public attitudes is documented by polls taken before and after Vietnam and Watergate. Support for Congress soared in the mid-1970s, although public support for the two branches became more balanced by about 1980. But then the Iran-contra episodes rekindled and strengthened the view in the late 1980s that the White House was violating the spirit of shared decision making. Congress was again put on notice by the American people to assert itself!

Congress definitely tried to reassert itself in the mid- to late-1970s. Did a new array of checks and balances cripple the presidency and undermine its potential for creative leadership? Did Congress overreact to Vietnam and Watergate and in the process create an "imperial Congress," as conservative critics charge? We examine these questions in the rest of this chapter. We explore how Congress tried to reclaim its policy-making powers and the impact of this on the presidency. We also examine how Reagan and Bush have tried to protect presidential powers and the prestige of the presidency.

"Kingsley says if he were President, he'd tell Congress to either put up or shut up."

Drawing by Stan Hunt; © 1978 The New Yorker Magazine, Inc.

The Imperial Presidency Argument

Back in the 1970s many critics held that, because of abuse of power by presidents, especially abuse of the war powers and secrecy, the presidency had become an imperial institution. In his book *The Imperial Presidency*, historian and former John Kennedy adviser Arthur M. Schlesinger, Jr., argued that presidential power was so expanded and misused by 1972 that it threatened our constitutional system.[7]

Schlesinger claimed that an imperial presidency had been created as a result of America's wartime experiences, particularly Vietnam.

Proponents of the "imperial presidency" view contend that the difficulty stems in part from ambiguity concerning the president's power as commander in chief; it is an undefined *office*, not a *function*. Schlesinger and others acknowledge that Nixon and Johnson did not create the imperial presidency; they merely built on some of the more questionable practices of their predecessors. But observers contend there is a distinction between the *abuse* and the *usurpation* of power. Abraham Lincoln, FDR, and Harry Truman temporarily usurped power in wartime. Johnson and Nixon abused power, even in peacetime, by claiming absolute powers to be a part of their office.

Secrecy has often been used to protect and preserve a president's national security power. It is argued that Nixon pushed the doctrine beyond acceptable limits. Before Eisenhower, Congress expected to get the information it sought from the executive branch. Instances of secrecy and executive privilege were the rare exceptions. By the early 1970s they had become the rule. And a Congress that knows only what the president wants it to know is not an independent body.

Political scientist Theodore Lowi contends that presidents have little choice but to be imperial, given the relationship between the development of the American national state and the significant practical role of the executive in that development. He suggests that Schlesinger's interpretation exaggerates the case of personal abuse of power by Nixon and others and underestimates the fact that the modern presidency is largely the construction of the Congress with the cooperation of the federal courts. He suggests that the vast growth of presidential power began with the coming of New Deal domestic programs and cannot be linked solely or even primarily with the expansion of the president's foreign policy powers. Although "there may be many specific cases of usurpation by modern presidents, these are extreme actions in pursuit of powers and responsibilities by and large willingly and voluntarily delegated to the president by Congress."[8]

Still, Schlesinger's book is a useful point of departure for discussing the alleged too-powerful presidency. The chief complaints involve such presidential activities as war making, emergency powers, diplomacy by executive agreement, and government by veto.

President Franklin D. Roosevelt, surrounded by congressional leaders, signs the Declaration of War against Japan on December 8, 1941. World War II was the last time a president signed a formal declaration of war.

PRESIDENTIAL WAR MAKING

The Constitution delegates to Congress the authority to *declare* the legal state of war (with the consent of the president), but in practice the commander in chief often starts or initiates war (or actions that lead to war). This power has been used by the chief executive time and time again. In 1846 Polk ordered American forces to advance into disputed territory; when Mexico resisted, Polk informed Congress that war existed by act of Mexico, and a formal declaration of war was soon forthcoming. McKinley's dispatch of a battleship to Havana, where it was blown up, helped precipitate war with Spain in 1898. The United States was not formally at war with Germany until late 1941, but prior to Pearl Harbor Roosevelt ordered the Navy to guard convoys to Great Britain and to open fire on submarines threatening the convoys. Since World War II presidents have sent forces without specific congressional authorization to Korea, Berlin, Vietnam, Lebanon, Grenada, Cuba, Libya—in fact, around the world.

Thus, from Washington's time on, by ordering troops into battle, the president has often decided when Americans will fight, and when they will not. When the cause has had political support, the president's use of this authority has been approved. Abraham Lincoln called up troops, spent money, set up a blockade, and fought the first few months of the Civil War without even calling Congress into session. More recently it became obvious that the president needed the power to respond to sudden attacks and to protect the rights and property of American citizens. The State Department described this enlarged mandate as follows:

> In the twentieth century the world has grown much smaller. An attack on a country far from its shores can impinge directly on the nation's security. . . . The Constitution leaves to the President the judgment to determine whether the circumstances of a particular armed attack are so urgent and the potential consequences so threatening to the security of the U.S. that he should act without formally consulting the Congress.[9]

But Congress became upset when it learned (several years after the fact) that in 1964 President Johnson won approval of his Vietnam initiatives on the basis of misleading information. In 1969 and 1970 a secret air war was waged in Cambodia with no formal congressional knowledge or authorization. The military also operated in Laos without formally notifying Congress. It was to prevent just such acts as these that the framers of the Constitution gave Congress the power to declare war; and many members of Congress believe that what happened in Indochina was the result of the White House's bypassing the constitutional requirements. But they also agree that presidential excesses came about because Congress either agreed with presidents or did nothing to stop them.

What the Johnson and Nixon war experiences also show is that at the beginning of hostilities, the country and Congress rally behind a president. As casualties mount and fighting continues, support usually falls off. In both Korea and Vietnam presidential failure to end the use of American ground forces led to increased political trouble. Eisenhower swept into power in 1952 saying, "I shall go to Korea" and thus arousing hope among voters that he would bring about an end to the Korean War. Nixon won in 1968 when Johnson was forced out over Vietnam. But even though Congress may have been misled during the Vietnam War, it enthusiastically supported the president and went along with his actions. Not until the war turned sour did senators and representatives begin to charge misrepresentation. Why, then, were they so easily talked into approving funds for the war? They continued to pass appropriations for it right up to April 1975. The more general lesson appears to be that the country and Congress (and the courts) tend to go along with a president's judgments about military action overseas.

There are additional reasons why no formal congressional declaration of war has been issued since 1941. During a state of war the president assumes certain legal prerogatives that Congress might not always be willing to grant. There are also international legal consequences of a formal declaration of war regarding foreign assets, the rights of neutrals, and so on, which our allies would not always be willing to recognize and which would be difficult to insist upon. Moreover, there is the psychological consequence of declaring war, compounded by the fact that, according to Article 2, Section 2, of the United Nations Charter, war is illegal except in self-defense.

EMERGENCY POWERS

From the early 1930s to the mid-1970s, Congress passed about 500 federal statutes collectively giving a president extraordinary powers. Once a state of emergency is declared, for example, a president can seize property, organize and control

---

Ratifying a Treaty

IN THE UNITED STATES
1. Treaty must be submitted to the Senate by President.
2. Senate leadership sends it to the Foreign Relations Committee and possibly the Armed Services and Intelligence Committees for action.
3. Foreign Relations Committee holds hearings.
4. Foreign Relations Committee votes on whether to recommend to the president that a treaty be ratified.
5. Recommendation then goes to the floor for full vote by the Senate. Approval requires a two-thirds vote.
6. President formally ratifies it. (Note that it is the president who ratifies a treaty, not the Senate.)

IN THE SOVIET UNION
Treaty is submitted to a full session of both houses of the Supreme Soviet, the Soviet parliament, and is ratified by a simple majority vote.

CHAPTER 16 / Congress and the President: The Politics of Shared Powers

the means of production, seize commodities, assign military forces abroad, declare martial law, and control all transportation and communications. A president might, in fact, control almost all aspects of citizens' lives. Abuses of presidential power under these emergency laws include detention of American citizens of Japanese ancestry during World War II, coverup of bombings in Cambodia, and directives to the FBI for illegal domestic surveillance and intelligence work.[10]

DIPLOMACY BY EXECUTIVE AGREEMENT

The growing use of **executive agreements,** as indicated in Table 16–2, shows their popularity with recent presidents. Before a president can ratify a **treaty,** two-thirds of the Senate must consent. But a president can enter into formal agreements with a foreign nation, by executive agreements, without senatorial approval. These agreements have been recognized as distinct from treaties since George Washington's day, and their use by the executive has been upheld by the courts. What has irked members of Congress throughout recent decades is that the Senate is often asked to approve international accords on only trivial matters. Critically important mutual-aid and military agreements have been arranged by the White House without its even informing Congress.

For example, while the Senate was approving treaties to preserve archeological artifacts in Mexico and maintain certain lights in the Red Sea, the president was using executive agreements to make vital decisions about United States presence in Vietnam, Laos, Korea, and Thailand. Several senators and others said these practices violated the Constitution's intent that Congress share in making foreign policy. And so the members of Congress began to look for ways to limit a president's executive agreement authority, as we shall discuss later.

Ironically, during the 1940s and 1950s conservative members of Congress tried to check the president's power to make executive agreements. In 1953 Senator John Bricker (R-Ohio) introduced a constitutional amendment that would have required Congress to approve all executive agreements. He was opposed by liberals, especially liberal political scientists and historians, who feared the Bricker amendment would reintroduce mindless **isolationism.** Bricker was opposed too by Eisenhower's secretary of state who called the amendment dangerous to our peace and security. In the wake of Vietnam, and especially during the Nixon administration, the shoe was on the other foot. The liberals, fearing an interventionist foreign policy, wanted to limit executive agreements.[11]

TABLE 16–2
Treaties and Executive Agreements, 1789–1986

PERIOD	TREATIES	EXECUTIVE AGREEMENTS	TOTALS
1789–1839	60	27	87
1840–1889	215	238	453
1890–1939	524	917	1441
1940–1973	364	6395	6759
1974–1979	102	2233	2335
1980–1985	101	1940	2041
	1366	11,750	13,116

Source: Congressional Research Service, Library of Congress.

CHAPTER 16 / Congress and the President: The Politics of Shared Powers

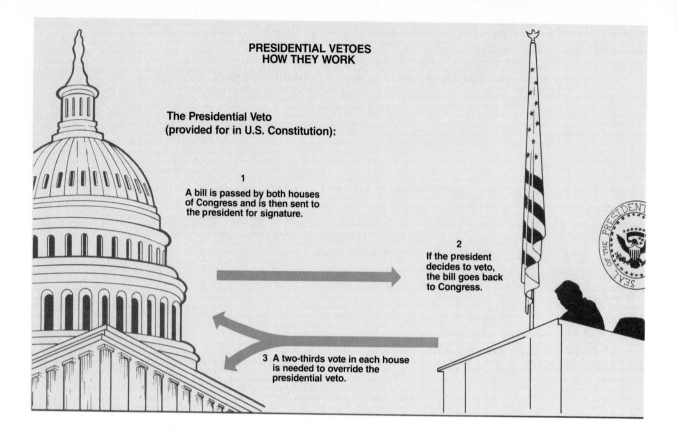

**PRESIDENTIAL VETOES
HOW THEY WORK**

**The Presidential Veto
(provided for in U.S. Constitution):**

1
A bill is passed by both houses of Congress and is then sent to the president for signature.

2
If the president decides to veto, the bill goes back to Congress.

3 A two-thirds vote in each house is needed to override the presidential veto.

GOVERNMENT BY PRESIDENTIAL VETO?

A president can veto a bill by returning it, together with specific objections, to the house in which it originated. Congress, by a two-thirds vote in each chamber, may then override the president's veto. Another variation of the veto is known as the **pocket veto.** In the ordinary course of events, if the president does not sign or veto a bill within ten weekdays after receiving it, it becomes law without the chief executive's signature. But if Congress adjourns within the ten days, the president—by taking no action—can kill the bill.

The veto's strength lies in the ordinary failure of Congress to get a two-thirds majority of both houses. Historically Congress has overridden less than 5 percent of presidents' vetoes. Yet a Congress that can repeatedly mobilize such a majority against a president can almost take command of the government. Such was the fate of Andrew Johnson in the late 1860s.

In ordinary times Congress will manipulate legislation to reduce the chance of a presidential veto. It can attach irrelevant but controversial provisions, called *riders*, to legislation the president considers vital. Presidents must either accept or reject the whole bill, for they do not have the power to delete individual items, that is, they do not have the **item veto.** In one appropriations bill, for example, law makers may combine badly needed funds for the armed forces with costly pork-barrel items. The president must take the bill as is or not at all.

For their part, presidents can also use the veto power in a positive way. They can announce that bills under consideration by Congress will be turned back unless certain changes are made. They can use the threat of vetoes against some bills Congress wants badly in exchange for other bills that they want. A presidential veto can also protect a national minority from hasty, unfair legislation

TABLE 16–3
Presidential Vetoes, 1789–1989

YEARS	PRESIDENT	REGULAR VETOES	OVER-RIDDEN	POCKET VETOES	TOTAL VETOES
1789–1797	George Washington	2	0	0	2
1797–1801	John Adams	0	0	0	0
1801–1809	Thomas Jefferson	0	0	0	0
1809–1817	James Madison	5	0	2	7
1817–1825	James Monroe	1	0	0	1
1825–1829	John Q. Adams	0	0	0	0
1829–1837	Andrew Jackson	5	0	7	12
1837–1841	Martin Van Buren	0	0	1	1
1841–1841	W. H. Harrison	0	0	0	0
1841–1845	John Tyler	6	1	4	10
1845–1849	James K. Polk	2	0	1	3
1849–1850	Zachary Taylor	0	0	0	0
1850–1853	Millard Fillmore	0	0	0	0
1853–1857	Franklin Pierce	9	5	0	9
1857–1861	James Buchanan	4	0	3	7
1861–1865	Abraham Lincoln	2	0	5	7
1865–1869	Andrew Johnson	21	15	8	29
1869–1877	Ulysses S. Grant	45	4	48	93
1877–1881	Rutherford B. Hayes	12	1	1	13
1881–1881	James A. Garfield	0	0	0	0
1881–1885	Chester A. Arthur	4	1	8	12
1885–1889	Grover Cleveland	304	2	110	414
1889–1893	Benjamin Harrison	19	1	25	44
1893–1897	Grover Cleveland	42	5	128	170
1897–1901	William McKinley	6	0	36	42
1901–1909	Theodore Roosevelt	42	1	40	82
1909–1913	William H. Taft	30	1	9	39
1913–1921	Woodrow Wilson	33	6	11	44
1921–1923	Warren G. Harding	5	0	1	6
1923–1929	Calvin Coolidge	20	4	30	50
1929–1933	Herbert Hoover	21	3	16	37
1933–1945	Franklin D. Roosevelt	372	9	263	635
1945–1953	Harry S. Truman	180	12	70	250
1953–1961	Dwight D. Eisenhower	73	2	108	181
1961–1963	John F. Kennedy	12	0	9	21
1963–1969	Lyndon B. Johnson	16	0	14	30
1969–1974	Richard M. Nixon[a]	26	7	17	43
1974–1977	Gerald R. Ford	48	12	18	66
1977–1981	Jimmy Carter	13	2	18	31
1981–1989	Ronald Reagan	39	9	39	78
1989–	George Bush	1	0	0	1
	TOTAL	**1,420**	**103**	**1,050**	**2,470**

Source: *Congressional Quarterly*, January 7, 1989, p. 7; and Louis Fisher, *The Politics of Shared Power* (Congressional Quarterly Press, 1981). Reprinted with permission from Congressional Quarterly, Inc.

[a] Two "pocket vetoes," overruled in the courts, are counted here as regular vetoes.

passed in the heat of the moment. But the veto is essentially a negative weapon of limited use to a president who has a positive program. For it is the *president* who is usually pressing for action.

The presidential veto power has stirred little controversy. Carter vetoed only thirty-one bills, Nixon vetoed forty-three, Ford, sixty-six, and Reagan, seventy-eight. Still, the occasional use of the pocket veto has stirred some criticism. Some members of Congress said our founders envisioned a more limited use of the veto. Other members of Congress, led by Senator Edward Kennedy, objected to Nixon's use of the pocket veto during short holiday recesses. The courts upheld Kennedy's contention that the pocket veto did not apply while Congress was in recess, but only when it had adjourned.

In fact, there is little that Congress can do when confronted with a presidential veto. It must either get enough votes to override the veto or modify the legislation and try again. As Table 16–3 suggests most presidents are able to make the vast majority of their regular vetoes stick. Congress, however, overrode 23 percent of Reagan's regular vetoes.[12]

Congress Reasserts Itself?

The end of the war in Vietnam, the 1974 impeachment hearings, and the resignation of President Nixon gave Congress new life.[13] It set about to recover lost authority and discover new ways to participate more fully in making national policy. Some of Congress's more notable efforts to reassert itself are examined next.

THE WAR OVER THE WAR POWERS

In 1973 Congress overrode Nixon's presidential veto and enacted the War Powers Resolution. Congress declared that henceforth the president can commit the armed forces of the United States only: (1) after a declaration of war by Congress; (2) by specific statutory authorization; or (3) in a national emergency created by an attack on the United States or its armed forces. After committing the armed forces under the third circumstance, the president is required to report to Congress within forty-eight hours. Unless Congress has declared war, the troop commitment will be ended within sixty days. The president is allowed another thirty days if the chief executive claims the safety of United States forces requires their continued use. A president is also obligated by this resolution to consult Congress "in every possible instance" before committing troops to battle. Moreover, at any time, by concurrent resolution *not subject to presidential veto*, Congress may direct the president to disengage such troops. Because of a 1983 court ruling, the question of whether Congress can remove the troops by concurrent resolution or legislative veto is now in doubt (see the discussion of the legislative veto later in this chapter).

Not everyone was pleased by the passage of the War Powers Resolution of 1973.[14] Nixon vetoed it because he said it encroached on presidential powers, but purists in Congress and elsewhere also say it is clearly unconstitutional, but for different reasons than Nixon's. They say it gives away a constitutional power plainly belonging to Congress—namely, the war making or war declaring power—for up to ninety days.

Still other observers, however much they may think this Resolution is defective, believe nonetheless that the War Powers legislation is of symbolic and institutional significance, because it reflected a new determination at the time in Congress. Presidents had been put on notice that commitment of American troops is subject to congressional approval. According to the Resolution, presidents have to persuade Congress and the nation that their actions are justified by the gravest of national emergencies.

Even so, all our recent presidents have opposed the War Powers Resolution as unwise and overly restrictive. They claim it gives Congress the right to force them to do what the Constitution says they do not have to do—withdraw American forces at some arbitrary moment. The War Powers Resolution has not been tested in the courts, and is unlikely to be, because it raises political questions judges generally seek to avoid.

How has the Resolution worked? Not well. Presidents have generally ignored it, although they have on a few occasions at least partially complied with some

The Troubled Life of the War Powers Resolution

When Congress passed the War Powers Resolution in 1973 it hoped the Resolution would pave the way for improved White House-Congressional cooperation when U.S. troops had to be used in emergency situations. In the years that followed, however, conflict and strain characterized these relations more than cooperation. Congress seldom believes it is properly consulted. Presidents Nixon, Ford, Carter, Reagan, and Bush all believed the War Powers Resolution was unconstitutional, impractical, or undesirable. All three branches have weakened the spirit of the War Powers Resolution. Presidents have often ignored it or complied with it in a minimal way. The Burger Court ruled on another measure that implicitly suggested a major provision of the Resolution was unconstitutional. Congress sometimes failed to follow through and use the Resolution. Time and again, when some members of Congress wanted to force the president into triggering the War Powers Resolution into effect, most members appeared overwhelmed by either the president or public support for the president's initiatives. In effect, Congress, thus far at least, has not been willing to force the hand of presidents in this area.

of the reporting or consultation features of the Resolution. Even leading members of Congress now question its effectiveness and say it needs to be revised, but they do not have the votes for the restructuring they see as necessary. These members know that Congress obviously will have a difficult time successfully arguing constitutional questions when U.S. troops are engaged in combat, especially when public opinion invariably sides with the president.

President Ford partially complied with the Resolution soon after it was passed when he sent Marines to free a merchant cargo ship that had been captured by Cambodians. Ford sent a report to Congress on the incident a few days later. In 1982 President Reagan reported to Congress, along the lines suggested in the Resolution, after he sent troops into Lebanon. Congress arranged a compromise favorable to the White House and sent it to Reagan for his signature. He made clear in a written statement that his compliance did not "cede any of the authority vested in me under the Constitution as President and as commander in chief. . . . Nor should my signing be viewed as any acknowledgement that the President's constitutional authority can be impermissibly infringed by statute."[15]

Ronald Reagan used the War Powers Resolution to send U.S. Navy ships to protect oil supplies under attack in the Persian Gulf.

In several other instances where he used the military in overseas operations, Reagan did not invoke the War Powers Resolution. He generally acted as though he did not need any authorization. How did Congress react? They never acted. Some members grumbled from time to time. Congressman Dante Fascell (D-Florida), chair of the House Foreign Affairs Committee, complained that Reagan was waltzing around the War Powers Resolution and was developing "a new way of going to war which totally bypasses the Constitution and its requirements that only Congress can declare war."[16] Reagan responded that he was acting in self-defense against terrorism. His State Department spokesperson said, "the deployment of anti-terrorist units . . . would seem to fall completely outside the scope of the [War Powers] Resolution."[17]

What then are the lessons of the War Powers Resolution of 1973? On the one hand, Congress reasserted itself and tried to get tough about unilateral presidential war making. On the other hand, presidents appeared to ignore it and viewed it merely as a nuisance. And now many members of Congess recognize that the approach was not effective and perhaps not wise.

Those who want to strengthen it and force presidents to comply with the letter of the Resolution don't have the votes to get their colleagues to confront the White House. Most Republicans (doubtless, in part because we have mainly had Republicans in the White House in recent years) would prefer to scrap the Resolution altogether, saying it has not worked, and it is not proper for Congress to undermine the hand of a president who necessarily, never mind what the Constitution may imply on the matter, has to act fast in today's military emergencies.

Another large group in Congress would like at some point to modify the War Powers Resolution to make it workable. This group of would-be reformers includes Senator Sam Nunn (D-Georgia) and Senator Robert Byrd (D-West Virginia). They would have Congress establish a special consultative group of about eighteen congressional leaders who would meet with the president before decisions are made committing American troops to situations where hostilities are probable. These reformers, believing that specific deadlines for completing military action are the wrong way to commit American troops or to force the hand of the commander in chief in military situations, would also remove the sixty and ninety day provisions from the War Powers Resolution. Nunn and the others say such automatic withdrawal provisions plainly give foreign governments and terrorist groups too much leverage for influencing United States policy options. They would rely instead on the Congress's power of the purse if presidents refuse to comply with the advice of Congress.

*Y*ou decide!

You are president. The director of the CIA and the head of the Joint Chiefs of Staff at the Pentagon advise you that a country in North Africa headed by an anti-American dictator has, with the help of the Soviet Union, assembled a team of scientists who are about to build an atomic bomb.

They also advise you that within that country a group who oppose the head of state believe that if they are given some weapons they can overthrow the government and establish one that would be friendly to the United States, would be more democratic, and would pledge not to introduce atomic weapons into the Middle East.

Many members of Congress oppose covert actions by the CIA. Should you, would you, authorize the CIA to assist the rebels in a covert way?

(Answer/Discussion is on page 421.)

But no events in recent years have provided the occasion for Congress to focus on revising the War Powers Resolution. Perhaps presidents will just go on ignoring it, and it will continue to atrophy in its nonuse.[18] President Bush and his advisors continue to prefer informal consultation with congressional leaders, as they did during the Panama turmoil in 1989. Bush opposes any restructuring of the War Powers Resolution and insists that briefings and compromises are the appropriate approach. Most members of Congress are inclined to agree. Some skeptical members respond, however, that a briefing is not consultation. After-the-fact consultation, they add, is really no consultation at all.

CURBING THE EMERGENCY POWERS

The National Emergencies Act of 1976 terminated, as of 1978, the extensive powers and authorities possessed by the president as a result of the continuing state of emergency in which the nation had been since the mid-1930s. It also established authority for the declaration of future emergencies in a manner that clearly defines the powers of the president and provides for regular congressional review. The act also calls upon presidents to inform Congress in advance and to identify those laws they plan to use when declaring a national emergency. A state of emergency so declared would automatically end after six months. But Congress must review the declaration of emergency powers at least every six months.

Congress hopes this legislation will ensure that emergency powers can be utilized only when legitimate emergencies actually exist, and then only with the safeguard of legislative review. As one senator reported to Congress: "Reliance on emergency authority, intended for use in crisis situations, would no longer be available in non-crisis situations. At a time when governments throughout the world are turning with increasing desperation to an all-powerful executive, this legislation is designed to insure that the United States travels a road marked by carefully constructed legal safeguards."[19]

CONGRESS AND THE INTELLIGENCE AGENCIES

For months during the summer of 1987, a joint congressional committee questioned Lt. Colonel Oliver North about White House involvement in evading congressional limits on action in Nicaragua.

Presidents have also been charged with abusing the intelligence and spying agencies. The Central Intelligence Agency (CIA) was established in 1947, when the threat of "world communism" led to a vast number of national security efforts. When the CIA was established, Congress recognized the dangers to a free society inherent in such a secret organization. Hence, it was stipulated that the CIA *was not to engage in any police work or to perform operations within the United States.*

From 1947 to the mid-1970s, no area of national policy making was more removed from Congress than CIA operations. In many instances Congress acted as if it really did not want to know what was going on. Said one senator: "It is not a question of reluctance on the part of CIA officials to speak to us. Instead it is a question of our reluctance, if you will, to seek information and knowledge on subjects which I personally, as a Member of Congress and as a citizen, would rather not have."[20] There is much evidence that both Congress and the White House were lax in supervising intelligence activities. By 1973, the CIA was accused of plotting assassinations, experimenting with mind-altering drugs, carrying out extensive foreign paramilitary operations, and, most important, spying on American citizens during the Watergate era.

Congress has tried to reassert control over the CIA. It now requires the Agency to report to two committees—the House and the Senate oversight committees—any plans for clandestine operations. In 1976, in an unprecedented exercise of power, Congress amended the Defense Appropriations Bill to terminate American covert intervention in Angola.

Presidents have criticized Congress for weakening the CIA—for going too far in making covert operations too difficult. President Carter especially pressed this case during the Iranian and Afghanistan crises of 1980. The Reagan administration gave to the CIA a new era of prominence and enhanced powers; its coordinating role in providing American assistance to the Nicaraguan contras is perhaps the most striking example.

Former CIA Director Stansfield Turner argues that congressional oversight has been useful. It forces, he contends, intelligence officers to exercise greater judiciousness and to maintain a healthy sense of the national temper. He also believes that congressional oversight strengthens the hand of the CIA director in controlling what has always been a notoriously independent agency.[21] On balance many observers conclude that for all the talk of greater congressional control, the CIA and the president have not been seriously hampered in carrying out what they deem necessary.[22]

After the Iran-contra scandals, Congress considered a variety of proposals to place additional curbs on the CIA. None became law. President Bush, a former director of the CIA, is not likely to take kindly to expanded congressional controls over it, yet he has promised to work with congressional leaders to keep them informed about CIA covert activities, as he is required to do under existing law. As one senator put it, he expects Bush will regularly comply with the spirit of the law, and that's fine. What the Senate does not want, the senator added, "is a return to the days when the administration says that 'timely notice' means whatever the president says it means."[23]

THE 1974 CONGRESSIONAL BUDGET AND IMPOUNDMENT CONTROL ACT

During the Nixon administration, some members of Congress used to joke that ours was a system of checks and balances all right: Congress wrote the checks and the White House kept the balance. They were referring to President Nixon's frequent use of the powers to impound funds appropriated by Congress.

By *impounding* funds a president forbids an executive branch agency to spend money even though it has been appropriated by Congress. **Impoundment** can take many forms. It may be necessary to accommodate a change in events (if a war ends) or to alter a managerial approach (to carry out a project more efficiently). Before Nixon, impoundments were infrequent and usually temporary; generally they involved small amounts of money. Nixon stretched the use of impoundment to new lengths. He claimed that the Democratic Congress was spending too much and causing huge deficits. Congress responded that Nixon was using impoundment to set policy and that he was violating the Constitution, which states: "No money shall be drawn from the Treasury, but in consequence of appropriations made by law." Congress took this to mean it had the final say in fiscal policy making. But Congress not only complained; it acted as well: It passed the 1974 Congressional Budget and Impoundment Control Act.

By this act Congress was trying to prevent presidential impoundments. It was also responding to the fact that since the days of FDR its influence over federal spending had diminished, while that of the Office of Management and Budget in the executive office of the president had increased. With no budget system of its own—only many separate actions and decisions—Congress had be-

"I want you to draft the bill with all your usual precision and flair. Explain its purposes, justify its expenditures, emphasize how it fits the broad aims of democratic progress. And one other thing: Can you make it sound like a tax cut?"

Drawing by Ed Fisher; © 1979 The New Yorker Magazine, Inc.

come dependent on the president's budget proposals. Members of Congress grew to appreciate, if not respect, the old saying: The one who controls the purse has the power.

The 1974 act created a permanent budget committee for each chamber of Congress, and a Congressional Budget Office (CBO). It provides budgetary and fiscal experts and computer services and gives Congress technical assistance in dealing with the president's proposals. Some members of Congress hoped the CBO would provide hard, practical data to guide the drafting of spending legislation. Others saw it as a potential "think tank" that might propose standards for spending and national priorities. In fact, the CBO is most frequently used to provide routine cost estimates of spending and tax bills and to keep track of the overall budget level.

Optimists hoped this budget reform act would force Congress into more systematic and timely action on budgetary legislation. They hoped, too, it would tie separate spending decisions in with fiscal policy objectives. Its budgetary time-table gives Congress three additional months to consider the president's recommendations. By May 15 of each year, Congress adopts a tentative budget that sets target totals for spending and taxes. These targets serve as guides for the committees considering detailed appropriations measures. By September 15 Congress is supposed to adopt a second resolution that either affirms or revises the earlier targets. If necessary to meet the final budget totals, this resolution must also dictate any changes in expenditures and revenues.[24]

How has the "reformed" budget process worked? The quality of information produced by the CBO has improved congressional deliberation on the budget; the new budget committees in each house have worked reasonably well and the budget resolutions have provided a vehicle for certain helpful debates on key economic issues. But overall the new budgetary process has not diminished the budgetary powers of the president. In fact, President Reagan dramatically used the "reconciliation" aspect of the process to push through major budget cuts. Although perfectly legal, this presidential use of the act was unanticipated by those who wrote it. The effect was to give Reagan, backed by majorities in both houses of Congress, an influence over the budget process that no president had exercised before. And it was contrary to what the writers of the act intended; indeed it was the very kind of presidential assertiveness Congress had hoped to limit. Reagan, however, enjoyed less success in controlling the budget after this remarkable first-year experience. Budget process politics became highly partisan in both houses of Congress, and legislative-executive budget relations often became strained.

The budgetary reforms of the 1970s have not done the job. Some progress has been made, but surely the fondest hopes of the reformers have not been achieved. Congress still fails to apply intelligent cuts to the "sacred cows" of welfare, subsidy, and defense spending. Far too much confusion still surrounds the budgetary process. The whole point of this new budget process was to force Congress to make choices, to put together in one place the spending claims and the revenues, and to decide what it wants. Many people believe the problem is structural and not the result of personal faults of members of Congress. Congress reflects local pressures, presidents reflect national pressures. All this is reflected in the budget process. Congress may well have to restructure itself to strengthen places where overall consensus can be built. But this would mean weakening subcommittees and curbing the recent tendencies to disperse power—something Congress is unlikely to do. If it cannot do this, Congress will very likely have to respond to the choices and priorities set by presidents.[25]

The impoundment control provisions of this new 1974 law have worked only slightly better than the budgetary process provisions. The 1974 Congressional Budget and Impoundment Act repealed the 1921 language used by Nixon to justify his impoundments. It also stipulated two new procedures—*rescissions* and *deferrals*—by which a president, at least temporarily, can override appropriations decisions or delay spending. A president may propose to cancel, or rescind, enacted appropriations or subsections of a larger appropriations bill, but unless Congress agrees (with a majority vote in both houses) to the rescission within forty-five days, the money must be spent by the executive branch.

All our recent presidents have used this provision, which has cut several billions from the budget, and Congress has usually gone along with the presidential suggestions for rescission. Some have complained, however, that this provision creates too much paperwork. Reports need to be sent to Congress even when a few thousand dollars are not spent for simple managerial and efficiency purposes. Others complain about the vagueness of the law. Still, this part of the law has reclaimed some of the diminished power of the purse for Congress.

The second provision, permitting the deferral of spending by the executive, has caused considerable confusion. According to the law, the president may propose to defer spending funds already appropriated for up to a year. The law only requires that the executive notify Congress of these deferrals and that new notifications be filed with Congress to continue a deferral into a second year. The law permits either the Senate or the House to overturn a deferral. But in 1983 the Supreme Court invalidated what was called "legislative vetoes" and in effect said, although in a broader ruling, that the only way to counter a president's deferral of funds was to pass a law doing so.

Before 1986 President Reagan, until then the only president to be affected by the 1983 Supreme Court ruling, was able to defer some spending and work out informal agreements with Congress to make the system work in a reasonably acceptable manner. At this point, however, Reagan and his new budget director began using the deferral more frequently and for larger spending projects. Both Congress and the federal courts protested that this was a violation of the law. When a federal district court ruled that the White House was wrong to halt an expenditure of more than $5 billion for housing and other matters, it in effect affirmed Congress's authority to shape federal spending. Meanwhile, some members of Congress proposed the repeal of the entire deferral provision, saying the deferral process is "a mess." But little change is expected.

By the 1990s national concern had turned from fears about the president's failure to spend money appropriated by Congress to fears that Congress would appropriate too much money. There seems to be little likelihood that Congress will propose an **item veto** to strengthen presidential powers to set aside congressional appropriations, and a Democratic Congress is not likely to enhance President Bush's powers. Nonetheless, these days questions are more likely to be raised about how to strengthen presidential control over spending rather than how to limit such authority.

BUDGET REFORM REVISITED: GRAMM–RUDMAN–HOLLINGS

After several years in which virtually no one believed the budget process had worked well, Congress, with White House support, voted to approve the Balanced Budget and Emergency Deficit Reduction Act of 1985 (popularly known by the names of its sponsors in the U.S. Senate, Gramm, Rudman, and Hollings). After years of being unable to cure the problem of deficit spending, Congress opted for what many call radical surgery. This new legislation sets maximum allowable deficit levels on a declining basis from 1986 to 1991, when the deficit was supposed to be at zero; Congress later set 1993 as the date to be at zero. The reduction of deficits was intended to be achieved through cancellation of budget authority and actual spending. An initial version of the bill had given the comptroller general of the General Accounting Office the final word in ordering the president to trim spending and reduce deficits. But a 1986 Supreme Court ruling (*Bowsher* v *Synar*, 478 U.S. 714) said that would violate the separation of powers doctrine because the comptroller general was in effect an officer of the Congress (because a vote of Congress could terminate or remove that official). Congress then reverted to a fallback position that required it to pass a resolution in both houses and send it to the president to order spending cuts. Certain spending, such as for Social Security or interest on the national debt, is exempt from this process but almost all domestic and military spending is subject to these cuts.

Even the sponsors of this budget-balancing measure called it a "bad idea whose time had come." But they insisted that it was needed to bring a dose of reality that would force hard choices about domestic spending, military spending, and taxes. It is far preferable, proponents argued, than the processes of the previous decade, during which no choices were made and annual deficits rose to over $200 billion and the national debt to over $1 trillion.

Critics of the Gramm–Rudman–Hollings act called it the worst form of congressional posturing and feared that it would bring about an unprecedented shift of power from the legislative to the executive branch. "With this additional power," wrote Senator Bill Bradley (D-New Jersey), a president, "if he plays hard ball, could dismantle the nondefense portion of the budget and wreak havoc with America's poor."[26] Others have noted other aspects of this measure that transfer power to the executive. For example, the proposal requires the president to bring future federal budgets into line with the deficit-reduction schedule by reducing, or even eliminating, cost-of-living allowances and similar automatic spending increases previously enacted in entitlement programs. But to allow a president to suspend such automatic increases or withhold other already appropriated funds is to grant to the White House the unilateral authority to limit or even extinguish whatever legal rights the recipients had to these increased payments.

In the long run, the Gramm–Rudman–Hollings approach to budgeting appears to limit Congress's ability to perform some of its critical policy clarification functions. This type of approach once again forces Congress to yield some of its authority to the executive in hopes of resolving our deficit problem. In the end Congress and the White House will doubtless have to make further cuts in spending as well as raise new revenues (formerly known as taxes).

CONFIRMATION POLITICS

The framers of the Constitution regarded the confirmation process and its advice and consent by the Senate as a check on executive power. Alexander Hamilton viewed it as a way for Congress to prevent the appointment of "unfit characters." Even today, the Senate and the president often struggle over control of top personnel in the executive and judicial branches. The Constitution leaves the question somewhat ambiguous: "The President . . . shall nominate, and by and with the advice and consent of the Senate, shall appoint Ambassadors, other public Ministers and Consuls, Judges of the Supreme Court, all other officers of the United States. . . ." Presidents, however, have never enjoyed exclusive control over hiring

CHAPTER 16 / *Congress and the President: The Politics of Shared Powers*

The Senate asserted itself to deny confirmation of Judge Robert Bork to the Supreme Court, despite character witnesses such as former President Gerald Ford and Senator Robert Dole. They later accepted Anthony Kennedy, shown here with the Court's only female member, Justice Sandra Day O'Connor.

and firing in the executive branch. The Senate jealously guards its right to confirm or reject major appointments; during the period of congressional government after the Civil War, presidents had to struggle to keep their power to appoint and dismiss. But for most of the twentieth century, presidents have gained a reasonable amount of control over top appointments. This has happened in part because public administration experts warned that a chief executive cannot otherwise be held accountable.

In recent years, however, the Senate has taken a somewhat tougher stand on presidential appointments. Senators are especially concerned about potential conflicts of interest. Time spent evaluating and screening presidential nominations has increased. "Our tolerance for mediocrity and lack of independence from economic interests is rapidly coming to an end," said one senator. Another summed it up this way: "Surely, we have learned that one item the government is short on is credibility." Screening has become somewhat tighter; all recent presidents have had several high-level appointees turned down. Both Bush and Reagan lost several potential nominees because of conflict-of-interest problems, and others were denied confirmation because of their policy views.

Perhaps the most celebrated recent rejection of a nominee occurred in 1989 when John Tower, President Bush's choice for Secretary of Defense, was turned down by a vote of 53 to 47. Tower, a prominent former senator, was accused of a drinking problem and having perhaps a too cozy tie to several defense contractors. Tower denied the charges, promised not to drink any kind of liquor if he was confirmed, but still failed to win confirmation. He was the first cabinet nominee to be rejected since 1959.

The Senate's role in the confirmation process was never intended to eliminate politics but rather to use politics as a safeguard. Some conservatives in recent years object that the Senate has rejected occasional nominees because of their political beliefs and thus interfered with the executive power of presidents. In such instances, so this complaint goes, the Senate's decision is not a reflection of the fitness of a nominee but rather of the political strength of the president.

Despite the importance of this constitutional power, the Senate has never established clear guidelines or a systematic process for screening presidential nominees. The Senate's participation during the past twenty-five years has become more thorough, more independent, and even somewhat more consistent. "Unfortunately, the process has also become more tedious, time-consuming, and intrusive for the nominees," according to one recent study. "For some, this price is too high, particularly in conjunction with the requirements of the Ethics in Government

President Bush "stood by his man" John Tower, even after damaging accusations in the confirmation hearings for his nomination as Secretary of Defense.

Act. For others, the process is annoying and distasteful but not enough of a roadblock to prevent them from going forward."[27]

To appoint someone to a *federal* position in a *state* (a U.S. attorney, for example), a president needs the approval of the senators from the state, especially if these senators are members of the president's party and that party controls the Senate. They need that approval because of a practice known as **senatorial courtesy:** the willingness of the Senate to confirm presidential appointments only if they are not "personally obnoxious"—that is, politically objectionable—to the senators from the state. Thus, for nearly all district court judgeships, many appellate court judgeships, and a variety of other positions, senators can exercise what is in fact a veto. This veto can be overridden only with great difficulty. Further, it is usually exercised in secret and is subject to little accountability. But the patronage is so important to senators that senatorial courtesy is likely to continue.

The confirmation provisions in the Constitution have fulfilled most of the intentions of the founders. The Senate has been able to use its power to reject unqualified nominees. It has sometimes also been able to prevent those with conflicts of interest from taking office. In addition, senators have been able to use the confirmation process to make their views known to prospective executive officials. Indeed, the very existence of the confirmation process deters presidents from appointing weak, questionable, or "unfit characters." Yet by and large presidents have still been able to appoint the people they want to important positions. During one session of Congress today, presidents regularly submit as many as 5000 civilian and over 100,000 military nominations for Senate confirmation.

THE LEGISLATIVE VETO

As yet another means of trying to strengthen itself as it struggled with the presidency, Congress in the 1970s and early 1980s often turned to the **legislative veto.** Using this device Congress would draft a law broadly but incorporate a provision allowing it to review the executive branch's implementation of the law. The legislative veto could be put into effect by a majority vote of one house, by both houses, or sometimes even by a single congressional committee, depending on how the law was written.

Whatever the form, the legislative veto allowed Congress to delegate general power and then take it away without having to secure presidential approval. In effect, it permitted Congress to legislate without exposing its handiwork to a presidential veto, as the framers intended. The Constitution stipulates that every bill, resolution, or vote for which the agreement of the Senate and the House of Representatives may be necessary shall be presented to the president for approval or veto. Joint resolutions were regularly submitted to the president; not so concurrent resolutions. In the past this made little difference, because concurrent or simple one-house resolutions were mainly used to express congressional opinion and had no force of law.

But the legislative veto was also used to keep presidents in check. Arms sales had to be submitted to Congress for its scrutiny. Presidential use of military troops abroad had to be reported to Congress and was subject to recall by unilateral congressional action. In short, upset by presidents who had either lied to or ignored Congress, a reassertive legislature attempted to use the legislative veto to recapture some of its authority.

In 1932, Congress passed a resolution allowing President Herbert Hoover limited authority to reorganize the executive branch agencies. The resolution stipulated that the president's proposals would not be put into effect for ninety days, during which time either house of Congress, by a simple resolution, could veto the proposal. For the next fifty-one years, the legislative veto became a standard practice.[28] Congress usually required sixty to ninety days in which to consider a proposed regulation. During that time either house could veto the regulation by passing a resolution. However, Congress sometimes simply required legislative approval *before* a regulation took effect.

Between 1932 and mid-1983 at least 210 pieces of legislation carried some form of legislative veto. About half of these were enacted between 1973 and 1983. The device was used to ensure that bureaucratic regulations conformed to congressional intentions. This was important to Congress because of the rapid increase of such regulations, which often have the same or nearly the same force as laws. In any given year in the late 1970s or early 1980s, Congress might have passed a few hundred public laws; but the administrators in about seventy executive branch agencies were responsible for twenty times as many regulations.

Then in June 1983 Chief Justice Warren Burger—speaking for a Supreme Court majority in a 7 to 2 decision (*INS* v. *Chadha*)—said that to maintain the separation of powers, the carefully defined limits on the power of each branch must not be eroded. The legislative veto was found unconstitutional. Said Burger: "With all the obvious flaws . . . we have not yet found a better way to preserve freedom than by making the exercise of power subject to the carefully crafted restraints spelled out in the Constitution."[29] In effect, the Court told Congress that to obtain more influence over an agency or the presidency, Congress should pass a law that accomplished this explicitly. In the words of dissenting Justice Byron White, the Court's decision "strikes down in one fell swoop provisions in more laws enacted by Congress than the Court has cumulatively invalidated in its history."

In this historic decision, the Court tried to curb a weapon that Congress had sometimes used effectively to intimidate executive branch officials. Clearly, the existence of the legislative veto stimulated compromise and understandings between executive and legislative officials. Some observers viewed the decision as just one in a long series of Supreme Court rulings that generally approve of and encourage an assertive and increasingly powerful presidency.

The long-range effect of this decision is unclear. Congress has been a little more explicit about the policy directions it sets. It is also exercising some options that make it clear to executive departments that if congressional committees are displeased by the actions of the departmental officials, congressional retribution in the form of reduced appropriations is likely. Congress has found ways to exercise the functional equivalent of a legislative veto.[30] By one estimate nearly 150 legislative vetoes have been signed into law since 1983. Further, there have been scores of informal agreements between the branches, such as the Bush/Congress agreement on aid to the Nicaraguan rebels.

These legislative vetoes and similar agreements survive, despite the Court's ruling, because they serve a purpose: They give the executive branch the flexibility it desires and that Congress might otherwise not provide, while allowing the Congress to retain a certain amount of ongoing control. "The legislative veto procedure represented a classic quid pro quo," says Louis Fisher of the Library of Congress. "It attempted to reconcile the interests of both branches: the desire of [executive] agencies for greater discretionary authority and the need of Congress to maintain control short of passing another public law."[31] Hence, legislative vetoes or agreements very similar to them are likely to be with us for the near future.

Constraints on the President: Post-Watergate Congressional Assertiveness

War Powers Resolution of 1973

Redefinition of national emergency powers

Curbs on CIA and FBI

1974 Congressional Budget and Impoundment Act

Slightly better use of the confirmation hearing process

Frequent use of legislative vetoes (until Supreme Court ruled them unconstitutional in 1983)

Growth of congressional staffs and research agencies

Curbs on executive agreements

Somewhat better oversight of executive branch program implementation

Greater congressional involvement in national security policy and arms trade deals

Establishment of independent counsels to investigate illegal or unethical behavior among top executive branch officials.

OTHER ACTIONS

Congress has also become more involved in general foreign policy. Shaking off years of inertia, Congress imposed a cutoff of aid to Vietnam and a bombing halt in Cambodia. As of 1972 it required the secretary of state to submit to Congress the final texts of executive agreements. It also restrained the Ford administration from getting involved in Angola. This was clearly a case of Congress's imposing its goals on the executive. Congress has also demanded, and won, a greater role in arms sales abroad and in determining U.S. involvement in Lebanon, Central America, and the Caribbean.

In addition, individual members of Congress are likely to travel around the world to international trouble spots, to conduct their own investigations and sometimes even their own negotiations. Presidents Ford, Carter, Reagan, and Bush became increasingly bothered by such second-guessing and attempts by Congress to interfere with presidential foreign policy making.[32] These and other actions were all efforts by Congress to reclaim its lost authority and to respond to a public that seemed to want power shared in a way that placed Congress on a more equal footing than had been the case under Presidents Johnson and Nixon.

The struggle between Congress—especially the Senate—and the president over the control of foreign policy making has even extended to attempts by the Senate to restrict a president's interpretation of a treaty. Although we might expect that the Senate and the president would want to provide maximum flexibility for the United States vis-à-vis other nations, in recent years the Senate has been more interested in pinning down the White House. When President Reagan construed the 1972 Antiballistic Missile Treaty with the Soviet Union as not banning tests of the Strategic Defense Initiative (SDI) antimissile defense system, some senators during the treaty ratification process tried to attach reservations to the INF (intermediate range nuclear force) missile treaty that would require Senate approval of any new interpretation of that treaty by the United States.

Not every effort by Congress has succeeded; nor has every effort guaranteed Congress a better or more creative role. Indeed, many well-intentioned reforms that sought to reclaim authority for the national legislature were merely congressional victories that stopped or inhibited presidents from carrying out their policy plans. Rarely did the reforms of the 1970s ensure that Congress would formulate better policy alternatives; more typically it meant that Congress could delay or modify what a president sought to achieve. And sometimes, it merely brought about a deadlock or stalemate.

AN ITEM VETO FOR THE PRESIDENT?

George Bush and several other presidents have called for a constitutional amendment permitting presidents to have **item veto** power—the right to veto particular subsections or items within major appropriations bills passed by Congress. Presidents can of course veto an entire bill, but they complain this is not very practical, especially just before a new fiscal year when the government needs funds to operate.

The item veto would work like this: Following a review of a major appropriations bill sent from Congress for presidential signature, the president might approve perhaps 94 percent of the spending, but object to the remaining 6 percent as wasteful, unnecessary, or inflationary. Or the president might just disagree with this type of spending. In any event, the White House would send back only those objectionable items to the two houses of Congress. Congress would have the right, according to most of the proposed item veto amendments, to override the president's veto of these items by the same two-thirds vote required to override a general presidential veto.

One of the major reasons advanced in support of the item veto is that presidents, although responsible for the budget and accountable for budget deficits, do not have adequate authority to fight deficit spending. If they had the item veto, supporters say, they could delete waste and "pork-barrel" spending primarily intended to help members of Congress win reelection. Pork-barrel items are often added to necessary appropriations bills at the last minute, and it is tough for other members of Congress to keep all such measures from sneaking into major appropriations bills. If the president could veto these items, they would usually not win two-thirds support in both chambers of Congress. Hence, waste would be reduced.

Recent presidents also say they need the item veto because Congress often passes crucial appropriations measures very near the end of congressional sessions. To veto an entire bill would force the government to shut down, and this is impossible. Also, clever legislators often add their own parochial measures to legislation the White House has struggled to win, thus making it unlikely that a president would dare veto the entire package.

Proponents note that forty-three state governors have the item-veto power, and it has worked well in the states. They also point out, correctly, that the American people in nearly every survey on this proposal favor giving this additional authority to presidents.

But perhaps the most compelling reason to support the item veto is the growing concern about the soaring federal debt and the seemingly never-ending annual deficits. Congress has the ultimate authority over the power of the purse but has not been able to curb enough spending, raise enough revenues, or bring about the proper balance to put our economic house in order. If Congress has acted irresponsibly and if presidents, for whatever reason, are generally unable to wield the general veto power, then why not, goes the argument, give the president this additional clout? For someone, somewhere, somehow has to provide deficit-slashing leadership.

Congress, not surprisingly, remains unconvinced. Most members of Congress see the item veto as an attempt by presidents to diminish the powers of the Congress and add further powers to the presidency. Many opponents of the item veto say it would end even the pretense of Congress acting as a coequal branch of government. In effect, they say, giving this power to the White House would allow presidents and their budget aides to "edit" the whole budget and rewrite appropriations legislation on a line-by-line basis.

Giving presidents the item veto could lead to undesirable levels of pressure tactics and political retribution. Imagine a president who needs just a few more votes for a prized space defense system or a war on poverty, and just a few holdouts remain. The White House could easily examine present or pending projects in the hold-out legislators' districts and then suggest that these members vote for the president's proposals in order to ensure that their own projects escape a possible item veto. Senior members in Congress have witnessed such high-pressure tactics when a Lyndon Johnson or a Ronald Reagan tried to "twist their arms" or threatened to use the existing general veto power. It doesn't take much imagination, they say, to consider how much more persuasive a president would be if such calls were buttressed with a veto stamp over individual projects and activities within their home states and districts.

Further, item veto critics say, a president already has a number of powers to help balance the budget and fight deficits. Since it is the president who prepares the budget, a president who really wants a balanced budget should produce one in the first place. Presidents also have the right, and ought to exercise it more regularly, to veto certain appropriations bills entirely. They also have the various options of sending measures back to Congress for rescission and deferral. Finally, they have the splendid power of the "bully pulpit," and this too can be used to keep Congress honest when it comes to wasteful spending.

Opponents also object to the item veto because they view it as an easy and convenient escape from the difficult political choices our elected officials must make. The problems the item veto supposedly addresses are more political and substantive than they are structural or constitutional. Congress and presidents should have the will to curb unneeded spending and to raise taxes and balance the budget. And they should be held accountable when they fail in these responsibilities. The item veto might make Congress even more irresponsible than it may already be by encouraging it to pass the buck even more often to the White House. At the same time, many people believe the item veto would provide more power than an effective president needs—and more power than an imperial or misguided president should have.[33]

Although there are heated views on both sides of this debate and we are likely to hear future presidents yearn for this power, we predict Congress won't budge from its present position for the many reasons we have just cited.

The President and Congress: The Continuing Struggle

Most informed observers now believe that Congress did not really gain back many of its alleged lost powers, and they are skeptical of Congress's ability to match the advantages of the presidency for setting the long-term policy direction of the nation. At least in his first term, Ronald Reagan demonstrated that a popular president who knew what he wanted to do could not only tremendously influence the national policy agenda but could also win considerable cooperation from the Congress.

Even before Reagan won the 1980 presidential election, public support for a restrengthened presidency was growing. Some people believed Congress (and the press) had overreacted to both Vietnam and Nixon's antics and abuses of power. Others believed Congress was correct to try to win back some of its powers, but felt it had gone a bit too far. Others could understand what Congress was doing, but soon realized that our system functions best when a strong positive president is willing to play a key role initiating legislative and budgetary proposals.

The American public may have lost confidence in its leaders, but it had not lost hope in the efficacy of strong, purposive leadership. Whether or not people believed in Ronald Reagan's policy priorities, many supported his view that the country needed a strong president who would strengthen the presidency and make the office a more vital center of national policy than it had been in the years immediately following the Watergate scandals.

A central question during this period was whether, in the wake of a somewhat diminished presidency, the Congress could furnish the necessary leadership to govern the country. Most people, including many members of Congress, did not think Congress could play that role. The routine answer now is that the United States needs a presidency of substantial power if we are to solve the trade, deficit, productivity, and other economic and national security problems we currently face. We live in a continuous state of emergency; instant terrorism and especially nuclear warfare can destroy our country. In addition, global competition of almost every sort highlights the need for swift and sure leadership, and a certain amount of efficiency and unity in our government. Many people realize too that weakening the presidency may, as often as not, strengthen the vast federal bureaucracy more than strengthen Congress.

It is clear today, far more than it was ten years or so ago, that the congressional reassertion efforts of the 1970s were more a groping and often unsystematic, if well-intentioned, attempt by Congress to be taken seriously than an effort to weaken the presidency. It did not take long for close observers to appreciate that when a president is unable to exercise authority and leadership, no one else is able to supply comparable purpose and initiative. Not only did we reaffirm the pre-Watergate view that history has shown the presidency to be the most effective instrument for innovation, experimentation, and progress, but a majority of Americans concurred that to the extent the country is governable on a national basis, it is governed from the White House by a president and his top advisers in cooperation with the Congress.

Reagan infused the presidency with more energy and effectiveness. He came to office with self-confidence, optimism, and a personal style that celebrated the promise of American success and achievements. He fully appreciated the symbolic and morale-building functions of the modern presidency. He also knew the power of ideas and themes, and he cleverly focused both his own energies and the attention of the nation on four or five fresh policy initiatives (such as tax cuts and tax reform, increased military spending, and reductions in what he claimed were unnecessary federal regulations). He also capitalized on his perceived landslide victory and claimed he had a mandate to alter national priorities. He used his appointment powers wisely as well.

The Imperial Congress Argument

Friends of Ronald Reagan and George Bush sometimes argue it is not an imperial presidency but rather an imperial Congress we should worry about. They say that since the president is the only elected officeholder in the nation answerable to the nation as a whole, the president is uniquely qualified to pursue foreign policy on behalf of the entire nation. Stretching what the framers of the Constitution actually said, those concerned about a too powerful Congress say the founders saw the wisdom of giving responsibility for foreign policy to the chief executive because Congress is poorly suited to *micromanage* U.S. foreign policy. (Micromanage, a favorite word of those who hold this point of view, is the ability to handle administrative or diplomatic details as opposed to general policy.) Because Congress's 535 members are too tied to parochial interests, the argument goes, Congress is too slow, too unwieldy, and too easily captured by either sectional interests or political-action committees when it tries to carry out what are properly executive functions. Congress, critics add, is more like a lawyer in representing its special clients, than it is like a judge, weighing the larger picture and the longer-term interests of the entire nation.[34]

Some proponents of the imperial Congress view contend that Congress needlessly embarrassed President Reagan and Oliver North by holding extensive hearings about the Iran-contra affair. They condemn Congress for legislating too many restrictions on foreign policy and arms sales. They believe too that presidents such as Bush should be permitted the nominees of their choice, such as John

Congress did not buy Richard Nixon's claim that "When the president does it, that means it is not illegal." Following congressional hearings on his involvement in the Watergate scandal, Nixon resigned.

Tower for the Secretary of Defense. After all, they say, the president won the national election and has the power of appointment and nomination. Congress should reject nominees only if they are unfit for the office, not because of differing policy or ideological views.

This school of thought also believes there is no need for independent counsels or special prosecutors. Let the president be judged by history—or by the voters at the next election. If a president does something unconstitutional, Congress has the power to impeach and convict a president. But if this is not the case, Congress should not interfere with presidents who are trying to lead, govern, and negotiate on behalf of the country. In short, Congress should seek to help rather than hinder our presidents. Better, they say, to follow the steady leadership of the president than the ever-changing whims of Congress.

There is much to be said for this argument, and it is a splendid counterpoint to the excesses of the imperial presidency argument. But what is missing in the imperial Congress literature is that a too powerful presidency can also pose dangers to the kind of society and the kind of government we want. We are bothered, and rightly so, when an occasional president such as Richard Nixon says: "When the president does it, that means it is not illegal." We are concerned as well that shortcuts that bypass the checks and balances of our constitutional system, and excessive secrecy by those who serve the president, do not, in the long run, strengthen the presidency. Such evasions usually weaken the presidency and the constitutional system of government, for rarely will a foreign policy stick unless the American people are behind it. And if Congress does not support a policy, the American people usually are not going to support it either.

The challenge that confronted the framers—how to reconcile the need for executive energy with republican liberty—is not only still with us, but it is exacerbated by the coming of the welfare, warfare, and regulatory states. The history of constitutionalism has always been the search for limitations on absolute power and for techniques of sharing power. Our American style of constitutionalism and separation of powers, especially in the absence of a major crisis, often means a slow-moving and sometimes inefficient decision-making system. It means a system that often hinders bold leadership rather than one that facilitates it. It is a system that plainly invites contention, division, debate, delay, and political conflict.

It is sometimes said that the intentions of the framers—and even important parts of the Constitution—are now obsolete and should no longer be our guides. Yet the framers were painfully aware of the horror and destructive consequences of warfare; that is why they decided that before the fate of the nation was put to risk, there ought to be debate, deliberation, and discussion. As the majority report from the Iran-contra hearings in Congress put it, "The theory of the Constitution is that policies formed through consultation and the democratic process are better, and wiser, than those formed without it."[35] The Constitution divided foreign policy making between Congress and the president. That division and the sharing it requires are fundamental to the system. An effective president will fashion policy with *the advice and consent of Congress*. An effective president will refrain from lying to Congress and from undeclared foreign policy operations. An effective president will ensure that the White House staff obeys the laws and understands the Constitution.

These are the lessons of past generations. The framers in 1787 knew well they were creating a unique, necessary, yet always potentially dangerous institution when they invented the presidency. This remains true today. What is needed, of course, is both a strong presidency *and* a strong Congress.

However much the public may want Congress to be a major partner with the president and a major check on the president, the public's support for Congress is always subject to deterioration. Power is dispersed in Congress. Its deliberations and quarrels are public. After a while, the public begins to view Congress as "the bickering branch," especially if a persuasive activist is in the White House.

Polls show, however, that people think Congress pays more attention to public views than does the president. Congress is a splendid forum that represents and registers the diversity of America. But that very virtue makes it difficult for Congress to provide leadership and difficult for it to challenge and bargain effectively with presidents. Not surprisingly, a wary public, dissatisfied with programs that do not work and policies that do not measure up to the urgencies of the moment, will look elsewhere, often to the president or to an aspiring presidential candidate.

It is no coincidence that the views about congressional versus presidential powers are related to which party controls these respective branches. In recent years Republicans have controlled the White House, and Democrats the Congress. Republicans, not surprisingly, tend to have a different view of the presidency now than they did when Truman, Kennedy, or Lyndon Johnson was president. Conversely, Democrats find a strong Congress more to their liking when Nixon, Ford, Reagan, or Bush is president than they did when their party was in office at 1600 Pennsylvania Avenue.

In addition, a theory of cyclical relations between the president and Congress has long been fashionable. It holds that there will be periods of presidential ascendancy followed by periods of congressional ascendancy. Usually these periods last a decade or more, and sometimes they are a generation in length. Analysis suggests that a moderate but real congressional resurgence did take place in the immediate post-Watergate years. But the responsibilities of the presidency these days, coupled with the complexities of foreign and economic policy, do not really permit any serious weakening of the office. Congress has regained some of its own lost power, and it has tried to curb the misuse and abuse of power, but it has not really weakened the presidency. Nor has Congress become imperial.

Many will continue to worry about future imperial presidents and about the possible alienation of the people from their leaders as complex issues continue to centralize responsibilities in the hands of the national government and the executive. Those who are concerned about these matters will not content themselves, nor should they, with the existing safeguards against the future misuse of presidential powers. It is not easy, however, to contrive devices that will check the president who would misuse powers without hamstringing the president who would use those same powers for purposive and democratically acceptable ends.

James Madison warned that our country could never trust "parchment barriers" to halt the encroaching spirit of power. In the end, constitutions live only if they embody the spirit, values, and deeply held civic beliefs of the people. As Walt Whitman reminded us, tyranny is always a possibility—if the people lose their supreme confidence in themselves and lose their spirit of defiance. Tyranny may always enter; there is no bar or charm against it. The only bar against it is a large, resolute breed of citizens.

Both the president and Congress have to recognize they are not supposed to be two sides out to "win" but two parts of the same government, both elected to pursue together the interests of the American people. Too much has been made by too many presidents and by too many scholars of that ancient but partial

On Consulting Congress

"The key is *prior consultation*, and if the executive chooses that route . . . Congress then can be seen as an ally not as a foe of the President in foreign affairs. But such consultation is not easy to come by. At a minimum it means regular bipartisan briefings; ad hoc consultative groups set up for whatever the particular issue may be; a regular parliamentary question and answer session with, if not the President, then the Secretary of State; consultation on policy *before, not after*, a policy has been formulated. . . . To come to brief the Congress and to call that briefing consultation is not the way to consult. In those instances, the executive is *informing* the Congress but not *consulting*. Similarly, to handle the Congress the way presidents often do with respect to arms control, for example, when they talk a lot about procedures but very little about substance; when they talk about atmosphere, but don't tell us what really is going on; that's not the way to consult either."

Source: Lee H. Hamilton, U.S. Representative from Indiana (D), "Congress and The Presidency in American Foreign Policy," *Presidential Studies Quarterly* (Summer 1988), pp. 510–11.

George Bush started his term in office with a harmonious relationship with the leaders of Congress and a pledge to avoid confrontation.

truth that only the president is the representative of all the people. Members of Congress do not represent the people exactly as a president does, but its two houses collectively represent them in ways a president cannot and does not.

In the end, the issue is not so much whether the presidency should be stronger than Congress, or vice versa. The real issue is that Congress and the presidency must both be strengthened to do the pressing work required for the well-being of the American people.

Summary

1. Congressional-presidential relations are not merely *constitutional* questions; they are also *political* struggles for the support of public opinion, as well as attempts to influence public policy. People may be far more attentive to presidents than to the operations of Congress, yet most Americans believe Congress should also have a major role in forming public policy.

2. During the 1970s Congress made notable efforts to reassert itself as a coequal policy-making branch. Congressional self-confidence increased as Congress reformed some of its practices and redefined certain presidential practices. During the 1980s the Reagan presidency was characterized by equally notable efforts to reassert old and gain additional presidential authority.

3. The separation of powers and necessity of sharing decision making, especially in foreign policy, produce a creative tension between the White House and Congress. Both presi-

dents and Congress have occasionally overstepped their roles in recent years; the process is never neat and tidy; complete accord is only sometimes achieved.

4. We have a system of checks and balances that is designed to be strong enough for effective leadership, but in which power is dispersed enough to ensure liberty. This delicate balance is constantly being readjusted.

5. Congressional reassertion took place in the immediate post-Watergate years. But the responsibilities of the presidency today, coupled with the complexities of foreign and economic policy, have not really permitted any serious weakening of the office. Congress has its work cut out for itself just strengthening and organizing itself to stay involved in national policy making. And presidents, as always, have their work cut out for them just trying to win influence in Congress and in the nation for the priorities and policies they think are best for the nation.

Further Reading

CECIL V. CRABB, JR., and PAT M. HOLT. *Invitation to Struggle: Congress, the President and Foreign Policy*, 3d ed. (Congressional Quarterly Press, 1989)

L. GORDON CROVITZ and JEREMY A. RABKIN, eds. *The Fettered Presidency: Legal Constraints on the Executive Branch* (American Enterprise Institute, 1989).

GEORGE EDWARDS III. *At The Margins: Presidential Leadership of Congress* (Yale University Press, 1989).

NIGEL BOWLES. *The White House and Capitol Hill.* (Oxford University Press, 1987).

LOUIS FISHER. *Constitutional Conflicts between Congress and the President* (Princeton University Press, 1985).

LOUIS FISHER. *The Politics of Shared Power: Congress and the Executive*, rev. ed. (Congressional Quarterly Press, 1987).

CHARLES O. JONES. *The Trusteeship Presidency: Jimmy Carter and

the United States Congress* (Louisiana State University Press, 1988).

LAWRENCE MARGOLIS. *Executive Agreements and Presidential Power in Foreign Policy* (Praeger, 1986).

MICHAEL L. MEZEY. *Congress, The President and Public Policy* (Westview, 1989).

ARTHUR M. SCHLESINGER, JR. *The Imperial Presidency* (Houghton Mifflin, 1973).

DAVID A. STOCKMAN. *The Triumph of Politics* (Harper & Row, 1986).

JAMES SUNDQUIST. *The Decline and Resurgence of Congress* (Brookings Institution, 1981).

See also *Congress and the Presidency*, published twice a year at American University and *Congressional Quarterly's* weekly reports.

Notes

1. Charles F. Hobson and Robert A. Rutland, eds., *The Papers of James Madison*, vol. 12 (University Press of Virginia, 1979), pp. 120–21.

2. Louis Fisher, *Constitutional Conflicts between Congress and the President* (Princeton University Press, 1985).

3. Leonard W. Levy, *Original Intent and the Framers' Constitution* (Macmillan Publishing Co., 1988), p. 30.

4. Roger H. Davidson and Walter J. Oleszek, *Congress and Its Members* (Congressional Quarterly Press, 1981), p. 282.

5. See George C. Edwards III, *Presidential Influence in Congress

(W. H. Freeman, 1980). See also his "Measuring Presidential Success in Congress: Alternative Approaches," *Journal of Politics* (Summer 1985), pp. 667–85.

6. William J. Keefe, *Congress and the American People*, 3rd ed. (Prentice Hall, 1988), p. 151.

7. Arthur M. Schlesinger, Jr., *The Imperial Presidency* (Houghton Mifflin, 1973).

8. Theodore Lowi, *The Personal President* (Cornell University Press, 1985), p. 179.

9. Leonard C. Meeker, "The Legality of U.S. Participation in the Defense of Vietnam," *Department of State Bulletin* (March 28, 1966), pp. 484–85.

10. For a discussion of abuses of power in U.S. intelligence agencies during the Cold War years, see Morton H. Halperin, Jerry J. Berman, Robert L. Borosage, and Christine M. Marwick, *The Lawless State* (Penguin, 1976); and David Wise, *The American Police State: The Government against the People* (Random House, 1976).

11. On executive agreements and treaties see Lawrence Margolis, *Executive Agreements and Presidential Power in Foreign Policy* (Praeger, 1986); and William L. Furlong and Margaret E. Scranton, *The Dynamics of Foreign Policymaking: The President, The Congress and the Panama Canal Treaties* (Westview Press, 1984).

12. On the veto power, see Robert Spitzer, *The Presidential Veto* (SUNY, 1988).

13. See James Sundquist, *The Decline and Resurgence of Congress* (Brookings Institution, 1981).

14. Ann Van Wynen Thomas and A. J. Thomas, Jr., *The War-Making Powers of the President* (Southern Methodist University Press, 1982).

15. Quoted in Christopher Madison, "Despite His Complaints Reagan Going Along with Spirit of War Powers Law," *National Journal* (May 19, 1984), p. 990.

16. Quoted in "In Wake of Libya, Skirmishing over War Powers," *Congressional Quarterly* (May 10, 1986), p. 1021.

17. Abraham D. Sofaer, "The War Powers Resolution and Antiterrorist Operations." Statement before the Subcommittee on Arms Control, International Security and Science, House Foreign Affairs Committee, April 29, 1986.

18. See Nancy N. Haanstad, "War Powers Resolution after the Persian Gulf: Death or Rebirth?" Paper delivered at the 1989 Annual Meeting of the Western Political Science Association Meetings, Salt Lake City, Utah, April 1, 1989.

19. Abraham Ribicoff, quoted in *National Emergencies Act, Report of the Committee on Government Operations, United States Senate* (U.S. Government Printing Office, 1976), p. 2.

20. Statement of Senator Leverett Saltonstall (R-Massachusetts), quoted in Henry Howe Ransom, *The Intelligence Establishment* (Harvard University Press, 1970), p. 169.

21. Stansfield Turner, *Secrecy and Democracy: The CIA in Transition* (Houghton Mifflin, 1985). See also John Oseth, *Regulating U.S. Intelligence Operations* (University of Kentucky Press, 1987); and Stephen J. Cimballa, ed., *Intelligence and Intelligence Policy in a Democratic Society* (Transnational, 1987).

22. See, for example, Bob Woodward, *Veil: The Secret Wars of the CIA* (Simon & Schuster, 1987).

23. Senator William Cohen, quoted in John Felton, "Wright Shelves Covert-Action Notice Bill," *Congressional Quarterly* (February 4, 1989), p. 224.

24. Three books describing the origins and early years of the 1974 Congressional Budget and Impoundment Control Act are Lance T. LeLoup, *The Fiscal Congress: Legislative Control of the Budget* (Greenwood Press, 1980); Allen Schick, *Congress and Money: Budgeting, Spending and Taxing* (Urban Institute, 1980); and Howard Shuman, *Politics and the Budget*, 2d ed. (Prentice Hall, 1988).

25. See Fisher, *Constitutional Conflicts between Congress and the President*; Allen Schick, *Crisis in the Budgetary Process* (American Enterprise Institute, 1986); and David A. Stockman, *The Triumph of Politics* (Harper & Row, 1986).

26. Bill Bradley, "Congress at Its Worst," *The Washington Post National Weekly Edition* (October 28, 1985), p. 29.

27. Christopher J. Deering, "Damned If You Do and Damned If You Don't: The Senate's Role in the Appointment Process," in G. Calvin Mackensie, ed., *The In-and-Outers: Presidential Appointees and the Problems of Transient Government in Washington* (Johns Hopkins Press, 1987), chap. 5.

28. Joseph Cooper and Patricia Hurley, "The Legislative Veto: A Policy Analysis," *Congress and the Presidency* (Spring 1983), pp. 25–46. See also Barbara Hinkson Craig, *The Legislative Veto* (Westview Press, 1983).

29. 77 L Ed 2d 317 (1983).

30. Daniel P. Franklin, "Why the Legislative Veto Isn't Dead," *Presidential Studies Quarterly* (Summer 1986), p. 499.

31. Quoted in Martin Tolchin, "The Legislative Veto, an Accommodation that Goes On and On," *The New York Times* (March 31, 1989), p. A8. See also Louis Fisher, *Constitutional Dialogues: Interpretation as Political Process* (Princeton University Press, 1988).

32. See their complaints developed at length by various authors in Gordon Jones and John Marini, eds., *The Imperial Congress* (Heritage Foundation/Claremont Institute, 1989).

33. For further elaboration of these arguments, see Thomas E. Cronin and Jeffrey Weill, "An Item Veto for Presidents?" *Congress and The Presidency* (Autumn, 1985), pp. 127–51.

34. These views are presented in detail in L. Gordon Crovitz and Jeremy Rabkin, eds., *The Fettered Presidency* (American Enterprise Institute, 1989); and Gordon Jones and John Marini, eds. *The Imperial Presidency* (Heritage Foundation/Claremont Institute, 1989).

35. *Report of the Congressional Committees Investigating the Iran-contra Affair* (Government Printing Office, 1987).

17

Judges:
The Balancing Branch

It was not an inspiring occasion. The few people present could hardly know they were witnessing the first meeting of what was to become the most important court in the world, the Supreme Court of the United States. It began on February 2, 1790. Chief Justice John Jay from New York, Justice James Wilson from Pennsylvania, and Justice William Cushing of Massachusetts were the only three of the original six appointees who made it through the muddy roads to New York City. They met in the Royal Exchange Building, an open-air market for butchers, which was the seat of the new federal government. The term lasted ten days, yet there were no cases to hear, and there was no quorum. The time was devoted to the admission of lawyers to practice before the Court.[1]

Four years later, Chief Justice John Jay resigned, in part because the federal court system lacked "energy, weight, and dignity," and in part to become governor of New York. But by the time of Chief Justice John Marshall (1801–1835), the Supreme Court had taken its place as a coequal third branch of the federal government. In fact, foreigners are often amazed at the power Americans give their judges, especially their federal judges. In 1834, after his visit to America, French aristocrat Alexis de Tocqueville wrote: "If I were asked where I place the American aristocracy, I should reply without hesitation . . . that it occupies the judicial bench and bar. . . . Scarcely any political question arises in the United States that is not resolved, sooner or later, into a judicial question."[2] A century later English laborite Harold Laski observed: "The respect in which federal courts and, above all, the Supreme Court are held is hardly surpassed by the influence they exert on the life of the United States."[3]

Should our judges play such a central role in our political life? Before answering, we must first understand *why* they have such great influence. One reason, as we saw in Chapter 2, is that in *Marbury* v. *Madison* John Marshall successfully claimed for judges the power of **judicial review,** that is, the power to interpret the Constitution authoritatively. Only a constitutional amendment or a later High

Chief Justice William Howard Taft and Members of the Supreme Court in the 1920s.

Court can modify the Court's doctrine. Justice Frankfurter once put it tersely: "The Supreme Court is the Constitution."

Besides exercising the power of judicial review, judges resolve disputes involving millions of dollars, decide conflicts among interests, supervise the criminal justice system, and make rules that affect the lives of millions of people. They are not only resolvers of legal conflicts; through their equity powers (see accompanying box), they have in effect become managers of schools, prisons, mental hospitals, and complex businesses. Sometimes, in fact, they decide the details of how these institutions should be run.

Still, the role of our judges is limited by the scope and nature of judicial power.

The Scope of Judicial Power

The American judicial process rests on an *adversary system*. A court of law is a neutral arena in which two parties argue their differences and present their points of view before an impartial arbiter. Whether the "fight theory" is or is not an adequate way to arrive at the truth, the fact is that it lies at the basis of our judicial system. The logic of the adversary system imposes formal restraints on the scope of judicial power, and its rhetoric leads us to conceive the role of the judge in a special way.

Judicial power is essentially *passive*. Judges cannot reach out and instigate a case. Furthermore, not all disputes are within the scope of judicial power. Judges decide only **justiciable disputes**—those that grow out of actual cases and are capable of settlement by legal methods. Not all constitutional disputes are justiciable. Some raise **political questions,** which require knowledge of a nonlegal character or the use of techniques not suitable for a court, or which are explicitly addressed by the Constitution to the Congress or the president. For example: Which of two competing state governments is the proper one? What does the Constitution mean when it provides that the national government should guarantee to each state a republican form of state government? Which group of officials of a foreign nation should be recognized by the United States as the government of that nation?[4] These are all political questions.

Judges are not supposed to use their power unless there is a real case or controversy. "It was never thought that, by means of a friendly suit, a party beaten in the legislature could transfer to the courts an inquiry as to the constitutionality of a legislative act."[5] (This, of course, is exactly what is done in nonfriendly suits. In such cases, however, the two parties have an interest in getting the full facts before the court.) In addition, litigants must have *standing to sue*; that is, they must have sustained or be in immediate danger of sustaining a direct and substantial injury. It is not enough merely to have a general interest in a subject or to believe that a law is unconstitutional.[6]

Of increasing importance in recent years are **class action suits** in which a small number of persons are allowed to represent all other persons similarly situated; for example, a suit in behalf of all students in a university, or all patients in a hospital, or all persons who bought a particular model of an automobile. "Would-be class action litigants must show that they are proper representatives for the class of persons they seek to champion, that the types of issues they wish to raise are common to the class, and they must be able to demonstrate how a remedy can be formed that will meet the needs of the class."[7]

DO JUDGES MAKE LAW?

"Do judges make law? Course they do. Made some myself," remarked Jeremiah Smith, judge of the New Hampshire Supreme Court.[8] Most judges, even today, are less candid. Judges obviously make law, but to admit it is somehow disturbing. Such statements do not conform to our notions of what a judge should do.

Why do we think judges should not make law? Many people equate a judge's role with that of a referee in a prizefight. We expect referees to be impartial and disinterested, to treat both parties as equals. We expect them to apply rules, not make them.

Laws are not made, however, in the same way as the rules of a sport, and herein lies the answer to our question. Not only *do* judges make law, but they *must*. Legislatures make law by enacting statutes, but judges apply statutes to concrete situations. In some cases general expressions are clearly applicable: "If anything is a vehicle, a motor-car is one."[9] But does the word *vehicle* in a statute include bicycles, airplanes, and roller skates? A judge is constantly faced with situations that possess some of the features of similar cases—but lack others. Statutes are drawn in broad terms: drivers shall act with "reasonable care"; no one may make "excessive noise" in the vicinity of a hospital; employers must maintain "safe working conditions." Such broad terms must be used because legislators cannot know exactly what will happen in the future.

These problems are intensified when judges are asked—as American judges are—to apply the Constitution, which was written two hundred years ago. The Constitution is full of generalizations: "due process of law," "equal protection of the laws," "unreasonable searches and seizures," "commerce among the several states." Recourse to the intent of the framers is not likely to help judges faced with cases involving electronic wiretaps, General Motors, or birth control pills.

Just because judges make policy, however, does not mean they are free to make it as they wish. They are subject to a variety of limits on what they decide—some imposed by the political system of which they are a part, some by their own professional obligations as lawyers. Among these constraints is the rule of **stare decisis,** the rule of precedent.

Types of Law

STATUTORY LAW
Formulated primarily by a legislature, but also includes treaties and executive orders; law that comes from authoritative and specific law-making sources.

COMMON LAW
Judge-made law that originated in England in the twelfth century, when royal judges traveled around the country settling disputes in each locality according to prevailing custom. The common law continues to develop according to the rule of *stare decisis*, which means "Let the decision stand." This is the rule of precedent, which implies that a rule established by a court is to be followed in all similar cases.

EQUITY
Used whenever common law remedies are inadequate. For example, if an injury done to property may do irreparable harm for which money damages cannot provide compensation, under equity a person may ask the judge to issue an injunction ordering the offending person not to take the threatening action. If the wrongdoer persists, he or she may be punished for contempt of court.

CHAPTER 17 / Judges: The Balancing Branch

Stare decisis pervades our judicial system. Judges are expected to abide by all previous decisions of their own courts and all rulings of superior courts. Although adherence to precedent is normal, the doctrine of stare decisis is not nearly so restrictive as some people think.[10]

Consider, for example, the father who, removing his hat as he enters a church, says to his son: "This is the way to behave on such occasions. Do as I do."[11] The son, like the judge trying to follow a precedent, has a wide range of possibilities open to him. How much of his father's behavior must be imitated? Does it matter if the hat is removed slowly or quickly? If the hat is put under the seat? If it is not replaced on the head inside the church? The judge can distinguish precedents by stating that a previous case does not control the immediate one because of differences in context. In addition, many areas of law have conflicting precedents, one of which can be chosen to support a decision for either party.

The doctrine of stare decisis is even less controlling in the field of constitutional law. Because the Constitution itself, rather than any one interpretation of it, is binding, the Court can reverse a previous decision it no longer wishes to follow, as it has done dozens of times. Supreme Court justices are therefore not seriously restricted by stare decisis. As the first Justice Harlan told a group of law students: "I want to say to you young gentlemen that if we don't like an act of Congress, we don't have too much trouble to find grounds for declaring it unconstitutional."[12]

Federal Justice

"The judicial Power of the United States," says Article III of the Constitution, "shall be vested in one supreme Court, and in such inferior Courts as the Congress may from time to time ordain and establish." Courts created to carry out this judicial power are called *Article III* or *constitutional courts*. Congress may also establish *Article I* or *legislative courts* to carry out the legislative powers the Constitution has granted to it. The main difference between a legislative and a constitutional court is that the judges of the former need not be appointed "to hold their Offices during good Behavior" and may be assigned other than purely judicial duties.

The Constitution requires a Supreme Court. It is a necessity if the national government is to have the power to frame and enforce laws superior to those of the states. The lack of such an agency to maintain national supremacy, to ensure uniform interpretation of national legislation, and to resolve conflicts among the states was one of the glaring deficiencies of the central government under the Articles of Confederation.

Congress decides whether there will be national courts in addition to the one Supreme Court ordained by the Constitution. (The Constitution also allows Congress to determine the size of the Supreme Court.) The first Congress divided the nation into districts and created lower national courts for each district. That decision, though often supplemented, has never been seriously questioned.

Types of Law (Cont'd.)

CONSTITUTIONAL LAW
Statements interpreting the United States Constitution that have been given Supreme Court approval.

ADMIRALTY AND MARITIME LAW
Law applicable to cases concerning shipping and waterway commerce on the high seas and on the navigable waters of the United States.

ADMINISTRATIVE LAW
Rules and decisions of administrators and judges as they relate to the authority of administrators.

CRIMINAL LAW
Defines crimes against the public order and provides for punishment. Government is responsible for enforcing criminal law, the great body of which is enacted by states and enforced by state officials in state courts; however, the criminal caseload of federal judges is growing.

CIVIL LAW
Governs the relations between individuals and defines their legal rights. However, the government can also be a party to a civil action. Under the Sherman Antitrust Act, for example, the federal government may initiate civil as well as criminal action to prevent violations of the law.

THE SUPREME COURT
Washington, D.C.

1 Courtyards
2 Solicitor General's Office
3 Lawyer's Lounge
4 Marshal's Office
5 Main Hall
6 Court Room
7 Conference Rooms

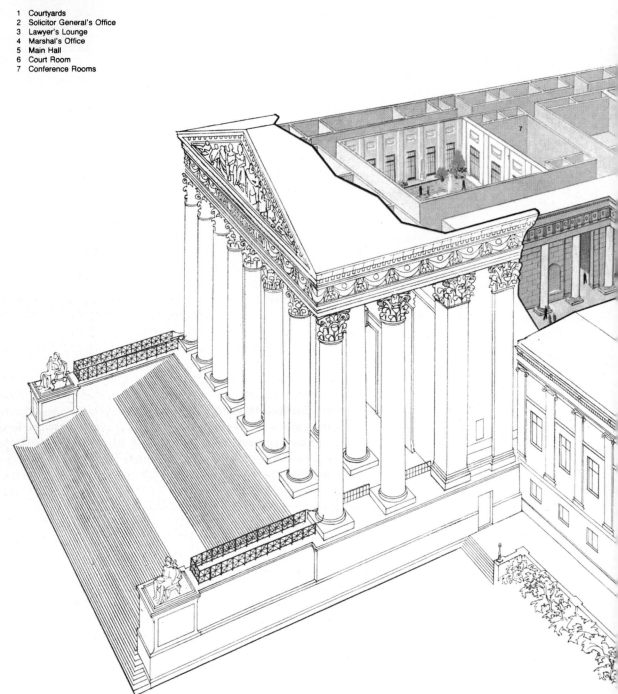

438

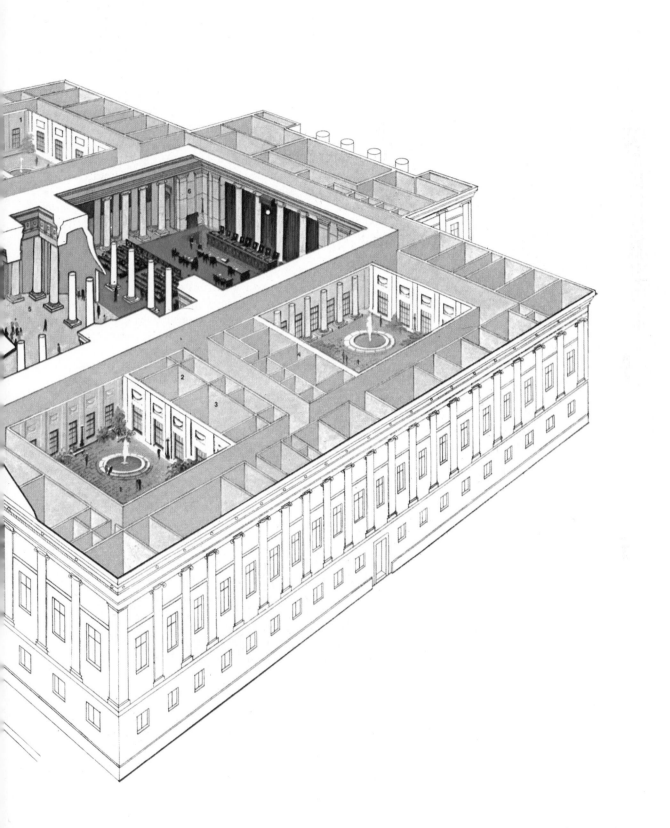

Examples of Special Article III Courts

In addition to Article III courts of general jurisdiction, Congress has created constitutional courts with special jurisdiction:

United States Court of Claims: Consists of sixteen judges, who have jurisdiction over all property and contract damage suits against the United States.

United States Court of International Trade (formerly U.S. Customs Court): Consists of nine judges who review rulings of customs collectors and conflicts arising under various tariff and trade laws.

United States Court of Appeals for the Federal Circuit: Consists of twelve judges who sit in panels of three to hear appeals of cases from all federal courts relating to patents, as well as to review decisions of the Patent Office and of the Court of International Trade.

Today the hierarchy of national courts of general jurisdiction consists of *district courts, courts of appeals,* and *one* Supreme Court. Although the Supreme Court and its justices receive most of the attention, the workhorses of the federal judiciary are the district courts within the states, in the District of Columbia, and in the territories. Each state has at least one district court. Larger states have as many as the demands of judicial business and the pressure of politics require (although no state has more than four).

Each district court is composed of at least one judge, but it may have as many as twenty-seven. District judges normally sit separately and hold court by themselves. There are eighty-nine district judges in the fifty states, plus one in the District of Columbia and one in the Commonwealth of Puerto Rico. All district judges are nominated by the president and confirmed by the Senate. District judges, like all Article III federal judges, hold office for life.

District courts are trial courts of *original jurisdiction.* They are the only federal courts that regularly employ **grand** (indicting) and **petit** (trial) **juries.** Many cases tried before district judges involve citizens of different states, and the judges apply the appropriate state laws. Otherwise, district judges are concerned with federal laws. For example, they hear and decide cases involving crimes against the United States—suits under the national revenue, postal, patent, copyright, trademark, bankruptcy, and civil rights laws.

District judges are assisted by clerks, bailiffs, stenographers, law clerks, court reporters, probation officers, and United States magistrates. All these officials are appointed by the judges. The 287 full-time and 168 part-time *federal magistrates* are becoming increasingly important. After being screened by panels composed of residents of the judicial districts, these magistrates are appointed for eight-year terms. Magistrates issue warrants for arrest, hold hearings to determine whether

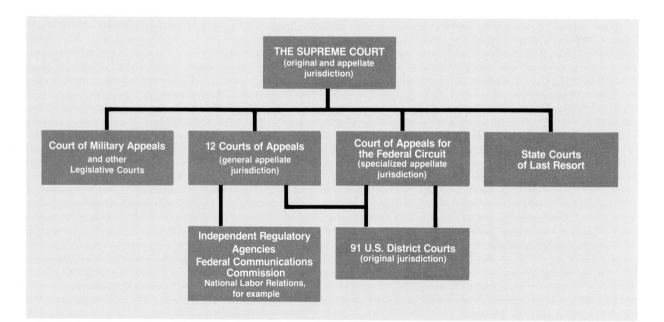

arrested persons should be held for action by the grand jury, and, if so, set bail. They hear motions subject to varying kinds of review by their district judges. They preside over civil trials—jury and nonjury—with the consent of both parties, and over nonjury trials for petty offenses with the consent of the defendants.[13]

United States marshals, appointed by the president and operating under the supervision of the attorney general, are assigned to each district court.

> Although their most dramatic exploits may be called to mind by references to names like Bat Masterson, Wyatt Earp, and David Neagle, or to events like the enforcement of civil rights legislation in the 1960's, the primary assistance to the Federal Judiciary provided by the marshals has been in the area of protection of the trial process, including the courtroom itself, and the service of writs issued by the judges.[14]

Except for the few cases that may be taken directly to the Supreme Court, a final decision of a district court is reviewable by a court of appeals. The United States is divided into twelve judicial circuits, one of which is the District of Columbia. Each has a court of appeals consisting of from six to twenty-eight permanent judgeships. The Court of Appeals for the Federal Circuit has national jurisdiction. Each court of appeals normally hears cases in panels of three but for especially important and controversial cases all judges may be present, that is, they may sit *en banc*.

Courts of appeals have only **appellate jurisdiction.** They review decisions of the district courts within their circuits and also some of the actions of the independent regulatory agencies, such as the Federal Trade Commission. These courts are powerful policy makers. Less than 1 percent of the cases from these courts are looked at carefully by the Supreme Court. As the policy role of federal courts has become a more prominent issue of national politics, more attention is being focused on these courts and the judges who serve on them.

STATE AND FEDERAL COURTS

In addition to this complex structure of federal courts, each state maintains a complete judicial system of its own. (Many large municipalities have judicial systems as complex as those of the states.) State courts have sole jurisdiction to try all cases not within the judicial power the Constitution grants to the United States.

This dual system of courts is not common—even among nations with federal systems of government. The two court systems are related, but they do not exist in a superior-inferior relationship. Except for the limited **habeas corpus** jurisdiction of the district courts—the power to release persons from custody if the judge is not satisfied that the person is being legally detained—the Supreme Court is the only federal court that may review state court decisions. And it may do so only under special conditions.

Other than the *original jurisdiction* the Constitution vests directly in the Supreme Court, no federal court has any jurisdiction except that granted to it by act of Congress. Congress also determines whether this judicial power of the United States will be exercised exclusively by federal courts or concurrently by both federal and state courts.

Examples of Article I or Legislative Courts

United States Court of Military Appeals: Consists of three civilian judges appointed for fifteen years each by the president with the consent of the Senate. This court, created by Congress under its grant of authority to make the rules and regulations for "land and naval Forces," applies military law, which is separate from the body of law that governs the rest of the federal court system.

Bankruptcy judges: Consists of almost 300 judges appointed by the courts of appeals to serve as adjuncts to the federal district courts for terms of fourteen years each. These judges handle bankruptcy matters subject to review by federal district judges.

Prosecution and Defense: Federal Lawyers

Judges decide cases; they do not prosecute persons. That job, on the federal level, falls to the Department of Justice: to the attorney general, the solicitor general, the ninety-one United States attorneys, and some 1200 assistant attorneys. The president, with the consent of the Senate, appoints a United States attorney for each district court. United States attorneys serve a four-year term but may be dismissed by the president at any time. These appointments are of great interest to senators, who exercise significant influence over the selection process through **senatorial courtesy.** Because the U.S. attorneys are almost always members of the president's political party, it is customary for them to resign if the opposition party wins the White House.

The attorney general, in consultation with the U.S. attorney in each district, appoints assistant attorneys. Some districts have only one; the largest, the Southern District of New York, has more than sixty-five. These attorneys, working with the U.S. attorney and assisted by the Federal Bureau of Investigation and other federal law-enforcement agencies, begin proceedings against those alleged to have broken federal laws. They also represent the United States in civil suits.

PROSECUTORS AND THE SOLICITER GENERAL

Prosecutors decide whether to charge an offense and which offense to charge. They have largely unreviewable discretion. "So long as the prosecutor has probable cause to believe that the accused committed an offense defined by statute, the decision whether or not to prosecute, and what charge to file or bring before a grand jury, generally rests entirely in his discretion."[15]

Prosecutors negotiate with **defendants** (usually through their lawyers) and often work out **plea bargains** whereby defendants agree to plead guilty to one offense to avoid having to stand trial for another, more serious one. Prosecutors make recommendations to judges about what sentences to impose.

Attorneys from the Department of Justice and from other federal agencies participate in well over half the cases on the Supreme Court's docket. Of special importance is the *solicitor general* (SG), who represents the government before the Supreme Court. When the solicitor general petitions the Supreme Court and asks it to review an opinion of a lower court, the Court is likely to do so. Moreover, no appeal may be taken by the United States to any appellate court without the approval of the solicitor general.[16] Although the solicitor general reports to the attorney general, the SG, sometimes called the "Tenth Justice," has traditionally been given some measure of independence from the White House. The Reagan administration, however, used the SG to carry its social policy agenda to the Supreme Court; for example, to try to persuade the justices to limit affirmative action and to restrict the right of women to have abortions.[17]

State attorneys general also play a special role before the Supreme Court. Their briefs, like those of the solicitor general, may be filed without the approval of the parties to litigation. Although not as successful as the solicitor general, state attorneys general have become more active participants in the debates before the Supreme Court.[18]

FEDERAL DEFENSE LAWYERS

The federal government also provides lawyers for poor defendants. Under the terms of the Criminal Justice Act of 1970, each district court has some discretion as to how to provide this assistance. Most districts use the traditional system of assigning a private attorney. Over forty districts, however, have opted to use the **public defender** system. These salaried public defenders operate under the general supervision of the Administrative Office of the United States Courts.

Congress has also created a private nonprofit organization—The Legal Services Corporation—to provide financial assistance to organizations that furnish legal help to the poor. The corporation has often been a center of controversy between those who would restrict its help to suing landlords, employers, husbands, or wives in traditional legal battles and those who would allow it to use class suits to challenge the status quo.

"Okay, who's the wiseguy?"

© *Schochet; reprinted from* Judicature.

How Federal Judges Are Selected

The Constitution empowers the president to select federal judges with the advice and consent of the Senate. Political reality imposes constraints on the president's discretion. The selection of a federal judge is actually a complex bargaining process. The principal figures involved are the candidates, the president, the "subpresidency for judicial selection"[19] consisting of key members of the Department of Justice, United States senators, the Standing Committee on the Federal Judiciary of the American Bar Association, and political-party leaders.

Prior to White House submission of nominees to the Senate, the president must observe the practice of senatorial courtesy. Senatorial courtesy gives a senator veto power over the appointment of a judge who is to sit in his or her state, if that senator is a member of the president's party. Even a senator from the opposition party must be consulted. When the Senate is controlled by partisan opponents of the president, the chief executive must negotiate with both senators from the state where the judge is to sit, regardless of party affiliation. If negotiations are deadlocked between the senators or between the senators and the Department of Justice, a seat may stay vacant for years.[20]

The rule of senatorial courtesy no longer applies to Supreme Court appointments and is not often applied to selection of judges for the courts of appeals, because these judges do not serve in any one senator's domain. This difference in selection politics means that district court judges often reflect values different from those of persons appointed to the courts of appeals or the Supreme Court.[21]

The American Bar Association's Committee on the Federal Judiciary plays a special role in the appointment process. Although its ratings do not bind a president or the Senate, any president is hesitant to submit for Senate confirmation a candidate rated "unqualified" by the ABA. During an earlier period, the American Bar Association was thought to introduce a conservative, "corporation lawyer" bias into the selection process. In recent years, however, conservative groups have mounted an attack on the ABA's role, contending it reflects a liberal bias and gives low ratings in order to "sand bag conservative nominees."[22]

THE SENATE AND ITS JUDICIARY COMMITTEE

The normal presumption is that the president should be allowed considerable discretion in the selection of federal judges. Despite this presumption, the Senate takes seriously its responsibility to confirm presidential nominations, especially if the party controlling the Senate is different from that of the president, as has been the case in recent years.

TABLE 17–1
Party Affiliation of Judges Appointed by Presidents from FDR to Reagan

PRESIDENT	PARTY	APPOINTEES FROM SAME PARTY
Roosevelt	Democrat	97%
Truman	Democrat	92%
Eisenhower	Republican	95%
Kennedy	Democrat	92%
Johnson	Democrat	94%
Nixon	Republican	93%
Ford	Republican	81%
Carter	Democrat	90%
Reagan	Republican	95%

Source: Sheldon Goldman, "Reagan's Judicial Legacy: Completing the Puzzle and Summing Up," *Judicature,* vol. 72 (April–May, 1989), pp. 318–330.

Nominations are processed through the Senate Judiciary Committee. This committee, or occasionally the full Senate, has rejected or refused to act on 29 of the 138 presidential nominations for Supreme Court justices, including 7 in this century.[23] Although the Senate usually confirms the Judiciary Committee's recommendations, floor debates over judicial nominees are not rare, especially in the case of Supreme Court nominations.[24]

THE ROLE OF PARTY, RACE, AND SEX

Presidents seldom nominate judges from the opposing party. Partisan considerations, although as significant as ever, are taken for granted, and partisan affiliation is rarely mentioned. Today journalists pay more attention to other characteristics, such as race and sex.

President Carter, who had no opportunity to appoint anyone to the Supreme Court, selected forty women, thirty-eight blacks, and sixteen Hispanics among his nominations to the lower federal courts—more minority members and women than all other presidents combined. President Reagan, although the first to appoint a woman to the Supreme Court, appointed fewer minority members or women than did President Carter, perhaps in part because fewer minorities and women could pass the Reagan administration's ideological screening (see the next section).

THE ROLE OF IDEOLOGY

Finding a party member is not enough. Presidents want to pick the "right" kind of Republican or "our" kind of Democrat. By and large they have been able to achieve this goal. Republican judges picked by Republican presidents tend to be judicial conservatives, and most Democratic judges picked by Democratic presidents are more likely to be liberals, with both of these orientations tempered by the fact that judges have had to go through a senatorial confirmation screen that in recent decades has been of the opposite persuasion from that of the White House.[25]

When the appointment is to the Supreme Court, the policy orientation of the nominee is likely to be foremost among presidential concerns. As President Abraham Lincoln told Congressman Boutewell when he appointed Salmon P. Chase to the Courts: "We wish for a Chief Justice who will sustain what has been done in regard to emancipation and legal tender."[26] Theodore Roosevelt voiced the same concern to appoint the "correct" person in a letter to Senator Lodge about Judge Oliver Wendell Holmes of the Massachusetts Supreme Judicial Court, whom he was considering for the Supreme Court: "Now I should like to know that Judge Holmes was in entire sympathy with our views, that is with your views and mine. I should hold myself guilty of an irreparable wrong to the nation if I should appoint any man who was not absolutely sane and sound on the great national policies for which we stand in public life."[27]

President Ronald Reagan's two terms made it possible for him to join Presidents Franklin D. Roosevelt and Dwight D. Eisenhower as the only presidents in modern times to appoint a majority of the federal bench. All told, Reagan appointed 346 lifetime judges. Like his predecessors, he was concerned about the ideologies of those he nominated, and his administration acted carefully and systematically to nominate only those whose views about the role of the courts and constitutional issues were consistent with Reagan's own.[28] Not only were a large number of judicial conservatives appointed, but many of them—because they are comparatively young—will have a long-lasting effect on judicial policy making well into the next century.

As President Bush's commitment to conservatism is less well established than Reagan's, conservatives and their organizations, such as the Heritage Foundation, the Pacific Legal Foundation, and the Federalist Society, are focusing their attention on Bush's judicial appointments. They are "turning on the heat over the next four years so that the Bush administration doesn't squander any opportunity to tip the U.S. Supreme Court further to the right or turn its back on President Reagan's legacy of appointing conservatives to the federal bench."[29]

JUDICIAL PHILOSOPHY: RESTRAINT VERSUS ACTIVISM

What about the candidates' "judicial philosophies"? Do prospective candidates believe in **judicial restraint,** or in **judicial activism?** Do candidates believe that judges should try to interpret the Constitution to reflect what the framers intended and what its words literally say? Or do they believe the Constitution cannot and should not be interpreted literally, but rather adapted to reflect current conditions and philosophies?

Judicial philosophy is closely related to political ideology. Throughout most of our history federal courts were more conservative than Congress, the White House, or the state legislatures. Prior to 1937 judicial self-restraint was the battle cry of liberals who objected to judges' striking down so many laws passed to protect labor and women and otherwise regulating the economy.

By the time of Richard Nixon, Ronald Reagan, and George Bush, the judicial shoe was on the other foot. Today, at least for the moment, conservatives are likely to be the advocates of judicial self-restraint. What is wanted, they argue, are judges who will let Congress, the president, and the state legislatures do what they want unless it clearly contravenes the precise words of the Constitution; for example, regulate or forbid abortions, adopt prayers for public schools, impose capital punishment, authorize police to engage in wire tapping, and so on.

It would be wrong to assume that judicial philosophy is nothing more than another way to argue about political ideology. Some conservatives, for example, favor judicial activism because they want current judges to reverse the last half century of precedents and actively seek to protect property rights from government regulation. Some liberals favor judicial restraint because they believe democracy

Factors Constraining Federal Judges

The Constitution
Precedent—*stare decisis*
Statutory law
Legal thought as found in books and law reviews
Opinions of other courts
Interest groups
Public opinion
Media opinion
Views of colleagues
Views of law clerks
Contemporary events and general social environment
Traditions of the law
Actions of the legislature, past and future
Actions of executives, past and future

Note: These factors are not listed in any particular order. Some weigh more heavily at one time than at another, and on some judges more than on others.

"It's nothing personal, Prescott. It's just that a higher court gets a kick out of overruling a lower court."

Copyright © 1967 by Sidney Harris. Reprinted from Saturday Review.

Number of Black Judges Appointed by Presidents from FDR to Reagan*

Court	Number of Judges	Appointing President
Supreme Court	1	Johnson
Courts of Appeals	1	Truman
	1	Kennedy
	2	Johnson
	9	Carter
	1	Reagan
District Courts	3	Kennedy
	5	Johnson
	6	Nixon
	3	Ford
	28	Carter
	6	Reagan
Special Courts	1	Johnson
	1	Eisenhower
Total:	68	

* Nine of these black judges were women. One was appointed by Johnson, seven by Carter, and one by Reagan.

Number of Women Judges Appointed to the Federal Bench

Court	Number of Judges	Appointing President
Supreme Court	1	Reagan
Court of Appeals	1	Roosevelt
	1	Johnson
	11	Carter
	6	Reagan*
District Courts	1	Truman
	1	Kennedy
	2	Johnson
	1	Nixon
	1	Ford
	29	Carter
	24	Reagan*
Special Courts	1	Coolidge
	1	Eisenhower
	1	Carter
	1	Reagan
Total	83	

* Reagan appointed two women to the district courts and subsequently elevated them to the appellate bench. They are counted here only as appointments to the court of appeals.

Source: Sheldon Goldman, "Reagan's Judicial Legacy: Completing the Puzzle and Summing Up," *Judicature*, vol. 72 (April–May, 1989), pp. 318–330.

will flourish when judges stay out of policy debates. Nonetheless, most of the country understands enough about the policy role of judges to recognize that the debates about the proper role of the courts and about how to interpret the Constitution are reflections of differing convictions about what policy outcomes are in the public interest. The debate over the Supreme Court's role today is less about activism and restraint than it is about competing conceptions of the proper balance between government authority and individual rights.

JUDICIAL LONGEVITY AND PRESIDENTIAL TENURE

Ideology and judicial philosophy affect not only presidents' nominations for the federal courts but also when sitting judges choose to retire. Because federal judges serve for life, they may be able to schedule their retirement to allow a president whose views they approve to nominate their successors. Chief Justice Taney stayed on the bench long after his health began to fail to prevent Lincoln from nominating a Republican. In 1929 Chief Justice Taft wrote: "I am older and slower and less acute and more confused. However, as long as things continue as they are, and I am able to answer in my place, I must stay on the court in order to prevent the Bolsheviki [Hoover—a Republican—was in the White House] from getting control."[30]

Although former Chief Justice Burger denied that he retired in 1986 in order to permit President Reagan to replace him with a constitutional conservative, his retirement did give President Reagan an opportunity to rejuvenate the conservative wing of the Court by promoting a then 61-year-old William Rehnquist (an articulate constitutional conservative) to replace the 78-year-old Burger. Reagan then picked another constitutional conservative, the 50-year-old Antonin Scalia, from the Court of Appeals for the District of Columbia to take the seat vacated by Rehnquist.[31]

THE BORK BATTLE

When Justice Powell, who had the swing vote on such critical issues as the scope of affirmative action and the extent of state power to regulate abortions, surprised most court watchers and announced his retirement in July 1987, he made it possible for Reagan to select a justice who could have a decisive vote on many issues.

With so much at stake the nation riveted on the appointment. President Reagan quickly nominated Judge Robert Bork, a member of the Court of Appeals for the District of Columbia and a noted jurist and legal scholar who for decades had attacked the judicial activism of the Warren and Burger Courts. Despite Bork's controversial writings on most current constitutional issues, his distinctive qualifications made it appear initially that he would be confirmed, even though the Senate was controlled by the Democrats. However, his nomination so offended many groups, especially women's and black organizations, that they organized a campaign to block the Bork nomination.

After almost four months of national debate, twelve days of extensive questioning by the members of the Senate Judiciary Committee, and twenty-three hours of debate on the Senate floor, the Senate voted 58 to 42 against Bork's confirmation. An angry President Reagan quickly sent to the Senate the name of Douglas H. Ginsburg, another judge from the Court of Appeals of the District of Columbia. Judge Ginsburg, a purported judicial conservative, had written little outside of his relatively few judicial opinions, and his votes on major constitutional issues were unknown. Although the Democratic members of the Senate Judiciary Committee made clear that they would carefully evaluate Judge Ginsburg's qualifications, it was anticipated that Judge Ginsburg would be confirmed, in part because of the political exhaustion of those who were fearful of the Reagan appointees, in part because of a lack of record on which to attack him. But after Judge Ginsburg's acknowledgment of past marijuana use created a storm of public protest, especially among conservatives, he withdrew his candidacy. The third time Reagan nominated a more mainstream conservative, Judge Anthony M. Kennedy from the Court of Appeals of the Ninth Circuit. After considerable searching through his judicial record by the Senate Judiciary Committee, the Senate unanimously confirmed Kennedy's appointment. He took his seat on the Court six months after Justice Powell's retirement.

The politics of judicial selection may shock those who like to think judges are picked strictly in terms of legal merit and without regard for party, race, sex, or ideology. But as a former Justice Department official has said: "When courts cease being an instrument for political change, then maybe the judges will stop being politically selected."[32]

CHANGING THE NUMBERS

Partisan politics also affects decisions about the number of federal judges. One of the first actions of a political party after gaining control of the White House and Congress is to increase the number of federal judgeships. However, when one party controls Congress and the other holds the White House, a stalemate is likely to occur, and relatively few new judicial positions will be created. During Andrew Johnson's administration, Congress went so far as to reduce the size of the Supreme Court to prevent the President from filling two vacancies. After Johnson left the White House, Congress returned the Court to its former size to permit Grant to fill the vacancies.

In 1937 President Roosevelt proposed an increase in the size of the Supreme Court by one additional justice for every member of the Court over 70, up to a total of fifteen members. Ostensibly, the proposal aimed to make the Court more efficient. In fact, Roosevelt and his followers were frustrated because the Court had declared much of the New Deal unconstitutional. Despite Roosevelt's popularity, this "court-packing scheme" aroused intense opposition. In the midst of the congressional debate, Justice Owen J. Roberts, who had previously voted with the conservative members of the Court against the New Deal, began to vote with the more liberal justices to sustain some important New Deal legislation. Because the Court was no longer an obstacle, Roosevelt's proposals to change its size failed. He lost the battle, but he won the war.

CHANGING JURISDICTION

Congressional control over the structure and jurisdiction of federal courts has been used to influence the course of judicial policy making. Although unable to get rid of Federalist judges by impeachment, the Jeffersonians abolished the circuit courts created by the Federalist Congress just prior to their losing control. In 1869 radical Republicans in Congress altered the Supreme Court's appellate jurisdiction in order to snatch from the Court a case it was about to review involving the constitutionality of some reconstruction legislation (*Ex parte McCardle*).[33]

Supreme Court nominee Robert Bork (top) was not confirmed by the Senate Judiciary Committee. Douglas Ginsburg (center) withdrew after conservatives were outraged by his past use of marijuana. Anthony Kennedy (bottom) was finally confirmed unanimously and is shown here taking the oath of office.

During the early years of the Reagan administration, there was a dramatic increase in the number of bills introduced in Congress either to eliminate the jurisdiction of all federal courts over cases relating to abortion, school prayer, and school busing, or to eliminate the appellate jurisdiction of the Supreme Court over such matters. These bills sparked a major debate about whether the Constitution gives Congress authority to take these actions and whether Congress ought to do so. As yet, persons angered by a particular line of decisions have not persuaded a majority of Congress to make what could amount to a fundamental shift in the nature of the relationship between Congress and the Supreme Court.

How the Supreme Court Operates

Supreme Court justices are in session from the first Monday in October through the end of June. They listen to oral arguments for two weeks and then adjourn for two weeks to consider the cases and write their opinions. Six justices must participate in each decision. Cases are decided by a majority. In the event of a tie vote, the decision of the lower court is sustained, although the case may be reargued.

At 10 A.M. on the days when the Supreme Court sits, the eight associate justices and the Chief Justice, dressed in their robes, file into the Court. As they take their seats—arranged according to seniority, with the chief justice in the center—the clerk of the Court introduces them as the "Honorable Chief Justice and Associate Justices of the Supreme Court of the United States." Those present in the courtroom are seated; and counsel take their places along tables in front of the bench. The attorneys for the Department of Justice, dressed in formal morning clothes, are at the right. The other attorneys are dressed conservatively; sport coats are not considered proper. This is all part of the high ritual of the Court:

> the majesty of its courtroom; the black robes of the justices; the ritual of its proceedings at oral argument and on decision day; the secrecy and isolation of its decision-making conferences; the formal opinions invoking the symbols of Constitution, precedent, constitutional guardians, from all other officials.[34]

WHAT CASES REACH THE SUPREME COURT?

When citizens vow they will take their cases to the highest court of the land, even if it costs their last penny, they underestimate the difficulty of securing Supreme Court review, overestimate the cost (although it costs plenty), and reveal a basic misunderstanding of the Court's role. The rules for appealing a case to the Supreme Court are established by act of Congress. Today all appellate cases come before the Court by means of a discretionary **writ of certiorari.** (Until 1988 there were a few types of cases the Supreme Court was obliged by law to review.) In addition, the Constitution stipulates the Supreme Court has *original jurisdiction* in a few specified situations. But the fact is the Supreme Court has control of its agenda and decides which cases it wants to consider. The justices closely review around 200 of the thousands of cases annually presented to them.

It is not enough, for example, that Jones thinks he should have won his case against Smith. There probably has already been at least one appellate review of the trial, either in a federal court of appeals or in a state supreme court. The

---

The Judicial Power of the United States

To hear and decide cases or controversies in law and equity if:

1. They arise under the Constitution, a federal law, or a treaty.
2. They arise under admiralty and maritime laws.
3. They arise because of a dispute involving land claimed under titles granted by two or more states.
4. The United States is a party to the case.
5. A state is a party to the case (but not if a suit was begun or prosecuted against a state by an individual or a foreign nation).
6. They are between citizens of different states.*
7. They affect the accredited representatives of a foreign nation.

* Congress has chosen to limit this "diversity jurisdiction" of federal courts, as it is called, to cases in which the amount in controversy exceeds $50,000.

Supreme Court will review Jones's case only if his claim has broad public significance. For instance, the rulings among the courts of appeals may conflict. By deciding Jones's case, the Supreme Court can establish which rule is to be followed throughout the judicial system or Jones's case may raise a constitutional issue on which a state supreme court has presented an interpretation with which the Court disagrees. The crucial factor in determining whether the Supreme Court will hear a case is its importance not to Jones, but to the operation of the governmental system as a whole.

The Court accepts cases under the "rule of four." If four justices are sufficiently interested in a petition for a writ of certiorari, the petition will be granted and the case brought forward for review. Denial of a writ of certiorari does not mean that the justices agree with the decision of the lower court, nor does it necessarily establish precedents. Refusal to grant such a writ may indicate all kinds of possibilities: the justices may not wish to become involved in a political "hot potato," or the Court may be so divided on an issue that it is not yet prepared to take a stand.[35]

THE BRIEFS AND ORAL ARGUMENT

Before a case is heard in open court, the justices receive printed briefs, perhaps hundreds of pages long, in which each side presents legal arguments, historical materials, and relevant precedents. In addition, the Supreme Court may receive briefs from **amici curiae**—friends of the court. These may be individuals, organizations, or government agencies who have an interest in the case and claim they have information of value to the Court. This procedure guarantees that the Department of Justice is represented if a suit between two private parties calls the constitutionality of an act of Congress into question.

Often organizations file amicus curiae briefs before the Supreme Court grants a writ of certiorari in order to lobby the Supreme Court to review the case. When they do so, it greatly enhances the probability that the court will take the case for review.[36] The friend of the court brief is also used by presidents, through the Department of Justice, to try to persuade the Supreme Court to change its mind about established constitutional doctrine.[37] A brief brought by a private party or interest group may help the justices by presenting an argument or point of law that the parties to the case have not raised. Often the briefs are filed as a means of "pressuring" the Court to reach a particular decision. In the *Bakke* case, in which the Supreme Court first dealt substantively with affirmative action issues, thirty-seven amicus briefs were filed for the university, sixteen for Bakke, and five that did not take sides. In *Webster* v. *Reproductive Health Services*, argued in the spring of 1989 and dealing with a Missouri law regulating abortions and a request from both Missouri and the solicitor general for the Court to reverse *Roe* v. *Wade,* seventy-eight amicus briefs were filed.

Formal oratory before the Supreme Court, perhaps lasting for several days, is a thing of the past. As a rule, counsel for each side is limited to a thirty-minute argument—sometimes less, sometimes more. Lawyers use a lectern to which two lights are attached. A white light flashes five minutes before time is up and when the red light goes on, the lawyer must stop, even in the middle of an "if."

The entire procedure is formally informal. Sometimes, to the annoyance of the attorneys, the justices talk among themselves or consult briefs or legal volumes during the oral presentation. Sometimes, if justices find a presentation particularly bad, they frequently and ostentatiously consult their watches.

Jurisdiction of the Supreme Court

ORIGINAL
In all cases affecting ambassadors, other public ministers, and consuls.

In cases in which a state is a party.

APPELLATE
In all other cases arising under the judicial power of the United States. The Supreme Court has appellate jurisdiction—power to review decisions of other courts—except when Congress determines otherwise.

The Liability Revolution: The Tort Law Explosion

In recent decades, and especially since the late 1980s, there has been an expansion in **tort law,** that part of civil law covering the liability of those whose conduct injures others and the compensation they must pay.

"Throughout most of American history, liability law has been an obscure legal byway . . . with little discernible effect on the wider society or economy."* Today liability has dramatically expanded and the targets are mainly manufacturers, physicians, hospitals, towns, and counties, and their insurance carriers.

Judges have played a leading role in this liability revolution, to the praise of some who believe judges have provided protection for the weak against the powerful, to the criticism of others who believe judges have usurped legislative responsibilities and impaired the effectiveness of our economy.

This is yet another example of the important role judges play: They not only resolve disputes between individuals but in so doing they are central policy makers.

* Walter Olson, "The Liability Revolution," *New Directions in Liability Law, Proceedings of the Academy of Political Science*, vol. 37, no. 1 (1988), p. 1.

The justices freely interrupt the lawyers to ask questions and to request additional information. If a lawyer seems to be having a difficult time, the justices may try to help him or her present a better case. Occasionally, the justices bounce arguments off a hapless attorney, and at one another. During oral argument in the school desegregation cases, for example, Justice Frankfurter was grilling an NAACP lawyer: "Are you saying that we can say that 'separate but equal' is not a doctrine that is relevant at the primary school level? Is that what you are saying?" he demanded.

Justice Douglas tried to help the lawyer out. "I think you are saying," he ventured, "that segregation may be all right in streetcars and railroad cars and restaurants, but . . . education is different from that."

The lawyer found the Douglas paraphrase to his liking. "Yes, sir," he replied. Douglas continued, "That is your argument, is it not? Isn't that your argument in this case?" Again a grateful "yes" from counsel.

Frankfurter, however, was not even moderately impressed. "But how can that be your argument . . . ?" he cried, and the lawyer was once again on his own.[38]

Justice Scalia is a particularly harsh questioner. "When Scalia prepares to ask a question he doesn't just adjust himself in his chair to get closer to the microphone like the others, he looks like a vulcher, zooming in for the kill. He strains way forward, pinches his eyebrows, and poses the question, like '. . . do you want us to believe. . . .' "[39] Stevens and Scalia, although of different perspectives, often sit together and chat with one another while the argument is going on. Justice Marshall "does a terrible job of keeping his mouth away from the mike when he's whispering."[40]

BEHIND THE CURTAINS—THE CONFERENCE

Wednesday afternoons and all day Friday the justices meet in conference. They have heard the oral arguments, read and studied the briefs, and examined the petitions. Before every conference each justice receives a list of the cases to be discussed. Each brings to the meeting a red leather book in which the cases and the votes of the justices are recorded. These conferences are secret affairs, although in recent years the secrecy has been penetrated. They are marked by informality and vigorous give-and-take. The chief justice presides. He usually opens the discussion by stating the facts, summarizing the questions of law, and making suggestions for disposing of the case. Each member of the Court is then asked, in order of seniority, to give his or her views and conclusions. Recently the justices have not bothered with formal votes because they express their views when they discuss the case.[41]

The dynamics of the conference are illustrated by the maneuvering in the case of *National League of Cities* v. *Usery*, taken up by the Court at its Friday, March 5, 1976, session.[42] (This case was reversed nine years later in *Garcia* v. *San Antonio Metro.*[43]) The question was whether the federal minimum wage law should be applied to municipal police and firefighters and other workers. In 1968, in *Maryland* v. *Wirtz*, the Court had upheld the application of this same law to state hospital workers and school employees. This would appear to be a binding precedent.

Chief Justice Burger opened the discussion by saying that for the time being he would pass, although his brethren, as the justices used to call each other until a year before the appointment of Justice O'Connor, knew he really would like to see *Wirtz* overruled. Justice Brennan, next in seniority, argued that the

Court was bound by the Wirtz precedent. Justice Potter Stewart told his colleagues that although he had dissented in *Wirtz*, he would not vote to overrule it unless five other justices wanted to do so. In other words, he did not want to be the one to cause a reversal. Justices White and Marshall agreed that the *Wirtz* precedent controlled. As the discussion went around the table, the vote was three for applying the federal law to city workers; Justice Stewart was prepared to go along and the chief justice was on the fence.

Justice Blackmun "wondered if there was some way to distinguish the case from *Wirtz* so that they could avoid the precedent."[44] There was a way to make a distinction between the two types of employees, agreed Justices Powell and Rehnquist. They were quite ready to overrule *Wirtz* and hold the federal law should not be applied to either state hospital workers or to city police and firefighters, if the rest of the justices would go along. Justice Stevens, the junior justice, said he thought *Wirtz* should prevail. Thus, there were five votes to uphold the law as applied to the additional state and municipal employees and to reinforce the *Wirtz* decision.

The discussion was not over. Justice White chided Justice Stewart for refusing to become the fifth vote to overturn a prior decision they both thought was wrong. Justice Stewart responded: "I think you are right, I'll vote the other way." But he said he was not going to vote for some underhanded formula; he wanted a clear ruling that *Wirtz* was being overruled. The chief justice now declared he would vote to overrule, so the vote became five to four to do so. He assigned Justice Rehnquist the responsibility for drafting an opinion for the Court.

OPINIONS

As a general rule, Supreme Court opinions state the facts, present the issues, announce the decision, and, most important, explain the reasoning of the Court. These opinions are the Court's principal method of expressing its views to the world. Perhaps the most important function of opinions is to instruct the judges of all other state and federal courts in the United States on how to decide similar cases in the future.

Judicial opinions may be directed at Congress or at the president. If the Court regrets that "in the absence of action by Congress, we have no choice but to . . ." or insists that "relief of the sort that petitioner demands can only come from the political branches of government," it is clearly asking Congress to act.[45] The justices also use opinions to communicate with the public. A well-handled opinion may increase support among specialized publics—especially lawyers and judges—and among the general population for a policy the Court is stressing. For this reason, the Court delayed declaring school segregation unconstitutional until unanimity could be secured. The justices understood that any sign of dissension on the bench on this major social issue would be an invitation to evade the Court's ruling.

ASSIGNING OPINIONS

Justices want to work on opinions that deal with significant issues, and the justice to whom an opinion is assigned knows that he or she must influence the outcome, for no vote in conference is final. Justices are free to change their minds if persuaded by the draft opinion. When voting with the majority, the chief justice decides who drafts the opinion. When the chief justice is in the minority, the senior

You decide!

A few years ago the Texas state legislature decided Texas taxpayers should no longer provide a free public education for the children of undocumented aliens.

Setting aside for a moment whether or not you think such a policy is desirable, in your judgment is there anything in the United States Constitution, especially in the equal protection clause (see Chapter 5), that should prevent the Texas legislature from making such a choice? (Answer/Discussion on page 453.)

"Do you ever have one of those days when everything seems unconstitutional?"

Drawing by Joe Mirachi; © 1974 The New Yorker Magazine, Inc.

justice among the majority makes the assignment, often to himself or herself. Justices are free to write **dissenting opinions** if they wish. If a justice agrees with the majority on how the case should be decided but differs on the reasoning, that justice may write a **concurring opinion.**

CIRCULATING DRAFTS

Writing an opinion for the Court is an exacting task. The document must win the support of at least four—even more, if possible—intelligent, strong-willed persons, all of whom may have voted the same way but for very different reasons. Assisted by the law clerks, the assigned justice writes a draft and sends it to colleagues for comments. If the justice is lucky, the majority will accept the draft, perhaps with only minor changes. If the draft is not satisfactory to the other justices, it must be redrafted and recirculated until a majority can reach agreement.

If the initial version is not acceptable to a majority, an elaborate bargaining process occurs. The opinion ultimately published is not necessarily the opinion the author would have liked to write. Like a committee report, it represents the common denominator. Holmes bitterly complained to Laski that he had written an opinion "in terms to suit the majority of the brethren, although they didn't suit me. Years ago I did the same thing in the interest of getting a job done. I let the brethren put in a reason that I thought bad and cut out all that I thought good and I have squirmed ever since, and swore that never again—but again I yield and now comes a petition for rehearing pointing out all the horrors that will ensue from just what I didn't want to say."[46]

The two major weapons justices can use against their colleagues are their votes and their willingness to write separate opinions attacking a doctrine the majority wishes to see adopted. A dissenting opinion is sometimes written and circulated for the stated purpose of convincing the majority. If the opinion writer is persuaded by the logic of the dissenter, the dissenting opinion may never be published. Even if this is not done, and it seldom is, the justice writing for the majority may be forced to give in to the demands of a colleague on his or her side as a price of keeping the majority together. Especially if the Court is closely divided, one justice may be in a position to demand that a given argument be included in, or removed from, the opinion as the price of his or her vote. Sometimes this can happen even if the Court is not closely divided. An opinion writer who anticipates that a decision will bring critical public reaction may very much wish to have it presented as the view of a unanimous Court and may be prepared to compromise to achieve unanimity. (See Table 17–2 for a comparison of dissent rates in various Courts.)

The internal battling over the opinion in *National League of Cities* v. *Usery* is typical of what happens in many cases. After the first round of voting, it appeared that Justice Brennan would assign the opinion, because he was the senior justice in what appeared to be the majority. But when Justice Stewart switched his vote, the chief justice was with the majority, so it now fell to him to assign the opinion, which he did—to Justice Rehnquist. As Justice Rehnquist circulated his draft, Justices Stevens and Brennan each sent around strong dissents. Justice Stewart's clerks hoped that they might be able to persuade him to change his mind, so they presented him with their own critical analysis of the Rehnquist draft. Despite the pressures, Justice Stewart stood fast with Rehnquist. Justice Blackmun was wavering, and how he would go would determine the outcome. Justice Rehnquist modified his draft to take Blackmun's views into account, to be sure that he kept Blackmun's vote. Justice Brennan was also working on Blackmun. In his dissent he had writ-

TABLE 17–2
Comparison of Dissent Rates

Justice	Number of Dissenting Opinions	Average per Term
"The Great Dissenters"		
W. Johnson, 1804–1834	30	1.0
J. Catron, 1837–1865	26	0.9
N. Clifford, 1858–1881	60	2.6
J. Harlan, 1877–1911	119	3.5
O. Holmes, 1902–1932	72	2.4
L. Brandeis, 1916–1939	65	2.9
H. Stone, 1925–1946	93	4.6
H. Black, 1937–1971	310	9.1
F. Frankfurter, 1939–1962	251	10.9
J. Harlan, 1955–1971	242	15.5
The Burger and Rehnquist Courts		
W. Douglas, 1969–1974	231	38.5
J. Stevens, 1975–1987	281	23.4
W. Brennan, Jr., 1969–1987	339	17.8
T. Marshall, 1969–1987	289	15.2
W. Rehnquist, 1971–1987	243	14.2
P. Stewart, 1969–1980	130	10.8
B. White, 1969–1987	207	10.8
H. Blackmun, 1971–1987	176	10.3
A. Scalia, 1986–1987	19	9.5
L. Powell, Jr., 1971–1987	144	9.0
S. O'Connor, 1981–1987	54	7.7
W. Burger, 1969–1986	111	6.5
A. Kennedy, 1987	3	3.0

Source: David M. O'Brien, *Storm Center: The Supreme Court in American Politics* (Norton, 1990).

William Hubbs Rehnquist, former Supreme Court Law clerk, Assistant Attorney General, Associate Justice of the Supreme Court (1971–1986), and now Chief Justice.

Answer/Discussion

Speaking through Justice William Brennan (*Plyler* v. *Doe*, 457 U.S. 202 1982), five members of the United States Supreme Court ruled that the law violated the equal protection clause because Texas had failed to show its action would, as alleged, protect the state from an influx of illegal immigrants, improve the overall quality of education, or save substantial sums of money. "If the state," wrote Justice Brennan, "is to deny a discrete group of innocent children the free public education it offers to other children residing within its borders, that denial must be justified by a showing that it furthers some substantial state interests. No such showing was made here." Chief Justice Burger, dissenting along with Justices White, Rehnquist, and O'Connor, wrote: "I agree without hesitation that it is senseless for an enlightened society to deprive any children—including illegal aliens—of an elementary education. However, the Constitution does not vest in this Court the authority to strike down laws because they do not meet our standards of desirable social policy, 'wisdom,' or 'common sense.' . . . Today's cases, I regret to say, present yet another example of unwarranted judicial action which in the long run tends to contribute to the weakening of our political process."

What dilemmas of democracy does this case illustrate?

Do you think this case might be decided differently the next time it, or a similar issue, comes before the Court, because of recent appointments of Justices Scalia and Kennedy to the Supreme Court?

ten: "I cannot recall another instance in the Court's history when the reasoning of so many decisions covering so long a span of time has been discarded in such a roughshod manner."[47] On the draft he sent to Justice Blackmun he wrote a personal note, "asking if there was anything that he could do to get his vote."[48]

Although Justice Blackmun was disturbed by the sarcastic tone of Brennan's opinion, he still had not made up his mind to stay with Rehnquist. He "toyed with concurring in the result only,"[49] which would have meant that Rehnquist would have been denied the fifth vote for his opinion, which was necessary to make it a controlling precedent. Finally, he decided merely to write a single-paragraph concurring opinion explaining that in different situations where the federal government has a greater interest than it did in this particular case, federal intervention into the affairs of state and local governments might be justified. But because his concurrence endorsed the Rehnquist opinion, that opinion became the opinion of the Court and thus a controlling precedent. (It was Justice Blackmun who nine years later wrote the opinion for the Court in *Garcia* v. *San Antonio Metro*, which overturned *National League of Cities* v. *Usery*.)

THE POWERS OF THE CHIEF JUSTICE

The ability of the chief justice to influence the Court has varied considerably.[50] Chief Justice Hughes ran the conferences like a stern schoolmaster, keeping the justices talking to the point, moving the discussion along, and doing his best to work out compromises. He tried to achieve unanimous votes in order to give

decisions greater weight. Chief Justice Stone, on the other hand, encouraged justices to state their own points of view and let the discussions wander. Chief Justice Burger devoted much of his time to judicial reform, speaking to bar and lay groups and trying to build political support for modernizing the judicial process. Chief Justice Rehnquist had fifteen years of Court experience prior to his appointment and had demonstrated personal warmth. What kind of chief justice he will be remains to be seen.[51] For as one scholar warns us, "The Chief Justiceship does not guarantee leadership. It only offers its incumbent an opportunity to lead. Optimum leadership inheres in the combination of the office and an able, persuasive, personable judge."[52]

THE RISE OF THE LAW CLERKS

Beginning in the 1930s federal judges began the practice of hiring the best recent graduates of law schools to serve as clerks for a year or two. As the judicial work load increased, more law clerks have been appointed. Today each Supreme Court justice is entitled to four clerks (circuit judges have three, and each court of appeals has "staff attorneys"). Clerks draft opinions and screen writs of certiorari, which determine the cases the Court will review. Justices often talk through their cases with their law clerks.

Law clerks are young and energetic, and they know how to use computers to do research and prepare drafts of opinions. As the number of law clerks and computers has increased, so has the number of concurring and dissenting opinions. Further, opinions are longer and have more substantive footnotes and elaborate citations of cases and law review articles. As Justice Harry A. Blackmun said about his colleague, Justice John Paul Stevens, "He uses hundreds of footnotes. Sometimes I think what he does is to outline his opinion, give it to his clerks and say, 'You put the footnotes in,' and of course there's an ego trip for the clerks and they have all kinds of footnotes."[53]

AFTER THE LAWSUIT IS OVER

Victory in the Supreme Court does not necessarily mean that winning parties get what they want. As a rule, the Court does not implement its own decision, but "remands" the case to the lower court with instructions to act in accordance with the Supreme Court's opinion. The lower court often has considerable leeway in interpreting the Court's mandate as it disposes of the case.

Although Congress or a president has occasionally "ignored" or "construed" a Supreme Court ruling to avoid its impact, decisions whose enforcement requires only the action of a central governmental agency usually become effective immediately. Thus, when the Supreme Court held that President Truman lacked constitutional authority to seize steel companies temporarily to avoid a shutdown during the Korean War, the president promptly complied. Of course, subsequent presidents have great discretion in determining how that particular precedent should be applied to their own behavior.

The impact of a particular ruling announced by the Supreme Court on the behavior of those who are not immediate parties to a lawsuit is even more uncertain. Many of the more important decisions require further action by administrative and elected officials before they become the effective law of the land. Sometimes Supreme Court decisions are simply ignored. Despite the Supreme Court's holding that it is unconstitutional for school boards to require prayers within schools,

Federal law clerks often rise to prominence, as in the case of Susan R. Estrich, who became a Harvard law professor and later campaign manager for Michael Dukakis; Elliot Richardson, former Attorney General; and Philip B. Kurland, dean of the law school at the University of Chicago.

CHAPTER 17 / Judges: The Balancing Branch

for example, some school boards continue their previous practices.[54] And for years after the Supreme Court held public school segregation unconstitutional, many school districts remained segregated.[55]

The most difficult Supreme Court decisions to implement are those that require the cooperation of large numbers of officials. For example, a Supreme Court decision announcing a new standard for warrantless searches is not likely to have an impact on the way police make arrests for some time, since not many police officers subscribe to the *United States Supreme Court Reports*. The process is more complex. Local prosecutors, state attorneys general, chiefs of police, and state and federal trial court judges must all participate to give "meaning" to Supreme Court decisions.

The Constitution may be what the Supreme Court says it is, but a Supreme Court opinion, for the moment at least, is what a trial judge or police officer or a prosecutor or a school board or a city council says it is.

Associate Justice Antonin Scalia, nominated by Ronald Reagan and confimed in 1986.

Judicial Power in a Democracy

An independent judiciary is one of the hallmarks of a free society. As impartial dispensers of equal justice under the law, judges should not be dependent on the executive, the legislature, the parties to the case, the electorate, or a mob outside the courtroom. But this very independence, essential to protect judges in their roles as legal umpires, raises basic problems when a democratic society decides—as has ours—also to make these same judges key policy makers. Perhaps in no other society do interests and individuals resort to litigation as much as they do in the United States as a means of making public policy.

The involvement of our courts in politics, especially the Supreme Court, in choosing among competing values has historically exposed the judiciary to political criticism. Throughout our history the Supreme Court has been attacked for engaging in "judicial legislation." This is nothing new. Yet the more active role of the federal courts in recent years in behalf of liberal causes and the Reagan and Bush administrations' frontal attack on that role have returned these issues to the forefront of public debate.

Since the end of World War II, federal courts under the Supreme Court's leadership have removed most of the constitutional restraints on government regulation of business. At the same time, they have imposed many more restraints in order to protect civil liberties and civil rights, especially for the poor and the black. Since 1943 the Supreme Court has declared unconstitutional more than fifty provisions of acts of Congress as well as more than 400 acts of state legislatures and city councils. (Overall, the Supreme Court has struck down 135 acts of Congress and almost 1000 pieces of state legislation and state constitutional provisions. In one 1983 decision, *INS* v. *Chadha*, it called into question 200 provisions of various federal laws.)

Whereas in earlier times the judges occasionally told public officials what they could not do, today they often tell them what they must do. For example, federal judges, often responding to class action complaints, have told Congress, state legislatures, and local officials that they must provide attorneys for the poor, and ensure adequate care for mental patients, modernize prisons, and even break up the telephone system (in this last case the Department of Justice initiated the action). Often the judges retain jurisdiction for years as they preside over the implementation of the decrees they have issued.[56] Closely related to this expansive interpretation of the requirement of constitutional law is the expansion in tort

Justice Thurgood Marshall, member of the Supreme Court since 1967, was the first black appointed to the nations's highest court.

liability that has opened wider the courts to persons who believe they have been injured by the actions of others, including the actions of public officials.[57] Judges have always been policy makers; it is not a matter of choice but of role. But today they also govern.

THE GREAT DEBATE OVER THE PROPER ROLE OF THE COURTS

Naturally, those who like what the judges have done tend to defend the propriety of the judges doing it. Judges should do what is right, and the assumption is frequently made that what is right and what is required by the Constitution are one and the same, even if such actions are not politically popular. They contend that courts have a duty to protect the long-range interests of the public as defined in the Constitution, even against the short-range wishes of the voters (but then what is and is not defined by the Constitution is the issue). Defenders of this kind of judicial role argue that if Congress, the White House, and the state legislatures are unable to resolve pressing problems and some are being denied justice and their constitutional rights, then the courts should do so. The Supreme Court, they say, should be "a leader in a vital national seminar that leads to the formulation of values for the American people."[58]

Critics of *judicial activism*, on the other side, contend that in recent years, the federal courts, in their zeal to protect the people, especially the poor, have become unhinged from their political moorings in the political and constitutional system. It was wrong for conservative justices prior to 1937 to strike down laws that did not conflict with the literal terms of the Constitution, they argue, so it is wrong for today's more liberal justices to do so. These critics argue that even if courts make the "right" decisions, it is not right for courts to take over the legislative responsibilities of the people's elected representatives.

Others claim that the debate between those who favor judicial restraint and those who favor judicial activism, oversimplifies the choices. They argue that judges should take a leadership role in some areas but a restrained role in others. They stand with Justice Harlan Stone, who, in his famous footnote four in his opinion in *Carolene Products*, argued that courts have a special duty to intervene (1) whenever legislation restricts the political process by which decisions are made or (2) whenever legislation restricts the rights of "discrete and insular minorities." In all other areas the political process should be allowed to work, and judges should not set aside legislation or interfere with administrative agencies merely because they would prefer some other policy or even some other interpretation of the Constitution.[59]

Since President Reagan was able to appoint so many conservative jurists and President Bush controls nominations for at least four years, it is probable that there will be a more conservative line of judicial decisions in the 1990s than there has been for several decades. It will be interesting to see if there is a reversion to the more traditional conservative support for and liberal skepticism about judicial power. When conservatives find federal judges more sympathetic to their perspective, they may become less skeptical about judicial activism, and liberals may once again become advocates of judicial restraint.

THE PEOPLE AND THE COURT

We no longer accept the explanation that it is right to give the power of judicial review to independent judges because their own policy views are irrelevant to the decisions they make. The absurdity of the assumption that they are merely

CHAPTER 17 / Judges: The Balancing Branch

carrying out the clear commands of the Constitution is indicated by the fact that the justices divide so frequently over what the Constitution means. More acceptable is the explanation that although judges do choose between competing values, they are not free to adopt whatever policies they wish. They are restricted by a variety of limitations, the most significant of which come from the political system of which the judges are a part.

Whether judges are liberal or conservative, defer to legislatures or not, try to apply the Constitution as the framers intended, or interpret it to conform to current values, there are linkages between what the judges do and what the people want done. The linkages are not direct, and the people never speak with one mind, but these linkages are the heart of the matter.[60] In the first place, the president and the Senate are likely to appoint justices whose decisions reflect contemporary values. When the people elected Carter, they got judges who reflected Carter's perspectives. When they elected Reagan, they got judges who reflected Reagan's values rather than Mondale's. Bush's judges reflect his views rather than Dukakis's. Although Bush's views about the Supreme Court may have had little to do with his winning the 1988 election, he made clear in his campaigns that if elected he would nominate judges of a more conservative bent than those Dukakis would choose. And Dukakis warned the voters against electing Bush because the next president might well have the chance to pick several Supreme Court justices and tip the balance on such key constitutional issues as affirmative action, abortion, and rights of persons accused of crime.

Even without a change in judicial personnel, changing currents of public opinion influence what the judges decide. This connection between the public and the Supreme Court does not come about because of Mr. Dooley's celebrated charge, "The Supreme Court follows the illiction returns."[61] On the contrary, after major **realigning elections,** when a new political coalition takes over the White House and/or Congress, the old regime stays on in the federal courts. Or, as one unknown wit put it: "The good presidents do dies with them, the bad lives on after them on the Supreme Court." Yet despite initial clashes, the new electoral coalitions eventually also "take over" the federal courts. Before too long, new interpretations of the Constitution reflect the dominant political ideology.

Judges have neither armies nor police to execute their rulings. Although Congress cannot reverse Supreme Court decisions as they relate to constitutional interpretations, and only four decisions have been reversed by formal constitutional amendment, the political system can alter the course of judicial policy making in other, only slightly more subtle ways. Decisions are binding on the parties to a particular case, but the policies involved in judicial decisions are effective and durable only to the extent that they are supported by a considerable portion of the electorate. To win a favorable Supreme Court decision is to win something of considerable political value, but the policies reflected by that decision may or may not alter the way people behave. If the Court's policies are too far out of step with the values of the country, the Court is likely to be "reversed."

The policy-making process is complex. What Congress and the White House and the state legislatures and police officers do has an effect on what the Supreme Court does, and what the Supreme Court does has an effect on what Congress and the White House and the state legislatures and the police do. Most importantly, what all these agencies do is related to what the various segments of "the people" want done. Consider, for example, the chain of developments that made the Constitution more reflective of the values of equal rights under the law. Changing economic and social conditions led to the growth of a black leadership, which in turn generated political power for blacks, which led presidents to care about what blacks wanted, which resulted in their appointing judges who reflected the

Justice William Brennan, On Constitutional Interpretation

There are those who find legitimacy in fidelity to what they call "the intention of the Framers." In its most doctrinaire incarnation, this view demands that Justices discern exactly what the Framers thought about the question under consideration and simply follow that intention in resolving the case before them. It is a view that feigns self-effacing deference to the specific judgments of those who forged our original social compact.

But in truth it is little more than arrogance cloaked in humility. It is arrogant to pretend that from our vantage we can gauge accurately the intent of the Framers on application of principle to specific, contemporary questions. Apart from the problematic nature of the sources, our distance of two centuries cannot but work as a prism refracting all we perceive.

One cannot help but speculate that the chorus of lamentations calling for interpretation faithful to "original intention"—and proposing nullification of interpretations that fail this quick litmus test—must inevitably come from persons who have no familiarity with the historical record. . . .

We current Justices read the Constitution in the only way we can: as 20th century Americans. We look to the history of the time of framing and to the intervening history of interpretation. But the ultimate question must be, what do the words of the text mean in our time? For the genius of the Constitution rests not in any static meaning it might have in a world that is dead and gone, but in the adaptability of its great principles to cope with current problems and current needs.

Source: Speech at Georgetown University, October 12, 1985. Reprinted in *The New York Times* (October 13, 1985), p. 36. Copyright © 1985 by The New York Times Company.

The Supreme Court today.

values of civil rights advocates. And this action led to action and reaction in city councils, school boards, and state legislatures. The judges certainly played a leadership role in the development of a national "civil rights" consensus, but where they led the people followed. Today we are in the midst of a continuing debate

TABLE 17–3
U.S. Supreme Court Declarations of Unconstitutionality of
Federal Statutes (in Whole or in Part)

Time Span	Chief Justice	Number of Declarations of Unconstitutionality	Comments
1798–1801	Jay	0	
	J. Rutledge	0	Weak, placid Court
	Ellsworth	0	
1801–1835	Marshall	1	1803: *Marbury* v. *Madison*
1836–1864	Taney	1	1857: *Dred Scott* v. *Sandford*
1864–1873	Chase	10	1870: *Legal Tender cases*
1874–1888	Waite	9	1833: *Civil Rights cases*[1]
1888–1910	Fuller	14 (15)	1895: *Income Tax cases*
1910–1921	White	12	1918: *Child Labor case*
1921–1930	Taft	12	1923: *Minimum Wage case*
1930–1936	Hughes	14	Of these, 13 came in 1934–36!
1936–1941	Hughes	0	The New Deal Court emerges following the "switch-in-time that saved nine" in 1937
1941–1946	Stone	2	New Libertarian emphasis
1946–1953	Vinson	1	Abstemious Court
1953–1969	Warren	25	High-water mark of Liberal-activism
1969–1986	Burger	34	First Amendment, Equal Protection, and Separation of Powers concerns
1986–present	Rehnquist	4	Conservative, Counter Revolution
Total		138	

Source: Adapted from Henry J. Abraham, *The Judicial Process*, 5th ed. (Oxford University Press, 1986), p. 294.

Note: Table is arranged chronologically in accordance with tenure of chief justices; as of July 1986.

[1] Consolidated five different cases in one opinion (here counted as one).

about what the Constitution "means" about affirmative action. The answer is being decided only in part by what the judges say it means.

"The people" speak in many ways and with many voices. The Supreme Court—and the other courts—represent and reflect the values of some of these people. Although the Court is not the defenseless institution portrayed by some commentators, and its decisions are as much shapers of public opinion as reflections of it, ultimately the power of the Court rests on retaining the support of most of the people most of the time. No better standard for determining the legitimacy of a governmental institution has been discovered.

Summary

1. Judges in the United States play a more active role in political life than they do in other democracies. Federal courts receive their jurisdiction directly from Congress, which must decide the constitutional division of responsibilities among federal and state courts.

2. Federal judges apply statutory law, common law, equity, admiralty and maritime law, and administrative law. They apply federal, criminal, and civil law. Although bound by procedural requirements, including *stare decisis*, they have to exercise discretion.

3. Partisanship and ideology are important factors in the selection of federal judges at all levels, and they ensure a linkage between the courts and the rest of the political system.

4. The Supreme Court, which has almost complete control over the cases it reviews as they come up from the state courts, the courts of appeals, and district courts, is a revered but somewhat mysterious branch of our government. Annu-

ally its nine justices dispose of thousands of cases, but most of their time is concentrated on the approximately 200 cases per year that establish guidelines for lower courts and the country.

5. A continuing concern of major importance is the reconciliation of the role of judges—especially those on the Supreme Court—as independent and fair dispensers of justice for the parties before them with their vital role as interpreters of the Constitution. This is an especially complex problem in our democracy because of the power of judicial review and the significant role courts play making public policy.

6. The debate about how judges should interpret the Constitution is almost as old as the Republic. Two hundred years after the Constitution was inaugurated the argument between those who contend judges should interpret the document literally and those who believe they cannot and should not has returned to the headlines.

Further Reading

HENRY J. ABRAHAM. *The Judiciary: The Supreme Court in the Governmental Process*, 7th ed. (Allyn and Bacon, 1987).

HENRY J. ABRAHAM. *Justices and Presidents: A Political History of Appointments to the Supreme Court*, 2d ed. (Oxford University Press, 1985).

MARK W. CANNON and DAVID O'BRIEN, eds. *Views from the Bench: The Judiciary and Constitutional Politics* (Chatham House, 1985).

BENJAMIN N. CARDOZO. *The Nature of the Judicial Process* (Yale University Press, 1921).

JOHN HART ELY. *Democracy and Distrust: A Theory of Judicial Review* (Harvard University Press, 1980).

JESSE H. CHOPER. *The Supreme Court and Its Justices: The Best of the ABA Journal* (The American Bar Association, 1987).

LOUIS FISHER. *Constitutional Dialogues: Interpretation as Political Process* (Princeton University Press, 1988).

STEPHEN C. HALPERN and CHARLES M. LAMB, eds. *Supreme Court Activism and Restraint* (Heath, 1982).

WILLIAM LASSER. *The Limits of Judicial Power: The Supreme Court in American Politics* (University of North Carolina Press, 1989).

LEONARD W. LEVY. *Original Intent and the Framers' Constitution* (Macmillian, 1988).

WALTER F. MURPHY and C. HERMAN PRICHETT. *Courts, Judges and Politics: An Introduction to the Judicial Process*, 4th ed. (Random House, 1986).

DAVID M. O'BRIEN. *Storm Center: The Supreme Court in American Politics*, 2nd ed. (W. W. Norton, 1990).

J. W. PELTASON. *Federal Courts in the Political Process* (Doubleday, 1955).

RICHARD A. POSNER. *The Federal Courts* (Harvard University Press, 1985).

BERNARD SCHWARTZ. *Super Chief: Earl Warren and His Supreme Court—A Judicial Biography* (New York University Press, 1983).

LAURENCE H. TRIBE. *God Save This Honorable Court: How the Choices of Supreme Court Justices Shape Our History* (Random House, 1985).

STEPHEN L. WASBY. *The Supreme Court in the Federal Judicial System*, 3d ed. (Nelson-Hall, 1988).

Notes

1. Henry J. Abraham, *The Judicial Process*, 5th ed. (Oxford University Press, 1986), p. 197.
2. Phillips Bradley, ed., *Democracy in America*, vol. 1 (Knopf, 1944), pp. 278–80.
3. Harold J. Laski, *The American Democracy* (Viking, 1948), p. 110.
4. *Luther v. Borden*, 7 Howard 1 (1849).
5. *Chicago Grand Trunk Railway Co.* v. *Wellman*, 143 U.S. 339 (1892).
6. Karen Orren, "Standing to Sue, Interest Group Conflict in the Federal Courts," *The American Political Science Review* (September 1976), pp. 723–741.
7. Phillip J. Cooper, *Hard Judicial Choices: Federal District Court Judges and State and Local Officials* (Oxford University Press, 1988), p. 15.
8. Quoted in Paul E. Freund, *On Understanding the Supreme Court* (Little, Brown, 1949), p. 3.
9. This discussion is based on H. L. A. Hart, *The Concept of Law* (Oxford University Press, 1961), chap. 7.
10. For one of the great classics, see Benjamin Cardozo, *The Nature of the Judicial Process* (Yale University Press, 1921).
11. Hart, *The Concept of Law*, pp. 121, 122.
12. Quoted by E. S. Corwin, *Constitutional Revolution* (Claremont and Associated Colleges, 1941), p. 38.
13. Steven Puro and Roger Goldman, "U.S. Magistrates: Changing Dimensions of First-Echelon Federal Judicial Officers," in Philip L. Dubois, ed., *The Politics of Judicial Reform* (Heath, 1982). See also Caroll Seron, "Magistrates and the Work of Federal Courts: A New Division of Labor," *Judicature* (April–May 1986), pp. 353–59; and Christopher E. Smith, "Who are the U.S. Magistrates"?, *Judicature* (October–November 1987), pp. 143–50.
14. Justice Stevens dissenting in *Pennsylvania Bureau of Correction* v. *United States Marshals Service*, 474 U.S. 348 (1985).
15. *Bordenkircher* v. *Hayes*, 434 U.S. 357 (1978). See also James Eisenstein, *Counsel for the United States: U.S. Attorneys in the Political and Legal Systems* (The Johns Hopkins Press, 1978); and *Wayte* v. *United States*, 470 U.S. 598 (1985).
16. Karen O'Connor, "The Amicus Curiae Role of the U.S. Solicitor General in Supreme Court Litigation," *Judicature* (December–January 1983), pp. 256–64; and Jeffrey A. Segal, "Amicus Curiae Briefs by the Solicitor General during the Warren and Burger Courts," *Western Political Quarterly* 41 (March 1988), pp. 134–44.
17. See Lincoln Caplan, *The Tenth Justice: The Solicitor General and the Rule of Law* (Knopf, 1987) for a critical analysis.
18. Thomas R. Morris, "States before the U.S. Supreme Court: State Attorneys General as Amicus Curiae," *Judicature*, vol. 70 (February–March 1987), p. 301.
19. Neil D. McFeeley, *Appointment of Judges: The Johnson Presidency* (University of Texas Press 1987), p. 1.
20. Harold W. Chase, *Federal Judges: The Appointing Process* (University of Minnesota Press, 1972), pp. 3–47; Paul Simon, "The Senate's Role in Judicial Appointments," *Judicature* (June–July 1986), pp. 55–58; and Elliot E. Slotnick, "Federal Judicial Recruitment and Selection Research: A Review Essay," *Judicature* (April–May 1988), p. 317–24.
21. Lettie McSpadden Wenner and Lee F. Dutter, "Contextual Influences on Court Outcomes," *Western Political Quarterly*, vol. 41 (March 1988), pp. 115–34; and Ronald Stidham and Robert A. Carp, "Exploring Regionalism in the Federal District Courts," *Publius*, vol. 18 (Fall 1988), pp. 113–25.
22. "Doubts about the ABA," *The Wall Street Journal*, editorial, April 11, 1989; Gordon J. Humphrey, "End ABA Role as Hanging Judge," *The Wall Street Journal* (March 22, 1989), A14; *Public Citizen* v. *Department of Justice*, 105 L.Ed. 2d 377 (1989).
23. Sheldon Goldman, "Judicial Selection and the Qualities That Make a Good Judge," *The Annals* (July 1982), p. 117–18. See also Elliot E. Slotnick, "The ABA Standing Committee on Federal Judiciary: A Contemporary Assessment," *Judicature* (March–April 1983), pp. 348ff and 385ff.
24. George Watson and John Stookey, "Supreme Court Confirmation Hearings: A View from the Senate," *Judicature* (December–January 1988), p. 193.
25. Robert A. Carp and C. K. Rowland, *Policymaking and Politics in the Federal District Courts* (University of Tennessee Press, 1983), p. 82.
26. Quotation from Lincoln in J. W. Peltason, *Federal Courts in the Political Process* (Doubleday, 1955); and Laurence H. Tribe, *God Save this Honorable Court: How the Choice of Supreme Court Justices Shapes Our History* (Random House, 1985). See also Henry J. Abraham, *Justices and Presidents: A Political History of Appointments to the Supreme Court*, 2d ed. (Oxford University Press, 1985).
27. Henry Cabot Lodge, *Selections from the Correspondence of Theodore Roosevelt and Henry Cabot Lodge*, vol. 1 (Scribner's, 1925), pp. 518–19.
28. Sheldon Goldman, "Reagan's Judicial legacy: Completing the Puzzle and Summing Up, *Judicature*, vol 72, no 6 (April–May 1989), pp. 318–330.
29. Jill Abramson, "Conservative Legal Groups Plan Efforts to Keep Bush Administration on Reagan's Judicial Path," *The Wall Street Journal* (November 21, 1988), p. A16.
30. Letter to Horace Taft, November 14, 1929, quoted in H. Pringle, *The Life and Times of William Howard Taft*, vol. 2 (Farrar, 1939), p. 967.
31. Sue Davis, "Federalism and Property Rights: An Examination of Justice Rehnquist's Legal Positivism," *The Western Political Quarterly* (June 1986), pp. 250–64.
32. Donald Santarelli, as quoted in Jerry Landauer, "Shaping the Bench," *The Wall Street Journal* (December 10, 1970), p. 1. See also Peltason, *Federal Courts in the Political Process*, p. 32.
33. Wallace 506 (1869).
34. Richard Johnson, *The Dynamics of Compliance* (Wiley, 1967), pp. 33–41. This summary of Johnson's comment is taken from David Adamany, "Legitimacy, Realigning Elections, and the Supreme Court," *Wisconsin Law Review* (1973), p. 792.
35. Sidney Ulmer, "The Supreme Court's Certiorari Decisions: Conflict as a Predictive Variable," *American Political Science Review* (December 1984), pp. 901–11.
36. Gregory A. Caldeira and John R. Wright, "Organized Interests and Agenda Setting in the U.S. Supreme Court, *American Political Science Review*, vol. 82 (December 1988), p. 1110.
37. Elder Witt, "Reagan Crusade before Court Unprecedented in Intensity," *Congressional Quarterly* (March 15, 1986), p. 616.
38. Daniel M. Berman, *It Is So Ordered: The Supreme Court Rules on School Segregation* (Norton, 1986), p. 227. For discussion of the debate before the Court as well as an analysis of all the issues of a major case from beginning to end, see Barbara Hinkson Craig, *Chadha: The Story of an Epic Constitutional Struggle* (Oxford University Press, 1988), pp. 203–14.
39. Joyce O'Connor, "Selections from Notes Kept on an Internship at the U.S. Supreme Court, Fall 1988," *Law, Courts, and Judicial Process* (Section Newsletter published by Department of Political Science, Purdue University), vol. 6 (Spring 1989), p. 44.
40. Ibid, p. 46.
41. William Rehnquist, *The Supreme Court: How It Was, How It Is* (William Morrow, 1987), pp. 289–90.
42. Bob Woodward and Scott Armstrong, *The Brethren* (Simon and Schuster, 1979), pp. 406–10.
43. *Garcia* v. *San Antonio Metropolitan Transit Authority*, 469 U.S. 528 (1985).

44. Woodward and Armstrong, *The Brethren*, p. 407.

45. Berman, *It Is So Ordered*, p. 114; Walter F. Murphy, *Elements of Judicial Strategy* (University of Chicago Press, 1964), p. 66; and O'Brien, *Storm Center*, pp. 262–72.

46. Mark De Wolfe Howe, ed., *Holmes-Laski Letters*, vol. 2 (Atheneum, 1963), pp. 124, 125.

47. 426 U.S. 833 (1976).

48. Woodward and Armstrong, *The Brethren*, p. 409.

49. Ibid., p. 410.

50. Robert J. Steamer, *Chief Justice: Leadership and the Supreme Court* (University of South Carolina Press, 1986). See also The White Burkett Miller Center of Public Affairs, *The Office of Chief Justice* (University of Virginia, 1984).

51. David W. Rohde and Harold J. Spaeth, "Ideology, Strategy and Supreme Court Decisions: William Rehnquist as Chief Justice," *Judicature*, vol. 72 (December–January 1989), pp. 247–50.

52. David Danelski, "The Influence of the Chief Justice in the Decisional Process of the Supreme Court," in Thomas P. Jahnige and Sheldon Goldman, eds., *The Federal Judicial System: Readings in Process and Behavior* (Holt, Rinehart Winston, 1968), p. 148.

53. Stuart Taylor, Jr., "When High Court's Away, Clerks' Work Begins," *The New York Times* (September 23, 1988), p. 22 y.

54. Stephen L. Wasby, *The Impact of the United States Supreme Court* (Dorsey Press, 1970).

55. J. W. Peltason, *Fifty-eight Lonely Men: Southern Federal Judges and School Desegregation* (University of Illinois Press), p. 19.

56. Phillip J. Cooper, *Hard Judicial Choices: Federal District Court Judges and State and Local Officials* (Oxford University Press, 1988), pp. 347–50.

57. Peter W. Huber, *Liability: The Legal Revolution and Its Consequences* (Basic, 1988).

58. Arthur S. Miller, "In Defense of Judicial Activism," in Stephen C. Halpern and Charles M. Lamb, eds., *Supreme Court Activism and Restraint* (Heath, 1982), p. 177. See also, by the Chief Justice of the West Virginia Supreme Court, Richard Neely, *How Courts Govern America* (Yale University Press, 1981).

59. *United States v. Carolene Products*, 304 U.S. 144 (1938). Variations on this basic position have been restated in dozens of recent books. Stephen C. Halpern and Charles M. Lamb, eds., *Supreme Court Activism and Restraint* (Heath, 1982), and Mark Tushnet, *Red, White, and Blue: A Critical Analysis of Constitutional Law* (Harvard University Press, 1988), provide balanced analysis from all perspectives. For another analysis of this great debate, see also Lief H. Carter, *Contemporary Constitutional Lawmaking* (Pergamon Press, 1985). For a sample of some recent books, see David J. Richards, *Toleration and the Constitution* (Oxford University Press, 1986); and Stephen Macedo, *The New Right* v. *The Constitution* (Cato, 1986). Leslie F. Goldstein, "Judicial Review and Democratic Theory: Guardian Democracy vs. Representative Democracy," *The Western Political Quarterly*, vol. 40 (September 1987), pp. 391–412, also contains bibliography.

60. Mark Silverstein and Benjamin Ginsberg, "The Supreme Court and the New Politics of Judicial Power," *Political Science Quarterly* (Fall 1987), pp. 371–88.

61. Finley Peter Dunne, "Mr. Dooley's Opinions," in *Bartlett's Familiar Quotations*, 14th ed. (Little, Brown, 1968), p. 890.

18

Bureaucrats: The Real Power?

The framers of the Constitution could hardly have anticipated the large and diverse national bureaucracy that exists today. Current federal employment (civilian and military) is considerably larger than the entire population of the thirteen states in 1789. Nor did the framers provide explicit guidance on the proper place of the federal bureaucracy in the American political system. The design of our political system makes it difficult for presidents to win control and cooperation from those who staff the executive branch departments.

President George Bush came into office in 1989 acutely aware that he faced repeated contests with Congress and countless interest groups for influence over the federal bureaucracy. Unlike several of his predecessors, Bush talks positively about the importance of the federal bureaucrats, and he urges pay increases for them. He also knows that his ability to win cooperation from the bureaucracy rests in large part on his appointing experienced and loyal cabinet and subcabinet officials for the various executive departments and agencies that comprise the federal bureaucracy.

Former President Reagan had come to Washington convinced that many of the Washington-based federal bureaucrats were more loyal to New Deal and Great Society programs than to his notions of scaling back the federal government—especially in domestic programs. He made known his philosophy: We need to get the bureaucracy off our backs and out of our pocketbooks. Early in his first term Reagan cut fringe benefits for federal workers. He rarely praised them; on the contrary, he strongly advocated **privatization** of federal programs. Privatization, a word everyone admits is clumsy and awkward, means relying more on private institutions and less on government to satisfy national goals. Examples of privatization are contracting out to private firms or nonprofit organizations for services that range from repairing the Navy's ships to delivering Meals-on-Wheels to the elderly. It has also been suggested that even our prisons and schools might be more efficiently operated by private sector firms guided by marketplace incentives. Reagan maintained that we would both reduce costs and receive better service if we greatly diminished our reliance on the federal bureaucracy. Not everyone agrees. Critics point to the contracting out of weapons systems as an example where efficiencies are realized in theory, but in actuality there are alleged waste, cost overruns and a woefully costly and perhaps inefficient system of government supervision of the whole defense procurement process.[1]

Reagan was credited with modernizing certain nuts-and-bolts managerial activities of the federal government, but criticized for too often seizing control of the bureaucracy by pushing aside hundreds of career public servants. Students of bureaucracy now believe that there was little or no evidence to support Reagan's conviction that the federal bureaucracy was a serious impediment to accomplishing his policy agenda. In short, "a principal failing of the Reagan administration lay in its apparent unwillingness to set aside its own management strategy to take a serious look at the problem of the long-term erosion of the capacity of the federal workplace . . . ," a legacy that the Bush administration has had to wrestle with in its first years in office.[2]

Reagan's complaints and strategies were familiar ones. Attacking the bureaucracy is as traditional as kissing babies and marching in Fourth of July parades. Candidates for public office frequently take aim at the federal bureaucracy and speak about it as an alien force or a foreign power. "Our government . . . is a horrible bureaucratic mess," said Jimmy Carter. "It is disorganized, wasteful, has no purpose and its policies are incomprehensible or devised by special interest groups with little regard for the welfare of the average citizen."

Members of Congress like to joke that there is a parlor game played in the nation's capital. "It's called 'Bureaucracy,'" they say. "And there is only one rule. The first one to move loses."

The public at large also dislikes or fears bureaucracy. Liberals say the federal bureaucracy is an overzealous guardian of the status quo and is too lazy or unimaginative to innovate or experiment. Conservatives fear a powerful national bureaucracy is too liberal and could bring about a social revolution. They also think the federal bureaucracy is too large, too powerful, and too unaccountable. People in the ideological center often fear the bureaucracy is not working at all. And nearly everyone is suspicious that there is too much waste and fat in government, especially having heard of $400 hammers, Defense Department procurement cost overruns, welfare fraud, and general inefficiencies. Such stereotypes may be as old as the nation (and probably a lot older, for bureaucracies have never been popular), but the skepticism and hostility toward public bureaucracies seem greater today than before.

The federal bureaucracy is an inviting target. There is hardly a citizen who has not been irritated, defeated, or offended at one time or another in dealing with the Internal Revenue Service, the Postal Service, the U.S. Army, the Department of Health and Human Services, or any of the dozens of national regulatory agencies such as the Food and Drug Administration or the Occupational Health and Safety Administration. Career public servants have no press secretary to tell their side of the story. But, as with much of the oversimplified campaign talk in American politics, the "bureaucrats-are-bums" speeches are often misleading. Of course, we have a lot of red tape and overlap in our public administration process—too much. And it is quite proper to ask whether bureaucracy and its methods have in some way stifled productivity. The real question is less the size or the existence of bureaucracy than whether the bureaucracy is responsive to the real needs and best interests of the country. We want to know whether the bureaucracy is accountable to the president, to Congress, and ultimately to the citizens. Finally, we wonder if the various bureaucratic entities perform their assigned functions efficiently.

"Bureaucrat"

The terms "bureaucrat" and "bureaucracy" are of recent origin. Initially referring to a cloth covering the desks or flat writing tables of French government officials in the eighteenth century, the term "bureau" came to be linked with a suffix signifying rule of government (as in "democracy" or "aristocracy").

Bureaucracy today can refer to a professional corps of officials organized in a pyramidal hierarchy and functioning under impersonal, uniform rules and procedures. In the social sciences the term usually does not carry the negative or pejorative associations of popular usage. It typically refers to the whole body of non-elective and non-presidentially appointed government officials.

We use the term in this chapter in a neutral and not a negative sense. However, many people use the word bureaucrat to describe an officious, blundering official engaged in slow operations, buck-passing, and wasteful redundancy. Roget's *Thesaurus* goes even further, linking bureaucracy to "officialism, red-tapism, red-tapery, red-tapedom, and Bumbledom."

"Frankly, trimming the bureaucracy has me worried. . . . It just means fewer people to handle all the red tape."

Reprinted with special permission of NAS, Inc.

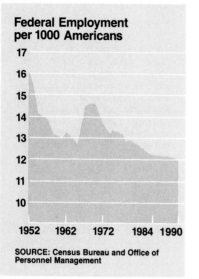
Who Are the Bureaucrats?

In this chapter we are mainly interested in the five million people (3 million civilians and about 2.1 million in uniform) who make up the executive branch of the federal government. Certain facts about these people need to be emphasized:

1. Only about 360,000 (or about 12 percent) of the career civilian employees work in the Washington area. The vast majority are employed in regional, field, and local offices scattered throughout the country and around the world. California alone has about 300,000 federal employees.

2. About 37 percent of the civilian employees work for the Army, the Navy, the Air Force, or for some other defense agency.

3. The welfare state may consume a sizable portion of our budget, but the size of the federal bureaucracy that administers it is relatively small. Only about 15 percent of the bureaucracy works for welfare agencies (such as the Social Security Administration or the Rural Electrification Administration), and about half of these work for the Department of Veteran Affairs.

4. Federal employees are not of one type. Indeed, in terms of social origin, education, religion, and other background factors, bureaucrats are more broadly representative of the nation than are legislators or politically appointed executives.[3]

5. Federal employment per 1000 people in the United States' population has decreased steadily over the past generation.

6. Bureaucrats work at an endless variety of jobs. Over 15,000 different personnel skills are represented in the federal government. Unlike Americans as a whole, however, most federal employees are white-collar workers: secretaries, clerks, lawyers, inspectors.

The vast number of bureaucrats are honest professionals, experts at their business. Bureaucrats are often criticized, but presidents and Congress ignore their advice at considerable risk. A compelling example is provided by the CIA's perceptive memos (many of them later published in the celebrated *Pentagon Papers*) arguing that the Vietnam War as President Johnson was intending to conduct it would be a disastrous failure. This was good advice, from an expert bureaucracy, that Johnson simply disregarded. The Reagan White House similarly chose to bypass and ignore top State department and CIA officials as well as laws passed by Congress on matters of Contra aid and arms sales to Iran in 1985 and 1986—actions Reagan and his aides later dearly regretted.

Bureaucrats, or career government employees, work in the executive branch, in the fourteen cabinet-level departments and more than fifty independent agencies embracing about 2000 bureaus, divisions, branches, offices, services, and other subunits. In size, five big agencies—the Departments of the Army, Navy, and Air Force, Veterans Affairs, and the Postal Service—tower over all the others. Most of the agencies are responsible to the president, but some are partly independent. Virtually all the agencies exist by act of Congress; legislators could abolish them either by passing a new law or by withholding funds.

FORMAL ORGANIZATION

The executive branch departments are headed by cabinet members called secretaries (except Justice, which is headed by the attorney general). The secretaries are directly responsible to the president. Although the departments vary greatly in

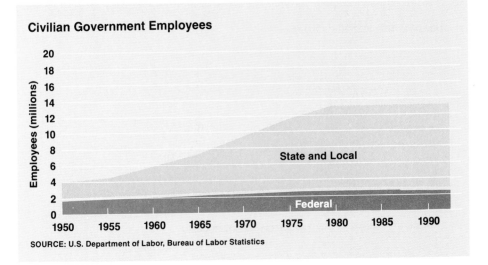

Civilian Government Employees

SOURCE: U.S. Department of Labor, Bureau of Labor Statistics

size, they have certain features in common: A deputy or an undersecretary takes part of the administrative load off the secretary's shoulders, and several assistant secretaries direct major programs. Like the president, the secretaries have various assistants who help them in planning, budget, personnel, legal services, public relations, and other staff functions. The departments are, of course, subdivided into bureaus and smaller units, but the basis for their division may differ. The most common basis is function. For example, the Commerce Department is divided into the Bureau of the Census, the Patent and Trademark Office, and so on. The basis may also be clientele (for example, the Bureau of Indian Affairs of the Interior Department), or work processes (for example, the Economic Research Service of the Agriculture Department), or geography (for example, the Alaskan Air Command of the Department of the Air Force).

The score or more of **government corporations,** such as the Tennessee Valley Authority and the Federal Deposit Insurance Corporation, may be described as a cross between business corporations and regular government agencies. Government corporations were designed to make possible a freedom of action and flexibility not always found in the regular agencies. These corporations have been freed from certain regulations of the Office of Management and Budget and the comptroller general. They have also had more leeway in using their own earnings as they please. Still, because the government owns the corporations it retains basic control over their activities.

The **independent agencies** consist of many types of organizations with differing degrees of independence. Broadly speaking, all agencies that are not corporations and that do not fall under the departments are called independent agencies. Many of these agencies, however, are no more independent of the president and Congress than the departments themselves. The huge General Services Administration is not represented in the cabinet, for example, but its director is responsible to the White House and its actions are closely watched by Congress.[4]

Another type of independent agency is the independent **regulatory board** or **commission**—agencies like the Securities and Exchange Commission, the National Labor Relations Board, and the Federal Reserve Board. Congress deliberately set up these boards to keep them somewhat free from White House influence; they exercise **quasilegislative and quasijudicial** functions. Congress has protected their independence in several ways: The boards are headed by three or more commissioners with overlapping terms; they often have to be bipartisan in

Bureaucracy entails endless filing of huge quantities of records.

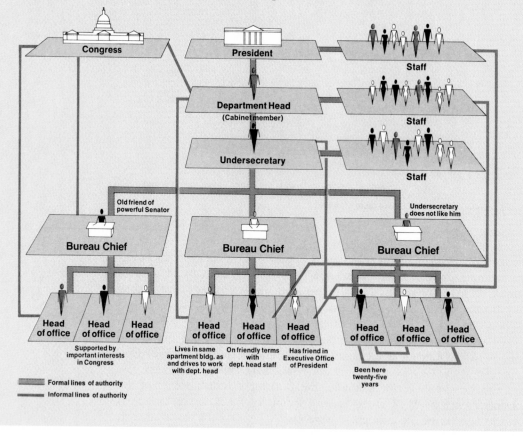

Formal and Informal Lines of a Bureaucratic Organization

Congress

President

Staff

Department Head
(Cabinet member)

Staff

Undersecretary

Staff

Old friend of powerful Senator

Undersecretary does not like him

Bureau Chief

Bureau Chief

Bureau Chief

Head of office

Head of office

Head of office

Head of office

Head of office

Head of office

Head of office

Head of office

Head of office

Supported by important interests in Congress

Lives in same apartment bldg. as and drives to work with dept. head

On friendly terms with dept. head staff

Has friend in Executive Office of President

Been here twenty-five years

Formal lines of authority

Informal lines of authority

membership; and they are appointed for fixed terms in office, some for only three years but others for up to fourteen years.

Within the departments, corporations, and independent agencies are many subordinate units. The standard name for the largest subunit is the **bureau,** although it is sometimes called an office, administration, or service. Bureaus are the working agencies of the federal government. In contrast to the big departments, which are often holding companies for a variety of agencies, the bureaus usually have fairly definite and clear-cut duties, as their names show: the Bureau of the Census in the Commerce Department, the Bureau of the Mint in the Treasury Department, the Bureau of Indian Affairs in the Interior Department, and the Bureau of Prisons in the Justice Department. Note that the U.S. Forest Service in Agriculture, the Social Security Administration in the Department of Health and Human Services, the Drug Enforcement Administration in Justice, and the National Park Service in Interior are also examples of what we here call a "bureau."

All this elaborate organization gives order to the business of administration. It assigns certain functions to certain units, places officials at the head of each unit and makes them responsible for performance, allows both specialization and coordination, permits ready communication, and in general makes our far-flung administration somewhat controllable and manageable. Yet this formal organization can be somewhat misleading. Informal ties are sometimes equally important.

Bureaucrats, like all people, differ—in attitude, motive, ability, experience, and political influence. Their very diversity leads to all kinds of complications. Relationships among officials in an agency may be based on influence rather than on formal authority, on expertise, or on political clout with constituency interest groups. Leadership may be lodged not at the top but in a variety of places. A certain group of officials may have considerable influence, whereas another group, with the same formal status, may have much less. Further, the loyalties of some officials may cut across the formal aims of the agency.

Informal organization can have a substantial effect on administration. A subordinate official in an agency might be especially close to the chief simply because they went to the same college or played poker together, or because the subordinate knows how to ingratiate himself with the chief. A staff official may have tremendous influence not because of formal authority but because experience, fairness, common sense, and personality make people turn to him or her for advice. In an agency headed by a chief who is weak or unimaginative, a vacuum may develop that encourages others to try to take over. Such informal organization and communication, cutting across regular channels, are inevitable in any organization—public or private, civilian or military.

The United States Civil Service: A Brief History

Until the middle of the nineteenth century, the federal civil service was based mainly on the spoils system. To ensure responsive government, it was believed new presidents should be free to put their own followers into office. This view was summarized in the famous American political expression "To the victor belongs the spoils." Besides, it was thought government should not be that complicated—almost anybody should be able to do the job. Later in the nineteenth century, however, a sharp reaction set in against this system. In response to a series of events, including the assassination of President James Garfield in 1881 by a disappointed office seeker, Congress passed the Pendleton Act. This set up a merit system under a three-person bipartisan board called the Civil Service Commission (which functioned from 1893 to 1978).[5]

The Civil Service Reform Act of 1978 abolished the Civil Service Commission and split its functions between two new agencies. The Office of Personnel Management (OPM) administers and enforces the civil service laws, rules, and regulations. An independent Merit Systems Protection Board and its staff is supposed to protect the integrity of the federal merit system and the rights of federal employees. It conducts special studies of the merit system, hears and decides charges of wrongdoing, considers employee appeals against adverse agency actions, and orders corrective and disciplinary actions against an executive agency or employee when appropriate. The independent special counsel of this Merit Systems Protection Board investigates prohibited personnel practices and prosecutes officials who violate civil service rules and regulations.

Senior government administrators work with the Office of Personnel Management in staffing their agencies. OPM acts as a central clearing house for recruiting, examining, and appointing government workers. It advertises for new employees, prepares and administers oral and written examinations throughout the country,

Answer/Discussion

Most bureaucrats, most of the time, follow guidelines provided either in the law or by their administrative superiors—but at times many factors come into play as bureaucrats have to exercise judgment and discretion. Many of the considerations listed on page 464 shape bureaucratic behavior implicitly rather than explicitly. Much of this chapter analyzes the question of bureaucratic accountability. Perhaps you will revise your "answer" by the time you finish this chapter.

and makes up a register of names of those who pass the tests. OPM has a policy of delegating to individual agencies the responsibility for hiring new personnel, subject to its standards. Individual agencies may promote people from within or transfer a civil servant already in the government. If, however, they wish to consider an "outsider," they request OPM to certify possible candidates from its roster of applicants. OPM typically certifies the top three applicants who have applied for the departmental or agency opening. Normally the agency then selects one of these. However, the agency can decide to make no appointment or to request other applicants if it thinks none of the three is qualified. These procedures are intended to protect the merit principle and to meet agencies' needs for qualified personnel. But in practice, the two objectives are not the same. Tradeoffs have to be made, particularly between central control by OPM and delegation of discretionary authority to the agencies. Further, pursuit of both objectives is enfeebled by introduction of yet additional and often incompatible objectives, for example, the veteran preference system.

THE HATCH ACT

In 1939 Congress passed an "Act to Prevent Pernicious Political Activities," usually called the **Hatch Act** after its chief sponsor, Senator Carl Hatch of New Mexico. In essence, this law bars federal civil service employees from becoming highly involved in elections. Because an increasing portion of the nation's workforce was on the government payroll, some people in the late 1930s saw a danger that civil servants would be able to shape, if not dictate, the election of presidents and members of Congress. The Hatch Act was designed to neutralize the federal civil service. Federal employees may vote, but they may not take an active part in partisan politics. The Supreme Court has ruled that such limitations are constitutional. The Hatch Act also makes it illegal to dismiss nonpolicy-making federal officials (those below cabinet and subcabinet rank) for partisan reasons.

The Hatch Act, say critics, is an outmoded ban that denies millions of federal employees the political rights all other Americans enjoy, and discourages political participation among the kinds of people who would otherwise be vigorous activists in party and election functions. Supporters of the Hatch Act quote Thomas Jefferson, who said the best way to achieve an impartial government and protect the rights of all federal workers is through a politically neutral civil service. Jefferson held that a government employee's attempts to influence the votes of others is inconsistent with the spirit of the Constitution. Supporters say the Hatch Act was passed to ensure impartiality and integrity, and to protect federal workers from coercion by superiors. Other defenders, fearing the growing influence of government employee unions, contend that a weakened Hatch Act could encourage these unions to extort from Congress both the right to strike and ever greater pay raises and fringe benefits.[6] Recent efforts to modify the Hatch Act have failed.

Bureaucracy in Action: The Classical or Textbook Model

Early in this century, several scholars developed a formal model of administration from which they derived certain principles:

1. *Unity of command.* Every officer should have a superior to whom to report and from whom to take orders.

2. *Chain of command.* There should be a firm line of authority running from the top down, and responsibility running from the bottom up.

3. *Line and staff.* The staff advises the executive but gives no commands, whereas the line has operating duties.

4. *Span of control.* A hierarchical structure should be established so that no individuals supervise more agencies directly than they can effectively handle.

5. *Decentralization.* Administrators when possible should delegate decisions and responsibilities to lower levels.

Woodrow Wilson.

Woodrow Wilson, while still a professor, adopted many of these views. He also argued that *politics* and *policy administration* should be carefully separated. Leave politics to Congress and management to administrators who adhere to the laws as passed by Congress. Followers of the noted German sociologist Max Weber contended that a properly run bureaucracy could be a model of efficiency. Together with Weber's idea, various textbook principles of public administration were thought to promote rational and impartial management.

According to the textbook model, bureaucrats should not have much discretion in making independent judgments. They should be closely controlled by established rules and regulations. Although this is not always true in practice, it is generally the case: Administrators are not free to make any rules they wish or to decide disputes any way they please. Several kinds of limitations exist:

1. The basic legislative power of Congress compels the agencies to identify the will of Congress and to interpret and apply laws as Congress would wish. Congress can amend a law to make its intent clearer, conduct oversight hearings and investigations, or restrict appropriations.

2. Congress has closely regulated the procedures to be followed by regulatory agencies. Under the Administrative Procedure Act of 1946, agencies must publicize their machinery and organization, must give advance information of proposed rules to interested persons, must allow such persons to present information and arguments, and must allow parties appearing before the agency to be accompanied by counsel and to cross-examine witnesses.

3. Under certain conditions final actions of agencies may be appealed to the courts.

4. Other federal agencies place limits on the administrators' activities; for example, the Office of Management and Budget (OMB) and the General Accounting Office (GAO). In addition to reviewing an agency's budget requests annually in the name of the president, the OMB has a management section to review management, organization, and administrative practices on a more or less continuous basis. The GAO conducts audits of agency spending, and it also investigates the effectiveness of alternative programs designed for similar ends.

Max Weber (1864–1920) was a noted German sociologist and theorist on bureaucracy and organizational behavior.

5. Administrators are also surrounded by informal political checks. They must keep in mind the demands of professional ethics, the advice and criticism of experts, and the attitudes of Congress, the president, interest groups, political parties, private persons, and so on. In the long run, these safeguards are the most important of all.

The textbook or classical model (sometimes also called "the rational person" approach) remains an influential ideal for those engaged in government administration. It describes a part of the reality of bureaucracy—*but only a part*. We need to emphasize here, however, that laws passed by Congress are not just important:

Applicants line up to apply for civil service jobs.

They are central. Most scholars and practitioners agree that the more they see of the bureaucracy, the more they appreciate that the agencies and the career public servants are very much the creatures of the enabling laws under which they work. So this textbook model is also, in part, the reality.

Bureaucrats as Administrators—Some Realities

Today we know we cannot separate the administration of policy from political conflicts over what the policy should be. Congress cannot possibly spell out exactly what needs to be done in every instance. Our political system is, as we have noted in earlier chapters, always marked by a fair amount of compromise and ambiguity. Put another way, often we can agree on something only by leaving the matter vague. Because this is so frequently the case, a considerable amount of discretion is usually left to the thousands of senior bureaucrats who administer federal programs and enforce government regulations.

Bureaucrats are heavily involved in the politics of national policy. Public employees are called upon for advice and policy judgments during the policy-making process. Suppose Congress passes a law setting federal standards for automobile safety and designates the Department of Transportation to carry out the program. Conflicts over standards—or politics—do not stop with the adoption of the law. Or suppose a president announces that we are about to wage war on drugs, and Congress designates the agencies to carry out certain programs and appropriates funds. Politics—conflicts over who is to get what and who is to do what—still need to be considered as the policy is applied to changing conditions. Hence, certain political decisions are merely transferred or delegated from the legislators to the bureaucrats.

PRESSURES AND PROBLEMS

Federal administrators must anticipate what is expected by their superiors, by fellow professionals, by Congress, by the courts, and by the dictates of conscience. Career administrators are in a good position to know when a program is not operating properly and what action is needed. But one of the major complaints about bureaucrats is that they do not go out of their way to make things better. The problem is that many bureaucrats often learn by hard experience that they are more likely to get into trouble by attempting to improve or change programs than they are if they just do nothing. Hardening of administrative arteries is more likely than administrative aggressiveness.

In those cases in which administrators *are* aggressive, they usually seek to increase the size and scope of their agencies. Often the fiercest battles in Washington are not over principles or programs but over territorial boundaries, personnel cuts, and fringe benefits: Career employees come to believe the health of their organization is vital to the public interest. Administrators sometimes become more skillful at building political alliances to protect their own organization than at building the alliances that may be needed to ensure the effectiveness of the programs their organization is supposed to administer.

Career government workers, like all those who work in complex organizations, tend to use the resources at their command on flashy programs, and to give priority to issues that help focus attention on their activities. For example, a few years ago we heard much of the Defense Department's efforts to "sell the

Pentagon," but except for the sheer size of its efforts, the Pentagon is not exceptional. All organizations, public and private, work to promote a favorable image.

Organizations, again both public and private, also tend to resist change and to resent "outside" direction whether by a president or by other external supervisors or boards. A department head in the government, in a large corporation, or in a university is likely to consider the president to be an outsider whose authority in matters affecting his or her bureau is always suspect.

ADMINISTRATORS AS POLITICAL ALLIANCE BUILDERS

In the real bureaucracy career administrators often become intricately involved in politics. They sometimes have more bargaining and alliance-building skills than the elected and appointed officials to whom they report. In one sense, agency leaders are at the center of action in Washington. Over time many administrative agencies come to resemble entrenched pressure groups in that they continually operate to advance *their own* interests.

Most career bureaucrats develop a keen sensitivity to the political pressures on their bureaus. It is impossible for them not to get caught up in a network of issue specialists and policy politicians that make up the thousand and one policy subgovernments in Washington. With the growth of federal programs has come an explosion in the number of policy aides on Capitol Hill, of Washington law firms that specialize in assisting clients who are interested in policy developments, and of the lobbyists (some say at least 30,000) who work with Congress and the federal bureaucracy to advance various economic and professional interests.[7] Groups that perceive real or potential harm to their interests cultivate the bureau chiefs and agency staffs of concern to their programs. They also work closely with the specific committees or subcommittees of Congress that authorize, appropriate, and oversee programs run by these key bureaucracies. One former cabinet member, testifying before a congressional committee, described the process this way:

> It is a fact, unknown to the general public, that some elements in Congress and some special interest lobbies have never really wanted the departmental Secretaries [cabinet members] to be strong. As everyone in this room knows but few people outside of Washington understand, questions of public policy nominally lodged with the Secretary are often decided far beyond the Secretary's reach by a trinity—not exactly a holy trinity—consisting of (1) representatives of an outside lobby, (2) middle-level bureaucrats, and (3) selected Members of Congress, particularly concerned with appropriations.
>
> In a given field these people may have collaborated for years. They may have formed deep personal and family friendships. They have traded innumerable favors. They have seen Secretaries come and go. . . . They have a durable alliance that cranks out legislation and appropriations in behalf of their special interest.[8]

Some bureaucrats become more entangled than others with these external coalitions. Bureau chiefs in particular become logical targets for the efforts of concerned interest groups. On the other hand, bureau chiefs, often recognizing the power of interest groups, frequently recruit them as allies in pursuing common goals. Sometimes bureau chiefs try to coopt potential adversaries among the interest groups by getting them appointed to governmental advisory committees or by arranging for certain contracts for that particular interest. The main point is that

Problems Faced by Women Bureaucrats

Although women constitute 48 percent of the federal career workforce, they are severely underrepresented in top positions. And they often complain that male supervisors tend to give preference to other males in hiring and promotions. Some women bureaucrats suggest that men progress more rapidly because they have more opportunities to "network" than women do.

Government Executive journal surveyed 156 of the women serving in the elite Senior Executive Service and found:

65% said they have the impression that their views were not respected as much as they would be if they were male.

63% said they have been mistaken for a secretary at a business meeting.

54% said they have felt that a male subordinate resisted taking direction from them because they were female.

30% said they felt that their personal lives were scrutinized more than those of their male colleagues.

21% said they have felt sexually harassed.

SOURCE: Bobbi Nodel, "Women in Government," *Government Executive* (August 1988), p. 13.

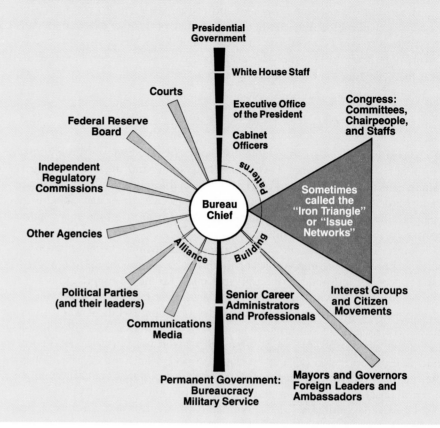

Bureau Chiefs and Their World

Presidential Government

White House Staff

Courts

Executive Office of the President

Federal Reserve Board

Cabinet Officers

Congress: Committees, Chairpeople, and Staffs

Independent Regulatory Commissions

Bureau Chief

Patterns

Sometimes called the "Iron Triangle" or "Issue Networks"

Other Agencies

Alliance Building

Political Parties (and their leaders)

Senior Career Administrators and Professionals

Interest Groups and Citizen Movements

Communications Media

Permanent Government: Bureaucracy Military Service

Mayors and Governors Foreign Leaders and Ambassadors

bureau leaders seldom ignore powerful interest groups. Pragmatic alliances are usually sought and established.

All interests are not equally represented in Washington. Even Ronald Reagan's first budget director, David Stockman, noted that the poor people's interests in the country fared much worse than other interests during the Reagan era budget cuts. Defense contractors, corporate farm interests, and those who can afford Washington "super-lawyers" to look after their tax benefits usually enjoy greater clout with the top bureaucrats as well as with congressional committees and their staffs.

What are the consequences of all this? First, it illustrates once again that the political system is composed of a wide variety of power centers. More specifically, it suggests that the executive branch is a many-splintered branch of government. Cabinet members and the White House have their work cut out for them, because such alliances cause the bureaucracy to resist change and direction from their appointed or elected political "superiors." Some view these external relations as a kind of administrative guerrilla warfare—and as a serious roadblock in the way of fulfilling electoral or party responsibility or of holding elected leaders to account. Others anticipate merely an inevitable clash over values in a system that provides ample opportunities for such clashes. After all, the bureaus themselves are merely one more forum for registering the many demands that make up the people's will.

Members of Congress pressure and cultivate bureau officials just as special interests nurture close ties with both Congress and bureau heads. Congress controls agency budgets and has the power to approve or deny requests for needed legislation. A bureau is especially careful to develop good relations with the members of the congressional committees and subcommittees handling its legislation and appropriations. The following exchanges at hearings illustrate this point:

Official of the Fish and Wildlife Service: Last year at the hearings . . . you were quite interested in the aquarium there [the Senator's state], particularly in view of the centennial coming up. . . .

Senator: That is right.

Official: Rest assured we will try our best to have everything in order for the opening of that centennial.

Subcommittee Chairman: I wrote you gentlemen . . . a polite letter about it . . . and no action was taken. . . . Now, Savannah may be unimportant to the Weather Bureau but it is important to me. . . .

Weather Bureau Official: I can almost commit ourselves to seeing to it that the Savannah weather report gets distribution in the northeastern United States [source of tourists for the subcommittee chairman's district].[9]

Administrators in Action: Case Studies

We have discussed the pressures and loyalties amid which bureaucrats must work. We have seen how bureaucrats build alliances; sometimes they become so powerful they defy presidents and Congress and seem to be little empires unto themselves.

The late J. Edgar Hoover, as chief of the FBI, was nominally subject to direction from the attorney general and the president of the United States. In fact, he was so popular with Congress and the public that he was practically immune from control. That immunity served the country poorly at times, such as when Hoover was able to wiretap Dr. Martin Luther King, Jr., or others he disliked, but it served the country well when Hoover was able to thwart President Nixon and his aides in certain of their illegal efforts to undermine political opponents. But how safe is a democracy when the administrative head of a major agency can defy even the elected president?

Of course, bureaucrats come in all shapes and sizes, with all kinds of political clout and alliances. Let us look at two case studies. One is real; the other is fictionalized yet realistic.

RICKOVER OF THE NAVY

The career of the late Admiral Hyman G. Rickover points up the sharp limits on the authority of presidents and cabinet members over some bureaucrats. Rickover served as an officer for 63 years, longer than any other naval officer in American history. Hailed for supervising the production of the nuclear-powered submarine, he often ignored red tape, bullied subordinates, intimidated superiors, and in general attacked the naval bureaucracy. For over thirty years Admiral Rickover worked with powerful members of Congress to build a nuclear-powered navy, often in complete and open defiance of the chief of naval operations, the secretary of defense, and the president. In fact, he outlasted fourteen secretaries of defense, fourteen secretaries of the navy, and at least ten chiefs of naval operations. Time and again Congress chose to listen to Rickover rather than to Rickover's bureaucratic superiors, even when they had vigorous backing from various presidents. Yet Rickover was an admiral in the U.S. Navy and as such was presumably subject to the authority of many of those whom he defied:

> On the face of it, there is something extraordinary about an engineer who is essentially an expert in nuclear propulsion playing such an important role in defense policy. Rickover, who has never held a major Navy command, has risen from captain to four-star admiral in two decades of doing exactly what he does now. On paper he is a bureaucrat whose two offices are so obscure that they are hard to find on government organization tables. As deputy commander of the nuclear power directorate in the Naval Sea Systems Command, and director of naval reactors in the Energy Research and Development Administration, Rickover has only about 250 employees in Washington plus another 100 or so in the field.
>
> Through these two posts, Rickover, backed by a loyal band of powerful congressmen, has wrought an astounding transformation of our naval forces. Since the *Nautilus* sent its epic message ("Under way on nuclear power") . . . Congress has entrusted Rickover with $27 billion to build what some Senators like to call "Rickover's Navy."[10]

President Jimmy Carter and the late Admiral Rickover.

One reason for Rickover's success was that his ships worked better than promised. Another reason was that he had unwavering support from the members of the Armed Services Committees of both the House and the Senate and from members of the Joint Committee on Atomic Energy. "Rickover's skill at cultivating Congress—he works the hallways of congressional office buildings as assiduously as any lobbyist for a cause—has given his supporters on the Hill a sense that they also played a key role in creating the nuclear fleet."[11] He was a frequent expert witness at congressional hearings and a notoriously tough manager with his employees.

BUREAU CHIEF GEORGE BROWN

The following case is fictional but based on actual experiences of a typical bureaucrat. (Note that not only is our main character, George Brown, fictitious, but so are the Bureau of Erosion and the Department of Conservation. Other agencies mentioned do exist.) It illustrates some of the painful choices bureaucrats have to make, whether they are in Washington or in the field.

George Brown is chief of the Bureau of Erosion in the Department of Conservation. He is in his mid-40s; his appointment to the post was a result of both ability and luck. When the old bureau chief retired, the president wanted to bring in an erosion expert from Illinois, but influential members of Congress pressed for the selection of a former member of the U.S. House of Representatives from a farm state. After deadlock and delay, and as a compromise, Brown, then a division head in the Bureau of Erosion, was promoted to bureau chief. A graduate of a midwestern agricultural college, Brown is a career official in the federal service and a member of the Senior Executive Service.

Early in March of Brown's second year in his new post, his boss, the secretary of conservation, summoned him and the other bureau heads to an important conference. The secretary informed the group that he had just attended a cabinet meeting in which the president had called on each department to make at least a 10 percent cut in spending in the coming fiscal year. The president, the secretary reported, was convinced that there was a great popular demand for federal fiscal restraint.

CHAPTER 18 / Bureaucrats: The Real Power?

Brown quickly calculated what this cutback would mean for his agency. For several years the Bureau of Erosion had been spending about $800 million a year to help farmers protect their farmland. Could it get along on about $700 million, and where could savings be made? Returning to his office, Brown called a meeting of his personnel, budget, and management officials, and his four division chiefs. After several hours of discussion it was agreed that savings could be effected only by decreasing the scope of the program—which would involve ending the jobs of about 1500 of the bureau's employees. Brown asked his subordinates to prepare a list of employees who were the least useful to the bureau. He would decide which to drop after checking with the affected members of Congress.

A few weeks later Brown presented a $710 million budget to Secretary Jones, who approved it and passed it along to the White House. The president then went over the figures in a conference with the director of the Office of Management and Budget, and a few weeks later the White House transmitted the budget for the whole executive department, incorporating the Erosion Bureau's $710 million, to Congress.

Meanwhile Brown was running into trouble. News of the proposed budget cut had leaked immediately to the bureau's personnel in the field. Nobody knew who would be dropped if the cut went through, and some officials were already looking around for other positions. Morale fell. Hearing of the cut, farmers' representatives in Washington notified local farm organizations throughout the country. Soon Brown began to receive letters asking that certain services be maintained. Members of the farm bloc in Congress were also becoming restless.

Shortly after the president's budget went to Congress, Representative Smith of Kansas asked Brown to meet with him. Smith was chairperson of the Subcommittee on Agriculture and related agencies of the House Appropriations Committee and thus was a powerful factor in congressional treatment of the budget. Brown immediately went up to the Hill. Smith began talking in an urgent tone. He said he had consulted his fellow subcommittee members, both Democratic and Republican, and they all agreed that the Erosion Bureau's cut must not go through. The farmers needed the usual $800 million and even more especially because of severe drought conditions in some sections of the country. They would practically rise up in arms if the program were reduced. Members of Congress from agricultural areas, Smith went on, were under tremendous pressure. Leaders of farm groups in Washington were mobilizing the farmers everywhere. Besides, Smith said, the president was unfair in cracking down on the farm program; he did not understand agricultural problems, and he failed to understand that programs designed to increase agricultural output were the best way to reduce our trade imbalance. Besides, the cuts in federal programs should be made elsewhere.

Then Smith came to the point. Brown, he said, must vigorously oppose the budget cut. Hearings on appropriations would begin in a few days, and Brown as bureau chief would of course testify. At that time he must state that the cut would hurt the bureau and undermine its whole program. Brown would not have to volunteer this statement, Smith said. He could just respond to leading questions put by committee members. Brown's testimony, Smith thought, would help clinch the argument against the cut, because the committee would respect the judgment of the administrator closest to the problem.

Smith informed Brown that other bureaucrats were fighting to save their appropriations. Obviously, said Smith, they are counting on public reaction to get them exemptions from the 10 percent cutback. Brown would be foolish not to do the same.

Brown was in an embarrassing position. He had submitted his estimates to the secretary of conservation and to the president and it was his duty to back

Bureaucrats at work: (top) the U.S. Bureau of the Census; (bottom) the Internal Revenue Service. One group is storing data; the other is disposing of excess mailing debris.

"This is brief, clear, concise, and to the point. Try again, and remember, this is a U.S. government office."

Reprinted with permission from Federal Times.

them up. The rules of the game demanded, moreover, that agency heads defend budget estimates submitted to Congress, whatever their personal feelings might be. The president had appointed him to his position, and had a right to expect loyalty. On the other hand, he was on the spot with his own agency. The employees all expected their chief to look out for them. Brown had developed happy relations with "the field," and he squirmed at the thought of having to let more than a thousand employees go. What would they think when they heard him defend the cut? More important, he wanted to maintain friendly relations with the farmers, the farm organizations, and the farm bloc in Congress. Finally, Brown was committed to his program. He grasped its true importance, whereas the president's budget advisers were less likely to understand it. And he knew that his pet project—aid to rural poverty areas in Appalachia—would probably be sacrificed, because it was not supported by a powerful constituency.

Brown turned for advice to an old friend in the Office of Management and Budget. This friend urged him to defend the president's budget. He appealed to Brown's professional pride as an administrator and career public servant. He reminded him that the chief executive must have control of the budget, and that agency heads must subordinate their own interests to the executive program. He said the only way to balance the budget would be for all agencies to make program cuts. As for the employees to be dropped—well, that was part of the game. A lot of them could get jobs in defense agencies; civil service would protect their status. Anyway, they would understand Brown's position. In a parting shot he mentioned the president had Brown in mind for bigger things.

The next day Brown had lunch with a senator, wise and experienced in Washington ways, who had helped him get his start in government. The senator was sympathetic. But there was no doubt about what Brown should do, the senator said. He should follow Representative Smith's plan, of course, being as diplomatic as possible about it. This way he would protect his position with those who would be most important in the long run.

"After all," the senator said, "presidents come and go, parties rise and fall, but Smith and those other members of Congress will be here a long time, and so will these farm organizations. They can do a lot for you in future years. And remember one other thing: These people are elected representatives of the people. Constitutionally, Congress has the power to spend money as it sees fit. Why should you object if they want to spend an extra 70 or 80 million?"

Leaving the Dirksen Senate Office Building, Brown realized his dilemma was worse than ever. The arguments on both sides were persuasive. He felt hopelessly divided in his loyalties and responsibilities. The president expected one thing of him. Congress (he was sure Smith reflected widespread sentiment on Capitol Hill) expected another. As a career man and professional administrator, he sided with the president; as head of an agency, however, he wanted to protect his team and his programs. His future? Whatever decision he made, he was bound to upset important people and interests.

After much soul searching, Brown decided the issue involved more than loyalties, ambitions, and programs. Ultimately it boiled down to two questions: First, to whom was he, Brown, legally and administratively responsible? Formally, of course, to the chief executive who appointed him and who was accountable to the people for the actions of the administration. And second, which course of action did he think was better for the welfare of all the people? Looking at the question this way, he believed the president was right in asking for fiscal restraint. As a taxpayer and consumer himself, Brown knew of the strong sentiment for doing something about the federal budget deficits. To be sure, Congress must make the final decision. Yet to make the decision, Brown reflected, Congress had to know the attitude of the administration, and the administration should speak with one voice for the majority of the people, or it should not be speaking out at all. With mixed feelings Brown decided to support the president. Being a seasoned alliance builder, however, he hedged his bets somewhat. He came out strongly for the president's budget, yet at the same time he sent to friendly members of Congress some questions to be asked of himself in future hearings, so he might be able to give some hints of the impact of the cutbacks. He also circulated to some of these same members of Congress an analysis of the impact of personnel and funding cuts in their states and districts.

The case studies just considered lead to three important generalizations:

Drawing by Engleman, August 16, 1976, Federal Times.

1. Bureaucrats are people, not robots, and as people they are subject to many influences.
2. Bureaucrats do not respond merely to orders from the top but to a variety of motives stemming from their own personalities, formal and informal organization and communication, their political attitudes, their educational and professional backgrounds, and the political context in which they operate.
3. Bureaucrats are important in government. Some of them have considerable discretion and make decisions of great significance. The cumulative effect of all their policies and actions on our daily lives is enormous.

What the Public Thinks of Bureaucrats

Cynical citizens think "government employees have got it made, and they know it." In general, the American people think federal bureaucrats are paid too much to do too little and that too many people are on the public payroll. About two-thirds believe government wastes a lot of their tax money. Further, a survey of the public-at-large indicates that most Americans believe federal employees do not work as hard as those who hold similar nongovernmental jobs (see Table 18–1).

These findings are not surprising. Big bureaucracy in the abstract—especially when it is out of sight in some remote capital—is unpopular; it engages in so many activities that most people find something it does offensive (like taxing them, inspecting them, conscripting them, and so on). Big bureaucracy has been

TABLE 18–1
Contrasting Criticisms of Federal Workers

Bureaucrats as Paper-Shuffling Clerks Are:	Bureaucrats as the Real Power in Washington Are:
1. Timid and indecisive	1. A self-anointed elite in our nation's capital
2. Flabby, overpaid, and lazy	2. An oppressive foreign power
3. Ruled by inertia	3. The fourth branch of government
4. Unimaginative	4. Intolerably meddlesome
5. Devoted to rigid procedures	5. A demanding giant
6. Slow to accept new ideas	6. The permanent government
7. Slow to abandon unsuccessful policies	7. Super-Bureaucrats who wield vast power
8. Impersonal and lacking individuality	8. Enormously powerful to do great injury
9. Red tape artists	9. Intrusive, arrogant empire builders
10. On "one long coffee break"	

defined as that part of the government people dislike. If someone is not directly concerned about a program one way or the other, it is easy for that person to say the national government should stay in Washington and mind its own business!

"It's very much a love-hate affair. Government is both problem and solution. Civil servants, as individuals, are appreciated, but as a class of people they are held in low esteem."[12] The public generally does approve of the general conduct of most of the federal employees with whom it comes in contact. Seventy percent of the public who have had dealings with the government say they were pleased or very pleased by the performance of those federal employees they actually met and dealt with on a face-to-face basis. Relatively few people say they were *displeased* by their contact with federal workers.[13] This suggests that in contrast to public scorn for bureaucrats and bureaucracy in the abstract, the typical American actually appreciates and approves of the conduct of such people as postal service delivery persons, forest rangers they met on camping trips, Veterans Affairs Department officials who helped their ailing uncles, or the U.S. Department of Agriculture county field agents who help with the local 4-H programs. They also admire astronauts, marines, FBI agents, and Coast Guard officers, all of whom are also federal employees.

One of the paradoxes of public attitudes toward bureaucrats is that some of the time we criticize federal employees for working too little, for being lazy, or for lacking initiative—for failing to abide by the so-called work ethic. Yet at the same time we view federal workers as too powerful, and we accuse them of intervening in or regulating our lives far too much.

Can bureaucrats in reality be both timid and empire builders? In fact, there are enough bureaucrats to fulfill all kinds of contrasting stereotypes—so perhaps it is possible to hold both views about them, despite the seeming contradiction.

Even federal employees themselves gripe about the system. Although top federal employees say they *like* the challenge of their work, the opportunity to participate in forming and managing important policies, and the quality of people with whom they work, as indicated in the margin box, these workers *dislike* the rigidity, the red tape, and many of the frustrations of dealing with interest groups and politicians.

Since 1962, federal employees have had the right to form unions or associations that represent them in seeking to improve government personnel policies, and about a third of them have joined such unions. Some of the more important unions representing federal employees today are the American Federation of Government Employees, the National Treasury Employees Union, the National Association of Government Employees, and the National Federation of Federal Employees. Unlike unions in the private sector, these groups lack the right to strike and are not able to bargain militantly over pay and benefits. What can they do? They attempt to negotiate better personnel policies and practices for federal workers, and they also represent federal bureaucrats during grievance and disciplinary proceedings. Further, they testify before Congress on measures affecting personnel changes.

Federal bureaucrats are aware that the public is not fond of them. However, this situation might change if more people took the time to learn about what the federal bureaucracy does, and if more politicians resist giving those "bureaucrats-are-bums" talks that win such ready applause. Still, the public will probably go on blaming the bureaucracy for rising taxes and for all the waste or crazy regulations about which they read in the newspapers.

Since 1789, Americans have always been skeptical of big government. We still like to think of ourselves as a nation of rugged individualists, and we cherish a lean government. Bureaucrats—especially Washington-based bureaucrats—are a symbol of losing that dream. To think of the bureaucracy is to think of our dependence on others, our inability to solve things at the neighborhood level, and our impersonal way of trying to solve so many of today's problems.

Finally, bureaucrats have become the favorite punching bag—a convenient scapegoat—for members of Congress or for reporters who have to place the blame on someone for things that go wrong in government. An irreverent and influential journal in the nation's capital, *The Washington Monthly*, rails against clumsy bureaucracy in every issue. *Fortune* magazine and the *Wall Street Journal* often feature stories critical of the federal bureaucracy.

Plainly, the "organization man" or the "bureaucratic man" has never been a hero in America. The lone cowboy, rugged individualist, or risk-taking entrepreneur is the cultural hero for most of us.

The Case against Big Bureaucracy and Its Waste

Americans generally view big government as bad. We equate bigness with remoteness, injustice, incompetence, and unresponsiveness. We also assume that the bigger government gets, the more it wastes.

Perhaps the most criticized aspect of the federal bureaucracy is that career public employees seem to enjoy the closest thing to permanent tenure; they are almost as secure in their jobs as if they were confirmed for the Supreme Court. For all practical purposes, critics say, federal workers can neither be fairly punished nor justly rewarded for performing well. Hence, most of them perform the bare minimum.

Senator William Roth displays the high-priced toilet seat Lockheed Corporation was going to charge the government $640 for; the price was later adjusted to $100 each.

Few ever get fired. The government's rate of discharge for inefficiency is said to be less than one-seventh of 1 percent. And of that one-seventh of 1 percent, a substantial number are reinstated after appeals in the federal courts. Even the occasional reductions-in-force (known as RIFs) during the Reagan years involved few people: mostly those encouraged to retire a bit earlier than they otherwise would have.

When Jefferson was president, the federal government employed 2120 persons: Indian commissioners, postmasters, collectors of customs, tax collectors, marshals, lighthouse keepers, and clerks. Today the president heads an executive branch of, as noted earlier, about 3 million civilians and over 2 million military employees, who work in at least 2000 units of federal administration. Critics say the federal bureaucracy is growing at an alarming rate and that by the year 2000 it will control nearly every aspect of our lives. Figures can indeed be presented that make the federal establishment look like a mushrooming giant. For example:

1. In 1929 federal spending amounted to about 2.5 percent of the gross national product (GNP). Today the federal share is over 24 percent of the GNP.

2. The estimated annual cost of federally mandated paperwork is at least $40 billion.

3. In the last twenty years or so, more than 250 new federal agencies or bureaus have sprung into being; less than two dozen have been disbanded. One example is the recently created office to fight the war on illegal drugs in the United States.

4. The national government owns one-third of the nation's land—and nearly 50 percent of the land west of Denver, Colorado. The Department of Defense

HOW THE PUBLIC JUDGES FEDERAL BUREAUCRATS

Q. Overall, who do you think works harder—people in federal government jobs, or people in similar jobs outside the government?

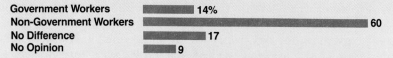

Government Workers	14%
Non-Government Workers	60
No Difference	17
No Opinion	9

Q. How about the number of people employed by the federal government: In general, do you think the federal government employs too many people or too few people to do the work that must be done?

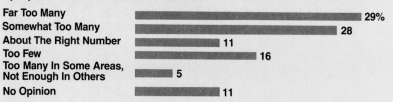

Far Too Many	29%
Somewhat Too Many	28
About The Right Number	11
Too Few	16
Too Many In Some Areas, Not Enough In Others	5
No Opinion	11

Q. Do you believe that federal employees are paid more, less or about the same as people in similar jobs outside the government?

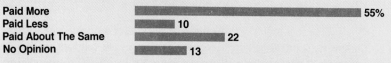

Paid More	55%
Paid Less	10
Paid About The Same	22
No Opinion	13

Q. (*Asked of people who say they have had at least some dealings with a federal government agency in the past year*) Overall, would you say you were pleased with the conduct of the government worker or workers you dealt with, or not? . . . Would you say you were very pleased/displeased, or just pleased/displeased?

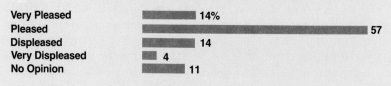

Very Pleased	14%
Pleased	57
Displeased	14
Very Displeased	4
No Opinion	11

SOURCE: Figures are from a national telephone poll of 1167 people taken by the *Washington Post*, January 16, 1983, section A, p. 80.

alone owns land equivalent to the size of the state of Virginia. The government holds title to more than 400,000 buildings that cost well over $100 billion. It pays well over $800 million a year for rent for another 54,000 buildings.

5. President Kennedy, in 1961, was the first president to have a budget of over $100 billion. It is now well over $1000 billion.

6. Several studies today find that for every worker on the federal civilian payroll as many as three or four workers may earn their livings indirectly from the federal government (as consultants and contractors). In other words, there may be about 8 to 10 million "invisible federal employees" as the government contracts out more of its work in order to keep its employment levels steady.

7. Another way the federal government conceals its growth is by shifting its work to the state and local governments. The federal government provides for about one-fourth of total spending at the state and local levels. Although no one knows exactly how many jobs this creates at those levels, estimates run as high as 5 million (of the 12 million state and local government jobs).

CHAPTER 18 / Bureaucrats: The Real Power?

No wonder people often conclude the government is trying to do too many things and make too many decisions, in too great detail, on too many subjects, for too many separate purposes. Some have advocated "birth control" for bureaucracy and federal programs. One person even suggested that before Congress can enact a new law, it should be required to repeal two existing ones. The central problem with the bureaucracy, critics add, is not that it exists, but that we have failed to subject it to the control and discipline alleged to operate in the private sector. In private business "the workings of self-interest are tempered and channeled by market disciplines, such as competition and consumer choice, and by public restraints, such as antitrust laws."[14] A corporation president who served as secretary of the treasury said one of the lessons he learned about working in government was "that the tests of efficiency and cost-effectiveness which are the basic standards of business, are in government not the only—and frequently not even the major—criteria."[15] President Ford put it this way: "One of the enduring truths of the nation's capital is that bureaucrats *survive*. Agencies don't fold their tents and quietly fade away after their work is done. They find Something New to Do. Invariably, that Something New involves more people with more power and more paperwork—all involving more expenditures."[16]

Critics say too that the incentive system in the national bureaucracy seems to promote growth and inefficiency. Growth improves chances for promotion and higher salaries. After a while a significant portion of time in a bureaucracy is devoted to its own expansion. In short, one of the most common complaints is that our national civil servants seldom have any incentive to save taxpayers money. On the contrary, everything seems to tempt them in the opposite direction.

Another charge leveled against the bureaucrats is that they extend the authority granted to them beyond the intention of Congress. However, they often do so not because they are "hungry for power," but because once a program is established, the people assigned to it tend to be committed to the "cause." In the Office of Civil Rights in the Department of Education, for example, appointments generally go to those concerned about protecting the rights of women and minorities. That is their assigned task, and in their zeal to get those things done, they strengthen their authority. Those assigned to the Bureau of Narcotics are likely to be persons convinced that enforcement of the federal laws against narcotics is of supreme importance; in carrying out their duties, they sometimes go beyond their vested authority. Further, and perhaps most to the point, those groups outside the government who want the laws to be enforced and their programs carried forward will place pressure on the agencies. Women's groups and minority advocacy groups carefully watch the Office of Civil Rights, for instance.

Herbert Kaufman, a student of bureaucracies, set out a few years ago to study whether any old government agencies ever die. He began by looking at 175 agencies in selected areas of the national government that existed in 1923, and then traced them for the next fifty years. All but twenty-seven were alive and well in 1973. In the meantime scores of new agencies had been created to work in these same areas. Death of a bureaucracy is the exception rather than the rule. The birth of new units continued regardless of whether a Democrat or a Republican occupied the White House. New bureaucracies seem to be encouraged either by sudden shifts in economic conditions or international tensions or by a "built-in thrust that . . . assists the even finer division of labor in organizations."[17] Excessive workloads in existing agencies, pressure by groups who believe a new agency will be more sympathetic to their point of view, and a variety of societal change factors all work in the direction of creating more units of government.

How wasteful is the federal government? A Reagan-appointed commission, composed mainly of corporate leaders, concluded that more than $400 billion could be saved in just three years. To do this, the Grace Commission (formally, the President's Private Sector Survey on Cost Control) made nearly 2500 recommendations that called for, among other things, strengthening presidential veto powers to cut programs, introducing common-sense private-sector business and accounting practices into federal procurement and management procedures, and ending countless programs and policies that lead to expensive fringe benefits and subsidy programs. The Grace Commission would end military commissaries, sell off the National and Dulles, Washington, D.C. area, airports, get the Veterans Affairs Department out of the hospital-construction business, impose much higher user fees for Coast Guard and national park services, and sharply reduce most of the fringe benefits and early-retirement arrangements for government employees.

The federal government is, this commission said, the nation's largest borrower, lender, employer, insurer, landowner, tenant, and landlord. It is responsible, they said, for the medical care received by 47 million people per year, and it provides 95 million subsidized meals each day. In an effort to arouse the nation's 82 million taxpayers, "the true victims of government waste," their report concluded that the federal government was both big and poorly run. Waste and inefficiency abound in virtually every governmental program.

The Grace Commission alleged, among other things, that the Veterans Affairs Department spends twice as much per hospital bed as the private sector, that half the government's computers are obsolete, that the General Services Administration employs seventeen times as many people to manage its facilities as comparable private-sector firms, and that military and civil service retirees received from three to six times the total lifetime pension benefits compared to their private-sector counterparts.

Commission chairperson J. Peter Grace, chief executive officer of a large American corporation, says the commission did not come up with easy solutions, "but the solutions don't get any easier by ignoring the problem." He especially faults Congress for most of the waste. His report's general recommendations are twofold: Strengthen presidential control over the bureaucracy, and move much of what the government is now doing back to the private sector. "Remember that Congressional instinct is to spend, never to save. We need to administer shock treatment to our elected representatives and let them know that their continued fiscal irresponsibility can no longer be tolerated. Much like the character in the movie *Network*, we're asking you to join with us in telling them that 'We're mad as hell, and we're not going to take it anymore!' "[18]

The Grace Commission was praised by President Reagan, who proceeded to use it effectively as an election year tool in 1984. However, Reagan implemented few of the Grace Commission suggestions. He did, however, pick up on the themes of privatization by imposing various user fees. He also continued to appeal for public support for an item veto for the president.

The Grace Commission allegations of waste and cost overruns were less warmly greeted by Congress, the bureaucrats, and various students of government. Both the General Accounting Office and the Congressional Budget office said the horror stories exaggerated the problems of the federal government. Moreover, many of the recommendations were politically unfeasible.

Nearly everyone agrees that the government should charge a fair (meaning higher) price for the electricity it generates, the crop irrigation it provides, the inland waterways it operates, and the grazing rights and firewood it almost gives

Answer/Discussion

Not too many years ago civil servants were required to prove their loyalty to the United States by taking oaths that they were not Communists. Such oaths raise serious First Amendment questions. Unannounced drug testing raises serious Fourth Amendment questions. The idea that a group of people should be subjected to random searches without reasonable individual cause was resisted at the outset of our life as a nation.

When Congress, or the president or head of a federal agency, does require testing as a condition of employment, even if evidence of drug use would not be used to dismiss employees, they need to persuade skeptical judges that this was not an "unreasonable" search and seizure.

The Supreme Court recently ruled in two 1989 decisions involving railway workers and U.S. Customs Service employees that mandatory blood and urine tests may be required for certain workers without a showing of "individualized suspicion." Writing for the Court in the railway workers' case, Justice Anthony Kennedy said: "The government's interest in testing [even] without a showing of individual suspicion is compelling. Employees subject to the tests discharge duties fraught with such risks of injury to others that even a momentary lapse of attention can have disastrous results.

The two cases dealt with post-accident testing of railway personnel on duty at the time of a major accident and with customs officials who carry firearms, handle classified information, or work to intercept drugs. Random, unannounced drug testing of all federal employees, or even of those in policy-making positions, presents different constitutional issues. The Bush administration has argued that such testing is both desirable and constitutional. Supporters of privacy rights and civil liberties are uncomfortable with carrying this policy too far. Drug testing, some concede, may be necessary for certain individuals—airline pilots and crews of ships, for example—where public safety is genuinely involved. But it is not needed and would be an unconstitutional deprivation of privacy rights under the Fourth Amendment, they say, as a general policy.

CHAPTER 18 / Bureaucrats: The Real Power?

away. "A citizens' campaign urging Congress to resist pork-barrel pressures and other wasteful tendencies could be a very useful thing—if it were built on realistic expectations of both savings and consequences," observes an editorial writer for *The Washington Post*. "But a campaign built on a false perception—the belief that better government management could make a big dent in the deficit—will only frustrate honest efforts in Congress and the administration to come to grips with the problem."[19]

One critic took the Grace Commission to task for grossly exaggerating and wildly misleading the general public. Steven Kelman of Harvard University's John F. Kennedy School of Government agreed that the government does produce a given output less efficiently than the private sector, yet "If I had to hazard a guess, I would say that the government might typically use, not four times or 17 times as many resources as the private sector to produce a given output, but perhaps 1.2 times."[20] Those responsible for the activities in question, Kelman adds, generally pay attention to costs and ways to keep them down. Critics like Grace, he says, are too quick to conclude that policies and programs are wasteful when they believe the programs are not worthwhile. In these cases, the real disagreement is over policies, not administration.[21]

Even the critics of the Grace Commission concede that a considerable saving could be realized with improved accounting methods, increased user fees, and continued contracting of noncore government functions out to private organizations, especially if the same products can be produced more cheaply that way.

What is the long-run impact of reports like the Grace findings? Efforts to "combat waste" by introducing additional rules and additional layers of control are likely to hinder good performance, and may, as the example of the procurement system suggests, not even reduce costs. Yet it is exactly the headline-grabbing horror stories, such as the ones in which the Grace Commission specialized, that lead more than anything to the development of ever-newer rules and clearance points. In this sense, the Grace Commission may have betrayed the "war on waste" it set out to wage.[22]

The Case for Bureaucracy

Perhaps we often ask too much of our government; perhaps we ask it to solve problems that are impossible to solve. Our expectations are high, even when we know government is making big promises it cannot back up with performance. The central problem of big government is the myth that it can solve every problem and meet every challenge. This problem is exacerbated by the rising demands placed upon it by nearly every interest group in America.

Bureaucracy is a function not only of governments, but also of corporations and universities. It is a fact of life. The size of the federal bureaucracy has remained fairly stable for at least the past generation despite population growth and the expansion of federal programs.

What about **red tape?** One person's red tape is another's proper procedures. Red tape may be viewed as a hopeless tangle of rules and regulations that keep public servants from doing anything but stamping and shuffling papers. Or these same rules and regulations may be said to ensure that public servants act impartially. A student who is told by her dean that she cannot drop a course after eight weeks without a penalty may complain about "red tape" and unfeeling bureaucrats. But the rule was adopted so that all students would be treated alike, so the dean

Red Tape

The term comes from the ribbon English civil servants once used to tie up and bind legal documents. It has become a despised symbol of having to wait in lines as officials check files or consult with their supervisors or lose important documents. Today, along with taxes and death, we think of red tape as inevitable—a symbol of bureaucratic inefficiency. Of course, one person's red tape is another's prudent system or proper cautiousness.

A useful book on red tape was written by Herbert Kaufman, *Red Tape: Its Origins, Uses and Abuses* (Brookings Institution, 1977). Fortunately, it's just 100 pages!

would not be able to allow only students he or she likes to drop the course. In other words, red tape stems in large part from our desire not to give public servants too much discretion, and to hold them accountable. After all, they are spending other people's money.

A comparison of our bureaucracy with most bureaucracies in the world suggests we should be grateful for the service we do get from our public employees. The U.S. Postal Service provides a good example. Although it is criticized as being the last dinosaur, it is faster, more efficient, and less costly than any comparable service in the world. Another example is the United States tax system: It is the most effective such system in the world.

Further, not all bureaucracies keep getting bigger. Some get bigger, some remain stable, and others actually shrink. The growth that does occur is often due to population or workload expansion rather than Parkinson's Law of bureaucratic "empire building." Little evidence is available to support contentions that bigness necessarily creates inefficiency and rigidity. Some studies even come to the opposite conclusion. Surely the success of IBM and General Electric in the private sector and the Universities of California and Michigan in the public sector suggest some virtues of bigness.

Compared to most other nations U.S. government employment has not grown much at all. Government employment in Sweden grew by more than 20 percent in the past generation, and by over 11 percent in Italy and Germany during the same period. There has been little growth in U.S. government employment during the last twelve years. Moreover, government employment as a percentage of total employment in the U.S. is 20 to 50 percent lower than in these western European democracies. Forty years ago, there were about nineteen federal civil servants for every 1000 Americans; now there are less than twelve per 1000. Defenders of the size of government also note that the proportion of our economic output consumed or distributed by the national government has increased only a few percentage points during the past two generations.

Finally, hundreds of federal career public servants have helped achieve notable savings in government operations and have been honored by recent administrations with various presidential awards. In 1989 Congress, with President Bush's encouragement (Reagan had vetoed a similar measure), passed legislation to ensure further protection for **whistle blowers**—federal employees who publicly reveal waste or mismanagement in their agencies. In the past occasional federal employees had been punished or transferred to highly undesirable jobs when they blew the whistle. A top Pentagon employee testified before Congress about huge cost overruns on the C–5A troop transport during the Nixon administration—an act that so angered President Nixon that he ordered Defense officials to "get rid of that————." The 1989 legislation grants relief to bureaucrats who can show that whistle blowing was a contributing factor in their demotion or firing. It also allows these whistle-blowing civil servants to appeal their cases in the federal courts. At a time when everyone is concerned with eliminating waste in government, especially in its procurement processes, Congress and George Bush acted to strengthen further the incentives for bureaucrats to serve the public interest.

Still, what is probably the best-equipped, highly trained, and, possibly, the most efficient national bureaucracy in the world, operating in one of the most technologically advanced societies, remains the target of public criticism. And perhaps the skepticism is healthy. In a way, it is yet another check and balance in our system of constraints on those who wield public power.

Big Bureaucracy—How Responsive Is It?

One of the most complex questions concerning public bureaucracies is whether they are responsive enough to the citizens. Being *responsive* means being answerable as well as being quick to respond to treating someone sympathetically. How responsive an agency is depends on the perceptions of the person involved. A person who has to stand in a long line, whether at the post office or at a welfare agency, often complains about unresponsive bureaucrats. Or someone who has a new or novel problem that a federal bureaucrat treats "by the book" rather than by providing personalized service, also develops a critical view.

Bureaucracies necessarily have to develop routines and standard operating procedures. They do so in order to increase efficiency and productivity. They also do so because they are striving to achieve fairness and evenhandedness. But on occasion such "red tape" reduces flexibility. Just about everyone has at one time or another been turned away from the local post office because a package to be mailed was too large, or too small, or in the wrong kind of container. It is hard on such occasions to hold back our anger. Why can't they be flexible? Why can't they be reasonable? Why can't they deal with me in a personal way?

The procedures that allow the post office, the Army, or the IRS to perform efficiently for large numbers sometimes also diminish the ability of these organizations to respond to the personalized needs of individuals. Routines help to prevent chaos and allow government behavior to be consistent, uniform, and just. The inevitable and necessary result of big bureaucracy is often a tradeoff: Responsiveness—quick, personalized, individualized, and sympathetic service—often must be sacrificed for the sake of orderly and impersonal routines.

A related question is whether certain problems ought to be handled by mechanisms other than bureaucracies. Political leaders of all persuasions now recognize that we sometimes turn problems over to government bureaucracies when perhaps there is a more effective way to solve them. For example, can the government effectively regulate health-care costs through bureaucracies, or should we allow the economic market mechanism to handle such policy matters? Perhaps something inherent in bureaucratic procedures makes public bureaucracy less appropriate for certain types of activities. Perhaps some programs or policies are best left to the private sector, or to state and local governments, or to the market system. This may be especially true of international trade policies, the government role in high-technology industries, and various energy policies. However, the privatization of public programs can sometimes mean only shifting from one bureaucracy (public) to another (private).

In the final analysis, the question of *bureaucratic responsiveness* is extremely difficult to disentangle from the question of *bureaucratic accountability*. In determining the responsiveness of the Navy, or of the FBI, we must also ask to whom they should be most responsive—which is similar to asking who should oversee and control them. Let us consider now who controls, and who should control, the federal bureaucrats.

Controlling the Bureaucrats: Who and How?

To whom *should* the bureaucrats (sometimes called the "powercrats") be accountable: themselves, organized interest groups, the majority who elected the president,

You decide!

How can private and public organizations' employees learn from one another? Can management and leadership strategies used by IBM, Hewlett Packard, or Prentice Hall be as easily used in the public sector? You decide!

(Answer/Discussion on page 486.)

or the majority as reflected by Congress? Plainly, most Americans would like the bureaucracy to be responsive to the public interest. *But defining the public interest is the crucial problem.* Both the president and Congress claim to speak in behalf of the public interest. Moreover, to whom bureaucrats should be accountable is an inherently political question. Certain forms of accountability favor some groups and interests over others. Support of bureaucratic accountability to the White House, for example, depends in large measure on the supporters' partisanship toward the president. Republicans not surprisingly favor strong presidential control over the bureaucracy when Republicans occupy the White House. Following are some of the realities and some of the recent suggestions for making bureaucrats more responsive and accountable.

PRESIDENTS AND BUREAUCRATS

One school of thought says the president should clearly be in charge, for the chief executive is responsive to the broadest constituency. The president, it is argued, must see that popular needs and expectations are converted into administrative action. When the nation elects a conservative president, such as Ronald Reagan, who favors major cutbacks in federal programs and restricted governmental intervention in the economy, these policies can be carried out only if the bureaucracy responds. The majority's wishes can be translated into action only if the bureaucrats support presidential policies.

Yet, as we have seen, under the American system of checks and balances a single political majority winning a presidential election does not acquire control of the national government, or even of the executive branch itself. Under our Constitution the president is not the undisputed master of the executive structure. Congress sets up the agencies, broadly determines their organization, provides money, and establishes the ground rules under which they operate. Congress constantly reviews the activities of the bureaucrats in appropriation hearings, special investigations, or informal inquiries. And, as we have also seen, the Senate must confirm most of the important cabinet-level leaders. In fact, presidents come into an ongoing system over which they have relatively little control—or relatively little leeway to shape the bureaucracy and make it responsive to their view of the public interest. Still, some presidential control over the bureaucracy may be exercised through the powers of *appointment, reorganization,* and *budgeting.* More specifically, a president can attempt to control the bureaucracy by appointing or promoting sympathetic personnel, mobilizing public opinion and congressional pressure to foster responsiveness, structurally changing the administrative apparatus, controlling the budget, using extensive personal persuasion, and, if the preceding fail, shifting a bureaucracy's assignment to another department or agency (although this usually requires congressional approval).

Presidents are allowed about 5000 political appointments to top positions within the executive branch. However, many of these are confidential assistants or highly specialized aides to cabinet officers. Moreover, many require confirmation by the Senate and thus are not exclusively a president's choice. Some reformers suggest that a president's hand could be strengthened if the chief executive were able to make two or three times as many political appointments.

Assistant Secretaries—A Weak Link But there is more to control than having the president appoint more people. The question is: Do those who are appointed have much to say once they are in office? Although presidents can usually recruit to their cabinets persons of prominence and influence, they find it much harder

CHAPTER 18 / Bureaucrats: The Real Power?

to hire outstanding persons at the assistant secretary level. Presidents depend in part on the assistant secretaries to infuse into the federal bureaucracy the views and values of the White House. These citizen-leaders are also expected to serve as links between the people who elect the presidents and the civil servants. Many people, however, are not willing to give up or interrupt their professional or business careers to become assistant secretaries: Over the last several years the position has become one of relatively low pay, little prestige in Washington, short tenure, and high cost to one's family. As a result presidents often fill these slots with relatively young people who, from the day they arrive in Washington, are looking for their next jobs. As a result, these assistant secretaries, or people in comparable appointed posts, are forced to wear "kid gloves" with those they are supposed to regulate, because it is from them that their next jobs are most likely to come. Others who tend to become assistant secretaries have strong ideological convictions but little experience in administration and congressional politics. Still others use the position as a transition to retirement.

Once in Washington these presidential appointees have to deal with civil servants who know their "bosses" will not be there long. Most civil servants have virtually secure jobs, and all they have to do to ignore presidentially selected assistant secretaries is to wait them out for a year or two. Moreover, in and around Washington, government workers comprise a powerful political group; assistant secretaries who try to significantly alter the policy directions of those who are supposedly under their supervision may do so at considerable political and legal peril.

President Carter did succeed in making some alterations in the higher reaches of the civil service. One of the changes brought about by the Civil Service Reform Act of 1978 was the creation of a Senior Executive Service. This service, or pool of about 7000 career (plus some noncareer) officials, can be filled without senatorial confirmation, and its individual members are subject to transfer from one agency to another according to an administration's wishes. The creation of the Senior Executive Service was intended to alleviate the feeling on the part of presidents that the senior career bureaucrats—especially those enmeshed in iron-triangle networks—are not responsive to the goals and policy preferences of the White House. With this new service presidents and their political appointees can have greater flexibility in selecting, promoting, and rewarding with financial bonuses those in the top career service who are productive and responsive. Up to half of the senior career executives in an agency could, in theory, get bonuses each year of up to 20 percent of their base salaries. Other financial incentives are also available; for example, 5 percent of the executives in the service could be named to special ranks in which they could each earn a bonus of $10,000 for distinguished work in a given year. On the other hand, nonproductive executives could be put back into the ranks of the regular civil service, with severe reductions in pay and responsibilities.

The Civil Service Reform Act of 1978 was viewed with skepticism and even some alarm as it was first being implemented.[23] Observers feared it would create an executive service that would be put to political use. Others worried that without strong White House support, the noble intentions of the act would not be achieved. President Carter was enthusiastic about the new plan, but President Reagan was noticeably less interested. Reagan was more preoccupied with cutting budgets and, where possible, cutting personnel. For a variety of reasons, the Senior Executive Service has not lived up to its creators' expectations. Many analysts now say it has had no significant impact on the federal workers it was supposed to help. Because of federal budgetary problems, most of the financial bonuses and related incentives have been held back. Morale in the senior ranks of the federal bureau-

"Think of it. Presidents come and go, but WE go on forever!"

Reprinted by permission of NEA, Inc.—Berry's World.

cracy is the same or worse than it was before it was adopted. The White House, however, has enjoyed an increase in flexibility of assignments, and Reagan and Bush have shrewdly used this to their advantage to influence and discipline the upper reaches of the executive branch.

PRESIDENTIAL CONTROL OVER THE BUREAUCRACY

Ever since Franklin Roosevelt strengthened the staffs of the presidency, the president's budget bureau, currently called the Office of Management and Budget, has been a key resource in helping to manage the executive branch. The OMB's primary task is to prepare the president's annual budget. A budget usually becomes the major vehicle for shaping a president's policy priorities. It is the place (and the process) that determines which programs will get more funds, which will be cut, and which will remain the same. Departments and agencies all over Washington fight to win larger chunks of the president's budget projections. The OMB supervises the preparation of the budget and hence assists very directly in the formulation of policy. The OMB is the closest thing a president has to an interest-free perspective on weighing and evaluating the merits of the countless proposals and pleas that constantly pour in upon the White House.

Ninety-six percent of the OMB's staff are career officials trained to evaluate ongoing projects and new spending requests. The OMB's top officials, of course, are presidential appointees, and they are often among a president's most important advisers. Together the OMB officials help a president make critical decisions not only about the budget but also about management practices, collaborative efforts among government agencies, and legislative planning. The OMB and its predecessor organization (the old Bureau of the Budget) have been actively involved in making sure that both the departments and Congress are informed of the president's legislative preferences.[24] All in all, the OMB plays an important role in expanding the policy and administrative options open to a president.[25]

Some writers call for a more radical overhaul of the civil service system. One observer, for example, would end career-long tenure in federal positions and allow for appointments for only six to twelve years, depending on a person's specialty. Tenure creates dead wood, they say, and periodic reexamination of a person's qualifications would greatly increase productivity and responsiveness. Although specialization is vital to modern organization, rotation (either from outside government or within government) might loosen up stiffened joints, bring new blood to agencies, and encourage a sense of breadth rather than fixed routines. It might even break up the "iron triangle"—alliances among senior civil servants, members of Congress, and outside client interest groups.

A related proposal deals with the heart of the democratic process. It is concerned not with making bureaucrats more effective but with ensuring that they are responsive to the electorate that elects the president. The emphasis here is on a vastly increased number of patronage positions, and much less reliance on the so-called merit system. One veteran observer of the Washington bureaucracy has complained that the greatest obstacle to reform of the civil service is that most people think it is better to have a system based on merit hiring than one based on political patronage. "But the fact is that getting a government job has only the most modest relation to merit." He adds, "Veterans get five free points added to their civil service exam score; disabled veterans get an extra ten. For nonveterans the trick is to get their names requested [from the Office of Personnel Management] by the agency filling the job, and the way to do that is to know

---

Why Presidents Reorganize the Bureaucracy

Shake up an organization to increase managerial control

Simplify or streamline the bureaucracy or a specific agency

Reduce costs by lessening overlap, duplication, inefficiencies

Symbolize priorities by signaling new responsibilities in new agencies

Improve program effectiveness by bringing separate but logically related programs to the same agency

Improve policy integration by placing competitive or conflicting interests within a single organization

Downgrade the importance of a program a president seeks to weaken.

CHAPTER 18 / Bureaucrats: The Real Power?

someone inside the agency. People already in the system are the first to know about a job opening, and knowing both the applicant and the job, they can tailor the job description to fit the person they want to hire. So the civil service is a patronage ring based not on politics but on friendship."[26] Thus, he calls the existing system a buddy system, and urges this unorthodox but intriguing proposal:

> It is wisely assumed that a patronage system will result in a government run by unqualified people. Let's take a look at that assumption. Why do political employees *have* to be unqualified? A politically appointed typist could be required to type the same number of words per minute as the civil service typist. Remember that merit appointment and promotion are not the reality in the present civil service, it's only make believe. Friendship and a military background have a lot more to do with hiring and advancement.
>
> Isn't it possible that government jobs might best be filled by politicians who are intersted in putting together an administration that will do a good enough job to get them re-elected? The same principle applies to most of the decisions government employees make. Why shouldn't they be made on a partisan basis if the motive behind them is doing a good enough job to be re-elected?[27]

Not surprisingly, neither Congress nor most career bureaucrats look with favor on this proposal. With the Watergate scandals of recent memory, and with the general indifference, if not contempt, most people have for our political parties, it is probable that most Americans would oppose this proposal as well. Plainly, however, it holds considerable appeal for those who have to work directly on behalf of a president.

Presidents as chief executives also have the power to reorganize the executive branch. Recent presidents tried to employ these powers, but they achieved few of their aims. President Nixon wanted to abolish six departments (Labor, Commerce, Transportation, Agriculture, Housing and Urban Development, and Health, Education and Welfare) and replace them with four new departments organized in broader categories, such as natural resources, human resources, and economic development. Nixon said this restructured national bureaucracy could provide coherent planning, resolve interdepartmental conflicts, and deliver services more efficiently. Congress and major interest groups disagreed. So did various department heads and career officials within the existing departments. Congressional committee leaders are always aware that if they restructure the federal administration, they may have to reorganize their own committee system. This would upset the balance of power in Congress. In short, changing the shape of administration is more than a matter of efficiency and economy. It also involves *policy outcomes*: Who gets what, how, and why.

President Carter learned these same realities. His ambitious plans for reshaping and reorganizing the federal bureaucracy came to little. Most of his ideas for sweeping organizational change, including the idea of a natural resources cabinet department, fell victim to the same political forces that had dealt the death blow to Nixon's reorganization efforts.

Ronald Reagan came to the White House pledging to abolish both the Education and Energy departments, but failed to do so. Instead, he ended up adding a Department of Veterans Affairs. He also proposed changing the Commerce Department into a Department of Trade. Reagan found out what most of his predecessors learned: although everybody favors sensible reorganization, difficulties and controversies arise when you get specific because the specifics may upset the already-established balance of power in the Washington power system.

Chief Executive versus White House Mouse

Students sometimes think presidents sit high atop the executive branch pyramid, barking out commands. Occasionally this is the case, but the degree to which a president can win cooperation or compliance varies enormously. And presidents can often be just as frustrated as parents are with their teenage offspring. Listen to the sad story of the White House mouse who had climbed inside a wall of the Oval Office and died there. The odor became offensive just as President Carter was about to greet a visiting diplomat.

An emergency call went out to the General Services Administration (the agency that maintains and oversees federal property), but the GSA refused to respond. The dead mouse, GSA officials said, had obviously come in from outside the building and was therefore the responsibility of the Department of the Interior. Interior officials, however, objected; they contended the mouse was not their concern because it was now inside the White House and their jurisdiction was merely the outside grounds.

Well, an exasperated Carter finally ordered officials from both agencies to his office where he angrily told them, "I can't even get a damn mouse out of my office. . . ." So how was the problem solved? By a two-agency White House supervised task force, of course.

Congress has a number of means of exercising control over the bureaucracy: by participating in the budget process, appropriating funds, confirming personnel, authorizing new programs or new shifts in direction, conducting investigations and hearings, reorganizing authority, and publicly rebuking the officials in a particular agency.

The foundation of bureaucratic power is, of course, a bureaucrat's information and expertise. Ordinarily, bureaucrats know much more than anyone else about their programs and the consequences of what they are doing. Recognizing this, Congress may request agency heads to make initial proposals and to provide cost and price estimates. It has imposed stiff penalties for providing misleading information—as a means of reducing bureaucratic deception.

Still, Congress is under fire, at least in some quarters, for encouraging the growth of bureaucracy and for deliberately allowing it to remain somewhat out of control. Members of Congress, so this reasoning goes, profit from the growth and complexity of the bureaucracy. It is to their state and district members of Congress that most constituents, especially business people, turn for help as they battle federal red tape and complications. Hence, as the federal bureaucracy and its programs grow, so too does the influence of members of Congress. Members of Congress, in fact, get big political mileage by interceding in federal agencies on behalf of their constituents.

The federal budget is a massive compilation that is distributed to Congress for debate and decision.

> The brutal fact is that only a small minority of our 535 congressmen would trade the present bureaucratic structure for one which was an efficient, effective agent of the general interest—the political payoffs of the latter are lower than those of the former. Congressional talk of inefficient, irresponsible, out-of-control bureaucracy is typically just that—talk—and when it is not, it usually refers to agencies under the jurisdiction of other congressmen's committees. Why do reformers continually ignore the fact that Congress has all the power necessary to enforce the "people's will" on the bureaucracy? The Congress can abolish or reorganize an agency. The Congress can limit or expand an agency's jurisdiction, or allow its authority to lapse entirely. The Congress can slash an agency's appropriations. The Congress can investigate. The Congress can do all these things, but individual congressmen generally find reasons not to do so.[28]

Basic to this point of view is the complaint that Congress does not pay enough attention to how its laws are administered, and that it delegates too much authority to bureaucrats. Congress, it is charged, anxious whenever possible to avoid conflict, adopts such sweeping legislation and delegates so much authority to the bureaucracy that bureaucrats, in effect, have become the nation's lawgivers.

But could Congress pass laws with very precise wording all the time? It would get too bogged down in the necessary details to complete its work. For example, imagine Congress is concerned that there be enough truck lines in operation to ensure prompt transportation service for shippers, but not so many as to lead to ruinous competition. If it should attempt to specify the exact circumstances under which a new truck route should be licensed, the statute would have to read as follows:

> Keokuk, Iowa, needs four truck lines unless the new superhighway that they have been talking about for ten years gets built. Then they will need five unless, of course, Uncle Charlie's Speedy Express gets rid of its Model

T and gets two tractors and vans. Then they will only need three as long as two freight trains a day also stop there.

On the other hand, Smithville, Tennessee, needs eight truck lines unless. . . .[29]

Of course, Congress seldom writes laws like these. Instead, it declares its policy in general terms and empowers the Interstate Commerce Commission to license new truck lines when such action would be warranted by "public convenience and necessity." The regulatory commissioners then judge the situation in Keokuk and Smithville and make specific rules.

But how can we get rid of wasteful and obsolete programs? Many people agree that too many federal programs are allowed to continue indefinitely, whether or not they are accomplishing what they were meant to do. If the country's needs and priorities change, programs should be adjusted or abolished accordingly. One attempted reform, adopted in most state governments, is a **sunset process.** Sunset laws place government agencies or programs on limited life cycles, and force them to justify their existence every six or seven years. Sunset review processes have been set up in most states. Their chief purpose is to weed out ineffective programs and make room for new ones. The technique derives its name from a group in Colorado that proposed that "the sun should set" on programs that have outlived their original purpose or whose benefits are outweighed by other considerations. The burden would be on the bureaucrats to perform well, so that in six or seven years they can prove themselves worthy of staying in business.

Sunset legislation is opposed by those who say it is too simple for the complicated and subtle evaluation work that needs to be done. Still others argue that sunset laws require enormous amounts of time and paperwork for bureaucrats to justify their existence every few years. The state experience with sunset procedures has generally been disappointing.

Remember that it is not Congress as a whole that shares the direction over the bureaucracy with the president. More accurately, it is individual members to whom Congress has delegated its authority. These people, primarily committee and subcommittee chairs, usually specialize in the appropriations and policies of a particular cluster of agencies—often the agencies serving constituents in their own districts. Some legislators stake out a claim over more general policies. Members of Congress, who see presidents come and go, come to think they know more about agencies than the president does (and sometimes this is the case). Although Congress as an institution may prefer to have presidents in charge of the executive branch so that it can hold them responsible for its operation, some congressional leaders prefer to seal off "their" agencies from presidential direction in order to maintain their own influence over public policy. Sometimes this is institutionalized—the Army chief of engineers, for example, is given authority by law to plan public works and report to Congress without going through the president.

Another factor works in favor of the Congress. Every day thousands of bureaucrats are involved in making thousands of decisions. A president has limited time, limited resources, and limited political influence over many of these agencies. Presidents and their staffs can become involved only in matters of significant political interest. Members of Congress, with an institutional staff of over 30,000, however, can operate in areas far from the presidential spotlight.[30]

So, who controls the bureaucrats? Presidents and members of Congress strive to do so, each in its own way. Interest groups also influence the way the bureaucracy operates. For their part career bureaucrats say they are responsive to the laws and statutes they work under and to their own standards of professional-

A committee hearing on the budget.

ism and responsibility. Plainly, there is no one answer to the question of who or what controls the bureaucracy. And because of this, there is a never-ending search for improved means of ensuring bureaucratic accountability. This search, and experiments with countless instruments—such as reorganizations, civil service reforms, sunset practices, budgetary planning, and oversight hearings—will always be with us—as they should be.

Summary

1. We regularly condemn our bureaucracy and our bureaucrats, yet we continue to turn to them to solve our toughest problems and to render more and better services. A survey of our bureaucratic agencies, then, is also a survey of how our political system has tried to identify many of our most important national goals.

2. The American bureaucracy does not strictly adhere to the textbook model of management organization. This is because our bureaucracy is not fully subordinate to any branch of government. It has at least two immediate bosses: Congress and the president. It must pay considerable attention as well to the courts and their rulings, and, of course, to well-organized interest groups and public opinion. In many ways the bureaucracy is a semi-independent force—a fourth branch of government—in American politics.

3. Debates and controversy over big government and big bureaucracy, and over how to reorganize them and how to eliminate waste in them, will continue. Meanwhile, most experts agree that the range and importance of the bureaucracy will expand in the years ahead. However, compared with many other nations and their centralized bureaucracies, the hand of the bureaucracy rests more gently and less oppressively on Americans than on other peoples.

4. Who and how the government hires and what discretion or powers it grants its employees will always be controversial topics. Morale has been low in recent years. Government personnel officers say the negative image of public service is a barrier to attracting new recruits for important federal jobs. Still, to work in the career public service is often to have the opportunity to serve people, to solve problems, and to try to bring about a better society. Efforts to make the bureaucracy more responsive and more accountable are enduring struggles, and they are issues raised in every presidential election. But there are never any final answers or quick fixes.

Further Reading

Lawrence Dodd and Richard Schott. *Congress and the Administrative State* (Wiley, 1979).

Anthony Downs. *Inside Bureaucracy* (Little, Brown, 1967).

James Eccles. *The Hatch Act and the American Bureaucracy* (Vantage Press, 1981).

Charles T. Goodsell. *The Case for Bureaucracy*, 2d ed. (Chatham House, 1985).

J. Peter Grace. *War on Waste: President's Private Sector Survey on Cost Control* (Macmillan, 1984).

Philip B. Heymann. *The Politics of Public Management* (Yale University Press, 1988).

Herbert Kaufman. *The Administrative Behavior of Federal Bureau Chiefs* (Brookings Institution, 1981).

Jack H. Knott and Gary J. Miller. *Reforming Bureaucracy: The Politics of Institutional Choice* (Prentice Hall, 1987).

Charles H. Levine, ed. *The Unfinished Agenda for Civil Service Reform* (Brookings Institution, 1985).

Dennis D. Riley. *Controlling the Federal Bureaucracy* (Temple University Press, 1987).

Francis E. Rourke. *Bureaucracy, Politics and Public Policy* (Little, Brown, 1983).

Harold Seidman and Robert Gilmour. *Politics, Position, and Power*, 4th ed. (Oxford University Press, 1986).

Stephen Skowronek. *Building a New American State: The Expansion of National Administrative Capacities, 1877–1920* (Cambridge University Press, 1982).

Bruce Smith and James Carroll, eds. *Improving the Accountability and Performance of Government* (Brookings Institution, 1982).

Richard J. Stillman. *The American Bureaucracy* (Nelson Hall, 1987).

John T. Tierney. *The U.S. Postal Service* (Auburn House, 1988).

Douglas Yates. *Bureaucratic Democracy* (Harvard University Press, 1982).

Three useful journals are *Journal of Policy Analysis and Management*; the *Public Administration Review*, and *Government Executive*.

Notes

1. For contending views of this debate see E. S. Savas, *Privatizing the Public Sector* (Chatham House, 1987), and Robert Kuttner, "False Profit," *The New Republic* (February 6, 1989), pp. 21–23.

2. Peter M. Benda and Charles H. Levine, "Reagan and the Bureaucracy: The Bequest, the Promise, and the Legacy," in Charles O. Jones, ed., *The Reagan Legacy* (Chatham House, 1988), p. 139.

3. For discussions of the representative character of the federal bureaucracy, see Samuel Krislov and David H. Rosenbloom, *Representative Bureaucracy and the American Political System* (Praeger, 1981).

4. For a discussion of these and the whole range of administrative agencies, see Harold Seidman and Robert Gilmour, *Politics, Position and Power: From the Positive to the Regulatory State*, 4th ed. (Oxford University Press, 1986), chap. 11. On government corporations, see John T. Tierney, "Government Corporations and Managing the Public's Business," *Political Science Quarterly* (Spring 1984), pp. 73–94.

5. For an analysis of the use and abuse of the civil service system in the early twentieth century, see Stephen Skowronek, *Building a New American State* (Cambridge University Press, 1982).

6. On the general subject of federal pay, see Robert W. Hartman and Arnold R. Weber, eds., *The Rewards of Public Service: Compensating Top Federal Officials* (Brookings Institution, 1980). See also Robert Hartman, *Pay and Pensions for Federal Workers* (Brookings Institution, 1983).

7. See the useful discussion of this in Hugo Heclo, "Issue Networks and the Executive Establishment," in Anthony King, ed., *The New American Political System* (American Enterprise Institute, 1978), pp. 87–124.

8. John W. Gardner, testimony before the U.S. Senate Committee on Government Operations, *Executive Reorganization Proposals, Hearings* (U.S. Government Printing Office, 1971), pp. 57–58. See also R. Douglas Arnold, *Congress and the Bureaucracy* (Yale University Press, 1979).

9. Quoted in Aaron Wildavsky, *The Politics of the Budgetary Process*, 4th ed. (Little, Brown, 1984), pp. 80, 81. See also Lawrence Dodd and Richard Schott, *Congress and the Administrative State* (Wiley, 1979).

10. Juan Cameron, "Admiral Rickover's Final Battle," *Fortune* (November 1976), p. 193. © 1976 Time Inc. For a critical view of Rickover's defiance of his superiors and his cozy relations with well-placed members of Congress, see Elmo R. Zumwalt, Jr., *On Watch: A Memoir* (Quadrangle, 1976), chap. 5.

11. Cameron, "Admiral Rickover's Final Battle," p. 200.

12. Karlyn H. Keene and Everett C. Ladd, "What the Public Says," *Government Executive* (January 1988), p. 11.

13. See *The Washington Post* (July 16, 1983), section A, p. 8. Similar positive findings are discussed in Goodsell, *The Case for Bureaucracy*, chap. 2.

14. Tom Alexander, "Why Bureaucracy Keeps Growing," *Fortune* (May 7, 1979), p. 164. See also Frederic V. Malek, *Washington's Hidden Tragedy: The Failure to Make Government Work* (Free Press, 1978).

15. W. Michael Blumenthal, "Candid Reflections of a Businessman in Washington," *Fortune* (January 29, 1979), p. 41.

16. Gerald R. Ford, *A Time to Heal: The Autobiography of Gerald R. Ford* (Harper & Row/Reader's Digest, 1979), p. 272.

17. Herbert Kaufman, *Are Government Organizations Immortal?* (Brookings Institution, 1976), p. 67. See also Richard Stillman, *The American Bureaucracy* (Nelson Hall, 1987), chaps. 1–3.

18. J. Peter Grace, *Burning Money: The Waste of Your Tax Dollars* (Macmillan, 1984), p. 172; and J. Peter Grace, "The Problem of Big Government" *Imprimis* (January 1988), pp. 1–7.

19. Jodie T. Allen, "The Grace Book," *The Washington Post National Weekly Edition* (January 7, 1985), p. 28.

20. Steven Kelman, "The Grace Commission: How Much Waste in Government?" *The Public Interest* (Winter 1985), p. 78.

21. Ibid., p. 78.

22. Ibid., p. 82.

23. Mark Huddleston, "The Carter Civil Service Reforms: Some Implications for Political Theory and Public Administration," *Political Science Quarterly* (Winter 1981–1982), pp. 607–21; and Bruce Buchanan, "The Senior Executive Service: How Can We Tell If It Works?" *Public Administration Review* (May–June 1981), pp. 349–58.

24. For useful studies of these functions of the OMB, see Larry Berman, *The Office of Budget and Management and the Presidency, 1921–1979* (Princeton University Press, 1979); and Howard Shuman, *Politics and the Budget* (Prentice-Hall, 1988).

25. Of course, the OMB does not always win, nor is it always right. See David Stockman, *The Triumph of Politics* (Harper & Row, 1986).

26. Charles Peters, *How Washington Really Works* (Addison-Wesley, 1980), pp. 47–48.

27. Ibid., pp. 48–49.

28. Morris P. Fiorina, "Flagellating the Federal Bureaucracy," *Society* (March/April 1983), p. 73.

29. Martin Shapiro, *The Supreme Court and Administrative Agencies* (Free Press, 1968), p. 4.

30. See Richard Cohen, "The King of Oversight," *Government Executive* (September 1988), pp. 16–18; and Don Lee, "Shear Audacity: 13 Years of the Golden Fleece Award," *Government Executive* (April 1988), pp. 28–30.

19
Making Public Policy

The playwright George Bernard Shaw suggested that progress comes about because of unreasonable people. Reasonable people, he said, adjust themselves to reality and cope with what they find. Unreasonable people dream of a different and better place and try to adapt the world to these ideals. Discontent or unreasonableness is often the first step in the development of a person, as well as in that of a nation. George Washington and his friends were decidedly unreasonable—from the British point of view—in the 1770s, just as those millions of Chinese students and their allies seemed unreasonable to the top government leaders in Beijing in 1989. Women suffragists, civil rights advocates, and social-issue activists often seem unreasonable—troublemakers or incurable idealists.

Many major policy changes in the United States have originated with those impatient with the old ways of doing things. These people are often the catalysts who move gifted coalition-building politicians and reasonable policy entrepreneurs to change policy through laws or court decisions.

But many policy changes also come from the grass roots, not just from Washington. Ideologues, business leaders, labor unionists, state and local officials, farmers, ethnic advocates, consumer spokespersons, religious leaders, scholars, representatives of foreign nations, pundits, and just plain citizens either want policy changes from government, or they want to prevent things from changing. Members of the government—elected leaders, appointed bureaucrats, and civil servants—can also be viewed as having an interest in the transformation of public policy. As a result, the nation's capital is both a germinating as well as a terminating stage in the process of policy change.

Public policy is the substance of what government does. More specifically, it is the set of declared intentions and follow-up actions our elected officials take to meet human needs and resolve conflict within society. But public policy can also be what a government decides to ignore or not do. This chapter examines some distinctive approaches to the national policy-making process. The four chapters that follow examine the most important policy functions of the national government: foreign, defense, domestic, and regulatory public policy.

The Boundaries of Public Policy

To understand the policy-making process we must first recognize that policy debate in the United States occurs within well-established boundaries. We tend to have the impression that the pursuit of any policy idea in America is at least a possibility. However, like any political system, the American system of policy making has constraints on what we might call the breadth of policy choice. This set of choices defines the most comprehensive parameters of political and policy possibility. There are distinct boundaries to a society's beliefs, thoughts, creativity, and imagination that limit and otherwise shape its policies. In the United States, some choices are within the boundaries of permissible policy discussion while others are not. Choices that may exist theoretically outside this boundary constitute possibilities that are completely foreign to the American political system. For example, the elimination of private property or extensive national economic planning are not policy choices within the historical boundaries of the American political system.[1] In addition to the boundaries of political acceptability created by our political culture and ideology (see Chapter 7), there are also constraints imposed by the structure of the American policy-making system. "The story of American public policy is in large measure a struggle by policymakers to develop and implement effective programs within the context of an elaborate and resiliently incoherent government structure."[2]

Of course, it is one thing to acknowledge the existence of such boundaries, yet quite another to determine their limits with precision. Such a determination is made more difficult by changes in the construction of such boundaries that occur through political development. In the American system, one such set of boundaries might be defined as the liberal tradition of Lockean individualism.[3] The liberal tradition advocates a strong belief in personal freedom, individual rights, limited government, and personal property. The economic system in America, or simply put, the market, also serves as a boundary that includes some choices and excludes others. The noted political economist Charles E. Lindblom refers to the market as a prison because it limits the viable options for policy development in the United States.[4] As a result of the control that American business has over the health of the economy, elected officials strive to develop policies favorable to a productive business climate. This means not only that business is in a privileged position when it comes to influencing public policy, but also that certain policies are seldom seriously considered by government officials.

The existence of such boundaries should be recalled when we explain the particular course of policy development in the United States and when we speculate about the prospects for policy change.

Getting Things Done in Washington: The Players

If we follow national policy making as it is reported on television or in the newspapers, we rarely see more than bill-signing ceremonies, press conferences, or formal speeches. And we hear mainly about conflicts between the branches, or disarray within a branch. Congress, we may be told, refuses to go along with the president on some foreign-aid package, or the Supreme Court overrules a provision of the Gramm–Rudman–Hollings Budget Balancing Act of 1986. Or the president vetoes a minimum wage bill passed by Congress. Although these contests capture our interest much like sporting events, they are the superficial eye-catching events.

"Please understand. I don't sell access to the government. I merely sell access to the guys who *do* sell access to the government."

Drawing by Ed Fisher; © 1986 The New Yorker Magazine, Inc.

Lobbyists and consultants are part of the Washington scene and exert a powerful influence on the members of Congress.

Washington journalism feeds on such contests because they make for more interesting copy than the numerous small cooperative and collaborative efforts to make policy. But box scores indicating how many of the president's legislative measures pass Congress often conceal as much as they reveal. They do not really tell us why a president has or has not been successful. Nor do they tell us much about the quality of measures proposed, passed, and rejected. A president with an eye solely on the box score, for example, can avoid endorsing measures that are unlikely to pass. Moreover, a higher success rate may be due more to rapidly increasing federal revenues than to presidential leadership. Conversely, lower success rates may be better attributed to the problems inherent in divided government, when the executive and legislature are controlled by different parties, than by a failure of presidential leadership.

Beneath and behind "the governing class," thousands of individuals are at work in the Washington policy-making process. They help articulate issues, resolve conflicts, and facilitate cooperation across institutions. Only by understanding these people can we appreciate the patterns of national policy making. Sometimes just being in the right place at the right time enables an individual to contribute to policy decisions. Usually, however, people who make a difference have formal positions, needed knowledge, access to power-holders, or some combination of these. Specialists from various professional communities are often looked to for advice in the early stages, when policy makers are assigning relative importance to various competing issues. Of course, one must also be familiar with the rules of the Washington public-policy process. In other words, not everyone who would like to influence the policy-making process may necessarily have the resources, experience, or wherewithal to do so.

Senior congressional committee staff positions, once a patronage payoff to campaign aides, are increasingly filled by highly qualified policy entrepreneurs. The ability of these professional staffs to analyze information for hearings and legislation gives them influence on policy making. They often become a kind of "shadow government" linking Congress, the executive branch, interest groups, and different constituencies around the nation. Federal biomedical policy, for example, has often been made by a small group of medical researchers, philanthropists, and members of Congress assisted by staffers in Congress and the White House.

Then, of course, come the lobbyists. Lobbyists have been in Washington as long as there have been lobbies—but never as many as today. Although about 5000 lobbyists are formally registered with Congress, it is widely estimated that about 30,000 to 40,000 people in Washington (or people who frequent Washington on a regular basis) do some sort of lobbying at any given time. "Washington is rife with institutions whose leaders are ushered through decision makers' doors and taken seriously not because of who they are but because of the multitudes they speak for or the respected institutions they represent," reports the *National Journal*.[5] The margin box lists some of the lobbying or advocacy institutions considered to be "influential" in Washington.

Representatives of state and local governments are increasingly present in Washington to get hearings for their points of view. These governments send an official or hire consultants to represent their interests and to ensure that issues of great concern to them are not ignored. The number of offices representing individual governors or state legislatures in Washington has grown to several dozen; in addition, lobbying officials work for the National Governors Association and the National Conference of State Legislators. The National League of Cities is an effective lobbying instrument for the special concerns of municipal governments.

Even individual cities now have lobbyists representing their interests to the Washington establishment.

Joining them are the new legions of professional *political consultants* who come to Washington during the election cycle and stay on afterward to advise their successful candidates who have become elected officials. Because of their polling and advertising skills and access to the mass media, professional consultants are a valuable resource to politicians and other members of the Washington community who seek to persuade and influence.

Washington is full of unelected *policy politicians* who have served long periods within a given policy area and in a variety of governmental as well as nongovernmental positions. The career ladders of these specialists are neither tidy nor predictable. An economist at the OMB may move to the nongovernmental Brookings Institution and a few years later go back to government service heading the Congressional Budget Office. An aide to a senator may go to HUD and then back to an elective state government position. Later the aide may return to cabinet posts at HUD, Defense, or Justice, then become ambassador to Great Britain, again become a cabinet officer, and then once again an ambassador. A young lawyer may work in the office of the secretary at the Department of Defense, then join the White House National Security Council Staff, leave to become counsel for the Senate Armed Services Committee, three years later enter private practice in Washington, D.C., three years later become undersecretary of the navy, and then return to private practice. These individuals have walked through the so-called "revolving door" that connects government service to private practice.

These illustrations are by no means unusual. Mobility in Washington is extensive, and career ladders diverse. As a result, complex networks of friendships, influence, and loyalties characterize the policy-making process.[6]

One of the more fascinating aspects of Washington politics is the way in which policy activists in different branches of government, or associated with various nongovernmental organizations (such as research institutes, foundations, lobbyist units, or media), join forces in working alliances. Policy subsystems grow up around a set of interrelated issues, as much a response to the process of getting things done as to the issues themselves. Age and formal position are less important than information, imagination, energy, and persistence. Policy activists learn how to capture support from members of Congress and senior White House aides. This is easy sometimes, since certain members of Congress, as well as White House aides, are always looking for new ideas with which to promote their careers. The role of the policy entrepreneur as a key element in the policy-making process cannot be overemphasized.[7]

Competing Models of Policy Making

There are numerous approaches to the study of public policy making. The choice of which approach is most appropriate depends on what policies are being considered, on the particular stage of the process selected for analysis, and on the analyst's political values. Nevertheless, there is a certain amount of agreement that distinct stages in the policy-making process can be identified.

1. *Problem identification*: What is the problem? How is the problem defined and by whom? How does the problem fit with existing policy categories and rankings of goals? Does the government need to help out, intervene, regulate, or make some kind of decision? Should the issue or problem be

Influential Institutions
ABC News
AFL-CIO
American Bankers Association
American Civil Liberties Union
American Farm Bureau Federation
American Federation of Government Employees
American Federation of State, County and Municipal Employees
American Hospital Association
American Medical Association
American Petroleum Institute
American Security Council
Associated Press
Business Roundtable
CBS News
Chamber of Commerce of the United States
Independent Bankers Association of America
Independent Petroleum Association of America
International Brotherhood of Teamsters
League of Women Voters
NAACP
National Association of Home Builders
National Association of Manufacturers
National Association of Realtors
National Education Association
National Federation of Independent Business
National Governors' Association
National League of Cities
National Rifle Association
National Wildlife Federation
NBC News
The New York Times
Newsweek
Sierra Club
Time
Tobacco Institute
Union of Concerned Scientists
United Auto Workers
United Food and Commercial Workers International Union
U.S. Conference of Mayors
Wall Street Journal
The Washington Post
Wilderness Society

placed on the agenda of government? For example, if air pollution is making people sick somewhere, is this a matter for governmental attention? What forces will determine whether or not the problem/issue will reach the attention of government officials?

2. *Policy formulation*: What should be done? How can we best assess the alternatives, including benefits, costs, and equity? Who should be involved in the planning and design of the policy? For example, if air pollution requires government action, what action is preferable? Policy analysts need to consider all the alternatives, but they must remember that alternatives must realistically be able to be implemented in our country.

3. *Policy adoption*: Who needs to act? What branch of government should get involved? What constitutional, legal, or political requirements must be met? How specific or how general must the decision be? For example, should Congress pass a clean air act, or should some regulatory body like the Environmental Protection Agency be asked to hold hearings on the matter and come up with recommendations? Or should this matter be one for presidential leadership requiring an executive order and major addresses to the public?

4. *Policy implementation*: Once it is adopted, how should the policy be carried out? At what level of government will the policy be most effectively implemented? How much should be spent where, and how? How will the process of administration affect the effectiveness of the policy? For example, which level of government will yield the greatest compliance with new clean air standards? How will the "successful implementation of the policy" be defined and by whom?

5. *Policy evaluation*: Is the policy working? How is the effectiveness or impact of the policy measured? Who evaluates the policy? What are the consequences of policy evaluation and congressional oversight? For example, are antipollution laws really improving air quality? Or are Bush's antidrug abuse measures making any headway?

Policy making can occur in any branch of government, and it can be carried out by a series of political participants, not just lawmakers. Note, too, policy making cannot be separated entirely from administration, and, as we saw in Chapter 18, appointed public officials often have as much influence as elected officials. Policy making is influenced by the political, economic, and social values of the people participating in each of the policy stages. Also, it is clearly influenced by interest groups of all kinds, especially by highly organized and well-financed groups and associations that can afford to maintain lobbyists in Washington, D.C.

Among the variety of approaches used to study policy making in the United States are the *rational person* model, the *power elite* model, the *interest group* or *Madisonian* model, the *policy systems model*, and the *incremental* or *gradualist* model. Although these are not the only explanations of how the system operates, examining them yields a variety of useful insights on how policy is shaped in the United States.

THE RATIONAL PERSON MODEL

Even though the rational person model is primarily a textbook abstraction, it is a helpful model to analyze public policy. The rational person model is sometimes called public-choice theory, deductive theory, rational choice theory, or even an economics approach to policy decision making. Rational policy makers try to protect or maximize their own personal interests or what they think is in the public or collective interest. Groups may also behave rationally by striving to protect their interests and advance those policies that they think will benefit them or society. The rational choice approach suggests a calculating strategy: Participants constantly ask how much they or their values will gain or lose from government action or inaction, and how much effort and time they should spend lobbying and building a constituency.

They do so by making "reasoned choices about the desirability of adopting different courses of action to resolve public problems."[8] These choices are based on the principle that no policy should be adopted if its costs (broadly speaking) outweigh its benefits. All other things being equal, a policy maker should select the policy that maximizes benefits over costs.

Faced with an issue, rational participants will first clarify their goals or objectives and rank them. They will then list all the important possible solutions and investigate the likely results of each. After considering the costs and benefits of each likely outcome, they then choose the policy whose consequences most closely matches their goals.[9]

Barriers to rational decision making include the absence of consensus about which values or goals should be maximized; conflicting costs and benefits that cannot be compared; conflicts between societal goals and the personal rewards for individuals or groups; the inevitability of incomplete information; and the inherent uncertainty about the consequences of policy alternatives.

However, even if these barriers were eliminated or modified, critics of rational decision making charge there is little that is actually rational about it. Contrary to expectations rational choice does not eliminate politics from the process of policy making. It does not turn policy making into an exacting science of goal maximization and efficiency. Rather, rational decision making may serve only to hide the politics inherent in the construction of rational categories of analysis. "Reasoned analysis" is necessarily political: "The categories of thought behind reasoned analysis are themselves constructed in political struggle . . ."[10] Despite the promise of rational decision making and its analytic usefulness, it fails to deliver us from the reality that the essence of policy making is about the struggle over ideas and values.[11]

THE POWER ELITE MODEL

The power elite approach generally interprets what happens in the policy arena as the product of the political influence of powerful economic interests. The charge is that we have a government of the rich, by the friends of the rich, and for the rich. If 5 percent of U.S. families control 30 percent of the wealth, it is because our public policies favor the wealthy. If the defense budget expands at a time when the problems of poverty, education, health care, and homelessness are widely viewed as our top priorities, it is because the interests of the military-industrial complex prefer a defense buildup to the expansion of social programs.

The power elite approach advises that we should study government inaction as much as government action, because powerful business interests are often able to keep certain issues off the government's agenda. And these powerful interests generally do not want any kind of governmental interference in the economy unless they stand to gain from it. In short, the power elite approach believes there is a "ruling class" in America whose influence and power are based upon the national corporate economy and the institutions that the economy nourishes,

---

Influential Policy Research "Think Tanks"

Listed here are just a few of the growing number of policy research centers in this country. Scholars and analysts at these institutes write books, prepare studies and reports, and make their findings available to Washington decision makers and the general public.

The Brookings Institution
RAND Corporation
The Urban Institute
American Enterprise Institute
The Heritage Foundation
Carnegie Endowment for International Peace
The Hoover Institution, Stanford University
Institute for Advanced Studies, Princeton University
Center for Strategic and International Studies, Georgetown University
John F. Kennedy School of Government, Harvard University
Woodrow Wilson School of Public Affairs, Princeton University
The Cato Institute
Institute for Policy Studies
The Twentieth Century Fund
American Federation of Scientists

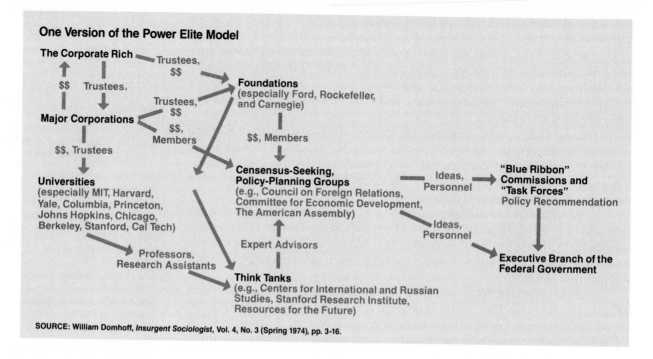

One Version of the Power Elite Model

The Corporate Rich — Trustees, $$

$$ ↕ Trustees,

Major Corporations — Trustees, $$

$$, Members

$$, Trustees

Foundations (especially Ford, Rockefeller, and Carnegie)

$$, Members

Universities (especially MIT, Harvard, Yale, Columbia, Princeton, Johns Hopkins, Chicago, Berkeley, Stanford, Cal Tech)

Professors, Research Assistants

Censensus-Seeking, Policy-Planning Groups (e.g., Council on Foreign Relations, Committee for Economic Development, The American Assembly)

Expert Advisors

Think Tanks (e.g., Centers for International and Russian Studies, Stanford Research Institute, Resources for the Future)

Ideas, Personnel

Ideas, Personnel

"Blue Ribbon" Commissions and "Task Forces" Policy Recommendation

Executive Branch of the Federal Government

SOURCE: William Domhoff, *Insurgent Sociologist*, Vol. 4, No. 3 (Spring 1974), pp. 3-16.

such as the defense establishment. Congress, presidents, and regulatory agencies are generally viewed as serving the interests of the powerful, monied class.[12]

The power elite model, although often described as one that visualizes the controllers of the economy as powerful, is actually somewhat compatible with the notion that many conservatives have of the way things get done in the United States. They sometimes think of the power elite as the big unions, the big media, the big bureaucracy, and others who, in alliance with the "Eastern Establishment," force upon common people programs and goals contrary to what the majority wish. This might be called a "populist-conservative" approach; it has been represented in part by the telepreacher Reverend Pat Robertson of Virginia, tax cutters Paul Gann and the late Howard Jarvis of California, and others who are also persuaded that a "ruling class" determines how policies are made and administered.

An important variant of the power elite approach suggests business has a "privileged position" in American politics.[13] According to this view, the power of business is not due to large campaign contributions (although business does make them), advertising campaigns (although business does use them) or to traditional pressure group politics (although business does lobby). Rather, the privileged position of business stems from the fact that the prosperity of the American economy and with it the well-being of elected politicians requires that government both respond to and anticipate the needs of business and act accordingly. This theory is based on the premise that the American electorate votes retrospectively on the basis of their evaluations of the economy. Since politicians want to stay in office they have a strong incentive to do whatever it takes to keep the economy healthy. Business activity determines the health of the economy; therefore, politicians are inclined to give business most of what it wants from government, frequently, so the argument goes, without business even having to ask for it. Thus, the electoral connection that links the interests of politicians to the demands and interests of their respective constituencies creates a set of incentives in which the interests of business dominate the policy-making process.

Another approach, often confused with the power elite theories, is a Marxist model. Marxists contend policy development and outcomes, especially for the working and poor classes, occur only as placating devices to lessen the likelihood of unrest and preserve the stability of a basically unfair system.[14] In this view, the formal provisions for a democratic system of policy making are subverted by the requirements for development of modern capitalism.[15]

Critics of the more general power elite approach say if researchers start with the assumption that elites account for policy change or lack of change, they are likely to find evidence to support it. But if they start with the assumption that the policy process is more complicated, they will find evidence of a more complicated and subtle set of influences.[16] As a result, studies of the power elite are suspect on the grounds they frequently assume, rather than empirically establish, the existence of an elite.

THE INTEREST GROUP (OR PLURALIST OR MADISONIAN) MODEL

The oldest theory of American politics, and the one most widely held, is that our politics and public policies are the product of the struggle among competing interest groups. This is the explanation of James Madison in the famous *Federalist 10*. You should read it carefully; it is in the Appendix of this book. This Madisonian model underlies much of the explanation of this book. Madison said it so well that we will elaborate no further here, although, as you will note, the Madisonian model is inherent in the incrementalist model explained below.

Recently, some scholars have concluded that the Madisonian theory overstates the role of interest groups and underestimates the role of public bureaucracies. Indeed, it largely ignores the role of the state and the autonomy its members may have for asserting their own interests in the policy-making process.[17] They now suggest the need to study the relative power and political strategies of the large public bureaucracies in Washington. This approach suggests bureaucracies are concerned with larger budgets and the expansion of programs. In addition, there are strong pressures for them to do something in a given arena before another agency acts instead. These factors shape the relationship that a bureaucracy has with a president and the Congress during the process of policy formation and also affect the way policies are implemented.

Adherents of this view recommend that students of public policy pay close attention to the way the bureaucracy functions and the way bureaucrats become involved in the various stages of the policy-making process. Critics of this view hold that while it might appear bureaucrats are exercising great influence on the policy-making process, they are really acting on behalf of clientele groups and other organized interests with whom bureaucracies are in daily contact.

THE POLICY SYSTEMS MODEL

A more ambitious yet more general approach is offered by those who want to place all the factors and all the stages of the process into a systems framework. They claim everything is interrelated and a full understanding of how policies are made or changed can come only from a comprehensive look at these relationships. Borrowing from engineering and biological models, these researchers examine the inputs of the policy system and stress the way the process translates inputs into outputs, and then how the outputs—laws—are converted into policy outcomes, or improvements in people's lives. Attention to these processes of policy making reveals "the way policies are made affects the content of public policy."[18] The diagram on page 502 conveys much of the policy systems model.

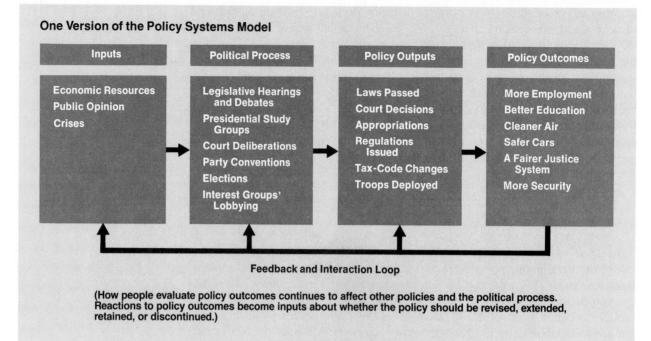

One Version of the Policy Systems Model

Inputs	Political Process	Policy Outputs	Policy Outcomes
Economic Resources Public Opinion Crises	Legislative Hearings and Debates Presidential Study Groups Court Deliberations Party Conventions Elections Interest Groups' Lobbying	Laws Passed Court Decisions Appropriations Regulations Issued Tax-Code Changes Troops Deployed	More Employment Better Education Cleaner Air Safer Cars A Fairer Justice System More Security

Feedback and Interaction Loop

(How people evaluate policy outcomes continues to affect other policies and the political process. Reactions to policy outcomes become inputs about whether the policy should be revised, extended, retained, or discontinued.)

Note that the feedback loop linking policy outcomes with the other aspects of the system implies that policy results, and how the public reacts to the results, will in turn affect other policies. A systems model is most valuable as an organizational and conceptual tool for policy research and analysis. It is less valuable in predicting which policies will or will not be produced by the system.

Critics say this approach ignores the content of public policy, thereby diminishing its value and relevance for the analysis of real political problems. In addition, critics allege this approach assumes changes in the process will always yield changes in the content of public policy. In fact, tinkering with the formal processes of decision making may not be sufficient to produce significantly different policies. Other factors, such as the requirements for economic development or the interests of public bureaucrats may be more important determinants of policy outcomes than formal structures.

THE INCREMENTALIST MODEL

Incrementalism, which flows from the Madisonian model, is perhaps the most popular approach to the process of public policy making and for explanations of that process. Incrementalism suggests problems can be solved only, or best, through small changes or adjustments. Does incrementalism mean there is no single, right, comprehensive answer to a problem? No. The incrementalist system can sometimes allow for a single answer, yet it requires that this answer be arrived at gradually.

Unlike the rational person model, the incrementalist model suggests that only some alternatives are examined. More attention is devoted to seeking mutual agreement about what small steps can be taken than to finding a single, comprehensive answer. Policy makers engage in incremental decision making for a number of reasons. The time, money, and information are not available to consider all the alternatives to the present policy. Policy makers prefer to stick with known policies rather than risk the uncertain consequences of new programs. The routines and sunk costs of a particular program provide a strong disincentive for radical policy change on an annual basis. Finally, incrementalism is simply an easier way for decision makers to reach policy agreements.[19] In addition to these personal incentives, the American system of separation of powers and dispersed authority promotes piecemeal policy change. Planning comprehensively is difficult in a system such as ours, which is glued together with alliance politics, majorities of the moment, and constant compromising.

Still, thinking comprehensively is not impossible in our system. However, in order to get something done and enforced, many different and often differing people must reach a consensus—with much compromising and bargaining. We have to get by so many potential veto points and groups that the resulting policy proposals are almost always different from what the sponsors desired.

Policy makers bend over backward to design programs that cultivate interest-group support and neutralize possible opponents. This results, not surprisingly, in watered-down objectives and laws that are extremely general and vague. To be sure, laws are often complex and detailed; yet they are deliberately written to permit a diversity of interpretations. Their ambiguity and vagueness make it possible to build the political coalitions necessary for the adoption of such public policies.

Defenders of the incrementalist model suggest that, with a more gradualist perspective about how the policy-change process works, we should "come to value not only those persons and events that rock the boat, that increase the pressures upon decision-makers to act, but also those persons who think deeply about problems, who search for and invent alternatives, and who keep alternative solutions alive and available to decision-makers."[20] So, in addition to the impatient and sometimes unreasonable cranks who call attention to the need for change, it is these policy brokers, adaptors, incubators, and issue entrepreneurs whose energy and ingenuity lay the groundwork for elected officials to bring about needed policy change.

In recent years direct governmental intervention in the form of a command-and-control approach has come under sharp attack as not always the only or best way to solve important problems. In its place the market approach has been hailed as a potentially more effective way to address these difficulties. To control pollution, for example, either the Environmental Protection Agency can enforce regulations for hundreds of thousands of different businesses, or we can make adjustments in the tax system to give industries an economic incentive to avoid pollution. During the Reagan years steps were taken to **privatize** various social programs (e.g., housing, employment training, prisons, and hospitals) and to build more effective private-public partnerships.[21]

Transferring authority to states and localities also encourages incrementalism. With such strategies Washington officials are in effect saying: "Let local elites decide what is proper policy in their locality. Let us not interfere." Some people contend, and they are partly correct, efficiency and a smaller federal bureaucracy should be prime concerns. But decentralization and "disaggregation" (dividing up policy making into fragmented, functional units) are also means of getting Congress and federal bureaucrats to give up their power over federal funds. Thus, local policy making is still another way for Washington officials to make people happy. Yet it is often at the expense of national objectives, comprehensive planning, and swift action. Historically, state responsibility for social programs, for example education and welfare, has often led to significant interstate disparities in funding and in the provision of services.

Even when the national government is unified in its views, localities are often able to delay or modify federal policies by local administrative manipulations. The diversity and intricacies created by federalism make it difficult for the national government to implement effectively public policy through state and local authorities. The states are not organized the same way, for example, they are divided into subunits differently. The presence of effective decision makers and policy entrepreneurs varies greatly across the states as do a state's financial capacity, responsibility, and commitment to particular programs.[22]

One charge against incrementalism as the way policy should be made is that it serves to conserve the present solutions to problems even after better alternatives are available. As a statement of how decisions are made, incrementalism is also the target of criticism, especially in the area of budgetary policy. Studies that claim to show incremental patterns of expenditures when entire agencies are analyzed reveal nonincremental patterns when the budgets are disaggregated into programs. In addition, only certain policy areas may be characterized by incremental decision making. Newer or more marginal programs may not be subject to incremental decision making at all. Finally, incrementalism fails to be an effective general explanation of how public policy is made because it does not explain how and when programs make big changes—or big losses—in their budgets and directions.[23]

Most of the models just outlined have some evidence to back them up, but it seems obvious that no single approach will explain everything. By and large, policies are shaped by a combination of events, the availability of resources, past experience, and the ideas of concerned public officials and activist citizens. Elections, public opinion, and competition among groups and bureaucracies, as well as struggles among the branches of government and the particular requirements of modern industrial capitalism, all influence the way policies are defined and settled. We now turn to a more detailed examination of what takes place in some of the key stages of the policy-making process.

National Policy Formation

AGENDA-BUILDING

Have you ever wondered why one subject seems to be in the headlines for weeks, or why suddenly something that has been talked about for decades is enacted into law? Why do we seem to be a nation with one or two issues dominating all the discussions and then overnight they disappear? Sometimes the answer is obvious. A catastrophic event, like the Challenger space shuttle tragedy that caused the death of seven astronauts, led to congressional hearings, presidential commission proceedings, investigative news stories, and books about our space program. Similarly, the Exxon oil spill off the coast of Alaska led to new thinking about shipping regulations, environmental standards, and liability requirements. But then there are other public policies that take years to enact. The issue of national health insurance for the elderly was on the national political agenda for twenty years before Medicare was passed in 1965. Why was the Civil Rights Act of 1964 so long in the making? Why after years of discussion was there finally tax reform in 1986? Questions like these require that we consider the process by which political issues come to receive the serious attention of government officials. This is often referred to as the process of national agenda-building.[24]

If we look closely, we find a variety of factors and people are involved in the process of agenda-building: events, crises, changes in expert opinion, changes in mass opinion, interest group agitation, and greater involvement by elected

Retired Surgeon General Everett Koop was instrumental in initiating government programs to deal with the AIDS crisis.

CHAPTER 19 / Making Public Policy

officials and their staffs. There are other possible determinants of the national agenda as well: the definition and redefinition of political problems, the identification of performance gaps in public policy, changes in knowledge (especially changes in technology), changes in dominant ideas or paradigms, the breakdown of a government program, or a problem produced by the government.[25] Indeed, public policy can be its own cause. Policy begets more policy. "[P]olicies feed on each other; the more there are, the more there have to be in order to cope with new circumstances, effects on other policies, and unexpected consequences."[26] Thus, the expansion of American national government can be seen not only as a solution to many social ills, but also as the occasion for greater policy demands and initiating opportunities. In recent years, political scientists have focused more attention on the agenda-building or idea-generation part of the policy-making process.

As noted a "crisis" or "catastrophic event" can play an important role in capturing the serious attention of government officials and in securing a place on the national agenda for a particular problem. The crisis—an oil spill, new information on the spread of AIDS, urban riots, and so forth—is more likely to attract the attention of government policy makers if a number of conditions are met. The crisis must not be a one-time event, but rather defined in terms of long-term prospects for its reoccurrence. The event must touch directly upon an important aspect of individual life. In addition, widespread consensus on the cause of the crisis must exist if the problem is to have a good chance of making the policy agenda. A crisis that affects a collective or public good, such as national defense, air quality, or transportation, has a higher probability of reaching the agenda. Finally, the public and government officials must be convinced that action can be taken on the crisis. Where helplessness is perceived, the issue may receive widespread media coverage but will not make it to the national agenda.

Who sets the agenda? According to classical theories of representation, our elected representatives should exercise the most influence in the making of laws and policies. Elected officials obviously play major roles in raising, debating, and acting upon issues in ways that are meant to solve problems and improve the nation. Yet both politicians and the media have so much else to do and are by definition generalists that in practice the agenda-building function is often performed by other participants in the policy process.

The media play a role in policy making by bringing critical issues before the public.

MASS MEDIA AGENDA-SETTING

It is often asserted that the mass media has a profound influence upon creating or setting the public agenda—the set of issues of most concern to the public. This assertion has an intuitive appeal given popular assumptions about the power of the media to influence how we think and what we think about. Careful studies, however, find the influence of the media is not as powerful as we sometimes think. The media is most influential on individuals who are less informed, have few friends, and a high need for structure (see Chapter 12).

This is both a frightening and an optimistic finding. The media has the greatest effect on those who are the most helpless in an increasingly information-based society. The good news is the media apparently does not have much of an effect (at least as it is currently understood) on well-informed citizens. Finally, when we look for media agenda-setting effects based on the characteristics of the issue, we find that effects are most pronounced when the issue has widespread agreement, has only an indirect effect on the individual, is national in character, and does not raise personally sensitive questions for the individuals. Thus on issues that profoundly affect an individual the media's impact on issue salience

Ralph Nader's reports and testimony before Congress have led to legislation on consumer and environmental protection.

and awareness will be minimal.[27] However, despite these specific limits to media influence, those issues that receive extended coverage in the national news become more important to viewers, while those that are ignored lose credibility. This means drug abuse, the deficit, energy shortages, and the homeless, for example, will become priority issues for the public only if they receive considerable attention from the news media.[28]

THE ROLE OF POLICY ENTREPRENEURS

In addition to politicians and the media other people also perform a role in defining important issues and advocating that they receive governmental attention. They point to problems and perhaps write about them and organize groups to petition for change. It may be a scientist who has come up with a better way to prevent heart disease or cancer or AIDS; it may be an inventor who has better ideas about a weapon or transportation system; it may be a professor who has suggestions for better ways to encourage competition and deregulation. A close examination of the agenda-building process suggests that a considerable amount of work is often needed before elected officials will become involved in a policy question. As a result, somebody first has to clarify the problem and offer options, choices, and alternatives—or merely call attention to the problem as a problem in the first place.

Policy entrepreneurs play a crucial role in articulating demands, issues, or problems to government policy makers. An entrepreneur can be an individual on the outside trying to get an issue into the political system or an individual on the inside trying to mobilize support for a policy. Classic examples of outside entrepreneurs include Upton Sinclair and food processing, Michael Harrington and poverty, Ralph Nader and automobile safety, and Rachel Carson and environmental protection. Members of Congress also serve as entrepreneurs to elevate some issues to the national agenda. Senator Estes Kefauver used committee hearings to publicize efforts to regulate the safety of drugs, Senator Edmund Muskie aided efforts at pollution control, and Congresswoman Leonore Sullivan promoted food stamps.

Policy entrepreneurs are an influential part of the policy-formation process because they are willing to invest their resources—time, energy, expertise, reputation, and money—in the advocacy of an issue. They supply political issues to government officials, play a key role in attaching a definition to the issue, help mobilize the public and create critical political coalitions, prioritize and highlight political demands, and link identified problems with possible solutions thus facilitating the ease with which new issues can be accommodated on the political agenda.[29]

THE ISSUE-ATTENTION CYCLE

Whether or not an issue will receive an effective policy response from government officials is also dependent upon the public's reaction to it. However, the public's attention span is short. Shifting public moods and the need for publicity encourage elected officials to adopt new policies rather than restructure old ones. Rallying support for a new program is easier than cutting back ongoing programs. Too many beneficiaries—those who receive money from the programs and those who administer the programs—will fight any changes in programs already on the books. Thus, reworking or even rethinking old programs becomes subordinate to taking what might be called an "add-on" approach to policy making. In other words, "Each of these new problems suddenly leaps into prominence, remains there for a short time, and then—though still largely unresolved—generally fades from the center of public attention."[30] Public boredom often sets in when large numbers of people realize the cost of solving a particular problem would be high indeed. (Boredom may be one of the most underrated forces in history.)

Policy makers, especially in a democracy, do not like to make anybody mad if they can help it. They would rather enlarge the size of the national economic pie and give new groups funds than redistribute what is currently there.[31] Like fathers and mothers—and university administrators—anybody who has the responsibility for allocating scarce resources would rather make everybody happy than take an allowance back from one child and give it to another, or take funds from one university department and redistribute them to another. If a group that is presently getting "the short end of the stick" lacks political clout, it is likely *not* to get its fair share of the economic goods of the society.

THE POLITICS OF NON-ACTION OR INACTION

Policy is certainly not formed in a vacuum. Organized interests representing varied points of view press claims and counterclaims. Some groups and persons clearly enjoy more access, more opportunities to get their cases heard, and greater possibilities for vetoing measures than others. Still, we cannot explain with certainty why some issues become national controversies and others do not.

According to some critics, what is even more important than who makes decisions is how many important matters fail to get the attention they deserve.[32] Matters of great importance to some people sometimes do not even get on the public agenda. Indeed, there are many ways in which issues can be prevented from reaching the national political agenda. These so-called "non-decisions" can occur at numerous places throughout the process of policy making. Individuals may be prevented from perceiving a cause for a grievance or want; likewise, even if perceived, the grievance may not be formulated into a demand. If a demand is formulated it may not be effectively expressed to government officials. Of course, even if well presented, there is no guarantee, as we've seen, that government officials will give the issue serious consideration. Once a demand has achieved agenda status it may still face the problem of non-decision making. A negative decision could be reached on the issue in question because of the biases of the key people in governmental organizations.[33] Even an apparently successful resolution of an issue may not turn out as planned. The resolution of the issue may vary from completely efficacious policy to entirely symbolic action. It is also possible that even when the policy has been favorably and efficaciously resolved, it will not be implemented effectively.

It should come as no surprise that there are many problems to which government has not effectively responded. On the one hand this may indicate that an effective response by government is not possible or, on the other hand, that an effective response is not forthcoming for a wide variety of political reasons. However, the absence of government activity in some area does not mean the government is without a policy in that area: Inaction is still a policy. Inattention to an issue can be as important as decisive action. Indifference to racial or sexual discrimination is clearly policy—very important policy for those affected by it. A former White House domestic adviser (currently a U.S. senator from New York), Daniel P. Moynihan, once called for a policy of "benign neglect" toward minority problems, not, presumably, because he was indifferent to racial discrimination but because he thought less governmental assertiveness was a better way to handle discrimination. In short, everything has political consequences, including doing nothing. Inaction by some policy makers often forces an issue to another part of the political system.

"There are days, Hank, when I don't know who's president, what state I'm from, or even if I'm a Democrat or a Republican, but, by God, I still know how to bottle up a piece of legislation in committee."

Drawing by Stan Hunt; © 1977 The New Yorker Magazine, Inc.

Senator Daniel P. Moynihan was a close advisor to Presidents Kennedy, Johnson, Nixon, and Carter, and is still a major influence in Congress.

All branches of the national government—as well as the bureaucracy, media, and interest groups—seem to take turns initiating policy changes. The Supreme Court's holding in *Brown* v. *Board of Education* (1954) is a classic example of a landmark civil rights policy decision with implications for the other components of the political system. This court decision, itself the result of a variety of economic, social, and political changes in the country, in turn triggered actions and reactions that ricocheted back to the Court.

SHARED INSTITUTIONAL LEADERSHIP

Separation of powers usually ensures that when things become clogged in one part of the system, a safety valve can be found elsewhere—sometimes in the courts, sometimes in a president, sometimes in regulatory agencies. Groups pressing for policy changes seek to exert influence where they are most likely to succeed. People with large sums of money to contribute to political campaigns are more likely to have influence with Congress and the presidency than with the courts. Those lacking substantial funds and a political base may find it more effective to resort to litigation. The NAACP's Legal Defense and Education Fund, Inc., for example, has won numerous cases in its long-term efforts to improve the legal protection of African Americans. Litigation is also a weapon in the arsenal of consumer and community groups working for reform today. It does, however, require money.

Just as Congress delegates extensive legislative power to the president, the chief executive delegates policy-making power to administrators. Obviously, a secretary of state can have a distinct influence on policy, as can other department heads and bureau, division, and section chiefs. In a sense, there is no level in the administrative hierarchy at which discretion ends.[34] At any time the most routine matter may be called to the public's attention by a newspaper columnist or a member of Congress. The matter will then be given consideration by a bureau or department chief—perhaps even by the White House. In short, thousands of people throughout the government (and millions more outside, such as editors, lobbyists, and activist citizens) exert direct pressure on legislators, legislation, and policy.

The extent to which presidents wield legislative power turns not only on their formal constitutional powers but also on their political powers. How good is their timing? How active and articulate are their lieutenants—their cabinet members and key agency heads? How close are their relations with congressional leaders? Can they mobilize public opinion? Does their influence reach into states and districts throughout the country? Do their parties control Congress? Presidents' effectiveness turns also on their professional reputations as politicians. Their words and actions are closely watched. Do they reward those who help them and punish those who do not? How well do they bargain with other power centers? Are they on top of the struggle for power, submerged in it, or remote from it? Presidents' political skill and political power are interrelated. Their influence over others derives from what the latter think of them and their power.[35]

Politics, Policy Making, and the Budget

The implementation of public policies requires money. Nothing reflects the growth in public policy in America along with the rise of big government more clearly than the change in the amounts and methods of spending by the federal government.

Presidents and Total Deficits, 1934–1989

Roosevelt	$197 billion
Truman	4.4
Eisenhower	15.8
Kennedy	11.9
Johnson	42.0
Nixon	68.7
Ford	124.6
Carter	181.0
Reagan	2825.0

Source: U.S. Department of Commerce, Office of Management and Budget, and *Congressional Quarterly Weekly Report* (February 20, 1988).

As recently as 1933 the federal government spent only $4 billion, about $30 per capita. In 1990 the respective figures were well over $1300 billion and about $4500. The machinery for spending has changed, too. At one time spending was loosely administered. Records show, for example, that in the early republic Nicholas Johnson, a Navy agent of Newburyport, Massachusetts, was handed several thousand dollars to supply "Cpt. Brown for recruiting his Crew."[36] Today Mr. Johnson would have to make out detailed forms and wait for a check.

Where does the money go? Much of it, of course, goes for national defense. In 1990 26 percent went to national security; 15 percent to interest on the national debt; 11 percent to grants for states and localities; 43 percent to direct benefit payments for individuals (such as social security, education, and other major social programs), and 5 percent for all other federal operations. Another way of understanding how the money is spent is to consider federal outlays as a percentage of the nation's gross national product or GNP. Between fiscal years 1981 and 1987 spending on entitlement programs stabilized at around 10.8 percent, spending for defense went up from 5.3 percent in 1981 to 6.4 percent by 1987, payments on the deficit went up as a percentage of GNP from 2.3 percent in 1981 to 3.1 percent in 1987, and non-defense discretionary spending declined from 5.7 in 1981 to 3.7 by 1987.[37]

Years ago federal revenues and outlays were so small that national taxing and spending had little impact on the overall economy. Today the federal government cannot drain billions of dollars from certain areas of the economy and pump them back into others without profoundly effecting the economy of the nation and the world. Much of the federal budget is "uncontrollable" in the sense that any major policy changes in most areas would be nearly impossible, politically speaking. Some people estimate this portion of the budget at about 74 percent.[38] The most important uncontrollable portions of the budget are the large entitlement programs for social welfare such as Social Security, Medicare, unemployment benefits, outstanding contracts, and other fiscal obligations. The most controllable part of the budget is defense spending. However, as we've seen, defense spending grew as a percentage of gross national product during the Reagan era. The effect of a budget comprised largely of uncontrollable expenditures and an administration committed to increases in defense spending is a sharply reduced capacity to target monies to any new federal programs. George Bush has found the budgetary situation inherited from his predecessor to be a real straightjacket on the development of new policies and it makes it difficult for him to live up to his promise of being the "environmental and education President."

FORMULATING THE BUDGET

As we have seen, Congress must authorize the spending of funds and appropriate the dollars, but the initiation of appropriations is now the responsibility of the president. The first step in preparing a federal budget is for the various departments and agencies to estimate their needs.[39] This process starts early. While Congress is debating the budget for the fiscal year immediately ahead, the agencies are making estimates for the following year. The estimating job is handled largely by officers under the direction of agency chiefs. Agency officials must take into account not only their needs as they see them but also the overall presidential program and the probable reactions of Congress. Departmental budgets are detailed; they include estimates on expected needs for personnel, supplies, office space, and the like.

"Should we live miserably or die comfortably?"

By permission of Bill Mauldin and Wil-Jo Associates, Inc.

The Office of Management and Budget (OMB), a staff agency of the president, handles the next phase. Budget examiners in the OMB examine each agency budget to see if it is in accord with the president's plans. Hearings are then held to give agency people a chance to clarify and defend their estimates. The OMB director and OMB aides, who make the final decision, sometimes prune the agencies' requests rather severely.

Finally, the director goes to the White House with a single consolidated set of estimates of both revenue and expenditures, the product of perhaps a year's work. The president takes a few days to review these figures. The budget director also helps the president prepare a budget message that will stress key aspects of the budget and tie it in with broad national plans. In January, soon after Congress convenes, the budget and the message are ready for the legislature and the public.

PROCESSING BUDGET PROPOSALS

Under the Constitution only Congress can appropriate funds. Yet, today Congress essentially follows the lead of the president in making national budget decisions. In 1974 Congress adopted the Budget Reform Act, which was (as we discussed in Chapter 16) intended to give it a more effective role in the budget process. That act specifies that when submitting proposals, the president must include proposed changes in tax laws, estimates of amounts of revenue lost through existing preferential tax treatments, and five-year estimates of the costs of new and continuing federal programs. The act also calls on the president to seek authorizing legislation for a program a year before asking Congress to fund it.

Preparing budget proposals is only the beginning. As we discussed earlier, the new Gramm–Rudman–Hollings budget procedures require Congress to make important changes in the way it participates in the budget process. According to that legislation, federal deficits must shrink by several billion dollars each year until they reach zero in 1993. Failure to hit the deficit targets will trigger automatic spending cuts in federal programs. No automatic cuts are permitted in social security, interest on the national debt, or such aid to low-income persons as Medicaid, Aid to Families with Dependent Children, veterans' compensation, and veterans' pensions.

A few other programs, such as unemployment assistance and student loans, will be subject to some but not sweeping across-the-board cuts. But most nondefense federal spending programs will be cut across the board. And defense programs will also be cut an equal amount. These automatic cuts have to be made in March of each year, depending on how closely the estimated deficit targets match the desired levels as of the previous October. Congress, however, is authorized to suspend the balanced-budget requirements if the economy dips into recession.

CHECKING EXPENDITURES

After Congress has appropriated money, it reserves the right to check the way the money is being spent. The General Accounting Office (GAO) is headed by the comptroller general, who is appointed by the president with the approval of the Senate for a fifteen-year term. The GAO, with over 5400 employees, now uses spot sampling methods to check vouchers and makes its audits in the field rather than in Washington. Although the comptroller general has the authority to disallow expenditures, approval is no longer needed for the disbursement of funds. In the past twenty years, the GAO has taken on broader responsibilities in investigating and even evaluating programs. It is increasingly checking up on the adequacy and effectiveness, as well as the honesty, of a program's performance.[40]

Policy Implementation

Once a policy is adopted, how should it be carried out? After the president has signed a bill into law or a regulatory agency has made its rules, the government must act.[41] Legislation or administrative decisions are not self-implementing. Effective implementation calls for a strategy.

Although other parts of the policy process are reasonably well publicized, the process of implementation is often hidden within the bureaucracy. By the time the implementation of a program begins the public may be satisfied to let the bureaucrats do their job and policy entrepreneurs may have already moved on to other issues and problems. As a result, implementation occurs without much public attention or political scrutiny. A number of federal programs fail to accomplish their desired goals because of problems that show up during the implementation phase. Kennedy's economic-reform programs in Latin America, Johnson's Model Cities program, Nixon's and Ford's crime-control programs, Carter's human-rights initiatives in foreign policy, and Reagan's tax cuts, which were supposed to have the effect eventually of balancing the budget, all faced problems that were not fully understood until well after the programs had been put into operation. When such failures occur, it is relatively easy to blame the original legislation rather than examine what happened after the bill became law. Of course, poorly written legislation and badly conceived policy yield poor results. But policy analysts have begun to realize that even the best legislation can fail because of problems encountered during implementation.[42] Sometimes these difficulties lead to the outright failure of a program, but more often they mean excessive delay, watered-down goals, or costs far above those originally expected.

THE DIFFICULTY WITH IMPLEMENTING FEDERAL POLICIES

More is at stake in the process of policy implementation than the literal translation of goals into practice. Indeed, it is during this stage that many key decisions are made by those individuals and organizations engaged in the implementation of a policy. The coalition of supporters that comes together to get a bill through Congress often does not stay together after the bill has been enacted. Furthermore, Congress often passes ambiguous legislation that conceals serious policy differences. Rather than set clear goals, Congress—reflecting differences among the supporters of the policies—sets general or vague goals, and then passes on the responsibility for interpretation to the bureaucrats. Legislators are frequently more concerned with the symbolic potency of a piece of legislation than with its substantive content. As a result, the agencies responsible for implementing the policy are given considerable latitude to translate symbolic claims into specific directives.[43] Bureaucrats are blamed for confusion, yet they are merely trying to carry out deliberately unclear policies, and they must act in a political atmosphere characterized by conflict and competing groups.

Consider civil rights legislation, for example. Often the differences among women's groups, black groups, Hispanic groups, employer groups, and trade unions are momentarily resolved and a bill becomes law. But after the bill has been enacted, the coalition falls apart, and the resulting pressures are felt on the agencies trying to implement the policies. Employers insist, for example, the agencies' regulations are unrealistic and interfere with their rights; women's groups argue the agencies are failing to enforce the law vigorously; black groups claim the agencies favor the women's groups but ignore the wishes of the blacks, and so on. The more controversial the issue, the greater the chance of delay as powerful interest groups clash over a program and force bureaucrats charged with implementation to move cautiously.[44]

The implementation process involves a long chain of decision points that must be cleared before a program can be successfully carried out. At each decision point there is a public official or community leader who has the power to advance— or delay—the program. The more decision points a program needs to clear, the greater the chance of failure or delay.[45] Special problems result if the successful implementation of a national program depends on the cooperation of state and local officials. One state or community may be eager to help; another may be opposed to a program and try to stop it.

POLICY IMPLEMENTATION

Like so much of politics, successful policy implementation cannot be guaranteed. Success in this stage of policy making will depend upon the creation of stable routines for implementation that can adjust to changing circumstances, the quality of the working relationship between implementors at various levels, the degree of conflict invoked by the policy, and the general level of public support for the program. In a study of the implementation process, political scientists Daniel A. Mazmanian and Paul A. Sabatier have identified conditions for effective implementation. They suggest "a statute or other policy decision seeking a substantial departure from the status quo will achieve its desired goals" under these conditions:

1. The enabling legislation or other legal directive mandates policy objectives that are clear and consistent or at least provide substantive criteria for resolving goal conflicts.

2. The enabling legislation incorporates a sound theory identifying the principal factors and causal linkages affecting policy objectives and gives implementing officials sufficient jurisdiction over target groups and other points of leverage to attain, at least potentially, the desired goals.

3. The enabling legislation structures the implementation process so as to maximize the probability that implementing officials and target groups will perform as desired. This involves assignment to sympathetic agencies with adequate hierarchical integration, supportive decision rules, sufficient financial resources, and adequate access to supporters.

4. The leaders of the implementing agency possess substantial managerial and political skills and are committed to statutory goals.

5. The program is actively supported by organized constituency groups and by a few key legislators (or a chief executive) throughout the implementation process, with the courts being neutral or supportive.

6. The relative priority of statutory objectives is not undermined over time by the emergence of conflicting public policies or by changes in relevant socioeconomic conditions that weaken the statute's causal theory or political support.[46]

Policy Evaluation

Is the policy working? As noted, the adoption of a policy is only the beginning of the process. After Congress passes a law and the president signs it, implementation takes place. But what happens next? Who decides whether it is working or not? The answer—or so it often seems—is everybody and nobody.

Program supporters and administrators tend to exaggerate the success of their favorite programs in order to justify the funds allocated to them. Bureaus and agencies often cast their proposals so as to persuade, not to evaluate. Program "evaluation" reports coming into the White House or Congress from the bureaucracy have long been suspect. In this sense, evaluation is never entirely nonpolitical: It will be used by one party or branch of government against another. Evaluation will also be used by one department or agency against another.[47] Also, delays and deficiencies in evaluation may occur because an agency wants to hide the real cost of its operations. Still, it is difficult and expensive to develop outcome or impact measures. It is hard to relate expenditures to outcomes, or to be precise about what has caused social change, even if change can be noticed or measured. We do not have the means to readily judge the value of what is being produced by government.

Political and social scientists have turned their attention to the product side of public policy. Instead of being concerned only with what affects government, or with what goes on inside government, they are paying attention to what social or economic change results from governmental actions. The test of a program is not input but outcome: "It is interesting, and at times important, to know how much money is spent on schools in a particular neighborhood or city. But the crucial question is how much do the children learn. Programs are for people, not for bureaucracies."[48] However, in order to make a program work for the people, politicians, administrators, and professional policy analysts have to pay careful attention to what bureaucracies are doing and how they are doing it. As one scholar has put it, evaluation research has three faces or purposes—even though they are not always mutually supportive: "(1) Learning about the program's operations and effects; (2) Controlling the behavior of those responsible for implementation; and (3) Influencing the response of outsiders."[49]

Why have Congress and the White House not insisted on more systematic planning and evaluation? Short-term political incentives seem to propel their energies in the opposite direction: Pass now, plan later! Presidents, especially, are always eager for fast results. They say they were elected not to study policies but to get things done and to put ideas into operation. As Congress has been eclipsed by the executive in more and more policy-formulation areas, there has been a move to strengthen it as a focus for program oversight. Congress holds hearings and discussions; legislators and administrators visit actual program sites; and measures of policy output are collected and occasionally even analyzed. However, even its staunchest defenders readily admit Congress performs this responsibility with only modest success.

The Legislative Reorganization Act of 1946 assigned to each standing committee of Congress the responsibility to "exercise continuous watchfulness" over how agencies administer laws. *Legislative oversight* is neither constant nor systematic, however. Comprehensive oversight of all federal programs would demand all the time of the staff and members of Congress. Members of Congress exercise the oversight function when they are particularly upset with executive branch officials and when it serves their constituents in a direct way. Certain standing committees have created specific oversight subcommittees.

Congressional committees not only draw up and pass laws, but they also have the responsibility to watch how the laws are carried out.

Another way in which evaluation takes place is through *presidential commissions.* Cabinet level commissions are common. Such diverse issues and problems as the NASA Challenger explosion, pornography, educational excellence, trade imbalances, social security, government waste, the MX missile, and Pentagon procurement methods have all been the subject of national commissions in recent years. The Presidential Commission on the space shuttle Challenger accident and the Grace Commission on government waste, whose official title was the President's Private Sector Survey on Cost Control, and a commission on pay for top public officials are some of the better known evaluation panels.[50] The annual budgeting process run out of the Office of Management and Budget (OMB) in the executive branch as well as the auditing process handled by the General Accounting Office (GAO) that reports to Congress also offer annual opportunities for program evaluation.

Of course, program evaluation is not limited to the government. The nation's major newspapers and magazines as well as academic journals frequently publish articles evaluating programs. Through special reports or exposés, television journalists focus the nation's attention on a wide variety of policies such as drug abuse, environmental pollution, poverty, immigration, and financial irregularities at H.U.D. Individuals like Ralph Nader and interest groups like the AFL-CIO, the U.S. Chamber of Commerce, and the NAACP also engage in program evaluation that may strongly influence governmental decisions.

Evaluating programs, however, is as much a political as a technical challenge. Of course, everyone will agree that something is wrong with Defense Department procurement when the cost of buying a weapons system is much more than Congress anticipated. But many evaluations involve choices between costs and benefits, a problem for which there is no expert answer. Is the welfare program worth the expenditure? Should we abolish subsidies to farmers? Has the auto emission-control program produced good or bad results in the nation? Are grants for students to attend medical schools worthwhile? No experts can tell us whether or not these programs are "successful," because the answers depend, in part, on political values. We have no choice but to rely on the democratic system, on politicians chosen by popular vote, to resolve such questions. This is why policy making and implementation are so complex, important, and frustrating.

Summary

1. Public policy is the substance of what government does and what government decides not to do. Public policy is never made in any fixed or final way, but is always in the process of being made. Public policy is often expressed only in part by a law, then by a court decision interpreting that law, then by a law modifying the court decision, then by an agency regulation implementing that law, then by a presidential executive order, and then by another law of Congress, and so on. There are, however, boundaries on what sort of policies may be developed in the United States due to tradition, political culture, ideology, and institutional structure.

2. Policy making in the United States is neither simple nor tidy. There is not a "top down" structure of authority, so policy is not made "on high." Rather, policy takes form gradually, and large numbers of people help formulate a new response to a public problem. Policies usually change slowly, reflecting gradual changes in public opinion. Mass public-opinion change is often the consequence of campaigns by political, professional, and scientific elites to alter the ways in which people define problems and policy options. How we define policy problems influences whether or not they will be taken seriously by government officials and the ways in which they will be addressed by laws, executive orders, administrative rules, or court decisions.

3. Policy outcomes are the consequences for society, the "so-what" or "bottom line" of what the government is doing and how it affects citizens. Policy making can be studied through six stages: the identification of a problem, the creation of an agenda for institutional action, the formulation of solutions, the adoption or enactment of a new policy response, the implementation or application of the policy, and the evaluation of the policy.

4. Our policy-making processes permit large numbers of groups and individuals to battle both to protect their own private interests and to enhance the public interest. Our political system, like all large systems, is weighted in favor of the status quo and against swift or sweeping change. But those who know better ways of doing things and are willing to take part in the pulling and hauling of the policy-making process can make a difference. Knowledge, political skills, and the ability to build coalitions of like-minded supporters and to attract press coverage are preconditions for changing public policy.

5. Making public policy cannot be easily described in the abstract. How policies change depends on what kinds of policies are being discussed and who and how many persons they affect. The four chapters that follow describe and analyze foreign, military, economic and social, and regulatory policy.

Further Reading

STEVEN KELMAN. *Making Public Policy: A Hopeful View of American Government* (Basic Books, 1987).

JOHN W. KINGDON. *Agendas, Alternatives and Public Policies* (Little, Brown, 1984).

LAURENCE E. LYNN, JR. *Managing Public Policy* (Little, Brown, 1987).

DANIEL A. MAZMANIAN and PAUL A. SABATIER. *Implementation and Public Policy* (Scott, Foresman, 1983).

ROBERT T. NAKAMURA and FRANK SMALLWOOD. *The Politics of Policy Implementation* (St. Martin's Press, 1980).

RICHARD E. NEUSTADT and ERNEST R. MAY. *Thinking in Time: The Uses of History for Decision Makers* (Free Press, 1986).

DENNIS J. PALUMBO. *Public Policy in America* (Harcourt Brace Jovanovich, 1988).

GUY PETERS. *American Public Policy*, 2d ed. (Chatham House, 1986).

NELSON W. POLSBY. *Political Innovation in America* (Yale University Press, 1984).

DAVID B. ROBERTSON and DENNIS R. JUDD. *The Development of American Public Policy* (Scott, Foresman/Little Brown, 1989).

RANDALL B. RIPLEY. *Policy Analysis in Political Science* (Nelson-Hall, Inc., 1985).

HEDRICK SMITH. *The Power Game: How Washington Really Works.* (Random House, 1988).

DEBORAH A. STONE. *Policy Paradox and Political Reason* (Scott, Foresman/Little Brown, 1988).

AARON WILDAVSKY. *The New Politics of the Budgetary Process* (Scott, Foresman, 1988).

Notes

1. A persuasive variant of this perspective is presented in Ira Katznelson, "Rethinking the Silences of Social and Economic Policy," *Political Science Quarterly* 101, no. 2 (1986), pp. 307–25.

2. David B. Robertson and Dennis R. Judd, *The Development of American Public Policy* (Scott, Foresman, 1989), p. viii.

3. This idea comes from the seminal study by Louis Hartz, *The Liberal Tradition in America* (Harcourt, Brace, 1955).

4. See Charles E. Lindblom, "The Market as Prison," *Journal of Politics* 44 (May 1982), pp. 324–36.

5. Burt Solomon, "How Washington Works," *National Journal* (June 6, 1986), p. 1428.

6. See Hugh Heclo, "Issue Networks and the Executive Establishment," in Anthony King, ed., *The New American Political System* (American Enterprise Institute, 1978), chap. 3; and Edward O. Lauman and David Knoke, *The Organizational State* (University of Wisconsin Press, 1987).

7. See Nelson W. Polsby, *Political Innovation in America: The Politics of Policy Initiation* (Yale University Press, 1984).

8. William N. Dunn, *Public Policy Analysis: An Introduction* (Prentice Hall, Inc., 1981), p. 226.

9. For a general introductory example, see Peter H. Aranson, *American Government: Strategy and Choice* (Winthrop, 1981). For more sophisticated treatments of rational choice theory, see Brian Barry and Russell Hardin, ed., *Rational Man and Irrational Society?* (Sage, 1982); and Jon Elster, ed., *Rational Choice* (New York University Press, 1986). See also the journal *Public Choice*.

10. Deborah A. Stone, *Policy Paradox and Political Reason* (Scott, Foresman/Little, Brown, 1988), p. 306.

11. See Robert B. Reich, ed., *The Power of Public Ideas* (Ballinger, 1988); and Steven Kelman, *Making Public Policy: A Hopeful View of American Government* (Basic Books, 1987).

12. C. Wright Mills made the classic statement of this view in *The Power Elite* (Oxford University Press, 1956). For another look at elite influence, see Thomas R. Dye, *Who's Running America? The Conservative Years* (Prentice Hall, 1986). See also John Manley, "Neo-Pluralism: A Class Analysis of Pluralism I and Pluralism II," *American Political Science Review* (June 1983), pp. 368–83.

13. The now classic treatment of this theme is by Charles E. Lindblom, *Politics and Markets* (Basic Books, 1977).

14. The most effective treatment of this theme remains, Frances Fox Piven and Richard Cloward, *Regulating the Poor: The Functions of Public Welfare* (Vintage Books, 1971). Also consider interpretations in Edwards S. Greenberg, *The American Political System: A Radical Approach*, 4th ed. (Little, Brown, 1986); and Robert Heilbroner, *Marxism: For and Against* (Norton, 1980).

15. For a general treatment of American government from this perspective, see Ira Katznelson and Mark Kesselman, *The Politics of Power*, 3d edition (Harcourt Brace Jovanovich, 1987).

16. A study that skillfully examines a range of complicated questions about power relationships is John Gavanta, *Power and Powerlessness* (University of Illinois Press, 1980). For a rebuttal to elite and neo-elite theory in defense of pluralism, see Nelson W. Polsby, *Community Power and Political Theory: A Further Look at Problems of Evidence and Inference*, 2d ed. (Yale University Press, 1980).

17. For a persuasive account of policy making in America that pays careful attention to the state, see Theda Skocpol, "Bringing the State Back In: Strategies of Analysis in Current Research," in *Bringing the State Back In*, P. Evans, D. Rueschemeyer, and T. Skocpol, eds. (Cambridge University Press, 1985), pp. 3–27. For conventional treatments of bureaucratic politics, see Graham T. Allison, *Essence of Decision* (Little, Brown, 1971); and Morton H. Halperin, *Bureau-*

cratic Politics and Foreign Policy (Brookings Institution, 1974).

18. Thomas R. Dye, *Understanding Public Policy*, 6th ed. (Prentice Hall, Inc., 1987), p. 25.

19. Ibid., pp. 36–37.

20. Polsby, *Political Innovation in America: The Politics of Policy Initiation*, p. 174.

21. See E. S. Savas, *Privatization: The Key to Better Government* (Chatham House, 1987).

22. On the limits of localism in the American polity, see E. W. Kelley, *Policy and Politics in the United States* (Temple University Press, 1987).

23. See B. Guy Peters, *American Public Policy: Promise and Performance*, 2d ed. (Chatham House, 1986), pp. 120–22.

24. The most important empirical study of national agenda-building is by John W. Kingdon, *Agendas, Alternatives, and Public Policies* (Little, Brown, 1984).

25. These determinants of agenda-building are analyzed in Mark P. Petracca, "Agenda-Building and National Policy Formation." Ph.D. dissertation, University of Chicago, 1986. See also John Zaller, "The Role of Elites in Shaping Public Opinion." Ph.D. dissertation, University of California, 1984.

26. Aaron Wildavsky, *Speaking Truth to Power: The Art and Craft of Policy Analysis* (Little, Brown, 1979), p. 82.

27. These findings are reviewed in Petracca, "Agenda-Building and National Policy Formation," chap. 4.

28. See Shanto Iyengar and Donald R. Kinder, *News That Matters* (University of Chicago Press, 1987).

29. See Kingdon, *Agendas, Alternatives, and Public Policies*; Polsby, *Political Innovation in America*; and Paul Light, *The President's Agenda* (Johns Hopkins University Press, 1982).

30. Anthony Downs, "Up and Down with Ecology—The Issue-Attention Cycle," *The Public Interest* (Summer 1972), p. 38. But see also B. Guy Peters and Brian W. Hogwood, "In Search of the Issue-Attention Cycle," *Journal of Politics* (February 1985), pp. 238–53, which clarifies and expands on Downs's classic essay; and Christopher J. Bosso, *Pesticides and Politics: The Lifecycle of a Public Issue* (University of Pittsburgh Press, 1987).

31. For a discussion of some of the implications of interest-group and logrolling special claims, see Mancur Olson, *The Rise and Decline of Nations* (Yale University Press, 1982).

32. Robert Paul Wolff, *The Poverty of Liberalism* (Beacon Press, 1968); Peter Bachrach and Morton Baratz, *Power and Poverty* (Oxford University Press, 1970); M. A. Crensen, *The Un-Politics of Air Pollution* (Johns Hopkins Press, 1971); and Charles E. Lindblom, "Another State of Mind," *American Political Science Review* 76 (March 1982), pp. 9–21.

33. See E. E. Schattschneider, *The Semi-Sovereign People* (The Dryden Press, 1975).

34. See Theodore J. Lowi, *The End of Liberalism*, 2d ed. (W. W. Norton, 1979).

35. Richard E. Neustadt, *Presidential Power*, rev. ed. (Wiley, 1980),

chap. 3. See also Bert Rockman, *The Leadership Question* (Praeger, 1984); and Samuel Kernell, *Going Public* (Congressional Quarterly Press, 1986).

36. L. D. White, *The Federalists* (Macmillan, 1948), p. 341.

37. See David Rapp, "Deficit Limits Reagan's Options in 1989 Budget," *Congressional Quarterly Weekly Report* (February 20, 1988), pp. 327–331.

38. See Peters, *American Public Policy*, p. 113.

39. For a discussion of the budgetary cycle, see Aaron Wildavsky, *The New Politics of the Budgetary Process* (Scott, Foresman, 1988). See also Howard Shuman, *Politics and the Budget*, 2d ed. (Prentice Hall, 1988).

40. For a study of changes in the GAO and its operations, see Wallace Earl Walker, *Changing Organizational Culture: Strategy, Structure, and Professionalism in the U.S. General Accounting Office* (University of Tennessee Press, 1986).

41. See Eugene Bardach, *The Implementation Game: What Happens after a Bill Becomes a Law* (MIT Press, 1977). Other general works on implementation include, Daniel A. Mazmanian and Paul A. Sabatier, *Implementation and Public Policy* (Scott, Foresman, 1983); George C. Edwards, III, *Implementing Public Policy* (Congressional Quarterly Press, 1980); and Robert T. Nakamura and Frank Smallwood, *The Politics of Policy Implementation* (St. Martin's Press, 1980).

42. Many political scientists and economists who study policy implementation publish their findings in the following quarterly publications: *Policy Sciences, The Journal of Policy Analysis and Management*, and *The Policy Studies Journal*. The Brookings Institution and the American Enterprise Institute for Public Policy Research, nonprofit, nongovernmental research organizations located in Washington, D.C., publish a wide variety of books and reports on policy.

43. See Murray Edelman, *Political Language*; and Murray Edelman, *Politics as Symbolic Action* (Academic Press, 1971).

44. These themes are elaborated upon by Dennis J. Palumbo, *Public Policy in America* (Harcourt Brace Jovanovich, 1988), pp. 102–06.

45. Jeffrey Pressman and Aaron Wildavsky, *Implementation* (University of California Press, 1973).

46. Daniel A. Mazmanian and Paul A. Sabatier, *Implementation and Public Policy*, pp. 41–42. Also consider the assessment by Randall P. Ripley and Grace A. Franklin, *Policy Implementation and Bureaucracy* (Dorsey Press, 1986).

47. Wildavsky, *Speaking Truth to Power*, chap. 9.

48. Daniel P. Moynihan, "Policy vs. Program in the '70s," *The Public Interest* (Summer 1970), p. 100.

49. Edie N. Goldberg, "The Three Faces of Evaluation," *Journal of Policy Analysis and Management* 2 (Summer 1983), p. 516.

50. See R. W. Apple, Jr. "Keeping Hot Potatoes Out of the Political Kitchen" *The New York Times* (February 2, 1989), p A.13.

20
Making
Foreign Policy

As the 1990s began peoples and governments around the world appeared to be undergoing momentous changes. Millions of Chinese students, often backed up by workers, took to the streets of Beijing and other cities to demand greater freedom and rights. In Moscow a Congress of "People's Deputies," some of them chosen democratically, criticized the nation's leader to his face. And Soviet scholars and journalists were criticizing not only Stalin, but publicly questioning the role of the patron saint of Soviet communism, Lenin himself! Latin America was witnessing a resurgence of democratic aspirations as a number of dictators quit or were toppled. In Poland the communist government was compelled to recognize workers' rights, and especially the workers' organization, *Solidarity*; in doing so Poland became a model of democratic aspirations for other countries in Eastern Europe. NATO, celebrating its fortieth birthday, faced new challenges and new opportunities. American and Soviet leaders were vying with each other in proposing arms reductions. All this prompted a rethinking of American foreign policy.

Why such seemingly momentous changes? How fundamental were they? And how long would they last? Some Republican party leaders in the United States claimed that the hard-line policies of the Reagan-Bush era had forced the Soviets to curb their hard-line foreign policy and moderate their domestic and international policies. Peace leaders in the United States believed the Soviet leadership was recognizing the popular support for arms reduction both in the United States and the Soviet Union, even while the Bush administration was proceeding cautiously.

As to the questions of how fundamental these changes were and how long they might last, these were urgent questions for the Bush administration. After proceeding cautiously during his first months in office, in the spring of 1989 President Bush appeared ready to compromise with Moscow on arms reduction and other matters. But the White House and the State Department faced a number of practical obstacles, such as the impact of Soviet-American detente on United States allies in both the Western and Eastern hemispheres. Long time "Moscow-

517

The student protests in Tiananmen Square, China, were echoed by Chinese students studying at American universities, who demonstrated in support of the pro-democracy movement.

watchers" in the United States also feared that the democratic momentum in the Soviet Union might not last long. They noted that historically the Russians had alternated between periods of rigid dictatorship and moments of anarchy, and they saw the possibility that an excessive movement toward liberation in the Soviet Union might produce a strong counteraction, and with it a return by Moscow to a hard-line in international affairs. Leaders of the American peace movement, on the other hand, feared the United States would not respond sufficiently to what they viewed as a major and irreversible turn in Soviet affairs—a turn toward a much more relaxed foreign policy abroad and toward less militant communist propaganda.

Perhaps the most important and exciting link among all these developments abroad was the people's yearning for freedom and democracy. For Americans, beginning the commemoration of the bicentennial of the drafting of the Bill of Rights in the spring of 1989, this was perhaps the most significant development in relation to American foreign policy. Although Americans had discovered that we must proceed cautiously in trying to impose our values on other peoples, as in Vietnam, it is also clear that the Bill of Rights and our civil rights movement have stood as symbols for many peoples abroad, including those under dictatorships. It was significant, for example, that Chinese students, before the fateful crackdown, paraded a huge "goddess of Democracy" statue that seemed modeled after the American Statue of Liberty through the streets of Beijing, much to the annoyance of the authorities.

If the American Bill of Rights and the continuing rights revolution in America have indeed served as a model for revolutions and protests throughout the world, it is a reminder to American foreign policy makers that what Americans do in the realm of liberty or freedom is far more important than what Americans say abroad. Americans also discovered again that the road toward democracy abroad is a rocky and sometimes tragic one, as it was in the United States right before and during the Civil War. We will long remember, for example, that fateful June 1989 weekend when courageous students and their allies in China stood their ground for democracy in Tiananmen Square, only to be slaughtered by the soldiers. Their "goddess of Democracy" statue they had so proudly carried into the square was crumpled into the dust and blood. Many of those students had studied our Declaration of Independence, our Bill of Rights, our civil rights movement and Gandhi's movement in India. They had dreamed dreams of a more open society. Those dreams, we believe, cannot be suppressed for long.

Defining and Defending Our Vital Interests

Since World War II the United States has become involved in world affairs in a way and to a degree unprecedented in our history. Whether we like it or not, our involvement is growing, primarily because we must pursue our security interests in an interlocked "global" world. As the world's principal economic trader, we need markets for our products. We also depend on imported raw materials.

Our political values and interests are also a factor: We want peace. We favor human rights. And we have a special relationship with those nations that share our commitment to representative democracy, or at least our common Western heritage of liberty and equality.

Our foreign policy leaders, whether Democratic or Republican, see American power as a vital means of shaping not only a more decent but also a more secure world. At the heart of our national security policy has been a recognition of the reality of Soviet power, and of the fact that the Soviets, at least in the past, have viewed the world differently than we have. This may be changing, as relationships with China, Japan, a new Europe, and the **third world** (developing nations outside the traditional influence of the superpowers, for example, in Africa and Latin America) increasingly hold central places on our foreign policy agenda.

The chief objective of American foreign policy has been to protect and promote the national security and economic well-being of the United States. But promoting our vital interests provides only hazy guidelines for those who must make foreign policy on a day-to-day basis. Furthermore, Americans differ on what constitutes our national interest (note the differing views in Table 20–1).

TABLE 20–1
Survey of U.S. Foreign Policy Goals

	PERCENT ANSWERING "VERY IMPORTANT"	
	PUBLIC	LEADERS
1. Protecting the jobs of American workers	78%	43%
2. Securing adequate supplies of energy	69	72
3. Worldwide arms control	69	83
4. Combatting world hunger	63	60
5. Reducing U.S. trade deficit with foreign countries	62	n.a.*
6. Containing communism	57	43
7. Defending U.S. allies' security	56	78
8. Matching Soviet military power	53	59
9. Strengthening the United Nations	46	22
10. Protecting the interests of American business abroad	43	32
11. Promoting and defending human rights in other countries	42	44
12. Helping to improve the standard of living of less developed nations	37	46
13. Protecting weaker nations against foreign aggression	32	29
14. Helping to bring a democratic form of government to other nations	30	29

Source: Data from Gallup Poll. Table adapted from John E. Reilly, ed., *American Public Opinion and U.S. Foreign Policy 1987* (Chicago Council on Foreign Relations, 1987), p. 12.

* n.a. = not asked

Few would question the need to defend our country, to survive, to protect our institutions and our values. Controversy arises, however, in determining the means to these ends. For example, to what extent should we intervene in the affairs of other nations in order to maintain international stability or the flow of resources to our economy? Our concern about the status of human rights and democratic institutions in foreign lands also enhances both the challenge and complexities facing our foreign policy makers.

In the early nineteenth century, the Monroe Doctrine defined the western hemisphere as an area of vital interest to our country, and we have often used force to prevent any perceived threats to our security in this hemisphere.[1] Beginning with the Spanish-American War we began to be involved elsewhere. President Woodrow Wilson wanted the United States to assume a more active role in the world in order to champion the cause of freedom and to encourage the rise of democratic nations. Wilsonian "internationalism"—sometimes also called idealism, globalism, or moralism—has been a powerful recurring strain in our foreign policy ever since. Jimmy Carter's human rights initiatives were in this tradition.[2] President Harry Truman's **Truman Doctrine** was more a blend of idealism and realism, yet it clearly required international involvement. It promised our support to all free peoples who faced totalitarian aggression. Truman doubtless had Europe in mind, but some supporters of this *internationalist* brand of foreign policy were willing to intervene nearly anywhere in the world in order to create an international order congruent with American values.

Pragmatists contend that it is just such broad, sweeping definitions of our vital interests that lead us to overextend ourselves and involve us in conflicts such as Korea, Vietnam, and Lebanon. Policy makers, they say, should disregard ideology and shape foreign policy on rational, "realistic" calculations: What are our national interests? And are we able to defend them? The *realists* say we should intervene in world affairs *only* if *our* vital interests are at stake, and if the other country is the victim of overt, outside aggression, not just an internal rebellion. Still, realists would generally have the United States work with any ally, regardless of that country's internal politics, whereas idealists prefer that we work only with "good" governments.[3]

The limits of a unilateral American role in reforming the world and defending freedom against aggressors are evident: A single country can or should do only so much. But old questions remain and new ones arise. Is the Persian Gulf, for example, vital to our national interests? And if it is, can we effectively intervene to ensure its stability? Do the political conditions in Panama, Mexico, Korea, or Colombia affect the United States, and if so, to what extent? Should the Monroe Doctrine be applied to oppose the intervention by foreign nations into the internal affairs of Western Hemisphere countries? How does the Cold War influence our options? What are our foreign policy strategies? What are the politics and options that shape foreign policy making in the United States?

Winston Churchill, Franklin D. Roosevelt, and Joseph Stalin at Yalta in 1945.

The Cold War and Its Legacy

Basic to any understanding of our contemporary foreign and defense policies is a recognition of the impact of the Cold War. For a time in the 1970s the policy of **detente**—an easing of strained relations between nations—between the United States and the USSR was seen as heralding the beginning of a new era of Soviet-American relations. But, in fact, the Cold War left a legacy that continues to be the dominant factor in our foreign policy making[4]—even with the remarkable Gorbachev initiations and the INF treaty of 1988.

Although many people think the Cold War began after World War II, some scholars believe its roots lie in the troubled course of Soviet-American relations after the Russian Revolution of 1917. Americans considered the Bolsheviks to be immoral revolutionaries and believed communism threatened both democracy and the world order envisioned by Woodrow Wilson. Great Britain and France joined the United States in open hostility to the new Soviet leaders; they even intervened briefly in that country's affairs. (The United States sent 5000 troops into Russia in 1918 soon after the revolution—a fact most Americans forget, but Soviet officials never do.) American leaders followed a policy of diplomatic non-recognition toward the Soviet government until 1933.

Although relations between the East and the West warmed slightly by the 1930s, the Soviet Union still felt isolated. The Soviets worried especially about Germany; they could not forget the 20 million casualties of World War I. Moscow's warnings about the dangers of Hitler's Germany went mostly unheeded by Western leaders. The inaction, and even appeasement, by some Western nations further isolated the Soviet Union, leaving it once again feeling vulnerable to German attack. The term **appeasement** describes concessions made to a potential enemy in the hope of preventing aggression. Britain's 1938 Munich agreement with Adolf Hitler to accept the partition of Czechoslovakia in exchange for a vague guarantee of peace was an example. Soviet leader Joseph Stalin, fearing his nation would be unable to repulse a Nazi attack, knowing he would have little assistance from the West, and not caring what happened to other countries, signed a nonaggression pact with Hitler in August 1939. But the Nazis soon attacked Poland, and World War II erupted in full force.

The West was outraged, and with reason, by this Soviet sellout. But in less than two years, Hitler also turned his military machine against the Russians, and the West and the Soviets faced Hitler as a common enemy. The wartime alliance between the United States and the USSR was an uneasy one. Although Stalin had advocated a European invasion by the Allies in 1941, this second front did not begin until 1944, after the Russians had sustained tremendous losses and had become bitter toward the West. To understand the origins of the Cold War, we must understand the aims of the United States and the Soviet Union as they emerged as superpowers at the end of World War II. Europe's economies had been crushed, and a power vacuum had to be filled. President Franklin D. Roosevelt saw a world based on the dominance of these two great nations, and therefore realized the necessity of maintaining an uneasy alliance with Stalin. Stalin's postwar priorities were to establish several pro-Soviet nations along its borders and to keep Germany divided and weak.

AFTER WORLD WAR II

In early 1945, with Hitler's defeat inevitable, Roosevelt, Stalin, and Winston Churchill met at Yalta (a port city in the southern Crimea on the Black Sea) to decide Europe's future. The agreement that emerged from these meetings has aroused controversy to this day. On the surface it appeared the three powers agreed on a set of democratic principles that would govern Europe's recovery. Many analysts now think, however, that the Yalta meetings simply allowed a Soviet sphere of influence in eastern Europe in exchange for Soviet cooperation in pursuing the war against Japan and in furthering Roosevelt's vision of the postwar world. Roose-

Joseph Stalin

Nikita Khrushchev

Leonid Brezhnev

Franklin D. Roosevelt

Harry S. Truman

John F. Kennedy

velt's death two months after Yalta signaled as well the death of cordial relations between the United States and the USSR. His successor, Harry Truman, soon embarked on a different path. Distrusting Soviet intentions, Truman and his advisers increasingly came to see Soviet-American competition as a conflict between two diametrically opposed ways of life. Possibilities for cooperation diminished.

Soviet intervention in eastern Europe, Iran, and Turkey reinforced U.S. views. Truman and his advisers developed the Truman Doctrine, mentioned earlier. The **Marshall Plan,** named after Secretary of State George C. Marshall, sought to rebuild Europe's economies with American economic assistance in the late 1940s and early 1950s. NATO—the North Atlantic Treaty Organization—was created in 1949 as a military alliance between the United States and western Europe. This was the strategy of **containment,** aimed at maintaining the international status quo and preventing any further Soviet territorial gains. Some of Truman's policies have been criticized as overextending the United States and as portraying Soviet-American relations as a simplistic struggle between good and evil rather than as traditional superpower competition. On the other hand, remember that the appeasement of Hitler remained fresh in policy makers' minds—"No More Munich!" was a fashionable saying—and that they did not want to make the same mistakes with Stalin. Truman's policies resulted in a military buildup and a state of constant readiness for war, coupled with a strong commitment to use American military force almost anywhere in the world. This was a notable departure from previous foreign policy.

By mid-1950 the United States was involved in the Korean War, and that set our overall foreign policy for the next twenty years. We believed we had no choice but to respond: Not to respond in Korea would have meant that our will and our commitments could be doubted, and that we might be challenged anywhere—or so our chief policy makers believed. With Eisenhower in the White House in the 1950s, our foreign policy changed somewhat, but the basic idea of containment remained. Eisenhower relied extensively on economic and military assistance and on covert operations by an expanded CIA to help overthrow unwanted governments, such as in Guatemala.[5] World order was still defined by the status quo and the **domino theory,** the idea that if one of our allies falls, a series of others may soon fall as well.

President John F. Kennedy, elected in late 1960, brought a fresh and youthful spirit to the country. He extended aid to newly independent nations and spoke boldly of a new and different world. Still, he was sharply anticommunist, so he built up nuclear weapons and military forces. He confronted the Soviets and their extending influence in Cuba (1961), Berlin (1961), and Vietnam.[6] He also acted decisively to oppose the Russians during the October 1962 Cuban Missile Crisis. Only in his third and last year did he hint at a possible detente with the Soviets.

VIETNAM

Lyndon Johnson's foreign policy became dominated by the Vietnam War, a conflict that must be viewed as a logical outgrowth of Cold War containment policy. Many American policy makers considered Vietnam to be a case of Soviet-controlled communist aggression. Critics charge it was primarily a revolutionary war deeply rooted in Vietnamese history.[7] Democratic institutions had few if any roots in Vietnam, and yet we became enmeshed in a war to prevent aggression and make the country safe for democracy. According to the domino theory, if Vietnam fell, so would the rest of Indo-China, Thailand, and then maybe the Philippines, and so on. Hence the United States had to make a stand in Vietnam so that it need not fight communists closer to home. President Johnson—in the Truman tradition—said in 1965 that if we failed to come to the aid of the South Vietnamese, we would be saying to the world that we "don't live up to our treaties and don't stand by our friends." No matter that South Vietnamese leaders might be corrupt, they were still our allies. Thus began our ever-escalating involvement in a war we hardly understood.

This is not the place to retell the story of the Vietnam War. It is enough to state that Vietnam, an undeclared war, was also our longest, and, next to the Civil War, it was our most controversial as well. As the war grew more costly and the chances for victory grew more remote, the American people began to express growing discontent with inflation, the draft that accompanied the war, and the rising number of American deaths. The average age of our combat soldiers was 19. More than 58,000 Americans died, 300,000 others suffered serious wounds. Massive bombing of North Vietnam failed to contain the opposition forces. The war divided the government, the Democratic party, the whole nation. It became a central issue in the 1968 election, as Nixon promised to end the war—but refused to say how.

These statues are adjacent to the Vietnam War Memorial in Washington, D.C., which is engraved with the names of U.S. service men and women killed in Vietnam.

NIXON AND DETENTE

Once in office, Nixon continued to act on most of the same assumptions as his predecessors. He and his chief national security adviser, Henry Kissinger, believed the way to end the war was to increase the costs of the war to the Soviets and Chinese. But they also realized Americans would not continue to back further escalation. Thus were born the two principles of the Nixon-Kissinger foreign policy: *Vietnamization*, which sought to let the South Vietnamese shoulder more and more of the fighting while the American troops disengaged; and *detente* with the Soviet Union, a downplaying of the threat of force and a new emphasis on cooperation, trade, and mutual arms limitations. The first principle (letting others fight in order to prevent the spread of communism) became known as the **Nixon Doctrine.**

The Nixon Doctrine specifically held that the United States would keep its treaty commitments. Moreover, we would provide a shield if a nuclear power threatened the freedom of a nation allied with us, or a nation whose survival we considered vital to our security and the security of the region as a whole. Finally, in cases involving other types of aggression, the United States would furnish military and economic assistance when requested and as appropriate. But the nation directly threatened was to assume the primary responsibility of providing the labor power for its own defense.[8]

Nixon presided over our exit from Vietnam; not long afterward, our former allies there fell to the opposition forces. Despite the reevaluation of our commitment to Vietnam, foreign policy makers in the 1970s still considered our role in the international system to be primarily in the context of Soviet-American competition. Nationalist movements in the third world were largely discounted as Soviet-inspired revolutions.

THE REAGAN DOCTRINE

Ronald Reagan came to the White House as a hawkish, anti-Soviet crusader. For more than a decade he had made campaign pledges to counter the massive Soviet military buildup and to take a much harder line in negotiations with the Soviets.

He had disapproved of the Kennedy, Nixon, Ford, and Carter test ban and arms negotiations and the SALT agreements. He was convinced—and frequently used the bully pulpit of the White House to try to convince the American public—that the United States should never trust the Soviet leaders. They would do anything, he said, to achieve their objectives, including deception, intensive spying, aggression, and massive nuclear and conventional military buildups. He accused the Soviet leaders of failing to abide by the SALT II agreements of the late 1970s. He called the Soviet Union the focus of evil in the world and an "evil empire." Critics said Reagan was in effect describing the Soviet leaders, if not their people, as diabolical, and that this was unlikely to create a mood conducive to negotiations.

Such criticism rarely bothered Reagan. He apparently believed, even after his several summit meetings with Soviet leader Mikhail Gorbachev, that the best way to deal with the Soviets was by publicly lashing out at them while also sending occasional signals that he was willing to negotiate. Reagan's longstanding views about the Soviet leaders and their goals modified, especially after Gorbachev had been in office for a while. Reagan the politician doubtless sensed, despite his own comfortable election victory in 1984, that both the American people and people around the world yearned for a rollback of nuclear arms. U.S.-USSR relations had sunk to their lowest point since the Cuban Missile Crisis in 1962.[9] Even while losing badly in 1984, the Democrats had been able to portray Ronald Reagan as a man who did not care about stopping the nuclear arms race. Reagan responded in two ways: He pushed even harder for his **Strategic Defense Initiative** (Star Wars program, discussed in the next chapter), and he told friends he really wanted to do something, before he left the White House, to quiet people's fears about the world's blowing up. His summit meetings with Gorbachev and the INF treaty of 1988 were the result.

Reagan himself avoided talking about a Reagan Doctrine, yet much of his foreign policy was based on the tenet of protecting our values by fighting communism. In a more extended form, Reagan's aides often phrased his philosophy as follows: Where genuine national liberation movements seek to recapture their countries from communist tyranny imposed from without, America reserves the right, and may even have the duty, to support those people.[10] Reagan administration efforts in Grenada (1983), Nicaragua, and Angola illustrate this kind of intervention. Reagan, following this same reasoning, also supported the Afghan "freedom fighters."

Reagan and Gorbachev shake hands after negotiating the INF Treaty in Moscow in 1988.

Elsewhere in its foreign policy dealings, the Reagan administration supported insurrectionist or opposition movements that sought to topple (or, in some cases, to regain their political rights from) authoritarian governments. Making its foreign policy fit a changing world, the Reagan administration, for example, eventually, if sometimes haltingly, supported moves to oust the leadership in Haiti and the Philippines and to put some pressure on the governments of Chile, South Korea, and South Africa. Too little, too late, critics often said. Still, the Reagan foreign policy team was often able to react more flexibly than most people expected. Reagan ended up putting pressure for democracy on governments of the right as well as the left. This emphasis on promoting democracy as the best ultimate guarantee of human rights rather than attacking specific human rights abuses was also a feature of the Reagan doctrine.

Perhaps it was in everyone's best interest that there was no one Reagan doctrine. Doctrines not only simplify the complex; they are often used to rally the public, or to embarrass the namesake administration as well. Indeed, Reagan had to shape and conduct his foreign policy in a climate of public opinion that often was opposed to what he may have preferred. Public opinion and Congress, in fact, restrained many of his more strident foreign policy views.

Despite these constraints, Reagan was a popular president in his second term—a time when most presidents witness a decline in public approval. And whenever he took vigorous action, such as the invasion of Grenada or the antiterrorist raids on Libya, he enjoyed public support.

FOREIGN POLICY IN THE BUSH ERA

George Bush came to the White House during a time of change and unusual opportunity. Even before Bush took office, Gorbachev challenged the new president to engage in further cutbacks of nuclear weapons and a new detente. A more unified Europe, acting more independent of the United States, and economic success in Japan and other Pacific Rim nations were fundamentally altering U.S. trading arrangements.

Although U.S.-USSR relations were the Bush administration's top priority, a new balance of power was evolving. Three nations—the United States, the USSR, and China—had assumed military leadership roles, and three regions—the United States, Japan, and Western Europe—were holding the balance of world economic power. Bush has had to work with these new realities.

With U.S.-Soviet relations more relaxed than at any time since World War II, many observers proclaimed that the Cold War was over. Peace between Iran and Iraq had been negotiated, and peace was also coming to several other parts of the world. Further, the quest for democratic rights was sweeping the world, from China to Chile to Hungary—and even to Moscow. Several European leaders yearned for a nuclear-free Europe.

The old order under the Cold War was always tense, yet relatively stable and predictable. Bush welcomed the new era, but he often responded slowly and, at least in his first year or so, he was often upstaged by Gorbachev's aggressive initiatives. Gradually, Bush and his foreign policy advisers put their stamp on U.S. foreign policy. Bush's style has been cautious and often painfully deliberate. Time and again, he has emphasized a bipartisan approach to relations with the USSR and Central America, stressing that while the executive branch is generally responsible for proposing and executing foreign policy, the legislature could support, modify, or even veto a course of action. He has been most careful to win

Views of Foreign Policy

THREAT OF WAR	
Say nuclear war is unlikely within the next 10 years	72%
Say Soviet military threat is constantly growing and presents a real, immediate danger	26%
VIEW OF MIKHAIL GORBACHEV	
Say he is different from previous Soviet leaders	79%
Say he wants better relations with the U.S. enough to make real concessions	64%
LONG RANGE SOVIET PRIORITIES	
Describe the Soviet Union as an aggressive nation that would start a war to get something it wants	57%
Say the Soviet Union is trying to dominate the world	50%
AMERICAN PRIORITIES	
Say George Bush has *not* been too slow in responding to foreign policy moves made by Gorbachev	52%
Say the biggest future threat facing the U.S. from overseas will be economic rather than military in nature	66%
Favor negotiations between the U.S. and the Soviet Union on the elimination of short range nuclear weapons in Europe	66%

Source: New York Times/CBS News Poll.
Based on telephone interviews with 1,073 adults nationwide conducted May 9–11,1989.
Copyright © 1989 by The New York Times Company. Reprinted by permission.

support from Democratic and Republican leaders in Congress before going public with a decision, for example, when he sent additional combat-ready troops into Panama in 1989.

Bush also came to office at a time when questions of world resources, global warming, and enormous population increases shaped the conduct of foreign policy.[11] Common interests and mutual problems had forced some traditional conflicts and rivalries aside, and resource scarcities created new ties and new alliances in the East and West, the North and South.

Bush, a veteran of various foreign policy assignments, moved cautiously in his first months in office, but he began to break away rather boldly from the Reagan rhetoric and sought to establish more positive relations with the Soviet Union. His proposals at NATO meetings and his travels to Eastern Europe helped him put his own stamp on foreign policy (see accompanying box). Nearly everyone now agrees that there are unusual opportunities for reducing international tensions.

Foreign Policy Strategies

How is a foreign policy objective actually implemented? As a major power the United States can choose a variety of options, but it usually employs the following six, or some combination of them.

CONVENTIONAL DIPLOMACY

Much of our day-to-day foreign policy is conducted by the Foreign Service and our ambassadors in face-to-face discussions in Washington and other capitals, at the United Nations, in Geneva (at arms talks), and elsewhere around the world (in regional or international organizations and world conferences). Even though such traditional diplomacy has acquired a less-than-shining image in this era of telecommunications and jet travel, it is still a vital, if slow, process by which nations can gain information, talk about mutual interests, and try to resolve bilateral and multilateral disputes.

Patience and incrementalism are the secret weapons of diplomacy. Reagan's Secretary of State George Shultz liked to refer to his own work as that of a

The first high-level talks of the new Bush administration took place in March 1989 in Vienna between Secretary of State James Baker (left) and Soviet Foreign Minister Eduard Shevardnadze (right).

"gardener" of diplomacy who persistently cultivated the soil of relations for some future bounty or breakthrough. "To a certain extent what you do all day is cope. A tremendous amount of policy comes about through the way little things you do all day long add up. . . ."[12]

Much of the conventional diplomacy that goes on through the work of our State Department and its $1.8 billion budget (1990) may not add up to important breakthroughs. Yet it is difficult to measure the value of diplomatic representation; for example, by placing a price tag on close personal relations with foreign officials, or on information gathered and arguments made to promote our interests around the world. Surely the closing of one embassy or the curtailment of our participation in one or even several international organizations is unlikely to cause major setbacks for our republic. "But less active diplomacy could mean less effective foreign policy or the 'loss' of a friendly nation—" warns Senator Charles McC. Mathias, Jr. (R-Maryland), "all for want of a cabled message containing a sound analysis of a crisis in one nation, or for want of timely meetings to cultivate contacts with future leaders of another."[13] Summit diplomacy is another form of conventional diplomacy.

FOREIGN AID

The United States regularly grants economic and military assistance to foreign countries—in part for humanitarian reasons and in part to further good relations with other nations. We have offered aid to over 100 countries directly and to a number of other nations through our contributions to various United Nations development funds. Since 1945 we have provided over $200 billion in economic assistance alone to foreign countries—a figure that looks and sounds impressive. Yet, these days, America devotes less of its gross national product to foreign aid and development than any other industrialized democracy. Most foreign aid goes to a few countries we deem to be of strategic importance—Israel, Egypt, Turkey, Pakistan, and El Salvador, for example. And nearly 80 percent of the nearly $20 billion spent annually is actually spent in the United States, where it must be used to pay for the purchases of American services and products. It thus constitutes a hefty subsidy for American companies and their employees.

Oscar Arias Sanchez, president of Costa Rica, proposed a peace plan for Central America for which he was awarded the Nobel Peace Prize.

Ever since we began giving serious amounts of foreign aid after World War II, many Americans and many members of Congress have vigorously opposed it. Save for those who support aid for Israel, no powerful interest groups or constituencies back foreign aid initiatives. Still, Republican and Democratic presidents alike keep asking Congress for increased funds for foreign aid. Successive presidents, despite differences of ideology and domestic priorities, have all wanted to maintain the leverage with key countries that economic and military assistance aid provides. Congress invariably trims these requests by between 15 and 30 percent, saying there is too much waste and that they resent giving away foreign aid paid for with borrowed money. Bush's Secretary of State James Baker asserts, in response, that foreign aid is less than 2 percent of the federal budget and adds: "We are asking for an investment to secure our vital national interests and a peaceful future."[14]

ECONOMIC SANCTIONS

The United States has frequently practiced the art of economic pressure in response to a nation's unwillingness to abide by what we perceive to be international law or proper relations. The United States grain embargo against the Soviet Union in the wake of the Soviet Union's invasion of Afghanistan is a classic example of our use of economic sanctions. The Reagan administration waged economic warfare against Nicaragua, and, pushed by Congress and public opinion, it also agreed to certain sanctions against South Africa. Economic pressure was put on Panama in the late 1980s. Tariffs and protectionism are yet another form of economic sanctions.

The popularity of economic sanctions has waxed and waned over the years, but they are still a potentially important weapon in the arsenal of diplomatic and foreign policy strategies. "Economic sanctions often emerge as the centerpiece when a balance is needed between actions that seem too soft or too strident. In these situations, sanctions are seldom regarded as the 'ideal' weapon; rather they are seen as the 'least bad' alternative."[15] Such sanctions are obviously not popular among the farmers or corporations who have to sacrifice part of their overseas economic markets to comply with government sanctions or controls. Nevertheless, the United States has employed this strategy at least seventy times since World War I.

POLITICAL COERCION

Occasionally our foreign policy officials decide that it is expedient to break diplomatic relations with, or otherwise isolate, a hostile country. This was our strategy toward the People's Republic of China during the 1950s and 1960s. Our relations with Iran and Libya have been of this kind in recent years. Our boycott of the 1980 Olympics in Moscow is another illustration of this strategy.

This approach is, however, a next to last resort (force is the last), because a complete break in diplomatic relations obviously establishes a hostile atmosphere and undermines our ability to reason with the nation in question or to use other diplomatic strategies to resolve conflicts.

COVERT OPERATIONS

President Eisenhower often used the CIA to engage in covert or quasimilitary ventures both to avoid deploying the military and also to advance our foreign policy interests. Every recent president has employed covert action to gain support and encourage our friends abroad. Covert activities are planned and executed to conceal the identity of the sponsor.

Covert action is distasteful to many Americans, who see it as incompatible with our basic principles of democracy. In the post-Vietnam years, Congress has insisted on being informed about such actions and has sought to retain a role in overseeing the goals and methods used in various CIA covert operations.[16]

MILITARY INTERVENTION

War, it is often said, is merely an extension of diplomacy. The United States has intervened with military action in other nations on the average of almost once a year since 1789, although usually in relatively minor or short-term events, such as Reagan's use of troops in Grenada and of Navy and Air Force fighter planes over Libya. (Of course, these may not be considered minor events by the target nations.)

Intervention with force is plainly the ultimate response in trying to resolve a conflict. Its success or failure depends on a number of factors. Two observers note, "Military intervention may work against certain small and even medium-sized countries (Grenada and Argentina), but it often seems too dangerous in instances where the threat of big-power confrontation lurks (Poland and Afghanistan), and military intervention often proves ineffective in the context of national civil wars (the United States in Vietnam; Israel in Lebanon)."[17]

Although these are the options available, their use is often conditioned by the character of both the politics of foreign policy making and our processes for deciding and implementing national security decisions.

The Politics of Making Foreign Policy

Foreign policy flows through the same institutional and constitutional structures as domestic policy. Public opinion, interest groups, members of Congress, elections, separation of powers, and federalism all affect the politics of making foreign policy. Yet they operate somewhat differently from the way they do in internal affairs. And, of course, foreign governments and international organizations also play an important role.

PUBLIC OPINION AND FOREIGN POLICY

Different foreign policy issues evoke different degrees of public interest and involvement. In crisis situations—such as the Cuban Missile Crisis or the U.S. raids on Libya in 1986—decisions are made by a small group of persons. Yet even in these situations presidents and their advisers know that what they decide will ultimately require support from the public and from Congress.

In noncrisis situations the public appears to consist of three subcategories. The largest, comprising perhaps as much as 75 percent of the adult population, is the **mass public.** This group knows little about foreign affairs, despite the subject's importance. The mass public concerns itself with foreign affairs mainly in conflict situations, especially those involving the actual or possible use of Ameri-

TABLE 20–2
American Public Ratings of Foreign Ties

The United States has formed ties of varying degrees with different nations in the world. For each of the countries listed below, would it be best in the long run for us to strengthen our ties with them, continue things about as they are, or lessen our commitments to them?

	STRENGTHEN TIES	CONTINUE AS NOW	LESSEN TIES	DON'T KNOW
Canada	54%	37%	1%	8%
Russia	47	20	23	11
England	45	43	3	8
West Germany	42	39	6	13
Mainland China	39	32	12	17
Japan	36	37	17	10
Israel	34	35	18	13
New Zealand	31	38	6	25
South Africa	28	22	34	17
Vietnam	21	26	35	17
Libya	11	14	58	17

Source: The Roper Organization, Inc. (February 1986).

can troops abroad. The second public is the **attentive public.** Comprising perhaps 15 to 20 percent of the population, it maintains an active interest in foreign policy. The **opinion makers** are the third and smallest public. They transmit information and judgments on foreign affairs and mobilize support in the other two publics.

Why are so many people indifferent or uninformed? First, foreign affairs are usually more remote than domestic issues. People have more firsthand information about unemployment or inflation than about Zimbabwean land reform or Turkish political problems. The worker in the factory and the boss in the front office know what labor-management relations are about, and they have strong opinions on the subject. They also may have strong opinions about gun control, capital punishment and abortion. They are likely to be less concerned about the internal struggles for power within Ethiopia or our policy on Cambodia—and probably feel that they could not do much about it anyway. Only when American soldiers, especially drafted soldiers, are being killed does the mass public become directly concerned with foreign affairs.

Lack of widespread concern, knowledge, and involvement in the politics of foreign policy should not be confused with lack of intense feelings about aspects of the international scene. Since World War II questions about our relations with other nations have been high on the list of public concerns. And when such issues as the Vietnam conflict or El Salvador and Nicaragua become domesticated—that is, when they visibly, directly, and immediately affect the people of the United States—the debate over them produces demonstrations, campaigns, and hearings: in other words, all the trappings of the ordinary political process.

PUBLIC MOODS: AN UNSTABLE BASE?

Fluctuating from no interest at all to intense feeling, the public reaction to foreign policy is sometimes based on moods. It is said the mass public oversimplifies the problems of foreign politics. It tends to reduce all issues to the one that is most urgent at the moment. It often thinks of the participants in terms of heroes and villains. It favors quick and easy remedies: Fire the secretary of state, or raise trade barriers, and all will be well. Although this "mood" theory has been challenged, it is conceded that Americans are extremely permissive with American foreign policy makers on international issues. However, even though members of the attentive public and the decision makers are also subject to mood responses and oversimplification, their responses tend to be more sophisticated.

Too much has been made, however, of the American people's ignorance about foreign policy in contrast to their knowledge of domestic issues. The instability of public moods, to the extent that it does exist, probably does not affect policy makers all that much. Issues are usually defined by policy makers; the public generally reacts to them. Policy makers, and events, shape the agenda. Still, public opinion determines the broad limits within which others make decisions.

The State Department makes an effort to keep people informed about those areas of policy it thinks should be talked about publicly, and makes an effort to keep itself informed about public opinion. Nevertheless, almost all negotiations in which our government has a major role are conducted in secret, and both the public and Congress are frequently kept at a distance.

SPECIAL INTERESTS AND FOREIGN POLICY

Interest groups and opinion leaders throughout society form an attentive public whose support is actively sought by official policy makers. They often have an influential voice in shaping foreign policy and serve as a national pulse for our decision makers.

The mass media are sometimes powerful in shaping public opinion, a fact reflected in frequent disputes between the media and government. Tension between the press and the State Department is an issue of long standing. The press becomes especially upset when the government uses classification or secrecy to bury its mistakes, yet press coverage of events in the Philippines, in South Africa, and in China, for example, put pressure on the White House and Congress to act differently than they might have otherwise acted.

Another segment of the attentive public consists of citizens' organizations dedicated to increasing public awareness of foreign policy. The Foreign Policy Association designs community and media programs to encourage citizens to study and discuss major controversies. The Council on Foreign Relations, sometimes called the cornerstone of the Eastern Establishment, publishes *Foreign Affairs* magazine and several books a year; it also provides a forum for bringing business leaders and government elites together for talks on new directions in foreign policy. Groups such as the World Federalists argue for world government. Defense contractors also sometimes try to promote certain kinds of foreign policies. Religious and ethnic groups are particularly interested in certain phases of foreign policy. Antinuclear war activists and those opposed to our involvement in Central America were active in recent years.

It is difficult to generalize about the impact of special-interest groups on American foreign policies. At moments of international crisis a president is usually able to mobilize so much public support that special groups find it difficult to exert much influence. Investigations into such areas of policy as trade, outside the crisis areas, find that special groups rarely have a decisive role in the formulation of foreign policy. Of course, what is more difficult to determine is the impact on policy caused by policy makers' *anticipations* of group reactions.

Ethnic interest groups sometimes play a role in foreign policy making. For example, Greece might sometimes be favored over Turkey in part because of the number of Greek-Americans and the strategic location in Congress of legislators especially attuned to them—as well as because of the strategic location of Greece. The same is sometimes true for Israel and Jewish-Americans.

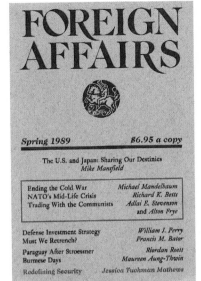

The public is kept well informed on foreign policy by various specialized publications.

FOREIGN COUNTRIES AND FOREIGN COMPANIES

Most countries, large and small, have long had embassies lobbying for their interests in Washington, D.C. Today, however, some countries, like Japan, have built up a powerful network of lawyers, lobbyists, and Washington-based publicists who are retained by Japanese companies and trade associations, as well as by the Japanese government, to defend their extensive economic interests in the United States. Lobbyists representing several newly industrial countries (South Korea, Taiwan, Hong Kong, Singapore, Brazil, and Mexico) have also beefed up their Washington representational efforts to fight U.S. protectionists and import quotas on textiles, shoes, and some of their other exports. These countries have learned "to tap as legal counsel and lobbyists a reservoir of former top U.S. government trade officials. And, these nations are mastering the art of mobilizing U.S. companies and investors who have a stake in trade with the Third World to work on their behalf in key congressional districts."[18] These and other nations have also learned to hire former congressional staffers and former White House staffers to help them make their cases before congressional committees and among administration decision makers.

PARTIES AND FOREIGN POLICY

Political parties do not usually play a major role in shaping foreign policy for two reasons. First, many Americans still prefer to keep foreign policy out of politics. Second, parties usually take less clear and candid stands on foreign policy than they do on domestic policy. All the party weaknesses discussed in Chapter 10 operate in full measure in foreign policy. Party platforms often obscure the issues instead of highlighting them, and many members of Congress fail to follow even a very general party line.

Should parties be concerned with foreign policy? At the end of World War II, sentiment grew stronger for a bipartisan approach to foreign policy. An ambiguous term, **bipartisanship** seems to mean (1) collaboration between the executive and the congressional foreign policy leaders of both parties; (2) support of presidential foreign policies by both parties in Congress; and (3) downplaying foreign policy issues in national elections and especially in presidential debates. In general, bipartisanship is an attempt to remove the issues of foreign policy from partisan politics.

Bipartisanship has appeal. In this era of frequent crises and divided government (when one party controls Congress and the other the White House), it seems to symbolize people's standing shoulder to shoulder as they face an uncertain and potentially hostile world. It provides more continuity of policy, and it ensures that a wider variety of leaders and interests are consulted in policy making. Psychologically, it helps to satisfy people's instincts to turn to one another for reassurance. Its motto—partisan politics stops at the water's edge—is comforting to the many Americans worried about disunity.

But the idea of bipartisanship sometimes comes under sharp attack. Some believe bipartisanship is merely a smokescreen for presidential domination of foreign policy. They suggest it obscures the fact that foreign policy is made by a relatively small, self-perpetuating elite of national security managers who are essentially partisan *and* unelected. Other critics charge that it denies a basic tenet of democracy: the right of a people to choose between alternative lines of action. According to this argument, people in a free society should be allowed and even encouraged to differ. In a democracy it is important not to stifle differences or to ignore them. Rather, there is a need to express the differences in a meaningful way, to find the will of the majority, and to permit the government to act and the opposition to oppose.

CONGRESS AND FOREIGN POLICY

It may seem strange to discuss our national legislative body as part of the attentive public rather than as part of the formal foreign policy establishment. But despite the importance of foreign policy, and even though Congress can block the president's policy and undermine the chief executive's decisions, Congress as an institution seldom directly makes foreign policy. The power of Congress is mainly consultative, although the legislature has taken the initiative in some trade and foreign economic and military assistance questions. As we discussed in Chapter 16, Congress has attempted to curb presidential war-making powers. It is also a link between the policy makers and the public. Congress wants a meaningful relationship—especially "meaningful consultation" with the president in matters of foreign relations.[19]

Individual members of Congress are sometimes included within the circle of those who make the decisions. For example, the leaders of the Senate Committee on Foreign Relations have been involved at times, although their main role is usually helping to educate the public, or educating the president on what will, or will not, run into congressional opposition. When out of sympathy with the policies of the president, key senators sometimes use this committee to focus attention on their differences.

During the 1930s and after World War II, the almost unanimous opinion of academics and the attentive public favored strengthening the hand of the president and limiting the role of Congress in the foreign policy area. It was generally believed that only the president had the knowledge, the political base, and the broad, global perspective from which to develop coherent foreign policies. Congress was thought to be too responsive to the parochial and uninformed attitudes of the public. When conservative leaders tried to alter constitutional arrangements in order to limit the president's power to make executive agreements and to implement treaties, they ran into solid opposition from the intellectual and academic elites. In 1964, Congress, by means of the Gulf of Tonkin Resolution, virtually relinquished war-making decision making in Vietnam to the president.

This sentiment was challenged in the 1970s, when there was so much opposition to the Vietnam policies of Presidents Johnson and Nixon that Congress, especially the Senate, became more assertive: the 1973 vote to cut off funds for bombing Cambodia, and War Powers Resolution of 1973, and countless amendments restricting arms sales and economic and military aid in the late 1970s were signs of a growing restiveness over presidential supremacy. The public again yearn today for strong presidential leadership; it also wants Congress and even public opinion to be consulted (see Tables 20–3 and 20–4).[20]

TABLE 20–3
Who Shapes U.S. Foreign Policy?

"How important a role do you think the following currently play in determining the foreign policy of the United States—a very important role, a somewhat important role, or hardly an important role at all?"

	PERCENT ANSWERING "VERY IMPORTANT"	
	PUBLIC	LEADERS
The President	70%	91%
Secretary of State	64	83
State Department	47	38
Congress	46	34
National Security Adviser	35	46
American Business	35	22
The Military	40	36
United Nations	29	2
The CIA	28	20
Public Opinion	23	15
Labor Unions	17	3

Source: John E. Reilly, ed., *American Public Opinion and U.S. Foreign Policy 1983* (Chicago Council on Foreign Relations, 1983), p. 33.

TABLE 20–4
Who Should Shape U.S. Foreign Policy?

"Do you feel the roles of the following should be more important than they are now, should be less important than they are now, or should be about as important as they are now?"

	PERCENT ANSWERING "MORE IMPORTANT"	
	PUBLIC	LEADERS
The President	39%	17%
Secretary of State	33	22
State Department	34	34
Congress	44	34
National Security Adviser	31	13
American Business	23	22
The Military	26	3
United Nations	37	33
The CIA	16	9
Public Opinion	54	36
Labor Unions	17	14

Source: John E. Reilly, *American Public Opinion and U.S. Foreign Policy 1983* (Chicago Council on Foreign Relations, 1983), p. 34.

CAN WE HAVE A DEMOCRATIC FOREIGN POLICY?

A great paradox exists in conducting the foreign relations of a modern democracy. In the last century Tocqueville wrote that foreign relations "demand scarcely any of the qualities which are peculiar to a democracy; they require, on the contrary, the perfect use of all those in which it is deficient."[21] One leading scholar observed more directly that policy makers in our democracy "either . . . must sacrifice what they consider good policy upon the altar of public opinion, or they must by devious means gain support for policies whose true nature is concealed from the public."[22] Critics have charged our leaders with misleading the people, the experts with misleading our leaders, and ideologies with blinding all of us, especially in Vietnam.

Where should we draw the line? How *do* our policy makers reconcile public rights with political realities? A democratic foreign policy is one in which policy makers are known and held accountable to the people. That is a tough test for any policy, but there are special liabilities in foreign policy: secrecy, the need to act with speed, a generally lower level of information among the general public, and, of course, the complexity of issues and options. Still, the American public wants to be consulted and informed—and ultimately it wants its leaders to be accountable to it.

In Vietnam our apparent policy was to stop communist expansion. Our policy makers guessed wrong in thinking gradual military pressure would deter the North. They miscalculated the character of the war as well as the commitment of those who opposed the Saigon government.[23] Finally, they tried to get out with some face-saving gestures. And because they recognized mistakes, or believed the American people and Congress might not support them in what they thought necessary, they sought to conceal difficulties.

Perhaps our biggest disappointment in Vietnam was that our institutions did not make up for these failings, or at least did not warn us of them sooner. Students of government must ask themselves: How can we organize our institutions and processes to prevent these human failings from exacting such a large toll again?

If we believe we were kept in the dark, then we ignore the fact that no group of citizens has ever had access to more information about a war than the American people had about Vietnam. We did not have all the information, and we surely had some misinformation, but because of a free press and independent judiciary, more was shown, written, and said about Vietnam than about any other war.

The Policy Machinery

It is the responsibility of those who formulate our foreign policies to determine the objectives vital to national interests and to devise programs to achieve those objectives. To the best of their ability and resources, these people must decide how to use (or not use) the instruments available to them: bargaining or negotiation, persuasion or propaganda, economic assistance or pressures, and the threat or actual use of armed force.

The responsibility for foreign policy was fixed in the Constitution at the national level. However, the powers over foreign relations are not divided cleanly or evenly. In England control over foreign relations had been given to the king and his ministers. Our framers tried to redress the balance a bit. Many of the powers given to Congress by the Constitution reflect the decision to take them away from the executive branch; the framers wanted to make what had been a prerogative of the executive into a more shared relationship with the legislature. Congress was given the power to declare war, to appropriate funds, and to make rules for the armed forces. But the president was left as commander in chief of the armed forces and was expected to negotiate treaties and receive and send ambassadors, that is, to recognize or refuse to recognize other governments. The courts have the power to interpret treaties, but by and large they have ruled that our relations with other nations are matters for the executive to negotiate. Executive domination of foreign policy is a fact of the political life of all nations, including democratic ones. To appreciate this phenomenon, let us look at the people within the executive departments who make up the foreign policy establishment.

Secretary of State James A. Baker

PRESIDENTIAL DECISION MAKING AND FOREIGN POLICY

The president's chief foreign policy adviser, according to what presidents say and according to formal statutes, is supposed to be the secretary of state. In some administrations, however, the *secretary of state* has often had to compete with the president's *national security adviser*. Just how much influence the secretary of state has depends largely on the president's personal desires. Presidents Harding, Coolidge, Hoover, Eisenhower, Ford and Reagan turned over to their secretaries of state considerable responsibility for making important decisions. Other presidents, for example, Wilson, both Roosevelts, Kennedy, Nixon, Carter and Bush, took a more active part themselves. Indeed, at times they were their own secretaries of state. Even so, important decisions on foreign policy are so numerous that both president and secretary of state play important roles.

Secretaries of state administer the State Department and fill multiple roles. They receive visits from foreign diplomats, attend international conferences, and usually head our delegation in the General Assembly of the United Nations. They also attempt to serve as the administration's chief coordinator of all governmental actions that affect our relations with foreign nations. Twice in this century secretaries of state have resigned because of policy differences with the presidents they served: William Jennings Bryan quit the Wilson administration, and Cyrus Vance resigned in the late 1970s over differences with Jimmy Carter.

At one time *only* the secretary of state was called upon for advice in formulating and implementing foreign policies. Today, because of the interdependence of foreign, economic, and domestic policies, a president calls on an increasing number of civilian and economic advisers. The day-to-day conduct of foreign affairs is now the business of several major departments and agencies: State, Defense, Treasury, Agriculture, Commerce, Labor, Energy, the Central Intelligence Agency, the Arms Control and Disarmament Agency, and others. The need for immediate reaction and preparedness has transferred more responsibilities directly to the president—and to a great extent to the senior White House aides who assist in coordinating information and advice.

In recent years the national security adviser to the president has become a key—and often the most important—adviser. John Kennedy had McGeorge Bundy, Richard Nixon had Henry Kissinger, Jimmy Carter had Zbigniew Brzezinski, and George Bush has retired Air Force General Brent Scowcroft. Presidents come to rely on these White House aides because of their proximity and because—or at least so presidents believe—these aides owe their prime loyalties to the president, and not to any department or program.

International communications now makes it possible for presidents and their national security advisers to communicate directly with foreign ministers and heads of state all around the globe. No longer do they have to conduct diplomacy through the Foreign Service or be dependent on overseas ambassadors. This reality has transformed the way in which foreign policy is conducted and has undercut and sometimes even threatened the prime role and mission of the State Department.

THE PRESIDENT'S FOREIGN POLICY STAFF

Secretaries, agency chiefs, and their senior subordinates are chosen by the president and are expected to support and carry out his decisions. Yet at the same time they retain a measure of independence; they naturally tend to reflect and defend the views of the departments and agencies they head. As a result, our presidents have found a need to appoint personal advisers whose loyalties lie solely with the chief executive. Because presidents view responsibility in a personal way, the special adviser has played a loosely defined role.

The key coordinating agency for the president is the National Security Council (NSC). Created by Congress, it is supposed to help presidents integrate foreign, military, and economic policies that affect national security.

THE NATIONAL SECURITY COUNCIL

The National Security Council, created in 1947, is the chief coordinating foreign policy staff at the White House. It serves directly under the president, and by law consists of the president, the vice-president, the secretary of state, and the secretary of defense. Recent presidents have sometimes included the director of the CIA,

CHAPTER 20 / Making Foreign Policy

the White House chief of staff, and the attorney general as ex officio members of the NSC.

The national security advisor, appointed by the president, has gradually emerged as one of the most powerful foreign policy makers, and has sometimes become a rival in influence to the secretary of state. Each president has shaped the NSC structure and adapted its staff procedures to suit his personal preferences, but over the years the National Security Council, an agency that is just supposed to provide information to the president, has also taken on major foreign-policy making and implementing roles.

Members of the joint House-Senate committee that investigated the Iran-contra affair.

INTELLIGENCE AND THE CIA

Policy makers must have some idea of the direction in which other nations are going to move in order to be able to assess and, if necessary, to counter those moves. In other words, they need high-level foreign policy intelligence. Therefore, those who gather and analyze material are among the most important assistants to the policy makers. They often become policy makers themselves.

What is the balance of power between government and rebel forces in El Salvador or Nicaragua? How many trained infantrymen are there in Czechoslovakia? What are the weapons and air strength of the North Korean military? Before policy makers can act on important issues, they have to know a great deal about other countries: their probable reactions to a particular policy, their strengths and weaknesses, and, if possible, their strategic plans and intentions.

Although most of the information comes from open sources, the term *intelligence work* conjures up visions of spies and undercover agents. Secret intelligence occasionally does supply crucial data. Intelligence work involves three operations: reporting, research, and transmission. *Reporting* is based on the close and systematic observation of developments the world over; *research* is the attempt "to establish meaningful patterns out of what was observed in the past and to get meaning out of what appears to be going on now"[25] and *transmission* is getting the right information to the right people at the right time.

Many agencies engage in intelligence work, among them the State Department's Bureau of Intelligence and Research, the Defense Intelligence Agency, the supersecret National Security Agency (which works on code breaking and electronic communications systems), the FBI, and the Central Intelligence Agency. These agencies form the United States Intelligence Board, which prepares intelligence surveys on most countries of the world.

CIA Director William H. Webster replaced the controversial William Casey, who died in 1987.

The CIA was created in 1947 to coordinate the gathering and analysis of information that flows into the various parts of our government from all over the world. Yet organization alone cannot ensure that our policy makers will know all they need to know. As an expert on intelligence operations has pointed out:

> In both the Pearl Harbor and Cuban crises there was plenty of information. But in both cases, regardless of what the Monday morning quarterbacks have to say, the data was ambiguous and incomplete. There was never a single, definitive signal that said, "Get ready, get set, go!" but rather, a number of signals that, when put together, tended to crystallize suspicion. The true signals were always embedded in the noise or irrelevance of the false ones.[26]

Employing more than 16,000 persons, the CIA spends more than $3 billion annually.

The CIA director, as head of our foreign intelligence community, oversees research, military intelligence operations, spy satellites, and U–2 and SR–71 exercises that may cost an additional $9 billion annually. (Another $12 billion is spent by the Defense Department in its intelligence needs.) Critics charge, with reason, that CIA operations amount to a secret foreign policy insulated from public control and public scrutiny. In a few nations the local CIA station chief has more staff, more agents, a larger budget, and more influence than the U.S. ambassador.

Since its creation in 1947, the CIA is credited with a number of covert activities and deposed governments, such as those in Iran (1953) and Guatemala (1954). The ill-fated 1961 Bay of Pigs invasion of Cuba was directed by the CIA. Later the CIA organized and trained anticommunist forces in Laos, and contributed considerable support to the anti-Allende forces in Chile. Because of its past record and because it must act when our government cannot officially intervene in another nation's affairs, there has been a growing tendency to credit (or blame) the CIA for all coups, purges, and revolts, whether or not it was actually involved.

In 1967 several CIA "front groups" were discovered supporting a variety of research and political-action programs, both domestic and foreign. In the mid-1970s it was revealed that the CIA had kept illegal files on 10,000 domestic dissidents within the United States. In the 1980s the CIA played an important role in U.S. involvement in Central American nations. Some observers think these activities represent an integral part of our diplomacy and preparedness. Others have denounced them as jeopardizing the values we are dedicated to defending.

The CIA's political leverage, its information, its secrecy, its speed in communication, its ability to act, and its enormous size make it a potent force.[27] Congress has resolved that this power will be used only by publicly accountable decision makers. Committees exist in both the Senate and the House whose primary purpose is to hold the CIA accountable to Congress, although earlier versions of these committees sometimes failed to do an adequate job.

UNITED STATES INFORMATION AGENCY

The United States Information Agency (USIA), established in 1953, has general responsibility for administering foreign information and cultural exchange programs. It administers the Fulbright scholars exchange program, the Voice of America, Radio Free Europe, and similar programs. It operates a worldwide satellite television network called WORLDNET, which permits the USIA to "tell the message of American democracy to the world." Through videoconferencing technology foreign news journalists meet and discuss issues with United States cabinet members, congressional leaders, scholars, and scientists.

The USIA is sometimes called the most technologically adroit propaganda machine in the world. It is also praised by officials in both political parties for its public diplomacy efforts and for its effective telling of the American story abroad. Voice of America radio news and feature programs are listened to all around the world and have won respect in places such as China where many people listen to its programs in both English and Chinese to learn not only about world events, but also what is going on in their own country. (People also listen to improve their English.) While most government programs had been cut back in the 1980s, the USIA had its budget doubled to $1 billion by 1990.

THE ROLE OF THE STATE DEPARTMENT

The U.S. State Department has been variously called "a fudge factory," a "machine that fails," and "a bowl of jelly." The prime duty of the State Department has always been the security of the nation. Although our armed forces remain the ultimate line of defense, the State Department is our first line. It is dedicated to a round-the-clock, world-wide effort to see that our troops and weapons do not need to be used except in genuine emergencies. It is also the central agency in the day-to-day management of foreign affairs. This executive department has six duties:

1. To negotiate with other nations and international organizations
2. To protect American citizens and interests abroad
3. To promote American commercial interests and enterprises
4. To collect and interpret intelligence
5. To represent an American "presence" abroad
6. To promote peace and human rights

As the diplomatic arm of a superpower, the State Department has responded to our new global concerns with continuous reorganization. Some critics insist, however, that the more it changes, the more it stays the same. Among the cabinet departments, State's annual budget is the lowest—less than 2 percent of that of the Department of Defense. Considering the State Department's role and prestige, its staff of 25,000 worldwide is small, especially compared with the nearly 3 million civilian and military officers in the Department of Defense. IBM employs about as many people abroad as the State Department has overseas.

THE ROLE OF THE FOREIGN SERVICE

The American Foreign Service is the eyes and ears of the United States in other countries. Although part of the State Department, the service represents the entire government and performs jobs for many other agencies. Its main duties are to carry out foreign policy as expressed in the directives of the secretary of state, gather data for American policy makers, protect Americans and American interests in foreign countries, and cultivate friendly relations with host governments and foreign peoples. In a very real sense diplomats are our first line of defense. Military power has always been something we fall back on when diplomats and diplomacy fail.

The Foreign Service is composed of Foreign Service officers, Foreign Service reserve officers, and Foreign Service staff officers. At the core of the service are the Foreign Service officers, comparable to the officers of the regular army in the military services.[28] They are a select, specially trained body who are expected to take assignments any place in the world on short notice. There are approximately 4500 such officers; in recent years fewer than 250 junior officers won appointment each year.

The Foreign Service is one of the most prestigious, and most criticized, career services of the national government. In recent years criticism of the Foreign Service has come as much from within as from outside. Most of the criticism claims the Foreign Service (1) stifles creativity; (2) attracts officers who are, or at least become, concerned more about *being* or *becoming* somebody than *doing* something; and (3) requires new recruits to wait fifteen to twenty years before being considered for positions of responsibility. The problems are recognized in Washington, and the task of improving the service continues. More women and minorities have been recruited in recent years. Certain managerial innovations have been tried. But the career service features of the Foreign Service—entry at the bottom, rank in the person rather than in the position, resistance to lateral entry, advancement through grades as determined by senior officers' evaluations, and the tendency toward self-government—make it resistant to change.

Criticism of the Foreign Service because of social-class homogeneity is probably overstated. More likely the structural characteristics of the State Department prevent independent reporting and creativity. There is an old saying in the Foreign Service that there are old Foreign Service officers and there are bold Foreign Service officers, but there are no old bold Foreign Service officers. So we can expect the Foreign Service exposés to keep coming. Its problems of overstaffing, empty jobs, and tedious apprenticeships are in fact common in most bureaucracies.[29]

International Organizations and the UN

The United States belongs to most important world organizations, and its representatives attend most major international conferences. These organizations and conferences are forums for American diplomacy. In addition to the United Nations and its related agencies, the United States is a member of more than 200 international organizations of various types. For example, in its own hemisphere the United States is a member of the Organization of American States (OAS), a regional agency of western hemisphere republics. We also belong to the sixteen-nation North Atlantic Treaty Organization (NATO).

The United Nations was set up by the victorious superpowers immediately after World War II in an effort to shape the postwar world and to promote peace. But when the superpowers, which of course included both the United States and the USSR, ceased to be friendly, the UN was doomed to political impotence. The liberal or idealist school of international relations believed the United Nations was destined to bring nations together, to maintain international peace and security, to achieve international cooperation in solving world problems, and to promote and encourage respect for human rights.

When it was founded the UN called for establishing conditions under which justice and respect for obligations arising from treaties and other sources of international law could be maintained. In the UN's first forty years, and directly against the provisions of Article 1 of the UN Charter, over 300 regional and civil wars throughout the world claimed up to 20 million lives. And, as wars continue in Africa, Central America, and Southeast Asia, the UN stands by, almost always helpless. Only occasionally does the UN play a constructive role in ceasefire or peacekeeping missions (as after Arab-Israeli wars, or during India-Pakistan clashes, and in Cyprus).

Public esteem in the United States for the UN, which has been low in recent years rose a bit when the UN was awarded a Nobel Peace Prize in 1988. Generally, however, the UN is viewed as drowning in a sea of words and suffocating under a rigid international civil service system. Even though it comprises three times as many countries today as when it was founded in 1945, the UN is characterized by timidity and bureaucracy. Even friendly critics say it has become an assembly line of mass produced resolutions that have little relevance to the substance of the problems under discussion.[30]

The UN, like every other agency of international politics, is dominated by the fact the world is divided into separate nations acting in their own self-interest as they define it. The United States, like most other nations, cites the UN Charter when it suits its short-term interest and ignores it when it does not. We grew impatient with the anti-U.S. propaganda occasioned by our involvement in Vietnam and by the UN condemnations of our involvement in Grenada and Nicaragua. Moreover, the Soviet Union's ability to line up nonaligned votes in the UN is greater today than ever. Probably the key element in the loss of faith in the UN by the United States is simply that the UN no longer so readily serves the interests of U.S. foreign policy as it did in the 1950s and 1960s.

One U.S. response has been to cut back our financial contributions to the UN. A legislative measure sponsored by Senator Nancy Kassebaum (R-Kans.) and signed into law by President Reagan effectively reduced our UN dues by one-fifth in 1987. That legislation also advised the UN to replace its principle of one-nation–one-vote on budgetary matters. Ideally, the United States wants the world body to introduce weighted voting, with power accorded to each nation on the basis of its financial contribution to the UN. U.S. officials often call the current system "taxation without representation" because it gives each of the 159 nations an equal say in determining the budget regardless of its contributions. In more recent years we have agreed to pay more of "our share" of UN funds. President Bush, a former U.S. ambassador to the UN, seems to be a more consistent supporter than was his predecessor.

Some conservatives have long opposed our involvement in the UN, fearing we risk being trapped or outvoted by the communists or by third-world nations. Critics across the political spectrum question whether it makes sense to give every UN member an equal vote in the UN's General Assembly regardless of its size, population, and contribution to the UN budget. (Britain, China, France, the Soviet Union, and the United States hold permanent seats in the UN's once-important Security Council, a fifteen-seat body.) Americans are plainly annoyed too by the anti-U.S. rhetoric heard in the General Assembly, by the UN's wasteful bureaucracy, and by its failure to keep the peace.[31]

U.S. foreign policy officials generally view the UN as both an expression of the world's desire for peace and the scene of certain passions that prevent peace. "Experience indicates that when nations need channels, when nations agree upon procedures, when they agree on much of the substance, the United Nations offers a valuable forum for making progress," says Secretary of State James A. Baker. "We support that, and we support the United Nations. Yet, in the final analysis, the United Nations can be neither a substitute for American leadership nor an excuse for a failure to try."[32]

Idealists believe the UN fails because we have had so little faith in it. They counsel us to expect more of it: *Stick with it and try to make it work.* Make it the world switchboard, whose job is to alert the world to our common problems long before they get out of control. Use its peace-keeping forces and its forums for conflict reduction, to make the world a safer place.

If the UN did not exist, something else like it would no doubt be devised to curb quarrels among independent sovereign nations. Even though less than half of the American public says the UN is doing a good job, about 80 percent believe we should remain in it—because they are convinced that we are better with it than without it.

NATO Member Nations

Belgium
Canada
Denmark
France*
Great Britain
Greece
Iceland
Italy
Luxembourg
The Netherlands
Norway
Portugal
Spain
Turkey
United States
West Germany

* Although France withdrew from NATO's military committee in the mid-1960s, it is otherwise an active member of NATO.

The Nobel UN

The 1988 Nobel Peace Prize was awarded, like four earlier ones, to a group related to the UN. This time the award recognized the UN's peacekeeping forces. The UN peacekeeping effort consists of some 11,000 troops and roughly 2000 support personnel. In recent years they have sought to end or reduce conflicts between Iran and Iraq, between Israel and Syria, between Israel and Lebanon, and between Greece and Turkey, among other conflicts. In many respects, the 1988 award honored Secretary General Javier Perez de Cuellar who proved to be a masterful negotiator. "The most important role of the secretary general is to help the parties in a dispute save face," Perez de Cuellar said. "When someone has to make a concession, it is easier to do it through the secretary general than directly to one's adversary." This Nobel Peace Prize helped, at least for awhile, to enhance worldwide esteem for the UN and its delicate missions.

Summary

1. American foreign policy during the past fifty years or more has been greatly influenced, and at times completely shaped, by our relations with the Soviet Union. To understand our foreign policy, we must first understand the continuing competition between these two major powers. Also, other economic and nuclear powers have emerged over the past twenty years thus further complicating even more the challenge of formulating wise and effective foreign policies.

2. Foreign policy is not made according to any set formula, but represents various traditions, organized interests, and constitutional processes. Precedent, if not our Constitution, has given the primary responsibility for making foreign policy to the chief executive. But presidents in turn are dependent on accidents of history, on advisers, and, in the long run, on Congress and the American people. When there are no obvious solutions to international problems, our decision makers must predict, act, and wait—sometimes successfully, but sometimes with unforeseeable and catastrophic consequences.

3. Our foreign policy interests are advanced by one or a combination of the following strategies or means: diplomacy, foreign aid, economic sanctions, political coercion (including breaking off of diplomatic relations), covert action, and military intervention.

4. Presidents can act swiftly and decisively. They are often in a good position to see the nation's long-run interests above the tugging of bureaucratic and special interests. They must face the people in elections, but not so often that they must slavishly follow public opinion. Yet the desired presidential accountability between elections can be achieved only if the people are willing to inform themselves and demand answers, explanations, and honest reporting from their leaders.

5. War is merely an extension of diplomacy. Perhaps future generations will be able to eliminate this alternative entirely, but in our own time leaders must deal with realities, not dreams; with the world as they see it, not as they wish it. Greater restraints upon decision makers might undermine our security, and fewer restraints might endanger our freedom. In the end, we have to be aware of the limits of our power to assist nations threatened by totalitarian systems and of the need to reappraise the balance of power among our institutions.

Further Readings

STEPHEN E. AMBROSE. *Rise to Globalism: American Foreign Policy, 1938–1986*, 5th ed. (Penguin, 1987).

DAVID A. BALDWIN. *Economic Statecraft* (Princeton University Press, 1985).

CECIL V. CRABB, JR. *The Doctrines of American Foreign Policy* (Louisiana State University Press, 1982).

GORDON A. CRAIG and ALEXANDER L. GEORGE. *Force and Statecraft: Diplomatic Problems of Our Time* (Oxford University Press, 1983).

I. M. DESTLER. *Making Foreign Economic Policy* (Brookings Institution, 1980).

ALEXANDER L. GEORGE. *Presidential Decision Making in Foreign Policy: The Effective Use of Information and Advice* (Westview, 1980).

LEE H. HAMILTON and DANIEL K. INOUYE, et al. *Iran-contra Affair*, Report of the Congressional Committees Investigating the Iran-contra Affair, H. Rpt 100–433 (U.S. Government Printing Office, 1987).

WALTER ISAACSON and EVAN THOMAS. *The Wise Men* (Simon & Schuster, 1986).

DANIEL J. KAUFMAN and JEFFREY S. MCKITRICK, eds. *U.S. National Security: A Framework for Analysis* (Lexington Books, 1985).

CARNES LORD. *The Presidency and the Management of National Security* (Free Press, 1988).

JOHN STEINBRUNER, ed. *Restructuring American Foreign Policy* (Brookings Institution, 1989).

See also *Foreign Affairs, Foreign Policy*, and *The National Interest*, journals published quarterly.

Notes

1. Cecil V. Crabb, Jr., *The Doctrines of American Foreign Policy* (Louisiana State University Press, 1982).

2. Gaddis Smith, *Morality, Reason and Power: American Diplomacy in the Carter Years* (Hill & Wang, 1986).

3. For a discussion of crusaders (idealists) and pragmatists (realists), see John Stoessinger, *Crusaders and Pragmatists*, 2d ed. (Norton, 1985).

4. Useful treatments of the Cold War and its legacy are Daniel Yergin, *Shattered Peace: The Origins of the Cold War and the National Security State* (Houghton Mifflin, 1978); Robert Dallek, *The American Style of Foreign Policy* (Alfred A. Knopf, 1983); and John Lewis Gaddis, *The Long Peace: Inquiries into the History of the Cold War* (Oxford University Press, 1987).

5. He also permitted the CIA to fly U–2 planes over the Soviet Union to gather intelligence—until one such flight was shot down with major consequences for U.S.-USSR relations. See Michael R. Beschloss, *MAYDAY: Eisenhower, Khrushchev, and the U–2 Affair* (Harper & Row, 1986).

6. See R. B. Smith, *An International History of the Vietnam War: The Kennedy Strategy* (St. Martin's Press, 1986); and George McT. Kahin, *Intervention* (Knopf, 1986).

7. See especially Frances Fitzgerald, *Fire in the Lake* (Atlantic-Little,

Brown, 1972); and Gabriel Kolko, *Anatomy of War: Vietnam, the United States, and the Modern Historical Experience* (Pantheon, 1986).

8. For Nixon's and Kissinger's own views, see Richard Nixon, *RN: The Memoirs of Richard Nixon* (Grosset and Dunlap, 1978); and Henry Kissinger, *The White House Years* (Little, Brown, 1979), pp. 223–25. See also Seymour M. Hersh, *The Price of Power: Kissinger in the Nixon White House* (Summit Books, 1983).

9. Richard W. Stevenson, *The Rise and Fall of Détente* (University of Illinois Press, 1985); Sanford J. Ungar, ed., *Estrangement: America and the World* (Oxford University Press, 1985); and Raymond L. Garthoff, *Détente and Confrontation: American-Soviet Relations from Nixon to Reagan* (Brookings Institution, 1985).

10. See, for example, Jeane Kirkpatrick, *The Reagan Doctrine* (The Heritage Foundation, 1984). But see the critique by Robert W. Tucker, *Intervention and the Reagan Doctrine* (Council on Religion and Foreign Affairs, 1985).

11. See, for example, Jessica Tuchman Mathews, "Redefining Security," *Foreign Affairs* (Spring 1989), pp. 162–77.

12. Don Oberdorfer, "The Mind of George Shultz," *The Washington Post National Weekly Edition* (February 17, 1986), p. 6.

13. Charles McC. Mathias, Jr., "Don't Straitjacket U.S. Diplomacy," *The New York Times* (June 26, 1986), p. 23.

14. Secretary of State James A. Baker, testimony before House Foreign Affairs Committee, February 21, 1989; U.S. Depart. of State Document No. 1147, p. 4.

15. Gary Clyde Hufbauer and Jeffrey J. Schott, "Economic Sanctions and Foreign Policy," *PS* (Fall 1985), p. 727. See also their longer study, *Economic Sanctions Reconsidered: History and Current Policy* (Institute for International Economics, 1985).

16. John Prados, *President's Secret Wars: CIA and Pentagon Covert Operations Since World War II* (Morrow, 1986).

17. Hufbauer and Schott, "Economic Sanctions and Foreign Policy," p. 728.

18. Bruce Stokes, "Developing Countries Join the Big Leagues in Washington Trade Lobbying," *National Journal* (January 25, 1986), p. 202.

19. See Cecil V. Crabb, Jr., and Pat M. Holt, *Invitation to Struggle: Congress, The President, and Foreign Policy*, 3d ed. (Congressional Quarterly Press, 1989).

20. See Thomas E. Cronin, "President, Congress, and Foreign Policy," in Charles Kegley and Eugene Witkopf, eds, *The Domestic Sources of American Foreign Policy* (St. Martin's Press, 1988), pp. 149–65.

21. Alexis de Tocqueville, *Democracy in America*, vol. I (Knopf, 1945), pp. 224–35.

22. Hans Morgenthau, "The Conduct of American Foreign Policy," *Parliamentary Affairs* (Winter 1949), p. 147.

23. For an excellent on-the-scene account of this miscalculation by a young Marine officer who fought there, see Philip Caputo, *A Rumor of War* (Holt, Rinehart & Winston, 1977). See also Leslie Gelb and Richard K. Betts, *The Irony of Vietnam: The System Worked* (Brookings Institution, 1979); and Harry G. Summers, Jr., *On Strategy: A Critical Analysis of the Vietnam War* (Presidio Press, 1983).

24. Carnes Lord, *The Presidency and the Management of National Security* (Free Press, 1988).

25. Sherman Kent, *Strategic Intelligence for American Policy* (Princeton University Press, 1949), especially p. 4. On the limits of intelligence activities, see Richard K. Betts, "Analysis, War, and Decision: Why Intelligence Failures Are Inevitable," *World Politics* (October 1978).

26. Roberta Wohlstetter, *Cuba and Pearl Harbor: Hindsight and Foresight* (Rand, 1965). p. 36.

27. For differing accounts of the CIA's influence and effectiveness, see John Ranelagh, *The Agency* (Simon & Schuster, 1986); Peter Maas, *Manhunt* (Random House, 1986); and Rhodri Jeffreys-Jones, *The CIA and American Democracy* (Yale University Press, 1989).

28. For a favorable treatment of the Foreign Service, see Andrew L. Steigman, *The Foreign Service of the United States* (Westview Press, 1985).

29. See the assessments by John M. Goshko, "Up or Out in the Foreign Service," *The Washington Post* (March 20, 1986) p. A13; and Christopher Madison, "The Morale Crisis at Foggy Bottom," *Government Executive* (February 1988), pp. 10–15.

30. See Peter R. Baehr and Leon Gordenker, *The United Nations: Reality and Ideal* (Praeger, 1984); and Shirley Hazzard, *Defeat of an Ideal: A Study of the Self Destruction of the United Nations* (Little, Brown, 1973).

31. See Charles Krauthammer, "Let It Sink," *The New Republic* (August 24, 1987), pp. 18–23.

32. James A. Baker, statement before the U.S. Senate, January, 1989, in U.S. Department of State, Bureau of Public Affairs, *Current Policy* No. 1146. p. 6.

21

Providing for the Common Defense

The Constitution of 1787 was written, ratified, and put into effect in good part because the framers and their friends feared for the security and survival of the new nation. They knew that action, unity, and sure leadership would be needed for future military emergencies. Today, presidents, Congress, and the public alike hope, work, and pray for a world in which our weapons and military forces may no longer be necessary, but our policy makers must deal with the world as it is.

Both Congress and the president are responsible for the common defense, and both have constitutional authority to discharge that responsibility. Congress appropriates the money and determines the size, structure, and organization of the fighting forces. The president is the commander in chief of these forces and initially determines how military power will be deployed. The president and Congress are jointly responsible for defining our defense objectives and ensuring that our deterrence and overall defense strategies are equal to the challenges from hostile nations. In defense, as in foreign policy, the president is often the key decision maker in emergencies.

Heated debates have taken place recently, as they have throughout our history, over what constitutes an effective national defense, especially over the controversial Strategic Defense Initiative (often called Star Wars) and how to respond to Gorbachev's bold initiatives. Other problems being debated by national defense policy makers are:

Are the Defense Department and the Joint Chiefs of Staff properly organized to provide the strategic direction needed to link long-range policies and military resources?

How can the procurement process deficiencies such as cost overruns, stretched-out development and delivery schedules, and unsatisfactory weapons performance be remedied?

How can the poor inter-Service coordination exhibited during the Vietnam conflict, the Iranian hostage rescue mission, and other military operations, be improved?

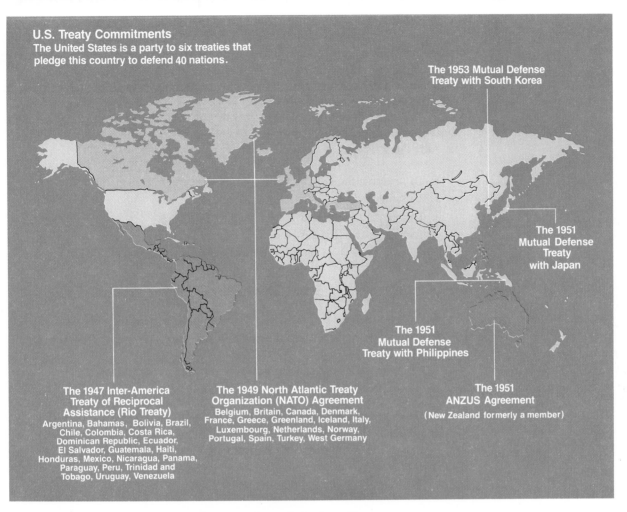

U.S. Treaty Commitments
The United States is a party to six treaties that pledge this country to defend 40 nations.

The 1953 Mutual Defense Treaty with South Korea

The 1951 Mutual Defense Treaty with Japan

The 1951 Mutual Defense Treaty with Philippines

The 1951 ANZUS Agreement
(New Zealand formerly a member)

The 1947 Inter-America Treaty of Reciprocal Assistance (Rio Treaty)
Argentina, Bahamas, Bolivia, Brazil, Chile, Colombia, Costa Rica, Dominican Republic, Ecuador, El Salvador, Guatemala, Haiti, Honduras, Mexico, Nicaragua, Panama, Paraguay, Peru, Trinidad and Tobago, Uruguay, Venezuela

The 1949 North Atlantic Treaty Organization (NATO) Agreement
Belgium, Britain, Canada, Denmark, France, Greece, Greenland, Iceland, Italy, Luxembourg, Netherlands, Norway, Portugal, Spain, Turkey, West Germany

How best can we prevent nuclear war: through further efforts on our current deterrence theories, reliance on the Strategic Defense Initiative, better conventional forces, more carriers and submarines, new technologies such as the Cruise and Stealth, through arms control, negotiations, and diplomacy?

What our national security goals are and how much money, personnel, and weapons are needed to provide for an effective national defense system are continually debated. Too often, however, most Americans leave this debate to a small number of informed officials, scientists, scholars, and the military. But the basic issues of defense policy are extremely important to every one of us: (1) What should be our national defense objectives? (2) How much should we spend on defense and how should that money be allocated? (3) How can we minimize the possibility of nuclear war? (4) Can we maximize our safety by threatening other nations, or is our security based on the principle of common security?

The Nation's Defense Objectives

The overriding mission of America's defense program is to deter a nuclear attack against the United States. We seek a peaceful world. We are also committed to defend western Europe, Japan, and several other nations and to protect our vital

U.S. Active Duty Military Personnel Abroad	
Total for All Locations	503,793
Ashore	447,998
Afloat	55,795
Major Locations Abroad	
Europe	344,120
Afloat	20,589
West Germany	249,753
United Kingdom	28,964
Italy	14,653
Spain	9,418
Turkey	5,174
Greece	3,746
Other	11,823
East Asia and Pacific	122,886
Afloat	19,197
Japan	46,663
South Korea	41,392
Philippines	14,534
Other	1,100
Western Hemisphere	21,848
Afloat	5,696
Panama	9,774
Guantanamo	2,274
Honduras	1,224
Other	2,880

Source: Department of Defense.

Active Military Personnel*	
Army	780,000
Air Force	635,000
Navy	615,000
Marines	205,000
Total	2,235,000
Nonactive Reserve Forces	
Army	1,300,000
Navy	305,000
Air Force	250,000
Marines	130,000
Total	1,985,000

* Defense Department projections for 1990, figures rounded off.

interests. Americans expect the president, Congress, and the military to do everything in their power to prevent war and to protect the United States and its allies from attack.

Our defense programs also enable us to conduct our routine diplomatic activities and allow us to have a presence around the world. Because we are a major military power, attention is paid to our positions and interests.

Our military and defense policies are intertwined with our foreign policy goals. Two hundred years after the beginning of the republic, these objectives include the following:

1. To preserve the United States as an independent nation.
2. To safeguard our institutions and values.
3. To maintain our ability to deter aggression.
4. To reduce the chances of nuclear war.
5. To protect as best as we can our supplies of strategic resources, energy, and food.
6. To help resolve regional conflicts and prevent the terrorism that threatens global peace.
7. To defend allied nations with whom we have mutual defense pacts.
8. To revitalize our bond with allies who share our traditions, values, and interests.
9. To build more rational relationships with potential adversaries.

The United States has been involved in military interventions of one kind or another on nearly 180 occasions, although only 5 of these occasions have been declared wars. Our last declaration of war was in 1941. American leaders sometimes use military forces for ends other than war. Since World War II alone we have alerted or deployed military units on more than 200 occasions to achieve specific goals that seemed important enough to warrant a show of military power.

U.S. DEFENSE SYSTEMS AND THE STRATEGIC DEBATE

Since the advent of nuclear weapons after World War II, America's primary defense against a Soviet attack has been the strategy of **deterrence** based on the threat of a massive retaliation. Effective deterrence is commonly measured by the usable strength of a survivable second-strike force. This means the United States wants such a large, diversified, and well-protected defense system that a Soviet first strike would not cripple our ability to retaliate decisively. We seek to prevent war by maintaining military forces and demonstrating the determination to use them, if needed, in ways that will persuade opponents that the cost of any attack on our interests will exceed the benefits they could hope to gain.

This strategy of mutual assured destruction is the core of American policy, and has been for a generation or more. Pentagon officials claim it has worked reasonably well. At least, they point out, it has succeeded in winning for the United States and our allies more than four decades of peace with our primary adversary—a period twice as long as the time span between World Wars I and II.

To be effective, deterrence must meet four tests:

Survivability: Our forces must be able to survive a preemptive attack with sufficient retaliatory strength to threaten losses that outweigh gains.

Credibility: Our threatened response to an attack must be of a form that the potential aggressor believes we could and would carry out.

Clarity: The action to be deterred must be sufficiently clear to our adversaries that the potential aggressor knows what is prohibited.

Safety: The risk of failure through accident, unauthorized use, or miscalculation must be minimized.[1]

This strategy of mutual assured destruction means that the only deterrent we have to keep an adversary from using nuclear weapons on us is our commitment to kill as many or more of them as they kill of us. This, for obvious reasons, has never been a wholly pleasing strategy. Many Americans, including most of our recent presidents, have been fundamentally dissatisfied with this defense strategy. Groups such as the Catholic bishops and other religious peace activists have condemned this posture and challenged the morality of relying on nuclear weapons to deter, much less to fight, a nuclear war. Advocates of the nuclear freeze, including many members of Congress and millions of citizens who voted for the freeze in state referendums in the early 1980s, have called on both the United States and the Soviet Union to halt production, testing, and deployment of nuclear weapons.

The most important challenge to the traditional deterrence strategies came from former President Reagan. In a 1983 address, Reagan called on American science to create a total defense against ballistic missiles, a defense of such qualitative difference that it could permit, he argued, a major shift in our defense systems. Nuclear strategy would no longer be based on offense, but rather on defense, no longer on assured destruction, but on assured survival. He put it this way:

> Up until now we have increasingly based our strategy of deterrence upon the threat of retaliation. But what if free people could live secure in the knowledge that their security did not rest on the threat of instant U.S. retaliation to deter a Soviet attack; that we could intercept and destroy strategic ballistic missiles before they reached our soil or that of our allies. I know this is a formidable task . . . but isn't it worth every investment necessary to free the world from the threat of nuclear war?[2]

Officially called the Strategic Defense Initiative (SDI), this proposal became popularly known as the "Star Wars" program. "Star Wars" began to be envisioned as one of the biggest research projects in American history, a multiyear $30 billion undertaking. Its long-range objective is the erection of a space "shield" to destroy enemy warheads after they are launched while they are in space flight, or as they reenter the atmosphere. The "shield" would not actually be a shield but rather a complex network of laser beams, particle beams, electromagnetic "slingshot" rail guns, and sensing, tracking, and aiming devices, all requiring highly sophisticated computer and satellite coordination at many different stages and levels.

Reagan was essentially saying that deterrence through the threat of mutual assured destruction should not be the basis for an enduring peace and that the threat to kill hundreds of millions of civilians as punishment for some unacceptable acts by a few government leaders was wrong. He was not the first American president to think this way. Every president going back to Harry Truman has sought an alternative to our primary defense strategy—yet no viable alternative has ever been developed.

What was the reaction to this SDI initiative? Although it was not entirely a new idea, the boldness and size of the project aroused the nation and triggered a national debate about defense strategy that is still going on in the Bush years.

"Before we talk about my daughter— where do you stand on Star Wars?"

Berry's World; reprinted by permission of NEA, Inc.

Conservative Reagan supporters hailed it as a means of taking advantage of American scientific and economic superiority to render Soviet nuclear weapons obsolete. Critics argued that the Star Wars program might cause the Soviet Union to increase its offensive nuclear attack forces to overcome this defense, to devise countermeasures to defeat it, and to perceive preemptive first strike as its best course of action. Critics also say that the technological inventions SDI would require are highly unlikely to work and would cost too much. They propose that the events surrounding the Challenger and Chernobyl disasters should caution us against grand wishful thinking—and about relying on technology.

Following is a summary of the principal points made by supporters and opponents of the SDI proposal:

Supporters say:

1. The United States should move away from deterrence based on the threat of nuclear retaliation and toward protection by complete, nationwide defense.

2. Even if a complete defense against nuclear weapons were unattainable, partial defenses are feasible and would reinforce deterrence by retaliation.

3. The United States enjoys both technological and economic advantages over the Soviets and ought to exploit these strengths.

4. At least while the SDI is in the research stage, it is essential that the United States not be constrained by arms control agreements that might limit research into the development and utility of strategic defenses.

5. Major new space-based technologies for defense appear to be possible and must be studied, if for no other reason than that the Soviets might develop them first. Even though some of the technologies may not work out, research can discover others that will. SDI is merely a research program; development decisions can be made later, after the technologies and their effectiveness have been established.

Opponents say:

1. The goal of a sure-proof defense is an illusion that cannot be achieved because the task is too difficult, it requires too many technological breakthroughs, and it will not be cost effective, especially if we strive for a near-perfect system. In addition, the Soviets will devise countermeasures that undermine deployment.

2. Although limited defenses, especially those of hardened military targets, are possible, they are enormously expensive. There are other ways of protecting these targets, such as mobility and redundancy, but they do not eliminate dependence on deterrence by second-strike nuclear retaliation.

3. The Soviets may respond to an American defense shield against their nuclear weapons with a variety of relatively low-cost measures including shortened launch times for missiles; increased numbers of missiles; increased numbers of warheads, decoys, and other penetration aids.

4. The cost of a multitiered space shield system will be enormous: $60 billion for research alone in the first decade, and estimates ranging from several hundred to $1000 billion for a final deployment of the full system.

5. A major U.S. program to develop SDI will only succeed if offensive forces are greatly reduced and constrained. Yet the SDI, if pursued unilaterally, could foreclose the possibility of negotiating joint reductions in nuclear arms.

6. The projected SDI is an attempt to apply military-technical solutions to what is basically a political problem between the United States and the USSR.[3]

7. SDI might encourage a first strike by the country possessing "Star Wars," or may lead an opposition nation into so thinking.

What is the status of the Star Wars program? It is still just a starry vision rather than an actual defense system. Congress went along with Reagan and funded, although somewhat scaled back from Reagan's requests, the early years of research. The Soviets told Reagan and now tell Bush they would like to see the United States abandon the goal of a space-based defensive system. Although they deny they used the SDI program as a bargaining chip, U.S. officials nonetheless have effectively used the program to gain certain concessions from the Soviets.

Several years and at least $15 billion after Reagan launched the Star Wars effort to render Soviet ballistic missiles "impotent and obsolete," the Bush administration, along with Congress, has sharply scaled back the efforts to implement the Reagan pledge. Technological and money problems are most often cited as the reasons. Instead of a massive space security shield that would protect major U.S. cities, Pentagon experts now champion the so-called "brilliant pebbles" concept of swarms of thousands of "smart" rocket interceptors in space to spot and destroy any incoming Soviet missiles. Secretary of Defense Richard Cheney said that this new approach plus budgetary limitations have made it necessary to postpone major decisions on the Strategic Defense Initiative. Yet if the brilliant pebbles approach turns out not to work, he said, continued research on the Star Wars approach would permit Congress and the president to decide sometime in the late 1990s whether to deploy a major space-based antimissile defense system.

How Much Is Enough?

Americans of every political view want a strong and effective defense. But considerable controversy arises about whether the Defense Department spends too much and about whether its weapons systems are reliable. Recent critics from both the right and the left say the Pentagon is a bureaucracy run wild and that its monies are not as wisely or effectively spent as they should be.[4] The Defense Department itself has charged many of the nation's biggest weapons contractors with poor design, inadequate quality controls, and excessive costs. In one recent year, 45 of the top 100 defense contractors were under criminal investigation.[5]

CONTROLLING THE DEFENSE BUDGET

During the peak of the Vietnam War effort, almost half the American people thought we were spending too much on defense. By 1980 many thought we were spending too little (Table 21–1). After Vietnam, expenditures for health, welfare, and education went way up. Those for national defense—at least as a proportion of the budget—went down. In the 1980s, these trends were reversed. Defense spending doubled in the 1981 to 1986 period, while many other areas of federal spending remained at about the same level.

Once again many people began to think we were spending too much on defense, and public concern over waste and sloppy purchasing practices in the Defense Department sharply increased. Critics of the approach pointed out that our investments must be carefully targeted to those areas most vital to national security, especially in strengthening our conventional forces, improving troop readiness, and upgrading the recruiting and training of military personnel.

The Top Defense Contractors
McDonnell Douglas
General Dynamics
Rockwell International
General Electric
Boeing
Lockheed
United Technologies
Hughes Aircraft
Raytheon
Grumman
Martin Marietta

Source: Department of Defense.

TABLE 21–1
Public Opinion and Defense Spending

	Is the U.S. spending too much, about right, or too little on defense?			
YEAR	TOO MUCH	ABOUT RIGHT	TOO LITTLE	NO OPINION
1989	49%	37%	11%	3%
1987	44	36	14	6
1986	47	36	13	4
1980	14	24	49	13
1976	36	32	22	10
1974	44	32	12	12
1971	49	31	11	9
1969	52	31	8	9

Source: Gallup poll index.

Critics of the increases doubted the wisdom of funding every new system on the Pentagon's shopping list. They noted that historically the most important factor in winning wars has been people; strategy and tactics come second, and expensive equipment often comes third.

As we enter the 1990s, defense spending has not only leveled off but has been subject to cutbacks. Weapons systems have been canceled or postponed, Navy ships have been retired, and the formerly envisioned goal of a 600-ship Navy, abandoned. The size of the Army has also been cut and several smaller bases closed. None of this retrenchment was easy, yet budgetary realities, coupled with Soviet cutbacks and the lack of popular support for increased military spending, forced Bush and the Pentagon to make hard choices. Ironically, yet predictably, members of Congress with major defense installations or defense contractors in their home districts vigorously protested many of these cutbacks, prompting Defense Secretary Cheney to observe that members of Congress wanted him to cut

Richard B. Cheney, appointed Secretary of Defense by President Bush in 1989, was a member of Congress from Wyoming and served previously in the Ford White House.

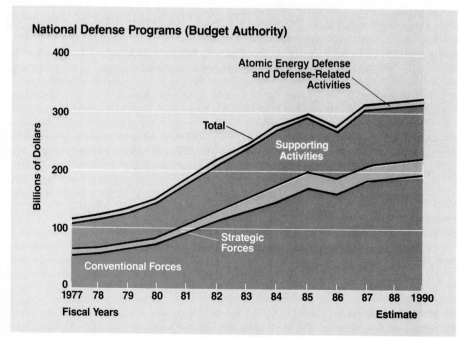

National Defense Programs (Budget Authority)

Atomic Energy Defense and Defense-Related Activities

Total

Supporting Activities

Strategic Forces

Conventional Forces

Billions of Dollars

400 — 300 — 200 — 100 — 0

1977 78 79 80 81 82 83 84 85 86 87 88 1990

Fiscal Years

Estimate

CHAPTER 21 / Providing for the Common Defense

the military budget without reducing funds for their favorite weapons system. "They can't have it both ways," said the Secretary, who is also a former member of Congress.

PRESSURES TO INCREASE DEFENSE SPENDING

One of the chief reasons presidents and Congress have such difficulty controlling the defense budget is that many people oppose any bold program of closing military bases or consolidating military operations. Base closings anger politicians, as well as local constituents and economic interests; and the Defense Department must hold extensive hearings before it can actually close a base. Further, weapons are a major American industry, and the industry and the members of Congress from such areas work hard to promote their products. Representatives from shipyard districts push for more submarines; those from Texas, St. Louis, or Seattle push for new planes. Then too, the logrolling arrangements that operate in other pork-barrel areas work here as well: you fatten my district, and I'll fatten yours. Even the fiercest antiwar doves in Congress can shout the loudest when a base closing or contract termination is suggested for their districts or states.

Government is usually the sole purchaser of most military hardware. The high technological levels of defense weaponry create high research and development costs, sometimes strung out over several years or a decade, that often cause high initial capital investments. The arms industry has the appearance of private enterprise operating in the commercial marketplace. But this is misleading, "for most of the big contractors operate as monopolies while the Pentagon is a monopsony, the sole customer. Competition is often artificial and does little to encourage quality, efficiency, or economy. For instance, the Navy can buy the F-18 only from McDonnell Douglas—or threaten, as it once did, to buy a different airplane from another company."[6] Pentagon officials say they occasionally find themselves with no place to turn.

Tensions also arise because military contractors must serve two contending masters: the Pentagon and taxpayers who want effective arms made at the lowest possible cost, and corporate shareholders who obviously want to make profits. Critics say that when these contending interests conflict, profits appear to take priority and the quality of arms suffers. All of this has led to a burgeoning staff of government inspectors who attempt to audit and measure manufacturers' efficiency and arms effectiveness.

How much defense spending is enough? A nation can never tell if defense expenditures are adequate until they are not—and then it is too late. Hence, when in doubt, the tendency is to spend more. Further, some of the best technical minds in the nation have been enticed into defense research and development work, and good minds can almost always come up with better, more expensive systems. The contracting structure of defense projects further escalates costs. It used to be that defense contracts operated on a cost-plus basis: A percentage of costs was designated as profits, to provide a direct incentive to decrease costs. Today (sometimes, but not always) contracts involve all costs plus a fixed fee, which provides little incentive to hold defense costs down.

The Defense Department spends approximately $300 billion a year. More than half the people employed by the national government work in the Defense Department. Nearly three-quarters of federal purchases of goods and services originate in the defense budget. Moreover, about 4000 defense installations are scattered across the country. Contracts in excess of $100 billion result in defense-related nongovernmental civilian employment of over 2 million. More than 1.5

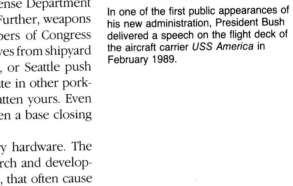

In one of the first public appearances of his new administration, President Bush delivered a speech on the flight deck of the aircraft carrier *USS America* in February 1989.

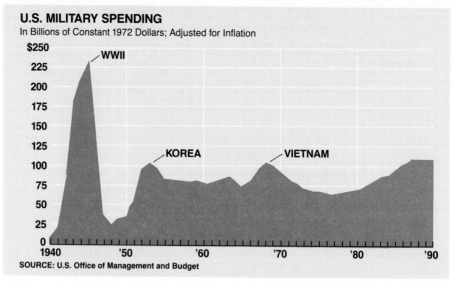

U.S. MILITARY SPENDING
In Billions of Constant 1972 Dollars; Adjusted for Inflation

SOURCE: U.S. Office of Management and Budget

million retired Defense Department personnel draw pensions and other fringe benefits. Clearly, the Defense Department's size and impact on our society raise questions about how it can be controlled.

According to the venerable foreign policy expert George Kennan, this vast flow of "military spending comes to constitute a vested interest on the part of all those who participate in it and benefit from it." The number of people who have a stake in the continuation of high defense spending is enormous, and their political punch is usually very powerful. "This includes not just the industrialists who get the money and the Pentagon purchasers who get the hardware and services," says Kennan, "but also all those who benefit from the arrangement in other ways: not only the uniformed personnel of the armed services but those who serve the Pentagon directly as civilian workers, and beyond them the many more who, as workers in defense plants or in other capacities, share in the spin-off from these vast expenditures."[7]

THE MILITARY-INDUSTRIAL COMPLEX

By its nature the defense industry is different from most other large industries in America. National defense is what economists call a "public good"; there is no way to exclude citizens from "consuming" national defense, whether they wish to pay for it or not. Thus, the government must provide for defense by taxing citizens. If it did not, most people would not pay, because they would figure they would receive the benefits anyway. Because the government is really the sole purchaser of defense, the defense industries—aerospace, electronics, and shipbuilding—rely heavily on government contracts for a large part of their business. In turn, the localities in which these industries are located, especially in the Sunbelt (Charleston, San Antonio, Colorado Springs, and San Diego, for example), rely heavily on defense spending for economic growth and stability. The defense industry is intertwined in the American economy; yet it responds to a different set of demands than other industries, and remains largely independent of private consumption and investment trends.

Critics sometimes charge that the military conspires with defense contractors and other strategic elites to maintain a vast network of bases and fleets around the world. They contend that the **military-industrial complex** has a life of its own, is too big to be managed or controlled, spends too large a share of our national wealth, and is dedicated to exaggerating the "Soviet menace."

Military leaders and many others generally deny the existence of a military-industrial complex. They point to the reduced size of the military and note that since its wartime peak in 1968, the number of military personnel has dropped from 3.5 million to about 2.2 million. Fewer people are in uniform now, they add, than at any time since 1950, and fewer U.S. troops are abroad than at any time since 1940. Furthermore, our active fleet has been reduced.

Even though we hear much about the military-industrial complex, it is not all-powerful, and it is not the only elite that operates in our democracy. There is also a scientific-intellectual elite, an agribusiness elite, a public employees elite, a trade union elite, and a number of other interest-group coalitions, all seeking to define the public interest.

Will U.S. Conventional Forces Be Strong Enough To Win?

Much of the debate over defense spending revolves around the question of *people* versus *weapons*. And central to this question is that of military personnel and their preparedness. We have to ask: If the country's army of volunteers has to go to war, could it fight and win, or would it be outnumbered and outfought?

THE ALL-VOLUNTEER FORCE

The means of maintaining our military forces have been debated since the beginning of the republic. As early as 1814 Daniel Webster asked his colleagues in Congress: "Where is it written in the Constitution . . . that you may take children from their parents, and parents from their children, and compel them to fight battles of any war in which the folly or the wickedness of government may engage it[self]?" The Constitution authorizes Congress to do what is "necessary and proper" in order to "raise and support armies," "to provide and maintain a navy," and "to provide for calling forth the militia." The problem is that America's role in the world has changed dramatically since 1789, as have our military needs. Although our boundaries once defined our national interest, our interests now reach around the globe.

Military conscription, or draft, was first instituted in 1862, during the Civil War. It was next used during World War I, when Congress passed the Selective Service Act. This act called for a draft of males between the ages of 21 and 30, although exemptions were allowed for certain public officials and for clergy. In both instances conscription ended when the conflicts ended. The first peacetime draft began in 1940, with the Selective Service and Training Act. By the time of Pearl Harbor in late 1941, men between the ages of 18 and 35 were eligible for the draft. When World War II ended, however, the draft continued, in various forms, for almost three decades. Soon after Vietnam, the all-volunteer force (AVF) was established by Congress. This force is to provide for our peacetime military personnel needs, although a draft would be reinstituted in time of war. Draft registration ended in 1975—to the delight of most young men—making the United States the first and only world power to maintain large-scale armed forces without some form of conscription.

Since its beginning, the all-volunteer force has been the center of controversy. Some experts contend the AVF has worked, that the quality and quantity of recruits

are as good or better than under the draft, and that the social costs are much lower. Other experts say quantity and quality have dropped; that the force is more and more made up of minorities or the disadvantaged, and that the AVF would be largely unable to defend our vital interests abroad.

Ten years ago, the military had problems attracting the desired number of recruits. All four services reported serious shortfalls; and active reserves were at only 80 percent strength. Furthermore, experienced personnel, physicians, technicians, and even pilots were in short supply in certain areas of the military. More recently, the nation has been running short of 18 year olds: the World War II baby boom is over; potential recruits in proportion to the total population are fewer than ever.

Total full-time, active personnel in all services is nearly 2.2 million. Minorities are overrepresented in the armed services, notably in the Army, where blacks comprise over 30 percent of the enlisted ranks (this sometimes gives rise to the contention that the all-volunteer force is becoming a mercenary army).[8] Women are underrepresented, although the proportion of women to men in the armed forces is growing.

The combat readiness of the AVF is the subject, understandably, of heated debate. Preparedness may be judged in part by the educational level of new recruits. About 80 percent of all new enlisted troops have graduated from high school, a higher level than the eligible pool. But maintaining this level requires extensive recruiting, and higher pay and fringe benefits. Another sign of overall troop quality, reenlistment, has also been reasonably good in recent years. Trends like these, of course, are often affected by economic conditions. High unemployment makes military service more attractive as compared to civilian employment; for many individuals it may actually be the only economically viable alternative. Long-term improvements such as higher pay and increased educational benefits are necessary to ensure the general strength and quality of the AVF.

Perhaps the most serious concern about the all-volunteer force is whether or not it is prepared for military combat. If there were a conflict requiring call-up of reserves and conscription, would we be able to produce enough combat-ready forces in time? Although some observers contend that conventional forces are obsolete in any large-scale conflict, such as a Soviet invasion of Europe, most insist we need conventional forces as a deterrent. The danger lies in becoming too reliant on "massive retaliation" and missiles, so that we would be forced to respond with nuclear weapons.[9]

THE POLITICS OF DRAFT REGISTRATION

The all-volunteer force was set up as a peacetime measure: If emergencies came, so would the draft. However, President Jimmy Carter won approval for the resumption of draft registration. Carter's original plan called for the registration of men and women within thirty days of their 18th birthdays. However, Congress refused to appropriate funds for the registration of women. Later the Supreme Court ruled Congress could, if it wished, call for the registration of men and not of women (this is the practice now).

Carter based his advocacy for registration on two grounds. First, in the wake of the then Soviet invasion of Afghanistan, registration would send a message to the Soviet Union demonstrating our resolve to resist Soviet aggression. Second, this new process would enable us to mobilize more quickly in wartime emergencies, by shortening the time period between initiation of conscription and full mobilization by as many as ninety days.

Some Americans opposed the draft registration process, because they believed it would inevitably lead to a draft. They also believed Carter was playing politics with this process and that it was entirely unneeded during peacetime. The Selective Service said registration would save less than two weeks in the event of mobilization. One political figure who spoke out against Carter's draft registration effort said it "destroys the very values that our society is committed to defending—namely our freedom."[10] That critic, Ronald Reagan, changed his mind once he got to the White House. And we still have the draft registration process. The Supreme Court has also upheld a law passed by Congress that makes male college students ineligible for federal scholarship aid if they have not registered for the draft.

SHOULD WE REVIVE THE DRAFT?

Some Americans favor substituting a draft for the present combination of volunteer enlistments and draft registration. Supporters of the draft generally include some conservatives, some members of the military establishment, such defense-conscious Democratic senators as Sam Nunn and Ernest Hollings, among others. They claim the armed services have not been able to attract an adequate number of recruits; those who do enlist, critics charge, are not sufficiently qualified to handle the modern, highly sophisticated weapons systems of today's armed forces. Further, supporters add, a draft would be much more equitable than the present system, correcting the disproportionately large minority membership in the services. Some draft advocates think the privilege of being an American justifies compulsory national service.

Another reason for returning to the draft is to lower defense spending. One of the largest single defense costs is for personnel. Also, as noted earlier, the declining number of teens in this era's pool of draftable males is another factor. But many Americans dispute the need for a draft—particularly the younger people most likely to be conscripted. Those opposed to the draft claim the all-volunteer force is working well. Not only can it fill its quotas, but the overall mental capability of its personnel is higher than that of conscripts. Also, draft opponents believe a peacetime draft contradicts the basic principles of liberty upon which America was founded.

WOMEN IN THE MILITARY

One of the more controversial questions today is whether women should join men in military combat. Women now comprise nearly 11 percent of the total enlistment in the armed forces. They graduate from military academies and they regularly move into many military jobs once reserved for men. And as the military becomes more mechanized and technical, the role of women may increase further. As one woman member of Congress put it, it doesn't take much muscle to launch an ICBM.

The rise of women in the military has not occurred without problems. Some males have refused to take orders from women officers. Some have refused to assign females to certain hazardous duties. In addition, at any given time about 5 percent of women in the military are pregnant. There have also been widespread complaints by women of sexual harassment. However, for many people the biggest problem is the question of women's role in combat. Women are currently excluded by law from combat duty in the Navy and Air Force. The Army and Marine Corps

These women found a career in the military and attended Officer Candidate School.

forbid the use of women in combat as a matter of established policy. The difficulty of course is in defining what is combat and what is not. Despite the legal and traditional barriers to the use of women in combat, some analysts say their large numbers and their increasing role in filling important positions make them destined to fight in any future war involving our military forces.

Women are destined to remain an integral part of our country's national defense. Although each of the four armed services currently has women serving as admirals and generals, women have generally not been allowed in those jobs that are critical for competitive promotion. This is slowly changing. And as long as the armed services continue to rely on volunteers to fill their personnel needs, they cannot afford to overlook such a major—indeed majority—demographic group. Women may face combat simply because it will be inescapable in wartime situations. Still, the country will have to undergo major changes in attitudes before large numbers of women are routinely used in combat situations. Meanwhile, the key to determining a proper role for women in the armed forces, a former secretary of defense has written, "is to move gradually toward expansion of the number of functions available to women, on a voluntary basis, and to insist that women accepted for such positions meet the same standards as the men who serve in them."[11]

Reorganizing for a More Effective Defense

Another major issue in recent years has been how to organize the Defense Department to ensure that it can provide both the strategic vision and the practical coordination between the military services that are necessary for maximum effectiveness. Congressional hearings, a presidential commission, and a shelf of books have focused on this problem during recent years. This has led to reorganization and new staffing patterns, especially in the Joint Chiefs of Staff.

To understand the current arrangements calls for a look at the organizational apparatus of defense policy making. The president, Congress, the National Security Council, and the State Department make overall policy and attempt to integrate our national security programs. But the day-to-day work of organizing for defense is the job of the Defense Department. The Pentagon, its headquarters, houses within its miles of corridors 25,000 top military and civilian personnel. The offices of several hundred generals and admirals are there, as is the office of the secretary of defense, symbolizing civilian control of the armed services.

Prior to 1947 there were two separate military departments, War and Navy. The difficulty of coordinating them during World War II led to demands for unification. In 1947 the Air Force, already an autonomous unit within the War Department, was made an independent unit. The three military departments—Army, Navy, and Air Force—were placed under the general supervision of the secretary of defense. The Unification Act of 1947 was a bundle of compromises between the Army, which favored a tightly integrated department, and the Navy, which wanted a loosely federated structure. It also reflected compromises between members of Congress who believed disunity and interservice rivalries were undermining our defense efforts, and those who feared that a unified defense establishment would defy civilian control and smother dissenting views. Unfortunately, all the act really accomplished was to bring the military services under a common organizational chart.

President Eisenhower felt strongly about the need to strengthen and centralize the Defense Department. Using his prestige as the victorious commander of the

Retired Air Force Lt. Gen. Brent Scowcroft, President Bush's national security advisor, held that post under President Ford and served as an advisor to Presidents Nixon, Carter, and Reagan.

CHAPTER 21 / Providing for the Common Defense

The Pentagon—headquarters for the Department of Defense and the Joint Chiefs of Staff. Built during World War II, the Pentagon is the world's largest office building. Constructed on swamps and landfill on the west bank of the Potomac River in northern Virginia, it has 20 miles of corridors. The Pentagon houses nearly 24,000 workers who tell time by 4200 clocks, drink water from 685 fountains, consume 30,000 cups of coffee daily, and place 200,000 phone calls a day on 87,000 phones connected by 100,000 miles of cable.

Allied Forces in World War II, he secured from Congress the Defense Department Reorganization Act. The act gave additional authority to the secretary of defense and the Joint Chiefs of Staff, especially its chair. But Congress continued to insist (and still does) that the appropriation of funds should be made directly to the specific services, even if it is funnelled to them through the office of the secretary of defense. Congress also insisted that the secretary of defense notify the House and Senate armed services committees when contemplating any major changes in combat functions. Congress also refused to repeal a provision, which Eisenhower called legalized insubordination, authorizing secretaries of a military department or members of the Joint Chiefs to make any recommendations they wish to Congress about Defense Department matters, even when their recommendations are contrary to department policy.

THE PROCUREMENT FRAUD SCANDAL

The great growth of defense spending in the 1980s fostered a get-rich-quick attitude among some defense contractors and defense consultants. At the heart of a 1988 government probe were "allegations that defense contractors spied on the Pentagon, on one another and even on other countries. They allegedly paid consultants to get classified information on program objectives, contract specifications, and their competitors' secret bids. Investigators say the consultants, often ex-Pentagon officials, sold access and brokered information to the highest bidder."[12]

The Pentagon probe of the cozy relationships between defense contractors and top Pentagon officials was quickly dubbed "Pentagate." Critics say that as military contracts became more lucrative some contractors began to do anything to win these contracts. The Defense Department awards at least $150 billion worth of contracts each year. It is also said the Defense Department's management was inefficient and the Justice Department's efforts to combat procurement abuses were similarly mismanaged.

The scandals became a campaign issue in the 1988 elections and numerous proposals for reorganizing the Pentagon and its procurement processes are still

You decide!

Do you favor a national program that would involve every young American around age 19 to serve the country for a year or two? Switzerland, Israel, and many European nations currently require a year or more of service to the nation. What are the pros and cons of such a proposed national service program? Should those who serve be entitled to subsidies for their higher education and reduced loans for their first homes? What incentives might be involved? Or would patriotism and altruism be motives enough? What are the policy and political implications?

(Answer/Discussion on page 559.)

BENEATH THE REVOLVING DOOR

PENTAGON

CONTRACTOR-PURCHASING TUNNEL

©1988 HERBLOCK

From Herblock at Large (Pantheon Books).

The Joint Chiefs of Staff in 1988 (left to right): General Alfred M. Gray, USMC, Admiral Carlisle A.H. Trost, USN, General Larry D. Welch, USAF, General Carl Edward Vuono, USA, Admiral William J. Crowe, USN, and General Robert T. Herres, USAF.

being debated in Congress and by Bush's Secretary of Defense Richard Cheney. Some members of Congress favor creating a "procurement czar" for all Pentagon acquisitions. Others urge stiff fines, long jail terms, and debarment from government contracts for those who violate existing bribery and bid-rigging laws.

THE CONFEDERATIONAL NATURE OF THE DEFENSE BUREAUCRACY

It is common to hear criticisms of the "Pentagon machine," the "national military establishment," or the "military mind." The defense bureaucracy is, however, best understood—as is any bureaucracy—as something less than a monolith. In practice, the Defense Department is comprised of four major components: (1) the Office of the Secretary of Defense and the civilians in the Department of Defense; (2) the organization of the Joint Chiefs of Staff; (3) the individual armed services (Army, Navy, Air Force, Marines); and (4) the intelligence community (Defense Intelligence Agency and National Security Agency).

Reflecting the fragmented nature of the larger American political system, defense policy is thrashed out in a day-to-day process of give and take among these constituent units in the Defense Department along with officials in the State Department, CIA, and the National Security Council at the White House. Insiders often stress that this policy-making structure is best thought of as a confederation or bargaining arena as opposed to a tight chain-of-command hierarchy. In fact, in recent years, a major issue has been the desirability of more centralized control and direction of the nation's defense bureaucracy.

MILITARY CHIEF OF STAFF: ESSENTIAL REFORM OR TOO MUCH CENTRALIZATION?

For decades there has been concern that the Joint Chiefs of Staff serve not to focus military planning but as an agency in which each military service chief defends his own service with the chair being so weak that little real leadership exists.

The Joint Chiefs of Staff (JCS) serve as the principal military advisers to the president, the National Security Council, and the secretary of defense. They include the military heads of the three armed services, the commandant of the Marine Corps, a chairman and a deputy chairman. The service chiefs are all appointed by the president with the consent of the Senate for four-year, nonrenewable terms. The chair of the JCS is appointed by the president with the consent of the Senate for a two-year term that may be renewed once.

The joint chiefs shape strategic plans, work out supply programs, review major supply and personnel requirements, formulate programs for training, make recommendations to the secretary of defense on the establishment of unified commands in strategic areas, and provide American representation on the military commissions of the United Nations, NATO, and the OAS.

The chair of the joint chiefs takes precedence over all other military officers. The chair presides over the meetings of the joint chiefs, prepares the agenda, directs the staff of some 400 officers in an overall JCS organization of about 2000 people, and informs the secretary of defense and the president of issues on which the joint chiefs have been unable to reach agreement.[13]

Disputes among military services involve more than professional jealousies. The technological revolution in warfare has rendered obsolete existing concepts

558

about military missions. In the past it made sense to divide command among land, sea, and air forces. Today technology makes a mockery of such distinctions. Defense research and development are constantly altering formerly established roles and missions. Yet the individual services are reluctant to give up their traditional functions, or to serve each others' crucial needs. The Navy, for example, is interested in waging sea warfare, not in running a freight service for the Army. Each branch supports weapons that bring it prestige. This often leads to such interservice rivalries as the Army and Air Force quarrel over who should provide air support for ground troops, and the Air Force and Navy dispute over land-versus sea-based missiles.

Sometimes interservice rivalries break out in Congress and the press. Organizations such as the Association of the United States Army, the Navy League, and the Air Force Association lobby openly on behalf of their particular services. Behind the scenes the military themselves are active. The president tries to keep interservice disputes inside the administration, but military commanders who believe administration policy threatens the national security have a problem. They are taught to respect civilian supremacy and to obey civilian superiors. But which civilian superiors? The president as commander in chief? Or should they report to Congress, which is also a civilian superior? A few officers resolve the dilemma of conflicting loyalties by resigning, so they can be free to carry their views to the nation. Sometimes military personnel who wish to dissent from official policy get their views to Congress by resorting to the Washington practice of "leaking" information to the press. And when testifying before congressional committees, officers can easily allow their views to come out especially when they are being questioned by members of Congress after they have given their formal, official views.

In 1982 former chair of the joint chiefs, General David Jones, called for strengthening the role of the chair of the JCS and increasing the organization's staff capability, and correspondingly reducing service involvement in joint actions. He also urged broadened training, experience, and rewards for officers assigned to JCS staff. He said service chairs are too often immobilized by their statesman-spokesman dilemma; that is, they are expected both to take the overall national view and also to remain advocates of their respective services. Jones believed the service chiefs were just too imbued with their services' traditions, doctrines, and disciplines to be objective about innovative proposals and needed military change.

Strategic defense policy, much like policy in any other area, is the result less of a collective process of rational inquiry than a mutual process of give and take. Whether strategic policies are worked out within the Defense Department, the White House, or Congress, the decisions result from a political process in which some measure of consensus is essential. And some conflict among the participants is not necessarily evil. The joint chiefs engage in the same type of logrolling tactics used in Congress. On budget issues they very often endorse all the programs desired by each service. When forced to choose on an issue of policy, the chiefs have traditionally compromised among the different service positions rather than attempt to develop a position based on a unified military point of view.

RESTRUCTURING THE JOINT CHIEFS OF STAFF

Before 1986 the Joint Chiefs of Staff were, collectively, all powerful. Together they advised the president and the secretary of defense. Because they functioned as a committee and could not act until they reached unanimous agreement, they

"No, no. When I say this new secret weapon can slip past their defenses undetected, I'm not referring to the Russians, I'm referring to Congress."

Drawing by Stevenson; © 1986 The New Yorker Magazine, Inc.

Answer/Discussion

Several members of Congress, including Senators Sam Nunn and James McCain, have introduced legislation calling for a system that would induce all males (some proposals include women too) to serve their nation for a year or two in exchange for educational grants for college education and favorable loan arrangements for buying a first home.

National polls indicate strong support for the concept of national service for everyone at some point in the young-adult period. Libertarians strenuously object to this as involuntary servitude. Others complain that it would be a mammoth "make work" project, even as they applaud the idea that people be encouraged to serve their country in either the military, the Peace Corps, or some domestic VISTA-type of community service.

President Bush proposed a limited YES (youth entering service) concept that would be largely financed and run by private sector charities and foundations. Some form of pilot project is likely to be funded by Congress in the early 1990s to test these concepts, but it is highly unlikely that a compulsory system of national service will be approved in the near future.

The debate over this proposal has promoted an excellent dialogue among educators and public officials.

For an in-depth analysis of many of these proposals, see Charles Moscos, *A Call to Civic Service* (Free Press, 1989).

often produced overly broad decisions. Critics viewed much of their work as wasteful, useless, and even dangerous.

The Department of Defense Reorganization Act of 1986, spearheaded by Senator Barry Goldwater, sought to change all that. This legislation, passed and signed into law in 1986, shifted considerable power to the chairman. Reporting through the secretary of defense, the chairman advises the president on military matters, exercises authority over the forces in the field, and is responsible for overall military planning. In theory, the chairman of the joint chiefs can even make a military decision if the chiefs of the other services oppose it. On paper at least, these other chiefs now serve the chairman merely as advisers, and even the chairman's deputy outranks the other service chiefs. The Reorganization Act of 1986 also strengthened the powers of the theater commanders who actually command forces in various parts of the world. It gave the chairman a mandate to encourage "jointness in military education and in other spheres to integrate the services for maximum effectiveness."

All of this made Admiral William J. Crowe, Jr., chairman of the joint chiefs in the late 1980s, the most powerful peacetime military officer in U.S. history.[14] The challenge for Crowe's successor, General Colin Powell, will be to make and enforce decisions that facilitate sensible coordination but do not prevent useful competition among the services. The clear goal is to overcome waste and provide the necessary cooperation for effective joint operations from the level of the Joint Chiefs of Staff down to field commanders in emergency situations.

In 1989 General Colin L. Powell was named Chairman of the Joint Chiefs of Staff by President Bush, an appointment that made him the first black officer to hold the nation's highest military post.

Arms Buildup and Arms Control

For centuries people have dreamed of a world in which conflicts could be resolved without force. However, as long as the United States exists in a world of sovereign, independent nations, it will look to its own defenses. Few Americans pay much attention to Soviet proposals to eliminate all nuclear weapons, even though many Americans wish that this could be achieved.

For the foreseeable future, as in the recent past, a reliance on the policy of deterrence (mutual assured destruction), despite its unappealing aspects, appears to be the policy America will employ. The Strategic Defense Initiative will take at least ten or fifteen years to develop an effective population defense, if one can be developed at all. Bush and his chief advisors have placed less emphasis on the Star Wars approach than did President Reagan. A more limited missile defense system intended to protect our retaliatory forces now has more support. Whatever the developments in the controversial Star Wars program, current deterrence programs would appear to be the future policy as well.

The Stealth bomber, the most expensive military aircraft ever built. A battle between Congress and the military erupted in 1989 over continued funding for this multibillion dollar project.

The buildup in the U.S. arsenal of weapons has been impressive in recent years. In fact the Reagan administration presided over the biggest peacetime military buildup in American history, although it is impossible to know if this buildup made the United States more secure. It is not clear, moreover, if this buildup can be maintained as it appears that defense spending will not increase at all during Bush's first term. The Army has 5000 M-1 tanks; a major new armored personnel carrier, the M-2 Bradley infantry vehicle; a new rocket artillery system; new helicopters, and air defense missiles. The Air Force, after years of on-again, off-again politics, finally has 100 B-1 bombers, more than 300 new F-15 fighter planes, and 1000 additional F-16 planes. Now it has the long-awaited Stealth aircraft that experts claim will make both our B-1 and Russian defenses for missiles obsolete. The Stealth bomber is shaped like a sting ray; it has a flying wing without the usual tubelike fuselage, to present minimal reflecting surfaces to searching radars. The Navy has sixty-five or more new combat surface vessels, about twenty-five new attack submarines, and more on the way.

The history of the MX missile illustrates how weapons policy is made today. Domestic, political, and technical considerations are often as important as national security needs, as the following suggests:

An MX missile is a large, multiple-warhead, extremely accurate nuclear weapon. The idea for an MX-type ICBM (Inter-Continental Ballistic Missile) arose in the 1960s. The original purpose of the MX was to fill a perceived need on the part of the United States to maintain a land-based missile capable of surviving an attack by the Soviet Union. In addition, the MX was meant to give the United States, for the first time, the ability to threaten large numbers of Soviet land-based missiles. The combination of these two factors, it was expected, would deter the USSR from launching a nuclear attack.

President Carter's MX plan called for deployment of the missiles on a so-called "race track" in Utah and Nevada. Each missile was to have its own fifteen-mile roadway loop connecting twenty-three separate concrete launching points. The missiles were to be intermittently shuffled from one launching point to another in order to keep the Soviets guessing as to their whereabouts. The plan was later abandoned in part because of widespread political opposition in Utah and Nevada. (One wag suggested that we merely put the MX on Amtrak trains. That way neither the USSR nor the United States would know where the MX missiles were—even with a schedule!)

President Reagan proposed placing 100 missiles in rows of two and three stretching in a fourteen-mile column. The theory behind this "dense pack" proposal was that a Soviet weapon detonating above an MX silo would destroy other incoming nuclear weapons before they reached their targets. The United States would then be able to launch the remaining MX missiles in retaliation. The dense pack proposal was rejected by Congress.

Reagan then appointed a blue-ribbon panel to try to break the political deadlock caused by congressional opposition to the various MX plans. It recommended, among other things, that the United States temporarily deploy 100 MX missiles in currently existing Minutemen missile silos. The commission also advised the United States to develop an unspecified number of smaller, single-warhead missiles to anchor America's long-term land-based defense.

Many of these recommendations were far-reaching in their implications. For example, they meant the entire complexion of U.S.-USSR arms control talks would have to be changed. Currently the two countries count missiles and missile launchers to determine each other's relative strength for arms control purposes. This system encourages both nations to build multiple-warhead missiles. Reagan's advisers also suggested that the United States eventually abandon large, multiple-warhead weapons in favor of small-warhead weapons. This led to a call for new arms control agreements to negotiate and redefine the acceptable strength of nuclear forces.

Predictably, the new MX plan generated opposition. Several senators and two former CIA directors said it would mean an escalation of the arms race. Former CIA director William Colby added that the MX would be considered by the Soviets as an offensive first-strike weapon, and hence it would send a dangerous message. Others claim that deploying the MX in existing Minutemen silos would render the missiles too vulnerable.

Although the MX won congressional approval, it did so by only slender majorities. And opponents of the MX did win commitments from Reagan to adjust his arms control negotiating strategy and to deploy a single-warhead missile system.

A launch of the "Peacekeeper" ICBM.

Richard Nixon and Leonid Brezhnev after signing a 1972 agreement to limit offensive nuclear arms.

Opposition to the costly MX program reappeared in the 1984 appropriations process, and the 1984 Democratic platform called for ending its production. But Reagan forged ahead, and the placing of MX missiles in silos began. Congress authorized fifty of them.

Even in 1990, Congress, the president, and the defense policy experts continue to debate how many and what kind of MX missiles to build, and where to put them. Some say we need bigger missiles with more warheads; others say it all costs too much. Others fear all of the systems are less stabilizing and less mobile than once promised, and less and less able to sustain widespread congressional support. Retired Air Force Lt. General Brent Scowcroft, now Bush's National Security Advisor, complained in 1986 that the MX had been decimated by compromises and budget cuts. We have spent a lot of money, he said, but haven't got a thing to show for it. Pentagon leaders now want to take fifty MX missiles out of silos and put them on rail cars. This may be done by 1992, if Congress can be persuaded.

U.S.-SOVIET ARMS NEGOTIATIONS

Proponents of arms control say the arms race itself is a fundamental cause of international tension. They warn of the immense risks of the deterrence system: human errors, failures in the warning network, growing risk of preemptive attack due to adoption of counterforce strategies, and breakdown of safeguards against nuclear proliferation. But they paint an even grimmer picture of a future without arms control: heightened tension as the result of the development of more devastating nuclear warheads and longer-ranged, more accurate delivery vehicles; threats of biological, chemical, and neutron-radiation weapons; constant surveillance by spy satellites; and ever-increasing defense budgets and commitments of human resources to weapons technology.

Some substantial arms control agreements already exist among the major world powers. As outlined in the following paragraphs, several treaties have been negotiated—some among several nations and a few between the United States and the USSR. *Disarmamemt* refers to actually reducing arms. *Arms control* refers to monitoring, mutually excluding certain weapons, requiring notification, imposing common ceilings that require no reduction, and similar agreements. Arms control strives to reduce the likelihood of war, to reduce the cost of defense, and to reduce the damage if war should occur.

A brief look at some past negotiations suggests the kinds of arms control efforts that may be possible in the future. In 1963 the United Kingdom, the Soviet Union, and the United States agreed on a treaty to ban nuclear explosions in the atmosphere or in any other place where there was danger of radioactive debris. The treaty permits nations to test underground and has an escape clause allowing any signer to withdraw on three months' notice. Its ratification by the United States and the Soviet Union, and the subsequent adherence to it by more than 100 nations, was viewed as a first step toward nuclear disarmament.

The test-ban treaty was followed in 1967 by the International Treaty on the Peaceful Uses of Outer Space, which bans the use of satellites as vehicles or platforms for launching nuclear weapons. In 1968 came the **Nonproliferation Treaty,** which pledges the nuclear powers not to disseminate nuclear devices to nonnuclear powers for at least twenty-five years, and the nonnuclear nations not to seek to acquire such devices.

The first **SALT (Strategic Arms Limitations Treaty)** agreement was signed by President Nixon and Leonid Brezhnev in May 1972. In this treaty the United States sought to place a freeze on the Soviets for five years, the time needed for the United States to catch up by developing the Trident submarine, MX missile, cruise missile, and B-1 bomber. SALT I was criticized by some people for giving the Soviets a considerable advantage both in numbers and megatonnage, but Henry Kissinger defended the treaty as freezing an inequality "we inherited" in order to gain time to reverse the situation.

In October 1974 President Gerald Ford met with Brezhnev in Vladivostok to decide in principle the general outline of SALT II accords. These accords set a limit on the number of offensive delivery vehicles (2400), and a sublimit on the number of launchers of strategic missiles equipped with multiple independently targetable reentry vehicles (MIRVs). No limits were to be placed on such other weapons as the cruise missiles, backfire planes, or strategic space defense systems. However, both sides soon decided that SALT II should place further limits on each other's new weapons, while not hindering their own weapons development. American cruise missiles and the Soviet backfire plane became the center of this controversy.

The Carter administration proposed that SALT II also put limits on "throw-weight" (the weight of the useful payload of the missile) and MIRVs, but this was met with strong Soviet opposition. As the SALT II agreements eventually took shape, it became apparent that they would have only a minimal effect on curbing the arms race. Carter was unsuccessful in winning Senate approval for SALT II. In any event, debate on SALT II was abruptly suspended in 1980 because of Soviet intervention in Afghanistan. Although the SALT II treaty was never ratified, the United States and the Soviet Union both agreed to stay within the limits spelled out in the treaty as long as the other side continued to do so. And to a large extent both sides did.

Jimmy Carter and Leonid Brezhnev exchange signed copies of the SALT II treaty in Vienna, June 18, 1979.

UNITED STATES–USSR INF TREATY—1988

At their fourth summit meeting over a three-year period Ronald Reagan and Mikhail Gorbachev signed a special agreement in 1988 reducing certain intermediate nuclear forces. The celebrated Intermediate Nuclear Forces (INF) treaty eliminated only a modest fraction of the world's nuclear stockpile, yet it sent an important signal to the world and perhaps has ushered in a new period of "realistic engagement" between the world's two superpowers. It represents the first time two superpowers have been able to agree on abolishing weapons rather than merely limiting their growth.

The INF treaty also provided for on-site inspection by the two military rivals, and both nations agreed to scrap many of their medium- and shorter-range missiles. Reagan, Bush, and other administration officials hailed this as a breakthrough in Soviet-American relations and argued that their defense buildup in the mid-1980s had allowed this small step in the direction of arms reduction to take place.

Critics of the INF treaty worry that reducing American medium- and short-range missiles in Europe without substantially keeping up our conventional forces there will reduce the credibility of NATO as a deterrent. Critics in Germany worry too that we may be leaving them to have a war fought in their area:

William Crowe, former chairman of the Joint Chiefs of Staff, and Sergei Akhromeyev, Chief of the General Staff of the Soviet Union, discuss their nations' military planning.

> The reasoning is as simple as it is critical. A war that is confined to Europe is one that might just happen. A war that is global will not happen, since it would destroy the superpowers along with Europe. Safety, then, has always consisted in the assurance of a common fate. But the INF agreement raises the distinct possibility that Europe—and, above all, Germany—may now have a separate fate.[15]

Despite extensive debate in the U.S. Senate, the United States ratified the INF treaty and a new engagement was set in motion. Gorbachev and Reagan won widespread praise for this diplomatic achievement. Strategic Arms Reduction Talks (START) continue between the two nations, yet there are sharp differences over how to restrict sea-launched cruise missiles, an area where the United States has a decided advantage it is unwilling to give up. Those talks are likely to go on for some time.

Security and Liberty: Not by Force Alone

What should be the role of the military in a democratic society? Although Americans have reasonably high confidence in the military, fear of the abuse of military force is deeply rooted in the American tradition. And the unpopularity of the Vietnam War, together with the belief that vast military expenditures are giving undue influence to the military and their allies in the industrial community, arouse concern about how to ensure civilian control over the so-called military-industrial complex.

The framers of 1787, recognizing that military domination is incompatible with free government, wove into the Constitution several precautions. The president, an elected official, is the commander in chief of the armed forces; with the Senate's consent the chief executive commissions all officers. No clear separation exists between military and civilian spheres of activity. In many cases the military decides what information must remain top secret. Members of Congress and the general public are thus sometimes at a disadvantage. With a large standing army and complicated intelligence and weapons systems invariably also come increased centralization of power and responsibility in the executive. A nation preoccupied with defense is sometimes tempted to suppress dissent and to label critics as unpatriotic or subversive.

Many members of Congress have tried to carve out an independent and thoughtful role in defense policy matters. Indicative is the Military Reform Caucus in the Congress, a bipartisan discussion forum that has brought together members and senators for the purpose of rethinking military budgets, programs, and priorities. Not long ago it was said, only partly with tongue in cheek, that most members of Congress couldn't care less about weapons systems and that most viewed the defense budget in terms of real estate and pork-barrel considerations that affected their home districts. Today this view is less persuasive. Military reformers in Congress stress the need for alternative defense priorities and programs and for a more generalist perspective in defense management.

This group endorses the changes in the Joint Chiefs of Staff discussed above. They urge reforming officer education and review of military doctrines, tactics, and force structures. Many of them call for a Navy rebuilt around the submarine rather than the aircraft carrier. They suggest the Air Force's primary purpose should be shifted from its preoccupation with winning through air power to greater support for the ground troops.

National debates about the military budget, deterrence strategies, missile defense systems, weapons systems, arms control, procurement processes, and force levels are commonplace in American politics, as they should be. The objectives of an ever more effective, yet ever more efficient, military-preparedness effort will guide these debates. Everyone recognizes, however, that true national security lies in something considerably more than troops and weapons. Still, providing for the nation's defense is recognized by almost everyone as a first requirement that must be satisfied before the nation can go about its other business.

CHAPTER 21 / Providing for the Common Defense

Summary

1. Providing for the nation's defense is one of the fundamental functions of the national government. Yet it is also one of the most costly and controversial functions. Nearly everything the nation's military does becomes enmeshed in politics—as it should.

2. Americans are often bewildered by the complicated weapons systems and the almost foreign language of U.S. defense strategies and military appropriations debates. The prevailing attitude of Americans toward defense spending and the military establishment is one of modified support. But we want to prevent war. We want military strength that will help achieve our foreign policy objectives. We are also concerned about the high cost of arms and the possibility of either a nuclear war or nuclear proliferation that some day will lead to war.

3. Our system is designed to provide civilian control over the military. This is always a challenge; presidents, Congress, and the secretaries of defense must weigh national security against competing claims. Although the military in any society has enormous potential for direct political involvement, this has not occurred in the United States.

4. Americans today are concerned about military preparedness and strength. Yet they are equally concerned with arms control and reducing the threat of a nuclear war. Even though military power alone may not guarantee international stability, it is generally viewed as a necessary condition for it. Americans are also optimistic that the Bush administration can continue to cut defense spending as the U.S., the Soviets, and Europe reduce the possibility of World War III.

Further Reading

JAMES FALLOWS. *National Defense* (Random House, 1981).

JACQUES GAMSLER. *Affording Defense* (MIT Press 1989).

ARTHUR T. HADLEY. *The Straw Giant, Triumph and Failure: America's Armed Services* (Random House, 1986).

ROBERT JERVIS. *The Illogic of American Nuclear Strategy* (Cornell University Press, 1984).

WILLIAM W. KAUFMAN. *A Reasonable Defense* (Brookings Institution, 1986).

PAUL KENNEDY. *The Rise and Fall of Great Powers* (Random House, 1987).

NICK KOTZ. *Wild Blue Yonder: Money, Politics and the B-1 Bomber* (Pantheon, 1988).

EDWARD N. LUTTWAK. *The Pentagon and the Art of War* (Simon & Schuster, 1985).

ROBERT S. MCNAMARA. *Out of the Cold* (Simon & Schuster, 1989).

ALLAN R. MILLETT, et al. *The Reorganization of the Joint Chiefs of Staff* (Pergamon-Brassey, 1986).

CHARLES C. MOSCOS. *A Call to Civic Service* (Free Press, 1989).

JOHN MUELLER. *Retreat from Doomsday: The Obsolescence of Major War* (Basic Books, 1989).

JEFFREY RECORD. *Revising U. S. Military Strategy: Tailoring Means to Ends* (Pergamon, 1984).

Notes

1. Caspar W. Weinberger, "U.S. Defense Strategy," *Foreign Affairs* (Spring 1986), p. 677.

2. Ronald Reagan, March 23, 1983, address.

3. This summary of points is adapted from Jeffrey Boutwell and F. A. Long, "The SDI and U.S. Security," in Franklin A. Long et al., eds., *Weapons in Space* (Norton, 1986), pp. 297–99. For other appraisals of the SDI-Star Wars proposal, see Keith B. Payne, *Strategic Defense: "Star Wars" in Perspective* (Hamilton Press, 1986); Gary L. Guertner and Donald M. Snow, *The Last Frontier: An Analysis of the Strategic Defense Initiative* (Lexington Books, 1986); and Union of Concerned Scientists, *The Fallacy of Star Wars* (Vintage, 1984).

4. See, for example, Edward N. Luttwak, *The Pentagon and the Art of War* (Simon & Schuster, 1985); Gary Hart and William Lind, *America Can Win* (Adler and Adler, 1986); and Arthur T. Hadley, *The Straw Giant* (Random House, 1986).

5. Richard Halloran, "Making Arms Makers Do It Right," *The New York Times* (June 15, 1986), p. F4.

6. Ibid.

7. George F. Kennan, *The Cloud of Danger* (Atlantic-Little, Brown, 1977), p. 13. See also Adam Yarmolinsky, *The Military Establishment* (Harper & Row, 1971).

8. But see Charles C. Moskos, "Success Story: Blacks in the Army," *The Atlantic Monthly* (May 1986), pp. 64–72.

9. William Bowman et al., eds., *The All-Volunteer Force After a Decade* (Pergamon Press, 1986).

10. Ronald Reagan, quoted in Stuart Taylor, Jr., "Draft Registration: Snags Emerge in Prosecutions," *The New York Times* (December 8, 1982), p. 10.

11. Harold Brown, *Thinking About National Security* (Westview, 1983), p. 253. See also the heated debate on women in the military, *USA Today* (January 6, 1988), opinion page, p. 10A.

12. "We've Got Some of These Guys Dead to Rights," *Business Week* (July 4, 1988), p. 31.

13. A dated but still useful study of the operations of the JCS is Lawrence J. Korb, *The Joint Chiefs of Staff: The First Twenty-five Years* (Indiana University Press, 1976).

14. See Arthur T. Hadley, "In Command," *New York Times Magazine* (August 7, 1988), pp. 19–22. See also Allan R. Millett, et al., *The Reorganization of the Joint Chiefs of Staff: A Critical Analysis* (Pergamon-Brassey, 1986).

15. Robert W. Tucker, "The INF Debate: The NOs Have It," *The National Interest* (Winter 1987/88), p. 116. But see also Richard Betts, "NATO's Mid-Life Crisis," *Foreign Affairs* (Spring 1989), pp. 37–52.

22

Making Economic and Social Policy

Our economy is primarily based on the principle that businesses, farms, and individuals are better qualified than government to decide how to produce income and how to spend it. Yet the existence of a large array of government subsidies, tax incentives, and regulations (such as those discussed in the next chapter) attests to the government's involvement as a shaper of economic and welfare policies.

All kinds of individuals and corporations benefit from government **subsidies.** Welfare programs for the needy may be the most publicized government assistance efforts, but "it is probably safe to assume that the preponderance of the benefits of many programs is garnered by profitable corporations and citizens in the top half of the nation's income distribution."[1]

How and when to use public funds to accomplish public purposes generates considerable disagreement. Conservatives say we need more economy in government and less government in the economy. Federal social welfare programs, they argue, are "giveaway programs" that undermine the values that made this nation great—the work ethic, family responsibility, and frugality. They advise us to cut back federal spending to avoid inflation and secure balanced budgets. Liberals respond that federal programs work, and that charges that federal programs are ineffective are based on ideological myths, not analytical facts. Moreover, they point out that it was conservative Reaganomics that gave us our huge federal deficits.[2]

The Politics of Taxation and Spending

Big government is expensive. Today federal, state, and local governments spend sums of money equal to about a third of the income of all Americans. The national government is the biggest spender of all. In recent years Washington has distributed more than all state and local governments combined. With tax collections of $1.06 trillion and a national budget of well over $1.1 trillion for 1990, our national government spends 23 percent of the gross national product (GNP), or nearly one dollar out of every four. We now have a national debt of over a trillion dollars, and we must pay more than $170 billion just for the interest payments on that debt.

Where does all this money come from? The federal government gets most of its funds from taxes. Other monies come from loans, special fees and fines, grants and gifts, and from administrative and commercial revenues. Despite these other sources most federal revenue is derived from personal and corporate income taxes and social insurance or payroll taxes. "In this world," Benjamin Franklin once said, "nothing is certain but death and taxes." Tax collecting is one of the oldest activities of government. Putting power over taxation into the hands of the people was a major achievement in the development of self-government. "No taxation without representation" has been a battle cry of people the world over.

The Constitution clearly provides that Congress "shall have power to lay and collect taxes, duties, imposts, and excises." But duties and **excise taxes** have to be levied *uniformly* throughout the United States; direct taxes have to be *apportioned among the states* according to population; and no tax can be levied on articles exported from any state. Except during the Civil War, for a century the federal government relied on the tariff for most of its revenue. This hidden tax, which many people mistakenly thought to be a tax on foreigners, fluctuated with the rise and fall of trade and tariff levels. Congress supplemented these taxes with excise taxes on the manufacture or sale of certain goods. In 1894 an income tax law was enacted (such a tax had been used during the Civil War but was given up shortly afterward). The 1894 tax was not drastic—only 2 percent on all income over $4,000. One opponent of the bill scorned it on the floor of the Senate as "an attempt to array the rich against the poor, the poor against the rich . . . Socialism, communism, *devilism*." The next year, the Supreme Court declared the tax unconstitutional on the grounds that it was a direct tax and therefore had to be apportioned among the states according to population.[3]

About twenty years later, in 1913, the Sixteenth Amendment was adopted. It authorized Congress "to lay and collect taxes on incomes, from whatever source derived, without apportionment among the several States, and without regard to any census or enumeration."[4]

Raising money is only one important objective of taxation. Regulating and, more recently, promoting economic growth are others. (We discuss taxation as a device to promote economic growth later.) In a broad sense all taxation regulates human behavior. A graduated income tax, for example, has a leveling tendency on incomes, and a tariff act affects foreign trade. Congress has used its taxing power to prevent or regulate certain practices. Years ago Congress, for instance, laid a 10 percent tax on the circulation of notes by state banks, which put an immediate end to such issues. In the Fiscal Budget for 1990 federal taxes include the following:

1. *Income taxes on individuals.* Taxes on individuals' incomes account for about 41 percent of the federal government's tax revenue. Over the years the income tax has grown increasingly complex, as Congress has responded to claims for differing kinds of exemptions and rates. But the tax has one great advantage in its flexibility: The schedule of rates can be raised or lowered in order to stimulate or restrain economic activity. The income tax is moderately progressive. People with high incomes generally pay larger

Tariffs as Taxes

Much debate exists over whether we should impose or raise tariffs on imported products such as steel and automobiles. Sometimes people say we should impose tariffs because foreign governments subsidize certain export industries which gives them a competitive advantage in international markets. Opponents of tariffs typically defend the importance of maintaining free international markets. It is important to realize a tariff is a tax on U.S. consumers. It is an additional cost to foreign producers of goods consumed in this nation. The additional cost is almost always passed on to consumers in the form of higher prices for both imported and domestically produced products. By imposing a tariff on imported goods, the United States is merely raising the prices on these goods.

fractions of their income than people with lower incomes, though many of the wealthy benefit from tax loopholes.[5] Despite recent efforts at tax reform, according to a Congressional Budget Office study, only the top 10 percent of the population received a significant net tax cut between 1977 and 1988; most of the other 90 percent paid a higher share of their income to Washington. At the extremes, the richest 1 percent received a net tax savings of 25 percent while the poorest tenth of workers saw 20 percent more of their incomes disappear into taxes.[6]

2. *Income taxes on corporations.* These account for 10 percent of the national government's tax revenues. As late as 1942 corporate income taxes amounted to more than individual income taxes, but returns from the latter increased more rapidly during World War II. Despite recent reforms in the tax code it is still possible for many of the nation's largest corporations to get away without paying any taxes on an annual basis.

3. *Social insurance or payroll taxes.* This is the second largest and most rapidly rising source of federal revenue, accounting for approximately 34 percent of all federal revenue. From a mere $4 billion in 1950, this tax raised over $360 billion in fiscal year 1990. These monies are collected mainly from payroll deductions to finance social security and other insurance programs. As economists point out, these taxes are highly regressive (see next section). Low-income people generally pay larger fractions of their income than do high-income people.

4. *Excise taxes.* These taxes account for 3 percent of federal revenue. Federal taxes on liquor, tobacco, gasoline, telephones, air travel, and other so-called luxury items totalled about $32 billion in 1990.

5. *Customs duties.* Although no longer the main source of federal income, in recent years these taxes provided an annual yield of more than $17 billion.

THE POLITICS OF TAXATION

Most of us complain our tax load is too heavy and someone else is not carrying a fair share. People with high incomes who are in the highest tax brackets naturally grumble. Low-income people point out that even a low tax may deprive them of the necessities of life. People in the middle-income brackets consider their situation the worst of all—their incomes are not high, but their taxes are.

What is the best type of tax? Some say the *graduated income tax*: It is relatively easy to collect, hits hardest those who are most able to pay, and hardly touches those at the bottom of the income ladder. Others say **excise taxes** are the fairest, because they are paid by people who are spending money for luxury goods and who thus obviously have money to spare. Further, by discouraging people from buying expensive goods, excise taxes sometimes have a deflationary effect in times of rising prices. On the other hand, excise taxes are more expensive to collect than income taxes. In some cases, moreover, such as the tax on tobacco, they may hit the poor the hardest. Excise taxes also face strong resistance from affected industries: tobacco, liquor, and airlines, for example.

Most controversial is the general **sales tax,** which is levied against the sales of all goods. Labor and liberal organizations call this form of tax **regressive** because lower-income citizens pay a higher proportion of their income in tax revenues than higher-income citizens. Proponents of the sales tax stress its potential antiinflationary effect and point to its successful use in a number of states.

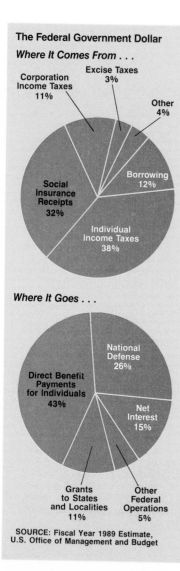

The Federal Government Dollar

Where It Comes From . . .

Corporation Income Taxes 11%
Excise Taxes 3%
Other 4%
Borrowing 12%
Individual Income Taxes 38%
Social Insurance Receipts 32%

Where It Goes . . .

National Defense 26%
Direct Benefit Payments for Individuals 43%
Net Interest 15%
Grants to States and Localities 11%
Other Federal Operations 5%

SOURCE: Fiscal Year 1989 Estimate, U.S. Office of Management and Budget

Talk of tax reform takes place every few years as people complain, usually with justification, that our tax system is unfair and confusing and that it is not doing what it is supposed to do. One of those years was 1986. After some major political battles Congress, as a result, enacted, and the president signed into law, a new tax system that brought more changes to the tax code than any in the previous seventy years.

Ideally, the function of tax legislation is to decide who shall pay how much to finance government spending. In practice, however, tax legislation over the years has also sought to promote economic growth of various kinds and to reward certain types of behavior, such as owning a home, contributing to charities, and investing in high-risk but desirable (from a national standpoint) energy or housing ventures. Cynics suggest too that from a member of Congress's point of view, tax legislation has the additional and important function of raising campaign funds. As long as tax legislation is under consideration in Congress, swarms of lobbyists are eager to attend expensive campaign dinners and to contribute generously to campaign coffers.[7]

Senator Bill Bradley (D-New Jersey) and President Reagan were among those who encouraged Congress to take on both the tax code and the vast number of interests who benefit from the scores of loopholes and tax preferences that were built into the pre-1987 tax system. In the early 1980s Senator Bradley began to build support in Congress and across the country for tax code changes that included lowering rates and eliminating most itemized tax deductions. Bradley understood that a growing number of Americans were upset by their lack of faith in and their inability to understand the United States tax process. For example, most middle-income people believed they paid more in taxes than many of their wealthy neighbors. He learned that citizens resented the thick hard-to-read book of tax instructions that arrives at tax time each year. "It's unfair. It's overly complex. It's distorting investment decisions," wrote Bradley, "encouraging people to put money into schemes to reduce their tax bills instead of enterprises to create jobs and to help our economy grow."[8]

Bradley and other supporters of tax reform urged dropping the tax rates from about fifteen categories to two or three. Even though the overall tax rates would come down, the taxable income base could be increased by the elimination of most existing tax deductions, or what is technically called tax expenditures. **Tax expenditures** are government revenue losses due to provisions of the federal tax laws that provide special tax incentives or benefits to individuals and businesses. These benefits, which totaled over $550 billion in the mid-1980s, arose from special exclusions, exemptions, or reductions from gross income, or from special credits, preferential tax rates, or deferrals of tax liability. Tax expenditures are so designated because they are one means by which the national government carries out public policy objectives. In most cases, they can be considered as an alternative to a direct-spending program. For example, investment in research and development is encouraged by allowing such costs to be deducted from a company's taxes. A program of direct federal grants could also achieve this objective.

Critics have often said that the rich got their welfare through these tax loopholes or tax expenditure schemes and that these get placed in the tax code more easily by members of Congress because they are not officially expenditures. In effect, however meritorious the objective they are encouraging, these tax benefits are a cost to government and cause a shortfall in revenues. They also have the

U.S. Tax Milestones

1989	Tax receipts total over $1 trillion.
1986	Tax reform enacted.
1983	Collection reaches about $600 billion.
1981	Inflation boosts collections to $407 billion; tax per capita $2687.
1950	Collections at $28 billion; tax per capita at $256.
1945	Wartime collections passed $43 billion.
1943	Withholding introduced.
1918	First $1 billion income tax collection.
1913	Income tax legalized by the Sixteenth Amendment.
1895	Income tax declared unconstitutional.
1894	Income tax revived.
1872	Tax discontinued. Most revenue raised by taxing liquor and tobacco.
1862	First income tax to support Civil War.
Prior to 1862	The government only taxed imports, slaves, and certain manufactured goods.

effect of providing benefits to the already financially advantaged. In many instances, they have also caused investors to waste resources on low-yield investments that carry large tax benefits; high-yield investments without such benefits, meanwhile, go unfunded. "The result is reduced national output, lower productivity, and sluggish economic growth."[9]

Tax reformers who advocated the flat tax or lower tax rates, or mere simplification of the tax code, came from all political persuasions. They believed the tax code of the recent past was no longer a progressive tax in that people of wealth could and did (with the help of their accountants and tax lawyers) significantly lower their tax brackets by taking advantage of many tax-expenditure or tax-shelter programs. Most tax reformers also believed tax rates were just too high and they were encouraging widespread tax cheating. According to even the Internal Revenue Service, nearly 19 percent of all taxes owed on legitimate earnings go uncollected.

The 1986 tax-reform package, though spurred on by Bradley's long-term advocacy and by Reagan's general endorsement, became a bipartisan effort in both houses of Congress. Tax "reformers" eventually agreed on the following principles: simplify the tax process; make it more fair; lower the marginal tax rates for individuals; slightly increase the tax burden on corporations; and encourage productive investments while discouraging wasteful investments in the economy. In the end, Congress reduced the number of tax brackets from fifteen to two, slightly raised personal and standard deductions, repealed scores of previously existing deductions, and limited certain other tax breaks. For example, in the past, when a businessperson took a customer to lunch, the entire expense used to be deductible. After the tax reform only 80 percent of the cost is deductible. Medical expenses and state and local sales taxes that were once deductible are only partially deductible in the current tax code.

Many business groups fought vigorously to stop the shift from business deductions, especially on investment credits, they had grown to enjoy under the previous tax code. Although they were successful in fighting off some of the proposed changes, businesses were defeated on many of the tax expenditures provided earlier. Their consolation was significantly lowered rates for individuals.

Has the new tax system made much of a difference? Most observers hailed the legislation as a notable improvement over the old system. Most taxpayers now pay lower income taxes. And millions of lower-income taxpayers have been taken off the tax rolls altogether. Most upper-middle-income people, in contrast, pay more. Most corporations now pay more, as their minimum tax has been raised to 25 percent. Some close watchers of tax politics warned, however, that the improvement might be temporary. Nothing has changed to prevent the political process that produced the earlier tax system from starting over again. "As lobbyists get back to action, and as members of Congress try to raise campaign funds, old loopholes will be reintroduced and new ones invented, and tax rates will start creeping up to offset the resulting loss of revenue," wrote Milton Friedman.[10]

THE POLITICS OF THE DEFICIT

When individuals are suddenly faced with emergency expenses too heavy to meet out of their regular incomes, they often have to borrow money. The same used to be true of government. During military and economic crises the federal government has gone heavily into debt. But recently we have also gone into great debt during a period of peace with a relatively healthy economy. We borrowed $23 billion during World War I, about $13 billion more during the 1930s, and $200 billion more during World War II. By 1991 the gross federal debt will be about $3 trillion. Borrowing costs money. Although the federal government can borrow at a relatively low rate, the interest on the federal debt is about $170 billion a year. The size of the debt and the interest payments alarms many Americans. How long can we allow the debt to grow at this rate? Two considerations must be kept in mind: The government owes most of the money to its own people rather than to foreign governments or people, although this is changing. Also, the economic strength and resources of the country are more significant than the size of the public debt. Still, the interest we pay to service the debt is a real cause for concern.

How, then, does the government borrow money? The Constitution says Congress may "borrow money on the credit of the United States"; it puts no limit on the extent or method of borrowing. Under congressional authorization the Treasury Department sells securities to banks, corporations, and individuals. Usually these securities take the form of long-term bonds or short-term Treasury notes. Some bonds may be cashed in at any time, others not until maturity. Because the United States government guarantees these bonds, they are in demand, especially by banks and investment companies.

Why do we have such huge deficits? These deficits are not the result of a weak economy, and they apparently cannot be cured simply by economic growth. The fact is that the United States is committed to spending more for defense and domestic programs than current tax revenues can afford, even though the economy is running at relatively full capacity. By tolerating unprecedented deficits in recent years, the Reagan administration was able to "create an austere political climate in which proposed cuts, not expected increments, focus the discussions of federal domestic programs."[11]

These budgetary limitations have clearly carried over to the new presidential administration despite campaign commitments by George Bush to increase funding for education, the homeless, drug-law enforcement, and the environment. The creation of such a massive deficit has been an effective way to stall, if not actually disassemble, the development of social welfare policy. As the 1988 election clearly showed, while Americans may be concerned about the deficit, they did not elect George Bush for his promises to do something about it. At the polls Americans are far more tolerant of the deficit than one might suppose.

But this is also creating a precarious political and economic situation that could put the nation in jeopardy if and when we face another recession. High deficits are objectionable for a variety of reasons. Together with huge national debt interest payments they put a damper on economic growth. It works this way: The annual deficit is now absorbing about 30 percent of all capital raised in the United States. For every dollar Uncle Sam borrows another dollar cannot be channeled into productive resources by corporations, small business operators, and home buyers. When interest rates are kept artificially high, many companies and would-be investors just will not borrow money they need to modernize factories, create jobs, and buy new homes.[12]

Our huge deficits in a time of relative economic prosperity also lessen our ability to rely on traditional economic remedies to revive the economy should the nation fall into another recession. Typically, during economic downturns the government has tried to increase demand for the goods and services that the nation has the capacity to produce. It does this by cutting taxes, stepping up government spending, and enlarging the budget deficit. This prescription helped us out of the depression of the 1930s, and many economists still view it as a plausible way to revive an ailing economy today. "But the huge buildup of deficits

Who Owns the Federal Debt?	
	Share of Total
U.S. government accounts (such as trust funds)	17%
Foreign owners	11
Federal Reserve banks	9
Commercial banks	11
State and local governments	10
Individuals, including savings-bond holders	9
Money market funds	2
Insurance companies	5
Corporations	3
Others, including S & Ls, pension funds, brokers, and nonprofit groups	24

Source: U.S. Department of the Treasury, 1985.

A group of senior citizens crowd around a table to sign a petition against any cuts in Medicare, Medicaid, or Social Security.

The Board of Governors of the Federal Reserve System, 1989: (seated) Manuel H. Johnson, Alan Greenspan, Martha R. Seger; (standing) John P. LaWare, Edward W. Kelley, Jr., H. Robert Heller, Wayne D. Angell.

and debt, combined with the growing weight of foreign trade and fluctuating exchange rates in a closely knit world economy, makes it difficult and even dangerous, perhaps impossible, for the United States to escape its burdens simply by increasing demand through still greater public or private borrowing," writes economist Leonard Silk. "The harvest would likely include greater inflation, a further loss of international competitiveness, more people out of work, and a worsening of protectionism, with dangerous implications for the world economy and polity."[13]

Managing the Economy

Does the government have the same direct control over the national economy that it has, say, over the military or national forests? No. Only if we had a socialized economy administered from Washington would we have a managed economy in that sense. In our economy a great deal of power is left to private individuals and enterprises. Yet the government keeps a firm hand on many of the gears and levers that control the economy's general direction and the rate at which it moves. These gears and levers are taxes, spending, and credit.

LESSONS OF THE GREAT DEPRESSION

Depression is a hard teacher, and the 1930s had a tremendous impact on American thinking about the role of government in the economy. Although we had had long, severe depressions before, for example, in the 1870s and 1890s, the Great Depression of 1929 brought mass misery. "One vivid, gruesome moment of those dark days we shall never forget," wrote one observer. "We saw a crowd of some fifty men fighting over a barrel of garbage which had been set outside the back door of a restaurant. American citizens fighting for scraps of food like animals!"[14]

Despite the efforts of the Roosevelt administration to cope with the Depression, it hung on. Faint signs of recovery could be seen in the mid-1930s, but the recession of 1937 to 1938 indicated that we were by no means out of the woods. Eight or nine million people were jobless in 1939. Then came the war, and unemployment seemed cured. Millions of people had more income, more security, and higher standards of living. Lord Beveridge in England posed a question that bothered many thoughtful Americans: "Unemployment has been practically abol-

Fed Board of Governors

Seven members appointed by the president and confirmed by the Senate. Terms are fourteen years. The president names one member as chairman for a four-year term.

WHAT IT DOES
Helps carry out policy for regulating the supply of money and credit

Sets reserve requirements for the depository institutions

Sets the discount rate on the Fed's loans to banks

Makes margin rules for purchases of securities on credit

Oversees major banks by regulating the nation's 6,146 bank holding companies

Inspects and regulates 1,052 state-chartered banks that are members of the reserve system

Monitors the economy

Deals with international monetary problems

Enforces consumer-credit laws

Supervises Federal Reserve banks

Source: *U.S. News & World Report* (January 27, 1986), p. 49. Copyright © 1986, US News & World Report.

CHAPTER 22 / Making Economic and Social Policy

ished twice in the lives of most of us—in the last war and in this war. Why does war solve the problem of unemployment which is so insoluble in peace?"[15] Worried that the economy might collapse after the war, thousands of people came up with plans to ensure jobs for all.

Some people think the Great Depression was caused by the **Federal Reserve System** and its mismanagement of the money supply. These people claim that had the Fed expanded the money supply in the early 1930s instead of keeping it constant and even reducing it, many of the bank failures and much of the misery of the Depression could have been avoided.

Others think the Depression lasted so long because the New Deal was hostile to business. Government intruded too long and too much into the economic life of the nation. Proponents of this theory urged the government to reduce spending, lower taxes, curb the power of labor, and generally leave business and the economy alone. Another large group said that the trouble with the New Deal was not that it had done too much but that it had done too little. This group's thinking was deeply influenced by the work of English economist **John Maynard Keynes.**[16] In visits to the United States during the 1930s, Keynes warned that if people did not consume enough or invest enough, national income would fall. The way to increase national income is to spend money on consumption goods (such as clothes or food or automobiles), or on investment goods (electronic chips and dock facilities), or on both. Finally, *in a recession government must do the spending and investing if private enterprise by itself will not or cannot.* Through the passage of the Employment Act of 1946, Congress accepted the Keynesian approach.

THE EMPLOYMENT ACT OF 1946

Passing a law specifically recognizing the major role of the national government in maintaining full employment was bound to be difficult.[17] Major business groups strongly opposed it. Enacted in February 1946, however, the act declared:

> It is the continuing policy and responsibility of the federal government to use all practicable means consistent with its needs and obligations and other essential considerations of national policy, with the assistance and cooperation of industry, agriculture, labor, and state and local governments, to coordinate and utilize all its plans, functions, and resources for the purpose of creating and maintaining, in a manner calculated to foster and promote free competitive enterprise and the general welfare, conditions under which there will be afforded useful employment, for those able, willing, and seeking to work, and to promote maximum employment, production, and purchasing power.

If this sounds like double talk, it is because the bill was a medley of compromises. In effect, the bill made the government responsible for maintaining high employment. Equally important, it established machinery to carry out that responsibility:

1. *The Council of Economic Advisers (CEA).* This body of three members appointed by the president with the consent of the Senate is located in the executive office of the president. It studies and forecasts economic trends, assesses the contribution of federal programs to maximum employment, and recommends to the president "national economic policies to foster and promote free competition, to avoid economic fluctuations or to diminish the effects thereof, and to maintain employment, production, and purchasing power."

Public Attitudes on Reducing Deficits

	Favor
Increase taxes on alcoholic beverages	83%
Limit defense spending	74
National lottery	64
National sales tax	31
Reduce Social Security COLAs	21
Limit Medicare payments	13
Tax Social Security benefits as ordinary income	10

Source: Times Mirror Corporation and The Gallup Organization, February 1989. (N = 2048)

You decide!

The United States became the world's number one debtor nation a few years ago. What does this mean, and why is this the case? What can be done about it, in your judgment?

(Answer/Discussion on page 575.)

2. *The Economic Report of the President.* Every January the president must submit to Congress an economic report based on the data and forecasts of the council. The report must include a program for carrying out the policy of the act; it can also include recommendations for legislation.

3. *Joint Economic Committee (JEC).* This committee of Congress composed of senators and representatives reports its findings and proposals in response to annual presidential recommendations. Aside from publishing various reports, the JEC tries to give Congress an overview of the economy. In this sense it is a planning and theory group in a legislature otherwise fiercely devoted to short-term, practical matters. The Senate and House Budget Committees also try to provide this kind of overview.

How has the Employment Act worked in practice? The CEA has emerged as a high-level presidential advisory body. Its chair serves both as an adviser to the president and as a spokesperson for the president before Congress and the country. The annual economic report and the budget message are major presidential statements on the role governmental fiscal policies will play in the economy. The JEC has usually played a useful role in developing information on important economic problems.[18] The various mechanisms of the act work reasonably well, but concern over trade imbalances and budget deficits have prompted recent presidents to set up an economic policy cabinet council in addition to the CEA. These cabinet-level coordinating units seek to provide policy options to the president and to coordinate the actions that result from economic decisions.[19] Good processes themselves, however, are no guarantee that the policies they generate will work well—if at all.

Fiscal Policy: Remedies

Nowadays the national government unquestionably has tremendous economic power. But both soaring government spending and deficits have raised a number of questions about how effectively the government is doing its job. Through two types of policy—**monetary policy** (control of the money supply) and **fiscal policy** (taxing and spending)—the government attempts to manage the economy's ups and downs, moderating both while allowing steady economic growth. This management power emerged earlier this century with such developments as the Federal Reserve System, the income tax, and the great growth of government spending.

Government management of the economy is still largely based on the theories of John Maynard Keynes: increasing aggregate demand by government spending during business slumps and curbing spending during booms. Politically, however, there is a problem: It is much easier to increase spending and government programs than it is to curb them. As a result, deficit spending is common. To stimulate demand, the government spends more money than it takes in. For many years this policy was thought to be beneficial to the economy, and it was convenient politically. However, the deficit has soared in recent years, and there have been no surpluses, even with economic growth. In fact, there has been only one year of surpluses in over twenty-five years.

Economists found that such policies, when accompanied by a loose-money policy by the Federal Reserve, resulted in a hidden cost: inflation. Even though taxpayers did not pay the entire cost of national programs, consumers did, as

"How do I spell 'relief'? T-A-X-C-U-T!"

Berry's World; reprinted by permission of NEA, Inc.

the pumped-up economy had too many dollars chasing too few goods. Although government spending is not responsible for all inflation, it has been a major contributor; as a result, more and more people have begun to look for new economic remedies.

SUPPLY-SIDE ECONOMICS

Ronald Reagan came to the White House preaching an alternative to Keynesian economics (but in fact he relied on deficit spending to prime the economy more than any other president). He pledged to balance the budget by cutting both taxes and government spending—the so-called **supply-side economics.** In simple terms, supply-side economics holds that large cuts in taxes will inspire productive investment so that the initial loss of federal revenues will be offset by the taxes generated from expanded private economic activity. Reagan maintained that by creating favorable conditions for businesses, investments would increase, companies would expand their operations, and more jobs would be created.

Once in office, President Reagan discovered that it was easier to cut taxes than federal spending and, in 1981, he pushed through Congress the largest tax cuts in our history. Critics of supply-side economics, including most economists, doubted that tax cuts alone would result in the economic expansion necessary to generate more tax revenues.

The extraordinary revenue growth forecast by supply-side economists in the early 1980s simply did not materialize. According to the supply siders, the implementation of major tax cuts would allow Americans to save more and to go to work in greater numbers. It would also encourage the economy to expand and more tax revenues to flow into the Treasury Department. But no extra savings were realized. And no significant increase in revenues resulted. Instead, the national savings rate remained low and corporations used their tax cuts to engage in a frenzy of mergers, producing few new jobs, little new investment, and only marginal economic growth. "Although it was never publicly admitted, the Reagan Administration had become 'born again Keynesians,' converted to easy money, large tax cuts, big increases in government spending, and huge deficits," writes economist Lester Thurow. "Midway through his first term of office President Reagan had adopted precisely the policies which he had spent a lifetime denouncing."[20]

MONETARISM

More significant than the supply-side approach in the Reagan years was the acceptance of the theory of *monetarism*. The core element of monetarism is the idea that prices, income, and economic stability are primarily the function of growth in the money supply. Monetarists contend the money supply is the key factor in affecting the economy's performance. Further, they argue that there should be restrained yet steady growth in the money supply, enough to encourage solid economic growth, but not inflation.

During the early 1980s the Federal Reserve Board, with the Reagan administration's encouragement, induced the longest and most severe post-World War II recession.[21] This seemed to succeed, at least temporarily, in reducing inflationary pressures. But unemployment soon reached 10 and 11 percent levels. The monetarist policy raised as many questions as it solved; it also divided many monetarists on such key questions as how long it should take to get from a position of high

Answer/Discussion

The United States had not been a debtor nation since 1914. But in recent years it has a billion plus deficit in investments. This means that foreigners owned more American investments than Americans had in foreign investments. This occurred because foreign investment in the United States soared in recent years, while American investments abroad increased only slightly.

The fact we are a debtor nation would be of little concern if this is a temporary condition. If it lasts for a few years, however, it is undesirable for several reasons. It means that an increasing amount of our national debt is owed to foreigners. And should foreigners take their money out of our economy and invest elsewhere, a great burden would be placed on the United States to finance the debt. It also constrains our ability to exercise the whole range of economic tools to deal with economic problems. For example, if we lower our interest rates and other Western nations do not, foreign investment would be driven away. Over the long run, the departure of the foreign investors probably would have the effect of increasing interest rates and diverting more money away from capital investments in the American economy. Efforts to get us out of this situation have included devaluation of the American dollar and coordination with other industrialized nations on interest rates. But more still will have to be done.

Authors of the budget-cutting act that bears their name (left to right): Senators Warren Rudman, Phil Gramm, and Ernest Hollings.

inflation to one with reasonable price stability: "It didn't say whether that reduction should occur in one year or in three or in five. It didn't say whether that reduction should be at a steady pace or should be faster at first or slower at first."[22]

THE BALANCED BUDGET AMENDMENT

The apparent inability of the federal government to balance its budget has led some politicians and economists to propose that it be constitutionally required to do so. The proposed balanced budget amendment (box on pages 576–577) would require Congress to adopt a budget in which projected spending is no larger than projected tax receipts. In addition, the amendment would limit the increase in taxes (and/or spending) in any fiscal year to the percentage increase in the gross national product (GNP) during the previous calendar year. The amendment has two escape clauses. Congress can waive the requirements of the amendment by a vote of two-thirds of all members of both houses. Also, the provisions of the amendment would not apply in any year in which a war has been declared.

Advocates of a balanced budget amendment (among them Ronald Reagan and George Bush) claim that such an amendment is necessary to correct what they call the "spending bias" that currently exists in government decision making. Senators such as Orrin Hatch (R-Utah), Strom Thurmond (R-South Carolina), and Dennis DeConcini (D-Arizona) claim there is a structural deficiency within our political system that causes higher levels of spending than is desired by the citizenry. Well-organized, powerful, and heavily financed special-interest groups sometimes overwhelm relatively weak taxpayer lobbies and regularly win on spending measures in Congress.[23]

Opponents of a balanced budget amendment say that such an amendment would reduce the flexibility of economic policy makers. It would virtually eliminate fiscal policy as a tool for managing the economy. Political leaders such as Senators Alan Cranston (D-California) and Daniel Patrick Moynihan (D-New York) say that often a federal budget deficit is an effective means of boosting the economy. In times of economic downturn, they say, government spending in excess of revenues can increase employment, generate investment, stimulate demand, and prevent a recession from deepening into a depression.

Opponents also say it is unwise to place an economic theory into the Constitution. The Constitution, they contend, should be a broad charter dealing with fundamental principles of governance, not a document with specific theories of economic management. Further, they contend, balancing the budget is a legislative as well as a political—not a constitutional—matter.

The balanced budget amendment is either a "fraud" or a "disaster," argue many opponents. It is a fraud in the sense that countless variables affect how much it will cost to run our national government and how much it will collect. Such changes as a drought in the south or a flood in California affect both sides of the budget—so much so it would be only an educated guess as to what federal revenues would be. If the balanced budget is adopted, Congress may very well have to resort to subterfuges to "pretend" it has balanced the books.

If the just described twisting of the intent is not accurate, and the amendment is actually used to cut back on federal expenditures to a level at which we can be sure that tax revenues will cover them, it will force alterations that themselves cause major social upheavals: Social security entitlements, military pay, veterans' benefits, and a host of other federal aid and educational benefits would have to be reduced, for instance.

*Y*ou decide!

Here is the actual wording of a proposed amendment to the U.S. Constitution that has the backing of several senators and members of Congress. Would you support it? If so, why? If not, why not? And what do you think are some of the reasons why people favor it or oppose it?

Resolved by the Senate and House of Representatives of the United States of America in Congress assembled (two-thirds of each House concurring therein), that the following article is proposed as an amendment to the Constitution of the United States, which shall be valid to all intents and purposes as part of the Constitution if ratified by the legislatures of three-fourths of the several states within seven years after its submission to the states for ratification:

Section 1. Prior to each fiscal year, the Congress shall adopt a statement of receipts and outlays for that year in which total outlays are not greater than total receipts. The Congress may amend such statement provided revised outlays are no greater than revised receipts. Whenever three-fifths of the whole number of both Houses shall deem it necessary, Congress in such statement may provide for a specific excess of outlays over receipts by a vote directed solely to the subject. The Congress and the President shall, pursuant to legislation or through the exercise of their powers under the first and second articles, ensure that actual outlays do not exceed the outlays set forth in such statement.

CHAPTER 22 / Making Economic and Social Policy

Perhaps more likely, the balanced budget amendment would change the "rules of the game" and would make it easier for social and economic conservatives to win more legislative battles. More votes would be required to adopt new programs, and some of these would require a two-thirds vote to appropriate money.

Government Subsidies: How and Why

Government **subsidies** provide economic assistance to certain targeted producers or consumers at the expense of others in the economy. Magazine and book publishers enjoy reduced postal rates on the grounds that this will enhance public knowledge and democratic discussion. Oil companies get certain tax write-offs on the grounds that we vitally need more oil to free ourselves of dependence on imported foreign oil. Farmers and ranchers, much beloved as the contemporary examples of old-fashioned rugged individualism, are protected by a dizzying array of federal assistance programs. The Chrysler Corporation and the U.S. Postal Service have received special treatment as well, because we place special value on their services and continued existence. College students are the beneficiaries of subsidies both directly and indirectly because of the widespread conviction that all of us benefit from their education.

Government promotion, or subsidies, are not a new creation. In his first annual address to Congress, George Washington called for a tariff to protect business. Alexander Hamilton, Washington's secretary of the treasury, proposed that government give financial assistance to new business ventures. In the 1790s the new government promoted commerce in numerous ways: by establishing a money system and a postal service, granting charters, enforcing contracts in court, and subsidizing roads and waterways. Significant public purposes can be and are achieved, such as conserving and developing energy; preserving vital nongovernmental sectors that fund and operate private hospitals, colleges, and charitable institutions; encouraging small businesses, and so on.

Some subsidies have outlived their purpose and today create unnecessary costs for taxpayers and consumers. They benefit narrow, well-organized interests, even though their costs are spread out among unorganized taxpayers. Many subsidies are hard to see because they take the form of tax preferences, loans, or protective regulations. Subsidies that have outlived their usefulness are often continued because of effective lobbying. Beneficiaries make strategic campaign contributions during elections and fight ruthlessly in other ways to hold on to their special advantages.

Computing how much is spent on subsidy programs is difficult because many federal subsidy programs are called something else. They may be called grants-in-aid, price supports, tax incentives, import quotas, stabilization programs, and loan guarantees. Government subsidy programs include:

1. *Cash benefits.* The government pays sugar beet and cane growers to protect the welfare of the domestic sugar industry, and it pays sheep raisers to improve the quality of American wool. Cash payments also help to support artists as well as the privately owned U.S. merchant marine.

2. *Tax incentives.* The recipients of these subsidies receive no cash; they are permitted to pay lower taxes than would normally be required. Tax incentives to business to encourage oil exploration and production are examples. So too is the tax deductibility of interest on homes occupied by their owners. Although the government makes no expenditure, it still loses revenue.

Proposed Amendment cont.

Section 2. Total receipts for any fiscal year set forth in the statement adopted pursuant to this article shall not increase by a rate greater than the rate of increase in national income in the year or years ending not less than six months nor more than twelve months before such fiscal year, unless a majority of the whole number of both Houses of Congress have passed a bill directed solely to approving specific additional receipts and such bill has become law.

Section 3. The Congress may waive the provisions of this article for any fiscal year in which a declaration of war is in effect.

Section 4. Total receipts shall include all receipts of the United States except those derived from borrowing and total outlays shall include all outlays of the United States except those for repayment of debt principal.

Section 5. The Congress shall enforce and implement this article by appropriate legislation.

Section 6. On and after the day this article takes effect, the amount of federal public limit as of such date shall become permanent and there shall be no increase in such amount unless three-fifths of the whole number of both Houses of Congress shall have passed a bill approving such increase and such bill has become law.

Section 7. This article shall take effect for the second fiscal year beginning after its ratification.

(Answer/Discussion on next page.)

3. *Credit subsidies.* These involve government participation in loan transactions that give lower rates of interest than prevailing market conditions would allow. Credit subsidies range from loans financing a student through college, to those financing a major public works project at a fraction of prevailing interest rates, to those financing New York City.

4. *Benefit-in-kind subsidies.* Recipients receive a product or service paid for by the government. Food stamps for the poor or Medicare for the elderly are examples.

There are other ways in which the federal government has a direct impact on the economy. The government sometimes sets tariffs on imports that allow domestic producers to earn higher profits than free markets would bring. In fact, almost all groups at one time or another have benefited from government help. Many business officials have sought government aid—to bail out numerous savings and loan banks or Chrysler, to support government-backed loans to railroads, to subsidize the merchant marine industry, and so on. Similarly, spokespersons for the poor seek a larger government role in providing health services, establishing a floor below which incomes are not allowed to fall, and subsidizing improved housing and employment opportunities. Governmental promotion can be used to help any group. But who shall be aided, in what way, and with what consequences, are the important questions.

Helping Business

A government that protects and enforces contracts enables owners of businesses to operate in a stable situation. A government that promotes a prosperous economy enables businesses to enjoy a large volume of sales and good profits. The kind of monetary policy established by government—for example, tight or easy money—is of direct interest to business. But the national government also supplies a number of specific services and assists individual sectors of the business community.

THE DEPARTMENT OF COMMERCE

The Department of Commerce is sometimes known as the nation's "service center" for businesses. Its secretary, nearly always a person with an extensive business background, is a spokesperson for business interests. Historically, the department has been at the center of government's efforts to promote economic growth and encourage business research and development. Its Social and Economic Statistics Administration reports on business activity and prospects at home and around the world. Its Bureau of the Census has been called the greatest fact-finding and figure-counting agency in the world. The Constitution requires that a national census be taken every ten years; the results supply valuable information on business and agricultural activity, incomes, occupations, employment, housing and home ownership, and government finances.

Its National Bureau of Standards (NBS) provides highly valued technical assistance to corporations such as GE, DuPont, and IBM. The NBS has helped companies study the structures of enzymes, look at submicroscopic flaws in jet-engine turbine blades, and probe the structure and properties of various materials used in biotechnology, electronics, fiber optics, and other fields.[24]

The Patent and Trademark Office (PTO) administers the patent system that Congress established to carry out its responsibilities "to promote the progress of . . . the useful arts . . ." under Article I of the Constitution. The PTO issues more than 82,000 patents each year to cover new and useful inventions that provide their owners certain exclusive rights for fourteen to seventeen years. It also issues trademarks to protect distinctive names for commercial purposes.

The Department of Commerce also undertakes basic research in ocean science and engineering, meteorology, and weather forecasting. Its National Oceanic and Atmospheric Administration is currently operating research on hurricane predictions, acid rain, marine fisheries, and a wide assortment of undersea research activities.

Treasury Secretary Nicholas Brady

THE DEPARTMENT OF THE INTERIOR

The Department of the Interior has long supported activities that assist mining and ranching interests, among others. Its Geological Survey undertakes research on the extent, distribution, and character of the nation's natural resources and on the geological processes, structures, and hazards that affect the development and use of virtually every aspect of the nation's physical lands. It appraises improved methods of mineral extraction and preparing new technologies for energy development.

The Bureau of Mines subsidizes basic and applied research to improve understanding of mining and to reduce the hazards involved in the mining industries. These services assist private-sector firms even as they promote such national interests as productivity and mine disaster prevention.

Helping Farmers

The impressive success and competitiveness of American agriculture owes much to the federal government and its subsidies, almost as much as to fertile soil, hard work, and the technology revolution. Agriculture is our largest industry—bigger than computers and automobiles or the movie and record industries. Agriculture and food-related businesses generate nearly one out of every five jobs in our private sector and account for almost 20 percent of the GNP and 15 percent of our exports. It is also the industry with the highest rate of productivity. In the past fifty years, agricultural productivity, substantially due to federal support for research in land grant institutions, has increased at a rate of about 6 percent a year.

Although our great agricultural production is the result of many factors, it reflects one of the more successful partnerships between government and private enterprise. The federal government has invested major sums in basic and applied agricultural research as well as in ways to apply this research on our farms. Much of this work is done through so-called land grant state universities and colleges. What is learned in the laboratories is tested on experimental farms. New techniques and products are then brought to farmers, primarily through the Agricultural Extension Services of these schools. Local county agents, part of the Agricultural Extension Service, are supported by a combination of national, state and local funds.

The Depression of the 1930s ravaged virtually every farmer. The New Deal helped to get farmers back on their feet by means of credit support, loans, and

Farmers demonstrating in Washington for the continuation of government support.

crop price supports. Major federal initiatives in irrigation and rural electrification fostered significant strides in productivity. Numerous loans and credit programs were established to help the farmers purchase needed equipment. Some of these programs have become self-financing, even though they were begun with public money. Other federal initiatives have been enacted to stabilize incomes and output with price supports and acreage controls.

Aid to farmers continues. The Department of Agriculture spent more than $30 billion for farm aid in one recent year. A single California farming operation received $20 million that year, part of a bumper crop of multimillion-dollar payments that the government doled out. A number of federal programs pay farmers to reduce production. One program buys out dairy production operations for five years, and another crop-reduction program takes marginally productive land out of use for ten years. These voluntary programs are intended to reduce food surpluses. It is estimated that between 30 and 45 million acres were taken out of production in these types of programs in recent years.

Although the farm subsidy program includes separate benefits for growing, or not growing, everything from tobacco to mohair, most of the money is spent on grain. The government spends billions to buy up, at a guaranteed minimum price, any surplus grain that was produced. Most of the burden falls on consumers, in the form of higher prices at the supermarket. In 1985 Congress cut back on much of this price support, but it offers direct cash payments to help farmers make up some of their lost income. These payment programs are intended to give farmers a decent standard of living, but they are paid according to volume grown. The rich get richer this way. Many federal subsidy programs pay farmers for not planting crops. It is the biggest farmers who are able not to grow the greatest quantity of food, and who have lots of land not to grow it on. That they should get the lion's share of farm welfare should come as no surprise.

The American farmers have had an enormously difficult time in recent years. Hundreds of thousands of farmers have simply closed their operations either because of bankruptcy or mortgage foreclosure. Meanwhile, as farmers pay more, the prices they receive are plummeting because the ballooning deficit distorts the value of the dollar worldwide. Yet the bleaker the farm situation becomes the greater the cry by farmers for more help: extensions on loans, bailouts of the farm credit system, and yet more subsidies or direct aid.

Plainly, the vast array of subsidies, loans, credits, and related programs of research and investment have helped successful American farmers increase productivity. Many economists point out, however, that not only do the big farmers gain the most from federal programs, but various federal government income transfers to farmers often hurt poor people by driving up the price of food. Thus, although helping farmers encourages productivity, it also increases poverty. Why do we do this? Farmers vote in large numbers. Further, not only are they organized, but, just like senior citizens and unions and the savings and loan industry and its friends, the farmers know how to present their case to Congress.[25]

PROTECTIONISM: HELPING OR HURTING?

America was once the dominant exporting nation, but our competitive edge eroded in the 1970s and 1980s. Today the United States must strive to be an equal among peers. America's biggest challenge is coming from Pacific Rim nations such as Japan, Korea, Taiwan, and Singapore. How did this happen? Our wages became higher and higher. Other nations became more productive. We designed our products for the large home market and then tried to export the same products with the same standards abroad. Other nations designed their products specifically for our market. Management wages in this country are three and four times those in competing nations. Most of our business executives are lawyers and advertising or accounting specialists; most executives in Japan are scientists and engineers. Many foreign governments have worked closely with industries in planning competitive products and helping to maximize export possibilities.

The two areas in which we continued, until recently, to have a competitive trading edge have also come under attack. Both our leadership and research in technology and our vast agricultural industry are now threatened by other nations who are fast moving up and doing what we do at lower costs and with a fresh assertiveness.

The costs to Americans are staggering. Thousands of plants have been closed. Hundreds of thousands of workers at steel mills, machine-tool factories, textile, and apparel manufacturing plants and in the computer, electronics, and communications industries have been laid off. In what is now becoming a familiar refrain, both industry and its unions blame their immediate problems on imports. Imports have doubled in recent years. In some clothing products, foreign competitors now enjoy more than half of our market.

The problem, in part, is not that we are importing too much, but that we are exporting too little. German cars, Japanese radios, and Indonesian textiles are fine products, provided we are productive enough to be able to pay for them. If other countries can produce better cars or shoes at a lower price, then we should deploy our labor and capital to do what we can do better. The question is whether there are still things we can do that will give us a competitive edge.

A hundred years ago, U.S. policymakers worried that we might someday not have enough incentives to keep people on the farms, yet we are now getting along fine with most Americans *not* being farmers. Will the same thing be said fifty or one hundred years from now about people working in factories and in manufacturing?

In 1971 the United States experienced its first trade deficit in more than a century. By 1990, our foreign trade imbalances grew to nearly $200 billion a year. Because the dollar was strong in the mid-1980s, foreign goods were less expensive to American buyers, causing an influx of imports, but American goods became prohibitively expensive in foreign markets. Another fact, not readily admitted by many Americans, is that the quality of American products left a lot to be desired, especially compared to available and less costly imports.

Congress and the president have come under continuing pressure from coalitions of industry, unions, and regional political leaders trying to save jobs and companies and communities from foreign competition. These pressures come not only from the textile and auto industries, but from glass, steel, shoe, lumber, electronics, book publishing, aluminum, farming, and domestic wine and spirit coalitions, to name just a few. Protectionists urge retaliation. They claim the United States' trade deficit justifies the imposition of **tariffs** and other trade sanctions. While urging Americans to "buy American" products, industries and unions regularly rush to Washington, D.C., urging Congress to enact tariffs and import quotas.

Grass-roots support of protectionism is demonstrated in this "Buy American" festival in Johnstown, Pennsylvania.

Protectionism sounds easy and workable as a solution to the trade deficit, yet the balance of trade deficit is only one of the many symptoms of more profound economic problems. Most economists almost always favor free trade and dislike protectionism. Protectionism, they say, prevents efficient use of resources. It merely postpones real solutions such as increased productivity and improved capital plant investments. It also inevitably invites retaliation from foreign countries.[26] Protectionism will only magnify most of the problems associated with America's trade problems.

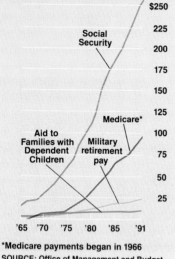
Over the years, when our businesses have been threatened owners and their employees have often successfully petitioned Congress to curb competitive imports. By imposing tariffs or negotiating trade agreements with other nations to restrict the quantities of cars, shoes, or motorcycles that are imported into the United States, the federal government maintains higher prices for these products—a situation that benefits (at least in the short run) domestic companies and their workers. The costs to American consumers, however, can be great. In recent years it has cost us between $25,000 and $1 million to produce a single job in certain industries.

Americans have usually favored free trade. Two hundred years ago Thomas Jefferson traveled to France to request that American whale oil, tobacco, and fish be allowed into that country without being subject to the intolerable tariff burdens the French had imposed. And over the years Americans have usually discovered that foreign trade is a two-way street: If we want people in a foreign market to buy our goods, we must be willing to buy theirs.

In the 1930s many nations experienced high unemployment, low production, and general economic misery. The United States was no exception. In an effort to aid ailing American industries, Congress passed the *Smoot-Hawley tariff act.* The act established the highest general tariff the United States had ever had. Supporters hoped high tariffs on imported goods would increase the demand for goods produced in the United States and thus help get the country out of the Depression. The exact opposite occurred. Other nations retaliated with high tariffs on American goods. Demand fell, heightening the Depression. In 1934 Congress gave the president power to negotiate mutual tariff reductions with other nations, subject to certain restrictions. By the early 1970s tariffs on industrial products had been substantially reduced. But restrictions on agricultural commodities remain, along with nontariff limitations such as quotas, minimum import prices, and prohibitions on the sale of certain products.

There is a general consensus to support the concerns of American industry and unions about "dumping." Certain nations have "dumped" products on our market (meaning they sell products here at below cost of manufacture) with the obvious intention of driving our producers out of the market and then later, after they dominate the market, raising their prices to profitable levels. Countries have also subsidized steel exported elsewhere in the world. Japan has protected several of its industries—producers of autos to baseball bats—by specifying standards that are virtually impossible for us to meet. Other nations have erected nontariff trade barriers, such as lengthy inspection procedures for imported goods.

The United States, of course, often reciprocates. In recent years we have imposed "voluntary" limits on Japanese automobiles and European steel imports. Further, as already indicated, the federal government has long subsidized agricultural exports in the form of price supports and inexpensive credit.

Opponents of these protectionist policies say that in the long run they cost us jobs rather than save them, and lead to higher prices. Protected American firms facing reduced competition from foreign firms are free to raise their prices. As demand falls, American manufacturers sell fewer products and are forced to lay off workers. Contrived protection of our industries also may lull an industry into complacent practices rather than encourage investment, renewal, and retooling that will lead to qualitative improvements necessary to remain competitive. Artificial protections also may mask the fact that we need to revitalize our educational system and merely postpone our recognition of the increasingly noncompetitive aspect of the American economy.

In short, protectionist measures are often merely another kind of subsidy—and often a subsidy that protects one industry at the expense of another. Protection-

Drawing by Wright for the Miami News.

CHAPTER 22 / Making Economic and Social Policy

ism is more expensive than taxpayers realize. Protectionism will rarely be the appropriate answer. Instead, the United States must continue, through hard negotiations with our trading partners, to remove unfair trade practices; encourage greater investments in what we have traditionally done well (science, technology, medical, and agricultural research, etc.); educate workers with better skills and executives with greater leadership abilities; and encourage labor-management experiments that can maximize productivity with an eye on higher quality products that will be highly prized abroad. Policy makers in the United States have sought to devalue the dollar and thereby make our products more accessible in foreign markets.[27]

Helping Retirees and the Disabled

Social security, the world's largest "insurance" program for retirees, survivors, and the disabled, covers over 90 percent of the American workforce and will cost about $350 billion by 1991. The program pays 36 million Americans every month, and 115 million people contribute to it. In recent years social security provided an estimated average payment of over $500 per month to a retired worker without dependents. Full benefits are paid to those between the ages of 65 and 70 who are not presently earning wages of more than a certain amount. After age 70 people are entitled to retirement benefits regardless of wage earnings. Since the Social Security Act was passed in 1935, the history of social security programs has largely been one of steady growth. The purpose of the program is to provide support for the aged in American society, and it has grown to include disability payments and Medicare. It is financed through compulsory "contributions" by workers and employers in the form of a payroll tax.

The first social security check was paid to Ida Fuller of Brattleboro, Vermont, in 1940. She had contributed $22 in payroll taxes between the beginning of 1937, when the system began, and the end of 1939, when she retired. Ms. Fuller's first monthly check was for $22.54. She continued to receive checks for thirty-four years, until her death in late 1974 (shortly after her 100th birthday). All told, Ida collected almost $21,000.

> For proponents and critics alike Ida Fuller's story captures much of the essence of the social security system. Critics can point out that Ida joined late, paid almost nothing, and received benefits nearly a thousand times as large as the taxes she paid in. Proponents can point with pride to a system providing a reliable stream of benefits to someone lucky enough to live as long as Ida did, and to the comfort and peace of mind social security gave her. They can also observe that though she received a high return on her contributions, the system was only a small cushion for her. History does not record her other sources of support, but she could not have lived thirty-four years sustained only by her social security checks.[28]

Until the 1970s growth was relatively noncontroversial, largely because "the costs were initially deceptively low," while benefits were steadily increasing, making the system politically painless.[29] The liberalization and expansion of benefits were made possible by the steady economic growth of the 1950s and 1960s. "The nature of the program in the short run has been such as to disguise the true cost of it, the true relation between costs and benefits, and the true principles by which benefits and costs have been distributed. The nature of policy making did little to correct, but instead reinforced, a complacent, poorly informed acceptance of the program."[30]

Financing Social Security

The National Commission on Social Security Reform (1983) was created by President Reagan to recommend ways to save the social security system. Its suggestions, adopted by Congress, were the result of compromise among many political leaders. Among the most important of the commission's suggestions were the following:

A six-month delay in the cost-of-living adjustment from July 1983 to January 1984. This provision saved the social security system an estimated $40 billion.

A rescheduling of previously approved increases in social security payroll taxes. Increases will take place sooner than legislated in existing law. This provision will save the system an estimated $40 billion.

A gradual increase in the retirement age. An increase in the benefit bonus for early retirement will be phased in gradually until 2010.

An extension of coverage to all newly hired federal workers. New federal employees will contribute to the social security system rather than to their own pension plans. Also, all employees of nonprofit organizations not covered at present will come under the social security system. Further, state and local governments now in the system will be prohibited from withdrawing. These steps will save $23 billion.

Subjecting for the first time benefits to income tax. One-half of all social security benefits of individuals with other income over $20,000 and families with earnings over $25,000 will be taxed. The expected $30 billion yield will be credited to the social security system.

In the 1930s, when the system was created, the life expectancy of Americans was about fifty-nine years. That figure has since risen to seventy-four. Most Americans now live longer and hence collect significantly more in social security benefits. Most Americans also face expensive medical costs in the later years of retirement. A steadily declining birthrate has placed the burden of supporting the social security system on fewer and fewer workers. Currently, for every three beneficiaries, ten employees contribute to the system. But by the year 2030 or so, the same ten employees will have to support about five social security recipients.

By the early 1980s this pay-as-you-go structure had plunged the system into a state of considerable financial uncertainty. Benefits, and especially the annual cost-of-living increases, were rapidly outstripping its reserves. Politicians in both parties, fearing the wrath of the 36 million or more social security recipients, skirted the issue of cutbacks or modifications in the system. Meanwhile senior Americans were growing very anxious about the system.

In 1983 the system was said to be losing $20,000 every minute—and estimates of projected shortages ranged as high as $1.5 trillion. That pending crisis forced President Reagan and Congress to take action. Reagan created a bipartisan National Commission on Social Security Reform. This fifteen-member group was charged with suggesting ways to solve and improve the system's financial problems. The commission proposed and Congress approved changes that have been so successful that the Social Security Trust Fund has moved from a deficit position to one that is generating a surplus. This surplus is generating a new political debate. Some conservatives want to return the surplus to the private sector; others want to restructure the benefits; still others suggest that social security payroll taxes be reduced; and others want to return to the pay-as-you-go system. The political realities are such that making changes in social security funding is very difficult, and it is not likely that any changes will be made in the next few years. But as the surplus grows, it will receive more and more attention.[31]

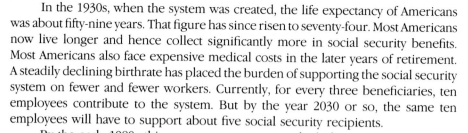

How Social Security Funds Will Grow
Data are Government Accounting Office projections.

SOURCE: Federal Old-age, Survivors' and Disability Insurance Trust Fund Board of Trustees, *The New York Times*, July 23, 1989.

Helping the Needy

Until the Great Depression the national government had no responsibility for taking care of people in need, except for veterans and a few special groups. America was thought to be a land of unlimited opportunities. When people failed to get ahead, people said, it was their own fault. The "worthy poor," widows and orphans, were taken care of through private or county relief. During the early twentieth century state governments extended relief to needy old people, the blind, and orphans, but the programs were limited. No work, no food was the ruling ethic. Then came the Great Depression. In the early 1930s nearly 15 million people were without jobs. Breadlines, soup kitchens, private charity, and meager state and local programs were pitifully inadequate gestures. The Roosevelt administration created an elaborate series of emergency relief programs. But what started as an emergency response to a temporary condition has become a permanent feature of our system. During the past fifty years the national government has progressively become more deeply involved in welfare activities. Most programs are administered by state and local governments but funded by the national government and thus subject to Washington's control. The complex tangle of programs has produced an administrative maze.

Today, federal **entitlement programs**—programs that provide a specified set of benefits as a matter of right to all individuals who meet statutory criteria— have become a significant provider to millions of Americans, perhaps as many as a third of American households. In one recent year, "more than 32 million individuals received payments under the old age and survivors insurance component of the social security program, almost 3 million received unemployment compensation in an average week, and 21.6 million received food stamps. In the health sector, 30 million people were enrolled in Medicare and 21.5 million in Medicaid. And many more Americans will receive additional entitlements benefits at some time in their lives, notably through social security and medicare."[32]

Although most people believe the national government should do something about poverty, few agree on what it should do. There is not even agreement about the dimensions of the problem: how many poor exist, who they are, and why they are poor. But it is clear that a substantial number of Americans, perhaps 40 million, do not have access to a "comfortable" lifestyle. These are often the hidden poor. They remain invisible to the majority of Americans because they exist in the dark slums of the city and in the mountains and valleys of rural America.

A third of the poor are from families in which the breadwinner has been without a job for a long time. (About 8 million people are unemployed in 1990.) Some of these families are headed by a father or a mother whose skills are so meager that he or she cannot support the family. A large portion of the poor live in families headed by a person at least 65 years of age or someone with little or no education. Because black Americans have been subject to discrimination and denied opportunities for education, a greater percentage of blacks than whites are poor. Nevertheless, 70 percent of the poor are white.

Almost everybody is unhappy about the present state of national welfare policies, especially the largest of the so-called categorical relief programs, Aid to Families with Dependent Children. (There is little criticism of programs providing help for the aged, the blind, or the disabled.) Conservatives argue that the drain on the taxpayer is beyond endurance, and that welfare creates and perpetuates dependency.[33] Liberals contend it is immoral for a rich nation to spend billions for defense, to subsidize wealthy farmers, and to assist business when millions are in want.[34] Liberals say too that welfare will in many cases improve opportunities for the poor and compensate for disadvantages imposed by society. Radicals argue that the poor are in poverty because of the deliberate design of the powerful or the natural workings of capitalism.

The famous exchange between F. Scott Fitzgerald and Ernest Hemingway continues to set the framework within which we debate welfare policies. Fitzgerald is reported to have said: "The rich are different from the poor." Hemingway responded: "Yes, they have more money." On the Fitzgerald side of the argument are some social scientists who believe we must make a distinction between those without money and the poor. A college student from a middle-class background, or a space scientist out of work, may be without much money, but he or she is not poor. To be poor is to be part of the "culture of poverty." This subculture, with its own system of values and behaviors, makes it possible for those living in poverty to exist but difficult for them to succeed in the larger society. "There is . . . a language of the poor, a psychology of the poor, a world view of the poor. To be impoverished is to be an internal alien, to grow up in a culture that is radically different from one that dominates the society."[35] Although modern-day Fitzgeralds vary in their political views, they tend to emphasize that poverty

Unemployment lines at Christmas time in Detroit.

Public Opinion and Government Antipoverty Efforts

There were many government programs in the 1960s to try to improve the condition of poor people. Do you think these programs generally made things better, worse, or do you think they didn't have much impact?

Made better	39%
Not much impact	38
Made worse	18

Do you think the federal government should spend money now on a similar effort to try to improve the condition of poor people in this country?

Should	66%
Other/No opinion	12
Should not	22

Source: CBS News-The New York Times poll (1986).

A mother on welfare (left) is struggling to provide a decent life for her child at a welfare hotel, where she says many parents are drug abusers. Joyce Floyd (center), a mental health aide, is a former resident of the hotel.

is unlikely to be reduced unless people are given the education, training, and skills they need to break out of the culture of poverty. They also tend to favor measures to increase the political power of the poor so that they can secure their share of society's resources. Those who take the Hemingway position say what the poor need most is money. With more money they will be able to provide decent housing, secure education for their children, and in time become capable of taking care of themselves.

During the last several decades we have had several waves of welfare reform. In broad terms, these reforms have had the following purposes:

1. *Trying to substitute work for welfare.* In November 1934 President Roosevelt wrote: "What I am seeking is the abolition of relief altogether. I cannot say so out loud yet but I hope to be able to substitute work for relief." He hoped that with economic recovery and full employment, people would move from relief to employment—and many did. But five presidents later, Richard Nixon announced: "What America needs now is not more welfare but more workfare."[36] More recent administrations also tried this. More jobs would benefit the temporarily unemployed. But the problem is that many of those on welfare are unemployable or unskilled.

2. *Trying to substitute social services.* In the early 1960s the major aim of reform was to provide professional help for those on welfare. It was believed that with this kind of assistance, those in need could learn to take care of themselves. Thus, if the problem appeared to be illness, a social worker or caseworker was to see to it that adequate health care was provided. If a family was about to lose its breadwinner because of a marital dispute, a caseworker would be assigned to see if the family could be kept together. The difficulty, however, is that there are not enough trained caseworkers to provide help for all those on welfare. In any event, experiments in which one group received services and another group merely received welfare payments demonstrated that the former group was not any less dependent on welfare than the latter.

3. *Trying to increase the political influence of the poor.* Some aims of President Johnson's War on Poverty were to mobilize the poor for political action, to involve the poor in community-action programs, and to create structures outside the regular channels the poor could use to claim a more adequate share of services.

4. *Trying to increase the cash income available to the very poor.* These reforms, the most recent, involve some kind of income maintenance program such as a family allowance, a negative income tax, or a guaranteed minimum annual income. Here the emphasis is on providing those in need with more dollars.

5. *Trying to produce more jobs and get lower income people off the tax rolls.* Ronald Reagan, George Bush, and their supporters in Congress argue that a rising tide lifts all boats and that their policies of stimulating private enterprise would, after a while, do more to help the poor than most of the social strategies programs promoted by liberals or Democrats. Thus the Reagan program cut food stamps and similar programs and emphasized tax cuts that would, they hoped, stimulate investment and business expansion, which, in turn, would produce a healthy economy, lower inflation, lower interest rates, and more jobs. When these programs failed to affect poverty, the Reagan administration, with Congress's approval, moved to get several million low-income citizens removed from tax-paying responsibility, which, in effect, was a subsidy approach.[37]

Many of the entitlement programs benefit middle-income groups. And these groups are politically alert and organized. A growing number of analysts of different political persuasions are now worried that the federal budget is "out of control." Congress finds it difficult to curtail entitlement programs. The federal deficit continues to grow, and the debate over providing assistance to the poor intensifies.

S ummary

1. During the past few years major efforts have been undertaken to reform the tax code (lowering tax rates and simplifying the tax system) and to devise economic policies (both fiscal and monetary) that will encourage economic growth but prevent inflation, high interest rates, and unemployment. Few policies have succeeded, but economists and political leaders continue to grope for a mix of the right economic strategies. Meanwhile, virtually everyone agrees that annual budgetary deficits and the soaring national debt are monumental problems.

2. One of the greatest challenges in a democracy is mobilizing the government so that it can respond to changing economic conditions, but in a way that keeps government accountable to the people. The problem in part is whether a system such as ours can act effectively when action is needed. But the problem is also knowing what to do and when to do it. Further, we no longer have a domestic economy autonomous from an international economy.

3. The role of government as promoter is not new. It is as old as the republic itself and our postal system. We have witnessed intense governmental concern with energy development, support of businesses such as Chrysler and the savings and loan banks, and human resource assistance programs.

4. Many disagree with efforts by the national government to improve the quality of life, to focus resources and attention on the problems of the poor, and to improve the cities. They view with distaste the bureaucracy required for these programs, allege that the programs cost far more than they might cost if administered at the local level, and claim that many of these programs create a dependency that undermines our traditional ethic of self-reliance. On the other hand, most of these problems developed because local, private, and voluntary sectors were overwhelmed by them and were unable to respond in a meaningful way.

5. The pressures are usually for more, not less, involvement by the national government. Once a subsidy or entitlement program is established, it is hard to get rid of. In one way or another the government subsidizes nearly every segment of our population. Which of these programs are justified and which are not is at the very heart of American politics. One person's subsidy is often viewed as the next person's boondoggle.

F urther Reading

JEFFREY H. BIRNBAUM and ALAN S. MURRAY. *Showdown at Gucci Gulch: Lawmakers, Lobbyists, and the Unlikely Triumph of Tax Reform* (Vintage, 1988).

PAUL BLUMBERG. *Inequality in an Age of Decline* (Oxford University Press, 1980).

FORREST CHISMAN and ALAN PIFER. *Government for the People— The Federal Social Role* (W.W. Norton, 1988).

WILLIAM GREIDER. *Secrets of the Temple: How the Federal Reserve Runs the Country* (Simon & Schuster, 1987).

HERMAN B. LEONARD. *Checks Unbalanced: The Quiet Side of Public Spending* (Basic Books, 1986).

DANIEL LEVINE. *Poverty and Society: The Growth of the American Welfare State in International Comparison* (Rutgers University Press, 1988).

PAUL LIGHT. *Artful Work: The Politics of Social Security Reform* (Random House, 1985).

THEODORE R. MARMOR and JERRY MASHAW, eds. *Social Security: Beyond the Rhetoric of Crisis.* (Princeton University Press, 1988).

CHARLES MURRAY. *Losing Ground: American Social Policy, 1950– 1980* (Basic Books, 1984).

BENJAMIN PAGE. *Who Gets What From Government* (University of California Press, 1983).

HOWARD SHUMAN. *Politics and the Budget*, 2d ed. (Prentice Hall, 1988).

LESTER THUROW. *The Zero-Sum Solution: Building a World Class American Economy* (Simon & Schuster, 1985).

MARGARET WEIR, ANN SHOLA ORLOFF, and THEDA SKOCPOL, eds. *The Politics of Social Policy in the United States* (Princeton University Press, 1988).

WILLIAM JULIUS WILSON. *The Truly Disadvantaged* (University of Chicago Press, 1987).

JOHN F. WITTE. *The Politics and Development of the Federal Income Tax* (University of Wisconsin Press, 1985).

Notes

1. Robert D. Reischauer, "The Federal Budget: Subsidies for the Rich," in Michael J. Boskin and Aaron Wildavsky, eds., *The Federal Budget: Economics and Politics* (Institute for Contemporary Studies, 1982), p. 236.
2. The debate over the federal government's role in social policy is a lively one. For conservative perspectives, see George Gilder, *Wealth and Poverty* (Bantam, 1981); and Charles Murray, *Losing Ground* (Basic, 1984). For liberal and left critiques, see John E. Schwartz, *America's Hidden Success* (Norton, 1984); Forrest Chisman and Alan Pifer, *Government for the People—The Federal Social Role* (Norton, 1987); and Frances Fox Piven and Richard A. Cloward, *Regulating the Poor* (Vintage Books, 1971).
3. *Pollock* v. *Farmer's Loan and Trust Co.*, 158 U.S. 601 (1895).
4. For studies on the origins of the income tax, see John F. Witte, *The Politics and Development of the Federal Income Tax* (University of Wisconsin Press, 1985); and Jerold L. Waltman, *Political Origins of the U.S. Income Tax* (University Press of Mississippi, 1985).
5. See Joseph A. Pechman, *Who Paid The Taxes, 1965–1985* (Brookings Institution, 1985).
6. George J. Church, "Are You Better Off?" *Time* (October 10, 1988), p. 29.
7. A lively story of tax reform is told by Jeffrey H. Birnbaum and Alan S. Murray, *Showdown at Gucci Gulch: Lawmakers, Lobbyists, and the Unlikely Triumph of Tax Reform* (Vintage, 1988).
8. Bill Bradley, *The Fair Tax* (Pocket Books, 1984), p. 11.
9. Henry J. Aaron and Harvey Galper, *Assessing Tax Reform* (Brookings Institution, 1985), p. 2.
10. "Tax Reform Lets Politicians Look For New Donors," *Wall Street Journal* (July 7, 1986), editorial page.
11. Paul E. Peterson, "The New Politics of Deficits," in John Chubb and Paul E. Peterson, eds., *New Directions in American Politics* (Brookings Institution, 1985), p. 365. For a perspective on how much bigger the deficit really is, see Phillip Longman, "How the Government Cooks the Books," *Washington Monthly* (July/August, 1987), pp. 47–52. For an alternative view, see Robert Eisner, *How Real Is the Federal Deficit?* (Free Press, 1986).
12. Aaron and Galper, *Assessing Tax Reform*, p. 8.
13. Leonard Silk, "Ailing Economy: Debt Buildup Called Cause," *The New York Times* (July 29, 1986), p. 34.
14. Quoted in F. L. Allen, *Since Yesterday* (Harper, 1940), p. 64.
15. W. H. Beveridge, *The Pillars of Security* (Macmillan, 1943), p. 51.
16. The debate over Keynes and his economic theories still takes place in the United States. See, for example, the special issue on Keynes in *The Economist* (American Enterprise Institute, June 1983); and Robert Eisner, *How Real Is the Federal Deficit?* (Free Press, 1986).
17. For the full history of the bill, see Stephen K. Bailey, *Congress Makes a Law* (Columbia University Press, 1950). For a history of national efforts at economic planning since the 1930s, see Otis L. Graham, *Toward a Planned Society* (Oxford University Press, 1976).
18. Herbert Stein, *Presidential Economics* (Simon & Schuster, 1985).
19. See Roger B. Porter, *Presidential Decision-Making: The Economic Policy Board* (Cambridge University Press, 1980). See also Ronald Brownstein and Dick Kirschten, "Cabinet Power," *The National Journal* (June 28, 1986), pp. 1582–89.
20. Lester C. Thurow, *The Zero-Sum Solution: Building a World Class American Economy* (Simon & Schuster, 1985), p. 30. See also Herbert Stein, *Presidential Economics* (Simon & Schuster, 1985).
21. On the Federal Reserve Board, see William Greider, *Secrets of the Temple* (Simon & Schuster, 1987); and Donald F. Kehl, *Leadership at the Fed* (Yale University Press, 1986).
22. Stein, *Presidential Economics*, p. 305.
23. See the debate on the amendment in *Congressional Digest* (October 1982).
24. Nell Henderson, "It's Not a Subsidy, Exactly; It's Technical Assistance," *The Washington Post National Weekly Edition* (July 7, 1986), p. 33.
25. An important study of agricultural support and political interest is William P. Browne, *Private Interests, Public Policy, and American Agriculture* (University Press of Kansas, 1988).
26. See the recent case against protectionism, for example, in Thurow, *Zero Sum Solution: Building a World Class American Economy*.
27. For a probing analysis of current trade policy, see David B. Yoffie, "American Trade Policy: An Obsolete Bargain?" in John E. Chubb and Paul E. Peterson, eds., *Can the Government Govern?* (Brookings Institution, 1989).
28. Herman B. Leonard, *Checks Unbalanced: The Quiet Side of Public Spending* (Basic Books, 1986), p. 51.
29. Martha Derthick, "No More Easy Votes for Social Security," *The Brookings Bulletin* (Fall 1979), p. 2.
30. Martha Derthick, *Policymaking for Social Security* (Brookings Institution, 1979), p. 413.
31. Paul Light, *Artful Work: The Politics of Social Security Reform* (Random House, 1985); see also Susan Lee and Mary Beth Grover, "Social Security Forces a $60 Billion Question," *The New York Times*, July 23, 1989, p. F5.
32. R. Kent Weaver, "Controlling Entitlements," in John Chubb and Paul Peterson, eds., *The New Directions in American Politics*, (Brookings Institution, 1985), p. 307.
33. Murray, *Losing Ground*.
34. Michael Harrington, *The Other America* (Penguin, 1963), pp. 23–24.
35. See, for example, Michael Harrington, *Taking Sides* (Holt, Rinehart, Winston, 1985); and Kenneth Dolbeare, *Democracy at Risk* (Chatham House, 1984).
36. Quoted in Daniel P. Moynihan, *The Politics of a Guaranteed Income: The Nixon Administration and the Family Assistance Plan* (Random House, 1973), p. 225.
37. See Gregory A. Fossedal, "Reagan's War on Poverty," *The New York Times* (May 28, 1986), p. A23.

23

The Politics of Regulation

What do lawn mowers, automobiles, telephones, smoke detectors, cereal ads, pornography, banks, natural gas companies, nuclear power plants, and workers' wages all have in common? They are all regulated in some way by the federal government. Because virtually every activity in the United States is supervised in one form or another, regulation today is a vast enterprise. And any activity as pervasive as this is bound to generate controversy.

Our regulatory arrangements were not arbitrarily created; the framers *explicitly* authorized Congress in the Constitution to regulate commerce among the states and with foreign nations. They came into existence to clean up meatpacking conditions such as those exposed in Upton Sinclair's *The Jungle*, to prevent the kind of pesticide contamination described in Rachel Carson's *Silent Spring*, and to respond to the lack of auto safety documented in Ralph Nader's *Unsafe at Any Speed*. Regulations exist both to encourage competition and to achieve valued social objectives. More recently, regulations have been enacted to protect us from raw sewage in rivers, lead in paint and gasoline, toxic wastes in the air, radon gas in our homes, and asbestos, cotton dust, and hazardous substances in toys and furniture.

Certain regulations have generated fierce resentment. Can we afford all these regulations? Are they driving people out of business? Do the costs outweigh the benefits? Political and business leaders in the 1970s and 1980s often said the United States was overregulated. Labor, consumers, and environmentalists disagreed, saying that in certain areas we needed more—not less—regulation.

Bush, while vice-president under Reagan, served as the lead agent for some of the dismantling of traditional regulation. When Bush came to the presidency, however, he faced heightened public concern over the shortcomings of national regulatory efforts. People complained about delays at airports, questioned federal safety regulations for the airline industry, criticized federal standards on hazardous waste, and were skeptical about the safety of money deposited in savings institutions.

Whereas the unfettering of industry and the federal bureaucracy from red tape was a priority of the Reagan presidency, President Bush was pressured on many fronts to reregulate, to toughen existing regulations, and even to impose new regulations.[1]

Who is right? Do we need more or less regulation? This chapter will treat these questions. It will explain what regulation is, analyze the different goals of regulatory activities, discuss some costs and their consequences, and examine the debate over the merits of regulatory efforts.

What Is Regulation?

Regulation occurs when the government steps in and alters the natural procedures of the open market to achieve some desired goal. The main regulatory role of government is to improve or supplant markets when they do not or cannot function effectively. In this sense regulation is a middle ground between socialism, or government ownership, and a "laissez-faire," or "hands-off," policy. The open market is characterized by self-adjustment, or natural regulation. Regulation by government interjects political goals and values into the economy in the form of rules that direct behavior in the marketplace.

All economies are sets of rules and regulations; there simply are no unregulated economies. The United States operates with a competitive market economy: Wages, prices, the allocation of goods and services, and the employment of resources are generally regulated by the laws of supply and demand. Put another way, we rely on private enterprise and market incentives to carry out most of our production and distribution.

A government regulation is a limitation imposed on the discretion of a person or an organization, and is backed up by government's use of police power. It means setting restraints on persons or groups, directly compelling them to take, or not take, certain actions.

Cleanup activity took many months after birds and other animals became covered with oil as a result of the tanker *Exxon Valdez* running aground in Alaska in March 1989.

TYPES OF REGULATION

Regulation is often broken down into two general categories or types: *economic* or traditional regulation and *social* or new regulation. *Economic regulation* generally refers to controlling the entry of individual firms into particular lines of business and setting the prices that firms in a particular industry may charge. Sometimes, too, it can refer to specifying the standards of service firms can offer. Such regulation began in the nineteenth century, when the Interstate Commerce Commission was established, and it has continued with the Federal Communications Commission and the Commodity Futures Trading Commission. It has usually been justified to correct inefficient markets and to limit one or a few firms who have been able to use their market power to discourage competition. Several of these regulatory agencies, and this type of regulation in general, have come under criticism in recent years; economic studies suggest that, because economic regulation has sometimes encouraged artificially high prices and barriers to entry in the industries it regulates, it is costly to consumers and to the economy as a whole.

Social regulation generally refers to government efforts to correct a wide variety of side effects, usually unintended, brought about by certain economic

CHAPTER 23 / The Politics of Regulation

activity. Health, safety, and environmental hazards are often the targets of social regulation. This type of regulation cuts across industry lines and aims at providing such goods as cleaner air and improved worker and consumer safety. In economic terms, producers regulated by social regulation must now pay for the "external costs" that once were free, such as using the atmosphere for waste disposal. These costs, however, are often passed along to the consumer, and the true cost of the product is more accurately reflected in its price. Some goods become too costly, and demand drops. Others become more popular (for instance, safe toys). In the end the goal of such regulation is a socially more beneficial allocation of resources. The Environmental Protection Agency (EPA), the Consumer Product Safety Commission, and the Occupational Safety and Health Administration (OSHA) are engaged in social regulation. Social regulation has also been widely criticized, as we discuss later in this chapter.

Regulatory efforts of the federal government are basically a twentieth-century development, although certain efforts, such as the Steamboat Inspection Service of 1837, would qualify in a general sense as a regulatory endeavor. By 1900 there were about five regulatory agencies; by 1933 about a dozen. Today, depending on how they are counted, over eighty regulatory organizations at the federal level employ nearly 100,000 federal civil servants. Congress has created both *executive branch* and *independent regulatory agencies*. Members of executive branch agencies serve at the pleasure of the president. Members of independent regulatory agencies are appointed by the president, confirmed by the Senate, and removable only for some specific "cause." Executive branch regulatory agencies include the Food and Drug Administration, the Office of Surface Mining, the National Highway Traffic Safety Administration, and the Comptroller of the Currency. Independent

TABLE 23–1
Some Regulatory Agencies and Their Missions

ORGANIZATION	YEAR ESTABLISHED	PRIMARY FUNCTION
Federal Trade Commission (FTC)	1914	Administers certain antitrust laws concerning advertising, labeling, and packaging to protect consumers from unfair business practices
Food and Drug Administration (FDA)	1931	Establishes regulations concerning purity, safety, and labeling accuracy of certain foods and drugs; issues licenses for manufacturing and distribution
Federal Communications Commission (FCC)	1934	Licenses civilian radio and television communication; licenses and sets rates for interstate and international communication
Animal and Plant Health Inspection Service	1953	Sets standards; inspects and enforces laws relating to meat, poultry, and plant safety
Environmental Protection Agency (EPA)	1970	Develops environmental quality standards; approves state environmental plans
Occupational Safety and Health Administration (OSHA)	1970	Develops and enforces worker safety and health regulations
Bureau of Alcohol, Tobacco and Firearms	1972	Enforces laws and regulates legal flow of these materials
Consumer Product Safety Commission (CPSC)	1972	Establishes mandatory product safety standards and bans sales of products that do not comply

These are examples of the nearly eighty services, commissions, agencies, or administrations that have a significant national regulatory function. Note that some, such as the FCC, are of the older, traditional type, and some, such as OSHA and the CPSC, are of the newer social type.

regulatory agencies, headed by a group usually composed of seven members, include the Federal Communications Commission, the Nuclear Regulatory Commission, and the Federal Reserve Board.

THE CASE FOR REGULATION

The philosophy behind regulation is simple: The marketplace often fails to provide the necessary protection for the achievement of certain valued goals such as personal safety and environmental health. Through government supervision of or intervention in potentially hazardous or abusive situations, all of society will benefit.

The costs of regulation are exaggerated, according to some observers. The gross national product (GNP) measures growth in goods and services but not the worth of a cleaner environment, a slower rate of natural resource depletion, or increased recreational opportunities. We too often overlook the advantages of clean air, a clear view, and so on.

Supporters of regulation also say it is necessary to protect specific groups as well as society as a whole. Consumers, for example, often lack sufficient power to act as a check on business, and minorities sometimes need assistance in wiping out discriminatory practices. Government regulation is needed to prevent pollution of the environment, unfair practices, discrimination, or exorbitant pricing. The same protection must be provided for innocent third parties. Supporters of regulation say residents of areas near industrial waste sites, for example, need government help to ensure the reasonable safety of their neighborhoods.

It is important to appreciate too that a lot of regulations were brought about because certain businesses wanted to make it difficult for new competitors to compete against them. Various airline, trucking, and banking regulations in the past, for example, clearly sought to make it easier for the existing commercial groups to continue their privileged status. Companies, of course, like regulation when it benefits them and detest it when it costs them money. Advocates of regulation do not oppose the free enterprise system. On the contrary, many believe regulation is the best instrument available for correcting the abuses of the system and thereby ensuring its survival. Some say the basic purpose of regulation is to ensure the continuation of a competitive atmosphere. If the government can prevent abuses by monopolies or correct market imperfections, economic competition will be enhanced for the benefit of all.

THE CASE AGAINST REGULATION

Opponents of extensive government regulation say that in most cases government regulation is not needed; market forces compel business to work for the benefit of consumers. The basic objectives are the same, opponents say: a clean, safe environment and an equitable and efficient economy. But differences arise over how best to achieve these objectives. Critics of regulation say the best mechanisms for attaining both economic and social goals are the free market and the forces of competition. With meaningful competition the consumer gets the most goods at the best price, and overall system output and efficiency are maximized.

Critics of regulation also say it is inefficient. The labyrinth of federal rules, they say, dampens productivity, fuels inflation, and blunts our competitive strength abroad. Further, they argue, public officials cannot know as much about the intricacies of any particular economic pursuit as do those engaged in the business on a daily basis. This lack of knowledge results in regulations that unduly hamper production and cost much more than the benefits they provide.

Government regulation is also often counterproductive, critics say. Many times, they claim, government regulations hurt the people they are intended to help, and vice versa. Some believe government actions often protect monopolies and cartels. Removing restrictions would make markets more equitable, to the benefit of consumers. Moreover, opponents of regulation suggest that some federal regulations penalize consumers, to whom the costs of regulations are usually passed along. For example, the extra costs of automobile safety and auto emission devices (sometimes as much as $2000) become part of the price paid by the purchaser of a car. Another criticism of regulation, from a strict economic standpoint, is that it diverts resources from potentially productive endeavors.

The regulation debate is not as clear-cut as it may appear. Few people call for unlimited government intervention in economic and social activity. Similarly, few people advocate absolute removal of government participation from the marketplace. Indeed, some people call for more regulation in some areas and less in others. Overall, the diversity of regulations makes generalizations difficult.

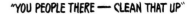

"YOU PEOPLE THERE — CLEAN THAT UP"

Copyright 1989 by Herblock in The Washington Post.

INCREASED REGULATION

Just a generation ago the national government had major regulatory responsibility in only a handful of policy areas—antitrust, financial institutions, transportation, and communications. But today dozens of commissions, agencies, services, and administrations limit or control what we can produce or do. About twenty of these are independent regulatory agencies. The other regulatory organizations, as discussed previously, are located within the executive departments.

Four major waves of regulatory legislation have occurred in American history: at the turn of the century, in the 1910s, in the 1930s, and in the late 1960s through 1980. In each case changing political intentions and forces gave rise to the legislation. Primary reasons for regulation have included: controlling monopoly and oligopoly, compensating for market imperfections, and defending the economically weak.

Controlling Monopoly and Oligopoly To achieve many economic goals, including the best allocation of resources, government must encourage competition. In a monopoly or oligopoly (discussed later) power is concentrated in the hands of only one or a few firms, and there is no competition. The government works to ensure competition through antitrust regulation. When monopoly and oligopoly exist, as in the case of power companies, for example, government regulation prevents these industries from taking advantage of the consumer. In some markets, government regulates prices and sets standards of performance.

Another market imperfection involves **natural monopolies.** A natural monopoly exists when it would be grossly inefficient to have competition in a particular industry. If competition existed in electric utilities, the price of power might be higher to the public than if just one company supplied all the power: Because of the size of its operation, and the vast capital investment needed, one company can be more efficient, and thus more economical, than many. When such a natural monopoly exists, the government regulates it.

Compensating for Market Imperfections The market does not always work to solve every problem, especially the problem of *externalities*, or side effects. Consider pollution. For a long time no price was imposed on a business for using air and

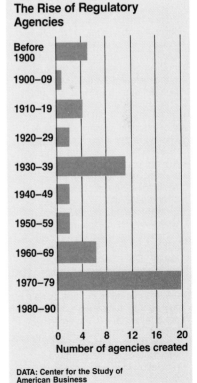

The Rise of Regulatory Agencies

DATA: Center for the Study of American Business

water to store or discharge toxic wastes. Therefore, market forces did not consider what it cost society to have its air and water polluted. Or take the case of commuters who use their cars to go to work. The more who do so, the more difficult it is for commuters to get to work. (That is why commuters frequently favor mass transportation—so that *other* people will use it and thus open the roadways for *them*.) Still, present market forces do not encourage taking a bus instead of a car to work.

When the market fails to set appropriate costs and benefits, pressures develop for the government to step in. The government can, for example, pass regulations that impose costs on air pollution.

Defending the Economically Weak   The government has involved itself directly in the economy to protect those who lack economic power. It has, for instance, worked to establish a minimum wage and to prevent such abuses as child labor. The government has also sought to control the conflict between labor and management and to protect workers' right to organize. In its role as protector of the weak, the government has sought to ensure equal opportunity (which we discussed in Chapter 5), and to protect the investor or consumer from fraud and unsafe products.

GOVERNMENT REGULATION: A FINGER IN EVERY PIE?

Although regulation has traditionally been defended as intervention to ensure more socially beneficial outcomes, it is sometimes criticized as imposing more costs on society than its benefits warrant. Even though we have many desired objectives—economic, social, and political—our resources are limited. A critical task of modern democratic government is to make wise, balanced choices among courses of action and competing objectives. Increasingly regulation is coming into conflict with other economic objectives: Critics charge it is contributing to higher inflation, lower productivity, and economic stagnation.[2] Proponents contend government regulation, though not perfect, has brought improvements in the areas of environmental quality, worker safety, and consumer protection.[3]

It should be pointed out that economists generally view regulation in the aggregate without much concern for distribution of costs. Political scientists, on the other hand, focus on who wins and who loses and the impact on business, consumers, and others who have a stake in the overall transactions. How desirable is it to have considerably cleaner air or considerably safer workplaces? Although it is relatively inexpensive to remove a large amount of air pollution, and therefore socially desirable, it becomes increasingly expensive to remove all or even almost all of it. To do so would require an allocation of resources that, from a taxpayer's point of view, might be better used for something else—whether new missiles or schools. Is there a socially optimal point of pollution control or worker safety beyond which it is too costly to go? The challenge for policy makers is to determine what this point is. In our political system, with its many competing interest groups, there is much difference of opinion on this matter.

Faced with this problem, Congress often legislates broad objectives for the regulatory agencies, which then set specific rules for meeting these goals. Agency regulations have been largely in the form of specific rules that a firm may not violate without being punished. Usually of the "command-control" type, they have been criticized as being arbitrary, costly, and inflexible. Recent presidents and their administrations have cut back some of these regulations. For example, OSHA trimmed over 1000 "nitpicking" regulations that governed such things as the shape of toilet seats.

Some economists have proposed regulating procedures that would make it less expensive for industries to meet requirements. The concept behind ideas such as performance standards or effluent fees is that the government should set requirements for pollution control or worker safety, but the means of reaching these goals should be left to the firms. For example, rather than factories being required to install expensive noise control facilities, workers could be required to wear hearing protectors.

The new regulatory techniques can be classified into four categories: (1) *market approaches*—reliance on the economic incentives of the free market to nudge industry in the direction of the public interest; (2) *performance standards*—replacement of regulations that spell out exactly how industry must meet a particular goal with broader statements that allow industry to choose the means; (3) *informational approaches*—requirements that manufacturers disclose complete information about their products, on the theory that consumers can then make intelligent choices; and (4) *self-regulation*—a government decision to do little more than help industry set its own voluntary standards.[4]

"I think we can agree, gentlemen, that one can respect Mother Nature without coddling her."

Drawing by Lorenz; © 1986 The New Yorker Magazine, Inc.

Regulating Business

Business has never been free of restrictive legislation, but during much of the latter part of the nineteenth century (as discussed in Chapter 7), our national policy was to leave business pretty much alone. With considerable freedom business leaders set about developing (as well as exploiting) a nation that was enormously rich in natural resources. The heroes of the 1870s and 1880s were not politicians but business magnates—the Rockefellers, Morgans, Carnegies, and Fricks. "From rags to riches" became the nation's motto.

Many businesspeople in the late nineteenth century were not just given freedom; they often were given prime sections of land to subsidize expansion of rail systems, tariffs to protect infant industries, and implicit—if not explicit—police assistance to prevent rapid unionization. Government actually helped to *promote* many of these businesses.

Toward the end of the century sharp depressions rocked the economy and threw people out of work. Millions labored long hours in factories and fields for meager wages. Muckrakers revealed that some of the most famous business leaders had indulged in shoddy practices and corrupt deals. A demand for government regulation sprang up, and a series of national and state laws were passed in an attempt to correct the worst abuses. Such laws were adopted on the pragmatic assumption that each problem could be handled as it arose. On balance, however, these laws still reflected a commitment to competitive markets. The government intervened only for the purpose of remedying the defects of the marketplace.

ANTITRUST POLICY

Social critics and populist reformers in the late nineteenth century believed consumers were being cheated, especially in the oil, sugar, whiskey, and steel industries where monopolies controlled goods and services. At the same time people began to have mixed feelings about big business. Americans, who have always been impressed by bigness—the tallest skyscraper, the largest football stadium, the biggest steel mill—the efficiency that often goes with it, have also been skeptical about the power and side effects of giant enterprises. We believe our economic system functions best under conditions of fair competition among many businesses. We would like to believe, too, that enterprising individuals can set themselves up in virtually any business. These mixed views have long been reflected in our attempts to prevent monopoly and the restraint of competition through **antitrust policy.** ("Trusts" are collusions or arrangements to reduce competition.)

In 1890 Congress responded to this new mood by passing the *Sherman Antitrust Act.* Designed to foster competition and stop the growth of private monopolies, the act made clear its intention "to protect trade and commerce against unlawful restraints and monopolies." Henceforth, persons making contracts, combinations, or conspiracies in restraint of trade in interstate and foreign commerce could be sued for damages, required to stop their illegal practices, and subjected to criminal penalities. The Sherman Antitrust Act had little immediate impact. Presidents made little attempt to enforce it, and the Supreme Court's early construction of the act limited its scope.[7]

During the administration of Woodrow Wilson, Congress added the *Clayton Act* to the antitrust arsenal. This act outlawed such specific abuses as charging different prices to different buyers in order to destroy a weaker competitor, granting rebates, making false statements about competitors and their products, buying up supplies to stifle competition, bribing competitors' employees, and so on. In addition, interlocking directorates (by which an officer or director in one corporation serves on the board of a competitor) were banned, and corporations were prohibited from acquiring stock (amended in 1950 to include assets) in competing concerns if such acquisitions substantially lessened interstate competition. Also, in 1914, Congress established the Federal Trade Commission (FTC), run by a five-person board, to enforce the Clayton Act and to prevent unfair competitive practices. The FTC was to be the "traffic cop" for competition.[8]

Still, antitrust activity continued to be weak during the 1920s. Times were prosperous: Republican administrations were actively probusiness. The FTC consisted of men who opposed government regulation of business. The Department of Justice, charged with enforcing the Sherman Act, paid little attention to it. During the Depression abuses were revealed, and popular resentment mounted against big business. At first the Roosevelt administration tried to fight the Depression by setting aside the antitrust laws. But by the late 1930s a period of trustbusting began in earnest. Since then the Supreme Court has shown a more sympathetic attitude toward the purposes of the Sherman Act, and the FTC has sometimes acted with more vigor.

But how effective has all this activity been? Have antitrust suits, FTC proceedings, and the fear of such reprisals kept our system competitive? It is difficult to tell. Some people think antitrust laws are out of date, in part because they were written when the major economic competitors in any industry were from this country alone. That has markedly changed in recent years.

Americans tend to think issues of domestic economic policy are solely within the jurisdiction of this government. But in recent years we have discovered that the economic fate of this nation and of its industries is tied closely to what happens elsewhere. For years we thought the automobile market in the United States was dominated by the Big Three (GM, Ford, and Chrysler), and that they could control the market and set the prices. But after they set the prices "too high," we discovered that firms located in Japan, Germany, and elsewhere can also make and sell cars: As a result, the Big Three look less Big. In fact, foreign corporations have captured

"As far as I'm concerned, they can do what they want with the minimum wage, just as long as they keep their hands off the maximum wage."

Drawing by Mankoff. © *1989 The New Yorker Magazine, Inc.*

increasing shares of our markets, and our corporations have moved more of their production facilities overseas. And more corporations have become multinational, seeking to benefit from the overlapping of national regulatory jurisdictions.

About one-third of our nation's manufacturing capacity is controlled by 50 companies, and about two-thirds of all manufacturing assets are owned by only 500 corporations. But monopolies as such have virtually disappeared from the economic arena. In place of monopolies two new threats to competition have emerged: the **oligopoly,** a situation in which a few firms dominate a market, such as in the automobile industry or the food processing industry; and the **conglomerate,** a situation in which a firm owns businesses in many unrelated industries.

Are the nation's antitrust laws, drawn up several decades ago, still practical for today's economy? This question evokes different responses. Some members of Congress and some former regulatory commissioners and Justice Department officials believe we need to design tighter penalties, impose more regulatory guidelines, and expand antitrust enforcement. But this is plainly a minority or nonexistent point of view in the Reagan and Bush administrations. At the Justice Department's Antitrust Division, about 300 lawyers work on cases brought to them in a general effort to protect the free enterprise system. Corporate conduct that may be illegal comes to their attention through complaints by competitors, customers, or suppliers.

Some outside observers say the Antitrust Division has done a fair job in recent years. Most think that it is understaffed and, considering its responsibilities, that it must work with too small a budget. Reagan and Bush want it that way. The Federal Trade Commission, also influenced by the Reagan years and by substantive budget cutbacks, is less aggressive. Many of the FTC's important cases are settled by negotiations. **Consent decrees** are orders to cease anticompetitive conduct (although things other than anticompetitive conduct are sometimes specified in consent decrees).[9]

Recent years witnessed a wave of corporate *mergers* involving one company's buying out another or two companies' pooling assets to form a larger single company. General Motors bought Hughes Aircraft. R. J. Reynolds absorbed Nabisco. GE and RCA merged. ABC became part of Capital Cities Communications. And Philip Morris merged with General Foods and Warner Communications merged with Time. Several airlines have also merged. In many instances, these mergers occurred among competing companies. In one recent five-year period, more than 10,000 mergers took place. Invariably such mergers raise the question of whether a specific merger will increase or decrease competition.

The Reagan and Bush administrations generally have adopted a permissive policy toward mergers, and few mergers have been prevented. The assumption is that most mergers are inherently good—not, as the common wisdom had it in the 1960s, that such mergers were suspect.[10]

CONTROLLING BIG BUSINESS

What should the government do about big business? Few policy makers agree on an answer. Some say we are doing too much—and even those who think we are doing too little do not agree on the solutions. Some economists, for example, see no need for new initiatives. They say the alleged damage done by big business is vastly overestimated, and that even the extent of concentration is exaggerated. They reject as pure myth the view that the United States has become a corporate state. They see the increasing size of business as an indication of increased economies of scale. Although the market is still as competitive as before, the companies are bigger. And we, as consumers, benefit from the technology provided by the large modern corporations.

Economist John Kenneth Galbraith, among others, agrees that bigness contributes to efficiency, provides the capital necessary for innovation, and spurs economic growth. But he also recognizes that abuses can occur when economic power is concentrated in the hands of a few corporate managers. Galbraith suggests three new tasks for government:

1. Provide assistance to the segment of our economy that is still considered to be competitive, for example, the corner grocery store or the independent TV repair shop.
2. Manage the economy directly by implementing wage-price controls in all the industries that are dominated by big business and big unions.
3. Control the direction of big business by restricting the use of resources in areas that are already overdeveloped; by setting limits on the use of technology, and by establishing stringent standards on the byproducts of industry, for example, pollution, *and* enforcing the standards once set.[11]

"But this would be socialism!" exclaim many economists and policy makers. No, says Galbraith; government already plays a major role in the development of individual firms and in the distribution of economic rewards among different industries. All Galbraith calls for, or so he claims, is the *redirection* of government subsidies. "If these proposals are socialism," he replies to his critics, "socialism already exists."

Still other reformers want to break up large corporations, not just regulate them. These individuals believe the market can work; all it needs is a chance. They are against bigness, charging that bigness leads to irresponsibility and misconduct.[12]

ANTITRUST ENFORCEMENT AND THE PHONE COMPANY

In 1975 American Telephone and Telegraph (AT&T) had been charged with monopolizing the telephone service and telephone equipment industry. The Justice Department claimed AT&T was using control of its twenty-two local phone companies to shut out competition in the long-distance and phone equipment sales markets. Antitrust laws were used in this instance by other business firms to break up AT&T. Pressures were not so much to protect consumers as to give other businesses an opportunity to sell telephones and long-distance services.

The huge antitrust case was settled in 1983, after costing AT&T over $360 million in legal fees over a seven-year period. Under the terms of the settlement, the twenty-two local phone companies owned by AT&T became reorganized into seven independent companies. AT&T was allowed to keep its long-distance operations, its equipment manufacturing and sales arms, and its research facilities. All other phone services, however, were divided among the local companies.

The long-term effects on telephone service and phone bills remain uncertain. Some analysts (including AT&T executives) think rates for local service will increase as smaller phone companies are forced to pass on increased costs to consumers. Critics of the AT&T "break-up" think this is government regulation at its worst. Altering and weakening the world's best telephone service just doesn't make sense, they say. The only people who will profit, they added, will be lawyers, bankers, stock brokers, and those who print stock certificates. Others think increased competition in the long-distance market will result in savings that will more than offset local rate increases. Initial developments suggest that more competition and lower rates on long-distance service have, in fact, been achieved. Still, there have been costs to the consumer: higher bills for local services, increased charges for connects and disconnects, and so on.

After the breakup of AT&T, telephone products and services became more numerous and sophisticated.

Regulating Labor-Management Relations

Government regulation of business is essentially restrictive. Most governmental laws and rules have curbed certain business practices and steered private enterprise into socially useful channels. But regulation cuts two ways. In the case of American workers, most laws in recent decades have tended not to restrict but rather to confer rights and opportunities. Actually, many labor laws do not touch labor directly; instead, they regulate its relations with employers.

LABOR AND THE GOVERNMENT

During the first half of this century, governmental protection and promotion were gradually extended over the whole range of labor activity and organization. This was the result of two basic developments: labor's growing political power, and the awareness of millions of Americans that a healthy and secure nation depends in large measure on a healthy and secure labor force.

Labor's basic struggle was for the right to organize. For many decades trade unions had been held lawful by acts of state legislatures, but the courts had chipped away at their status by legalizing certain antiunion devices. The most notorious was the **yellow-dog contract,** by which employers made new workers promise not to join labor organizations. If labor organizers later tried to unionize the workers, the employers, on the basis of the yellow-dog contract, could apply for court orders to stop the organizers. In 1932 labor secured the passage of the Norris-La Guardia Act, which made yellow-dog contracts unenforceable and granted labor the right to organize. By 1932 unions had won other kinds of protection from the federal government, especially over conditions of labor. Yet progress was slow. With the New Deal, Congress began to enact a series of laws to protect workers and their right to form trade unions.

PROTECTING WORKERS

Among the more important areas of federal regulation designed to protect workers are the following:

Top officials of the AFL-CIO in conference at their headquarters building two blocks from the White House.

1. *Public contracts.* The Walsh-Healy Act of 1936, as amended, requires that no worker employed under contracts with the national government in excess of $10,000 be paid less than the prevailing wage; and that he or she be paid overtime for all work in excess of eight hours per day or forty hours per week. Two contested questions today are how to determine what the prevailing wage is and whether or not to retain this provision inserted in the mid-1930s. Skilled craftworkers and union officials insist that the Davis-Bacon provision, as it is known, is still necessary to protect their standards of living and to ensure quality work on government projects. Others argue

that in the present-day context the prevailing wage requirement makes public work unreasonably expensive and that the provision merely gives craftworkers a special privilege at the expense of the taxpayers.

2. *Wages and hours.* The Fair Labor Standards Act of 1938 set a maximum work week of forty hours for all employers engaged in interstate commerce or in the production of goods for interstate commerce (with certain exemptions). Work beyond that amount must be paid for at one and one-half times the regular rate. Minimum wages, first set at 25 cents an hour, were progressively increased; from 1981 to 1989 the minimum wage was $3.35.

3. *Child labor.* The Federal Labor Standards Act prohibits child labor (under 16 years of age, or under 18 in hazardous occupations) in industries that engage in, or that produce goods for, interstate commerce.

4. *Industrial safety and occupational health.* The Occupational Safety and Health Act of 1970 created the first comprehensive federal industrial safety program. It gives the secretary of labor broad authority to set safety and health standards for workers of companies in interstate commerce.

PROTECTING UNIONS

Do unions need federal laws to protect their right to organize? The history of union efforts before 1933 suggests that organizing without federal protection was extremely difficult. Indeed, union membership and strength were waning fast until New Deal measures granted workers the right to organize and bargain collectively. The National Labor Relations Act of 1935 (usually called the Wagner Act) made these guarantees permanent. The preamble declared that workers in industries affecting interstate commerce (with certain exemptions) should have the right to organize and bargain collectively, and that inequality in bargaining power between employers and workers led to industrial strife and economic instability. The act made five types of action unfair for employers: (1) interfering with workers in their attempt to organize unions or bargain collectively; (2) supporting company unions (unions set up and dominated by the employer); (3) discriminating against members of unions; (4) firing or otherwise victimizing an employee for having taken action under the act; and (5) refusing to bargain with union representatives. The act was intended to prevent employers from using violence, espionage, propaganda, and community pressure to resist unionization.

To administer the act, a board of three (now five) members, holding overlapping terms of five years each, was set up. Under the act the National Labor Relations Board (NLRB), a regulatory commission, has the ticklish job of determining the appropriate bargaining unit, that is, whether the employees may organize by plant, by craft, or some other basis. The board operates largely through regional officers, who investigate charges of unfair labor practices and issue formal complaints; and through trial examiners, who hold hearings and submit reports to the board in Washington.

STRIKING A BALANCE

From the start the Wagner Act was controversial. It strengthened the unions and helped them seize greater economic and political power. In 1936 a committee of noted attorneys declared it unconstitutional. But in 1937 the Supreme Court, by a vote of five to four, upheld the constitutionality of the act. The fight then shifted to Congress, where senators and representatives attacked the NLRB through denunciations, investigations, and slashes in appropriations.

What caused all this uproar? First, from the outset the board vigorously applied the prolabor provisions of the act. Second, the board got caught in the struggle between the AFL (American Federation of Labor) and the CIO (Congress of Industrial Organizations). Whichever way it decided certain cases, it was bound to antagonize one labor faction or the other. Third, the purpose of the act was widely misunderstood. Employers and editorial writers charged that the act was biased too much in favor of labor, and that it went well beyond merely improving the workers' bargaining power.

Most unions were run honestly and responsively. Nevertheless, public opinion seemed to swing against labor after World War II. Both labor excesses and a wave of great industrywide strikes intensified demands that Congress equalize the obligations of labor and management. In 1946 the Republicans won majorities in both the House and Senate, paving the way for modification of the Wagner Act.

THE TAFT-HARTLEY ACT

The result of the Labor-Management Relations Act of 1947, commonly called the **Taft-Hartley Act.** This act applies (with certain exceptions) to industries dealing in interstate commerce. The act:

1. Outlaws the **closed shop** and permits the **union shop** only under certain conditions. (A closed shop requires an employer to hire and retain only union members in good standing. A union shop is one in which new employees must join the union within a stated period of time.)

2. Outlaws jurisdictional strikes (strikes arising from disputes between unions over whose members should perform a particular task); **secondary boycotts** (efforts by unions involved in disputes with employers to encourage other unions to boycott a fourth party—usually the employers—who, in response to such pressure, might put pressure on the original offending employers); excessive union dues or fees; and strikes by federal employees.

3. Makes it an unfair labor practice for unions to refuse to bargain with employers.

4. Permits employers and unions to sue each other in federal court for violation of contracts.

5. Allows the use of the **labor injunction** on a limited scale. (Such an injunction is a court order forbidding specific individuals or groups to perform acts the court considers harmful to the rights or property of an employer or community.)

6. Permits states to outlaw union shops. **Right-to-work laws,** which states could now adopt, typically make it illegal for **collective bargaining** agreements to contain closed shop, union shop, preferential hiring, or any other clauses calling for compulsory union membership.

The Taft-Hartley Act also set up machinery for handling disputes affecting an entire industry or a major part of it, if a stoppage would threaten national health or safety. When such a strike breaks out, the following steps are authorized:

1. The president appoints a special board to investigate and report the facts.

2. The president may then instruct the attorney general to seek, in a federal court, an eighty-day injunction against the strike.

You decide!

Since 1938 the federal government has maintained a floor on wages in order to achieve a minimal socially acceptable standard of living for all protected workers without eliminating too many jobs. The minimum wage is defended as the most direct, comprehensive means of increasing the earnings of the working poor. But several people have proposed that there should be a subminimum wage for youth—perhaps $2.50 or $3.00 an hour. What do you think about this proposal? What do you think the benefits and disadvantages would be?

(Answer/Discussion on page 602.)

Answer/Discussion

Youth unemployment is a problem. It is usually at least double that of the adult population; for black teenagers, it is several times that of all adults. A subminimum wage would encourage some employers to put more younger people to work; it would probably also create some jobs.

But, if there were a subminimum wage, young people would often displace older workers because they would be cheaper to hire. The minimum wage was $3.35 from 1981 through 1989. The minimum wage recently has not kept up with inflation. After adjusting for inflation, the 8 million or more workers paid the current minimum wage in effect have had their income reduced nearly 30 percent in recent years. This debate over a subminimum wage for teenagers distracts attention from the more important issue of the substantial erosion in the minimum wage for all. Still a case can be made that a two-tier minimum wage should be tried for a period.

Jack Bavis, president of the Airline Pilot's Association, on the picket line with his union during the strike against Eastern Airlines.

3. If the court agrees that national health or safety is endangered, it grants this injunction.

4. If the parties have not settled the strike within the eighty days, the board informs the president of the employer's last offer of settlement.

5. The NLRB takes a secret vote among the employees to see if they will accept the employer's last offer.

6. If no settlement is reached, the injunction expires, and the president reports to Congress with such recommendations as the chief executive may wish to make.

The Taft-Hartley Act has been invoked against strikes in vital sectors of the economy, such as atomic energy, coal, shipping, steel, and telephone service. Sometimes a president and the secretary of labor attempt to mediate strikes without resorting to the act. The effectiveness of this act is difficult to assess because legislation is only one of the many factors that affect industrial peace. Still, the basic issue remains unresolved. Strikes are part of the price we pay for the system of **collective bargaining.** But under what conditions does the price become so high that the federal government should intervene, stop the strike, and force a settlement?

The policies of **collective bargaining** are part of a broader set of issues. Labor is deeply concerned with the traditional conditions of work, such as hours, wages, and pensions. But it must also deal with the issue of job security, which is now threatened by technological change and automation. Business faces not only rising costs but intense foreign competition. All this means labor leaders are having to deal as best they can with such problems as the erosion of workers' wages, benefits, and even job security.

Unions have been losing strength for some decades. During the 1980s, for a variety of reasons, they suffered some notable political and policy losses. For example, President Reagan defeated a strike by the Professional Air Traffic Controllers Organization (PATCO), and then proceeded to destroy that union. He also appointed people to the National Labor Relations Board (the board legally mandated to *protect* the rights of workers to organize unions) who were strongly critical of unions. The Reagan Administration, although friendly to the Teamster's Union which had endorsed it, investigated a number of union officials from other unions that had actively endorsed and campaigned for Mondale in the 1984 elections.[13]

Labor in some areas is helping management raise productivity in exchange for lifetime jobs and institutional security for the union. The National Labor Relations Board has approved such arrangements between General Motors and the UAW. The UAW helps GM design work practices to use with new technology for producing the Saturn car, which will compete with low-priced imports. In return, GM pledges to hire UAW members from other plants to staff new plants, and thus ensures that the UAW will be the bargaining agent. In this particular instance GM and UAW employees jointly design the work systems and workers are given a greater voice in operations; certain traditional work rules and job classifications are thus relaxed. Critics on the right, such as the National Right to Work Committee, and critics on the left, such as old-line labor leaders, oppose these collaborative efforts. But such innovations, aimed at making companies more competitive, are part of a new trend. Moreover, in recent years, "federal judges have avoided a literal interpretation of decades-old labor laws which established rules for adversary relations, if that meant outlawing a cooperative venture.[14]

Regulation to Protect the Environment

The issue of pollution vividly illustrates the regulatory dilemma. Critics of strict controls on air, water, and noise pollution say our pursuit of a clean environment has damaged our economy and will continue to cause unemployment. They call attention, for example, to the disastrous consequences of the shutdown of an industry (or even of one large company). Proponents of tough antipollution laws have argued that we must now pay the price for decades of environmental abuse. They further contend that the longer we delay, the greater the costs to society—both in dollars and in lives.

Private companies and individuals tend to ignore pollution. If there is no cost attached to polluting the air or befouling a stream, firms will find it economically advantageous to do so. Because we all benefit from a pollution cleanup, whether we pay for it or not, it is not in any one party's interest to pay the cost. Consequently, the government must step in to control environmental damage. Although people usually agree that the government should do something about pollution, they agree far less about what it should do, how much it should do, to whom it should do it, and who should pay the cost. These questions take on increased importance because of the special nature of the pollution issue. Today the immediate cost of pollution control tends to fall on the polluter, so we would expect opposition from industry. The benefits on the other hand, go to everyone. Thus, the issue evokes concentrated opposition but diffuse or weak support.

Historically, environmental issues were discussed by local and state governments. In a study of the pollution question, one political scientist found that municipal *in*action had been a regular response to the air pollution problem in communities throughout the nation: "The federal government has taken on new responsibilities in the field of pollution abatement not so much because these local officials demand it, but because these lower levels of government have often failed to take action themselves."[15]

Using its power as a promoter, the federal government finances research into control devices and assists states both in maintaining their own pollution-control programs and in building waste-treatment facilities. The primary federal agencies concerned with the environment are the Council on Environmental Quality and the Environmental Protection Agency (EPA). Other federal agencies also regulate the environment, including the Interior Department, the Food and Drug Administration, and the Departments of Energy and Transportation. The Council on Environmental Quality, in the executive office of the president, develops and recommends policy options to the president and Congress. The Environmental Protection Agency is responsible for enforcing federal environmental laws and regulations.

The federal government today administers rules and regulations covering many forms of pollution—air, water, and noise—as well as dangers to the environment from harmful chemicals. Arguments about pollution control rarely concern whether to act or not; rather, they ask *what price* we are willing and able to pay for a clean environment and how best to achieve it.[16] Laws already on the books cost the average homeowner an extra $15 to $20 a month in electricity costs. Some private interests, including the automotive industry and the chemical industry, have been hit hard by pollution-control laws.[17]

Is pollution control too costly? Environmentalists point to the high costs of

Environmental Protection Agency head William K. Reilly testifying before the Senate Commerce Committee about the *Exxon Valdez* oil spill. With him are U.S. Coast Guard Captain Richard Larrabee and Transportation Secretary Samuel Skinner.

pollution itself. Dirty air and water and hazardous chemicals affect health care costs and worker productivity. It is estimated, for example, that one out of five workers in the asbestos industry may develop cancer; certain other job situations pose similar dangers.

Legislative action in environmental control has been extensive. The National Environmental Policy Act of 1969 set up the controversial requirement of **environmental impact statements.** The law requires the filing of statements assessing the potential effects of federal actions on the environment. This has been interpreted to require most projects utilizing federal funds to file such statements. Since 1970 thousands of statements have been filed. Critics claim environmental impact statements simply represent more government interference in the private sector. Supporters contend the statements have pointed out major flaws in projects and have led to cost savings along with greater environmental awareness.

THE CLEAN AIR ACT

One of the most significant pieces of environmental legislation is the 1970 amendment to the Air Quality Act of 1967. The 1970 Clean Air Act establishes national quality standards for states, strict pollution guidelines for automobiles, and regulations concerning stationary sources of pollution. It has been harshly criticized by business and industry, who contend that substantial changes are needed to ease its economic and regulatory burden. Environmentalists claim the act, even with its admitted weaknesses, has substantially improved the quality of the air. Further, the American public supports such a tough law; recent polls indicate that an overwhelming majority of Americans opposed changes that would make the antipollution law less strict.

DISPOSING OF TOXIC WASTE

An EPA "sewergate" scandal focused American attention on a uniquely modern problem: disposing of toxic waste. The United States produces more than 280 million metric tons of hazardous waste a year. Much of this waste is deposited in landfills, from where it seeps into and contaminates ground water. Toxic wastes create other types of health hazards as well: "Love Canal" and "Times Beach" have now joined Three Mile Island on the list of least desirable addresses in the United States.

Love Canal, a residential community in Niagara Falls, New York, was evacuated when health officials linked unusually high death rates and illness there to chemicals leaking from an old industrial dump. Times Beach, Missouri, suffered a similar fate. Officials discovered that unpaved roads there had been sprayed with Dioxin, which is not only one of the most toxic synthetic substances but also a suspected cause of cancer. The beleaguered EPA took the unprecedented move of buying the town of Times Beach. The agency paid out $36.7 million and evacuated the residents of the community.

Toxic waste disposal is rapidly replacing nuclear energy as the dominant environmental issue. The apparent move away from the construction of nuclear power plants—and increased public awareness—may help to solve the separate problem of disposal of nuclear wastes. Referendums passed in several states have placed stricter limitations on the establishment of nuclear waste dump sites. The Nuclear Regulatory Commission (NRC) has also gradually become more active in overseeing potential hazards of nuclear power plants.

Every day tons of toxic chemicals are spewed into our air.

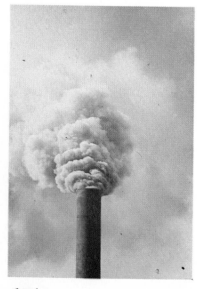

CHAPTER 23 / The Politics of Regulation

THE ACID RAIN DEBATE

More than 50,000 synthetic chemicals now exist, and 1000 new ones are created each year. Although most of them have beneficial effects, some are known to cause sickness and death to humans. Others are suspected of such effects. For years they have been used without much control, without regard for their effects on humans, and without regard for what they might do a few days or a few weeks later—as they infiltrate the atmosphere and rivers.

Until a few years ago the debate over "acid rain" focused on whether or not there was a problem. Today scientific consensus is that sulfur dioxide and other air pollutants belched from coal-burning utility boilers and other industries in the Midwest are damaging northeastern and Canadian lakes and water supplies, and are probably contributing to the damage of forests in the American South and elsewhere.

The challenge for policy makers is what to do and how to do it. Several measures proposed in Congress would mandate major power plants to install "scrubbers," complex equipment that removes sulfur dioxide from smokestacks. These measures usually direct states to develop their own strategies for meeting specified reductions. Industries and utilities have the option of switching to low sulfur coal, cleaning the coal before using it, or resorting to these scrubbers. Purchasing the scrubbers, however, is expensive. And switching to low sulfur coal means eliminating thousands of mining jobs in the East. Each of the options thus involves considerable costs and political liabilities. Regional politics are also involved, as one recent report describes:

> . . . the benefits of reducing acid rain would accrue primarily to the North-east, while the billions of dollars in costs would land on the Midwest—from the loss of high-sulfur coal jobs and the considerable financial investment in pollution control. The West is somewhat sympathetic to control, which would benefit its low-sulfur coal industry, but not to a national subsidy program that would spread the cost burden beyond the Midwest.[18]

The political fights over approaches to solving the acid rain problem have divided the mining unions, the utilities, the Democratic and Republican parties, the coal associations, and the governors. Sharp differences of view also separate the United States and Canada. This problem will not be solved easily: It will be costly, it will take a long time, and it will require strict enforcement and regulation at the state, national, and international levels. Scientific and economic considerations will continue to be important, and political factors will continue to influence both the legislative and regulatory policies that are hammered out in this problem area.

THE REAGAN IMPACT ON ENVIRONMENTAL REGULATION

Until the Reagan presidency, protection of the environment was not particularly a partisan issue. Both Democrats and Republicans had responded to the intense concern of the American people about pollution, carcinogens, and hazardous wastes that cause sickness, injury, and death. Reagan, however, appointed many regulators who were hostile to the environmentalist agenda. Although they revised or changed few of the major environmental statutes, the different outlooks, combined with serious cutbacks, led to a marked change in how provisions of the law were applied and implemented. The Reagan administration tried to cut the

From Herblock Through the Looking Glass (W. W. Norton, 1984).

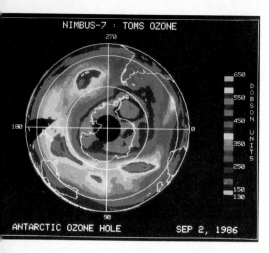

A map of the ozone hole over the Antarctic. In October 1986 the hole expanded to an area about the size of the United States.

toxic substances program, curbed the regulation of deadly air pollutants, and set a deliberate policy to proceed slowly with the cleanup of hazardous wastes. They cut the air quality and water quality programs and initially opposed all efforts to control acid rain. "Under-staffed, under-funded and under-Reagan" became the lament of those concerned with environmental regulation.[19]

No doubt, Reagan was acting in response to those, especially in the business community, who believed that during the previous fifteen years the government had gone overboard in its impulse to protect the environment. Reagan had campaigned on a series of pledges to cut back needless regulations and lessen the interference of the federal government in the private sector. His policies were consistent with his earlier stands. Reagan clearly achieved much of what he set out to do in this area, just as he succeeded in vastly increasing military spending and reducing federal income taxes, which he had also pledged to do. Yet his achievements in this area are less likely to enhance his reputation as a national leader; the American people were critical of Reagan's indifference to concerns about the environment.

George Bush campaigned in 1988 as an "environmentalist," yet he failed to win the support of most of the politically active environmentalist groups. But many environmental leaders were pleased by his appointment of conservation activist William Riley to head the important Environmental Protection Agency. Bush's appointments in the Interior Department won far less praise. Still, initial decisions in the Bush administration suggest Bush is more willing than Reagan to listen to the environmentalist point of view. He appears to sense that whether it is the polluted Boston Harbor, the Exxon oil spill off Alaska, or the Army Corps of Engineers' push for more dams, the increasing public concern about damage to the environment requires more of a Theodore Roosevelt than a Ronald Reagan approach in the 1990s.

Each of the issues just discussed represents the fundamental problem at the heart of environmental regulation: the problem of priorities. In a system such as ours, one that aspires to ensure free enterprise, the government tries to balance economic and environmental concerns. It attempts to guarantee the health and safety of its citizens and preserve the natural beauty of America for future generations. At the same time it tries not to inhibit developments vital to improving the standard of living for all Americans.

Regulating Occupational Safety and Health: A Case Study

One of the most criticized federal regulatory agencies has been in the Occupational Safety and Health Administration (OSHA), a unit in the Department of Labor. If you have read about OSHA in the newspapers, you have doubtless come across some report of its endless rules or its allegedly arrogant or patronizing warnings to business operators. OSHA has thousands of rules that can be found in the Code of Federal Regulations. It employs some 2000 persons, about half of whom are safety and health inspectors.

OSHA was set up because the public perceived that too many people were becoming disabled, or were dying, from work-related accidents. As of 1970 over 14,000 people were dying each year in industrial accidents, and an estimated 100,000 a year were being permanently disabled in workplace injuries. The mandate of OSHA is nothing less than to protect the health and safety of more than 60

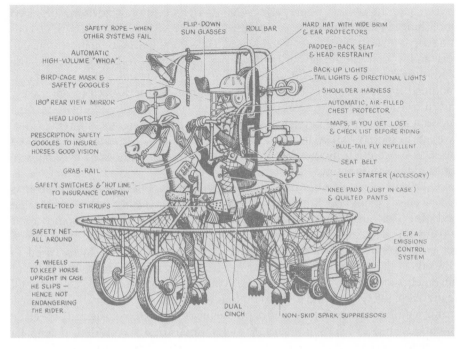

SAFETY ROPE - WHEN OTHER SYSTEMS FAIL
AUTOMATIC HIGH-VOLUME "WHOA" -
BIRD-CAGE MASK & SAFETY GOGGLES
180° REAR VIEW MIRROR
HEAD LIGHTS
PRESCRIPTION SAFETY GOGGLES TO INSURE HORSES GOOD VISION
GRAB-RAIL
SAFETY SWITCHES & "HOT LINE" - TO INSURANCE COMPANY
STEEL-TOED STIRRUPS
SAFETY NET ALL AROUND
4 WHEELS TO KEEP HORSE UPRIGHT IN CASE HE SLIPS - HENCE, NOT ENDANGERING THE RIDER

FLIP-DOWN SUN GLASSES
ROLL BAR
HARD HAT WITH WIDE BRIM & EAR PROTECTORS
PADDED-BACK SEAT & HEAD RESTRAINT
BACK-UP LIGHTS - TAIL LIGHTS & DIRECTIONAL LIGHTS
SHOULDER HARNESS
AUTOMATIC, AIR-FILLED CHEST PROTECTOR
MAPS, IF YOU GET LOST & CHECK LIST BEFORE RIDING
BLUE-TAIL FLY REPELLENT
SEAT BELT
SELF STARTER (ACCESSORY)
KNEE PADS (JUST IN CASE) & QUILTED PANTS

E.P.A. EMISSIONS CONTROL SYSTEM

DUAL CINCH
NON-SKID SPARK SUPPRESSORS

Cowboy after OSHA. Mythical supersafe cowboy illustrates what many businesspeople think of the practicality of federal health and safety rules. Union leaders, meanwhile, complain regulation is lax.

J. N. Devin in National Safety News

million workers in about 5 million workplaces. It is also asked to issue compulsory safety and health standards and to monitor compliance. To achieve these objectives, OSHA is empowered to inspect businesses and to issue notices of violation and fines.

CRITICISM OF OSHA

In business circles OSHA quickly became a "four-letter word." Many business executives criticize OSHA's standards as having only nuisance value. They also contend that inspectors are not familiar enough with their operations to make criticisms. Further, they believe many of the OSHA regulations do not protect the workers. They think, too, that the costs of many OSHA changes have had an inflationary effect. General Motors, for example, claims to have spent over $100 million to meet OSHA standards.

In the first years of OSHA, small businesses (55 percent of industrial fatalities occur in businesses employing twenty-five or fewer workers) complained that OSHA made rules that were too numerous, too complex, and too technical. Further, the costs of compliance are supposedly prohibitive for small business operators and raise the costs of production to unacceptable levels. Some businesses even said they had to close down; others said they might have to close down because of OSHA and similar governmental regulations.

Labor groups were OSHA's major source of support in its early years. But labor officials have often criticized OSHA for being a "toothless watchdog," and not strict enough. Too much attention was given to trivial violations, and fines were too small. Still, labor believed workers could use OSHA to force an employer to correct unsafe conditions.

Nevertheless, the backlash from business interests was intense. Proposals sprang up in Congress to exempt small businesses from OSHA's provisions. President Ford repeatedly condemned OSHA, saying at one point he'd like to throw

Risky Businesses

Annual fatalities per 100,000 workers:	
Mining	30
Construction	23
Agriculture, forestry, and fishing	20
Transportation, communications, and public utilities	19

Injuries and illnesses per 100 full-time workers:	
Meatpacking	33
Mobile home manufacturing	30
Vending machine manufacturing	28
Structural wood manufacturing	27
Raw cane sugar processing	26
Prefabricated wood building	26
Rubber recycling	25

Source: Department of Labor, as reported in *The New York Times* (January 10, 1988), p. E5.

OSHA "into the ocean." Some of President Carter's economic advisers suggested abolishing it. President Reagan campaigned for office saying he would curb OSHA's tendency to harass businesses—and he did. He wanted OSHA to be more conciliatory and to concentrate on major industries and major workplace hazards. The whole tone of OSHA changed in the Reagan years. It streamlined its restrictions, modified its enforcement policies, reduced its number of inspectors, and nearly cut in half its dollar amount of penalties. Critics in the labor and environmental movements said Reagan virtually dismantled the agency. Even the Supreme Court worked to modify OSHA; it held that OSHA's practices of making unannounced inspections of all businesses for violations, even though authorized by Congress, violated the Constitution.

OSHA has not been as bad as its critics maintain, but neither has it been as effective as it should be. It deserves credit for its action against polyvinyl chloride and other serious threats to workers' health. And OSHA deserves some credit too for the decrease in work-related injuries and illnesses, from about eleven for every worker in 1972 to about eight in the late 1980s. OSHA has tried to concentrate its limited energies on severe health hazards and make more use of an emergency power to restrict use of dangerous substances. It has dropped many trivial safety rules and focused on four major industries (construction, heavy manufacturing, transportation, and petrochemicals) that are considered especially hazardous. It also keeps pressure on a few industries it considers potentially dangerous, such as auto repair, dry cleaning, and building materials. Today it uses more simply written guidelines, and a simplified paperwork as well.

Later in the Reagan years, OSHA appeared to get a bit tougher. OSHA hit several industrial giants such as Chrysler, Ford, Union Carbide, General Dynamics, and Caterpillar Tractor with fines of six figures or more. But behind many of OSHA's fines, critics said, were court decisions, critical internal reports, congressional investigations, or union complaints spelling out the lax investigations of OSHA's inspectors.

OSHA apparently takes action only when a company's problems are severe. In 1988, for example, OSHA proposed fining Pepperidge Farms, a subsidiary of the Campbell Soup Company, $14 million for exposing workers to dangers at a plant in Pennsylvania. The company maintained these were unjustified fines, yet fifty workers at the plant had developed carpal tunnel syndrome, an inflammation of the sheaths around nerve endings in the fingers, wrists, and shoulders. Twenty-six of the workers had to undergo surgery. According to reports, the injuries came from repeatedly putting together sandwich cookies in an unsafe procedure. All this came about after a six-month OSHA investigation recorded 389 violations of record keeping and safety standards at the plant that employs 1500 people. Management "chose to ignore its own experts and employees while more and more employees suffered crippling injury," said the head of OSHA.[20]

As the OSHA overhaul proceeds, more controversies are bound to arise. They cannot be avoided as the government faces up to some tough issues of industrial health in a world of complex technology. Workers are exposed to a host of substances whose effects on human health are not fully understood. Even when something is known to be toxic, the precise degree of risk—or an acceptable amount of exposure—is hard to calculate, and the costs of full protection can run very high. And the harmful effects of many substances (such as asbestos and cotton dust) do not appear until years later, making proof of causation more difficult and the establishment of regulations more tenuous.

OSHA's problems stem in part from the fact that it is an attempt by government to intervene in the private sector by using command-control types of devices (that is, by dictating do this, or don't do that) rather than economic incentives. Liberals as well as conservatives now hold that even though it should be costly for businesses not to adopt safety standards, the details of administration should usually be worked out by the businesses themselves rather than by a government agency.

Regulatory Outcomes and Issues

Positive accomplishments of regulation are usually overlooked. Considerable progress has been made in air pollution control. Lead paint poisonings and accidental aspirin poisonings have markedly decreased as a result of new regulatory efforts. Childproof bottle tops, automobile seat belts, and federally insured bank accounts are all byproducts of federal regulation. The prevention of thalidomide babies can be credited to regulatory activity, as can the banning of many cancer-producing pesticides.

Positive accomplishments are, of course, somewhat offset by the costs. Thus, there has been a lower rate of new drug development and introduction since the 1962 amendments to the Food and Drug Act were passed. There is also little doubt that get-tough pollution regulations have added to the costs of many products. Other studies argue that the Interstate Commerce Commission virtually killed the railroad industry and that Federal Communications Commission regulations caused drab uniformity in television programming.

The major problems and criticisms of regulation are as follows:

1. *Regulation Distorts and Disrupts the Operation of the Market.* Sometimes governmental intervention upsets the normal adjustment processes of the market and thus encourages higher prices, misallocation of resources, and inefficiency.

2. *Regulation Can Discourage Competition.* Some forms of regulation (often the kind desired by industry) actually have the reverse of their desired effect. This is especially true where the government grants operating licenses and charters and seeks to maintain a certain level of quality or stability in the market. (This used to exist in trucking and air travel, where the federal government exerted control over entry into markets.) Regulatory red tape has also been charged with discouraging entry into industries and driving small businesses out.

3. *Regulation May Discourage Technological Development.* It is argued that if people perceive that the reward for an innovation is a new set of rules and a struggle for permission to use a new product, they may not find it worth the effort to innovate.

4. *Regulatory Agencies Are Often "Captured" by the Industries They Regulate.* It is suggested, especially by those on the political left, that some regulatory bodies are controlled by the big businesses they are supposed to be regulating. This is a popular view among those who consider big business to be a great power in our society. Although it may describe the view of a few of the older regulatory bodies, it has been downplayed by several scholars.[21]

The newer regulatory bodies are probably less "captured" because they deal with many industries and have intentionally been made harder to capture. Also public-interest groups are increasingly on the lookout for potential conflicts

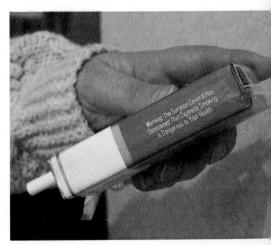

Government regulations require that cigarettes carry a label warning of the health hazards from smoking.

of interest in nominees to regulatory boards. A number of presidential nominees to regulatory positions have been defeated, or their names have been withdrawn, because of opposition of this kind. General standards have been suggested against which to measure these nominees. These include the following:

1. Nominees should be persons of integrity, whose past records demonstrate they have conducted their affairs honestly and have conscientiously complied with the law.
2. Nominees should be committed to basic principles of accountability in the executive branch, such as strong conflict of interest regulations, financial disclosure, open meetings, and checks on inordinate influence by regulated interests over agency policy.
3. Nominees should be knowledgeable about the industries they will regulate.

Still, some evidence of the capture thesis does exist in the "revolving door" situation, where federal regulators leave their jobs to take high-paying posts with the industries they previously regulated. There is evidence too that some people consider jobs in regulatory agencies as stepping stones to lucrative careers in private industry—and the industries obviously benefit in several ways from hiring some of the more able regulators.

Regulation Increases Costs to Industry and to the Consumer   Federal regulations, as noted earlier, are costly. Probusiness estimates claim that overall federal regulations cost well over $500 for every man, woman, and child in the United States. Such figures are disputed by many labor and consumer advocates who say health and safety standards are the best investment we can make. Every life and every limb we save, and every disease we prevent, represents not only a human achievement but also a reduction in the nation's enormous hospital and medical bills. The cost of neglecting health and safety requirements can be calculated in terms of loss of worker productivity and in such insurance costs as workers' compensation. Further, regulation provides new jobs in industry—perhaps as many as a million jobs in just the last few years. Plainly, however, the side you take in the debate over the costliness of federal regulations depends on where you sit—that is, on whether you favor labor or management, producer or consumer, energy developer or ecologist.

Regulation Has Often Been Introduced without Cost-Benefit Analysis   Many critics say too little attention is given to the questions of whether the benefits of a particular piece of regulation are great enough to justify its cost. Is it worth it to restrict new drugs if some who would benefit may die, even if the side effects are not yet well known? Is it worth it to clean up automobile emissions 95 percent if the cost is many times that of an 85 percent cleanup? The answers to these questions may be yes, but Congress and regulatory agencies are criticized for failing to ask, let alone answer, various questions of this type.[22]

Regulatory Agencies Lack Qualified Personnel   Critics of regulation and some heads of regulatory agencies themselves, say regulators lack the expertise to do their jobs properly. Regulatory agencies complain they need larger budgets to do their jobs properly. Regulatory agencies complain they need larger budgets to attract more qualified staff. Critics argue, too, that government should not meddle in complex chemical or technological industries about which it knows little.

Drawing by Richter; © 1988 The New Yorker Magazine, Inc.

The Deregulation Debate

For the last thirty years every president has proposed a program for regulatory reform. Economists from the conservative "University of Chicago school," on the one side, to the most liberal pro-Ted Kennedy and pro-Mario Cuomo school, on the other, are all but unanimous in their view that much regulation is unnecessary and that some of its uses the wrong strategy. Although **deregulation** and regulatory reform have different meanings to different people, the terms are generally used to describe a cutback in the amount of regulation attempted by the federal government. Even if various parties agree that reform is needed, they find it more difficult to agree on what specific actions to take.

DEREGULATING TRANSPORTATION

No industry has undergone as extensive deregulation as has the transportation industry. Airlines, trucking, and railroads have all recently been granted more freedom in conducting their operations. Enough time has now elasped so that we may analyze the reasons behind transportation deregulation, the key provisions of each particular deregulation act, and the effects on each specific industry.

Airline Deregulation   The Civil Aeronautics Board (CAB) was established by the federal government in 1938 to protect airlines from unreasonable competition by controlling rates and fares. Critics of CAB regulation charged that airlines were competing only in the frequency and convenience of flights and in the services they offered on flights. Because there was no competition over price, consumers were being forced to pay high rates for services they may not have desired. Others claimed CAB regulation of fares may have been keeping them higher than they would have been under more competitive conditions. It was also charged that new routes were being opened up very slowly under CAB supervision.

In light of these and other considerations, Congress passed the Airline Deregulation Act in the fall of 1978.[23] The act sought to phase out the CAB (which was legislated out of existence in 1985), relax restrictions on airline fares and routes, and authorize federal subsidies to airlines serving certain unprofitable markets.

In the early years of airline deregulation, the industry faced difficult economic conditions. Also one of the first results of deregulation was that many medium-sized cities lost service as larger carriers found it more profitable to use their aircraft in other markets. However, after a while, some of these cities had service restored by smaller airlines using smaller planes. But in the meantime, this shift caused scheduling problems at major airports—problems that were compounded by the strike and firing of the federal air traffic controllers in 1981. Also, airlines raised fares on routes over which they had monopolies in order to subsidize lower fares on more competitive routes. Finally, critics of airline deregulation charge that safety precautions and maintenance suffered as a result of cutthroat competition and the ease with which new airlines could enter the market.

Although there were some transitional problems as deregulation got under-way, overall it has resulted in generally lower fares, greater choice of routes and fares in most markets, and more efficient use of assets by the industry.[24] It has also resulted in less good service and higher fares for many smaller or medium size cities. Deregulation has also, unfortunately, produced a chaotic maze of pricing inequities.

Some charge that airline deregulation may be an indirect cause of fewer safety inspections, leading to accidents such as this, in which a cargo door blew out in midair and several passengers were sucked out of the plane.

Still, on balance, deregulation of the airlines has been judged a success by both the airlines and many students of the industry. Economic regulation invariably grants significant benefits to specific groups, yet there are costs as well. What are the lessons for other industries? In the long run, "deregulation may have many benefits, but in the short run, some groups may suffer substantially. The most important task of would-be deregulators is to assess both the credits and debits on the deregulation ledger. There are always winners and losers in any change, be it social, political, economic, or a combination of the three," write three students of this field. "For the airline industry, deregulation seems, on balance, to have provided more benefits than costs."[25]

The long-term effects of airline deregulation are likely to be positive. Eventually, analysts hope, the marketplace will determine the level of service. If an airline is overcharging passengers on a route, a competitor will eventually steal those travelers away by offering better or lower-priced service. In the long run, deregulation should strengthen the industry by forcing companies to streamline operations in order to survive in a competitive market.

Trucking and Railroad Deregulation   Deregulation of the trucking and railroad industries soon followed airline deregulation. In 1980 the railroad industry was in poor condition—as it had been for several decades, especially in the East. Many railroads were in serious financial trouble; two went bankrupt. In addition, many observers believed the Interstate Commerce Commission (ICC), which had regulated the railroads since 1887, was being too rigid in interpreting and enforcing federal regulations. Moreover, a growing body of economic evidence suggested that regulation was causing great inefficiencies and that market forces could generate better service to shippers and travelers at lower prices.

The trucking industry was much healthier. In fact, many observers said the industry was too healthy. ICC regulations had limited the entry of new competitors into trucking and had kept rates high. Competition was generally low, allowing trucking companies to charge relatively high rates for hauling cargo. Both the trucking industry itself and the Teamsters Union opposed deregulation, fearing it would alter this mutually beneficial situation. Calls for deregulation came primarily from business leaders who were forced to pay high rates to have their goods transported.

In 1980 Congress passed the Staggers Rail Act to deregulate railroads and the Motor Carrier Act to relax supervision of trucking. Both acts loosened restrictions on entry into their respective industries, made it easier for railroads and trucking companies to abandon unprofitable activities, and allowed each industry more freedom in setting rates.

The effects of deregulation on both industries have been broadly similar and, by most accounts, positive. In the case of trucking, the primary benefit of deregulation has been to increase profitability. In addition, new firms are entering the industry. Railroad deregulation has led to discounted rates, more competition, improved service, and service innovations.

The deregulation of the transportation industry illustrates the practical application of abstract economic theory. This form of deregulation signaled a return to relying on the marketplace to achieve what regulation intended to do in the first place. Recent legislation deregulating the transportation sector has enhanced competition and reduced prices by putting pressure on firms to operate more efficiently. And while the government may not have acted quickly enough in some instances to provide the additional safety resources to meet the changed needs of the airline and trucking industries, deregulation has had mostly positive effects.[26]

BANKING DEREGULATION

The relatively successful deregulation of airlines, railroads, and trucking has encouraged the relaxation of federal supervision over other industries as well. One such industry is banking. The banking industry has long been protected by the federal government. The trauma caused by the numerous bank failures during the Great Depression led to controls and regulations designed to ensure that such a shock would never recur. In addition, many economists point out the banking industry performs a special role in the economy and therefore warrants special treatment. Because banks and other financial institutions control the flow of money, the lifeblood of the economy, some observers believe the federal government must supervise the industry in order to guarantee that the flow is uninterrupted.[27]

Regulation of the banking industry has consisted mainly of protective devices. The federal government established the Federal Deposit Insurance Corporation (FDIC) to insure bank deposits up to a specified amount. (The FDIC has had to assist hundreds of banks that failed or required major assistance in recent years.) The Federal Savings and Loan Insurance Corporation (FSLIC) that performs a similar function for savings and loans institutions has had even more problems and its lax regulations have caused a scandal. In addition, financial institutions were barred from performing certain financial services. Banks and savings and loans institutions have been prevented from offering speculative investment services, for fear they would cover bad investments with the deposits of innocent third-party customers.

As a result of the deregulation movement, the directors of the FDIC and the FSLIC shifted responsibility for insuring bank and savings and loan deposits to private companies. Also, the distinctions between financial institutions and securities firms are beginning to diminish. Investment firms such as Merrill Lynch now offer certain banking services. Even retailers such as Sears now compete with banks for deposits. Banking officials say deregulation is needed so that banks can compete with these new adversaries. And they are now allowed to compete in many areas.

The massive savings and loan crisis of the late 1980s and early 1990s has raised serious questions about whether the federal government failed to regulate this industry enough. Hundreds of banks have gone bankrupt, and the federal government, under George Bush, has had to respond with a massive bailout program that will cost the industry and taxpayers hundreds of billions of dollars over the next several years. The effects on the entire economy of these failures in the banking industry are such that the federal government will have to play a much greater role here than elsewhere. It is one thing for a railroad or airline like Eastern Airlines to go bankrupt, but quite another for hundreds of large financial institutions to shut down. Thus, reregulation, not deregulation, is the likely reality in the savings and loan industry.

Treasury Secretary Nicholas Brady (second from the left) presents the Bush administration plan for rescuing the savings and loan industry to members of the Senate Banking Committee. It was passed by Congress and signed into law by President Bush in 1989.

EVALUATING DEREGULATION

Deregulation appears to be working better in some areas than in others. In the area of drug deregulation, the results are mixed. The Food and Drug Administration, especially since 1981, relaxed the requirements for introducing new medicines. Those in the drug industry applaud these efforts. They urge that as a result of deregulation the public gets better medicines faster and cheaper. Opponents con-

"I've deregulated Arthur, but he still doesn't run very efficiently."

Drawing by Handelsman; © 1989 The New Yorker Magazine, Inc.

tend, however, and with some growing evidence, that the accelerated approval process is endangering public health by prematurely allowing potentially hazardous drugs on the market.[28]

Advocates of deregulation say consumers are capable of making intelligent choices and are profiting from the lower prices and expanded services brought about by deregulation. Opponents contend deregulation results in such confusion in the marketplace that consumers cannot make sensible choices. In the airline business, they say, even experienced travel agents often cannot figure out the cheapest way to go "from here to there."

One other point: In our federal system the mere fact that the national government stops regulating an industry does not mean that the particular industry will be unregulated. On the contrary, when the national government ceases regulating it sometimes fifty different state regulations take over, making it even more difficult for that industry to operate on a large scale.[29] (This is why businesspeople themselves sometimes call for more, not less, national regulation. They often prefer one set of national regulations for auto safety to fifty different state ones.)

In the debate about deregulation it is desirable to separate those problems associated with transition from regulation to deregulation. There are always problems becoming adjusted to new ways. Every change hurts some and benefits others. The questions are whether in the long run deregulation benefits more people than does regulation, and which people it does benefit and which it does hurt.

In general the overall effects of deregulation trends, especially as they affect traditional economic regulation, appear to be positive. Deregulation has forced some industries to become more efficient. Consumers have had better services at less cost. Also, and not insignificantly, in a democracy such as ours, deregulation has made transfers of wealth visible rather than hidden. Under government regulation, transfers of wealth (that is, benefits or profits from certain arrangements that get established and protected) are often the result of hidden subsidies. Prices of regulated goods are kept artificially high in order to finance losses on goods whose prices are kept artificially low due to government controls. Under deregulation, prices are more in accord with costs. Subsidies must be authorized by Congress and are therefore subject to public scrutiny.

Summary

1. Regulation in America is neither socialism nor laissez-faire policy but rather a kind of pervasive intervention into the private sector built upon a commitment to a market economy. Although we often think of politics as the pursuit of private power and private interests, it is plainly also an effort to define the public interest. We set up regulatory agencies in an effort to interpret the public interest and to achieve various goals.

2. Even though their members are nominated by the president, their powers derived from legislative delegation, and their decisions subject to review by the courts, independent regulatory agencies have a scope of responsibility in the American economy that sometimes exceeds that of the three regular branches of government.

3. Even though few people have kind words to say about regulation, we will doubtless have more of it in the future. Regulation is a means of controlling or eliminating some of the abuses and problems generated by the private economy while avoiding government ownership and the risks of too much centralization. Increasing regulation is an inevitable byproduct of a complex, industrialized, high-technology society.

4. A deregulation movement designed to get the government out of the regulation of certain businesses took place in the late 1970s and early 1980s. Liberals sometimes favor deregulation if they believe it will foster more competition. Conservatives generally favor deregulation that will get federal regulators off their backs in areas such as affirmative action, safety and health, and environmental and consumer-protection standards. There are always winners and losers with deregulation. Businesses would like further deregulation of OSHA and EPA, but this would be vigorously opposed by labor and environmental interests. The major broadcast networks want more regulation of the cable industry, which has taken away much of their business in recent years. Predictably, the cable companies prefer deregulation. Of one thing we can be certain: Controversy in regulatory politics will always be with us.

Further Reading

Paul Asch. *Consumer Safety Regulation* (Oxford, 1988).

Anthony E. Brown. *The Politics of Airline Deregulation* (University of Tennessee Press, 1987).

Martha Derthick and Paul J. Quirk. *The Politics of Deregulation* (Brookings Institution, 1985).

Marshall Goodman and Margaret Wrightson. *Managing Regulatory Reform: The Reagan Strategy and Its Impact* (Praeger, 1987).

Richard A. Harris and Sidney M. Milkis. *The Politics of Regulatory Change: A Tale of Two Agencies* (Oxford, 1989).

Alfred Kahn. *The Economics of Regulation* (MIT Press, 1988).

Robert A. Katzmann. *Regulatory Bureaucracy: The Federal Trade Commission and Antitrust Policy* (MIT Press, 1980).

Robert A. Leone. *Who Profits: Winners, Losers, and Government Regulation* (Basic Books, 1986).

Robert E. Litan and William D. Nordhaus. *Reforming Federal Regulation* (Yale University Press, 1983).

Kenneth J. Meier. *Regulation: Politics, Bureaucracy, and Economics* (St Martin's Press, 1985).

Steven Morrison and Clifford Winston. *The Economic Effects of Airline Deregulation* (Brookings Institution, 1986).

Alan Stone. *Regulation and Its Alternatives* (Congressional Quarterly Press, 1982).

Martin Tolchin and Susan J. Tolchin. *Dismantling America: The Rush to Deregulate* (Houghton Mifflin, 1983).

Isaac Turiel. *Indoor Air Quality and Human Health* (Stanford University Press, 1985).

Norman J. Vieg and Michael E. Knott, eds. *Environmental Policy in the 1980s: Reagan's New Agenda* (Congressional Quarterly Press, 1984).

Notes

1. Richard L. Berke, "Deregulation Has Gone Too Far Many Telling New Administration," *The New York Times* (December 11, 1988), pp. 1 and 23.

2. See, for example, Milton Friedman and Rose Friedman, *Free to Choose* (Harcourt Brace Jovanovich, 1980); Murray L. Weidenbaum, *Business, Government and the Public* (Prentice Hall, 1977); and Murray L. Weidenbaum and Robert DeFina, *The Cost of Federal Regulation of Economic Activity* (American Enterprise Institute Reprint, May 1978).

3. See, for example, *Benefits of Environmental, Health and Safety Regulation* (Committee on Governmental Affairs, U.S. Senate, 1980); Steven Kelman, "Regulation that Works," *The New Republic* (November 25, 1978), pp. 16–19; and Timothy B. Clark, "The Costs and Benefits of Regulation," *National Journal* (December 1, 1979), pp. 2023–27.

4. Timothy Clark, "New Approaches to Regulatory Reform—Letting the Market Do the Job," *National Journal* (August 11, 1979), p. 1316.

5. See Arthur Andersen & Co., *Cost of Government Regulation Study* (Business Roundtable, 1979); and Murray L. Weidenbaum, *The Future of Business Regulation* (AMACON, 1979).

6. See Robert E. Litan and William D. Nordhaus, *Reforming Federal Regulation* (Yale University Press, 1983).

7. On the historical development of, the purpose for, and the underlying reasoning behind antitrust, see George Thompson and Gerald Brady, *Antitrust Fundamentals* (West, 1979).

8. On the origins of the FTC and the role of Louis B. Brandeis, see Thomas K. McCraw, *Prophets of Regulation* (Belknap, 1984), chap. 3.

9. Robert J. Mackay, James C. Miller, III, and Bruce Yandle, eds., *Public Choice and Regulation: A View from Inside the Federal Trade Commission* (Hoover Institution Press, 1987).

10. See Mark Clayton, "Critics Say Justice Department Has Become Too Lax on Antiturst," *Christian Science Monitor* (July 8, 1987), p. 19.

11. John Kenneth Galbraith, *Economics and Public Purpose* (Houghton Mifflin, 1973), pp. 221–22. See also Walter Adams and James V. Brock. *The Bigness Complex* (Pantheon, 1986).

12. See, for example, Ralph Nader et al., *Taming the Giant Corporation* (Norton, 1976).

13. Michael Goldfield, *The Decline of Organized Labor in the United States* (University of Chicago Press, 1987), p. 6.

14. "The NLRB Strikes a Blow for Worker Participation," *Business Week* (June 16, 1986), p. 36.

15. Matthew A. Crenson, *The Un-Politics of Air Pollution* (Johns Hopkins University Press, 1971), p. 10.

16. See John C. Whitaker, *Striking a Balance* (American Enterprise Institute/Hoover Institution, 1976), and Walter A. Rosenbaum, *Environmental Politics and Policy* (Congressional Quarterly Press, 1985).

17. See, for example, Robert Crandall et al., *Regulating the Automobile* (Brookings Institution, 1986), chaps. 3 to 5.

18. Rochelle L. Stanfield, "The Acid Rainmakers," *National Journal* (June 14, 1986), p. 1500–03.

19. Mchael E. Kraft and Norman J. Vieg, "Environmental Policy in the Reagan Presidency," *Political Science Quarterly* (Fall 1984), pp. 415–39.

20. "Pepperidge Farm Faces Fine in Worker Injuries," *The New York Times* (November 15, 1988), p. A11.

21. James Q. Wilson, "The Dead Hand of Regulation," *The Public Interest* (Fall 1971), p. 47; and Paul Quirk, *Industry Influence in Federal Regulatory Agencies* (Princeton University Press, 1981).

22. For some useful books on this, see Robert A. Leone, *Who Profits: Winners, Losers, and Government Regulation* (Basic Books, 1986), and Thomas C. Schelling, ed., *Incentives for Environmental Protection* (MIT Press, 1983).

23. See the public document that helped pave the way for this act: *Civil Aeronautics Board Practices and Procedures, Report of the Subcommittee on Administrative Practice and Procedure of the Committee on the Judiciary, U.S. Senate* (U.S. Government Printing Office, 1975.)

24. Steven Morrison and Clifford Winston, *The Economic Effects of Airline Deregulation* (Brookings Institution, 1986).

25. Larry N. Gerston, Cynthia Fraleigh, and Robert Schwab, "Whatever Happened to the 'Friendly Skies'?: Deregulation of the Airline Industry." Paper delivered at the 1987 Western Political Science Association Meetings, Anaheim, California, March, 1987, p. 42.

26. Martha V. Gottron, ed., *Regulation: Process and Politics* (Congressional Quarterly Press, 1982). See also Leon N. Moses and Ian Savage, eds., *Transportation Safety in an Age of Deregulation* (Oxford University Press, 1989).

27. Alan Stone, *Regulation and Its Alternatives* (Congressional Quarterly Press, 1982), p. 46.

28. See Martin Tolchin and Susan J. Tolchin, *Dismantling America: The Rush to Deregulate* (Houghton Mifflin, 1983).

29. See, for example, Kenneth J. Meier, "The Politics of Consumer Protection." Paper delivered at the Western Political Science Association Meetings, March 28–30, 1985, Las Vegas, Nevada, and Martha M. Hamilton, "Just Because It Melts, That Doesn't Mean It's Cheese," *The Washington Post National Weekly Edition* (April 21, 1986), pp. 6–7.

24

The Democratic Faith

The founding generation fought an eight-year revolution to secure their rights and liberty. Then they wrestled first at the Constitutional Convention and later in the first Congress to write a Constitution and to draft a Bill of Rights that would protect the rights to life, liberty, and self-government for themselves and for those who would come later. But they knew, as we also know, that passive allegiance to these ideas and rights is never enough. Every generation must see itself as having a duty to nurture these ideals by actively reconstructing and renewing the community and nation of which they are a part.

The framers knew well the story of Athens. They were familiar with Pericles and his famed funeral oration in which he said that the person who takes no part in public affairs is a useless person, a good-for-nothing. The city's business, as Pericles and many Athenians saw it, was everyone's business. Athens had flourished as a shining beacon of what a civilized city might be, but it floundered after a time, when greed, self-centeredness, and a smugness set in. As time went on the Athenians wanted security more than they wanted liberty and freedom, and they yearned for a comfortable life. In the end they lost it all—security, comfort, *and* freedom. When they wanted not to give to society, but rather for society to give to them, when the freedom they most wished was freedom from their responsibility to the city, then Athens ceased to be free. "Responsibility was the price every man must pay for freedom. It was to be had on no other terms."[1]

If you are to be a citizen of the United States in the truest meaning of the term, your dreams must go beyond personal ambition and the accumulation of material goods. Our country needs citizens who understand that their own well-being is tied to the well-being of their neighbors, their community, their country. True citizens are committed to a continuous rebuilding and reweaving of their society's social and political fabric.

Our theme in this last chapter is simple: *Leadership is important, but an active, committed citizenry that can assume leadership itself is even more important.* Freedom and obligation go together. Liberty and duty, that's the deal. The answer to our nation's problems lies not in producing a perfect Constitution or a few larger-than-life leaders. The answer lies in educating a nation of citizen leaders who, regardless of their professional and private ambitions, will at the very least make the concerns of the Republic and humankind their avocation.

We are not complete persons, as the Athenians would remind us, unless we are reacting to and expressing ourselves through politics. We should be participating in public affairs not out of social or civic duty or the prospect of a particular reward. It is for the completion of self, for our growth and self-definition in relation to others, and as an expression of our concern for those others, that all of us must act politically.[2]

More than any other form of government, the kind of democracy that has emerged under our Constitution requires a certain kind of faith—and a certain kind of skepticism. It requires faith concerning the common human enterprise, a belief that if the people are informed and caring, they can be trusted with their own self-government, and an optimism that when things begin to go wrong, the people can be relied upon to set them right.

A healthy skepticism is needed as well. Democracy requires us to be questioning of our leaders and never too trusting of any group with too much power. Although we prize majority rule, we are skeptical enough to ask whether a majority is always right. Democracy requires us to be constantly concerned about whether we really tolerate and protect the rights and opinions of others, and about whether democratic processes are in fact serving the principles of liberty, equality, and justice. In short, the democratic faith rests upon a peculiar blend of faith in the people and skepticism of them.

Thomas Jefferson, our best-known champion of the democratic faith, believed in the common sense of humankind and in the flowering of the human spirit. Jefferson believed deeply that every government degenerates when it is trusted to rulers alone. The people themselves, he wrote, are the only safe depositories of government. His was a robust commitment to popular control, to representative processes, and to accountable leadership. But he was no believer in the simple participatory democratic system of ancient Greece or revolutionary France. The people, too, must have their power checked and balanced.

The customary government of humankind has been authoritarian or tyrannical. Throughout history, including the present, most people have lived in societies in which a small group at the top have imposed their will on the others. Today some authoritarian governments justify their actions by saying people are too weak to govern themselves; they need to be ruled. Others claim to be true representatives of all the people. But neither in Castro's Cuba nor in the military regime of North Korea, neither in the People's Republic of China nor in South Africa, do ordinary people have a voice in the types of decisions Americans routinely make: Who should go to college, or work in the fields, or serve in the army? How much money should be spent for schools, Stealth fighter planes, or environmental protection?

It is only by intense thought, great commitment, countless sacrifices, and an enduring faith in democracy that liberty and equality have prevailed—at least to the extent they have—in the United States. The celebrated efforts and faith that were necessary to create this democratic republic are fully as necessary to sustain it in our own time.

Thomas Jefferson

"The Athenians are here, Sire, with an offer to back us with ships, money, arms, and men—and, of course, their usual lectures about democracy."

Drawing by Ed Fisher; © 1983 The New Yorker Magazine, Inc.

The Case for Government by the People

The essence of our Constitution is that it both grants power to and withholds power from the national government. Fearing national weakness and popular disorder, the framers wanted to grant the government enough power to do its basic jobs, such as maintaining national defense and financial stability. Yet, valuing above all the principle of individual liberty, the framers also wanted to protect the people from too much government. They wanted a limited government—but one that would work. The solution was to make government responsive to the people–yet not too responsive.

The first step was to distribute power among the three branches of government: legislative, executive, and judicial (*separation of powers*). The second was to leave extensive authority with state and local governments (*federalism*). Then the framers took a third step, the most brilliant and successful of all. Public officials were provided with different and competing constituencies to satisfy (*checks and balances*). The framers also assumed that the constitutents themselves would be divided (*pluralism*): Northerners versus Southerners, rich versus poor, city people versus country people. Finally, as the ultimate protection of the people's liberties, in 1791 the founders in Congress and in the state legislatures added the Bill of Rights to the Constitution.

This was not, of course, a very efficient system. Yet efficiency was not the main goal; the framers wanted a *safe government*. As the decades passed, the national government came under greater and greater pressure to perform effectively. The twentieth century in particular brought American involvement in vast global wars, depressions, and huge migrations of Europeans and Hispanics and Asians. There were also migrations of blacks and other rural people into northern cities, industrialization, and technological changes in transportation, communications, medicine, and education. Divided governments always have trouble pulling themselves together, but the American experiment had even more trouble. It is easy for leaders to "pass the buck." Certain arrangements also increased the power

Independence Hall, Philadelphia

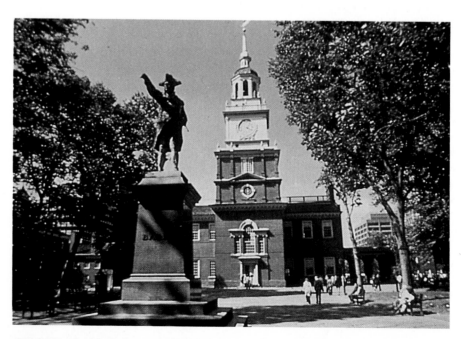

CHAPTER 24 / The Democratic Faith

of political minorities: the filibuster in the Senate, for example, or the Supreme Court's power to declare national or state laws unconstitutional. The power of organized minorities to obstruct sharpened the whole question of a representative republic. If leaders acting for a majority of people could not act—could not pass a gun-control law, for example, or obtain a constitutional amendment protecting the rights of women—was this really government *by the people*?

Most Americans now want a government that is *efficient* and *effective*—that gets things done. We want to maintain our commitment to liberty and freedom. We want a government that acts for the majority but also protects minorities. We want to safeguard our nation in a world full of change and violence. We live in an era of rising demands on resources and declining supply, of widening concepts of the rights of the poor, the elderly, and others. Do we expect too much from government? Of course we do!

Democracy is a system of checks and balances. It continually balances values and competing dreams. We have to balance all individual liberties against the collective security and needs of society; we must also balance certain individual liberties against other individual liberties. The question is always which *rights* of which people are to be protected by what means and at what price.

Participation and Representation

In essence, the challenge to the future of democracy is whether we can make our *representative* process work. No political problem is more complicated than this. For one thing, exact representation is impossible in the literal sense. Every man and woman has a host of conflicting desires, fears, hopes, and expectations, and no government can represent them all. Moreover, even if millions of voters could be represented in their billions of interests, the question would remain as to how they would be represented. Through direct representation, such as a New England town meeting? Through economic or professional associations, such as labor unions or political-action committees? Through a coalition of minority groups? Through a direct popular majority? All these, and other alternatives can be defended as proper forms of representation in a pluralist democracy.

Some propose to bypass this thorny problem of representation by vastly increasing the role of direct popular participation in decision making. What many people would regard as the most perfect form of democracy exists when every person within a given group has a full and equal opportunity to participate in all decisions and in all processes of influence, persuasion, and discussion that bear on that decision. Direct participation in decision making, its advocates contend, will serve two major purposes. It will enhance the dignity, self-respect, and under-standing of individuals by giving them responsibility for the decisions that shape their lives. And it will act as a safeguard against antidemocratic and undemocratic forms of government and prevent the replacement of democracy by dictatorship or tyranny. This idea rests on a theory of self-protection that says interests can be represented, furthered, and defended best by those whom they concern directly.

Experience with many forms of participatory democracy, however, suggests that it has limitations as a form of decision making. In an age of burgeoning population, increasingly complex economic and social systems, and enormously wide-ranging decision-making units of government, direct participation can work only in smaller communities or at the neighborhood level. As a practical matter, people simply cannot put in endless hours taking part in every decision that affects their lives. (There is an old joke that the problem with socialism is that it takes too many evenings!)

Participatory democracy still has a great role in smaller units—in the running of colleges, communes, poverty organizations, local party committees, and the like. And perhaps the idea of participation should be greatly extended, for example, to greater control by workers over the running of factories. But we must distinguish between democracy as participation and a greater role for participation in a democracy. One course of action is to enlarge the role of participation in representation; that is, to broaden the power of all people to take part in local decision making and in choosing their representatives in larger units of government. And this brings us back to the hard questions of indirect representation.

If we must have representatives, who shall represent whom? Although this question can be answered in countless ways, in practice there are two basic ways to organize representation. By electing representatives in a *multitude of local districts*, it is possible to build into representative institutions—the American Congress, for example—most *minority* interests and attitudes found throughout the nation. The other way is through an election system that emphasizes majority representation. This can be achieved by creating a *nationwide electorate* that elects one representative (the American president, for example) or by developing a strong two-party system that knits all the local constituencies into coalitions that can *elect* and *sustain national majorities*. A nation does not have to choose between these alternatives. It can have both, as does the United States.

Which is better: a government that represents coalitions of minorities, or a government that represents a relatively clear-cut majority and has no obligation to the minority? The answer depends on what one expects from government. A system that represents coalitions of minorities usually reflects the trading, competition, and compromising that must take place in order to reach agreement among the various groups. Such a government has been called *broker rule*; the government acts essentially as a go-between, as a mediator among organized groups that have definite policy goals. Under broker rule leaders cannot get too far ahead of the groups; they must tack back and forth, shifting in response to changing group pressures. Instead of acting for a united popular majority with a fairly definite program, either liberal or conservative, the government tries to satisfy all major interests by giving them a voice in decisions and sometimes a veto over actions. In the pushing and hauling of political groups, the government is continually involved in delicate balancing acts.

Some critics believe in full representation of minority groups—in broker rule—but point out that fair representation has not been achieved in the American system. They point to the extent of nonvoting and other forms of nonparticipation in politics; the fact that low-income persons are less well organized in groups than upper-income persons; the bias of the stronger organized groups toward the status quo; the lack of competition among much of the news and opinion media, combined with the domination of television and the press by a few corporations; and the virtual monopoly of party politics by the two major parties, which do not always offer the voters meaningful alternatives. In the governmental system itself, critics note the devices in Congress that block majority will and overrepresent certain minorities; the distortion of representation embodied in the electoral college; and the power of the Supreme Court to invalidate laws demanded by popular majorities acting through the legislative and executive branches.

These charges may be exaggerated, but they cannot be denied, as this book shows. Those who believe in fairer representation, however, can point to fairly steady improvement in recent years; for example, changes in election laws to simplify and extend voting, to enforce one-person–one-vote standards, and to regulate campaign finance, and some progress in Congress to strengthen majority rule.

By this point in the book you undoubtedly appreciate that democracy has to mean much more than popular government and unchecked majority rule. A democracy needs competing politicians with competing conceptions of the public interest. A vital democracy, living and growing, places its faith in the voters, faith that they will not just elect people who will mirror their views, but that they will elect leaders who will exercise their best judgment—"faith that the people will not condemn those whose devotion to principle leads them to unpopular courses, but will reward courage, respect honor, and ultimately recognize right."[3]

The Role of the Politician

Americans have mixed views about their elected officials. We realize they are skillful at compromising, mediating, negotiating, "brokering"—and that governing often requires these qualities. But can there be too much of a good thing? Americans suspect politicians of being ambitious, conniving, unprincipled, opportunistic, and even corrupt—"just into politics for what they can get out of it for themselves." Not long ago a board game similar to *Monopoly* was invented and marketed with the cynical title *Lie, Cheat and Steal: The Game of Political Power*.

Yet we often find individual office holders are responsive, bright, hardworking, and friendly (even though we may suspect they are simply trying to get out the vote). And our liking often turns into reverence after these same politicians depart or die. Surely Washington, Lincoln, Eisenhower, and John F. Kennedy are acclaimed today. Harry Truman liked to say that a statesman is merely a politician who has been dead for about ten years.

Of course, we must put the problem in perspective. In all democracies the public may expect too much from politicians. Further, people naturally dislike those who wield power. Public office holders, after all, tax us, regulate us, and conscript us. We dislike political compromisers, bargainers, and ambitious opportunists—even though we may need such people to get things done.

One of us has been conducting surveys in recent years on what people think of *the typical American politician*. Eighty percent of the responses are negative. Consider these responses: The typical American politician is "male, middle-age, and usually a lawyer," authoritarian, power hungry, on an ego trip, slick, two-faced, outgoing, glib-talkative, superficial, evasive, self-serving, an opportunist, manipulative, preoccupied with getting elected, "listens to voters when he thinks they might be angry enough to vote him out of office," and promises too much.

When asked to describe *the ideal American politician*, people responded very differently. Common responses were as follows: The ideal American politician is honest, humble, patriotic, compassionate, sensitive to the needs of others, well-informed, competent, fair-minded, objective, intellectually honest, a good listener, candid, a good mediator, self-confident, inspiring, "a candidate of the people, not of the money," courageous enough to stand up to special interests—people "who do not want power but lead because they are called upon to exercise their talents for the public good," and "do the job and get out when finished."

Why the gap between our expectations about the typical and the ideal politician? The gap exists in part because we have overly high expectations. We want politicians to be perfect, to have all the answers, and to have all the right (in our minds) opinions. It is impossible for anyone to live up to these ideals. Politicians, like all individuals, live in a real world in which perfection may be a goal—but compromises, ambition, fund-raising, and self-promotion are necessary. Our "ideal leaders" are usually dead. Time makes myths and irons out the wrinkles. We

Poking Fun at Politicians

"Don't vote, it only encourages them!"

"Thank God only one of them can win!"

"Old politicians never die, they just evade away."

"A politician is a person who approaches every question with an open mouth."

"Politicians are there when they need you."

"Politicians divide their time between running for office and running for cover."

"Political promises go in one year and out the other."

"In one African country it is said that people can rise to public office only when they shoot a rhinoceros. In this country, people can only win public office if they shoot the bull."

"Let's run through this once more—and, remember, you choke up at Paragraph Three and brush away the tear at Paragraph Five."

Drawing by D. Reilly; © 1988 The New Yorker Magazine, Inc.

Assessments of Various Professions' Honesty and Ethical Standards	
	Percent Answering Very High
Druggists, pharmacists	66
Clergymen	60
College teachers	54
Medical doctors	53
Dentists	51
Engineers	48
Policemen	47
Bankers	26
Funeral directors	24
Journalists	23
TV reporters, commentators	22
Newspaper reporters	22
Building contractors	22
Senators	19
Lawyers	18
Business executives	16
Congressmen	16
Local officeholders	14
Labor union leaders	14
Real estate agents	13
Stockbrokers	13
State officeholders	11
Insurance salesmen	10
Advertising practitioners	7
Car salesmen	6

Source: *The Gallup Poll*, November 16, 1988.

want politicians to solve our worst problems, but we also want them to be the scapegoats for all the things we dislike about government: taxes, regulations, and any limitations on our freedom.

Politicians are absolutely necessary to run a democracy—certainly the American republic whose fragmented powers require politicians to mediate among factions, build coalitions, and compromise among and within branches of government to produce policy. But are such politicians adequate? Do we not also need *leaders* who can rise above everyday "wheeling and dealing" and lead the nation through great crises—or, better yet, plan ahead to avert such crises?

What Kind of Political Leadership?

Can we generalize about the leadership abilities of those who are elected today? Although the concept of leadership—like many other concepts in political science—is broad and hazy, we can break it down to distinguish among *agitators*, *coalition builders*, and *office holders*.

TYPES OF LEADERS

Agitators, or people who instigate movements, arouse people's consciousness of their needs and problems, raise their hopes and expectations, organize or take leadership of political and social movements, and mobilize grass-roots pressure on government from the outside. Movement leaders are often considered crusaders or even prophets, whether they are abolitionists, women's suffrage leaders, anti-slavery leaders such as William Lloyd Garrison, or conservatives such as California's crusading tax cutter the late Howard Jarvis.[4]

Coalition builders are usually intent on winning elections, whereas agitators are more concerned with mobilizing groups of people who may or may not take part in elections. Coalition builders must knit together a variety of groups inside the process and movements in order to build a majority that can carry elections. Hence, such leaders tend to be power brokers, widening their political appeals as broadly as possible without becoming *too* thin or flabby, accommodating single-interest or single-cause groups or movements with intense concerns, and building compromise party platforms.

Office holders are in a mixed position to exercise leadership: They have the authority that goes with their offices, but they must try not to alienate elements of the electoral majority they will need at the next election. They dare not be too far ahead of their times. Their behavior under these circumstances may be closely affected by the political system. Presidents, for example, may wish not to worry about their electoral majorities until the last years of their terms, but they have to consider the midterm elections for senators and representatives. Because members of Congress have to think about winning the next election in a year or two, they are almost constantly working to secure their electoral home base. Senators, with their six-year tenures, can think in somewhat longer terms.

The relationship between John F. Kennedy, office holder, and Martin Luther King, Jr., movement leader, exemplifies the diversity of leadership. Even though Kennedy raised civil rights issues during his campaign for the presidency in 1960, he never accorded them top priority in his program; rather, he held off making major civil rights proposals until he could get his economic program through Congress. In the meantime King and other black leaders were protesting, demonstrating, encountering violence, appealing to northern and southern public opinion, and putting intense pressure on Kennedy and other federal officials to protect their civil rights and especially to put through legislation that would protect their right to vote. As a result of this kind of *movement* pressure, Kennedy by 1963 was appealing to Congress for civil rights legislation. He worked closely with King and other civil rights leaders through his brother Robert, the attorney general, and at the same time tried to maintain old-time Democratic party coalitions of northerners and white southerners. Movement leaders like King put pressure on the government from the outside—while also working with Attorney General Robert Kennedy and others from the inside. After JFK's assassination, office holders like President Lyndon B. Johnson, together with congressional leaders, built a broad coalition of blacks, liberals, and moderate whites that helped to put the Civil Rights Act of 1964 and the Voting Rights Act of 1965 into law.[5]

POLITICIANS AS BROKERS

Most American politicians hardly aspire to such grand leadership roles as movement founders or coalition builders. They work at the grass roots as city council members, sheriffs, state legislators, district attorneys, and county commissioners. As such they are popular targets for cartoonists and others who picture them as ridiculous, confused, and addled—and above all as ignorant and incompetent. Most of these portraits, especially the last two, are caricatures. The average politician in office has an alert, shrewd, calculating mind.

Thinking About Leadership

An adequate democratic theory recognizes that democracy is not self-executing. A democracy needs leaders who have a sense of the past and who are willing to share their varying conceptions of the public interest.

Even though one of the most universal cravings of our time is a hunger for creative and compelling leadership, defining creative leadership is a challenge in itself. Leadership can be understood only in the context of both leaders and followers—a leader without followers is a contradiction in terms. Leadership is also *situational* and *contextual*. A person is often effective in only one kind of situation. Leadership is not necessarily transferable. James Madison, for example, was a brilliant political and constitutional theorist. He was also a superb founding politician. Still, he was not a particularly able presidential leader. The leadership required to lead a marine platoon up a hill in battle is different from the leadership needed to change racist, sexist attitudes in city or community governments. The leadership required of a campaign manager differs from that required of a candidate. Leaders of thought are not always effective as leaders of action.

Although leaders are often skilled managers, they often need more than just managerial skills. Managers do things *the right way*, whereas leaders are more concerned, or perhaps more preoccupied, with doing *the right thing*; that is, they are more concerned with the longer range, with the purposes and ends of a society or an organization. Put another way, managers are concerned with efficiency, and with keeping things going, especially routines and standard operating procedures. Leaders, on the other hand—in addition to having certain managerial skills—also are inventors, risk takers, and entrepreneurs. Further, they are morale builders who can infuse values and purpose into the mission of their community or nation.

Observations on John F. Kennedy by Martin Luther King, Jr.

"The basic thing about him—he had the ability to respond to creative pressure."

"I never wanted—and I told him this—to be in the position that I couldn't criticize him if I thought he was wrong."

"And Kennedy said, 'it often helps me to be pushed.'"

"When he saw the power of the movement, he didn't stand there arguing about it. He had the vision and wisdom to see the problem in all of its dimensions and the courage to do something about it."

Source: T. George Harris, "The Competent American," *Look* (November 17, 1964).

Proud to Be a Politician

Must a politician gain public office by denouncing his or her own profession? From the tone of many recent congressional races it would appear that this is a growing trend. Journalist Charles McDowell of the *Richmond Times-Dispatch* noted this trend on the PBS series "The Lawmakers," and suggested that such a tactic . . . "demeans an honorable and essential profession—that of the politician." McDowell proposed that every member of Congress be required to take the following oath:

"*I affirm that I am a politician. That I am willing to associate with other known politicians. That I have no moral reservations about committing acts of politics. Under the Constitution, I insist that politicians have as much right to indulge in politics as preachers, single-issue zealots, generals, bird-watchers, labor leaders, big business lobbyists, and all other truth-givers.
I confess that, as a politician, I participate in negotiation, compromise, and tradeoffs in order to achieve something that seems reasonable to a majority. And, although I try to be guided by principle, I confess that I often find people of principle on the other side, too.
So help me God.*"

Four presidents who exhibited very different leadership styles: John F. Kennedy, Lyndon B. Johnson, Dwight D. Eisenhower, and Harry S. Truman.

Leaders have those indispensable qualities of contagious self-confidence, unwarranted optimism, and incurable idealism that attract others, and mobilize them to undertake tasks they never dreamed they could accomplish. In short, transcending or **transforming leaders** empower others, and enable many of their followers to become leaders in their own right. Most of the significant breakthroughs in our nation (as well as in our communities) have been made (or shaped) by people who, while seeing all the complexities and obstacles ahead of them, believed in themselves and in their purposes so much that they refused to be overwhelmed and paralyzed by self-doubts. They were willing to gamble, to take risks, to look at things in a fresh way, and often to invent new rules.[6]

Leaders must recognize the fundamental—unexpressed as well as felt—wants and needs of potential followers. By bringing followers to a fuller consciousness of their needs, they help convert the resulting hopes and aspirations into practical demands on other leaders (especially leaders in government). Leaders must also sense when people are ready for action. A leader in a democracy consults and listens while educating followers and attempting to renew the goals of an organization.

Leaders must also be sensitive to the distinctions between *power* and *authority*. Power is the strength or raw force to exercise control or coerce someone to do something. Authority is power that is accepted as legitimate by subordinates or constituents. The whole issue of leadership raises countless questions about participation in and acceptance of power in superior-subordinate, or leader-led, relationships. How best can leaders earn and sustain moral and social acceptance for their authority? Americans generally prize participation in all kinds of organizations, especially in civic and political life. Yet a part of us yearns for charismatic leaders—decisive, attractive leaders who will simplify problems and relieve us of the burdens of leadership. Ironically, however, savior figures and charismatic leaders often—indeed almost always—create distance, not participation.

Ultimately two overriding kinds of political leadership exist: transactional leadership and transformational leadership. The **transactional leader** engages in an exchange, usually a short-term bargain: "I'll vote for your bill if you'll vote for mine." Or "You raise money for my campaign and I'll help get your daughter a state job after I'm elected." Most political office holders practice transactional leadership as a practical necessity. It is the common means of doing business. The transforming leader is the person who, as we discussed earlier, so engages

Leadership for a Change

with followers as to bring them to heightened political consciousness and activity, and in the process converts many of them into leaders in their own right.[7]

The transforming leader is usually preoccupied with the longer term and is, as a rule, less interested in selfish gains than in community or societal improvements. The transforming leader is also in many ways an educator or teacher who points out the possibilities and the hopes and dreams of a people. Is it possible for most elected political officials to exercise transforming leadership? Does transforming leadership require a special set of circumstances, or a special set of personal qualities, or possibly certain kinds of constitutional and structural arrangements?

POLITICIANS AS LEADERS

One reason we are often so skeptical or even cynical toward politicians is that we fail to appreciate the importance of politics and the limits or constraints within which politicians must work. Office holding politicians are in many ways **Act III leaders.** Most plays have three acts. In politics, different tasks or different periods often seem to require different kinds of political leaders.

Act I leaders are the *crowd gatherers* or *agitators*. They stir things up and thus are often viewed as cranks and troublemakers—Patrick Henry, Sam Adams, and Tom Paine, for example. Also in this category are John Brown (in the pre-Civil War days), Rap Brown (in the early civil rights protests of the 1960s), Saul Alinsky (in urban protests), and Edward Abbey and the radical environmentalists of the present era.

Act II leaders are *coalition builders*. Often unelected and even unelectable, they galvanize movements and coalitions in such a way that politicians heed their messages. Martin Luther King, Jr., Susan B. Anthony, and the leaders of the contemporary balanced-budget amendment and nuclear freeze movements are examples.

Act III leaders typically are *the elected officials*. Some have highly publicized and sometimes even glamorous careers; but theirs are also often the hardest, least secure, and least rewarding careers. They have to be ambitious, and willing to assume frantic lifestyles. Yet they also have to be brokers, ever-sensitive to the policy views of pluralities and majorities. As elected representatives they cannot be too innovative. They usually have to be balancers and bargainers, and to reconcile competing claims of what is in "the public interest." Act III types have to follow public opinion as well as mold or shape it. They are usually more constrained than other kinds of political leaders. They depend on Act I and II leaders for fresh ideas and novel approaches to public problems.

If elected politicians often seem bewildered in dealing with controversial issues in these confusing times, so are the rest of us. If elected officials sometimes make mistakes, so do the rest of us. If they sometimes postpone things rather than directly confront them, so do we all. The late Senator Everett Dirksen of Illinois offered a helpful perspective on politicians:

> Politics is not something you can afford to leave to "other people." Since politics is the art of ordering the affairs of men through government, it should be the vocation of the very best in this Republic and the avocation of all.
>
> There have been many who seem to equate politics with that which is bad, that which is corrupt, that which is venal, and that which is corrosive of our moral fiber. I find that throughout history most such disparaging remarks are made by those who never dared seek elective office.

What Are the Most Important Qualities of a Leader?

No one knows—so much depends on the context, the challenge, and the need. Still, the following qualities or skills are often cited as critically important. (But none of these guarantees leadership effectiveness.)

Self-knowledge
Self-confidence
Optimism/hope
Self-discipline
Sensitivity/empathy
Stamina/energy
Tenacity/persistence
Integrity
Vision
Imagination
Judgment
Risk taking
Morale building
Coalition building
Negotiating/mediating
Communicating
Breadth/creativity
Concern for results
Sense of humor
Enjoyment of people

On Leadership

Mary Parker Follett back in 1923 wrote a book that summed it up well: "He is a leader who gives form to the inchoate energy in every man. The person who influences me most is not he who does great deeds but he who makes me feel I can do great deeds."* That is, the leader guides the group and is at the same time guided by the group. No one can truly lead except from within. Leaders interpret our experience to us. Leaders give form to things vague, things latent, to mere tendencies and aspirations. They integrate, create communities of trust and empower the best in us not by dominating us but by expressing us and our collective energies and ideals and our yearning for liberty, freedom and social justice.

* Mary Parker Follett, *The New State* (Longman's, 1923), pp. 229–30.

This participant at a national convention is acting on the philosophy expressed by his T-shirt.

To scorn all politicians and to decry their actions is to scorn those who elect them and support them—namely the citizen-elector.[8]

The American people will never be completely satisfied with their politicians, nor should they be. The ideal politician is truly a fictional character, for the ideal politician would be able to please absolutely everyone and to make conflicts absolutely disappear. Such a person could exist only in an extremely small community in which all the people shared the same ideas, ideals, and interests. But American liberties invite diversity and, therefore, conflict. Politicians as well as the people they represent have different ideas about what is best for the nation. After all, who is really to say what is good for anyone else—let alone for *everyone* else? That's why we have politicians and politics. To understand this is to better appreciate the delicate and crucial responsibilities entrusted to our elected Act III politicians.[9]

Democratic Leadership

Our challenge of reconciling democracy and leadership is part definitional and part attitudinal. Too often in the past we have held a view of leaders as hierarchical, male, and upon whom followers are overly dependent. That conception is antithetical to our democratic aspirations. A nation of subservient followers can never be a democratic one. A democratic nation requires educated, skeptical, caring, engaged, and conscientious citizen-leaders.

Such a democratic citizen-leader appreciates that power wielded justly today may be wielded corruptly tomorrow. The democratic citizen-leader is moved to protest when he or she knows a policy is wrong or when other citizens find their rights diminished. This leader appreciates that criticism of official error is not criticism of our country. Citizen-leaders recognize as well that democracy rests solidly upon a mixed view of human nature. Our capacity for justice, as Reinhold Niebuhr observed, makes democracy possible. But our inclination to injustice makes democracy necessary.

Democratic politics is the forum or arena for excellence and responsibility, where—by acting together—citizens become free. In this sense, politics is not a necessary evil, it is a realistic good. It is the preoccupation of free people, and its existence is a test of freedom.

Thus democratic leadership can be enabling and facilitating. Leadership, thought of as an engagement among equals, a collegial collaboration, can empower and liberate people, and enlarge their options, choices, and freedoms. The answer for our republic lies not in producing a handful of great, charismatic, Mt. Rushmore leaders, but in educating a citizenry who can boast that we are no longer in need of great leaders because we have become a nation of citizens who believe one person can make a difference, and that every person should regularly try.

The Democratic Faith

The ultimate test of a democratic system is the legal existence of an *officially recognized opposition*. A cardinal characteristic of a democracy is that it not only recognizes the need for the free organization of opposing views but even positively encourages this organization. Freedom for political expression and dissent is basic—even freedom for nonsense to be spoken so that good sense not yet recognized gets a chance to be heard.

Crucial to the democratic faith is the belief that a democracy cherishes the free play of ideas. Only where the safety valve of public discussion is available and where almost any policy is subject to perpetual questioning and challenge can there be the assurance that both minority and majority rights will be served. To be afraid of public debate is to be afraid of self-government.

"Rulers always have and always will find it dangerous to their security to permit people to think, believe, talk, write, assemble, and particularly to criticize the government as they please," says Supreme Court Justice William J. Brennan, "but the language of the First amendment indicates the framers weighed the risk involved in such freedoms and deliberately chose to stake this government's security and life upon preserving liberty to discuss public affairs intact and untouched by government."[10]

We hold with Jefferson that there is nothing in the country so radically wrong that it cannot be cured by good newspapers and sound schoolmasters. Inform and educate the citizenry, and a major hurdle is overcome. Jefferson had boundless faith in education. He believed that people are rationally endowed by nature with an innate sense of justice; the average person has only to be informed to act wisely. In the long run, said Jefferson, only an educated and enlightened democracy can hope to endure.

We are a restless, dissatisfied, and searching people. We are our own toughest critics. Our political system is far from perfect, but it still is an open system. People can fight city hall. People who disagree with policies in the nation can band together and be heard. We know only too well that the American Dream is never something fully attained, and it is certainly not something inherited: It is always something to be achieved. Ultimately, we the people will determine whether we can make a government by the people work. We need enormous stamina and democratic faith to do so.

Our future will be shaped by those who care about making and preserving our political rights and freedoms. Our individual liberties will never be assured unless there are people willing to take considerable personal responsibility for the progress of the whole community, and people willing to exercise their determination and democratic faith. Carved in granite on one of the long corridors in a building on the Harvard University campus are these words of American poet Archibald MacLeish: "How shall freedom be defended? By arms when it is attacked by arms; by truth when it is attacked by lies, by democratic faith when it is attacked by authoritarian dogma. Always, in the final act, by determination and faith."

Millions of Americans tour through the great monuments in our nation's capital each year. They admire the beauty and are always impressed by the memorials to Washington, Jefferson, Lincoln, and the Vietnam veterans, the Capitol, the Supreme Court, and the White House. The strength of the nation, however, resides not in these official buildings but in the hearts, minds, and behavior of citizens. If we lose faith, stop caring, stop participating, and stop believing in the possibilities of self-government, the monuments "will be meaningless piles of stone, and the venture that began with the Declaration of Independence, the venture familiarly known as America will be as lifeless as the stone."[11]

One thing is certain amid all the debates over what the Constitution and the Bill of Rights mean, or should mean. The celebrations and the traumas, the advances and failures, the processes and institutions of "a government by the people"—as contrasted with something called "the state" in other lands—are

Why People Run for Political Office

To solve problems and promote the "American Dream"—enhancing liberty and justice

To advance fresh ideas and approaches

To "throw some rascal out" whose views you dislike

To gain a voice in policy making

To serve as a party spokesperson

To acquire political influence and a platform from which to influence public opinion

To gain prominence and power

To satisfy ego needs

To gain the opportunity to learn, grow, travel, and meet all kinds of people

To be where the "action is"—involved in the thick of government and political life—campaigning, debating, drafting laws, reconciling diverse views, and making the system responsive.

Why People Shy Away from Running for Public Office

Loss of privacy for you and your family

Less time to spend with families or favorite pastimes

Less income than in many business or professional occupations

Exposure to partisan and media criticism

Campaigning involves many things most people would rather not do—like marching in countless parades, attending county fairs, going to endless political dinners, banquets, service club meetings, and so on

Rewards of serving in office appear meager

Fear that one may have to compromise one's principles because of the complexity of our adversarial system

Campaigning can often be expensive

Some people don't want to show their ambitions, and they don't like conflict and divisiveness

Some people think the constitutional structure and the party systems we now have make it nearly impossible to exercise meaningful leadership

Walt Whitman

inseparable from the daily lives and hopes and needs of 250 million Americans. No one has expressed this argument more eloquently than Walt Whitman, in his "By Blue Ontario's Shore":

> O I see flashing that this America is only you and me,
> Its power, weapons, testimony, are you and me.
> Its crime, lies, thefts, defections, are you and me,
> Its Congress is you and me, the officers, capitols, armies, ships are you and me.
> Its endless gestation of new states are you and me,
> The war (that war so bloody and grim, the war I will henceforth forget), was you and me,
> Freedom, language, poems, employments, are you and me,
> Past, present, future, are you and me,
> I dare not shirk any part of myself,
> Nor any part of America good or bad. . . .

Notes

1. Edith Hamilton, *The Echo of Greece* (W.W. Norton, 1957), p. 47.
2. Adapted from Kenneth M. Dolbeare and Patricia Dolbeare, *American Ideologies* (Markham Publishing, 1971).
3. John F. Kennedy, *Profiles in Courage* (Pocket Books, 1956), p. 108.
4. See, for example, Charles Madison, *Critics and Crusaders* (Holt, 1947); Saul Alinsky, *Rules for Radicals* (Random House, 1972); and Harvey Goldberg, ed., *American Radicals: Some Problems and Personalities* (Monthly Review Press, 1957). On Howard Jarvis, see Jarvis, *I'm Mad as Hell!* (Times Books, 1979). See also Edward N. Kearney, *Mavericks in American Politics* (MIMIR Publishers, 1976).
5. See Herbert S. Parmet, *The Presidency of John F. Kennedy* (Dial Press, 1983). See also Stephen B. Oates, *Let the Trumpet Sound! The Life of Martin Luther King, Jr.* (Harper & Row, 1982); and Harris Wofford, *Of Kennedys & Kings* (Farrar, Straus & Giroux, 1980).
6. See Thomas E. Cronin, "Thinking and Learning About Leadership," *Presidential Studies Quarterly* (Winter 1984), pp. 22–34.
7. These distinctions are outlined in detail in James MacGregor Burns, *Leadership* (Harper & Row, 1978), chaps. 1 and 2.
8. Quoted in Conrad Joyner, *The American Politician* (University of Arizona Press, 1971). See also many of the essays in Paul Tillett, ed., *The Political Vocation* (Basic Books, 1965).
9. See Bernard Crick, *In Defense of Politics*, rev. ed. (Pelican Books, 1983), and Stimson Bullitt, *To Be a Politician*, rev. ed. (Yale University Press, 1977).
10. William J. Brennan, Commencement Address, Brandeis University (May 18, 1986).
11. John W. Gardner, *Self-Renewal* (Norton, 1981), Preface, p. xiv.

Appendix

The Declaration of Independence

Drafted mainly by Thomas Jefferson, this document adopted by the Second Continental Congress, and signed by John Hancock and fifty-five others, outlines the rights of man and the rights to rebellion and self-government. It declared the independence of the colonies from Great Britain, justified rebellion, and listed the grievances against George the III and his government. What is memorable about this famous document is not only that it declared the birth of a new nation, but that it set forth, with eloquence, our basic philosophy of liberty and representative democracy.

IN CONGRESS, JULY 4, 1776
(The unanimous Declaration of the Thirteen United States of America)

PREAMBLE

When, in the course of human events, it becomes necessary for one people to dissolve the political bands which have connected them with another, and to assume, among the powers of the earth, the separate and equal station to which the laws of nature and of nature's God entitle them, a decent respect to the opinions of mankind requires that they should declare the causes which impel them to the separation.

New Principles of Government

We hold these truths to be self-evident; that all men are created equal, that they are endowed by their Creator with certain unalienable rights, that among these are life, liberty, and the pursuit of happiness.

That, to secure these rights, governments are instituted among men, deriving their just powers from the consent of the governed;

That whenever any form of government becomes destructive of these ends, it is the right of the people to alter or to abolish it, and to institute new government, laying its foundation on such principles, and organizing its powers in such form, as to them shall seem most likely to effect their safety and happiness. Prudence, indeed, will dictate that governments long established should not be changed for light and transient causes; and accordingly all experience hath shown that mankind are more disposed to suffer while evils are sufferable, than to right themselves by abolishing the forms to which they are accustomed. But when a long train of abuses and usurpations, pursuing invariably the same object, evinces a design to reduce them under absolute despotism, it is their right, it is their duty, to throw off such government, and to provide new guards for their future security.

Reasons for Separation

Such has been the patient sufferance of these colonies; and such is now the necessity which constrains them to alter their former systems of government. The history of the present king of Great Britain is a history of repeated injuries and usurpations, all having in direct object the establishment of an absolute tyranny over these states. To prove this, let facts be submitted to a candid world.

He has refused his assent to laws, the most wholesome and necessary for the public good.

He has forbidden his governors to pass laws of immediate and pressing importance unless suspended in their operation till his assent should be obtained; and when so suspended, he has utterly neglected to attend to them.

He has refused to pass other laws for the accommodation of large districts of people, unless those people would relinquish the right of representation in the legislature, a right inestimable to them, and formidable to tyrants only.

He has called together legislative bodies at places unusual, uncomfortable, and distant from the depository of their public records, for the sole purpose of fatiguing them into compliance with his measures.

He has dissolved representative houses repeatedly, for opposing, with manly firmness, his invasions on the rights of people.

He has refused, for a long time after such dissolutions, to cause others to be elected; whereby the legislative powers, incapable of annihilation, have returned to the people at large for their exercise; the state remaining, in the mean time, exposed to all the dangers of invasion from without and convulsions within.

He has endeavored to prevent the population of these states; for that purpose obstructing the laws of naturalization of foreigners, refusing to pass others to encourage their migration hither, and raising the conditions of new appropriations of lands.

He has obstructed the administration of justice, by refusing his assent to laws for establishing judiciary powers.

He has made judges dependent on his will alone for the tenure of their offices, and the amount and payment of their salaries.

He has erected a multitude of new

offices, and sent hither swarms of officers to harass our people and eat out their substance.

He has kept among us, in times of peace, standing armies, without the consent of our legislature.

He has affected to render the military independent of, and superior to, the civil power.

He has combined with others to subject us to a jurisdiction foreign to our constitution and unacknowledged by our laws, giving his assent to their acts of pretended legislation:

For quartering large bodies of armed troops among us;

For protecting them, by a mock trial, from punishment for any murders which they should commit on the inhabitants of these states;

For cutting off our trade with all parts of the world;

For imposing taxes on us without our consent;

For depriving us, in many cases, of the benefits of trial by jury;

For transporting us beyond seas, to be tried for pretended offenses;

For abolishing the free system of English laws in a neighboring province, establishing therein an arbitrary government, and enlarging its boundaries, so as to render it at once an example and fit instrument for introducing the same absolute rule into these colonies;

For taking away our charters, abolishing our most valuable laws, and altering, fundamentally, the forms of our governments;

For suspending our own legislatures, and declaring themselves invested with power to legislate for us in all cases whatsoever.

He has abdicated government here, by declaring us out of his protection and waging war against us.

He has plundered our seas, ravaged our coasts, burned our towns, and destroyed the lives of our people.

He is at this time transporting large armies of foreign mercenaries to complete the works of death, desolation, and tyranny already begun with circumstances of cruelty and perfidy scarcely paralleled in the most barbarous ages and totally unworthy of the head of a civilized nation.

He has constrained our fellow-citizens, taken captive on the high seas, to bear arms against their country, to become the executioners of their friends and brethren, or to fall themselves by their hands.

He has excited domestic insurrections among us, and has endeavored to bring on the inhabitants of our frontiers the merciless Indian savages, whose known rule of warfare is an undistinguished destruction of all ages, sexes, and conditions.

In every stage of these oppressions we have petitioned for redress in the most humble terms; our repeated petitions have been answered only by repeated injury. A prince whose character is thus marked by every act which may define a tyrant is unfit to be the ruler of a free people.

Nor have we been wanting in attention to our British brethren. We have warned them, from time to time, of attempts by their legislature to extend an unwarrantable jurisdiction over us. We have reminded them of the circumstances of our emigration and settlement here. We have appealed to their native justice and magnanimity; and we have conjured them, by the ties of our common kindred, to disavow these usurpations, which would inevitably interrupt our connections and correspondence. They, too, have been deaf to the voice of justice and of consanguinity. We must, therefore, acquiesce in the necessity which denounces our separation, and hold them, as we hold the rest of mankind, enemies in war, in peace, friends.

We, therefore, the representatives of the United States of America, in General Congress assembled, appealing to the Supreme Judge of the world for the rectitude of our intentions, do, in the name and by authority of the good people of these colonies, solemnly publish and declare, that these united colonies are, and of right ought to be, free and independent states; that they are absolved from all allegiance to the British crown, and that all political connection between them and the state of Great Britain is, and ought to be, totally dissolved; and that, as free and independent states, they have full power to levy war, conclude peace, contract alliances, establish commerce, and do all other acts and things which independent states may of a right do. And, for the support of this declaration, with a firm reliance on the protection of Divine Providence, we mutually pledge to each other our lives, our fortunes, and our sacred honor.

*T*he *Federalist*, No. 10, James Madison

The Federalist, No. 10, written by James Madison soon after the Constitutional Convention, was prepared as one of several dozen newspaper essays aimed at persuading New Yorkers to ratify the proposed constitution. One of the most important basic documents in American political history, it outlines the need for and the general principles of a democratic republic. It also provides a political and economic analysis of the realities of interest group or faction politics.

To the People of the State of New York: Among the numerous advantages promised by a well-constructed union, none deserves to be more accurately developed than its tendency to break and control the violence of faction. The friend of popular governments, never finds himself so much alarmed for their character and fate, as when he contemplates their propensity to this dangerous vice. He will not fail, therefore, to set a due value on any plan which, without violating the principles to which he is attached, provides a proper cure for it. The instability, injustice, and confusion introduced into the public councils, have, in truth, been the mortal diseases under which popular governments have everywhere perished; as they continue to be the favourite and fruitful topics from which the adversaries to liberty derive their most specious declamations. The valuable improvements made by the American constitutions on the popular models, both ancient and modern, cannot certainly be too much admired; but it would be an unwarrantable partiality, to contend that they have as effectually obviated the danger on this side, as was wished and expected. Complaints are everywhere heard from our most considerate and virtuous citizens, equally the friends of public and private faith, and of public and personal liberty, that our governments are too unstable; that the public good is disregarded in the conflicts of rival parties; and that measures are too often decided, not according to the rules of justice, and the rights of the minor party, but by the superior force of an interested and overbearing majority. However anxiously we may wish that these complaints had no foundation, the evidence of known facts will not permit us to deny that they are in some degree true. It will be found, indeed, on a candid review of our situation, that some of the distresses under which we labour have been erroneously charged on the operation of our governments; but it will be found, at the same time, that other causes will not alone account for many of our heaviest misfortunes; and, particularly, for that prevailing and increasing distrust of public engagements, and alarm for private rights, which are echoed from one end of the continent to the other. These must be chiefly, if not wholly, effects of the unsteadiness and injustice, with which a factious spirit has tainted our public administrations.

By a faction, I understand a number of citizens, whether amounting to a majority or minority of the whole, who are united and actuated by some common impulse of passion, or of interest, adverse to the rights of other citizens, or to the permanent and aggregate interests of the community.

There are two methods of curing the mischiefs of faction: the one, by removing its causes; the other, by controlling its effects.

There are again two methods of removing the causes of faction: the one, by destroying the liberty which is essential to its existence; the other, by giving to every citizen the same opinions, the same passions, and the same interests.

It could never be more truly said, than of the first remedy, that it was worse than the disease. Liberty is to faction what air is to fire, an aliment without which it instantly expires. But it could not be a less folly to abolish liberty, which is essential to political life, because it nourishes faction, than it would be to wish

the annihilation of air, which is essential to animal life, because it imparts to fire its destructive agency.

The second expedient is as impracticable, as the first would be unwise. As long as the reason of man continues fallible, and he is at liberty to exercise it, different opinions will be formed. As long as the connection subsists between his reason and his self-love, his opinions and his passions will have a reciprocal influence on each other; and the former will be objects to which the latter will attach themselves. The diversity in the faculties of men, from which the rights of property originate, is not less an insuperable obstacle to an uniformity of interests. The protection of these faculties is the first object of government. From the protection of different and unequal faculties of acquiring property, the possession of different degrees and kinds of property immediately results; and from the influence of these on the sentiments and views of the respective proprietors, ensues a division of the society into different interests and parties.

The latent causes of faction are thus sown in the nature of man; and we see them everywhere brought into different degrees of activity, according to the different circumstances of civil society. A zeal for different opinions concerning religion, concerning government, and many other points, as well of speculation as of practice; an attachment to different leaders ambitiously contending for pre-eminence and power; or to persons of other descriptions whose fortunes have been interesting to the human passions, have, in turn, divided mankind into parties, inflamed them with mutual animosity, and rendered them much more disposed to vex and oppress each other, than to cooperate for their common good. So strong is this propensity of mankind, to fall into mutual animosities, that where no substantial occasion presents itself, the most frivolous and fanciful distinctions have been sufficient to kindle their unfriendly passions and excite their most violent conflicts. But the most common and durable source of factions, has been the various and unequal distribution of property. Those who hold, and those who are without property, have ever formed distinct interests in society. Those who are creditors, and those who are debtors, fall under a like discrimination. A landed interest, a manufacturing interest, a mercantile interest, a moneyed interest, with many lesser interests, grow up of neces-

sity in civilized nations, and divide them into different classes, actuated by different sentiments and views. The regulation of these various and interfering interests forms the principal task of modern legislation, and involves the spirit of the party and faction in the necessary and ordinary operations of the government.

No man is allowed to be a judge in his own cause; because his interest will certainly bias his judgment, and, not improbably, corrupt his integrity. With equal, nay, with greater reason, a body of men are unfit to be both judges and parties at the same time; yet what are many of the most important acts of legislation, but so many judicial determinations, not indeed concerning the right of single persons, but concerning the rights of large bodies of citizens? And what are the different classes of legislators, but advocates and parties to the causes which they determine? Is a law proposed concerning private debts? It is a question to which the creditors are parties on one side, and the debtors on the other. Justice ought to hold the balance between them. Yet the parties are, and must be, themselves the judges; and the most numerous party, or, in other words, the most powerful faction, must be expected to prevail. Shall domestic manufactures be encouraged, and in what degree, by restrictions on foreign manufactures? are questions which would be differently decided by the landed and the manufacturing classes; and probably by neither with a sole regard to justice and the public good. The apportionment of taxes, on the various descriptions of property, is an act which seems to require the most exact impartiality; yet there is, perhaps, no legislative act, in which greater opportunity and temptation are given to a predominant party to trample on the rules of justice. Every shilling, with which they overburden the inferior number, is a shilling saved to their own pockets.

It is in vain to say, that enlightened statesmen will be able to adjust these clashing interests, and render them all subservient to the public good. Enlightened statesmen will not always be at the helm; nor, in many cases, can such an adjustment be made at all, without taking into view indirect and remote considerations, which will rarely prevail over the immediate interest which one party may find in disregarding the rights of another, or the good of the whole.

The inference to which we are brought is, that the *causes* of faction cannot be removed; and that relief is only to be sought in the means of controlling its *effects*.

If a faction consists of less than a majority, relief is supplied by the republican principle, which enables the majority to defeat its sinister views, by regular vote. It may clog the administration, it may convulse the society; but it will be unable to execute and mask its violence under the forms of the Constitution. When a majority is included in a faction, the form of popular government, on the other hand, enables it to sacrifice to its ruling passion or interest, both the public good and the rights of other citizens. To secure the public good, and private rights, against the danger of such a faction, and at the same time to preserve the spirit and the form of popular government, is then the great object to which our inquiries are directed. Let me add, that it is the great desideratum, by which alone this form of government can be rescued from the opprobrium under which it has so long laboured, and be recommended to the esteem and adoption of mankind.

By what means is this object attainable? Evidently by one of two only. Either the existence of the same passion or interest in a majority, at the same time, must be prevented; or the majority, having such coexistent passion or interest, must be rendered, by their number and local situation, unable to concert and carry into effect schemes of oppression. If the impulse and the opportunity be suffered to coincide, we well know that neither moral nor religious motives can be relied on as an adequate control. They are not found to be such on the injustice and violence of individuals, and lose their efficacy in proportion to the number combined together; that is, in proportion as their efficacy becomes needful.

From this view of the subject, it may be concluded, that a pure democracy, by which I mean a society consisting of a small number of citizens, who assemble and administer the government in person, can admit of no cure for the mischiefs of faction. A common passion or interest will, in almost every case, be felt by a majority of the whole; a communication and concert, results from the form of government itself; and there is nothing to check the inducements to sacrifice the weaker party, or an obnoxious individual. Hence, it is, that such democracies have ever been spectacles of turbulence and contention; have ever been found incompatible with personal security, or the

rights of property; and have in general been as short in their lives, as they have been violent in their deaths. Theoretic politicians, who have patronized this species of government, have erroneously supposed, that by reducing mankind to a perfect equality in their political rights, they would, at the same time, be perfectly equalized and assimilated in their possessions, their opinions, and their passions.

A republic, by which I mean a government in which the scheme of representation takes place, opens a different prospect, and promises the cure for which we are seeking. Let us examine the points in which it varies from pure democracy, and we shall comprehend both the nature of the cure and the efficacy which it must derive from the union.

The two great points of difference, between a democracy and a republic, are, first, the delegation of the government, in the latter, to a small number of citizens, elected by the rest; secondly, the greater number of citizens, and greater sphere of country, over which the latter may be extended.

The effect of the first difference is, on the one hand, to refine and enlarge the public views, by passing them through the medium of a chosen body of citizens, whose wisdom may best discern the true interest of their country, and whose patriotism and love of justice, will be least likely to sacrifice it to temporary or partial considerations. Under such a regulation, it may well happen, that the public voice, pronounced by the representatives of the people, will be more consonant to the public good, than if pronounced by the people themselves, convened for the purpose. On the other hand the effect may be inverted. Men of factious tempers, of local prejudices, or of sinister designs, may by intrigue, by corruption, or by other means, first obtain the suffrages, and then betray the interest of the people. The question resulting is, whether small or extensive republics are most favourable to the election of proper guardians of the public weal; and it is clearly decided in favour of the latter by two obvious considerations.

In the first place, it is to be remarked that, however small the republic may be, the representatives must be raised to a certain number, in order to guard against the cabals of a few; and that however large it may be, they must be limited to a certain number, in order to guard against the confusion of a multitude. Hence, the number of representatives in

the two cases not being in proportion to that of the constituents, and being proportionally greatest in the small republic, it follows, that if the proportion of fit characters be not less in the large than in the small republic, the former will present a greater option, and consequently a greater probability of a fit choice.

In the next place, as each representative will be chosen by a greater number of citizens in the large than in the small republic, it will be more difficult for unworthy candidates to practise with success the vicious arts, by which elections are too often carried; and the suffrages of the people being more free, will be more likely to centre in men who possess the most attractive merit, and the most diffusive and established characters.

It must be confessed, that in this, as in most other cases, there is a mean, on both sides of which inconveniences will be found to lie. By enlarging too much the number of electors, you render the representatives too little acquainted with all their local circumstances and lesser interests; as by reducing it too much, you render him unduly attached to these, and too little fit to comprehend and pursue great and national objects. The federal constitution forms a happy combination in this respect; the great and aggregate interests being referred to the national, the local and particular to the state legislatures.

The other point of difference is, the greater number of citizens, and extent of territory, which may be brought within the compass of republican, than of democratic government; and it is this circumstance principally which renders factious combinations less to be dreaded in the former, than in the latter. The smaller the society, the fewer probably will be the distinct parties and interests composing it; the fewer the distinct parties and interests, the more frequently will a majority be found of the same party; and the smaller the number of individuals composing a majority, and the smaller the compass within which they are placed, the more easily will they concert and execute their plans of oppression. Extend the sphere, and you take in a greater variety of parties and interests; you make it less probable that a majority of the whole will have a common motive to invade the rights of other citizens; or if such a common motive exists, it will be more difficult for all who feel it to discover their own strength, and to act in unison with each other. Besides other impediments, it may be remarked, that where there is a consciousness of unjust or dishonourable purposes, communication is always checked by distrust, in proportion to the number whose concurrence is necessary.

Hence, it clearly appears, that the same advantage, which a republic has over a democracy, in controlling the effects of faction, is enjoyed by a large over a small republic—is enjoyed by the union over the states composing it. Does this advantage consist in the substitution of representatives, whose enlightened views and virtuous sentiments render them superior to local prejudices, and to schemes of injustice? It will not be denied that the representation of the union will be most likely to possess these requisite endowments. Does it consist in the greater security afforded by a greater variety of parties, against the event of any one party being able to outnumber and oppress the rest? In an equal degree does the increased variety of parties, comprised within the union, increase the security? Does it, in fine, consist in the greater obstacles opposed to the concert and accomplishment of the secret wishes of an unjust and interested majority? Here, again, the extent of the union gives it the most palpable advantage.

The influence of factious leaders may kindle a flame within their particular states, but will be unable to spread a general conflagration through the other states; a religious sect may degenerate into a political faction in a part of the confederacy; but the variety of sects dispersed over the entire face of it, must secure the national councils against any danger from that source: a rage for paper money, for an abolition of debts, for an equal division of property, or for any other improper or wicked project, will be less apt to pervade the whole body of the union than a particular member of it; in the same proportion as such a malady is more likely to taint a particular county or district, than an entire state.

In the extent and proper structure of the union, therefore, we behold a republican remedy for the diseases most incident to republican government. And according to the degree of pleasure and pride we feel in being republicans, ought to be our zeal in cherishing the spirit, and supporting the character of federalists.

*T*he *Federalist*, No. 51, James Madison

The Federalist, No. 51, also written by Madison, is a classic statement in defense of separation of powers and republican processes. Its fourth paragraph is especially famous and is frequently quoted by students of government.

To what expedient, then, shall we finally resort, for maintaining in practice the necessary partition of power among the several departments as laid down in the Constitution? The only answer that can be given is that as all these exterior provisions are found to be inadequate the defect must be supplied, by so contriving the interior structure of the government as that its several constituent parts may, by their mutual relations, be the means of keeping each other in their proper places. Without presuming to undertake a full development of this important idea I will hazard a few general observations which may perhaps place it in a clearer light, and enable us to form a more correct judgment of the principles and structure of the government planned by the convention.

In order to lay a due foundation for that separate and distinct exercise of the different powers of government, which to a certain extent is admitted on all hands to be essential to the preservation of liberty, it is evident that each department should have a will of its own; and consequently should be so constituted that the members of each should have as little agency as possible in the appointment of the members of the others. Were this principle rigorously adhered to, it would require that all the appointments for the supreme executive, legislative, and judiciary magistracies should be drawn from the same fountain of authority, the people, through channels having no communication whatever with one another. Perhaps such a plan of constructing the several departments would be less difficult in practice than it may in contemplation appear. Some difficulties, however, and some additional expense would attend the execution of it. Some deviations, therefore, from the principle must be admitted. In the constitution of the judiciary department in particular, it might be inexpedient to insist rigorously on the principle: first, because peculiar qualifications being essential in the members, the primary consideration ought to be to select that mode of choice which best secures these qualifications; second, because the permanent tenure by which the appointments are held in that department must soon destroy all sense of dependence on the authority conferring them.

It is equally evident that the members of each department should be as little dependent as possible on those of the others for the emoluments annexed to their offices. Were the executive magistrate, or the judges, not independent of the legislature in this particular, their independence in every other would be merely nominal.

But the great security against a gradual concentration of the several powers in the same department consists in giving to those who administer each department the necessary constitutional means and personal motives to resist encroachments of the others. The provision for defense must in this, as in all other cases, be made commensurate to the danger of attack. Ambition must be made to counteract ambition. The interest of the man must be connected with the constitutional rights of the place. It may be a reflection on human nature that such devices should be necessary to control the abuses of government. But what is government itself but the greatest of all reflections on human nature? If men were angels, no government would be necessary. If angels were to govern men, neither external nor internal controls on government would be necessary. In framing a government which is to be administered by men over men, the great difficulty lies in this: you must first enable the government to control the governed; and in the next place oblige it to control itself. A dependence on the people is, no doubt, the primary control on the government; but experience has taught mankind the necessity of auxiliary precautions.

This policy of supplying, by opposite and rival interests, the defect of better motives, might be traced through the whole system of human affairs, private as well as public. We see it particularly displayed in all the subordinate distributions of power, where the constant aim is to divide and arrange the several offices in such a manner as that each may be a check on the other—that the private interest of every individual may be a sentinel over the public rights. These inventions of prudence cannot be less requisite in the distribution of the supreme powers of the State.

But it is not possible to give to each department an equal power of self-defense. In republican government, the legislative authority necessarily predominates. The remedy for this inconveniency is to divide the legislature into different branches; and to render them, by different modes of election and different principles of action, as little connected with each other as the nature of their common functions and their common dependence on the society will admit. It may even be necessary to guard against dangerous encroachments by still further precautions. As the weight of the legislative authority requires that it should be thus divided, the weakness of the executive may require, on the other hand, that it should be fortified. An absolute negative on the legislature appears, at first view, to be the natural defense with which the executive magistrate should be armed. But perhaps it would be neither altogether safe nor alone sufficient. On ordinary occasions it might not be exerted with the requisite firmness, and on extraordinary occasions it might be perfidiously abused. May not this defect of an absolute negative be supplied by some qualified connection between this weaker department and the weaker branch of the stronger department, by which the latter may be led to support the constitutional rights of the former, without being too much detached from the rights of its own department?

If the principles on which these observations are founded be just, as I persuade myself they are, and they be applied as a criterion to the several State constitutions, and to the federal Constitution, it will be found that if the latter does not perfectly correspond with them, the for-

mer are infinitely less able to bear such a test.

There are, moreover, two considerations particularly applicable to the federal system of America, which place that system in a very interesting point of view.

First. In a single republic, all the power surrendered by the people is submitted to the administration of a single government; and the usurpations are guarded against by a division of the government into distinct and separate departments. In the compound republic of America, the power surrendered by the people is first divided between two distinct governments, and then the portion allotted to each subdivided among distinct and separate departments. Hence a double security arises to the rights of the people. The different governments will control each other, at the same time that each will be controlled by itself.

Second. It is of great importance in a republic not only to guard the society against the oppression of its rulers, but to guard one part of the society against the injustice of the other part. Different interests necessarily exist in different classes of citizens. If a majority be united by a common interest, the rights of the minority will be insecure. There are but two methods of providing against this evil: the one by creating a will in the community independent of the majority—that is, of the society itself; the other, by comprehending in the society so many separate descriptions of citizens as will render an unjust combination of a majority of the whole very improbable, if not impracticable. The first method prevails in all governments possessing an hereditary or self-appointed authority. This, at best, is but a precarious security; because a power independent of the society may as well espouse the unjust views of the major as the rightful interests of the minor party, and may possibly be turned against both parties. The second method will be exemplified in the federal republic of the United States. Whilst all authority in it will be derived from and dependent on the society, the society itself will be broken into so many parts, interests and classes of citizens, that the rights of individuals, or of the minority, will be in little danger from interested combinations of the majority. In a free government the security for civil rights must be the same as that for religious rights. It consists in the one case in the multiplicity of interests, and in the other in the multiplicity

of sects. The degree of security in both cases will depend on the number of interests and sects; and this may be presumed to depend on the extent of country and number of people comprehended under the same government. This view of the subject must particularly recommend a proper federal system to all the sincere and considerate friends of republican government, since it shows that in exact proportion as the territory of the Union may be formed into more circumscribed Confederacies, or States, oppressive combinations of a majority will be facilitated; the best security, under the republican forms, for the rights of every class of citizen, will be diminished; and consequently the stability and independence of some member of the government, the only other security, must be proportionally increased. Justice is the end of government. It is the end of civil society. It ever has been and ever will be pursued until it be obtained, or until liberty be lost in the pursuit. In a society under the forms of which the stronger faction can readily unite and oppress the weaker, anarchy may as truly be said to reign as in a state of nature, where the weaker individual is not secured against the violence of the stronger; and as, in the latter state, even the stronger individuals are prompted, by the uncertainty of their condition, to submit to a government which may protect the weak as well as themselves; so, in the former state, will the more powerful factions or parties be gradually induced, by a like motive, to wish for a government which will protect all parties, the weaker as well as the more powerful. It can be little doubted that if the State of Rhode Island was separated from the Confederacy and left to itself, the insecurity of rights under the popular form of government within such narrow limits would be displayed by such reiterated oppressions of factious majorities that some power altogether independent of the people would soon be called for by the voice of the very factions whose misrule had proved the necessity of it. In the extended republic of the United States, and among the great variety of interests, parties, and sects which it embraces, a coalition of a majority of the whole society could seldom take place on any other principles than those of justice and the general good; whilst there being thus less danger to a minor from the will of a major party, there must be less pretext, also, to provide for the security of the former, by introducing into the government a will not dependent on the latter, or, in other words, a will independent of the society itself. It is no less certain that it is important, notwithstanding the contrary opinions which have been entertained, that the larger the society, provided it lie within a practicable sphere, the more duly capable it will be of self-government. And happily for the *republican cause*, the practicable sphere may be carried to a very great extent by a judicious modification and mixture of the *federal principle*.

*T*he Federalist, No. 78, Alexander Hamilton

The Federalist, No. 78, written by Alexander Hamilton, explains and praises the provisions for the judiciary in the newly drafted Constitution. Notice especially how Hamilton asserts that the courts have a key responsibility in determining the meaning of the Constitution as fundamental law. Hamilton is outlining here the doctrine of *judicial review* as we now know it.

We proceed now to an examination of the judiciary department of the proposed government.

In unfolding the defects of the existing Confederation, the utility and necessity of a federal judicature have been clearly pointed out. It is the less necessary to recapitulate the considerations there urged as the propriety of the institution in the abstract is not disputed; the only questions which have been raised being relative to the manner of constituting it, and to its extent. To these points, therefore, our observations shall be confined.

The manner of constituting it seems to embrace these several objects: 1st. The mode of appointing the judges. 2nd. The tenure by which they are to hold their places. 3rd. The partition of the judiciary authority between different courts and their relations to each other.

First. As to the mode of appointing the judges: this is the same with that of appointing the officers of the Union in general and has been so fully discussed in the two last numbers that nothing can be said here which would not be useless repetition.

Second. As to the tenure by which the judges are to hold their places: this chiefly concerns their duration in office, the provisions for their support, the precautions for their responsibility.

According to the plan of the convention, all judges who may be appointed by the United States are to hold their offices *during good behavior*; which is conformable to the most approved of the State constitutions, and among the rest, to that of this State. Its propriety having been drawn into question by the adversaries of that plan is no light symptom of the rage for objection which disorders their imaginations and judgments. The standard of good behavior for the continuance in office of the judicial magistracy is certainly one of the most valuable of the modern improvements in the practice of government. In a monarchy it is an excellent barrier to the despotism of the prince; in a republic it is a no less excellent barrier to the encroachments and oppressions of the representative body. And it is the best expedient which can be devised in any government to secure a steady, upright, and impartial administration of the laws.

Whoever attentively considers the different departments of power must perceive that, in a government in which they are separated from each other, the judiciary, from the nature of its functions, will always be the least dangerous to the political rights of the Constitution; because it will be least in a capacity to annoy or injure them. The executive not only dispenses the honors but holds the sword of the community. The legislature not only commands the purse but prescribes the rules by which the duties and rights of every citizen are to be regulated. The judiciary, on the contrary, has no influence over either the sword or the purse; no direction either of the strength or of the wealth of the society, and can take no active resolution whatever. It may truly be said to have neither FORCE nor WILL but merely judgment; and must ultimately depend upon the aid of the executive arm even for the efficacy of its judgments.

This simple view of the matter suggests several important consequences. It proves incontestably that the judiciary is beyond comparison the weakest of the three departments of power; that it can never attack with success either of the other two; and that all possible care is requisite to enable it to defend itself against their attacks. It equally proves that though individual oppression may now and then proceed from the courts of justice, the general liberty of the people can never be endangered from that quarter; I mean so long as the judiciary remains truly distinct from both the legislature and the executive. For I agree that "there is no liberty if the power of judging be not separated from the legislative and executive powers." And it proves, in the last place, that as liberty can have nothing to fear from the judiciary alone, but would have everything to fear from its union with either of the other departments; that as all the effects of such a union must ensue from a dependence of the former on the latter, notwithstanding a nominal and apparent separation; that as, from the natural feebleness of the judiciary, it is in continual jeopardy of being overpowered, awed, or influenced by its co-ordinate branches; and that as nothing can contribute so much to its firmness and independence as permanency in office, this quality may therefore be justly regarded as an indispensable ingredient in its constitution, and, in a great measure, as the citadel of the public justice and the public security.

The complete independence of the courts of justice is peculiarly essential in a limited Constitution. By a limited Constitution, I understand one which contains certain specified exceptions to the legislative authority; such, for instance, as that it shall pass no bills of attainder, no *ex post facto* laws, and the like. Limitations of this kind can be preserved in practice no other way than through the medium of courts of justice, whose duty it must be to declare all acts contrary to the manifest tenor of the Constitution void. Without this, all the reservations of particular rights or privileges would amount to nothing.

Some perplexity respecting the rights of the courts to pronounce legislative acts void, because contrary to the Constitution, has arisen from an imagination that the doctrine would imply a superiority of the judiciary to the legislative power. It is urged that the authority which can declare the acts of another void must necessarily be superior to the one whose acts may be declared void. As this doctrine is of great importance in all the American constitutions, a brief discussion of the grounds on which it rests cannot be unacceptable.

There is no position which depends on clearer principles than that every act of a delegated authority, contrary to the tenor of the commission under which it is exercised, is void. No legislative act, therefore, contrary to the Constitution, can be valid. To deny this would be to affirm that the deputy is greater than his principal; that the servant is above his master; that the representatives of the people are superior to the people themselves; that men acting by virtue of powers may do not only what their powers do not authorize, but what they forbid.

If it be said that the legislative body are themselves the constitutional judges of their own powers and that the construction they put upon them is conclusive upon the other departments it may be answered that this cannot be the natural presumption where it is not to be collected from any particular provisions in the Constitution. It is not otherwise to be supposed that the Constitution could intend to enable the representatives of the people to substitute their *will* to that of their constituents. It is far more rational to suppose that the courts were designed to be an intermediate body between the people and the legislature in order, among other things, to keep the latter within the limits assigned to their authority. The interpretation of the laws is the proper and peculiar province of the courts. A constitution is, in fact, and must be regarded by the judges as, a fundamental law. It therefore belongs to them to ascertain its meaning as well as the meaning of any particular act proceeding from the legislative body. If there should happen to be an irreconcilable variance between the two, that which has the superior obligation and validity ought, of course,

to be preferred; or, in other words, the Constitution ought to be preferred to the statute, the intention of the people to the intention of their agents.

Nor does this conclusion by any means suppose a superiority of the judicial to the legislative power. It only supposes that the power of the people is superior to both, and that where the will of the legislature, declared in its statutes, stands in opposition to that of the people, declared in the Constitution, the judges ought to be governed by the latter rather than the former. They ought to regulate their decisions by the fundamental laws rather than by those which are not fundamental.

This exercise of judicial discretion in determining between two contradictory laws is exemplified in a familiar instance. It not uncommonly happens that there are two statutes existing at one time, clashing in whole or in part with each other and neither of them containing any repealing clause or expression. In such a case, it is the province of the courts to liquidate and fix their meaning and operation. So far as they can, by any fair construction, be reconciled to each other, reason and law conspire to dictate that this should be done; where this is impracticable, it becomes a matter of necessity to give effect to one in exclusion of the other. The rule which has obtained in the courts for determining their relative validity is that the last in order of time shall be preferred to the first. But this is a mere rule of construction, not derived from any positive law but from the nature and reason of the thing. It is a rule not enjoined upon the courts by legislative provision but adopted by themselves, as consonant to truth and propriety, for the direction of their conduct as interpreters of the law. They thought it reasonable that between the interfering acts of an *equal* authority that which was the last indication of its will should have the preference.

But in regard to the interfering acts of a superior and subordinate authority of an original and derivative power, the nature and reason of the thing indicate the converse of that rule as proper to be followed. They teach us that the prior act of a superior ought to be preferred to the subsequent act of an inferior and subordinate authority; and that accordingly, whenever a particular statute contravenes the Constitution, it will be the duty of the judicial tribunals to adhere to the latter and disregard the former.

It can be of no weight to say that the courts, on the pretense of a repugnancy, may substitute their own pleasure to the constitutional intentions of the legislature. This might as well happen in the case of two contradictory statutes; or it might as well happen in every adjudication upon any single statute. The courts must declare the sense of the law; and if they should be disposed to exercise WILL instead of JUDGMENT, the consequence would equally be the substitution of their pleasure to that of the legislative body. The observation, if it prove anything, would prove that there ought to be no judges distinct from that body.

If, then, the courts of justice are to be considered as the bulwarks of a limited Constitution against legislative encroachments, this consideration will afford a strong argument for the permanent tenure of judicial offices, since nothing will contribute so much as this to that independent spirit in the judges which must be essential to the faithful performance of so arduous a duty.

This independence of the judges is equally requisite to guard the Constitution and the rights of individuals from the effects of those ill humors which the arts of designing men, or the influence of particular conjunctures, sometimes disseminate among the people themselves, and which, though they speedily give place to better information, and more deliberate reflection, have a tendency, in the meantime, to occasion dangerous innovations in the government, and serious oppressions of the minor party in the community. Though I trust the friends of the proposed Constitution will never concur with its enemies in questioning that fundamental principle of Republican government which admits the right of the people to alter or abolish the established Constitution whenever they find it inconsistent with their happiness; yet it is not to be inferred from this principle that the representatives of the people, whenever a momentary inclination happens to lay hold of a majority of their constituents incompatible with the provisions in the existing Constitution would, on that account, be justifiable in a violation of those provisions; or that the courts would be under a greater obligation to connive at infractions in this shape than when they had proceeded wholly from the cabals of the representative body. Until the people have, by some solemn and authoritative act, annulled or changed the established form, it is binding upon themselves collectively, as well as individually; and no presumption, or even knowledge of their sentiments, can warrant their representatives in a departure from it prior to such an act. But it is easy to see that it would require an uncommon portion of fortitude in the judges to do their duty as faithful guardians of the Constitution, where legislative invasions of it had been instigated by the major voice of the community.

But it is not with a view to infractions of the Constitution only that the independence of the judges may be an essential safeguard against the effects of occasional ill humors in the society. These sometimes extend no farther than to the injury of the private rights of particular classes of citizens, by unjust and partial laws. Here also the firmness of the judicial magistracy is of vast importance in mitigating the severity and confining the operation of such laws. It not only serves to moderate the immediate mischiefs of those which may have been passed but it operates as a check upon the legislative body in passing them; who, perceiving that obstacles to the success of iniquitous intention are to be expected from the scruples of the courts, are in a manner compelled, by the very motives of the injustice they mediate, to qualify their attempts. This is a circumstance calculated to have more influence upon the character of our governments than but few may be aware of. The benefits of the integrity and moderation of the judiciary have already been felt in more States than one; and though they may have displeased those whose sinister expectations they may have disappointed, they must have commanded the esteem and applause of all the virtuous and disinterested. Considerate men of every description ought to prize whatever will tend to beget or fortify that temper in the courts; as no man can be sure that he may not be tomorrow the victim of a spirit of injustice, by which he may be a gainer today. And every man must now feel that the inevitable tendency of such a spirit is to sap the foundations of public and private confidence and to introduce in its stead universal distrust and distress.

That inflexible and uniform adherence to the rights of the Constitution, and of individuals, which we perceive to be indispensable in the courts of justice, can certainly not be expected from judges who hold their offices by a temporary commission. Periodical appointments, however regulated, or by whomsoever made, would, in some way or other, be fatal to their necessary independence. If the power of making them was committed either to the executive or legislature there would be danger of an improper complaisance to the branch which possessed it; if to both, there would be an unwillingness to hazard the displeasure of either; if to the people, or to persons chosen by them for the special purpose, there would be too great a disposition to consult popularity to justify a reliance that nothing would be consulted but the Constitution and the laws.

There is yet a further and a weighty reason for the permanency of the judicial offices which is deducible from the nature of the qualifications they require. It has been frequently remarked with great propriety that a voluminous code of laws is one of the inconveniences necessarily connected with the advantages of a free government. To avoid an arbitrary discretion in the courts, it is indispensable that they should be bound down by strict rules and precedents which serve to define and point out their duty in every particular case that comes before them; and it will readily be conceived from the variety of controversies which grow out of the folly and wickedness of mankind that the records of those precedents must unavoidably swell to a very considerable bulk and must demand long and laborious study to acquire a competent knowledge of them. Hence it is that there can be but few men in the society who will have sufficient skill in the laws to qualify them for the stations of judges. And making the proper deductions for the ordinary depravity of human nature, the number must be still smaller of those who unite the requisite integrity with the requisite knowledge. These considerations apprise us that the government can have no great option between fit characters; and that a temporary duration in office which would naturally discourage such characters from quitting a lucrative line of practice to accept a seat on the bench would have a tendency to throw the administration of justice into hands less able and less well qualified to conduct it with utility and dignity. In the present circumstances of this country and in those in which it is likely to be for a long time to come, the disadvantages on this score would be greater than they may at first sight appear; but it must be confessed that they are far inferior to those which present themselves under the other aspects of the subject.

Upon the whole, there can be no room to doubt that the convention acted wisely in copying from the models of those constitutions which have established *good behavior* as the tenure of their judicial offices, in point of duration; and that so far from being blamable on this account, their plan would have been inexcusably defective if it had wanted this important feature of good government. The experience of Great Britain affords an illustrious comment on the excellence of the institution.

Year	Candidates	Party	Popular Vote	Electoral Vote
1789	**George Washington**			69
	John Adams			34
	Others			35
1792	**George Washington**			132
	John Adams			77
	George Clinton			50
	Others			5
1796	**John Adams**	Federalist		71
	Thomas Jefferson	Democratic-Republican		68
	Thomas Pinckney	Federalist		59
	Aaron Burr	Democratic-Republican		30
	Others			48
1800	**Thomas Jefferson**	Democratic-Republican		73
	Aaron Burr	Democratic-Republican		73
	John Adams	Federalist		65
	Charles C. Pinckney	Federalist		64
1804	**Thomas Jefferson**	Democratic-Republican		162
	Charles C. Pinckney	Federalist		14
1808	**James Madison**	Democratic-Republican		122
	Charles C. Pinckney	Federalist		47
	George Clinton	Independent-Republican		6
1812	**James Madison**	Democratic-Republican		128
	DeWitt Clinton	Federalist		89
1816	**James Monroe**	Democratic-Republican		183
	Rufus King	Federalist		34
1820	**James Monroe**	Democratic-Republican		231
	John Quincy Adams	Independent-Republican		1
1824	**John Quincy Adams**	Democratic-Republican	108,740 (30.5%)	84
	Andrew Johnson	Democratic-Republican	153,544 (43.1%)	99
	Henry Clay	Democratic-Republican	47,136 (13.2%)	37
	William H. Crawford	Democratic-Republican	46,618 (13.1%)	41
1828	**Andrew Jackson**	Democratic	647,231 (56.0%)	178
	John Quincy Adams	National Republican	509,097 (44.0%)	83
1832	**Andrew Jackson**	Democratic	687,502 (55.0%)	219
	Henry Clay	National Republican	530,189 (42.4%)	49
	William Wirt	Anti-Masonic		7
	John Floyd	National Republican	33,108 (2.6%)	11
1836	**Martin Van Buren**	Democratic	761,549 (50.9%)	170
	William H. Harrison	Whig	549,567 (36.7%)	73
	Hugh L. White	Whig	145,396 (9.7%)	26
	Daniel Webster	Whig	41,287 (2.7%)	14
1840	**William H. Harrison**	Whig	1,275,017 (53.1%)	234
	Martin Van Buren	Democratic	1,128,702 (46.9%)	60
1844	**James K. Polk**	Democratic	1,337,243 (49.6%)	170
	Henry Clay	Whig	1,299,068 (48.1%)	105
	James G. Birney	Liberty	63,300 (2.3%)	
1848	**Zachary Taylor**	Whig	1,360,101 (47.4%)	163
	Lewis Cass	Democratic	1,220,544 (42.5%)	127
	Martin Van Buren	Free Soil	291,163 (10.1%)	
1852	**Franklin Pierce**	Democratic	1,601,474 (50.9%)	254
	Winfield Scott	Whig	1,386,578 (44.1%)	42
1856	**James Buchanan**	Democratic	1,838,169 (45.4%)	174
	John C. Fremont	Republican	1,335,264 (33.0%)	114
	Millard Fillmore	American	874,534 (21.6%)	8
1860	**Abraham Lincoln**	Republican	1,865,593 (39.8%)	180
	Stephen A. Douglas	Democratic	1,381,713 (29.5%)	12
	John C. Breckinridge	Democratic	848,356 (18.1%)	72
	John Bell	Constitutional Union	592,906 (12.6%)	79
1864	**Abraham Lincoln**	Republican	2,206,938 (55.0%)	212
	George B. McClellan	Democratic	1,803,787 (45.0%)	21
1868	**Ulysses S. Grant**	Republican	3,013,421 (52.7%)	214
	Horatio Seymour	Democratic	2,706,829 (47.3%)	80
1872	**Ulysses S. Grant**	Republican	3,596,745 (55.6%)	286
	Horace Greeley	Democratic	2,843,446 (43.9%)	66
1876	**Rutherford B. Hayes**	Republican	4,036,571 (48.0%)	185
	Samuel J. Tilden	Democratic	4,284,020 (51.0%)	184
1880	**James A. Garfield**	Republican	4,449,053 (48.3%)	214
	Winfield S. Hancock	Democratic	4,442,035 (48.2%)	155
	James B. Weaver	Greenback-Labor	308,578 (3.4%)	

Year	Candidates	Party	Popular Vote	Electoral Vote
1884	**Grover Cleveland**	Democratic	4,874,986 (48.5%)	219
	James G. Blaine	Republican	4,851,931 (48.2%)	182
	Benjamin F. Butler	Greenback-Labor	175,370 (1.8%)	
1888	**Benjamin Harrison**	Republican	5,444,337 (47.8%)	233
	Grover Cleveland	Democratic	5,540,050 (48.6%)	168
1892	**Grover Cleveland**	Democratic	5,554,414 (46.0%)	277
	Benjamin Harrison	Republican	5,190,802 (43.0%)	145
	James B. Weaver	People's	1,027,329 (8.5%)	22
1896	**William McKinley**	Republican	7,035,638 (50.8%)	271
	William J. Bryan	Democratic; Populist	6,467,946 (46.7%)	176
1900	**William McKinley**	Republican	7,219,530 (51.7%)	292
	William J. Bryan	Democratic; Populist	6,356,734 (45.5%)	155
1904	**Theodore Roosevelt**	Republican	7,628,834 (56.4%)	336
	Alton B. Parker	Democratic	5,084,401 (37.6%)	140
	Eugene V. Debs	Socialist	402,460 (3.0%)	
1908	**William H. Taft**	Republican	7,679,006 (51.6%)	321
	William J. Bryan	Democratic	6,409,106 (43.1%)	162
	Eugene V. Debs	Socialist	420,820 (2.8%)	
1912	**Woodrow Wilson**	Democratic	6,286,820 (41.8%)	435
	Theodore Roosevelt	Progressive	4,126,020 (27.4%)	88
	William H. Taft	Republican	3,483,922 (23.2%)	8
	Eugene V. Debs	Socialist	897,011 (6.0%)	
1916	**Woodrow Wilson**	Democratic	9,129,606 (49.3%)	277
	Charles E. Hughes	Republican	8,538,211 (46.1%)	254
1920	**Warren G. Harding**	Republican	16,152,200 (61.0%)	404
	James M. Cox	Democratic	9,147,353 (34.6%)	127
	Eugene V. Debs	Socialist	919,799 (3.5%)	
1924	**Calvin Coolidge**	Republican	15,725,016 (54.1%)	382
	John W. Davis	Democratic	8,385,586 (28.8%)	136
	Robert M. La Follette	Progressive	4,822,856 (16.6%)	13
1928	**Herbert C. Hoover**	Republican	21,392,190 (58.2%)	444
	Alfred E. Smith	Democratic	15,016,443 (40.8%)	87
1932	**Franklin D. Roosevelt**	Democratic	22,809,638 (57.3%)	472
	Herbert C. Hoover	Republican	15,758,901 (39.6%)	59
	Norman Thomas	Socialist	881,951 (2.2%)	
1936	**Franklin D. Roosevelt**	Democratic	27,751,612 (60.7%)	523
	Alfred M. Landon	Republican	16,681,913 (36.4%)	8
	William Lemke	Union	891,858 (1.9%)	
1940	**Franklin D. Roosevelt**	Democratic	27,243,466 (54.7%)	449
	Wendell L. Wilkie	Republican	22,304,755 (44.8%)	82
1944	**Franklin D. Roosevelt**	Democratic	25,602,505 (52.8%)	432
	Thomas E. Dewey	Republican	22,006,278 (44.5%)	99
1948	**Harry S Truman**	Democratic	24,105,812 (49.5%)	303
	Thomas E. Dewey	Republican	21,970,065 (45.1%)	189
	J. Strom Thurmond	States' Rights	1,169,063 (2.4%)	39
	Henry A. Wallace	Progressive	1,157,172 (2.4%)	
1952	**Dwight D. Eisenhower**	Republican	33,936,234 (55.2%)	442
	Adlai E. Stevenson	Democratic	27,314,992 (44.5%)	89
1956	**Dwight D. Eisenhower**	Republican	35,590,472 (57.4%)	457
	Adlai E. Stevenson	Democratic	26,022,752 (42.0%)	73
1960	**John F. Kennedy**	Democratic	34,227,096 (49.9%)	303
	Richard M. Nixon	Republican	34,108,546 (49.6%)	219
1964	**Lyndon B. Johnson**	Democratic	43,126,233 (61.1%)	486
	Barry M. Goldwater	Republican	27,174,989 (38.5%)	52
1968	**Richard M. Nixon**	Republican	31,783,783 (43.4%)	301
	Hubert H. Humphrey	Democratic	31,271,839 (42.7%)	191
	George C. Wallace	American Independent	9,899,557 (13.5%)	46
1972	**Richard M. Nixon**	Republican	46,632,189 (61.3%)	521
	George McGovern	Democratic	28,422,015 (37.3%)	17
1976	**Jimmy Carter**	Democratic	40,828,587 (50.1%)	297
	Gerald R. Ford	Republican	39,147,613 (48.0%)	240
1980	**Ronald Reagan**	Republican	42,941,145 (51.0%)	489
	Jimmy Carter	Democratic	34,663,037 (41.0%)	49
	John B. Anderson	Independent	5,551,551 (6.6%)	
1984	**Ronald Reagan**	Republican	53,428,357 (59%)	525
	Walter F. Mondale	Democratic	36,930,923 (41%)	13
1988	**George Bush**	Republican	48,881,011 (53%)	426
	Michael Dukakis	Democratic	41,828,350 (46%)	111

Glossary
of Key Terms

We have tried to write a readable book about American politics and government. We realize, however, that certain legal terms and political science phrases may not be familiar to our readers. To make such words or phrases, which appear in the text in boldface, more understandable, we have compiled this glossary to define them. We welcome suggestions for additions.

Act III leaders Typically, office holders and elected politicians who are skilled in bargaining and brokerage politics—in reconciling competing conceptions of the public interest and making the necessary compromises so that government can work. The notion of Act III implies that these leaders often depend on other kinds of leaders to set the agenda, to mobilize public opinion, and to begin the movements and even the early stages of coalition building that precede law making and policy making.

Administrative law Law relating to the authority and procedures of administrative agencies, as well as to the rules and regulations issued by those agencies.

Admiralty and maritime law Law derived from the general maritime law of nations, modified by Congress. Applicable not only on the high seas but also on all navigable waterways in the United States.

Advisory Commission on Intergovernmental Relations A permanent national bipartisan board created by Congress in 1959 to monitor the operation of and to recommend improvements for the U.S. federal system. ACIR is composed of representatives from the executive and legislative branches of the federal, state, and local governments, as well as members from the general public.

Affirmative action Remedial actions originally relating to employment but now also covering college and university admissions, contracting, and other areas designed to overcome effects of past societal and individual discrimination against minorities and women.

Amendment Addition to or deletion from a constitution or law.

Amici curiae (friend of the court) brief A brief filed by an individual or organization with the permission of the court. It provides arguments in addition to those presented by the immediate parties to the case.

Annapolis convention A convention held in August 1786 that issued the call to Congress and the states for what became the Constitutional Convention. The Annapolis Convention itself, attended by delegates from five states, was called to consider problems of trade and navigation.

Anti-Federalists Persons opposed to more nationally centralized government in general, and to the ratification of the 1787 Philadelphia Constitution in particular.

Antitrust policy The several federal laws (of which the Sherman Antitrust Act of 1890 is most prominent), supplemented by state laws, that try to prevent one or a few business firms from dominating a particular market.

Appeasement Term used to describe concessions made to a potential military opponent.

Appellate jurisdiction Authority to review decisions of lower courts and administrative tribunals.

Articles of Confederation The first constitution of the newly independent American states. It was drafted in 1777, ratified in 1781, and replaced by the present Constitution in 1789.

Assigned counsel system Arrangement whereby attorneys are provided for persons accused of crime who are unable to hire their own lawyers. The judge assigns a member of the bar to provide counsel to a particular defendant.

Attentive public Those who follow public affairs fairly carefully; those who read newspapers and magazines to keep informed.

Autocracy Government in which all power is concentrated in one person.

Bad tendency doctrine Interpretation of the First amendment that would permit legislatures to make illegal speech that can reasonably be said to have a tendency to cause people to engage in illegal action.

Baker v. Carr A 1962 Supreme Court ruling that legislative apportionment could be challenged and reviewed by federal courts.

Bicameralism The principle of the two-house legislature.

Bicameral legislature Two-house legislature; form for forty-nine of the states, as well as for the U.S. Congress.

Bill of attainder Legislative act that inflicts punishment on either named individuals or on a readily identifiable group.

Binding arbitration See *Compulsory (and binding) arbitration*.

Bipartisanship Policy that emphasizes cooperation and a united front between the major political parties.

Bipolarity A world situation in which two major superpowers dominate world politics.

Block grant Broad grant of funds made by one level of government to another for specific program areas—for example, health programs or crime prevention.

Bureau Generally, the largest subunit of a government department or agency.

Bureaucrat Government official; normally, one who gains office by appointment rather than election.

Categorical formula grant Grant of funds made by one level of government to another, to be used for specified purposes and in specified ways.

Caucus (local party) Meeting of party members in a ward or town to choose party officials and/or candidates for public office and to decide questions of policy (e.g., platforms).

Caucus (legislative) or conference Meeting of the members of a party in a chamber of legislature to select the party leadership in that chamber and to take party positions on pending legislative issues.

Centralists Those who favor national rather than state or local action.

Checks and balances Constitutional grant of powers that enables each of the three branches of government—legislative, executive, and judicial—to stop some of the acts of the other branches and ensures each branch a sufficient role in the actions of the others so that no one branch may dominate. The branches must work together if governmental business is to be performed.

City-manager plan Same as council-manager plan. A city hires a professional manager to administer city departments and agencies. In most cities, the city manager reports directly to the city council.

Civil law The legal code regulating conduct between private persons. Under civil law, governments provide the forum for the settlement of disputes between private parties in such matters as contracts and business relations.

Class action suit Lawsuit brought by a person or group of persons in behalf of all persons similarly situated. The class may consist of a few persons or of thousands of persons. An example of a class action would be a suit by one person against an airline, alleging overcharges in behalf of that person and all others charged the same price for the same flight.

Clear and present danger doctrine Interpretation of the First amendment first announced by Justice Holmes. This doctrine would not let laws that directly or indirectly restrict freedom of speech be applied unless the particular speech, article, or book in question is made or published such that there is a clear and present danger that the speech will lead to acts that the government may make illegal.

Closed shop Labor arrangement in which an employer must hire only those people who are continuing union members.

Cloture Procedure for terminating debate (especially filibusters) in the U.S. Senate.

Coattail effect Influence a popular or unpopular candidate has on the electoral success or failure of other candidates on the same party ticket.

Collective bargaining Method whereby representatives of the union and the employer determine wages, hours, and other conditions of employment through direct negotiation.

Commerce clause The clause of the Constitution giving Congress the power to regulate all business activities that affect more states than one and also prohibiting states from unduly burdening or discriminating against business activities of other nations or states.

Commission charter Form of city government in which a group of commissioners (usually five) serve as the city council and act as heads of departments in the municipal administration.

Common law Body of judge-made law developed as judges decided cases; part of the English and American systems of justice.

Comparable worth The idea that jobs should be paid at the same rate if they require comparable skills and contributions, even if market considerations make it possible to secure employees for one job at a lower rate than for another. The notion of comparable worth is advocated by those who believe jobs traditionally dominated by women—as nurses, secretaries, and elementary school teachers, for example—are held down in wage rates compared to equivalent type jobs traditionally dominated by men—as plumbers and janitors, for example—because of discrimination and role stereotyping.

Compulsory (and binding) arbitration Process whereby a dispute between management and a union is settled by an impartial third party. When the law dictates that a stalemated labor dispute must be turned over to an outside arbitrator, the process is called *compulsory arbitration*. When union and management are required by law to accept the decision of the arbitrator, it is called *binding arbitration*.

Concurrent powers Powers the Constitution gives to both the national and state governments.

Concurring opinion An opinion in which a Supreme Court justice agrees with the decision of the majority or plurality, but for reasons different from those of the majority or plurality.

Confederation Government created when nation-states, by compact, create a new government and delegate certain powers to it. In contrast to a federation, a confederation does not have power to regulate the conduct of individuals directly.

Conference committee Committee appointed by the presiding officers of each house of the legislature to adjust differences on a particular bill. The report of the conference committee back to each chamber cannot be amended but must be accepted or rejected as it stands.

Conglomerate Firm that owns businesses in many unrelated industries.

Connecticut Compromise Agreement by delegates to the Constitutional Convention to give each state two senators, regardless of population. This would offset the decision to allocate representatives in the House of Representatives among the states according to population. This compromise between the less and more populous states was the price required by the less populous states for agreeing to the new Constitution.

Consent decree Order issued by either a regulatory commission or a court in which a party, though not conceding guilt, agrees to modify future behavior. It is often used by the Federal Trade Commission to require business firms to cease alleged anticompetitive or illegal practices.

Conservatism Philosophical approach to the role of government that generally opposes governmental regulation of the economy and favors local or state governmental action over federal governmental action. Both Barry Goldwater in 1964 and Ronald Reagan in the 1980s were major proponents of this approach.

Conspiracy Combination between two or more persons for the purpose of committing an unlawful act or an act that is lawful by itself but unlawful when done by the concerted action of two or more persons.

Constitution The fundamental rules that determine how those who govern are selected, the procedures by which they operate, and the limits to their powers.

Constitutional convention The convention in Philadelphia in 1787 (May 25 to September 17) that framed the Constitution of the United States. It invented the presidency and electoral college, and the federalism and separation of powers features that are still the central elements of American government. This convention's draft then had to be ratified by nine states before it was adopted in 1788.

Constitutional government Government that enforces recognized and regularly applied limits on the powers of those who govern.

Constitutional home rule State constitutional authorization for local governmental units to conduct their own affairs.

Constitutional law In an American context, the authoritative interpretations of the meaning of the Constitution of the United States; such interpretations are chiefly found in the opinions of the U.S. Supreme Court.

Containment Foreign policy strategy pursued to some extent by all post-World War II presidential administrations—but especially by the Truman administration. Its basic aim was to prevent the industrial or emerging powers of Europe or the Middle East from falling under the control of the Soviet Union.

Convention See *Party convention*.

Council-manager plan Form of city government in which the city council hires a professional administrator to manage city affairs; also known as the city-manager plan.

Curtiss-Wright case (*U.S. v. Curtiss-Wright*, 1936) Supreme Court case upholding the sovereignty of the national government in foreign affairs and declaring the president to be its prime agent.

Dealignment Refers to the decline in attachment and loyalty to the two major political parties, and is an alternative to party realignment, which refers to shifting loyalties from one of the political parties to another.

Decentralists Those who favor state or local action rather than national.

De facto segregation Racial segregation that results from non-governmental practices.

Defendant In a civil action, the party defending himself or herself against charges brought by the plaintiff. In a criminal action, the person charged with the offense.

De jure segregation Racial segregation that results from governmental actions. See also *Jim Crow laws*.

Delegate One view of the role of a member of a legislature. It holds that, as delegates, legislators should represent the views of constituents even when the legislators may personally hold different views.

Demagogue Leader who gains power by means of impassioned appeals to the prejudices and emotions of the masses.

Democracy Government by the people, either directly or indirectly, with free and frequent elections.

Deregulation Efforts to reduce or eliminate governmental controls, rules, or regulation of economic activity. Typically, deregulation implies allowing more of a market or "hands off" approach as opposed to detailing federal rules or specifications to guide some industrial operations.

Detente Relaxation of tension with another nation; conciliation or settlement with another nation.

Deterrence The U.S. defense policy of taking steps to prevent a nuclear attack by an adversary, commonly measured by the U.S. capacity to survive a first strike by the Soviets and still respond with a massive retaliation that would impose such costs on the Soviets that they would not consider the first strike. This capacity has to be effective enough to discourage any initial attack.

Deviating election Election in which the party out of power wins, but underlying voting patterns remain unchanged.

Direct primary Election, open to all members of the party, in which voters choose the persons who will be the party's nominees in the general election.

Direct transmission satellite Communications satellite that transmits messages to individual receiving sets in homes or offices.

Discharge petition Petition that, if signed by a majority of the members of the House of Representatives, will pry a bill from committee and bring it to the floor for consideration.

Dissenting opinion An opinion in which a judge explains why he or she disagrees with the decision of the majority.

Doctrine of Dual Federalism View that national and state governments are equal sovereigns, each granted certain powers by the Constitution with the Supreme Court to serve as arbitrator in case of conflicts between them.

Domino theory Doctrine that assumes if some key nation or region falls into Communist control, a string of other nations will subsequently fall. President Eisenhower and later presidents used this theory to describe the situation in Indochina.

Double jeopardy Trial or punishment for the *same* crime by the *same* government. Such a practice is forbidden by the Constitution.

Due process clauses Clauses in the Fifth and Fourteenth amendments that state that the national (Fifth) and the state (Fourteenth) governments shall not deprive any person of life, liberty, or property without due process of law.

Economies of scale The assumption that larger size makes possible lower per unit costs and thus more efficiency.

Electoral college In general, the procedures established by the Constitution for the election of the president and vice-president. More specifically, the gathering in each state of electors from that state who formally cast their ballots for their parties' candidates for president and vice-president. Largely a formality.

Eminent domain Power of governments to take private property for public use. The Constitution requires governments to provide just compensation for property so taken.

Entitlement programs Programs such as Social Security, Aid to Families with Dependent Children, Medicare, and unemployment insurance to which qualified citizens are "entitled" by definitions in national legislation.

Environmental impact statement A statement required by federal law from all agencies for any project using federal funds that assesses the potential effect of a federal action on the environment. Many states also require EIRs.

Equal protection clause Clause in the Fourteenth amendment that forbids any state (by interpretation, the Fifth amendment imposes the same limitation on the national government) to deny to any person within its jurisdiction the equal protection of the laws. This is the major constitutional restraint on the power of governments to discriminate against persons because of race, national origin, or sex.

Equal Rights Amendment (ERA) Constitutional amendment proposed by Congress in 1972, designed to guarantee women equality of rights under the law. Although ratified by thirty-five states, the additional three states necessary for ratification failed to approve the amendment by the June 30, 1982, deadline. An ERA-type amendment is likely to be proposed again by Congress.

Equal-time requirement Requirement of Congress and Federal Communications Commission that radio and television licencees must give opposing candidates for public office equal air time.

Equity Judicial remedy used whenever suits for money damages do not provide adequate justice.

Establishment clause Clause in the First amendment that states that Congress (by interpretation, the Fourteenth amendment imposes the same limitation on state legislatures) shall make no law respecting an establishment of religion. It has been interpreted by the Supreme Court to forbid governmental support to any or all religions.

Ethnocentrism Belief in the superiority of one's nation or ethnic group; an overriding concern or preoccupation with one's own group.

Excise tax Consumer tax on a specific kind of merchandise, such as tobacco.

Executive agreement International agreement made by a president that has the force of a treaty. It does not need the approval of the Senate.

Executive Office of the President Cluster of staff agencies created by the Reorganization Act of 1939 to help the president. Currently the Executive Office includes an Office of Management and Budget, the Council of Economic Advisers, the National Security Council, and a number of specialized offices.

Executive privilege The claim by presidents that they have the discretion to decide that the national interest will be better served if certain information in the custody of the executive departments is withheld from the public, including the courts and Congress. In *United States* v. *Nixon* the Supreme Court ruled that even though presidents are entitled to the privilege, the privilege is not unlimited, and its extent is subject to judicial determination.

Ex post facto law Retroactive criminal law.

Express powers Powers specifically granted to one of the branches of the national government by the Constitution.

Extradition Legal process whereby an alleged criminal offender is surrendered by the officials of one state to officials of the state in which the crime is alleged to have been committed.

Faction Organized group of politically active persons, usually less than a majority, seeking to realize group goals in competition with other groups.

Fairness doctrine Doctrine, written into law and interpreted by the Federal Communications Commission, that imposed on radio and television licensees an obligation to ensure that differing viewpoints were presented about controversial issues or persons. Repealed by the FCC in 1987.

Federal Reserve System The private-public banking regulatory system, created by Congress in 1913, to establish banking practices and regulate currency in circulation and the amount of credit available. It is comprised of twelve regional banks, and its major responsibilities are supervised by a seven-member presidentially appointed Federal Reserve Board of Governors in Washington, D.C.

Federalism Constitutional arrangement whereby power is divided by a constitution between a national government and constituent governments, called states in the U.S. The national and the constituent governments both exercise direct authority over individuals.

The Federalist Series of essays favoring the new Constitution. Written by Alexander Hamilton, John Jay, and James Madison in 1787 and 1788, during the debate over ratification.

Federalists Persons who supported the Constitution before its ratification in 1787 to 1788. After ratification a Federalist party developed under the leadership of Alexander Hamilton, Washington's first secretary of the treasury. Federalists like John Adams and John Marshall generally favored a strong central government and a fiscal policy of assuming state debts and establishing a national bank.

Fighting words Words that by their very nature inflict injury upon those to whom they are addressed.

Filibuster Holding the floor of the U.S. Senate to delay proceedings and thereby prevent a vote on a controversial issue.

Fiscal policy Government's use of its financial powers, such as raising taxes or cutting spending to promote economic growth and stability. Decisions on fiscal strategy are made by Congress and the president.

Floating debt Short-term government loans, in the form of bank notes or tax-anticipation warrants, that are paid out of current revenues.

Four Freedoms American goals proclaimed by Franklin D. Roosevelt in his annual message to Congress, January 6, 1941: freedom of speech and expression, freedom of worship, freedom from want, and freedom from fear.

Fourth world Those nations that are among the poorest in the world and whose per capita standard of living is among the lowest of any nations.

Franchise The right to vote.

Full faith and credit clause Clause in the Constitution requiring each state to recognize the civil judgments rendered by the courts of the other states.

General property tax Tax levied by local (and some state) governments on real or personal, tangible property—the major portion of which is on the estimated value of one's home and land.

General search warrants These are prohibited by the Constitution. A search warrant must specify the place to be searched and the objects to be seized in order to protect people from unreasonable government intrusion.

Gerrymandering Drawing an election district in such a way that one party or group has a distinct advantage. The strategy is to provide a close but safe margin in numerous districts while concentrating (and hence wasting) the opposition's vote in a few districts.

Government corporation Cross between a business corporation and a government agency, created to secure greater freedom of action for a particular program.

Grand jury A jury comprising twelve to twenty-three persons who, in private, hear evidence presented by the government to determine whether persons shall be required to stand trial.

Great Society President Lyndon Johnson's vision of this country in which federal money was granted to states and localities to improve housing, mass transportation, and education.

Gross national product (GNP) The monetary value of all goods and services produced in the nation in a given year.

Habeas corpus See *Writ of habeas corpus.*

Hatch Act Federal statute barring federal employees from active participation in certain kinds of politics and protecting them from being fired on partisan grounds.

Ideology Interrelated or integrated set of attitudes and beliefs about political values and the role of power and government.

Ideologue Person who has a relatively fixed and highly integrated set of attitudes and beliefs about the role of government as it affects individuals and public policy.

Immunity Exemption from prosecution based on evidence secured as the result of testimony compelled by a government agency.

Implied limitations Doctrine regarding constitutional construction of state constitutions. It holds that powers not granted to municipal corporations are denied to such corporations.

Implied powers Powers given to Congress, by the Constitution, that allow Congress to do whatever is necessary and proper in order to carry out one of the express powers or any combination of them.

Impoundment Presidential refusal to allow an agency to spend funds authorized and appropriated by Congress.

Incrementalism Theory of public policy and public administration that deemphasizes comprehensiveness and insists that governmental decisions are and should be made piecemeal.

Independent agency Sometimes used interchangeably with "independent regulatory agency" to refer to an agency that is not part of the legislative, executive, or judicial branch, such as the Interstate Commerce Commission. The term also refers to a nonregulary agency that is not part of a cabinet department such as the National Aeronautics and Space Administration.

Indiana ballot See *Party column ballot.*

Inflation Rise in the general level of prices, which is the same thing as a fall in the value of money.

Information affidavit Certification by a public prosecutor that there is evidence to justify bringing named individuals to trial.

Inherent powers Those powers of the national government in the field of foreign affairs that the Supreme Court has declared do not depend upon constitutional grants but rather grow out of the very existence of the national government.

Initiative petition Procedure whereby a certain number of voters may, by petition, propose a law and get it submitted to the people for a vote. Initiative may be direct (if the proposed law is voted on directly by the people) or indirect (if the proposal is submitted first to the legislature and then to the people, if the legislature rejects it).

Intangible property Wealth indicated by cash, stocks, bonds, savings accounts, partnerships, money funds, and so on, in contrast to wealth in the form of such physical objects as land, houses, automobiles, and jewels.

Interest group A collection of people who share some common interest or attitude and seek to influence government for specific ends. Interest groups will usually work within the framework of government and employ tactics such as lobbying to achieve their goals.

Interlocking directorate Situation in which the same persons serve as members of the boards of directors of competing companies.

Interstate compacts Agreements among the states. The Constitution requires that most such agreements be approved by Congress.

Isolationism The attitude (somewhat in fashion in the 1930s) that the U.S. should retreat from world affairs and curb the tendency to intervene abroad—especially in military conflicts.

Item veto Authority of the executive (usually the governor of a state) to veto parts of a legislative bill without having to veto the entire bill. Presidents do not have the power of the item veto.

Jim Crow laws Laws that require public facilities and places of public accommodation, including those privately owned and operated, to be segregated by race.

Joint committee Committee composed of members of both houses of a legislature. Such committees are intended to speed up legislative action.

Judicial activism Variously defined. One definition is the philosophy proposing that judges cannot decide cases strictly by applying the literal words of the Constitution or by discerning the intention of the framers, but that they could and should openly recognize that judicial decision making is choosing among conflicting values. Judges should so interpret the Constitution as to keep it reflecting the current values of the American people. Judicial activism is used to contrast with judicial restraint.

Judicial restraint Variously defined. One definition is the philosophy proposing that, in deciding cases, judges should declare unconstitutional only those legislative actions and executive actions that clearly violate the words of the Constitution or the intent of the framers, and that constitutional changes should be left to the formal amendatory process.

Judicial review The authority, spelled out by Chief Justice Marshall in *Marbury* v. *Madison* (1803), of judges when deciding cases to examine statutes and the actions of executive officials in order to determine their validity, according to the judges' interpretation of the Constitution.

Jus sanguinis Citizenship acquired through citizenship of parents.

Jus soli Citizenship acquired through place of birth.

Justiciable disputes Disputes that, in contrast to political questions, raise questions about legality and that are appropriate for resolution before a court of law.

Keynes, John Maynard English economist whose views have dominated economic thinking in recent decades.

Labor injunction Court order forbidding specific individuals or groups from performing certain acts, such as striking, that the court considers harmful to the rights and property of others.

Lame duck Official serving out a term of office after defeat for reelection and before the inauguration of a successor.

Legislative home rule Power given by the legislature to local governments that eliminates the need for local governments to go back to the legislature for additional grants of power. However, state law still takes precedence over local ordinances, and powers given to the local governments by the legislature may be rescinded.

Legislative veto Until it was declared unconstitutional by the Supreme Court in 1983, a provision in a law reserving to Congress, or to a chamber or committee of Congress, the power to reject by majority vote an act or regulation of a department or agency of the national government.

Libel Written defamation of another person. Especially in the case of public officials and public figures, the constitutional tests designed to restrict libel actions are very rigid.

Liberalism Philosophical approach to the role of government that generally favors governmental action, especially to help the underdog and achieve equal opportunity for all.

Libertarianism Philosophical approach to the role of government that favors as limited a government as possible and believes in free-market economics and a noninterventionist foreign policy.

Lobby/lobbying To conduct activities aimed at influencing public officials and the policies they enact. This is, of course, part of the citizen's right to petition the government.

Lobbyist Person who acts for an organized interest group or association or corporation to try to influence policy decisions and positions in the executive and—especially—legislative branches.

Long ballot Ballot that came into general use in the late 1820s. Based on the belief that voters should elect all, or nearly all, the people who governed them. It is criticized as being unwieldy and confusing because it contains too many offices and candidates.

Lottery A form of voluntary taxation used by more than half of the states and the District of Columbia; it involves distributing prizes by lot or random chance to the buyers of winning tickets. State income from lotteries typically amounts to less than 3 or 4 percent of state revenue; lotteries do, however, generate income without raising taxes. They are also sometimes defended as means of reducing the amount of illegal gambling and of minimizing the influence of organized crime.

Maintaining election Election that shows a continuation of a pattern of partisan support.

Majority floor leader Legislature position held by an important party member selected by the majority party in caucus or conference. The majority floor leader helps frame party strategy and tries to keep the membership in line. In the U.S. Senate the majority leader (in consultation with the minority floor leader) determines the agenda and has strong influence in committee selection.

Marshall Plan The American program to assist European economic recovery following World War II.

Massachusetts ballot See *Office group ballot.*

Mass public The general public, including a large segment of the population that is often uninformed about the details of political controversy and policy debates.

Mayor-council charter The oldest and most common form of city government, consisting of either a weak mayor and city council or a strong mayor and council.

McCulloch v. *Maryland* (1819) Celebrated Supreme Court decision that established the doctrine of national supremacy and the principle that the implied powers of the national government are to be generously interpreted.

Medicaid A joint state and federal assistance program for impoverished individuals who do not qualify for the national medicare program. Medicare ensures that the federal government pays up to 80 percent of the cost of medical care for the elderly whose nursing home and hospital costs exceed their social security and meager pension incomes.

Messianic spirit Belief in the future deliverance or saving of a people or a nation. The notion that a people are select, singled out for a special destiny.

Metropolis City regarded as the center or central community

of a particular area. The city is generally an important one with a population of over 500,000.

Midterm party conference National meeting, presently of Democratic party members, held halfway through a presidential term, designed to activate the party and bring its platform up to date.

Military-industrial complex Alleged alliance between top military and industrial leaders, who have a common interest in arms production.

Minority floor leader Party leader in each house of a legislature, elected by the minority party as spokesperson for the opposition.

Misdemeanor Offense of lesser gravity than a felony, for which punishment may be a fine or imprisonment for a relatively brief time, usually less than a year.

Missouri Plan System for selecting judges that combines features of the appointive and elective methods. The governor makes an initial appointment from a list of persons—usually three—presented by a panel of lawyers and laypersons (the panel is usually appointed by the chief judge of the state court of last resort). After the judge has served for a year, the electorate is asked at the next general election whether or not the judge should be retained in office. If a majority vote yes, the judge serves the rest of the term. At the end of the term, if a judge wishes to serve again, his or her name is once again presented to the electorate.

Monetary policy National government policy that seeks to change the interest, credit, or stock market rates. The Federal Reserve Board, for example, uses "tight money" policies to restrain and prolong boom periods and to fight inflation. "Loose money" policies—making credit and money more freely—are used to fight recessions or a depression.

Movement A large body of people united around a central idea whose goal is to change attitudes or institutions, not just policies. Movements tend to feel "left out" of government and may sometimes resort to extreme measures to advance their cause.

Multipolar Refers to a world in which many nations shape world political developments and influence world affairs.

National Security Council Planning and advisory board that confers with the president on matters relating to national security. Permanent members include the president, vice-president, secretary of state, secretary of defense, and the chair of the joint chiefs of staff.

National supremacy Constitutional doctrine that whenever conflict occurs between the constitutionally authorized actions of the national government and those of a state or local government, the actions of the national government take priority.

Naturalization Process by which persons acquire citizenship in a country other than the nation of their birth.

Natural monopoly Condition that exists when it would be inefficient to have competition in a particular industry, as in the case of a power company.

Necessary and proper clause Clause of the Constitution setting forth the implied powers of Congress. It states that Congress, in addition to its enumerated powers, has the power to make all laws necessary and proper for carrying out all powers vested by the Constitution in the national government.

Neoconservatives A pragmatic form of traditional liberalism that accepts some of the welfare state but believes affirmative action has gone too far; also wants a more assertive, anticommunist foreign policy.

Neoliberals   People who are left-of-center ideologically yet distrustful or skeptical of large bureaucracies and traditional welfare strategies; they believe in relying on the marketplace and favor middle-of-the-road tax and defense policies.

New Jersey Plan   Plan presented by Paterson of New Jersey at the Constitutional Convention as a counterproposal to the Virginia Plan. The New Jersey Plan proposed only modifications in the Articles of Confederation and provided for a confederation built around powerful state governments.

New judicial federalism   The practice of some state courts of using the bill of rights in their state constitution to provide more protection for some rights than is provided by Supreme Court interpretation of the Bill of Rights in the Constitution.

Nixon Doctrine   Policy suggested by President Nixon in the early 1970s that would have the U.S. come to the assistance of allies and friendly nations, but only if they themselves would do the main fighting.

Nonprobability sampling   A method of polling in which the public is invited to write or call in, as opposed to random sampling, in which the respondents are selected at random.

Nonproliferation Treaty   International agreement under which nuclear powers pledge not to distribute nuclear devices to nonnuclear powers.

Obscenity   Work that taken as a whole appeals to a prurient interest in sex by depicting sexual conduct as specifically defined by legislation or judicial interpretation in a patently offensive way, and that lacks serious literary, artistic, political, or scientific value.

Office group ballot   Method of voting in which all candidates are listed under the office for which they are running. Sometimes called the Massachusetts ballot or the office-block ballot.

Office of Management and Budget (OMB)   Presidential staff agency that serves as a clearinghouse for budgetary requests and management improvements.

Oligarchy   Government controlled by a small segment of the people, who are chosen on the basis of wealth or power.

Oligopoly   Situation in which a few firms dominate an industry.

Ombudsman   Office in Sweden and elsewhere that handles citizen complaints against the government.

On appeal   Order formerly issued by the Supreme Court to review those decisions of the lower courts, federal and state, that Congress has stipulated the Supreme Court is required to review.

Opinion maker   Person who influences how the general public views policy problems—for example, an elected official, editor, writer, and teacher.

Override   An action by Congress to try to reverse a presidential veto (a veto by the president of legislation) by means of a two-thirds vote in both chambers of the Congress. Veto overrides are rare; they are successful only about 3 percent of the time.

Palko Test   A test established by the Supreme Court in the case of *Palko* v. *Connecticut* (1937). The test determines which provisions of the Bill of Rights should be "incorporated" into the Fourteenth amendment as a limitation on state and local governments: namely, those provisions that relate to rights that are so important that neither "liberty nor justice would exist if they were sacrificed."

Party column ballot   Method of voting in which all candidates are listed under their party designations, which makes it easy for the voters to cast votes for all the candidates of one party. Sometimes called the Indiana ballot.

Party convention   A meeting of party delegates to pass on matters of policy and in some cases to select party candidates for public office. Conventions are held on county, state, and national levels.

Party primary   Election for choosing party nominees that is open to members and supporters of the party making the nomination.

Party realignment   Fundamental change in the economic, racial, social, sectional, and other electoral foundations of a party as it seeks to maintain its competitive position in elections.

Patronage   Dispensing government jobs to persons who belong to the winning political party.

Personal property   As opposed to real estate—houses and land—this refers to household goods, jewelry, stocks, and bonds.

Petit jury   The ordinary jury for the trial of a civil or criminal action. So called to distinguish it from the grand jury.

Plaintiff   Party who brings a civil action or sues to obtain a legal remedy from a court for injury to his or her rights.

Plea bargaining   Negotiations between prosecutor and defendant aimed at getting the defendant to plead guilty in return for prosecutor's agreeing to reduce the seriousness of the crime for which the defendant will be convicted.

Pluralistic power structure   The notion that even though some people do have more influence than others, that influence is shared among many people and tends to be limited to particular issues and policy areas.

Pocket veto   Special veto power exercised by a chief executive after a legislative body has adjourned. Bills that a chief executive refuses to sign at this time do not become law. In effect, by such an action, a governor or president "puts the bill in his or her pocket," and the bill thus dies.

Police powers   Powers of a government to regulate persons and property in order to promote the public health, welfare, and safety. In the U.S., the states, but not the national government, have such general police power.

Political Action Committee (PAC)   The political arms of organized interests. PACs have become major agencies through which to finance congressional campaigns.

Political culture   The widely shared political beliefs, values, and norms most citizens share concerning the relationship of citizens to government and to one another.

Political machine   Organized subgroup within a party, consisting of a political boss and supporting ward and precinct workers who get out the vote and perform a variety of "services" for local constituents between elections.

Political questions   Constitutional questions that judges refuse to answer because to do so would involve judicial encroachment upon the authority of Congress or the president. For example: Congress determines if a sufficient number of states have ratified a constitutional amendment within a reasonable time; Congress determines which states have the required republican form of government; and the president determines which foreign governments are to be recognized by the U.S. Because the Supreme Court determines which constitutional questions are political and which are justiciable, this limitation on the authority of the courts is self-defined.

Political socialization Processes by which we develop our political attitudes, values, and behavior.

Poll tax Payment by a person, formerly required in some states, as a condition for voting.

Populists Adherents of a movement and political party of the 1880s and 1890s. Their geographical base was rural—in the Midwest, South, and Southwest especially. Waging "reformist" efforts against the banks, railroads, and other establishments, Populists raised issues that influenced the Progressive movement and the Democratic party after 1892.

Power elite Term originally used by sociologist C. Wright Mills to describe the small group of people he believed rule the country because of their socioeconomic status.

Preferred position doctrine Interpretation of the First amendment that holds that no law restricting expression is constitutional unless the government can demonstrate convincingly to a court that the law is absolutely necessary to prevent serious injury to the public well-being.

Presidential primaries Statewide primaries in which rank-and-file party members choose the delegates to the national party convention and may indicate their choice for the party's presidential nominee.

President pro tempore Officer of the U.S. Senate chosen from the ranks—usually the senior member of the majority party. Serves as president of the Senate in the absence of the vice-president.

Principle democrats Persons more concerned with the goals and values of "government by the people" than with the procedures used to reach those goals.

Prior restraint Restraint imposed prior to a speech's being made, a newspaper's being published, or a motion picture's being shown. The restraint may be of various kinds—for example, a requirement that a license be granted or that the approval of a censorship board be given.

Privatization The contracting out to the "for profit" private sector "public services" that are typically provided by public organizations. Trash collection, ambulance, and fire protection services have been the most common privatizations of public services. The objectives are to obtain the public services at lower costs, and sometimes to shrink the public bureaucracy to encourage additional efficiencies.

Pro bono Term used to refer to the work lawyers (or other professionals) do to serve the public good and for which they either receive no fees or decline fees.

Procedural due process Constitutional requirement that governments proceed by proper means.

Process democrats Persons who believe that if proper procedures are followed in running the government, the more likely it is that sound and democratic policy will result. (All democrats believe in both good processes and principles, they differ over the balance between the two.)

Program oversight Process of monitoring and evaluating the details of how a program is being, or has been, carried out.

Progressives Adherents of a "good government" movement in the first two decades of this century that advocated measures that would open up the system and weaken party bosses. They favored nonpartisan elections, participatory primaries, and direct elections of senators. The Progressive party, especially active from 1912 through the mid-1920s, emerged as a visible part of the Progressive movement.

Progressive tax A tax whereby upper-income citizens pay a higher proportion of their incomes in tax revenues than do lower-income citizens.

Project grant Federal funds given for specified purposes and based on the merits of applications.

Public defender Public officer whose job is to provide legal assistance to those persons accused of crimes who are unable to hire their own attorneys.

Public opinion Cluster of views and attitudes held by people on a significant issue. Because any complex society has many groups, it is more precise to talk about publics, subpublics, and public opinions than about a single public opinion.

Public policy The substance of what government does. More generally, the intentions of a government and the subsequent follow-up actions to implement laws and other decisions of governmental bodies.

Public/special authority Special government agencies frequently found in metropolitan areas, set up to undertake such highly specialized functions as overseeing mass transit, an interstate harbor complex, or a regional airport.

Quasilegislative and quasijudicial Phrase coined by the Supreme Court to permit noncourt and nonlegislative bodies to decide disputes and make rules. Decisions must, however, be subject to court review and rules must be within the general guidelines established by the legislature.

Quota sampling Accounting for the variables in the population and assigning a quota for each variable to produce a representative cross section.

Random sampling Creating a representative sample through random selection—for example, by shuffling housing tracts and interviewing individuals in every fifth, tenth, or fifteenth house.

Rational basis test Test used to measure laws for compliance with the requirements of the equal protection clause. This test is applied to laws that do *not* affect a suspect classification of fundamental rights. Such laws need only a rational basis in fact.

Realigning election Election in which the basis partisan commitments of a significant segment of the electorate change, as in 1932.

Real property Land and buildings.

Reapportionment Redrawing of legislative district lines to recognize the existing population distribution.

Recall Election held to determine whether or not an official should be removed from office before the end of his or her term. A certain number of voters must petition to hold a recall election.

Recidivists One who habitually relapses into crime.

Redistributive policy Governmental policy that seeks to use tax revenues in such a way as to help those who have less. In effect, tax monies from the upper and middle classes are channeled into programs that assist lower income or truly needy people by redistributing some of society's wealth.

Red tape Procedures and forms used to carry out policies and governmental functions. The term often expresses dissatisfaction with especially slow and formal rules and procedures.

Reduction veto The power of a governor in a few states to reduce a particular money-providing measure approved by the state legislature.

Referendum Practice of submitting to popular vote measures passed by the legislature or proposed by initiative. Use of the referendum may be required or optional.

Regressive tax   Tax that weighs most heavily on those least able to pay.

Regulation   Governmental order having the force of law and designed to control or govern the behavior of a business, union, or similar organizations and individuals.

Regulatory board or commission   Agency responsible for enforcing particular statutes. Generally such an agency has quasi-legislative and quasijudicial functions as well as executive powers.

Representative democracy   See *Republic*.

Republic   Form of government that derives its powers directly or indirectly from the people. Those chosen to govern are accountable, directly or indirectly, to those whom they govern. In contrast to a direct democracy, in which the people make rules directly, in a republic the people select representatives who make the rules.

Republican form of government   See *Republic*.

Restrictive covenant   A restriction in a deed limiting to whom property may be sold and how it may be used.

Revenue sharing   Program whereby federal funds are provided to state and local governments to be spent largely at the discretion of the receiving governments.

Right-to-work law   Provision in state laws that prohibits arrangements between a union and an employer requiring membership in a union as a condition for getting or keeping a job.

Runoff election   Election held when no candidate receives a required percentage of the vote in an earlier election. Usually held between the two candidates who received the most votes in the first election.

Safe seat   Electoral office, usually in legislature, for which the party or the incumbent is so strong that reelection is almost taken for granted.

Sales tax   General tax on sales transactions.

Salience   Significance of an event or issue.

SALT (Strategic Arms Limitation Treaty)   An agreement between the U.S. and Soviet governments to limit both defensive and offensive weapons systems.

Sampling error   The degree to which a sample is distorted and does not represent the "polling universe" to be measured.

Secondary boycott   Concerted effort by a union involved in a dispute with an employer to place pressure on a third party, who—in response to such pressure—might put pressure on the workers' employer. Such boycotts are forbidden by the 1947 Taft-Hartley Act.

Sedition   Attempting to overthrow the government by force or to interrupt its activities by violence.

Seditious   Term used to describe speech that advocates the forceful overthrow of the government. The Supreme Court has ruled that Congress may make seditious speech a crime, but no one may be punished for seditious speech unless it can be shown that he or she specifically urged people to engage in concrete acts of violence.

Selective incorporation   The doctrine that some, but not all, provisions of the Bill of Rights should be included within the Fourteenth Amendment as a limitation on state and local governments.

Senate majority leader   Elected leader of the majority party in the U.S. Senate. This person functions as the chief agenda setter and usually as the most important power broker in the U.S. Senate. George J. Mitchell, Robert Dole, Robert Byrd, Mike Mansfield, and Lyndon Johnson have served in this influential position in the past thirty years.

Senatorial courtesy   Custom in the U.S. Senate of (1) referring the names of prospective appointees, especially federal judges, to senators from the states in which the appointees reside; and (2) withdrawing any nominees these senators deem objectionable, especially if senators are from the same party as the nominating president.

Separation of powers   Constitutional division of power among legislative, executive, and judicial branches. The legislative branch is assigned the power to make laws; the executive is charged with the power to apply the laws; and the judiciary receives the power to interpret laws.

Severance tax   Tax on the privilege of "severing" natural resources such as coal, oil, and timber, charged to the companies doing the extracting or severing.

Shays's Rebellion   Rural rebellion of 1786 to 1787 protesting mortgage foreclosures in western Massachusetts. Led by Daniel Shays, it brought conservative support for a stronger national government.

Shield law   Law establishing a legal right for reporters and other representatives of the media to refuse, under certain circumstances, to respond to orders of legislative committees or court subpoenas to reveal sources of information.

Socialism   Philosophical approach to the role of government that favors national planning and public ownership of business.

Social stratification   Sociological theory suggesting that the upper class, or the wealthy, wield extensive influence over the decisions and policies made by governments at all levels.

Speaker   Presiding officer in the House of Representatives, formally elected by the House but actually selected by the majority party. The Speaker's powers include referring legislation to committees, making appointments to the House Rules Committee, recognizing members who wish to speak, ruling on questions of parliamentary procedure, and appointing special conference committees. There is a similar office in state legislatures.

Spoils system   A way of rewarding those who support victorious candidates with profitable contracts or jobs in government.

Standard Metropolitan Statistical Area (SMSA)   A central city—or twin cities—of at least 50,000 people, along with those surrounding counties that are economically and socially dependent on the city.

Stare decisis   The rule of precedent, whereby a rule of law contained in a judicial decision is commonly viewed as binding on judges whenever the same question is presented.

Star Wars   See *Strategic Defense Initiative*.

Statism   Belief in the rights of the state over those of the individual—the opposite of the American tradition that the individual is exalted above the state.

Statutory law   Law enacted by a legislature.

Strategic Defense Initiative (SDI)   *Also known as Star Wars*. Proposed in 1983 by President Ronald Reagan, this system seeks to discover and construct a defensive "shield" against incoming nuclear missiles. The shield would be made of laser and electronic devices that would destroy such missiles launched to attack the U.S.

Strong mayor-council   Form of local government in which the public directly elects the mayor as well as the city council. However, the mayor appoints the department heads, with the approval of the council, and in effect serves as the chief executive officer for the city and its administration.

Subsidy   Governmental support that can take many forms— reduction of taxes, government loans, special protections, outright cash, or credit assistance. Subsidies are designed to encourage a particular type of private-sector action.

Substantive due process   Constitutional requirement that governments act reasonably and that the substance of the laws themselves be reasonable.

Subpoena   Court order to present oneself before an official agency. A subpoena duces tecum is a court order to present specific documents.

Suburbs   Residential areas or communities in the outlying regions around a city.

Sunset process   Legislative review process that calls for the termination of a program after a certain number of years, often six or seven, unless it is carefully examined, certified to be doing what it was intended to do, and repassed by the legislature. Many states have adopted this practice. The word comes from the expression that "the sun should set" on programs that have outlived their usefulness.

Sunshine law   Law requiring governmental agencies, under certain circumstances and usually subject to certain exceptions, to operate in public.

Supply-side economics   Economic strategy of stimulating production through tax cuts or reduced governmental regulation.

Suspect classifications   Racial or national origin classifications created by law and subject to careful judicial scrutiny. Likely to be declared unconstitutional unless they can be justified by overwhelmingly desirable state purposes that can be achieved in no other way.

Taft-Hartley Act   Passed by Congress in 1947, an act that elaborates the terms of labor-management bargaining, the conditions under which strikes can occur, and related aspects of union organization.

Tariff   Tax levied on imports in order to help protect a nation's industries, labor, or farmers from foreign competition. It can also be used merely to raise additional revenue.

Tax expenditure   Loss of tax revenue due to provisions of the federal tax laws that allow special exclusions, exemptions, or deductions, or that provide special credit, preferential rates of tax, or deferrals of tax liability.

Third world   Those nations that are relatively poor but that are seeking to modernize and develop.

Three-Fifths Compromise   North-South agreement at the Constitutional Convention of 1787 to count only three-fifths of the slave population in determining representation in the House of Representatives.

Ticket splitting   Practice of voting for candidates at the ballot box with little or no regard to their parties, with the result that one voter may vote for a Democrat for governor and a Republican for Congress, or vice versa.

Titular leader   Nominal leader; leader by title only. The defeated presidential nominee is referred to as the titular leader of the party out of power, but the role is more honorary than it is a realistic power base.

Tort law   Law, primarily judge made, dealing with damages to compensate people for legal wrongs done to them.

Transactional leader   A leader who deals in the short term and, generally, for self-interest. One who engages in exchanges and bargains as in a quid pro quo fashion.

Transforming leader   A leader who helps liberate followers so they can achieve higher aspirations and longer range goals. A leader who so engages with followers as to heighten their political awareness and their own abilities for leadership.

Treason   Carefully defined for the U.S. by the Constitution to consist *only* of levying war against the U.S., adhering to its enemies, or giving the latter aid and comfort. Moreover, no person can be convicted of treason unless the accused confesses in open court or unless two witnesses testify in court that they saw the acts of treason being committed.

Treaty   A formal agreement between two or more sovereign nations. According to the U.S. Constitution, once a president has negotiated a treaty with a foreign nation, it must win a two-thirds vote of approval by the Senate before being sent back to the White House for ratification by the president. Although the Constitution does not specify how a treaty is terminated, the Supreme Court has ruled that a president can terminate a treaty unilaterally, that is, without the Senate's approval.

Truman Doctrine   Policy, sponsored by President Harry Truman in 1947, aimed at halting Communist expansion in southeastern Europe. It called for American support and funds for all free peoples so that they might resist being taken over by outside forces of repression.

Trustee   One view of the function of a member of a legislature. It holds that, as trustees, legislators may believe that they were sent to Washington or the state capitals to think and vote independently for the general welfare—and not as their constituents determine.

Unicameral legislature   One-house legislature, Nebraska and almost all cities use this form.

Union shop   "Union-security" provision found in some collective bargaining agreements requiring all employees to become members of the union within a short period—usually thirty days after being hired—and to remain members as a condition of employment.

Unitary system   Government with power concentrated by the constitution in the central government.

Unitary tax   A state tax on a company's worldwide profits, typically based on a formula that takes into account payroll, property, and sales in the state as well as some percentage of out-of-state or worldwide receipts and profits. It is a controversial tax that is heatedly debated around the country: Some states view it as a legitimate means to secure added revenue, whereas other states avoid or repeal it as a means of luring companies to relocate into their states.

Unit rule   Requirement that the whole delegation to a party convention cast its vote as the majority decides.

Universe   The entire population of a group about which information is sought.

User charges   Fees charged directly to individuals who use certain public services on the basis of service consumed. Sometimes called a user fee or user tax.

Virginia Plan   Proposal at the Constitutional Convention that provided for a strong legislature with representation in each house determined by population. It thus favored the large states.

Watergate   The general name given to a set of both major and minor violations of the law committed by Nixon administration officials and their "friends" in 1972—including obstruction of justice or covering up of crimes that took place when the National Democratic Committee headquarters was broken into in 1972. The Committee was then located in the Watergate Office Building adjacent to the fashionable Watergate Hotel in Washington, D.C. Other incidents involved misusing the Internal Revenue Service, the Central Intelligence Agency, and the FBI; the breaking in and entering of a psychiatrist's office; and perpetrating various "dirty tricks" on some of President Nixon's election opponents in the 1972 presidential election. Nixon was eventually forced out of office because of these events, and several of his advisers were indicted and served jail sentences.

Weak mayor-council   Form of local government in which the mayor must share most of the executive powers of a city with other elected or appointed boards and commissions. The mayor in weak-mayor cities is often mainly a ceremonial leader.

Whip   Party leader who is the liaison between the leadership and the rank and file in the legislature.

Whistle blowers   Federal employees who publicly reveal waste or mismanagement in government agencies.

White primary   Under the pretense that it was not governmental action, officials of the Democratic party in the South used to admit to its primaries only white persons. In the South in those days candidates of the Democratic party were the only ones with any chance of winning in the following general election; blacks were thus excluded from the only election that counted. The white primary in all its various forms was declared unconstitutional by the Supreme Court in *Smith* v. *Allwright* (1944).

Winner-take-all   In American presidential elections, the winner of the popular vote in a state receives all the electoral votes of that state.

Workfare   A program at the state, and sometimes also local, level that either mandates or strongly encourages able-bodied welfare recipients to accept public-service jobs or similar low-paying private-sector jobs that would help free them of their dependency on welfare subsidies.

Writ of certiorari   Writ used by the Supreme Court to review decisions of lower courts, federal and state, that are within the discretionary appellate jurisdiction of the Supreme Court. It is a formal device regularly used to bring a case up to the Court.

Writ of habeas corpus   Court order requiring jailers to explain to a judge why they are holding a prisoner in custody.

Writ of mandamus   Court order directing an official to perform a nondiscretionary, or ministerial, act as required by law.

Yellow-dog contract   Contract by an antiunion employer that forces prospective workers to promise they will not join a union after employment.

Zero-based budgeting (ZBB)   A budgeting procedure popularized by former President Carter that forces an agency or department to reevaluate its existing programs and performance. According to this procedure, agencies must specify alternative levels of service and rank their highest priorities.

Zoning   The use of city laws to classify land uses and assign land to certain uses—for example, residential, commercial, or industrial.

Photographs

Chapter 16: 406. AP/Wide World Photos. 407. UPI/Bettmann Newsphotos. 409. Carol Powers/The White House. 411. AP/Wide World Photos. 417. AP/Wide World Photos. 418. AP/Wide World Photos. 434 (left). AP/Wide World Photos. 423 (right). AP/Wide World Photos. 423 (bottom). AP/Wide World Photos. 430. UPI/Bettmann Newsphotos. 431. John Ficara/Woodfin Camp & Associates.

Chapter 17: 434. A. Tannenbaum/Sygma. 435. Copyright by Harris & Ewing. 447 (top to bottom). AP/Wide World Photos; AP/Wide World Photos; UPI/Bettmann Newsphotos. 453. The Supreme Court Historical Society. 454 (top to bottom). AP/Wide World Photos; AP/Wide World Photos; Courtesy of Philip Kurland. 455 (top). J. L. Atlan/Sygma. 455 (bottom). The Supreme Court Historical Society. 458. UPI/Bettmann Newsphotos.

Chapter 18: 462. AP/Wide World Photos. 469 (top). The Bettmann Archive. 469 (bottom). Culver Pictures. 470. UPI/Bettmann Newsphotos. 474. National Archives. 475. AP/Wide World Photos. 479. AP/Wide World Photos. 490. Dennis Brack/Black Star. 491. AP/Wide World Photos.

Chapter 19: 494. AP/Wide World Photos. 496. Terry Ashe/Uniphoto. 504. AP/Wide World Photos. 505 (bottom). Copyright May 8, 1989, *U.S. News & World Report*. 505 (top). From *Newsweek*, May 22, 1989. © Newsweek, Inc. All rights reserved. Reprinted by permission. 506. Terry Ashe/Uniphoto. 507. AP/Wide World Photos. 513. AP/Wide World Photos.

Chapter 20: 517. AP/Wide World Photos. 518. AP/Wide World Photos. 520. UPI/Bettmann Newsphotos. 521. UPI/Bettmann Newsphotos. 522. Library of Congress. 523. T. Cronin. 524. Tass/Sovfoto. 526. AP/Wide World Photos. 527. AP/Wide World Photos. 535. Michael Evans/Sygma. 537 (top). AP/Wide World Photos. 537 (bottom). Courtesy of Central Intelligence Agency.

Chapter 21: 544. Courtesy U.S. Military Academy, West Point. 550. Russell Roederer. 551. AP/Wide Woold Photos. 554 (top). Library of Congress. 554 (bottom). The Granger Collection. 555. DAVA. 556. AP/Wide World Photos. 557. UPI/Bettman Newsphotos. 558. Official Department of Defense photograph by Russell Roederer. 560 (top). AP/Wide World Photos. 560. (bottom). U.S. Air Force Photo. 561. U.S. Air Force Photo. 562. AP/Wide World Photos. 563 (top). UPI/Bettmann Newsphotos. 563 (bottom). AP/Wide World Photos.

Chapter 22: 566. Teresa Zabala/Uniphoto. 571. AP/Wide World Photos. 572. Courtesy Federal Reserve System; photo by Brooks. 576. AP/Wide World Photos. 579. AP/Wide World Photos. 580. Arthur Grace/Sygma. 581 (top). T. Cronin. 581 (bottom). Lynn Johnson/Black Star. 585. Junebug Clark/Photo Researchers. 586. AP/Wide World Photos.

Chapter 23. 589. AP/Wide World Photos. 590. AP/Wide World Photos. 599 (top). Courtesy of AT&T. 599 (bottom). Courtesy of *The AFL/CIO News.* 602. AP/Wide World Photos. 603. AP/Wide World Photos. 606. NASA. 609. Van Bucher/Photo Researchers. 611. AP/Wide World Photos. 613. AP/Wide World Photos.

Chapter 24: 616. New York Convention and Visitors Bureau. 617. The Granger Collection. 618. Philadelphia Convention and Visitors Bureau. 624. UPI/Bettmann Newsphotos. 626. Jim Clark. 628. The Granger Collection.

Index

Abbey, Edward, 625
Abernathy, Ralph, 216
Abortion, 50, 169, 446
ABSCAM scandals, 373
Act III leaders, 625
Acting president, 399
Adams, Abigail, 7
Adams, John, 3, 7, 29, 143, 173, 186, 234, 376
Adams, John Quincy, 234, 326
Adams, Samuel, 7, 15, 16, 801
Administrative model, classical, 393, 468–69
Administrative Procedure Act, 469
Advisory Commission on Civil Disorders, 107
Advisory Commission on Intergovernmental Regulations, 62
Affirmative action, 125–26
cases related to, 126, 127
Afghanistan, 529
Age:
as suspect classification, 114
and voting, 285
Agencies (see Regulation; Regulatory commissions)
Agenda setting
mass media and, 505–6
public policy and, 504–5
Agitators, political leaders as, 622, 625
Agnew, Spiro T., 399
Agriculture, farm subsidies, 579–80
Aid to Families with Dependent Children, 62, 510, 585
Ailes, Roger, 323
Airline deregulation, 611–12
Airline Deregulation Act, 611
Air Quality Act, 604
Alaskan oil spill, 277
Alcatraz Island, 214
Aliens, political refugees, 134–35
All-volunteer force, 553–54
Amendment process, 37–43
political implications, ERA example, 42–43
proposing amendments, 38–39
ratifying amendments, 39–42
American Association of Retired Persons (AARP), 190
American Bar Association, 443
American Civil Liberties Union, 183, 197
American Coalition for Traditional Values, 224
American Creed, 159
American Dream, 161–65, 384
challenges to, 163–65
elements of, 161–63
messianic spirit and, 163
American Farm Bureau Federation, 191
American Federation of Labor Congress of Industrial Organizations (AFL-CIO):
formation of, 191
as political machine, 203
American Independent party, 242, 243

American Indian Movement (AIM), 214
Americans for Democratic Action (ADA), 193
American Telephone & Telegraph, divestitures, 598–99
Amicus curiae briefs, 197, 449
Amnesty International, 183
Anderson, John, 242, 243, 326
Angola, 524
Annapolis convention, 6
Anthony, Susan B., 625
Antiballistic Missile Treaty, 426
Anti-Federalists, 234
Constitution and, 14–16
Anti-lynching movement, 217
Anti-Saloon League, 201
Anti-tax movement, 212–13
Antitrust policy, 595–96
Clayton Act, 596
consent decrees, 597
in current economy, 597
Sherman Antitrust Act, 596
Appeasement, 521
Appellate jurisdiction, 441
Appleby, Joyce, 5
Appointment powers, president, 386
Arms buildup, 560–62
MX missile, plans for, 561–62
weapons in, 560–61
Arms control, 523, 562–64
disarmament, 562
Intermediate Nuclear Forces (INF) treaty, 563–64
Nonproliferation Treaty, 562
SALT I, 562–63
SALT II, 563
Arrest:
exclusionary rule, 145–46
probable cause and, 143–44
rights of accused, 148–52
bail, 149, 151
double jeopardy limitation, 151
example of, 148–50
impartial jury, 150
national constitution and, 151–52
plea bargaining, 150
punishment and, 151
right to remain silent, 146
speedy and public trial, 150
search and seizure, 143–45
third degree, 146–47
writ of habeas corpus, 147–48
Articles of Confederation, 6, 39, 48
Asian Americans:
groups of, 111, 112
migration patterns, 111–12
Assembly (see Freedom of assembly)
Association (see Freedom of association)
Association of Southern Women for the Prevention of Lynching, 217
Asylum status, political refugees, 134–35
Attentive public, 530

Attorney general, 442
Autocracy, 19

Bad tendency doctrine, 79
Bagley, Sarah, 219
Bail, 149, 151
Bail Reform Act of 1984, 149
Baker, Howard H., Jr., 307
Baker, James, 527
Bakke, Allan, 126
Bakke case, 126, 449
Bakker, Jim, 224
Balanced Budget Amendment, 39, 576–77
opponents/proponents of, 576
Balanced Budget and Emergency Deficit Reduction Act of 1985, 421
Balanced government, 9
Banking deregulation, 613
Barber, James David, 400–401
Barron v. Baltimore, 72
Bay of Pigs, 538
Beard, Charles A., 12
Benefit-in-kind subsidies, 578
Bentham, Jeremy, 84
Bentsen, Lloyd, 304, 322, 325, 336, 339
Bicameral legislature, 343
Bilingual education, 111
Bill of Rights, 25, 39, 72, 147, 164
American roots of, 4–5
drafting of, 16–17
historical roots of, 4
nationalization of, 73
Second Bill of Rights, 167–68
selective incorporation, 73
state bills of rights, 74
Bills, in lawmaking process, 363–65
Bipartisanship:
criticism of, 532
foreign policy, 525, 532
meaning of, 532
Black equality movement, 214–18
civil rights movement, 216–17
current activity, 218
historical view, 215–17
KKK as countermovement, 217
(see also Racial equality; Segregation)
Blackmun, Harry A., 451, 453, 454
Blacks, voting patterns, 289
Block grants, 62, 63–64
Board of Governors, 387
Bode, Ken, 309
Boorstin, Daniel, 158
Borah, William, 104
Bork, Robert, 121, 158, 182, 380, 446
Bowsher v. Synar, 422
Boycotts, secondary, 601
Bradley, Bill, 172, 339, 358, 422, 569, 570
Bradley, Tom, 289
Brandeis, Louis, 50, 145
Breaux, John, 254
Brennan, William J., 113, 450, 452, 627
Brezhnev, Leonid, 562–63

Bricker, John, 413
British governmental system, compared to American system, 32–34
Broder, David, 309
Bronson, Ruth Muskrat, 213
Brookings Institution, 497
Brown, John, 625
Brown, Ronald H., 158, 218, 245, 330
Brown v. Board of Education, 116, 125, 508
Bryan, William Jennings, 21, 536
Bryce, James, 21
Brzezinski, Zbigniew, 536
Buchanan, Pat, 309
Buckley v. Valeo, 96, 206, 333
Budget:
checking expenditures, 510–11
controllable/uncontrollable parts of, 509
defense spending, 549–51
federal spending, composition of, 509
formulation of, 509–10
Gramm-Rudman-Hollings Act, 421–22
impoundment control, 419–21
proposals, processing of, 510
Budget deficit, 570–72
impact of, 571–72
politics of, 570–71
reasons for, 571
Bull Moose party, 235, 242, 243
Bundy, McGeorge, 536
Bureau of the Census, 578
Bureaucracy:
accountability issue, 485
administrative model, classical, 468–69
bureaus, 466
civil service, 467–68
criticism of, 463, 479, 481–82
government corporations, 465
Grace Commission, 482–83
independent agencies, 465
organization of, 464–67
formal organization, 464–66
informal organization, 467
privatization and, 462–63
proponents, 483–84
red tape and, 483–84
regulatory commissions, 465–66
responsiveness issue, 485
sunset process, 491
wastefulness issue, 479–82
Bureaucrats:
as administrators, 470–71
as alliance builders, 471–72
appointments, 486–87
congressional control, 490–91
diversity and, 467
job as permanent tenure, 479
presidential control, 486–89
profile of, 464
public opinion of, 477–79
Bureau of Indian Affairs, 108
Bureau of Intelligence and Research, 537

Bureau of Mines, 579
Bureaus, 466
Burger, Warren, 83, 89, 90–91, 424, 446, 450, 454
Burke, Edmund, 357
Burr, Aaron, 234, 314
Bush, George, 57, 158, 168, 173, 177, 193, 212, 225, 236, 237, 253, 255, 264, 281, 291, 303, 325, 336, 380, 398, 462, 525–26, 576
Business Roundtable, 192
Byrd, Robert C., 308, 417

Cabinet, functions of, 396–97
Cable Act of 1984, 87
Cable television, freedom of speech, 87–88
Calhoun, John C., 57
Calvin, John, 4
Campaign:
   congressional, 315–18
   presidential, 322–24
Campaign finance, 331–35
   evaluation of reforms, 333
   freedom of association and, 95–96
   future view, 335–36
   political action committees, 334–35
   regulation efforts, 331–33
Candidate selection process:
   caucus, 240, 241
   conventions, 240, 241
   direct primaries, 240–41
   national nominating convention, 241–42
Capitalism:
   versus political equality, 179–82
   rise of, 166–67
Capital punishment, 151
Cardozo, Benjamin, 73
Carmichael, Stokely, 217
Carnal Knowledge, 91
Carson, Rachel, 589
Carter, Hodding, 309
Carter, Jimmy, 232, 236, 320, 321, 327, 328, 329, 554
Cash benefits, 577
Categorical-formula grants, 62
Caucus, presidential candidate selection, 240–41, 320
Central Intelligence Agency (CIA), 418–19
   foreign policy and, 528, 537–38
Centralists, 56
Centrality of political speech, 82
Chase, Salmon P., 444
Checks and balances:
   Constitution and, 18, 27–28
   meaning of, 18
   presidency and, 401–2
Cheney, Richard, 549, 558
Chicanos, 109
Chief Justice, powers of, 453–54
Child labor, 600
Child, Lydia Maria, 215
Child Protection and Obscenity Act of 1988, 91
China, 277, 518, 525
Chinese people, 111
Christian Broadcasting Network, 224
Christian Voter's Victory Fund, 197
Church/state separation, establishment clause, 74–76
Cities, federal grants, 66

Citizenship:
   aliens
      admission to U.S., 133–35
      rights of, 137–38
      undocumented aliens, 135–37
   jus sanguinis principle, 132
   jus soli principle, 132
   naturalization, 132
   rights of American citizens, 132–33
      to live in U.S., 133
      to travel abroad, 133
   Slaughter House cases, 133
Civil Aeronautics Board, 611
Civil Rights Acts:
   listing of major laws, 123
   1964, 59, 64, 107, 116, 120
      Title II, 122–23
      Title VI, 123–24
   1968, 125
   1988, 125
Civil rights movement, 216–17
Civil service, 467–68
   agencies related to, 467–68
   Hatch Act, 468
   historical view, 467
Civil Service Commission, 467
Civil Service Reform Act, 467, 487
Civil War, 48
Class action suits, 124, 436
Class bias issue, voting, 289–90
Classical model, bureaucracy, 468–69
Clayton Act, 596
Clean Air Act, 65, 604
Clear and present danger doctrine, 80
Cleveland, Grover, 235, 326
Closed shop, 601
Cloture rule, 354
Coalition-building
   political leaders and, 622, 625
   presidential role, 390
Coalition of Labor Union Women (CLUW), 222
Coattail effect, 281, 315, 409
Coelho, Tony, 371
Coercion, political, 528
Colby, William, 561
Cold War, 381, 520–21, 525
   historical view, 521
Coles, Robert, 270
Collective bargaining, 601, 602
Collins, Frank, 93
Columbia University, 8
Commerce clause, 59, 122
Commerce, Department of, 578–79
Commercial speech, freedom of, 88
Commission on Campaign Costs, 332
Commission on Party Structure and Delegate Selection, 259
Commission on Presidential Debates, 326
Committee on Civil Rights, 217
Committee of Eleven, 10
Committee for Non-Violent Action (CNVA), 226
Committee on Political Education (COPE), 197, 199, 203
Committee for a Sane Nuclear Policy (SANE), 226
Commodity Futures Trading Commission, 590
Commoner, Barry, 226
Common Security concept, 226–27
Communication satellites, 296

Comparable worth, 48
Comptroller of the Currency, 591
Comstock, Anthony, 91
Concurrent powers, 53
Concurring opinions, Supreme Court, 452
Confederations, 48
Conference, Supreme Court, 450–51
Conference Board, 192
Conference committees, 17
   Congress, 370
Confirmation politics, 422–24
Conglomerate, 597
Congress:
   bicameral nature of, 343
   bureaucrats/bureaucracy and, 490–91
   Constitution and, 407–8
   criticisms of, 346–47, 370–73
   defenders of, 373
   district boundaries, 356
   dual nature of, 347
   election to, 355–56
   foreign policy and, 532–33
   functions of, 349
   historical view, 343–44
   House of Representatives, 350–52
   House/Senate coordination, 369–70
   lawmaking process, 363–65
   legislators
      characteristics of, 354–55
      as law maker, 358–63
      as representative, 357–58
   powers of, 347–49
   Senate, 352–54
   workings of, 345–46, 366
   (see also Congress and president; Congressional committees; Congressional elections; House of Representatives; Senate; specific topics)
Congressional Budget and Impoundment Control Act, 419–21
Congressional Budget Office, 420, 497
Congressional committees:
   chairs, 367
   choosing members of, 365–66
   committee investigations, 369
   conference committees, 370
   diversity of, 366–67
   seniority system, 367–69
   standing committees, 365
   subcommittees, 365, 366, 367
   types of, 365
Congressional elections:
   campaigning
      House of Representatives, 315–17
      Senate, 317–18
   future view, 339–40
   incumbency advantage, 356
   1988 results, 338
Congressional Record, 359
Congress and president:
   confirmation politics, 422–24
   emergency powers, 412–13, 418
   executive agreements, 413
   future view, 431–32
   imperial Congress view, 429–30
   impoundments, 419–21
   influence of president, 408–10
   intelligence agencies, 418–19
   veto
      item veto, 414, 426–28

   legislative veto, 424–25
   pocket veto, 414
   presidential veto, 414–16
   war making, 411–12, 416–17
   White House proposals, 389
Congress of Racial Equality (CORE), 216
Connecticut Compromise, 10–11
Consensus, public opinion, 275
Consent decrees, 597
Conservatism, 173–77
   neoconservatives, 176–77
   New Right, 175–76
   position of, 174–75, 182–83
   roots of, 173–74
   types of conservatives, 174–75
Conspiracy, 96–97
Constitution:
   amendment process, 37–43
   Articles of Confederation, 6
   Bill of Rights, 16–17
   checks and balances, 18, 27–28
   Congress and, 407–8
   constitutional elaboration, 34–35
   customs/usage and, 36
   Federalist/Antifederalist split, 14–16
   federalist nature of, 17–18, 47–56
   flexibility/rigidity concepts, 36–37
   judicial interpretation, 36–37
   judicial review, 28–31
   judicial system and, 437
   power and, 26
   ratification, 13–16
   "second constitution," 230–31
   separation of powers, 17–18, 26–27
   states and, 55–56
   supremacy clause, 10
   unwritten Constitution, 34
Constitutional Convention:
   Annapolis convention, 6
   compromises of, 9
   Connecticut Compromise, 10–11
   consensus and, 9
   delegates to, 7–8
   dissent and conflict, 10–11
   framers, characteristics of, 2–4, 11–13
   philosophy of, 9
   Virginia Plan, 10
Constitutional government:
   critics of, 18
   democracy in, 19–23
   meaning of, 19
Consumer Product Safety Commission, 591
Consumer protection, 50
Containment, 522
Content neutral, 82
Contract clause, property rights, 138
Conventions, 320
   candidate selection process, 240, 241
   national presidential convention, 245
   (see also National convention)
Cooperative lobbying, 204
Corporations:
   corporate income taxes, 568
   political influence and, 180–81
Corrupt Practices Act, 332
Corwin, Edward S., 28
Council of Economic Advisors, 387, 573
Council on Environmental Quality, 603

Council on Foreign Relations, 193, 531
County committees, 247
Court of appeals, 440, 441
Courts (see Judicial system)
Covert operations, 528, 538
Cranston, Alan, 254, 576
Credit Mobilier scandals, 205
Credit subsidies, 578
Criminal Justice Act, 442
Criminal justice system:
    civil liberties and, 155–56
    criticisms of, 152–54
    discrimination and, 154–55
Criminals (see Arrest)
Crisis management, presidential role, 382–83
Cross-cutting requirements, federal grants, 64
Cross-over sanctions, federal grants, 64
Crowe, William J., Jr., 560
C-SPAN, 296, 306
Cuban Missile Crisis, 522, 529
Cubans, 109
Cuomo, Mario, 158, 254, 339
Curtiss-Wright case, 387
Cushing, William, 434

Dahl, Robert, 166
Daley, Richard J., 247, 259
Dart, Justin, 200
Dawkins, Pete, 318
"Day After, The," 273–74
Deadly force, 144
Death penalty, 151
Deaver, Michael K., 308
Debates, presidential candidates, 326–27
Debs, Eugene, 21
Decentralists, 56
Decentralized structure, political parties, 237, 247
Declaration of Independence, 19, 23, 101
De facto segregation, 118
Defendants, 442
Defense Appropriations Bill, 419
Defense Department, 556–60
    components of, 558
    historical view, 556–57
    Joint Chiefs of Staff, 558–60
    policy making, 559
    procurement fraud scandal, 557–58
    reorganization of, 560
Defense Department Reorganization Act, 557, 560
Defense Intelligence Agency, 537
Defense policy:
    arms buildup, 560–62
    arms control, 562–64
    basic issues, 544–45
    budget, 549–51
    debates on, 564
    Defense Department, 556–60
    deterrence, 546
    goals of, 545–46
    military contractors, 551–52
    military-industrial complex, 552–53
    military service, 553–56
    mutual assured destruction, 546–47
    Strategic Defense Initiative (SDI), 547–48
Deferrals, 421

De jure segregation, 118
Demagogues, 9
Democracy:
    basic premises of, 19–20
    case for, 618–19
    democratic goals, 20–21
    elections, elements of, 22–23
    foreign policy and, 534–35
    meaning of, 18–19
    officially recognized opposition as test of, 626–27
    participatory democracy, 619–20
    as political means, 22
    politician, role in, 621, 626
    principle democrats, 22, 23
    process democrats, 22, 23
Democratic Leadership Council, 260
Democratic Republicans, 234
Democrats:
    historical view, 234
    Jeffersonian Republicans, 28
    party renewal, 261–62
    compared to Republicans, 248–49, 251–55
    strategies to regain power, 265
Dennis v. United States, 98
Deregulation, 611–14
    airline deregulation, 611–12
    banking deregulation, 613
    effects of, 614
    evaluation of, 613–14
    interest groups, 208
    trucking/railroad deregulation, 612
Detente, 520, 523
Deviating elections, 281
Dewey, Thomas E., 253
Diamond, Martin, 12
Dickinson, John, 8
Dingell, John, 199
Diplomacy, foreign policy and, 526–27
Direct primaries, 240–41
    differences between states, 241
Dirksen, Everett McKinley, 69, 801
Discharge petition, 365
Discrimination:
    criminal justice system, 154–55
    employment discrimination, 123–24
    housing and, 124–25
    Jim Crow laws, 115
    places of public accommodation, 122–23
    private discriminatory conduct, 121–22
    segregation, 115–18
    tests of, 115
Dissenting opinions, Supreme Court, 452
District of Columbia, 44
District courts, 440–41
District judges, 440
Doctrine of dual federalism, 61
Dole, Elizabeth, 294
Dole, Robert, 294, 339, 353
Domestic insurrection, 54–55
Domestic policy, presidential role, 389
Domino theory, 522
Donaldson, Sam, 309
Double jeopardy limitation, 151
Douglass, Frederick, 215, 219
Douglas, William O., 87, 153, 450
Downey, Tom, 358

Draft:
    draft registration, 554–55
    revival proposal, 555
Dred Scott case, 30
Drug testing, 145
DuBois, W.E.B., 217
Due process:
    procedural due process, 139–40
    right of privacy, 142–43
    substantive due process, 140–42
Dukakis, Michael, 172, 254, 255, 291, 303, 306, 323, 328
Dukakis, Mike, 254, 255
Dumping, 582
Dupont, Pete, 253

Economic interest groups, 191–92
Economic Interpretation of the Constitution, An (Beard), 12
Economic policy:
    balanced budget amendment, 576–77
    budget deficit, 570–72
    Employment Act of 1946, 573–74
    entitlement programs, 585–87
    fiscal policy, 574–84
    Great Depression, lessons of, 572–73, 584
    Keynesian economics, 573, 574, 575
    monetarism, 575
    monetary policy, 574
    presidential role, 387
    protectionism, 580–83
    Social Security system, 583–84
    subsidies, 577–78
    supply-side economics, 575
    taxation, 566–70
Economic regulation, 590
Economic Report of the President, 574
Economic sanctions, 527–28
Education Act of 1972, 116
Eighth Amendment, 40, 149, 151
Eisenhower, Dwight, 22, 236, 251, 252, 263, 390, 552
Elections:
    campaigning
        House of Representatives, 315–17
        Senate, 317–18
    candidate selection process, 240–42
    democratic elements of, 22–23
    forecasting and polling, 278–80
    interest groups and, 197–98
    mass media and, 303–7
    political action committees, 198–201
    running for office, 314–15
    (see also Presidential elections)
Electoral college:
    mechanism of, 324–25
    politics of, 325–26
Electronic devices, search and seizure issue, 145
Eleventh Amendment, 61
El Salvador, 530
Emergencies, presidential power, 412–13, 418
Emergency Highway Energy Conservation Act of 1974, 64
Emerson, Ralph Waldo, 162
Eminent domain, property rights, 139
Employment Act of 1946, 573–74

Employment discrimination, 123–24
    law against, 123–24
Entitlement programs, 585–87
    criticisms of, 585
    welfare reform, 586
Environmental protection, 603–6
    acid rain debate, 605
    agencies for, 603
    Bush and, 606
    Clean Air Act, 604
    costs of pollution control, 603–4
    Reagan impact on, 605–6
    toxic waste disposal, 604–5
Environmental Protection Agency, 591, 603, 606
Equal Employment Opportunity Commission, 124
Equality, 164
    as democratic goal, 20–21
    liberal view, 171
    use of term, 102–3
    (see also Equal rights)
Equal Opportunity Act of 1982, 64
Equal Protection Clause, 126
    tests of
        quasi-suspect classifications, 113–14
        rational basis test, 112–13
        suspect classifications, 113, 114
Equal rights:
    ethnic minority groups and, 109–12
    Native Americans, 108
    racial equality, 104–8
    voting rights, 103–4, 118–21
    women's rights, 103–4
Equal Rights Amendment (ERA), 40, 205, 220, 222
Equal Time Provision, 326
Equal-time requirement, 86
Ervin, Sam, 289
Eskew, Carter, 318
Essay on Liberty (Mill), 78
Establishment clause, Lemon test, 75, 76
Ethics in Government Act, 386, 423–24
Evers, Medgar, 216
Excise taxes, 567, 568
Exclusionary rule, 145–46
Executive agreements, 383, 413
Executive Office of the President, 393, 393–96
    Cabinet, 396–97
    Office of Management and Budget, 394–95
    White House staff, 393–94
Executive privilege, 36, 84
Express powers, 52
Externalities, regulation and, 593–94
Extradition, 55–56

Factionalism, 18
    Madison on, 187
    (see also Interest groups; Movements)
Fair Housing Amendments Act, 125
Fair Labor Standards Act of 1938, 61, 600
Fairness Commission, 260
Fairness doctrine, 86
Falwell, Jerry, 90, 175, 224, 225
Family Educational Rights Act of 1974, 142

Family influences:
  political socialization, 270–71
  voting, 283
Farm subsidies, 579–80
Fascell, Dante, 417
Federal Communications Commission (FCC), 86, 590, 609
Federal Corrupt Practices Act, 205
Federal Deposit Insurance Corporation (FDIC), 465, 613
Federal Election Campaign Act of 1971, 206, 247, 332, 335
Federal Election Commission, 331, 333, 334, 373
Federal grants:
  block grants, 62, 63–64
  categorical-formula grants, 62
  federal regulation of, 64–65
  iron triangles, 63
  politics of, 63
  project grants, 62
  Reagan/Bush administrations and, 63–64, 65
  revenue sharing, 62–63
Federalism:
  advantages of
    control of tyranny, 48, 50
    experimentation and, 50
    government/public proximity, 50–51
    unity without uniformity, 48
  alternatives to, 48
  Constitution and, 14–16, 48, 51
  dual federalism, 61
  federal courts and, 60–61
  federal system, components of, 47
  interstate constitutional relations, 54–55
  levels of, 65–66
  limitations on government and, 53–55
  McCulloch v. Maryland, 57–59
  meaning of, 17–18
  national governmental powers, 52
  nationalist interpretation, 56–58
  politics and, 66–68
  states powers, 52–53, 69
Federalist Society, 445
Federalist, The, 13, 186
  No. 10, 48, 50, 186–187, 233, 501
  No. 47, 27
  No. 51, 26, 350
  No. 57, 373
  No. 78, 28, 30
Federal magistrates, 440
Federal Register, 197
Federal Regulation of Lobbying Act, 206
Federal Reserve Board, 465
Federal Reserve System, Great Depression and, 573
Federal Trade Commission, 596, 597
Feiner v. New York, 94
Ferraro, Geraldine A., 222, 285, 322
Fifteenth Amendment, 60, 103, 104, 105, 118, 119
Fifth Amendment, 73, 182
  due process clause, 139–43
Fighting words, 79, 89–90, 93
Filibuster, 18, 353–54
Filipinos, 111–12
First Amendment, 73, 396
  establishment clause, 74–76
  fairness doctrine, 86
  freedom of assembly, 93–95
  freedom of association, 95

freedom of the press, 83–86
freedom of religion, 76–78
freedom of speech, 78–93
seditious speech, 79, 97–98
subversive conduct, 96–97
  (*see also* individual rights)
Fiscal policy, 574–84
Floor leaders, House of Representatives, 351
Foley, Tom, 254
Food and Drug Administration, 591, 613
Ford, Gerald, 232, 236, 399
Foreign Affairs, 531
Foreign aid, 527
Foreign policy:
  agencies/departments related to, 536
  appeasement, 521
  Bush era, 525–26
  Central Intelligence Agency and, 528, 537–38
  Cold War, 520–21
  Congress and, 426
  containment, 522
  democratic foreign policy issue, 534–35
  detente, 520, 523
  domino theory, 522
  foreign companies and, 531
  Foreign Service, 539
  historical view, 520
  interest groups and, 193–94, 530–31
  national security advisor, 536
  National Security Council and, 536–37
  Nixon Doctrine, 523
  objectives of, 519–20
  politics of
    bipartisanship, 525, 532
    Congress and, 532–33
    foreign countries/companies, 531
    public opinion, 529–30
    special interests, 530–31
  post World War II, 521–22
  presidential role, 387, 535–36
  pragmatists' view of, 520
  Reagan Doctrines, 523–25
  realists' view of, 520
  secretary of state, 535–36
  State Department, 539
  strategies
    coercion, 528
    covert operations, 528, 538
    diplomacy, 526–27
    economic sanctions, 527–28
    foreign aid, 527
    military intervention, 528–29
  Truman Doctrine, 520
  United Nations, 540–41
  United States Information Agency and, 538
  Vietnam, 522–23
Foreign Policy Association, 531
Foreign Service, 539
  criticisms of, 539–40
  functions of, 539
Four Freedoms, 21
Fourteenth Amendment, 60, 72, 73, 104, 105, 112, 118, 125
  citizenship, 132–38
  discrimination, 115–16
  due process clause, 139–43
  equal protection, 112–14
  equal rights, 102–12

private discriminatory practices, 121–27
right to vote, 118–21
segregation, 115–18
states' manipulation of, 119–20
  (*see also* specific topics)
Fourth Amendment, unreasonable search and seizure, 143–45
Fourth Virginia Resolve, 9
Fowler, Wyche, 263
Franchise, 9
Frankfurter, Felix, 148, 450
Franklin, Benjamin, 8, 9, 24
Freedmen's Bureau, 104
Freedom:
  as democratic goal, 20–22
  Four Freedoms, 21
Freedom of assembly, 93–95
  peaceful violation of law, 95
  property classifications and, 94–95
Freedom of association, 95
  campaign finance, 95–96
  Hatch Acts, 95
Freedom of Information Act of 1966, 84
Freedom of the press, 83–86
  executive privilege and, 84
  versus fair trials, 85
  Freedom of Information Act of 1966, 84
  compared to freedom of speech, 83
  information withheld by press, 84
  shield laws, 85
  sunshine laws, 83–84
Freedom of religion, 76–78
  free exercise clause, 78
Freedom of speech, 78–93, 164
  cable television, 87–88
  commercial speech, 88
  constitutional tests
    bad tendency doctrine, 79
    centrality of political speech, 82
    clear and present danger doctrine, 80
    content neutral, 82
    least drastic means, 82
    overbreadth, 82
    preferred position doctrine, 81
    prior restraint, 81
    vagueness doctrine, 81–82
  fighting words, 79, 89–90, 93
  handbills/sound trucks/billboards, 88
  libel, 90
  mails, 85–86
  motion pictures, 86
  obscenity, 90–91
  picketing, 88
  pornography, 92
  radio/television, 86–87
  seditious speech, 79, 97–98
  symbolic speech, 89
  terms/definitions related to, 79
Free Exercise Clause, 78
Free Soilers, 198, 243
Friedan, Betty, 222
Friedman, Milton, 358
Frost, Martin, 199
Fuller, Ida, 583
Full faith and credit clause, 55
Fundamental rights, 114
Furman v. Georgia, 151

Galbraith, John Kenneth, 358, 598
Gann, Paul, 500

Garcia v. San Antonio Metro, 61, 450, 453
Garfield, James, 467
Garrison, William Lloyd, 215, 622
Gender, and voting, 285
General Accounting Office (GAO), 469, 510–11, 514
General search warrants, 144
General Services Administration, 465
Geological Survey, 579
Gephardt, Richard, 339, 358
Gerrymandering, 119, 356
Gingrich, Newt, 358
Ginsburg, Douglas H., 446–47
Gitlow v. New York, 73
Glenn, John, 307
Goldwater, Barry, 174, 175–76, 237, 251, 253, 262, 263, 560
Gompers, Samuel, 203
Gonzalez, Henry B., 110
Goode, Wilson, 289
Gorbachev, Mikhail, 226, 277, 524, 563
Gore, Albert, 320, 358, 369
Government corporations, 465
Grace Commission, 482–83, 514
Grace, J. Peter, 482
Graham, Bob, 318
Gramm, Phil, 254, 353
Gramm-Rudman-Hollings Act, 421–22, 510
Grand jury, 440
  criticism of, 153–54
Grass-roots:
  lobbying, 188
  political parties, 246–48
Gray, William, 120, 200
Great Depression, 56, 67, 69, 167, 177, 235, 283, 584, 613
  causes of, 573
  current economic policy and, 572–73, 584
Great Society programs, 67, 176
Greenpeace, 211
Green, William, 203
Grenada, 524, 528, 529
Gross national product (GNP), 576, 592
Group theory, 189–91
Grove City College v. Bell, 116
Guatemala, 522, 538
Gulf of Tonkin Resolution, 533

Habeas corpus, 441
Haig, Alexander, 253
Hamilton, Alexander, 2–4, 6, 8, 10, 13, 14, 28, 173, 233, 422, 577
Hancock, John, 7, 16
Handbills/sound trucks/billboards, freedom of speech, 88
Harlan, John, 125
Harrington, Michael, 506
Harrison, Benjamin, 205, 326
Harrison, William Henry, 234
Hart, Gary, 328
Hatch Acts, 95
Hatch, Carl, 468
Hatch, Orrin, 576
Hatfield, Mark, 251
Hawkins, Paula, 318
Hayes, Rutherford, 326
Heart of Atlanta Motel v. United States, 123
Helms, Jesse, 175
Henry, Patrick, 7, 16, 343, 625
Heritage Foundation, 445

High-pressure politics, 24
Highway Safety Act, 193
Hispanics, 135–36
  classifications of, 109
  militancy of, 109–10
Hitler, Adolf, 521
Hollings, Ernest, 555
Holmes, Oliver Wendell, 61, 85, 145, 445
Hoover, Herbert, 21
Hoover, J. Edgar, 473
House of Commons, 34
House of Lords, 34
House of Representatives, 350–52
  campaigning for seat, 315–17
  committees of, 365
  floor leaders, 351
  powers of, 348
  procedure in, 350
  Rules Committee, 351–52
  speaker of the house, 350–51
  whips, 351
Housing discrimination, law against, 124–25
Housing and Urban Development, Department of, 125
Hughes, Justice, 453
Hunt, James, 260

Idealism, 520
Ideology:
  American Dream, 161–65
  as cause and effect, 177
  historical development, 166–68
  meaning of, 159
  political socialization and, 272
  (see also Political ideology)
Illegal aliens, 135–37
Illegitimacy, as suspect classification, 113
Immigration Acts:
  1924, 133
  1986, 136
Immigration and Naturalization Service (INS), 132, 134–35
Immunities, 55
Impeachment, as Constitutional elaboration, 34–35
Imperial Congress view, 429–30
Imperial presidency view, 410–11
Implied powers, 52, 58
Impoundment, 36
  forms of, 419
  legal restriction of, 419–21
Income taxes, 567, 568
Incrementalist model, public policy, 502–4
Incumbents, Congress, advantages to, 356
Independent agencies, 465
Independents, voters, 286
Indictment, criminal, 149–50
Individualism, 19, 160, 272
IndoChinese refugees, 112
Industrial capitalism, 166
Informational approaches, to regulation, 595
INF treaty (see Intermediate Nuclear Forces (INF) treaty)
Inherent powers, 52
INS v. Chadha, 424, 455
Intelligence agencies, 418–19
  operations of, 537
  types of, 537
  (see also Central Intelligence Agency (CIA))

Interest group model, public policy, 501
Interest groups:
  current status of, 188–89
  economic interest groups, 191–92
  foreign policy oriented groups, 193–94, 531
  group theory, 189–91
  growth of, 188–89
  impact, factors in, 194–96
  lobbying, 201–8
  political action committees, 198–201
  public interest groups, 193
  regulatory issues, 208
  single-cause groups, 194, 205
  techniques used
    election activities, 197–98
    litigation, 196–97
    persuasion, 196
    rule making, 197
  types of, 188, 192
Interior, Department of, 579
Intermediate Nuclear Forces (INF) treaty, 426, 521, 563–64
Internationalism, 520
International Treaty on the Peaceful Uses of Outer Space, 562
Interstate commerce, 59
Interstate Commerce Commission, 491, 590, 609, 612
Interstate compacts, 56
Iran, 538
Iran-Contra scandals, 23, 369, 380, 399, 410, 419, 429
Iron triangles, 63
Isolationism, 381, 413
Issue-attention cycle, public policy, 506–7
Item veto, 414, 421, 426–28

Jackson, Andrew, 234, 240, 257
Jackson, Jesse, 44, 172, 251, 254, 260, 328, 339
Jackson, Robert, 78, 155
Japanese, 111
Jarvis, Howard, 500, 622
Javits, Jacob, 251
Jay, John, 11, 14, 434
Jeffersonian Republicans, 28, 29
Jefferson, Thomas, 3, 7, 10, 19, 26, 29, 37, 57, 233, 234, 468, 617
Jim Crow laws, 115
John Birch Society, 193
Johnson, Andrew, 35, 447
Johnson, Lyndon, 107, 187, 216, 238, 251, 300, 396, 412, 427, 522
Johnson, Richard M., 325
Joint Chiefs of Staff, 558–60
  reorganization of, 559–60
Joint Economic Committee, 574
Jones, David, 559
Judges:
  appointment of, 443–47
  disputes settled by, 435, 436
  district judges, 440
  judicial activism, 445, 455, 456
  judicial philosophy, 444–46
  judicial restraint, 445, 456
  judicial review, 434–35
  lawmaking and, 436
  party control factors, 447
  public influences on, 456–59
  role of, 434–36
  selection of
    ABA role, 443

Bork example, 446–47
  ideology in, 444–45
  judicial philosophy in, 445–46
  party/race, 444
  Senate Judiciary Committee, 443–44
  tenure, length of, 446
Judicial activism, 445, 455, 456
Judicial restraint, 445, 456
Judicial review, 28–31, 434–35, 456
  Marbury v. Madison, 29–31
  origins of, 28–29
Judicial system:
  as adversary system, 435
  changing jurisdiction, 447–48
  Constitution and, 437
  court system
    court of appeals, 440, 441
    district courts, 440–41
    state courts, 441
    Supreme Court, 437, 440
  democracy and, 455–56
  federal lawyers, 442–43
  legislative courts, 437
  power and, 435–36
  stare decisis, 436–37
Judiciary Act of 1789, 34
Juries:
  grand jury, 440
  impartial jury, 150
  jury trial, 701–3
  petit jury, 440
Jurisdiction of courts:
  appellate, 441
  changing jurisdiction, 447–48
  habeas corpus, 441
  original, 440
Jus sanguinis principle, 132
Jus soli principle, 132

Kammen, Michael, 3
Kaplan, David A., 88
Kassebaum, Nancy, 541
Katz v. United States, 145
Kaufman, Herbert, 481
Kefauver, Estes, 506
Kelman, Steven, 483
Kemp, Jack, 253, 294, 339
Kennedy, Anthony M., 61, 75, 486, 447
Kennedy, Edward M., 193, 254, 265, 305, 415
Kennedy, John F., 106, 236, 251, 300, 326, 396, 522, 622
Kennedy, Paul, 402
Kennedy, Robert, 216, 251, 258
Kerner Committee, 107
Kerner, Otto, 107
Keynesian economics, 573, 574, 575
Keynes, John Maynard, 573, 574
Khomeini, Ayatollah, 93
Khrushchev, Nikita, 552
King, Martin Luther, Jr., 93, 95, 106, 120, 216, 258, 473, 622, 625
Kings College, 8
Kirkland, Lane, 203
Kirk, Paul G., 262
Kissinger, Henry, 523, 536, 563
Koreans, 111
Korean War, 412, 522
Kristol, Irving, 176–77, 300
Ku Klux Klan (KKK), 60
  anti-lynching movement and, 217

Labor:
  AFL-CIO, 191–92
  as political machine, 203

Labor injunction, 601
Labor-management relations, 599–602
  historical view, 599–600
  legislation to protect workers, 599–600
  unions, 600–602
  yellow-dog contracts, 599
Labor-Management Relations Act of 1947, 601
Ladd, Everett Carll, 160
LaFollette, Robert, 21, 197
Lallaye, Tim, 224
Laski, Harold, 21, 434
Lautenberg, Frank, 318
Lau v. Nichols, 111
Law clerks, role of, 454
Lawmaking:
  bills, 363–65
  item veto proposal, 426–28
  judicial system and, 436–37
  legislators' role, 358–63
  presidential veto, 414–16
Lawyers, federal, 442–43
Leadership (see Political leadership)
League of Cities v. Usery, 61
League of Women Voters, 221, 222, 326
Least drastic means, 82
Lee, Richard Henry, 7
Legal tender, 138
Legislative inquiry, 369
Legislative Reorganization Act, 513
Legislative veto, 421, 424–25
Legislators:
  as delegates of district, 357
  influences on
    colleagues, 359
    congressional staff, 360
    ideology, 358
    political party, 361–62
    president, 362–63
    voters, 358–59
  as representatives, 357–58
  as trustees, 357
Legislature, bicameralism, 9–10
  (see also Congress)
Lemon test, establishment clause, 75, 76
Lemon v. Kurtzman, 75
Lewis, John L., 199
Libel, freedom of speech issue, 90
Liberalism, 170–73
  criticism of, 172–73
  neoliberals, 172
  position of, 170–71, 182–83
  types of liberals, 172
Libertarianism, 165, 178–79
  critics of, 179
  position of, 178–79
Liberty:
  as democratic goal, 20–22
  political culture and, 159–60
Libya, 529
Lieberman, Joseph, 318
Lightner, Candy, 211
Lincoln, Abraham, 21, 57, 162, 235, 277, 412, 444
Lindbergh, Charles A., 226
Lindblom, Charles, 180
Lippmann, Walter, 298
Lobbying, 201–8
  cooperative lobbying, 204
  historical view, 201
  labor as political machine, 203
  opponents/proponents of, 207–8
  process of, 202–3
Logrolling arrangements, 551

Lott, Trent, 263
Love Canal, 604
Lowi, Theodore, 411
Lugar, Richard, 358
Luther, Martin, 4

McCarthy, Eugene, 251, 258
McConnell, Mitch, 206
McCulloch, James William, 57
McCulloch v. Maryland, 57
McGovern-Fraser Commission, 259
McGovern, George, 176, 236, 237, 252, 259
McKinley, William, 205
Madison, James, 1–3, 4, 8, 9, 13, 14, 16–17, 26, 27, 29, 39, 48, 155, 186, 204, 208, 234, 343–44, 373, 406, 431, 501
Mails, freedom of speech, 85–86
Maintaining elections, 281
Majority leaders, Congress, 351, 352
Majority rule, 18, 27, 34
Malcolm X, 216
Mapp v. Ohio, 145
Marbury v. Madison, 29, 434
Marbury, William, 29
Marine Protection Amendments of 1977, 64
Market approaches, to regulation, 595
Marshall, George C., 522
Marshall, James, 29–30
Marshall, John, 57, 58, 72, 138, 434, 450
Marshall Plan, 522
Marshall, Thurgood, 127, 145
Martin, Luther, 8, 58
Marx, Karl, 177
Maryland Act for the Liberties of the People, 5
Maryland v. Wirtz, 450–51
Maslin, Paul, 318
Mason, George, 15
Massachusetts Body of Liberties of 1641, 5
Mass mailing, 189
Mass media:
    agenda setting, 505–6
    control of media, 297–98
    elections and, 303–7
        Bush/Dukakis election, 295, 303–4
        influence of media, 303–5
        media consultants, 305–6
        technology and, 305–7
    influences of
        political socialization, 272–73
        public opinion, 297–98
    journalists political bias, 300, 308–10
    new media, 296
    newspapers, 299–300
    opinion leadership and, 299
    power of, 296–97, 307–8, 310
    president and, 390–91, 396–98
    public opinion and, 298–99
    television news, 298, 300–02
    use of term, 295
Mass public, 529–30
Mathias, Charles McC., Jr., 527
Mayflower, 4
Mazmanian, Daniel A., 512
Meany, George, 203
Media (*see* Mass media)
Medicaid, 62, 510, 585
Medicare, 578, 585
Memoirs v. Massachusetts, 91

Merit Systems Protection Board, 467
Messianic spirit, of American, 163
Metzenbaum, Howard, 254
Midterm party conference, 261
Military intervention, 528–29
Military service, 553–56
    all-volunteer force, 553–54
    draft registration, 554–55
    historical view, 553
    women in, 555–56
Miller v. California, 90–91
Mill, John Stuart, 78, 183
Minimum wage, 600
Minority floor leader, 351
Miranda v. Arizona, 147
Mitchell, George, 254, 339
Mondale, Walter, 203, 285, 301, 322, 328
Monetarism, 575
Monetary policy, 574
Monopoly:
    antitrust policy, 595–96
    natural monopolies, 593
    regulation, 593
Monroe Doctrine, 520
Monroe, James, 343
Morale-building, presidential role, 384–85
Moral Majority, 175, 176, 183, 193, 224, 225, 290
Moral philosophers, framers as, 13
Morris, Gouverneur, 8, 377
Mothers Against Drunk Driving (MADD), 183, 211
Motion pictures, freedom of speech, 86
Motor Carrier Act, 612
Mott, Lucretia, 219
Movements:
    antitax movement, 212–13
    black movement, 214–18
    Constitution and, 227–28
    definition of, 211
    development of, 211–12
    goals of, 211
    compared to interest groups, 211
    Native American movement, 213–14
    New right, 223–25
    peace movement, 225–26
    women's movement, 210, 218–23
Moyers, Bill, 309
Moynihan, Daniel Patrick, 300, 507, 576
Multiple independently targetable reentry vehicles, 563
Murdock, Rupert, 298
Muskie, Edmund, 506
MX missile, 514
    plans for, 561–62

Nader, Ralph, 188, 193, 197, 506, 589
National Association for the Advancement of Colored People (NAACP), 216
National Association of Colored Women, 220
National Bureau of Standards, 578
National Commission on Social Security Reform, 584
National Conference of State Legislatures, 496
National Congress of American Indians (NCAI), 213
National convention:
    delegates to, 320–21

historical view, 321
procedures of, 322
National Emergencies Act of 1976, 418
National Federation of Business and Professional Women (NFBPW), 220
National government:
    expansion of
        Constitutional basis, 59–60
        politics of growth, 67–69
        reactions to, 68–69
    necessary and proper clause, 52
    powers of, 52
    supremacy clause, 52
National Governors Association, 496
National Highway Traffic Safety Administration, 591
National Indian Youth Council (NIYC), 214
Nationalist interpretation, of federalism, 56–58
National Labor Relations Act of 1935, 600
National Labor Relations Board, 465, 600, 602
National League of Cities, 496
National League of Cities v. Usery, 450, 452, 453
National nominating convention, 241–42
National Organization for Women (NOW), 42, 196–97, 221
National party leadership, 245–46
National Rifle Association (NRA), 183, 194, 202
National Right to Work Committee, 602
National security advisor, 534, 536
    foreign policy, 536
National Security Agency, 537
National Security Council, 395, 558
    foreign policy and, 536–37
National supremacy, 58
National Traffic and Motor Vehicle Safety Act, 193
National Unity party, 242
National Woman's Party (NWP), 220
Nation, Carrie, 201
Native Americans:
    Native American movement, 213–14
        historical view, 213–14
        modern militancy, 214
    poverty status of, 108
    rights of, 108
Naturalization, 132
Necessary and proper clause, 52
Neoconservatives, 176–77
Neoliberals, 172
Neustadt, Richard, 36
New Christian Right, 224
New Deal, 21, 164, 170, 174, 176, 236, 251, 379, 387, 447, 579
New Deal liberals, 172
New judicial federalism, 74
New Right, 175, 175–76, 223–25, 225
    growth of movement, 223–24
    Moral Majority, 224, 225
Newspapers, 299–300
    political impact of, 299–300
New York Times v. Sullivan, 90
Nicaragua, 524, 530
1988 election:
    congressional election results, 338
    interpretation of, 336–37
    key factors in, 336–37

mass media and, 295, 303–4
presidential debates, 326–27
Nineteenth Amendment, 40, 104, 118, 119, 235
Nixon Doctrine, 523
Nixon, E.D., 216
Nixon, Richard M., 35, 232, 236, 251, 263, 299, 326, 399
Nomination, candidates, 241–42
Nonprobability sampling, 278
Nonproliferation Treaty, 562
North Atlantic Treaty Organization (NATO), 522, 540
North, Oliver, 429
Nuclear Regulatory Commission, 604
Nunn, Sam, 172, 254, 339, 353, 356, 417, 555

Oaker, Mary Rose, 200
Obscenity, freedom of speech issue, 90–91
Occupational Safety and Health Administration, 591, 606–9
    criticisms of, 606, 607–9
    formation of, 606–7
O'Connor, Sandra Day, 61, 386, 450
Office holders, political leaders as, 622, 625
Office of Management and Budget (OMB), 387, 469
    functions of, 394–95, 488
Office of Personnel Management, 467–68
Office of Surface Mining, 591
O'Hara, James, 259
Oligarchy, 19
Oligopoly, regulation, 593, 597
Olmstead v. United States, 145
O'Neill, Thomas P. "Tip," 351
Opinion leadership:
    mass media and, 299
    public and, 530
Opinions, Supreme Court, 451–52
Oral arguments, Supreme Court, 449–50
Original jurisdiction, 440, 448
Otis, James, 143
Overbreadth, 82

Pacific Legal Foundation, 445
Pacifists, 212
Packwood, Bob, 199, 206
Paine, Thomas, 7, 625
Palko v. Connecticut, 73
Parks, Rosa, 106, 216
Parliament, British, 34
Partial preemption, federal grants, 65
Participatory democracy, 619–20
Partisans, voters, 285
Party leadership, president, 391–92
Party platforms, 248–49
Party Unity Score, 257
Patent and Trademark Office, 579
Paterson, William, 8, 10
Patronage system, political parties, 240
Paul, Ron, 178
Payner, Jack, 146
Peaceful picketing, 88
Peace movement, 225–26
    Common Security concept, 226–27
    historical view, 225–26
Pearl Harbor, 277, 553

Pelosi, Nancy, 200
Pendleton Act, 467
Pentagate, 557
Pentagon, 556
Pentagon Papers, 464
Performance standards, and regulation, 595
Personal property, 164
Persuasive power, presidential role, 390
Petit jury, 440
Phillips, Kevin, 300
Picketing, freedom of speech, 88
Plea bargaining, 150, 442
Plessy v. Ferguson, 105, 115–16, 125
Pocket veto, 414
Poland, 517
Police powers, 138
Policy entrepreneurs, role of, 506
Policy making (*see* Public policy)
Policy politicians, 497
Policy systems model, public policy, 501–2
Political action committees (PACs), 188, 198–201
  campaign money, 200–201
  influence of, 199
Political consultants, 497
Political culture:
  American values and, 159–61
  use of term, 159
Political ideology:
  conservatism, 173–77
  liberalism, 170–73
  libertarianism, 178–79
  nature of, 169
  political equality versus capitalism, 179–82
  socialism, 177–78
  tolerance and, 182–83
Political leadership:
  agitators, 622, 625
  broker role, 623
  coalition builders, 622–25
  office holders, 622, 625
  transactional leaders, 624
  transforming leaders, 624, 625
Political parties:
  candidate selection process, 240–42
  characteristics of, 236–37
  criticisms of, 248, 257
  decentralized structure, 237, 247
  decline of, 232–33, 255–57
  Democrats/Republicans, comparison of, 248–49, 251–55
  functions of, 237–42
  grass roots level parties, 246–48
  historical view, 233–34
    Democrats, 234
    Republican Party, 235–36
  influence on legislators, 361–62
  membership weaknesses, 250
  national party leadership, 245–46
  party affiliation, 285–86
  party platforms, 248–49
  party reform, 258–61
  party renewal, 261–62
  patronage system, 240
  progress and, 250–51
  realignment, 262–66
  as "second constitution," 230–31
  spoils system, 235
  third parties, 242–45
  two-party system compared to multi-party system, 244
Political process, democracy and, 22
Political refugees, 134–35

Political socialization, 270–73
  family influences, 270–71
  ideology and, 272
  media influences, 272–73
  religious influences, 273
  school influences, 271–72
Poll tax, 119
Pollution (*see* Environmental protection)
Populists, 119, 166
Pornography, freedom of speech issue, 92
Poverty:
  culture of poverty, 585
  entitlement programs, 585–87
  as suspect classification, 114
Powell, Lewis, 114, 126, 141, 240
Power elite model, public policy and, 499–501
Preferred position doctrine, 81
Prerogative theory, 400
Presidency:
  administrative role, 393
  appointment powers, 386
  bureaucrats/bureaucracy and, 486–89
  character and personality of president, 400–401
  checks and balances, 401–2
  coalition-building, 390
  crisis management, 382–83
  criticisms of, 399–400
  domestic policy, 389
  economic policy, 387
  executive agreements, 383
  Executive Office of the President, 393–96
  expanded role, 382
  expectations of American people, 378–79, 382, 402
  foreign policy, 387, 535–36
  ideal model for, 403–4
  imperial presidency view, 410–11
  job of, 380–82, 383
  legislators and, 362–63
  media and, 396–98
  morale-building, 384–85
  party leadership, 391–92
  persuasive power, 390
  powers of, 380–81
  press conferences, 390–91
  priority setting, 386–87, 389
  qualifications for office, 378
  strong presidents, view of, 379–80, 428–29
  symbolic significance, 384–85
  (*see also* Congress and president)
Presidential Commission on Obscenity and Pornography, 90
Presidential commissions, 514
Presidential Commission on the Space Shuttle Challenger Accident, 514
Presidential debates:
  historical view, 326
  1988 election, 326–27
Presidential elections:
  campaign, 322–24
  campaign finance, 331–35
  caucuses, 320
  conventions, 320
  electoral college, 324–26
  mass media and
    Bush/Dukakis election, 295, 303–4
    media consultants, 305–6
  national convention, 320–22

1988 election, interpretation of, 336–37
  presidential debates, 326–27
  primaries, 319–20
    pros/cons of, 327–29
  reform proposals
    campaign finance, 335–36
    electoral college, 330–31
    nominating process, 329–30
  vice-presidential nominee, 322
  view for 1990s, 338–40
  (*see also* Campaign finance; Candidate selection process)
Presidential power:
  executive privilege, 36
  impoundment of funds, 36
Presidential veto, 414–16
Press (*see* Freedom of the press)
Press conferences, presidential, 390–91
Preventive Detention Act, 149
Primaries, 319–20
  characteristics of, 319–20
  pros/cons of, 327–29
  reform proposals, 329–30
Principle democrats, 22, 23
Priority setting, presidential role, 386–87, 389
Prior restraint, 81
Privacy, right of, 142–43
Privacy Act of 1974, 142
Privatization, 503
  of federal programs, 462
Procedural due process, 139–40
  expanded interpretation, 140
Process democrats, 22, 23
Procurement fraud scandal, 557–58
Professional Air Traffic Controllers Organization, 602
Progressive Era, 235
Progressive party, 243, 666
Project grants, 62
Property rights:
  contract clause, 138
  eminent domain, 139
  meaning of, 138
Proposing amendments, 38–39
Prosecutors, role of, 442
Prosser, Gabriel, 215
Protectionism, 580–83
Pruneyard Shopping Center v. Robins, 94
Public accommodation, discrimination in places of, 122–23
Public defender system, 443
Public interest groups, 193
Public Interest Research Groups (PIRGs), 193
Public opinion:
  of bureaucrats, 477–79
  characteristics of, 275
  foreign policy and, 529–30
  formation of, 274
  mass media and, 297–98
  public
    attentive public, 530
    mass public, 529–30
    opinion makers, 530
  public mood and, 530
  stability/fluidity of, 276–77
  Supreme Court decisions, 456–59
  voting and, 291
Public opinion polls, 275
  interpretation of, 279–80
  measurement aspects, 278
  questions, construction of, 278–79

Public policy:
  boundaries of, 495
  budget
    checking expenditures, 510–11
    formulation of, 509–10
    proposals, processing of, 510
  evaluation of, 513–14
  formation of
    agenda building, 504–5
    agenda setting by media, 505–6
    issue-attention cycle, 506–7
    by policy entrepreneurs, 506
  implementation
    difficulties related to, 511–12
    failure of, 511
    guidelines for, 512
  inaction, politics of, 507
  incrementalist model, 502–4
  interest group model, 501
  meaning of, 494
  participants in, 495–97
  policy systems model, 501–2
  power elite model, 499–501
  rational person model, 498–99
  shared institutional leadership, 508
  stages in process, 497–98
Puerto Ricans, 109
Puritans, theocracy of, 4–5

Quasi-suspect classifications, 113–14
Quayle, Dan, 294–95, 304, 322, 398

Race, and voting, 285
Racial equality:
  amendments related to, 104
  historical evaluation of, 104–8
  (*see also* Black equality movement; Segregation)
Radical Right, 175
Radio Free Europe, 538
Radio/television, freedom of speech, 86–87
Random sampling, 278
Rangel, Charles, 199
Ratifying amendments, 39–42
Rational basis test, 112–13
Rational person approach:
  bureaucracy, 468–69
  public policy, 498–99
Reagan Doctrines, 523–25
Reagan, Ronald, 57, 62–63, 173, 193, 232, 236, 237, 263, 300, 379, 396, 427, 428–29, 445, 576
Realigning election, 281, 457
Realignment, political parties, 262–66
Recall, right to, 161
Recycling law, 50
Red Lion Broadcasting Co. v. Federal Communications Commission, 87
Red tape, bureaucracy and, 483–84
Reform, political parties, 258–61
Regressive tax system, 568
Regulation:
  antitrust policy, 595–96
  big business and, 597–98
  deregulation, 611–14
  economic regulation, 590
  enforcement, AT&T case, 598–99
  environmental protection, 603–6

Regulation (*continued*)
externalities and, 593–94
historical view, 591
labor-management relations, 599–602
meaning of, 590
monopoly, 593
occupational health/safety regulation, 606–9
oligopoly, 593, 597
opponents/proponents of, 592–93, 594, 609–10
proposals for new methods, 595, 598
purposes of, 593–94
social regulation, 590–91
types of agencies, 591–92
Regulatory commissions, 465–66
appointments, 466
quasilegislative/quasijudicial functions, 465–66
Rehnquist, William H., 74, 78, 145, 149, 386, 446, 452, 454
Religion:
church/state separation, 74–76
freedom of religion, 76–78
free exercise clause, 78
Religious influences:
political socialization, 273
voting, 284–85
Representative, congressional role, 357–58
Representative democracy, 19
Republican form of government, states, 54
Republicans:
compared to Democrats, 248–49, 251–55
historical view, 235–36
party renewal, 262
Rescissions, 421
Restrictive covenants, 125
Revenue Act of 1971, 332
Revenue sharing, 62–63
Reverse discrimination, 126
Revolutionary War, 5–6, 12
Rhodes, John, 346
Richards, Richard, 246
Richmond v. Corson, 127
Rickover, Hyman G., 473–74
Right of privacy, 142–43
Right to recall, 161
Right to remain silent, 146
Right to vote (*see* Voting rights)
Right-to-work laws, 601
Riley, William, 606
Robb, Charles, 172, 254, 339
Roberts, Justice, 447
Robertson, Pat, 224, 225, 253, 285, 500
Robinson, Michael J., 304
Rockefeller, Nelson, 252, 253, 332, 399
Roe v. Wade, 42, 449
Roosevelt, Franklin D., 21, 57, 133, 167, 170, 174, 235, 298, 300, 379, 389, 390, 400, 447
Roosevelt, Theodore, 21, 57, 235, 242, 243, 445
Rossiter, Clinton, 159
Rule of four, 449
Rules Committee, 351–52
Runaway convention, 39
Runoff election, 330

Sabatier, Paul A., 512
Sabin, Pauline Morton, 201

Safire, William, 309
Sales tax, 568
Salinger, Pierre, 309
SALT I (Strategic Arms Limitation Treaty), 562–63
SALT II, 563
Sampling error, 278
San Antonio School District v. Rodriguez, 114
Sanford, Terry, 263
Sawyer, Diane, 309
Scalia, Antonin, 74, 386, 446, 450
Schlafly, Phyllis, 42, 224
Schlesinger, Arthur M., Jr., 410–11
School desegregation, 118
School influences, political socialization, 271–72
Schweiker, Richard S., 373
Scowcroft, Brent, 536, 562
Search and seizure:
arrests, 143–44
deadly force, 144
electronic devices, use of, 145
searches, 145
drug testing, 145
by public officials, 144–45
search warrants, 144
Secondary boycotts, 601
Second Bill of Rights, 167–68, 174
Secretary of state, 535–36
foreign policy, 535–36
Section 1983, 60–61
Securities and Exchange Commission, 465
Sedition Act of 1798, 97, 98
Seditious speech, 79, 97–98
Segregation, 115–18
antisegregation movement, 216
de facto segregation, 118
de jure segregation, 118
end of, *Brown v. Board of Education*, 116
Plessy v. Ferguson, 115–16
separate-but-equal concept, 115–16
Selective incorporation, 73
Selective Service Act, 553
Selective Service and Training Act, 553
Self-determination, 20
Self-regulation, 595
Senate, 352–54
campaigning for seat, 317–18
cloture rule, 354
committees of, 365
confirmation power, 422–24
federal judge selection, 443–45
filibuster, 353–54
majority leader, 352
policy committee, 352
political environment, 353
powers of, 348
procedure in, 352
senatorial courtesy, 424, 442, 443
Senate Committee on Foreign Relations, 533
Senate Judiciary Committee, 443–44
Senatorial courtesy, 424, 442, 443
Seneca Falls Women's Rights Convention, 103
Senior Executive Service, 487
Seniority system, Congress, 367–69
Sentencing Reform Act of 1984, 151
Separation of powers, 508
Constitution and, 26–27
meaning of, 17–18

Seventeenth Amendment, 235, 345, 350
Sex classifications, 113–14
Shays, Daniel, 6, 18
Shays's Rebellion, 7, 48
Shelby, Richard, 254
Shelley v. Kraemer, 125
Sherman Antitrust Act, 596
Shield laws, 85
Shultz, George, 526
Silk, Leonard, 572
Simon, Paul, 172
Simpson, Alan, 294
Simpson-Rodino Act, 136
Sinclair, Upton, 506, 589
Single-cause groups, 194, 205
1628 Petition of Rights, 4
Sixteenth Amendment, 567
Sixth Amendment, 150
Slaughter House Cases, 133
Slavery:
antislavery movement, 215–16
as constitutional convention issue, 11
slave uprisings, 215
Smith Act of 1940, 97–98
Smith, J. Allen, 12
Smith v. Allwright, 119
Smoot-Hawley Tariff Act, 582
Social class, voting patterns and, 288–90
Social and Economic Statistics Administration, 578
Socialism, 177–78
critics of, 178
position of, 178
Social regulation, 590–91
Social Security Act of 1935, 583
Social Security system, 583–84
historical view, 583–84
pay-as-you-go system, 584
problems of, 584
Social Security Trust Fund, 584
Social Security taxes, 568
Soft money, 247
Solicitor general, 442
Solzhenitsyn, Alexander, 163–64
Southern Christian Leadership Conference (SCLC), 106, 216
Soviet Union, 521
detente, 520, 523
Special interests (*see* Interest groups)
Speech (*see* Freedom of speech)
Spencer, Stuart, 294
Spirit of American Government, The (Smith), 12
Spoils system, 235
Squier, Robert, 318
Staebler, Neil O., 331
Staggers Rail Act, 612
Stalin, Joseph, 521
Standing committees, Congress, 365
Stanton, Elizabeth Cady, 219
Star Wars (*see* Strategic Defense Initiative (SDI))
State attorneys, 442
State committees, 246–47
State courts, 441
State Department, 527, 530, 539
functions of, 539
States:
bill of rights, 74
Constitutional prohibitions, 53
Constitutional provisions
extradition, 55–56
full faith and credit clause, 55

immunities, 55
interstate compacts, 56
criminals, double jeopardy limitation, 151–52
dual federalism, 61
federal grants
federal regulations, 64–65
reduction of, 66
future view, 69
powers of, 52–53
ratification of amendments, 39–42
republican form of government, 54
States' rights interpretation, of federalism, 57
States' Rights party, 243
Statism, 20
Statistical methods, in polling, 278
Stevens, John Paul, 240, 454
Stevenson, Adlai E., 323
Stewart, Potter, 122, 451, 452
Stockman, David, 472
Stone, Harlan, 57, 454, 456
Strategic Arms Limitation Treaty (*see* SALT (Strategic Arms Limitation Treaty))
Strategic Arms Reduction Talks (START), 564
Strategic Defense Initiative (Star Wars), 169, 426, 524, 544
Strikes, 601–2
Student Nonviolent Coordinating Committee (SNCC), 216
Subcommittees, Congress, 365, 366, 367
Subsidies, 566, 577–78
farm subsidies, 579–80
functions of, 577
historical view, 577
types of, 577–79
Substantive due process, 140–42
Subversive conduct, 96–97
Sullivan, Leonore, 506
Sullivan, Louis, 225
Sunset process, 491
Sunshine laws, 83–84
Superdelegates, 232
Super Tuesday, 320, 328
Supply-side economics, 575
Supremacy clause, 10, 52
Supreme Court, 437, 440
amicus curiae briefs, 449
cases heard, 448–49
Chief Justice, powers of, 453–54
conference, 450–51
debate on role of, 456
implementation of rulings, 454–55
law clerks, 454
opinions of, 451–52
assignment of, 451
concurring opinions, 452
dissenting opinions, 452
uses of, 451
writing of, 452–53
oral arguments, 449–50
ritual in, 448
rule of four, 449
writ of certiorari, 448
Supreme Court decisions:
bad tendency doctrine, 79
campaign finance, 96
clear and present danger doctrine, 80
establishment clause, 74–76
exclusionary rule, 145–146
executive privilege, 84

Supreme Court decisions (*continued*)
  freedom of assembly, 94
  freedom of press, 83–87
  freedom of religion, 76–78
  freedom of speech, 79–82, 89–91, 98
  habeas corpus, 147–48
  intergovernmental relations, 73
  national supremacy, 72, 73
  obscenity, 90–91
  preferred position doctrine, 81
  rights of accused, 147, 149, 151
  Roe v. Wade, 42
  segregation, 115–16
  unreasonable search and seizure, 145
  (*see also* Supreme Court; specific Supreme Court cases)
Suspect classifications, 113, 114
  age as, 114
  illegitimacy as, 113
  poverty as, 114
  sex classifications, 113–14
Swaggert, Jimmy, 224
Symbolic significance, presidential role, 384–85
Symbolic speech, 89

Taft-Hartley Act, 196, 601–2
Taft, Robert A., 253, 446
Talbert, Mary B., 217
Taney, Justice, 446
Tarkanian, Jerry, 61
Taxation, 566–70
  Congressional power and, 59
  corporate income taxes, 568
  criticism of system, 569–70
  excise taxes, 567–68
  income taxes, 567–68
  objectives of, 567
  regressive tax system, 568
  sales tax, 568
  social security taxes, 568
  tax expenditures, 569
  tax incentives, 577
  tax reform (1986), 569–70
Tax Reform Act of 1986, 202
Television news, 298, 300–302
  control of, 302
  critics of, 301, 302
  political impact of, 300–302
Temperance Movement, 103
Tennessee Valley Authority, 465
Tenth Amendment, 57, 61, 73
Tesh, Sylvia, 205
Theocracy, 4–5
Third degree, 146–47
Third parties, 242–45
  doctrinal party, 242–43
  issue party, 243
  political personality based party, 243
Third world, 519
Thirteenth Amendment, 60, 104, 105, 122

Thomas, Norman, 226
Three Mile Island, 604
Thurmond, Strom, 243, 576
Thurow, Lester, 575
Tilden, Samuel, 326
Times Beach, 604
Tocqueville, Alexis de, 21, 434, 534
Tolerance, political ideology and, 182–83
Tower, John, 380, 386, 429–30
Toxic waste disposal, 604–5
Trade deficit, 581
Trading:
  dumping, 582
  protectionism, 580–83
  tariffs, 581–82
  trade deficit, 581
Transactional leaders, 624
Transforming leaders, 624, 625
Treason, use of term, 96
Treaties:
  Antiballistic Missile Treaty, 426
  Nixon Doctrine and, 523
  Nonproliferation Treaty, 562
  North Atlantic Treaty Organization (NATO), 522
  SALT I, 562–63
  SALT II, 563
Trucking/railroad deregulation, 612
Truman Doctrine, 520
Truman, Harry, 162, 172, 256, 279, 390
Trustee, congressional role, 357
Tubman, Harriet, 215
Turner, Stansfield, 419
Tweed, Boss, 258
Twelfth Amendment, 325
Twenty-fifth Amendment, 399
Twenty-first Amendment, 40
Twenty-fourth Amendment, 119
Twenty-second Amendment, 399
Twenty-sixth Amendment, 118, 259

Ultraconservatism, 175
Undocumented aliens, 135–37
Unification Act of 1947, 556
Unions, 600–602
  collective bargaining, 601, 602
  losses to, 602
  strikes, 601–2
  Taft-Hartley Act, 601–2
  union shop, 601
  Wagner Act, 600
Unitary systems, 48
United Nations, 176, 536, 540–41
  opposition to, 541
  origin of, 540
  public view of, 540–41
United States Information Agency, foreign policy and, 538
United States marshalls, 441
United States Sentencing Commission, 151
United States Supreme Court Reports, 455

United States v. Darby, 57
United States v. Nixon, 84
United States v. Salerno, 149
Unit rule, 259
Universe, 278
University of California Regents v. Bakke, 126
Unwritten Constitution, 34

Vagueness doctrine, 81–82
Van Buren, Martin, 231, 234, 257, 325
Vance, Cyrus, 536
Vardman, James, 104
Veterans Affairs, Department of, 489
Veto:
  item veto, 414, 426–28
  legislative veto, 424–25
  pocket veto, 414
  presidential veto, 414–16
Vice-president:
  amendments related to, 399
  roles of, 398
  selection alternatives, 399
  selection of, 322
Vietnam War, 177, 236, 251, 369, 412
  escalation of, 523
  major failure of, 534–35
  roots of, 522
Viguerie, Richard A., 224
Virginia and Kentucky Resolutions, 28
Virginia Plan, 10
Voice of America, 538
Voter Education Project (VEP), 216
Voters, influence on legislators, 358–59
Voting:
  group influences
    age, 285
    family, 283
    gender, 285
    race, 285
    religion, 284–85
  independents, 286
  nonvoters, 287–91
    class bias issue, 289–90
    nonvoting groups, 288–89
    reasons for, 187–88
    solutions to, 290
  partisans, 285
  patterns in, 280–81, 283
  public opinion and, 291
Voting rights:
  blacks, 119–20
  states, 118
  women, 104, 119
Voting Rights Act of 1965, 115, 120–21, 287

Wages, minimum wage, 600
Wallace, George, 242, 243
Wallace, Henry, 243
Walsh-Healy Act of 1936, 599
War making, presidential power, 411–12, 416–17

War on Poverty, 174
War Powers Resolution of 1973, 416–18, 533
Warren, Earl, 89, 176, 385–86
Warren, Mercy, 15
Washington, George, 1–3, 5, 6, 8, 10, 16–17, 24, 233, 257, 325, 376–77, 381, 384, 406, 577
Washington Monthly, The, 172, 479
Washington v. Davis, 115
Watergate, 23, 154, 232, 284, 299, 332, 379, 399, 410
Watergate Committee, 369
Weber, Max, 469
Webster, Daniel, 58, 139, 553
Webster v. Reproductive Health Services, 449
Weicker, Lowell, 318
Welfare:
  criticisms of, 585
  welfare reform, 586
Wells-Barnett, Ida Bell, 217
Weyrich, Paul, 224
Whips, 351
Whistle blowers, 484
White, Byron, 74, 84
White House staff, 393, 393–94
White, Joe Slade, 305
White primary, 119
White, Theodore, 308
Willard, Emma, 219
Willard, Frances, 201
Will, George, 309
Wilson, James, 15, 377, 434
Wilson, Woodrow, 21, 36, 235, 240, 469, 520, 521, 596
Winner-take-all, 243
Wirth, Tim, 358
Women:
  in military, 555–56
  voting behavior, 285
Women's movement, 210, 218–23
  Equal Rights Amendment, 221–22
  historical view, 218–20
  National Organization for Women, 221
  suffrage movement, 103–4
  voting rights, 104
World Federalists, 531
WORLDNET, 538
World War II, 177
Wounded Knee, 214
Wright, Frances, 219
Wright, Jim, 371
Writ of certiorari, 448
Writ of habeas corpus, 147–48
Writ of mandamus, 29, 30

Yalta Conference, 521
Yellow-dog contracts, 599
Young Americans for Freedom (YAF), 193

Zenger, Peter, 5

WASHINGTON
Centers of Decision and Landmarks

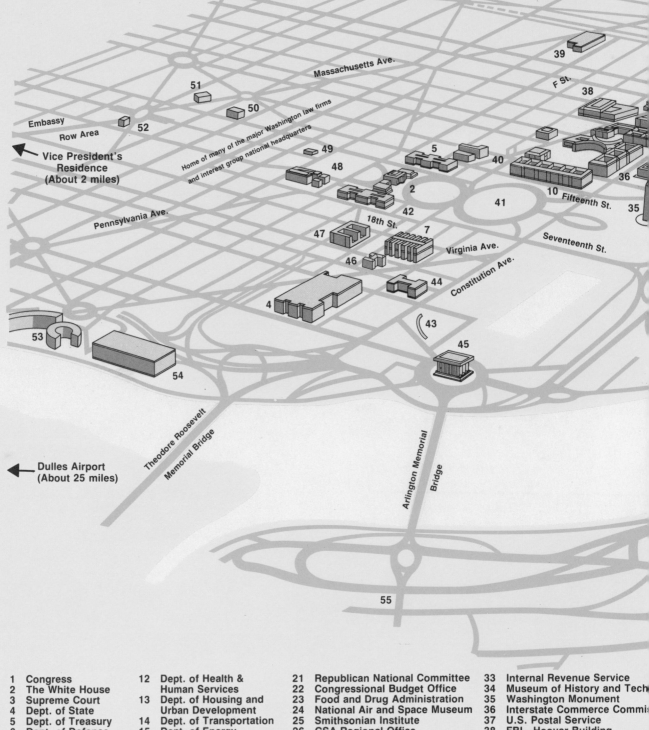

Massachusetts Ave.

F St.

39

38

51

50

Embassy
Row Area

52

Home of many of the major Washington law firms
and interest group national headquarters

49

48

5

40

Vice President's
Residence
(About 2 miles)

←

2

10   Fifteenth St.

36

Pennsylvania Ave.

42

41

35

18th St.

47

7

46

44

Virginia Ave.

Seventeenth St.

Constitution Ave.

4

43

53

45

54

Theodore Roosevelt
Memorial Bridge

Dulles Airport
(About 25 miles)

←

Arlington Memorial
Bridge

55

1	Congress	12	Dept. of Health & Human Services	21	Republican National Committee	33	Internal Revenue Service
2	The White House			22	Congressional Budget Office	34	Museum of History and Tech.
3	Supreme Court	13	Dept. of Housing and Urban Development	23	Food and Drug Administration	35	Washington Monument
4	Dept. of State			24	National Air and Space Museum	36	Interstate Commerce Commi...
5	Dept. of Treasury	14	Dept. of Transportation	25	Smithsonian Institute	37	U.S. Postal Service
6	Dept. of Defense	15	Dept. of Energy	26	GSA Regional Office	38	FBI—Hoover Building
7	Dept. of Interior	16	Dept. of Education	27	Bureau of Engraving & Printing	39	General Accounting Office
8	Dept. of Justice	17	Senate Office Buildings	28	Jefferson Memorial	40	National Press Club
9	Dept. of Agriculture	18	Hall of States	29	Union Station (Railroad)	41	The Ellipse
10	Dept. of Commerce	19	Library of Congress	30	National Art Gallery Bldgs.	42	Executive Office of the Presi...
11	Dept. of Labor		Congressional Research Service	31	Federal Trade Commission		Office of Management and Budget
		20	House Office Buildings	32	Museum of Natural History		Council of Economic Advisers
							National Security Council